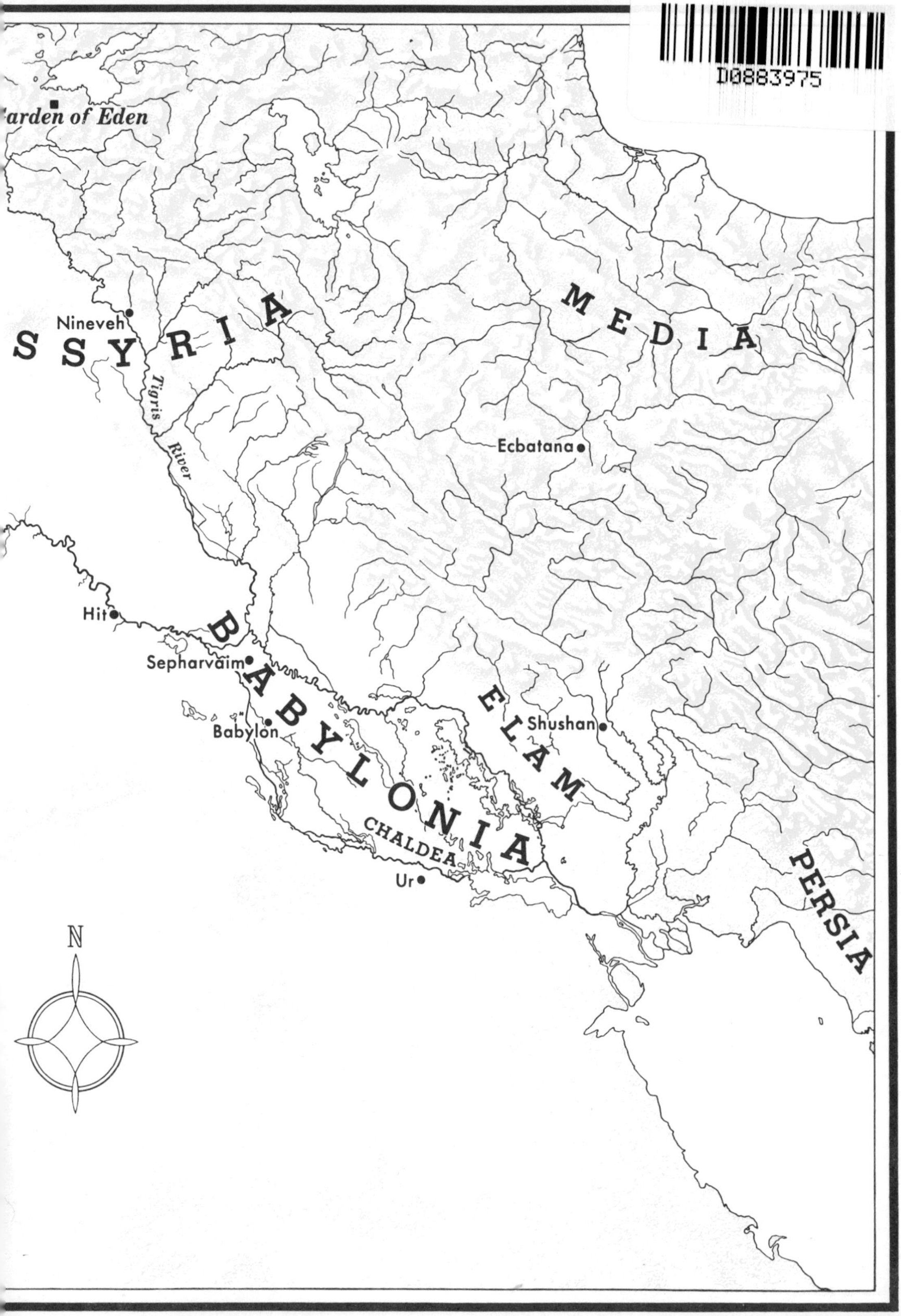

Garden of Eden
Nineveh
ASSYRIA
Tigris River
MEDIA
Ecbatana
Hit
Sepharvaim
BABYLONIA
Babylon
ELAM
Shushan
CHALDEA
Ur
PERSIA
N

"ALL SCRIPTURE IS INSPIRED OF GOD AND BENEFICIAL"

"All Scripture is inspired of God and beneficial for teaching, for reproving, for setting things straight, for disciplining in righteousness, that the man of God may be fully competent, completely equipped for every good work."
—2 Timothy 3:16, 17.

PUBLISHERS
WATCHTOWER BIBLE AND TRACT SOCIETY OF NEW YORK, INC.
INTERNATIONAL BIBLE STUDENTS ASSOCIATION
Brooklyn, New York, U.S.A.

First Edition
2,000,000 Copies

Unless otherwise stated, all Scripture quotations in this book are from the *New World Translation of the Holy Scriptures,* 1961 edition.

Made in the United States of America

CONTENTS

		PAGE
"All Scripture Is Inspired of God and Beneficial"		7
BIBLE BOOK NUMBER		
1	Genesis	13
2	Exodus	19
3	Leviticus	25
4	Numbers	30
5	Deuteronomy	36
6	Joshua	42
7	Judges	46
8	Ruth	51
9	1 Samuel	53
10	2 Samuel	59
11	1 Kings	64
12	2 Kings	69
13	1 Chronicles	75
14	2 Chronicles	79
15	Ezra	85
16	Nehemiah	88
17	Esther	91
18	Job	95
19	Psalms	101
20	Proverbs	106
21	Ecclesiastes	111
22	Song of Solomon	115
23	Isaiah	118
24	Jeremiah	124
25	Lamentations	130
26	Ezekiel	132
27	Daniel	138
28	Hosea	143
29	Joel	146
30	Amos	148
31	Obadiah	151

BIBLE BOOK NUMBER		PAGE
32	Jonah	153
33	Micah	155
34	Nahum	158
35	Habakkuk	161
36	Zephaniah	163
37	Haggai	166
38	Zechariah	168
39	Malachi	172
40	Matthew	175
41	Mark	181
42	Luke	186
43	John	192
44	Acts	198
45	Romans	204
46	1 Corinthians	208
47	2 Corinthians	213
48	Galatians	216
49	Ephesians	219
50	Philippians	222
51	Colossians	224
52	1 Thessalonians	227
53	2 Thessalonians	230
54	1 Timothy	232
55	2 Timothy	235
56	Titus	237
57	Philemon	239
58	Hebrews	241
59	James	246
60	1 Peter	249
61	2 Peter	252
62	1 John	254
63	2 John	256
64	3 John	258
65	Jude	259
66	Revelation	261

STUDY PAGE

1 A Visit to the Promised Land . . . 269
2 Time and the Holy Scriptures . . . 277
3 Measuring Events in the Stream of Time . . . 283
4 The Bible and Its Canon . . . 298
5 The Hebrew Text of the Holy Scriptures . . . 304
6 The Greek Text of the Holy Scriptures . . . 314
7 The Bible in Modern Times . . . 319
8 Advantages of the "New World Translation" . . . 326
9 Archaeology Supports the Inspired Record . . . 331
10 The Bible—Authentic and True . . . 337

The Inspired Scriptures Bring Eternal Benefits . . . 349

Charts, Maps and Illustrations:

The Bible's Inspired Penmen and Their Writings . . . 12
Genesis—Inspired and Beneficial . . . 18
Some Legal Precedents in Deuteronomy . . . 41
Natural Regions of the Promised Land . . . 272
Typical Cross Sections of the Promised Land . . . 273
The Year of the Israelites . . . 280
Main Events of Jesus' Earthly Sojourn . . . 286
Chart of Outstanding Historical Dates . . . 292
Table of the Books of the Bible . . . 297
Outstanding Early Catalogues of the Christian Greek Scriptures . . . 302
Sources for the Text of the New World Translation of the Hebrew Scriptures . . . 308
Sources for the New World Translation of the Christian Greek Scriptures . . . 309
Some Leading Papyrus Manuscripts . . . 312
Some Leading Vellum Manuscripts . . . 313
Some Leading Bible Translations in Seven Principal Languages . . . 321
The Moabite Stone . . . 333
King Sennacherib's Prism . . . 334
The Nabonidus Chronicle . . . 335
Outstanding Prophecies Concerning Jesus and Their Fulfillment . . . 343
Examples of Other Bible Prophecies Fulfilled . . . 345
Some Quotations and Applications of the Hebrew Scriptures by Writers of the Greek Scriptures . . . 346

"All Scripture Is Inspired of God and Beneficial"

"ALL Scripture is inspired of God." These words at 2 Timothy 3:16 identify God, whose name is Jehovah, as the Author and Inspirer of the Holy Scriptures. How satisfyingly delightful the inspired Scriptures are! What an amazing fund of true knowledge they provide! They are indeed "the very knowledge of God" that has been sought after and treasured by lovers of righteousness in all ages.—Prov. 2:5.

2 One of these seekers of knowledge was Moses, the visible leader and organizer of God's nation of Israel, who described divine instruction to be as refreshing "as the dew, as gentle rains upon grass and as copious showers upon vegetation." Then there was David, valiant fighter and upholder of Jehovah's name, who prayed: "Instruct me, O Jehovah, about your way. I shall walk in your truth." There was peaceful Solomon, builder of one of the most glorious structures ever to stand on this earth, the house of Jehovah in Jerusalem, who evaluated Bible wisdom in these words: "Having it as gain is better than having silver as gain and having it as produce than gold itself. It is more precious than corals, and all other delights of yours cannot be made equal to it."—Deut. 32:2; Ps. 86:11; Prov. 3:14, 15.

3 Jesus the Son of God set the highest value on God's word, declaring, "Your word is truth." To his followers he said: "If you remain in my word, you are really my disciples, and you will know the truth, and the truth will set you free." (John 17:17; 8:31, 32) Powerful indeed is this word that Jesus received from his Father. It is God's word. After his death and resurrection and ascension to Jehovah's own right hand in the heavens, Jesus made further revelation of his Father's word, including a delightful description of God's blessings for mankind in the paradise earth, and then God instructed the apostle John: "Write, because these words are faithful and true." All the words of the inspired Scriptures are "faithful and true," bringing immeasurable benefits to those who heed them.—Rev. 21:5.

4 How do these benefits come about? The complete expression of the apostle Paul at 2 Timothy 3:16, 17 supplies the answer: "All Scripture is inspired of God and beneficial for teaching, for reproving, for setting things straight, for disciplining in righteousness, that the man of God may be fully competent, completely equipped for every good work." The inspired Scriptures, then, are beneficial for teaching right doctrine and right conduct, setting things straight in our minds and lives, and reproving and disciplining us so that we may walk humbly in truth and righteousness. By submitting ourselves to the teaching of God's Word we may become "God's fellow workers." (1 Cor. 3:9) There is no greater privilege on earth today than for one to be busy in God's work as the 'fully competent and completely equipped man of God.'

1. How does the Bible identify its Author, and what kind of knowledge do the Scriptures provide?
2. How did Moses, David and Solomon evaluate Bible wisdom?
3. What value do Jesus and God himself place on the divine word?
4. For what are the inspired Scriptures beneficial?

FIRM FOUNDATION FOR FAITH

5 For this, faith is needed. Faith is not to be confused with the watered-down credulity that is so prevalent today. Many people think that any kind of belief—sectarian, evolutionary or philosophical—is sufficient. However, the man of God must "keep holding the pattern of healthful words . . . with the faith and love that are in connection with Christ Jesus." (2 Tim. 1:13) His faith must be real and alive, for "faith is the assured expectation of things hoped for, the evident demonstration of realities though not beheld." It must be grounded in a firm belief in God and his rewards for those who please him. (Heb. 11:1, 6) This faith is to be obtained only through diligent study of God's Word, the Bible. It is founded in deep love for the Bible and for the God of the Bible, Jehovah, and his Son Jesus Christ. There is only one such living faith, even as there is only one Lord Jesus Christ and one God and Father of all, Jehovah.—Eph. 4:5, 6.

6 We need to know what God's Word is, where it came from, its authority and purpose and its power for righteousness. Gaining appreciation of its glorious message, we will have faith. Moreover, we shall come to love the Bible and its Author so fervently that nothing will ever be able to stifle that faith and love. It is the Scriptures, which include the sayings of Jesus Christ, that build a firm foundation for faith. True faith will be of the kind that will endure test and bitter trial, persecutions, and

5. What is faith, and how only may it be obtained?
6. True faith is of what quality?

materialistic advances and philosophies of a godless society. It will triumph gloriously right through into God's new world of righteousness. "This is the conquest that has conquered the world, our faith."—1 John 5:4.

7 In order to gain and hold on to faith, we need to apply ourselves to building love and appreciation for God's Word, the inspired Scriptures. The Scriptures are God's incomparable gift to mankind, a storehouse of spiritual treasures whose depth of wisdom is unfathomable, and whose power for enlightening and stimulating to righteousness exceeds that of all other books ever written. As we dig down to gain knowledge of God's Word, we will be led to exclaim with the apostle Paul: "O the depth of God's riches and wisdom and knowledge!" To know the inspired Scriptures and their Author is to enter into the pathway of eternal joy and pleasantness.—Rom. 11:33; Ps. 16:11.

JEHOVAH—A COMMUNICATING GOD

8 In speaking of the glory of Jehovah's name, David exclaimed: "You are great and are doing wondrous things; you are God, you alone." (Ps. 86:10) Jehovah has done many "wondrous things" for mankind on earth, and among these is the communicating of his Word to them. Yes, Jehovah is a communicative God, a God who lovingly expresses himself for the benefit of his creatures. How thankful we should be that our Creator is no aloof potentate, shrouded in mysteries and unresponsive to the needs of lovers of righteousness on earth! As he will also do in the New World to come, Jehovah resides even now with those who exercise faith and love toward him, in the relation of a kind Father communicating good things to his inquiring children. (Rev. 21:3) Our heavenly Father is not like the demon gods, who must be represented by fearsome dumb idols. Gods of metal and stone have no fatherly relationship with their benighted worshipers. They can communicate nothing of benefit to them. Truly, "those making them will become just like them."—Ps. 135:15-19; 1 Cor. 8:4-6.

9 Jehovah is the "God merciful and gracious, slow to anger and abundant in loving-kindness and truth." (Ex. 34:6) Out of the abundance of his loving-kindness he has communicated an abundance of truth to mankind. This is all sound counsel for the guidance of mankind and includes prophecy to lighten one's paths to future blessings. "For all the things that were written aforetime were written for our instruction, that through our endurance and through the comfort from the Scriptures we might have hope." (Rom. 15:4) Out of the realms above, from heaven itself, have come these reliable communications to instruct mankind in the realms below.—John 8:23.

10 Jehovah has never communicated in an unknown tongue, but always in the language of mankind, the living tongue of his faithful witnesses. (Acts 2:5-11) To Adam, Noah, Abraham, Moses and the Hebrew prophets, Jehovah spoke in mankind's first language, now known as Hebrew. Hebrew continued to be used for as long as it could be understood, even as late as the time of Saul of Tarsus, to whom the resurrected Jesus spoke in that language. (Acts 26:14) When the Aramaic language of the Chaldean Babylonians took hold among the Israelites of the captivity, some communications then came from God in Aramaic, for the people understood that language. (Ezra 4:8–6:18; 7:12-26; Dan. 2:4–7:28) Later, when Greek was the international language and the principal language of his witnesses, Jehovah's communications were made and preserved in that tongue. The sayings preserved in the Bible are Jehovah's communications, spoken always in a living tongue for the benefit of humble, truth-loving men on earth.

11 Since Jehovah is the Creator of that amazing instrument the tongue, which, together with the mouth and throat, forms all the intricacies of speech sounds for each of the many systems of languages, it may be said that Jehovah is the Former of all language. His authority over the language of mankind was demonstrated by his miracle performed at the Tower of Babel. (Ex. 4:11; Gen. 11:6-9; 10:5; 1 Cor. 13:1) No tongue or language is strange to Jehovah. He not only gave man the original Hebrew tongue, but by his creation of the instrument of speech he provided the basis for Aramaic and Greek and for all the 2,796 different languages now being spoken by mankind.[a]

THE LANGUAGE OF TRUTH

12 Regardless of the system of human language used by Jehovah, in all instances he has communicated in the language of truth, not in religious mysticisms. It is a language simple and easy to understand. (Zeph. 3:9) Earthly man can understand only three-dimensional

a According to the French Academy. See *The Encyclopedia Americana*, 1956, Vol. 16, page 731.

7. What rewards come with the finding of Bible wisdom?
8. (a) Why should we be thankful that Jehovah is a communicative God? (b) In what way does he contrast with the demon gods?
9. What kind of communications have come from God in the realms above?
10. In what tongues has Jehovah made communications, and why?
11. Why may it be said that Jehovah is the Former of all language?
12, 13. (a) How has Jehovah made his communications easy to understand? (b) Give examples.

matters, that is, objects that have height, breadth and length, and which are set in the stream of time. Therefore, Jehovah has represented things invisible by typical representations that the mind of man can comprehend. As an example, there was the tabernacle designed by God and erected by Moses in the wilderness. Under inspiration Paul used its three-dimensional symbols to explain glorious realities that are in heaven itself.—Heb. 8:5; 9:9.

13 Another example: Jehovah in heaven, who is spirit, does not literally sit on a thronelike chair. However, to us mere men, bound by visible realities, God expresses himself by such a visible symbol to convey understanding. When he commences heavenly court proceedings, it is just as when a king on earth begins proceedings by taking his seat on a throne. —Dan. 7:9-14.

EASILY TRANSLATED

14 Since the Bible has been written in these down-to-earth, easily understandable terms, it is possible to translate its symbols and actions clearly and accurately into most modern-day languages. The original power and force of truth are preserved in all translations. Simple everyday words, such as "horse," "war," "crown," "throne," "husband," "wife" and "children," communicate accurate thought clearly in every language. This is in contrast to human philosophical writings, which do not lend themselves to accurate translation. Their complicated expressions and up-in-the-air terminology often cannot be conveyed precisely in another tongue.

15 The Bible's power of expression is far superior. Even when God communicated judgment messages to nonbelievers, he did not use philosophical language, but, rather, everyday symbols. This is shown at Daniel 4:10-12. Here the kingdom of the self-glorifying pagan king was described in some detail under the symbol of a tree, and then, by means of actions involving this tree, future happenings were accurately foretold. All of this is clearly conveyed in translations into other languages. Jehovah has lovingly made communications in this way, in order that "the true knowledge will become abundant." How wonderfully this has aided in understanding prophecy in this "time of the end"!—Dan. 12:4.

LINE OF COMMUNICATION

16 Someone may ask, What has been the means of communication? This may well be illustrated by a modern-day example. Communications lines have (1) the utterer or originator of the message, (2) the transmitter, (3) the media through which the message passes, (4) the receiver and (5) the hearer. In telephone communications we have (1) the telephone user originating the communication; (2) the telephone transmitter, which converts the message into electrical impulses; (3) the telephone lines carrying the electrical impulses to the destination; (4) the receiver reconverting the message from impulses to audibility and (5) the hearer. Likewise in heaven, (1) Jehovah God originates his utterances, and then (2) his official Word or Spokesman, now known as Jesus Christ, transmits the message; (3) God's holy spirit is the active force that is used as the medium to carry the communication earthward; (4) God's prophet on earth is the receiver of the message; and (5) he then publishes it for the benefit of God's people. Just as on occasions today a courier may be sent to deliver an important message, so Jehovah at times chose to use spirit messengers, or angels, to carry some communications from the heavens to his servants on the earth.—Gal. 3:19; Heb. 2:2.

PROCESS OF INSPIRATION

17 The expression "Inspired of God" in the title of this book is translated from the Greek *The·op'neu·stos*, meaning "God-breathed." It is God's own spirit, his active force, that he has 'breathed' on faithful men, causing them to compile and write the Sacred Scriptures. This process is known as inspiration. The prophets and other faithful servants of Jehovah who became subject to inspiration had their minds borne along by means of active force. This means they received from God messages or pictures of purpose that became firmly fixed in the circuits of their minds. "For prophecy was at no time brought by man's will, but men spoke from God as they were borne along by holy spirit."—2 Pet. 1:21; John 20:21, 22.

18 While these men of God were awake and fully conscious, or while they were asleep in a dream, his spirit firmly implanted the message emanating from the divine origin of the line of communication. Upon receiving the message, it was the prophet's responsibility to relay it in word form to others. When Moses and other faithful prophets return in the resurrection, they will no doubt be able to confirm the accuracy of the preserved records of their writings, because their appreciative re-created minds will still hold the original communications clearly

14, 15. Why is the Bible, in contrast to human philosophical writings, easily translatable into other tongues? Illustrate.

16. How may Jehovah's channel of communication be outlined?

17. What Greek word is translated "Inspired of God," and how does its meaning help us to understand the process of inspiration?

18. How deeply were the inspired messages impressed on their human receivers?

in memory. In like manner, the apostle Peter was so deeply impressed by the vision of the transfiguration, that he could write vividly concerning its magnificence more than thirty years afterward.—Matt. 17:1-9; 2 Pet. 1:16-21.

THE AUTHOR AND HIS FINGER

19 All human authors have used fingers to write, in ancient times by means of a pen or stylus, and in modern times by means of a typewriter or pen. What has been produced through these fingers is said to have been authored by the mind of their owner. Did you know that God has a finger? This is so, for Jesus spoke of God's spirit as His "finger." When Jesus cured a demon-possessed man so that he regained his power of speech and his sight, religious foes blasphemed the means by which Jesus had cast out the demon. According to Matthew, Jesus said to them: "If it is by means of God's spirit that I expel the demons, the kingdom of God has really overtaken you." (Matt. 12:22, 28) Luke adds to our understanding by quoting Jesus as saying on a like occasion: "If it is by means of God's finger I expel the demons, the kingdom of God has really overtaken you." (Luke 11:20) On an earlier occasion the magic-practicing priests of Egypt were forced to admit that the plagues on Egypt were an exhibition of Jehovah's superior power, acknowledging: "It is the finger of God!" —Ex. 8:18, 19.

20 In harmony with these uses of the word "finger," it can be appreciated that "God's finger" has great power and that this designation well applies to his spirit as he used it in the writing of the Bible. So the Scriptures inform us that by means of "God's finger" he wrote the Ten Commandments on the two tablets of stone. (Ex. 31:18; Deut. 9:10) When God used men to write the various books of the Holy Bible, his symbolic finger, or spirit, was likewise the directive force behind the pen of those men. God's holy spirit is unseen, but it has been active in a marvelous way, with the visible, tangible result that mankind has received the treasured gift of God's Word of truth, *His* Bible. There is no question that the Bible's Author is Jehovah God, the heavenly Communicator.

THE INSPIRED COLLECTION BEGINS

21 As has been seen, Jehovah "proceeded to give Moses two tablets of the Testimony, tablets of stone written on by God's finger." (Ex. 31:18) This writing comprised the Ten Commandments, and it is of interest that this document officially presents the divine name, Jehovah, eight times. In that same year, 1513 B.C.E., Jehovah commanded Moses to start making permanent records. So began the writing of the Sacred Scriptures. (Ex. 17:14; 34:27) God also commanded Moses to construct the "ark of the testimony," or "ark of the covenant," a chest of beautiful workmanship, in which the Israelites were to preserve this most treasured communication. (Ex. 25:10-22; 1 Ki. 8:6, 9) The design of the Ark, and of the tabernacle that housed it, was supplied by Jehovah; and the chief workman, Bezalel, was filled "with the spirit of God in wisdom, in understanding and in knowledge and in every sort of craftsmanship," in order to complete his work after the divine pattern.—Ex. 35:30-35.

22 In making known his purposes, God "spoke on many occasions and in many ways" over a long period of time. (Heb. 1:1) The penmen who wrote down his Word did so from 1513 B.C.E. to about A.D. 98, or during about 1,610 years. The one Author, Jehovah God, used about forty of these scribes or human secretaries. All of these co-writers were Hebrews and thus members of the nation "entrusted with the sacred pronouncements of God." (Rom. 3:2) Eight of them were Christian Jews who knew Jesus personally or through his apostles. The inspired Scriptures written before their time had borne witness concerning the coming of Messiah or Christ. (1 Pet. 1:10, 11) Although called from many walks of life, these earthly Bible writers, from Moses to the apostle John, all shared in upholding the sovereignty of Jehovah God and proclaiming his purposes in the earth. They wrote in Jehovah's name and by the power of his spirit.—Jer. 2:2, 4; Ezek. 6:3; 2 Sam. 23:2; Acts 1:16; Rev. 1:10.

23 Several of these writers include in their records compilations from eyewitness documents made by earlier writers, who were not all inspired. Moses, for example, compiled most of Genesis from such eyewitness accounts, as Samuel did in writing the book of Judges. Jeremiah compiled First and Second Kings, and Ezra wrote First and Second Chronicles, in this way. The holy spirit guided these compilers in determining which portions of older human documents should be incorporated, thus authenticating these compilations as being reliable. From the time of their compilation forward these extracts from older documents became

---

19. What is God's "finger," as proved by what scriptures?
20. How has this "finger" operated, and with what result?
21. (a) How did the writing of the Scriptures commence? (b) In what way did Jehovah provide for their preservation?
22. (a) How many authors are there of the inspired Scriptures, and how long did the writing take? (b) Who were the Bible's co-writers, and what is known about them?
23. What earlier records did they use, and how did these become inspired Scripture?

part of the inspired Scriptures.—Gen. 2:4; 5:1; 2 Ki. 1:18; 2 Chron. 16:11.

24 In what order did the sixty-six Bible books come to us? What part of the endless stream of time do they cover? After describing the creation of the heavens and the earth, and the preparation of the earth as man's home, the Genesis account takes up the beginnings of human history from the creation of the first man in 4026 B.C.E. The Sacred Writings then narrate important events down until shortly after 443 B.C.E. Then, after a gap of more than four hundred years, they pick up the account again in 3 B.C.E., taking it on to about A.D. 98. Thus, from a historical viewpoint, the Scriptures span a period of 4,123 years.

25 The chart on page 12 will assist in understanding the background of the Bible writers and the sequence in which the Bible writings came to us.

THE COMPLETE "BOOK" OF DIVINE TRUTH

26 The Sacred Scriptures, as a collection from Genesis to Revelation, form one complete Book, one complete library, all inspired by the one supreme Author. They should not be divided into two parts, so that one part is given less value. The Hebrew Scriptures and the Christian Greek Scriptures are essential to each other. The latter supplements the former to make the one complete Book of divine truth. The sixty-six Bible books, *all together,* form the one library of the Holy Scriptures.—Rom. 15:4.

27 It is a mistake of tradition to divide God's written Word into two sections, calling the first section, from Genesis to Malachi, "The Old Testament," and the second section, from Matthew to Revelation, "The New Testament." At 2 Corinthians 3:14 the popular King James Version Bible tells of the "reading of the old testament," but here the apostle is not referring to the ancient Hebrew Scriptures in their entirety. Nor does he mean that the inspired Christian writings constitute a "new testament [covenant]." The apostle is speaking of the law covenant, which was recorded by Moses in the Pentateuch and which makes up only a part of the pre-Christian Scriptures. For this reason he says in the next verse, "when Moses is read." The word "testament," which occurs a number of times in the King James Version Bible, has uniformly been rendered "covenant" in most modern translations.—Matt. 26:28; 2 Cor. 3:6, 14, *NW, RS, AS.*

28 That which has been recorded and preserved as the Holy Scriptures is not to be tampered with. (Deut. 4:1, 2; Rev. 22:18, 19) The apostle Paul writes on this point: "However, even if we or an angel out of heaven were to declare to you as good news something beyond what we declared to you as good news, let him be accursed." (Gal. 1:8; see also John 10:35.) All of Jehovah's word of prophecy must be fulfilled in due course. "So my word that goes forth from my mouth will prove to be. It will not return to me without results, but it will certainly do that in which I have delighted, and it will have certain success in that for which I have sent it."—Isa. 55:11.

EXAMINING THE SCRIPTURES

29 In the following pages the sixty-six books of the Sacred Scriptures are examined in turn. The setting of each book is described and information given concerning the writer, the time of writing and the period covered. Proof is also presented to show that the book is authentic and that it rightly belongs as part of the inspired Scriptures. This proof may be found in the words of Jesus Christ or in the inspired writings of other servants of God. Very often the authenticity of the book is shown by undeniable fulfillments of Bible prophecy or by internal evidence from the book itself, such as its harmony, honesty and candor. Supporting evidence may be taken from archaeological finds or reliable secular history.

30 As the contents of each book are described, the endeavor is to make the powerful message of the Bible writer stand out in such a way as to instill in the heart of the reader a deep love for the inspired Scriptures and their Author, Jehovah God, and thus to enhance appreciation of the living message of God's Word in all its practicalness, harmony and beauty. The contents of the book are set out under paragraph subheadings. This is for convenience in study and does not mean that these are arbitrary subdivisions for the books of the Bible. Each book is in itself an entity, making a valuable contribution to the understanding of the divine purposes.

31 In concluding each book the discussion points out why this portion of the inspired Scriptures is "beneficial for teaching, for reproving, for setting things straight, for disciplining in righteousness." (2 Tim. 3:16) The fulfillments of prophecy, where these are indicated by the inspired testimony of later Bible writers, are considered. In each instance, the

24, 25. (a) What period of history is covered in the Bible? (b) Point out some interesting facts found in the chart on page 12.
26. In what way are the Scriptures one complete book?
27. Why are the expressions "Old Testament" and "New Testament" misnomers?
28. What assurance is given as to Bible prophecies?
29. As each Bible book is examined in turn, what introductory information is provided in this book?
30. In what way are the contents of each Bible book presented?
31. (a) What information is then presented to show why each book is beneficial? (b) What glorious theme is kept to the fore throughout these discussions?

book's contribution to developing the overall theme of the Bible is shown. The Bible is no myth. It contains the only living message for mankind. From the first book, Genesis, to the last book, Revelation, the inspired Scriptures testify to the purpose of the Creator of the Universe, Jehovah God, to sanctify his name by the Kingdom ruled by his Seed. Therein lies the glorious hope for all lovers of righteousness.—Matt. 12:18, 21.

32 After considering the sixty-six Bible books themselves, we devote some space to giving background information on the Bible. This includes studies on the geography of the Promised Land, the timing of the events of the Bible, Bible translations, archaeological and other supporting evidences of the authenticity of the Bible, and proof of the Bible catalogue. Other valuable information and tables also appear in this section. All of this is designed to heighten appreciation of the Bible as the most practical and beneficial book on earth today.

33 The divine Author has spoken to mankind at great length. He has shown great depth of love and Fatherly interest in benefiting his children on earth. What a remarkable collection of inspired documents he has provided for us in the Holy Scriptures! Truly, these form a treasure beyond compare, an extensive library of 'divinely breathed' information, far exceeding in wealth and in scope the writings of mere men. Devotion to the study of God's Word will not become "wearisome to the flesh," but, rather, it will bring eternal benefits in knowing "the saying of Jehovah [which] endures forever."—Eccl. 12:12; 1 Pet. 1:24, 25.

32. What other information is provided to heighten appreciation of the Bible?

33. As what may the Bible be described, and of what benefit is its study?

THE BIBLE'S INSPIRED PENMEN AND THEIR WRITINGS
(In Date Order)

Order	*Writers*	*Occupations*	*Writings Completed*	*Writings*
1.	Moses	Scholar, shepherd, prophet and leader	1473 B.C.E.	*Genesis* (compiled from eleven ancient documents, and the Joseph account); *Exodus; Leviticus; Job; Numbers; Deuteronomy; Psalms* 90 (91).
2.	Joshua	Military general	c. 1433 B.C.E.	*Joshua.*
3.	Samuel	Levite, judge and prophet	before c. 1080 B.C.E.	*Judges* (compiled from several documents); *Ruth;* part of *First Samuel.*
4.	Gad	Prophet	c. 1040 B.C.E.	Part of *First Samuel; Second Samuel* (both with Nathan).
5.	Nathan	Prophet	c. 1040 B.C.E.	See above (with Gad).
6.	David	King, musician	1037 B.C.E	Many of the *Psalms.*
7.	Asaph	Singer		Some *Psalms;* other *Psalms,* ascribed to the sons of Korah.
8.	Heman	Wise man		*Psalm* 88.
9.	Ethan	Wise man		*Psalm* 89.
10.	Solomon	King	c. 1000 B.C.E.	Most of *Proverbs; Song of Solomon; Ecclesiastes; Psalm* 127.
11.	Agur			*Proverbs* chapter 30.
12.	Lemuel	King		*Proverbs* chapter 31.
13.	Jonah	Prophet	c. 852 B.C.E.	*Jonah.*
14.	Joel	Prophet	c. 820 B.C.E.	*Joel.*
15.	Amos	Herdsman, prophet	c. 811 B.C.E.	*Amos.*
16.	Hosea	Prophet	after 745 B.C.E	*Hosea.*
17.	Isaiah	Prophet	c. 732 B.C.E.	*Isaiah.*
18.	Micah	Prophet	before 716 B.C.E.	*Micah.*
19.	Zephaniah	Prince, prophet	before 648 B.C.E.	*Zephaniah.*
20.	Nahum	Prophet	before 633 B.C.E.	*Nahum.*
21.	Habakkuk	Prophet	c. 628 B.C.E.	*Habakkuk.*
22.	Obadiah	Prophet	c. 607 B.C.E.	*Obadiah.*
23.	Ezekiel	Priest, prophet	591 B.C.E.	*Ezekiel.*
24.	Jeremiah	Priest, prophet	c. 580 B.C.E.	*First* and *Second Kings* (compiled from documents of the kingdoms of Judah and Israel); *Jeremiah; Lamentations.*
25.	Daniel	Prince, ruler and prophet	536 B.C.E.	*Daniel.*
26.	Haggai	Prophet	521 B.C.E.	*Haggai.*
27.	Zechariah	Prophet	519 B.C.E.	*Zechariah.*
28.	Mordecai	Prime minister	c. 474 B.C.E.	*Esther.*
29.	Ezra	Priest, copyist, administrator	c. 460 B.C.E.	*First* and *Second Chronicles* (compiled from state chronicles of Judah and Israel, and others); *Ezra.*
30.	Nehemiah	Court official, governor	after 443 B.C.E.	*Nehemiah.*
31.	Malachi	Prophet	after 443 B.C.E.	*Malachi.*
32.	Matthew	Tax collector, apostle	c. A.D. 41	*Matthew.*
33.	James	(Brother of Jesus), overseer	before A.D. 62	*James.*
34.	Mark	Missionary	c. A.D. 60-65	*Mark.*
35.	Luke	Physician, missionary	c. A.D. 61	*Luke; Acts.*
36.	Peter	Fisherman, apostle	c. A.D. 64	*First* and *Second Peter.*
37.	Paul	Missionary, apostle, tentmaker	c. A.D. 65	*First* and *Second Thessalonians; Galatians; First* and *Second Corinthians; Romans; Ephesians; Philippians; Colossians; Philemon; Hebrews; First* and *Second Timothy; Titus.*
38.	Jude	(Brother of Jesus), disciple	c. A.D. 65	*Jude.*
39.	John	Fisherman, apostle	c. A.D. 98	*Revelation; John; First, Second* and *Third John.*

Bible Book Number One— Genesis

Writer:	**Moses**
Place Written:	**Wilderness**
Writing Completed:	**1513 B.C.E.**
Time Covered:	**46,026-1657 B.C.E.**

IMAGINE picking up a book of only fifty short chapters and finding in the first page or two the only accurate account of the earliest history of man and a record showing the relation of man to God, his Creator, as well as to the earth with its myriads of creatures! In these few pages you gain, too, a deep insight into God's purpose in putting man on earth. Reading a little farther, you discover why man dies and the reason for his present troubled condition, and you are enlightened to receive a real basis for faith and for hope, even to identifying God's instrument for deliverance—the Seed of promise. The remarkable book that contains all these things is Genesis, the first of the sixty-six books of the Bible.

² *Genesis* means "origin; generation; coming into existence," the name being taken from the Greek *Septuagint* translation of this book. In the Hebrew manuscripts the title is the opening word *Beʹre·shithʹ*, "in the beginning" (Greek, *en ar·kheiʹ*). It has been said that the original Hebrew name for the book was *Se·fer Maʽa·sehʹ Beʹre·shithʹ*, meaning "Book of Work in the Beginning." Genesis is the first book of the Pentateuch (Greek for "five rolls" or "fivefold volume"). These were originally one book called the Torah ("Law") or "the book of the law of Moses," but were later divided into the five rolls for easier handling.—Josh. 23:6; Ezra 6:18.

³ Jehovah God is the Author of the Bible, but he inspired Moses to compile and write the book of Genesis. We say "compile" because it is evident that Moses possessed written documents preserved by his forefathers as precious, valuable records of the origins of mankind. The Bible refers to eleven of these, the Hebrew word being *to·le·dothʹ* (Greek, *genʹe·sis*), which, according to the noted Hebrew scholar Gesenius, means "history." A study of the writing style of ancient times reveals that such historical documents were ended with a colophon or conclusion, setting out the name of the writer or owner of the document. Hence, we are able to identify the eleven "histories" in Genesis by these colophons that conclude them. Who wrote these documents?

⁴ Adam, who received the creation account from God, was interested in a record for his family, the human race. He wrote the first two documents, which end with colophons at Genesis 2:4 and 5:1, 2. These writings were carried through the Flood by Noah, who wrote the next "history," and then eight other men shared in adding to and preserving the records. Written between 4026 and 1728 B.C.E., in locations as varied as near the garden of Eden, the mountains of Ararat, Mesopotamia and Palestine, they carry history down to Jacob, whose twelve sons became the foundations of the nation of Israel.

⁵ It was in the wilderness of Sinai in 1513 B.C.E. that Moses compiled these documents under inspiration. (2 Tim. 3:16; John 5:39, 46, 47) Where did Moses obtain the information for the last part of Genesis? Since his great-grandfather Levi was the half brother of Joseph, these details would be accurately known within his own family. Levi's life may even have overlapped that of Moses' father, Amram. Further, Jehovah's spirit would again assure the correct recording of this portion of the Scriptures.—Ex. 6:16, 18, 20; Num. 26:59.

⁶ There is no question as to who wrote Genesis. "The book of the law of Moses" and similar references to the first five books of the Bible, of which Genesis is one, are to be found often from the time of Moses' successor Joshua onward. In fact, there are some two hundred references to Moses in twenty-seven of the later Bible books. Moses' writership has never been questioned by the Jews. The Christian Scriptures make frequent mention of Moses as the writer of "the law," the crowning testimony being that of Jesus Christ. Moses wrote at Jehovah's direct command and under his inspiration.—Ex. 17:14; Josh. 8:31; Dan. 9:13; Luke 24:27, 44.

---

1. What are some of the vital topics covered in Genesis?
2. What is the meaning of the name "Genesis," and of what is it the first part?
3. (a) Who is the Author of Genesis? (b) How can it be said that Moses was inspired to "compile" as well as to "write" this book?
4. Who wrote the documents used by Moses, and how far do these carry the history of mankind?
5. (a) Where and when did Moses compile the record? (b) How could Moses have obtained the material he incorporated in the last part of Genesis?
6. What internal Bible evidence proves Moses' writership?

7 Some skeptics have asked, But how were Moses and his predecessors able to write? Was not writing a later human development? Recently a great mass of archaeological discoveries have produced much external evidence concerning man's early ability to write. The well-known archaeologist Sir Charles Marston states: "In Mesopotamia, Asia Minor, Egypt, Syria, and Persia, excavators have been finding whole libraries of clay tablets, covered with writing, in the cuneiform or wedge-shaped characters, and in other scripts."[a] Excavations by Sir Leonard Woolley on the site of Ur of the Chaldeans have produced evidence that in his view writing goes back to nearly 4,000 years B.C.E. Still another authority says: "One of the most remarkable facts which has emerged from archaeological research, is that the art of writing began in the earliest historical times known to man."[b]

8 In many other respects Genesis has proved to be amazingly consistent with proved facts. It is only Genesis that gives a true and factual account of the Flood and its survivors, though accounts of the Flood and survival by means of one man (in most cases as a result of his building a boat) are found in the legends of all branches of the human family. The Genesis account also locates the beginnings of the dwellings of the different branches of mankind, stemming from the three sons of Noah—Shem, Ham and Japheth. Says Dr. Melvin G. Kyle, of Xenia Theological Seminary, Missouri, U.S.A.: "That from a central point, somewhere in Mesopotamia, the Hamitic branch of the race migrated to the south-west, the Japhetic branch to the north-west, and the Semitic branch 'eastward' toward the 'land of Shinar' is indisputable."[c]

9 The authenticity of Genesis as part of the divine record is shown also by its internal harmony, as well as its complete agreement with the remainder of the inspired Scriptures. Its candor reflects a writer who feared Jehovah and loved truth, and who unhesitatingly wrote of the sins of both the nation and those prominent in Israel. Above all, the unswerving accuracy with which its prophecies have come to fulfillment, as will be shown toward the end of this chapter, marks Genesis as an outstanding example of a writing inspired by Jehovah God. —Gen. 9:20-23; 37:18-35; Gal. 3:8, 16.

CONTENTS OF GENESIS

10 **A history of the heavens and the earth** (1:1–2:4). Reaching back through billions of years of time, Genesis opens with impressive simplicity: "In the beginning God created the heavens and the earth." Significantly, this opening sentence identifies God as the Creator and his material creation as the heavens and the earth. In majestic, well-chosen words the first chapter continues on to give a general account of the creative work relative to the earth. This is accomplished in six time periods called "days," each beginning with an evening, when the creative work for that period is undefined, and ending in the brightness of a morning, as the glory of the creative work becomes clearly manifest. The light, the expanse of the atmosphere, dry land and vegetation, the luminaries to divide day and night, fish and fowl, land animals and finally man, all appear in God's creative order. God here makes known his law governing kinds, the impassable barrier making it impossible for one kind to evolve into another. Having made man in his own image, God announces his threefold purpose for man on earth: to fill it with righteous offspring, to subdue it, and to have in subjection the animal creation. The first "history" ends at the opening of the seventh "day," which is blessed and pronounced sacred by Jehovah, who now proceeds 'to rest from all his work that he has made.'

11 **The book of Adam's history** (2:5–5:2). This gives a closeup or magnified view of God's creative work as regards man. It describes the garden of Eden and its location, states God's law of the forbidden tree, relates Adam's naming of the animals and then gives the account of Jehovah carrying out the first marriage by forming a wife from Adam's own body and bringing her to Adam. However, the woman eats the forbidden fruit, persuades her husband to join her in rebellion, and so Eden becomes defiled through disobedience. God immediately points to the means by which his purpose will be accomplished: "And Jehovah God proceeded to say to the serpent [Satan, the invisible instigator of the rebellion]: ' . . . And I shall put enmity between you and the woman and between your seed and her seed. He will bruise you in the head and you will bruise him in the heel.' " (3:14, 15) Man is expelled from the garden, to live in pain and sweatful toil among

a *The Bible Is True,* 1934, page 47.
b *New Discoveries in Babylonia About Genesis,* 1936, P. J. Wiseman, page 35.
c *Biblical History in the Light of Archaeological Discovery,* 1934, D. E. Hart-Davies, page 5.

7. What evidence testifies to man's early ability to write?
8. What secular confirmation is there of the Flood and of the Bible account of three branches to the human race?
9. What other evidences testify to the authenticity of Genesis?
10. What is related concerning God's creation in the first "history" in Genesis?
11. (a) What magnified view does the second "history" give concerning man? (b) What important purpose is here made known?

thorns and thistles. Finally, he must die and return to the ground from which he had been taken. Only his offspring can hope in the promised Seed.

12 The ravages of sin continue outside Eden. Cain, the first man-child born, becomes the murderer of his brother Abel, a faithful servant of Jehovah. Jehovah banishes Cain to the land of Fugitiveness, where he brings forth a generation later completely wiped out by the Flood. Adam now has another son, Seth, who becomes father to Enosh; at this time men begin to call on the name of Jehovah in hypocrisy.

13 **The history of Noah** (5:3–6:9a). Adam dies at 930 years of age. The genealogy through Seth is here given. Outstanding among these descendants of Seth is Enoch, who sanctifies Jehovah's name by "walking with the true God." The next man of notable faith is Enoch's great-grandson Noah, born 1,056 years after Adam's creation. About this time something occurs to increase the violence in the earth. Angels of God forsake their heavenly habitation to marry the good-looking daughters of men. This unauthorized cohabitation produces a hybrid race of giants known as the Nephilim ("Fellers"), who make a name, not for God, but for themselves. Jehovah therefore announces to Noah that he is going to wipe out man and animal because of the continuing badness of mankind. Only Noah finds favor with Jehovah.

14 **The history of Noah's sons, Shem, Ham and Japheth** (6:9b–10:1a). Noah becomes father to Shem, Ham and Japheth. As violence and ruination continue in the earth, Jehovah reveals to Noah that he is about to sanctify his name by means of a great flood and he commands Noah to build an ark of preservation, giving him detailed building plans. Noah promptly obeys, gathers in his family of eight persons, together with beasts and birds, and in the 600th year of his life (2370 B.C.E.) the floodwaters descend. The downpour continues for forty days, until even the tall mountains are covered by as much as fifteen cubits (more than twenty-two feet) of the waters. When, after one solar year, Noah is finally able to lead his family out of the ark, his first act is to offer a great sacrifice of thanksgiving to Jehovah.

15 Jehovah now blesses Noah and his family and commands them to fill the earth with their offspring. God's decree gives permission to eat meat, but demands abstinence from blood, which is the soul or life of the flesh, and requires the execution of a murderer. God's covenant nevermore to bring a deluge upon the earth is confirmed by the appearance of the rainbow in the heavens. Later, Ham shows disrespect for Jehovah's prophet Noah. Learning of this, Noah curses Ham's son Canaan, but he adds a blessing showing that Shem will be specially favored and that Japheth also will be blessed. Noah dies at 950 years of age.

16 **The history of Shem** (10:1b–11:10a). Noah's three sons carry out God's command to multiply, producing seventy families, the progenitors of the present human race. Nimrod, grandson of Ham, is not counted in, because he becomes "a mighty hunter in opposition to Jehovah." He sets up a kingdom and starts to build cities. At this time all the earth has one language. Instead of scattering over the earth to populate and cultivate it, men decide to build a city and a tower with its top in the heavens so that they can make a celebrated name for themselves. However, Jehovah thwarts their intention by confusing their language, and so scatters them. The city is called Babel ("Confusion").

17 **The history of Terah** (11:10b–11:27a). This history traces the important line of descent from Shem to Terah's son Abram, supplying also the chronological links.

18 **The history of Ishmael the son of Abraham** (11:27b–25:12). Instead of seeking a name for himself, Abram exercises faith in God. He leaves Ur of the Chaldeans at God's command and becomes a temporary resident in the land of Canaan at seventy-five years of age, sanctifying the name of Jehovah before his household and the people in that land.[a] Because of his faith and obedience he comes to be called "Jehovah's friend [lover]," and God establishes his covenant with him. (Jas. 2:23; 2 Chron. 20:7; Isa. 41:8) God protects Abram and his wife during a brief stay in Egypt. Back in Canaan, Abram shows his generosity and peaceableness by allowing his nephew and fellow worshiper Lot to select the best part of the land. Later, he rescues Lot from four kings who have captured him, and then, returning from the fight, he meets Melchizedek king of Salem, who as priest of God blesses Abram, and to whom Abram pays tithes.

19 God later appears to Abram, announcing

a Genesis 12:8; 13:4, *NW* footnotes, 1953 Edition.

12. What further developments close out the second "history"?
13. What does Noah's "history" reveal?
14. How does Jehovah now sanctify his name?
15. What does Jehovah now command, and covenant, and what events fill out Noah's life?
16. What does "the history of Shem" relate as to Jehovah's supremacy?
17. Why is "the history of Terah" important?
18. How does Abram come to be called "Jehovah's friend," and what blessings does he receive?
19. How does God enlarge his covenant, and for what reason does Jehovah change the names of Abram and Sarai?

himself as Abram's shield and enlarging on his covenant promise by revealing that Abram's seed will become as the stars of heaven for number. Abram is told that his seed will suffer affliction for four hundred years, but will be delivered by God, with judgment upon the afflicting nation. When Abram is eighty-five years old, Sarai his wife, still childless, gives him her Egyptian maidservant Hagar, that he may have a child by her. Ishmael is born and is viewed as the possible heir. However, Jehovah purposes differently. When Abram is ninety-nine years old Jehovah changes his name to Abraham and Sarai's name to Sarah, and promises that Sarah will bear a son. The covenant of circumcision is given to Abraham, and he immediately has his household circumcised.

20 God now announces to his friend Abraham his determination to destroy Sodom and Gomorrah because of their heavy sin. Angels of Jehovah warn Lot and help him to flee from Sodom with his wife and two daughters. However, his wife, lingering to look back at the things behind, becomes a pillar of salt. In order to procure offspring, Lot's daughters get their father intoxicated with wine, and through intercourse with him they bear two sons, who become the fathers of the nations of Moab and Ammon.

21 God protects Sarah from contamination by Abimelech of the Philistines. The promised heir Isaac is born when Abraham is a hundred years old and Sarah about ninety. Some five years after this the nineteen-year-old Ishmael pokes fun at Isaac, the heir, resulting in the dismissal of Hagar and Ishmael, with God's approval. Some years later God tests Abraham by commanding him to sacrifice his son Isaac on one of the mountains of Moriah. Abraham's great faith in Jehovah does not waver. He attempts to offer up his son and heir, but is stopped by Jehovah, who provides a ram as a substitute sacrifice. Jehovah again confirms his promise to Abraham, saying that he will multiply Abraham's seed like the stars of heaven and the grains of sand that are on the seashore. He shows that this seed will take possession of the gate of his enemies, and that all nations of the earth will certainly bless themselves by means of the Seed.

22 Sarah dies at the age of 127 and is buried in a field that Abraham buys from the sons of Heth. Abraham now sends his chief household servant to obtain a wife for Isaac from the country of his relatives. Jehovah guides the servant to the family of Nahor's son Bethuel, and arrangements are made for Rebekah to return with him. Rebekah goes willingly, with her family's blessing, and becomes the bride of Isaac. Abraham, on his part, takes another wife, Keturah, who bears him six sons. However, he gives these gifts and sends them away and makes Isaac his sole heir. Then, at the age of 175, Abraham dies.

23 **The history of Isaac the son of Abraham** (25:13–25:19a). As Jehovah had foretold, Isaac's half-brother Ishmael becomes the head of a great nation, founded upon his twelve chieftain-sons listed in this history.

24 **The history of Esau, that is to say, Edom** (25:19b–36:1). For twenty years Rebekah remains barren, but, as Isaac keeps on entreating Jehovah, she gives birth to twins, Esau and Jacob, of whom Jehovah had told her the older would serve the younger. Isaac is now sixty years old. Esau becomes a lover of hunting. Failing to appreciate the covenant with Abraham, he returns from the hunt one day and sells his birthright to Jacob for a mere swallow of stew. He also marries two Hittite women (and later an Ishmaelite), who become a source of bitterness to his parents. With his mother's assistance, Jacob disguises himself as Esau in order to obtain the firstborn's blessing. Esau, who had not revealed to Isaac that he had sold the birthright, now plans to kill Jacob; so Rebekah advises that Jacob flee to Haran to her brother Laban. Before he leaves, Isaac blesses him again, and instructs him to take, not a pagan wife, but one from his mother's household. At Bethel, on his way to Haran, Jehovah appears to him in a dream, reassuring him and confirming the covenant promise toward him.

25 At Haran, Jacob works for Laban, marrying his two daughters, Leah and Rachel. Though this polygamous marriage is brought on him by a trick of Laban, God blesses it by giving Jacob twelve sons and a daughter through the wives and their two handmaidens, Zilpah and Bilhah. God sees to it that the flocks of Jacob increase greatly, and then instructs him to return to the land of his fathers. He is pursued by Laban, but they make a covenant at the place called Galeed and The Watchtower (Hebrew, *ham-Mits·pah'*).[a] Resuming the journey, Jacob is reassured by angels and grapples at night with an angel, who finally blesses him and changes his name from Jacob to Israel. He

[a] Genesis 31:48, 49, *NW* footnotes, 1953 Edition.

20. What noteworthy happenings climax Lot's life?
21. What test does Abraham meet successfully in connection with the Seed, and what does Jehovah further reveal in confirming his promise?
22. What care does Abraham exercise in providing Isaac a wife, and how is Isaac made sole heir?
23. What is contained in "the history of Isaac"?
24. How do Esau and Jacob view the covenant with Abraham, and with what results?
25. (a) How does Jacob come to have twelve sons? (b) Why does the birthright pass from Reuben to Joseph?

peacefully negotiates a meeting with Esau and travels on to Shechem. Here his daughter Dinah is violated by the Hivite chieftain's son. Her brothers Simeon and Levi take revenge by slaughtering the men of Shechem. This displeases Jacob, because it gives him, as a representative of Jehovah, a bad name in the land. God tells him to go to Bethel to make an altar there. On the trek out of Bethel Rachel dies while bearing to Jacob his twelfth son Benjamin. Reuben violates Rachel's handmaid Bilhah, the mother of two of Jacob's sons, and for this forfeits the birthright, which passes to Joseph as Rachel's firstborn son. Soon afterward Isaac also dies at 180 years of age, and Esau and Jacob bury him.

26 **The history of Esau the father of Edom** (36:2-9). Esau and his household move to the mountainous region of Seir, the accumulated wealth of Esau and Jacob being too great to permit their dwelling together any longer.

27 **The history of Jacob** (36:10–37:2a). This eleventh and final "history," belonging to Jacob, lists the posterity of Esau in Edom, the sheiks and the kings. Jacob continues dwelling in Canaan.

28 **The concluding portion of Genesis** (37:2b–50:26). This is concerned with Jacob and his twelve sons, especially Joseph. Because of Jehovah's favor and some dreams that he causes Joseph to have, the older brothers come to hate Joseph. They scheme to kill him, but finally sell him to some passing Ishmaelite merchants. Dipping Joseph's striped garment in the blood of a goat, they present it to Jacob as evidence that the young lad of seventeen has been killed by a wild beast. Joseph is taken to Egypt and sold to Potiphar, the chief of Pharaoh's bodyguard.

29 Chapter 38 digresses momentarily to give the account of the birth of Perez to Tamar, who, by strategy, causes Judah her father-in-law to perform marriage that should have been performed by his son toward her. This account again underlines the extreme care with which the Scriptures record each development leading to the production of the Seed of promise. Judah's son Perez becomes one of the ancestors of Jesus.—Luke 3:23, 33.

30 Meanwhile Jehovah blesses Joseph in Egypt, and he becomes great in Potiphar's household. However, difficulty pursues him when he refuses to reproach God's name by fornication with Potiphar's wife, and he is falsely accused and thrown into prison. There he is used by Jehovah in interpreting the dreams of two fellow prisoners, Pharaoh's cupbearer and baker. Later, when Pharaoh has a dream that greatly worries him, Joseph's ability is called to his attention, so that he is quickly brought to Pharaoh from his prison hole. Giving the credit to God, Joseph interprets the dream to forecast seven years of plenty, to be followed by seven years of famine. Pharaoh recognizes "the spirit of God" upon Joseph, and appoints him prime minister to handle the situation. Now thirty years of age, Joseph administers wisely by storing up foodstuffs during the seven years of plenty. Then during the worldwide famine that follows, he sells the grain to the peoples of Egypt and of other nations who come to Egypt for food.

31 Eventually Jacob sends his ten older sons to Egypt for grain. Joseph recognizes them, but they do not recognize him. Holding Simeon as hostage, he demands that they bring their youngest brother back with them on the next trip for grain. When the nine sons return with Benjamin, Joseph reveals himself, expresses forgiveness toward the ten guilty ones, and instructs them to get Jacob and move to Egypt for their welfare during the famine. Accordingly, Jacob, with sixty-six of his offspring, moves down to Egypt. Pharaoh gives them the best of the land, the land of Goshen in which to dwell.

32 As Jacob draws close to death, he blesses Ephraim and Manasseh, the sons of Joseph, and then calls his own twelve sons together to tell them what will happen to them "in the final part of the days." He now gives in detail a series of prophecies, all of which have since come to remarkable fulfillment.[a] Here he foretells that the scepter of rulership will remain in the tribe of Judah until the coming of Shiloh (meaning "the one whose it is"), the promised Seed. After thus blessing the heads of the twelve tribes and giving command concerning his own future burial in the Land of Promise, Jacob dies at the age of 147 years. Joseph continues to care for his brothers and their households until his own death at 110 years of age, at which time he expresses his faith that God will again bring Israel into their land, and requests that his bones, too, be taken to that Land of Promise.

WHY BENEFICIAL

33 As the "beginning" of the inspired Word of God, Genesis is of inestimable benefit in intro-

a *The Watchtower*, 1962, pages 360-374, 392-408.

26. What is discussed in the second "history of Esau"?
27. What is found in the "history of Jacob"?
28. What events lead to Joseph's becoming a slave in Egypt?
29. Why is the account of Perez' birth important?
30. How does Joseph become prime minister of Egypt?
31. What events surround the moving of Jacob's household to Egypt?
32. What important series of prophecies does Jacob make on his deathbed?
33. (a) What basis does Genesis provide for understanding the later Bible books? (b) To what proper objective does Genesis point?

ducing and explaining the glorious purposes of Jehovah God. What a basis it provides for understanding the later Bible books! Within its broad scope it describes the beginning and end of the righteous world in Eden, the development and disastrous flushing out of the first world of ungodly people and the rise of the present evil world. Outstandingly, it sets the theme for the entire Bible, namely, the sanctification of Jehovah's name through the Kingdom ruled by the Seed. It shows why man dies. From Genesis 3:15 forward, and especially in the record of God's dealings with Abraham, Isaac and Jacob, it holds forth the hope of life in the new world under the Kingdom of the Seed. It is beneficial in pointing out the proper objective for all mankind—to be integrity-keepers and sanctifiers of Jehovah's name.—Rom. 5:12, 18; Heb. 11:3-22, 39, 40; 12:1; Matt. 22:31, 32.

34 The Christian Greek Scriptures make reference to every prominent event and person recorded in the book of Genesis. Moreover, as shown throughout the entire Scriptures, the prophecies recorded in Genesis have been unerringly fulfilled. One of these, the "four hundred years" of affliction on Abraham's seed, commenced when Ishmael mocked Isaac in 1913 B.C.E. and ended with the deliverance from Egypt in 1513 B.C.E.[a] Examples of other meaningful prophecies and their fulfillment are shown here in the table. Also of immense benefit in building faith and understanding are the divine principles first stated in Genesis. The prophets of old, as well as Jesus and his disciples, frequently referred to and applied passages from the book of Genesis. We will do well to follow their example, and a study of the accompanying table should assist in this.

35 Genesis very clearly reveals God's will and purpose concerning marriage, the proper relationship of husband and wife, and the principles of headship and family training. Jesus himself drew on this information, quoting both the first and second chapters of Genesis in his one statement: "Did you not read that he who created them from the beginning made them male and female and said, 'For this reason a man will leave his father and his mother and will stick to his wife, and the two will be one flesh'?" (Matt. 19:4, 5; Gen. 1:27; 2:24) The record in Genesis is essential in providing the genealogy of the human family and also in calculating the time that man has been on this earth.—Chapters 5, 7, 10, 11.

GENESIS – INSPIRED AND BENEFICIAL

Genesis Texts	*Principle*	*References from Other Writers*
1: 27; 2: 24	Sacredness, permanence of marriage bond	Matt. 19: 4, 5
2: 7	Man is a soul	1 Cor. 15: 45
2: 22, 23	Headship	1 Tim. 2: 13; 1 Cor. 11: 8
9: 4	Sacredness of blood	Acts 15: 20, 29
20: 3	Adultery wrong	1 Cor. 6: 9
24: 3; 28: 1-8	Marry only believer	1 Cor. 7: 39
28: 7	Obedience to parents	Eph. 6: 1
	Prophecies Fulfilled	
12: 1-3; 22: 15-18	Abraham's seed is Christ	Gal. 3: 16
14: 18	Melchizedek typifies Christ	Heb. 7: 13-15
16: 1-4, 15	Pictorial meaning of Sarah, Hagar, Ishmael, Isaac	Gal. 4: 21-31
17: 11	Pictorial meaning of circumcision	Rom. 2: 29
28: 12	Ladder of communication with heaven	John 1: 51
49: 1-28	Jacob's blessing on the twelve tribes	Josh. 14: 1–21: 45
49: 9	Lion that is of the tribe of Judah	Rev. 5: 5
Other Texts Used by Prophets, Jesus and Disciples in Illustration, Application or as Example, Further Proving Authenticity of Genesis		
1: 1	God created heaven and earth	Isa. 45: 18; Rev. 10: 6
1: 26	Man made in God's image	1 Cor. 11: 7
1: 27	Man made, male and female	Matt. 19: 4; Mark 10: 6
2: 2	God rested on seventh day	Heb. 4: 4
3: 1-6	Serpent deceived Eve	2 Cor. 11: 3
3: 20	All mankind from original pair	Acts 17: 26
4: 8	Cain killed Abel	Jude 11; 1 John 3: 12
4: 9, 10	Abel's blood	Matt. 23: 35
Chaps. 5, 10, 11	Genealogy	Luke, chap. 3
5: 21	Enoch	Jude 14
5: 29	Noah	Ezek. 14: 14; Matt. 24: 37
6: 13, 17-20	Flood	Isa. 54: 9; 2 Pet. 2: 5
12: 1-3, 7	Abrahamic covenant	Gal. 3: 15-17
15: 6	Faith of Abraham	Rom. 4: 3; Jas. 2: 23
15: 13, 14	Sojourn in Egypt	Acts 7: 1-7
18: 1-5	Hospitality	Heb. 13: 2
19: 24, 25	Sodom and Gomorrah destroyed	2 Pet. 2: 6; Jude 7
19: 26	Wife of Lot	Luke 17: 32
20: 7	Abraham a prophet	Ps. 105: 9, 15
21: 9	Ishmael taunts Isaac	Gal. 4: 29
22: 10	Abraham attempts to offer up Isaac	Heb. 11: 17
25: 23	Jacob and Esau	Rom. 9: 10-13; Mal. 1: 2, 3
25: 32-34	Esau sells birthright	Heb. 12: 16, 17
37: 28	Joseph sold into Egypt	Ps. 105: 17
41: 40	Joseph made prime minister	Ps. 105: 20, 21

36 Also of real benefit to the student of the Scriptures is the study of patriarchal society that Genesis affords. Patriarchal society was

a See Study 3, paragraph 10.

34. By reference to the accompanying chart show that Genesis contains (a) meaningful prophecies, and (b) valuable principles.
35. What important information does Genesis contain on marriage, genealogy and the count of time?

36. Name some principles and practices of patriarchal society that are important to understanding the Bible.

the community form of family government that operated among God's people from Noah's day until the Law was given at Mount Sinai. Many of the details incorporated in the law covenant were already being practiced in patriarchal society. Such principles as community merit (Gen. 18:32), community responsibility (Gen. 19:15), sanctity of blood and of life (Gen. 9:4-6), capital punishment (Gen. 19:25) and God's hatred of the glorifying of men (Gen. 11:4-8) have affected mankind throughout history. Many legal practices and terms throw light on later events, even down to the days of Jesus. Patriarchal law governing the custody of persons and property (Gen. 31:38, 39; 37:29-33; John 10:11, 15; 17:12; 18:9), the manner of conveying property (Gen. 23:3-18), the law governing the inheritance of one who received the right of the firstborn (Gen. 48:22) —all these must be understood if we are to get a clear background to the meaning of the Bible. Other practices of patriarchal society incorporated in the Law were sacrifices, circumcision (given first to Abraham), making of covenants, brother-in-law marriage (Gen. 38:8, 11, 26) and use of oaths to confirm a matter.—Gen. 22:16; 24:3.[a]

[37] Genesis, the opening book of the Bible, provides many lessons in integrity, faith, faithfulness, obedience, respect, good manners and courage. Here are a few examples: Enoch's faith and courage in walking with God in the face of violent enemies; Noah's implicit obedience and activity as a preacher; Abraham's faith, determination and endurance, his sense of responsibility as a family head and teacher of God's commands to his children, his generosity and love; Sarah's submissiveness to her husband-head and her industriousness; Jacob's concern for the promise of God and his mildness of temper; Joseph's obedience to his father, his moral uprightness, his courage, his good conduct in prison, his respect for superior authorities, his humility in giving glory to God and his merciful forgiveness of his brothers; the consuming desire of all these men to sanctify Jehovah's name. These exemplary traits stand out in the lives of those who walked with God during the long period of 2,369 years from the creation of Adam to the death of Joseph, as covered in the book of Genesis.

[38] Truly, the account in Genesis is beneficial in building up faith, presenting as it does such magnificent examples of faith, that tested quality of faith that reaches out for the city of God's building and creation, his Kingdom government that he long ago began to prepare through his Seed of promise, the leading sanctifier of Jehovah's great name.—Heb. 11:8, 10, 16.

a *The Watchtower*, 1952, pages 432-445.

37. What lessons, valuable to Christians, may be learned through the study of Genesis?

38. In building faith, to what does Genesis point forward?

Bible Book Number Two— Exodus

Writer:	**Moses**
Place Written:	**Wilderness**
Writing Completed:	**1512 B.C.E.**
Time Covered:	**1657-1512 B.C.E.**

THE soul-stirring account of momentous signs and miracles that Jehovah enacted in delivering his name people from the afflictions of Egypt, his organizing them as his special property as "a kingdom of priests and a holy nation," and the beginning of Israel's constitutional history—these are the highlights of the Bible book of Exodus. In Hebrew it is called *Weʼel'leh sheʼmoth,* meaning "Now these are the names," or simply *Sheʼmoth,* "Names," according to its first words. The modern-day name comes from the Greek *Septuagint Version,* where it is called *Exodos,* which has been Latinized to *Exodus,* meaning "Going Forth" or "Departure." That Exodus is a continuation of the account in Genesis is shown by the opening word "Now" (literally, "And"), and by the relisting of the names of Jacob's sons, as taken from the fuller record of Genesis 46:8-27.

[2] The book of Exodus reveals God's magnificent name, JEHOVAH, in all the brilliance of its glory and sanctity. As he proceeded to demonstrate the depth of meaning of his name, God told Moses, "I SHALL PROVE TO BE WHAT I SHALL PROVE TO BE," and added that he should

1. (a) What are the highlights of Exodus? (b) What names have been given the book, and of what account is it a continuation?

2. What does Exodus reveal concerning the name JEHOVAH?

tell Israel, "I SHALL PROVE TO BE (Hebrew אהיה, *Ehyéh*) has sent me to you." The name JEHOVAH (יהוה, YHWH) is thought by some authorities to be the causative form of this verb. Certainly Jehovah's mighty and fearsome acts that he now proceeded to bring to pass on behalf of his people Israel magnified and clothed that name in a resplendent glory, making it a memorial "to generation after generation," *the name* to be revered for an eternity of time. It is of all things most beneficial that we know the wonderful history surrounding that name, and worship the only true God, the One who declares, "I am Jehovah."[a]—Ex. 3:14, 15; 6:6.

³ Moses is the writer of Exodus, as indicated by its being the second volume of the Pentateuch. The book itself registers three instances of Moses' making a written record at the direction of Jehovah. (Ex. 17:14; 24:4; 34:27) Jesus and the writers of the Christian Scriptures quote or refer to Exodus more than forty times, as when Jesus said: "Moses gave you the Law, did he not?" Exodus was written in the wilderness of Sinai, in the year 1512 B.C.E., a year after the sons of Israel had left Egypt. It covers a period of 145 years, from the death of Joseph in 1657 B.C.E. to the erection of the tabernacle of Jehovah's worship in 1512 B.C.E. —John 7:19; Ex. 1:6; 40:17.

⁴ Considering that the events of Exodus occurred around 3,500 years ago, there is a surprising amount of archaeological and other external evidence testifying to the accuracy of the record. Egyptian names are correctly used in Exodus, and titles mentioned correspond with Egyptian inscriptions. Archaeology shows that it was an Egyptian custom to allow foreigners to live in Goshen. It was the custom for the upper classes, which would include Pharaoh's daughter, to bathe in the Nile River. Bricks have been found, made with and without straw, probably dating back to the Egyptian oppression of the Israelites. Also, magicians were prominent in Egypt's heyday.—Ex. 8:22; 2:5; 5:6, 7, 18; 7:11.

⁵ Monuments show that the Pharaohs personally led their charioteers into battle, and Exodus indicates that the Pharaoh of Moses' day followed this custom. How great must have been his humiliation! But how is it that ancient Egyptian records make no reference to the Israelites' sojourn in their land, or to the calamity that befell Egypt? Archaeology has shown that it was the custom for a new Egyptian dynasty to erase anything uncomplimentary in previous records. They never recorded humiliating defeats. The blows against the gods of Egypt—such as the Nile god, the frog god and the sun god—which discredited these false gods and showed Jehovah to be supreme, would not be suited to the annals of a proud nation.—Ex. 14:7-10; 15:4.[b]

⁶ Moses' forty years of service as a shepherd under Jethro would acquaint him with living conditions and locations of water and food in the area, thus well qualifying him to lead the exodus. The authenticity of Moses' account is seen in the corroboration of the sites along the route of travel. The Egyptian store cities of Pithom and Raamses have been identified by archaeologists, the location of the former now being called Tell Maskhûta. Marah (now ʽAin Huwarah), where a basin still contains bitter waters as in the days of Israel, and Elim (now Wadi Gharandel) have also been located. Mount Sinai (Horeb) is now known as Jebel Musa (the "Mountain of Moses") in Arabic. It appears that Israel followed much of the land route long used by labor gangs mining copper and turquoise in going from the Nile to the Sinai mountains. Without a firsthand knowledge of the topography of the territory, it would have been impossible to write the account of the travels of Israel as Moses does in the book of Exodus.—Ex. 1:11; 13:20; 15:23, 27.

⁷ The account of the construction of the tabernacle on the plains before Sinai fits in with local conditions. The laver of copper was made from the metal mirrors that the women brought with them from Egypt, samples of which have been dug up in Egypt by archaeologists. One scholar states: "In form, structure, and materials, the tabernacle belongs altogether to the wilderness. The wood used in the structure is found there in abundance."[c] Whether they concern names, customs, religion, places, geography or materials, the accumulation of external evidences confirms the inspired Exodus account, now close to 3,500 years old.—Ex. 38:8; 26:14.

⁸ Later Bible writers referred to Exodus constantly, showing its prophetic significance and value. Over 900 years later Jeremiah wrote of "the true God, the great One, the mighty One, Jehovah of armies being his name," who pro-

---

a Exodus 3:14, *NW* footnote, 1953 Edition; *"Let Your Name Be Sanctified,"* pages 88-92.

b *Archaeology and Bible History,* 1950, J. P. Free, page 98.

c *Exodus,* 1874, F. C. Cook, page 247.

---

3. (a) How do we know Moses to be the writer? (b) When was Exodus written, and what period does it cover?
4, 5. What archaeological evidence supports the Exodus account?
6. What does the description of the route of travel indicate as to the authenticity of Exodus?
7. What other evidences, including the tabernacle construction, confirm Exodus as inspired?
8. How is Exodus shown to be interwoven with the rest of the Scriptures as inspired and beneficial?

ceeded to bring his people Israel out of Egypt "with signs and with miracles and with a strong hand and with a stretched-out arm and with great fearsomeness." (Jer. 32:18-21) More than 1,500 years later, Stephen based much of the stirring testimony that led to his martyrdom on the information in Exodus. (Acts 7:17-44) The life of Moses is cited for us as an example of faith at Hebrews 11:23-29, and Paul makes other frequent references to Exodus in drawing examples and warnings for us today. (Acts 13:17; 1 Cor. 10:1-6, 11, 12; 2 Cor. 3:7-16) This all helps us to appreciate how the parts of the Bible are interwoven one with another, each portion sharing in the revelation of Jehovah's purpose in a way that is beneficial.

CONTENTS OF EXODUS

9 **Jehovah commissions Moses, reveals his Memorial Name** (1:1–4:31). After naming the sons of Israel who have come down into Egypt, Exodus next records the death of Joseph. In time a new king arises over Egypt. When he sees that the Israelites keep on "multiplying and growing mightier at a very extraordinary rate," he adopts repressive measures, including forced labor, and tries to reduce Israel's male population by ordering the destruction of all newborn male children. (1:7) It is under these circumstances that a son is born to an Israelite of the house of Levi. This child is the third in the family. When he is three months old, his mother hides him in a papyrus ark among the reeds by the bank of the Nile River. He is found by the daughter of Pharaoh, who likes the boy and adopts him. His own mother becomes his nursemaid, so that he grows up in an Israelite home. Later on he is brought to Pharaoh's court. He is named Moses, meaning "Drawn Out; Saved Out of Water."—Ex. 2:10, *NW* footnote, 1953 Edition; Acts 7:17-22.

10 This Moses is interested in the welfare of his fellow Israelites. He kills an Egyptian for mistreating an Israelite. As a result he has to flee, and so he comes into the land of Midian. There he marries Zipporah the daughter of Jethro, the priest of Midian. In time he becomes father to two sons, Gershom and Eliezer. Then, at the age of eighty, after he has spent forty years in the wilderness, Moses is commissioned by Jehovah for a special service in sanctification of Jehovah's name. One day while shepherding Jethro's flock near Horeb, "the mountain of the true God," Moses sees a thornbush aflame without being consumed. When he goes to investigate, he is addressed by an angel of Jehovah, who tells him of God's purpose to bring His people "the sons of Israel out of Egypt." (Ex. 3:1, 10) Moses is to be used as Jehovah's instrument in freeing Israel from Egyptian bondage.—Acts 7:23-35.

11 Moses then asks how he is to identify God to the sons of Israel. It is here, for the first time, that Jehovah makes his name known in a special relationship, associating it with his specific purpose and establishing it as a memorial. "This is what you are to say to the sons of Israel, 'I SHALL PROVE TO BE has sent me to you . . . Jehovah the God of your forefathers, the God of Abraham, the God of Isaac and the God of Jacob, has sent me to you.'" His name Jehovah will now stand as assurance that he will cause to come to pass his purposes in connection with his name people. To this people, the descendants of Abraham, he will give the land promised to their forefathers, "a land flowing with milk and honey."—Ex. 3:14, 15, 17.

12 Jehovah explains to Moses that the king of Egypt will not let the Israelites go free, but that He will first have to strike Egypt with all his wonderful acts. Moses' brother Aaron is given to him as spokesman, and they receive three signs to perform to convince both Israelites and Egyptians that they come in the name of the God 'who proves to be.' While on the way to Egypt, Moses' son has to be circumcised to prevent a death in the family, reminding Moses of God's requirements. Moses and Aaron gather the older men of the sons of Israel, and inform them of Jehovah's purpose to bring them out of Egypt and take them to the Promised Land. They perform the signs, and the people believe and accept them.

13 **The blows on Egypt** (5:1–10:29). Moses and Aaron now go in to Pharaoh and announce that Jehovah the God of Israel has said: "Send my people away." In scornful tone proud Pharaoh replies: "Who is Jehovah, so that I should obey his voice to send Israel away? I do not know Jehovah at all and, what is more, I am not going to send Israel away." (5:1, 2) Instead of freeing the Israelites, he imposes harder tasks on them. However, Jehovah renews his promises of deliverance, again tying this in with the sanctification of his name: "I am Jehovah . . . I shall indeed prove to be God to you . . . I am Jehovah."—6:6-8.

14 The sign Moses performs before Pharaoh, by having Aaron throw down his rod to become a big snake, is imitated by the magic-practicing priests of Egypt. Although their snakes are swallowed up by Aaron's big snake, still Phar-

9. Under what circumstances is Moses born and reared?
10. What events lead to Moses' being commissioned for special service?
11. In what special sense does Jehovah now make known his name?
12. What does Jehovah explain to Moses as to freeing the Israelites, and how do the people accept the signs?
13. What results from Moses' first encounter with Pharaoh?
14. How are the Egyptians compelled to recognize "the finger of God"?

aoh's heart becomes obstinate. Jehovah now proceeds to bring ten successive heavy blows upon Egypt. First, their river Nile and all the waters of Egypt turn to blood. Then a plague of frogs comes upon them. These two blows are imitated by the magic-practicing priests, but not the third blow, that of gnats on man and beast. They have to recognize that this is "the finger of God." However, Pharaoh will not send Israel away.—8:19.

15 The first three blows come upon Egyptians and Israelites alike, but from the fourth one on, only the Egyptians are afflicted, Israel standing distinct under Jehovah's protection. This fourth blow is heavy swarms of gadflies. Then comes pestilence upon all the livestock of Egypt, followed by boils with blisters on man and beast, so that even the magic-practicing priests are unable to stand before Moses. Jehovah again lets Pharaoh's heart become obstinate, declaring to him through Moses: "But, in fact, for this cause I have kept you in existence, for the sake of showing you my power and in order to have my name declared in all the earth." (9:16) Moses then announces to Pharaoh the next blow, "a very heavy hail," and here the Bible registers for the first time that some among Pharaoh's servants fear Jehovah's word and act on it. The eighth and ninth blows follow in quick succession, an invasion of locusts and a gloomy darkness, so that the obstinate, enraged Pharaoh threatens Moses with death if he tries to see his face again.—9:18.

16 **The passover and striking of the firstborn** (11:1–13:16). Jehovah now declares, "One plague more I am going to bring upon Pharaoh and Egypt"—the death of the firstborn. He orders that the month of Abib be the first of the months for Israel. On the tenth day they are to take a sheep or goat, a male, one year old, unblemished, and kill it on the fourteenth day. On that evening they must take the blood of the lamb and splash it on the two doorposts and the upper part of the doorway, and then stay inside the house and eat the roasted lamb, of which not one bone is to be broken. They are to have no leaven in the house, and must eat in haste, dressed and equipped for marching. It is to serve as a memorial, a festival to Jehovah throughout their generations, to be followed by the seven-day feast of unleavened cakes, in all the meaning of which their sons must be fully instructed. (Later, Jehovah gives further instructions concerning these feasts and commands that all firstborn males belonging to Israel, both men and beasts, must be sanctified to him.)

17 Israel does as Jehovah commands. Then disaster strikes! At midnight Jehovah kills all the firstborn of Egypt, while passing over and delivering the firstborn of Israel. "Get out from the midst of my people," shouts Pharaoh. And 'the Egyptians begin to urge the people' to get away quickly. (12:31, 33) They do not leave empty-handed, for they ask for and receive from the Egyptians articles of silver and gold and clothing. They march out of Egypt in battle formation, to the number of 600,000 able-bodied men, together with their families and a vast mixed company of non-Israelites, as well as a numerous stock of animals. This marks the end of 430 years of dwelling in Canaan and Egypt, and is indeed a night to be memorialized.—Ex. 12:40, *LXX*, also *NW* footnote, 1953 Edition; Gal. 3:17.

18 **Jehovah's name sanctified at the Red Sea** (13:17–15:21). Guiding them by day in a pillar of cloud and by night in a pillar of fire, Jehovah leads Israel out by way of Succoth. Again Pharaoh grows obstinate, chasing them with his chosen chariots of war and trapping them, so he thinks, at the Red Sea. Moses reassures the people, saying: "Do not be afraid. Stand firm and see the salvation of Jehovah, which he will perform for you today." (14:13) Jehovah then makes the sea go back, forming an escape corridor whereby Moses leads the Israelites safely to the eastern shore. Pharaoh's mighty hosts rush in after them, only to be trapped and drowned in the returning waters. What a climactic sanctification of Jehovah's name! What grand cause for rejoicing in him! That rejoicing is then expressed in the Bible's first great song of victory: "Let me sing to Jehovah, for he has become highly exalted. The horse and its rider he has pitched into the sea. My strength and my might is Jah, since he serves for my salvation. . . . Jehovah will rule as king to time indefinite, even forever." —15:1, 2, 18.

19 **Jehovah makes law covenant at Sinai** (15:22–34:35). In successive stages, as guided by Jehovah, Israel travels toward Sinai, the mountain of the true God. When the people murmur about the bitter water at Marah, he makes it sweet for them. Again, when they murmur about the lack of meat and bread, he provides them quails in the evening and the sweetish "manna," like dew on the ground in the morning. This manna is to serve as bread for the Israelites for the next forty years. Also, for the first time in history, Jehovah orders the observance of a rest day or sabbath, having them pick up twice the quantity of manna on

---

15. Which blows afflict only the Egyptians, and why only does Jehovah permit Pharaoh to continue?
16. What does Jehovah command concerning the passover and the feast of unleavened cakes?
17. What events mark this as a night to be memorialized?
18. What climactic sanctification of Jehovah's name takes place at the Red Sea?
19. What events mark the journey toward Sinai?

the sixth day and withholding the supply on the seventh. He also produces water for them at Rephidim and fights for them against Amalek, having Moses record his judgment that Amalek will be completely wiped out.

20 Moses' father-in-law Jethro then brings him his wife and two sons. The time has now come for better organization in Israel, and Jethro contributes some good practical counsel. He advises Moses not to carry the whole load himself, but to appoint capable God-fearing men to judge the people as chiefs of thousands, hundreds, fifties and tens. Moses does this, so that now only the hard cases come to him.

21 Within three months after the exodus Israel camps in the wilderness of Sinai. Jehovah here promises them: "And now if you will strictly obey my voice and will indeed keep my covenant, then you will certainly become my special property out of all other peoples, because the whole earth belongs to me. And you yourselves will become to me a kingdom of priests and a holy nation." The people vow: "All that Jehovah has spoken we are willing to do." (19:5, 6, 8) Following a period of sanctification for Israel, Jehovah comes down on the third day upon the mountain in fire, causing it to smoke and tremble.

22 Jehovah then proceeds to give the Ten Words or Ten Commandments. These stress exclusive devotion to Jehovah, forbidding other gods, image worship and the taking up of Jehovah's name in a worthless way. The Israelites are commanded to render service six days and then to keep a sabbath to Jehovah, and to honor father and mother. Laws against murder, adultery, stealing, testifying falsely and covetousness complete the Ten Words. Then Jehovah goes on to set judicial decisions before them, instructions for the new nation that cover slavery, assault, injuries, compensation, theft, damage from fire, false worship, seduction, mistreatment of widows and orphans, loans and many other matters. Sabbath laws are given and three annual festivals arranged for the worship of Jehovah. Moses then writes down the words of Jehovah, sacrifices are offered and half the blood sprinkled on the altar. The book of the covenant is read to the people and, upon their again attesting their willingness to obey, the rest of the blood is sprinkled on the book and all the people. Thus Jehovah makes the law covenant with Israel through the mediator Moses.—Heb. 9:19, 20.

23 Moses then goes up to Jehovah in the mountain to receive the Law. During forty days and nights he is given many instructions concerning the materials for the tabernacle, the details of its furnishings, minute specifications for the tabernacle itself and the design for the priestly garments, including the plate of pure gold, inscribed "Holiness belongs to Jehovah," on Aaron's turban. The installation and service of the priesthood are detailed, and Moses is reminded that the sabbath will be a sign between Jehovah and the sons of Israel "to time indefinite." Moses is then given the two tablets of the Testimony written on by the 'finger of God.' —Ex. 28:36; 31:17, 18.

24 In the meantime the people become impatient and ask Aaron to make a god to go ahead of them. Aaron does this, forming a golden calf, which the people worship in a "festival to Jehovah." (32:5) Jehovah speaks of exterminating Israel, but Moses intercedes for them, though he shatters the tablets in his own blazing anger. The sons of Levi now stand up on the side of pure worship, slaughtering 3,000 of the revelers. Jehovah also plagues them. After Moses implores God to continue leading them, he is told he may glimpse the glory of God, and is instructed to carve two additional tablets on which Jehovah will again write the Ten Words. When he goes up into the mountain the second time, Jehovah proceeds to declare to him the name of Jehovah as He goes passing by: "Jehovah, Jehovah, a God merciful and gracious, slow to anger and abundant in loving-kindness and truth, preserving loving-kindness for thousands." (34:6, 7) Then he states the terms of his covenant, and Moses writes it down as we have it today in Exodus. When Moses comes down from Mount Sinai again the skin of his face emits rays because of Jehovah's revealed glory, so that he has to put a veil over his face.—2 Cor. 3:7-11.

25 **Construction of the tabernacle** (35:1–40:38). Moses then calls Israel together and transmits Jehovah's words to them, telling them of the privilege of the willinghearted to contribute and that of the wisehearted to do the work on the tabernacle. Soon it is reported to Moses: "The people are bringing much more than what the service needs for the work that Jehovah has commanded to be done." (36:5) Under Moses' direction workmen filled with Jehovah's spirit proceed to build the tabernacle and its furnishings and to make all the garments for the priests. One year after the exodus the

20. How is better organization effected?
21. What promise does Jehovah next make, but on what conditions?
22. (a) What commandments are contained in the "Ten Words"? (b) What other judicial decisions are set before Israel, and how is the nation taken into the law covenant?
23. What instructions does Jehovah provide Moses in the mountain?
24. (a) What sin do the people commit, and with what result? (b) How does Jehovah next reveal his name and glory to Moses?
25. What does the record relate concerning the tabernacle and the further manifestation of Jehovah's glory?

tabernacle is completed and erected on the plain before Mount Sinai. Jehovah shows his approval by covering the tent of meeting with his cloud and by filling the tabernacle with his glory, so that Moses is not able to enter the tent. This same cloud by day, and a fire by night, mark Jehovah's guidance of Israel during all their journeyings. It is now the year 1512 B.C.E., and here the record of Exodus ends, with the name of Jehovah gloriously sanctified through his marvelous works performed in behalf of Israel.

WHY BENEFICIAL

26 Preeminently, Exodus reveals to us and establishes our faith in Jehovah as the great Deliverer, Organizer and Fulfiller of his magnificent purposes. This faith is added to as we study the many references to Exodus in the Christian Greek Scriptures, indicating fulfillments of many features of the law covenant, the assurance of a resurrection, Jehovah's provision to sustain his people, and precedents for Christian relief work, counsel on consideration for parents and requirements for gaining life, and how to view retributive justice. The Law was finally summarized as commanding the showing of love for God and fellowman.—Matt. 22:32—Ex. 4:5; John 6:31-35 and 2 Cor. 8:15—Ex. 16:4, 18; Matt. 15:4 and Eph. 6:2—Ex. 20:12; Matt. 5:26, 38, 39—Ex. 21:24; Matt. 22:37-40.

27 At Hebrews 11:23-29 we read of the faith of Moses and his parents. By faith he left Egypt, by faith he celebrated the passover and by faith he led Israel through the Red Sea. The Israelites got baptized into Moses and ate spiritual food and drank spiritual drink, looking forward to the spiritual rock-mass, Messiah or Christ, but still they did not have God's approval, for they put God to the test and became idolaters, fornicators and murmurers. Paul explains that this has an application for Christians today: "Now these things went on befalling them as examples, and they were written for a warning to us upon whom the ends of the systems of things have arrived. Consequently let him that thinks he is standing beware that he does not fall."—1 Cor. 10:1-12; see also Hebrews 3:7-13.

28 Much of the deep spiritual significance of Exodus, together with its prophetic application, is given in Paul's writings, especially in Hebrews chapters 9 and 10. "For since the Law has a shadow of the good things to come, but not the very substance of the things, men can never with the same sacrifices from year to year which they offer continually make those who approach perfect." (Heb. 10:1) We are interested, therefore, in knowing the shadow and understanding the reality. Christ "offered one sacrifice for sins perpetually." He is described as "the Lamb of God." Not a bone of this "Lamb" was broken, just as in the type. The apostle Paul comments: "Christ our passover has been sacrificed. Consequently let us keep the festival, not with old leaven, neither with leaven of injuriousness and wickedness, but with unfermented cakes of sincerity and truth." —Heb. 10:12; John 1:29 and 19:36—Ex. 12:46; 1 Cor. 5:7, 8—Ex. 23:15.

29 Jesus became the mediator of a new covenant, as Moses had been mediator of the law covenant. The contrast between these covenants is also clearly explained by the apostle Paul, who speaks of the 'handwritten document of decrees' having been taken out of the way by Jesus' death on the torture stake. The resurrected Jesus as High Priest is "a public servant of the holy place and of the true tent, which Jehovah put up, and not man." The priests under the Law rendered "sacred service in a typical representation and a shadow of the heavenly things" according to the pattern that was given by Moses. "But now Jesus has obtained a more excellent public service, so that he is also the mediator of a correspondingly better covenant, which has been legally established upon better promises." The old covenant became obsolete and was done away with as a code administering death. Those Jews not understanding this are described as having their perceptions dulled, but those believers who appreciate that spiritual Israel has come under a new covenant can "with unveiled faces reflect like mirrors the glory of Jehovah," being adequately qualified as its ministers. With cleansed consciences these are able to offer up their own "sacrifice of praise, that is, the fruit of lips which make public declaration to his name."—Col. 2:14; Heb. 8:1-6, 13; 2 Cor. 3:6-18; Heb. 13:15; Ex. 34:27-35.

30 Exodus magnifies Jehovah's name and sovereignty, pointing forward to a glorious deliverance of the Christian nation of spiritual Israel, to whom it is said: "You are 'a chosen race, a royal priesthood, a holy nation, a people for special possession, that you should declare abroad the excellencies' of the one that called you out of darkness into his wonderful light. For you were once not a people, but are now God's people." Jehovah's power as demonstrated in gathering his spiritual Israel out of

26. (a) How does Exodus establish faith in Jehovah? (b) How do Greek-Scripture references to Exodus add to this faith?
27. Of what benefit to the Christian is the historical record in Exodus?
28. How have the shadows of the Law and the passover lamb been fulfilled?
29. (a) Contrast the law covenant with the new covenant. (b) What sacrifices do spiritual Israelites now offer to God?
30. The deliverance of Israel and the magnifying of Jehovah's name in Egypt foreshadowed what?

the world to magnify his name is no less miraculous than the power he showed on behalf of his people in ancient Egypt. In keeping Pharaoh in existence to show him His power and in order that His name might be declared, Jehovah foreshadowed a far greater testimony to be accomplished through His Christian witnesses.—1 Pet. 2:9, 10; Rom. 9:17; Rev. 12:17.

31 Thus we can say from the Scriptures that the nation formed under Moses pointed forward to a new nation under Christ and to a kingdom that will never be shaken. In view of this, we are encouraged to "render God sacred service with godly fear and awe." Just as Jehovah's presence covered the tabernacle in the wilderness, so he promises to be eternally present with those who fear him: "Look! The tent of God is with mankind, and he will reside with them, and they will be his peoples. And God himself will be with them. . . . Write, because these words are faithful and true." Exodus is indeed an essential and beneficial part of the Bible record.—Ex. 19:16-19—Heb. 12:18-29; Ex. 40:34—Rev. 21:3, 5.

31. What does Exodus foreshadow as to a kingdom and Jehovah's presence?

Bible Book Number Three— *Leviticus*

Writer:	**Moses**
Place Written:	**Wilderness**
Writing Completed:	**1512 B.C.E.**
Time Covered:	**1 month (1512 B.C.E.)**

THE most common name for the third book of the Bible is Leviticus, which comes from *Le·vi·ti·kon'* of the Greek *Septuagint Version* by way of the Latin *Vulgate's Le·vi'ti·cus.* This name is fitting, even though the Levites are given only passing mention (at 25:32, 33), for the book consists chiefly of the regulations of the Levitical priesthood, which was chosen from the tribe of Levi, and the laws that the priests taught the people: "For the lips of a priest are the ones that should keep knowledge, and the law is what people should seek from his mouth." (Mal. 2:7) In the Hebrew text the book is named from its opening expression, *Way·yi·qra',* that is, "And he proceeded to call." Among the later Jews the book also was called "Law of the Priests" and "Law of Offerings."—Lev. 1:1, *NW* footnote, 1953 Edition.

2 There is no question but that Moses wrote Leviticus. The conclusion or colophon states: "These are the commandments that Jehovah gave Moses." (27:34) A similar statement is found at Leviticus 26:46. The evidence previously noted that proves Moses to have written Genesis and Exodus also supports his writership of Leviticus, as the Pentateuch was originally one scroll. Moreover, Leviticus is joined to the preceding books by the conjunction "And." The strongest of all testimony is found in the fact that Jesus Christ, as well as other inspired servants of Jehovah, frequently quote or refer to the laws and principles in Leviticus and attribute them to Moses.—Lev. 23:34, 40-43—Neh. 8:14, 15; Lev. 14:1-32—Matt. 8:2-4; Lev. 12:2—Luke 2:22; Lev. 12:3—John 7:22; Lev. 18:5—Rom. 10:5.

1. (a) Why is the name "Leviticus" fitting? (b) What other names have been given to the book?
2. What evidence supports Moses' writership?

3 What time period does Leviticus cover? The book of Exodus concludes with the setting up of the tabernacle "in the first month, in the second year, on the first day of the month." The book of Numbers opens with Jehovah's speaking to Moses "on the first day of the second month in the second year of their coming out of the land of Egypt." It follows, therefore, that not more than a lunar month could have elapsed for the few events of Leviticus, most of the book consisting of laws and regulations.—Ex. 40:17; Num. 1:1; Lev. 8:1–10:7; 24:10-23.

4 When did Moses write Leviticus? It is reasonable to conclude that he kept a record of events as they took place and wrote down God's instructions as he received them. This is implied by God's command to Moses to write down the doom of the Amalekites right after Israel had defeated them in battle. An early date is also suggested by certain matters in the book. For example, the Israelites were commanded to bring animals that they wanted to use for food to the entrance of the tent of meeting for slaughtering. This command would be given and recorded shortly after the installation of the priesthood. Many instructions are given for guiding the Israelites during their

3. What time period is covered by Leviticus?
4. When was the book written?

wilderness journey. All of this points to Moses' writing Leviticus during 1512 B.C.E.—Ex. 17:14; Lev. 17:3, 4; 26:46.

5 Why was Leviticus written? Jehovah had purposed to have a holy nation, a sanctified people, set apart for his service. While from the time of Abel faithful men of God had been offering sacrifices to Jehovah, first with the nation of Israel did Jehovah now give explicit instructions regarding sin offerings and other sacrifices. These, as explained in detail in Leviticus, made the Israelites aware of the exceeding sinfulness of sin and impressed upon their minds how displeasing it made them to Jehovah. These sacrifices of the Law served, therefore, as a tutor leading the Jews to Christ, showing them the need of a Savior and at the same time serving to keep them as a people separate from the rest of the world. Especially did God's laws regarding ceremonial cleanness serve the latter purpose.—Lev. 11:44; Gal. 3:19-25.

6 As a new nation journeying toward a new land, Israel needed proper direction. It was still less than a year from the exodus, and the living standards of Egypt as well as its religious practices were fresh in mind. Marriage of brother and sister was common in Egypt. False worship was carried on in honor of many gods, some of them animal gods. Now this large congregation was on its way to Canaan, where life and religious practices were equally degrading. But look again at the encampment of Israel. Swelling the congregation were many pure or part Egyptians, a mixed multitude living right in among the Israelites and who had been born of Egyptian parents, raised and schooled in the ways, religion and patriotism of the Egyptians. Many of these had undoubtedly indulged in detestable practices in their homeland only a short time before. How necessary that they now receive detailed guidance from Jehovah!

7 Leviticus bears the stamp of divine inspiration throughout. Mere humans could not have devised its wise and just laws and regulations. Its statutes regarding diet, diseases and treatment of dead bodies were written thousands of years before medical men discovered the connection between microorganisms and disease. The Jewish priests appear to have been the first to practice quarantining the sick. God's law regarding animals unclean for eating would protect them while they traveled. It would safeguard them against trichinosis from pigs, tularemia from rabbits, psittacosis from parrots, tapeworms from fish, germ infection or parasites from animals found already dead, and septicemia and parasites from blood. The laws concerning dead animals would protect them against bubonic plague, spotted fever or typhus fever and against water contamination, typhoid fever and cholera. These practical laws were to direct their religion and their lives, that they might remain a holy nation and reach and inhabit the promised land of milk and honey. History shows that the regulations provided by Jehovah gave the Jews a definite advantage over other peoples in the matter of health.

8 The fulfillment of the prophecies and types in Leviticus further proves its inspiration. Both sacred and profane history record the fulfillment of the Leviticus warnings about the consequences of disobedience. Among other things, it foretold that mothers would eat their own children because of famine. Jeremiah indicates that this was fulfilled at the destruction of Jerusalem in 607 B.C.E., and Josephus tells of its happening at the city's later destruction, A.D. 70. The prophetic promise that Jehovah would remember them if they repented found its fulfillment in their return from Babylon in 537 B.C.E. (Lev. 26:29, 41-45; Lam. 2:20; 4:10; Ezra 1:1-6) Further testifying to the inspiration of Leviticus are quotations other Bible writers make from it as inspired Scripture. In addition to those previously noted in establishing Moses as the writer, please see Matthew 5:38, 43; 12:4; 2 Corinthians 6:16 and 1 Peter 1:16.

9 The book of Leviticus consistently magnifies Jehovah's name and sovereignty. No less than thirty-six times its laws are credited to Jehovah. The name "Jehovah" itself appears, on an average, ten times in each chapter, and time and again obedience to God's laws is inculcated by the reminder, "I am Jehovah." A theme of *holiness* runs throughout Leviticus, which mentions this requirement more often than any other Bible book. The Israelites were to be holy because Jehovah is holy. There were also varying degrees of holiness or separateness to Jehovah as regards persons, places and times. For example, certain days and years were more holy than other days and years, with the day of atonement and the Jubilee year being the holiest.

10 In line with its emphasis on holiness, the book of Leviticus stresses the part that the shedding of blood, that is, the sacrifice of a

5. What purpose was served by the laws concerning sacrifices and ceremonial uncleanness?
6. Why was detailed guidance from Jehovah now a special need?
7. In what way do the regulations of Leviticus bear the stamp of divine authorship?
8. How do the prophetic contents of the book further prove inspiration?
9. How does the book magnify Jehovah's name and holiness?
10. What is stressed in connection with sacrifices, and what penalties for sin are noted?

life, played in the forgiveness of sins. The animal sacrifices were limited to creatures that were both domestic and clean. For certain sins confession, restoration and the payment of a penalty were required in addition to a sacrifice. For still other sins the penalty was death.

CONTENTS OF LEVITICUS

11 Leviticus consists mostly of legislative writing, much of which is also prophetic. In the main the book follows a topical outline, and may be divided into eight sections, which follow one another quite logically.

12 **Regulations for sacrifices** (1:1–7:38). The various sacrifices fall into two general categories: *blood,* consisting of cattle, sheep, goats and fowl; and *bloodless,* consisting of grain. The *blood* sacrifices are to be offered as either (1) burnt, (2) communion, (3) sin or (4) guilt offerings. All four have these three things in common: the offerer must bring it himself to the entrance of the tent of meeting, he must lay his hands upon it, and then the animal is to be slaughtered. Following the sprinkling of the blood, the carcass must be disposed of according to the kind of sacrifice. Let us now consider the *blood* sacrifices in turn.

13 (1) Burnt offerings may consist of a young bull, ram, goat, turtledove or male pigeon, depending upon the means of the offerer. It is to be cut in pieces and, except for the skin, is to be burned in its entirety upon the altar. In the case of a turtledove or a pigeon the head must be nipped off but not severed and the crop and feathers must be removed.—1:1-17; 6:8-13; 5:8.

14 (2) The communion sacrifice may be either a male or a female, of the cattle or of the flocks. Only its fatty parts will be consumed upon the altar, a certain portion going to the priest and the rest being eaten by the offerer. It is well termed a communion sacrifice, for by it the offerer shares a meal or has communion, as it were, with Jehovah and with his priest.—3:1-17; 7:11-36.

15 (3) A sin offering is required for unintentional sins, or sins by mistake. The type of animal offered depends upon whose sin is being atoned for—that of the priest, the people as a whole, a chieftain or an ordinary person. Unlike the voluntary burnt and communion offerings for individuals, the sin and guilt offerings are mandatory.—4:1-35; 6:24-30.

16 (4) Guilt offerings are required to cover personal guilt due to unfaithfulness, deception or robbery. In some instances guilt requires confession and a sacrifice according to one's means. In others, compensation equivalent to the loss plus 20 percent and the sacrifice of a ram is required. In this section of Leviticus dealing with the offerings, the eating of blood is emphatically and repeatedly forbidden.—5:1–6:7; 7:1-7, 26, 27; 3:17.

17 The *bloodless* sacrifices are to consist of grain and to be offered either whole roasted, coarse ground or as fine flour, prepared in various ways, such as baked, done on a griddle or fried in deep fat, and to be offered with salt and oil and at times with frankincense, but they must be wholly free of leaven or honey. With some sacrifices a portion will belong to the priest.—2:1-16.

18 **Installation of the priesthood** (8:1–10:20). The time now comes for a great occasion in Israel, the installation of the priesthood. Moses handles it in all its detail, just as Jehovah commanded him. "And Aaron and his sons proceeded to do all the things that Jehovah had commanded by means of Moses." (8:36) After the seven days occupied with the installation, there comes a miraculous and faith-strengthening spectacle. The whole assembly is present. The priests have just offered up sacrifice. Aaron and Moses have blessed the people. Then, look! "Jehovah's glory appeared to all the people, and fire came out from before Jehovah and began consuming the burnt offering and the fatty pieces upon the altar. When all the people got to see it, they broke out into shouting and went falling upon their faces." (9:23, 24) Indeed, Jehovah is worthy of their obedience and worship!

19 Yet there are transgressions of the Law. For example, Aaron's sons Nadab and Abihu offer illegitimate fire before Jehovah. "At this a fire came out from before Jehovah and consumed them, so that they died before Jehovah." (10:2) In order to offer acceptable sacrifice and enjoy Jehovah's approval, people and priest alike must follow Jehovah's instructions. Right after this, God gives the command that priests must not drink alcoholic beverages while serving at the tabernacle, implying that Aaron's two sons may have sinned because of being under the influence of liquor.

20 **Laws on cleanness** (11:1–15:33). This section deals with ceremonial and hygienic cleanness. Certain animals, both domestic and wild, are unclean. All dead bodies are unclean and

11. How may the book be outlined?
12. What kinds of blood sacrifices are there, and how must they be offered?
13-16. (a) Outline the requirements for (1) burnt offerings, (2) communion sacrifices, (3) sin offerings and (4) guilt offerings. (b) In this section of Leviticus, what is repeatedly forbidden?
17. How are bloodless sacrifices to be offered?
18. With what faith-strengthening spectacle is the installation of the priesthood climaxed?
19. What transgression takes place, to be followed by what?
20, 21. What regulations cover cleanliness and proper hygiene?

cause those who touch them to become unclean. The birth of a child, which involves spilling of blood, also brings uncleanness and requires separation and special sacrifices.

21 Certain skin diseases, such as Hansen's disease, anciently called leprosy, also cause ceremonial uncleanness, and cleansing is to apply, not only to persons, but even to clothing and houses. Quarantining is required. Menstruation and seminal emissions likewise result in uncleanness, as do running sores, such as those of venereal diseases. Separateness is required in these cases and, on recovery, the washing of the body or offering of sacrifices or both.

22 **Day of atonement** (16:1-34). This is an outstanding chapter, for it contains the instructions for Israel's most important day, the day of atonement, which falls on the tenth day of the seventh month. It is a day to afflict the soul (most likely by fasting) and on it no secular work will be permitted. It begins with the offering of a young bull for the sins of Aaron and his household, the tribe of Levi, followed by the offering of a goat for the rest of the nation. After the burning of incense some of the blood of each is to be brought, in turn, into the Most Holy of the tabernacle, to be sprinkled before the Ark's cover. Later the animal carcasses must be taken outside the camp and burned. On this day also a live goat is to be presented before Jehovah, and upon it all the sins of the people are to be pronounced, after which it is to be led off into the wilderness. Then two rams must be offered as burnt offerings, one for Aaron and his household and the other for the rest of the nation.

23 **Statutes on blood and other matters** (17:1–20:27). This section sets out many statutes for the people. Once again blood is prohibited in the most explicit statement on blood to be found anywhere in the Scriptures. (17:10-14) It may properly be used on the altar, but not for eating. Detestable practices such as incest, sodomy and bestiality are forbidden. There are regulations for the protection of the afflicted, the lowly and the alien, and the command, "You must love your fellow as yourself. I am Jehovah." (19:18) The social and economic well-being of the nation is guarded, and spiritual dangers, such as the worship of Molech and spiritism, are outlawed with death as the penalty. Again God emphasizes separateness for his people: "And you must prove yourselves holy to me, because I Jehovah am holy; and I am proceeding to divide you off from the peoples to become mine."—20:26.

22. (a) Why is chapter 16 outstanding? (b) What is the atonement day procedure?
23. (a) Where do we find the Bible's most explicit statement on blood? (b) What other regulations follow?

24 **The priesthood and festivals** (21:1–25:55). The next three chapters deal chiefly with Israel's formal worship: the statutes governing the priests, their physical qualifications, whom they may marry, who may eat holy things, and the requirements for sound animals to be used in sacrifices. Three national seasonal feasts are commanded, providing occasions to "rejoice before Jehovah your God." (23:40) As one man the nation thus will turn attention, praise and worship to Jehovah, strengthening its relationship with him. These are feasts to Jehovah, annual holy conventions. The passover, along with the festival of unfermented cakes, is set for early spring, Pentecost or the festival of weeks to follow in the late spring, and the atonement day and eight-day festival of booths or ingathering in the fall.

25 In chapter 24 instruction is given concerning the bread and oil to be used in the tabernacle service. There follows the incident in which Jehovah rules that anyone abusing "the Name"—yes, *the* Name Jehovah—must be stoned to death. He then states the law of punishment in kind, "eye for eye, tooth for tooth." In chapter 25 regulations are found regarding the seventh-year sabbath, or rest year, and the Jubilee every fiftieth year. In this year liberty must be proclaimed in all the land, and hereditary property sold or surrendered during the past forty-nine years must be restored. Laws protecting the rights of the poor and of slaves are given. In this section the number "seven" appears prominently—the seventh day, the seventh year, festivals of seven days, a period of seven weeks, and the Jubilee, to come after seven times seven years.

26 **Consequences of obedience and disobedience** (26:1-46). The book of Leviticus reaches its climax in this chapter. Jehovah here lists the rewards for obedience and the punishments for disobedience. At the same time he holds out hope for the Israelites if they humble themselves, saying: "I will remember in their behalf the covenant of the ancestors whom I brought forth out of the land of Egypt under the eyes of the nations, in order to prove myself their God. I am Jehovah."—26:45.

27 **Miscellaneous statutes** (27:1-34). Leviticus concludes with instructions on handling vow offerings, on the firstborn for Jehovah and on the tenth part that becomes holy to Jehovah. Then comes the brief colophon: "These are the commandments that Jehovah gave Moses as commands to the sons of Israel in Mount Sinai."

24. What does Leviticus outline as to priestly qualifications and seasonal feasts?
25. (a) How is it shown that "the Name" must be held in honor? (b) What regulations involve the number "seven"?
26. In what does the book reach its climax?
27. How does the book conclude?

WHY BENEFICIAL

28 As a part of the inspired Scriptures, the book of Leviticus is of great benefit to Christians today. It is of wonderful help in appreciating Jehovah, his attributes and his ways of dealing with his creatures, as he so clearly demonstrated with Israel under the law covenant. Leviticus states many basic principles that will always apply, and contains many prophetic patterns, as well as prophecies, that are faith-strengthening to consider. Many of its principles are restated in the Christian Greek Scriptures, some of them being directly quoted. Seven outstanding points are discussed below.

29 (1) *Jehovah's sovereignty.* He is the Lawgiver, and we as his creatures are accountable to him. Rightly he commands us to be in fear of him. As the Universal Sovereign he brooks no rivalry, be that in the form of idolatry, spiritism or other forms of demonism.—Lev. 18:4; 25:17; 26:1; Matt. 10:28.

30 (2) *Jehovah's name.* His name is to be kept holy, and we dare not bring reproach upon it by words or by actions.—Lev. 22:32; 24:10-16; Matt. 6:9.

31 (3) *Jehovah's holiness.* Because he is holy, his people must also be holy, that is, sanctified or set apart for his service. This includes keeping separate from the godless world around us. —Lev. 11:44; 20:26; Jas. 1:27; 1 Pet. 1:15, 16.

32 (4) *The exceeding sinfulness of sin.* It is God who determines what is sin, and we must strive against it. Sin always requires an atoning sacrifice. In addition, it also requires of us confession, repentance and making amends to the extent possible. For certain sins there can be no forgiveness.—Lev. 4:2; 5:5; 20:2, 10; 1 John 1:9; Heb. 10:26-29.

33 (5) *The sanctity of blood.* Because blood is sacred, it may not be taken in any form. The only use permitted for blood is as an atonement for sin.—Lev. 17:10-14; Acts 15:29; Heb. 9:22.

34 (6) *Relativity in guilt and punishment.* Not all sins and sinners were considered in the same light. The higher the office, the greater the responsibility and penalty for sin. Willful sin was punished more severely than unintentional sin. Penalties were often graded according to ability to pay. This principle of relativity also applied in fields other than sin and punishment, such as in ceremonial uncleanness.—Lev. 4:3, 22-28; 5:7-11; 6:2-7; 12:8; 21:1-15; Luke 12: 47, 48; Jas. 3:1.

35 (7) *Justice and love.* Summing up our duties toward our fellowman, Leviticus 19:18 says: "You must love your fellow as yourself." This takes in everything: It precludes showing partiality, stealing, lying, slandering, and it requires showing consideration to the handicapped, the poor, the blind and the deaf.—Lev. 19:9-18; Rom. 13:8-13.

36 Also proving that Leviticus is outstandingly "beneficial for teaching, for reproving, for setting things straight, for disciplining in righteousness" in the Christian congregation, are the repeated references made to it by Jesus and his apostles, notably Paul and Peter. These called attention to the many prophetic patterns and shadows of things to come. As Paul noted, "the Law has a shadow of the good things to come." It sets forth "a typical representation and a shadow of the heavenly things." —Heb. 10:1; 8:5.

37 The tabernacle, the priesthood and the sacrifices all had typical significance, especially in connection with the annual atonement day. Paul, in his letter to the Hebrews, helps us to identify the spiritual counterparts of these things in relation to the "true tent" of Jehovah's worship. (Heb. 8:2) Chief priest Aaron typifies Christ Jesus "as a high priest of the good things that have come to pass through the greater and more perfect tent." (Heb. 9:11; Lev. 21:10) The blood of the animal sacrifices foreshadows the blood of Jesus, which obtains "everlasting deliverance for us." (Heb. 9:12) The innermost compartment of the tabernacle, the Most Holy, into which the high priest entered once a year on atonement day to present the sacrificial blood, is a "copy of the reality," "heaven itself," to which Jesus ascended "to appear before the person of God for us."—Heb. 9:24; Lev. 16:14, 15.

38 The actual sacrificial victims, sound, unblemished animals offered as burnt or sin offerings, represent the perfect unblemished sacrifice of the human body of Jesus Christ. (Heb. 9:13, 14; 10:1-10; Lev. 1:3) Paul also interestingly discusses the feature of the atonement day where the carcasses of animals for the sin offering were taken outside the camp and burned there. (Lev. 16:27) "Hence Jesus also," writes Paul, "suffered outside the gate. Let us, then, go forth to him outside the camp, bearing the reproach he bore." (Heb. 13:12, 13) By such inspired interpretation, the ceremonial procedures outlined in Leviticus take on added significance, and we can indeed begin to compre-

---

28. Of what benefit is the book to Christians today?
29-31. How does Leviticus emphasize respect for Jehovah's (a) sovereignty, (b) name, and (c) holiness?
32-34. What principles are outlined as to (a) sin, (b) blood, and (c) relative guilt?
35. How does Leviticus sum up our duties toward our fellowman?
36. What further proves the book to be beneficial for the Christian congregation?
37. What fulfillments of types are described in Hebrews?
38. How were the typical sacrifices fulfilled in Jesus?

hend how marvelously Jehovah there made awesome shadows pointing forward to realities that could be made plain only by the holy spirit. (Heb. 9:8) Such proper understanding is vital for those who are to benefit by the provision for life that Jehovah makes through Christ Jesus, the "great priest over the house of God."—Heb. 10:19-25.

39 Like Aaron's priestly "household," Jesus Christ as high priest has associated with him underpriests. These are spoken of as "a royal priesthood." (1 Pet. 2:9) Leviticus clearly points to and explains the sin-atoning work of Jehovah's great High Priest and King and the requirements laid upon the members of his "household," who are spoken of as "happy and holy," and as being 'priests of God and of the Christ, and ruling as kings with him for the thousand years.' What blessings that priestly work will accomplish in lifting obedient mankind up to perfection, and what happiness that heavenly kingdom will bring by restoring peace and righteousness to the earth! Surely, we must all thank the holy God, Jehovah, for his arrangement of a High Priest and King, and of a royal priesthood to declare abroad his excellencies in sanctification of his name! Truly, Leviticus blends in wonderfully with "all Scripture" in making known Jehovah's Kingdom purposes.—Rev. 20:6.

39. How does Leviticus blend in with "all Scripture" in making known Jehovah's Kingdom purposes?

Bible Book Number Four— Numbers

Writer: Moses
Place Written: Plains of Moab
Writing Completed: 1473 B.C.E.
Time Covered: 1512-1473 B.C.E.

THE events of the Israelites' wilderness trek have been recorded in the Bible for our benefit today. As the apostle Paul said: "Now these things became our examples, for us not to be persons desiring injurious things." (1 Cor. 10:6) The vivid record in Numbers impresses upon us that survival depends on sanctifying Jehovah's name, obeying him under all circumstances and showing respect for his representatives. His favor does not come because of any goodness or merit in his people, but out of his great mercy and undeserved kindness.

2 The name "Numbers" has reference to the numbering of the people that took place first at Mount Sinai and later on the plains of Moab, as recorded in chapters 1-4 and 26. This name has been carried over from the title *Nu'me·ri* in the Latin *Vulgate* and is derived from *A·rith·moi'* in the Greek *Septuagint.* However, the Jews more fittingly call the book *B^emid·bar',* which means "In the wilderness." The Hebrew word *mid·bar* indicates an open place, empty of cities and towns. It was in the wilderness to the south and to the east of Canaan that the events of Numbers took place.

3 Originally, Numbers was part of the fivefold volume including the books from Genesis to Deuteronomy. Its first verse opens with the conjunction "And," tying it in with what went before. Thus, it must have been written by Moses, the writer of the preceding records. This is also clear from the statement in the book that "Moses kept recording," and by the colophon, "These are the commandments and the judicial decisions that Jehovah commanded by means of Moses."—33:2; 36:13.

4 The Israelites had departed from Egypt a little more than a year previously. Taking up the account in the second month of the second year after the exodus, Numbers covers the next thirty-eight years and nine months, from 1512 to 1473 B.C.E. (Num. 1:1; Deut. 1:3) Though not fitting into this time period, the events related in chapters 7 and 9:1-15 are included as background information. The earlier portions of the book were no doubt written as the events occurred, but it is evident that Moses could not have completed Numbers until toward the end of the fortieth year in the wilderness, early in the calendar year 1473 B.C.E.

5 Of the authenticity of the account there can be no doubt. Mount Sinai, from which Israel began its journey northward toward the Promised Land, is still there, rising to an imposing 7,363 feet. Of the generally arid land in which they journeyed after leaving Sinai, Moses said that it was a "great and fear-inspiring wilderness," and it is true even today that the scat-

1. Why were the events of Numbers recorded, and what do they impress on us?
2. To what does the name "Numbers" refer, but what more fitting title did the Jews give to the book?
3. What proves Moses' writership?
4. What period of time is covered, and when was the book completed?
5. What features testify to the book's authenticity?

tered inhabitants are constantly on the move in search of pastures and water. (Deut. 1:19) Furthermore, the detailed instructions concerning encampment of the nation, the order of march and the trumpet signals to govern camp affairs, testify that the account was indeed written "in the wilderness."

6 Even the fearful report of the spies when they returned from their expedition into Canaan, to the effect that "the fortified cities are very great," is borne out by archaeological testimony. (Num. 13:28) Modern-day discoveries have shown that the inhabitants of Canaan at that time had consolidated their hold by a series of forts stretching across country in several places, from the plain of Esdraelon in the north to Gerar in the south. Not only were the cities fortified, but they were usually built on the tops of hills, with towers rising above their walls, making them most impressive to people like the Israelites, who had lived for generations in the flat land of Egypt.

7 Nations of the world are prone to whitewash their failures and magnify their conquests, but, with an honesty that bespeaks historical truth, the Numbers account tells that Israel was completely routed by the Amalekites and the Canaanites. (14:45) It straightforwardly confesses that the people proved faithless and treated God without respect. (14:11) With remarkable candor, God's prophet Moses exposes the sins of the nation, of his nephews and of his own brother and sister. Nor does he spare himself, for he tells of the time that he failed to sanctify Jehovah when water was provided at Meribah, so that he forfeited the privilege of entering the Promised Land.—3:4; 12:1-15; 20:7-13.

8 That the account is a genuine part of the Scriptures that are inspired by God and beneficial is borne out by the fact that nearly all its major events, as well as many other details, are directly referred to by other Bible writers, many of whom highlight their significance. For example, Joshua (4:12; 14:2), Jeremiah (2 Ki. 18:4), Nehemiah (9:19-22), Asaph (Ps. 78:14-41), David (Ps. 95:7-11), Isaiah (48:21), Ezekiel (20:13-24), Hosea (9:10), Amos (5:25), Micah (6:5), Luke in his record of Stephen's discourse (Acts 7:36), Paul (1 Cor. 10:1-11), Peter (2 Pet. 2:15, 16), Jude (verse 11) and John in recording Jesus' words to the Pergamum congregation (Rev. 2:14), all draw on the record in Numbers, as did Jesus Christ himself.—John 3:14.

9 What purpose, then, does Numbers serve? Truly its account is of more than historical value. Numbers emphasizes that Jehovah is the God of order, requiring exclusive devotion of his creatures. This is vividly impressed on the reader's mind as he observes the numbering, testing and sifting of Israel, and sees how the nation's disobedient and rebellious course is used to emphasize the vital need of obeying Jehovah.

10 The record was preserved for the benefit of the generations to come, just as Asaph explained, "that they might set their confidence in God himself and not forget the practices of God but observe his own commandments," and that "they should not become like their forefathers, a generation stubborn and rebellious, a generation who had not prepared their heart and whose spirit was not trustworthy with God." (Ps. 78:7, 8) Over and over again the events of Numbers were recounted in the Psalms, which were sacred songs among the Jews, and so were often repeated as being beneficial to the nation.—Psalms 78, 95, 105, 106, 135, 136.

CONTENTS OF NUMBERS

11 Numbers logically falls into three parts. The first of these, concluding at chapter 10, verse 10, covers events taking place while the Israelites were still encamped at Mount Sinai. The next part, concluding with chapter 21, tells what happened during the next thirty-eight years and a month or two more, while they were in the wilderness and until they arrived at the plains of Moab. The final part, through chapter 36, is concerned with events on the plains of Moab, as the Israelites prepared for their entry into the Promised Land.

12 **Events at Mount Sinai** (1:1–10:10). The Israelites have already been in the mountainous region of Sinai for about a year. Here they have been molded into a closely knit organization. At Jehovah's command a census is now taken of all the men twenty years old and upward. The tribes are found to range in size from 32,200 able-bodied men in Manasseh up to 74,600 in Judah, making a total of 603,550 men qualified to serve in the army of Israel, besides the women and children—a camp probably numbering two million or more. The tent of meeting is situated, along with the Levites, in the center of the camp. In assigned places on each side are camped the other Israelites, in three-tribe divisions, each tribe having instructions as to the order of march when the camp is to move. Jehovah issues the instructions,

6. How do archaeological finds support the record?
7. What stamp of honesty does the record bear?
8. How do other Bible writers testify to the inspiration of Numbers?
9. What does the book emphasize concerning Jehovah?
10. For whose benefit was the record preserved, and why?
11. Into what three parts may the contents of the book be divided?
12. How large is the Israelite encampment at Sinai, and how is the camp organized?

and the record says: "The sons of Israel proceeded to do according to all that Jehovah had commanded Moses." (2:34) They obey Jehovah and show respect for Moses, God's visible representative.

13 The Levites are then set apart for Jehovah's service, as a ransom for the firstborn of Israel. They are divided into three groups, according to their descent from the three sons of Levi: Gershon, Kohath and Merari. Locations in the camp and service responsibilities are determined on the basis of this division. From thirty years of age on, they are to do the heavy work of transporting the tabernacle. To get the lighter work done, provision is made for others to serve starting at twenty-five years of age. (Reduced in David's time to twenty years of age.)—1 Chron. 23:24-32; Ezra 3:8.

14 That the camp may be kept pure, instructions are given for quarantining those who become diseased, for making atonement for acts of unfaithfulness, for resolving cases in which a man might become suspicious of the conduct of his wife, and for assuring right conduct on the part of those set apart by vow to live as Nazirites to Jehovah. Since the people are to have the name of their God upon them, they must deport themselves in accord with his commandments.

15 Filling in some details from the previous month (Num. 7:1, 10; Ex. 40:17), Moses next tells of the contributions of materials made by the twelve chieftains of the people over a period of twelve days from the time of the inauguration of the altar. There was no competition or seeking of self-glory in it; each one contributed exactly what the others did. All must now keep in mind that over these chieftains, and over Moses himself, there is Jehovah God, who speaks instructions to Moses. They must never forget their relationship to Jehovah. The passover is to remind them of Jehovah's wondrous deliverance from Egypt, and they celebrate it here in the wilderness at the appointed time, one year after leaving Egypt.

16 In the same way that he had directed Israel's movement out of Egypt, Jehovah continues to lead the nation in its travels by a cloud that covers the tent of the Testimony by day, and by the appearance of fire there by night. When the cloud moves, they move. When the cloud remains over the tabernacle, they remain encamped, whether for a few days or a month or longer, for the account tells us: "At the order of Jehovah they would encamp, and at the order of Jehovah they would pull away. They kept their obligation to Jehovah at the order of Jehovah by means of Moses." (Num. 9:23) As the time for departure from Sinai draws near, trumpet signals are arranged both to assemble the people and to direct the various divisions of the encampment on their wilderness trek.

17 **Events in the wilderness** (10:11–21:35). At last, on the twentieth day of the second month, Jehovah lifts the cloud from over the tabernacle, thus signaling Israel's departure from the region of Sinai. With the ark of Jehovah's covenant in their midst, they set out for Kadesh-barnea, 150 air miles to the north. As they march by day, Jehovah's cloud is over them. Each time the Ark goes out, Moses prays to Jehovah to arise and scatter his enemies, and each time it comes to rest he prays Jehovah to return "to the myriads of thousands of Israel."—10:36.

18 However, trouble arises in the camp. On the trip north to Kadesh-barnea there are at least three occasions of complaining. To quell the first outbreak, Jehovah sends a fire to consume some of them. Then the "mixed crowd" sets Israel to bemoaning that they no longer have as food the fish, cucumbers, watermelons, leeks, onions and garlic of Egypt, but only manna. Moses becomes so distressed that he asks Jehovah to kill him off rather than let him continue as male nurse to all this people. Considerately, Jehovah takes away some of the spirit from Moses and puts it upon seventy of the elder men, who proceed to assist Moses as prophets in the camp. Then meat comes in abundance. As had happened once before, a wind from Jehovah drives in quails from the sea, and the people greedily seize great supplies, selfishly hoarding them. Jehovah's anger blazes against them, striking down many because of their selfish craving.—Ex. 16:2, 3, 13.

19 The troubles continue. Failing properly to view their younger brother Moses as Jehovah's representative, Miriam and Aaron find fault with him over his wife, who has recently come into the camp. They demand more authority, comparable to that of Moses, though "the man Moses was by far the meekest of all the men who were upon the surface of the ground." (Num. 12:3) Jehovah himself sets the matter straight, letting it be known that Moses occupies a special position, and striking Miriam, the apparent instigator of the complaint, with lep-

13. According to what arrangement are the Levites assigned to service?
14. What instructions are given to ensure the purity of the camp?
15. (a) In connection with the inauguration of the altar, what contributions were made? (b) What relationship must Israel remember, and of what is the passover to remind them?
16. How does Jehovah lead the nation, and what trumpet signals are arranged?
17. Describe the procedure of march.
18. What complaining breaks out on the way to Kadesh-barnea, and how does Jehovah adjust theocratic procedure in the camp?
19. How does Jehovah deal with the faultfinding of Miriam and Aaron?

rosy. Only by Moses' intercession is she later healed.

[20] Arriving at Kadesh, Israel camps at the threshold of the Promised Land. Jehovah now instructs Moses to send spies to scout out the land. Entering from the south, they travel north clear to "the entering in of Hamath," walking five hundred or more miles in forty days. (13:21) When they return with some of the rich fruitage of Canaan, ten of the spies faithlessly argue that it would be foolish to go up against so strong a people and such great fortified cities. Caleb tries to quiet the assembly with a favorable report, but without success. The rebellious spies strike fear into the Israelites' hearts, claiming the land to be one that "eats up its inhabitants" and saying, "All the people whom we saw in the midst of it are men of extraordinary size." As murmurings of rebellion sweep through the camp, Joshua and Caleb plead, "Jehovah is with us. Do not fear them." (13:32; 14:9) However, the assembly begins to talk of pelting them with stones.

[21] Then Jehovah intervenes directly, saying to Moses: "How long will this people treat me without respect, and how long will they not put faith in me for all the signs that I performed in among them?" (14:11) Moses implores him not to destroy the nation, as Jehovah's name and fame are involved. Jehovah therefore decrees that Israel must continue to wander in the wilderness until all those registered among the people, from twenty years old and up, have died off. Only Caleb and Joshua will be permitted to enter the Land of Promise. In vain the people try to go up on their own initiative, only to suffer a terrible defeat meted out by the Amalekites and Canaanites. What a high price the people pay for their disrespect of Jehovah and his loyal representatives!

[22] Truly, they have much to learn in the way of obedience. Fittingly, Jehovah gives them further laws highlighting this need. He lets them know that, when they come into the Promised Land, atonement must be made for mistakes, but the deliberately disobedient must be cut off without fail. Thus, when a man is found gathering wood in violation of the sabbath law, Jehovah commands: "Without fail the man should be put to death." (15:35) As a reminder of the commandments of Jehovah and the importance of obeying them, Jehovah instructs that they wear fringes on the skirts of their garments.

[23] Nevertheless, rebellion breaks out again. Korah, Dathan, Abiram and two hundred and fifty prominent men of the assembly gather in opposition to the authority of Moses and Aaron. Moses puts the issue to Jehovah, saying to the rebels, 'Take fire holders and incense and present them before Jehovah, and let him choose.' (16:46) Jehovah's glory now appears to all the assembly. Swiftly he executes judgment, causing the earth to split apart to swallow up the households of Korah, Dathan and Abiram, and sending out a fire to consume the two hundred and fifty men, including Korah, offering the incense. The very next day the people begin to condemn Moses and Aaron for what Jehovah did, and again He scourges them, wiping out fourteen thousand seven hundred complainers.

[24] In view of these events, Jehovah commands that each tribe present a rod before him, including a rod with Aaron's name for the tribe of Levi. The next day Aaron is shown to be Jehovah's choice for the priesthood, for his rod alone is found to be in full bloom and bearing ripe almonds. It is to be preserved in the ark of the covenant "for a sign to the sons of rebelliousness." (Num. 17:10; Heb. 9:4) After further instructions for the support of the priesthood by means of tithes and concerning the use of cleansing water with the ashes of a red cow, the account returns us to Kadesh. Here Miriam dies and is buried.

[25] Again at the threshold of the Land of Promise the assembly gets to quarreling with Moses because of the lack of water. Jehovah counts it as quarreling with Him, and appears in his glory, commanding Moses to take the rod and bring out water from the crag. Do Moses and Aaron now sanctify Jehovah? Instead, Moses twice strikes the crag in anger. The people and their livestock get water to drink, but Moses and Aaron fail to give the credit to Jehovah. Though the heartbreaking wilderness journey is almost over, they both incur Jehovah's displeasure and are told they will not enter the Land of Promise. Aaron dies on Mount Hor and his son Eleazar takes over the duties of high priest.

[26] Israel turns to the east and seeks to go through the land of Edom, but is rebuffed. While making a long detour around Edom, the people get into trouble again as they complain against God and Moses. They are tired of the manna and they are thirsty. Because of their rebelliousness Jehovah sends poisonous serpents among them, so that many die. At last, when Moses intercedes, Jehovah instructs him to make a fiery copper serpent and place it on a signal pole. Those who have been bitten but

20, 21. What events give rise to Jehovah's decree that Israel must wander forty years in the wilderness?
22. In what ways is the importance of obedience emphasized?
23. What is the outcome of the rebellion of Korah, Dathan and Abiram?
24. What sign does Jehovah perform to end this rebelliousness?
25. How do Moses and Aaron fail to sanctify Jehovah, and with what result?
26. What events mark the detour around Edom?

who gaze at the copper serpent are spared alive. Heading north, the Israelites are impeded, in turn, by the belligerent kings Sihon of the Amorites and Og of Bashan. Both of these they defeat in battle, and Israel occupies their territories to the east of the Rift Valley.

27 **Events on the plains of Moab** (22:1–36:13). In eager anticipation of their entry into Canaan, the Israelites now gather on the desert plains of Moab, north of the Dead Sea and to the east of the Jordan across from Jericho, over 230 miles from Mount Sinai. Seeing this vast encampment spread out before them, the Moabites feel a sickening dread. Their king Balak, in consultation with the Midianites, sends for Balaam to use divination and put a curse on Israel. Although God directly tells Balaam, "You must not go with them," he wants to go. (22:12) He wants the reward. Finally he does go, only to be stopped by an angel and to have his own she-ass miraculously speak to rebuke him. When at last Balaam gets around to making pronouncements about Israel, God's spirit comes to be upon him, so that his four proverbial utterances prophesy only blessings for God's nation, even foretelling that a star would step forth out of Jacob and a scepter rise out of Israel to subdue and destroy.

28 Having infuriated Balak by his failure to curse Israel, Balaam now seeks the king's good graces by suggesting that the Moabites use their own females in enticing the men of Israel to share in the lewd rites involved in the worship of Baal. (31:15, 16) Here, right on the border of the Promised Land, the Israelites begin to fall away to gross immorality and the worship of false gods. As Jehovah's anger blazes forth in a scourge, Moses calls for drastic punishment of the wrongdoers. When Phinehas, son of the high priest, sees the son of a chieftain bring a Midianite woman into his tent right inside the camp, he goes after them and kills them, striking the woman through her genital parts. At this the scourge is halted, but not before twenty-four thousand die from it.

29 Jehovah now commands Moses and Eleazar to take a census of the people again, as had been done nearly thirty-nine years earlier at Mount Sinai. The final count shows that there has been no increase in their ranks. To the contrary, there are 1,820 fewer men registered. None remain that had been registered at Sinai for army service, except Joshua and Caleb. As Jehovah had indicated would happen, all of them had died in the wilderness. Jehovah next gives instructions concerning the division of the land as an inheritance. He repeats that Moses will not enter the Land of Promise because of the failure to sanctify Jehovah at the waters of Meribah. (20:13; 27:14, *NW* footnotes, 1953 Edition) Joshua is commissioned as successor to Moses.

30 Through Moses, Jehovah next reminds Israel of the importance of his laws concerning sacrifices and feasts and of the seriousness of vows. He also has Moses settle the account with the Midianites, because of their part in seducing Israel over Baal of Peor. All the Midianite males are slain in battle, along with Balaam, and only virgin girls are spared, 32,000 of these being taken captive along with plunder that includes 808,000 animals. Not one Israelite is reported missing in battle. The sons of Reuben and of Gad, who are stock raisers, request to settle in the territory east of Jordan, and, after they agree to help in conquering the Promised Land, the request is granted, so that these two tribes, together with half the tribe of Manasseh, are given this rich tableland as their possession.

31 After a review of the stopping places on the forty-year journey, the record again focuses attention on the need for obedience to Jehovah. God is giving them the land, but they must become His executioners, driving out the depraved, demon-worshiping inhabitants and destroying every last trace of their idolatrous religion. The detailed boundaries of their God-given land are stated. It is to be divided among them by lot. The Levites, who have no tribal inheritance, are to be given forty-eight cities with their pasture grounds, six of these to be cities of refuge for the unintentional manslayer. Territory must remain within the tribe, never being transferred to another tribe by marriage. If there is no male heir, then the daughters who receive an inheritance—for example, the daughters of Zelophehad—must marry within their own tribe. (27:1-11; 36:1-11) Numbers concludes with these commandments of Jehovah through Moses, and with the sons of Israel poised at last to enter the Land of Promise.

WHY BENEFICIAL

32 Jesus referred to Numbers on several occasions, and his apostles and other Bible writers clearly demonstrate how meaningful and beneficial is its record. The apostle Paul specifically compared Jesus' faithful service to that of

27. How does Jehovah overrule Balak's plans in connection with Balaam?
28. What subtle snare is brought on Israel at Balaam's suggestion, but how is the scourge halted?
29. (a) What is revealed by the census at the end of the fortieth year? (b) What preparation is now made for entry into the Promised Land?
30. How is the account with Midian settled, and what territory assignment is made east of Jordan?
31. (a) On entering the land, how must Israel continue to show obedience? (b) What instructions are given regarding tribal inheritances?
32. In what ways are Jesus and his sacrifice typified in Numbers?

Moses, which is largely recorded in Numbers. (Heb. 3:1-6) Also, in the animal sacrifices, and in the sprinkling of the ashes of the young red cow of Numbers 10:2-9, we again see pictured the far grander provision for cleansing through the sacrifice of Christ.—Heb. 9:13, 14.

33 Similarly, Paul showed that the bringing forth of water from the rock in the wilderness is full of meaning for us, saying: "They used to drink from the spiritual rock-mass that followed them, and that rock-mass meant the Christ." (1 Cor. 10:4; Num. 20:7-11) Fittingly, it was Christ himself who said: "Whoever drinks from the water that I will give him will never get thirsty at all, but the water that I will give him will become in him a fountain of water bubbling up to impart everlasting life." —John 4:14.

34 Jesus also made direct reference to an incident recorded in Numbers that foreshadowed the marvelous provision that God was making through him. "Just as Moses lifted up the serpent in the wilderness," he said, "so the Son of man must be lifted up, that everyone believing in him may have everlasting life."—John 3:14, 15; Num. 21:8, 9.

35 Why were the Israelites sentenced to wander forty years in the wilderness? For lack of faith, is the answer. The apostle Paul gave powerful admonition on this point: "Beware, brothers, for fear there should ever develop in any one of you a wicked heart lacking faith by drawing away from the living God; but keep on exhorting one another each day." Because of their disobedience, because of their faithlessness, those Israelites died in the wilderness. "Let us therefore do our utmost to enter into [God's] rest, for fear anyone should fall in the same pattern of disobedience." (Heb. 3:7–4:11; Num. 13:25–14:38) In warning against ungodly men who speak abusively of holy things, Jude referred to Balaam's greed for reward and to Korah's rebellious talk against Jehovah's servant Moses. (Jude 11; Num. 22:7, 8, 22; 26:9, 10) Balaam was also referred to by Peter as one "who loved the reward of wrongdoing," and by the glorified Jesus in his revelation through John as one who 'put before Israel a stumbling block of idolatry and fornication.' Certainly the Christian congregation today should be warned against such unholy ones. —2 Pet. 2:12-16; Rev. 2:14.

36 When immorality arose in the Corinthian congregation, Paul wrote them about "desiring injurious things," referring specifically to Numbers. He admonished: "Neither let us practice fornication, as some of them committed fornication, only to fall, twenty-three thousand of them in one day." (1 Cor. 10:6, 8; Num. 25:1-9; 31:16)[a] What about the occasion when the people complained that obeying God's commands entailed personal hardship and that they were dissatisfied with Jehovah's provision of the manna? Concerning this Paul says: "Neither let us put Jehovah to the test, as some of them put him to the test, only to perish by the serpents." (1 Cor. 10:9; Num. 21:5, 6) Then Paul continues: "Neither be murmurers, just as some of them murmured, only to perish by the destroyer." How bitter the experiences of Israel as a result of their murmuring against Jehovah, his representatives and his provisions! These things that *"went on* befalling them as examples" should stand forth as a clear warning to all of us today, so that we may *go on* serving Jehovah in the fullness of faith.—1 Cor. 10:10, 11; Num. 14:2, 36, 37; 16: 1-3, 41; 17:5, 10.

37 Numbers also provides the background against which many other Bible passages can be better understood.—Num. 28:9, 10—Matt. 12:5; Num. 15:38—Matt. 23:5; Num. 6:2-4—Luke 1:15; Num. 4:3—Luke 3:23; Num. 18:31 —1 Cor. 9:13, 14; Num. 18:26—Heb. 7:5-9; Num. 17:8-10—Heb. 9:4.

38 What is recorded in Numbers is indeed inspired of God, and it is beneficial in teaching us the importance of obedience to Jehovah and respect for those whom he has made overseers among his people. By example it reproves wrongdoing, and by happenings with prophetic import it directs our attention to the One whom Jehovah has provided as the Savior and Leader of his people today. It provides an essential and instructive link in the record leading to the establishment of Jehovah's righteous kingdom in the hands of his great Mediator and High Priest, Jesus Christ.

a See *The Watchtower,* 1952, page 223.

33. Why is the bringing forth of water in the wilderness of interest to us today?
34. How did Jesus show that the copper serpent had prophetic meaning?
35. (a) Of what should Christians beware, as illustrated by the Israelites in the wilderness, and why? (b) In their letters, to what examples of greed and rebellion did Jude and Peter refer?
36. Against what injurious practices did Paul warn, and how may we today benefit by his counsel?
37. Illustrate how Numbers helps us in understanding other Bible passages.
38. In what particular ways is the book of Numbers beneficial, and to what does it direct our attention?

Bible Book Number Five— Deuteronomy

Writer:	**Moses**
Place Written:	**Plains of Moab**
Writing Completed:	**1473 B.C.E.**
Time Covered:	**2 months (1473 B.C.E.)**

THE book of Deuteronomy contains a dynamic message for Jehovah's people. After wandering in the wilderness for forty years, the sons of Israel now stood on the threshold of the Land of Promise. What lay ahead of them? What were the peculiar problems that they would face on the other side of the Jordan? What would Moses finally have to say to the nation? Also we may ask, Why is it beneficial for us today to know the answers to these questions?

2 The answers are to be found in the words that Moses spoke, and which he recorded in the fifth book of the Bible, Deuteronomy. Though it reiterates much from the earlier books, Deuteronomy is important in its own outstanding way. Why so? It adds emphasis to the divine message, being provided at a time in the history of Jehovah's people when they really needed dynamic leadership and positive direction. They were about to enter the Promised Land under a new leader. They needed encouragement to go forward, and at the same time they needed divine warning to enable them to take the right course leading to Jehovah's blessing.

3 In accord with the need, Moses was moved mightily by Jehovah's spirit to make a forthright appeal to Israel to be obedient and faithful. Throughout the entire book he emphasizes that Jehovah is the Most High God, who exacts exclusive devotion, desires his people to 'love him with all their heart and all their soul and all their vital force.' He is "the God of gods and the Lord of lords, the God great, mighty and fear-inspiring, who treats none with partiality nor accepts a bribe." He tolerates no rivalry. To obey him means life, to disobey, death. Jehovah's instruction, as given in Deuteronomy, was just the preparation and counsel that Israel needed for the momentous tasks that lay ahead of them. It is also the kind of admonition we need today, so that we may keep walking in the fear of Jehovah, sanctifying his name in the midst of a corrupt world.—Deut. 10:12-22; 5:9, 10; 6:4-6.

4 The name "Deuteronomy" comes from th[e] title in the Greek *Septuagint* translation, *Deu·te·ro·no'mi·on,* which combines *deu'teros,* mean[-]ing "second," with *no'mos,* meaning "law." I[t] therefore means "Second Law." The Jewis[h] rabbis call it *Mish·neh' hat·To·rah',* which i[s] translated "Repetition (Duplicate or Double[)] of the Law." Often they simply refer to it a[s] *Mish·neh',* meaning "Repetition." It appear[s] that both the *Septuagint* translators and th[e] rabbis adopted this meaningful name from Deuteronomy 17:18, which instructs the futur[e] king in Israel to "write for himself this repe[-]tition of the law [Greek, *deu·te·ro·no'mi·on*] i[n] a book, from that which is in the custody o[f] the priests, the Levites." (*LXX*)[a] Later, i[n] Deuteronomy 27:1-8, Moses commanded th[e] Israelites to write "the words of this law" upon stones when they entered the Promise[d] Land. Which "law"? When Joshua carried ou[t] this command in Mount Ebal, he wrote "th[e] repetition of the law [Greek, *deu·te·ro·no'mi·on*] of Moses, in the presence of the childre[n] of Israel." (Josh. 8:32, *LXX*)[a] Fittingly, he use[d] the law in Deuteronomy, which was a revisio[n] of the law given at Mount Sinai, adapted t[o] the Israelites' new land and circumstances.

5 This being the fifth roll or volume of th[e] Pentateuch, the writer must have been th[e] same as for the preceding four books, namely, Moses. The opening statement identifies Deuteronomy as "the words that Moses spoke t[o] all Israel," and later expressions, such a[s] "Moses wrote this law" and "Moses wrote thi[s] song," clearly prove his writership. His name appears nearly forty times, usually as authority for the statements made. The first person, referring to Moses, is used predominantly throughout. The concluding chapter was added after Moses' death, most likely by Joshua or by Eleazar the high priest.—Deut. 1:1; 31:9, 22, 24-26.

6 When did the events of Deuteronomy take

a *LXX,* Thomson's translation; see also *NW* footnotes.

1. What questions may be asked in connection with Israel's entry into the Promised Land?
2. In what outstanding way is Deuteronomy important?
3. What does Moses emphasize throughout the book, and why is this important to us today?
4. What is the significance of the name "Deuteronomy," and how did Joshua make use of the book in obedience to Moses' command?
5. What proves Moses to have been the writer?
6. (a) What time period is covered? (b) By when was the book practically completed?

place? At the outset, the book itself states that "in the fortieth year, in the eleventh month, on the first of the month, Moses spoke to the sons of Israel." On completion of the record in Deuteronomy, the book of Joshua takes up the account three days before the crossing of the Jordan, which was "on the tenth of the first month." (Deut. 1:3; Josh. 1:11; 4:19) This leaves a period of two months and one week for the events of Deuteronomy. However, thirty days of this nine-week period were spent mourning the death of Moses. (Deut. 34:8) This means that practically all the events of Deuteronomy must have occurred in the eleventh month of the fortieth year. By the close of that month the writing of the book must also have been practically complete, with Moses' death coming early in the twelfth month of the fortieth year, or early in 1473 B.C.E.

7 The proofs already submitted for the authenticity of the other four books of the Pentateuch hold also for Deuteronomy, which is the fifth book thereof. It is also one of the four books in the Hebrew Scriptures most often cited in the Greek Scriptures, the others being Genesis, Psalms and Isaiah. There are eighty-three of these citations, and only six of the books in the Christian Greek Scriptures omit alluding to it.[a]

8 Jesus himself gives the strongest testimony in support of Deuteronomy. At the outset of his ministry he was three times tempted by the Devil, and three times he came back with the answer, "It is written." Written where? Why, in the book of Deuteronomy, which Jesus quoted (from 8:3; 6:16, 13) as his inspired authority: "Man must live, not on bread alone, but on every utterance coming forth through Jehovah's mouth." "You must not put Jehovah your God to the test." "It is Jehovah your God you must worship, and it is to him alone you must render sacred service." (Matt. 4:1-11) Later, when the Pharisees came testing him with regard to God's commandments, Jesus quoted in reply "the greatest and first commandment" from Deuteronomy 6:5. (Matt. 22: 37, 38; Mark 12:30; Luke 10:27) Jesus' testimony conclusively stamps Deuteronomy as authentic.

9 Moreover, the events and statements in the book fit exactly the historical situation and surroundings. The references to Egypt, Canaan, Amalek, Ammon, Moab and Edom are faithful to the times, and place-names are accurately stated.[b] Archaeology continues to bring proof upon proof to light as to the integrity of Moses' writings. Henry H. Halley writes: "Archaeology has been speaking so loudly of late that it is causing a decided reaction toward the conservative view [that Moses wrote the Pentateuch]. The theory that writing was unknown in Moses' day is absolutely exploded. And every year there are being dug up in Egypt, Palestine and Mesopotamia, evidences, both in inscriptions and earth layers, that the narratives of the [Hebrew Scriptures] are true historical records. And 'scholarship' is coming to have decidedly more respect for the tradition of Mosaic authorship."[c] Thus external evidence vindicates Deuteronomy, and all the Pentateuch, as being a genuine, authentic record made by God's prophet Moses.

CONTENTS OF DEUTERONOMY

10 The book is mainly composed of a series of discourses that Moses delivered to the sons of Israel on the plains of Moab opposite Jericho. The first of these concludes in chapter 4, the second runs to the end of chapter 26, the third continues through chapter 28, and another discourse extends to the end of chapter 30. Then, after Moses makes final arrangements in view of his approaching death, including the commissioning of Joshua as his successor, he records a most beautiful song to Jehovah's praise, followed by a blessing on the tribes of Israel.

11 **Moses' first discourse** (1:1–4:49). This provides a historical introduction to what follows. Moses first reviews Jehovah's faithful dealings with his people. He is telling them to go in and take possession of the land promised to their forefathers, Abraham, Isaac and Jacob. He recounts how Jehovah coordinated the activity of this theocratic community at the outset of the wilderness trek by having him, Moses, select wise, discreet and experienced men to act as chiefs of thousands, of hundreds, of fifties and of tens. There was splendid organization, watched over by Jehovah, as they "went marching through all that great and fear-inspiring wilderness."—1:19.

12 Moses now recalls their sin of rebellion when they heard the report of the spies returning from Canaan and complained that Jehovah hated them because, they charged, he had brought them up out of Egypt only to abandon them to the Amorites. For their lack of faith, Jehovah told that evil generation that none of them, except Caleb and Joshua, would see the good land. At this they again behaved

a *The Interpreter's Bible,* 1953, Vol. 2, page 311.
b Deut. 3:9, *NW* footnote, 1953 Edition.
c *Pocket Bible Handbook,* 1944, Henry H. Halley, page 47.

7. What shows the book to be authentic?
8. What conclusive testimony by Jesus bears out this authenticity?
9. What external evidences vindicate Deuteronomy?
10. Of what is Deuteronomy composed?
11. How does Moses introduce his first discourse?
12. What events surrounding the initial spying out of Canaan does he next recall?

rebelliously, getting all heated up and making their own independent assault on the enemy, only to have the Amorites chase them like a swarm of bees and scatter them.

13 They traveled in the wilderness down toward the Red Sea, and during thirty-eight years all the generation of the men of war died off. Jehovah then commanded them to cross over and take possession of the land north of the Arnon, saying: "This day I shall start to put the dread of you and the fear of you before the peoples beneath all the heavens, who will hear the report about you; and they will indeed be agitated and have pains like those of childbirth because of you." (2:25) Sihon and his land fell to the Israelites, and then Og's kingdom was occupied. Moses assured Joshua that Jehovah would fight for Israel in the same way in overcoming all the kingdoms. He then asked God if he himself might by any means pass over to the good land beyond Jordan, but Jehovah continued to refuse this, telling him to commission, encourage and strengthen Joshua.

14 Moses now lays great emphasis on God's law, warning against adding to or taking away from His commandments. Disobedience will bring disaster: "Only watch out for yourself and take good care of your soul, that you may not forget the things that your eyes have seen and that they may not depart from your heart all the days of your life; and you must make them known to your sons and to your grandsons." (4:9) They saw no form when Jehovah stated the Ten Words to them under fearsome circumstances in Horeb. It will be ruination to them if they now turn to idolatry and image worship, for, as Moses said, "Jehovah your God is a consuming fire, a God exacting exclusive devotion." (4:24) He it was who had loved their forefathers and chosen them. There is no other God in the heavens above or on the earth beneath. Obey Him, Moses exhorts, "that you may lengthen your days on the soil that Jehovah your God is giving you, always."—4:40.

15 After concluding this powerful speech, Moses proceeds to set apart Bezer, Ramoth and Golan as cities of refuge to the east of the Jordan.

16 **Moses' second discourse** (5:1–26:19). This is a call to Israel to hear Jehovah, who spoke with them face to face at Sinai. Note how Moses restates the Law with some necessary adjustments, thus adapting it for their new life across the Jordan. It is no mere recounting of regulations and ordinances. Every word shows that the heart of Moses is full of zeal and devotion to his God. He speaks for the welfare of the nation. Obedience to the law is stressed throughout—obedience from a loving heart, not by compulsion.

17 First, Moses repeats the Ten Words, the Ten Commandments, and tells Israel to obey them, not turning to the right or to the left, that they may lengthen their days in the land, and become very many. "Listen, O Israel: Jehovah our God is one Jehovah." (6:4) Heart, soul and vital force must be given to loving Him, and they must teach their sons and tell them of the great signs and miracles that Jehovah performed in Egypt. There are to be no marriage alliances with the idolatrous Canaanites. Jehovah has chosen them to become his special property, not because they are populous, but because he loves them and will keep his sworn statement to their forefathers. They must shun the snare of demon religion, destroy the images out of the land and hold to Jehovah, truly "a great and fear-inspiring God." —7:21.

18 Jehovah humbled them for forty years in the wilderness, teaching them that man lives, not by manna or bread, but by every expression of Jehovah's mouth. During all those years of correction their clothing did not wear out, nor did their feet become swollen. Now they are about to enter a land of wealth and plenty! However, they must watch against the snares of materialism and self-righteousness and remember that Jehovah is 'the giver of power to make wealth' and the dispossessor of the wicked nations. Moses then recounts occasions when Israel provoked God. Remember how Jehovah's anger blazed against them in the wilderness, with plague and fire and slaughter! Remember their ruinous worship of the golden calf, which resulted in Jehovah's hot anger and the remaking of the tablets of the Law! (Ex. 32:1-10, 35; 17:2-7; Num. 11:1-3, 31-35; 14:2-38) Surely they must now serve and cling to Jehovah, who had loved them for their fathers' sakes and had constituted them "like the stars of the heavens for multitude."—Deut. 10:22.

19 Israel must keep "the whole commandment" and they must without fail obey Jehovah, loving him as their God and serving him with all their heart and all their soul. (11:8, 13) Jehovah will back up and reward them if they obey him. However, they must apply themselves and diligently teach their sons. The choice before Israel is clearly stated: obedience leads to blessing, disobedience to malediction. They must not "walk after other gods." (11:26-

13. On what basis did Moses assure Joshua of victory?
14. What emphasis does Moses place on God's law and on exclusive devotion?
15. What arrangement for cities of refuge is then made east of Jordan?
16. What does Moses' second discourse stress?
17. How must Israel reciprocate the love that Jehovah has shown them?
18. Against what does Moses now exhort the Israelites to guard themselves?
19. What choice is clearly stated, and what laws are outlined for the nation?

28) Moses then outlines specific laws affecting Israel as they move in to take possession of the Land of Promise. There are (1) laws touching religion and worship; (2) laws relating to administration of justice, government and war; and (3) laws regulating the private and social life of the people.

20 (1) *Religion and worship* (12:1–16:17). When the Israelites enter the land, every vestige of false religion—its high places, altars, pillars, sacred poles and images—must be absolutely destroyed. They must worship only in the place where Jehovah their God chooses to put his name, and there they must rejoice in him, all of them. Regulations on eating of meat and sacrifices include repeated reminders that they must not eat blood. "Simply be firmly resolved not to eat the blood . . . You must not eat it, in order that it may go well with you and your sons after you, because you will do what is right in Jehovah's eyes." (12:16, 23-25, 27; 15:23) Moses now launches into an outspoken condemnation of idolatry. Israel must not even inquire into the ways of false religion. If a prophet is proved to be false, he must be put to death, and apostates—even one's dear relative or friend, yes, even entire cities—must likewise be devoted to destruction. Next come regulations on clean and unclean food, the payment of tenths and the care of the Levites. The interests of debtors, the poor and bond slaves are to be lovingly protected. Finally, Moses reviews the annual festivals as times to thank Jehovah for his blessing: "Three times in the year every male of yours should appear before Jehovah your God in the place that he will choose: in the festival of the unfermented cakes and the festival of weeks and the festival of booths, and none should appear before Jehovah empty-handed."—16:16.

21 (2) *Justice, government and war* (16:18–20:20). First of all, Moses gives the laws affecting judges and officers. Justice is the important thing, bribes and perverted judgment being hateful to Jehovah. The procedures in establishing evidence and handling legal cases are outlined. "At the mouth of two witnesses or of three witnesses the one dying should be put to death." (17:6) Laws are stated concerning kings. Provision is made for the priests and Levites. Spiritism is outlawed as "detestable to Jehovah." (18:12) Looking far into the future, Moses declares: "A prophet from your own midst, from your brothers, like me, is what Jehovah your God will raise up for you—to him you people should listen." (18:15-19) However, a false prophet must die. This section closes with laws concerning cities of refuge and the avenging of blood, qualifications for military exemptions and the rules of war.

22 (3) *Private and social life* (21:1–26:19). Laws touching the everyday life of the Israelites are set forth on such matters as a person found slain, marriage to captive women, the right of the firstborn, a rebellious son, the staking of criminals, evidence of virginity, sex crimes, castration, illegitimate sons, treatment of foreigners, sanitation, payment of interest and vows, divorce, kidnaping, loans, wages and harvest gleanings. The limit for beating a man is to be forty strokes. A bull must not be muzzled while threshing. The procedure for brother-in-law marriage is outlined. Accurate weights must be used, for injustice is detestable to Jehovah.

23 Before concluding this fervent discourse, Moses recalls how Amalek struck the weary Israelites from the rear, as they fled from Egypt, and Moses commands Israel to "wipe out the mention of Amalek from under the heavens." (25:19) When they enter into the land, they must offer the firstfruits of the soil with rejoicing, and also the tithes with the thankful prayer to Jehovah: "Do look down from your holy dwelling, the heavens, and bless your people Israel and the soil that you have given us, just as you swore to our forefathers, the land flowing with milk and honey." (26:15) If they carry out these commandments with all their heart and soul, Jehovah, on his part, will 'put them high above all the other nations that he has made, resulting in praise and reputation and beauty, while they prove themselves a people holy to Jehovah their God, just as he has promised.'—26:19.

24 **Moses' third discourse** (27:1–28:68). In this the older men of Israel and the priests are associated with Moses, as he recites at length Jehovah's curses for disobedience and the blessings for faithfulness. This gives dire warnings concerning the fearful results of unfaithfulness. If Israel as his holy people keep listening to the voice of Jehovah their God they will enjoy wonderful blessings, and all the peoples of the earth will see that Jehovah's name is called upon them. However, if they fail in this, Jehovah will send upon them the curse, confusion and rebuke. They will be stricken by loathsome diseases, by drought and by famine; their enemies will pursue and enslave them, and they will be scattered and annihilated out of the land. These curses, and more, will come upon them if they "will not take care to carry out all the words of this law that are written

20. What points highlight the laws concerning worship?
21. What laws are given relating to justice, and what important prophecy does Moses utter?
22. Laws governing what private and social matters are discussed?
23. What does Moses show will result from obeying God's commandments?
24. What blessings and cursings does the third discourse set before Israel?

in this book so as to fear this glorious and fear-inspiring name, even Jehovah, [their] God."—28:58.

25 **Moses' fourth discourse** (29:1–30:20). Moses as mediator now concludes Jehovah's covenant of the repeated law with the nation of Israel. This incorporates the repetition of the Law, with its up-to-date revisions, that will guide Israel as they enter the Land of Promise. The solemn oath accompanying the covenant drives home the nation's responsibilities. Finally, Moses calls the heavens and the earth to witness, as he places before them life and death, the blessing and the malediction, and exhorts: "You must choose life in order that you may keep alive, you and your offspring, by loving Jehovah your God, by listening to his voice and by sticking to him; for he is your life and the length of your days, that you may dwell upon the ground that Jehovah swore to your forefathers Abraham, Isaac and Jacob to give to them."—30:19, 20.

26 Chapter 31 relates how, after writing the Law and giving instructions concerning the regular public reading of it, Moses commissions Joshua, telling him to be courageous and strong, and then how Moses prepares a memorial song and completes the writing of the words of the Law and arranges for it to be placed at the side of the ark of the covenant of Jehovah. After that Moses speaks the words of the song to all the congregation as a final exhortation. Finally, before going up Mount Nebo to die, he pronounces blessing on the sons of Israel, though not mentioning Simeon.

27 **The song of Moses** (32:1-47). How appreciatively does this song open, identifying the refreshing Source of Moses' instruction! "My instruction will drip as the rain, my saying will trickle as the dew, as gentle rains upon grass and as copious showers upon vegetation. For I shall declare the name of Jehovah." Yes, attribute greatness to "our God," "the Rock." Make known his perfect activity, his just ways, his faithfulness, righteousness and uprightness. It was shameful that Israel acted ruinously, though Jehovah encircled them in an empty, howling desert, safeguarding them as the pupil of his eye and hovering over them as an eagle over its fledglings. He made his people fat, calling them Jeshurun, "Upright One," but they incited him to jealousy with strange gods and became "sons in whom there is no faithfulness." Vengeance and retribution are Jehovah's. He puts to death and makes alive. When he sharpens his glittering sword and his hand takes hold on judgment, he will indeed pay back vengeance to his adversaries. What confidence this should inspire in his people and in all men of goodwill! As the song says in climax, it is a time to "be glad, you nations, with his people." What worldly poet could ever approach the exalted beauty, power and depth of meaning of this song to Jehovah?

28 **Moses' blessing** (32:48–33:29). Moses is now given final instructions concerning his death, but he is not yet through with his theocratic service. First, he must bless Israel, and in doing this he again extols Jehovah, the King in Jeshurun, as beaming forth with his holy myriads. By name the tribes receive individual blessings, and then Moses praises Jehovah as the eminent One: "A hiding place is the God of ancient time, and underneath are the indefinitely lasting arms." From a heart brimming with appreciation, he then speaks his final words to the nation: "Happy you are, O Israel! Who is there like you, a people enjoying salvation in Jehovah?"—33:29.

29 After viewing the Land of Promise from Mount Nebo, Moses dies and Jehovah buries him in Moab, his tomb being unknown and unhonored till this day. He lived to be 120 years of age, but "his eye had not grown dim, and his vital strength had not fled." Jehovah had used him to perform great signs and miracles and, as the final chapter reports, there had not yet "risen up a prophet in Israel like Moses, whom Jehovah knew face to face."—34:9, 10.

WHY BENEFICIAL

30 As the concluding book of the Pentateuch, Deuteronomy ties together all that has gone before in declaring and sanctifying the great name of Jehovah God. He is God alone, exacting exclusive devotion and tolerating no rivalry by demon gods of false religious worship. In this day all Christians must give earnest attention to the great principles underlying God's law and obey him, so that they will be free of his curse as he sharpens his glittering sword for execution of vengeance on his adversaries. His greatest and first commandment must become the guiding post in their lives: "You must love Jehovah your God with all your heart and all your soul and all your vital force."—6:5.

31 The rest of the Scriptures frequently refer to Deuteronomy to enrich appreciation of the divine purposes. In addition to his quotations in answering the Tempter, Jesus made many other references. (Deut. 5:16—Matt. 15:4; Deut. 17:6—Matt. 18:16 and John 8:17) These continue into Revelation, where the glorified Jesus

25. (a) What covenant does Moses now conclude with Israel? (b) What choice does he place before them?
26. What final arrangements does Moses make before his death?
27. What powerful message is contained in Moses' song?
28. How is Jehovah exalted in Moses' final blessing?
29. In what ways was Moses outstanding?
30. How does Deuteronomy provide a fitting conclusion to the Pentateuch?
31. How do other inspired scriptures draw on Deuteronomy in enriching appreciation of God's purposes?

finally warns against adding to or taking away from the scroll of Jehovah's prophecy. (Deut. 4:2—Rev. 22:18) Peter quotes from Deuteronomy in clinching his powerful argument that Jesus is the Christ and the Prophet greater than Moses whom Jehovah promised to raise up in Israel. (Deut. 18:15-19—Acts 3:22, 23) Paul quotes from it with reference to rewards for workers, thorough investigation at the mouth of witnesses and the instruction of children.—Deut. 25:4—1 Cor. 9:8-10 and 1 Tim. 5:17, 18; Deut. 13:14 and 19:15—1 Tim. 5:19 and 2 Cor. 13:1; Deut. 5:16—Eph. 6:2, 3.

32 Not only the writers of the Christian Scriptures, but also God's servants of pre-Christian times drew instruction and encouragement from Deuteronomy. We do well to follow their example. Consider the implicit obedience of Moses' successor Joshua during the invasion of Canaan, such as in devoting conquered cities to destruction, taking no spoil as did Achan. (Deut. 20:15-18 and 21:23—Josh. 8:24-27, 29) Gideon's elimination of those "afraid and trembling" from his army was in obedience to the Law. (Deut. 20:1-9—Judg. 7:1-11) It was out of faithfulness to the law of Jehovah that the prophets in Israel and Judah spoke boldly and courageously in condemnation of those backsliding nations. Amos provides an excellent example of this. (Deut. 24:12-15—Amos 2:6-8) Indeed, there are literally hundreds of examples tying Deuteronomy in with the rest of God's Word, thus showing that it is an integral and beneficial part of the harmonious whole.

33 The very essence of Deuteronomy breathes praise to the Sovereign God, Jehovah. It stresses throughout: 'Worship Jehovah; render him exclusive devotion.' Though the Law is no longer binding upon Christians, yet its underlying principles have not been abrogated. (Gal. 3:19) How much true Christians can learn from this dynamic book of God's law, with its progressive teaching, its candor and simplicity of presentation! Why, even the nations of the world have recognized the excellence of Jehovah's Supreme Law, writing many of the regulations of Deuteronomy into their own lawbooks. The accompanying table gives interesting examples of laws that they have drawn on or applied in principle.

34 Moreover, this "repetition of the law," the *deu·te·ro·no'mi·on*, points to and heightens appreciation of God's kingdom. How so? While on earth the king-designate Jesus Christ was thoroughly acquainted with the book and applied it, as his skillful references to it show. In spreading his Kingdom rule over all the earth, he will govern according to the right *principles* of this same "law," and all who come to bless themselves in him as the Kingdom "Seed" will have to obey these principles. (Gen. 22:18; Deut. 7:12-14) It is beneficial and advantageous to start obeying them now. Far from being out of date, this 3,500-year-old "law" speaks to us today in dynamic tones, and it will keep on speaking right on into the new world of God's kingdom. May Jehovah's name continue to be sanctified among his people in the application of all the beneficial instruction of the Pentateuch, which so gloriously reaches its climax in Deuteronomy—certainly an inspired and inspiring part of "all Scripture"!

32. In what respect are Joshua, Gideon and the prophets a fine example to us?
33. (a) What is the very essence of Deuteronomy? (b) What does the accompanying table show as to the worldly nations' recognition of principles of God's law?
34. What connection is there between this "repetition of the law" and God's kingdom?

SOME LEGAL PRECEDENTS IN DEUTERONOMY[a]

	Chapters and Verses
I. Personal and family laws	
A. Personal relations	
1. Parents and children	5: 16
2. Marriage relations	22: 30; 27: 20, 22, 23
3. Laws of divorce	22: 13-19, 28, 29
B. Property rights	22: 1-4
II. Constitutional laws	
A. Qualifications and duties of the king	17: 14-20
B. Military regulations	
1. Exemptions from military service	20: 1, 5-7; 24: 5
2. Minor officers	20: 9
III. The judiciary	
A. Duties of judges	16: 18, 20
B. Supreme court of appeal	17: 8-11
IV. Criminal laws	
A. Crimes against the state	
1. Bribery, perverting justice	16: 19, 20
2. Perjury	5: 20
B. Crimes against morality	
1. Adultery	5: 18; 22: 22-24
2. Unlawful marriage	22: 30; 27: 20, 22, 23
C. Crimes against the person	
1. Murder and assault	5: 17; 27: 24
2. Rape and seduction	22: 25-29
V. Humane laws	
A. Kindness toward animals	25: 4; 22: 6, 7
B. Consideration for the unfortunate	24: 6, 10-18
C. Building safety code	22: 8
D. Treatment of dependent classes, including slaves and captives	15: 12-15; 21: 10-14; 27: 18, 19
E. Philanthropic provisions for the needy	14: 28, 29; 15: 1-11; 16: 11, 12; 24: 19-22

a *Israel's Laws and Legal Precedents,* 1907, C. F. Kent, pages vii to xviii.

Bible Book Number Six— Joshua

Writer: **Joshua**
Place Written: **Canaan**
Writing Completed: **c. 1433 B.C.E.**
Time Covered: **1473—c. 1433 B.C.E.**

THE year is 1473 B.C.E. The scene is most dramatic and thrilling. The Israelites, encamped on the plains of Moab, are poised for their entry into Canaan, the Promised Land. This territory on the other side of Jordan is inhabited by numerous petty kingdoms, each with its own private army. They are divided among themselves and weakened through years of corrupt domination by Egypt. Yet, to the nation of Israel, the opposition is formidable. The many fortified walled cities, such as Jericho, Ai, Hazor and Lachish, have to be taken if the land is to be subdued. A critical time lies ahead. Decisive battles must be fought and won, with Jehovah himself entering in with powerful miracles in behalf of his people, in order to fulfill his promise to settle them in the land. Unquestionably, these stirring events, so outstanding in Jehovah's dealings with his people, will have to be recorded, and that by an eyewitness. What better man could there be for this than Joshua himself, the one appointed by Jehovah as successor to Moses!—Num. 27:15-23.

2 The choice of Joshua, both as leader and as a recorder of the events about to take place, is most appropriate. He has been a very close associate of Moses throughout the previous forty years in the wilderness. He has been "the minister of Moses from his young manhood on," showing him to be qualified as a spiritual as well as a military leader. (Num. 11:28; also Ex. 24:13; 33:11; Josh. 1:1) In the year Israel left Egypt, 1513 B.C.E., he was captain of the armies of Israel in the defeat of the Amalekites. (Ex. 17:9-14) As the loyal companion of Moses and a fearless army commander, he was the natural choice to represent the tribe of Ephraim in the dangerous mission of spying out Canaan along with eleven others. His courage and faithfulness on this occasion had assured his entry into the Promised Land. (Num. 13:8; 14:6-9, 30, 38) Yes, this man Joshua, the son of Nun, is "a man in whom there is spirit," a man who "followed Jehovah wholly," a man "full of the spirit of wisdom." No wonder that "Israel continued to serve Jehovah all the days of Joshua."—Num. 27:18; 32:12; Deut. 34:9; Josh. 24:31.

3 From the standpoint of his experience, training and tested qualities as a true worshiper of Jehovah, Joshua was certainly in position to be used as one of the writers of the 'Scriptures inspired by God.' Joshua is no mere legendary figure, but a real-life servant of Jehovah. He is mentioned by name in the Christian Greek Scriptures. (Acts 7:45; Heb. 4:8) Interestingly, in the year 1888 (A.D.) some 320 clay tablets were found at a place called Tel el Amarna in Egypt, one of which actually contains the name Joshua, and apparently some give accounts by Canaanite, Amorite and Jebusite chiefs of his invasion of the land.[a] It is logical that, just as Moses was used to write concerning the events of his lifetime, so his successor Joshua would be used to write down the events that he himself witnessed. That the book was written by a contemporary is shown by Joshua 6:25. Jewish tradition credits Joshua with writership, and the book itself states: "Then Joshua wrote these words in the book of God's law."—Josh. 24:26.

4 At the time of Jericho's destruction Joshua placed a prophetic curse on the rebuilding of the city, which had a remarkable fulfillment in the days of Ahab king of Israel, some five hundred years later. (Josh. 6:26; 1 Ki. 16:33, 34) Along with prophecy, archaeology also gives convincing testimony as to the genuineness of Joshua's account. Excavations at the site of ancient Jericho confirm, not only the five hundred years of desolation, but many details of the city's destruction.[b] Archaeologists have now identified or excavated a great number of the cities mentioned in Joshua. Jericho and Hazor both show signs of devotion to fiery destruction. (Josh. 6:2, 24; 11:10, 11) The Tel el Amarna tablets, already mentioned, reflect some of the fear that gripped all Canaan at that time. For example, they contain a letter sent to Egypt from the king of Jerusalem, which says: "The Khabiru are devastating all the lands of

a *The Bible Comes Alive,* 1950, Sir Charles Marston, page 64.
b See Study 9, paragraph 8.

1. What situation confronts Israel in 1473 B.C.E.?
2. Why is the choice of Joshua, both as leader and as recorder, appropriate?
3. What proves Joshua to have been a real-life servant of Jehovah, as well as the writer of this book?
4. How has the accuracy of the book of Joshua been proved both by the fulfillment of prophecy and by archaeological finds?

the king. . . . If no troops arrive, the lands of the king my lord are lost." Also: "Now the Khabiru are seizing the cities of the king. There is no local ruler left to the king my lord; all are lost."[a] The letters also mention the attack on Hazor and its king. The conquest of Canaan certainly marked a striking fulfillment of the prophecy of Jehovah concerning Israel: "This day I shall start to put the dread of you and the fear of you before the peoples beneath all the heavens, who will hear the report about you; and they will indeed be agitated and have pains like those of childbirth because of you." —Deut. 2:25; Josh. 2:9, 11; 5:1; 9:24.

5 The book of Joshua covers a period of about forty years, from the entry into Canaan in 1473 to approximately 1433 B.C.E., in which year Joshua probably died. The very name "Joshua" (Hebrew, *Yᵉho·shúʽa*), meaning "Jehovah is Salvation," is most fitting in view of Joshua's role as visible leader in Israel during the conquest of the land. He gave all the glory to Jehovah as Deliverer. In the *Septuagint* the book is called *Ie·soús* (the Greek equivalent of *Yᵉho·shúʽa*), and from this the name "Jesus" has been derived. In his fine qualities of courage, obedience and integrity, Joshua was truly a splendid prophetic type of "our Lord Jesus Christ."

CONTENTS OF JOSHUA

6 The book falls into four natural sections: (1) Crossing into the Promised Land, (2) the conquest of Canaan, (3) apportioning the land and (4) Joshua's farewell exhortations. The entire account is vividly told and packed with thrilling drama.

7 **Crossing into the Promised Land** (1:1–5:12). Knowing of the tests ahead, Jehovah gives assurance and sound counsel to Joshua at the outset: "Only be courageous and very strong . . . This book of the law should not depart from your mouth, and you must in an undertone read in it day and night, in order that you may take care to do according to all that is written in it; for then you will make your way successful and then you will act wisely. Have I not commanded you? Be courageous and strong . . . for Jehovah your God is with you wherever you go." (1:7-9) Joshua gives credit to Jehovah as the real leader and commander, and immediately sets about preparing to cross the Jordan as commanded. The Israelites accept him as Moses' successor and pledge loyalty. Onward, then, to the conquest of Canaan!

8 Two men are dispatched to spy out Jericho. Rahab the harlot seizes the opportunity to show goodwill toward Jehovah and his people by hiding the spies at the risk of her life. In return, the spies swear that she will be spared when Jericho is destroyed. The spies carry back the report that all the inhabitants of the land have grown disheartened because of the Israelites. The report being favorable, Joshua moves immediately to the Jordan River, which is at flood stage. Jehovah now gives tangible evidence that he is backing up Joshua and that, just as in Moses' time, there is "a living God" in the midst of Israel. (3:10) As the priests carrying the ark of the covenant step into the Jordan, the waters from upstream are heaped up, allowing the Israelites to pass over on dry ground. Joshua takes twelve stones from the middle of the river as a memorial, and sets another twelve stones in the river, where the priests are standing, after which the priests pass over and the waters return to flood stage.

9 Once across, the people encamp at Gilgal, between the Jordan and Jericho, and here Joshua sets up the memorial stones as a witness to the generations to come, and "in order that all the peoples of the earth may know Jehovah's hand, that it is strong; in order that you may indeed fear Jehovah your God always." (4:24) (Joshua 10:15 indicates that Gilgal is thereafter used as a base camp for some time.) It is here that the sons of Israel are circumcised, since there had been no circumcising during the wilderness journey. The passover is celebrated, the manna ceases and at last the Israelites begin to eat the produce of the land.

10 **Conquest of Canaan** (5:13–12:24). Now the first objective lies within striking distance. But how to take this "tightly shut up" walled city of Jericho? Jehovah himself details the procedure, sending the "prince of the army of Jehovah" to instruct Joshua. (5:14) Once a day for six days they must march around the city, with the men of war in the lead, followed in procession by priests blowing rams' horns and others carrying the ark of the covenant. On the seventh day they must go around seven times. Joshua faithfully relays the orders to the people. Exactly as commanded, the armies of Israel march around Jericho. No word is spoken. There is no sound but the tramping of feet and the blowing of horns by the priests. Then, on the final day, after the completion of

a *Modern Discovery and the Bible*, 1949, A. Rendle Short, page 155.

5. (a) What period is covered by the book of Joshua? (b) Why is the name "Joshua" appropriate?
6. Into what natural sections does the book fall?
7. What encouragement and counsel does Jehovah give Joshua at the outset?
8. (a) How does Rahab show goodwill? (b) How does Jehovah show himself to be "a living God" in the midst of Israel?
9. What next happens at Gilgal?
10. How does Jehovah instruct Joshua concerning the capture of Jericho, and what dramatic action follows?

the seventh circuit, Joshua signals them to shout. Shout they do, "a great war cry," and the walls of Jericho fall down flat! (6:20) As one man they rush the city, capturing it and devoting it to fiery destruction. Only the faithful Rahab and her household find deliverance.

11 Then on westward to Ai! Confidence in another easy victory turns to dismay, as the men of Ai put to rout the three thousand Israelite soldiers sent up to capture the city. What has happened? Has Jehovah forsaken them? Joshua anxiously inquires of Jehovah. In reply Jehovah discloses that, contrary to his command to devote everything in Jericho to destruction, someone in the camp has disobeyed, stealing something and hiding it. This uncleanness must be removed from the camp before Israel can continue to prosper with Jehovah's blessing. Under divine guidance, Achan the evildoer is discovered, and he and his household are stoned to death. With Jehovah's favor restored, the Israelites now move against Ai. Once again Jehovah himself reveals the strategy to be used. The men of Ai are lured out of their walled city and find themselves trapped in an ambush. The city is captured and devoted to destruction with all its inhabitants. (8:26-28) No compromise with the enemy!

12 In obedience to Jehovah's command through Moses, Joshua next builds an altar in Mount Ebal and writes on it the "repetition of the law." (8:32, *LXX*) Then he reads the words of the Law, together with the blessing and the malediction, to the assembly of the entire nation as they stand, half in front of Mount Gerizim and the other half in front of Mount Ebal. —Deut. 11:29; 27:1-13.

13 Alarmed at the speedy progress of the invasion, a number of the petty kingdoms of Canaan unite in an effort to halt Joshua's advance. However, 'the Gibeonites, when they hear what Joshua has done to Jericho and Ai, act with shrewdness.' (Josh. 9:3, 4) Under pretense of being from a land distant from Canaan, they enter into a covenant with Joshua "to let them live." When the ruse is discovered, the Israelites honor the covenant but make the Gibeonites "gatherers of wood and drawers of water," like the 'lowest slaves,' thus fulfilling Noah's inspired curse on Canaan, the son of Ham.—Josh. 9:27; Gen. 9:25.

14 This defection of the Gibeonites is no small matter, for "Gibeon was a great city . . . greater than Ai, and all its men were mighty ones." (Josh. 10:2) Adoni-zedek, king of Jerusalem, sees in this a threat to himself and the other kingdoms in Canaan. An example must be made to stop further desertion to the enemy. So Adoni-zedek and four other kings (those of the city kingdoms of Hebron, Jarmuth, Lachish and Eglon) organize and war against Gibeon. Honoring his covenant with the Gibeonites, Joshua marches up all night to their aid, and routs the armies of the five kings. Once again Jehovah enters into the fight, using superhuman powers and signs with devastating results. Mighty hailstones rain down from heaven, killing more of the enemy than the swords of the Israelite army. And then, wonder of wonders, 'the sun keeps standing still in the middle of the heavens and does not hasten to set for about a whole day.' (10:13) Thus mopping-up operations can be completed. The worldly-wise may try to discount this miraculous event, but men of faith accept the divine record, well aware of Jehovah's power to control the forces of the universe and direct them according to his will. For a fact, "Jehovah himself was fighting for Israel."—10:14.

15 After slaying the five kings, Joshua devotes Makkedah to destruction. Passing on quickly to the south, he utterly destroys Libnah, Lachish, Eglon, Hebron and Debir, cities in the mountains and hills between the Salt and Great Seas. By now news of the invasion has spread the length of Canaan. Up in the north the alarm is sounded by Jabin, king of Hazor. Far and wide, to both sides of the Jordan, he sends out the call to mass for united action against the Israelites. As they encamp by the waters of Merom, below Mount Hermon, the assembled forces of the enemy are "as numerous as the grains of sand that are on the seashore." (11:4) Again Jehovah assures Joshua of victory and outlines the battle strategy. And the result? Another crushing defeat for the enemies of Jehovah's people! Hazor is burned with fire, and its allied cities and their kings are devoted to destruction. Thus Joshua extends the area of Israelite domination through the length and breadth of Canaan. Thirty-one kings have been defeated.

16 **Apportioning the land** (13:1–22:34). Despite these many victories, with many key fortified cities destroyed and organized resistance broken for the time being, "to a very great extent the land yet remains to be taken in possession." However, Joshua is now close to eighty years of age and there is also another big job to be done—that of apportioning the land as inheritances for nine full tribes and the half tribe of Manasseh. Reuben, Gad and half the tribe of Manasseh have already received their inheritance of land to the east of Jordan,

11. How is the initial reverse at Ai remedied?
12. What divine command does Joshua next carry out?
13. What results from the Gibeonites' acting "with shrewdness"?
14. How does Jehovah demonstrate at Gibeon that he is fighting for Israel?
15. Describe the course of the invasion, and its climax at Hazor.
16. What assignments of land are then made?

and the tribe of Levi is to receive none, "Jehovah the God of Israel" being their inheritance. (13:33) With the help of Eleazar the priest, Joshua now makes the assignments to the west of the Jordan. The eighty-five-year-old Caleb, eager to fight Jehovah's enemies to the last, requests and is assigned the Anakim-infested region of Hebron. (14:12-15) After the tribes receive their inheritances by lot, Joshua requests the city of Timnath-serah in the mountains of Ephraim, and this is given him "at the order of Jehovah." (19:50) The tent of meeting is set up at Shiloh, which is also in the mountainous region of Ephraim.

17 Six cities of refuge for the unintentional manslayer are set aside, three on each side of the Jordan. Those to the west of the Jordan are Kedesh in Galilee, Shechem in Ephraim, and Hebron in the mountains of Judah. Those on the east are Bezer in Reuben's territory, Ramoth in Gilead and Golan in Bashan. These are given "a sacred status." (20:7) Forty-eight cities with their pasture grounds are assigned by lot from the tribal allocations as cities of residence for the Levites. These include the six cities of refuge. Thus Israel "proceeded to take possession of [the land] and to dwell in it." Just as Jehovah had promised, so "it all came true."—21:43, 45.

18 The men of war from the tribes of Reuben, Gad and the half tribe of Manasseh, who have continued with Joshua up to this time, now return to their inheritances across the Jordan, carrying with them Joshua's exhortation to faithfulness and his blessing. On the way, as they come close to the Jordan, they erect a great altar. This precipitates a crisis. Since the appointed place for Jehovah's worship is at the tent of meeting in Shiloh, the western tribes fear treachery and disloyalty, and prepare for battle against the supposed rebels. However, bloodshed is averted when it is explained that the altar is not for sacrifice but only to serve as "a witness between us [Israel to the east and to the west of the Jordan] that Jehovah is the true God."—22:34.

19 **Joshua's farewell exhortations** (23:1–24:33). 'And it comes about many days after Jehovah has given Israel rest from all their enemies all around, when Joshua is old and advanced in days,' that he calls all Israel together for inspiring farewell exhortations. (23:1) Humble to the end, he gives Jehovah all the credit for the great victories over the nations. Let all now continue faithful! "Be very courageous to keep and to do all that is written in the book of the law of Moses by never turning away from it to the right or to the left." (23:6) They must shun the false gods, and 'be on constant guard for their souls by loving Jehovah their God.' (23:11) There must be no compromise with the remaining Canaanites, no marriage or interfaith alliances with them, for this will bring down Jehovah's blazing anger.

20 Assembling all the tribes at Shechem, and calling out their representative officers before Jehovah, Joshua next relates Jehovah's personal account of his dealings with his people from the time he called Abraham and brought him into Canaan until the conquest and occupation of the Land of Promise. Again he warns against false religion, calling on Israel to "fear Jehovah and serve him in faultlessness and in truth." Yes, "serve Jehovah"! Then he puts the issue with utmost clarity: "Choose for yourselves today whom you will serve, whether the gods that your forefathers . . . served or the gods of the Amorites in whose land you are dwelling. But as for me and my household, we shall serve Jehovah." With conviction reminiscent of Moses, he reminds Israel that Jehovah "is a holy God; he is a God exacting exclusive devotion." So, away with the foreign gods! The people are thus stirred to declare as one man: "Jehovah our God we shall serve, and to his voice we shall listen!" (24:14, 15, 19, 24) Before dismissing them, Joshua makes a covenant with them, writes these words in the book of God's law and sets up a great stone as a witness. Then Joshua dies at the good old age of 110 years and is buried in Timnath-serah.

WHY BENEFICIAL

21 As you read Joshua's farewell exhortations concerning faithful service, does it not make your blood tingle? Do you not echo the words of Joshua that he uttered more than 3,400 years ago: "As for me and my household, we shall serve Jehovah"? Or if you serve Jehovah under conditions of trial or isolation from other faithful ones, do you not draw inspiration from Jehovah's words to Joshua uttered at the beginning of the march into the Land of Promise: "Only be courageous and very strong"? Moreover, do you not find inestimable benefit in following His admonition to 'read [the Bible] in an undertone day and night, in order to make your way successful'? Surely, all who follow these wise admonitions will find them outstandingly beneficial.—24:15; 1:7-9.

22 The events so vividly recorded in the book of Joshua are more than just ancient history.

17. What provision is made for cities of refuge and for cities of residence for the Levites?
18. What crisis develops between the eastern and the western tribes, but how is this resolved?
19, 20. (a) What farewell exhortations does Joshua give? (b) What issue does he put before Israel, and how does he emphasize the right choice to make?
21. What wise admonitions in the book of Joshua are of outstanding benefit today?
22. What essential qualities of true worship are highlighted?

They highlight godly principles—preeminently, that implicit faith and obedience to Jehovah are vital to his blessing. The apostle Paul records that by faith "the walls of Jericho fell down after they had been encircled for seven days," and that because of faith "Rahab the harlot did not perish with those who acted disobediently." (Heb. 11:30, 31) James likewise cites Rahab as a beneficial example for Christians in producing works of faith.—Jas. 2:24-26.

23 The unusual supernatural events recorded at Joshua 10:10-14, when the sun kept motionless and the moon stood still, as well as the many other miracles that Jehovah performed in behalf of his people, are powerful reminders of Jehovah's ability and purpose to bring a final extermination of all wicked opposers of God. Gibeon, the scene of battle in both Joshua's and David's times, is connected by Isaiah with Jehovah's rising up in agitation for this extermination, "that he may do his deed—his deed is strange—and that he may work his work—his work is unusual."—Isa. 28:21, 22.

24 Do the events of Joshua point forward to God's kingdom? Certainly they do! That the conquest and settlement of the Promised Land are to be tied in with something far greater was indicated by the apostle Paul: "For if Joshua had led them into a place of rest, God would not afterward have spoken of another day. So there remains a sabbath resting for the people of God." (Heb. 4:1, 8, 9) They press onward to make sure of their "entrance into the everlasting kingdom of our Lord and Savior Jesus Christ." (2 Pet. 1:10, 11) As shown by Matthew 1:5, Rahab became an ancestress of Jesus Christ. The book of Joshua thus provides another vital link in the record leading down to the production of the Kingdom Seed. It provides firm assurance that Jehovah's Kingdom promises will come to certain fulfillment. Speaking of God's promise made to Abraham, Isaac and Jacob, and repeated to the Israelites, their descendants, the record states concerning Joshua's day: "Not a promise failed out of all the good promise Jehovah had made to the house of Israel; it all came true." (Josh. 21:45; Gen. 13:14-17) Likewise, with Jehovah's "good promise" concerning the righteous kingdom of heaven—it shall all come true!

23. What powerful reminders are contained in Joshua?
24. How does the book of Joshua tie in with the Kingdom promises, and what assurance does it give that these will 'all come true'?

Bible Book Number Seven— Judges

Writer: **Samuel**
Place Written: **Israel**
Writing Completed: **c. 1100 B.C.E.**
Time Covered: **c. 1433-1190 B.C.E.**

HERE is a page of Israel's history that is packed full of action, seesawing between disastrous entanglements with demon religion and Jehovah's merciful deliverances of his repentant people by divinely appointed judges. Faith-inspiring are the mighty deeds of Othniel, Ehud, Shamgar and the other judges who followed. As the writer of Hebrews said: "The time will fail me if I go on to relate about Gideon, Barak, Samson, Jephthah, . . . who through faith defeated kingdoms in conflict, effected righteousness, . . . from a weak state were made powerful, became valiant in war, routed the armies of foreigners." (Heb. 11:32-34) To round out the number of twelve faithful judges of this period, there are also Tola, Jair, Ibzan, Elon and Abdon. (Joshua and Samuel were also judges, though the latter is usually referred to as a prophet.) Jehovah fought the judges' battles for them, and his spirit enveloped them as they performed their deeds of prowess. They gave all the credit and glory to their God.

2 In the *Septuagint* the book is called *Kritaí*, and in the Hebrew Bible it is *Sho·phᵉtim'*, which is translated "Judges." *Sho·phᵉtim'* is derived from the verb *sha·phat'*, meaning to "judge, vindicate, punish, govern," which well expresses the office of these theocratic appointees of "God the Judge of all." (Heb. 12:23) They were men raised up by Jehovah on specific occasions to deliver his people from foreign bondage.

3 When was Judges written? Two expressions in the book help us in finding the answer. The first is this: "But the Jebusites keep on dwelling . . . in Jerusalem down to this day." (Judg.

1. In what ways was the period of the judges noteworthy?
2. In what way is the Hebrew name of the book appropriate?
3. When was Judges written?

1:21) Since King David threw the Jebusites out of Jerusalem in the eighth year of his reign, or in 1070 B.C.E., Judges must have been written before that date. (2 Sam. 5:4-7) The second expression occurs four times: "In those days there was no king in Israel." (Judg. 17:6; 18:1; 19:1; 21:25) Hence the record was written down at a time when there *was* a "king in Israel," that is, after Saul became the first king in 1117 B.C.E. It must therefore be dated between 1117 and 1070 B.C.E.

4 Who was the writer? Unquestionably, he was a devoted servant of Jehovah. It is Samuel who stands out alone as the principal advocate of Jehovah's worship at this transition time from the judges to the kings, and he is also the first of the line of faithful prophets. As such, Samuel would be the logical one to record the history of the judges.

5 How long a period does Judges cover? This can be calculated from 1 Kings 6:1, which shows that Solomon began to build the house of Jehovah in the fourth year of his reign, which was also "the four hundred and eightieth year after the sons of Israel came out from the land of Egypt." ("Four hundred and eightieth" being an ordinal number, it represents 479 full years.) The known time periods included in the 479 years are forty years under Moses in the wilderness (Deut. 8:2), forty years of Saul's reign (Acts 13:21), forty years of David's reign (2 Sam. 5:4, 5) and the first three full years of Solomon's reign. Subtracting this total of 123 years from the 479 years of 1 Kings 6:1, there remain 356 years for the period between Moses and Saul.[a] The events actually recorded in the book of Judges, extending from the death of Joshua down to the time of Samuel, cover about 240 years of this 356-year period.

6 The authenticity of Judges is beyond doubt. The Jews have always recognized it as part of the Bible canon. Writers of both the Hebrew and the Greek Scriptures have drawn on its record, as at Psalm 83:9-18; Isaiah 9:4; 10:26 and Hebrews 11:32-34. In candor, it hides nothing of Israel's shortcomings and backslidings, while at the same time exalting the infinite loving-kindness of Jehovah. It is Jehovah, and no mere human judge, who receives the glory as Deliverer in Israel.

7 Further, archaeological finds continue to supply supporting proofs of the genuineness of Judges. For example, the Hittites, mentioned in Judges 1:26 and 3:5, were an "undiscovered" people until this last century, when the extensive Hittite civilization was again brought to light.[b] Archaeology has also revealed how it would be possible for Samson to topple the temple of Dagon. Excavations at ancient Gaza brought to light two stone bases close together in the center upon which the two main pillars of such a temple stood. On these pillars rested the main beams that supported the entire house. Thus the pillars were conveniently situated for Samson to force them out of the perpendicular and achieve his object.

8 Most striking, however, are archaeological finds on the nature of the Baal religion of the Canaanites. Apart from the Bible references, little was known of Baalism until the ancient Canaanite city of Ugarit was excavated in 1929.[c] Here Baal religion was revealed as featuring materialism, extreme nationalism and sex worship. Each Canaanite city had its Baal sanctuary on one of the "high places," with an image, an altar and a phallic symbol of the god. Detestable human sacrifices bloodied these shrines. When the Israelites became contaminated by Baalism, they likewise offered up their sons and daughters. (Jer. 32:35) There was a sacred pole representing Baal's mother, Asherah. The fertility goddess, Ashtoreth, Baal's wife, was worshiped by lewd sex rites, both men and women being kept as "consecrated" temple prostitutes. It is no wonder that Jehovah had commanded extermination for Baalism and its bestial adherents. "Your eye must not feel sorry for them; and you must not serve their gods."—Deut. 7:16.

CONTENTS OF JUDGES

9 The book divides up logically into three sections. The first two chapters describe the conditions in Israel at the time. Chapters 3 to 16 describe the deliverances of twelve of the judges. Chapters 17 to 21 then describe some events involving internal strife in Israel.

10 **Conditions in Israel at the time of the judges** (1:1–2:23). The tribes of Israel are de-

a Most modern translations testify that the "about four hundred and fifty years" of Acts 13:20 do not correspond with the period of the judges, but precede it; they cover the period from Isaac's birth in 1918 B.C.E. to the division of the Land of Promise in 1467 B.C.E. The order in which the judges are mentioned in Hebrews 11:32 is different from that in the book of Judges, but this fact does not necessarily indicate that the events in Judges do not follow in chronological sequence, for certainly Samuel did not follow David.

b *The Hittites, Story of a Forgotten Empire,* Dr. A. H. Sayce.

c *Light from the Ancient Past,* 1946, J. Finegan, pages 146-148.

4. Who was the writer?
5. How may the time period of Judges be calculated?
6. What proves the book's authenticity?
7, 8. (a) How does archaeology support the record in Judges? (b) Why did Jehovah rightly decree extermination for Baal worshipers?
9. Into what sections does the book logically divide?
10. What background is provided by the two opening chapters?

scribed as they spread out to settle in their assigned territories. However, instead of completely driving out the Canaanites, they put many of them to forced labor, permitting them to dwell among them. Therefore Jehovah's angel declares, "They must become snares to you, and their gods will serve as a lure to you." (2:3) Thus, when a new generation arises that does not know Jehovah or his works, they soon abandon him to serve the Baals and other gods. Because Jehovah's hand is against them for calamity they get "in very sore straits." Because of their stubbornness and refusal to listen even to the judges, Jehovah does not drive out a single one of the nations he has left to test Israel. This background is a help to understanding subsequent events.—2:15.

11 **Judge Othniel** (3:1-11). In distress because of their captivity to the Canaanites, the sons of Israel begin to call on Jehovah for aid. He first raises up Othniel as judge. Does Othniel judge by human power and wisdom? No, for we read: "The spirit of Jehovah now came upon him" to subdue his enemies. "After that the land had no disturbance for forty years."

12 **Judge Ehud** (3:12-30). When the sons of Israel have been subject to Moab's king Eglon for eighteen years, Jehovah again hears their calls for aid, and raises up Judge Ehud. Gaining secret audience with the king, left-handed Ehud snatches his homemade sword from beneath his cloak and plunges it deep into fat Eglon's belly. Israel rallies quickly to Ehud's side in the fight against Moab, and the land again enjoys God-given rest, for eighty years.

13 **Judge Shamgar** (3:31). Shamgar saves Israel by striking down six hundred Philistines. That the victory is by Jehovah's power is indicated by the weapon he uses—a mere cattle goad.

14 **Judge Barak** (4:1–5:31). Israel next becomes subject to the Canaanite king Jabin and his army chief Sisera, who boasts nine hundred chariots with iron scythes. As Israel again begins to cry out to Jehovah, He raises up Judge Barak, ably supported by the prophetess Deborah. So that Barak and his army may have no cause to boast, Deborah makes known that the battle will be by Jehovah's direction, and she prophesies: "It will be into the hand of a woman that Jehovah will sell Sisera." (4:9) Barak calls together men of Naphtali and Zebulun to Mount Tabor. His army of ten thousand then descends to do battle. Strong faith wins the day. 'Jehovah begins to throw Sisera and all his war chariots and all the camp into confusion,' overwhelming them by a flash flood in the valley of Kishon. "Not as much as one remained." (4:15, 16) Jael, wife of Heber the Kenite, to whose tent Sisera flees, climaxes the slaughter by nailing Sisera's head to the ground with a tent peg. "Thus God subdued Jabin." (4:23) Deborah and Barak exult in song, extolling the invincible might of Jehovah, who caused even the stars to fight from their orbits against Sisera. Truly, it is a time to "bless Jehovah"! Forty years of peace follow.

15 **Judge Gideon** (6:1–9:57). The sons of Israel again do bad, and the land is devastated by raiding Midianites. Jehovah, through his angel, commissions Gideon as judge, and Jehovah himself adds assurance with the words, "I shall prove to be with you." (6:16) Gideon's first courageous act is to break down Baal's altar in his home city. The combined armies of the enemy now cross over into Jezreel, and 'Jehovah's spirit envelops Gideon' as he summons Israel to battle. (6:34) By the test of exposing a fleece to the dew on the threshing floor, he receives a twofold sign that God is with him.

16 Jehovah tells Gideon that his army of thirty-two thousand is too many, and may give cause for human bragging about victory. The fearful are first sent home, to leave but ten thousand. (Judg. 7:3; Deut. 20:8) Then, by the water-drinking test, all but an alert and watchful three hundred are eliminated. Gideon reconnoiters the Midianite camp at night and is reassured on hearing a man interpret a dream to mean that "this is nothing else but the sword of Gideon . . . The true God has given Midian and all the camp into his hand." (Judg. 7:14) Gideon worships God, then sets his men in three bands around the Midianite camp. The calm of night is suddenly shattered by the trumpeting of horns, by the flashing of torches and by Gideon's three hundred shouting, "Jehovah's sword and Gideon's!" (7:20) The enemy camp breaks into pandemonium. They fight one against another and take to flight. Israel gives chase, slaughtering them and killing their princes. Israel now asks Gideon to rule over them, but he refuses, saying, "Jehovah is the one who will rule over you." (8:23) However, he makes an ephod out of the war booty, which later comes to be overly venerated and hence to be a snare to Gideon and his household. The land has rest for forty years during Gideon's judgeship.

17 After Gideon's death, Abimelech, one of his sons by a concubine, seizes power and murders

---

11. By what power does Othniel judge, and with what result?
12. How does Jehovah use Ehud in bringing deliverance to Israel?
13. What shows that Shamgar's victory is by God's power?
14. What dramatic events are climaxed by the victory song of Barak and Deborah?
15, 16. What sign does Gideon receive of Jehovah's backing, and how is this fact further emphasized in the final defeat of the Midianites?
17. What doom befalls the usurper Abimelech?

his seventy half brothers. Jotham, Gideon's youngest son, is the only one to escape, and he proclaims Abimelech's doom from his refuge in Mount Gerizim, in "the parable of the trees." This likens Abimelech's "kingship" to that of a lowly bramble. Abimelech soon gets caught up in internal strife in Shechem, and is humbled in being killed by a woman, who makes a direct hit with a millstone thrown from the tower of Thebez, smashing his skull.—Judg. 9:53; 2 Sam. 11:21.

18 **Judges Tola and Jair** (10:1-5). These are next to effect deliverances in Jehovah's power, judging for twenty-three and twenty-two years respectively.

19 **Judge Jephthah** (10:6–12:7). As Israel persists in turning to idolatry, Jehovah's anger again blazes against them. They now suffer oppression from the Ammonites and the Philistines. Jephthah is recalled from exile to lead Israel in the fight. But who is the real judge in this controversy? Jephthah's own words supply the answer: "Let Jehovah the Judge judge today between the sons of Israel and the sons of Ammon." (11:27) As Jehovah's spirit now comes upon him he vows that, on returning from Ammon in peace, he will devote to Jehovah the one that shall first come out of his house to meet him. Jephthah subdues Ammon with a great slaughter. As he returns to his home in Mizpah, it is his own daughter who first comes running to meet him with joy at Jehovah's victory. Jephthah fulfills his vow—no, not by pagan human sacrifice according to Baal rites, but by devoting this only daughter to perpetual service in Jehovah's house to His praise.

20 The men of Ephraim now protest that they were not called on to fight against Ammon, and they threaten Jephthah, who is compelled to drive them back. In all, 42,000 Ephraimites are slaughtered, many of them at the fords of the Jordan, where they are identified by their failure to pronounce the password "Shibboleth" correctly. Jephthah continues to judge Israel for six years.

21 **Judges Ibzan, Elon and Abdon** (12:8-15). Though little is mentioned concerning these, the periods of their judging are stated as seven, ten and eight years.

22 **Judge Samson** (13:1–16:31). Once again Israel falls captive to the Philistines. This time it is Samson that Jehovah raises up as judge. His parents devote him as a Nazirite from birth, and this requires that no razor shall ever come upon his hair. As he grows up, Jehovah blesses him, and 'in time Jehovah's spirit starts to impel him.' (13:25) The secret of his strength lies, not in human muscle, but in power supplied by Jehovah. It is when "Jehovah's spirit [becomes] operative upon him" that he is empowered to slay a lion with his bare hands and later to repay Philistine treachery by striking down thirty of their number. (14:6, 19) As the Philistines continue to act treacherously in connection with Samson's marriage to a Philistine girl, he takes three hundred foxes and, turning them tail to tail, puts torches between their tails and sends them out to burn the grainfields, vineyards and olive groves of the Philistines. Then he accomplishes a great slaughter of the Philistines, "piling legs upon thighs." (15:8) The Philistines persuade his fellow Israelites, men of Judah, to bind Samson and deliver him to them, but again 'Jehovah's spirit becomes operative upon him,' and his fetters melt, as it were, from off his hands. Samson strikes down a thousand of those Philistines—"one heap, two heaps!" (15:14-16) His weapon of destruction? The moist jawbone of an ass. Jehovah refreshes his exhausted servant by causing a miraculous spring of water to break forth at the scene of battle.

23 Samson next lodges a night at a prostitute's house in Gaza, where the Philistines quietly surround him. However, Jehovah's spirit again proves to be with him, as he arises at midnight, pulls out the city gate and its side posts and carries them clear to the top of a mountain before Hebron, about thirty miles away. After this he falls in love with the treacherous Delilah. A willing tool of the Philistines, she nags him until he discloses that his Nazirite devotion to Jehovah, as symbolized in his long hair, is the real source of his great strength. While he sleeps, she has his hair snipped off. This time it is in vain that he awakes to do battle, for "it was Jehovah that had departed from him." (16:20) The Philistines grab him, bore out his eyes, and set him to grinding as a slave in their prison house. As it comes time for a great festival in honor of their god, Dagon, the Philistines bring Samson out to provide amusement for them. Failing to attach value to the fact that his hair is again growing luxuriantly, they allow him to be stationed between the two mighty pillars of the Dagon temple. Samson calls on Jehovah: "Lord Jehovah, remember me, please, and strengthen me, please, just this once." Jehovah *does* remember him. Samson grasps the pillars and 'bends himself with power'—Jehovah's power—"and the house went falling . . . , so that the

18. What does the record tell of Judges Tola and Jair?
19. (a) What deliverance does Jephthah bring? (b) What vow to Jehovah does he faithfully perform? How?
20. What events lead to the "Shibboleth" test?
21. Which three judges next receive mention?
22, 23. (a) What mighty acts does Samson perform, and by what power? (b) How is he finally overcome by the Philistines? (c) What events culminate in Samson's greatest feat, and who remembers him in this hour?

dead that he put to death in his own death came to be more than those he had put to death during his lifetime."—16:28-30.

24 We now come to chapters 17 to 21, which describe some of the internal strife that unhappily plagues Israel during this time. These events take place quite early in the period of the Judges, as is indicated by mention of Jonathan and Phinehas, grandsons of Moses and Aaron, as being still alive.

25 **Micah and the Danites** (17:1–18:31). Micah, a man of Ephraim, sets up his own independent religious establishment, an idolatrous "house of gods," complete with carved image and a Levite priest. Tribesmen of Dan come by on their way to seek an inheritance in the north. They plunder Micah of his religious paraphernalia and priest, and march far north to destroy the unsuspecting city of Laish. In its place they build their own city of Dan and set up Micah's carved image. Thus, they follow the religion of their own independent choice all the days that Jehovah's house of true worship continues in Shiloh.

26 **Benjamin's sin at Gibeah** (19:1–21:25). The next recorded event gives rise to Hosea's later words: "From the days of Gibeah you have sinned, O Israel." (Hos. 10:9) Returning home with his concubine, a Levite from Ephraim lodges overnight with an old man in Gibeah of Benjamin. Good-for-nothing men of the city surround the house, demanding to have intercourse with the Levite. However, they accept his concubine instead and abuse her all night. She is found dead on the threshold in the morning. The Levite takes her body home, carves it into twelve pieces and sends these into all Israel. The twelve tribes are thus put to the test, as to whether they will punish Gibeah and so remove the immoral condition from Israel. Benjamin condones this vile crime. The other tribes congregate to Jehovah at Mizpah, where they resolve to go up by lot against Benjamin at Gibeah. After two sanguinary setbacks, Israel succeeds by an ambush and practically annihilates the tribe of Benjamin, only six hundred men escaping to the crag of Rimmon. Later Israel regrets that one tribe has been chopped off. Occasion is found to provide wives for the surviving Benjamites from among the daughters of Jabesh-gilead and of Shiloh. This closes out a record of strife and intrigue in Israel. As the concluding words of Judges repeat, "In those days there was no king in Israel. What was right in his own eyes was what each one was accustomed to do."—Judg. 21:25.

24. What events are recounted in chapters 17 to 21, and when did they take place?
25. How do some Danites set up an independent religion?
26. How is internal strife in Israel climaxed at Gibeah?

WHY BENEFICIAL

27 Far from being merely a record of strife and bloodshed, the book of Judges exalts Jehovah as the great Deliverer of his people. It shows how his incomparable mercy and long-suffering are expressed toward his name people when they come to him with repentant hearts. Judges is most beneficial in its forthright advocacy of Jehovah's worship and its powerful warnings concerning the folly of demon religion, interfaith and immoral associations. Jehovah's severe condemnation of Baal worship should impel us to stand clear of the modern-day equivalents of materialism, nationalism and sex delinquency.—Judg. 2:11-18.

28 An examination of the fearless and courageous faith of the judges should stir in our hearts a like faith. No wonder they are mentioned with such glowing approval at Hebrews 11:32-34! They were fighters in vindication of Jehovah's name, but not in their own strength. They knew the source of their power, Jehovah's spirit, and they humbly acknowledged it. Likewise, we today can take up "the sword of the spirit," God's Word, confident that he will empower us as he did Barak, Gideon, Jephthah, Samson and the others. Yes, we can be as strong spiritually as Samson was physically in overcoming mighty obstacles, if we will but pray to Jehovah and lean upon him so as to have his spirit.—Eph. 6:17, 18; Judg. 16:28.

29 The prophet Isaiah refers to Judges in two places to show how Jehovah will, without fail, shatter the yoke that his enemies place upon his people, just as he did in the days of Midian. (Isa. 9:4; 10:26) This reminds us also of the song of Deborah and Barak, which concludes with the fervent prayer: "Thus let all your enemies perish, O Jehovah, and let your lovers be as when the sun goes forth in its mightiness." (Judg. 5:31) And who are these lovers? Jesus Christ himself shows them to be the Kingdom heirs, in using a parallel expression at Matthew 13:43: "At that time the righteous ones will shine as brightly as the sun in the kingdom of their Father." Thus Judges points forward to the time when the righteous Judge and Kingdom Seed, Jesus, exercises power. By means of him Jehovah will bring glory and sanctification to His name, in harmony with the psalmist's prayer concerning the enemies of God: "Do to them as to Midian, as to Sisera, as to Jabin at the torrent valley of Kishon . . . that people may know that you, whose name is Jehovah, you alone are the Most High over all the earth."—Ps. 83:9, 18; Judg. 5:20, 21.

27. What powerful warnings in Judges apply also in this day?
28. How may we today profit by the good example of the judges?
29. How does Judges point forward to the sanctification of Jehovah's name through the Kingdom Seed?

Bible Book Number Eight— Ruth

Writer:	**Samuel**
Place Written:	**Israel**
Writing Completed:	**c. 1090 B.C.E.**
Time Covered:	**11 years (judges)**

THE book of Ruth is a delightful drama from the early domestic life of Israel that blossoms into the beautiful love story of Boaz and Ruth. However, it is no mere love idyll. Its purpose is not to entertain. The book highlights Jehovah's purpose to produce a Kingdom heir, and exalts his loving-kindness. (Ruth 1:8; 2:20; 3:10) The expansive quality of Jehovah's love is seen in his selecting a Moabitess girl, a former worshiper of the pagan god Chemosh who converted to the true religion, to become an ancestress of Jesus Christ. Ruth is one of four women mentioned by name in the genealogy from Abraham to Jesus. (Matt. 1:3, 5, 16) Ruth, along with Esther, is one of the two women after whom Bible books are named.

2 "Now it came about in the days when the judges administered justice . . ." With these opening words the book of Ruth launches into its thrilling narrative. By these words it is understood that the book itself was written later, in the time of the kings of Israel. However, the events took place much earlier, probably around 1300 B.C.E., covering a period of about eleven years. Though the name of the writer is not stated, very likely it was Samuel, who also appears to have written Judges, and who was the outstanding faithful figure at the start of the period of the kings. Since the closing verses indicate that David was already becoming prominent, this would place the writing at about 1090 B.C.E. Samuel, who was well acquainted with Jehovah's promise of a "lion" from the tribe of Judah, and who had been used by Jehovah in anointing David of that tribe to be king in Israel, would be deeply interested in making a record of the genealogy down to David.—Gen. 49:10; 1 Sam. 16:1, 13; Ruth 2:4; 4:13, 18-22.

3 The canonical authority of Ruth has never been challenged. Sufficient confirmation of it was given when Jehovah inspired the listing of Ruth in the genealogy of Jesus at Matthew 1:5. Ruth has always been recognized by the Jews as part of the Hebrew canon. It is not surprising, then, that fragments of the book have been found among the other canonical books in the Dead Sea Scrolls discovered between 1947 and 1953. Moreover, Ruth harmonizes completely with Jehovah's Kingdom purposes, as well as with the requirements of the law of Moses. Though marriage with idol-worshiping Canaanites and Moabites was forbidden to the Israelites, this did not exclude "foreigners" such as Ruth who embraced Jehovah's worship. The law on repurchase and brother-in-law marriage is observed in all its detail.—Deut. 7:1-4; 23:3, 4; 25:5-10.

1. (a) Why is the book of Ruth more than just a love story? (b) What special mention is given Ruth in the Bible?
2. When did the events of Ruth take place, when was the book written, and by whom?
3. What facts confirm the canonicity of Ruth?

CONTENTS OF RUTH

4 **Ruth's decision to stick with Naomi** (1:1-22). The story opens during a season of famine in Israel. A man of Bethlehem, Elimelech, crosses the Jordan with his wife, Naomi, and two sons, Mahlon and Chilion, to settle for a time in the land of Moab. There the sons marry Moabite women, Orpah and Ruth. Tragedy breaks the family circle, first in the death of the father, and later in the death of his two sons. Three childless widowed women are left, with no seed to Elimelech. Hearing that Jehovah has again turned his attention to Israel by giving his people bread, Naomi decides to journey back to her native Judah. The daughters-in-law set out with her. Naomi pleads with them to return to Moab, petitioning Jehovah's loving-kindness in providing them husbands from their own people. Finally Orpah "returned to her people and her gods," but Ruth, sincere and strong in her conversion to the worship of Jehovah, sticks with Naomi. Her decision is beautifully expressed in the words: "Where you go I shall go, and where you spend the night I shall spend the night. Your people will be my people, and your God my God. Where you die I shall die, and there is where I shall be buried. May Jehovah do so to me and add to it if anything but death should make a separation between me and you." (1:15-17) Thus Ruth really lives up to the meaning of her name, "friendship." However, the widowed and childless Naomi, whose name means "My Delight," suggests for herself the name Mara, meaning "Bitterness."

4. What decision faces Ruth, and what does her choice indicate as to her form of worship?

5 **Ruth gleans in the field of Boaz** (2:1-23). On arrival in Bethlehem, Ruth obtains Naomi's permission to glean in the barley harvest. Boaz, the owner of the field, an elderly Jew and near kinsman of her father-in-law, Elimelech, notices her during the first day. Though God's law grants her gleaner's rights, Ruth shows meekness by asking permission to work in the field. (Lev. 19:9, 10) This is readily granted, and Boaz tells her to glean only with his young men until the harvest ends. Saying that he has heard of her loyal conduct toward Naomi, he encourages her with the words: "May Jehovah reward the way you act, and may there come to be a perfect wage for you from Jehovah the God of Israel, under whose wings you have come to seek refuge." (Ruth 2:12) That evening Ruth generously shares the fruits of her labor with Naomi, and explains that her success in gleaning is due to the goodwill of Boaz. Naomi sees in this the hand of Jehovah, saying: "Blessed be he of Jehovah, who has not left his loving-kindness toward the living and the dead. . . . The man is related to us. He is one of our repurchasers." (2:20) Yes, Boaz is a near relative, who can legally raise up offspring for Naomi in the name of the dead Elimelech. Ruth continues to glean in the fields of Boaz until the harvest of the barley and of the wheat come to an end.

6 **Boaz, as repurchaser, marries Ruth** (3:1–4:22). Having grown too old herself for bearing offspring, Naomi now instructs Ruth to substitute for her in marriage by repurchase. At so important a season it was customary for the landowner himself to supervise personally the winnowing out of the grain, and this he would do in the evening, to catch the breezes that blew after a hot day. Boaz would be sleeping at the threshing floor, and that is where Ruth finds him. She comes quietly to him, uncovers him at his feet and lies down. On his awaking at midnight, she identifies herself, and requests him to spread his skirt over her in legal proposal of marriage. Boaz declares, "Blessed may you be of Jehovah, my daughter," and commends her for not going after the young men out of passion or greed. Far from being one who would make a proposal of impure relationship, Ruth makes a reputation as "an excellent woman." (3:10, 11) However, as he now tells her, there is another repurchaser more closely related than himself; he will consult with this one in the morning. Ruth keeps lying at his feet until early morning. Then he presents her with a gift of grain and she returns to Naomi, who anxiously inquires as to the outcome.

7 Boaz goes up early to the city gate to seek the repurchaser. Taking ten of the older men of the city as witnesses, he gives this next of kin first opportunity to purchase all that had belonged to Elimelech. Will he do this? His immediate answer is "Yes" when it appears that he can increase his wealth. However, when he learns of the requirement of marriage by repurchase with Ruth, he becomes fearful of his own inheritance, and then legally signifies his refusal by drawing off his sandal. In the Bible record he remains nameless, receiving only dishonorable mention as "So-and-so." Before the same witnesses, Boaz then purchases Ruth as his wife. Is this for any selfish reason? No, but that "the name of the dead man may not be cut off." (4:10) All the onlookers call down Jehovah's blessing on this loving arrangement, and wonderful indeed does that blessing prove to be! Ruth bears a son to Boaz in his old age, and Naomi becomes nurse to the child. He is called "a son . . . to Naomi," and is named Obed.—4:17.

8 The closing verses of Ruth give the genealogy from Perez, through Boaz, to David. Some critics have argued that not all the generations are listed, as the time span is too great for so few persons. Is this true? Or was each one blessed with great longevity, and with a son in his old age? The latter conclusion appears to be the correct one, emphasizing that the production of the promised Seed is by Jehovah's arrangement and undeserved kindness, and not by the power of natural man. On other occasions Jehovah exercised his power in a similar way, as with the births of Isaac, Samuel and John the Baptist.—Gen. 21:1-5; 1 Sam. 1:1-20; Luke 1:5-24, 57-66.

WHY BENEFICIAL

9 This delightful record is certainly beneficial, helping to build strong faith in lovers of righteousness. All the principals in this exciting drama showed outstanding faith in Jehovah, and they "had witness borne to them through their faith." (Heb. 11:39) They became fine examples for us today. Naomi exhibited deep confidence in the loving-kindness of Jehovah. (Ruth 1:8; 2:20) Ruth willingly left her homeland to pursue the worship of Jehovah; she proved herself to be loyal, submissive and a willing worker. It was Boaz' keen appreciation of Jehovah's law, his humble acquiescence in doing Jehovah's will, as well as his love for the faithful Naomi and the industrious Ruth,

5. What fine qualities does Ruth display, and how does Boaz encourage her?
6. How does Ruth request marriage by repurchase, and what response does Boaz make?
7. How does Boaz negotiate the marriage, and what blessing results?
8. What further indicates that the production of the Seed of promise is by Jehovah's arrangement?
9. In what respects are the principal persons in the drama of Ruth fine examples for us today?

that led him to perform his privilege of marriage by repurchase.

10 Jehovah's provision of marriage, and in this instance marriage by repurchase, was used to his honor. Jehovah was the Arranger of the marriage of Boaz and Ruth, and he blessed it according to his loving-kindness, using it as a means of preserving unbroken the royal line of Judah leading to David, and finally to the Greater David, Jesus Christ. Jehovah's watchful care in producing the Kingdom heir according to his legal provision should strengthen our assurance and make us look forward with confidence to the fulfillment of all the Kingdom promises. It should stimulate us to be busy in the modern-day harvest work, confident of a perfect wage from Jehovah, the God of spiritual Israel, under whose 'wings we have come to seek refuge' and whose Kingdom purposes are advancing so gloriously to their fruition. (Ruth 2:12) The book of Ruth is another essential link in the record leading up to that kingdom!

10. Why should the record in Ruth strengthen our confidence in the Kingdom promises?

Bible Book Number Nine— 1 Samuel

Writers:	**Samuel, Gad, Nathan**
Place Written:	**Israel**
Writing Completed:	**c. 1077 B.C.E.**
Time Covered:	**c. 1190-1077 B.C.E.**

IN THE year 1117 B.C.E. there came a momentous change in Israel's national organization. A human king was appointed! This happened while Samuel was serving as Jehovah's judge and prophet in Israel. Though Jehovah had foreknown and foretold it, still the change to a monarchy, as demanded by the people of Israel, came as a stunning blow to Samuel. Devoted as he had been to Jehovah's service from birth, and filled as he was with reverential recognition of Jehovah's kingship, Samuel foresaw disastrous results for his fellow members of God's holy nation. Only at Jehovah's direction did Samuel give in to their demands. "Upon that Samuel spoke to the people about the rightful due of the kingship and wrote it in a book and deposited it before Jehovah." (1 Sam. 10:25) Thus there came to an end the era of the judges, and there began the era of human kings that would see Israel rise to unprecedented power and prestige, only to fall finally into disgrace and divorcement from Jehovah's favor.

2 Who would qualify to make the divine record of this momentous period? Fittingly, Jehovah chose the faithful Samuel to start the writing. "Samuel" means "Name of God," and he was indeed outstanding as an upholder of Jehovah's name in those days. It appears that Samuel wrote the first twenty-four chapters of the book. Then, at his death, Gad and Nathan took up the writing, completing the last five years of the record down to Saul's death. This is indicated by 1 Chronicles 29:29, which reads: "As for the affairs of David the king, the first ones and the last, there they are written among the words of Samuel the seer and among the words of Nathan the prophet and among the words of Gad the visionary." Unlike Kings and Chronicles, the books of Samuel make practically no reference to earlier records, and thus Samuel, Gad and Nathan are confirmed as the writers. All three of these men held positions of trust as prophets of Jehovah and were opposed to the idolatry that had sapped the strength of the nation.

1. What great change in the organization of the nation of Israel came in 1117 B.C.E., and what conditions were to follow thereafter?
2. Who wrote First Samuel, and what were their qualifications?

3 The two books of Samuel were originally one roll or volume. The first time the division into two books was made was on the publication of this part of the Greek *Septuagint Version* within the last three centuries B.C.E., when First Samuel was called First Kings. This division and name were adopted by the Latin *Vulgate* and continue in Catholic Bibles to this day. That First and Second Samuel originally formed one book is shown by the Masoretic note to 1 Samuel 28:24, which states that this verse is in the middle of the book of Samuel. The book was no doubt completed soon after Saul's death in 1077 B.C.E. Samuel died shortly before this, perhaps about 1080 B.C.E. Hence it appears that First Samuel covers a period of approximately 113 years, from about 1190 to 1077 B.C.E.

3. (a) How did First Samuel come to be a separate Bible book? (b) When was it completed, and what period does it cover?

4 Evidences abound as to the accuracy of the record. Geographical locations fit the events described, and archaeology brings further convincing testimony. For example, it was between 1926 and 1929 that a Danish expedition excavated the remains of Shiloh. They revealed that the city was destroyed about the time of the Philistine victory over Israel, described in 1 Samuel 4:1-11. In 1933 an American group of archaeologists, digging on the site that was once Gibeah, unearthed evidence identifying Saul's citadel, where the king sat "in the seat by the wall." (1 Sam. 20:25) Jonathan's successful attack on a Philistine garrison at Michmash, which led to the complete rout of the Philistines, was repeated in World War I by a British Army officer, who routed the Turks by following the landmarks described in Samuel's inspired record.—1 Sam. 14:4-14.[a]

5 However, there are even stronger proofs of the inspiration and authenticity of the book. It contains the striking fulfillment of Jehovah's prophecy that Israel would ask for a king. (Deut. 17:14; 1 Sam. 8:5) Years later, Hosea confirmed its record, quoting Jehovah as saying, "I proceeded to give you a king in my anger, and I shall take him away in my fury." (Hos. 13:11) Peter implied that Samuel was inspired when he identified Samuel as a prophet who had 'plainly declared the days' of Jesus. (Acts 3:24) Paul quoted 1 Samuel 13:14 in briefly highlighting the history of Israel. (Acts 13:20-22) Jesus himself stamped the account with authenticity, in asking the Pharisees in his day: "Have you not *read* what David did when he and the men with him got hungry?" He then related the account of David's asking for the showbread. (Matt. 12:3; 1 Sam. 21:1-6) Ezra also accepted the account as genuine, as already mentioned.—1 Chron. 29:29.

6 This being the original account of David's activities, every mention of David throughout the Scriptures confirms the book of Samuel as being part of God's inspired Word. Some of its events are even referred to in titles of the psalms of David, as at Psalm 59 (1 Sam. 19:11), Psalm 34 (1 Sam. 21:13, 14) and Psalms 57 and 142 (1 Sam. 22:1). Thus the internal evidence of God's own Word testifies conclusively to the authenticity of First Samuel.

a *The Bible as History,* 1958, Werner Keller, pages 175-178 N.Y. Ed., pages 178-181 London Ed.

4. How has the accuracy of the record in First Samuel found striking confirmation?
5. How do other Bible writers testify to the genuineness of the record?
6. What other internal Bible evidence shows First Samuel to be authentic?

CONTENTS OF FIRST SAMUEL

7 The book covers in part or whole the lifespans of four of Israel's leaders: Eli the high priest, Samuel the prophet, Saul the first king, and David who was anointed to be the next king.

8 **Eli's judgeship and the youthful Samuel** (1:1–4:22). As the account opens we are introduced to Hannah, the favorite wife of Elkanah, a Levite. She is childless, and is scorned on this account by his other wife, Peninnah. While the family is making one of its yearly visits to Shiloh, where the ark of Jehovah's covenant is located, Hannah prays fervently to Jehovah for a son. She promises that if her prayer is answered, she will devote the child to the service of Jehovah. God answers her prayer, and she bears a son, Samuel. As soon as he is weaned, she brings him to the house of Jehovah and places him in the care of the high priest Eli, as one 'lent to Jehovah.' (1:28) Hannah then expresses herself in a jubilant song of thanksgiving and happiness. The boy becomes "a minister of Jehovah before Eli the priest." —2:11.

9 All is not well with Eli. He is old, and his two sons have become good-for-nothing scoundrels that do "not acknowledge Jehovah." (2:12) They use their priestly office to satisfy their greed and immoral lusts. Eli fails to correct them. Jehovah therefore proceeds to send divine messages against the house of Eli, warning that "there will not come to be an old man in your house" and that both of Eli's sons will die on the one day. (1 Sam. 2:30-34; 1 Ki. 2:27) Finally, He sends the boy Samuel to Eli with an ear-tingling judgment message. Thus young Samuel is accredited as prophet in Israel. —1 Sam. 3:1, 11.

10 In due course Jehovah executes this judgment by bringing up the Philistines. As the tide of battle turns against the Israelites, they bring the ark of the covenant from Shiloh to their army encampment with loud shouting. Hearing the shouting and learning that the Ark had been brought inside the camp, the Philistines strengthen themselves and win a startling victory, completely routing the Israelites. The Ark is captured, and Eli's two sons die. His heart atremble, Eli hears the report. At mention of the Ark he falls backward off his seat and dies of a broken neck. Thus ends his forty-year judgeship. Truly, "Glory has gone away from Israel," for the Ark represents Jehovah's presence with his people.—4:22.

7. The history contained in the book concerns the lives of which leaders in Israel?
8. What are the circumstances of Samuel's birth and of his becoming "a minister of Jehovah"?
9. How does Samuel come to be prophet in Israel?
10. How does Jehovah execute judgment on Eli's house?

11 **Samuel judges Israel** (5:1–7:17). Now the Philistines, too, have to learn to their great sorrow that the ark of Jehovah must not be used as a good-luck charm. When they bring the Ark into Dagon's temple at Ashdod, their fish god falls flat on his face. On the next day Dagon again falls down flat at the threshold, this time with his head and both palms cut off. This starts the superstitious practice of 'not treading upon the threshold of Dagon.' (5:5) The Philistines hurry the Ark off to Gath, and then to Ekron, but all to no avail! Torments come in the form of panic, piles and a plague of mice. The Philistine axis lords, in final desperation as the death toll mounts, return the Ark to Israel on a new wagon drawn by two milch cows. At Beth-shemesh disaster befalls some of the Israelites because they look upon the Ark. (1 Sam. 6:19; Num. 4:6, 20) Finally, the Ark comes to rest in the house of Abinadab in the Levite city of Kiriath-jearim.

12 For twenty years the Ark remains in the house of Abinadab. Samuel, grown to manhood, urges Israel to put away the Baals and the Ashtoreth images and to serve Jehovah with all their heart. This they do. As they gather to Mizpah to worship, the axis lords of the Philistines seize the opportunity for battle. Caught off guard, Israel calls on Jehovah through Samuel. A loud noise of thunder from Jehovah throws the Philistines into confusion, and the Israelites, strengthened by sacrifice and by prayer, gain a smashing victory. From that time on, 'the hand of Jehovah continues to be against the Philistines all the days of Samuel.' (7:13) However, there is no retirement for Samuel. All his life he keeps judging Israel, making a yearly circuit from Ramah, just north of Jerusalem, to Bethel, Gilgal and Mizpah. In Ramah he builds an altar to Jehovah.

13 **Israel's first king, Saul** (8:1–12:25). Samuel has grown old in Jehovah's service, but his sons do not walk in their father's ways, for they accept bribes and pervert judgment. At this time the older men of Israel approach Samuel with the demand: "Now do appoint for us a king to judge us like all the nations." (8:5) Greatly disturbed, Samuel seeks Jehovah in prayer. Jehovah answers: "It is not you whom they have rejected, but it is I whom they have rejected from being king over them. . . . And now listen to their voice." (8:7-9) First, however, Samuel must warn them of the dire consequences of their rebellious request: regimentation, taxation, loss of freedom, and eventually bitter sorrow and crying to Jehovah. Undeterred in their wishes, the people demand a king.

14 Now we meet Saul, a son of Kish of the tribe of Benjamin, and by far the handsomest and tallest man in Israel. He is directed to Samuel, who honors him at a feast, anoints him and then introduces him to all Israel at an assembly at Mizpah. Though Saul at first hides among the luggage, he is finally presented as Jehovah's choice. Samuel once again reminds Israel of the rightful due of kingship, writing it in a book. However, it is not until his victory over the Ammonites, which relieves the siege at Jabesh in Gilead, that Saul is taken to heart by all the people, so that they confirm his kingship at Gilgal. Samuel again exhorts them to fear, serve and obey Jehovah, and calls on Jehovah to send a sign in the form of unseasonal thunders and rain in harvesttime. In a frightening demonstration Jehovah shows his anger at their rejection of him as King.

15 **Saul's fatal sins** (13:1–15:35). As the Philistines continue to harass Israel, Saul's courageous son Jonathan strikes down a Philistine garrison. To avenge this, the enemy sends a huge army, 'like the sand of the seashore' for number, and encamp at Michmash. Unrest sweeps the Israelite ranks. If only Samuel would come to give us Jehovah's direction! Impatient at waiting for Samuel, Saul presumptuously combines the priesthood with kingship, offering up the burnt sacrifice himself. Suddenly Samuel appears. Brushing aside Saul's lame excuses, he pronounces Jehovah's judgment: "And now your kingdom will not last. Jehovah will certainly find for himself a man agreeable to his heart; and Jehovah will commission him as a leader over his people, because you did not keep what Jehovah commanded you."—13:14.

16 Jonathan, zealous for Jehovah's name, again attacks a Philistine outpost, this time with only his armor-bearer, and quickly strikes down about twenty men. An earthquake adds to the enemy's confusion. They are routed, with Israel in full pursuit. However, the full force of the victory is weakened by Saul's rash oath forbidding the warriors to eat before the battle is over. The men tire quickly and then sin against Jehovah by eating freshly killed meat without taking time to drain the blood. Jonathan, on his part, has refreshed himself from a honeycomb before hearing of the oath, which he boldly denounces as a hindrance. He is redeemed from death by the people, because of the great salvation he has performed in Israel.

17 Now it comes time to carry out Jehovah's

---

11. How does the Ark prove to be no "good-luck charm"?
12. What blessings result from Samuel's advocacy of right worship?
13. How does Israel come to reject Jehovah as their King, and of what consequences does Samuel warn?
14. How does Saul come to be established in the kingship?
15. What outstanding sin leads to Saul's failure?
16. Saul's rashness results in what difficulties?
17. What further rejection of Saul follows his second fatal sin?

judgment on the despicable Amalekites. (Deut. 25:17-19) They are to be completely wiped out. Nothing is to be spared, man or beast. No spoil is to be taken. Everything must be devoted to destruction. However, Saul disobediently preserves Agag, the Amalekite king, and the best of the flocks and herds, ostensibly to sacrifice to Jehovah. This so displeases the God of Israel that he inspires Samuel to express a second rejection of Saul. Disregarding Saul's face-saving excuses, Samuel declares: "Does Jehovah have as much delight in burnt offerings and sacrifices as in obeying the voice of Jehovah? Look! To obey is better than a sacrifice . . . Since you have rejected the word of Jehovah, he accordingly rejects you from being king." (1 Sam. 15: 22, 23) Saul then reaches out to beseech Samuel and rips the skirt off his coat. Samuel assures him that Jehovah will just as surely rip the kingdom from Saul and give it to a better man. Samuel himself picks up the sword, executes Agag and turns his back on Saul, never to see him again.

18 **David's anointing, his valor** (16:1–17:58). Jehovah next directs Samuel to the house of Jesse in Bethlehem of Judah to select and anoint the future king. One by one the sons of Jesse pass in review but are rejected. Jehovah reminds Samuel: "Not the way man sees is the way God sees, because mere man sees what appears to the eyes; but as for Jehovah, he sees what the heart is." (16:7) Finally, Jehovah indicates his approval of David, the youngest, described as "ruddy, a young man with beautiful eyes and handsome in appearance," and Samuel anoints him with oil. (16:12) Jehovah's spirit now comes upon David, but Saul develops a bad spirit.

19 The Philistines again make inroads into Israel, putting forward their champion, Goliath, a giant more than nine feet tall, so monstrous that his coat of mail weighs 126 pounds and his spearhead fifteen pounds. (17:5, 7, *NW* footnotes, 1955 Edition) Day after day this Goliath blasphemously and contemptuously challenges Israel to choose a man and let him come out and fight, but none reply. Saul quakes in his tent. However, David comes to hear the Philistine's taunts. With righteous indignation and inspired courage, David exclaims: "Who is this uncircumcised Philistine that he has to taunt the battle lines of the living God?" (17: 26) Rejecting Saul's armor as untried, David goes out to do battle, equipped only with a shepherd's staff, a sling and five smooth stones. Regarding a match with this young shepherd boy as beneath his dignity, Goliath calls down evil on David. The confident reply rings out: "You are coming to me with a sword and with a spear and with a javelin, but I am coming to you with the name of Jehovah of armies." (17:45) One well-aimed stone from David's sling crumples the champion of the Philistines to the ground—dead! Running to him, in full view of both armies, David draws the giant's sword and uses it to cut off its owner's head. What a great deliverance from Jehovah! What rejoicing in the camp of Israel! With their champion dead, the Philistines take to flight, with the jubilant Israelites in hot pursuit.

20 **Saul's pursuit of David** (18:1–27:12). David's fearless action in behalf of Jehovah's name opens up a wonderful friendship for him. This is with Jonathan, son of Saul and the one naturally in line for the kingdom, who comes "to love him as his own soul," so that the two conclude a covenant of fidelity. (18:1-3) As David's fame comes to be celebrated in Israel, Saul angrily seeks to kill him, even while giving him his daughter Michal in marriage. Saul's enmity grows more and more insane, so that at last David has to make his escape with Jonathan's loving assistance. The two weep at parting, and Jonathan reaffirms his loyalty to David, saying: "May Jehovah himself prove to be between me and you and between my offspring and your offspring to time indefinite." —20:42.

21 In his flight from the embittered Saul, David and his small band of famished supporters come to Nob. Here the priest Ahimelech, on receiving assurance that David and his men are clean from women, permits them to eat the holy showbread. Now armed with the sword of Goliath, he flees to Gath in Philistine territory, where he feigns insanity. Then he goes on to the cave of Adullam, then to Moab, and later, at the advice of Gad the prophet, back to the land of Judah. Fearful of an uprising in favor of David, the insanely jealous Saul has Doeg the Edomite slaughter the priestly population of Nob, only Abiathar escaping to join David. He becomes priest for the group.

22 As a loyal servant of Jehovah, David now wages effective guerrilla warfare against the Philistines. However, Saul continues his all-out campaign to get David, gathering his men of war and hunting him "in the wilderness of Engedi." (24:1) David, the beloved of Jehovah, always manages to keep one step ahead of the pursuers. On one occasion he has opportunity to strike down Saul, but he refrains, simply cutting off the skirt of Saul's coat in evidence that he has spared his life. Even this harmless

18. On what basis does Jehovah choose David?
19. What early victory does David gain in Jehovah's name?
20. How does Jonathan's attitude toward David contrast with that of Saul?
21. What events mark David's flight from Saul?
22. How does David demonstrate loyalty to Jehovah and respect for His organization?

act strikes David at heart, for he feels he has acted against the anointed of Jehovah. What a fine respect he has for Jehovah's organization!

23 Though Samuel's death is now recorded (25:1), his successor scribe keeps the account moving. David requests Nabal, of Maon in Judah, to provide him food in return for befriending his shepherds. Nabal only 'screams rebukes' at David's men, and David sets out to punish him. (25:14) Realizing the danger, Nabal's wife Abigail secretly takes provisions to David and appeases him. David blesses her for this discreet act and sends her back in peace. When Abigail informs Nabal of what has taken place, his heart is stricken, and ten days later he dies. David himself now marries the gracious and beautiful Abigail.

24 For a third time Saul takes up the fanatical pursuit of David, and once again he experiences David's mercy. "A deep sleep from Jehovah" falls upon Saul and his men. This enables David to enter the camp and take Saul's spear, but he refrains from thrusting out his hand "against the anointed of Jehovah." (26:11, 12) David is forced a second time to flee to the Philistines for refuge, and they give him Ziklag as dwelling. From here he keeps up his sorties against others of Israel's enemies.

25 **Saul's suicidal end** (28:1–31:13). The axis lords of the Philistines move a combined army to Shunem. Saul, in a countermove, takes up his position at Mount Gilboa. He frantically seeks guidance, but can get no answer from Jehovah. If only Samuel could be contacted! Disguising himself, he goes to seek out a spirit medium at En-dor, behind the Philistine lines. Finding her, he begs her to contact Samuel for him. Anxious to jump to conclusions, Saul assumes that the apparition called up by the medium is the dead Samuel. However, "Samuel" has no comforting message for the king. Tomorrow he will die and, true to Jehovah's words, the kingdom will be taken from him. In the other camp the axis lords of the Philistines are going up to the battle. Seeing David and his men among them, they become suspicious and send them home. David's men arrive back in Ziklag just in time! A raiding band of Amalekites has made off with the family and possessions of David and his men, but chase is given, and all are recovered without harm.

26 Battle is now joined at Mount Gilboa, resulting in a disastrous defeat for Israel and giving the Philistines control of strategic areas of the land. Jonathan and other sons of Saul are slain, and the mortally wounded Saul kills himself with his own sword—a suicide. The victorious Philistines hang the bodies of Saul and his three sons on the walls of the city of Beth-shan, but they are removed from this disgraceful position by the men of Jabesh-gilead. The calamitous reign of Israel's first king has reached its disastrous end.

23. How does Abigail win peace with David, finally to become his wife?
24. How does David again spare Saul's life?
25. What third fatal sin does Saul commit?
26. How does the calamitous reign of Israel's first king end?

WHY BENEFICIAL

27 What a history is contained in First Samuel! Starkly honest in every detail, it exposes at once both the weakness and the strength of Israel. Here were four leaders in Israel, two who heeded the law of God and two who did not. Note how Eli and Saul were failures, as the former neglected to act and the latter acted presumptuously, overstepping God's law. On the other hand, Samuel and David showed a love for Jehovah's way from their youth on, and they prospered accordingly. What valuable lessons we find here for all overseers! How necessary for these to be firm, watchful of cleanliness and order in Jehovah's organization, respectful of his arrangements, fearless, even-tempered, courageous and lovingly considerate of others! (1 Sam. 2:23-25; 24:5, 7; 18:5, 14-16) Note also that the two who were successful had the advantage of a good theocratic training from their youth upward and that they were courageous from an early age in speaking Jehovah's message and guarding the interests entrusted to them. (3:19; 17:33-37) May all youthful worshipers of Jehovah today become young "Samuels" and "Davids"!

28 Clearly to be remembered among all the beneficial words of this book are those that Jehovah inspired Samuel to utter in judgment of Saul for his failure to "wipe out the mention of Amalek from under the heavens." (Deut. 25:19) The lesson that 'obedience is better than sacrifice' is repeated in various settings at Hosea 6:6, Micah 6:6-8 and Mark 12:33. It is essential that we today benefit by this inspired record, in fully and completely obeying the voice of Jehovah our God! Obedience in recognizing the sanctity of blood is also drawn to our attention at 1 Samuel 14:32, 33. Eating flesh without properly draining the blood was considered as "sinning against Jehovah." This also applies to the Christian congregation, as made plain at Acts 15:28, 29.

29 The focal point of First Samuel is the pitiful error of a nation that came to view God's

27. (a) Wherein did Eli and Saul fail? (b) In what respects are Samuel and David fine examples for overseers and for youthful ministers?
28. How is obedience stressed, and what counsel of First Samuel is repeated later by other Bible writers?
29. The book illustrates the consequences of what national error on the part of Israel? With what warning to self-willed persons?

rule from heaven as impractical. (1 Sam. 8:5, 19, 20; 10:18, 19) The pitfalls and futility of human rulership are graphically as well as prophetically portrayed. (8:11-18; 12:1-17) Saul is revealed at the outset as a modest man who had God's spirit (9:21; 11:6), but his judgment darkened and his heart became bitter as love of righteousness and faith in God diminished. (14: 24, 29, 44) His early record of zeal was annulled by his later acts of presumptuousness, disobedience and infidelity to God. (1 Sam. 13:9; 15:9; 28:7; Ezek. 18:24) His lack of faith bred insecurity, festering into envy, hate and murder. (1 Sam. 18:9, 11; 20:33; 22:18, 19) He died as he had lived, a failure to his God and to his people, and as a warning to any who might become "self-willed" as he did.—2 Pet. 2:10-12.

30 However, there is the contrast of the good. For example, note the course of the faithful Samuel, who served Israel all his life without fraud, partiality or favor. (1 Sam. 12:3-5) He was eager to obey from his boyhood on (3:5), polite and respectful (3:6-8), dependable in performing his duties (3:15), unswerving in his dedication and devotion (7:3-6; 12:2), willing to listen (8:21), ready to uphold Jehovah's decisions (10:24), firm in his judgment regardless of personalities (13:13), strong for obedience (15:22), persistent in fulfilling a commission (16:6, 11) and one having a favorable report from others. (2:26; 9:6) Not only should his youthful ministry encourage young ones to take up the ministry today (2:11, 18), but his continuance without retirement to the end of his days should uphold those weary with age. —7:15.

31 Then there is the splendid example of Jonathan. He showed no hard feelings at the fact that David was anointed to the kingship that he might have inherited. Rather, he recognized David's fine qualities and made a covenant of friendship with him. Similar unselfish companionships can be most upbuilding and encouraging among those today who faithfully serve Jehovah.—23:16-18.

32 For women, there is the example of Hannah, who accompanied her husband regularly to the place of Jehovah's worship. There, in prayer to Jehovah, she showed that her main interest in bearing a son was not to seek personal advantage, but in order that the child might serve God. Wonderful indeed was her reward in seeing him embark on a lifetime of fruitful service to Jehovah. (1:11, 21-23, 27, 28) Further, there is the example of Abigail, who displayed a womanly submission and "sensibleness" that won David's praise, so that later she became his wife.—25:32-35.

33 David's love for Jehovah is movingly expressed in the Psalms that David composed while being hounded in the wilderness by Saul, the backsliding "anointed of Jehovah." (Ps. 34: 7, 8; 52:8; 57:1, 7, 9) And with what heartfelt appreciation did David sanctify Jehovah's name as he hurled defiance at the taunter Goliath! "I am coming to you with the name of Jehovah of armies . . . This day Jehovah will surrender you into my hand, . . . and people of all the earth will know that there exists a God belonging to Israel. And all this congregation will know that neither with sword nor with spear does Jehovah save, because to Jehovah belongs the battle, and he must give you men into our hand." (1 Sam. 17:45-47) David, the courageous and loyal "anointed of Jehovah," magnified Jehovah as God of all the earth and the only true Source of salvation. May we ever follow this fearless example!

34 What has First Samuel to say about the development of God's Kingdom purposes? Ah, this brings us to the real highlight of this Bible book! For it is here that we meet David. Just as his name means "Beloved," so David was loved of Jehovah and chosen as the "man agreeable to his heart," the one fit to be king in Israel. (13:14) Thus the kingdom passed to the tribe of Judah, in harmony with Jacob's blessing at Genesis 49:9, 10, and the kingship was due to remain in the tribe of Judah until the ruler to whom the obedience of all people belongs should come.

35 Moreover, David's name is associated with that of the Kingdom Seed, who was also born in Bethlehem, of David's line. (Matt. 1:1, 6; 2:1; 21:9, 15) That one is the glorified Jesus Christ, the "Lion that is of the tribe of Judah, the root of David," and "the root and the offspring of David, and the bright morning star." (Rev. 5:5; 22:16) Reigning in Kingdom power, this "son of David" will show all the steadfastness and courage of his illustrious forebear in fighting God's enemies to their downfall and sanctifying Jehovah's name in all the earth. How strong our confidence in this Kingdom Seed!

30. What qualities of Samuel may be cultivated with profit by modern-day ministers?
31. In what was Jonathan a fine example?
32. What fine womanly traits are to be observed in Hannah and in Abigail?
33. David's fearless love and loyalty should impel us to what course?
34. How do Jehovah's Kingdom purposes further unfold in connection with David?
35. How did David's name come to be associated with that of the Kingdom Seed, and what qualities of David will that Seed yet show?

Bible Book Number Ten— 2 Samuel

Writers: **Gad and Nathan**
Place Written: **Israel**
Writing Completed: **c. 1040 B.C.E.**
Time Covered: **1077—c. 1040 B.C.E.**

THE nation of Israel was in despair over the disaster of Gilboa and the resulting inroads of the victorious Philistines. The leaders of Israel and the flower of its young men lay dead. In this setting the young "anointed of Jehovah," David the son of Jesse, moved fully onto the national scene. Thus commences the book of Second Samuel, which might well be called a book of Jehovah and David. Its narrative is filled with action of every sort. We are carried from the depths of defeat to the pinnacle of victory, from the distresses of a strife-torn nation to the prosperity of a united kingdom, from the vigor of youth to the wisdom of advanced years. Here is the intimate account of David's life, as he sought to follow Jehovah with all his heart. It is an account that should cause searchings of heart on the part of every reader, that he may strengthen his own relationship and standing with his Creator.

2 Actually, Samuel's name is not even mentioned in the record of Second Samuel, the name being given to the book only because of its having been originally one roll or volume with First Samuel. The prophets Nathan and Gad, who completed the writing of First Samuel, continued on in writing all of Second Samuel. (1 Chron. 29:29) They were well qualified for this task. Not only had Gad been with David when he was a hunted outlaw in Israel, but toward the end of David's forty-year reign he was still actively associated with the king. Gad was the one used to pronounce Jehovah's displeasure on David for unwisely numbering Israel. (1 Sam. 22:5; 2 Sam. 24:1-25) Overlapping and extending beyond the period of Gad's lifetime was the activity of Nathan the prophet, a close associate of David. It was his privilege to make known Jehovah's significant covenant with David, the covenant for the Kingdom. He it was who courageously and under inspiration pointed out David's great sin involving Bath-sheba and the penalty for it. (2 Sam. 7:1-17; 12:1-15) Thus Jehovah used Nathan, whose name means "Gift; Given," and Gad, whose name means "Good Fortune," to record the inspired and beneficial information in Second Samuel. These unassuming historians did not seek to preserve memory of themselves, as no information is given of their ancestry or personal lives. They sought only to preserve the record inspired of God, for the benefit of future worshipers of Jehovah.

3 Second Samuel takes up the narrative of accurate Bible history following the death of Saul, Israel's first king, and carries it along to near the end of David's forty-year reign. Thus, the period covered is from 1077 to about 1040 B.C.E. The fact that the book does not record David's death is strong evidence that it was written about 1040, or just prior to his death.

4 For the same reasons put forth with regard to First Samuel, the book of Second Samuel must be accepted as part of the Bible canon. Its authenticity is beyond question. Its very candor and frankness, not even glossing over King David's sins and shortcomings, is a strong circumstantial evidence in itself. Archaeological discoveries have verified many of the details of Second Samuel. For example, the pool of Gibeon is mentioned at 2 Samuel 2:12-17 as being the starting point of an encounter between the servants of David and Ish-bosheth, Saul's son. Archaeologist J. B. Prichard, associate of the University of Pennsylvania Museum, has recently located the exact site of the ancient pool of Gibeon at El-jib in the Hashemite Kingdom of Jordan. This was quite large, the well being thirty-seven feet across at the top, and with a water-drawing room eighty-two feet below the surface.[a]

5 However, the strongest evidence for the authenticity of Second Samuel is to be found in the fulfilled prophecies, particularly those relating to the kingdom covenant with David. God promised David: "Your house and your kingdom will certainly be steadfast to time in-

a The New York *Times*, Sept. 22, 1957.

1. Against what background does Second Samuel open, and how does its account develop?
2. (a) How did the book come to be called "Second Samuel"? (b) Who were the writers, what were their qualifications, and what record only did they seek to preserve?
3. What period is covered by the book, and when was its writing completed?
4. (a) For what reasons must Second Samuel be accepted as part of the Bible canon? (b) How does archaeology support the record?
5. What is the strongest reason for accepting Second Samuel as inspired Scripture?

definite before you; your very throne will become one firmly established to time indefinite." (2 Sam. 7:16) Jeremiah, even in the evening time of the kingdom of Judah, mentioned the continuity of this promise to the house of David, with the words: "This is what Jehovah has said, 'There will not be cut off in David's case a man to sit upon the throne of the house of Israel.'" (Jer. 33:17) This prophecy has not gone unfulfilled, for Jehovah later brought forth from Judah "Jesus Christ, son of David," as both Bible and profane history so clearly testify.—Matt. 1:1.

CONTENTS OF SECOND SAMUEL

6 **Early events of David's reign** (1:1–4:12). Following Saul's death at Mount Gilboa, an Amalekite fugitive from the battle comes hurrying to David at Ziklag with the report. Hoping to curry favor with David, he fabricates the story that it is he himself that took Saul's life. Instead of commendation, the Amalekite receives only the reward of death, for he has condemned himself by testifying to striking "the anointed of Jehovah." (1:16) The new king, David, now composes a dirge, "The Bow," in which he laments the deaths of Saul and Jonathan. This rises to a beautiful climax in its touching expression of David's overflowing love for Jonathan: "I am distressed over you, my brother Jonathan, very pleasant you were to me. More wonderful was your love to me than the love from women. How have the mighty ones fallen and the weapons of war perished!"—1:26, 27.

7 At Jehovah's direction, David and his men move their households to Hebron in the territory of Judah. Here the elders of the tribe come to anoint David as their king in 1077 B.C.E. General Joab becomes the most prominent of David's supporters. However, as a rival for the kingship over the nation, Ish-bosheth, a son of Saul, is anointed by General Abner. There are periodic clashes between the two opposing forces until Abner defects to David's camp. He takes with him to David Saul's daughter Michal, for whom David has long previously paid the marriage price. However, in revenge for the slaying of his brother, Joab finds an occasion for killing Abner. David is greatly distressed at this, disclaiming any responsibility. Soon thereafter Ish-bosheth himself is murdered as he is "taking his noonday siesta." —4:5.

8 **David king in Jerusalem** (5:1–6:23). Though he has already ruled as king in Judah for seven years and six months, David now becomes undisputed ruler, and representatives of the tribes anoint him as king over all Israel. This is his third anointing (1070 B.C.E.). One of David's first acts as ruler of the entire kingdom is to capture the stronghold of Zion in Jerusalem from the entrenched Jebusites, surprising them by way of the water tunnel. David then makes Jerusalem his capital city. Jehovah of armies blesses David, making him greater and greater. Even Hiram, rich king of Tyre, sends David valuable cedars and also workmen to construct a house for the king. David's family increases, and Jehovah prospers his reign. There are two more encounters with the warlike Philistines. In the first of these, Jehovah breaks through the enemy for David at Baal-perazim, giving him the victory. In the second, Jehovah performs another miracle by making a "sound of a marching in the tops of the baca bushes," indicating that Jehovah is going ahead of Israel to rout the armies of the Philistines. (5:24) Another outstanding victory for Jehovah's forces!

9 Taking 30,000 men with him, David sets out to bring the ark of the covenant from Baale-judah (Kiriath-jearim) to Jerusalem. As it is being brought along with great music and rejoicing, the wagon on which it is riding gives a lurch, and Uzzah, who is walking alongside, reaches out to steady the sacred Ark. "At that Jehovah's anger blazed against Uzzah and the true God struck him down there for the irreverent act." (6:7) The Ark comes to rest at the house of Obed-edom, and during the next three months Jehovah richly blesses the household of Obed-edom. After three months David comes to take the Ark in the right manner the rest of the way. With joyful shouting, music and dancing, the Ark is brought into David's capital. David gives vent to his great joy in dancing before Jehovah, but his wife Michal takes exception to this. David insists: "I will celebrate before Jehovah." (6:21) In consequence Michal remains childless until her death.[a]

10 **God's covenant with David** (7:1-29). We now come to one of the most important events in David's life, one that is directly connected with the central theme of the Bible, the sanctification of Jehovah's name by the kingdom of his Seed. This event arises out of David's desire to build a house for the ark of God. Living in a beautiful house of cedars himself, he indicates to Nathan his desire to build a house for Jehovah's ark of the covenant. Through Nathan, Jehovah reassures David of his loving-

6. How does David react on hearing news of the deaths of Saul and Jonathan?
7. What other events mark the early part of David's reign?
8. How does Jehovah prosper David's reign over all Israel?

a *The Watchtower*, 1962, pages 511, 512.

9. Describe the events connected with bringing the Ark up to Jerusalem.
10. What covenant and promise of Jehovah next come to our attention?

kindness toward Israel and establishes with him a covenant that will abide for all time. However, it will not be David, but his seed that will build the house for Jehovah's name. In addition, Jehovah makes the loving promise: "And your house and your kingdom will certainly be steadfast to time indefinite before you; your very throne will become one firmly established to time indefinite."—7:16.

11 Overcome by Jehovah's goodness, as expressed through this kingdom covenant, David pours out his thankfulness for all of God's loving-kindness: "What one nation in the earth is like your people Israel, whom God went to redeem to himself as a people and to assign himself a name and to do for them great and fear-inspiring things? . . . and you yourself, O Jehovah, have become their God." (7:23, 24) Fervently he prays for the sanctification of Jehovah's name and for the house of David to become firmly established before Him.

12 **David extends Israel's dominion** (8:1–10:19). However, David is not left to rule in peace. Wars are yet to be fought. David proceeds to strike down the Philistines, the Moabites, the Zobahites, the Syrians and the Edomites, extending Israel's boundary to its God-ordained limits. (2 Sam. 8:1-5, 13-15; Deut. 11:24) He then turns his attention to the house of Saul in order that, for the sake of Jonathan, he might express loving-kindness toward any remaining. Ziba, a servant of Saul, calls to his attention a son of Jonathan, Mephibosheth, who is lame in the feet. Immediately, David requires that all of Saul's goods be turned over to Mephibosheth and that his land be cultivated by Ziba and his servants to provide food for Mephibosheth's house. Mephibosheth himself, however, is to eat at the table of David.

13 When the king of Ammon dies, David sends ambassadors to Hanun his son with expressions of loving-kindness. Hanun's counselors, however, accuse David of sending them to spy out the land, and so they humiliate them and send them back half naked. Angered by this affront, David sends Joab with his army to avenge the wrong. Dividing his forces, he easily routs the Ammonites and the Syrians who had come up to their help. The Syrians regroup their forces, only to be defeated once again by the armies of Jehovah under the command of David, with the loss of 700 charioteers and 40,000 horsemen. Here is further evidence of Jehovah's favor and blessing on David.

14 **David sins against Jehovah** (11:1–12:31). The following spring David again sends Joab into Ammon to lay siege to Rabbah, while he himself remains in Jerusalem. One evening he happens to observe from his rooftop the beautiful Bath-sheba, wife of Uriah the Hittite, as she is bathing. Bringing her to his house, he has relations with her, and she becomes pregnant. David tries to cover up by bringing Uriah back from the fighting at Rabbah, and sending him down to his house to refresh himself. However, Uriah refuses to please himself and have relations with his wife while the Ark and the army are "dwelling in booths." In desperation David sends Uriah back to Joab with a letter saying: "Put Uriah in front of the heaviest battle charges, and you men must retreat from behind him, and he must be struck down and die." (11:11, 15) In this way Uriah dies. After Bath-sheba's period of mourning is passed, David immediately takes her to his house, where she becomes his wife, and their child, a son, is born.

15 This is bad in Jehovah's eyes. He sends the prophet Nathan to David with a message of judgment. Nathan tells David of a rich man and a poor man. The one had many flocks, but the other had one female lamb, which was a pet in the family and "as a daughter to him." However, when it came to making a feast, the rich man took, not a sheep from his own flocks, but the female lamb of the poor man. Incensed at hearing this, David exclaims: "As Jehovah is living, the man doing this deserves to die!" Back come Nathan's words: "You yourself are the man!" (12:5, 7) He then pronounces prophetic judgment that David's wives will be violated publicly by another man, that his house will be plagued by internal warfare and that his child by Bath-sheba will die.

16 In sincere sorrow and repentance, David openly acknowledges: "I have sinned against Jehovah." (12:13) True to Jehovah's word, the offspring of the adulterous union dies after seven days' illness. (Later, David has another son by Bath-sheba; this one they call Solomon, meaning "Peaceable." However, Jehovah sends through Nathan to call him also Jedidiah, meaning "Beloved of Jah.") Following his soul-shaking experience, David is called by Joab to come to Rabbah, where the final assault is being made ready. Having captured the city's water supply, Joab respectfully leaves to the king the honor of capturing the city itself.

17 **David's domestic difficulties** (13:1–18:33). David's household troubles get started when Amnon, one of David's sons, falls passionately

11. With what prayer does David express thankfulness?
12. What wars does David fight, and what kindness does he show to Saul's house?
13. By what further victories does Jehovah show that he is with David?
14. What sins does David commit over Bath-sheba?
15. How does Nathan pronounce prophetic judgment on David?
16. (a) What meanings attach to the names of David's other son by Bath-sheba? (b) What is the final outcome of the assault on Rabbah?
17. What internal troubles start to afflict David's household?

in love with Tamar, the sister of his half-brother Absalom. Amnon feigns illness and asks that the beautiful Tamar be sent to care for him. He violates her, and then comes to hate her intensely, so that he sends her away in humiliation. Absalom plans vengeance, biding his time. About two years later he prepares a feast to which Amnon and all the other sons of the king are invited. When Amnon's heart becomes merry with wine, he is caught off guard and put to death at Absalom's order.

18 Fearing the king's displeasure, Absalom flees to Geshur, where he lives in semi-exile for three years. Meanwhile, General Joab schemes to bring about a reconciliation between David and his son. He arranges for a wise woman of Tekoa to pose a fictitious situation before the king concerning retribution, banishment and punishment. When the king passes judgment, the woman reveals the true reason for her presence, in that the king's own son Absalom is in banishment in Geshur. David recognizes that Joab has planned this, but gives permission for his son to return to Jerusalem. It is another two years before the king consents to see Absalom face to face.

19 Despite David's loving-kindness, Absalom soon works up a conspiracy to seize the throne itself from his father. Absalom is outstandingly handsome among all the valiant men of Israel, and this makes him ambitious and proud. Each year the shearings of his luxuriant head of hair weigh almost four pounds. (14:26, *NW* footnote, 1955 Edition) By various crafty maneuvers, Absalom begins to steal the hearts of the men of Israel. Finally, the conspiracy comes out into the open. Gaining his father's permission to go to Hebron, Absalom there announces his rebellious purpose and calls for the support of all Israel in his uprising against David. As great numbers flock to his rebel son's side, David flees from Jerusalem with a few loyal supporters, typical of whom is Ittai the Gittite, who declares: "As Jehovah is living and as my lord the king is living, in the place where my lord the king may come to be, whether for death or for life, there is where your servant will come to be!"—15:21.

20 While in flight from Jerusalem, David learns of the treachery of one of his most trusted counselors, Ahithophel. He prays: "Turn, please, the counsel of Ahithophel into foolishness, O Jehovah!" (15:31) Zadok and Abiathar, priests loyal to David, and Hushai the Archite are sent back to Jerusalem to watch and report on Absalom's activities. Meanwhile, in the wilderness, David meets Ziba, the attendant of Mephibosheth, who reports that his master is now expecting the kingdom to revert to the house of Saul. As David passes on, Shimei, of Saul's house, curses him and hurls stones at him, but David restrains his men from taking vengeance.

21 Back in Jerusalem, at Ahithophel's suggestion, the usurper Absalom has relations with his father's concubines "under the eyes of all Israel." This is in fulfillment of Nathan's prophetic judgment. (16:22; 12:11) Ahithophel also counsels Absalom to take a force of 12,000 men and hunt David down in the wilderness. However, Hushai, who has won his way into Absalom's confidence, recommends a different course, just as David has prayed. Judas-like, the frustrated Ahithophel goes home and strangles himself. Hushai secretly reports the usurper's plans to the priests Zadok and Abiathar, who, in turn, have the message relayed to David in the wilderness.

22 This enables David to cross the Jordan, and to choose the site of battle in the forest at Mahanaim. There he deploys his forces and commands them to treat Absalom gently. The rebels suffer a crushing defeat. As Absalom flees on a mule through the heavily wooded forest, his head gets caught in the lower branches of a massive tree, and there he hangs suspended in midair. Finding him in this predicament, Joab kills him, in utter disregard for the king's command. David's deep grief on hearing of the death of his son is reflected in his lament: "My son Absalom, my son, my son Absalom! O that I might have died, I myself, instead of you, Absalom my son, my son!" —18:33.

23 **Closing events of David's reign** (19:1–24:25). David continues to mourn bitterly until Joab urges him to resume his rightful position as king. He now appoints Amasa as head over the army in place of Joab. As he returns he is welcomed by the people, including Shimei, who asks and receives forgiveness. Mephibosheth also comes to plead his case, and David gives him an equal inheritance with Ziba. Once again, all Israel and Judah are united under David.

24 However, there are more troubles in store. Sheba, a Benjaminite, declares himself king and turns many aside from David. Amasa, ordered by David to gather men to put down the rebellion, is met by Joab and treacherously murdered. Joab then takes over the army and follows Sheba to Abel and lays siege to the city. Heeding the advice of a wise woman of the city, the inhabitants execute Sheba, and

18. By what subterfuge is Absalom restored from exile?
19. What conspiracy now comes into the open, and with what result to David?
20, 21. (a) What events accompany David's flight, and how is Nathan's prophecy fulfilled? (b) How does treacherous Ahithophel come to his end?
22. With what sorrow is David's victory tempered?
23. What arrangements mark David's return as king?
24. What further developments take place, involving the tribe of Benjamin?

Joab withdraws. Because of unavenged bloodguilt on Benjamin over Saul's slaying the Gibeonites, there comes to be a three-year famine in Israel. To remove the bloodguilt, seven sons of Saul's household are executed. Later, in battle with the Philistines again, David's life is barely saved by Abishai, his nephew. His men swear that he must no more go out to battle with them, "that you may not extinguish the lamp of Israel!" (21:17) Three of his mighty men then perform notably in striking down Philistine giants.

25 At this point, the writer breaks into the account with a song of David to Jehovah, paralleling the eighteenth Psalm, and expressing thanks for deliverance "out of the palm of all his enemies and out of Saul's palm." Joyfully he declares: "Jehovah is my crag and my stronghold and the Provider of escape for me. The One doing great acts of salvation for his king and exercising loving-kindness to his anointed one, to David and to his seed for time indefinite." (22:1, 2, 51) There follows the last song of David, in which he acknowledges, "The spirit of Jehovah it was that spoke by me, and his word was upon my tongue."—23:2.

26 Coming back to the historical record, we find listed the mighty men who belong to David, three of whom are outstanding. These are involved in an incident occurring when an outpost of the Philistines has been established in Bethlehem, David's hometown. David expresses the desire: "O that I might have a drink of the water from the cistern of Bethlehem that is at the gate!" (23:15) At that the three mighty men force their way into the Philistine camp, draw water from the cistern and carry it back to David. But David refuses to drink it. Instead, he pours it out on the ground, saying: "It is unthinkable on my part, O Jehovah, that I should do this! Shall I drink the blood of the men going at the risk of their souls?" (23:17) To him the water is the equivalent of the lifeblood they have risked for it. The thirty mightiest men of his army and their exploits are next listed.

27 Finally, David sins in numbering the people. Pleading with God for mercy, he is given the choice between three punishments: seven years of famine, three months of military defeats or three days of pestilence in the land. David replies: "Let us fall, please, into the hand of Jehovah, for many are his mercies; but into the hand of man do not let me fall." (24:14) The nationwide pestilence kills 70,000 persons, being stopped only when David, acting on Jehovah's instructions through Gad, purchases the threshing floor of Araunah, where he offers up burnt and communion sacrifices to Jehovah.

25. What is expressed in the songs of David next recorded?
26. What is stated concerning David's mighty men, and how does he show respect for their lifeblood?
27. What final sin does David commit? How is the resulting plague stopped?

WHY BENEFICIAL

28 There is much to be found in Second Samuel that is beneficial for the modern reader! Almost every human emotion is painted here in colors of the fullest intensity, those of real life. Thus, we are warned in striking terms of the disastrous results of ambition and revenge (3:27-30), of wrongful lust for another's marriage mate (11:2-4, 15-17; 12:9, 10), of traitorous action (15:12, 31; 17:23), of immoral courtship (13:10-15, 28, 29), of hasty judgment (16:3, 4; 19:25-30), and of disrespect for another's acts of devotion.—6:20-23.

29 However, by far the greatest benefit from Second Samuel is to be found on the positive side, by heeding its many excellent examples of right conduct and action. David is a model in his exclusive devotion to God (7:22), his humility before God (7:18), his exalting of Jehovah's name (7:23, 26), his proper viewpoint in adversity (15:25), his sincere repentance of sin (12:13), his faithfulness to his promise (9:1, 7), his keeping balance under trial (16:11, 12), his consistent reliance on Jehovah (5:12, 20) and his deep respect for Jehovah's arrangements and appointments. (1:11, 12) No wonder that David was called "a man agreeable to [Jehovah's] heart"!—1 Sam. 13:14.

30 The application of many Bible principles is also to be found in Second Samuel. Among these are the principles of community responsibility (3:29; 24:11-15), that good intentions do not alter God's requirements (6:6, 7), that headship in Jehovah's theocratic arrangement should be respected (12:28), that blood is to be regarded as sacred (23:17), that atonement is required for bloodguilt (21:1-6, 9, 14), that a wise one can avert disaster for many (2 Sam. 20:21, 22; Eccl. 9:15) and that loyalty to Jehovah's organization and its representatives must be maintained "whether for death or for life." —2 Sam. 15:18-22.

31 Most important of all, Second Samuel points forward to and gives brilliant foregleams of God's kingdom that he establishes in the hands of the "son of David," Jesus Christ. (Matt. 1:1) The oath that Jehovah made to David, whose name means "Beloved," concerning the permanence of his kingdom (2 Sam. 7:16) is cited at

28. What striking warnings are contained in Second Samuel?
29. What excellent examples of right conduct and action are to be found?
30. What principles are applied and illustrated in the book?
31. How does Second Samuel provide foregleams of God's kingdom, as testified in the Christian Greek Scriptures?

Acts 2:29-36 with reference to Jesus. That the prophecy, "I myself shall become his father, and he himself will become my son" (2 Sam. 7:14), really pointed forward to Jesus is shown by Hebrews 1:5. This was also testified to by Jehovah's voice speaking from heaven: "This is my Son, the beloved, whom I have approved." (Matt. 3:17; 17:5) Finally, the kingdom covenant with David is referred to by Gabriel in his words to Mary concerning Jesus: "This one will be great and will be called Son of the Most High; and Jehovah God will give him the throne of David his father, and he will rule as king over the house of Jacob forever, and there will be no end of his kingdom." (Luke 1:32, 33) How thrilling does the promise of the Kingdom Seed appear as each step in its development unfolds before our eyes!

Bible Book Number Eleven— 1 Kings

Writer: **Jeremiah**
Places Written: **Jerusalem and Israel**
Writing Completed: **c. 580 B.C.E.**
Time Covered: **c. 1040-917 B.C.E.**

THE conquests of David had extended Israel's domain to its God-given boundaries, from the river Euphrates in the north to the river of Egypt in the south. (2 Sam. 8:3; 1 Ki. 4:21) As the old king died, and his son Solomon came to rule in his stead, "Judah and Israel were many, like the grains of sand that are by the sea for multitude, eating and drinking and rejoicing." (1 Ki. 4:20) Solomon ruled with great wisdom, a wisdom that far surpassed that of the ancient Greeks. He built a magnificent temple to Jehovah. However, even Solomon fell away to the worship of false gods. At his death the kingdom was ripped in two, and a succession of wicked kings in the rival kingdoms of Israel and Judah acted ruinously, bringing distress to the people, just as Samuel had predicted. (1 Sam. 8:10-18) Of the fourteen kings who ruled in Judah and in Israel after Solomon's death and as reviewed in the book of First Kings, only two succeeded in doing right in Jehovah's eyes. Is this record, then, "inspired and beneficial"? Most certainly it is, as we shall see from its admonitions, its prophecies and types, and its relation to the dominant Kingdom theme of "all Scripture."

2 "The Book of Kings" was originally one roll or volume and was called *Se'pher M^e lach·im'* in Hebrew. The translators of the *Septuagint* called it *Bas·il·ei'on,* "Of Kingdoms," and were the first to divide it into two scrolls for convenience' sake. They were later called Third and Fourth Kings, which designation continues in the Catholic Bible to this day. However, they are now generally known as First and Second Kings. They differ from First and Second Samuel in naming previous records as source material for the compiler. Hence, these are not eyewitness records, though the records from which they were compiled undoubtedly were. The one compiler, in the course of the two books, refers fifteen times to "the book of the affairs of the days of the kings of Judah," eighteen times to "the book of the affairs of the days of the kings of Israel," and also to "the book of the affairs of Solomon." (1 Ki. 15:7; 14:19; 11:41) Though these other ancient records have been completely lost, the inspired compilation remains, as the beneficial account of First and Second Kings.

3 Who wrote the books of Kings? Their emphasis on the work of the prophets, especially Elijah and Elisha, indicates a prophet of Jehovah. Similarities of language, composition and style suggest the same writer as the book of Jeremiah. Many Hebrew words and expressions appear only in Kings and Jeremiah, and in no other Bible book. However, if Jeremiah wrote the books of Kings, why is he not mentioned therein? It was not necessary, for his work had already been covered in the book bearing his name. Moreover, Kings was written to magnify Jehovah and His worship, not to add to Jeremiah's reputation. Actually, Kings and Jeremiah are complementary for the most part, each filling in what the other omits. In addition, there are parallel accounts, as, for example, 2 Kings 24:18–25:30 and Jeremiah 39:1-10; 40:7–41:10; 52:1-34. Jewish tradition confirms that Jeremiah was the writer of First and Second Kings. No doubt he commenced the compilation of both books in Jerusalem, and it appears

1. (a) How did Israel's radiant prosperity degenerate into ruin? (b) Yet why may this record be described as "inspired and beneficial"?
2. How did the record of First and Second Kings come to be in two scrolls, and how were they compiled?
3. (a) Who undoubtedly wrote these books, and why do you so answer? (b) When was the writing completed, and what period is covered by First Kings?

that the second book was completed in Egypt about 580 B.C.E., since he refers to events of that year in the conclusion of his record. (2 Ki. 25:27) First Kings takes up the history of Israel from the end of Second Samuel, and carries it through to 917 B.C.E., when Jehoshaphat died.—1 Ki. 22:50.

4 First Kings takes its rightful place in the canon of the Holy Scriptures, being accepted by all authorities. Moreover, events in First Kings are confirmed by the secular histories of Egypt and Assyria.[a] Archaeology, too, supports many of the statements in the book. Excavations in Jericho have shown that the city was rebuilt some 500 years after its destruction, a prophecy uttered by Joshua also having a remarkable fulfillment at the time. (Josh. 6:26; 1 Ki. 16:33, 34)[b] At 1 Kings 7:45, 46 we read of Hiram's casting the copper utensils for Solomon's temple "in the District of the Jordan . . . between Succoth and Zarethan." Archaeologists digging on the site of ancient Succoth have unearthed fragments of slag there, as well as great slag heaps at the modern Ajlun, in the same area north of the Jabbok River. From their investigations they conclude that "in Solomon's time, this entire district of the Jordan valley hummed with industrial activity."[c]

5 References by other Bible writers and fulfillments of prophecies support the authenticity of First Kings. Jesus spoke of the events surrounding Elijah and the widow of Zarephath as historical realities. (Luke 4:24-26) He showed Elijah to be a type of John the Baptist: "This is 'Elijah who is destined to come.'" (Matt. 11:13, 14) Here Jesus was referring to the prophecy of Malachi, who spoke also of a future day: "Look! I am sending to you people Elijah the prophet before the coming of the great and fear-inspiring day of Jehovah."—Mal. 4:5.

CONTENTS OF FIRST KINGS

6 **Solomon becomes king** (1:1–2:46). The record of First Kings opens with David near death as he draws close to the conclusion of his reign of forty years. His son Adonijah, with the help of Joab the army chief and Abiathar the priest, conspires to take over the kingship. The prophet Nathan informs David of this, and indirectly reminds him that he has already designated Solomon to be king at his death. David therefore has Zadok the priest anoint Solomon as king, even while the conspirators are celebrating Adonijah's succession. David now charges Solomon to be strong and prove himself a man, and to walk in the ways of Jehovah his God, after which David dies and is buried in "the city of David." (2:10) In time Solomon banishes Abiathar and executes troublemakers Adonijah and Joab. Later, Shimei is executed when he does not show respect for the merciful provision made to save his life. The kingdom is now firmly established in the hands of Solomon.

7 **Solomon's wise rule** (3:1–4:34). Solomon forms a marriage alliance with Egypt by marrying Pharaoh's daughter. He prays to Jehovah for an obedient heart, in order to judge Jehovah's people with discernment. Because he does not request long life or riches, Jehovah promises to give him a wise and discerning heart and also riches and glory. Solomon early shows his wisdom when two women appear before him claiming the same child. Solomon orders: "Sever the living child in two" and give a half to each. At this the real mother pleads for the child's life, saying the other woman should have it. Solomon thus identifies the rightful mother, and she gets the child. Because of Solomon's God-given wisdom, all Israel prospers and is happy and secure. People from many lands come to hear his wise sayings.

8 **Solomon's temple** (5:1–10:29). Solomon recalls Jehovah's words to his father David: "Your son whom I shall put upon your throne in place of you, he is the one that will build the house to my name." (5:5) He therefore makes preparation for this. Hiram the king of Tyre, who was a lover of David, assists by sending cedar and juniper logs from Lebanon and by providing skilled workers. These, together with Solomon's conscripted workers, start work on the house of Jehovah in the fourth year of Solomon's reign, in the four hundred and eightieth year after the Israelites left Egypt. (6:1) No tools are used at the building site, as all the stones are prepared and fitted at the quarry before being brought to the temple site for assembly. The entire interior of the temple, first covered with cedar on the walls and juniper wood on the floor, is then beautifully overlaid with gold. Two figures of cherubs are made of oil-tree wood, each about fifteen feet high and fifteen feet from wing tip to wing tip, and these are placed in the innermost

[a] See Study 9, paragraph 10; also *The Bible as History,* 1956, Werner Keller, pages 228-233 N.Y. Ed., pages 223-228 London Ed.
[b] *The Story of Jericho,* 1948, John Garstang, pages 146-150.
[c] *The River Jordan,* 1945, Nelson Glueck, pages 145, 146.

4. How do secular history and archaeology confirm the record?
5. What inspired testimony proves the book's authenticity?
6. Under what circumstances does Solomon ascend the throne, and how does he become firmly established in the kingdom?
7. What prayer of Solomon does Jehovah answer, and with what result to Israel?
8. (a) How does Solomon go about building the temple? Describe some of its features. (b) What further building program does he carry out?

room. Other cherubs, along with palm-tree figures and blossoms, are engraved on the temple walls. At last, after more than seven years' work, the magnificent temple is completed. Solomon continues his building program: a house for himself, the House of the Forest of Lebanon, the Porch of Pillars, the Porch of the Throne and a house for Pharaoh's daughter. He also makes two great copper pillars for the porch of Jehovah's house, the molten sea for the court and the copper carriages, copper basins and golden utensils.

9 Now the time comes for the priests to bring up the ark of Jehovah's covenant, and to place it in the innermost room, the Most Holy, under the wings of the cherubs. As the priests come out, 'the glory of Jehovah fills the house of Jehovah,' so that the priests can no longer stand and minister. (8:11) Solomon blesses the congregation of Israel, and blesses and praises Jehovah. On bended knees, and with his palms spread out to the heavens, he prayerfully acknowledges that the heaven of the heavens cannot contain Jehovah, much less this earthly house he has built. He prays that Jehovah will hear all those fearing Him as they pray toward this house. Yes, even the foreigner from a distant land, "in order that all the peoples of the earth may get to know your name so as to fear you the same as your people Israel do." —8:43.

10 During the fourteen-day feast that follows, Solomon sacrifices 22,000 cattle and 120,000 sheep. Jehovah tells Solomon that he has heard his prayer and that he has sanctified the temple by putting his "name there to time indefinite." Now, if Solomon will walk in uprightness before Jehovah, the throne of his kingdom will continue. However, if Solomon and his sons after him leave Jehovah's worship and serve other gods, then, says Jehovah, "I will also cut Israel off from upon the surface of the ground that I have given to them; and the house that I have sanctified to my name I shall throw away from before me, and Israel will indeed become a proverbial saying and a taunt among all the peoples. And this house itself will become heaps of ruins."—9:3, 7, 8.

11 It has taken Solomon twenty years to complete the two houses, the house of Jehovah and the house of the king. Now he proceeds to build many cities throughout his domain, as well as ships to trade with distant lands. Thus it is that the queen of Sheba hears of the great wisdom that Jehovah has given Solomon, and comes to test him with perplexing questions. After hearing him and seeing the prosperity and happiness of his people, she exclaims: "I had not been told the half." (10:7) As Jehovah continues to show love to Israel, Solomon becomes "greater in riches and wisdom than all the other kings of the earth."—10:23.

12 **Solomon's unfaithfulness and death** (11:1-43). Contrary to Jehovah's command, Solomon takes many wives from other nations—seven hundred wives and three hundred concubines. (Deut. 17:17) His heart is drawn away to serve other gods. Jehovah tells him that the kingdom will be ripped away from him, not in his day, but in the day of his son. Nevertheless, a part of the kingdom, one tribe in addition to Judah, will be ruled over by Solomon's sons. God begins to raise up resisters to Solomon in nearby nations, and Jeroboam of the tribe of Ephraim also lifts himself up against the king. Ahijah the prophet tells Jeroboam that he will become king over ten tribes of Israel, and Jeroboam flees for his life to Egypt. Solomon dies after reigning for forty years, and his son Rehoboam becomes king in the year 997 B.C.E.

13 **The kingdom divided** (12:1–14:20). Jeroboam returns from Egypt and goes up with the people to ask Rehoboam for relief from all the burdens that Solomon had placed upon them. Listening to young men instead of to the wise counsel of the elders in Israel, Rehoboam increases the hardships. Israel rises in revolt and makes Jeroboam king over the northern ten tribes. Rehoboam, left with only Judah and Benjamin, gathers an army to fight the rebels, but at Jehovah's command turns back. Jeroboam builds Shechem as his capital, but he still feels insecure. He fears the people will return to Jerusalem to worship Jehovah, and so come under Rehoboam again. To prevent this he sets up two golden calves, in Dan and Bethel, and selects priests to direct the worship, not from the tribe of Levi, but from among the people in general.

14 While Jeroboam is sacrificing at the altar in Bethel, Jehovah sends a prophet to warn him that He will raise up a king from David's line named Josiah, who will take strong action against this altar of false worship. As a portent the altar is then and there ripped apart. The prophet himself is later killed by a lion for disobeying Jehovah's instruction not to eat or drink while on his mission. Adversity now begins to plague Jeroboam's house. His child

9. What manifestation of Jehovah and what prayer by Solomon mark the bringing in of the ark of the covenant?
10. With what promise and prophetic warning does Jehovah answer Solomon's prayer?
11. What becomes the extent of Solomon's riches and wisdom?
12. (a) In what does Solomon fail, and what seeds of revolt begin to appear? (b) What does Ahijah prophesy?
13. How does division come in the kingdom as Rehoboam begins his reign, and how does Jeroboam try to make his kingship secure?
14. What prophetic warning is sounded against Jeroboam's house, and what adversities come upon them?

dies as a judgment from Jehovah, and God's prophet Ahijah foretells that his house will be cut off completely because of his great sin in setting up false gods in Israel. After reigning twenty-two years, Jeroboam dies and his son Nadab becomes king in his place.

15 **In Judah: Rehoboam, Abijam and Asa** (14:21–15:24). Meanwhile, under Rehoboam, Judah is also doing bad in Jehovah's eyes, practicing idol worship. The king of Egypt invades and carries off many of the temple treasures. After ruling seventeen years, Rehoboam dies, and his son Abijam becomes king. He also keeps sinning against Jehovah, and dies after a three-year reign. Asa his son now rules, and, in contrast, serves Jehovah with a complete heart and removes the dungy idols out of the land. There is constant warfare between Israel and Judah. Asa obtains help from Syria, and Israel is forced to retire. Asa rules for forty-one years and is succeeded by his son Jehoshaphat.

16 **In Israel: Nadab, Baasha, Elah, Zimri, Tibni, Omri and Ahab** (15:25–16:34). What a wicked crowd! Baasha assassinates Nadab after he has reigned only two years, and follows through by annihilating the entire house of Jeroboam. He continues in false worship, and in fighting with Judah. Jehovah foretells that he will make a clean sweep of Baasha's house, as he has done with Jeroboam's. After Baasha's twenty-four-year reign, he is succeeded by his son Elah, who is assassinated two years later by his servant Zimri. As soon as he takes the throne, Zimri strikes down all the house of Baasha. When the people hear of it, they make Omri, the chief of the army, king, and come up against Tirzah, Zimri's capital. When he sees that all is lost, Zimri burns the king's house over himself, so that he dies. Now Tibni tries to reign as a rival king, but after a time the followers of Omri overpower and kill him.

17 Omri buys the mountain of Samaria and builds there the city of Samaria. He goes walking in all the ways of Jeroboam, offending Jehovah with idol worship. In fact, he is worse than all the others before him. After reigning twelve years he dies, and Ahab his son becomes king. Ahab marries Jezebel, the daughter of the king of Sidon, and then sets up an altar to Baal in Samaria. He exceeds in wickedness all those who have preceded him. It is at this time that Hiel the Bethelite rebuilds the city of Jericho at the cost of the life of his firstborn son and his youngest son. True worship is at its lowest ebb.

18 **Elijah's prophetic work in Israel.** (17:1–22:40). Suddenly a messenger from Jehovah appears on the scene. It is Elijah the Tishbite. Startling indeed his opening pronouncement to King Ahab!—"As Jehovah the God of Israel before whom I do stand is living, there will occur during these years neither dew nor rain, except at the order of my word!" (17:1) Just as suddenly, Elijah retires at Jehovah's direction to a valley east of the Jordan. Drought is on Israel, but ravens bring food to Elijah. When the valley stream dries up, Jehovah sends his prophet to Zarephath in Sidon to dwell there. Because of a widow's kindness to Elijah, Jehovah miraculously maintains her small supply of bread and oil so that she and her son do not die of hunger. Later the son becomes sick and dies, but at Elijah's plea Jehovah restores the child's life. Then, in the third year of the drought, Jehovah sends Elijah to Ahab again. Ahab accuses Elijah of bringing ostracism on Israel, but Elijah boldly tells Ahab: "You and the house of your father have," because of following the Baals.—18:18.

19 Elijah calls on Ahab to assemble all the prophets of Baal at Mount Carmel. No longer will it be possible to limp upon two opinions. The issue is drawn: Jehovah versus Baal! Before all the people the four hundred and fifty priests of Baal prepare a bull, set it on wood on the altar and pray for fire to come down and consume the offering. From morning to noon they call in vain on Baal, amid taunts from Elijah. They scream and cut themselves, but no answer! Next, the lone prophet Elijah builds an altar in the name of Jehovah and prepares the wood and bull for sacrifice. He has the people soak the offering and the wood three times with water, and then he prays to Jehovah: "Answer me, O Jehovah, answer me, that this people may know that you, Jehovah, are the true God." At that, fire flashes from heaven, consuming the offering, the wood, the altar stones, the dust and the water. When all the people see it, they immediately fall upon their faces and say: "Jehovah is the true God! Jehovah is the true God!" (18:37, 39) Death to the prophets of Baal! Elijah personally takes care of the slaying, so that not one escapes. Then Jehovah gives rain in Israel.

20 When the news of Baal's humiliation reaches Jezebel, she seeks to have Elijah killed. Out of fear he flees with his attendant to the wilderness, and Jehovah directs him to Horeb.

---

15. What events take place during the next three reigns in Judah?
16. What turbulent events now occur in Israel, and why?
17. (a) For what is Omri's reign noted? (b) Why does true worship fall to its lowest ebb during Ahab's reign?
18. What prophetic work does Elijah now commence in Israel, and how does he pinpoint the real reason for Israel's troubles?
19. How is the issue drawn, and Jehovah's supremacy proved?
20. (a) How does Jehovah appear to Elijah in Horeb, and what instruction and comfort does he provide? (b) What sin and crime are committed by Ahab?

Jehovah there appears to him—no, not spectacularly in a wind, or a quaking, or a fire, but with "a calm, low voice." (19:11, 12) Jehovah tells him to anoint Hazael as king of Syria, Jehu as king over Israel and Elisha as prophet in his place. He comforts Elijah with the news that seven thousand in Israel have not bent down to Baal. Elijah proceeds straightaway to anoint Elisha by throwing his official garment upon him. Ahab now wins two victories over the Syrians, but is rebuked by Jehovah for making a covenant with their king instead of killing him. Then comes the affair of Naboth, whose vineyard Ahab covets. Jezebel has Naboth framed by false witnesses and put to death, so that Ahab can take the vineyard. What an unforgivable crime!

21 Again Elijah appears. He tells Ahab that where Naboth has died, dogs will lick up his blood also, and that his house will be exterminated as completely as those of Jeroboam and Baasha. Dogs will eat up Jezebel in the plot of land of Jezreel. "Without exception no one has proved to be like Ahab, who sold himself to do what was bad in the eyes of Jehovah, whom Jezebel his wife egged on." (21:25) However, because Ahab humbles himself on hearing Elijah's words, Jehovah says that the calamity will not come in his days, but in the days of his son. Ahab now teams up with Jehoshaphat king of Judah in the fight against Syria, and they go out to battle contrary to the advice of Jehovah's prophet Micaiah. Ahab dies of wounds received in battle. As his chariot is washed down at the pool of Samaria, dogs lick up his blood, just as Elijah prophesied. Ahaziah his son becomes king of Israel in his place.

22 **Jehoshaphat reigns in Judah** (22:41-53). Jehoshaphat, who accompanied Ahab to the battle with Syria, is faithful to Jehovah like Asa his father, but he fails to clear out entirely the high places of false worship. After ruling for twenty-five years he dies, and Jehoram his son is king. To the north, in Israel, Ahaziah follows in his father's footsteps, offending Jehovah by his Baal worship.

WHY BENEFICIAL

23 Great benefit is to be derived from the divine instruction in First Kings. Consider, first, the matter of prayer, which so often comes to the fore in this book. Solomon, when faced with the tremendous responsibility of kingship in Israel, prayed humbly to Jehovah in the manner of a child. He asked merely for discernment and an obedient heart, but, in addition to wisdom in overflowing measure, Jehovah gave him also riches and glory. (3:7-9, 12-14) May we have assurance today that our humble prayers for wisdom and direction in Jehovah's service will not go unanswered! May we always pray fervently from the heart, with deep appreciation for all of Jehovah's goodness, as Solomon did at the temple dedication! (8:22-53) May our prayers always bear the stamp of implicit trust and confidence in Jehovah, as did the prayers of Elijah in time of trial, and when face to face with a demon-worshiping nation! Jehovah provides wonderfully for those who seek him in prayer.—17:20-22; 18:36-40.

24 Further, we should be warned by the examples of those who did not humble themselves before Jehovah. There was Adonijah, who thought he could bypass Jehovah's theocratic appointment (1:5; 2:24, 25); Shimei, who thought he could step out of bounds and back again (2:37, 41-46); the Solomon of later years, whose disobedience brought "resisters" from Jehovah (11:9-14, 23-26); and the kings of Israel, whose false religion proved disastrous (13:33, 34; 14:7-11; 16:1-4). Moreover, there was the wickedly covetous Jezebel, the power behind Ahab's throne, whose notorious example was used a thousand years later as the basis for a warning to the congregation in Thyatira: "Nevertheless, I do hold this against you, that you tolerate that woman Jezebel, who calls herself a prophetess, and she teaches and misleads my slaves to commit fornication and to eat things sacrificed to idols." (Rev. 2:20) Overseers must keep congregations clean and free of all Jezebel-like influences!

25 Jehovah's power of prophecy is clearly shown in the fulfillment of many predictions made in First Kings. For example, there is the remarkable forecast, made more than three hundred years in advance, that Josiah would be the one to rip apart Jeroboam's altar at Bethel. Josiah did it! (1 Ki. 13:1-3; 2 Ki. 23:15) However, most outstanding are the prophecies relating to the house of Jehovah, built by Solomon. Jehovah told Solomon that falling away to false gods would result in his 'cutting Israel off from the surface of the ground, and throwing away before him the house that he had sanctified to his name.' (1 Ki. 9:7, 8) At 2 Chronicles 36:17-21 we read how utterly true this prophecy proved to be. Moreover, Jesus showed that the later temple built by Herod the Great on the same site would suffer the same fate and for the same reason. (Luke 21:6) How true this also proved to be! Now in this twen-

21. (a) What doom does Elijah pronounce on Ahab and his house, and on Jezebel? (b) What prophecy is fulfilled at Ahab's death?
22. What characterizes the reigns of Jehoshaphat in Judah and Ahaziah in Israel?
23. What assurance and encouragement does First Kings provide with regard to prayer?
24. What warning examples are set forth in First Kings, and why, particularly, should overseers take note?
25. What prophecies of First Kings have had remarkable fulfillment, and how can remembrance of these aid in our instruction today?

tieth century we should remember these catastrophes and the reason, walking always in the ways of the true God.

26 The queen of Sheba came from her far country to marvel at Solomon's wisdom, the prosperity of his people and the glory of his kingdom, including the magnificent house of Jehovah. However, even Solomon confessed to Jehovah: "The heavens, yes, the heaven of the heavens, themselves cannot contain you; how much less, then, this house that I have built!" (1 Ki. 8:27; 10:4-9) But centuries later Jesus said: "Something more than Solomon is here." Christ Jesus had come, to build a far more glorious spiritual temple. (Matt. 12:42; 1 Pet. 2:5) To this One, greater than Solomon, Jehovah's promise holds true: "I also shall indeed establish the throne of your kingdom over Israel to time indefinite." (1 Ki. 9:5; Matt. 1:1, 6, 7, 16; Luke 1:32) First Kings provides a stimulating forevision of the glory of Jehovah's spiritual temple and of the prosperity, rejoicing and delightsome happiness of all who come to live under the wise rule of Jehovah's kingdom by Christ Jesus. Our appreciation of the importance of true worship and of Jehovah's wonderful provision of His kingdom by the Seed continues to grow!

26. What stimulating forevision of Jehovah's temple and kingdom is provided in this book?

Bible Book Number Twelve— 2 Kings

Writer: Jeremiah
Places Written: Jerusalem and Egypt
Writing Completed: c. 580 B.C.E.
Time Covered: 922—c. 580 B.C.E.

THE book of Second Kings continues to trace the turbulent course of the kingdoms of Israel and Judah. Elisha took up the mantle of Elijah, and was blessed with two parts of Elijah's spirit, performing sixteen miracles to Elijah's eight. He continued to prophesy doom for apostate Israel, where only Jehu provided a brief flash of zeal for Jehovah. More and more Israel's kings became bogged down in wickedness, until the northern kingdom finally crumbled before Assyria in 740 B.C.E. In the southern kingdom of Judah a few outstanding kings, notably Jehoshaphat, Jehoash, Hezekiah and Josiah, swept back the tide of apostasy for a time, but Nebuchadnezzar at last executed Jehovah's judgment by devastating Jerusalem, its temple and the land of Judah in 607 B.C.E. Thus Jehovah's prophecies were fulfilled and his word was vindicated!

2 Since Second Kings was originally part of the same roll with First Kings, what has already been said concerning Jeremiah's writership applies equally here, as do the proofs of the book's canonicity and authenticity. It was completed about 580 B.C.E., and covers the period beginning with the reign of Ahaziah of Israel in 922, and ending in the thirty-seventh year of Jehoiachin's exile, 580.—1:1; 25:27.

3 Archaeological finds supporting the record of Second Kings give further evidence of its genuineness. For example, there is the famous Moabite Stone, whose inscription describes the warfare between Moab and Israel, supporting 2 Kings 3:4, 5.[a] There is also the black basalt obelisk of the Assyrian Shalmaneser III, now on display in the British Museum, London, which gives in picture and cuneiform writing a contemporary history of Jehu's time, mentioning King Jehu by name. There are the clay and stone cuneiform tablets of Tiglath-pileser III, Shalmaneser V and Sargon II, unearthed from the temples of Assyria's past glory on the Tigris River, which relate a history parallel to that at 2 Kings 15:29; 16:7-18 and 17:6, 24-28.[b]

4 A clear proof of the authenticity of the book is to be found in the utmost candor with which it describes the execution of Jehovah's judgments upon his own people. As first the kingdom of Israel and then the kingdom of Judah go crashing into ruin, the telling force of Jehovah's prophetic judgment in Deuteronomy 28:15–29:28 is brought home to us. In the destruction of those kingdoms, "Jehovah's anger blazed against that land by bringing upon it the whole malediction written in this book." (Deut. 29:27; 2 Ki. 17:18; 25:1, 9-11) Other

1. What histories are related in Second Kings, and in vindication of what?
2. What may be said as to the writership and canonicity of the book, and what period is covered by it?
3. What remarkable archaeological finds support the book?

a See Study 9, paragraph 11.
b *The Bible as History*, 1956, Werner Keller, pages 239-255 N.Y. Ed., pages 232-247 London Ed.

4. With regard to prophecy, how does Second Kings show itself to be an integral part of the inspired Scriptures?

events recorded in Second Kings are prophetic of later happenings. At Luke 4:24-27, after Jesus refers first to Elijah and the widow of Zarephath, he then speaks of Elisha and Naaman, in showing why he himself was not accepted as a prophet in his home territory. Thus both First and Second Kings are seen to harmonize with the rest of the Holy Scriptures, of which they are indeed a part.

CONTENTS OF SECOND KINGS

5 **Ahaziah, king of Israel** (1:1-18). Suffering a fall in his home, this son of Ahab gets sick. He sends to inquire of Baal-zebub, the god of Ekron, whether he is to recover. Elijah, the prophet of Jehovah, intercepts the messengers and sends them back to the king, reproving him for not inquiring of the true God, and telling him that he will positively die. When the king sends out a chief with fifty men to take Elijah and bring him to the king, Elijah calls down fire from heaven to devour them. The same thing happens to a second chief with his fifty. A third chief and fifty are sent, and this time Elijah spares their lives. Elijah goes with them to the king and again pronounces sentence of death on Ahaziah. The king dies just as Elijah said he would. Then Jehoram the brother of Ahaziah becomes king over Israel, for Ahaziah has no son to take his place.

6 **Elisha succeeds Elijah** (2:1-25). The time comes for Elijah to be taken away. Elisha sticks with him on his journey from Gilgal to Bethel, to Jericho, and finally across the Jordan, whose waters Elijah parts by striking them with his official garment. As he sees a fiery war chariot and fiery horses come between them, and Elijah go up in a windstorm, Elisha receives the promised two parts in Elijah's spirit. He soon shows that "the spirit of Elijah" has settled down upon him. Taking up Elijah's fallen garment, he uses it to divide the waters again. He then heals the bad water at Jericho. Then, on the way to Bethel, small boys begin to jeer at him: "Go up, you baldhead! Go up, you baldhead!" (2:23) Elisha calls on Jehovah, and two she-bears come out of the woods and kill forty-two of these juvenile delinquents.

7 **Jehoram, king of Israel** (3:1-27). This king keeps on doing what is bad in Jehovah's eyes, sticking to the sins of Jeroboam. The king of Moab has been paying tribute to Israel, but now revolts, and Jehoram obtains the help of King Jehoshaphat of Judah and the king of Edom in going against Moab. On the way to the attack their armies come to waterless terrain and are about to perish. The three kings go down to Elisha to inquire of Jehovah his God. Because of faithful Jehoshaphat Jehovah rescues them and gives them the victory over Moab.

8 **Elisha's further miracles** (4:1–8:15). As her creditors are about to take her two sons into slavery, the widow of one of the sons of the prophets seeks help from Elisha. He miraculously multiplies the small supply of oil in her house so that she is able to sell enough to pay her debts. A Shunammite woman recognizes Elisha as a prophet of the true God, and she and her husband prepare a room for his use when he is in Shunem. Because of her kindness Jehovah blesses her with a son. Some years later the child becomes sick and dies. The woman immediately seeks out Elisha. He accompanies her to her home, and by Jehovah's power raises the child to life. Returning to the sons of the prophets at Gilgal, Elisha miraculously removes "death in the pot" by rendering poisonous gourds harmless. He then feeds a hundred men with twenty barley loaves, and yet they have "leftovers."—4:40, 44.

9 Naaman, the chief of the Syrian army, becomes afflicted with leprosy. A captive Israelite girl tells his wife that there is a prophet in Samaria that can cure him. Naaman journeys to Elisha, but, instead of attending to him personally, Elisha merely sends word for him to go and wash himself seven times in the Jordan River. Naaman is indignant at this apparent lack of respect. Are not the rivers of Damascus better than the waters of Israel? But he is prevailed upon to obey Elisha, and is cured. Elisha refuses to accept a gift as a reward, but later his attendant Gehazi runs after Naaman and asks for a gift in Elisha's name. When he returns and tries to deceive Elisha, he is struck with leprosy. Still another miracle is performed when Elisha makes an axhead float.

10 When Elisha warns the king of Israel of a Syrian plot to kill him, the king of Syria sends a military force to Dothan to capture Elisha. Seeing the city surrounded by the armies of Syria, Elisha's attendant becomes fearful. Elisha assures him: "Do not be afraid, for there are more who are with us than those who are with them." Then he prays to Jehovah to let his attendant see the great force that is with Elisha. 'And, look! the mountainous region is full of horses and war chariots of fire all around Elisha.' (6:16, 17) When the Syrians attack, the prophet again prays to Jehovah, and

5. What reproof and sentence does Elijah pass on Ahaziah, and why?
6. Under what circumstances does Elijah part from Elisha, and how is it soon shown that "the spirit of Elijah" has settled on him?
7. Because of what does Jehovah rescue Jehoshaphat and Jehoram?
8. What further miracles does Elisha now perform?
9. What miracles are performed in connection with Naaman, and the axhead?
10. How are the superior forces of Jehovah shown, and how does Elisha turn back the Syrians?

he Syrians are struck with blindness and led o the king of Israel. Instead of their being put o death, however, Elisha tells the king to pread a feast for them and send them home.

11 Later on, King Ben-hadad of Syria besieges ;amaria, and there is a great famine. The king f Israel blames Elisha, but the prophet predicts an abundance of food for the following lay. In the night Jehovah causes the Syrians o hear the sound of a great army, so that they lee, leaving all their provisions for the Is-aelites. After some time Ben-hadad becomes ick. On hearing a report that Elisha has come o Damascus, he sends Hazael to inquire if he vill recover. The king will die, says Elisha, and Iazael will become king in his place. Hazael nakes sure of this by himself killing the king ind taking over the kingship.

12 **Jehoram, king of Judah** (8:16-29). Mean-vhile, in Judah, Jehoshaphat's son Jehoram is iow king. He proves to be no better than the kings of Israel, doing bad in Jehovah's eyes. His wife is Ahab's daughter Athaliah, whose rother, also named Jehoram, is reigning in srael. At the death of Jehoram of Judah, his on Ahaziah becomes king in Jerusalem.

13 **Jehu, king of Israel** (9:1–10:36). Elisha ends one of the sons of the prophets to anoint ehu to be king over Israel and to commission im to strike down the entire house of Ahab. ehu loses no time. He sets out after Jehoram, king of Israel, who is recuperating from war vounds at Jezreel. The watchman sees the ieaving mass of men approaching, and at last ie reports to the king: "The driving is like the lriving of Jehu the grandson of Nimshi, for it s with madness that he drives." (9:20) In vain ehoram of Israel and the visiting Ahaziah of udah ride out to sue for peace. Jehu replies: 'What peace could there be as long as there ire the fornications of Jezebel your mother and ier many sorceries?" (9:22) As Jehoram turns o flee, Jehu shoots an arrow through his heart. His body is thrown there into the field of Na-oth, as further repayment for the innocent lood shed by Ahab. Later Jehu and his men ursue after Ahaziah, striking him down so hat he dies at Megiddo. Two kings die in Jehu's first lightning campaign.

14 Now it is Jezebel's turn! Playing the adul-teress to the last, she appears at her window n Jezreel in her most glamorous makeup. ehu is unimpressed. "Let her drop!" he calls o some attendants. Down she goes, her blood splattering the wall and the horses that tram-ple on her. When they go to bury her, they can find only skull, feet and the palms of her hands. In fulfillment of Elijah's prophecy, 'dogs have eaten her, and she has become as manure in the tract of land of Jezreel.'—2 Ki. 9:36, 37; 1 Ki. 21:23.

15 Next, Jehu orders the slaughter of the seventy sons of Ahab, and stacks their heads at the gate of Jezreel. All of Ahab's yes-men in Jezreel are struck down. Now, on to Israel's capital, Samaria! On the way he meets the forty-two brothers of Ahaziah, who are travel-ing to Jezreel, unaware of what is happening. They are taken and slain. But now there is a different kind of encounter. Jehonadab the son of Rechab comes out to meet Jehu. To Jehu's question, "Is your heart upright with me, just as my own heart is with your heart?" Jehona-dab replies, "It is." Jehu then makes him go along with him in his chariot to see first-hand his "toleration of no rivalry toward Je-hovah."—2 Ki. 10:15, 16.

16 On arrival in Samaria, Jehu annihilates everything left over of Ahab's, according to Jehovah's word to Elijah. (1 Ki. 21:21, 22) However, what of the detestable religion of Baal? Jehu declares, "Ahab, on the one hand, worshiped Baal a little. Jehu, on the other hand, will worship him a great deal." (2 Ki. 10:18) Calling all these demon worshipers to the house of Baal, he has them put on their garments of identification and makes sure there is no worshiper of Jehovah among them. Then he sends his men in to strike them down to the last man. Baal's house is demolished and the place turned into privies, which remain till Jeremiah's day. 'Thus Jehu annihilates Baal out of Israel.'—10:28.

17 However, even the zealous Jehu fails. In what? In that he continues to follow the golden calves that Jeroboam set up in Bethel and Dan. He does not "take care to walk in the law of Jehovah the God of Israel with all his heart." (10:31) But, because of his action against the house of Ahab, Jehovah promises that his descendants will reign over Israel to the fourth generation. In his days, Jehovah starts to cut off the eastern part of the king-dom, bringing Hazael of Syria against Israel. After reigning twenty-eight years Jehu dies and is succeeded by his son Jehoahaz.

18 **Jehoash, king of Judah** (11:1–12:21). The queen mother Athaliah is daughter to Jezebel

1. How are Elisha's prophecies concerning the Assyr-ans and Ben-hadad fulfilled?
2. What kind of king does Jehoshaphat's son Jehoram rove to be?
3. With what lightning campaign does Jehu follow up iis anointing?
4. How is Elijah's prophecy concerning Jezebel ful-illed?
15. What different kinds of encounters does Jehu make on the way to Samaria?
16. How thorough is Jehu's action against Ahab's house and against Baal?
17. In what does Jehu fail, and how does Jehovah start to bring punishment on Israel?
18. How is Athaliah's conspiracy in Judah thwarted, and what is noteworthy about Jehoash's reign?

in flesh and in spirit. Hearing of her son Ahaziah's death, she orders the execution of the entire royal family and takes over the throne. Only Ahaziah's baby son Jehoash escapes death when he is hidden away. In the seventh year of Athaliah's reign, Jehoiada the priest has Jehoash anointed as king and Athaliah put to death. Jehoiada directs the people in the worship of Jehovah, instructs the youthful king in his duties before God and arranges for repairing the house of Jehovah. By means of gifts Jehoash turns back an attack by Hazael the king of Syria. After he has ruled for forty years in Jerusalem, Jehoash is assassinated by his servants, and Amaziah his son begins to rule as king in place of him.

19 **Jehoahaz and Jehoash, kings of Israel** (13:1-25). Jehu's son Jehoahaz continues in idol worship, and Israel comes under the power of Syria, although Jehoahaz is not dethroned. Jehovah frees them in time, but the Israelites continue in Jeroboam's calf worship. At Jehoahaz' death, his son Jehoash takes his place as king in Israel, even while the other Jehoash is reigning in Judah. Jehoash of Israel continues in the idol worship of his father. At his death his son Jeroboam becomes king. It is during the reign of Jehoash that Elisha falls sick and dies, after making his final prophecy that Jehoash will strike down Syria three times, which is duly fulfilled. The final miracle accredited to Elisha takes place after his death, when a dead man is thrown into the same burial place, only to stand up alive as soon as he touches Elisha's bones.

20 **Amaziah, king of Judah** (14:1-22). Amaziah does what is upright in Jehovah's eyes, but fails to destroy the high places used for worship. He is defeated in war by Jehoash of Israel. After a twenty-nine-year reign, he is killed in a conspiracy. Azariah his son is made king in his place.

21 **Jeroboam II, king of Israel** (14:23-29). The second Jeroboam to be king in Israel continues in the false worship of his forefather. He reigns in Samaria for forty-one years and is successful in winning back Israel's lost territories. Zechariah his son becomes his successor on the throne.

22 **Azariah (Uzziah), king of Judah** (15:1-7). Azariah rules for fifty-two years. He is upright before Jehovah, but fails to destroy the high places. Later Jehovah plagues him with leprosy, and his son Jotham takes care of the roya duties, becoming king on Azariah's death.

23 **Zechariah, Shallum, Menahem, Pekahia and Pekah, kings of Israel** (15:8-31). Accordin to Jehovah's promise, the throne of Israel re mains in the house of Jehu to the fourt generation, Zechariah. (10:30) However, h reigns only six months, until an assassi strikes him down. Shallum, the usurper, last only one month. False worship, assassinatio and intrigue continue to plague Israel as king Menahem, Pekahiah and Pekah pass in proces sion. During Pekah's reign Assyria closes i for the kill. Hoshea assassinates Pekah, t become Israel's last king.

24 **Jotham and Ahaz, kings of Judah** (15:32 16:20). Jotham practices pure worship, but let the high places continue. Ahaz, his son, imitate the kings of neighboring Israel by practicin what is bad in Jehovah's eyes. Under attack b the kings of Israel and Syria, he appeals t the king of Assyria for help. The Assyrian come to his aid, capturing Damascus, and Aha goes there to meet the king of Assyria. Seein the altar of worship there, he has one erecte in Jerusalem according to the same pattern and begins sacrificing on it instead of on th copper altar at Jehovah's temple. His son Heze kiah becomes king of Judah as his successor

25 **Hoshea, last king of Israel** (17:1-41). Israe now comes under the power of Assyria. Hoshe rebels and seeks help from Egypt, but in th ninth year of his reign Israel is conquered b Assyria and carried into captivity. Thus end the ten-tribe kingdom of Israel. Why? "Becaus the sons of Israel had sinned against Jehova their God . . . And they continued to serv dungy idols, concerning which Jehovah ha said to them: 'You must not do this thing Therefore Jehovah got very incensed agains Israel, so that he removed them from hi sight." (17:7, 12, 18) The Assyrians bring i people from the east to settle the land, an these become 'fearers of Jehovah,' though the continue to worship their own gods. They be come the Samaritans.

26 **Hezekiah, king of Judah** (18:1–20:21). Heze kiah does what is right in Jehovah's eyes, ac cording to all that David his forefather ha done. He roots out false worship, tears dowr the high places and even destroys the coppe serpent Moses made, because the people now worship it. Sennacherib, king of Assyria, now

---

19. (a) What inroads does Syria continue to make during the reigns of Jehoahaz and Jehoash in Israel? (b) How does Elisha end his course as Jehovah's prophet?
20. Describe Amaziah's reign in Judah.
21. What occurs during the reign of Jeroboam II in Israel?
22. What is related here concerning Azariah's reign in Judah?
23. With what evils is Israel plagued as the Assyria menace arises?
24. After Jotham, how does Ahaz of Judah sin as t worship?
25. (a) How does Israel go into captivity, and why (b) Who become the Samaritans?
26, 27. (a) How does Hezekiah of Judah do right i Jehovah's eyes? (b) How does Jehovah answer praye in turning back the Assyrians? (c) What further ful fillment does Isaiah's prophecy have?

nvades Judah and captures many fortified ities. Hezekiah tries to buy him off with a ıeavy tribute, but Sennacherib sends his mesenger Rabshakeh, who comes up to the walls f Jerusalem and demands surrender and nocks Jehovah in the hearing of all the people. 'he prophet Isaiah assures faithful Hezekiah vith a message of doom against Sennacherib. 'This is what Jehovah has said: 'Do not be fraid.'" (19:6) As Sennacherib continues to hreaten, Hezekiah implores Jehovah: "And ow, O Jehovah our God, save us, please, out f his hand, that all the kingdoms of the earth nay know that you, O Jehovah, are God alone." —19:19.

27 Does Jehovah answer this unselfish prayr? First, through Isaiah, he sends the mesage that "the very zeal of Jehovah of armies" vill turn back the enemy. (19:31) Then, that ame night, he sends his angel to strike down 85,000 in the camp of the Assyrians. In the norning 'all of them are dead carcasses.' (19: 5) Sennacherib returns in defeat to Nineveh. 'here his god Nisroch fails him once more, or it is while he is bowed in worship that his wn sons kill him, in fulfillment of Isaiah's rophecy.—19:7, 37.

28 Hezekiah becomes deathly sick, but Jehoah again heeds his prayer and prolongs his ife another fifteen years. The king of Babylon ends messengers with gifts, and Hezekiah preumes to show them all his treasure house. saiah then prophesies that everything in his ouse will one day be carried to Babylon. Hezeiah then dies, renowned for his mightiness, nd for the tunnel that he built to bring Jerualem's water supply within the city.

29 **Manasseh, Amon and Josiah, kings of Judah** 21:1–23:30). Manasseh succeeds his father, Iezekiah, and reigns fifty-five years, doing ad in Jehovah's eyes on a large scale. He estores the high places of false worship, sets p altars to Baal and makes a sacred pole s Ahab did, and makes Jehovah's house a lace of idolatry. Jehovah foretells that he vill bring calamity on Jerusalem as he has lone on Samaria, "wiping it clean and turning t upside down." Manasseh also sheds innocent lood "in very great quantity." (21:13, 16) He s succeeded by his son Amon, who continues o do bad for two years, until struck down by ssassins.

30 The people now make Amon's son Josiah ing. During his thirty-one-year reign he briefly everses Judah's plunge toward destruction 'by walking in all the way of David his forefather.' (22:2) He begins repairs on the house of Jehovah, and there the high priest finds the book of the law. This confirms that destruction will come on the nation for its disobedience to Jehovah, but Josiah is assured that because of his faithfulness it will not come in his day. He purges the house of Jehovah and the entire land of demon worship and extends his idol-smashing activity to Bethel, where he destroys Jeroboam's altar in fulfillment of the prophecy at 1 Kings 13:1, 2. He reinstitutes the passover to Jehovah. "Like him there did not prove to be a king prior to him who returned to Jehovah with all his heart and with all his soul and with all his vital force, according to all the law of Moses." (23:25) Nevertheless, Jehovah's anger still burns because of Manasseh's offenses. Josiah dies in an encounter with the king of Egypt at Megiddo.

31 **Jehoahaz, Jehoiakim and Jehoiachin, kings of Judah** (23:31–24:17). After a three-month reign Josiah's son Jehoahaz is taken captive by the king of Egypt, and his brother Eliakim, whose name is changed to Jehoiakim, is placed on the throne. He follows in the wrong course of his forefathers, and becomes subject to Nebuchadnezzar king of Babylon, but rebels against him after three years. At his death his son Jehoiachin begins to reign. Nebuchadnezzar besieges Jerusalem, captures it and carries the treasures of the house of Jehovah to Babylon, "just as Jehovah had spoken" by Isaiah. (24:13; 20:17) Jehoiachin and thousands of his subjects are carried into exile in Babylon.

32 **Zedekiah, last king of Judah** (24:18–25:30). Nebuchadnezzar makes Jehoiachin's uncle, Mattaniah, king and changes his name to Zedekiah. He reigns eleven years in Jerusalem, and continues to do bad in Jehovah's eyes. He rebels against Babylon; so in Zedekiah's ninth year Nebuchadnezzar and his entire army come up and build a siege wall all around Jerusalem. After eighteen months the city is ravaged by famine. The walls are then breached, and Zedekiah is captured while trying to flee. His sons are slaughtered before him, and his eyes are blinded. In the next month all the principal houses of the city, including the house of Jehovah and the king's house, are put to flames and the city walls demolished. Most of the survivors are carried off captive to Babylon. Gedaliah is appointed governor over the few lowly ones who remain in the countryside of Judah. However, he is assassinated, and the people flee to Egypt. Thus from the seventh month of 607 B.C.E. the land lies utterly deso-

8. For what is Hezekiah renowned, but in what does e sin?
9. What idolatry does Manasseh institute, what caamity does Jehovah foretell, and what further sin does Ianasseh commit?
0. Why and how does Josiah return to Jehovah with ll his heart?
31. What setbacks befall Judah following Josiah's death?
32. What dramatic events lead up to the desolation of Jerusalem and of the land?

late. The final words of Second Kings tell of the favor the king of Babylon shows to Jehoiachin in the thirty-seventh year of his captivity.

WHY BENEFICIAL

33 Though it covers the fatal decline of the kingdoms of Israel and Judah, Second Kings sparkles with many individual examples of Jehovah's blessing on those who showed love for him and his right principles. Like the widow of Zarephath before her, the Shunammite woman received an abundant blessing for her hospitality shown to God's prophet. (4:8-17, 32-37) Jehovah's ability always to provide was shown when Elisha fed one hundred men from twenty loaves, even as Jesus was to perform similar miracles later. (2 Ki. 4:42-44; Matt. 14:16-21; Mark 8:1-9) Note how Jehonadab received a blessing in being invited to go along in Jehu's chariot to see the destruction of the Baal worshipers. And why? Because he took positive action in coming out to greet the zealous Jehu. (2 Ki. 10:15, 16) Finally, there are the splendid examples of Hezekiah and Josiah, in their humility and proper respect for Jehovah's name and law. (19:14-19; 22:11-13) These are splendid examples for us to follow.

34 Jehovah tolerates no disrespect for his official servants. When the delinquents mocked Elisha as the prophet of Jehovah, He brought swift recompense. (2:23, 24) Moreover, Jehovah respects the blood of the innocent. His judgment rested heavily on Ahab's house, not only because of Baal worship, but also because of the bloodshed that accompanied it. Thus Jehu was anointed to "avenge the blood of [Jehovah's] servants the prophets and the blood of all the servants of Jehovah at the hand of Jezebel." When judgment was executed against Jehoram, Jehovah reminded that it was on account of "the blood of Naboth and the blood of his sons." (9:7, 26) Likewise, it was Manasseh's bloodguilt that finally sealed Judah's doom. Adding to his sin of false worship, Manasseh 'filled Jerusalem with blood from end to end.' Not even the good reign of Josiah, and his putting away of all idolatry, could wipe out the community bloodguilt lasting over from Manasseh's reign. Years later, when Jehova began to bring his executioners up against Je rusalem, he declared it was because Manasse "filled Jerusalem with innocent blood, and Je hovah did not consent to grant forgiveness. (21:16; 24:4) Likewise, Jesus declared that th Jerusalem of the first century A.D. must peris because its priests were the sons of those wh shed the blood of the prophets, 'that there ma come upon them all the righteous blood spille on earth.' (Matt. 23:29-36) God warns the worl that he will avenge the innocent blood that ha been shed, and especially the blood "of thos slaughtered because of the word of God. —Rev. 6:9, 10.

35 The unerring sureness with which Jehova brings his prophetic judgments to fulfillment i also shown in Second Kings. Three leadin prophets are brought to our attention, Elijal Elisha and Isaiah. The prophecies of each on are shown to have striking fulfillments. (2 K 9:36, 37; 10:10, 17; 3:14, 18, 24; 13:18, 19, 25 19:32-36; 20:17; 24:13) Elijah is also confirme as a true prophet in his appearing with th prophet Moses and the Great Prophet, Jesu Christ, in the transfiguration on the mountai (Matt. 17:1-5) Referring to the magnificence c this occasion, Peter said: "Consequently w have the prophetic word made more sure; an you are doing well in paying attention to it a to a lamp shining in a dark place, until da dawns and a daystar rises, in your hearts. —2 Pet. 1:19.

36 The events recorded in Second Kings clear ly reveal that Jehovah's judgment against al practicers of false religion and all willful shed ders of innocent blood is extermination. Ye Jehovah showed favor and mercy to his peopl "for the sake of his covenant with Abrahan Isaac and Jacob." (2 Ki. 13:23) He preserve them "for the sake of David his servant. (8:19) He will show like mercy to those wh turn to him in this day. As we review the Bibl record and promises, with what deepening con fidence do we look forward to the Kingdom o the "son of David," Jesus Christ the Seed wherein bloodshed and wickedness will be n more!—Isa. 2:4; Ps. 145:20.

---

33. What fine examples are provided in Second Kings for us to follow?
34. What does Second Kings teach as regards respect for official servants, and as regards bloodguilt?
35. (a) How are Elijah, Elisha and Isaiah confirme to be true prophets? (b) In connection with Elijah what does Peter say as to prophecy?
36. Why did Jehovah show his people mercy, and ho is our confidence in the kingdom of the Seed deepened

Bible Book Number Thirteen— 1 Chronicles

Writer:	**Ezra**
Place Written:	**Jerusalem (?)**
Time of Writing:	**c. 460 B.C.E.**
Time Covered:	**1077-1037 B.C.E.**

IS FIRST Chronicles just a dry list of genealogies? Is it merely a repetition of the books of Samuel and Kings? Far from it! Here is an illuminating and essential part of the divine record—essential in the day of its writing in reorganizing the nation and its worship, and essential and beneficial in showing a pattern of divine worship for later days, including this present day. First Chronicles contains some of the most beautiful expressions of praise to Jehovah to be found in all Scripture. It provides wonderful foregleams of Jehovah's kingdom of righteousness, and is to be studied with profit by all who hope in that kingdom. The two books of Chronicles have been treasured by Jews and Christians alike through the ages. The Bible translator Jerome had such an exalted opinion of First and Second Chronicles that he considered them an "epitome of the Old Testament," and asserted that "they are of such high moment and importance, that he who supposes himself to be acquainted with the sacred writings, and does not know *them,* only deceives himself."[a]

2 The two books of Chronicles were originally one book or roll, which was later divided for convenience. Why was Chronicles written? Consider the setting. The captivity to Babylon had ended about seventy-seven years before. The Jews were resettled in their land. However, there was a dangerous trend away from Jehovah's worship at the rebuilt temple in Jerusalem. Ezra had been commissioned by the king of Persia to appoint judges and teachers of the law of God and to beautify the house of Jehovah. Accurate genealogical lists were necessary to assure that only legitimate persons served in the priesthood, and also to confirm the tribal inheritances whence the priesthood gained its support. In view of Jehovah's prophecies regarding the Kingdom, it was also vital to have a clear and dependable record of the lineage of Judah and of David.

3 Ezra was earnestly desirous of arousing the restored Jews from their apathy, and of infusing in them the realization that they were indeed the inheritors of Jehovah's covenanted loving-kindness. In the Chronicles, therefore, he set before them a full account of the nation's history, and of the origins of mankind, going back as far as the first man Adam. Since the kingdom of David was the focal point, he highlighted the history of Judah, omitting almost entirely the absolutely unredeeming record of the ten-tribe kingdom. He depicted Judah's greatest kings as engaged in building or restoring the temple and zealously leading in the worship of God. He pointed out the religious sins that led to the kingdom's overthrow, while emphasizing also God's promises of restoration. He stressed the importance of pure worship by focusing attention on the many details pertaining to the temple, its priests, the Levites, the masters of song, and so on. Whereas in Kings the prophet Jeremiah had stressed the prophetic element, the priest Ezra stressed the priestly element in Chronicles.

4 What is the evidence that Ezra wrote Chronicles? One strong reason has already been suggested, in its emphasis on the Levitical spirit. Ezra would give this emphasis, for he is described as a descendant "of Aaron the high priest—the said Ezra himself went up from Babylon; and he was a skilled copyist in the law of Moses." (Ezra 7:1-7) The closing two verses of Second Chronicles are the same as the opening two verses of Ezra, and Second Chronicles ends in the middle of a sentence that is finished in Ezra 1:3. The writer of Chronicles must therefore have been the writer also of Ezra. This is further borne out in that the style, language, wording and spelling of Chronicles and Ezra are the same. Some of the expressions in these two books are found in no other Bible books. Ezra, who wrote the book of Ezra, must also have written Chronicles. Jewish tradition supports this conclusion.

5 No one was better qualified than Ezra to compile this authentic and accurate history. "For Ezra himself had prepared his heart to consult the law of Jehovah and to do it and to teach in Israel regulation and justice." (Ezra 7:10) Jehovah aided him by holy spirit. The

a *Clarke's Commentary,* Volume II, page 574.

1. Why is First Chronicles an essential and beneficial part of the divine record?
2. Why was Chronicles written?
3. (a) What was Ezra desirous of infusing in the Jews? (b) Why did he highlight the history of Judah and the priestly element?
4. What evidence favors Ezra as the writer?
5. What were Ezra's spiritual and secular qualifications?

Persian world-ruler also recognized the wisdom of God in Ezra and commissioned him with wide civil powers in the jurisdictional district of Judah. (Ezra 7:12-26) Thus equipped with divine and imperial authority, Ezra could compile his account from the best available documents.

6 Ezra was a researcher extraordinary. He searched through older records of Jewish history that had been compiled by reliable prophets contemporary with the times, and by official recorders and keepers of public records. Some of the documents he consulted were State documents. Ezra cites at least fourteen such sources of information.[a] By these explicit citations Ezra honestly gave his contemporaries the opportunity to check his sources if they wished to do so, and this adds considerable weight to the argument for the credibility and authenticity of his word. We today can have confidence in the correctness of the books of Chronicles for the same reason that the Jews of Ezra's time had such confidence.

7 Since Ezra "went up from Babylon" in the seventh year of the Persian king, Artaxerxes I (Longimanus), which was 468 B.C.E., and Ezra makes no record of Nehemiah's significant arrival in 455, Chronicles must have been written between these dates, probably about the year 460, in Jerusalem. (Ezra 7:1-7; Neh. 2:1-18) The Jews of Ezra's day accepted Chronicles as a genuine part of 'all Scripture that is inspired of God and beneficial.' They called it *Di·bᵉréy Hay·yamím,* which means "The Affairs of the Days," that is, history of the days or times. Some two hundred years later the translators of the Greek *Septuagint* also included Chronicles as canonical. They divided the book into two, and supposing it to be supplementary to Samuel and Kings or to the entire Bible of that time, called it *Paraleipoménōn,* meaning "Of Things Omitted." Though the name is not particularly appropriate, still their action shows that they regarded Chronicles as authentic, inspired Scripture. In preparing the Latin *Vulgate* version, Jerome suggested: "We may more significantly call [them] the *Chronicon* of the whole divine history." It is from this that the title "Chronicles," meaning "History of Times," appears to have been derived. After listing its genealogies, First Chronicles is concerned mainly with the "times" of King David, 1077-1037 B.C.E.

[a] 1 Chronicles 27:24; 29:29; 2 Chronicles 9:29; 12:15; 13:22; 16:11; 20:34; 21:12; 24:27; 26:22; 32:32; 33:18, 19; 35:25.

6. Why may we have confidence in the correctness of Chronicles?
7. When was Chronicles written, who have regarded it as authentic, and what "times" does it cover?

CONTENTS OF FIRST CHRONICLES

8 This book of First Chronicles divides naturally into two sections: the first nine chapters, which deal primarily with genealogies, and the last twenty chapters, which cover events during the forty years from the death of Saul to the end of David's reign.

9 **The genealogies** (1:1–9:44). These chapters take in a sweep of thirty-seven or more centuries from Adam down to the tenth generation after Zerubbabel, at least late in the fourth century before Christ. (1:1; 3:19-24) The generations of Zerubbabel were added by a hand later than Ezra's. The extensive genealogies are based on earlier Bible books, on family and tribal archives and on census data, to which Ezra had access.—23:3, 27.

10 First, there are supplied the ten generations from Adam to Noah, and then the ten generations down to Abraham. Abraham's sons and their offspring, the posterity of Esau and of Seir, who lived in the mountainous region of Seir, and early kings of Edom are listed. From the second chapter, however, the record is concerned with the descendants of Israel, or Jacob, from whom the genealogy is first traced through Judah and then ten generations to David. (2:1-14) The listing is also made for the other tribes, with particular reference to the tribe of Levi and the high priests, and ending with a genealogy of the tribe of Benjamin, by way of introduction to the Benjamite King Saul, with whom the historical narrative in a strict sense then opens. Sometimes there may appear to be contradictions between Ezra's genealogies and other Bible passages. However, it must be kept in mind that certain persons were also known by other names, and that the passing of time and language changes could change the spelling of some names. Careful study removes most of the difficulties.

11 Ezra intersperses his genealogies here and there with bits of historical and geographical information that serve to clarify and to give important reminders. For example, in listing Reuben's descendants, Ezra adds an important piece of information: "And the sons of Reuben the first-born of Israel—for he was the first-born; but for his profaning the lounge of his father his right as first-born was given to the sons of Joseph the son of Israel, so that he was not to be enrolled genealogically for the right of the first-born. For Judah himself proved to

8. Into what two sections does the book of First Chronicles divide?
9. What is the basis of the extensive genealogies?
10. (a) What generations are first given? (b) What genealogy is logically traced at the start of the second chapter? (c) What other listings are made, ending in what?
11. Give examples of other useful information interspered in the record of genealogies.

be superior among his brothers, and the one for leader was from him; but the right as firstborn was Joseph's." (5:1, 2) Much is explained in these few words. Further, it is only in Chronicles that we learn that Joab, Amasa and Abishai were all nephews of David, which helps us to appreciate the various events surrounding them.—2:16, 17.

12 **Saul's unfaithfulness** (10:1-14). The narrative opens with the Philistines pressing the attack in the battle of Mount Gilboa. Three of Saul's sons, including Jonathan, are struck down. Then Saul is wounded. Not wishing to be taken by the enemy, he urges his armor-bearer: "Draw your sword and run me through with it, that these uncircumcised men may not come and certainly deal abusively with me." When his armor-bearer refuses, Saul kills himself. Thus Saul dies for acting "faithlessly against Jehovah concerning the word of Jehovah that he had not kept and also for asking of a spirit medium to make inquiry. And he did not inquire of Jehovah." (10:4, 13, 14) Jehovah gives the kingdom to David.

13 **David confirmed in the kingdom** (11:1–12:40). In time the twelve tribes assemble to David at Hebron and anoint him as king over all Israel. He captures Zion and goes on 'getting greater and greater, for Jehovah of armies is with him.' (11:9) Mighty men are put in charge of the army, by whom Jehovah saves "with a great salvation." (11:14) David receives united support as the men of war flock together with one complete heart to make him king. There is feasting and rejoicing in Israel.

14 **David and the ark of Jehovah** (13:1–16:36). David consults the national leaders, and they agree to move the Ark to Jerusalem from its abode of about seventy years at Kiriath-jearim. On the way, Uzzah dies for irreverently ignoring God's instructions, and the Ark is left for a time at the home of Obed-edom. (Num. 4:15) The Philistines resume their raids, but David crushingly defeats them twice, at Baal-perazim and at Gibeon. Instructed by David, the Levites now follow theocratic procedure in moving the Ark safely to Jerusalem, where it is put in a tent that David has pitched for it, amid dancing and rejoicing. There is an offering of sacrifice and singing, David himself contributing a song of thanks to Jehovah for the occasion. Its grand climax is reached in the theme: "Let the heavens rejoice, let the earth be joyful, and let them say among the nations, 'Jehovah himself has become king!'" (1 Chron. 16:31) What a stirring, faith-inspiring occasion! Later, this song of David is adapted as the basis for new songs, one of which is Psalm 96. Another is recorded in the first fifteen verses of Psalm 105.

15 **David and Jehovah's house** (16:37–17:27). An unusual arrangement now obtains in Israel. The ark of the covenant resides in a tent in Jerusalem where Asaph and his brothers are in attendance, while a few miles northwest of Jerusalem at Gibeon, Zadok the high priest and his brothers carry on the prescribed sacrifices at the tabernacle. Always mindful to exalt and unify Jehovah's worship, David indicates his desire to build a house for Jehovah's ark of the covenant. But Jehovah states that, not David, but his son, will build a house for Him, and that He will "certainly establish his throne firmly to time indefinite," showing loving-kindness as from a father to a son. (17:11-13) This marvelous promise by Jehovah—this covenant for an everlasting kingdom—moves David to the heart. His thankfulness overflows in petitioning that Jehovah's name will "prove faithful and become great to time indefinite," and that His blessing will be upon his house.—17:24.

16 **David's conquests** (18:1–21:17). Through David, Jehovah now carries out his promise to give the entire Promised Land to Abraham's seed. (18:3) In a rapid series of campaigns Jehovah gives "salvation to David" wherever he goes. (18:6) In smashing military victories David subdues the Philistines, strikes down the Moabites, defeats the Zobahites, forces the Syrians to pay tribute, and conquers Edom and Ammon, as well as Amalek. However, Satan incites David to sin by numbering Israel. Jehovah sends a pestilence in punishment, but mercifully brings an end to the calamity at Ornan's threshing floor, after 70,000 have been executed.

17 **David's preparation for the temple** (21:18–22:19). David receives angelic notice through Gad "to erect an altar to Jehovah on the threshing floor of Ornan the Jebusite." (21:18) After purchasing the location from Ornan, David obediently offers sacrifices there and calls upon Jehovah, who answers him "with fire from the heavens upon the altar of burnt offering." (21:26) David concludes that Jehovah wants his house built there, and sets to work in shaping the materials and assembling them, saying: "Solomon my son is young and delicate, and the house to be built to Jehovah is to be surpassingly magnificent for beauteous distinction to all the lands. Let me, then, make preparation for him." (22:5) He explains to Solomon that Jehovah has not permitted him to build the house, as he has been a man of wars and

12. What are the circumstances of Saul's death?
13. How does David prosper in the kingdom?
14. How does David fare in battle with the Philistines, and what faith-inspiring occasion gives rise to joyful song?
15. With what marvelous promise does Jehovah answer David's desire to build a house for unified worship?
16. What promise does Jehovah carry out through David, but how does David sin?
17. What preparation does David make for building Jehovah's house, and how does he encourage Solomon?

blood, and exhorts his son to be courageous and strong in this undertaking. "Rise and act, and may Jehovah prove to be with you." —22:16.

[18] **David organizes for Jehovah's worship** (23:1–29:30). A census is taken, this time according to God's will, for the reorganizing of the priestly and Levitical services, which latter services are here described in greater detail than anywhere else in the Scriptures. The divisions of the king's service are then outlined.

[19] Near the end of his eventful reign, David congregates the representatives of the entire nation, "Jehovah's congregation." (28:8) The king rises to his feet. "Hear me, my brothers and my people." He then speaks to them concerning the desire of his heart, "the house of the true God." In their presence he commissions Solomon: "And you, Solomon my son, know the God of your father and serve him with a complete heart and with a delightful soul; for all hearts Jehovah is searching, and every inclination of the thoughts he is discerning. If you search for him, he will let himself be found by you; but if you leave him, he will cast you off forever. See, now, for Jehovah himself has chosen you to build a house as a sanctuary. Be courageous and act." (28:2, 9, 10) He gives young Solomon the detailed architectural plans received by inspiration from Jehovah, and contributes toward the building an immense personal fortune in gold and silver, amounting to about $140,000,000 in modern value, that he has saved up for this purpose. With such a splendid example before them, the princes and the people respond by making a similar donation valued at more than $230,000,000.[a] They give way to rejoicing at this privilege.

[20] David then praises Jehovah in prayer, acknowledging that all this abundant offering has actually proceeded from His hand and petitioning his continued blessing on the people and upon Solomon. This final prayer of David reaches sublime heights in exalting Jehovah's kingdom and His glorious name: "Blessed may you be, O Jehovah the God of Israel our father, from time indefinite even to time indefinite. Yours, O Jehovah, are the greatness and the mightiness and the beauty and the excellency and the dignity; for everything in the heavens and in the earth is yours. Yours is the kingdom, O Jehovah, the One also lifting yourself up as head over all. The riches and the glory are on account of you, and you are dominating everything; and in your hand there are power and mightiness, and in your hand is ability to make great and to give strength to all. And now, O our God, we are thanking you and praising your beauteous name."—29:10-13.

[21] Solomon is anointed a second time, and begins to sit on 'the throne of Jehovah' in place of the aging David. After a reign of forty years, David dies "in a good old age, satisfied with days, riches and glory." (29:28) Ezra then concludes First Chronicles on a lofty note, emphasizing the superiority of David's kingdom over all the kingdoms of the nations.

WHY BENEFICIAL

[22] Ezra's fellow Israelites derived much benefit from his book. Having this compact history with its fresh and optimistic viewpoint, they appreciated Jehovah's loving mercies toward them on account of his loyalty to the kingdom covenant with King David and for his own name's sake. Encouraged, they were able to take up the pure worship of Jehovah with renewed zeal. The genealogies strengthened their confidence in the priesthood officiating at the rebuilt temple.

[23] First Chronicles was also of great benefit to the early Christian congregation. Matthew and Luke could draw on its genealogies in clearly establishing that Jesus Christ was the "son of David" and Messiah with legal right. (Matt. 1:1-16; Luke 3:23-38) In concluding his final witness, Stephen spoke of David's request to build a house for Jehovah and of Solomon's doing the building. Then he showed that "the Most High does not dwell in houses made with hands," indicating that the temple of Solomon's day pictured far more glorious heavenly things. —Acts 7:45-50.

[24] What of true Christians today? First Chronicles should build and stimulate our faith. There is much that we can copy in David's glowing example. How unlike the faithless Saul he was, in always inquiring of Jehovah! (1 Chron. 10:13, 14; 14:13, 14; 17:16; 22:17-19) In bringing up the ark of Jehovah to Jerusalem, in his psalms of praise, in his organizing of the Levites for service and in his request to build a glorious house for Jehovah—in all these ways he showed that Jehovah and His worship were first in mind. (16:23-29) He was no complainer. He did not seek special privileges for himself, but only to do Jehovah's will. Thus when Je

a Exodus 38:24; 1 Kings 20:39; *NW* footnotes, 1953 and 1955 Editions.

18. For what purpose is a census taken?
19. With what words does David commission Solomon, what plans does he provide, and what splendid example does he set?
20. What sublime heights are reached in David's final prayer?
21. On what lofty theme does First Chronicles end?
22. How were Ezra's fellow Israelites encouraged by this record?
23. How did Matthew, Luke and Stephen make good use of First Chronicles?
24. What in David's glowing example may we copy today?

hovah assigned the building of the house to his son, he wholeheartedly instructed his son, and gave of his time, his energy and his wealth in preparing for the work that would commence after his death. (29:3, 9) A splendid example of devotion indeed!—Heb. 11:32.

25 Then there are the climactic concluding chapters. The magnificent language with which David praised Jehovah and glorified his "beauteous name" should stir in us joyful appreciation of our modern-day privilege of making known the glories of Jehovah and his kingdom by Christ. (1 Chron. 29:10-13) May our faith and joy ever be like David's, as we express thankfulness for Jehovah's everlasting kingdom, by pouring ourselves out in His service. (17:16-27) Truly, First Chronicles makes the Bible theme of Jehovah's kingdom by his Seed scintillate more beauteously than ever, leaving us expectant of further thrilling disclosures of Jehovah's purposes.

25. To what appreciation of Jehovah's name and kingdom should this record stir us?

Bible Book Number Fourteen— 2 Chronicles

Writer:	**Ezra**
Place Written:	**Jerusalem (?)**
Writing Completed:	**c. 460 B.C.E.**
Time Covered:	**1037-537 B.C.E.**

SINCE First and Second Chronicles were originally one book, the arguments presented in the previous chapter as to background, writership, time of writing, canonicity and authenticity, apply to both books. According to the evidence presented, Ezra completed Second Chronicles about 460 B.C.E., probably in Jerusalem. It was Ezra's purpose to preserve historical materials that were in danger of being lost. He had the help of holy spirit, as well as a historian's ability to lay hold of and sort out details, so as to make an accurate and permanent record. He saved for the future that which he regarded as historical fact. Ezra's work was most timely, as now it was also necessary to collect together the entire body of sacred Hebrew writings that had been recorded over the centuries.

2 The Jews of Ezra's day were benefited greatly by Ezra's inspired chronicle. It was written for their instruction and to encourage endurance. Through the comfort from the Scriptures they could have hope. They accepted the book of Chronicles as part of the Bible canon. They knew it was trustworthy. They could check it by other inspired writings and by numerous secular histories cited by Ezra. Whereas they allowed the uninspired secular histories to perish, they carefully preserved Chronicles. The *Septuagint* translators included Chronicles as part of the Hebrew Bible.

3 Jesus Christ and the writers of the Christian Greek Scriptures accepted it as authentic and inspired. Jesus no doubt had in mind such incidents as recorded at 2 Chronicles 24:21 when denouncing Jerusalem as a killer and stoner of Jehovah's prophets and servants. (Matt. 23:35; 5:12; 2 Chron. 36:16) When James referred to Abraham as "Jehovah's friend," he no doubt had reference to Ezra's expression at 2 Chronicles 20:7. (Jas. 2:23) The book also contains prophecies that were unerringly fulfilled.—2 Chron. 20:17, 24; 21:14-19; 34:23-28; 36:17-20.

4 Archaeology also testifies to the authenticity of Second Chronicles. For example, the Bible record says that Solomon made a "very great quantity" of copper utensils for the house of Jehovah, in fact, so many that "the weight of the copper was not ascertained." (4:18) Critics have challenged whether this was possible. However, excavations near the Gulf of Aqaba, to the south of the Land of Promise, have led American archaeologist Nelson Glueck to describe Solomon as the "great copper king." He writes concerning Ezion-geber, the center of his copper industry, that it "represented a carefully integrated industrial complex" that "took a great deal of business ability, as well as architectural, engineering and metallurgical skill to construct. The entire town was a phenomenal industrial site. Ezion-geber was the Pittsburgh of old Palestine, in addition to being its most important seaport."[a] Other digging, on the site of ancient Babylon, has unearthed clay

1. When did Ezra complete Chronicles, and with what purpose in view?
2. Why is there no reason to doubt the accuracy of Chronicles?
3. How do other scriptures indicate Chronicles to be authentic?

a *The Other Side of the Jordan,* 1945, Nelson Glueck, pages 91-98.

4. What are some of the archaeological finds giving support to the record?

tablets dated the thirteenth year of Nebuchadnezzar's reign, one of which names Jehoiachin (actually *Yaukin,* as his name was then pronounced), along with his title as King of Judah.[a] This fits in well with the Bible account of his being taken captive to Babylon, in the eighth year of Nebuchadnezzar's reign.

5 The record of Second Chronicles traces events in Judah from the reign of Solomon, commencing in 1037 B.C.E., to Cyrus' decree in 537 B.C.E. to rebuild the house of Jehovah in Jerusalem. In this 500-year history, the northern ten-tribe kingdom is referred to only as it becomes involved in the affairs of Judah, and its destruction in 740 B.C.E. is not even mentioned. Why so? Because the priest Ezra was concerned only with Jehovah's worship at its rightful place, His house in Jerusalem, and with the kingdom of the line of David, with whom Jehovah made his covenant. Thus it is on the southern kingdom that Ezra concentrates attention in support of true worship and in expectation of the ruler to come out of Judah.—Gen. 49:10.

6 Ezra takes an uplifting viewpoint. Of the thirty-six chapters of Second Chronicles, the first nine are devoted to Solomon's reign, and six of these wholly to the preparation and dedication of the house of Jehovah. The record omits mention of Solomon's defection. Of the remaining twenty-seven chapters, fourteen deal with the five good kings who followed David's example of exclusive devotion to Jehovah's worship: Asa, Jehoshaphat, Jotham, Hezekiah and Josiah. Even in the other thirteen chapters, Ezra is careful to highlight the good points of the bad kings. He always emphasizes events relating to restoration and preservation of true worship. How stimulating!

CONTENTS OF SECOND CHRONICLES

7 **The glory of Solomon's reign** (1:1–9:31). As Second Chronicles opens we see Solomon the son of David growing in strength in the kingship. Jehovah is with him and keeps "making him surpassingly great." When he makes sacrifices at Gibeon, Jehovah appears to him at night, saying: "Ask! What shall I give you?" Solomon asks for knowledge and wisdom in order to govern Jehovah's people properly. Because of this unselfish request, God promises to give Solomon, not only wisdom and knowledge, but also wealth and riches and honor "such as no kings that were prior to you happened to have, and such as no one after you will come to have." So great is the wealth that flows into the city, that in time Solomon comes "to make the silver and the gold in Jerusalem like the stones."—1:1, 7, 12, 15.

8 Solomon conscripts 153,600 laborers for the work of building the house of Jehovah, and King Hiram of Tyre cooperates by sending timbers and a gifted workman. "In the fourth year of his reign" the building gets under way, and it is completed seven and a half years later, in 1027 B.C.E. The temple itself is fronted by a large porch that towers 180 feet high. Two immense copper pillars, one named Jachin, meaning "He Will Firmly Establish," and the other named Boaz, apparently meaning "In Strength," stand in front of the porch. (3:17) The house itself is comparatively small, being approximately ninety feet long, forty-five feet high and thirty feet broad, but it is covered with gold; its inner room, the Most Holy, is itself elaborately decorated with gold valued at over twenty-six million dollars. It also contains the two golden cherubs, one on each side of the room, whose wings stretch across and meet in the center.

9 In the inner courtyard there is a huge copper altar thirty feet long, thirty feet wide and fifteen feet high. As an indication of its size, a hall of those dimensions would seat about one hundred persons! Another striking object in the courtyard is the molten sea, an immense copper bowl resting on the backs of twelve copper bulls that look outward, three in each direction. This sea is capable of holding 29,400 gallons (U.S.A.) of water, which is used by the priests to wash themselves. Also located in the courtyard are ten small copper bowls resting on ornamented copper carriages, and in this water things having to do with burnt offerings are rinsed. They are filled from the molten sea, and wheeled to wherever the water is needed. In addition, there are the ten gold lampstands and many other utensils, some of gold and some of copper, for the temple worship.

10 Finally, after seven and a half years of work, the house of Jehovah is completed. (1 Ki. 6:1, 38) The day of its inauguration is the time to bring the symbol of Jehovah's presence into the innermost room of this gorgeous building. The priests bring "the ark of the covenant of Jehovah into its place, into the innermost room of the house, into the Most Holy, to underneath the wings of the cherubs." Then what happens? As the Levite singers and mu-

a *Biblical Archaeology,* 1957, G. Ernest Wright, page 177.

5. What time period is covered in Second Chronicles, and why is the history of Judah featured rather than that of the ten-tribe kingdom?
6. In what respects is Second Chronicles uplifting and stimulating?
7. How does Jehovah make Solomon "surpassingly great"?
8. How does the temple work proceed, and what are some details of its construction?
9. Describe the furnishings and the utensils of the courtyard and the temple.
10. What happens when the Ark is brought into the Most Holy?

sicians praise and thank Jehovah in united song, the house is filled with a cloud and the priests are not able to stand to minister because "the glory of Jehovah" fills the house of the true God. (2 Chron. 5:7, 13, 14) Thus Jehovah shows his approval of the temple and betokens his presence there.

11 A four-and-a-half-foot-high copper platform has been built for the occasion, and it is set in the inner courtyard near the huge copper altar. In this elevated position Solomon can be seen by the vast throngs that have assembled for the temple dedication. Following the miraculous manifestation of Jehovah's presence by the glory cloud, Solomon kneels before the crowd and offers a moving prayer of thanksgiving and praise, which includes a series of humble requests for forgiveness and blessing. In conclusion, he pleads: "Now, O my God, please, let your eyes prove to be opened and your ears attentive to the prayer respecting this place. O Jehovah God, do not turn back the face of your anointed one. O do remember the loving-kindnesses to David your servant."—6:40, 42.

12 Does Jehovah hear this prayer of Solomon? As soon as Solomon finishes praying, fire comes down from the heavens and consumes the burnt offering and the sacrifices, and "Jehovah's glory itself" fills the house. This leads all the people to prostrate themselves and thank Jehovah, "for he is good, for his loving-kindness is to time indefinite." (7:1, 3) A huge sacrifice is then made to Jehovah. A week-long feast of dedication is followed by the week-long feast of ingathering, and then a sabbath of refraining from work. After this happy, spiritually strengthening fifteen-day celebration, Solomon sends the people away to their homes "joyful and feeling good at heart." (7:10) Jehovah, too, is pleased. He reconfirms the kingdom covenant to Solomon, warning at the same time of the dire consequences of disobedience.

13 Solomon now carries on extensive construction work throughout his dominion, building not only a palace for himself, but also fortified cities, storage cities, chariot cities, cities for horsemen and everything he desires to build. It is a period of glorious prosperity and peace, because both the king and the people are mindful of Jehovah's worship. Even the queen of Sheba, from more than a thousand miles away, hears of the prosperity and wisdom of Solomon, and undertakes the long, arduous journey to come and see for herself. Is she disappointed? Not at all, for she confesses: "I did not put faith in their words until I had come that my own eyes might see; and, look! there has not been told me the half of the abundance of your wisdom. You have surpassed the report that I have heard. Happy are your men, and happy are these servants of yours." (9:6, 7) No other kings of the earth surpass Solomon in riches and wisdom. He reigns for forty years in Jerusalem.

14 **The reigns of Rehoboam and Abijah** (10:1–13:22). The harsh and oppressive rule by Solomon's son Rehoboam provokes the northern ten tribes under Jeroboam to revolt in 997 B.C.E. However, the priests and Levites that are in all Israel take their stand with Rehoboam, putting loyalty to the Kingdom covenant above nationalism. Rehoboam soon forsakes Jehovah's law, and Egypt's King Shishak invades, breaking into Jerusalem and stripping the house of Jehovah of its treasures. How sad that, scarcely more than thirty years after their construction, these gorgeously decorated buildings are stripped of their glory! The reason: The nation has "behaved unfaithfully toward Jehovah." Just in time Rehoboam humbles himself so that Jehovah does not bring them to complete ruin.—12:2.

15 At Rehoboam's death one of his twenty-eight sons, Abijah, is made king. Abijah's three-year reign is marked by bloody war with Israel to the north. Judah is outnumbered two to one, 400,000 troops against the 800,000 under Jeroboam. These figures are in keeping with the census taken in David's time. (1 Chron. 21:5) During the tremendous battles that follow, Israel's warriors are reduced to less than half, calf worshipers to the number of half a million being destroyed. The sons of Judah prove superior because they lean "upon Jehovah the God of their forefathers."—2 Chron. 13:18.

16 **God-fearing King Asa** (14:1–16:14). Abijah is succeeded by his son Asa. Asa is a champion of true worship. He campaigns to cleanse the land from image worship. But, look! Judah is threatened by an overwhelming military force of one million Ethiopians. Asa prays: "Help us, O Jehovah our God, for upon you we do lean, and in your name we have come against this crowd." Jehovah answers by giving him a smashing victory.—14:11.

17 The spirit of God comes upon Azariah to tell Asa: "Jehovah is with you as long as you prove to be with him; and if you search for him, he will let himself be found by you." (15:

11. What prayer does Solomon offer, and what does he petition?
12. How does Jehovah answer Solomon's prayer, and on what happy note does the fifteen-day celebration end?
13. (a) What construction work follows? (b) How does the queen of Sheba express herself on seeing Solomon's kingdom?
14. Why is Israel so soon stripped of her glory?
15. What bloody battles follow, and why does Judah prove superior against Israel?
16. How does Jehovah answer Asa's urgent prayer?
17. How is Asa encouraged to reform worship in Judah, but for what is he rebuked?

2) Greatly encouraged, Asa reforms worship in Judah, and the people make a covenant that anyone that will not search for Jehovah shall be put to death. However, when Baasha, king of Israel, erects barriers to stop the flow of Israelites into Judah, Asa commits a grave error by hiring Ben-hadad, king of Syria, to fight against Israel, instead of looking to Jehovah for help. For this Jehovah rebukes him. Despite this, Asa's heart proves "to be complete all his days." (15:17) He dies in the forty-first year of his reign.

18 **Jehoshaphat's good reign** (17:1–20:37). Asa's son Jehoshaphat continues the fight against image worship, and inaugurates a special educational campaign, with instructors traveling throughout the cities of Judah, teaching the people from the book of Jehovah's law. A time of great prosperity and peace follows, and Jehoshaphat continues "advancing and growing great to a superior degree." (17:12) But then he makes a marriage alliance with wicked King Ahab of Israel, and goes down to help him fight against the growing Syrian power, ignoring Jehovah's prophet Micaiah and barely escaping with his life when Ahab is killed in battle at Ramoth-gilead. Jehovah's prophet Jehu rebukes Jehoshaphat for making common cause with wicked Ahab. Thereafter Jehoshaphat appoints judges throughout the land, and instructs them to carry out their duties in the fear of God.

19 Now comes the climax of Jehoshaphat's reign. The combined forces of Moab, Ammon and the mountainous region of Seir move against Judah in overwhelming strength. Up they swarm through the wilderness of En-gedi. Fear strikes the nation. Jehoshaphat and all Judah, with "their little ones, their wives and their sons," stand before Jehovah and seek him in prayer. Jehovah's spirit comes upon Jahaziel the Levite, who calls to the assembled throngs: "Pay attention, all Judah and you inhabitants of Jerusalem and King Jehoshaphat! Here is what Jehovah has said to you, 'Do not you be afraid or be terrified because of this large crowd; for the battle is not yours, but God's. Tomorrow go down against them. . . . Jehovah will be with you.'" Rising early in the morning, Judah marches out with the Levite singers in the lead. Jehoshaphat encourages them: "Put faith in Jehovah . . . Put faith in his prophets and so prove successful." The singers joyfully extol Jehovah, "for to time indefinite is his loving-kindness." (20:13, 15-17, 20, 21) Jehovah manifests his loving-kindness in a marvelous way, setting an ambush against the invading armies so that they annihilate one another. Coming to the watchtower in the wilderness, the exultant Judeans see only dead carcasses. Truly, the battle is God's! To the end of his twenty-five-year reign Jehoshaphat keeps walking faithfully before Jehovah.

20 **Bad reigns of Jehoram, Ahaziah and Athaliah** (21:1–23:21). Jehoshaphat's son Jehoram starts off badly by killing all his brothers. However, Jehovah spares him because of His covenant with David. Edom begins to revolt. From somewhere Elijah sends a letter, warning Jehoram that Jehovah will strike his house a great blow and that he will die horribly. (21:12-15) True to the prophecy, the Philistines and the Arabs invade and loot Jerusalem, and the king dies of a loathsome intestinal disease, after an eight-year reign.

21 Jehoram's sole surviving son, Ahaziah (Jehoahaz), succeeds him, but is influenced for bad by his mother Athaliah, the daughter of Ahab and Jezebel. His reign is cut short after one year by Jehu's purge of the house of Ahab. At this, Athaliah murders her grandchildren and usurps the throne. However, one of Ahaziah's sons survives. He is the one-year-old Jehoash, who is smuggled into the house of Jehovah by his aunt Jehoshabeath. Athaliah reigns for six years, and then Jehoshabeath's husband, the high priest Jehoiada, courageously takes young Jehoash and has him proclaimed king, as one of the "sons of David." Coming to the house of Jehovah, Athaliah rips her clothing apart and cries, "Conspiracy! Conspiracy!" But to no avail. Jehoiada has her thrown out of the temple and put to death.—23:3, 13-15.

22 **Reigns of Jehoash, Amaziah and Uzziah start well, end badly** (24:1–26:23). Jehoash reigns for forty years, and, as long as Jehoiada is alive to exercise a good influence, he does right. He even takes an interest in the house of Jehovah and has it renovated. When Jehoiada dies, however, Jehoash is influenced by the princes of Judah to turn from Jehovah's worship to serve the sacred poles and idols. When God's spirit moves Zechariah the son of Jehoiada to rebuke the king, Jehoash has the prophet stoned to death. Soon afterward a small military force of Syrians invades, and the much larger Judean army is unable to turn them back, because they have "left Jehovah the God of their forefathers." (24:24) Now Jehoash's own servants rise up and assassinate him.

23 Amaziah succeeds his father Jehoash. He begins his twenty-nine-year reign well, but

18. (a) How does Jehoshaphat campaign for true worship, and with what results? (b) How does his marriage alliance almost lead to disaster?
19. At the climax of Jehoshaphat's reign, how does the battle prove to be God's?
20. What disasters mark Jehoram's reign?
21. What bad things result from Athaliah's domination in Judah, but how does Jehoiada succeed in restoring the throne of David?
22. How does Jehoash's reign start well but end badly?
23. What similar pattern does Amaziah follow?

later falls from Jehovah's favor because he sets up and worships the idols of the Edomites. "God has resolved to bring you to ruin," Jehovah's prophet warns him. (25:16) However, Amaziah becomes boastful and challenges Israel to the north. True to God's word, he suffers a humiliating defeat at the hands of the Israelites, after which conspirators rise up and put him to death.

24 Amaziah's son Uzziah follows in his father's footsteps. He reigns well for the greater part of fifty-two years, gaining fame as a military genius, as a builder of towers and as "a lover of agriculture." (26:10) He equips and mechanizes the army. However, his strength becomes his weakness. He becomes haughty and presumes to take over the priestly duty of offering incense in the temple of Jehovah. For this Jehovah smites him with leprosy. As a result he has to live apart, away from the house of Jehovah and also from the king's house, where his son Jotham judges the people in his place.

25 **Jotham serves Jehovah** (27:1-9). Unlike his father, Jotham does not "invade the temple of Jehovah." Instead 'he keeps doing what is right in Jehovah's eyes.' (27:2) During his sixteen-year reign he does much construction work, and successfully puts down a revolt of the Ammonites.

26 **Wicked King Ahaz** (28:1-27). Jotham's son Ahaz proves to be one of the wickedest of the twenty-one Judean kings. He goes to the extreme in offering his own sons as burnt sacrifices to heathen gods. Consequently Jehovah abandons him, in turn, to the armies of Syria, Israel, Edom and Philistia. So Jehovah humbles Judah because Ahaz 'lets unrestraint grow in Judah, and there is an acting with great unfaithfulness toward Jehovah.' (28:19) Going from bad to worse, Ahaz sacrifices to the gods of Syria because the Syrians prove superior to him in battle. He closes the doors of the house of Jehovah and replaces the worship of Jehovah with the worship of heathen gods. None too soon, Ahaz' reign ends after sixteen years.

27 **Faithful King Hezekiah** (29:1–32:33). Hezekiah son of Ahaz reigns for twenty-nine years in Jerusalem. His first act is to reopen and repair the doors of the house of Jehovah. Then he assembles the priests and Levites and gives them instructions to clean the temple and sanctify it for Jehovah's service. He declares that he wants to conclude a covenant with Jehovah to turn back His burning anger. Jehovah's worship is resumed in a grand way.

28 A tremendous passover is planned, but since there is no time to prepare it in the first month, the provision of the Law is taken advantage of, and it is celebrated in the second month of the first year of Hezekiah's reign. (2 Chron. 30:2, 3; Num. 9:10, 11) The king not only invites all Judah to attend, but Israel as well, and while some in Ephraim, Manasseh and Zebulun mock the invitation, others humble themselves and come to Jerusalem along with all Judah. Following the passover, the festival of unfermented cakes is held. What a joyous seven-day feast it is! So upbuilding, indeed, that they extend the feast another seven days. There is "great rejoicing in Jerusalem, for from the days of Solomon the son of David the king of Israel there was none like this in Jerusalem." (2 Chron. 30:26) The spiritually restored people follow up with a smashing campaign to rid both Judah and Israel of idolatry, while Hezekiah, on his part, restores the material contributions for the Levites and the temple services.

29 Then Sennacherib the king of Assyria invades Judah and threatens Jerusalem. Hezekiah takes courage, repairs the defenses of the city and defies the taunts of the enemy. Putting complete trust in Jehovah, he keeps praying for aid. Jehovah dramatically answers this prayer of faith. He proceeds "to send an angel and efface every valiant, mighty man and leader and chief in the camp of the king of Assyria." (32:21) Sennacherib returns home in shame. Even his gods cannot help him save face, for he is later on slain at their altar by his own sons. (2 Ki. 19:7) Jehovah miraculously extends Hezekiah's life and he comes to have great riches and glory, all Judah honoring him at his death.

30 **Manasseh and Amon reign wickedly** (33:1-25). Hezekiah's son Manasseh reverts to the wicked course of his grandfather Ahaz, undoing all the good accomplished during Hezekiah's reign. He builds up the high places, sets up the sacred poles and even sacrifices his sons to false gods. Finally, Jehovah brings the king of Assyria against Judah, and Manasseh is carried away captive to Babylon. There he repents of his wrongdoing. When Jehovah shows mercy by restoring him to his kingship, he endeavors to root out demon worship and restore true religion. However, when Manasseh dies after a long fifty-five-year reign, his son Amon ascends the throne and wickedly champions false wor-

24. How does Uzziah's strength become his weakness, and with what result?
25. Why does Jotham succeed?
26. To what unprecedented depths of wickedness does Ahaz descend?
27. How does Hezekiah resume Jehovah's worship?
28. What tremendous feast does Hezekiah hold in Jerusalem, and how do the people express their joy?
29. How does Jehovah reward Hezekiah's implicit trust in Him?
30. (a) To what wickedness does Manasseh revert, but what follows his repentance? (b) What marks Amon's short reign?

ship again. After two years, his own servants put him to death.

31 **Josiah's courageous reign** (34:1–35:27). Youthful Josiah, the son of Amon, makes a courageous attempt to restore true worship. He has the altars of the Baals and graven images pulled down, and repairs the house of Jehovah, where a copy of the law of Moses is found. Yet he is told that calamity will come on the land for the unfaithfulness that has already occurred, but not in righteous Josiah's day. In the eighteenth year of his reign he arranges an outstanding passover celebration. After a thirty-one-year reign Josiah meets his death in a vain attempt to prevent the Egyptian hosts from passing through the land on their way to the Euphrates.

32 **Jehoahaz, Jehoiakim, Jehoiachin, Zedekiah and Jerusalem's desolation** (36:1-23). The wickedness of the last four Judean kings quickly carries the nation to its disastrous end. Josiah's son Jehoahaz rules only three months, being removed by Pharaoh Necho of Egypt. He is replaced by his brother Eliakim, whose name is changed to Jehoiakim, and during whose reign Judah is subjugated by the new world power, Babylon. (2 Ki. 24:1) When he rebels, Nebuchadnezzar comes up to Jerusalem to punish him in 618 B.C.E., but Jehoiakim dies this same year, after reigning eleven years. He is replaced by his eighteen-year-old son Jehoiachin, who surrenders to Nebuchadnezzar after a reign of scarcely three months and is carried away captive to Babylon. Nebuchadnezzar now places a third son of Josiah, Jehoiachin's uncle Zedekiah, on the throne. Zedekiah reigns badly for eleven years, refusing to "humble himself on account of Jeremiah the prophet at the order of Jehovah." (2 Chron. 36:12) In large-scale unfaithfulness, priests and people alike defile the house of Jehovah.

33 Finally, Zedekiah rebels against Babylon's yoke, and this time Nebuchadnezzar shows no mercy. Jehovah's rage is full, and there is no healing. Jerusalem falls, its temple is looted and burned, and the survivors of the eighteen-month siege are carried as captives to Babylon. Judah is left desolate. Thus in this very year of 607 B.C.E. begins the desolation "to fulfill Jehovah's word by the mouth of Jeremiah, . . . to fulfill seventy years." (36:21) The chronicler then leaps this gap of nearly seventy years, to record in the last two verses the historic decree of Cyrus in 537 B.C.E. The Jewish captives are to be set free! Jerusalem must rise again!

WHY BENEFICIAL

34 Second Chronicles adds its powerful testimony to that of other witnesses concerning this eventful period, 1037-537 B.C.E. Moreover, it gives valuable supplementary information not found in other canonical histories, for example, at 2 Chronicles chapters 19, 20 and 29-31. Ezra's selection of material emphasized the fundamental and permanent elements in the history of the nation, such as the priesthood and its service, the temple and the kingdom covenant. This was beneficial in holding the nation together in hope of the Messiah and his kingdom.

35 The closing verses of Second Chronicles (36:17-23) give conclusive proof of the fulfillment of Jeremiah 25:12, and, in addition, show that a *full* seventy years must be counted from the complete desolation of the land to the restoration of Jehovah's worship at Jerusalem in 537 B.C.E. This desolation therefore begins 607 B.C.E., and not 586 B.C.E., as some Bible chronologies assert.—Jer. 29:10; 2 Ki. 25:1-26; Ezra 3:1-6.

36 Second Chronicles contains powerful admonitions for those walking in Christian faith. So many of the kings of Judah started well but then lapsed into wicked ways. We should be warned therefore not to be "the sort that shrink back to destruction, but the sort that have faith to the preserving alive of the soul." (Heb. 10:39) Even faithful King Hezekiah became haughty on recovering from his sickness, and it was only because he quickly humbled himself that he was able to avoid Jehovah's indignation. Second Chronicles magnifies Jehovah's wonderful qualities and extols his name and sovereignty. The entire history is presented from the standpoint of exclusive devotion to Jehovah. As it lays emphasis also upon the royal line of Judah, it strengthens our expectation of seeing pure worship exalted under the everlasting kingdom of Jesus Christ, the loyal "son of David."—Acts 15:16, 17.

31. What are the highlights of Josiah's courageous reign?
32. How do the last four kings lead Judah to its disastrous end?
33. (a) How does the seventy-year desolation begin, "to fulfill Jehovah's word"? (b) What historic decree is recorded in the last two verses?
34. What is emphasized in Ezra's selection of material, and how was this beneficial to the nation?
35. What important points are proved in the closing verses?
36. (a) What powerful admonitions are contained in Second Chronicles? (b) How does it strengthen expectation concerning the Kingdom?

Bible Book Number Fifteen— Ezra

Writer:	**Ezra**
Place Written:	**Jerusalem**
Writing Completed:	**c. 460 B.C.E.**
Time Covered:	**537-467 B.C.E.**

THE end of the prophesied seventy years of Jerusalem's desolation under Babylon was drawing near. True, it was Babylon's reputation that she never released her captives, but Jehovah's word would prove stronger than Babylonian might. Release of Jehovah's people was in sight. Jehovah's temple that had been laid low would be rebuilt and Jehovah's altar would again receive sacrifices of atonement. Jerusalem would again know the shout and praise of the true worshiper of Jehovah. Jeremiah had prophesied the length of the desolation, and Isaiah had prophesied how the release of captives would come about. Isaiah had even named Cyrus of Persia as 'the shepherd of Jehovah,' who would tumble haughty Babylon from her position as the third world power of Bible history.—Jer. 25:12; Isa. 44:28; 45:1, 2.

2 This disaster befell Babylon on the night of October 5-6, 539 B.C.E., as the Babylonian king Belshazzar and his grandees were drinking toasts to their demon gods. Adding to their pagan debauchery, they were using the holy vessels from Jehovah's temple as their cups of drunkenness! How fitting that Cyrus was there that night to fulfill the prophecy! "B.C. 539 Cyrus takes Babylon," says the *Westminster Dictionary of the Bible.* (1944 Ed., page 108) "In 539 B.C. Cyrus turned his attack against Nabonidus [father and coregent of Belshazzar], and the Babylonian army was defeated," says Werner Keller in *The Bible as History* (1956, page 310, N.Y. Ed.; page 297, London Ed.). To which *The Encyclopædia Britannica,* Eleventh Edition, Vol. 7, page 707, adds its testimony: "Why the war with Babylon, which had become inevitable, was delayed until 539, we do not know. Here too Cyrus in a single campaign destroyed a mighty state. The army of Nabonidus was defeated; Babylon itself attempted no resistance, but surrendered on the 16th Tishri . . . 539, to the Persian general Gobryas."

3 This date 539 B.C.E. is an absolute date, that is, a date fixed, proved and accepted by secular history. In the following year, beginning in 538, Cyrus began his first complete year as world ruler, and it was during this year, some time before the spring of 537, that Cyrus "caused a cry to pass through all his realm," authorizing the Jews to go up to Jerusalem to rebuild the house of Jehovah.[a] A faithful remnant journeyed back in time to set up the altar and offer the first sacrifices in the "seventh [Jewish] month," corresponding to September-October 537, seventy years to the month after Judah and Jerusalem's desolation by Nebuchadnezzar.—Ezra 1:1-3; 3:1-6.

4 Restoration! This provides the setting of the book of Ezra. The use of the first person, "I," in the narration from chapter 7, verse 28, onward clearly shows that the writer was Ezra. As "a skilled copyist in the law of Moses" and a man of practical faith who "prepared his heart to consult the law of Jehovah and to do it and to teach" it, Ezra was well qualified to record this history, even as he had recorded Chronicles. (Ezra 7:6, 10) Since the book of Ezra is a continuation of Chronicles, it is generally believed to have been written at the same time, about 460 B.C.E. It covers seventy years, from the time that the Jews were a broken, scattered nation marked as "sons of death," to the completion of the second temple and the cleansing of the priesthood after Ezra's return to Jerusalem.—Ezra 1:1; 7:7; 10:17; Ps. 102:20, *NW* footnote, 1957 Edition.

5 The Hebrew name Ezra means "The Help." The books of Ezra and Nehemiah were originally one scroll. (Neh. 3:32, *NW* footnote, 1955 Edition) Later the Jews divided this scroll, and called it First and Second Ezra. Modern Hebrew Bibles call the two books Ezra and Nehemiah, as do other modern Bibles. Part of the book of Ezra (4:8 to 6:18, and 7:12-26) was written in Aramaic, and the remainder in Hebrew, Ezra being skilled in both languages.

6 Ezra had been charged with carrying out

a *Babylonian Chronology,* 1956, Parker and Dubberstein, page 29.

1. What prophecies gave assurance of Jerusalem's restoration?
2. What were the time and occasion of Babylon's fall?
3. What proclamation by Cyrus made it possible to restore Jehovah's worship exactly seventy years after the desolation began?
4. (a) What is the setting of the book, and who wrote it? (b) When was it written, and what period does it cover?
5. What relation has the book of Ezra to the book of Nehemiah, and in what languages was it written?
6. With regard to Ezra's record, what has archaeology confirmed?

the imperial decree to instruct the Jews in the law of Jehovah. (7:25) Archaeological evidence supports the record in Ezra, showing that he performed this task thoroughly. For example, papyrus finds as far south as Elephantine, in southern Egypt, have been found to contain instructions from King Darius II of Persia to the Jews there, on how to observe the passover properly.[a] Concerning the canonicity of Ezra, W. F. Albright writes in his treatise *The Bible After Twenty Years of Archaeology:* "Archaeological data have thus demonstrated the substantial originality of the Books of Jeremiah and Ezekiel, of Ezra and Nehemiah beyond doubt; they have confirmed the traditional picture of events, as well as their order."

7 Though the book of Ezra may not be quoted or referred to directly by the Greek Scripture writers, yet there is no question about its place in the canon of the Bible, carrying as it does the record of Jehovah's dealings with the Jews down to the time of the assembling of the Hebrew catalogue, which work was largely accomplished by Ezra, according to Jewish tradition. Moreover, the book of Ezra so vindicates all the prophecies concerning the restoration as to prove that it is indeed an integral part of the divine record, with which it also harmonizes completely, honoring pure worship and sanctifying the great name of Jehovah God.

CONTENTS OF EZRA

8 **A remnant returns** (1:1–3:6). His spirit roused by Jehovah, Cyrus king of Persia issues the decree for the Jews to return and build the house of Jehovah in Jerusalem. He urges those Jews who may remain in Babylon to contribute freely toward the project, and arranges for the returning Jews to take back the utensils of the original temple. A leader from the royal tribe of Judah, and lineal descendant of King David, Zerubbabel (Sheshbazzar), is assigned as governor to lead the released ones, and Jeshua (or Joshua) is the high priest. (Ezra 1:8; 5:2; Zech. 3:1) A remnant of nearly fifty thousand faithful servants of Jehovah, including priests, Levites and non-Israelite slaves and temple workers, make the journey of about a thousand miles. By the seventh month, according to the Jewish calendar, they are settled in their cities, and then they gather at Jerusalem to offer sacrifices at the site of the temple altar and to celebrate the festival of booths in the fall of 537 B.C.E. Thus the seventy years' desolation ends exactly on time!

a *The Bible as History,* 1956, Werner Keller, page 318 N.Y. Ed., page 304 London Ed.

7. How is the book of Ezra shown truly to be a part of the divine record?
8. Describe the train of events leading to the end of the seventy years' desolation.

9 **Rebuilding the temple** (3:7–6:22). Materials are assembled, and in the second year of their return the foundation of the temple of Jehovah is laid amid shouts of joy, and amid the weeping of the older men who had seen the former house. The neighboring peoples, adversaries, offer to help with the construction, saying they are seeking the same God, but the Jewish remnant flatly refuse any alliance with them. The adversaries continually try to weaken and dishearten the Jews and frustrate their work, from the reign of Cyrus down to that of Darius. Finally, in the days of "Artaxerxes" (Magian Gaumata, 522 B.C.E., the usurper who preceded Darius), they have the work forcibly stopped by royal command. This ban continues "until the second year of the reign of Darius the king of Persia," which is over fifteen years after the laying of the foundation.—4:4-7, 24.

10 Jehovah now sends his prophets Haggai and Zechariah to arouse Zerubbabel and Joshua, and the building work is taken up with renewed zeal. Again the adversaries complain to the king, but the work goes on with unabated vigor. Darius I (Hystaspis), after referring to Cyrus' original decree, orders the work to continue without interference, and even commands the opposers to supply materials to facilitate construction. With continued encouragement from Jehovah's prophets, the builders complete the temple in less than five years. This is in the month Adar of the sixth year of Darius or near the spring of 516 B.C.E., and the entire construction has taken just about twenty years. (6:14, 15) The house of God is now inaugurated with great joy and with appropriate sacrifices. Then the people celebrate the passover and go on to hold "the festival of unfermented cakes seven days with rejoicing." (6:22) Yes, joy and rejoicing mark the dedication of this second temple to Jehovah's praise.

11 **Ezra returns to Jerusalem** (7:1–8:36). Almost fifty years elapse, bringing us down to 468 B.C.E., the seventh year of the Persian king, Artaxerxes I (known as "Longimanus," due to having his right hand longer than his left). The king grants the skilled copyist Ezra "all his request" with respect to a journey to Jerusalem to render much-needed aid there. In commissioning him, the king encourages the Jews to go with him, and grants Ezra silver and gold vessels for temple use, and provisions of wheat, wine, oil and salt. He exempts the

9. How does the temple work begin, but what happens in the years that follow?
10. (a) How does encouragement from God's prophets combine with the king's order in getting the work completed? (b) What joy marks the second temple dedication?
11. How does the king grant Ezra "all his request," and what is Ezra's response?

priests and temple workers from taxation. The king makes Ezra responsible to teach the people, and declares it to be a capital offense for anyone not to become a doer of the law of Jehovah and the law of the king. With thankfulness to Jehovah for this expression of his loving-kindness through the king, Ezra acts immediately on the commission.

[12] At this point Ezra commences his eyewitness account, writing in the first person. He assembles the returning Jews at the river Ahava for final instructions, and adds some Levites to the group of about 1,500 adult males already assembled. Ezra recognizes the dangers of the route to be taken, but declines to ask the king for an escort, lest it may be construed as showing lack of faith in Jehovah. Instead, he proclaims a fast and leads the camp in making entreaty to God. This prayer is answered, and the hand of Jehovah proves to be over them throughout the long journey. Thus they are able to bring their treasures (worth well over $5,000,000 at modern values) safely to the house of Jehovah in Jerusalem.—8:26, 27 and *NW* footnotes, 1955 Edition.

[13] **Cleansing the priesthood** (9:1–10:44). But not all has gone well during the sixty-nine years of dwelling in the restored land! Ezra learns of disturbing conditions, in that the people, the priests and the Levites have intermarried with the pagan Canaanites. Faithful Ezra is stunned. He lays the matter in prayer before Jehovah. The people confess their wrongdoing, and ask Ezra to "be strong and act." (10:4) He has the Jews put away the foreign wives that they have taken in disobedience to God's law, and the uncleanness is cleared out in the space of about three months. —10:8.

WHY BENEFICIAL

[14] The book of Ezra is beneficial, in the first place, in showing the unerring accuracy with which Jehovah's prophecies are fulfilled. Jeremiah, who had so accurately foretold Jerusalem's desolation, also foretold its restoration after seventy years. (Jer. 29:10) Right on time, Jehovah showed his loving-kindness in bringing his people, a faithful remnant, back again into the Land of Promise to carry on true worship.

[15] The restored temple again exalted Jehovah's worship among his people, and it stood as a testimony that he wonderfully and mercifully blesses those who turn to him with a desire for true worship. Though it lacked the glory of Solomon's temple, yet it served its purpose in harmony with the divine will. The material splendor was no longer there. It was also inferior in spiritual treasures, lacking, among other things, the ark of the covenant, the tables of the law and the supernatural light of Jehovah's presence.[a] Nor was the inauguration of Zerubbabel's temple comparable with that in Solomon's day. At most, about 50,000 persons were in attendance, compared with a far larger number on the first occasion, and the sacrifices of cattle and sheep were less than one percent of the sacrifices at Solomon's temple. No cloudlike glory filled the latter house, as it had the former, nor did fire descend from Jehovah to consume the burnt offerings. Both temples, however, served the important purpose of exalting the worship of Jehovah, the true God.

[16] This worship is also exalted in the temple described by the apostle Peter. Its foundation is Jesus Christ, "chosen, precious, with God." It is made up of "living stones" that are "built up a spiritual house for the purpose of a holy priesthood, to offer up spiritual sacrifices acceptable to God through Jesus Christ," and to "declare abroad the excellencies" of God, as his people. (1 Pet. 2:4-9) This grows into a temple of superlative glory, incomparable in beauty and desirableness, and whose splendor is unfading and above that of any material structure. It is the temple of worship that Jehovah himself builds up "to inhabit by spirit." —Eph. 2:19-22; Rev. 11:19.

[17] The book of Ezra contains lessons that are of highest value for Christians today. In it we read of Jehovah's people making willing offerings for his work. (Ezra 2:68; 2 Cor. 9:7) We are encouraged in learning of Jehovah's unfailing provision for and his blessing upon assemblies for his praise. (Ezra 6:16, 22) We see a fine example in the Nethinim, and other believing foreigners, as they go up with the remnant to give wholehearted support to Jehovah's worship. (2:43, 55) Consider, too, the humble repentance of the people when advised of their wrong course in intermarrying with pagan neighbors. (10:2-4) Bad associations led to divine disapproval. (9:14, 15) Joyful zeal for his work brought his approval and blessing. —6:14, 21, 22.

[18] Though a king no longer sat on Jehovah's throne at Jerusalem, the restoration aroused

12. How does Jehovah prove to be with Ezra's group during the journey?
13. How does Ezra act in removing uncleanness from among the Jews?
14. What does the book of Ezra show as to Jehovah's prophecies?
15. (a) How did the restored temple serve Jehovah's purpose? (b) In what respects did it lack the glory of the first temple?

a The Jewish *Mishnah* (Yoma, 21, 2).

16. But what other temple exceeds both these temples for glory?
17. What valuable lessons are to be found in the book of Ezra?
18. Why was the restoration of Jehovah's people an important step leading to the appearance of Messiah the King?

expectation that Jehovah would in due course produce his promised King in the line of David. The restored nation was now in position to guard the sacred pronouncements and worship of God until the time of Messiah's appearing. If this remnant had not responded in faith, in returning to their land, to whom would Messiah have come? Truly, the events of the book of Ezra are an important part of the history leading to the appearance of the Messiah and King! It is all most beneficial for our study today.

Bible Book Number Sixteen— Nehemiah

Writer:	**Nehemiah**
Place Written:	**Jerusalem**
Writing Completed:	**After 443 B.C.E.**
Time Covered:	**456—after 443 B.C.E.**

NEHEMIAH, whose name means "Jah Is Comfort," was a Jewish servant of the Persian king Artaxerxes I. He was cupbearer to the king. This was a position of great trust and honor, and one to be desired, for it gave access to the king at times when he was in a happy frame of mind and ready to grant favors. However, Nehemiah was one of those faithful exiles who preferred Jerusalem above any personal "cause for rejoicing." (Ps. 137:5, 6) It was not position or material wealth that was uppermost in Nehemiah's thoughts, but, rather, the restoration of Jehovah's worship.

2 In 456 B.C.E. those "left over from the captivity," the Jewish remnant that had returned to Jerusalem, were not prospering. They were in a lamentable condition. The wall of the city was rubble, and the people were a reproach in the eyes of their ever-present adversaries. Nehemiah was grieved. However, it was Jehovah's appointed time for something to be done about the walls of Jerusalem. Enemies or no enemies, Jerusalem with its protective wall must be built as a time marker in connection with a prophecy that Jehovah had given Daniel concerning the coming of Messiah. (Dan. 9:24-27) Accordingly, Jehovah directed events, using the faithful and zealous Nehemiah to carry out the divine will.

3 Nehemiah is undoubtedly the writer of the book that bears his name. The opening statement, "The words of Nehemiah the son of Hacaliah," and the fact that he wrote mostly in the first person, clearly prove this. Originally the books of Ezra and Nehemiah were one book, called "Ezra." Later, the Jews divided the book into First and Second Ezra, and later still Second Ezra became known as Nehemiah. An interval of about twelve years lies between the closing events of Ezra and the opening events of Nehemiah, whose history then covers the period of 456 till after 443 B.C.E.—Neh. 1:1; 5:14; 13:6.

4 The book of Nehemiah harmonizes with the rest of inspired Scripture, with which it rightfully belongs. It names eleven of the twelve gates in the restored Jerusalem, the remaining gate being named by Ezra at 2 Chronicles 25:23. There are also twelve gates in the Revelation vision of the heavenly Jerusalem. (Neh. 2:13, 14; 3:3, 6, 26, 28, 31, 32; 12:39; Rev. 21:21) Further, the book marks the beginning of the fulfillment of Daniel's prophecy that Jerusalem would be rebuilt, but not without opposition "in the straits of the times." (Dan. 9:25) Yes, in just fifty-two days; and archaeological investigation supports this in revealing a hurriedly built wall, made of unusually small stones cemented with clay plaster mixed with stone chips.[a]

5 What about the date of 455 B.C.E. for Nehemiah's journey to Jerusalem to rebuild the city wall? Testimony by the Greek historian Thucydides, who lived during the reign of Artaxerxes I, taken with the chronology of the Greek historian Diodorus Siculus of the first century B.C.E., pinpoints the beginning of Artaxerxes' rule as 474 B.C.E.[b] This would make

a *The Bible as History*, 1956, Werner Keller, page 317 N.Y. Ed., pages 303, 304 London Ed.
b *The Watchtower*, 1946, page 360, footnote.

1. What position of trust did Nehemiah hold, and what was uppermost in his mind?
2. What sorry condition grieved Nehemiah, but what appointed time was drawing near?
3. (a) What proves Nehemiah to be the writer, and how did the book come to be called "Nehemiah"? (b) What interval separates this book from the book of Ezra, and what years does the book of Nehemiah cover?
4. (a) How does the book harmonize with the rest of the Scriptures? (b) How does archaeology confirm the record?
5. (a) What testimony pinpoints the beginning of Artaxerxes' reign as 474 B.C.E.? (b) What date marks his twentieth year? (c) How do the books of Nehemiah and Luke tie in with Daniel's prophecy in a remarkable fulfillment of prophecy?

his twentieth year 455. Nehemiah 2:1-8 indicates it was in the spring of that year, in the Jewish month Nisan, that Nehemiah, the royal cupbearer, received from the king the command to restore and rebuild Jerusalem, its wall and its gates. Daniel's prophecy stated that sixty-nine weeks of years, or 483 years, would stretch from this command to the appearance of Messiah—a prophecy that was remarkably fulfilled at Jesus' anointing A.D. 29, another date that may be proved from secular and Biblical records.[a] (Dan. 9:24-27; Luke 3:1-3, 23) Indeed, the books of Nehemiah and Luke tie in remarkably with Daniel's prophecy in showing Jehovah God to be the Author and Fulfiller of true prophecy! Nehemiah is truly a part of the inspired Scriptures.

CONTENTS OF NEHEMIAH

6 **Nehemiah sent to Jerusalem** (1:1–2:20). Nehemiah is greatly troubled by a report from Hanani, who has returned to Shushan from Jerusalem bearing tidings of the severe plight of the Jews there and the broken-down state of the wall and gates. He fasts and prays to Jehovah as "the God of the heavens, the God great and fear-inspiring, keeping the covenant and loving-kindness toward those loving him and keeping his commandments." (1:5) He confesses Israel's sins, and petitions Jehovah to remember His people because of His name, even as He promised Moses. (Deut. 30:1-10) On the king's inquiring the reason for his gloomy countenance, Nehemiah tells him, and requests permission to return and rebuild Jerusalem and its wall. His request is granted, and immediately he journeys to Jerusalem. Following a nighttime inspection of the city wall to acquaint himself with the job ahead, he reveals his plan to the Jews, emphasizing God's hand in the matter. At this they say: "Let us get up, and we must build." (Neh. 2:18) When the neighboring Samaritans and others hear that the work has started they begin to deride and mock.

7 **The wall rebuilt** (3:1–6:19). Work on the wall begins on the third day of the fifth month, with the priests, the princes and the people sharing together in the labor. The city gates and the walls between are rapidly repaired. Sanballat the Horonite taunts: "What are the feeble Jews doing? . . . Will they finish up in a day?" To this, Tobiah the Ammonite adds his ridicule: "Even what they are building, if a fox went up against it, he would certainly break down their wall of stones." (4:2, 3) As the wall reaches half its height, the combined adversaries grow angry and conspire to come up and fight against Jerusalem. But Nehemiah exhorts the Jews to keep in mind "Jehovah the great and fear-inspiring One," and to fight for their families and their homes. (4:14) The work is reorganized to meet the tense situation, some standing guard with lances while others work with their swords on their hips.

8 However, there are also problems among the Jews themselves. Some of them are exacting usury from their fellow worshipers of Jehovah, contrary to His law. (Ex. 22:25) Nehemiah corrects the situation, counseling against materialism, and the people willingly comply. Nehemiah himself, during all his twelve years of governorship, from 455 to 443 B.C.E., never demands the bread due the governor, because of the heavy service upon the people.

9 The enemies now try more subtle tactics to stop the building. They invite Nehemiah to come down for a conference, but he replies that he cannot take time off from the great work that he is doing. Sanballat now charges Nehemiah with rebellion and planning to make himself king in Judah, and secretly hires a Jew to frighten Nehemiah into wrongfully hiding in the temple, to his reproach. Nehemiah refuses to be intimidated, and calmly and obediently goes about his God-assigned task. The wall is completed "in fifty-two days."—Neh. 6:15.

10 **Instructing the people** (7:1–12:26). There are but few people and houses within the city, because most of the Israelites are living outside according to their tribal inheritances. God directs Nehemiah to take a census of all the people that had returned from Babylon. The entire congregation amounts to 42,360 persons, together with 7,337 slaves and 245 singers. An eight-day assembly is next called at the public square by the Water Gate. Ezra opens the program from a wooden podium. He blesses Jehovah and then reads from the book of the law of Moses from daybreak until midday. He is ably assisted by other Levites, who explain the law to the people and continue 'reading aloud from the book, from the law of the true God, it being expounded, and there being a putting of meaning into it; and they continue giving understanding in the reading.' (8:8) Nehemiah urges the people to feast and rejoice and to appreciate the force of the words: "The joy of Jehovah is your stronghold."—8:10.

a *The Watchtower*, 1959, pages 489-492.

6. (a) What report causes Nehemiah to pray to Jehovah, and what request does the king grant? (b) How do the people of Jerusalem respond to Nehemiah's plan?
7. How does the work proceed, and what situation calls for reorganization?
8. How does Nehemiah handle problems among the Jews themselves?
9. (a) How does he meet subtle tactics to stop the building? (b) In what time is the wall completed?
10. (a) Where do the people live, and what does a census reveal? (b) What assembly is now called, and what is the first day's program?

11 On the second day of the assembly the heads of the people have a special meeting with Ezra to gain insight into the Law. They learn of the festival of booths that should be celebrated this very seventh month and immediately arrange to build booths for this feast to Jehovah. There is "very great rejoicing" as they dwell in booths for the seven days, hearing day by day the reading of the Law. On the eighth day they hold a solemn assembly, "according to the rule."—Neh. 8:17, 18; Lev. 23:33-36.

12 On the twenty-fourth day of the same month the sons of Israel again assemble and proceed to separate themselves from all the foreigners. They listen to a special reading of the Law and then a heart-searching review of God's dealings with Israel, presented by a group of the Levites. This takes as its theme: "Rise, bless Jehovah your God from time indefinite to time indefinite. And let them bless your glorious name, which is exalted above all blessing and praise." (Neh. 9:5) They proceed to confess the sins of their forefathers and humbly to petition Jehovah's blessing. This is in the form of a resolution that is attested by the seal of the nation's representatives. The entire group agree to keep free from intermarriage with the peoples of the land, to observe the sabbaths and to provide for the temple service and workers. One person out of every ten is selected by lot to dwell permanently in Jerusalem, inside the wall.

13 **The wall dedicated** (12:27–13:3). The dedication of the newly built wall is a time of song and happiness. It is the occasion for another assembly. Nehemiah arranges for two large thanksgiving choirs and processions to make a tour of the wall in opposite directions, finally joining in sacrifices at the house of Jehovah. Arrangements are made for material contributions to support the priests and Levites at the temple. A further Bible reading reveals that Ammonites and Moabites should not be permitted to come into the congregation, and hence they begin to separate all the mixed company from Israel.

14 **Purging out uncleanness** (13:4-31). After a period of absence in Babylon Nehemiah returns to Jerusalem and finds that new vices have crept in among the Jews. How quickly things have changed! The high priest Eliashib has even made a dining hall in the courtyard of the temple for the use of Tobiah, one of the enemies of God. Nehemiah wastes no time. He throws out Tobiah's furniture and has all the dining halls cleansed. He finds, too, that the material contributions of the Levites have been discontinued, so they are going outside Jerusalem to make a living. Commercialism runs rampant in the city. The sabbath is not observed. "You are adding to the burning anger against Israel by profaning the sabbath," Nehemiah tells them. (13:18) He shuts up the city gates on the sabbath to keep out the traders, and orders them away from the city wall. But there is an evil worse than this, something they had solemnly agreed not to do again. They have brought foreign, pagan wives into the city. Already the offspring of these unions no longer speak the Jewish language. Nehemiah reminds them that Solomon sinned because of foreign wives. On account of this sin, Nehemiah chases out the grandson of Eliashib the high priest.[a] Then he sets in order the priesthood and the work of the Levites.

15 Nehemiah ends his book with the simple and humble request: "Do remember me, O my God, for good."—13:31.

WHY BENEFICIAL

16 Nehemiah's godly devotion should be an inspiration to all lovers of right worship. He left a favored position to become a humble overseer among Jehovah's people. He even refused the material contribution that was his right, and roundly condemned materialism as a snare. The zealous pursuit and upkeep of Jehovah's worship was what Nehemiah advocated for the entire nation! (5:14, 15; 13:10-13) Nehemiah was a splendid example to us in being entirely unselfish, discreet, a man of action, and fearless for righteousness in the face of danger. (4:14, 19, 20; 6:3, 15) He had the proper fear of God, and was interested in building up his fellow servants in the faith. (13:14; 8:9) He vigorously applied the law of Jehovah, and especially as it related to true worship and the rejection of foreign influences, such as marriages with pagans.—13:8, 23-29.

17 Throughout the book it is evident that Nehemiah had a good knowledge of Jehovah's

a Some Jewish historians claim that this grandson of Eliashib was named Manasseh, and that, with his father-in-law Sanballat, he built the temple on Mount Gerizim, which became the center of Samaritan worship and where he officiated as priest during his lifetime. This is the mountain referred to by Jesus at John 4:21. —*The Second Temple in Jerusalem,* 1908, W. Shaw Caldecott, pages 252-255.

11. What special meeting is held on the second day, and how does the assembly proceed with rejoicing?
12. (a) What assembly is held later in the same month, with what theme? (b) What resolution is adopted? (c) How is it arranged to populate Jerusalem?
13. What assembly program marks the dedication of the wall, and what arrangements result?
14. Describe the vices arising during Nehemiah's absence, and the steps he takes to eliminate them.
15. What humble request does Nehemiah make?
16. In what ways is Nehemiah a splendid example of uncompromising and godly devotion?
17. How is he an example, also, in knowledge and in application of God's law?

aw, and he made good use of this. He invoked God's blessing because of Jehovah's promise at Deuteronomy 30:1-4, having full faith that Jehovah would act loyally on his behalf. (Neh. :8, 9) He arranged numerous assemblies, principally to acquaint the Jews with the hings written aforetime. In reading the Law, Nehemiah, and Ezra too, were diligent to make God's Word plain to the people, and to follow hrough by applying it.—8:8, 13-16; 13:1-3.

18 Nehemiah's complete reliance on Jehovah nd his humble petitions should encourage in s a like attitude of prayerful dependence on God. Note how his prayers glorified God, howed recognition of the sins of his people nd petitioned that Jehovah's name be sanctified. (1:4-11; 4:14; 6:14; 13:14, 29, 31) That his zealous overseer was a power for strength among God's people was shown by the readiness with which they followed his wise direcion, and the joy that they found in doing God's will along with him. An inspiring example indeed! However, in the absence of a wise overseer, how quickly did materialism, corruption and outright apostasy creep in! Surely this should impress on all overseers among God's people today the need to be alive, alert, zealous for the interests of their Christian brothers, and understanding and firm in leading them in the ways of true worship.

19 Nehemiah showed strong reliance on God's Word. Not only was he a zealous teacher of the Scriptures, but he also used them in establishing the genealogical inheritances and the service of the priests and Levites among God's restored people. (Neh. 1:8; 11:1–12:26; Josh. 14:1–21:45) This must have been of great encouragement to the Jewish remnant. It strengthened their confidence in the grand promises previously given concerning the Seed and the greater restoration to come under his kingdom. It is hope in the Kingdom restoration that stimulates God's servants to fight courageously for the Kingdom interests and to be busy in building true worship throughout the earth.

8. What lessons should Nehemiah's prayerful leaderhip impress on all overseers?

19. (a) How did Nehemiah use God's Word to strengthen confidence in the Kingdom promises? (b) How does a similar hope stimulate God's servants today?

Bible Book Number Seventeen— Esther

Writer: **Mordecai**
Places Written: **Shushan, Elam**
Writing Completed: **c. 474 B.C.E.**
Time Covered: **c. 484-474 B.C.E.**

SIMPLY told, here is the story of Ahasuerus king of Persia, thought by some to be Xerxes I, whose disobedient wife Vashti is replaced by the Jewess Esther, cousin of the court official Mordecai. The Amalekite Haman plots the death of Mordecai and all the Jews, but is hanged on his own stake while Mordecai is advanced to be prime minister and the Jews are delivered.

2 Of course, there are those who want to say that the book of Esther is neither inspired nor beneficial, but simply a beautiful legend. They base their claim on the absence of God's name. While it is true that God is not directly mentioned, yet in Hebrew there appear to be four separate instances of an acrostic of the tetragrammaton, the initial letters of four successive words spelling out YHWH (Hebrew יהוה), or Jehovah. These initials are made especially prominent in at least three ancient Hebrew manuscripts, and are also marked in the Masorah by red letters. (See *New World Translation* footnotes, 1955 Edition, on Esther 1:20; 5:4, 13 and 7:7. Also at 7:5 there is apparently an acrostic on the divine pronouncement "I shall prove to be.")

3 Throughout the record it is strongly evident that Mordecai both accepted and obeyed the law of Jehovah. He refused to bow down to honor a man who was one of God's enemies, an Amalekite whom God had marked for extermination. (Esther 3:1, 5; Deut. 25:19; 1 Sam. 15:3) Mordecai's expression at Esther 4:14 indicates that he expected deliverance from Jehovah, and that he had faith in divine direction of the entire course of events. Esther's fasting, together with the other Jews, for three days before she went in to the king shows reliance upon God. (Esther 4:16) His maneu-

1. What story unfolds in the book of Esther?
2. (a) Why have some questioned the inspiration of the book? (b) Yet in what form does God's name appear to be used?

3. What events indicate faith in and prayer to God, as well as God's maneuvering of matters?

vering of events is also suggested in Esther's finding favor in the eyes of Hegai, the guardian of the women, and in the king's sleeplessness on the night that he called for the official records and found that Mordecai had not been honored for his past good deed. (2:8, 9; 6:1-3) There is undoubtedly a reference to prayer in the words, "the matters of the fasts and their cry for aid."—9:31.

4 Many facts establish the record as authentic and factual. It was accepted by the Jewish people, who called the book simply *the M^{e}gil·lah'*, meaning "Roll; Volume." It appears to have been included in the Hebrew canon by Ezra, who would certainly have rejected a fable. To this day the Jews keep the feast of Purim, or "Lots," in celebration of the great deliverance in Esther's time. The book presents Persian manners and customs in a lifelike way, and in harmony with the known facts of history and archaeological discoveries. It is interesting to note from history that Xerxes held a great feast and council of war in the third year of his reign before setting out against Greece, and that he returned in the seventh year. If Ahasuerus is Xerxes, this is in accord with the Bible record and explains why there was such a delay in choosing Vashti's successor as queen. (1:3; 2:16)[a] French archaeologists excavating the site of the castle Shushan have found the descriptions in the book of Esther exact to the smallest detail.

5 This exactness is also to be noted in the account itself, in its careful naming of court officials and attendants, giving even the names of Haman's ten sons. Mordecai's and Esther's lineage is traced back to Kish of the tribe of Benjamin. (2:5-7) References are made to the official records of the Persian government. (2:23; 6:1; 10:2) The language of the book is late Hebrew, with many Persian and Aramaic words and expressions added, which style matches that of Chronicles, Ezra and Nehemiah, thus harmonizing completely with the period in which it was written.

6 It is thought that the events of Esther are set in the days when the mighty Persian empire was at its peak, and cover about ten years of the reign of Ahasuerus (Xerxes I). The time period, extending down to 474 B.C.E., is indicated by the contemporary history of Thucydides, supported by the later chronology of Diodorus.[b] Mordecai, eyewitness and principal actor in the drama, was the writer of the book; the intimate and detailed account shows that the writer must have lived through these events in Shushan the palace.[c] Though he is not mentioned in any other Bible book, there is no question that Mordecai was an actual individual of history. Interestingly, an undated cuneiform text has been found, and is described by A. Ungnad of Germany as referring to Marduka (Mordecai) as a high official at the court of Susa (Shushan) during the reign of Xerxes I.[d] It was here at Shushan that Mordecai no doubt recorded the events of Esther immediately after they took place, that is, in 474 B.C.E.

CONTENTS OF ESTHER

7 **Queen Vashti deposed** (1:1-22). It is the third year of the reign of Ahasuerus. He holds a mighty banquet for the officials of his empire. It lasts 180 days. Next there is a grand feast for all the people in Shushan, lasting seven days. At the same time Vashti his queen holds a banquet for the women. The king boasts of his riches and glory, and, merry with wine, calls on Vashti to come and show her loveliness to the peoples and the princes. Queen Vashti keeps refusing. On the advice of court officials, who point out that this bad example can cause the king to lose face throughout the empire, Ahasuerus removes Vashti as queen and publishes documents calling on all wives to "give honor to their owners," and every husband to "be continually acting as prince in his own house."—1:20, 22.

8 **Esther becomes queen** (2:1-23). Later on the king appoints commissioners to seek out the most beautiful virgins in all the 127 provinces of the empire, and to bring them to Shushan, where they are to be prepared by beauty treatment for presentation to the king. Among the young women selected is Esther. Esther is a Jewish orphan girl, "pretty in form and beautiful in appearance," who has been reared by her cousin Mordecai, an official in Shushan the castle. (2:7) Esther's Jewish name Hadassah means "Myrtle" or "Joy," and the Persian form Esther means "Fresh Myrtle." Hegai, the

a *Ancient Cities*, 1886, William Burnet Wright, page 211.

b *Christology of the Old Testament*, Ernst Wm. Hengstenberg, translated from the German by Reuel Keith, D.D., from the First Edition, 1836-1839, Vol. 2, pages 389-391.

c M'Clintock and Strong's *Cyclopædia*, 1882, Vol. III, page 310.

d A. Ungnad, "Keilinschriftliche Beiträge zum Buch Esra und Ester," *Zeitschrift für die alttestamentliche Wissenschaft*, LVIII (1940-1941), 240-244.

4. How is the record established as authentic and factual?
5. What exactness gives the account a note of genuineness, and with what period does the language harmonize?
6. (a) What time period is indicated for the book? (b) What does the evidence suggest as to the writer, and the place and the time of writing?
7. What crisis develops at Ahasuerus' banquet, and what action does the king take as a result?
8. (a) What events lead up to Esther's becoming queen? (b) What plot does Mordecai uncover, and what record is made thereof?

guardian of the women, is pleased with Esther and gives her special treatment. No one knows that she is a Jewess, for Mordecai has instructed her to keep this a secret. The young women are brought in to the king in turn. He selects Esther as his new queen, and a banquet is held to celebrate her coronation. Shortly afterward Mordecai hears of a conspiracy to assassinate the king, and has Esther make it known to him "in Mordecai's name." (2:22) The plot is uncovered, the conspirators are hanged and a record is made in the royal annals.

9 **Haman's conspiracy** (3:1–5:14). About four years pass by. Haman, a descendant of the Amalekite king Agag whom Samuel slew, becomes prime minister. (1 Sam. 15:33) The king exalts him, and orders all his servants in the king's gate to bow before Haman. These include Mordecai. However, Mordecai refuses to so honor this descendant of the enemies of God. (Ex. 17:14, 16) Haman is filled with rage, and, finding out that Mordecai is a Jew, sees in this the grand opportunity to get rid of Mordecai and all the Jews once and for all. The lot ("Pur") is cast to determine a good day for annihilating the Jewish race. Using his favor with the king, Haman charges lawlessness against the Jews and asks that their destruction be ordered in writing. Haman offers a contribution of ten thousand silver talents (equivalent to $12,144,000) toward financing the slaughter.[a] The king consents, and written orders, sealed with the king's ring, are sent throughout the empire, setting Adar the thirteenth as the day for the genocide of the Jews.

10 On hearing the law, Mordecai and all the Jews go to mourning in sackcloth and ashes. There is "fasting and weeping and wailing." (Esther 4:3) On being informed by Mordecai of the Jews' plight, Esther at first hesitates to intercede. Death is the penalty for appearing uninvited before the king. However, Mordecai shows his faith in Jehovah's power by declaring that if Esther fails them she will die anyway and deliverance will "stand up for the Jews from another place." Moreover, may it not be that Esther has become queen "for a time like this"? (4:14) Seeing the issue, she agrees to take her life in her hands, and all the Jews in Shushan fast with her for three days.

11 Then Esther appears before the king, dressed in her royal best. She gains favor in his eyes and he holds out to her his golden scepter, sparing her life. She now invites the king and Haman to a banquet. During the feast the king urges her to make known her petition, assuring that it will be granted, "to the half of the kingship," whereupon she invites the two to a further banquet the following day. (5:6) Haman goes out joyful. But there in the king's gate is Mordecai! Again he refuses to do him honor or quake before him. Haman's joy turns to anger. His wife and friends suggest he build a stake fifty cubits high, and get an order from the king to hang Mordecai on it. Haman has the stake built immediately.

12 **The tables turned** (6:1–7:10). That night the king cannot sleep. He has the book of the records brought and read to him, and discovers that he has not rewarded Mordecai for saving his life. Later, the king asks who is in the courtyard. It is Haman come to ask the king's warrant for Mordecai's death. The king asks Haman how one who pleases the king should be honored. Thinking that the king has him in mind, Haman outlines a lavish program of honor. But the king commands him: "Do that way to Mordecai the Jew"! Haman has no alternative but to clothe Mordecai in regal splendor, seat him on the king's horse and lead him round the public square of the city calling out ahead of him. Humiliated, Haman hurries home mourning. His wife and friends have no comfort to offer. Haman is doomed!

13 It is now time for Haman to attend the banquet with the king and Esther. The queen declares that she and her people have been sold, to be destroyed. Who has dared to perpetrate this wickedness? Says Esther: "The man, the adversary and enemy, is this bad Haman." (7:6) The king rises up in a rage and walks out into the garden. Alone with the queen, Haman pleads for his life, and the king, returning, is further infuriated at seeing Haman on the queen's couch. He forthwith orders Haman's execution on the stake he has prepared for Mordecai—fifty cubits high!—Ps. 7:16.

14 **Mordecai promoted, the Jews delivered** (8:1–10:3). The king gives Esther all of Haman's possessions. Esther makes known to Ahasuerus her relationship to Mordecai, whom the king promotes to Haman's previous position, giving him the royal signet ring. Again, Esther risks her life in going in before the king to request the undoing of the written decree to destroy the Jews. However, "the laws of Persia and Media" cannot be annulled! (1:19) The king therefore gives Esther and Mordecai authority to write a new law, and seal it with the king's ring. This written order, sent

[a] Esther 3:9, *NW* footnote, 1955 Edition.

9. How does Mordecai anger Haman, and what royal decree does the latter obtain against the Jews?
10. How do Mordecai and Esther proceed with faith in Jehovah's power?
11. How does Esther use her favor with the king, but what does Haman plot against Mordecai?
12. What turn in events results in Ahasuerus' honoring Mordecai, to Haman's humiliation?
13. What does Esther reveal at the banquet, leading to what doom for Haman?
14. How does the king reward Esther and Mordecai, and with what written decree does he favor the Jews?

throughout the empire in the same way as the previous one, grants the Jews the right 'to congregate themselves and stand for their souls, to annihilate and kill and destroy all the force of the people and jurisdictional district that are showing hostility to them, little ones and women, and to plunder their spoil' on the same day that Haman's law goes into effect.—8:11.

15 When the appointed day, the thirteenth of Adar, comes, not a man can stand before the Jews. On Esther's petitioning the king, the fighting is continued on the fourteenth day in Shushan. All together, 75,810 of the enemies are killed throughout the empire, including 810 in Shushan the castle. Among these are Haman's ten sons, who are killed the first day and hanged on stakes the second day. No plunder is taken. On the fifteenth of Adar there is rest and the Jews give way to banqueting and rejoicing. Mordecai now gives written instructions for the Jews to observe this feast of "Pur, that is, the Lot," every year on the fourteenth and fifteenth of Adar, and this they do to the present day. (9:24) Mordecai is magnified in the kingdom and uses his position as second to King Ahasuerus "for the good of his people and speaking peace to all their offspring."—10:3.

WHY BENEFICIAL

16 While no other Bible writer makes any direct quotation from Esther, the book is completely in harmony with the rest of the inspired Scriptures. In fact, it provides some splendid illustrations of Bible principles that are stated later in the Christian Greek Scriptures, and which apply to Jehovah's worshipers in all ages. A study of the following passages will not only show this to be so, but will be upbuilding to Christian faith: Esther 4:5—Philippians 2:4; Esther 9:22—Galatians 2:10. The charge made against the Jews, that they did not obey the king's laws, is similar to the charge raised against the early Christians. (Esther 3:8, 9; Acts 16:21; 25:7) True servants of Jehovah meet such charges fearlessly and with prayerful reliance on divine power to deliver, after the splendid pattern of Mordecai, Esther and their fellow Jews.—Esther 4:16; 5:1, 2; 7:3-6; 8:3-6; 9:1, 2.

17 As Christians we should not think that our situation is different from that of Mordecai and Esther. We, too, live under the "superior authorities" in an alien world, and they continue to demand more and more of our time, effort and allegiance. It is our desire to be law-abiding citizens in whatever country we reside, but at the same time we want to draw the line correctly between 'paying back Caesar's things to Caesar, and God's things to God.' (Rom. 13:1; Luke 20:25) Prime Minister Mordecai and Queen Esther set good examples of devotion and obedience in their secular duties. (Esther 2:21-23; 6:2, 3, 10; 8:1, 2; 10:2) However, Mordecai fearlessly drew the line at obeying the royal command to bow low before the despicable Amalekite, Haman. Moreover, he saw that appeal was made to seek legal redress when Haman conspired to destroy the Jews.—3:1-4; 5:9; 4:6-8.

18 All the evidence points to Esther as being part of the Holy Bible, "inspired of God and beneficial." Even without mentioning God or his name, it provides us sterling examples of faith. Mordecai and Esther were no mere figments of some storyteller's imagination, but real servants of Jehovah God, persons who placed implicit confidence in Jehovah's power to save. Though they lived under "superior authorities" in a foreign land, they used every legal means to defend the interests of God's people and their worship. We today can follow their examples in "the defending and legally establishing of the good news" of God's kingdom of deliverance.—Phil. 1:7.

---

15. (a) What is the outcome of the fighting, and what feast does Mordecai institute? (b) To what position is Mordecai exalted, and to what end does he use this authority?
16. What divine principles and worthy patterns do Christians find in the book of Esther?
17. How did Mordecai and Esther exemplify the proper course in subjecting themselves to God and the "superior authorities"?
18. (a) What proves the book of Esther to be "inspired of God and beneficial"? (b) How does it encourage the defense of God's Kingdom interests?

Bible Book Number Eighteen— Job

Writer: **Moses**
Place Written: **Wilderness**
Writing Completed: **c. 1473 B.C.E.**
Time Covered: **Between 1657-1473 B.C.E.**

ONE of the oldest books of the inspired Scriptures! A book that is held in the highest esteem, and that is often quoted, yet one that is least understood by mankind! Why was this book written, and what value does it have for us in this twentieth century? The answer is indicated in the meaning of Job's name: "Object of Hostility." Yes, this book takes up the important questions: Why do the innocent suffer? and, Why does God permit wickedness in the earth? We have the record of Job's suffering and his great endurance for our consideration in answering these questions. It has all been written down, just as Job requested.—19:23, 24.

2 Job has become synonymous with patience and endurance. But was there such a person as Job? There can be only one answer, in spite of all the efforts of the Devil to remove this sterling example of integrity from the pages of history. Job was an actual person! Jehovah names him along with his witnesses Noah and Daniel, whose existence is unquestioned. (Ezek. 14:14, 20) The ancient Hebrew nation regarded Job as a real person. The Christian writer James points to Job's example of endurance. (Jas. 5:11) Only a true-life example, not a fictitious one, would carry weight, convincing worshipers of God that integrity can be maintained under all circumstances. Moreover, the intensity and feeling of the speeches recorded in Job testify to the reality of the situation.

3 That the book of Job is authentic and inspired is also proved in that the ancient Hebrews always included it in their Bible canon, a fact remarkable in that Job himself was not of the commonwealth of Israel. In addition to the references by Ezekiel and James, the book is also quoted by the apostle Paul. (Job 5:13; 1 Cor. 3:19) Powerful proof of the book's inspiration is given in its amazing harmony with the proved facts of the sciences. How could it be known that Jehovah is "hanging the earth upon nothing," when all the ancients had the most fantastic notions as to how the earth was supported? (Job 26:7) Some thought it was flat and stood on pillars, others believed that a god named Atlas held it up, and still others that it was balanced on the back of an elephant that stood on a turtle that swam in a universal cosmic sea. Why does not Job line up with such nonsense? Obviously because Jehovah the Creator supplied the truth by inspiration. The many other descriptions of the earth and its wonders and of the wild animals and birds in their natural habitats are so accurate that only Jehovah God could be the Author and Inspirer of the account.[a]

4 Job lived in Uz, located, according to some geographers, in the Syrian desert north of the land occupied by the Edomites and east of the land promised to Abraham's offspring. The Sabeans were on the south, the Chaldeans on the east. (Job 1:1, 3, 15, 17) The time of Job's trial was long after Abraham's day. It was at a time when there was "no one like him in the earth, a man blameless and upright." (1:8) This appears to be the period between the death of Joseph (1657 B.C.E.), a man of outstanding faith, and the time of Moses, who was born in 1593 B.C.E. Job excelled in pure worship at this period of Israel's contamination by the demon worship of Egypt. Furthermore, the practices mentioned in the first chapter of Job, and God's acceptance of Job as a true worshiper, point to patriarchal times rather than to the later period, from 1513 B.C.E. on, when God dealt exclusively with Israel under the Law. (Amos 3:2; Eph. 2:12) Thus, allowing for Job's long life, it appears that the book covers a period between 1657 and 1473, the year of Moses' death, being completed by Moses sometime after Job's death and while the Israelites were in the wilderness.—Job 1:8; 42:16, 17.

5 Why do we say Moses was the writer? This is according to the oldest tradition, among both Jewish and early Christian scholars. The vigorous authentic style of Hebrew poetry used in the book of Job makes it evident that it was an original composition in Hebrew, the language of Moses. It could not have been a translation from another language such as Arabic.

1. What does Job's name mean, and what questions does this book answer?
2. What proves Job to have been a real person?
3. What evidences testify to the inspiration of the account?

a *The Watchtower,* 1955, pages 133, 134; 1962, pages 165-168, 293-296, 421-424, 485-488; 1963, pages 89-94.

4. Where and when was the drama enacted, and when was the writing of the book completed?
5. What indicates Moses' writership?

Also, the portions in prose bear stronger resemblance to the Pentateuch than to any other writings in the Bible. The writer must have been an Israelite, as Moses was, because the Jews "were entrusted with the sacred pronouncements of God." (Rom. 3:1, 2) After he had reached maturity, Moses spent forty years in Midian, not far from Uz, where he could obtain the detailed information recorded in Job. Later, when he passed near Job's homeland, during Israel's forty-year wilderness journey, Moses could learn of and record the concluding details in the book.

6 *The Encyclopedia Americana* refers to Job as "the supreme masterpiece of ancient Hebrew literature." However, the book is much more than a literary masterpiece. Job is outstanding among the books of the Bible in exalting Jehovah's power, justice, wisdom and love. It reveals most clearly the primary issue before the universe. It illuminates much that is said in other books of the Bible, especially Genesis, Exodus, Ecclesiastes, Luke, Romans and Revelation. (Compare Job 1:6-12; 2:1-7 with Genesis 3:15; Exodus 9:16; Luke 22:31, 32; Romans 9:16-19 and Revelation 12:9; also Job 1:21; 24:15; 21:23-26; 28:28 respectively with Ecclesiastes 5:15; 8:11; 9:2, 3; 12:13.) It provides the answers to many of life's questions. It is certainly an integral part of the inspired Word of God, to which it contributes much in the way of beneficial understanding.

CONTENTS OF JOB

7 **Prologue to the book of Job** (1:1-5). This introduces us to Job, a man "blameless and upright, and fearing God and turning aside from bad." Job is happy, having seven sons and three daughters. He is a materially rich landholder with numerous flocks and herds. He has many servants, and is "the greatest of all the Orientals." (1:1, 3) However, he is not materialistic, for he does not depend on his material possessions. He is also rich spiritually, rich in good works, willing at all times to help someone afflicted or in distress, or to give a garment to anyone needing it. (29:12-16; 31:19, 20) All respect him. Job worships the true God, Jehovah. He refuses to bow down to the sun, moon and stars as did the pagan nations, but is faithful to Jehovah, keeping integrity to his God and enjoying a close relationship to him. (29:7, 21-25; 31:26, 27; 29:4) Job serves as priest for his family, offering up burnt sacrifices regularly, in case they have sinned.

8 **Satan challenges God** (1:6–2:13). Marvelously the curtain of invisibility is drawn back, so that we can get a view of heavenly things. Jehovah is seen presiding over an assembly of the sons of God. Satan also appears among them. Jehovah calls attention to his faithful servant Job, but Satan challenges Job's integrity, charging that Job serves God because of material benefits received. If God will allow Satan to take these away, Job will turn away from his integrity. Jehovah accepts the challenge, with the restriction that Satan must not touch Job himself.

9 Many calamities start to befall the unsuspecting Job. Raids by Sabeans and Chaldeans remove his great riches. A storm kills his sons and daughters. This severe test fails to make Job curse God or turn away from him. Rather, he says, "Let the name of Jehovah continue to be blessed." (1:21) Satan, defeated and proved a liar on this count, appears again before Jehovah and charges: "Skin in behalf of skin, and everything that a man has he will give in behalf of his soul." (2:4) Satan claims that, if permitted to touch Job's body, he could make Job curse God to his face. With permission to do everything short of taking Job's life, Satan strikes him with a dreadful disease. His flesh becomes "clothed with maggots and lumps of dust," and his body and breath foul-smelling to his wife and relatives. (7:5; 19:13-20) Indicating that Job has not broken his integrity, his wife urges him: "Are you yet holding fast your integrity? Curse God and die!" Job rebukes her and does not "sin with his lips." —2:9, 10.

10 Satan now raises up three companions, who come to comfort Job. They are Eliphaz, Bildad and Zophar. At a distance they do not recognize Job, but then they proceed to raise their voices and weep and toss dust on their heads. Next, they sit before him on the earth without speaking a word. After seven days and nights of this silent "comfort," Job finally breaks silence in opening a lengthy debate with his would-be sympathizers.

11 **The debate: round one** (3:1–14:22). From this point the drama unfolds in sublime Hebrew poetry. Job calls down evil on the day of his birth and wonders why God has permitted him to go on living.

12 In response, Eliphaz accuses Job of lacking integrity. The upright have never perished, he avers. He recalls a night vision in which a voice told him that God has no faith in his servants, especially those of mere clay, the dust of the earth. He indicates that Job's suffering is a discipline from Almighty God.

6. In what respects is the book of Job much more than a literary masterpiece?
7. In what situation do we find Job as the book opens?
8. (a) How does Satan come to challenge Job's integrity? (b) How does Jehovah accept the challenge?
9. (a) What severe tests fall on Job? (b) What proves that he keeps integrity?
10. What silent "comfort" does Satan next provide?
11-13. How does Job open the debate, what accusation does Eliphaz make, and what is Job's spirited reply?

13 Job spiritedly replies to Eliphaz. He cries ut as any creature would because of persecuion and distress. Death would be a relief. He pbraids his companions for scheming against im and protests: "Instruct me, and I, for my art, shall be silent; and what mistake I have ommitted make me understand." (6:24) Job ontends for his own righteousness before God, the Observer of mankind."—7:20.

14 Bildad now voices his argument, implying hat Job's sons have sinned and that Job himelf is not upright, else he would be heard by God. He instructs Job to look to the former enerations and to the things searched out by heir forefathers as a guide.

15 Job replies, admitting God is not unjust. Neither does God have to account to man, for he is "doing great things unsearchable, and wonderful things without number." (9:10) Job cannot win against Jehovah as his opponentat-law. He can only implore God's favor. And yet, is there any benefit in seeking to do what s right? "One blameless, also a wicked one, he s bringing to their end." (9:22) There is no righteous judgment in the earth. Job fears he will lose his case even with God. He needs a mediator. He asks why he is being tried, and mplores God to remember that he is made 'out of clay." (10:9) He appreciates God's past kindnesses, but says God will only be more greatly vexed if he argues, even though he is n the right. Could he but expire!

16 Zophar now enters the debate. He says in effect: Are we children, to listen to empty talk? You say you are really clean, but if only God would speak he would reveal your guilt. He asks Job: "Can you find out the deep things of God?" (11:7) He advises Job to put away hurtful practices, for blessings will come to those who do this, whereas "the very eyes of the wicked will fail."—11:20.

17 Job cries out with strong sarcasm: "For a fact you men are the people, and with you wisdom will die out!" (12:2) He may be a laughingstock, but he is not inferior. If his companions would look to the creations of God, even these would teach them something. Strength and practical wisdom belong to God, who controls all things, even to "making the nations grow great, that he may destroy them." (12:23) Job finds delight in arguing his case with God, but as for his three "comforters"—"you men are smearers of falsehood; all of you are physicians of no value." (13:4) It would be wisdom on their part to keep silent! He expresses confidence in the justness of his case and calls on God to hear him. He turns to the thought that "man, born of woman, is short-lived and glutted with agitation." (14:1) He soon passes, as a blossom or a shadow. You cannot produce someone clean out of someone unclean. In praying that God would keep him secret in Sheol until His anger turns back, Job asks: "If an able-bodied man dies can he live again?" In answer he expresses strong hope: "I shall wait, until my relief comes."—14:13, 14.

14, 15. What is Bildad's argument, and why does Job fear he will lose his case with God?
16, 17. (a) What smug advice does Zophar give? (b) How does Job evaluate his "comforters," and what strong confidence does he express?

18 **The debate: round two** (15:1–21:34). In opening the second debate, Eliphaz ridicules Job's knowledge, saying he has 'filled his belly with the east wind.' (15:2) Again he disparages Job's claim of integrity, holding that neither mortal man nor the holy ones in the heavens can hold faith in Jehovah's eyes. He indirectly accuses Job of trying to show himself superior to God, and practicing apostasy, bribery and deceit.

19 Job retorts that his companions are 'troublesome comforters with windy words.' (16:2, 3) If they were in his place, he would not revile them. He greatly desires to be justified, and looks to Jehovah, who has his record and will decide his case. Job finds no wisdom in his companions. They take away all hope. Their "comfort" is like saying night is day. The only hope is to 'go down to Sheol.'—17:15, 16.

20 The argument is becoming heated. Bildad now is bitter, for he feels Job has compared his friends to beasts with no understanding. He asks Job, 'Will the earth be abandoned for your sake?' (18:4) He warns Job that he will fall into a terrible snare, as an example to others. He will have no progeny to live after him.

21 Job answers: "How long will you men keep irritating my soul and keep crushing me with words?" (19:2) He has lost family and friends, his wife and household have turned away from him, and he himself has only escaped 'with the skin of his teeth.' (19:20) He trusts in the appearance of a redeemer to settle the issue in his behalf, so that he will at last "behold God." —19:25, 26.

22 Zophar, like Bildad, feels hurt at having to listen to Job's "insulting exhortation." (20:3) He repeats that Job's sins have caught up with him. The wicked always receive punishment from God, and they have no rest, says Zophar, even while enjoying prosperity.

23 Job replies with a withering argument: If God always punishes the wicked thus, why is

18, 19. (a) With what ridicule does Eliphaz open the second round of debate? (b) How does Job regard his companions' "comfort," and for what does he look to Jehovah?
20, 21. What bitterness does Bildad express, what does Job protest, and where does he show his trust to be?
22, 23. (a) Why does Zophar feel hurt, and what does he say about Job's alleged sins? (b) With what withering argument does Job reply?

it that the wicked keep living, grow old, become superior in wealth? They spend their days in good times. How often does disaster come upon them? He shows that rich and poor die alike. In fact, a wicked man often dies "carefree and at ease," while a righteous man may die "with a bitter soul."—21:23, 25.

24 **The debate: round three** (22:1–25:6). Eliphaz returns savagely to the attack, ridiculing Job's claim of blamelessness before the Almighty. He brings lying slander against Job, claiming that he is bad, has exploited the poor, has held back bread from the hungry and has mistreated widows and fatherless boys. Job's private life is not as pure as he claims, Eliphaz says, and this explains Job's bad condition. But "if you return to the Almighty," intones Eliphaz, "he will hear you."—22:23, 27.

25 Job in reply refutes Eliphaz' outrageous charge, saying that he desires a hearing before God, who is aware of his righteous course. There are those who oppress the fatherless, the widow and the poor and who commit murder, theft and adultery. They may seem to prosper for a while, but they will get their reward. They will be brought to nothing. "So really now, who will make me out a liar?" Job challenges.—24:25.

26 Bildad makes a brief retort to this, pressing his argument that no man can be clean before God. Zophar fails to take part in this third round. He has nothing to say.

27 **Job's concluding argument** (26:1–31:40). In a final dissertation, Job completely silences his companions. (32:12, 15, 16) With great sarcasm he says: "O how much help you have been to one without power! . . . How much you have advised one that is without wisdom!" (26:2, 3) Nothing, however, not even Sheol, can cover up anything from God's sight. He describes God's wisdom in outer space, the earth, the clouds, the sea and the wind, all of which man has observed. These are but the fringes of the Almighty's ways. They are hardly a whisper of the Almighty's greatness.

28 Triumphant in argument, he declares: "Until I expire I shall not take away my integrity from myself!" (27:5) Contrary to their charges, God will reward integrity by seeing that the things stored up by the wicked in their prosperity will be inherited by the righteous.

29 Man knows where the treasures of earth (silver, gold, copper) come from, "but wisdom itself—from where does it come?" (28:20) He has sought for it among the living; he has looked into the sea; it cannot be bought with gold or silver. God is the one who understands wisdom. He sees to the ends of the earth and the heavens, apportions out the wind and the waters, and controls the rain and the storm clouds. Job concludes: "Look! The fear of Jehovah—that is wisdom, and to turn away from bad is understanding."—28:28.

30 The afflicted Job next presents the history of his life. He desires to be restored to his former intimate status with God, when he was respected even by the leaders of the town. He was a rescuer of the afflicted and eyes to the blind ones. His counsel was good, and people waited upon his words. But now, instead of having an honorable standing, he is laughed at even by those younger in days, whose fathers were not even fit to be with the dogs of his flock. They spit on him and oppose him. Now in his greatest affliction they give him no rest.

31 Job describes himself as a dedicated man and asks to be judged by Jehovah. "He will weigh me in accurate scales and God will get to know my integrity." (31:6) Job defends his past actions. He has not been an adulterer, nor a schemer against others. He has not neglected to help the needy. He has not trusted in material wealth, even though he was rich. He has not worshiped the sun, moon and stars, nor any inanimate creation, for "that too would be an error for attention by the justices, for I should have denied the true God above." (31:28) Job invites his opponent-at-law to file charges against the true record of his life.

32 **Elihu speaks** (32:1–37:24). Meanwhile Elihu, a descendant of Buz, the son of Nahor, and hence a distant cousin of Abraham, has been listening to the debate. He has waited because of feeling that those of greater age should have greater knowledge. It is not age, however, but God's spirit that gives understanding. Elihu's anger blazes at Job's "declaring his own soul righteous rather than God," but gets even hotter at his three companions for their deplorable lack of wisdom in pronouncing God wicked. Elihu has "become full of words," and God's spirit compels him to give vent to these, but without partiality or 'bestowing titles on earthling man.'—Job 32:2, 3, 18-22; Gen. 22:20, 21.

33 Elihu speaks in sincerity, acknowledging

24, 25. (a) What lying slander does Eliphaz self-righteously bring against Job? (b) What refutation and challenge does Job make in answer?
26. What more do Bildad and Zophar have to say?
27. How does Job now extol the Almighty's greatness?
28. What forthright statement does Job make on integrity?
29. How does Job describe wisdom?
30. What restoration does Job desire, but what is his present status?
31. In whose judgment does Job express confidence, and what does he say as to the true record of his life?
32. (a) Who is it that now speaks? (b) Why does his anger blaze against Job and his companions, and what compels him to speak?
33. Wherein has Job erred, yet what favor will God show him?

God as his Creator. He points out that Job has been more concerned with his own vindication than with God's. It was not necessary for God to answer all of Job's words, as if he had to justify his actions, and yet Job had contended against God. However, as his soul draws close to death, God favors him with a messenger, saying: "Let him off from going down into the pit! I have found a ransom! Let his flesh become fresher than in youth; let him return to the days of his youthful vigor." (Job 33:24, 25) The righteous will be restored!

34 Elihu calls on the wise ones to listen. He reproves Job for saying there is no profit in being an integrity-keeper: "Far be it from the true God to act wickedly, and the Almighty to act unjustly! For according to the way earthling man acts he will reward him." (34:10, 11) He can remove the breath of life, and all flesh will expire. God judges without partiality. Job has been putting his own righteousness too much to the fore. He has been rash, not deliberately so, but "without knowledge"; and God has been long-suffering with him. More needs to be said for *God's* vindication. God will not take his eyes away from the righteous, but will reprove them. "He will not preserve anyone wicked alive, but the judgment of the afflicted ones he will give." (36:6) Since God is the supreme Instructor, Job should magnify His activity.

35 In the awe-inspiring atmosphere of a gathering storm, Elihu speaks of the great things done by God and of His control of natural forces. To Job he says: "Stand still and show yourself attentive to the wonderful works of God." (37:14) Consider the golden splendor and fear-inspiring dignity of God, far beyond human finding out. "He is exalted in power, and justice and abundance of righteousness he will not belittle." Yes, Jehovah will regard those who fear him, not those "wise in their own heart."—37:23, 24.

36 **Jehovah answers Job** (38:1–42:6). Job had asked God to speak to him. Now Jehovah majestically answers out of the windstorm. He sets before Job a series of questions that are in themselves an object lesson in man's littleness and God's greatness. "Where did you happen to be when I founded the earth? . . . who laid its cornerstone, when the morning stars joyfully cried out together, and all the sons of God began shouting in applause?" (38:4, 6, 7) That was long before Job's time! One after another, questions are raised that Job cannot answer, as Jehovah points to earth's sea, its garment of cloud, the dawn, the gates of death, and light and darkness. "Have you come to know because at that time you were being born, and because in number your days are many?" (38:21) And what about the storehouses of snow and of hail, the storm and the rain and the dewdrops, the ice and the hoarfrost, the mighty heavenly constellations, the lightnings and cloud layers, and the beasts and the birds?

37 Job humbly admits: "Look! I have become of little account. What shall I reply to you? My hand I have put over my mouth." (40:4) Jehovah commands Job to face the issue. He poses a further series of challenging questions that exalt his dignity, superiority and strength, as displayed in his natural creations. Even Behemoth and Leviathan are much more powerful than Job! Completely humbled, Job acknowledges his wrong viewpoint, and admits he spoke without knowledge. Seeing God now, not by hearsay but with understanding, he makes a retraction and repents "in dust and ashes."—42:6.

38 **Jehovah's judgment and blessing** (42:7-17). Jehovah next charges Eliphaz and his two companions with not speaking truthful things about Him. They must provide sacrifices, and have Job pray for them. After this, Jehovah turns back the captive condition of Job, blessing him in double amount. His brothers, sisters and former friends return to him with gifts, and he is blessed with twice as many sheep, camels, cattle and she-asses as previously. He again has ten children, his three daughters being the prettiest women in all the land. His life is miraculously extended by 140 years, so that he comes to see four generations of his offspring, dying "old and satisfied with days."—42:17.

WHY BENEFICIAL

39 The book of Job exalts Jehovah and testifies to his unfathomable wisdom and power. (12:12, 13; 37:23) In this one book God is called the "Almighty" thirty-one times, which is more often than in all the rest of the Scriptures. The account extols His eternity and exalted position (10:5; 36:4, 22, 26; 40:2; 42:2); his justice, loving-kindness and mercy (36:5-7; 10:12; 42:12). It stresses Jehovah's vindication above man's salvation. (33:12; 34:10, 12; 35:2; 36:24; 40:8) Jehovah, the God of Israel, is shown to be also the God of Job.

---

34. (a) What further reproofs does Elihu give? (b) Rather than Job's righteousness being magnified, what needs to be said?
35. (a) To what should Job give attention? (b) To whom will Jehovah show favor?
36. What object lesson does Jehovah himself now give Job, and by what series of questions?
37. What further series of questions humbles Job, and what is he compelled to admit and do?
38. (a) How does Jehovah dispose of Eliphaz and his companions? (b) What favor and blessing does he bestow on Job?
39. In what various ways does the book exalt and extol Jehovah?

40 The record in Job magnifies and explains the creative work of God. (38:4–39:30; 40:15, 19; 41:1; 35:10) It recognizes the Genesis statement that man is made from the dust, and that he returns to it. (Job 10:8, 9; Gen. 2:7; 3:19) It uses the terms "redeemer," "ransom" and "live again," thus giving a foreglimpse of teachings prominent in the Christian Greek Scriptures. (Job 19:25; 33:24; 14:13, 14) Many of its expressions have been drawn on or paralleled by the prophets and Christian writers. Compare, for example, Job 7:17—Psalm 8:4; Job 9:24—1 John 5:19; Job 10:8—Psalm 119:73; Job 12:25—Deuteronomy 28:29; Job 24:23—Proverbs 15:3; Job 26:8—Proverbs 30:4; Job 28:12, 13, 15-19—Proverbs 3:13-15; Job 39:30—Matthew 24:28.

41 Jehovah's righteous standards of living are set forth in many passages. The book strongly condemns materialism (Job 31:24, 25), idolatry (31:26-28), adultery (31:9-12), gloating (31:29), injustice and partiality (31:13; 32:21), selfishness (31:16-21) and dishonesty and lying (31:5), showing that a person who practices these things cannot gain God's favor and eternal life. Elihu gives a fine example of deep respect and modesty, together with boldness, courage and exaltation of God. (32:2, 6, 7, 9, 10, 18-20; 33:6, 33) Job's own exercise of headship, consideration of his family and hospitality provide also a fine lesson. (1:5; 2:9, 10; 31:32) However, Job is remembered most for his integrity-keeping and patient endurance, setting an example that has proved to be a faith-strengthening bulwark for God's servants throughout the ages and especially in these faith-trying times. "You have heard of the endurance of Job and have seen the outcome Jehovah gave, that Jehovah is very tender in affection and merciful."—Jas. 5:11.

42 Though Job was not one of the seed of Abraham, to whom the Kingdom promises were given, yet the record concerning his integrity does much to clarify understanding of Jehovah's Kingdom purposes. The book is an essential part of the divine record, for it reveals the fundamental issue between God and Satan, which involves man's integrity to Jehovah as his Sovereign. (Job 36:24) It shows that the angels, who were created before the earth and man, are also spectators and very much interested in this earth and the outcome of the controversy. (1:6-12; 2:1-5; 38:6, 7) It indicates that the controversy existed before Job's day and that Satan is an actual spirit person; if Moses wrote the book of Job, the expression *has-Sa·tan'* appears here for the first time in the Hebrew text of the Bible, giving further identity to the "original serpent." (Job 1:6; Rev. 12:9) The book also proves that God is not the cause of mankind's suffering, sickness and death, and explains why the righteous are persecuted, while the wicked and wickedness are permitted to continue. It shows that Jehovah is interested in pushing the issue to its final settlement.

43 Now is the time when all who want to live under God's Kingdom rule must answer Satan "the accuser" in integrity. (Rev. 12:10, 11) Even in the midst of 'puzzling trials,' integrity-keepers must continue praying for God's name to be sanctified, and for his kingdom to come and stamp out Satan and all his derisive seed. That will be God's "day of fight and war," to be followed by the relief and blessings in which Job hoped to share.—1 Pet. 4:12; Matt. 6:9, 10; Job 38:23; 14:13-15.

---

40. (a) How does the record magnify and explain God's creative works? (b) How does it give a foreglimpse of and harmonize with the teachings of the Christian Greek Scriptures?

41. (a) What theocratic standards are emphasized in Job? (b) In what is God's servant Job preeminently a fine example to us today?

42. What fundamental Kingdom issue is clarified in the book, and what interesting aspects of this issue are explained?

43. In harmony with the divine revelations in the book of Job, what course must now be followed by all who seek God's Kingdom blessings?

Bible Book Number Nineteen—Psalms

Writers:	**David and others**
Place Written:	**Undetermined**
Writing Completed:	**c. 460 B.C.E.**
Time Covered:	**Undetermined**

PSALMS was the inspired songbook of true worshipers of Jehovah in ancient times, a collection of one hundred and fifty sacred songs, set to music and arranged for the public worship of Jehovah God in his temple at Jerusalem. These are songs of praise to Jehovah, and, not only that, they also contain prayers of supplication for mercy and help, as well as expressions of trust and confidence. They abound with thanksgivings and exultations, and with exclamations of great, yes, superlative joy. Some are recapitulations of history, contemplating Jehovah's loving-kindness and his great deeds. They are packed full with prophecies, many of which have had remarkable fulfillments. They contain much instruction that is beneficial and upbuilding, all of it clothed in lofty language and imagery that stirs the reader to the very depths. The Psalms are a sumptuous spiritual meal, beautifully prepared and spread invitingly before us.

2 What is the significance of the book's title, and who wrote the Psalms? In the Hebrew Bible the book is called *Se′pher T*^{e}*hil·lim′*, meaning "Book of Praises," or simply *T*^{e}*hil·lim′*, that is, "Praises." This is the plural form of *T*^{e}*hil·lah′*, meaning "A Praise" or "Song of Praise," found in the superscription of Psalm 145. The name "Praises" is most appropriate, as the book highlights praise to Jehovah. Our title "Psalms" comes from the Greek *Septuagint* translation *Psal·moi′*, denoting songs sung with a musical accompaniment. The word is also found at a number of places in the Greek Scriptures, such as at Luke 20:42 and Acts 1:20. A psalm is a sacred song or poem used in the praise and worship of God.

3 Many of the psalms have headings, or superscriptions, and these often name the writer. Seventy-three headings bear the name of David, "the pleasant one of the melodies of Israel." (2 Sam. 23:1) Twelve psalms are ascribed to Asaph, evidently including his sons also, as some of these speak of events later than Asaph's day. (Psalms 79 and 80; 1 Chron. 16: 4, 5, 7; Ezra 2:41) Eleven psalms are attributed to the sons of Korah. (1 Chron. 6:31-38) Psalm 127 is Solomon's, and Psalm 72 is regarding him. In addition to mentioning "the sons of Korah," Psalm 88 also accredits Heman in its superscription, and Psalm 89 names Ethan as the writer. Psalm 90 is attributed to Moses, and Psalm 91 is probably Moses' as well. Two-thirds of the psalms are thus ascribed to various writers.

4 The Psalms comprise the Bible's largest single book. As evidenced by Psalms 90 and 137, it was long in the writing, at least from the time Moses wrote (1513-1473 B.C.E.) until after the restoration from Babylon and probably Ezra's day (537—c. 460 B.C.E.). Thus the writing is seen to span approximately one thousand years. The time covered by the contents is much greater, though, starting from the time of the creation and epitomizing the history of Jehovah's dealings with his servants down to the time of the composition of the last of the psalms.

5 The book of Psalms is one that reflects organization. David himself refers to "the processions of my God, my King, into the holy place. The singers were in front, the players on stringed instruments after them; in between were the maidens beating tambourines. In congregated throngs bless God, Jehovah." (Ps. 68: 24-26) This explains the oft-repeated expression "To the director" in the superscriptions, as well as the many poetic and musical terms. Some superscriptions explain the use or purpose of the psalm, or what kind of chorus is to sing it. (Psalms 6, 16, 30, 32, 39, 53, 88, 120 and *NW* footnotes, 1957 edition) For at least thirteen of David's psalms, the events spurring their composition are briefly related, such as at Psalms 7, 18 and 51. Thirty-four of the psalms are entirely without superscriptions. The little word *Selah*, occurring seventy-one times in the main text, thought by some to mean "Lift Up," indicates probably a pause in the singing, and hence need not be pronounced in reading the Psalms.—See Psalm 46.

---

1. What is the book of Psalms, and what does it contain?
2. (a) What titles have been applied to the book, and with what meanings? (b) What is a psalm?
3. What do the superscriptions tell as to the writers?
4. What time period is covered by the writing?
5. (a) How does the book of Psalms reflect organization? (b) What further information is supplied by the superscriptions? (c) Why is it not necessary to pronounce the word *Selah* in reading the Psalms?

6 From ancient times, the book of Psalms has been divided into five separate books or volumes, as follows: Psalms 1-41, Psalms 42-72, Psalms 73-89, Psalms 90-106, Psalms 107-150. The prevailing opinion is that these five books are different collections of psalms made at various times. It appears that the first collection was made by David. The families of Asaph and the sons of Korah possibly had their own collections at first, these later being merged with other Davidic psalms. Two other kings of Judah, the reformers Hezekiah and Josiah, are believed to have had a hand in later collections when they revived the service of the Levites at the temple. (2 Chron. 29:25-30; 31:2; 35:4, 5, 15) It appears that Ezra, the priest and "skilled copyist in the law of Moses," was the one used by Jehovah to collect the book of Psalms in its present form and include it in the Hebrew canon.—Ezra 7:6, 7.

7 The progressive growth of the collection also explains why some of the psalms are repeated in the different sections, such as Psalms 14 and 53; 40:13-17 and 70; 57:7-11 and 108:1-5. Each of the five sections closes with a blessing pronounced on Jehovah, or "doxology," the first four of these including responses by the people, and the last one being the entire Psalm 150.

8 A very special style of composition is employed in nine psalms, called "acrostic" because of its alphabetical structure. (Psalms 9, 10, 25, 34, 37, 111, 112, 119 and 145) In this structure the first verse or verses of the first stanza begin with the first letter of the Hebrew alphabet, *aleph* (א), the next verse(s) with the second letter, *beth* (ב), and so on through the entire Hebrew alphabet of twenty-two characters. This may have been designed to aid the memory—just think of the temple singers having to remember songs as long as Psalm 119! Interestingly, an acrostic of Jehovah's name is found at Psalm 96:11, the first half of this verse in Hebrew consisting of four words the initial letters of which words are the four Hebrew consonants of the tetragrammaton, YHWH (יהוה).

9 These sacred, lyrical poems are written in unrhymed Hebrew verse and display unsurpassed beauty of style and rhythmical flow of thought. They speak directly to the mind and heart. They paint vivid pictures. The wonderful breadth and depth, in both the subject matter and the strong emotions expressed, are due in part to David's extraordinary life experiences, which provide background to many of the psalms. Few men have lived so varied a life, as a shepherd boy, a lone warrior against Goliath, a court musician, an outlaw among loyal friends and among traitors, a king and conqueror, a loving father beset with division in his own household, one who twice experienced the bitterness of serious sin and yet was ever an enthusiastic worshiper of Jehovah and lover of His law. Against such a background, it is little wonder that Psalms runs the entire scale of human emotions! Contributing to its power and beauty are the poetic parallelisms and contrasts so characteristic of Hebrew verse.—Ps. 1:6; 22:20; 42:1; 121:3, 4.

10 The authenticity of these most ancient songs to Jehovah's praise is amply testified to by the Bible itself, which shows that the Psalms were used in temple worship. (1 Chron. 15:19-21, 28; 16:5, 6, 42; 2 Chron. 5:12, 13; 7:6; 20:21, 22; 29:25, 28, 30; Ezra 3:10, 11; Neh. 12:27, 40-43) David himself said in his last song: "The spirit of Jehovah it was that spoke by me, and his word was upon my tongue." It was this spirit that had operated upon him from the day of his anointing by Samuel. (2 Sam. 23:2; 1 Sam. 16:13) Additionally, the apostles quoted from the Psalms "scripture . . . which the holy spirit spoke beforehand by David's mouth," and, in a number of quotations from the Psalms, the writer to the Hebrews referred to them either as statements spoken by God or by the words "just as the holy spirit says." —Acts 1:16; 4:25; Heb. 1:5-14; 3:7; 5:5, 6.

11 Coming to the strongest proof of authenticity, we quote Jesus as the risen Lord, in saying to the disciples: "These are my words which I spoke to you . . . that all the things written in the law of Moses and in the Prophets and Psalms about me must be fulfilled." Jesus was there grouping the entire Hebrew Scriptures in the way adopted by the Jews and well known to them. His mention of the Psalms included the whole of the third group of Scriptures, called the *Hagiographa* (or "Holy Writings"), of which the Psalms was the first book. This is confirmed by what he said a few hours earlier to the two on their way to Emmaus, when "he interpreted to them things pertaining to himself in *all* the Scriptures."—Luke 24:44, 27.

CONTENTS OF PSALMS

12 **Book One** (Psalms 1-41). All of these are directly ascribed to David except Psalms 1, 2, 10 and 33. Psalm 1 strikes the keynote at the

6. (a) Into what separate volumes has Psalms been divided, and how did this come about? (b) Who collected Psalms in its present form?
7. What other features of these collections are to be noted?
8. Explain and illustrate the acrostic style of composition.
9. (a) Because of what background do many of the psalms make a direct appeal to mind and heart? (b) What else contributes to their power and beauty?
10. What testifies to the authenticity of Psalms?
11. How is this testimony crowned by Jesus' own statements?
12. How does Psalms quickly strike up a theme of "happiness," as well as the Kingdom theme?

utset, as it pronounces happy the man deghting in Jehovah's law, contemplating it day nd night in order to follow it, in contrast with ngodly sinners. This is the first pronounceient of "happiness" found in Psalms, there eing twenty-four all together. After this reeshing appetizer, we turn to Psalm 2 and at nce come to strong meat. This opens with a hallenging question, and tells of the combined tand of all the kings and high officials of earth against Jehovah and against his anointed one." ehovah laughs at them in derision, and then peaks to them in hot anger, saying: "I, even I, ave installed my king upon Zion, my holy nountain." He is the one who will break and ash in pieces all opposition. You other kings nd rulers, "serve Jehovah with fear," and cknowledge His Son lest you perish! (Vss. 2, , 11) Thus the Psalms quickly strike up the Kingdom theme of the Bible.

13 In this first collection, prayers, both of etition and of thanksgiving, are prominent. salm 8 contrasts Jehovah's greatness and nan's smallness, and Psalm 14 exposes the olly of godless people. Psalm 19 shows how he wonderful creation of Jehovah God delares his glory, and verses 7 to 14 extol the ewarding benefits of keeping God's perfect aw, which is later reflected on a grander scale n Psalm 119. Psalm 23 is universally accepted s one of the masterpieces of all literature, but t is even more magnificent in the beautiful simplicity of its expression of loyal trust in ehovah. O that we may all 'dwell in the ouse of Jehovah, the Great Shepherd, to the ength of days'! (23:1, 6) Psalm 37 gives good counsel to God-fearing people who live among evildoers, and Psalm 40 expresses the delight of doing God's will, even as David did it.

14 **Book Two** (Psalms 42-72). This section starts with eight Korahite psalms. Psalms 42 and 43 are both attributed to the sons of Korah since together they are in reality one poem in three stanzas, linked together by a recurring verse. (42:5, 11; 43:5) Psalm 49 emphasizes the need for a ransom for mankind, and points to God as the one strong enough to furnish it. Psalm 51 is a prayer of David, uttered after his terrible sin with Bath-sheba, the wife of Uriah the Hittite, and shows his genuine repentance. (2 Sam. 11:1–12:24) This section closes with a psalm "regarding Solomon," praying for his peaceful reign and for Jehovah's blessing to go with him.—Ps. 72.

15 **Book Three** (Psalms 73-89). At least two of these, Psalms 74 and 79, were composed following the destruction of Jerusalem in 607 B.C.E. They lament this great catastrophe, and implore Jehovah to help his people 'for the sake of the glory of his name.' (79:9) Psalm 78 recounts the history of Israel from the time of Moses until David "began to shepherd them according to the integrity of his heart" (vs. 72), and Psalm 80 points to Jehovah as the real "Shepherd of Israel." (Vs. 1) Psalms 82 and 83 are strong pleas to Jehovah to execute his judgments against his enemies and the enemies of his people. Far from being vindictive, these petitions are to the end "that people may search for your name, O Jehovah . . . that people may know that you, whose name is Jehovah, you alone are the Most High over all the earth." (83:16, 18) Last in this section comes Psalm 89, highlighting "Jehovah's expressions of loving-kindness," as shown preeminently in his kingdom covenant made with David. This is for an everlasting Heir to David's throne, ruling to time indefinite before Jehovah!—Vss. 1, 34-37.

16 **Book Four** (Psalms 90-106). Like Book Three, this contains seventeen psalms. It begins with the prayer of Moses, setting in sharp relief God's eternal existence and the short lifespan of mortal man. Psalm 92 extols Jehovah's superior qualities, and then there is that grand group, Psalms 93-100, that commence with the stirring cry, "Jehovah himself has become king!" Hence "all you people of the earth" are called upon to "sing to Jehovah, bless his name . . . For Jehovah is great and very much to be praised." "Jehovah is great in Zion." (93:1; 96:1, 2, 4; 99:2) Psalms 105 and 106 thank Jehovah for his wondrous deeds on behalf of his people, and for his faithfully keeping his covenant with Abraham in giving his seed the land, despite their countless murmurings and backslidings.

17 Of unusual interest is Psalm 104. This extols Jehovah for the dignity and splendor with which he has clothed himself, and describes his wisdom as displayed in his many works and productions on earth. Then the theme of the entire book of Psalms is set forth with full force, as the exclamation appears for the first time: "Praise Jah, you people!" (Vs. 35) This call to true worshipers to render Jehovah the praise due his name is, in Hebrew, just one word *Hal^elu-Yah'* or "Hallelujah," which latter form is familiar to people all over the earth today. From this verse on, the expression occurs twenty-three times, a number of psalms both opening and closing with it.

13. What else does the first collection make prominent?
14. What need is emphasized in Book Two of the Psalms, and what prayers of David are featured?
15. What does Book Three state regarding Israel's history, Jehovah's judgments and his Kingdom covenant?
16. How does the fourth book exalt Jehovah's kingship and his keeping covenant?
17. Of what unusual interest is Psalm 104, and what theme is repeated from this point on?

18 **Book Five** (Psalms 107-150). In Psalm 107 we have a description of Jehovah's deliverances, accompanied by the melodious refrain: "O let people give thanks to Jehovah for his loving-kindness and for his wonderful works to the sons of men." (Vss. 8, 15, 21, 31) Psalms 113 to 118 are the so-called Hallel Psalms, sung by the Jews at the great annual feasts following the return from Babylon.

19 Psalm 117 is powerful in its simplicity, being the shortest of all chapters in the Bible. Psalm 119 is the longest of all psalms and Bible chapters, counting a total of 176 verses in its twenty-two alphabetic stanzas of eight verses each. All but two of these verses (90 and 122) refer in some way to the word or law of Jehovah God, repeating several or all of the expressions (law, reminder, orders, commandment, judicial decisions) of Psalm 19:7-14 in each stanza. The word of God is mentioned a total of 207 times by one or the other of the following ten expressions: Way(s), reminder(s), orders, commandments, saying(s), law, judicial decision(s) or judgment, righteous(ness), regulation(s) or statute, and word(s).

20 Next, we find another group of psalms, the fifteen 'Songs of the Ascents,' Psalms 120-134. Translators have rendered this expression in various ways, because its meaning is not fully understood. It comes from a root word expressing the thought "to ascend or mount upwards." Some say that these songs were sung by the worshipers traveling or "ascending" up to Jerusalem for the annual festivals, the trip to the capital being regarded as an ascent because the city was situated high up in the mountains of Judah. However, it may well refer to "stairsteps," where the singers stood at the temple on Mount Moriah, or perhaps to the exalted contents of the psalms. David especially had a deep appreciation of the need for God's people to unite in worship. He rejoiced to hear the invitation: " 'To the house of Jehovah let us go' . . . to which the tribes have gone up, . . . to give thanks to the name of Jehovah." On that account he earnestly sought for the peace, security and prosperity of Jerusalem, praying: "For the sake of the house of Jehovah our God I will keep seeking good for you." —122:1, 4, 9.

21 Psalm 132 tells of David's oath to give himself no rest until he has found an appropriate resting-place for Jehovah, as represented in the ark of the covenant. After the Ark has been set up in Zion, Jehovah is described in beautiful poetic phrase as saying that he has chose Zion, "my resting place forever; here I sha dwell, for I have longed for it." He recognize this central place of worship, "for there Jeh vah commanded the blessing." "May Jehova bless you *out of Zion.*"—132:1-6, 13, 14; 133:3 134:3. See also Psalm 48.

22 Psalm 135 extols Jehovah as the prais worthy God who does all his delight, in con trast to the vain and empty idols, whos makers will become just like them. Psalm 13 is for responsive singing, each verse conclu ing: "For his loving-kindness is to time in definite." Such responses are shown to hav been used on many occasions. (1 Chron. 16:41 2 Chron. 5:13; 7:6; 20:21; Ezra 3:11) Psalm 13 relates the longing for Zion that dwelt in th hearts of the Jews when captive in Babylon and also testifies that they did not forget th songs or psalms of Zion though they were fa from their homeland. Psalm 145 exalts Jeh vah's goodness and kingship, showing that h "is guarding all those loving him, but all th wicked ones he will annihilate." (Vs. 20) Ther as a rousing conclusion, Psalms 146 to 15 strike up again the glorious theme of the boo each psalm beginning and ending with th words, "Praise Jah, you people!" This melod of praise rises to a grand crescendo in th 150th Psalm, where thirteen times in the spac of six verses it calls on all creation to prais Jehovah.

WHY BENEFICIAL

23 Because of their perfection of beauty an style, the psalms of the Bible are to be in cluded among the greatest literature in an language. However, they are much more tha literature. They are a living message from th Supreme Sovereign of all the universe, Jeh vah God himself. They give deep insight int the fundamental teachings of the Bible, speak ing first and foremost of Jehovah, its Author He is clearly shown to be the Creator of th universe and everything in it. (8:3-9; 90:1, 2 100:3; 104:1-5, 24; 139:14) The name "Jehovah" is indeed magnified in the book of Psalms where it appears more than 740 times. Ad ditionally, the abbreviated form "Jah" is to b found forty-three times, so that all together th divine name is mentioned more than five times on the average, in each Psalm. Moreover, Je hovah is spoken of more than 350 times a *Elohim,* or "God." Jehovah's rulership as su preme is shown in references to him as "Sov ereign Lord" in a number of psalms.—68:20 69:6; 71:5; 73:28; 140:7; 141:8.

18. (a) What refrain highlights Psalm 107? (b) What are the so-called Hallel Psalms?
19. How do Psalms 117 and 119 contrast, and what are some of the features of the latter?
20, 21. (a) What are the 'Songs of the Ascents'? (b) How do they express David's appreciation of the need for united worship?
22. (a) How is Jehovah's praiseworthiness extolled? (b) How does the glorious theme of the book rise to a crescendo in the concluding psalms?
23. (a) What living message is contained in Psalms? (b) How are Jehovah's name and sovereignty exalted?

24 In contrast with the eternal God, mortal man is shown to be born in sin and in need of a redeemer, and as dying and returning to "crushed matter," going down into Sheol, the common grave of all mankind. (6:4, 5; 49:7-20; 51:5, 7; 89:48; 90:1-5; 115:17; 146:4) The book of Psalms emphasizes the need for heeding the law of God and trusting in Jehovah. (1:1, 2; 62:8; 65:5; 77:12; 115:11; 118:8; 119:97, 105, 165) It warns against presumptuous and concealed sins (19:12-14; 131:1) and counsels honest and healthful associations. (15:1-5; 26:5; 101:5) It shows that right conduct brings Jehovah's approval. (34:13-15; 97:10) It holds out bright hope in saying that "salvation belongs to Jehovah," and that in the case of those fearing him, he will "deliver their soul from death itself." (3:8; 33:19) This brings us to the prophetic aspect.

25 The Psalms are virtually packed with prophecies, pointing forward to Jesus Christ, the "son of David," and the role he would play as Jehovah's Anointed One and King. As the Christian congregation sprang into life on the day of Pentecost, A.D. 33, the holy spirit began to enlighten the apostles as to the fulfillment of these prophecies. On that very day Peter quoted repeatedly from Psalms in building up the theme of his famous talk. This had to do with an individual: "Jesus the Nazarene." The latter part of his argument is based almost entirely on quotations from the Psalms proving that Christ Jesus is the Greater David and that Jehovah would not leave his soul in Hades but would raise him from the dead. No, "David did not ascend to the heavens," but, as he foretold at Psalm 110:1, his Lord did. Who is David's Lord? Peter reaches his great climax and forcefully answers: "This Jesus whom you impaled"!—Acts 2:14-36; Ps. 16:8-11; 132:11.

26 Was Peter's speech, based on the Psalms, beneficial? The fact that as a direct result about three thousand were baptized and added to the Christian congregation the same day speaks for itself.—Acts 2:41.

27 Shortly after, at a special gathering, the disciples appealed to Jehovah, quoting Psalm 2: 1, 2 and saying that this had been fulfilled in the united opposition of the rulers against "your holy servant Jesus, whom you anointed." And the account goes on to say that they were "all filled with the holy spirit."—Acts 4:23-31.

28 Look, now, at the letter to the Hebrews. In the first two chapters we find a number of quotations from the Psalms, respecting Jesus' superiority over the angels as God's heavenly enthroned Son. Paul shows from Psalm 22:22 and other references that Jesus has a congregation of "brothers," part of Abraham's seed and "partakers of the heavenly calling." (Heb. 2: 10-13, 16; 3:1) Then, commencing at Hebrews 6:20 and on through chapter seven, the apostle enlarges on the further office that Jesus occupies as "high priest according to the manner of Melchizedek forever." This refers to God's oath-bound promise at Psalm 110:4, to which Paul makes reference time and again in proving the superiority of Jesus' priesthood over that of Aaron. He shows how this priesthood operates for the benefit especially of Jesus' "brothers," those who share with him in the Kingdom covenant and who will be made "priests of God" and will "rule as kings with him for the thousand years."—Heb. 7:21, 25-28; Rev. 20:6.

29 Further, at Hebrews 10:5-10, we are told of Jesus' fine appreciation of the sacrificial course that was God's will for him and of his determination to carry out that will. This is based on David's words at Psalm 40:6-8. This exemplary spirit of devotion is of the greatest benefit for us all to consider and to copy so as to win God's approval.—See also Psalm 116:14-19.

30 The course that Jesus took, culminating in that terrible ordeal he endured on the torture stake, was foretold in the Psalms in remarkable detail. This included offering him vinegar to drink, the casting of lots for his outer garments, the cruel suffering to his hands and feet, the mockery and the still more bitter mental anguish of that agonizing cry: "My God, my God, why have you forsaken me?" (Matt. 27: 34, 35, 43, 46; Ps. 22:1, 7, 8, 14-18; 69:20, 21) As indicated by John 19:23-30, even during those hours Jesus must have drawn much comfort and guidance from the Psalms, knowing that all these scriptures had to be fulfilled down to the last detail. Jesus knew that the Psalms also spoke concerning his resurrection and exaltation. He doubtless had all these things in mind when leading in "singing praises" or psalms with his apostles on the last night before his death.—Matt. 26:30.

31 Thus Psalms clearly identifies the "son of David" and Kingdom Seed to be Christ Jesus, who is now exalted as both king and priest in the heavenly Zion. Space does not permit to

24. What is said concerning mortal man, and what sound counsel is given?
25. (a) With what is Psalms virtually packed? (b) How did Peter use Psalms in identifying the Greater David?
26. How did Peter's speech prove to be beneficial?
27. How did "the holy spirit" interpret Psalm 2?
28. (a) By the use of Psalms, what argument does Paul develop in Hebrews chapters 1 to 3? (b) How does Psalm 110:4 provide a basis for Paul's discussion of the Melchizedekian priesthood?
29. What exemplary example of devotion should we heed, as stated in the Psalms and explained at Hebrews 10:5-10?
30. How did the Psalms foretell Jesus' course in detail, and how must he have drawn comfort from them?
31. What does Psalms foretell in connection with the Kingdom Seed and Jesus' congregation?

describe in detail all the passages from Psalms that are quoted in the Greek Scriptures as fulfilled in this Anointed One of Jehovah, but a few more examples are here listed: Ps. 78:2—Matt. 13:31-35; Ps. 69:4—John 15:25; Ps. 118: 22, 23—Mark 12:10, 11 and Acts 4:11; Ps. 34: 20—John 19:33, 36; Ps. 45:6, 7—Heb. 1:8, 9. Also, Jesus' congregation of true followers is foretold in the Psalms, not as individuals, but as a group taken into God's favor from all nations to share in a work of praise to Jehovah's name.—Ps. 117:1—Rom. 15:11; Ps. 68:18 —Eph. 4:8-11; Ps. 95:7-11—Heb. 3:7, 8; 4:7.

32 Our study of the Psalms adds much to our appreciation of the kingship of Jehovah God, which he exercises through the promised Seed and Kingdom Heir, to his glory and sanctification. May we ever be among those loyal ones who exult in 'the glorious splendor of Jehovah's dignity,' and who are spoken of in Psalm 145, "A praise, of David": "About the glory of your kingship they will talk, and about your mightiness they will speak, to make known to the sons of men his mighty acts and the glory of the splendor of his kingship. Your kingship is a kingship for all times indefinite and your dominion is throughout all successive generations." (145:5, 11-13) True to the prophetic psalm, the splendor of God's established kingdom by Christ is even now being made known to the sons of men in all nations. How thankful we should be for that kingdom and its King! Appropriate, indeed, are the closing words of the Psalms: "Every breathing thing —let it praise Jah. Praise Jah, you people!" —150:6.

32. (a) What does the study of Psalms reveal as to Jehovah's sanctification and Kingdom purposes? (b) In appreciation of his kingship, how should we express loyalty and thankfulness?

Bible Book Number Twenty— Proverbs

Speakers:	**Solomon, Agur, Lemuel**
Place Written:	**Undetermined**
Writing Completed:	**c. 716 B.C.E.**
Time Covered:	**Undetermined**

WHEN Solomon, the son of David, became king of Israel in 1037 B.C.E., he prayed to Jehovah for "wisdom and knowledge" to "judge this great people." In response, Jehovah gave him 'knowledge and wisdom and an understanding heart.' (2 Chron. 1:10-12; 1 Ki. 3:12; 4:30, 31) As a result, Solomon came to "speak three thousand proverbs." (1 Ki. 4:32) Some of this spoken wisdom was recorded in the Bible book of Proverbs. Since his wisdom was really that which "God had put in his heart," then in studying Proverbs we are in fact studying the wisdom of Jehovah God. (1 Ki. 10:23, 24) These proverbs sum up eternal truths. They are just as up to date now as when they were first uttered.

2 The reign of Solomon was an appropriate time for providing this divine guidance. Solomon was said to "sit upon Jehovah's throne." The theocratic kingdom of Israel was at its height, and Solomon was favored with surpassing "royal dignity." (1 Chron. 29:23, 25) It was a time of peace and plenty, a time of security. (1 Ki. 4:20-25) However, even under that theocratic rule, the people still had their personal problems and difficulties due to human imperfections. That the people would look to wise King Solomon to help them solve their problems is understandable. (1 Ki. 3:16-28) In the course of pronouncing judgment in these many cases, he uttered proverbial sayings that fitted the many circumstances of life arising from day to day. These brief but impressive sayings were greatly treasured by those who desired to regulate their lives in accordance with the will of God.

3 The record does not say that Solomon *wrote* the Proverbs. However, it says that he '*spoke*' proverbs, also that "he . . . made a thorough search, that he might arrange many proverbs in order," thus showing that he had an interest in preserving proverbs for later use. (1 Ki. 4:32; Eccl. 12:9) In the time of David and Solomon there were official secretaries in the lists of court officials. (2 Sam. 20:25; 2 Ki. 12:10) Whether these scribes in his court wrote and collected his proverbs we do not know, but the expressions of any ruler of his caliber would be highly regarded and recorded. It is generally agreed that the book is a collection compiled from other collections.

1. What wisdom is to be found in the book of Proverbs?
2. Why was Solomon's time an appropriate one in which to provide this divine guidance?

3. How did Proverbs come to be compiled?

4 The book of Proverbs is generally divided into five divisions. These are: (1) Chapters 1-9, opening with the words, "The proverbs of Solomon the son of David"; (2) Chapters 10-24, described as the "Proverbs of Solomon"; (3) Chapters 25-29, which division begins: "These also are the proverbs of Solomon that the men of Hezekiah the king of Judah transcribed"; (4) Chapter 30, introduced as "The words of Agur the son of Jakeh"; and (5) Chapter 31, which comprises "The words of Lemuel the king, the weighty message that his mother gave to him in correction." Solomon was thus the originator of the bulk of the proverbs. As to Agur and Lemuel, there is nothing definite as to their identity. Some commentators suggest that Lemuel may have been another name for Solomon.

5 When was Proverbs compiled? The greater part was no doubt written down during Solomon's reign (1037-997 B.C.E.), before his apostasy. Due to the uncertainty as to the identity of Agur and Lemuel, it is not possible to date their material. Since one of the collections was made in the reign of Hezekiah (745-716 B.C.E.), it could not have been before his reign that the final collecting was done. Were the last two divisions also collected under King Hezekiah's purview? In answer there is an illuminating footnote to Proverbs 31:31 in the *New World Translation of the Hebrew Scriptures:* "At the end of this book of Proverbs M [Masoretic Hebrew Text] displays the three letters or trigrammaton חזק (*Hheth, Zayin, Qoph*), three Hebrew letters that are found in the name Hezekiah that appears at Proverbs 25:1. This trigrammaton would therefore stand as King Hezekiah's signature to the copy-work done by his men, his scribes, to signify that the work had been completed."—1957 Edition.

6 In Hebrew Bibles the book was first called by the opening word in the book, *mi·sheleiʹ*, meaning "proverbs." However, this is just the plural number, construct state, of the Hebrew noun *mâ·shâlʹ*, which noun carries the deeper meaning of "simile, similitude, comparison, parable." These terms nicely describe the contents of the book, which are pithy sayings designed to make the hearer think. The English title, from the Latin *Proverbia*, is also descriptive of the contents. It means "For Words," that is, few words standing for many words, presenting the whole idea "in a nutshell." The brief form not only makes the proverbs easy to follow and interesting, but in this form they are easily taught, learned and remembered. The idea sticks.

4. (a) How is the book of Proverbs generally divided? (b) Who originated the bulk of the proverbs?
5. When was Proverbs written and compiled?
6. What is a proverb, and why are the Hebrew and English titles of the book fitting?

7 The style of expression in the book is also most interesting. It is in Hebrew poetic style. The structure of most of the book is parallel poetry. This does not make the ends of lines or verses rhyme or sound alike. It consists in making rhythmic lines give parallel thoughts or ideas. Its beauty and power of instruction lie in this thought rhythm. The thoughts may be synonymous or contrasting, but the power of the parallel is there to give extension to the thought, to enlarge upon the idea and to make sure of conveying the meaning in the thought. Examples of the synonymous parallelism are to be found at Proverbs 11:25; 16:18; and 18:15; and of the more abundant contrasting parallelism at Proverbs 10:7, 30; 12:25; 13:25 and 15:8. Another type of structure is found right at the end of the book. (31:10-31) The twenty-two verses there are arranged so that, in Hebrew, each one begins with the succeeding letter of the Hebrew alphabet, this being the "acrostic" style that is used also in a number of the Psalms. For beauty this style has no parallel in ancient writings.

8 The authenticity of Proverbs is also shown in the wide use made of it by the early Christians in stating rules of conduct. James was apparently very familiar with Proverbs, and used its basic principles in the fine counsel he gave for Christian conduct. (See Proverbs 14:29; 17:27 and James 1:19, 20; Proverbs 3:34 and James 4:6; Proverbs 27:1 and James 4:13, 14.) Direct quotations from Proverbs are also to be found in the following passages: Romans 12:20—Proverbs 25:21, 22; Hebrews 12:5, 6—Proverbs 3:11, 12; 2 Peter 2:22—Proverbs 26:11.

9 In addition, Proverbs shows itself to be in harmony with the rest of the Bible, thus proving it to be a part of "all Scripture." It presents striking unity of thought when compared with the Law of Moses, Jesus' teaching and the writings of his disciples and apostles. (See Proverbs 10:16—1 Corinthians 15:58 and Galatians 6:8, 9; Proverbs 12:25—Matthew 6:25; Proverbs 20:20—Exodus 20:12 and Matthew 15:4.) Even when touching on such points as the readying of the earth for human habitation, there is oneness of thinking with other Bible writers as to the scientific fact that masses of water were involved.—Prov. 3:19, 20; Gen. 1:6, 7; Job 38:4-11; Ps. 104:5-9.

10 Also testifying to the book's divine inspiration is its scientific accuracy, whether the proverb involves chemical, medical or health

7. What should be noted about the style of Proverbs?
8. How does the use made of Proverbs by the early Christians testify to its authenticity?
9. How does Proverbs harmonize with other Bible teachings?
10, 11. What further testifies to the book's divine inspiration?

principles. Proverbs 25:20 tells of acid-alkali reactions. Proverbs 31:4, 5 agrees with the latest scientific findings that alcohol does not aid but slows the reaction time and the thinking processes. Wine is now known to dilate the coronary vessels and to be a stimulant for a failing heart. (31:6) Many doctors and nutritionists recommend honey. (24:13) Modern psychosomatic observations are not new to Proverbs. "A heart that is joyful does good as a curer."—17:22; 15:17.

11 Indeed, Proverbs' coverage of every human need and situation is so complete as to have caused one authority to state: "There is no relation in life which has not its appropriate instruction, no good or evil tendency without its proper incentive or correction. The human consciousness is everywhere brought into immediate relation with the Divine, . . . and man walks as in the presence of his Maker and Judge . . . Every type of humanity is found in this ancient book; and though sketched three thousand years ago, is still as true to nature as if now drawn from its living representative."—Smith's *Bible Dictionary,* 1879, Vol. III, page 2616.

CONTENTS OF PROVERBS

12 **The First Section** (1:1–9:18). This is a connected poem made up of short discourses as though from a father to a son that deal with the need for wisdom to guide the heart, or motive, and to direct desire. It teaches the value of wisdom and its blessings: happiness, pleasantness, peace and life. (1:33; 3:13-18; 8:32-35) It contrasts this with the lack of wisdom and its results: suffering and finally death. (1:28-32; 7:24-27; 8:36) Considering the infinite cases and possibilities of life, it gives one a basic study in human conduct and the present and future consequences of that conduct. The words at Proverbs 1:7 set the pattern for the entire book: "The fear of Jehovah is the beginning of knowledge." All actions must show that Jehovah is taken into consideration. There is constant repetition of the need not to forget God's laws, to keep his commandments close and not to forsake them.

13 The prominent threads that run through the fabric are "practical wisdom," "knowledge," "fear of Jehovah," "discipline" and "discernment." Warnings are given against bad company, rejecting Jehovah's discipline and improper relations with strange women. (1:10-19; 3:11, 12; 5:3-14; 7:1-27) Twice, wisdom is described as being in public places, thus obtainable, available. (1:20, 21; 8:1-11) It i personified and speaks appealingly to the in experienced ones, even throwing some light o the creation of the earth. (1:22-33; 8:4-36 What an amazing book this is! This sectio closes out on its starting theme, that "the fea of Jehovah is the start of wisdom." (9:10 Throughout, it argues that recognition of Je hovah in all our ways, together with our ad herence to his righteousness, can guard u against so much that is undesirable and bles us eternally with life.

14 **The Second Section** (10:1–24:34). Here w find many choice, unconnected maxims tha apply wisdom to the complex situations of life By teaching us the proper applications it aim to promote greater happiness and pleasan living. Contrasts in the parallelisms make thes teachings stand out in our minds. Here is partial list of the subjects that are considere in just chapters 10, 11 and 12:

- love vs. hatred
- wisdom vs. foolishness
- honesty vs. cheating
- faithfulness vs. slander
- truth vs. falsehood
- generosity vs. holding back
- diligence vs. slackness
- walking in integrity vs. crooked ways
- good counsel vs. no skillful direction
- capable wife vs. shameful wife
- righteousness vs. wickedness
- modesty vs. presumptuousness

Considering this list in relation to daily living must convince us that Proverbs really is practical book!

15 The remainder of this section (13:1–24:34 continues with its reminders of Jehovah's standards, so that we may have insight an discernment. A list of the great variety o human situations dealt with will show what broad coverage this book gives. It is most bene ficial to have this Bible counsel on: pretense presumptuousness, keeping one's word, shrewd ness, associations, child correction and train ing, man's view of what is right, being slow t anger, favor to the afflicted, fraud, prayer ridicule, contentment with life's necessities pride, unjust profit, bribery, contention, self control, isolation, silence, partiality, quarreling humility, luxury, care of a father and a mother intoxicating beverages, weights and measures qualities of a wife, gifts, borrowing, lending kindness, confidence, property lines, building up the household, envy, retaliation, vanity, mil answer, meditation and true companionship Quite a wealth of counsel to go to for soun

12. (a) What connected poem makes up the First Section? (b) What does it teach concerning wisdom and human conduct? (c) How does Proverbs 1:7 set the pattern for the entire book?
13. Trace the prominent threads that run through this section.
14. What contrasting parallelisms make the practica teachings of Proverbs stand out?
15. What wealth of counsel does Proverbs give in th small things, as well as in the big things?

uidance on everyday affairs! To some, a num-
er of these items may seem unimportant, but
erein we note that the Bible considers more
han just the "big" things. There is no neglect
f our needs in small things. In this, Proverbs
; of inestimable value.

16 **The Third Section** (25:1–29:27). Upbuild-
ıg counsel is given on such matters as honor,
atience, enemies, dealing with stupid persons,
aving fun, flattery, jealousy, hurt caused by a
riend, hunger, slander, attention to responsiility, interest, confession, results of wicked
ule, arrogance, the blessings of righteous rule,
hild delinquency, treatment of servants, in-
ight, vision, and others.

17 **The Fourth Section** (30:1-33). This is "the
eighty message" attributed to Agur. After a
umble admission of his own unimportance, the
riter makes reference to the inability of man
o create the earth and the things in it. He calls
od's Word refined and a shield. He asks that
he lying word be put far away from him and
hat he be given neither riches nor poverty. He
escribes an impure, proud and greedy genera-
ion that calls down evil upon its parents. Four
hings that have not said "Enough!" are iden-
ified, along with four things that are too won-
erful to know. An adulterous woman's brazen
elf-acquittal is given. Then there are described
our things under which the earth cannot en-
ure, four small things instinctively wise and
our things that excel in their moving along.
y apt comparisons he warns that "the
queezing out of anger is what brings forth
uarreling."—30:33.

18 **The Fifth Section** (31:1-31). Here is an-
ther "weighty message," that of Lemuel the
ing. This is in two styles of writing. The first
art discusses the ruin to which one can come
hrough a bad woman, warns how liquor can
ervert judgment and calls for righteous judg-
ıent. The acrostic in the latter part is devoted
o a classic description of a good wife. In some
etail it considers her value, pointing out that
he is trusted, is rewarding to her owner, in-
ustrious, an early riser, a careful buyer, kind
o the poor, exercising foresight, speaking with
visdom, alert, respected by her children and
raised by her husband. Above all, she fears
ehovah.

WHY BENEFICIAL

19 The beneficial purpose of Proverbs is tated in the opening verses: "For one to know wisdom and discipline, to discern the sayings of understanding, to receive the discipline that gives insight, righteousness and judgment and uprightness, to give to the inexperienced ones shrewdness, to a young man knowledge and thinking ability." (1:2-4) In harmony with that stated purpose, the book highlights knowledge, wisdom and understanding, each of which is beneficial in its particular way.

20 (1) *Knowledge* is man's great need, for it is not good for man to fall into ignorance. One can never acquire accurate knowledge without the fear of Jehovah, for knowledge starts with that fear. Knowledge is to be preferred to choice gold. Why? Through knowledge the righteous are rescued; it holds us back from hastening into sin. How we need to search for it, to take it in! Precious it is. So "incline your ear and hear the words of the wise ones, that you may apply your very heart to my knowledge."—22:17; 1:7; 8:10; 11:9; 18:15; 19:2; 20:15.

21 (2) *Wisdom,* the ability to use knowledge aright to the praise of Jehovah, "is the prime thing." Acquire it. Its Source is Jehovah; so life-giving wisdom has its start in knowing and fearing Jehovah God. That is the great secret of wisdom. So fear God, not man. Wisdom personified issues her proclamation, urging all to reform their ways. Wisdom cries aloud in the very streets. Jehovah calls out to all those inexperienced ones and those in want of heart to turn aside and feed themselves with wisdom's bread. Then they will be happy with little, along with fear of Jehovah, rather than with an abundance without such fear. Many are the blessings of wisdom; greatly beneficial, its effects. Wisdom and knowledge—these are preliminary fundamentals for thinking ability, the kind that will safeguard us. As honey is beneficial and pleasant, so is wisdom. It is of more value than gold; it is a tree of life. People perish without wisdom, for it preserves life; it means life.—4:7; 1:7, 20-23; 2:6, 7, 10, 11; 3:13-18, 21-26; 8:1-36; 9:1-6, 10; 10:8; 13:14; 15:16, 24; 16:16, 20-24; 24:13, 14.

22 (3) Besides knowledge and wisdom, *understanding* is vital; hence "with all that you acquire, acquire understanding." Understanding is the ability to see a thing in its connected parts; it means discernment, always with God in mind, for man cannot lean upon his own understanding. How utterly impossible to have understanding or discernment if one works in opposition to Jehovah! Keenly we must seek understanding as a hidden treasure, to make it our own. To understand we must have knowl-

6. What upbuilding counsel is given in the Third ection?
7. (a) What "weighty message" does Agur convey? b) What different sets of four things does he describe? c) By what apt comparisons does he warn against nger?
8. What does King Lemuel have to say about (a) a bad voman, and (b) a good wife?
9. How does Proverbs itself make known its beneficial urpose?

20. What does Proverbs say about knowledge?
21. What is the divine teaching concerning wisdom?
22. What safeguard is to be found in understanding?

edge. The search that the understanding one makes for knowledge is rewarded, and wisdom is in front of him. He is safeguarded from this world's innumerable pitfalls, such as from the countless bad people who might try to ensnare one to walk with them in the way of darkness. Thanks be to Jehovah God—the Source of life-giving knowledge, wisdom and understanding!—4:7; 2:3, 4; 3:5; 15:14; 17:24; 19:8; 21:30.

23 In harmony with the beneficial purpose of Proverbs, the book presents an abundance of wise, inspired counsel to help us keep understanding and to safeguard the heart, "for out of it are the sources of life." (4:23) Following is a selection of the wise counsel stressed throughout the book.

24 *The wicked and the righteous contrasted:* The wicked one will be caught in his crooked ways, and his treasures will not save him in the day of fury. The righteous one is in line for life and will be rewarded by Jehovah.—2:21, 22; 10:6, 7, 9, 24, 25, 27-32; 11:3-7, 18-21, 23, 30, 31; 12:2, 3, 7, 28; 13:6, 9; 14:2, 11; 15:3, 8, 29; 29:16.

25 *The need for clean morals:* Solomon warns continually against immorality. Adulterous persons will receive a plague, dishonor, and their reproach will not be wiped out. "Stolen waters" may seem sweet to a youth, but the prostitute descends to death and takes her inexperienced victims with her. Those who fall into the deep pit of immorality are denounced by Jehovah.—2:16-19; 5:1-23; 6:20-35; 7:4-27; 9:13-18; 22:14; 23:27, 28.

26 *The need for self-control:* Drunkenness and gluttony are condemned. All who will have God's approval must practice moderation in eating and drinking. (20:1; 21:17; 23:21, 29-35; 25:16; 31:4, 5) Those who are slow to anger are abundant in discernment and greater than a mighty man that captures a city. (14:17, 29; 15:1, 18; 16:32; 19:11; 25:15, 28; 29:11, 22) Self-control is also needed to avoid envy and jealousy, which is rottenness in one's bones.—14:30; 24:1; 27:4; 28:22.

27 *Wise and unwise use of speech:* Crooked speech, the slanderer, the false witness and the falsifier will be uncovered in the congregation, for they are detestable to Jehovah. (4:24; 6:16-19; 11:13; 12:17, 22; 14:5, 25; 17:4; 19:5, 9; 20:17; 24:28; 25:18) If one's mouth speaks good things, it is a source of life; but the mouth of the foolish person precipitates his ruin. "Death and life are in the power of the tongue, and he that is loving it will eat its fruitage." (18:21) Slander, deceitful speech, flattery and hasty words are condemned. It is the course of wisdom to speak truth, to honor God.—10:11, 13, 14; 12:13, 14, 18, 19; 13:3; 14:3; 16:27-30; 17:27, 28; 18:6-8, 20; 26:28; 29:20; 31:26.

28 *The folly of pride and the need for humility:* The proud person elevates himself to a height that he really does not have, so that he crashes. The proud in heart are detestable to Jehovah, but he gives humble ones wisdom, glory, riches and life.—3:7; 11:2; 12:9; 13:10; 15:33; 16:5, 18, 19; 18:12; 21:4; 22:4; 26:12; 28:25, 26; 29:23.

29 *Diligence, not slothfulness:* Many are the descriptions of a lazy person. He should go to the ant for a lesson and become wise. Ah, but the diligent one—he will prosper!—1:32; 6:6-11; 10:4, 5, 26; 12:24; 13:4; 15:19; 18:9; 19:15, 24; 20:4, 13; 21:25, 26; 22:13; 24:30-34; 26:13-16; 31:24, 25.

30 *Right association:* It is folly to associate with those who do not fear Jehovah, with wicked or stupid ones, with hot-tempered people, with talebearers or with gluttons. Rather, associate with wise persons, and you will become still wiser.—1:10-19; 4:14-19; 13:20; 14:7; 20:19; 22:24, 25; 28:7.

31 *Need for reproof and correction:* "The one whom Jehovah loves he reproves," and those who pay heed to this discipline are on the way to glory and life. He who hates reproof will come to dishonor.—3:11, 12; 10:17; 12:1; 13:18; 15:5, 31-33; 17:10; 19:25; 29:1.

32 *Counsel on being a good wife:* Repeatedly the Proverbs warn against a wife's being contentious and acting shamefully. The discreet, capable God-fearing wife has the law of loving-kindness on her tongue; whoever finds such a wife gets goodwill from Jehovah.—12:4; 18:22; 19:13, 14; 21:9, 19; 27:15, 16; 31:10-31.

33 *The rearing of children:* Teach them God's commandments regularly so that they "do not forget." Bring them up from infancy in the instruction of Jehovah. Do not spare the rod when it is needed; as an expression of love, the rod and reproof give a boy wisdom. Those who rear children God's way will have wise children who will bring rejoicing and much pleasure to father and mother.—4:1-9; 13:24; 17:21; 22:6, 15; 23:13, 14, 22, 24, 25; 29:15, 17.

34 *Responsibility to help others:* This is often stressed in the Proverbs. The wise one must

23. What kind of wise counsel will next be discussed?
24. What is stated concerning the wicked and the righteous?
25. How does Proverbs warn against immorality?
26. What is said concerning self-control?
27. (a) What is unwise use of speech? (b) Why is the wise use of our lips and tongue so vital?
28. What harm does pride bring, but what benefits result from humility?
29. How is laziness to be regarded, and of what value is diligence?
30. How does Proverbs stress right association?
31. What is the wise counsel concerning reproof?
32. What fine admonition is provided on being a good wife?
33. What beneficial advice is presented on child training?
34. Of what advantage is it to take responsibility in helping others?

pread knowledge about for the benefit of thers, and in doing so he is really lending to ehovah, who guarantees repayment.—11:24-26; 5:7; 19:17; 24:11, 12; 28:27.

35 *Reliance upon Jehovah:* Proverbs gets to ıe heart of our problems in counseling comlete trust in God. We must take notice of Jeovah in all our ways. A man may plan his ourse, but Jehovah must direct his steps. The ame of Jehovah is a strong tower, into which ıe righteous run and gain protection. Hope in ehovah and go to his Word for guidance. -3:1, 5, 6; 16:1-9; 18:10; 20:22; 28:25, 26; 0:5, 6.

36 How beneficial for teaching and disciplinıg ourselves and others is the book of Proverbs! No phase of human relationship seems) be overlooked. Is there one that isolates imself from his fellow worshipers of God? 18:1) Is one in a high position coming to conlusions before hearing both sides of a mater? (18:17) Is one a dangerous joker? (26:18, 9) Does one tend to be partial in his ways? 28:21) The tradesman in his store, the farmer ı his field, the husband and wife and child—all eceive wholesome instruction. Parents are elped so they can expose the many snares ırking in the path of youth. Wise ones can each the inexperienced ones. The proverbs are ractical wherever we live; the book's instruction and counsel never go out of date. "The ook of Proverbs," once said American educaor William Lyon Phelps, "is more up to date than this morning's newspaper."[a] Up to date, practical and beneficial for teaching is the book of Proverbs because it is inspired of God.

37 Being beneficial for setting things straight, the book of Proverbs, spoken largely by Solomon, turns men to Almighty God. So, too, did Jesus Christ, the one referred to at Matthew 12:42 as "something more than Solomon."

38 How thankful we can be that this preeminently wise One is Jehovah's choice as the Kingdom Seed! His throne it is that "will be firmly established by righteousness itself," for a peaceful reign far more glorious even than that of King Solomon. Concerning that Kingdom rule it will be said, "Loving-kindness and trueness—they safeguard the king; and by loving-kindness he has sustained his throne." That will open up an eternity of righteous government for mankind, concerning which the Proverbs also say: "Where a king is judging the lowly ones in trueness, his throne will be firmly established for all time." Thus we come to appreciate with joy that the Proverbs not only light our pathway to knowledge, wisdom and understanding, and to everlasting life, but, more important, they magnify Jehovah as the Source of true wisdom, which he dispenses through Christ Jesus, the Kingdom Heir. Proverbs adds much to our appreciation of God's kingdom and the righteous principles by which it will be governed.—Prov. 25:5; 16:12; 20:28; 29:14.

a *Treasury of the Christian Faith,* 1949, edited by Stuber and Clark, page 48.

5. What counsel does Proverbs give in getting to the ery heart of our problems?
3. From what viewpoints may Proverbs be described s up-to-date, practical and beneficial?
37. How does Proverbs harmonize with the teachings of the Greater Solomon?
38. How does Proverbs add to our appreciation of God's kingdom and its righteous principles?

Bible Book Number Twenty-one— Ecclesiastes

Writer:	**Solomon**
Place Written:	**Jerusalem**
Writing Completed:	**c. 1000 B.C.E.**
Time Covered:	**Undetermined**

THE book of Ecclesiastes was written for a lofty purpose. Solomon, as leader of a peole dedicated to Jehovah, had the responsibility o hold them together in faithfulness to their edication. He sought to fulfill this responsiility by means of the wise counsel of Ecclesiastes.

2 In Ecclesiastes 1:1 he refers to himself as "the congregator." The word in the Hebrew language is *Qo·hel'eth,* and in the Hebrew Bible the book is given that name. The Greek *Septuagint* gives the title as *Ekklesiastés,* meaning "One who sits or speaks in an ecclesia; a member thereof," from which is derived the English name Ecclesiastes. However, *Qohel'eth* is more aptly translated "The Congregator," and this is also a more fitting designation for Solomon. It conveys Solomon's purpose in writing the book.

For what lofty purpose was Ecclesiastes written?
. How is this purpose expressed in the book's Hebrew ame, thus making this more appropriate than the reek and English names?

3 In what sense was King Solomon a congregator, and to what did he do congregating? He was a congregator of his people, the Israelites, and also of others of goodwill. He congregated all these to the worship of his God, Jehovah. Previously he had built Jehovah's temple in Jerusalem, and at its dedication he had called together or congregated all of them to the worship of God. (1 Ki. 8:1) Now, by means of Ecclesiastes, he sought to congregate his people to worthwhile works, and away from the vain, fruitless works of this world.—Eccl. 12:8-10.

4 Though Solomon is not specifically named, several passages are quite conclusive in establishing him as the writer. The congregator introduces himself as "the son of David" who "happened to be king over Israel in Jerusalem." This could apply only to King Solomon, for his successors in Jerusalem were kings over Judah only. Moreover, as the congregator writes: "I myself have greatly increased in wisdom more than anyone that happened to be before me in Jerusalem, and my own heart saw a great deal of wisdom and knowledge." (1:1, 12, 16) This fits Solomon. Ecclesiastes 12:9 tells us that "he pondered and made a thorough search, that he might arrange many proverbs in order." King Solomon spoke three thousand proverbs. (1 Ki. 4:32) Ecclesiastes 2:4-9 tells of his building program, vineyards, gardens and parks, irrigation system, arranging of menservants and maidservants, accumulating of silver and gold and other accomplishments. All of this was true of Solomon. When the queen of Sheba saw it, she said: "I had not been told the half." —1 Ki. 10:7.

5 The book identifies Jerusalem as the place of writing in saying that the congregator was king "in Jerusalem." The time must have been about the year 1000 B.C.E., well along in Solomon's forty-year reign, after he had engaged in the numerous pursuits referred to in the book, but before his fall into idolatry. By then he would have gained extensive knowledge of this world's occupations and its striving after material gains. At the time he would still be in God's favor and under his inspiration.

6 How can we be sure that Ecclesiastes is "inspired of God"? Some may query its inspiration in that it does not once mention the divine name, Jehovah. However, it certainly advocates the true worship of God, and repeatedly uses the expression *ha·El·o·him'*, "the [true] God." Another objection may be raised because there are no direct quotations from Ecclesiastes in the other Bible books. However, the teachings presented and the principles laid down in the book are entirely in harmony with the remainder of the Scriptures. *Clarke's Commentary*, Volume III, page 799, states: "The book, entitled *Koheleth,* or *Ecclesiastes,* has ever been received, both by the Jewish and Christian Church, as written under the *inspiration* of the Almighty; and was held to be properly a part of the sacred canon."

7 Worldly-wise "higher critics" have claimed that Ecclesiastes is not Solomon's writing or a genuine part of "all Scripture," saying that its language and its philosophy are of a later date. They ignore the fund of information that Solomon would accumulate through his progressive development of international trade and industry, as well as through his many foreign wives and other contacts with the outside world. (1 Ki. 3:1; 4:30, 34; 9:26-28; 10:1, 23, 24) As F. C. Cook in his *Bible Commentary*, Volume IV, page 622, writes: "The daily occupations and chosen pursuits of the great Hebrew king must have carried him far out of the sphere of ordinary Hebrew life, thought and language."

8 However, are outside sources really needed to argue the canonicity of Ecclesiastes? An examination of the book itself will reveal, not only its inward harmony, but also its harmony with the rest of the Scriptures, of which it is indeed a part.

CONTENTS OF ECCLESIASTES

9 **The vanity of man's way of life** (1:1–3:22) The opening words sound the theme of the book: " 'The greatest vanity!' the congregator has said, 'the greatest vanity! Everything is vanity!' " What profit is there in mankind's toil and labor? Generations come and go, the natural cycles repeat on earth, and "there is nothing new under the sun." (1:2, 3, 9) The congregator has set his heart to seek and explore wisdom, with regard to the calamitous occupations of the sons of men, but he finds that, in wisdom and in folly, in exploits and in hard work, in eating and in drinking, everything is "vanity and a striving after wind." He comes to 'hate life,' a life of calamity and materialistic pursuits.—1:14; 2:11, 17.

10 For everything there is an appointed time —yes, God has 'made everything pretty in its time.' He wants his creatures to enjoy life on earth. "I have come to know that there is nothing better for them than to rejoice and to

3. In what sense was Solomon a congregator?
4. How is Solomon established as the writer?
5. Where and when must the book have been written?
6. What objections have been raised as to the book's inspiration, but how may these be refuted?

7. What in Solomon's background made him eminently qualified to write this book?
8. What is the strongest argument for the canonicity of the book?
9. What does the congregator find as to the occupations of the sons of men?
10. What is God's gift, but what eventuality befalls sinful man?

do good during one's life; and also that every man should eat and indeed drink and see good for all his hard work. It is the gift of God." But, alas! To sinful mankind there is the same eventuality as with the beasts: "As the one dies, so the other dies; and they all have but one spirit, so that there is no superiority of the man over the beast, for everything is vanity."—3:1, 11-13, 19.

11 **Wise counsel for those who fear God** (4:1–7:29). Solomon congratulates the dead, because they are free of "all the acts of oppression that are being done under the sun." Then he continues to describe vain and calamitous works. He also wisely counsels that "two are better than one" and that "a threefold cord cannot quickly be torn in two." (4:1, 2, 9, 12) He gives fine advice on the congregating of God's people: "Guard your feet whenever you go to the house of the true God; and let there be a drawing near to hear." Do not be hasty in speaking before God; let 'your words prove to be few,' and pay what you vow to God. "Fear the true God himself." When the poor are oppressed, remember that "one that is higher than the high one is watching, and there are those who are high above them." The mere servant, he observes, will have sweet sleep, but the rich man is too worried to sleep. Yet he has come naked into the world, and for all his hard work, he can carry nothing out of the world.—5:1, 2, 4, 7, 8, 12, 15.

12 A man may receive riches and glory, but what is the use of living "a thousand years twice over" if he has not seen what is good? It is better to take to heart the serious issues of life and death than to associate with the stupid "in the house of rejoicing"; yes, better to receive the rebuke of the wise one, for as the crackling "sound of thorns under the pot, so is the laughter of the stupid one." Wisdom is advantageous. "For wisdom is for a protection the same as money is for a protection; but the advantage of knowledge is that wisdom itself preserves alive its owners." Why, then, has the way of mankind become calamitous? "The true God made mankind upright, but they themselves have sought out many plans."—6:6; 7:4, 6, 12, 29.

13 **The one eventuality to all** (8:1–9:12). "Keep the very order of the king," advises the congregator, but he observes that it is because sentence against bad work has not been executed speedily that "the heart of the sons of men has become fully set in them to do bad." (8:2, 11) He himself commends rejoicing, but there is another calamitous thing! All kinds of men go the same way—to the dead ones! The consciousness of the living is that they will die, "but as for the dead, they are conscious of nothing at all . . . All that your hands find to do, do with your very power, for there is no work nor devising nor knowledge nor wisdom in Sheol, the place to which you are going." —9:5, 10.

14 **Practical wisdom and man's obligation** (9:13–12:14). The congregator speaks of other calamities, such as "foolishness . . . in many high positions." He also sets forth many proverbs of practical wisdom, and he declares that even "youth and the prime of life are vanity" unless —yes, unless true wisdom is heeded: "Remember, now, your grand Creator in the days of your young manhood." Otherwise, old age will merely return one to the dust of the earth, to the accompaniment of the congregator's words: "The greatest vanity! . . . Everything is vanity." He himself has taught the people knowledge continually, for "the words of the wise ones are like oxgoads," spurring on to right works, but, as to worldly wisdom, he warns that "to the making of many books there is no end, and much devotion to them is wearisome to the flesh." Then the congregator brings the book to its grand climax, summing up all that he has discussed on vanity and wisdom: "The conclusion of the matter, everything having been heard, is: Fear the true God and keep his commandments. For this is the whole obligation of man. For the true God himself will bring every sort of work into the judgment in relation to every hidden thing, as to whether it is good or bad."—10:6; 11:1, 10; 12:1, 8-14.

WHY BENEFICIAL

15 Far from being a book of pessimism, Ecclesiastes is studded with bright gems of divine wisdom. When enumerating the many accomplishments that he labels vanity, Solomon does not include the building of Jehovah's temple on Mount Moriah in Jerusalem, nor the pure worship of Jehovah. He does not describe God's gift of life as vanity, but shows that it was for the purpose of man's rejoicing and doing good. (3:12, 13; 5:18-20; 8:15) The calamitous occupations are those that ignore God. A father may lay up wealth for his son, but a disaster destroys all and nothing remains for him. Far better it would have been to provide an enduring inheritance of spiritual riches. It is calamitous to possess an abundance and not be able to enjoy it. Calamity overtakes all

11. What wise counsel does the congregator give the God-fearing man?
12. What advice is given on the serious issues of life, and on the advantage of wisdom over money?
13. What does the congregator advise and commend, and what does he say concerning the place where man is going?

14. (a) What practical wisdom does the congregator stress? (b) What is the conclusion of the matter?
15. How does Solomon distinguish between calamitous occupations and worthwhile works?

the worldly rich when they "go away" in death, with nothing in their hand.—5:13-15; 6:1, 2.

16 At Matthew 12:42, Christ Jesus referred to himself as "something more than Solomon." Since Solomon pictured Jesus, do we find the words of Solomon in his book *Qo·hel'eth* to be in harmony with the teachings of Jesus? We find many parallels! For example, Jesus underlined the extensive scope of the work of God in saying, "My Father has kept working until now, and I keep working." (John 5:17) Solomon also refers to God's works: "And I saw all the work of the true God, how mankind are not able to find out the work that has been done under the sun; however much mankind keep working hard to seek, yet they do not find out. And even if they should say they are wise enough to know, they would be unable to find out."—Eccl. 8:17.

17 Jesus set the pattern in making a vow of dedication to God, saying, "Look! I am come . . . to do your will, O God," and he paid that vow. (Heb. 10:7) Solomon also encourages us: "What you vow, pay." (Eccl. 5:2-7) Both Jesus and Solomon encouraged true worshipers to congregate. (Matt. 18:20; Eccl. 4:9-12; 5:1) Jesus' comments on "the conclusion of the system of things" and "the appointed times of the nations" are in harmony with the statement by Solomon that "for everything there is an appointed time, even a time for every affair under the heavens."—Matt. 24:3; Luke 21:24; Eccl. 3:1.

18 Above all, Jesus and his disciples join with Solomon in warning of the pitfalls of materialism. Wisdom is the true protection, for it "preserves alive its owners," says Solomon. "Keep on, then, seeking first the kingdom and his righteousness, and all these other things will be added to you," says Jesus. (Eccl. 7:12; Matt. 6:33) At Ecclesiastes 5:10 it is written: "A mere lover of silver will not be satisfied with silver, neither any lover of wealth with income. This too is vanity." Very similar is the counsel that Paul gives at 1 Timothy 6:6-19 on the theme that "the love of money is a root of all sorts of injurious things." There are similar parallel passages on other points of Bible instruction.—Eccl. 3:17—Acts 17:31; Eccl. 4:1—Jas. 5:4; Eccl. 5:1, 2—Jas. 1:19; Eccl. 6:12—Jas. 4:14; Eccl. 7:20—Rom. 3:23; Eccl. 8:17—Rom. 11:33.

19 When Solomon wrote this book, as "king over Israel in Jerusalem," he could write: "There is nothing new under the sun." But by means of Christ Jesus "new things have come into existence." Not least of these new things is the Kingdom rule of God's beloved Son, who in the flesh was a descendant of wise King Solomon. That rule will mean a "new earth" for believing humankind. (Eccl. 1:9; 2 Cor. 5:17; Col. 1:13; Rev. 21:1-5) What Solomon wrote for the guidance of his subjects in his typical kingdom is of vital interest to all who now rest their hope in God's kingdom under Christ Jesus. Under its rule mankind will live by the same wise principles that the congregator set forth, and will rejoice eternally in God's gift of happy life. Now is the time to be congregated in Jehovah's worship, in order to realize to the full the joys of life under his kingdom.—Eccl. 3:12, 13; 12:13, 14.

16. How does *Qo·hel'eth* harmonize with the teachings of Jesus?
17. What other parallels are to be found in Jesus' and Solomon's words?
18. In giving what warnings do Jesus and his disciples join with Solomon?
19. What "new things" have appeared, and with what happy prospect may we therefore congregate in Jehovah's worship today?

Bible Book Number Twenty-two— Song of Solomon

Writer:	**Solomon**
Place Written:	**Jerusalem**
Writing Completed:	**c. 1020 B.C.E.**
Time Covered:	**Undetermined**

"THE whole world was not worthy of the day in which this sublime Song was given to Israel." Thus the Jewish "rabbi" Akiba, who lived in the first century of the Christian era, expressed his appreciation for the Song of Solomon.[a] The book's title is a contraction of the opening words, "The superlative song, which is Solomon's." According to the Hebrew word-for-word text it is "the song of songs," denoting superlative excellence, similar to the expression "the heavens of the heavens" for the highest heavens. (Deut. 10:14) It is not a collection of songs, but one song, "a song of the utmost perfection, one of the best that existed, or had ever been penned."[b]

[2] King Solomon of Jerusalem was the writer of this song, as is borne out by its introduction. He was highly qualified to write this supremely beautiful example of Hebrew poetry. (1 Ki. 4:32) It is an idyllic poem loaded with meaning and most colorful in its description of beauty. The reader who can visualize the Oriental setting will appreciate this still more. (Song of Sol. 4:11, 13; 5:11; 7:4) The occasion for its writing was a unique one. The great King Solomon, glorious in wisdom, mighty in power and dazzling in the luster of his material wealth, which evoked the admiration even of the queen of Sheba, could not impress a simple country girl with whom he fell in love. Because of the constancy of her love for a shepherd boy the king lost out. The book, therefore, could rightly be called The Song of Solomon's Frustrated Love. Jehovah God inspired him to compose this song for the benefit of Bible readers of the ages to follow. He wrote it in Jerusalem. Perhaps this was about 1020 B.C.E., some years after the temple had been completed. By the time he wrote the Song, Solomon had "sixty queens and eighty concubines," compared with "seven hundred wives, princesses, and three hundred concubines" at the end of his reign. —Song of Sol. 6:8; 1 Ki. 11:3.

[a] *Mishnah,* in the Sixth Division under "Yadaim," section 3, ¶5.
[b] *Clarke's Commentary,* Vol. III, page 841.

1. In what respect is this "the song of songs"?
2. (a) Who was the writer, what were his qualifications, and why could the book be called a song of "frustrated love"? (b) Where was the book written, and what is its probable date?

[3] The canonicity of the Song of Solomon was wholly unchallenged in early times. It was regarded as an integral and inspired portion of the Hebrew canon long before the Christian era. It was embodied in the Greek *Septuagint* translation. Josephus inserted it in his catalogue of the sacred books. Therefore, it has the same evidence for its canonicity as is commonly adduced for any other book of the Hebrew Scriptures.

[4] Some, however, have questioned the book's canonicity on the ground that there is no reference to God in it. The absence of any mention of God would not disqualify the book any more than the mere presence of the word "God" would make it canonical. The fact is that the divine name does appear in its abbreviated form at chapter 8, verse 6, where love is said to be "the flame of Jah." The book unquestionably forms a part of those writings to which Jesus Christ referred with approval when he said: "You are searching the Scriptures, because you think that by means of them you will have everlasting life." (John 5:39) Moreover, its powerful portrayal of the exquisite quality of mutual love, such as exists, in a spiritual sense, between Christ and his "bride," marks the Song of Solomon for its unique place in the Bible canon.—Rev. 19:7, 8.

CONTENTS OF THE SONG OF SOLOMON

[5] The material of the book is presented by a series of conversations. There is a constant change of speakers. The characters with speaking parts are Solomon the king of Jerusalem, a shepherd, his beloved Shulammite, her brothers, court ladies and women of Jerusalem. They are identified by what they say or by what is said of them. The drama unfolds near Shunem, or Shulem, about fifty-five miles north of Jerusalem, where Solomon is camped with his court entourage. It expresses a touching theme—the love of a country girl of the village of Shulem for her shepherd companion.

3. What is the evidence for the book's canonicity?
4. (a) Does the absence of the word "God" argue against its being canonical? (b) What marks it for its unique place in the Bible canon?
5. (a) How are the characters in the drama identified? (b) What touching theme is expressed?

6 **The Shulammite maiden in Solomon's camp** (1:1-14). The maiden appears in the royal tents into which the king has brought her, but she is anxious only to see her shepherd lover. With longing for her loved one she speaks out as if he were present. The ladies of the court who wait on the king, the "daughters of Jerusalem," look curiously at the Shulammite, because of her swarthy complexion. She explains that she is sunburned through caring for her brothers' vineyards. She then speaks to her lover as though she were free and asks where she might find him. The court ladies bid her to go out and pasture her flock by the tents of the shepherds.

7 Solomon comes forward. He is unwilling to let her go. He praises her beauty and promises to adorn her with "circlets of gold" and "studs of silver." The Shulammite resists his advances and lets him know that the only love she can feel is for her beloved.

8 **The shepherd lover appears** (1:15–2:2). The Shulammite's lover makes his way into Solomon's camp and encourages her. He pours out his love upon her. The Shulammite yearns for the nearness of her dear one and the simple pleasure of dwelling at one with him out in the fields and woods.

9 The Shulammite is a modest girl. "A mere saffron of the coastal plain I am," she says. Her shepherd lover thinks her to be without compare, saying: "Like a lily among thorny weeds, so is my girl companion among the daughters."—2:1, 2.

10 **The maiden longs for her shepherd** (2:3–3:5). Separated again from her lover, the Shulammite shows how she esteems him above all others, and she tells the court women that they are under oath not to try to arouse in her unwanted love for another. The Shulammite remembers the time when her shepherd answered her call and invited her to the hills in springtime. She sees him climbing upon the mountains, leaping with joy. She hears him cry out to her: "Rise up, come, O girl companion of mine, my beautiful one, and come away." However, her brothers, who were not sure of her steadiness, got angry and set her to work in guarding the vineyards. She declares, "My dear one is mine and I am his," and pleads for him to hurry to her side.—2:13, 16.

11 The Shulammite describes her detainment in Solomon's camp. At night in bed she longs for her shepherd. Again she reminds the daughters of Jerusalem that they are under oath not to awaken in her unwanted love.

12 **The Shulammite in Jerusalem** (3:6–5:1). Solomon returns to Jerusalem in regal splendor, and the people admire his cortege. The shepherd lover does not fail her in this critical hour. He follows and gets in touch with the Shulammite, who is veiled. He strengthens his beloved with warm expressions of endearment. She tells him she wants to get free and leave the city, and then he bursts into an ecstasy of love: "You are altogether beautiful, O girl companion of mine." (4:7) A mere glimpse of her makes his heart beat faster. Her expressions of endearment are better than wine, her fragrance like that of Lebanon and her skin like a paradise of pomegranates. The maiden invites her dear one to come into "his garden," and he accepts. Friendly women of Jerusalem encourage them: "Eat, O companions! Drink and become drunk with expressions of endearment!"—5:1.

13 **The maiden's dream** (5:2–6:3). The Shulammite tells the court women of a dream, in which she hears a knock. Her dear one is outside, pleading for her to let him in. But she is in bed. When she finally gets up to open the door, he has disappeared into the night. She goes out after him, but he cannot be found. The watchmen mistreat her. She obligates the court ladies to tell her lover if they see him that she is lovesick. They ask her what makes him so outstanding. She launches into an exquisite description of him, saying he is "dazzling and ruddy, the most conspicuous of ten thousand." (5:10) The court women ask her of his whereabouts. She says he has gone to shepherd among the gardens.

14 **Solomon's final advances** (6:4–8:4). King Solomon approaches the Shulammite. Again he tells her how beautiful she is, more lovely than "sixty queens and eighty concubines," but she rejects him. She is here only because an errand of service had brought her near his camp in Shulem. 'What do you see in me?' she asks. Solomon takes advantage of her innocent question to tell her of her beauty, from the soles of her feet to the crown of her head, but the maiden resists all his arts. Courageously she declares her devotion to her shepherd, crying out for him. For the third time she reminds the daughters of Jerusalem that they are under oath not to awaken love in her against her will. Solomon lets her go home. He has lost out in his quest for the Shulammite's love.

6. What conversation takes place between the maiden and the court ladies of Solomon's camp?
7. What advances does Solomon make, but with what success?
8. How does the maiden's lover encourage her? For what does she yearn?
9. How do the girl and her lover appraise her beauty?
10. What does the maiden recall concerning her love?
11. Of what oath does she again remind the daughters of Jerusalem?
12. What further encouragement does her lover give when she is taken by Solomon to Jerusalem?
13. What dream does the maiden have, and how does she describe her lover to the court ladies?
14. Despite all his arts, how does Solomon lose out in his quest?

15 **The Shulammite returns** (8:5-14). Her brothers at Shulem see her approaching, but she is not alone. She is "leaning upon her dear one." She calls to mind having met her lover under an apple tree, and declares the unbreakableness of her love for him. Some of her brothers' earlier comments about their concern over her when a "little sister" are mentioned, but she declares she has proved herself a mature and stable woman. Let her brothers now consent to her marriage. King Solomon can have his thousand vineyards! She is content with her one vineyard, for she loves one who is exclusively dear to her. In her case this love is as strong as death and its blazings as "the flame of Jah." Insistence on exclusive devotion "as unyielding as Sheol" has triumphed and has led to the glorious heights of union with her shepherd lover.—8:5, 6.

WHY BENEFICIAL

16 What lessons are taught in this Song of love that the man of God might find beneficial today? Faithfulness to one's lover and integrity to godly principles are clearly shown. The Song teaches that virtue and innocence in a true lover are things invincible to temptation. It teaches that genuine love remains unconquerable, inextinguishable, unpurchasable. Christian young men and women, husbands and wives, can benefit from this fitting example of integrity when temptations arise and allurements present themselves.

17 But this inspired Song is also most beneficial for the Christian congregation as a whole. It was recognized as part of the inspired Scriptures by the Christians of the first century, one of whom wrote: "All the things that were written aforetime were written for our instruction, that through our endurance and through the comfort from the Scriptures we might have hope." (Rom. 15:4) This same inspired writer, Paul, could well have had in mind the Shulammite girl's exclusive love for her shepherd when he wrote to the Christian congregation: "For I am jealous over you with a godly jealousy, for I personally promised you in marriage to one husband that I might present you as a chaste virgin to the Christ." Paul also wrote of the love of Christ for the congregation as that of a husband for a wife. (2 Cor. 11:2; Eph. 5:23-27) Jesus Christ is not only the Fine Shepherd for them, but he is also their King who holds out to his anointed followers the indescribable joy of "marriage" with him in the heavens.—John 10:11; Rev. 19:9.

18 Certainly these anointed followers of Christ Jesus can benefit much from the example of the Shulammite girl. They also must be loyal in their love, unenticed by the materialistic glitter of the world and keeping balance in their integrity clear through to the attainment of the reward. They have their minds set on the things above and 'seek first the Kingdom.' They welcome the loving endearments of their Shepherd, Jesus Christ. They are overjoyed in knowing that this dear one, though unseen, is close beside them, calling on them to take courage and conquer the world. Having that unquenchable love, as strong as "the flame of Jah," for their Shepherd King, they will indeed overcome and be united with him as fellow heirs in the glorious kingdom of the heavens. Thus will Jah's name be sanctified!—Matt. 6:33; John 16:33.

15. (a) With what request does the maiden return to her brothers? (b) How has exclusive devotion triumphed?
16. What valuable lessons are taught in this Song?
17. (a) How does Paul show this Song to have been written for the instruction of the Christian congregation? (b) Why may he well have had it in mind in writing to the Corinthians and the Ephesians? (c) What interesting comparisons may be made with inspired writings of John?
18. In what way may the anointed followers of Christ Jesus benefit from the example of the Shulammite girl?

Bible Book Number Twenty-three— Isaiah

Writer:	**Isaiah**
Place Written:	**Jerusalem**
Writing Completed:	**c. 732 B.C.E.**
Time Covered:	**c. 775-732 B.C.E.**

THE menacing shadow of the cruel Assyrian monarch hung heavy over the other empires and lesser kingdoms of the Middle East. The whole area was alive with talk of conspiracy and confederation. (Isa. 8:9-13) Apostate Israel to the north would soon fall victim to this international intrigue, while Judah's kings to the south were reigning precariously. (2 Kings, chaps. 15 to 21) New weapons of war were being developed and put into action, adding to the terror of the times. (2 Chron. 26:14, 15) Where could anyone look for protection and salvation? Although the name of Jehovah was on the lips of the people and the priests in the little kingdom of Judah, their hearts turned far off in other directions, first to Assyria and then down to Egypt. (2 Ki. 16:7; 18:21) Faith in Jehovah's power waned. Where it was not outright idolatry, there prevailed a hypocritical way of worship, based on formalism and not the true fear of God.

2 Who, then, would speak for Jehovah? Who would declare his saving power? "Here I am! Send me," came the ready response. The speaker was Isaiah, who had already been prophesying before this. It was 775-774 B.C.E., the year that leprous King Uzziah died. (Isa. 6:1, 8) The name Isaiah means "Salvation of Jehovah," which is the same meaning, though written in the reverse order, of the name Jesus ("Jehovah Is Salvation"). From start to finish, Isaiah's prophecy highlights this fact, that Jehovah is salvation.

3 Isaiah was the son of Amoz (not to be confused with Amos, another prophet from Judah). (Isa. 1:1) The Scriptures are silent as to his birth and death, though tradition has him sawn asunder by wicked King Manasseh. (Compare Hebrews 11:37.) His writings show him stationed in Jerusalem with his wife, a prophetess, and at least two sons with prophetic names. (Isa. 7:3; 8:1, 3) He served during the time of at least four kings of Judah: Uzziah, Jotham, Ahaz and Hezekiah; evidently beginning at least by 775 B.C.E. (before Uzziah's death) and continuing at least till 732 B.C.E. (Hezekiah's fourteenth year), or no less than forty-three years. No doubt he had also committed his prophecy to writing by this date. (Isa. 1:1; 6:1; 36:1) Other prophets of his day were Micah in Judah and, to the north, Hosea and Oded.—Mic. 1:1; Hos. 1:1; 2 Chron. 28:6-9.

4 That Jehovah commanded Isaiah to write down prophetic judgments is established by Isaiah 30:8: "Now come, write it upon a tablet with them, and inscribe it even in a book, that it may serve for a future day, for a witness to time indefinite." The Jews recognized Isaiah as the writer and included the book as the first book of the Major Prophets (Isaiah, Jeremiah and Ezekiel).

5 Though some have pointed to the book's change of style from chapter 40 onward as indicating a different writer, or "Second Isaiah," the change in subject matter should be sufficient to explain this. There is much evidence that Isaiah wrote the entire book that bears his name. For example, the oneness of the book is indicated by the expression, "the Holy One of Israel," which appears twelve times in chapters 1 to 39, and thirteen times in chapters 40 to 66, a total of twenty-five times, whereas it appears only six times throughout the rest of the Hebrew Scriptures. The apostle Paul also testifies to the unity of the book by quoting from all parts of the prophecy and crediting the whole work to one writer, Isaiah. —Compare Romans 10:16, 20; 15:12 with Isaiah 53:1; 65:1; 11:1.

6 Interestingly, in the year 1947 (A.D.) some ancient documents were brought out of the darkness of a cave in the wilderness of the Hashemite Kingdom of Jordan. These were the Dead Sea Scrolls, which included the prophecy of Isaiah. This is beautifully written in well-preserved Hebrew and is some 2,000 years old,

1. What situation confronted the Middle East, and Israel and Judah in particular, in the eighth century B.C.E.?
2. (a) Who answered the call to speak for Jehovah, and when? (b) What is significant about this prophet's name?
3. (a) What is known concerning Isaiah? (b) Over what period did he prophesy, and who were other prophets of his day?
4. What indicates that Isaiah was the writer of the book?
5. What testifies to the unity of the book?
6. How does the Dead Sea Scroll of Isaiah give convincing proof (a) that our Bibles today represent the original inspired writing, and (b) that the entire book was written by the one Isaiah?

dating from the first or second century B.C.E. Its text is thus one thousand years older than the Masoretic text on which modern translations of the Hebrew Scriptures are based and yet, except for some minor variations of spelling, it is identical with the Masoretic text. Here is convincing proof that our Bibles today contain the original inspired message of Isaiah. Moreover, these ancient scrolls refute the critics' claims of two "Isaiahs," since chapter 40 begins on the last line of the column of writing containing chapter 39, the opening sentence being completed in the next column. Thus the copyist was obviously unaware of any supposed change in writer or of any division in the book at this point.

7 There is abundant proof of the authenticity of Isaiah's book. Aside from Moses, no other prophet is more often quoted by the Christian Bible writers. There is likewise a wealth of historical and archaeological evidence that proves it genuine, such as the historical records of the Assyrian monarchs, including Sennacherib's hexagonal prism in which he gives his own account of the siege of Jerusalem.[a] (Isaiah, chaps. 36 and 37) The deserted heap of ruins that was once Babylon still bears silent witness to the fulfillment of Isaiah 13:17-22. There was a living testimony in each one of the thousands of Jews that marched back from Babylon, freed by a king whose name, Cyrus, had been penned by Isaiah some 150 years before the king was born. Whether the Jewish historian Josephus' claim that Cyrus was shown this prophetic writing be true or not, it is significant that Cyrus, on freeing the Jewish remnant, spoke of being commissioned by Jehovah to do so.—Isa. 44:28; 45:1; Ezra 1:1-3.

8 Outstanding in the book of Isaiah are the Messianic prophecies. Isaiah has been called "the Evangelist prophet," so numerous are the predictions fulfilled in the events of Jesus' life. Chapter 53, for long a "mystery chapter," not only to the Ethiopian eunuch referred to in Acts chapter 8, but to the Jewish people as a whole, foretells so vividly the treatment accorded Jesus, that it is like an eyewitness account. Here are some Greek Scripture citations that, starting from Isaiah 53:1 and continuing to the end of the chapter, show in order just one of the prophetic fulfillments from each verse: John 12:37, 38; John 18:40; Mark 9:12; Matthew 8:16, 17; 1 Peter 2:24; 1 Peter 2:25; Acts 8:32; Acts 8:33; Matthew 27:57-60; Hebrews 7:27; Romans 5:18; Luke 22:37. Who but God could be the source of such accurate forecasting?

a Study 9, paragraphs 13, 14.

7. What abundant proof is there concerning the book's authenticity?
8. How is inspiration proved by fulfillment of the Messianic prophecies?

CONTENTS OF ISAIAH

9 The first six chapters give the setting in Judah and Jerusalem and relate Judah's guilt before Jehovah and Isaiah's commissioning. Chapters 7 to 12 deal with threatened enemy invasions and the promise of relief by "the prince of peace" commissioned by Jehovah. Chapters 13 to 35 contain a series of pronouncements against many nations and forecast of salvation to be provided by Jehovah. Historic events of Hezekiah's reign are described in chapters 36 to 39. The remaining chapters, 40 to 66, have as their theme the release from Babylon, the return of the Jewish remnant and the restoration of Zion.

10 **Isaiah's message "concerning Judah and Jerusalem"** (1:1–6:13). See him there in sackcloth and sandals, as he stands in Jerusalem and cries out: Dictators! People! Listen! Your nation is sick from head to toe, and you have wearied Jehovah with your bloodstained hands upraised in prayer. Come, set matters straight with him, that scarlet sins may be made white like snow. In the final part of the days the mountain of Jehovah's house will be lifted up, and all nations will stream to it for instruction. No more will they learn war. Jehovah will be raised on high and sanctified. But at present Israel and Judah, though planted a choice vine, produce grapes of lawlessness. They make good bad and bad good, for they are wise in their own eyes.

11 "I, however, got to see Jehovah, sitting on a throne lofty and lifted up," says Isaiah. Along with the vision comes Jehovah's commission: "Go, and you must say to this people, 'Hear again and again.'" For how long? "Until the cities actually crash in ruins."—6:1, 9, 11.

12 **Threatened enemy invasions and promise of relief** (7:1–12:6). Jehovah uses Isaiah and his sons as prophetic 'signs and miracles' to show that first the combine of Syria and Israel against Judah will fail but in time Judah will go into captivity with only a remnant returning. A maiden will become pregnant and bear a son. His name? Immanuel (meaning, "With Us Is God"). Let the combined enemies against Judah take note! "Gird yourselves, and be shattered to pieces!" There will be hard times, but then a great light will shine upon God's people. For a child has been born to us, "and

9. Into what divisions do the contents of Isaiah fall?
10. (a) Why does Isaiah call on the nation to set matters straight? (b) What does he prophesy for the final part of the days?
11. Along with what vision does Isaiah receive his commission?
12. (a) How are Isaiah and his sons used as 'prophetic signs'? (b) What outstanding promise is given in Isaiah chapter nine?

his name will be called Wonderful Counsellor, Mighty God, Eternal Father, Prince of Peace." —7:14; 8:9, 18; 9:6.

13 "Aha, the Assyrian," Jehovah cries, "the rod for my anger." After using that rod against "an apostate nation" God will cut down the insolent Assyrian himself. Later, "a mere remnant will return." (10:5, 21) See now a sprout, a twig from the stump of Jesse (David's father)! This "twig" will rule in righteousness, and by him there will be enjoyment for all creation, with no harm or ruin, "because the earth will certainly be filled with the knowledge of Jehovah as the waters are covering the very sea." (11:9) With this one as signal for the nations a highway goes out from Assyria for the returning remnant. There will be exultation in drawing water from the springs of salvation and making melody to Jehovah.

14 **Pronouncing Babylon's doom** (13:1–14:27). Isaiah now looks past the Assyrian's day into the time of Babylon's zenith. Listen! The sound of numerous people, the uproar of kingdoms, of nations gathered together! Jehovah is mustering the army of war! It is a dark day for Babylon. Amazed faces flame and hearts melt. The pitiless Medes will tumble Babylon, "the decoration of kingdoms." She is to become an uninhabited desolation and a haunt of wild creatures "for generation after generation." (13:19, 20) The dead in Sheol are stirred to receive the king of Babylon. Maggots become his couch and worms his covering. What a comedown for this 'shining one, the son of the dawn'! (14:12) He aspired to God's throne but has become a carcass thrown out, as Jehovah sweeps Babylon with the broom of annihilation. No name, no remnant, no progeny, no posterity are to remain!

15 **International desolations** (14:28–23:18). Isaiah now points back to Philistia along the Mediterranean Sea and then to Moab, southeast of the Dead Sea. He directs his prophecy up beyond Israel's northern boundary to Syrian Damascus, dips deep south into Ethiopia and moves up the Nile into Egypt, with God's judgments producing desolation all along the way. He tells of Assyrian King Sargon, the predecessor of Sennacherib, sending commander Tartan against the Philistine city of Ashdod, east of Jerusalem. At this time Isaiah is told to strip and go naked and barefoot for three years. Thus he vividly portrays the futility of trusting in Egypt and Ethiopia, who, with "buttocks stripped," will be led captive by the Assyrian.

16 A lookout upon his watchtower sees the fall of Babylon and her gods, and adversities for Edom. Jehovah himself addresses Jerusalem's boisterous people who are saying, "Let there be eating and drinking, for tomorrow we shall die." 'Die you shall,' says Jehovah. (22:13, 14) The ships of Tarshish, too, are to howl and Sidon is to be ashamed, for Jehovah has given counsel against Tyre, to "treat with contempt all the honorable ones of the earth." —23:9.

17 **Jehovah's judgment and salvation** (24:1–27:13). But look now at Judah! Jehovah is emptying the land. People and priest, servant and master, buyer and seller—all must go, for they have bypassed God's laws and broken the indefinitely lasting covenant. But in time he will turn his attention to the prisoners and gather them. He is a stronghold and refuge. He will set a banquet in his mountain and swallow up death forever, wiping tears from off all faces. "This is our God," sings Isaiah. "This is Jehovah." (25:9) Judah has a city with salvation for walls. Continuous peace is for those trusting in Jehovah, "for in Jah Jehovah is the Rock of times indefinite." But the wicked "simply will not learn righteousness." (26:4, 10) Jehovah will slay his adversaries, but he will restore Jacob.

18 **God's indignation and blessings** (28:1–35:10). Woe to Ephraim's drunkards whose "decoration of beauty" must fade! But Jehovah is to "become as a crown of decoration and as a garland of beauty" to the remnant of his people. (28:5) However, the braggarts of Jerusalem look to a lie for refuge, rather than to the tried and precious foundation stone in Zion. A flash flood will wash them all away. Jerusalem's prophets are asleep and God's book is sealed to them. Lips draw close, but hearts are far away. Yet the day will come when the deaf will hear the words of the book. The blind will see and the meek rejoice.

19 Woe to those who go down to Egypt for refuge! This stubborn people want smooth, deceptive visions. They will be cut off, but Jehovah will restore a remnant. These will see their Grand Instructor, and they will scatter their images, calling them, "Mere dirt!" (30:22) Jehovah is Jerusalem's true Defender. A king will rule in righteousness, together with his princes. He will bring in peace, quietness and security to time indefinite. Treachery will cause the messengers of peace to weep bitterly, but to his own people the Majestic One, Jehovah, is Judge,

13. (a) What fate awaits the insolent Assyrian? (b) What will result from the rule of the "twig" from Jesse?
14. What comedown is foretold for Babylon?
15. What international desolations does Isaiah prophesy?
16. What calamities are seen for Babylon, Edom, Jerusalem's boisterous ones, and for Sidon and Tyre?
17. What judgment and restoration are foretold for Judah?
18, 19. (a) What contrasting woes and joys are proclaimed for Ephraim and Zion? (b) In what capacities is Jehovah to save and govern his people?

Statute-giver and King, and he himself will save them. No resident will then say: "I am sick."—33:24.

20 Jehovah's indignation must break out against the nations. Carcasses will stink and mountains will melt with blood. Edom must be desolated. But for Jehovah's repurchased ones, the desert plain will blossom, and "the glory of Jehovah, the splendor of our God," will appear. (35:2) The blind, the deaf and the dumb will be healed, and the Way of Holiness will be opened for the redeemed of Jehovah, as they return to Zion with rejoicing.

21 **Jehovah turns back Assyria in Hezekiah's day** (36:1–39:8). Is Isaiah's exhortation to rely on Jehovah practical? Can it stand the test? In the fourteenth year of Hezekiah's reign, Sennacherib of Assyria makes a scythelike sweep through Palestine and diverts some of his troops to try to intimidate Jerusalem. His Hebrew-speaking spokesman Rabshakeh hurls taunting questions at the people lining the city's walls: 'What is your confidence? Egypt? A crushed reed! Jehovah? There is no god that can deliver from the king of Assyria!' (36:4, 6, 18) In obedience to the king, the people give no answer.

22 Hezekiah prays to Jehovah for salvation for His name's sake, and Isaiah answers that Jehovah will put his hook in the Assyrian's nose and lead him back the way he has come. An angel strikes 185,000 Assyrians dead and Sennacherib scurries back home, where his own sons murder him in his pagan temple.

23 Hezekiah becomes deathly ill. However, Jehovah miraculously causes the shadow produced by the sun to retreat, as a sign that Hezekiah will be healed, and fifteen years are added to Hezekiah's life. In thankfulness he composes a beautiful psalm of praise to Jehovah. When hypocritical "glad-you-are-better" greetings come from Babylon, Hezekiah indiscreetly shows the royal treasures to the messengers. As a result Isaiah prophesies that everything in his house will one day be carried to Babylon.

24 **Jehovah comforts his witnesses** (40:1–44:28). The opening word "Comfort" well describes the rest of Isaiah. A voice in the wilderness cries out: "Clear up the way of Jehovah, you people!" (40:3) There is good news for Zion. Jehovah shepherds his flock, carrying young lambs in his bosom. From lofty heavens he looks down on earth's circle. To what can he be compared for greatness? He gives full power and dynamic energy to the tired and weary who hope in Him. He declares the molten images of the nations to be wind and unreality. His chosen one will be as a covenant for the peoples and a light of the nations to open blind eyes. Jehovah says to Jacob, "I myself have loved you," and calls to sunrising, sunset, north and south: 'Give up! Bring back my sons and my daughters.' (43:4, 6) With court in session, he orders the nations to produce witnesses to clear their gods. Israel's people are Jehovah's witnesses, his servant, testifying that he is God and Deliverer. To Jeshurun ("Upright One," Israel) he promises his spirit and then casts shame on the makers of see-nothing, know-nothing images. Jehovah is the Repurchaser of his people; Jerusalem will again be inhabited and its temple rebuilt.

25 **Vengeance upon Babylon** (45:1–48:22). For the sake of Israel Jehovah names Cyrus (Hebrew: *Khóresh*) to vanquish Babylon. Men will be made to know that Jehovah alone is God, the Creator of the heavens, the earth and man upon it. He mocks Babylon's gods, Bel and Nebo, for only He can tell the finale from the beginning. The virgin daughter of Babylon is to sit in the dust, dethroned and naked, and the multitude of her counselors will be burned up like stubble. Jehovah tells the 'iron-necked, copper-headed' Israelite idol worshipers that they could have peace, righteousness and prosperity by listening to him, but 'there is no peace for the wicked ones.'—48:22.

26 **Zion comforted** (49:1–59:21). Giving his servant as a light of the nations, Jehovah cries to those in darkness: "Come out!" (49:9) Zion will be comforted and her wilderness will become like Eden, the garden of Jehovah, overflowing with exultation, rejoicing, thanksgiving and the voice of melody. Jehovah will make the heavens go up in smoke, the earth wear out like a garment and its inhabitants die like a mere gnat. So why fear the reproach of mortal men? The bitter goblet that Jerusalem has drunk must now pass to the nations that have trampled on her.

27 'Wake up, O Zion, and rise from the dust!' See the messenger, bounding over the mountains with good news and calling to Zion, "Your God has become king!" (52:1, 7) Get out of the unclean place and keep yourselves clean, you in Jehovah's service. The prophet now describes 'Jehovah's servant.' He is a man despised, avoided, carrying our pains and yet accounted

20. What indignation is to break out against the nations, but what blessing awaits the restored remnant?
21. The Assyrian hurls what taunts at Jerusalem?
22. How does Jehovah answer Hezekiah's prayer, and fulfill Isaiah's prophecy?
23. (a) What occasions Hezekiah's composing a psalm to Jehovah? (b) What indiscretion does he commit, resulting in what prophecy by Isaiah?
24. (a) What news of comfort does Jehovah proclaim? (b) Can the gods of the nations compare with Jehovah for greatness, and what witness does he call for?
25. What are men to come to know by Jehovah's judgments on Babylon and her false gods?
26. How will Zion be comforted?
27. What good news is proclaimed to Zion, and what is prophesied concerning 'Jehovah's servant'?

as stricken by God. He was pierced for our transgressions, but he healed us by his wounds. Like a sheep brought to the slaughter, he did no violence and he spoke no deception. He gave his soul as a guilt offering to bear the errors of many people.

28 As husbandly owner, Jehovah tells Zion to cry out joyfully because of her coming fruitfulness. Though afflicted and tempest-tossed, she will become a city of sapphire foundations, ruby battlements, and gates of fiery glowing stones. Her sons, taught by Jehovah, will enjoy abundant peace, and no weapon formed against them will be successful. "Hey there, all you thirsty ones!" cries Jehovah. If they come, he will conclude with them his "covenant respecting the loving-kindnesses to David"; he will give a leader and commander as a witness to the national groups. (55:1-4) God's thoughts are infinitely higher than man's, and his word will have certain success. Eunuchs keeping his law, no matter of what nationality, will receive a name better than sons and daughters. His house will be called a house of prayer for all the peoples.

29 As the High and Lofty One, whose name is holy, Jehovah tells the sex-crazy idolaters that he will not contend with Israel to time indefinite. Their pious fasts are cover-ups for wickedness. The hand of Jehovah is not too short to save, nor his ear too heavy to hear, but it is 'the very errors of you people that have become the things causing division between you and your God,' says Isaiah. (59:2) That is why they hope for light and grope in darkness. On the other hand, Jehovah's spirit upon his faithful covenant people guarantees that his word will remain in their mouth to all future generations, irremovably.

30 **Jehovah beautifies Zion** (60:1–64:12). "Arise, O woman, shed forth light, for . . . the very glory of Jehovah has shone forth." In contrast, thick gloom envelops the earth. (60:1, 2) At that time Zion will lift her eyes and become radiant and her heart will quiver as she sees the resources of the nations coming to her on a heaving mass of camels. Like clouds of flying doves they will flock to her. Foreigners will build her walls, kings will minister to her, and her gates will never close. Her God must become her beauty and he will swiftly multiply one into a thousand and a small one into a mighty nation. God's servant exclaims that Jehovah's spirit is upon him, anointing him to tell this good news. Zion gets a new name, My Delight Is in Her (Hephzibah), and her land is called Owned as a Wife (Beulah). (62:4, *NW* footnotes, 1958 Edition) The order goes out to bank up the highway back from Babylon and to raise a signal in Zion.

31 Out of Bozrah in Edom comes one in blood-red garments. In his anger he has stamped down people in a wine trough, spurting blood. Jehovah's people feel keenly their unclean condition and offer a poignant prayer, saying, 'O Jehovah, you are our Father. We are the clay and you are our Potter. Do not be indignant, O Jehovah, to the extreme. We are all your people.'—64:8, 9.

32 **"New heavens and a new earth"!** (65:1–66:24). The people who have abandoned Jehovah for gods of Good Luck and Destiny will starve and suffer shame. God's own servants will rejoice in abundance. Look now! Jehovah is creating new heavens and a new earth. What joyfulness and exultation are to be found in Jerusalem and her people! Houses will be built and vines planted, while wolf and lamb feed as one. There will be no harm or ruin.

33 The heavens are his throne and the earth is his footstool, so what house can men build for Jehovah? A nation is to be born in one day and all lovers of Jerusalem are invited to rejoice as Jehovah extends to her peace just like a river. Against his enemies he will come as a very fire, stormwind chariots paying back his anger with sheer rage, and flames of fire against all disobedient flesh. Messengers will go out among all nations and to faraway islands to tell of his glory. His new heavens and earth are to be permanent. Permanent will be those serving him, and their offspring also. It is either this or everlasting death.

WHY BENEFICIAL

34 Viewed from every angle the prophetic book of Isaiah is a most beneficial gift from Jehovah God. It beams forth the lofty thoughts of God. (Isa. 55:8-11) Public speakers of Bible truths can draw on Isaiah as a treasure-house of vivid illustrations that strike home with forcefulness like that of Jesus' parables. He powerfully impresses us with the foolishness of the man who uses the same tree both for fuel and for making an idol of worship. He makes us feel the discomfort of the man on the couch that is too short and whose sheet is too narrow, and hear the heavy slumbering of the prophets who are like dumb dogs, too lazy to bark. So, then, may we 'search for ourselves

---

28. How is the coming blessedness of Zion described, and in connection with what covenant?
29. What does Jehovah tell the idolaters, but what assurance does he give his people?
30. How does Jehovah beautify Zion, as illustrated by what new names?
31. Who comes from Edom, and what prayer do God's people utter?
32. In contrast with those who abandon Jehovah, at what may his own people exult?
33. What rejoicing, glory and permanence are foretold for lovers of Jerusalem?
34. What are some of the vivid illustrations that add power to Isaiah's message?

in the book of Jehovah and read out loud.' (Isa. 44:14-20; 28:20; 56:10-12; 34:16) In this way we can appreciate the powerful message that Isaiah has for this day.

35 The prophecy focuses particularly on God's kingdom by Messiah. Jehovah himself is the supreme King, and he it is that saves us. The apostle John refers to Isaiah's vision of Jehovah's kingly glory. (Isa. 33:22; 6:1-4; John 12:41) But what of Messiah himself? The angel's announcement to Mary concerning the child that would be born showed that Isaiah 9:6, 7 was to be fulfilled in his receiving the throne of David; "and he will rule as king over the house of Jacob forever, and there will be no end of his kingdom." (Luke 1:32, 33) Matthew 1:22, 23 shows that Jesus' birth by a virgin was a fulfillment of Isaiah 7:14 and identifies him as "Immanuel." Some thirty years later John the Baptist came preaching that "the kingdom of the heavens has drawn near." All four evangelists quote Isaiah 40:3 to show that this John was the one 'calling out in the wilderness.' (Matt. 3:1-3; Mark 1:2-4; Luke 3:3-6; John 1:23) At his baptism Jesus became the Messiah, the Anointed of Jehovah and the twig or root of Jesse to rule the nations. On him they must rest their hope, in fulfillment of Isaiah 11:1, 10.—Rom. 15:8, 12.

36 See how Isaiah continues to identify Messiah the King! Jesus read his commission from an Isaiah scroll (similar no doubt to the recently discovered Dead Sea scroll) to show that he was Jehovah's Anointed, and then proceeded to "declare the good news of the kingdom of God, because," as he said, "for this I was sent forth." (Luke 4:17-19, 43; Isa. 61:1, 2) The four Gospel accounts are full of details as to Jesus' earthly ministry and his manner of death as foretold in Isaiah chapter 53. Though they heard the good news of the Kingdom and saw his marvelous works, the Jews did not get the meaning because of their unbelieving hearts, in fulfillment of Isaiah 6:9, 10; 29:13 and 53:1. (Matt. 13:14, 15; John 12:38-40; Acts 28:24-27; Rom. 10:16; Matt. 15:7-9; Mark 7:6, 7) He was a stone of stumbling to them, but became the foundation cornerstone that Jehovah laid in Zion and upon which he builds his spiritual house in fulfillment of Isaiah 8:14 and 28:16. —Luke 20:17; Rom. 9:32, 33; 10:11; 1 Pet. 2:4-10.

37 The apostles of Jesus Christ continued to make good use of Isaiah's prophecy, applying it to the ministry. For example, in showing that preachers are needed in order to build faith, Paul quotes Isaiah in saying: "How comely are the feet of those who declare good news of good things!" (Rom. 10:15; Isa. 52:7; see also Romans 10:11, 16, 20, 21.) Peter, also, quotes Isaiah in showing the permanence of the good news: "For 'all flesh is like grass, and all its glory is like a blossom of grass; the grass becomes withered, and the flower falls off, but the saying of Jehovah endures forever.' Well, this is the 'saying,' this which has been declared to you as good news."—1 Pet. 1:24, 25; Isa. 40:6-8.

38 Gloriously does Isaiah paint the Kingdom hope for the future! Look! It is the "new heavens and a new earth," wherein "a king will reign for righteousness itself" and princes will rule for justice. What cause for joyfulness and exultation! (Isa. 65:17, 18; 32:1, 2) Again, Peter takes up the glad message of Isaiah: "But there are new heavens and a new earth that we are awaiting according to [God's] promise, and in these righteousness is to dwell." (2 Pet. 3:13) This wondrous Kingdom theme comes to full glory in the closing chapters of Revelation. —Isa. 66:22, 23; 25:8; Rev. 21:1-5.

39 Thus, the book of Isaiah, while containing scathing denunciations of Jehovah's enemies and of those hypocritically professing to be his servants, points in exalted tones to the magnificent hope of Messiah's kingdom whereby His great name will be sanctified. It does much to explain the wondrous truths of Jehovah's kingdom and to warm our hearts in joyful expectation of "salvation by him."—Isa. 25:9; 40:28-31.

35. How does the book focus attention on the kingdom by Messiah, and on the forerunner, John the Baptist?
36. What further rich prophetic fulfillments clearly identify Messiah the King?
37. How did Jesus' apostles quote and apply Isaiah?
38. What glorious Kingdom theme is painted in Isaiah, to be taken up later by other Bible writers?
39. To what magnificent hope does Isaiah point?

Bible Book Number Twenty-four—Jeremiah

Writer:	Jeremiah
Places Written:	Jerusalem and Egypt
Writing Completed:	c. 580 B.C.E
Time Covered:	647—c. 580 B.C.E.

THE prophet Jeremiah lived during dangerous and turbulent times. He was commissioned by Jehovah in the year 647 B.C.E., the thirteenth year of the reign of God-fearing King Josiah of Judah. While repairing the house of Jehovah, the king had found the book of the law of Jehovah. He worked hard at enforcing this, but could at most only temporarily turn back the falling away to idolatry. Josiah's grandfather Manasseh, who had reigned for fifty-five years, and his father Amon, who had been assassinated after a reign of just two years, had both done wickedly. They had encouraged the people in impure orgies and gruesome rites, so that they had become accustomed to offering incense to the "queen of the heavens" and human sacrifices to demon gods. Manasseh had filled Jerusalem with innocent blood.—Jer. 1:2; 44:19; 2 Ki. 21:6, 16, 19-23; 23:26, 27.

2 Jeremiah's task was no easy one. He had to serve as Jehovah's prophet in foretelling the desolation of Judah and Jerusalem, the burning of the magnificent temple of Jehovah and the captivity of his people—catastrophes almost unbelievable! His prophesying in Jerusalem had to continue forty years, through the reigns of bad Kings Jehoahaz, Jehoiakim, Jehoiachin (Coniah) and Zedekiah. (Jer. 1:2, 3) Later, in Egypt, he had to prophesy concerning the idolatries of the captive Jews there. His book was completed about 580 B.C.E. The time covered by Jeremiah is thus an eventful period of about sixty-seven years.—Jer. 52:31.

3 In Hebrew the name of the prophet and of his book is *Yir·m^e·yah'* or *Yir·m^e·ya'hu,* meaning, possibly, "Yah loosens [the womb]." The book occurs in all the catalogues of the Hebrew Scriptures and its canonicity has never been questioned. The dramatic fulfillment of the prophecy during Jeremiah's own lifetime attests fully to its authenticity. Moreover, Jeremiah is referred to several times by name in the Christian Greek Scriptures. (Matt. 2:17, 18; 16:14; 27:9) That Jesus had studied the book of Jeremiah is evident from the fact that in his cleansing of the temple he combined the language of Jeremiah 7:11 with that of Isaiah 56:7. (Mark 11:17; Luke 19:46) Because of Jesus' boldness and courage some people even thought him to be Jeremiah. (Matt. 16:13, 14) Jeremiah's prophecy of a new covenant (31:31-34) is referred to by Jesus at Luke 22:20 and by Paul at Hebrews 8:8-12 and 10:16, 17. Paul quotes Jeremiah 9:24 in saying: "He that boasts, let him boast in Jehovah." (1 Cor. 1:31) At Revelation 18:21 there is an even more forceful application of Jeremiah's illustration (51:63, 64) of Babylon's downfall.

4 Ancient historians confirm that the events described in the prophecy not only took place but did so exactly at the times stated by Jeremiah. For example, in referring to the fall of Jerusalem, Josephus wrote: "Now the city was taken on the ninth day of the fourth month, in the eleventh year of the reign of Zedekiah."[a] —Compare Jeremiah 52:5-7.

5 Archaeological data also give strong support to the record in Jeremiah. "The city was broken through . . . [and] Zedekiah the king of Judah and all the men of war . . . began to run away and to go out by night from the city by the way of the garden of the king, by the gate between the double wall." (Jer. 39:2, 4) The details of this route can now be reconstructed as a result of excavations in the area. Excavations since A.D. 1926 have established the fact that many towns and fortresses of Judah were destroyed at the time of the Babylonian invasion and not rebuilt.—Jer. 34:22.[b]

6 We possess a more complete biography of Jeremiah than of any of the other ancient prophets, with the exception of Moses. Jeremiah reveals much about himself, his feelings and his emotions, indicating an intrepid boldness and courage, mingled with humility and tenderness of heart. He was not only a prophet, but also a priest, a compiler of Scripture and an accurate historian. By birth he was the son

a *Antiquities of the Jews,* Flavius Josephus, X, 8.
b *The Bible as History,* 1956, Werner Keller, pages 291-293 N.Y. Ed., pages 279-281 London Ed.

1. When and by whom was Jeremiah commissioned?
2. What was his task, and what eventful years did his prophesying cover?
3. (a) How were the canonicity and authenticity of the book established in Hebrew times? (b) What further testimony on this is to be found in the Christian Greek Scriptures?
4. What do historians confirm?
5. How does archaeology support the record?
6. (a) What is known concerning Jeremiah himself? (b) What may be said as to his style of writing?

of priest Hilkiah of Anathoth, a priest's city in the country to the north of Jerusalem, "in the land of Benjamin." (1:1) Jeremiah's style of writing is clear, direct and easily understood. Illustrations and pictorial imagery abound, and the book consists of both prose and poetry.

CONTENTS OF JEREMIAH

7 The material is not arranged chronologically, but, rather, according to subject matter. Thus the account makes many changes as to time and surrounding circumstances. Finally, the desolation of Jerusalem and Judah is described in stark detail in chapter 52. This not only shows the fulfillment of much of the prophecy, but also provides the setting for the book of Lamentations, which follows.

8 **Jehovah commissions Jeremiah** (1:1-19). Is it because Jeremiah wanted to be a prophet, or because he came from a priestly family, that he is commissioned? Jehovah himself explains: "Before I was forming you in the belly I knew you, and before you proceeded to come forth from the womb I sanctified you. Prophet to the nations I made you." It is an assignment from Jehovah. Is Jeremiah willing to go? In humility he offers the excuse, "I am but a boy." Jehovah reassures him: "Here I have put my words in your mouth. See, I have commissioned you this day to be over the nations and over the kingdoms, in order to uproot and to pull down and to destroy and to tear down, to build and to plant." Jeremiah must not be afraid. "They will be certain to fight against you, but they will not prevail against you, for 'I am with you,' is the utterance of Jehovah, 'to deliver you.'" —1:5, 6, 9, 10, 19.

9 **Jerusalem an unfaithful wife** (2:1–6:30). What message does the word of Jehovah bring to Jeremiah? Jerusalem has forgotten her first love. She has left Jehovah, the source of living waters, and prostituted herself with strange gods. From a choice red vine she has been changed into "the degenerate shoots of a foreign vine." (2:21) Her skirts have been bloodied with the souls of the poor innocent ones. Even prostitute Israel has proved more righteous than Judah. God calls on these renegade sons to return, because he is their husbandly owner. But they have been as a treacherous wife. They may return if they will take away their disgusting things and circumcise their hearts. "Raise a signal toward Zion," for Jehovah will bring a calamity from the north. (4:6) Crash upon crash! As a lion out of his thicket, as a searing wind through the wilderness, with chariots like a stormwind, so will Jehovah's executioner come.

10 Go roving through Jerusalem. What do you see? Only transgressions and unfaithfulness! The people have denied Jehovah, and his word in Jeremiah's mouth must become a fire to devour them like pieces of wood. Just as they have left Jehovah to serve a foreign god, so He will make them serve strangers in a foreign land. Stubborn ones! They have eyes but cannot see, and ears but cannot hear. How horrible! Prophets and priests actually prophesy in falsehood, "and my own people have loved it that way," says Jehovah. (5:31) Calamity approaches from the north, yet "from the least one of them even to the greatest one of them, every one is making for himself unjust gain." They are saying, '"Peace! Peace!" when there is no peace.' (6:13, 14) But suddenly the despoiler will come. Jehovah has made Jeremiah a metal tester among them, but there is nothing but dross and rejected silver. They are entirely bad.

11 **Warning that temple is no protection** (7:1–10:25). The word of Jehovah comes to Jeremiah and he is to make proclamation at the temple gate. Hear him as he cries out to those entering in: You are bragging about the temple of Jehovah, but what are you doing? Oppressing the fatherless and widow, shedding innocent blood, walking after other gods, stealing, murdering, committing adultery, swearing falsely and making sacrifices to Baal! Hypocrites! You have made Jehovah's house "a mere cave of robbers." (7:11) Recall what Jehovah did to Shiloh. (1 Sam. 2:12-14; 3:11-14; 4:12-22) He will do the same to your house, O Judah, and he will throw you out, just as he threw out Ephraim (Israel) to the north.

12 This people is past praying for. Why, they are even making cakes to sacrifice to the "queen of the heavens"! Truly, "this is the nation whose people have not obeyed the voice of Jehovah its God, and have not taken discipline. Faithfulness has perished." (Jer. 7:18, 28) Judah has set disgusting things in Jehovah's house, and has burned her sons and daughters on the high places of Topheth in the valley of Hinnom. Look! It will be called "the valley of the killing," and their dead bodies will become food for fowl and beast. Rejoicing and exultation must cease out of Judah and Jerusalem.

13 They were hoping for peace and healing, but look, terror! Scattering, extermination and lamentation will result from their stubborn-

7. How is the subject matter of the prophecy arranged?
8. How did Jeremiah become a prophet, and how does Jehovah reassure him?
9. (a) In what has Jerusalem been unfaithful? (b) How will Jehovah bring calamity?
10. (a) What word does Jeremiah have for stubborn Jerusalem? (b) Of what use are their cries of "Peace!"?
11. Why must Jerusalem meet up with the same fate as Shiloh and Ephraim?
12. Why is Judah past praying for?
13. Instead of peace, what is to overtake Judah and her adopted gods?

ness. 'Jehovah is the living God and the King to time indefinite.' As for the gods that did not make the heavens and the earth, there is no spirit in them. They are a vanity and a work of mockery, and they will perish. (10:10-15) Jehovah will sling out the inhabitants of the earth. Listen! A great pounding from the land of the north that is to desolate the cities of Judah. The prophet acknowledges: 'It is not in earthling man to direct his course,' and prays for correction, that he may not be reduced to nothing.—10:23.

14 **The covenant breakers cursed** (11:1–12:17). Judah has disobeyed the words of its covenant with Jehovah. It is in vain for them to call for aid. Jeremiah must not pray for Judah, because Jehovah "has set a fire blazing" against this once luxuriant olive tree. (11:16) As Jeremiah's fellow citizens of Anathoth conspire to destroy him, the prophet turns to Jehovah for strength and help. Jehovah promises vengeance on Anathoth. Jeremiah asks, Why is it that the way of the wicked has succeeded? Jehovah assures him: 'I will uproot and destroy the disobedient nation.'—12:17.

15 **Jerusalem irreformable and doomed** (13:1–15:21). Jeremiah recounts how Jehovah commanded him to put a linen belt on his hips and then hide it in a crag by the Euphrates. When Jeremiah came to dig it up, it had been ruined. "It was not fit for anything." Thus Jehovah illustrated his determination to bring to ruin "the pride of Judah and the abundant pride of Jerusalem." (13:7, 9) He will dash them together in their drunkenness, like large jars filled with wine. "Can a Cushite change his skin? or a leopard its spots?" (13:23) Just so, Jerusalem is irreformable. Jeremiah must not pray for these people. Even if Moses and Samuel came before Jehovah to intercede for them he would not listen, for he has determined to devote them to destruction. Jehovah strengthens Jeremiah against his reproachers. He finds and eats Jehovah's words, resulting in 'exultation and rejoicing of heart.' (15:16) It is a time, not for idle joking, but for trusting in Jehovah, who has promised to make him a fortified copper wall against the people.

16 **Jehovah will send fishers and hunters** (16:1–17:27). In view of the impending desolation, Jehovah commands Jeremiah: "You must not take for yourself a wife, and you must not come to have sons and daughters in this place." (16:2) It is no time to mourn or banquet with the people, for Jehovah is about to hurl them out of the land. Then Jehovah also promises to send 'fishers to fish them and hunters to hunt them,' and by his accomplishing all this "they will have to know that [his] name is Jehovah." (16:16, 21) The sin of Judah is engraved on their heart with an iron stylus, yes, with a diamond point. "The heart is more treacherous than anything else and is desperate," but Jehovah can search the heart. None can deceive him. Those apostatizing "have left the source of living water, Jehovah." (17:9, 13) If Judah will not sanctify the sabbath day, Jehovah will devour her gates and towers with fire.

17 **The potter and the clay** (18:1–19:15). Jehovah commands Jeremiah to go down to the potter's house. There he observes how the potter turns back a spoiled vessel of clay, making it into another vessel as he pleases. Jehovah then declares himself to be the Potter to the house of Israel, with power to pull down or to build up. Next, he tells Jeremiah to take a potter's flask to the valley of Hinnom and there pronounce calamity from Jehovah, because the people have filled the place with innocent blood, burning their sons in the fire as whole burnt offerings to the Baal. Jeremiah must then break the flask in symbol of Jehovah's breaking Jerusalem and the people of Judah.

18 **No quitting under persecution** (20:1-18). Irritated by Jeremiah's bold preaching, the temple commissioner Pashhur puts him in stocks for a night. On his release Jeremiah foretells Pashhur's captivity and death in Babylon. Grieved by the derision and reproach leveled against him, Jeremiah contemplates quitting. However, he cannot keep silent. The word of Jehovah comes to be 'in his heart like a burning fire shut up in his bones,' so that he is compelled to speak. Though cursing the day of his birth, yet he can cry out: "Sing to Jehovah, you people! Praise Jehovah! For he has delivered the soul of the poor one out of the hand of evildoers."—20:9, 13.

19 **Jehovah's indignation against the rulers** (21:1–22:30). In answer to an inquiry from Zedekiah, Jeremiah notifies him of Jehovah's rage against the city: The king of Babylon will lay siege against it, and it will be destroyed by pestilence, sword, famine and fire. Jehoahaz (Shallum) will die in exile, Jehoiakim will have the burial of a he-ass, and his son Jehoiachin

14. Why is Jeremiah forbidden to pray for Judah, and how does Jehovah strengthen his prophet in an hour of danger?
15. (a) By what illustrations does Jehovah make known that Jerusalem is irreformable, and the judgment against her irreversible? (b) What results to Jeremiah from eating Jehovah's words?
16. (a) How serious are the times, and by what command does Jehovah give this emphasis? (b) How will they come to know Jehovah's name, and why does their sin not deceive him?
17. What does Jehovah illustrate by the potter and his clay vessels?
18. What hard experience does Jeremiah have, but does this silence him?
19. Of what does Jeremiah notify Zedekiah?

(Coniah) will be hurled out of Judah to die in Babylon.

20 **Hope in a "righteous sprout"** (23:1–24:10). Jehovah promises real shepherds to replace the false shepherds and a "righteous sprout" out of the stock of David, a king who "will certainly reign and act with discretion and execute justice and righteousness in the land." His name? "He will be called, Jehovah Is Our Righteousness." He will gather the dispersed remnant. (23:5, 6) If the prophets had stood in Jehovah's intimate group, they would have caused the people to hear and turn back from their bad way. Instead, says Jehovah, they "cause my people to wander about because of their falsehoods." (23:22, 32) "Look! Two baskets of figs." Jeremiah uses the good and the bad figs to illustrate a faithful remnant returning to their land in God's favor, and another class perishing in captivity.—24:1, 5, 8.

21 **Jehovah's controversy with the nations** (25:1-38). This chapter is a summary of judgments that appear in greater detail in chapters 45 to 49. By three parallel prophecies Jehovah now pronounces calamity for all the nations on earth. First, Nebuchadnezzar is identified as Jehovah's servant to devastate Judah and the surrounding nations, "and these nations will have to serve the king of Babylon seventy years." Then it will be Babylon's turn, and she will become "desolate wastes to time indefinite."—25:1-14.

22 The second prophecy is the vision of the 'cup of wine of Jehovah's rage.' Jeremiah must take this cup to the nations, and "they must drink and shake back and forth and act like crazed men" because of Jehovah's destruction coming against them. First, to Jerusalem and Judah! Then on to Egypt, back to Philistia, across to Edom, up to Tyre, to lands near and far, "and all the other kingdoms of the earth that are on the surface of the ground; and the king of Sheshach himself will drink after them." They shall drink and puke and fall. None will be spared.—25:15-29.

23 In the third prophecy Jeremiah rises to magnificent poetic heights. "From on high Jehovah himself will roar . . . against all the inhabitants of the earth." A noise, a calamity, a great tempest! "And those slain by Jehovah will certainly come to be in that day from one end of the earth clear to the other end of the earth." No lamenting, no funerals. They will be as manure on the ground. The false shepherds will be slaughtered, along with the majestic ones of their flock. There is no escape for them. Listen to their howling! Jehovah himself "is despoiling their pasturage . . . because of his burning anger."—25:30-38.

24 **Jeremiah vindicated against false prophets** (26:1–28:17). The rulers and people conspire to put Jeremiah to death. Jeremiah makes his defense. It is the word of Jehovah that he has spoken. If they kill him, they will kill an innocent man. The verdict: Not guilty. The older men introduce the precedents of the prophets Micah and Urijah in contrasting Jeremiah's course. Jehovah next commands Jeremiah to make bands and yokes, put them upon his neck, and then send them to the nations round about as symbols that they must serve the king of Babylon for three generations of rulers. Hananiah, one of the false prophets, opposes Jeremiah. He declares that the yoke of Babylon will be broken within two years and pictures this by breaking the wooden yoke. Jehovah underlines his prophecy by having Jeremiah put on iron yokes, and by foretelling that Hananiah must die that year. He does.

25 **Comfort for the exiles in Babylon** (29:1–31:40). Jeremiah writes to the exiles taken to Babylon with Jehoiachin (Jeconiah): Settle down there, for there is coming a period of seventy years of exile before Jehovah brings you back. Jehovah commands Jeremiah to write of their return in a book: Jehovah will break their yoke and "they will certainly serve Jehovah their God and David their king, whom I [Jehovah] shall raise up for them." (30:9) Rachel must hold her voice back from weeping, for her sons "will certainly return from the land of the enemy." (31:16) And now, a reassuring declaration by Jehovah! He will conclude with the houses of Judah and Israel a new covenant. Far grander this than the covenant they have broken! Jehovah will write his law deep down inside, on their hearts. "And I will become their God, and they themselves will become my people." From the least to the greatest all will know Jehovah, and he will forgive their error. (31:31-34) Their city will be rebuilt as something holy to Jehovah.

26 **Jehovah's kingdom covenant sure** (32:1–34:22). During Nebuchadnezzar's final siege of Jerusalem, Jeremiah is under restraint.

---

20. What does Jeremiah prophesy concerning a "righteous sprout," and what is illustrated by the two baskets of figs?
21. How does Jehovah use Babylon as his servant, but what, in turn, will be her fate?
22. Who must drink of the cup of Jehovah's rage? With what result?
23. In what great calamity will Jehovah's burning anger be expressed?
24. (a) What conspiracy is formed against Jeremiah, what is his defense, and what precedents are referred to in acquitting him? (b) How does Jeremiah enact the coming Babylonian bondage, and what prophecy concerning Hananiah comes true?
25. (a) What message does Jeremiah send to the exiles in Babylon? (b) With whom will Jehovah conclude a new covenant, and how will this prove to be grander than the former covenant?
26. How is the certainty of Israel's restoration emphasized, and what news does the word of Jehovah bring?

However, as a sign that Jehovah will certainly restore Israel, Jeremiah buys a field in Anathoth and puts the deeds aside in an earthenware vessel. The word of Jehovah now brings good news: Judah and Jerusalem will rejoice again and Jehovah will fulfill his kingdom covenant with David. But you, O Zedekiah, be warned that the king of Babylon will burn this city with fire and you yourself will go in captivity to Babylon. Woe to the slaveowners who agreed to free their slaves, but who have violated their covenant!

27 **Jehovah's promise to Rechab** (35:1-19). In the days of King Jehoiakim Jehovah sends Jeremiah to the Rechabites. These took refuge in Jerusalem at the first approach of the Babylonians. Jeremiah offers them wine to drink. They refuse it because of the command of their forefather Jonadab, given over 250 years earlier. A striking contrast, indeed, to the unfaithful course of Judah! Jehovah promises them: "There will not be cut off from Jonadab the son of Rechab a man to stand before me always."—35:19.

28 **Jeremiah rewrites the book** (36:1-32). Jehovah orders Jeremiah to write down all the words of his prophecies to date. He dictates these to Baruch, who then reads them aloud in the house of Jehovah on a fast day. King Jehoiakim sends for the roll, and, on hearing a part, angrily tears it up and pitches it into the fire. He commands the arrest of Jeremiah and Baruch, but Jehovah conceals them and tells Jeremiah to write a duplicate roll.

29 **Jerusalem's last days** (37:1–39:18). The record returns to the reign of Zedekiah. The king asks Jeremiah to pray to Jehovah on Judah's behalf. The prophet refuses, saying Jerusalem's doom is certain. Jeremiah attempts to go to Anathoth, is seized as a deserter, beaten, and imprisoned many days. Zedekiah then sends for him. Is there word from Jehovah? To be sure there is! "Into the hand of the king of Babylon you will be given!" (37:17) Angered by his persistent prophecies of doom, the princes throw Jeremiah into a miry cistern. Ebed-melech the Ethiopian, a eunuch in the king's house, kindly intercedes for him, so that Jeremiah is rescued from a lingering death but remains in detention in the Courtyard of the Guard. Again Zedekiah calls Jeremiah before him, only to be told: Surrender to the king of Babylon, or face captivity and the destruction of Jerusalem!

27. What promise does Jehovah make to the Rechabites, and why?
28. What makes necessary the rewriting of the book of Jeremiah's prophecies?
29. (a) What persistent prophecies does Jeremiah make? (b) How does Ebed-melech's course contrast with that of the princes?

30 The siege of Jerusalem lasts eighteen months, and then the city is broken through in the eleventh year of Zedekiah. The king flees with his army, but is overtaken. His sons and the nobles are slain before his eyes, and he is blinded and carried to Babylon in fetters. The city is burned and laid in ruins, and all except a few poor people are taken into exile to Babylon. By Nebuchadnezzar's order, Jeremiah is released from the courtyard. Before his release he tells Ebed-melech of Jehovah's promise to deliver him, 'because he trusted in Jehovah.' —39:18.

31 **Final events at Mizpah and in Egypt** (40:1–44:30). Jeremiah remains at Mizpah with Gedaliah, whom the Babylonians make governor over the remaining people. After two months Gedaliah is murdered. The people seek Jeremiah's advice, and he relays God's word to them: 'Jehovah will not uproot you from this land. Do not be afraid because of the king of Babylon. If, however, you go down to Egypt you will die!' Down to Egypt they go, taking Jeremiah and Baruch with them. At Tahpanhes in Egypt, Jeremiah makes known Jehovah's judgment of doom: The king of Babylon will set his throne in Egypt. It is in vain for Israel to worship the gods of Egypt and to resume sacrifice to the "queen of the heavens." Have they forgotten how Jehovah desolated Jerusalem for its idolatry? Jehovah will bring calamity on them in the land of Egypt, and they will not return to Judah. As a sign Jehovah is giving Pharaoh Hophra himself into the hand of his enemies.

32 **Baruch's lot** (45:1-5). Baruch is distressed at hearing Jeremiah's repeated prophecies of doom. He is told to think first of Jehovah's work of building up and tearing down rather than of himself. He will be saved through all the calamity.

33 **Jehovah's sword against the nations** (46:1–49:39). Jeremiah tells of Babylon's victories over Egypt at Carchemish and elsewhere. Though the nations be exterminated, Jacob will remain, but will not go unpunished. "The sword of Jehovah" will come against the Philistines, against proud Moab and bragging Ammon, against Edom and Damascus, Kedar and Hazor. The bow of Elam will be broken.

34 **Jehovah's sword against Babylon** (50:1–51:64). Jehovah speaks concerning Babylon: Tell it among the nations. Hide nothing. Bab-

30. What calamity now befalls Jerusalem, but how do Jeremiah and Ebed-melech fare?
31. How do the remaining people fail to heed Jeremiah's advice, and what judgment of doom does Jeremiah make known in Egypt?
32. What assurance is given Baruch?
33. Against whom will "the sword of Jehovah" come?
34. (a) What will happen to the golden cup, Babylon? (b) How, therefore, must God's people act?

lon has been captured and her gods shamed. Flee out of her. This forge hammer that has smashed the nations of all the earth has herself been broken. "O Presumptuousness," the oppressor of captive Israel and Judah, know that Jehovah of armies is their Repurchaser. Babylon will become a haunt of howling animals. "Just as with God's overthrow of Sodom and of Gomorrah . . . no man will dwell there." (50:31, 40) Babylon has been a golden cup in Jehovah's hand to make the nations drunk, but suddenly she has fallen so that she herself is broken. Howl over her, you people. Jehovah has aroused the spirit of the kings of the Medes to bring her to ruin. The mighty men of Babylon have ceased to fight. They have become like women. The daughter of Babylon will be trodden down solid like a threshing floor. "They must sleep an indefinitely lasting sleep, from which they will never wake up." The sea has come up and covered Babylon with a multitude of waves. "Get out of the midst of her, O my people, and provide each one his soul with escape from the burning anger of Jehovah." (51:39, 45) Listen to the outcry, to the great crash from Babylon! Their weapons of war must be shattered, for Jehovah is a God of recompenses. Without fail he will repay.

35 Jeremiah commands Seraiah: Go to Babylon and read aloud these words of the prophecy against Babylon. Then tie a stone to the book and pitch it into the midst of the Euphrates. "And you must say, 'This is how Babylon will sink down and never rise up because of the calamity that I am bringing in upon her.'" —51:64.

36 **Résumé of Jerusalem's fall** (52:1-34). This account is almost identical with that previously covered at 2 Kings 24:18-20; 25:1-21, 27-30.

WHY BENEFICIAL

37 This inspired prophecy is altogether upbuilding and beneficial. Look at the courageous example of the prophet himself. He was fearless in proclaiming an unpopular message to a godless people. He spurned fellowship with the wicked. He appreciated the urgency of Jehovah's message, giving himself wholeheartedly to Jehovah's work and never quitting. He found God's Word to be like a fire in his bones, and it was the exultation and rejoicing of his heart. (15:16-20; 20:8-13) May we ever be as zealous for the word of Jehovah! May we also give loyal support to God's servants, as Baruch did to Jeremiah. The sincere obedience of the Rechabites is also a splendid example to us, and so is Ebed-melech's kindly consideration for the persecuted prophet.—36:8-19, 32; 35:1-19; 38:7-13; 39:15-18.

38 The word of Jehovah that came to Jeremiah was fulfilled with astounding accuracy. This certainly strengthens faith in Jehovah's power of prophecy. Take, for example, the prophecy fulfillments that Jeremiah himself survived to see, such as: The captivity of Zedekiah and destruction of Jerusalem (Jer. 21:4-10; 39:6-9); the dethronement and death in captivity of King Shallum (Jehoahaz) (Jer. 22:11, 12; 2 Ki. 23:30-34; 2 Chron. 36:1-4); the taking captive of King Coniah (Jehoiachin) to Babylon (Jer. 22:25-27; 2 Ki. 24:15, 16); and the death within one year of the false prophet Hananiah. (Jer. 28:16, 17) All these prophecies, and more, were fulfilled just as Jehovah had foretold. Later prophets and servants of Jehovah also found Jeremiah's prophecy authoritative and beneficial. For example, Daniel discerned from the writings of Jeremiah that Jerusalem's desolation must be seventy years, and Ezra drew attention to the fulfillment of Jeremiah's words at the end of the seventy years.—Dan. 9:2; 2 Chron. 36:20, 21; Ezra 1:1; Jer. 25:11, 12; 29:10.

39 On the occasion of the last supper with his disciples Jesus not only indicated the fulfillment of Jeremiah's prophecy concerning the new covenant with the house of Israel, but he also showed this had a connection with God's kingdom. Thus he referred first to "the new covenant by virtue of my blood," whereby their sins were forgiven and they were gathered as Jehovah's spiritual nation, and then went on to say, "And I make a covenant with you, just as my Father has made a covenant with me, for a kingdom." (Luke 22:20, 29; Jer. 31:31-34) This Davidic covenant for a kingdom is referred to at a number of places in Jeremiah's prophecy. Amid all the denunciations of faithless Jerusalem, Jeremiah pointed out this ray of hope: "'Look! There are days coming,' is the utterance of Jehovah, 'and I will raise up to David a righteous sprout. And a king will certainly reign and act with discretion and execute justice and righteousness in the land.'" Yes, a king called "Jehovah Is Our Righteousness."—Jer. 23:5, 6.

40 Again Jeremiah speaks of a restoration: "And they will certainly serve Jehovah their God and David their king, whom I shall raise up for them." (30:9) Finally, he tells of the

35. What sign assures Babylon's fall?
36. What résumé now follows?
37. (a) What example of courageous zeal do we find in Jeremiah? (b) In what respects are Baruch, the Rechabites and Ebed-melech also fine examples for us?
38. How does a consideration of Jeremiah strengthen faith in Jehovah's power of prophecy?
39. (a) What two covenants, as referred to also by Jesus, are highlighted in Jeremiah's prophecy? (b) What Kingdom hope is proclaimed?
40. The return of a remnant from Babylon, as foretold by Jeremiah, gives assurance of what?

good word that Jehovah has spoken concerning Israel and Judah, to the effect that "in those days and at that time I shall make sprout for David a righteous sprout," so as to multiply his seed and so that there will be "a son ruling as king upon his throne." (33:15, 21) As surel as a remnant returned from Babylon, so wi the kingdom of this righteous "sprout" ex cute justice and righteousness in all the eart —Luke 1:32.

Bible Book Number Twenty-five— Lamentations

Writer:	**Jeremiah**
Place Written:	**Near Jerusalem**
Writing Completed:	**607 B.C.E.**
Time Covered:	**Undetermined**

THIS book of the inspired Scriptures is certainly well named. It is a lament expressing deep sorrow over that calamitous happening in the history of God's chosen people, the destruction of Jerusalem in 607 B.C.E. by Nebuchadnezzar, king of Babylon. In Hebrew this book is named by its first word, *Ei·khah'!*, meaning "How!" The translators of the Greek Septuagint Bible called the book *Thre'noi*, which means "Dirges; Laments." The Talmud uses the term *Qi·noth'*, which means "Dirges; Elegies." It was Jerome, writing in Latin, who named it *La·men·ta·tion'es*, from which our English title comes.

2 In English versions of the Bible, Lamentations is placed after Jeremiah, but in the Hebrew canon it is usually found in the Hagiographa, or Writings, along with the Song of Solomon, Ruth, Ecclesiastes and Esther—a small group collectively known as the five *Meg·il·loth'* (Rolls). In some modern Hebrew Bibles it is placed between Ruth or Esther and Ecclesiastes, but in ancient copies it is said to have followed Jeremiah, as it does in our Bible today. Some believe Jeremiah and Lamentations were originally one volume.

3 The book does not name the writer. However, there is little doubt it was Jeremiah. In the Greek *Septuagint Version* the book carries this preface: "And it came to pass, after Israel was taken captive, and Jerusalem made desolate, that Jeremias sat weeping, and lamented with this lamentation over Jerusalem, and said . . ." (Bagster) Jerome considered these words spurious and omitted them from his version. However, the ascribing of Lamentations to Jeremiah is the accepted tradition of the Jews and is confirmed by the *Syriac Version*, the Latin *Vulgate*, the Targum of Jonathan and the Talmud, among others.

4 Some critics have tried to prove that Jere miah did not write Lamentations. Howeve *The One Volume Bible Commentary* cites a evidence of Jeremiah's writership "the vivi descriptions of Jerusalem in chapters 2 and 4 which are evidently the pen-pictures of an eye witness; likewise the strongly sympathetic tem per and prophetic spirit of the poems through out, as well as their style, phraseology, an thought, which are all so characteristic of Jere miah."[a] There are many parallel expressions i Lamentations and Jeremiah, such as that o the extreme sorrow of 'eyes running down wit waters (tears)' (Lam. 1:16; 2:11; 3:48, 49; Je 9:1; 13:17; 14:17) and those of disgust at th prophets and priests because of their corrup tion. (Lam. 2:14; 4:13, 14; Jer. 2:34; 5:30, 31 14:13, 14) The passages at Jeremiah 8:18-2 and 14:17, 18 show that prophet to be quit capable of the mournful style of Lamentations

5 The time of writing is generally agreed t have been soon after the fall of Jerusalem 607 B.C.E. The horror of the siege and th burning of the city was still fresh in Jere miah's mind, and his anguish is vividly ex pressed. One commentator remarks that n single facet of sorrow is fully exploited in an given place but each returns again and agai in the several poems. Then he says: "This tu mult of thought is one of the very stronges evidences that the book stands close to th events and emotions it purports to commu nicate."[b]

6 The construction of Lamentations is o great interest to the Bible scholar. There ar five chapters, or rather, five lyrical poems. Th first four are acrostics, with each verse begin

a 1942, edited by J. R. Dummelow, page 483.
b *Studies in the Book of Lamentations*, 1954, Norma K. Gottwald, page 31.

1. How is the book of Lamentations well named?
2. How has it been grouped and placed in the Bible?
3, 4. What evidence is there for Jeremiah's writership?
5. By what reasoning do we arrive at the time o writing?
6. What is interesting in the book's style and construction?

ing successively with one of the twenty-two etters of the Hebrew alphabet. However, the hird chapter has sixty-six verses, so that hree successive verses begin with the same etter before passing on to the next letter. The fth poem is not acrostic, though it does have wenty-two verses.

7 Lamentations expresses overwhelming grief t the siege, capture and destruction of Jeru- alem by Nebuchadnezzar, and is unsurpassed n any literature for its vividness and pathos. 'he writer expresses deep sorrow over the esolation, misery and confusion that he views. 'amine, sword and other horrors have brought readful suffering to the city, all of it because f the sins of the people, the prophets and the riests, and as a direct penalty from God. Iowever, hope and faith in Jehovah remain, nd to him go the prayers for restoration.

CONTENTS OF LAMENTATIONS

8 "O how she has come to sit solitary, the city hat was abundant with people!" Thus **the first oem** opens its lament. The daughter of Zion vas a princess, but her lovers have abandoned ter and her people have gone into exile. Her ates are laid desolate. Jehovah has punished er for the abundance of her transgressions. She has lost her splendor. Her adversaries have aughed over her collapse. She has gone down n a wondrous manner and has no comforter, nd her remaining people are hungry. She sks: "Does there exist any pain like my pain?" She stretches out her hands and says: "Jeho- 'ah is righteous, for it is against his mouth hat I have rebelled." (1:12, 18) She calls on Jehovah to bring calamity on her exulting nemies, even as he has done on her.

9 "O how Jehovah in his anger beclouds the laughter of Zion!" **The second poem** shows that t is Jehovah himself that has thrown down to arth the beauty of Israel. He has caused fes- ival and sabbath to be forgotten, and has cast off his altar and sanctuary. O the pathetic ights in Jerusalem! "My eyes have come to heir end in sheer tears. My intestines are in a erment. My liver has been poured out to the very earth, on account of the crash of the laughter of my people." (2:11) To what shall ne liken the daughter of Jerusalem? How shall ne comfort the daughter of Zion? Her own prophets proved worthless and unsatisfying. Now passersby laugh scorn at her: "Is this the ity of which they used to say, 'It is the per- ection of prettiness, an exultation for all the earth'?" (2:15) Her enemies have opened their mouth and whistled and ground their teeth, saying, 'This is the day we have hoped for to swallow her down.' Her children faint for famine, and women eat their own offspring. Corpses litter the streets. "In the day of the wrath of Jehovah there proved to be no escapee or survivor."—2:16, 22.

10 **The third poem,** of sixty-six verses, stresses Zion's hope in God's mercy. By many meta- phors the prophet shows that it is Jehovah who has brought the captivity and desolation. In the bitterness of the situation the writer asks God to remember his affliction, and expresses faith in the loving-kindness and mercies of Jehovah. Three successive verses begin with "Good," and show the propriety of waiting for salvation from Jehovah. (3:25-27) Jehovah has caused grief, but he will also show mercy. But for now, despite confession of rebellion, Jehovah has not forgiven; he has blocked the prayers of his people and made them "mere offscouring and refuse." (3:45) With bitter tears the prophet recalls that his enemies hunted for him as for a bird. However, Jehovah drew near to him in the pit and said: "Do not be afraid." He calls on Jehovah to answer the reproach of the enemy: "You will pursue in anger and annihi- late them from under the heavens of Jehovah." —3:57, 66.

11 "O how the gold that shines becomes dim, the good gold!" **The fourth poem** bemoans the faded glory of Jehovah's temple, whose stones are poured out in the streets. The precious sons of Zion have become of little value, like jars of earthenware. There is neither water nor bread, and those raised in luxury "have had to em- brace ash heaps." (4:5) The punishment is even greater than that for the sin of Sodom. The Nazirites, once 'purer than snow and whiter than milk,' have become "darker than black- ness itself" and are all shriveled up. (4:7, 8) Better to have been slain by the sword than by the famine, at a time when women have boiled their own children! Jehovah has poured out his burning anger. The unbelievable has hap- pened—the adversary has come into the gates of Jerusalem! And why? "Because of the sins of her prophets, the errors of her priests," who poured out righteous blood. (4:13) The face of Jehovah is not toward them. However, the error of the daughter of Zion has come to its finish and she will not again be carried into exile. Now it is your turn, O daughter of Edom, to drink the bitter cup of Jehovah!

12 **The fifth poem** opens with an appeal to Je-

---

7. What grief does Jeremiah express, but what hope remains?
8. What desolation is described in the first poem, but how does the daughter of Zion express herself?
9. (a) From whom has this calamity come on Jerusa- em? (b) How does Jeremiah speak of the scorn heaped on her, and of the terrible conditions in the city?

10. Of what qualities of God does the writer make mention, as a basis for hope?
11. In what ways has Jehovah's burning anger been poured out on Zion, and why?
12. What humble appeal is made in the fifth poem?

hovah to remember his orphaned people. It is their forefathers that have sinned, and whose error they must now bear. Mere servants rule over them, and they are tortured by pangs of hunger. The exultation of their heart has ceased and their dancing has been changed into mourning. They are sick at heart. Humbly they acknowledge Jehovah: "As for you, O Jehovah, to time indefinite you will sit. Your throne is for generation after generation." They cry out: "Bring us back, O Jehovah, to yourself, and we shall readily come back. Bring new days for us as in the long ago. However, you have positively rejected us. You have been indignant toward us very much."—5:19-22.

WHY BENEFICIAL

13 The book of Lamentations expresses Jeremiah's complete confidence in God. In the very depths of sorrow and crushing defeat, with absolutely no hope of comfort from any human source, the prophet looks forward to salvation by the hand of the great God of the universe, Jehovah. Lamentations should inspire all true worshipers toward obedience and integrity, while at the same time providing a fearsome warning concerning those who disregard the greatest name and what it stands for. History does not show another ruined city lamented in such pathetic and touching language. It is certainly of benefit in describing the severity of God toward those who continue to be rebellious, stiffnecked and unrepenting.

13. What confidence does Lamentations express, yet why is it beneficial in showing the severity of God?

14 Lamentations is also beneficial in showi the fulfillment of a number of divine warnin and prophecies. (Lam. 1:2—Jer. 30:14; La 2:15—Jer. 18:16; Lam. 2:17—Lev. 26:17; La 2:20—Deut. 28:53) Also note that Lamentatio provides vivid testimony to the fulfillment Deuteronomy 28:63-65. Moreover, the book co tains a number of references to other parts the sacred Scriptures. (Lam. 2:15—Ps. 48: Lam. 3:24—Ps. 119:57) Daniel 9:5-14 corrob rates Lamentations 1:5 and 3:42 in showi that the calamity came on account of t people's own transgressions.

15 Heartrending indeed is the tragic plight Jerusalem! Amid all this, however, Lament tions voices confidence in Jehovah's lovin kindness and mercy, and that he will reme ber Zion and bring her back. (3:31, 32; 4:2 It expresses hope in "new days" like the da of long ago, when Kings David and Solom reigned in Jerusalem. There is still Jehovah covenant with David for an everlasting kin dom! "His mercies will certainly not come an end. They are new each morning." And th will continue toward those who love Jehov until, under his righteous Kingdom rule, eve creature that lives will exclaim in thankf ness: "Jehovah is my share."—Lam. 5:2 3:22-24.

14. What divine warnings and prophecies are shown Lamentations to be fulfilled, and how does it tie in wi other inspired writings?
15. To what "new days" does Lamentations point fo ward?

Bible Book Number Twenty-six— Ezekiel

Writer:	**Ezekiel**
Place Written:	**Babylon**
Writing Completed:	**591 B.C.E.**
Time Covered:	**613-591 B.C.E.**

IN THE year 617 B.C.E. Jehoiachin king of Judah surrendered Jerusalem to Nebuchadnezzar, who took the foremost people of the land and the treasures of the house of Jehovah and of the king's house to Babylon. Among the captives were the king's family and the princes, the valiant and mighty men and craftsmen and builders, and Ezekiel the son of Buzi the priest. (2 Ki. 24:11-17; Ezek. 1:1-3) With heavy hearts, these exiled Israelites had completed their weary journey of approximately 1,000 miles from a land of hills, springs and valley to one of vast level plains. Now they lived b the river Chebar in the midst of a mighty en pire, surrounded by a people of strange cu toms and of pagan worship. Nebuchadnezza permitted them to have their own houses, kee servants and engage in business. (Ezek. 8: Jer. 29:5-7; Ezra 2:65) If industrious, the could become prosperous. Would they fall int the traps of Babylonian religion and materia ism? Would they continue to rebel against J hovah? Would they accept their exile as di cipline from him? They would meet new test in the land of their exile.

1. What were the circumstances of the exiles in Babylon, and what new tests did they face?

2 During these critical years leading down to the destruction of Jerusalem, Jehovah did not deprive himself or the Israelites of the services of a prophet. Jeremiah was stationed in Jerusalem itself, Daniel was right in the palace of the king in Babylon and Ezekiel was the prophet to the Jewish exiles by the river Chebar. Ezekiel was both priest and prophet, a distinction he enjoyed with Jeremiah and, later, Zechariah. (Ezek. 1:3) Throughout his book he is addressed ninety-two times as "son of man," a point of significance when studying his prophecy, because, in the Greek Scriptures, Jesus is also referred to as "Son of man" more than eighty times. His name Ezekiel (in Hebrew *Yᵉhhez·qel'*) means "God Strengthens." It was in the fifth year of Jehoiachin's exile, 613 B.C.E., that Ezekiel was commissioned by Jehovah as prophet. We read of him still at his work in the twenty-seventh year of the exile, twenty-two years later. (1:1, 2; 29:17) He was married, but his wife died on the day that Nebuchadnezzar began his final siege of Jerusalem. (24:2, 18) The date and manner of his own death are unknown.

3 That Ezekiel actually wrote the book that bears his name and that it has a rightful place in the canon of Scripture is not in dispute. It was included in the canon in Ezra's day and appears in the catalogues of early Christian times, notably that of Origen. Its authenticity is also testified to by the striking similarity between its symbolisms and those of Jeremiah and the Revelation.—Ezek. 24:2-12—Jer. 1:13-15; Ezek. 23:1-49—Jer. 3:6-11; Ezek. 18:2-4—Jer. 31:29, 30; Ezek. 1:5, 10—Rev. 4:6, 7; Ezek. 5:17—Rev. 6:8; Ezek. 9:4—Rev. 7:3; Ezek. 2:9; 3:1—Rev. 10:2, 8-10; Ezek. 23:22, 25, 26—Rev. 17:16; 18:8; Ezek. 27:30, 36—Rev. 18:9, 17-19; Ezek. 37:27—Rev. 21:3; Ezek. 48:30-34—Rev. 21:12, 13; Ezek. 47:1, 7, 12—Rev. 22:1, 2.

4 Further proof of authenticity is to be found in the dramatic fulfillment of Ezekiel's prophecies against neighboring nations, such as Tyre, Egypt and Edom. For example, Ezekiel prophesied that Tyre would be devastated, and this was partly fulfilled when Nebuchadnezzar took the city after a siege of thirteen years. (Ezek. 26:2-21) At that time the Tyrians transferred with the bulk of their treasures to a small island half a mile from the mainland. However, Jehovah's judgment was that Tyre should be *completely* destroyed. He had foretold through Ezekiel: "I will scrape her dust away from her and make her a shining, bare surface of a crag. . . . Your stones and your woodwork and your dust they will place in the very midst of the water." (26:4, 12) This was all fulfilled more than 250 years later, when Alexander the Great moved against Tyre. The historian Arrian relates that Alexander's soldiers scraped up all the debris of the ruined mainland city and threw it into the sea, making a great causeway, about 200 feet wide, that reached out to the island city. Then, with an intricate siegework, they scaled the 150-foot-high walls to take the city in 332 B.C.E. Thousands were killed and many more were sold into slavery. As Ezekiel had also predicted, Tyre became the 'bare surface of a crag and a drying yard for dragnets.' (26:14)[a] On the other side of the Promised Land, the treacherous Edomites were also annihilated, in fulfillment of Ezekiel's prophecy. (25:12, 13; 35:2-9)[b] And, of course, Ezekiel's prophecies about the destruction of Jerusalem and Israel's restoration also proved to be accurate.—17:12-21; 36:7-14.

5 In the early years of his prophetic career Ezekiel proclaimed God's certain judgments against unfaithful Jerusalem and warned the exiles against idolatry. (14:1-8; 17:12-21) The captive Jews were showing no real signs of repentance. Their responsible men made a practice of consulting Ezekiel, but they paid no attention to the messages from Jehovah that he conveyed to them. They went right ahead with their idolatry and materialistic practices. The loss of their temple, their holy city and their dynasty of kings came as a terrific shock, but it awakened only a few to humility and repentance.—Psalm 137.

6 Ezekiel's prophecies in the later years emphasized the hope of restoration. They also took Judah's neighbor nations to task for exulting over her downfall. Their own humiliation, together with Israel's restoration, would sanctify Jehovah before their eyes. In summary, the purpose of the captivity and of the restoration was: You people, both of the Jews and of the nations, will have to know that I am Jehovah. This sanctification of Jehovah's name is highlighted throughout the book, there being at least sixty occurrences of the expression: "You [or, they] will have to know that I am Jehovah."

CONTENTS OF EZEKIEL

7 The book falls naturally into three sections. The first, chapters 1 to 24, contains warnings

a *The Watchtower,* 1959, pages 310-312.
b *The Watchtower,* 1957, pages 489-492.

2. (a) Which three prophets were outstanding during these critical years? (b) Significantly, how is Ezekiel addressed, and what does his name mean? (c) During what years did Ezekiel prophesy, and what is known of his life and his death?
3. What can be said as to Ezekiel's writership, and as to the canonicity and authenticity of the book?
4. What dramatic fulfillments have Ezekiel's prophecies seen?
5. How did the Jews react to Ezekiel's early prophecies?
6. What do Ezekiel's later prophecies emphasize, and how is the sanctification of Jehovah's name highlighted?
7. Into what three natural sections do the contents fall?

of the certain destruction of Jerusalem. The second section, chapters 25 to 32, contains prophecies of doom to several pagan nations. The last section, chapters 33 to 48, consists of prophecies of the restoration, culminating in the vision of a new temple and holy city. The prophecies are dated and set down in chronological order, with the exception of those to the pagan nations.

8 **Jehovah commissions Ezekiel as watchman** (1:1–3:27). In his initial vision, in 613 B.C.E., Ezekiel sees a violent wind from the north, together with a cloud mass and quivering fire. Out of it come four winged living creatures, with faces of a man, a lion, a bull and an eagle. They have the appearance of burning coals, and each is accompanied, as it were, by a wheel in the midst of a wheel of fearful height, with rims full of eyes. They move in any direction in constant unity. Above the heads of the living creatures is the likeness of an expanse, and above the expanse a throne on which is "the appearance of the likeness of the glory of Jehovah."—1:28.

9 Jehovah calls on the prostrate Ezekiel: "Son of man, stand up." He then commissions him as prophet to Israel and to the rebellious nations round about. Whether they heed or not is beside the point. At least they will know that a prophet of the Lord Jehovah has been in their midst. Jehovah makes Ezekiel eat the roll of a book, which becomes like honey for sweetness in his mouth. He tells him: "Son of man, a watchman is what I have made you to the house of Israel." (2:1; 3:17) Ezekiel must faithfully give the warning, or die.

10 **Enacting the siege of Jerusalem** (4:1–7:27). Jehovah tells Ezekiel to engrave a sketch of Jerusalem on a brick. He must stage a mock siege against it as a sign to Israel. To impress the point, he is to lie before the brick 390 days on his left side and 40 days on his right side, while subsisting on a very meager diet. That Ezekiel actually acts out the scene is indicated by his plaintive appeal to Jehovah for a change of cooking fuel.—4:9-15.

11 Jehovah has Ezekiel portray the calamitous end of the siege by shaving off his hair and beard. A third of this he must burn, a third hack with a knife and a third scatter to the wind. Thus, at the end of the siege, will Jerusalem's inhabitants die by famine and pestilence, and by the sword, and the rest be scattered among the nations. Jehovah will make her a devastation. Why? Because of the offensiveness of her depraved and detestable idolatry. Wealth will buy no relief. In the day o Jehovah's fury they will throw their silver i the streets, "and they will have to know tha I am Jehovah."—7:27.

12 **Ezekiel's vision of apostate Jerusalem** (8:1 11:25). It is now 612 B.C.E. In a vision Ezeki is transported to faraway Jerusalem, where h sees the detestable things that are happening i Jehovah's temple. In the courtyard there is disgusting symbol inciting Jehovah to jealous Boring through the wall, Ezekiel finds sevent of the elder men worshiping before wall carv ings of loathsome beasts and dungy idol They excuse themselves by saying: "Jehova is not seeing us. Jehovah has left the land. (8:12) At the north gate women are weepin over the pagan god Tammuz. But that is no all! Right in the entrance of the temple itsel there are twenty-five men, with backs turne on the temple, worshiping the sun. They ar profaning Jehovah to his face, and he wil surely act in his rage!

13 Now look! Six men appear with smashin weapons in their hands. Among them is seventh clothed with linen, with a recorder inkhorn. Jehovah tells this man in linen t pass through the midst of the city and put mark on the foreheads of the men sighing an groaning over the detestable things being don in its midst. Next, he tells the six men to mov in and kill off everyone, "old man, young ma and virgin and little child and women," o whom there is no mark. This they do, startin with the old men before the house. The man i linen reports: "I have done just as you hav commanded me."—9:6, 11.

14 Ezekiel again sees the glory of Jehovah rising above the cherubs. A cherub thrusts ou fiery coals from between the wheelwork, an the man in linen takes them and scatters them over the city. Ezekiel has a final view of th twenty-five sun worshipers in their foolish mistaken security. As for the scattered ones o Israel, Jehovah promises to regather them an give them a new spirit. But what of these wicked false worshipers in Jerusalem? "Upo their head I shall certainly bring their ow way," says Jehovah. (11:21) The glory of Je hovah is seen ascending from over the city and Ezekiel proceeds to tell the vision to th exiled people.

15 **Further prophecies in Babylon concerning Jerusalem** (12:1–19:14). Ezekiel becomes th actor in another symbolic scene. During th

8. What does Ezekiel see in his initial vision?
9. What is involved in Ezekiel's commission?
10. What sign to Israel does Ezekiel enact?
11. (a) How does Ezekiel portray the calamitous end of the siege? (b) Why will there be no relief?
12. What detestable things are seen by Ezekiel in his vision of apostate Jerusalem?
13. What orders do the man in linen and the six mer with weapons carry out?
14. What does the vision finally show as to Jehovah's glory and his judgments?
15. By what further illustration does Ezekiel show the certainty of Jerusalem's going into captivity?

ytime he brings out of his house his luggage r exile, and then at night he goes through a le in the wall of the city with his face cov- ed. He explains this to be a portent: "Into ile, into captivity they will go." (12:11) Those upid prophets who walk after their own irit! They are crying, "There is peace!" when ere is no peace. (13:10) Even if Noah, Daniel id Job were in Jerusalem, they could not de- ver a soul but themselves.

16 The city is like a worthless vine. The wood no good for making poles, not even pegs! It burned at both ends and scorched in the iddle—useless. How faithless and worthless is Jerusalem become! Born from the land of e Canaanites, she was picked up by Jehovah an abandoned infant. He reared her and itered into a marriage covenant with her. He ade her beautiful, "fit for royal position." .6:13) But she has become a prostitute, turn- g to the nations as they pass by. She has orshiped their images and burned her sons in e fire. Her end will be destruction at the ands of these same nations, her paramours. he is worse than her sisters Sodom and Sa- aria. Even so, Jehovah, the merciful God, will ake atonement for her and restore her ac- ording to his covenant.

17 Jehovah gives the prophet a riddle and ien relates the interpretation. It illustrates e futility of Jerusalem's turning to Egypt for elp. A great eagle (Nebuchadnezzar) comes nd plucks the top (Jehoiachin) of a lofty edar, bringing him to Babylon, and plants in is place a vine (Zedekiah). The vine turns its ranches toward another eagle, Egypt, but is successful? It is torn out by the roots! Jeho- ah himself will take a tender twig from the fty treetop of the cedar and transplant it pon a high and lofty mountain. There it will row into a majestic cedar as a residing place or "all the birds of every wing." All will have know that Jehovah has done it.—17:23, 24.

18 Jehovah reproves the Jewish exiles for ieir proverbial saying: "Fathers are the ones hat eat unripe grapes, but it is the teeth of the ons that get set on edge." No, "the soul that sinning—it itself will die." (18:2, 4) The ighteous one will keep living. Jehovah takes o delight in the death of the wicked. His de- ight is to see the wicked turn from his evil 'ays and live. As for the kings of Judah, like oung lions they have been snared by Egypt nd by Babylon. Their voice will "no more e heard on the mountains of Israel."—19:9.

19 **Denunciations against Jerusalem** (20:1–23:49). Time has moved on to 611 B.C.E. Again the elders among the exiles come to Ezekiel to inquire of Jehovah. What they hear is a recital of Israel's long history of rebellion and depraved idolatry and a warning that Jehovah has called for a sword to execute judgment against her. He will make Jerusalem "a ruin, a ruin, a ruin." But, glorious hope! Jehovah will hold the kingship ("the crown") for the one who comes with "the legal right" and will give it to him. (21:27) Ezekiel reviews the detestable things done in Jerusalem, "the bloodguilty city." The house of Israel has become like "scummy dross" and is to be gathered into Jerusalem and liquefied there as in a furnace. (22:2, 18) The unfaithfulness of Samaria (Israel) and Judah is illustrated by two sisters. Samaria as Oholah prostitutes herself to the Assyrians and is destroyed by her lovers. Judah as Oholibah does not learn a lesson, but does even worse, prostituting herself first to Assyria and then to Babylon. She will be utterly destroyed, "and you people will have to know that I am the Lord Jehovah."—23:49.

20 **The final siege of Jerusalem commences** (24:1-27). It is 609 B.C.E. Jehovah announces to Ezekiel that the king of Babylon has besieged Jerusalem on this tenth day of the tenth month. He compares the walled city to a widemouthed cooking pot with its "choice" inhabitants as the flesh therein. Heat it up! Boil out all the uncleanness of Jerusalem's abominable idolatry! On that same day Ezekiel's wife dies, but, in obedience to Jehovah, the prophet does not mourn. This is a sign that they must not mourn at Jerusalem's destruction, for it is a judgment from Jehovah, that they may know who he is. Jehovah will send an escapee to advise of the destruction of "the beautiful object of their exultation," and until he arrives Ezekiel must speak no more to the exiles. —24:25.

21 **Prophecies against the nations** (25:1–32:32). Jehovah foresees that the surrounding nations will rejoice at Jerusalem's downfall and use it as an occasion for casting reproach on the God of Judah. They shall not go unpunished! Ammon will be given to the Orientals, and Moab also. Edom will be made a devastated place, and great acts of vengeance will be executed against the Philistines. All of them "will have to know that I am Jehovah when I bring my vengeance on them."—25:17.

;. How is the worthlessness of Jerusalem pictured, ut why will there be a restoration?
7. What does Jehovah show by the riddle of the eagle nd the vine?
8. (a) What principles does Jehovah state in reproving he Jewish exiles? (b) What judgment awaits the kings f Judah?
19. (a) Against the background of ruin, what hope does Ezekiel make known? (b) How does he illustrate the unfaithfulness of Israel and Judah and its result?
20. To what is besieged Jerusalem likened, and what potent sign does Jehovah give with regard to his judgment on her?
21. How will the nations have to know Jehovah and his vengeance?

22 Tyre receives special mention. Proud of her thriving commerce, she is like a pretty ship in the midst of the seas, but soon she will lie broken in the depths of the waters. "I am god," boasts her leader. (28:9) Jehovah has his prophet deliver a dirge concerning the king of Tyre: As a beauteous anointed cherub he has been in Eden, the garden of God, but Jehovah will put him out of his mountain as profane and he will be devoured by a fire from within. Jehovah also will be sanctified in his bringing destruction on scornful Sidon.

23 Jehovah now tells Ezekiel to set his face against Egypt and its Pharaoh and to prophesy against them. "My Nile River belongs to me, and I—I have made it for myself," brags Pharaoh. (29:3) He and the Egyptians that believe in him will also have to know that Jehovah is God, and the lesson will be administered by a forty-year desolation. Ezekiel here inserts some information actually revealed to him later, in 591 B.C.E. Jehovah will give Egypt to Nebuchadnezzar as compensation for his service in wearing down Tyre. (Nebuchadnezzar took very little spoil at Tyre, since the Tyrians escaped with most of their wealth to their island city.) In a dirge Ezekiel makes known that Nebuchadnezzar will despoil the pride of Egypt, "and they also will have to know that I am Jehovah."—32:15.

24 **Watchman to the exiles; restoration foretold** (33:1–37:28). Jehovah reviews with Ezekiel his responsibility as watchman. The people are saying, "The way of Jehovah is not adjusted right." So he must make it clear to them how wrong they are. (33:17) But now it is 607 B.C.E., the fifth day of the tenth month.[a] An escapee arrives from Jerusalem to tell the prophet: "The city has been struck down!" (33:21) Ezekiel, now free again to speak to the exiles, tells them that any thoughts they have of rescuing Judah are futile. Though they come to Ezekiel to hear Jehovah's word, he is to them just like a singer of love songs, like one with a pretty voice playing well on a stringed instrument. They pay no attention. However, when it comes true, they will know that a prophet has been in their midst. Ezekiel rebukes the false shepherds who have forsaken the flock to feed themselves. Jehovah the perfect Shepherd will gather the scattered sheep and bring them to a fat pasturage on the mountains of Israel. There he will raise up over them one shepherd, 'even his servant David.' (34:23) Jehovah himself will become their God. He will make a covenant of peace and pour upon them rains of blessing.

25 Ezekiel again prophesies desolation for Mount Seir (Edom). However, the devastated places of Israel will be rebuilt, for Jehovah will have compassion for his holy name, to sanctify it before the nations. He will give his people a new heart and a new spirit, and their land will again become "like the garden of Eden." (36:35) Ezekiel now sees a vision of Israel represented as a valley of dry bones. Ezekiel prophesies over the bones. Miraculously they begin to have flesh, breath and life again. Just so will Jehovah open the burial places of captivity in Babylon and restore Israel to its land again. Ezekiel takes two sticks representing the two houses of Israel, Judah and Ephraim. In his hand they become one stick. Thus, when Jehovah restores Israel, they will be united in a covenant of peace under his servant "David."

26 **The attack by Gog of Magog on restored Israel** (38:1–39:29). Then will come invasion from a new quarter! Drawn out to the attack by the tantalizing peace and prosperity of Jehovah's restored people, Gog of Magog will make his frenzied attack. He will rush in to engulf them. At this Jehovah will rise in the fire of his fury. He will set each one's sword against his brother's, and bring on them pestilence and blood and a flooding downpour of hailstones, fire and sulphur. They will go down knowing that Jehovah is "the Holy One in Israel." (39:7) His people will then light fires with the enemies' shattered war equipment and bury the bones in "the Valley of Gog's Crowd." (39:11) Carrion birds will eat their flesh and drink their blood. Henceforth Israel will dwell in security, with no one to make them tremble, and Jehovah will pour out his spirit on them.

27 **Ezekiel's vision of the temple** (40:1–48:35). We come to the year 593 B.C.E. It is the fourteenth year since the destruction of Solomon's temple, and the repentant ones among the exiles are in need of encouragement and hope. Jehovah transports Ezekiel in a vision to the land of Israel and sets him down on a very high mountain. Here, in vision, he sees a temple and "the structure of a city to the south." An angel instructs him to "tell everything that you are seeing to the house of Israel." (40:

[a] While the Masoretic text says that the escapee arrived from Jerusalem in the twelfth year, other manuscripts read "eleventh year," and the text is so translated by Lamsa, Moffatt and in *An American Translation.*

22. What special mention does Tyre receive, and how will Jehovah be sanctified in connection with Sidon?
23. What will Egypt have to know, and how will this come about?
24. (a) What is Ezekiel's responsibility as watchman? (b) At news of Jerusalem's fall, what message does Ezekiel proclaim to the exiles? (c) What promise of blessing is highlighted in chapter 34?
25. (a) Why and how will Jehovah make the land like Eden? (b) What is illustrated by the vision of the dry bones? by that of the two sticks?
26. Why does Gog of Magog attack, and with what result?
27. What does Ezekiel see in a visionary visit to the land of Israel, and how does God's glory appear?

Then he shows Ezekiel all the details of the mple and its courtyards, measuring the walls, e gates, the guard chambers, the dining oms and the temple itself, with its Holy and ost Holy. He takes Ezekiel to the east gate. .nd, look! the glory of the God of Israel was ming from the direction of the east, and his ice was like the voice of vast waters; and the rth itself shone because of his glory." (43:2) e angel fully instructs Ezekiel concerning e House (or temple), the altar and its sacri- es, the rights and duties of the priests, the vites and the chieftain, and the apportioning the land.

28 The angel brings Ezekiel back to the en- ance of the House, where the prophet sees ter going forth from the threshold of the ouse toward the east, by the south side of the tar. It starts as a trickle, but gets bigger and gger until it becomes a torrent. Then it flows to the Dead Sea, where fish come to life and fishing industry springs up. On either side of e torrent, trees provide food and healing for e people. The vision then gives the inheri- nces of the twelve tribes, not overlooking the ien resident and the chieftain, and describes e holy city to the south, with its twelve gates med after the tribes. The city is to be called a most glorious name: "Jehovah Himself There."—48:35.

WHY BENEFICIAL

29 The pronouncements, the visions and the omises that Jehovah gave to Ezekiel were all ithfully related to the Jews in exile. While any scoffed at and ridiculed the prophet, me did believe. These benefited greatly. They ere strengthened by the promises of restora- on. Unlike other nations taken into captivity, ey preserved their national identity, and Je- vah restored a remnant, as he foretold, in 7 B.C.E. (Ezek. 28:25, 26; 39:21-28; Ezra 2:1; 1) They rebuilt the house of Jehovah and re- wed true worship there.

30 The principles set out in Ezekiel are also valuable to us today. Apostasy and idolatry, upled with rebellion, can only lead to Jeho- ah's disfavor. (Ezek. 6:1-7; 12:2-4, 11-16) Each e will answer for his own sin, but Jehovah ill forgive the one who turns back from his rong course. He will be granted mercy and will keep living. (18:20-22) God's servants must be faithful watchmen like Ezekiel, even in difficult assignments and under ridicule and reproach. We must not let the wicked die unwarned, with their blood upon our heads. (3:17; 33:1-9) Shepherds of God's people bear a heavy responsibility to care for the flock. —34:2-10.

31 Outstanding in the book of Ezekiel are the prophecies concerning the Messiah. He is referred to as the one "who has the legal right" to the throne of David and to whom it must be given. In two places he is spoken of as "my servant David," also as "shepherd," "king" and "chieftain." (21:27; 34:23, 24; 37:24, 25) Since David was long since dead, Ezekiel was speaking of the one who was to be both David's Son and Lord. (Ps. 110:1; Matt. 22:42-45) Ezekiel, like Isaiah, speaks of the planting of a tender twig that will be put on high by Jehovah. —Ezek. 17:22-24; Isa. 11:1-3.

32 It is of interest to compare Ezekiel's temple vision with the Revelation vision of the "holy city Jerusalem." There are differences to be noted; for example, Ezekiel's temple is separate and to the north of the city, while Jehovah himself is the temple of the city of Revelation. In each case, however, there is the flowing forth of the river of life, the trees bearing monthly crops of fruit and leaves for healing, and the presence of the glory of Jehovah. Each vision makes its contribution toward appreciating Jehovah's kingship and his provision of salvation for those who render him sacred service.—Ezek. 43:4, 5—Rev. 21:11; Ezek. 47:1, 8, 9, 12—Rev. 22:1-3.

33 The book of Ezekiel emphasizes that Jehovah is holy. It makes known that the sanctification of Jehovah's name is more important than anything else. " 'I shall certainly sanctify my great name, . . . and the nations will have to know that I am Jehovah,' is the utterance of the Lord Jehovah." As the prophecy shows, he will sanctify his name by destroying all profaners of that name, including Gog of Magog. Wise are all those who now sanctify Jehovah in their lives by meeting his requirements for acceptable worship. These will find healing and eternal life by the river that flows from his temple. Transcendent in glory and exquisite in beauty is the city that is called "Jehovah Himself Is There"!—Ezek. 36:23; 38:16; 48:35.

. What does the vision show concerning the stream at proceeds forth from the House, and what is re- aled as to the city and its name?
. In what way did the Jewish exiles benefit by ekiel's prophecy?
. What principles set out in Ezekiel are valuable to today?

31. What prophecies foretell the coming of the Messiah?
32. How does Ezekiel's temple vision compare with the Revelation vision of the "holy city"?
33. What does Ezekiel emphasize, and what will result to those who now sanctify Jehovah in their lives?

Bible Book Number Twenty-seven— Daniel

Writer:	**Daniel**
Place Written:	**Babylon**
Writing Completed:	**536 B.C.E.**
Time Covered:	**618-536 B.C.E.**

IN THIS day when all nations of earth stand on the brink of disaster, the book of Daniel brings to attention prophetic messages of momentous import. Whereas the Bible books of Samuel, Kings and Chronicles are based on eyewitness records of the history of God's typical kingdom (the Davidic dynasty), Daniel focuses on the nations of the world and gives forevisions of the "power struggle" of the great dynasties from Daniel's time down till the "time of the end." This is world history written in advance. It leads up to an absorbing climax in showing what comes to pass "in the final part of the days." Like Nebuchadnezzar, the nations have to learn the hard way "that the Most High is Ruler in the kingdom of mankind," and that finally he gives it to one "like a son of man," the Messiah and Leader, Christ Jesus. (Dan. 12:4; 10:14; 4:25; 7:13, 14; 9:25; John 3:13-16) By paying close attention to the prophetic fulfillments of the inspired book of Daniel we will appreciate more fully Jehovah's power of prophecy and his assurances of protection and blessing for his people.—2 Pet. 1:19.

2 The book is named after its writer. "Daniel" (Hebrew: *Dâ·nî·yel'*) means "God Is [My] Judge" or "God's Judge." Ezekiel, who lived at the same time, confirms that Daniel was an actual person, naming him along with Noah and Job. (Ezek. 14:14, 20; 28:3) Daniel dates the beginning of his book as "the third year of the kingship of Jehoiakim the king of Judah." This was 618 B.C.E., Jehoiakim's third year as *tributary king* to Nebuchadnezzar.[a] Daniel's prophetic visions continued down to Cyrus' third year, about 536 B.C.E. (Dan. 1:1; 2:1; 10:1, 4) What eventful years were covered by Daniel's life-span! His early days were spent under God's kingdom in Judah. Then as a teen-age prince, along with his noble Judean companions, he was taken to Babylon to live through the rise and fall of that third world power of Bible history. However, that was not the end, for Daniel survived to serve as government official in the fourth world power of Medo-Persia. Daniel must have lived nearly one hundred years.

3 The book of Daniel has always been included in the Jewish catalogue of inspired Scriptures. Fragments of Daniel have been found among those of the other canonical books in the Dead Sea Scrolls, some of which have already been dated back to the second or first century B.C.E.[b] However, an even more important proof of the book's authenticity is to be found in the references to it in the Christian Greek Scriptures. Jesus specifically names Daniel in his prophecy on "the conclusion of the system of things," wherein he makes several quotations from the book.—Dan. 9:27; 11:31 and 12:11—Matt. 24:15 and Mark 13:14; Dan. 12:1—Matt. 24:21; Dan. 7:13, 14—Matt. 24:30.

4 Though "higher critics" of the Bible have called in question the historicalness of Daniel's book, archaeological finds over the years have completely routed their assertions. For example, these critics leveled scorn at Daniel's statement that Belshazzar was king in Babylon at the time that Nabonidus was reputed to be ruler. (Dan. 5:1) Archaeology has now established beyond question that Belshazzar was an actual person and that there was a dual rulership in Babylon for many years. For example, they have unearthed a tablet, dated in the twelfth year of Nabonidus, containing an oath made in the name of Nabonidus, the king, and Belshazzar, the king's son, thus showing that Belshazzar ranked with his father.[c] This is also of interest in explaining why Belshazzar offered to make Daniel "the third one in the kingdom" if he could interpret the handwriting on the wall. Nabonidus would be considered the first, Belshazzar the second, and Daniel came to be heralded as the third ruler. (Dan 5:16, 29) One authority now says: "Cuneiform allusions to Belshazzar have thrown so much light upon the role which he played that his

a *Clarke's Commentary,* Vol. IV, pages 562, 563.

b *The Biblical Archaeologist,* Vol. XVII, 1954, No. 1 page 16.

c *Archaeology and the Bible,* 1949, George A. Barton page 483.

1. What kind of history is contained in Daniel, and what does it highlight?
2. What confirms Daniel to be an actual person, and during what eventful period did he prophesy?
3. What proves the canonicity and authenticity of the book?
4. How has archaeology put the "higher critics" to flight?

lace in history stands clearly revealed. There re many texts which indicate that Belshazzar lmost equaled Nabonidus in position and restige. Dual rulership during most of the last Jeo-Babylonian reign is an established fact. Jabonidus exercised supreme authority from is court in Tema in Arabia, while Belshazzar cted as coregent in the homeland with Bab- lon as his center of influence. It is evident that elshazzar was not a feeble viceroy; he was ntrusted with 'the kingship.' "[a]

5 Some have tried to discredit Daniel's ac- ounts of the fiery furnace and the lions' pit chapters 3 and 6), saying that these are leg- ndary inventions. However, remarkable con- rmations have again come from the archaeol- gists, digging in the ruins at Babylon. One iscovery was thought to be a brick kiln, until n inscription at the base was found to read: This is the place of burning where men who lasphemed the gods of Chaldea died by fire." n another place a deep pit was unearthed, earing the inscription: "The place of execution here men who angered the king died torn by vild animals." Though these are not neces- arily the identical places mentioned in the ook of Daniel, they confirm that such places xisted in Daniel's time.[b]

6 *The Westminster Dictionary of the Bible* icely sums up the situation with the book of aniel, in these words: "The asserted historical naccuracies in Daniel are not statements which re disproved by history, but only statements hich have seemed difficult to harmonize with he meager accounts of secular historians. The sserted historical inaccuracies have, moreover, een steadily diminishing before the increasing nowledge of the times of Cyrus. . . . The rowth of our knowledge of this period shows ow cautious one should be in doubting the istorical accuracy of the Biblical records." –1944, page 130.

7 The Jews included his book, not with the rophets, but with the Writings. However, he English Bible follows the catalogue order f the Greek *Septuagint* and the Latin *Vulgate* y placing Daniel between the major and the ninor prophets. There are actually two parts o the book. The first of these, chapters one to ix, gives in chronological order the experiences f Daniel and his companions in governmental ervice from 617 to 538 B.C.E. (Dan. 1:1, 21) The second part, comprising chapters seven to welve, is written in the first person by Daniel himself as recorder and describes private visions and angelic interviews that Daniel had from 553[c] to 536 B.C.E. (Dan. 7:2, 28; 8:2; 9:2; 12:5, 7, 8) The two parts together make up the one harmonious book of Daniel.

a *The Yale Oriental Series · Researches*, Vol. XV, 1929.
b *Dead Men Tell Tales*, 1946, Harry Rimmer, pages 25-327.

. What other inscriptions have given support to the ecord?
. What has the growth of knowledge shown concerning his period?
. What two parts make up the book?

CONTENTS OF DANIEL

8 **Preparation for State service** (1:1-21). In 617 B.C.E. Daniel comes to Babylon with the captive Jews. The sacred utensils from Jerusalem's temple come also, to be stored in a pagan treasure-house. Daniel and his three Hebrew companions are among the royal Judean youths chosen for a three-year course of training in the king's palace. Resolved in his heart not to pollute himself with the king's pagan delicacies and wine, Daniel proposes a ten-day test of a vegetable diet. The test turns out in favor of Daniel and his companions, and God gives them knowledge and wisdom. Nebuchadnezzar appoints the four to stand before him as counselors. The last verse, which may have been added long after the preceding portion was written, indicates that Daniel was still in royal service some eighty years after his going into exile, or about 538 B.C.E.

9 **Dream of the dreadful image** (2:1-49). In the second year of his kingship as world ruler, 606-605 B.C.E., Nebuchadnezzar is agitated by a dream. On awakening he is unable to remember it and calls in his magic-practicing priests to tell him the dream and its interpretation. He offers them great gifts, but they protest that no one but the gods can show the king the thing that he is asking. The king becomes furious and orders the wise men to be put to death. Since the four Hebrews are included in this decree, Daniel asks for time to reveal the dream. They pray to Jehovah for guidance. Jehovah reveals the dream and its meaning to Daniel, who then goes before the king and says: "There exists a God in the heavens who is a Revealer of secrets, and he has made known to King Nebuchadnezzar what is to occur in the final part of the days." (2:28) Daniel describes the dream. It is about an immense image. Its head is of gold, its breasts and arms of silver, its belly and thighs of copper and its legs of iron, with feet partly iron, partly clay. A stone strikes and crushes the image and becomes a large mountain to fill the whole earth. What does this mean? Daniel makes known that the king of Babylon

c According to *The Westminster Dictionary of the Bible*, 1944, page 64, and *Babylonian Chronology*, 1956, Parker and Dubberstein, pages 13, 29, Belshazzar began to reign as coregent in the third regnal year of Nabonidus (Nabunaid), which was 553 B.C.E.; Daniel 7:1.

8. What leads to Daniel and his companions' entering Babylonian governmental service?
9. What dream and interpretation does God reveal to Daniel, and how does Nebuchadnezzar show his appreciation?

is the head of gold. After his kingdom there will follow a second, a third and a fourth kingdom. Finally, "the God of heaven will set up a kingdom that will never be brought to ruin. . . . It will crush and put an end to all these kingdoms, and it itself will stand to times indefinite." (2:44) In gratitude and appreciation the king extols Daniel's God as a "God of gods" and makes Daniel and his companions administrators in the kingdom.

10 **Three Hebrews survive the fiery furnace** (3:1-30). Nebuchadnezzar erects a mighty image of gold, ninety feet high, and orders the rulers of the empire to assemble for its dedication. At the sound of special music all are to fall down and worship the image. Any who fail to do so are to be thrown into the burning fiery furnace. It is reported that Daniel's three companions, Shadrach, Meshach and Abednego, have failed to comply. They are brought before the enraged king, where they boldly testify: "Our God whom we are serving is able to rescue us. . . . the image of gold that you have set up we will not worship." (3:17, 18) Filled with fury, the king orders the furnace to be heated seven times more than customary, and to bind the three Hebrews and throw them in. As they do this, the executioners are killed by the fiery flame. Nebuchadnezzar becomes frightened. What is this he sees in the furnace? Four men are walking about unharmed in the midst of the fire and "the fourth one is resembling a son of the gods." (3:25) The king calls on the three Hebrews to step out of the fire. Out they come, unsinged. As a result of their courageous stand for true worship, Nebuchadnezzar proclaims freedom of worship for the Jews throughout the empire.

11 **Dream of the "seven times"** (4:1-37). This dream appears in the record as Daniel's transcription of a state document of Babylon. It was written by the humbled Nebuchadnezzar. Nebuchadnezzar first acknowledges the might and kingdom of the Most High God. Then he relates a frightening dream and how it was fulfilled upon himself. He saw a tree that reached to heaven and provided shelter and food for all flesh. A watcher called out: 'Chop the tree down. Band its stump with iron and copper. Let seven times pass over it, and it will be known that the Most High is Ruler in the kingdom of mankind and sets up over it the lowliest one of mankind.' (4:14-17) Daniel interpreted the dream, making known that the tree represented Nebuchadnezzar. A fulfillment of this prophetic dream soon followed. At a time of expressing great pride the king was afflicted with madness, and lived as a beast in the field for seven years. After that his sanity was restored and he acknowledged Jehovah's supremacy.

12 **Belshazzar's feast: handwriting interpreted** (5:1-31). It is the fateful night of October 5-6, 539 B.C.E. King Belshazzar, coregent of Babylon with his father Nabonidus, makes a big feast for a thousand of his grandees. The king, under the influence of wine, calls for the sacred gold and silver vessels from Jehovah's temple and from these they drink in their debauchery while praising their pagan gods. Immediately a hand appears and writes a cryptic message on the wall. The king is terrified. His wise men cannot interpret the writing. Finally Daniel is brought in. The king offers to make him the third one in the kingdom if he can read and interpret the writing, but Daniel tells him to keep his gifts to himself. Then he goes on to make known the writing and its meaning: "MENE, MENE, TEKEL and PARSIN. . . . God has numbered the days of your kingdom and has finished it. . . . you have been weighed in the balances and have been found deficient. . . . your kingdom has been divided and given to the Medes and the Persians." (5:25-28) That very night Belshazzar is killed, and Darius the Mede receives the kingdom.

13 **Daniel in the lions' pit** (6:1-28). High officials in Darius' government frame mischief against Daniel by having the king pass a law that places a thirty-day prohibition on making a petition to any god or man other than the king. Anyone disobeying is to be thrown to the lions. Daniel refuses to obey this law affecting his worship and turns to Jehovah in prayer. He is thrown into the lions' pit. Miraculously, Jehovah's angel shuts the mouths of the lions, and next morning King Darius is glad to find Daniel unharmed. The enemies are now fed to the lions, and the king issues a decree to fear the God of Daniel, as "he is the living God." (6:26) Daniel prospers in government service on into the reign of Cyrus.

14 **Visions of the beasts** (7:1–8:27). We return to the "first year of Belshazzar," whose reign began in 553 B.C.E. Daniel receives a private dream, which he records in Aramaic. He sees four huge and fearsome beasts appear each in its turn. The fourth is unusually strong, and a small horn comes up among its other horns "speaking grandiose things." (7:8) The Ancient of Days appears and takes his seat. "Thousand

---

10. What results from the three Hebrews' bold stand against image worship?
11. What frightening dream involving "seven times" did Nebuchadnezzar have, and was it fulfilled upon him?
12. During what debauchery does Belshazzar see the fateful handwriting, how does Daniel interpret it, and how is it fulfilled?
13. How is a plot against Daniel thwarted, and what decree does Darius then issue?
14. In a private dream, what vision does Daniel have concerning four beasts and the rulership of the kingdom?

ousands" minister to him. "Someone like a n of man" comes before him and is "given lership and dignity and kingdom, that the oples, national groups and languages should serve even him." (7:10, 13, 14) Daniel then ceives the interpretation of the vision of the ur beasts. They represent four kings, or kingms. From among ten horns on the fourth ast a small horn arises. It becomes mighty d makes war on the holy ones. However, the avenly Court steps in to give "the kingdom d the rulership and the grandeur of the ngdoms under all the heavens . . . to the peoe who are the holy ones of the Supreme One." 7:27.

[15] Two years later, long before Babylon's ll, Daniel sees another vision, which he rerds in Hebrew. A he-goat with a conspicuous rn between its eyes struggles with, and overmes, a proud ram that has two horns. The -goat's great horn is broken and four lesser rns come forth, and out of one of these mes a little horn that becomes great, even to fying the army of the heavens. A period of 300 days is foretold until the holy place is to brought into its "right condition." (8:14) briel explains the vision to Daniel. The ram ands for the kings of Media and Persia. The -goat is the king of Greece, whose kingdom ll be broken into four. Later, a king of fierce untenance will stand up "against the Prince princes." Since the vision "is yet for many ys," Daniel must keep it secret for the prest.—8:25, 26.

[16] **Messiah the Leader foretold** (9:1-27). "The st year of Darius . . . of the Medes" finds Danexamining Jeremiah's prophecy. Realizing at the foretold seventy-year desolation of rusalem is nearing its close, Daniel prays to hovah in confession of his own and Israel's ns. (Dan. 9:2-4; Jer. 29:10) Gabriel appears, to ake known that there will be "seventy weeks . . to terminate the transgression, and to ish off sin, and to make atonement for ror." Messiah the Leader will come at the d of sixty-nine weeks, after which he will be t off. The covenant will be kept in force for e many till the end of the seventieth week, d, finally, there will be desolation and an termination.—Dan. 9:24-27.

[17] **North vs. south, Michael stands up** (10:1–:13). It is "the third year of Cyrus," and nce about 536 B.C.E., not long after the Jews' turn to Jerusalem. After a three weeks' fast, aniel is by the bank of the river Hiddekel. (Dan. 10:4; Gen. 2:14) An angel appears to him and explains that the 'prince of Persia' opposed his coming to Daniel, but that "Michael, one of the foremost princes," helped him. He now relates to Daniel a vision that is for "the final part of the days."—Dan. 10:13, 14.

[18] As it opens, this enthralling vision speaks of the Persian dynasty and a coming struggle with Greece. A mighty king will stand up with extensive dominion, but his kingdom will be broken into four. Eventually there will be two long lines of kings, the king of the south as opposed to the king of the north. The power struggle will surge back and forth. These incorrigibly bad kings will keep speaking a lie at one table. "At the time appointed," the warfare will flare up again. There is to be a profaning of God's sanctuary, and "the disgusting thing that is causing desolation" is to be set in place. (11:29-31) The king of the north will speak marvelous things against the God of gods and give glory to the god of fortresses. When "in the time of the end" the king of the south engages with the king of the north in a pushing, the king of the north will flood over into many lands, entering also "into the land of the Decoration." Disturbed by reports out of the east and north, he will rage forth and plant "his palatial tents between the grand sea and the holy mountain of Decoration." So, "he will have to come all the way to his end, and there will be no helper for him."—11:40, 41, 45.

[19] The grand vision continues: Michael will stand up 'in behalf of the sons of God's people.' There is to be "a time of distress" unprecedented in human history, but those found written in the book will escape. Many will awake from the dust to everlasting life, "and the ones having insight will shine like the brightness of the expanse." They will bring many to righteousness. Daniel is to seal up the book "until the time of the end." "How long will it be to the end of the wonderful things?" The angel mentions time periods of three and a half times, 1,290 days and 1,335 days, and that only "the ones having insight will understand." Happy are such ones! Finally, the angel holds out to Daniel the reassuring promise that he will rest, and stand up for his lot "at the end of the days."—12:1, 3, 4, 6, 10, 13.

WHY BENEFICIAL

[20] All who are determined to maintain integrity in an alien world do well to consider the fine example of Daniel and his three com-

What vision does Daniel have featuring a he-goat d a two-horned ram? How does Gabriel explain it?
What causes Daniel to pray to Jehovah, and what es Gabriel now make known concerning "seventy eks"?
Under what circumstances does an angel again pear to Daniel?
18. What prophetic history of the king of the north and the king of the south does Daniel now record?
19. What things follow on Michael's standing up 'in behalf of the sons of God's people'?
20. What fine examples of integrity and prayerful reliance on Jehovah are to be found in the book of Daniel?

panions. No matter how vicious the threat, these continued to live by divine principles. When their lives were in peril, Daniel acted "with counsel and sensibleness" and with respect for the king's superior authority. (2:14-16) When the issue was forced, the three Hebrews preferred the burning fiery furnace to an act of idolatry, and Daniel preferred the lions' den to foregoing his privilege of prayer to Jehovah. In each instance Jehovah granted protection. (3:4-6, 16-18, 27; 6:10, 11, 23) Daniel himself provides a splendid example of prayerful reliance on Jehovah God.—2:19-23; 9:3-23; 10:12.

21 Daniel's visions are thrilling and faith-strengthening to consider. First, consider the four visions concerning the world powers: (1) There is the vision of the dreadful image, whose head of gold represents the king of Babylon, after whom three other kingdoms rise, as pictured in the other parts of the image. These are the kingdoms that are crushed by the "stone," which in its turn becomes "a kingdom that will never be brought to ruin," God's kingdom. (2:31-45) (2) There follow Daniel's private visions, the first being that of the four beasts, representing "four kings." These are like a lion, a bear, a leopard with four heads, and a beast with big teeth of iron and, among its horns, a small horn. (7:1-8, 17-28) (3) Next, there is the vision of the ram (Medo-Persia), the he-goat (Greece) and the small horn. (8:1-27) (4) Finally, we have the vision of the king of the south and the king of the north. World historians agree that Daniel 11:5-19 accurately describes the rivalry between the Egyptian and Seleucid offshoots of Alexander's Grecian Empire between 323 and 190 B.C.E. From verse 20 the prophecy continues to trace the course of successor nations of the south and north. Jesus' reference to "the disgusting thing that is causing desolation" (Dan. 11:31) in his prophecy on the end of the world shows that this power struggle of the two "kings" continues right down to "the conclusion of the system of things." How comforting the prophecy's assurance that in the "time of distress such as has not been made to occur since there came to be a nation until that time," Michael himself will stand up in behalf of God's people, even as he came to the angel's help!—11:20–12:1; 10:13, 20, 21[a]

22 Then, there is Daniel's prophecy of the "seventy weeks," after sixty-nine weeks of which "Messiah the Leader" was to appear. Remarkably, 483 years (69 times 7 years) after Artaxerxes (Longimanus), in his twentiet year, sent forth the command to rebuild Jer salem with its wall and this command wa carried out, Jesus of Nazareth was baptized i the Jordan River and anointed with holy spiri so becoming Christ (that is, Anointed On Hebrew: Messiah).[b] That was in the ye 29 (A.D.). Thereafter, as Daniel also foretol there came an "extermination" when Jerusale was desolated A.D. 70.—Dan. 9:24-27; Luke 21-23; 21:20.

23 In Nebuchadnezzar's dream concerning th chopped-down tree, as recorded by Daniel i chapter 4, it is related that the king, wh boasted of his own achievements and had co fidence in his own might, was humbled by J hovah God. He was made to live as a beast the field until he recognized "that the Mo High is Ruler in the kingdom of mankind, an that to the one whom he wants to he gives it (4:32) Are we today going to be like Neb chadnezzar, boasting in our achievements an placing our confidence in the might of men, s that God has to mete out punishment to u or will we wisely acknowledge that he is th Ruler in the kingdom of men, and place ou confidence in his kingdom?

24 The Kingdom hope is emphasized throug out the book of Daniel in a faith-inspiring way Jehovah God is shown as the Supreme So ereign who sets up a kingdom that will neve be brought to ruin and that will crush all othe kingdoms. (2:19-23, 44; 4:25) Even the paga kings Nebuchadnezzar and Darius were com pelled to acknowledge Jehovah's supremac (3:28, 29; 4:2, 3, 37; 6:25-27) Jehovah is exalte and glorified as the Ancient of Days who judge the Kingdom issue and gives to "someone lik a son of man" the everlasting "rulership an dignity and kingdom, that the peoples, nation groups and languages should all serve eve him." It is "the holy ones of the Supreme One that share with Christ Jesus, "the Son of man, in the Kingdom. (Dan. 7:13, 14, 18, 22; Mat 24:30; Rev. 14:14) He is Michael, the gre prince, who exercises his Kingdom power t crush and put an end to all the kingdoms this old world. (Dan. 12:1; 2:44; Matt. 24:3, 21 Rev. 12:7-10) The understanding of these prop ecies and visions should encourage lovers o righteousness to bestir themselves and rov through the pages of God's Word to find th truly "wonderful things" of God's Kingdo purposes that are revealed to us through th inspired and beneficial book of Daniel.—Da 12:2, 3, 6.

a *"Your Will Be Done on Earth,"* 1958, pages 220-323.

b Nehemiah 2:1-8; see also footnote b, page 92.

21. What four visions are recorded concerning the world powers, and why is it faith-strengthening to consider these today?

22. How did Daniel's prophecy of the "seventy weeks" have a remarkable fulfillment?

23. What lesson do we learn from the humbling Nebuchadnezzar?

24. (a) How is the Kingdom hope emphasized throug out Daniel? (b) What should this book of prophec encourage us to do?

...ible Book Number Twenty-eight— Hosea

Writer:	**Hosea**
Place Written:	**Samaria (District)**
Writing Completed:	**After 745 B.C.E.**
Time Covered:	**Before 811— after 745 B.C.E.**

...HE last twelve books of the Hebrew Scriptures are commonly referred to in English-...eaking countries as "The Minor Prophets." ...he expression in common use in Germany, ...he Little Prophets," would seem to be more ...ppropriate, for these books are certainly not ...inor in importance, although their combined ...ngth is still less than that of Isaiah or Jere-...iah. In the Hebrew Bible they were consid-...ed as one volume and called the "Book of ...e Twelve." Their collection together in this ...anner was probably for the purpose of pres-...vation, since a single small roll might have ...en easily lost. As in the case with each of ...ese twelve books, the first one is named after ...s writer, Hosea, whose name means "Salva-...on; Deliverance."

2 In the book bearing his name little is re-...aled directly concerning Hosea except that ... was the son of Beeri. His prophecies con-...rn Israel almost exclusively, Judah being ...entioned only in passing; and while Jeru-...lem is not mentioned by Hosea, Israel's dom-...ant tribe, Ephraim, is spoken of by name ...irty-seven times and Israel's capital, Samaria, ...x times.

3 The first verse of the book tells us that ...osea served as Jehovah's prophet for an un-...ually long time, from near the end of the ...ign of Israel's King Jeroboam II on into the ...ign of Hezekiah of Judah. That is from some ...me before 811 until after 745 B.C.E., a min-...ium of sixty-six years. However, his time of ...ophetic service no doubt spread over some ...ars into the reigns of Jeroboam and Heze-...ah. During this time Amos, Isaiah, Micah and ...ded were other faithful prophets of Jehovah. —Amos 1:1; Isa. 1:1; Mic. 1:1; 2 Chron. 28:9.

4 The authenticity of the prophecy is con-...rmed by its being quoted a number of times ... the Christian Greek Scriptures, and is at-...sted by Jesus himself when he quotes Ho-...a 10:8 in pronouncing judgment on Jeru-...lem: "Then they will start to say to the mountains, 'Fall over us!' and to the hills, 'Cover us over!' " (Luke 23:30) This same passage is partially quoted at Revelation 6:16. Matthew (2:15) quotes Hosea 11:1 in showing the fulfillment of the prophecy: "Out of Egypt I called my son." Hosea's prophecy of the restoration of *all* Israel was fulfilled in that many from the ten-tribe kingdom joined with Judah before its captivity and their descendants were among those who returned after the exile. (Hos. 1:11; 2 Chron. 11:13-17; 30:6-12, 18, 25; Ezra 2:70) From the time of Ezra the book has occupied its rightful place in the Hebrew canon as "the word of Jehovah by Hosea." —Hos. 1:2.

5 Why did Jehovah send Hosea as his prophet to Israel? It was because of Israel's unfaithfulness and contamination with Baal worship, in violation of Jehovah's covenant. In the Promised Land Israel had become an agricultural people, but in doing so they adopted not only the Canaanites' way of life but also their religion with its worship of Baal, a god symbolic of the reproductive forces of nature. In Hosea's day Israel had turned completely from the worship of Jehovah to a riotous, drunken ceremonial that included immoral relations with temple prostitutes. Israel attributed prosperity to Baal. She was disloyal to Jehovah, unworthy of him, and must therefore be disciplined. Jehovah was going to show her that her material possessions were not from Baal and so he sent Hosea to warn Israel what failure to repent would mean. After Jeroboam II died, Israel faced her most terrible period. A reign of terror, with a number of rulers being assassinated, continued down until the Assyrian captivity in 740 B.C.E. During this time two factions fought each other, one wanting to form an alliance with Egypt, and the other, with Assyria. Neither group trusted in Jehovah.

6 Hosea's style of writing is revealing. He is often tender and sensitive in his wording and repeatedly emphasizes Jehovah's loving-kindness and mercy. He dwells on each small sign of repentance that he sees. His language is at other times abrupt and impulsive. What he lacks in rhythm he makes up in force and

2. (a) By what names are the last twelve books of ...e Hebrew Scriptures sometimes called? (b) What is ...own about Hosea, and whom does his prophecy con-...rn?
... For how long did Hosea prophesy, and who were ...her prophets of this period?
... What quotations and prophetic fulfillments prove the ...thenticity of Hosea?
5. Because of what unfaithfulness did Jehovah punish Israel?
6. What is revealing about Hosea's style of writing?

power. He expresses very strong feeling and changes thought rapidly.

7 At the outset of his prophetic career Hosea was commanded to take "a wife of fornication." (1:2) Certainly Jehovah had a purpose in this. Israel had been to Jehovah like a wife who had become unfaithful, committing adultery, fornication. Yet he would show his love for her and try to recover her. Hosea's wife Gomer could accurately illustrate this. It is understood that after the birth of the first child she became unfaithful and apparently bore the other children in adultery. (2:5-7) This is indicated by the record's stating she "bore to *him* [Hosea] a son," but omitting any reference to the prophet in connection with the birth of the other two children. (1:3, 6, 8) Chapter 3, verses 1-3, seems to speak of Hosea's taking back Gomer, purchasing her as though a slave, and this ties in with Jehovah's taking back his people after they repented from their adulterous course.

8 The ten-tribe northern kingdom of Israel, to whom the words of Hosea's prophecy are principally directed, was also known as "Ephraim," after the name of the dominant tribe in the kingdom. These names, Israel and Ephraim, are used interchangeably in the book.

CONTENTS OF HOSEA

9 **Israel's adulterous course illustrated** (1:1–3:5). Hosea's "wife of fornication" bears the prophet a son, Jezreel. Later she has two other children, a daughter, Lo-ruhamah, meaning "She Was Not Shown Mercy," and a son, Lo-ammi, meaning "Not My People." These two names Jehovah gave to indicate he would "no more show mercy again to the house of Israel," and to emphasize his rejection of them as a whole as his people. (1:6, 9) Yet the sons of Judah and Israel, as "sons of the living God," are to be gathered in unity under one head, "because great will be the day of Jezreel." (1:10, 11) Cleansed of adulterous Baal worship, God's people will return to Him as their husband. (2:16) Jehovah will give security to Israel and will engage her to him for time indefinite in righteousness, in justice, in loving-kindness, in mercies and in faithfulness. In harmony with the name Jezreel (meaning "God Will Sow Seed"), Jehovah promises: "I shall certainly sow her like seed for me in the earth, . . . and I will say to those not my people: 'You are my people'; and they, for their part, will say: 'You are my God.'" (2:23) Like a wife repentant from her adultery, "Israel will come back and certainly look for Jehovah their God, and fo[r] David their king."—3:5.

10 **Prophetic judgments against Ephraim (an[d] Judah)** (4:1–14:9). The first verse of chapter [4] gives the setting for the prophetic warning[s] that follow: "Jehovah has a legal case wit[h] the inhabitants of the land, for there is n[o] truth nor loving-kindness nor knowledge o[f] God in the land." What will result from thi[s] condition? "Because the knowledge is what yo[u] yourself have rejected, I shall also reject yo[u] from serving as a priest to me; and becaus[e] you keep forgetting the law of your God, [I] shall forget your sons, even I," says Jehovah. (4:1, 6) The very spirit of fornication ha[s] caused Israel to wander away. There will be a[n] accounting for harlotrous Israel and Judah, bu[t] they will seek Jehovah when they find them[-] selves "in sore straits."—5:15.

11 Hosea pleads with the people: "Let us re[-] turn to Jehovah, for . . . he will heal us." Je[-] hovah delights in loving-kindness and divin[e] knowledge rather than in sacrifices and burn[t] offerings, but the loving-kindness of Ephraim and Judah is "like the dew that early goe[s] away." (6:1, 4) Ephraim is "like a simple[-] minded dove without heart." They go to Egyp[t] and to Assyria for aid rather than to Jehovah. (7:11) It is woe to them. Why? They are loa[f-] ing about, scheming bad things, overstepping Jehovah's covenant and transgressing agains[t] his law. "For it is wind that they keep sowing, and a stormwind is what they will reap." (8:7) Jehovah will remember their error and giv[e] attention to their sins. "They will becom[e] fugitives among the nations." (9:17) Israel i[s] a degenerating vine whose heart has becom[e] hypocritical. Instead of sowing seed in righ[-] teousness and reaping in accord with loving[-] kindness, Israel has plowed wickedness an[d] reaped unrighteousness. "Out of Egypt I calle[d] my son," reminds Jehovah. (11:1) Yes, he love[d] Israel from his boyhood, but Israel has su[r-] rounded Him with lying and deception. Jehova[h] counsels: "To your God you should return, keeping loving-kindness and justice; and le[t] there be a hoping in your God constantly." —12:6.

12 In the thirteenth chapter Hosea sums u[p] all that has gone before regarding Israel['s] early promise and Jehovah's tender care, Is[-] rael's forgetfulness and the nation's finall[y] turning against Jehovah. Jehovah declares: "[I] proceeded to give you a king in my anger, an[d] I shall take him away in my fury." (13:11) But, then, there will be restoration: "From th[e]

7. What is illustrated in Gomer's unfaithfulness and her later recovery?
8. What names are used interchangeably in the book?
9. What do the names of Gomer's children indicate as to how Jehovah would deal with Israel?
10. What is to result from the nation's rejection [of] knowledge?
11. How does Hosea plead with the people, but why [is] it woe to them?
12. (a) Of what has Israel been forgetful? (b) Wh[at] restoration is promised?

hand of Sheol I shall redeem them; from death I shall recover them. Where are your stings, O Death? Where is your destructiveness, O Sheol?" (13:14) However, horrible indeed will be the fate of rebellious Samaria.

13 The book concludes with the heartrending plea: 'Do come back, O Israel, to Jehovah your God, for you have stumbled in your error. Seek pardon, and offer in return the young bulls of your lips. Jehovah will show you mercy and love. He will become like refreshing dew to you, and you will blossom as the lily and the olive tree.' The wise and discreet will understand these things: "For the ways of Jehovah are upright, and the righteous are the ones who will walk in them; but the transgressors are the ones who will stumble in them."—14:1-6, 9.

WHY BENEFICIAL

14 The book of Hosea strengthens faith in Jehovah's inspired prophecies. Everything that Hosea prophesied concerning Israel and Judah came true. Israel was deserted by her lovers among the idolatrous neighbor nations and reaped the whirlwind of destruction from Assyria in 740 B.C.E. (Hos. 8:7-10; 2 Ki. 15:20; 17:3-6, 18) However, Hosea had foretold that Jehovah would show mercy to Judah and save her, but not by military might. This was fulfilled when Jehovah's angel slew 185,000 of the Assyrians threatening Jerusalem. (Hos. 1:7; 2 Ki. 19:34, 35) Nevertheless, Judah was included in the judgment of Hosea 8:14: "And I shall certainly send fire into his cities and it must devour the dwelling towers of each one," a forecast that had terrible fulfillment when Nebuchadnezzar laid waste Judah and Jerusalem, 609-607 B.C.E. (Jer. 34:7; 2 Chron. 36:19) Hosea's many prophecies of restoration were fulfilled when Jehovah collected together Judah and Israel and 'they went up out of the land' of their captivity in 537 B.C.E.—Hos. 1:10, 11; 2:14-23; 3:5; 11:8-11; 13:14; 14:1-9; Ezra 3:1-3.

15 References to Hosea's prophecy by the writers of the Christian Greek Scriptures are also most beneficial for our consideration today. For example, Paul makes a powerful application of Hosea 13:14 in discussing the resurrection: "Death, where is your victory? Death, where is your sting?" (1 Cor. 15:55; see also Revelation 20:13.) In emphasizing Jehovah's undeserved kindness as expressed toward vessels of mercy, Paul quotes from Hosea 1:10 and 2:23: "It is as he says also in Hosea: 'Those not my people I will call "my people," and her who was not beloved "beloved"; and in the place where it was said to them, "You are not my people," there they will be called "sons of the living God."'" (Rom. 9:25, 26) Peter paraphrases these same passages from Hosea in saying: "For you were once not a people, but are now God's people; you were those who had not been shown mercy, but are now those who have been shown mercy."—1 Pet. 2:10.

16 Thus, Hosea's prophecy is seen to have been fulfilled, not only in the return of a remnant in Zerubbabel's day, but also in Jehovah's merciful gathering of a spiritual remnant who become 'beloved sons of the living God.' By inspiration Hosea saw the requirements for these. It is not an appearance of worship with formal ceremony, but in the words of Hosea 6:6 (which Jesus repeated at Matthew 9:13 and 12:7): "In loving-kindness I have taken delight, and not in sacrifice; and in the knowledge of God rather than in whole burnt offerings."

17 The illustration of the adulterous wife that was so vividly acted in Hosea's own life shows that Jehovah abhors those who turn from him into ways of idolatry and false worship, thus committing spiritual adultery. Any who have stumbled in error must come back to Jehovah in true repentance and 'offer in return the young bulls of their lips.' (Hos. 14:2; Heb. 13:15) These may rejoice with the remnant of the spiritual sons of Israel in the fulfillment of the Kingdom promise of Hosea 3:5: "Afterwards the sons of Israel will come back and certainly look for Jehovah their God, and for David their king; and they will certainly come quivering to Jehovah and to his goodness in the final part of the days."

---

13. What plea ends the book, and who will walk in Jehovah's ways?
14. What accurate fulfillments of Hosea's prophecy are to be noted?
15. How do writers of the Christian Greek Scriptures apply quotations from the book of Hosea?
16. What words of Hosea did Jesus repeat as showing Jehovah's requirements for worship?
17. (a) What is necessary for any who stumble into spiritual adultery? (b) What joyful Kingdom promise is contained in Hosea?

Bible Book Number Twenty-nine— Joel

Writer: Joel
Place Written: Judah
Writing Completed: c. 820 B.C.E. (?)
Time Covered: Undetermined

WAVE upon wave, a horde of insects desolates the land. Fire ahead of them and flame behind complete the devastation. Everywhere there is famine. The sun turns into darkness and the moon into blood, for the great and fear-inspiring day of Jehovah is at hand. He commands to thrust in the sickle and gather the nations in their crowds for destruction. However, some "will get away safe." (Joel 2:32) The consideration of these dramatic events makes Joel's prophecy both intensely interesting and of great benefit to us.

2 The book is introduced as "the word of Jehovah that occurred to Joel the son of Pethuel." The Bible tells us nothing more than this about Joel himself. It is the prophetic message that is emphasized and not its writer. The name "Joel" (Hebrew: *Yô·'él'*) is understood to mean "Jehovah Is God." It has the same meaning as "Elijah," but with the two parts of the word in the reverse order. Joel's firsthand familiarity with Jerusalem, its temple and the details of temple service may indicate that he wrote his book in Jerusalem or Judah.—Joel 1:9, 13, 14; 2:1, 15, 16, 32.

3 When was the book of Joel written? This cannot be stated with certainty. The language of the prophecy indicates that the locust plague is pictorial, and, indeed, Bible history contains no mention of an insect plague of such devastating proportions occurring in Canaan. The description of Jehovah's judgment of the nations in the plain of Jehoshaphat suggests that Joel wrote his prophecy some time after Jehovah's great victory on behalf of King Jehoshaphat of Judah in the valley of Beracah, and hence after Jehoshaphat became king 938 B.C.E. (Joel 3:2, 12; 2 Chron. 20:22-26) Amos begins his prophecy by quoting abruptly from the text of Joel, indicating that Joel's prophecy was written before that of Amos, who prophesied about 811 B.C.E. (Joel 3:16; Amos 1:2) An early date is also indicated by the book's position in the Hebrew canon. A number of authorities suggest the beginning of the reign of King Jehoash of Judah, 903-863 B.C.E. However, a majority favor the reign of King Uzziah, 826-774 B.C.E. In *The Bible Commentary,* 1886, Vol. VI, page 494, F. C. Cook, with reference to prophets who were Bible writers after 997 B.C.E., says: "Joel then, we may consider, was the earliest prophet of the kingdom of Judah, a contemporary of Hosea in the northern kingdom, and followed in quick succession in Judah by Isaiah, who quotes a sentence from him (xiii. 6), and by Micah."[a] Hence a date of approximately 820 B.C.E. is suggested for Joel's prophecy.

4 The authenticity of the prophecy is proved by quotations and references to it in the Christian Greek Scriptures. On the day of Pentecost Peter spoke of "the prophet Joel" and applied one of his prophecies. Paul quoted the same prophecy and showed its fulfillment toward both Jew and Greek. (Joel 2:28-32; Acts 2:14-21; Rom. 10:13) In earlier times Joel's prophecies against neighbor nations were all fulfilled. The great city of Tyre was destroyed by Nebuchadnezzar and, later, the island city, by Alexander the Great, and is now only a small fishing village. Philistia likewise perished. Edom became a wilderness. (Joel 3:4, 19) The Jews never questioned the canonicity of Joel and placed the book second among the Minor Prophets.

5 M'Clintock and Strong's *Cyclopœdia* refers to Joel as the "pattern of the prophets." He repeats for emphasis and uses striking similes. Locusts are called a nation, a people and an army. Their teeth are like those of lions, their appearance like horses and their sound like chariots of an army drawn up for battle. *The Interpreter's Bible* quotes an authority on locust control as saying: "Joel's description of a locust invasion has never been surpassed for its dramatic accuracy of detail."[b] Listen now as Joel prophesies of the fear-inspiring day of Jehovah.

CONTENTS OF JOEL

6 **Insect invasion strips the land; day of Jehovah near** (1:1–2:11). What a terrible vision of

1. What dramatic events highlight Joel's prophecy?
2. What do we know of Joel and the circumstances of his prophesying?
3. For what reasons is a date of about 820 B.C.E. suggested for the prophecy?

a See also M'Clintock and Strong's *Cyclopœdia,* 1882, page 939.
b 1956, Vol. VI, page 733.

4. What proves its authenticity?
5. In what way is the prophecy strikingly expressive?
6. What terrible vision does Joel first see?

calamity Joel sees! A devastating onslaught by the caterpillar, the locust, the creeping unwinged locust and the cockroach. Vines and fig trees have been stripped bare, and starvation stalks the land. There are no grain or drink offerings for the house of Jehovah. Joel warns the priests and ministers of God to repent. "Alas for the day," he cries out, "because the day of Jehovah is near, and like a despoiling from the Almighty One it will come!" (1:15) Animals wander in confusion. Flames have scorched the pastureland and trees, and the wilderness has been seared by fire.

7 Sound the alert! "Blow a horn in Zion, O men, and shout a war cry in my holy mountain." (2:1) The day of Jehovah is near, a day of darkness and thick gloom. Look! A people numerous and mighty. They turn the Eden-like land into a desolate wilderness. Nothing escapes. Like horses and with a sound like chariots on the mountaintops they run. Like a people in battle order they rush the city, climbing on walls and houses and through the windows. The land is agitated and the heavens rock. Jehovah is in command of this numerous military force. "The day of Jehovah is great and very fear-inspiring, and who can hold up under it?" —2:11.

8 **Turn to Jehovah; spirit to be poured out** (2:12-32). But something can be done to stem the invasion. Jehovah counsels: "Come back to me with all your hearts, . . . rip apart your hearts, and not your garments; and come back to Jehovah your God." (2:12, 13) A horn blast summons the people to solemn assembly. If they return to him, "Jehovah will be zealous for his land and will show compassion upon his people." (2:18) There will be blessings and forgiveness, and the invader will be turned back. Rather than a time for fear, it is a time to be joyful and rejoice, for there will be fruit and grain and new wine and oil. Jehovah will compensate for the years that his great military force of locusts has eaten. His promise is: "You will certainly eat, eating and becoming satisfied, and you will be bound to praise the name of Jehovah your God, who has done with you so wonderfully." (2:26) They will learn that Jehovah alone is their God in the midst of Israel.

9 "And after that it must occur that I shall pour out my spirit on every sort of flesh," says Jehovah, "and your sons and your daughters will certainly prophesy. As for your old men, dreams they will dream. As for your young men, visions they will see. And even on the menservants and on the maidservants in those days I shall pour out my spirit." There will be terrifying portents in sun and moon before the coming of the day of Jehovah. Yet some will survive. "It must occur that everyone who calls on the name of Jehovah will get away safe." —2:28-32.

10 **Nations to be judged in "plain of Jehoshaphat"** (3:1-21). Jehovah will bring back the captives of Judah and Jerusalem. The nations will be gathered, and Tyre, Sidon and Philistia will pay dearly for reproaching and enslaving Jehovah's people. Listen to Jehovah as he challenges the nations: "Sanctify war! Arouse the powerful men! Let them draw near! Let them come up, all the men of war!" (3:9) Let them beat plowshares into swords and come up to the low plain of Jehoshaphat (meaning "Jehovah Is Judge"). His command rings out: "Thrust in a sickle, for harvest has grown ripe. . . . The press vats actually overflow; for their badness has become abundant. Crowds, crowds are in the low plain of the decision, for the day of Jehovah is near." (3:13, 14) Sun and moon become dark. Jehovah roars out of Zion, causing heaven and earth to rock, but he proves to be a refuge and fortress for his own people. They will have to know that he is Jehovah their God.

11 What paradisaic plenty will be seen "in that day"! (3:18) The mountains will drip wine, the hills will flow with milk, and the stream beds with abundant water. A refreshing spring will go forth from the house of Jehovah. Egypt and Edom, who have shed innocent blood in Judah, will become desolate wastes, but Judah and Jerusalem will be inhabited to time indefinite, "and Jehovah will be residing in Zion."—3:21.

WHY BENEFICIAL

12 Some commentators have described Joel as a "prophet of gloom." However, from the point of view of God's own people he appears as the proclaimer of glorious tidings of deliverance. The apostle Paul emphasizes this thought at Romans 10:13, saying: "For 'everyone who calls on the name of Jehovah will be saved.'" (Joel 2:32) There was a striking fulfillment of Joel's prophecy on the day of Pentecost. On that occasion Peter was inspired to explain that the miraculous gift of tongues was the evidence of the outpouring of God's spirit as foretold by Joel. (Acts 2:1-21; Joel 2:28, 29, 32) Peter laid great stress on the prophetic import of Joel's words: "And everyone who calls on the

7. How is Jehovah's invading military force described?
8. (a) How only may the invasion be stemmed? (b) What compensation does Jehovah promise?
9. What heart-stirring prophecy follows?
10. What is to take place at the low plain of Jehoshaphat?
11. How does Joel then describe the blessings to follow from Jehovah?
12. What prophetic import of Joel did Peter stress at Pentecost?

name of Jehovah will be saved."—Acts 2:21, 39, 40.

13 Striking similarities between the locust plague described by Joel and the plague prophesied in Revelation (chapter nine) indicate that they are both part of the same overall prophetic message. Again the sun is darkened, the locusts resemble horses prepared for battle, they make a sound like that of chariots and have teeth like those of lions. (Joel 2:10, 4, 5; 1:6; Rev. 9:2, 7-9) Joel's prophecy at 2:31, which tells of the sun turning into darkness, is paralleled as an event by Isaiah 13:9, 10 and Revelation 6:12-17, and also by Matthew 24:29, 30, where Jesus shows the prophecy to apply at the time he comes as the Son of man with power and great glory. The words of Joel 2:11, "the day of Jehovah is great and very fear-inspiring," are apparently referred to at Malachi 4:5. Parallel descriptions of this 'day of darkness and thick gloom' are also to be found at Joel 2:2 and Zephaniah 1:14, 15.

13. (a) What indicates that Joel and Revelation are both part of the same overall prophetic message? (b) What parallels are to be found with other prophecies?

14 The prophecy of Revelation looks forward to the day of "the salvation and the power and the kingdom of our God." (Rev. 12:10) Joel also prophesies of that time, showing that, when the great "day of Jehovah" comes upon the nations, those who call on him for protection and deliverance "will get away safe." "Jehovah will be a refuge for his people." Edenic prosperity will be restored: "And it must occur in that day that the mountains will drip with sweet wine, and the very hills will flow with milk, and the very stream beds of Judah will all flow with water. And out of the house of Jehovah there will go forth a spring." In presenting these bright promises of restoration, Joel also magnifies the sovereignty of Jehovah God and appeals to those of sincere heart on the basis of His great mercy: "Come back to Jehovah your God, for he is gracious and merciful, slow to anger and abundant in loving-kindness." All who heed this inspired appeal will reap eternal benefits.—Joel 2:32; 3:16, 18; 2:13.

14. What passages in Joel magnify Jehovah's sovereignty and his loving-kindness?

Bible Book Number Thirty— Amos

Writer:	**Amos**
Place Written:	**Judah**
Writing Completed:	**c. 811 B.C.E.**
Time Covered:	**Undetermined**

NOT a prophet nor the son of a prophet, but a raiser of sheep and a nipper of figs of sycamore trees—this was Amos when Jehovah called him and sent him to prophesy, not only to his own nation of Judah, but particularly to the northern kingdom of Israel. He was one of the prophets mentioned at 2 Kings 17:13, 22, 23. He came from Tekoa in Judah, about six miles south of Bethlehem and about a day's journey from the southern border of the ten-tribe kingdom of Israel.—Amos 1:1; 7:14, 15.

2 The opening verse of his prophecy states that it was during the days of Uzziah the king of Judah, and of Jeroboam (II) the son of Joash, the king of Israel, that he began his career as prophet, two years before an earthquake of unusual note. This places the prophecy within the fifteen-year period 826-811 B.C.E., during which the reigns of these two kings overlapped. The prophet Zechariah mentions the disastrous earthquake in the days of Uzziah, at which time the people fled in fear. (Zech. 14:5) The Jewish historian Josephus states that this earthquake occurred at the time Uzziah presumptuously attempted to offer up incense in the temple. He says it made a huge crack in the temple so that sunlight shone on the king's face as he was stricken with leprosy.[a]

1. Who was Amos?
2. How may the time of the prophecy be determined?

3 The name Amos means "Being a Load" or "Carrying a Load." While he carried messages burdened with woe to Israel and Judah (and also to numerous heathen nations), yet he also bore a message of comfort concerning the restoration of Jehovah's people. There was every reason for pronouncing a burden of woe in Israel. Prosperity, luxurious living and licentiousness were the order of the day. The people had forgotten the law of Jehovah. Their

a *Antiquities of the Jews,* ix, 10.

3. (a) Why was Amos' message of woe timely? (b) How did he magnify Jehovah's sovereignty?

apparent prosperity blinded them to the fact that, like overripe fruit, they were already in the process of decay leading to destruction. Amos prophesied that in just a few short years the ten-tribe kingdom would go into exile beyond Damascus. In this he magnified the righteousness and sovereignty of Jehovah, whom he refers to twenty-one times as "the Lord Jehovah."—Amos 1:8, *NW* footnote, 1960 Edition; 5:27.

4 The fulfillment of this and other prophecies attests to the authenticity of Amos. The prophet also foretold that the enemy nations round about Israel—the Syrians, the Philistines, the Tyrians, the Edomites, the Ammonites and the Moabites—would all be devoured by the fire of destruction. It is a matter of history that each of these enemy strongholds was in time broken. The ways of Judah and Israel were even more reprehensible, because they left Jehovah for the practice of false worship. The last stronghold of Israel, the fortified city of Samaria, after being besieged by the Assyrian army under Shalmaneser, fell in the year 740 B.C.E. (2 Ki. 17:1-6) Judah did not profit from what happened to her sister, and she was destroyed in 607 B.C.E.

5 Amos condemned Israel for its luxurious living, because the rich were defrauding the poor to build their "houses of ivory," in which they wined and dined themselves sumptuously. (Amos 3:15; 5:11, 12; 6:4-7) Archaeologists have uncovered the evidence of this prosperity. In his book *The Bible as History,* Werner Keller writes: "From the same period [that of Jeroboam II] come a number of beautifully carved ivories, some of which are expensively embellished with gold and semiprecious stones and ornamented with colorful powdered glass. They show mythological motifs borrowed from Egypt, such as Harpocrates on the lotus flower or figures of gods, like Isis and Horus, or cherubs. At that time all over Israel granaries and storehouses were being built to hold goods of all descriptions whose supply exceeded demand."[a] The following is stated in *Harper's Bible Dictionary,* 1952, page 295: "The famous Samaria ivories include thousands of fragments which have been cleaned, studied, and recorded . . . These small objects, fashioned in the 9th or 8th centuries B.C., put moderns in touch with what . . . the prophet Amos knew of the 'ivory houses' and the ivory-trimmed furnishings and paneled palaces of King Ahab. (Amos 3:15; 6:4) These ivory fragments, among the most valuable finds in the costly excavations in Samaria, once formed borders and inlay for couches, thrones, and stools."

6 That the book of Amos belongs in the Bible canon there can be no doubt. Clinching its authenticity are Stephen's paraphrase of three verses at Acts 7:42, 43 and James' quotation from the book at Acts 15:15-18.—Amos 5:25-27; 9:11, 12.

CONTENTS OF AMOS

7 **Judgments against the nations** (1:1–2:3). "Jehovah—out of Zion he will roar." (1:2) Amos proceeds to warn of His fiery judgments against the nations. Damascus (Syria) has threshed Gilead with iron threshing instruments. Gaza (Philistia) and Tyre have handed over Israelite captives to Edom. In Edom itself mercy and brotherly love have been lacking. Ammon has invaded Gilead. Moab has burned the bones of the king of Edom for lime. Jehovah's hand is against all these nations, and he says: "I shall not turn it back."—1:3, 6, 8, 9, 11, 13; 2:1.

8 **Judgment against Judah and Israel** (2:4-16). Nor will Jehovah turn his anger back from Judah. They have transgressed by "rejecting the law of Jehovah." (2:4) And Israel? Jehovah favored Israel by bringing them up out of the land of Egypt. He annihilated the formidable Amorites for them and gave them the good land. He raised up Nazirites and prophets among them, but they made the Nazirites break their vow and commanded the prophets: "You must not prophesy." (2:12) Therefore Jehovah is making their foundations sway like a wagon loaded with newly cut grain. As for their mighty men, they will flee naked.

9 **The accounting with Israel** (3:1–6:14). By striking illustrations Amos drives home the point that the fact of his prophesying proves that Jehovah has spoken. "For the Lord Jehovah will not do a thing unless he has revealed his confidential matter to his servants the prophets. . . . The Lord Jehovah himself has spoken! Who will not prophesy?" (3:7, 8) Amos *does* prophesy against the luxury-loving despoilers dwelling in Samaria. Jehovah will snatch them off their splendid couches, and their houses of ivory will perish.

10 Jehovah recounts his chastisements and corrections of Israel. Five times he reminds them: "You did not come back to me." Therefore, O Israel, "get ready to meet your God."

---

a 1956, New York Ed., page 242; London Ed., page 236.

4. The fulfillment of what prophecies testifies to the authenticity of Amos?
5. How does archaeology support the record?
6. What clinches the book's authenticity?
7. Amos warns of Jehovah's judgments against what nations?
8. Why is Jehovah's judgment also proclaimed against Judah and Israel?
9. What proves that Jehovah has spoken, and against whom does Amos specially prophesy?
10. Of what does Jehovah remind Israel, and what day of woe is due to come?

(4:6-12) Amos takes up a prophetic dirge: "The virgin, Israel, has fallen; she cannot get up again. She has been forsaken upon her own ground; there is no one raising her up." (5:2) However, Jehovah, the Maker of wonderful things in heaven and earth, keeps calling Israel to search for him and keep living. Yes, "search for what is good, and not what is bad, to the end that you people may keep living." (5:4, 6, 14) But what will the day of Jehovah mean to them? It will be a day of woe. Like a torrent it will sweep them to exile beyond Damascus, and the ivory-decked houses of their sprawling feasts will be turned to rubble and debris.

11 **Amos prophesies in spite of opposition** (7:1-17). Jehovah shows his prophet a plummet set in the midst of Israel. There will be no further excusing. He will devastate the sanctuaries of Israel and rise up against the house of Jeroboam with a sword. Amaziah the priest of Bethel sends to Jeroboam II, saying: "Amos has conspired against you." (7:10) He tells Amos to go to Judah to do his prophesying. Amos makes clear his authority, saying: "Jehovah proceeded to take me from following the flock, and Jehovah went on to say to me, 'Go, prophesy to my people Israel.'" (7:15) Amos then foretells calamity for Amaziah and his household.

12 **Oppression, punishment and restoration** (8:1–9:15). Jehovah shows Amos a basket of summer fruit. He condemns Israel's oppression of the poor and swears "by the Superiority of Jacob" that they will have to mourn on account of their bad works. "'Look! There are days coming,' is the utterance of the Lord Jehovah, 'and I will send a famine into the land, a famine, not for bread, and a thirst, not for water, but for hearing the words of Jehovah.'" (8:7, 11) They will fall to rise up no more. Whether they dig down into Sheol or climb up to the heavens, Jehovah's own hand will take them. The sinners of his people will die by the sword. Then, a glorious promise! "In that day I shall raise up the booth of David that is fallen, and I shall certainly repair their breaches. . . . I shall certainly build it up as in the days of long ago." (9:11) So prosperous will they grow that the plowman will overtake the harvester before he can gather in his bumper crops. Permanent will be these blessings from Jehovah!

WHY BENEFICIAL

13 Bible readers today can benefit by noting the reason for the warnings that Amos' prophecy proclaimed to Israel, Judah and their near neighbors. Those who reject the law of Jehovah, defraud and oppress the poor, and are greedy, immoral and practice idolatry, cannot have Jehovah's approval. But those who turn away from such things and repent Jehovah forgives, and to them he shows mercy. We are wise if we separate from corrupting associations in this evil world and heed Jehovah's admonition: "Search for me, and keep living." —5:4, 6, 14.

14 At the time of his martyrdom Stephen cited Amos. He reminded the Jews that it had been Israel's idolatry with foreign gods, such as Moloch and Rephan, that had brought on the captivity. Did those Jews benefit by hearing Amos' words repeated? No! Enraged, they stoned Stephen to death, and so placed themselves in line for further calamity at the destruction of Jerusalem, A.D. 70.—Amos 5:25-27; Acts 7:42, 43.

15 It is beneficial to consider the fulfillment of the many prophecies in Amos, not only those that were fulfilled in the punishment of Israel, Judah and the other nations, but also the prophecies of the restoration. True to Jehovah's word through Amos, the captives of Israel returned in 537 B.C.E. to build and inhabit their desolated cities and plant their vineyards and gardens.—Amos 9:14; Ezra 3:1.

16 However, there was a glorious and upbuilding fulfillment of Amos' prophecy in the days of the apostles. In discussing the gathering of non-Israelites into the Christian congregation, James, under inspiration, makes clear that this was foretold in the prophecy at Amos 9:11, 12. He indicates that the 'rebuilding of the booth of David that had fallen down' finds fulfillment in connection with the Christian congregation, "in order that those who remain of the men may earnestly seek Jehovah, together with people of all the nations, people who are called by my name, says Jehovah." Here, indeed, was the Scriptural support for the new development, as related by Simon Peter—that God was taking out of the nations "a people for his name."—Acts 15:13-19.

17 Jesus Christ, the head of this Christian congregation, is elsewhere identified as the "son of David," who inherits the "throne of David his father" and rules in an everlasting kingdom. (Luke 1:32, 33) Thus the prophecy of Amos points forward to the fulfillment of the Kingdom covenant with David. The concluding

11. By what authority does Amos insist on prophesying against Israel?
12. What famine is foretold for Israel, but with what glorious promise does the prophecy end?
13. How may we today benefit by Amos' warnings?
14. Did the Jews of Stephen's time benefit by these reminders?
15. What prophecies of restoration are beneficial to consider?
16. How did James indicate a fulfillment of Amos 9:11, 12 in connection with the Christian congregation?
17. What prosperity and permanence does Amos foretell in connection with God's kingdom?

words of Amos not only give a marvelous vision of overflowing prosperity at the time of raising up "the booth of David," but they also underline the permanence of God's kingdom: "'And I shall certainly plant them upon their ground, and they will no more be uprooted from their ground that I have given them,' Jehovah your God has said." Earth will abound with everlasting blessings as Jehovah fully restores "the booth of David"!—Amos 9:13-15.

Bible Book Number Thirty-one— Obadiah

Writer:	**Obadiah**
Place Written:	**Undetermined**
Writing Completed:	**c. 607 B.C.E.**
Time Covered:	**Undetermined**

IN JUST twenty-one verses Obadiah, the shortest book of the Hebrew Scriptures, proclaims a judgment of God that resulted in the end of a nation, while foretelling the triumph of the kingdom of God. The introductory words simply state: "The vision of Obadiah." When and where he was born, of what tribe, the details of his life—none of this is told. Clearly, the identity of the prophet is not the important thing; the message is, and rightly so, because, as Obadiah himself declared, it is 'a report from Jehovah.'

2 The report focuses its chief attention on Edom. Extending south from the Dead Sea along the Arabah, the land of Edom, also known as Mount Seir, is a rugged country of lofty mountains and deep ravines. These mountains, composed of sandstone, red granite, porphyry and chalky limestone, jut up to 3,500 feet above the adjacent Arabah. The district of Teman was renowned for the wisdom and courage of its people. Edom's capital, Sela (Hebrew: "Rock"), later apparently known as Petra (Greek: "Rock"), was situated securely in a ravine honeycombed with caverns and shut in by mountains, with ample water flowing through the chasm, but desert outside. The very geography of the land made its inhabitants feel secure and proud.

3 The Edomites were descendants of Esau, who was the brother of Jacob, whose name was changed to Israel, and so they were closely related to the Israelites; so much so that they were viewed as 'brothers.' (Deut. 23:7) Yet Edom's conduct had been anything but brotherly. Shortly before the Israelites entered the Promised Land Moses sent to the king of Edom requesting permission to pass peaceably through his land, but, in a display of hostility, the Edomites coldly refused and backed up their refusal with a display of force. (Num. 20:14-21) Though subjugated by David, they later conspired with Ammon and Moab against Judah in the days of Jehoshaphat, revolted against Jehoshaphat's son King Jehoram, took charge of Israelite captives from Gaza and Tyre, and raided Judah in the days of King Ahaz to take even more captives.—2 Chron. 20:1, 2, 22, 23; 2 Ki. 8:20-22; Amos 1:6, 9; 2 Chron. 28:17.

4 This hostility reached a peak in 607 B.C.E., when Jerusalem was desolated by the Babylonian hordes. Not only did the Edomites watch approvingly, but they urged on the conquerors to make the desolation complete. "Lay it bare! Lay it bare to the foundation within it!" they shouted. (Ps. 137:7) When lots were cast over the booty, they were among those to share the loot; and when escapees of the Jews tried to flee out of the land, they blocked the roads and handed them over to the enemy. It is this violence at the time of Jerusalem's destruction that evidently is the basis for the denunciation recorded by Obadiah, and it was no doubt written while Edom's despicable act was still fresh in mind. (Obad. 11, 14) Since Edom itself was apparently captured and plundered by Nebuchadnezzar within five years after Jerusalem's destruction, the book must have been written before then; 607 B.C.E. is suggested as the most likely date.

5 Obadiah's prophecy against Edom was fulfilled—all of it! In reaching its climax the prophecy states: "The house of Esau [must become] as stubble; and they must set them ablaze and devour them. And there will prove

1. What shows the message to be important, rather than the messenger?
2. On what country does the prophecy focus, and what made its inhabitants feel secure?
3. Had the Edomites acted as brothers to Israel?

4. (a) What dispicable action evidently provided the basis for Obadiah's denunciation of Edom? (b) What evidence suggests 607 B.C.E. as the most likely date of writing?
5. (a) What proves the record to be authentic and true? (b) How did Obadiah fulfill the requirements of a true prophet, and why is his name appropriate?

to be no survivor to the house of Esau; for Jehovah himself has spoken it." (Obad. 18) Edom lived by the sword and she died by the sword, and no trace of her descendants remains. Thus the record is proved to be authentic and true. Obadiah had all the credentials of a true prophet: He spoke in the name of Jehovah, his prophecy honored Jehovah, and it came true as subsequent history proved. His name, which in Hebrew is *'O·bad·yah'*, appropriately means "Servant of Jah."

CONTENTS OF OBADIAH

6 **Judgment upon Edom** (Vss. 1-16). At Jehovah's command Obadiah makes known his vision. The nations are summoned to join in war against Edom. "Rise up, you people, and let us rise up against her in battle," God commands. Then, directing his remarks to Edom itself, he assesses her position. Edom is just a small one among the nations and despised, yet she is presumptuous. She feels safe lodged in among the lofty crags, sure that no one can bring her down. Nevertheless, Jehovah declares that, even if her dwelling were as high as the eagle's, even if she were to nest among the stars themselves, from there he would bring her down. She is due for punishment.

7 What is going to happen to her? If thieves were to despoil Edom, they would take only what they wanted. Even grape gatherers would leave some gleanings. But what lies ahead for the sons of Esau is worse than this. Their treasures will be completely ransacked. The very allies of Edom will be the ones to turn on her. Those who have been her close friends will catch her in a net as one without discernment. Her men known for wisdom and her warriors known for valor will be no help in the time of her calamity.

8 But why this severe punishment? It is because of the violence that they have done to the sons of Jacob, their brothers! They have rejoiced at the fall of Jerusalem, and have even joined with the invaders in dividing up the plunder. In strong denunciation, as if Obadiah is witnessing the vile deeds, Edom is told: You ought not to rejoice at your brother's distress. You ought not to hinder the flight of his escapees and hand them over to the enemy. The day of Jehovah's reckoning is near, and you will be called to account. The way you have done is the way it will be done to you.

9 **Restoration for the house of Jacob** (Vss. 17-21). In contrast, the house of Jacob is due for restoration. Men will return to Mount Zion. They will devour the house of Esau as fire does stubble. They will take hold of the land to the south, the Negeb, the mountainous region of Esau and the Shephelah; to the north they will possess the land of Ephraim, Samaria and on as far as Zarephath; to the east they will get the territory of Gilead. Proud Edom must cease to be, Jacob must be restored, and "the kingship must become Jehovah's."—Vs. 21.

WHY BENEFICIAL

10 Attesting to the surety of the fulfillment of this message of judgment against Edom, Jehovah had similar pronouncements made by others of his prophets. Outstanding among them are the ones recorded at Joel 3:19; Amos 1:11, 12; Isaiah 34:5-7; Jeremiah 49:7-22; Ezekiel 25:12-14; 35:2-15. The earlier pronouncements obviously make reference to acts of hostility in times past, while the ones of later date evidently are indictments of Edom for her unpardonable conduct, referred to by Obadiah, at the time the Babylonians seized Jerusalem. It will strengthen faith in Jehovah's power of prophecy if we examine how the foretold calamities befell Edom. Moreover, it will build confidence in Jehovah as the God who always brings to pass his stated purpose.—Isa. 46:9-11.

11 Obadiah had foretold that "the very men in covenant with" Edom, those "at peace with" her, would be the ones to prevail against her. Jeremiah (27:3, 6) had specified that Babylon's king Nebuchadnezzar would seize the land of Edom. Babylon's peace with Edom was short-lived. In the fifth year after Jerusalem's destruction, when Nebuchadnezzar's military forces swept through Ammon and Moab they apparently subjugated Edom also. Nevertheless, a century and a half after Nebuchadnezzar's invasion of the land confident Edom still hoped to make a comeback, and concerning it Malachi 1:4 reports: "Because Edom keeps saying, 'We have been shattered, but we shall return and build the devastated places,' this is what Jehovah of armies has said, 'They, for their part, will build; but I, for my part, shall tear down.'" Despite Edom's efforts at recovery, by late in the fourth century B.C.E. the Nabataeans were firmly established in the land, with Petra as their own capital. Having been pushed out of their land, the Edomites dwelt in the southern part of Judea, which they had seized shortly after the Jews went into captivity. This territory came to be called Idumaea. They never succeeded in reconquering the land of Seir. Instead, they received further punishment, largely at the hands of the descendants

6. How does Jehovah speak of Edom, and from where will he bring her down?
7. To what extent is Edom to be despoiled?
8. Why is the punishment so severe?
9. What restoration is foretold?
10. What other prophecies foretold Edom's doom, and why will it be beneficial to consider these along with Obadiah?
11, 12. (a) How did those "at peace with" Edom come to prevail against her? (b) By what stages did Edom come to be "cut off to time indefinite"?

of the repatriated Jews. "Jacob" and "Joseph" proceeded to devour "the house of Esau as stubble."—Obad. 18.

[12] In the second century B.C.E. Judas Maccabeus overthrew the Edomites at Acrabattene and at Hebron. Not long after that the remaining Edomites were subjugated by the Jewish king John Hyrcanus, were forced to submit to circumcision and thus were absorbed into the Jewish domain under a Jewish governor. During the time of Roman rule Simon of Gerasa attacked them, virtually depopulating the country of Idumaea and stripping it bare. What survivors there were largely perished when the Romans seized Jerusalem, and their name in time disappeared from history.[a] It was as Obadiah had foretold: "You will have to be cut off to time indefinite. . . . And there will prove to be no survivor to the house of Esau." —Obad. 10, 18.

a Josephus, *Antiquities of the Jews*, x, 9, ¶7; xii, 8, ¶1, 6; xiii, 9, ¶1; *Wars of the Jews*, iv, 9, ¶7.

[13] In contrast with Edom's desolation, the Jews were restored to their homeland in 537 B.C.E. under the governorship of Zerubbabel, rebuilt the temple in Jerusalem and became firmly established in the land.

[14] How evident it is that pride and presumptuousness lead to calamity! Let all who proudly exalt themselves and cruelly gloat over the hardship that comes upon the servants of God take warning from the fate of Edom. Let them acknowledge, as did Obadiah, that "the kingship must become Jehovah's." The laws, purposes and principles of Jehovah never change. Those who fight against Jehovah and his covenant people will be completely cut off to time indefinite, but Jehovah's majestic kingdom and eternal kingship will stand vindicated forever!

13. What happened to the Jews, in contrast to Edom?
14. (a) What warning is to be found in Edom's fate? (b) What should all acknowledge, as did Obadiah, and why?

Bible Book Number Thirty-two— Jonah

Writer:	**Jonah**
Place Written:	**Undetermined**
Writing Completed:	**c. 852 B.C.E.**
Time Covered:	**Undetermined**

JONAH—foreign missionary of the ninth century B.C.E.! How did he view his assignment from Jehovah? What new experiences did this open up for him? Did he find the people in his assignment receptive? How successful was his preaching? The dramatic record of the book of Jonah answers these questions. Written at a time when Jehovah's "chosen nation" had broken covenant with Him and fallen into pagan idolatry, the prophetic record shows that God's mercy is not limited to any one nation, not even to Israel. Moreover, it exalts Jehovah's great mercy and loving-kindness, in contrast to the lack of mercy, patience and faith so often observed in imperfect man.

[2] The name Jonah (Hebrew: *Yô·nâh'*) means "Dove." He was the son of the prophet Amittai of Gath-hepher in Galilee of the tribe of Zebulun. At 2 Kings 14:23-25 we read that Jeroboam the king of Israel extended the boundary of the nation according to the word that Jehovah spoke through Jonah. This would place the time of Jonah's prophesying at about 852 B.C.E., the year of the accession of Jeroboam II of Israel and many years before Assyria, with its capital at Nineveh, began to dominate Israel.

1. What questions are answered in the book of Jonah, and what does it show as to Jehovah's mercy?
2. What is known concerning Jonah, and about what year did he prophesy?

[3] There is no question that the entire account of Jonah is factual and authentic. The "Perfecter of our faith, Jesus," referred to Jonah as an actual person and gave the inspired interpretation of two of the prophetic happenings in Jonah, thus showing the book to contain true prophecy. (Heb. 12:2; Matt. 12:39-41; 16:4; Luke 11:29-32) Jonah has always been placed by the Jews among their canonical books and is regarded by them as historical. Josephus referred to it as such. The description of the size of Nineveh as "a city . . . with a walking distance of three days" fits well with ancient records and archaeological investigations. The sixty-mile circumference of the ancient city and suburbs corresponds with a three-day journey on foot. (Jonah 3:3)[b] Jonah's own candor in describing his mistakes and weaknesses,

b *Clarke's Commentary*, Vol. IV, page 703.

3. What proves the account to be factual and authentic?

without any attempt to gloss over them, also marks the record as genuine.

4 What about the "great fish" that swallowed Jonah? There has been considerable speculation as to what kind of fish this may have been. M'Clintock and Strong's *Cyclopœdia* (1881, Vol. 10, page 973) mentions the huge white shark (*Carcharias vulgaris*), a dreaded enemy of sailors, as "quite able to swallow a man whole." It quotes authorities to show that whole bodies of men and one of a horse have been found in the bellies of these sharks. There are also other denizens of the deep with large mouths and stomachs. *Nature Magazine*, February, 1945, page 99, describes one of them as follows: "The sperm whale has a tremendous mouth, capable of swallowing seals, sharks or a man . . . it can bite a whaling boat in half."

5 Though it may have been one of a number of kinds of fish, the Bible record that it was a "great fish" is sufficient for our information. Incidentally, it appears Jonah has not been alone in having an experience such as this. French scientist M. de Parville, in *Journal des Debats*, 1914, gives the detailed account of a sailor who spent the best part of a day in the stomach of a whale and survived the ordeal.[a]

CONTENTS OF JONAH

6 **Jonah assigned to Nineveh, but runs away** (1:1-16). "And the word of Jehovah began to occur to Jonah the son of Amittai, saying: 'Get up, go to Nineveh the great city, and proclaim against her that their badness has come up before me.'" (1:1, 2) Does Jonah relish this assignment? Not one bit! He runs away in the opposite direction, taking a ship for Tarshish, now Spain. Jonah's ship meets up with a great storm. In fear, the mariners call for aid, "each one to his god," while Jonah sleeps in the ship's hold. (1:5) After arousing Jonah, they cast lots in an attempt to discover who is responsible for their plight. The lot falls upon Jonah. It is now that he makes known to them that he is a Hebrew, a worshiper of Jehovah, and that he is running away from his God-given task. He invites them to hurl him into the sea. After making further efforts to bring the ship through, they at last pitch Jonah overboard. The sea stops its raging.

7 **Swallowed by "a great fish"** (1:17–2:10). "Now Jehovah appointed a great fish to swallow Jonah, so that Jonah came to be in the inward parts of the fish three days and three nights." (1:17) He prays fervently to Jehovah from inside the fish. "Out of the belly of Sheol" he cries for help, and declares he will pay what he has vowed, for "salvation belongs to Jehovah." (2:2, 9) At Jehovah's command the fish vomits Jonah onto the dry land.

8 **Preaching in Nineveh** (3:1–4:11). Jehovah renews his command to Jonah. No longer does Jonah evade his assignment, but goes to Nineveh. There he marches through the city streets and cries: "Only forty days more, and Nineveh will be overthrown." (3:4) His preaching is effective. A wave of repentance sweeps through Nineveh, and its people begin to put faith in God. The king proclaims that man and beast must fast and be clothed in sackcloth. Jehovah mercifully spares the city.

9 This is more than Jonah can bear. He tells Jehovah he knew all along that He would show mercy and that is why he ran away to Tarshish. He wishes he could die. Thoroughly disgruntled, Jonah encamps to the east of the city and waits to see what will happen. Jehovah appoints a bottle-gourd plant to come up as shade over his moody prophet. Jonah's rejoicing at this is short-lived. Next morning Jehovah appoints a worm to smite the plant, so that its comforting protection is replaced by exposure to a parching east wind and a broiling sun. Again he wishes he could die. Self-righteously he justifies his anger. Jehovah points out his inconsistency: Jonah felt sorry for one bottle-gourd plant but is angry because Jehovah now feels sorry for the great city of Nineveh.

WHY BENEFICIAL

10 Jonah's course of action and its outcome should stand as a warning to us. He ran away from God-given work; he should have put his hand to the task and trusted in God to uphold him. (Jonah 1:3; Luke 9:62; Prov. 14:26; Isa. 6:8) When he got going in the wrong direction he showed a negative attitude in failing to identify himself freely to the mariners as a worshiper of "Jehovah the God of the heavens." He had lost his boldness. (Jonah 1:7-9; Matt. 5:15, 16; Eph. 6:19, 20) Jonah's self-centeredness led him to regard Jehovah's mercy toward Nineveh as a personal affront; he tried to save face by telling Jehovah that he had known all along that this would be the outcome—so why send him as prophet? He was reproved for this disrespectful, complaining attitude, so we should benefit from his experience and refrain from finding fault with Jehovah's showing

a *Awake!*, April 8, 1952, pages 27, 28.

4, 5. What kind of fish may have swallowed Jonah? Yet, what is sufficient for our information?
6. How does Jonah react to his assignment, and with what result?
7. What is Jonah's experience with the "great fish"?
8. How effective is Jonah's preaching in Nineveh?
9. How does Jonah react to Jehovah's expressing mercy on the city, and how does Jehovah expose the prophet's inconsistency?
10. What attitude and course of Jonah should stand as a warning to us?

mercy or with his way of doing things.—Jonah 4:1-4, 7-9; Phil. 2:13, 14; 1 Cor. 10:10.

11 Overshadowing everything else in the book of Jonah is its portrayal of the magnificent qualities of Jehovah's loving-kindness and mercy. Jehovah showed loving-kindness toward Nineveh in sending his prophet to warn of impending destruction, and he was ready to show mercy when the city repented—a mercy that permitted Nineveh to survive more than two hundred years until its destruction by the Medes and Chaldeans about 633 B.C.E. He showed mercy toward Jonah in delivering him from the storm-tossed sea and in providing the gourd to "deliver him from his calamitous state." By providing and then taking away the protecting gourd, Jehovah made known to Jonah that he will show mercy and loving-kindness according to his own good pleasure. —Jonah 1:2; 3:2 4, 10; 2:10; 4:6, 10, 11.

12 At Matthew 12:38-41, Jesus showed that Jonah's three days and three nights in "the belly of Sheol" and his return therefrom constituted a prophetic sign of Jesus' going down into the grave and his resurrection by Jehovah's power. (Jonah 1:17; 2:2, 10) (According to the Jewish method of measuring time and the facts in fulfillment of Jesus' case, this period of "three days and three nights" allows for one full twenty-four-hour day [from sundown to sundown] plus parts of the preceding and following days. The Bible indicates that Jesus' "three days" in the tomb amounted to about thirty-six hours.[a])

11. How are Jehovah's loving-kindness and mercy illustrated in the book?
12. What remarkable prophetic sign is provided in Jonah?

13 In this same reference, Jesus refers to his burial and resurrection as "the sign of Jonah the prophet" and says that this is the only sign that will be given to "a wicked and adulterous generation." He contrasts the repentance of the Ninevites with the hardness of heart and outright rejection he experienced from the Jews during his own ministry, saying: "Men of Nineveh will rise up in the judgment with this generation and will condemn it; because they repented at what Jonah preached, but, look! something more than Jonah is here." (See also Matthew 16:4 and Luke 11:30, 32.) "Something more than Jonah"—what did Jesus mean by these words? He was referring to himself as the greatest prophet of all, the One sent by Jehovah to preach: "Repent, for the kingdom of the heavens has drawn near." (Matt. 4:17) First to the Jews, and later to the Gentile nations, this call has gone forth. Like the repentant Ninevites who were blessed through the preaching of Jonah, so men of the Gentile nations have had the glorious opportunity of hearing the good news of God's kingdom that was first preached by Jesus, "the Son of man." These also may share in Jehovah's abundant and merciful provision for extended life, for truly "salvation belongs to Jehovah." —Rom. 15:8-12; Jonah 2:9.

a *The Watchtower*, 1944, pages 86-92; *Awake!*, May 22, 1960, pages 27, 28.

13. (a) What else does Jesus say concerning "the sign of Jonah"? (b) How did "something more than Jonah" appear, having what connection with Jehovah's kingdom and salvation?

Bible Book Number Thirty-three— Micah

Writer:	**Micah**
Place Written:	**Judah**
Writing Completed:	**Before 716 B.C.E.**
Time Covered:	**c. 774-716 B.C.E.**

THINK of a man of maturity, one who has spent many years in faithful service to Jehovah. Think of a bold man, one who could tell the rulers of his nation, "You haters of what is good and lovers of badness, . . . you the ones who have also eaten the organism of my people, and have stripped their very skin from off them." Think of a humble man, one giving all credit for his powerful utterances to Jehovah, by whose spirit he spoke. Would you not enjoy the acquaintance of a man like that? What a wealth of information and sound counsel he could impart! The prophet Micah was such a man. We still have access to his choice counsel in the book that bears his name.—Mic. 3:2, 3, 8.

1. What kind of man was Micah?

2 As is true of many of the prophets, very little is said concerning Micah himself in his book; it was the message that was important. The name Micah (Hebrew: *Mi·khah'*) means "Who Is like Jah?" He served as prophet during the reigns of Jotham, Ahaz and Heze-

2. What is known concerning Micah and the period of his prophesying?

kiah (774-716 B.C.E.), which made him a younger contemporary of the prophets Isaiah and Hosea. (Isa. 1:1; Hos. 1:1) The exact period of his prophesying is uncertain, but at most it was fifty-eight years. His prophecies of Samaria's ruin must have been given before the city's destruction 740 B.C.E. and the entire writing completed by the end of Hezekiah's reign, 716 B.C.E. (Mic. 1:1) He was a rural prophet from the village of Moresheth in the fertile Shephelah southwest of Jerusalem. His familiarity with rural life is shown in the kind of illustrations he used to drive home the points of his declarations.—2:12; 4:12, 13; 6:15; 7:1, 4, 14.

3 Micah lived in dangerous and significant times. Fast-moving events were foreboding doom for the kingdoms of Israel and Judah. Moral corruption and idolatry had gone to seed in Israel, and this brought the nation destruction from Assyria, evidently during Micah's own lifetime. Judah swung from doing right in the reign of Jotham to duplicating Israel's wickedness in Ahaz' rebellious reign, and then to a recovery during the reign of Hezekiah. Jehovah raised up Micah to warn his people strongly of what he was bringing upon them. Micah's prophecies served to corroborate those of Isaiah and Hosea.—2 Ki. 15:32–20:21; 2 Chronicles, chaps. 27-32; Isa. 7:17; Hos. 8:8; 2 Cor. 13:1.

4 There is an abundance of evidence to show the authenticity of the book of Micah. It has always been accepted by the Jews in the Hebrew canon. Jeremiah 26:18, 19 refers directly to Micah's words (3:12): "Zion will be plowed up as a mere field, and Jerusalem herself will become mere heaps of ruins." This prophecy was accurately fulfilled in 607 B.C.E. when the king of Babylon razed Jerusalem, "so as to cause ruin." (2 Chron. 36:19) A similar prophecy about Samaria, that it would become "a heap of ruins of the field," was likewise fulfilled. (Mic. 1:6, 7) Not only was Samaria ruined by the Assyrians in 740 B.C.E. when they took the northern kingdom of Israel into captivity (2 Ki. 17:5, 6), but it also suffered devastations by Alexander the Great (331 B.C.E.) and by the Jews under John Hyrcanus two hundred years later. Of this last occasion one authority states: "The victor demolished it, attempting to efface all proofs that a fortified city had ever stood on the hill."[a]

5 Archaeological evidence also adds its voice in support of the fulfillments of Micah's prophecy. Samaria's destruction by the Assyrians is confirmed in Sargon's inscription; he boasted that he had captured two hundred Israelite chariots and deported 27,290 people from Samaria.[b] The invasion of Judah in Hezekiah's reign, as foretold by Micah, was well chronicled by Sennacherib. (Mic. 1:6, 9; 2 Ki. 18:13) He had a large four-paneled relief made on the wall of his palace at Nineveh depicting the capture of Lachish. On his prism he states: "I laid siege to 46 of his strong cities . . . I drove out [of them] 200,150 people. . . . Himself I made a prisoner in Jerusalem his royal residence, like a bird in a cage." He also lists tribute paid to him by Hezekiah.[c]

6 Putting the inspiration of the book beyond all doubt is the outstanding prophecy of Micah 5:2, which foretells the birthplace of the Messiah. (Matt. 2:4-6) There are also passages that are paralleled by statements in the Christian Greek Scriptures.—Mic. 7:6, 20; Matt. 10:35, 36; Luke 1:72, 73.

7 While Micah may have been from the rurals of Judah, he certainly was not a "country boy" in ability to express himself. Some of the finest expressions in God's Word are to be found in his book. Chapter six is written in striking dialogue. Abrupt transitions grip the reader's attention as he moves swiftly from one point to another, from cursing to blessing and back again. (Mic. 2:10, 12; 3:1, 12; 4:1) Vivid figures of speech abound: At Jehovah's going forth, "the mountains must melt under him, and the low plains themselves will split apart, like wax because of the fire, like waters being poured down a steep place."—1:4; see also 7:17.

8 The book is divided into three sections, each section beginning with a "Hear," and containing rebukes, warnings of punishment and promises of blessing.

CONTENTS OF MICAH

9 **Section One** (1:1–2:13). Jehovah is coming forth from his temple to punish Samaria for her idolatry. He will make her "a heap of ruins" and "pour down into the valley her stones," while crushing to pieces her graven images. There will be no healing for her. Judah, too, is guilty and will suffer invasion "to the gate of Jerusalem." Those scheming harmful things are condemned and will lament: "We have positively been despoiled!"—1:6, 12; 2:4.

a *The Westminster Dictionary of the Bible,* 1944, page 528.

b *Archaeology and the Bible,* 1949, G. A. Barton, page 466.

c Study 9, paragraphs 13, 14.

3. In what significant times did Micah serve, and why did Jehovah commission him as prophet?
4. What proves the authenticity of the book?
5. How does archaeology testify to the fulfillment of Micah's prophecies?
6. What puts the inspiration of the book beyond all doubt?
7. What may be said of Micah's power of expression?
8. What is contained in each of the three sections of the book?
9. What punishments are decreed against Samaria and Judah?

10 Abruptly Jehovah's mercy comes into focus as, in Jehovah's name, the prophet declares: "I shall positively gather Jacob . . . In unity I shall set them, like a flock in the pen, like a drove in the midst of its pasture; they will be noisy with men."—2:12.

11 **Section Two** (3:1–5:15). Micah continues: "Hear, please, you heads of Jacob and you commanders of the house of Israel." A scathing denunciation is leveled against these "haters of what is good and lovers of badness" who oppress the people. They have "smashed to pieces their very bones." (3:1-3) Included with them are the false prophets who give no true guidance, causing God's people to wander. More than human courage is needed to proclaim this message! But Micah confidently states: "I myself have become full of power, with the spirit of Jehovah, and of justice and mightiness, in order to tell to Jacob his revolt and to Israel his sin." (3:8) His denunciation of the bloodguilty rulers reaches a scathing climax: "Her own head ones judge merely for a bribe, and her own priests instruct just for a price, and her own prophets practice divination simply for money." (3:11) Therefore Zion will be plowed like a field and Jerusalem become nothing more than a heap of ruins.

12 Again in sudden contrast, the prophecy turns to "the final part of the days" to give a grand, moving description of the restoration of Jehovah's worship at his mountain. Many nations will go up to learn Jehovah's ways, for his law and word will proceed out of Zion and out of Jerusalem. They will learn war no more, but each one will sit under his vine and fig tree. They will be unafraid. Let the peoples follow each one its god, but true worshipers will walk in the name of Jehovah their God, and he will rule over them as king forever. First, however, Zion must go into captivity to Babylon. Only at her restoration will Jehovah pulverize her enemies.

13 Micah now foretells that the ruler in Israel "whose origin is from early times" will come out of Bethlehem Ephrathah. He will rule as a 'shepherd in the strength of Jehovah' and be great, not just in Israel, but "as far as the ends of the earth." (5:2, 4) The invading Assyrian will have but fleeting success, for he will be turned back and his own land laid waste. The "remaining ones of Jacob" will be like "dew from Jehovah" among the people and like a lion for courage among nations. (5:7) Jehovah will root out false worship and execute vengeance upon the disobedient nations.

14 **Section Three** (6:1–7:20). A striking court scene is now presented in dialogue. Jehovah has "a legal case" with Israel, and he calls on the very hills and mountains as witnesses. (1:1) He challenges Israel to testify against him, and recounts his righteous acts in their behalf. What does Jehovah require of earthling man? Not a multitude of animal sacrifices, but, rather, "to exercise justice and to love kindness and to be modest in walking with your God." (6:8) This is just what is lacking in Israel. Instead of justice and kindness there are "wicked scales," violence, falsehood and trickery. (6:11) Instead of walking in a modest way with God, they are walking in the wicked counsels and idol worship of Omri and Ahab, who reigned in Samaria.

15 The prophet deplores the moral decay of his people. Why, even their "most upright one is worse than a thorn hedge." (7:4) There is treachery among intimate friends and within households. Micah does not lose heart. "It is for Jehovah that I shall keep on the lookout. I will show a waiting attitude for the God of my salvation. My God will hear me." (7:7) He warns others not to rejoice over Jehovah's punishment of His people, for deliverance will come. Jehovah will shepherd and feed Israel and "show him wonderful things," making the nations afraid. (7:15) In closing his book, Micah fittingly uses the meaning of his name to praise Jehovah for his delightsome loving-kindness. Yes, 'who is a God like Jehovah?' —7:18.

WHY BENEFICIAL

16 Almost 2,700 years ago the prophesying of Micah proved most 'beneficial for reproving,' for King Hezekiah of Judah responded to his message and led the nation to repentance and religious reformation. (Mic. 3:9-12; Jer. 26:18, 19; compare 2 Kings 18:1-4.) Today this inspired prophecy is even more beneficial. Hear, all professing worshipers of God, Micah's plain warnings against false religion, idol worship, lying and violence! (Mic. 1:2; 3:1; 6:1) Paul corroborates these warnings at 1 Corinthians 6:9-11, saying that true Christians have been washed clean and that no one who indulges in such practices will inherit God's kingdom. Simply and clearly Micah 6:8 states that Jehovah's

---

10. How does Jehovah's mercy come into focus?
11. (a) What denunciation is now leveled against the rulers of Jacob and Israel? (b) How does Micah acknowledge the source of his courage?
12. What grand prophecy is given for "the final part of the days"?
13. What kind of ruler will come out of Bethlehem, and like what will the "remaining ones of Jacob" become?
14. (a) With the use of what illustration does section three begin? (b) What requirements of Jehovah has Israel failed to meet?
15. (a) What does the prophet deplore? (b) What fitting conclusion does the book have?
16. (a) How did the prophecy prove beneficial in Hezekiah's day? (b) What powerful admonitions does it contain for this present day?

requirement is for man to walk with Him in justice, kindness and modesty.

17 Micah delivered his message among a people so divided that 'a man's enemies were the men of his household.' True Christians often preach in similar circumstances, and some even meet with betrayals and bitter persecutions within their own family relationship. Always they need to wait patiently on Jehovah, the 'God of their salvation.' (Mic. 7:6, 7; Matt. 10:21, 35-39) In persecutions, or when faced with a difficult assignment, those who rely courageously on Jehovah will, like Micah, "become full of power, with the spirit of Jehovah," in telling forth His message. Micah prophesied that such courage would be especially evident in "the remaining ones of Jacob." These would be like 'a lion among the nations, in the midst of many peoples,' and at the same time like refreshing dew and showers from Jehovah. These qualities were certainly manifest in the 'remnant of Israel (Jacob)' who became members of the Christian congregation of the first century.—Mic. 3:8; 5:7, 8; Rom. 9:27; 11:5, 26.

18 Jesus' birth at Bethlehem, in fulfillment of Micah's prophecy, not only confirms the divine inspiration of the book, but illuminates the context of the verse as prophetic of the coming of the kingdom of God under Christ Jesus. He is the One who appears out of Bethlehem ("the House of Bread") with life-giving benefits for all who exercise faith in his sacrifice. He it is that does "shepherding in the strength of Jehovah" and that becomes great and spells peace to the ends of the earth among the restored, unified flock of God.—Mic. 5:2, 4; 2:12; John 6:33-40.

19 Great encouragement is to be found in Micah's prophecy concerning "the final part of the days," when "many nations" seek instructions from Jehovah. "And they will have to beat their swords into plowshares and their spears into pruning shears. They will not lift up sword, nation against nation, neither will they learn war any more. And they will actually sit, each one under his vine and under his fig tree, and there will be no one making them tremble; for the very mouth of Jehovah of armies has spoken it." Abandoning all false worship, they join with Micah in affirming: "We, for our part, shall walk in the name of Jehovah our God to time indefinite, even forever." Truly Micah's prophecy is faith-inspiring in providing a forevision of these momentous happenings. It is outstanding, too, in exalting Jehovah as the eternal Sovereign and King. How thrilling the words: "Jehovah will actually rule as king over them in Mount Zion, from now on and into time indefinite"!—Mic. 4:1-7; 1 Tim. 1:17.

17. What encouragement does the prophecy provide for those who serve God under persecution and difficulty?
18. What is the prophecy tied in with God's Kingdom rule by means of Christ Jesus?

19. (a) What faith-inspiring encouragement is provided for those who live in "the final part of the days"? (b) How does Micah exalt Jehovah's sovereignty?

Bible Book Number Thirty-four— *Nahum*

Writer:	**Nahum**
Place Written:	**Judah**
Writing Completed:	**Before 633 B.C.E.**
Time Covered:	**Undetermined**

"THE pronouncement against Nineveh." Nahum's prophecy opens with these ominous words. But why did he make this declaration of doom? What is known of ancient Nineveh? Her history is summarized by Nahum in three words: "city of bloodshed." (Nah. 3:1) Nineveh lay on the east bank of the Tigris River, at the confluence of the Khosr. It was heavily fortified by walls and moats, and was the capital of the Assyrian Empire in the latter part of its history. However, the origin of the city goes back to the days of Nimrod, the "'mighty hunter in opposition to Jehovah.' . . . he went forth into Assyria and set himself to building Nineveh." (Gen. 10:9-11) Nineveh thus had a bad beginning. She became specially renowned during the reigns of Sargon, Sennacherib, Esarhaddon and Ashurbanipal, in the closing period of the Assyrian Empire. By wars and conquests she enriched herself with loot, and became famed on account of the cruel, inhuman treatment that her rulers meted out to the multitude of captives. Says C. W. Ceram, on page 266 of his book *Gods, Graves and Scholars* (German, 1958): "Nineveh was impressed on the consciousness of mankind by little else than murder, plunder, suppression, and the violation of the weak; by war and all manner of physical violence; by the deeds of a sanguinary dynasty

1. What is known of ancient Nineveh?

of rulers who held down the people by terror and who often were liquidated by rivals more ferocious than themselves."

2 What of Nineveh's religion? She worshiped a great pantheon of gods, many of them imported from Babylon. Her rulers invoked these gods as they went out to destroy and exterminate, and her greedy priests egged on her campaigns of conquest, looking forward to rich repayment from the booty. In his book *Ancient Cities* (1886, page 25) W. B. Wright says: "They worshiped strength, and would say their prayers only to colossal idols of stone, lions and bulls whose ponderous limbs, eagle wings, and human heads were symbols of strength, courage, and victory. Fighting was the business of the nation, and the priests were incessant fomenters of war. They were supported largely from the spoils of conquest, of which a fixed percentage was invariably assigned them before others shared, for this race of plunderers was excessively religious."

3 Nahum's prophecy, though short, is packed with interest. All that we know of the prophet himself is contained in the opening verse: "The book of the vision of Nahum the Elkoshite." His name (Hebrew: *Na·hhum'*) means "Comfort; Comforter." His message was certainly no comfort to Nineveh, but to God's true people it spelled sure and lasting relief from an implacable and mighty foe. It is of comfort, too, in that almost alone of Jehovah's prophets, Nahum makes no mention of the sins of his own people. Though the site of Elkosh is now unknown, it seems probable that the prophecy was written in Judah. (Nah. 1:15) The fall of Nineveh, which occurred about 633 B.C.E., was still future when he recorded his prophecy, and he compares this event to the fall of No-amon (Thebes, in Egypt) that took place shortly before this. (Nah. 3:8) Hence Nahum must have written his prophecy sometime during this period.

4 The style of the book is distinctive. It contains no superfluous words. Its vigor and realism are in keeping with its being part of the inspired writings. Nahum excels in descriptive, emotional and dramatic power, dignified expression, clearness of imagery and graphically striking phraseology. (1:2-8, 12-14; 2:4, 12; 3: 1-5, 13-15, 18, 19) Most of the first chapter appears to be in the style of an acrostic poem. (Nah. 1:10, *NW* footnote, 1960 Ed.) Nahum's style is enriched by the singleness of his theme. He has utter abhorrence for Israel's treacherous foe. He sees nothing but the doom of Nineveh.

2. Of what kind was her religion?
3. (a) In what way is the meaning of Nahum's name appropriate? (b) To what period does his prophecy belong?
4. What qualities of writing are apparent in the book?

5 The authenticity of Nahum's prophecy is proved by the accuracy of its fulfillment. In Nahum's day, who else but a prophet of Jehovah would have dared to forecast that the proud capital of the Assyrian world power could be breached at the "gates of the rivers," her palace dissolved and she herself become "emptiness and voidness, and a city laid waste"? (Nah. 2:6-10) The events that followed showed that the prophecy was indeed inspired of God. The annals of the Babylonian king Nabopolassar describe the capture of Nineveh by the Medes and Babylonians: "By the bank of the Tigris they marched against Nineveh: a mighty assault they made upon the city, . . . a great havoc of the chief men was made. . . . The spoil of the city, a quantity beyond counting, they plundered, and turned the city into a mound and a ruin."[a] So complete was the ruin of Nineveh that even its site was forgotten for many centuries. Some critics came to ridicule the Bible on this point, saying that Nineveh could never have existed.

6 However, adding further to the evidence of Nahum's authenticity, the site of Nineveh was discovered and excavations were begun there A.D. 1843-1846. The mound of the ruined city is one of the largest in Mesopotamia, and it is estimated that 14,000,000 tons of earth would have to be moved to excavate it completely. What has been unearthed in Nineveh? Much that supports the accuracy of Nahum's prophecy! For example, her limestone streets still show ruts made by the wheels of her war chariots, her monuments and inscriptions testify to her cruelties and there are the remains of colossal statues of lions, many of them having human heads. No wonder Nahum spoke of her as "the lair of lions"!—2:11.

7 The canonicity of Nahum is shown by the book's being accepted by the Jews as part of the inspired Scriptures. It is completely in harmony with the rest of the Bible. The prophecy is uttered in the name of Jehovah, to whose attributes and supremacy it bears eloquent testimony.

CONTENTS OF NAHUM

8 **Pronouncement of Jehovah against Nineveh** (1:1-15). "Jehovah is a God exacting exclusive devotion and taking vengeance." With these words the prophet sets the scene for the "pronouncement against Nineveh." (1:1, 2) Though Jehovah is slow to anger, see him now as he expresses vengeance by wind and storm. Moun-

[a] *The Interpreter's Bible,* 1956, Vol. VI, page 694.

5. What proves the authenticity of Nahum's prophecy?
6. What has been uncovered at the site of ancient Nineveh that vindicates the accuracy of the book?
7. What supports the canonicity of the book?
8. What doom is pronounced for Nineveh, but what good news for Judah?

tains rock, hills melt and the earth heaves. Who can stand before the heat of his anger? Nonetheless, Jehovah is a stronghold for those who seek refuge in him. But Nineveh is doomed. She will be exterminated by a flood, and "distress will not rise up a second time." (1:9) Jehovah will blot out her name and her gods. He will bury her. In refreshing contrast there is good news for Judah! What is it? A publisher of peace calls on them to celebrate their festivals and pay their vows, for the enemy, the "good-for-nothing person," is doomed. "In his entirety he will certainly be cut off."—1:15.

9 **Foreview of Nineveh's destruction** (2:1–3:19). Nahum issues a taunting challenge to Nineveh to reinforce herself against an oncoming scatterer. Jehovah will regather his own, 'the pride of Jacob and of Israel.' See the shield and crimson garb of his men of vital energy and the fiery iron fittings of his "war chariot in the day of his getting ready"! War chariots "keep driving madly" in the streets, running like lightnings. (2:2-4) Now we get a prophetic view of the battle. The Ninevites stumble and hasten to defend the wall, but to no avail. The river gates open, the palace dissolves and the slave girls moan and beat upon their hearts. The fleeing men are commanded to stand still, but no one turns back. The city is plundered, and laid waste. Hearts melt. Where now is this lair of lions? The lion has filled his cave with prey for his whelps, but Jehovah declares: "Look! I am against you." (2:13) Yes, Jehovah will burn up Nineveh's war machine, send a sword to devour her young lions and cut off her prey from the earth.

10 "Woe to the city of bloodshed . . . full of deception and of robbery." Hear the lash of the whip and the rattling wheel. See the dashing horse, the leaping chariot, the mounted horseman, the flame of the sword and the lightning of the spear—and then, the heavy mass of carcasses. "There is no end to the dead bodies." (3:1, 3) And why? It is because she has ensnared nations with her prostitutions and families with her sorceries. A second time Jehovah declares: "Look! I am against you." (3:5) Nineveh will be exposed as an adulteress and despoiled, her fate being no better than that of No-amon (Thebes), whom Assyria took into captivity. Her fortresses are like ripe figs, "which, if they get wiggled, will certainly fall into the mouth of an eater." (3:12) Her warriors are like women. Nothing can save Nineveh from fire and sword. Her guardsmen will flee like a locust swarm on a sunny day, and her people will be scattered. The king of Assyria will know that there is no relief, nor is there healing for this catastrophe. All those hearing the report will clap their hands, for all have suffered from the badness of Assyria.

WHY BENEFICIAL

11 The prophecy of Nahum illustrates some fundamental Bible principles. The opening words of the vision repeat God's reason for giving the second of the Ten Commandments: "Jehovah is a God exacting exclusive devotion." Immediately thereafter he makes known the certainty of his "taking vengeance against his adversaries." Assyria's cruel pride and pagan gods could not save her from the execution of Jehovah's judgment. We can be confident that in due course Jehovah will likewise mete out justice to all the wicked. "Jehovah is slow to anger and great in power, and by no means will Jehovah hold back from punishing." Thus Jehovah's justice and supremacy are exalted against the background of his extermination of mighty Assyria. Nineveh did become "emptiness and voidness, and a city laid waste!" —Nah. 1:2, 3; 2:10.

12 In contrast to this 'entire cutting off' of Nineveh, Nahum announces restoration for 'the pride of Jacob and of Israel.' (Nah. 2:2) Jehovah also sends happy tidings to his people: "Look! Upon the mountains the feet of one bringing good news, one publishing peace." These tidings of peace have a connection with God's kingdom. How do we know this? It is apparent because of Isaiah's use of the same expression, but to which he adds the words: "the one bringing good news of something better, the one publishing salvation, the one saying to Zion: 'Your God has become king!' " (Nah. 1:15; Isa. 52:7) In turn, the apostle Paul at Romans 10:15 applies the expression to those whom Jehovah sends forth as Christian preachers of good news. These ones proclaim the "good news of the kingdom." (Matt. 24:14) True to the meaning of his name, Nahum provides much "Comfort" for all who seek the peace and salvation that come with God's kingdom. All of these will surely realize that 'Jehovah is good, a stronghold in the day of distress for those seeking refuge in him.'—Nah. 1:7.

9. What prophetic view do we get of the defeat of Nineveh?
10. As what is Nineveh exposed, and how is her end further described?
11. What fundamental Bible principles are illustrated in Nahum?
12. What restoration does Nahum announce, and how may his prophecy be linked with the Kingdom hope?

Bible Book Number Thirty-five—Habakkuk

Writer:	**Habakkuk**
Place Written:	**Judah**
Writing Completed:	**c. 628 B.C.E.**
Time Covered:	**Undetermined**

HABAKKUK is another of the "minor" prophets of the Hebrew Scriptures. However, his vision and pronouncement inspired of God are by no means minor in significance to God's people. Encouraging as well as strengthening, his prophecy sustains God's servants in time of stress. The book highlights two sublime truths: Jehovah God is the Universal Sovereign, and the righteous live by faith. The writing serves also as a warning to opposers of God's servants and to those who hypocritically profess to be His people. It sets a pattern for enduring faith in Jehovah, who is worthy of all songs of praise.

2 The book of Habakkuk opens: "The pronouncement that Habakkuk the prophet visioned." Who was this prophet? Habakkuk (Hebrew: *Hha·baq·qûq'*), whose name means "Embrace," that is, of love. Whether he was a Levitical temple musician cannot be stated definitely, although this has been inferred from the subscription at the end of the book: "To the director on my stringed instruments."

3 When did Habakkuk make his prophetic pronouncements? The above-mentioned subscription and the words "Jehovah is in his holy temple" indicate that the temple in Jerusalem was still standing. (2:20) This, together with the message of the prophecy, suggests that it was spoken not long before Jerusalem's destruction in 607 B.C.E. But how many years before? It must have been after the reign of God-fearing King Josiah, 659-628 B.C.E. The prophecy itself provides the clue in foretelling an activity that the people in Judah will not believe even if it is related. What is this? It is the raising up of the Chaldeans (Babylonians) by God to punish faithless Judah. (1:5, 6) This would fit the early part of the reign of idolatrous King Jehoiakim, a time when disbelief and injustice were rampant in Judah. Jehoiakim had been put on the throne by Pharaoh Nechoh and the nation was within Egypt's sphere of influence. Under such circumstances the people would feel they had cause to discredit any possibility of invasion from Babylon. But Nebuchadnezzar defeated Pharaoh Nechoh in the battle of Carchemish in 625 B.C.E., thus breaking the power of Egypt. The prophecy would therefore have been delivered before that event. So the indications point to the beginning of Jehoiakim's reign (begun in 628 B.C.E.), making Habakkuk a contemporary of Jeremiah.

4 How can we know that the book is inspired of God? Ancient catalogues of both Jews and Christians list the book as part of the canon of the Scriptures. The apostle Paul recognized the prophecy as part of the inspired Scriptures and makes a direct quotation of Habakkuk 1:5, referring to it as something "said in the Prophets." (Acts 13:40, 41) He made several references to the book in his letters. Certainly the fulfillment of Habakkuk's utterances against Judah and Babylon marks him as a true prophet of Jehovah, in whose name and for whose glory he spoke.

5 The book of Habakkuk is made up of three chapters. The first two chapters relate the strength of the Chaldeans, the grief awaiting the Babylonian nation that multiplies what is not its own, that makes evil gain for its house, that builds a city by bloodshed and that worships the carved image. The third chapter deals with the magnificence of Jehovah in the day of battle, and is unrivaled in the power and vibrancy of its dramatic style. This chapter is in the form of a poem and has been called "one of the most splendid and magnificent within the whole compass of Hebrew poetry."[a]

CONTENTS OF HABAKKUK

6 **The prophet's dialogue with Jehovah** (1:1-17). Faithlessness in Judah has provoked questions in Habakkuk's mind. "How long, O Jehovah, must I cry for help, and you do not hear?" he asks. "Why are despoiling and violence in front of me?" (1:2, 3) Law grows numb, the wicked one is surrounding the righteous one, and justice goes forth crooked. Because of this Jehovah will carry on an activity that will cause

a *The Twelve Minor Prophets,* 1868, E. Henderson, page 285.

1. What sublime truths are highlighted in the prophecy of Habakkuk?
2. What information is given about the writer?
3. What circumstances affecting Judah help to indicate the time of writing?
4. What proves the book to be inspired of God?
5. Briefly summarize the contents of the book.
6. What is the condition in Judah, and what amazing activity will Jehovah therefore carry on?

amazement, something that the "people will not believe although it is related." He is actually "raising up the Chaldeans"! Frightful indeed is the vision that He gives of this fierce nation as it comes swiftly. It is devoted to violence, and gathers up captives "just like the sand." (1:5, 6, 9) Nothing will stand in its way, not even kings and high officials, for it laughs at them all. It captures every fortified place. All this is for a judgment and a reproving from Jehovah, the "Holy One."—1:12.

7 **The vision of the five woes** (2:1-20). Habakkuk waits attentively for God to speak. Jehovah answers: "Write down the vision, and set it out plainly upon tablets." Even if it seems to be delayed, it will without fail come true. Jehovah comforts Habakkuk with the words: "As for the righteous one, by his faithfulness he will keep living." (2:2, 4) The self-assuming foe will not reach his goal, even though he keeps gathering to himself nations and peoples. Why, these are the very ones who will take up against him the proverbial saying of the five woes:

8 "Woe to him who is multiplying what is not his own." He himself will become something to pillage. He will be despoiled "because of the shedding of blood of mankind and the violence to the earth." (2:6, 8) "Woe to the one that is making evil gain for his house." His cutting off of many peoples will cause the very stones and woodwork of his house to cry out, high as he may set his nest. (2:9) "Woe to the one that is building a city by bloodshed." His peoples will toil only for fire and nothingness, declares Jehovah. "For the earth will be filled with the knowing of the glory of Jehovah as the waters themselves cover over the sea." —2:12, 14.

9 'Woe to the one who in anger makes his companion drunk so as to see his parts of shame.' Jehovah will make him drink from the cup of His right hand, bringing him disgrace in place of glory "because of the shedding of blood of mankind and the violence done to the earth." Of what use is a carved image to its maker—are not such valueless gods speechless? (2:15, 17) "Woe to the one saying to the piece of wood: 'O do awake!' to a dumb stone: 'O wake up! It itself will give instruction'!" In contrast to these lifeless gods, "Jehovah is in his holy temple. Keep silence before him, all the earth!"—2:19, 20.

10 **Jehovah in the day of battle** (3:1-19). In solemn prayer Habakkuk graphically recalls the fearsome activity of Jehovah. At his appearing "his dignity covered the heavens; and with his praise the earth became filled." (3:3) His brightness was like the light, and pestilence kept going before him. He stood still, shaking up the earth, causing the nations to leap and the eternal mountains to be smashed. Jehovah went riding like a mighty warrior with naked bow and with chariots of salvation. Mountains and the watery deep were agitated. Sun and moon stood still, and there were the light of arrows and the lightning of his spear as he marched through the earth threshing the nations in anger. He went forth for the salvation of his people and of his anointed one, and for the laying bare of the foundation of the wicked one, "clear up to the neck."—3:13.

11 The prophet is overwhelmed by this vision of the might of Jehovah's former work and of his coming world-shaking activity. "I heard, and my belly began to be agitated; at the sound my lips quivered; rottenness began to enter into my bones; and in my situation I was agitated, that I should quietly wait for the day of distress, for his coming up to the people, that he may raid them." (3:16) However, Habakkuk is determined that, regardless of the bad times that must be faced—no blossom on the fig tree, no yield on the vines, no flock in the pen—still he will exult in Jehovah and be joyful in the God of his salvation. He concludes his song of ecstasy with the words: "Jehovah the Sovereign Lord is my vital energy; and he will make my feet like those of the hinds, and upon my high places he will cause me to tread."—3:19.

WHY BENEFICIAL

12 Recognizing Habakkuk's prophecy as beneficial for teaching, the apostle Paul quoted from chapter two, verse four, on three different occasions. When stressing that the good news is God's power for salvation to everyone having faith, Paul wrote the Christians in Rome: "For in it God's righteousness is being revealed by reason of faith and toward faith, just as it is written: 'But the righteous one—by means of faith he will live.'" When writing the Galatians, Paul stressed the point that blessing comes through faith: "That by law no one is declared righteous with God is evident, because 'the righteous one will live by reason of faith.'" Paul also wrote in his letter to the Hebrews that Christians must show a live, soul-preserving faith, and he again referred to Jehovah's words to Habakkuk. However, he not only quotes Habakkuk in saying, "my righteous one will live by reason of

7. How does Jehovah comfort Habakkuk?
8, 9. Against what kind of persons are the five woes of the vision directed?
10. What fearsome activity accompanies Jehovah's appearing in the day of battle?
11. How does the vision affect Habakkuk, but what is his determination?
12. What beneficial application of Habakkuk 2:4 did Paul make?

faith," but also his further words, according to the Greek *Septuagint:* "If he shrinks back, my soul has no pleasure in him." Then he sums up by saying: We are "the sort that have faith to the preserving alive of the soul."—Rom. 1:17; Gal. 3:11; Heb. 10:38, 39.

13 Habakkuk's prophecy is most beneficial today to Christians who need vital energy. It teaches reliance upon God. It is also beneficial for warning others of God's judgments. The warning lesson is forceful: Do not consider God's judgments as being too delayed; they will "without fail come true." (Hab. 2:3) Without fail the prophecy of Judah's destruction by Babylon came true, and without fail Babylon itself was captured, the Medes and Persians taking the city in 539 B.C.E. What a warning to believe God's words! Thus the apostle Paul found it beneficial to quote Habakkuk (1:5, *LXX*) when he warned the Jews of his day not to be faithless: "See to it that what is said in the Prophets does not come upon you, 'Behold it, you scorners, and wonder at it, and vanish away, because I am working a work in your days, a work that you will by no means believe even if anyone relates it to you in detail.'" (Acts 13:40, 41) The faithless Jews would not heed Paul, even as they had not believed Jesus' warning of Jerusalem's destruction; they suffered the consequences for their faithlessness when Rome's armies devastated Jerusalem A.D. 70.—Luke 19:41-44.

14 Likewise, today, Habakkuk's prophecy encourages Christians to hold strong faith, while living in a world filled with violence. It helps them to teach others and to answer the question people all over the world have asked, Will God execute vengeance on the wicked? Note again the words of the prophecy: "Keep in expectation of it; for it will without fail come true. It will not be late." (Hab. 2:3) Whatever the commotions that occur in the earth, the anointed remnant of Kingdom heirs recall Habakkuk's words concerning Jehovah's past acts of vengeance: "You went forth for the salvation of your people, to save your anointed one." (3:13) Jehovah is indeed their "Holy One," from long ago, and the "Rock" who will reprove the unrighteous and give life to those whom he embraces in his love. All who love righteousness may rejoice in his kingdom and sovereignty, saying: "As for me, I will exult in Jehovah himself; I will be joyful in the God of my salvation. Jehovah the Sovereign Lord is my vital energy."—1:12; 3:18, 19.

13. The accurate fulfillment of Habakkuk's prophecies against Judah and Babylon emphasize what as to God's judgments?

14. (a) How does Habakkuk's prophecy encourage Christians today to hold strong faith? (b) As stated in the prophecy, what joyful confidence may lovers of righteousness now have?

Bible Book Number Thirty-six— Zephaniah

Writer:	**Zephaniah**
Place Written:	**Judah**
Writing Completed:	**Before 648 B.C.E.**
Time Covered:	**Undetermined**

EARLY in the reign of King Josiah of Judah (659-628 B.C.E.), at a time when Baal worship was running rampant and "the foreign-god priests" or Chemarim,[a] a group of black-robed temple keepers, were taking a lead in this unclean worship, the people of Jerusalem must have been startled by the message proclaimed by the prophet Zephaniah. Though he was probably a descendant of King Hezekiah and hence related to the royal house of Judah, Zephaniah was highly critical of conditions in the nation. (1:1) His message was one of doom. God's people had become disobedient, and only Jehovah could restore them to pure worship and bless them so that they might serve as "a name and a praise among all the peoples of the earth." (3:20) Zephaniah pointed out that only by divine intervention might one "be concealed in the day of Jehovah's anger." (2:3) How appropriate his name *Tsephan·yah'* (Hebrew), meaning "Jehovah Has Concealed"!

2 Zephaniah's efforts bore fruit. King Josiah, who had ascended the throne at the age of eight, started in the twelfth year of his reign "to cleanse Judah and Jerusalem." He rooted out false worship, repaired "the house of Jehovah," and reinstituted the celebration of the passover. (2 Chronicles, chaps. 34 and 35) King

a Zephaniah 1:4, *NW* footnote, 1960 Edition.

1. (a) Why was Zephaniah's message appropriate to his time? (b) How did the meaning of his name fit the situation?

2. How did Zephaniah's efforts bear fruit, but why was this only temporary?

Josiah's reforms were only temporary, however, for he was succeeded by three of his sons and one of his grandsons, all of whom did "bad in the eyes of Jehovah." (2 Chron. 36:1-12) This was all in fulfillment of Zephaniah's words: "I will give attention to the princes, and to the sons of the king, and to . . . those who are filling the house of their masters with violence and deception."—Zeph. 1:8, 9.

3 From the above it appears that "the word of Jehovah . . . occurred to Zephaniah" sometime before 648 B.C.E., the twelfth year of Josiah. Not only does the first verse identify him as speaking in Judah, but the detailed knowledge he shows of the localities and customs of Jerusalem argue for his residence in Judah. The message contained in the book is twofold, being both threatening and consoling. For the most part it centers around the day of Jehovah, a day of terror that is imminent, but at the same time it foretells that Jehovah will restore a humble people that "actually take refuge in the name of Jehovah."—1:1, 7-18; 3:12.

4 The authenticity of this book of prophecy cannot be successfully disputed. Jerusalem was destroyed in 607 B.C.E., more than forty years after Zephaniah had foretold it. We have not only secular history's word for this, but the Bible itself contains internal proof that this happened exactly as Zephaniah had prophesied. Shortly after Jerusalem's destruction, Jeremiah wrote the book of Lamentations, describing the horrors he had witnessed while they were still vividly in mind. A comparison of several passages bears out that Zephaniah's message is indeed "inspired of God." Zephaniah (2:2) warns of the need for repentance "*before* there comes upon you people the burning anger of Jehovah," whereas Jeremiah (Lam. 4:11) refers to something that has already happened when he says, "Jehovah . . . *has poured out* his burning anger." Zephaniah (1:17) foretells that Jehovah "*will cause* distress to mankind, and they *will* certainly *walk* like blind men . . . And their blood *will* actually *be poured out* like dust." Jeremiah (Lam. 4:14) speaks of this as an accomplished fact: "They *have wandered* about as blind in the streets. They *have become polluted* with blood."—See also Zeph. 1:13—Lam. 5:2; Zeph. 2:8, 10—Lam. 1:9, 16 and 3:61.

5 History likewise reports the destruction of the heathen nations, Moab, Ammon and Assyria, including its capital Nineveh, just as Zephaniah had foretold at God's direction. Even as the prophet Nahum foretold Nineveh's destruction (1:1; 2:10), so Zephaniah declared that Jehovah "will make Nineveh a desolate waste, a waterless region like the wilderness." (2:13) This destruction was so complete that scarcely two hundred years later the historian Herodotus wrote of the Tigris as "the river upon which the town of Nineveh formerly stood."[a] About A.D. 150 the Greek writer Lucian wrote that "not a trace of it remains."[b] *The Westminster Dictionary of the Bible* (1944), pages 428, 429, states that the invading armies "were greatly aided by a sudden rise of the Tigris, which carried away a great part of the city wall and rendered the place indefensible. So complete was the desolation that in Greek and Roman times the departed Nineveh became like a myth. Yet all the while part of the city lay buried under mounds of apparent rubbish." On page 402 the same volume shows that Moab was also destroyed as prophesied: "Nebuchadnezzar subjugated the Moabites. (Jos. *Antiq.* x 9,7) They disappear henceforth from history as a nation, though still existing as a race." Josephus also reports the subjugation of Ammon.

6 The Jews have always given Zephaniah its rightful place in the canon of inspired Scriptures. Its declarations uttered in Jehovah's name have been notably fulfilled, to Jehovah's vindication.

CONTENTS OF ZEPHANIAH

7 **Day of Jehovah at hand** (1:1-18). The book opens on a note of doom. " 'I shall without fail finish everything off the surface of the ground,' is the utterance of Jehovah." Nothing will escape, of man or of beast. Baal worshipers, foreign-god priests, rooftop worshipers of the heavens, those who mix Jehovah's worship with Malcham's, those drawing back from Jehovah and those not interested in seeking him—all must perish. The prophet commands: "Keep silence before the Lord Jehovah; for the day of Jehovah is near." (1:2, 7) Jehovah himself has prepared a sacrifice. Princes, violent ones, deceivers and the indifferent at heart—all will be sought out. Their wealth and possessions will be brought to nothing. The great day of Jehovah is near! It is "a day of fury, a day of distress and of anguish, a day of storm and of desolation, a day of darkness and of gloomi-

a M'Clintock and Strong's *Cyclopædia,* 1883, Vol. VII, page 112.

b *Gods, Graves, and Scholars,* 1958, by C. W. Ceram, page 281.

3. When and where did he prophesy, and what twofold message does the book contain?
4. What proves the prophecy to be authentic and inspired of God?
5. How does history show the prophecy to have been accurately fulfilled?
6. Why, then, does it take a rightful place in the Bible canon?
7. What will the great day of Jehovah mean for his enemies?

ness, a day of clouds and of thick gloom." The blood of those sinning against Jehovah will be poured out like dust. "Neither their silver nor their gold will be able to deliver them in the day of Jehovah's fury." The fire of his zeal will devour the whole earth.—1:15, 18.

8 **Seek Jehovah; nations to be destroyed** (2:1-15). Before that day passes like the chaff let the meek "seek Jehovah . . . Seek righteousness, seek meekness," and it may be you will be "concealed in the day of Jehovah's anger." (2:3) The utterance of Jehovah continues, pronouncing woe on the land of the Philistines, which is later to become a "region for the remaining ones of the house of Judah." Proud Moab and Ammon will be desolated like Sodom and Gomorrah, "because they reproached and kept putting on great airs against the people of Jehovah of armies." Their gods will perish with them. (2:7, 10) Jehovah's "sword" will slay also the Ethiopians. What of Assyria, with its capital Nineveh, to the north? It will become a barren wilderness and a dwelling for wild animals, yes "an object of astonishment," so that "everyone passing along by her will whistle" in amazement.—2:15.

9 **Rebellious Jerusalem called to account; humble remnant blessed** (3:1-20). It is woe, also, to Jerusalem, the rebellious and oppressive city! Her princes, "roaring lions," and her prophets, "men of treachery," have not trusted in her God, Jehovah. He will call for a full accounting. Will she fear Jehovah and accept discipline? No, for they act "promptly in making all their dealings ruinous." (3:3, 4, 7) It is Jehovah's judicial decision to gather the nations and pour out upon them all his burning anger, and all the earth will be devoured by the fire of his zeal. But, wonderful promise! Jehovah will "give to peoples the change to a pure language, in order for them all to call upon the name of Jehovah, in order to serve him shoulder to shoulder." (3:9) The haughtily exultant ones will be removed, and a humble remnant that does righteousness will find refuge in Jehovah's name. Joyful cries, cheers, rejoicing and exultation break out in Zion, for Jehovah the King of Israel is in their midst. This is no time to be afraid or to let hands drop down, for Jehovah will save and exult over them in his love and joy. "'For I shall make you people to be a name and a praise among all the peoples of the earth, when I gather back your captive ones before your eyes,' Jehovah has said."—3:20.

8. (a) How may protection be found? (b) What woes are pronounced against the nations?
9. (a) Why is it woe to Jerusalem, and what is Jehovah's judicial decision upon the nations? (b) On what joyful note does the prophecy end?

WHY BENEFICIAL

10 King Josiah, for one, heeded Zephaniah's warning message and benefited from it greatly. He embarked on a great campaign of religious reform. This also brought to light the book of the law that had been lost when the house of Jehovah fell into disrepair. Josiah was grief-stricken at hearing the consequences for disobedience read to him from this book, which confirmed at the mouth of another witness, Moses, what Zephaniah had been prophesying all along. Josiah now humbled himself before God, with the result that Jehovah promised him that the foretold destruction would not come in his day. (Deuteronomy, chaps. 28-30; 2 Ki. 22:8-20) The land had been spared disaster! But not for long, for Josiah's sons failed to follow the good example he set. However, for Josiah and his people, their paying attention to "the word of Jehovah that occurred to Zephaniah" proved highly beneficial indeed.

11 In his famous Sermon on the Mount, Christ Jesus, God's greatest prophet, supported Zephaniah as a true prophet of God by speaking words that are strikingly similar to Zephaniah's counsel at chapter 2, verse 3: "Seek Jehovah, all you meek ones of the earth . . . Seek righteousness, seek meekness." Jesus' admonition was: "Keep on, then, seeking first the kingdom and his righteousness." (Matt. 6:33) Those who seek first God's kingdom must guard against the indifference that Zephaniah warned about when he spoke of "those who are drawing back from following Jehovah and who have not sought Jehovah and have not inquired of him," and "who are saying in their heart, 'Jehovah will not do good, and he will not do bad.'" (Zeph. 1:6, 12) In his letter to the Hebrews (10:30, 37-39) Paul likewise tells of a coming day of judgment, warns against shrinking back, and adds: "Now we are not the sort that shrink back to destruction, but the sort that have faith to the preserving alive of the soul." It is not to the quitters or the unappreciative ones, but to those who meekly and earnestly seek Jehovah in faith, that the prophet says: "Probably you may be concealed in the day of Jehovah's anger." Zephaniah's prophecy leaves no question as to the suddenness with which that day will break upon the unsuspecting.—Zeph. 2:3; 1:14, 15; 3:8.

12 Here, then, is a message foreboding destruction for those who sin against Jehovah, but providing bright foregleams of blessings for those who repentantly "seek Jehovah." These may take courage, for, says Zephaniah,

10. Of what benefit was the prophecy in King Josiah's days?
11. How does Zephaniah tie in with the Sermon on the Mount and Paul's letter to the Hebrews in giving sound admonition?
12. What basis for courage does Zephaniah give for those who "seek Jehovah"?

"the king of Israel, Jehovah, is in the midst of you." It is no time for Zion to be afraid or to let hands drop down in inactivity. It is a time to trust in Jehovah. "As a mighty One, he will save. He will exult over you with rejoicing. He will become silent in his love. He will be joyful over you with happy cries." Happy, too, those who 'seek first his kingdom,' in anticipation of his loving protection and eternal blessing! —3:15-17.

Bible Book Number Thirty-seven— Haggai

Writer:	**Haggai**
Place Written:	**Jerusalem Rebuilt**
Writing Completed:	**521 B.C.E.**
Time Covered:	**112 days (521 B.C.E.)**

HAGGAI was his name, a prophet and "messenger of Jehovah" was his position, but what was his origin? Who was he? Haggai is the tenth of the "minor" prophets, and he was the first of the three that served after the Jews returned to their homeland in 537 B.C.E., the other two being Zechariah and Malachi. Haggai's name (Hebrew: *Hhag·gai'*) means "Festive." This may indicate he was born on a feast day. However, one Bible commentator says that he was given this name "in anticipation of the joyous return from exile."[a] Some suggest that "Haggai" may be an abbreviation of "Hag·gi'ah" (as at 1 Chronicles 6:30), which name means "Festival of Jehovah (or Jah)."

2 As handed down by Jewish tradition, it is reasonable to conclude that Haggai was born in Babylon and returned to Jerusalem with Zerubbabel and High Priest Joshua. Haggai served side by side with the prophet Zechariah, and at Ezra 5:1 and 6:14 the two are shown encouraging the sons of the Exile to resume temple building. He was a prophet of Jehovah in two respects, in that he both exhorted the Jews to fulfill their duties toward God and foretold, among other things, the shaking of all nations.—Hag. 2:6, 7.

3 Why did Jehovah commission Haggai? For this reason: In 537 B.C.E. Cyrus had issued the decree permitting the Jews to return to their homeland to rebuild the house of Jehovah. But it was now 521 B.C.E. and the temple was far from being completed. All these years they had let the obstacles of enemy opposition and materialism prevent them from realizing the very purpose of their return.—Ezra 1:1-4; 3:1-6, 8-10.

4 As the record shows, no sooner had the foundation of the temple been laid than "the people of the land were continually weakening the hands of the people of Judah and disheartening them from building, and hiring counselors against them to frustrate their counsel." (Ezra 4:4, 5) This continued all the remaining years of Cyrus, through the reigns of Cambyses and the usurper Magian Gaumata, and into the reign of Darius Hystaspis, who began to rule in 522 B.C.E. It was in the second year of his reign, that is, 521 B.C.E., that Haggai began to prophesy, and this encouraged the Jews to resume their temple building. At that a letter was sent to Darius by the neighboring governors asking for a ruling on the matter; Darius revived the decree of Cyrus and supported the Jews against their enemies.

5 There was never any question among the Jews about Haggai's prophecy belonging to the Hebrew canon, and this is also supported by the reference to him in Ezra 5:1 as prophesying "in the name of the God of Israel," as well as in Ezra 6:14. That his prophecy is part of 'all Scripture inspired of God' is proved by Paul's quoting it at Hebrews 12:26: "Now he has promised, saying: 'Yet once more I will set in commotion not only the earth but also the heaven.' "—Hag. 2:6.

6 Haggai's prophecy consists of four messages given over a period of 112 days, the time being figured according to the length of Jewish months, as shown in the chronology tables published by Parker and Dubberstein (1956). His style is simple and direct, and his emphasis on Jehovah's name is particularly noteworthy. In his thirty-eight verses he mentions Jehovah's name thirty-four times, fourteen times in the expression, "Jehovah of armies." He leaves no doubt that his message is from Jehovah: "Haggai the messenger of Jehovah went on to say

a *Bible Cyclopædia,* 1910, A. R. Fausset, page 267.

1, 2. What information is given about the prophet Haggai, and what was his twofold message?
3. What had the Jews failed to realize as to the purpose of their return from captivity?
4. What had hindered the temple building, but what developments took place when Haggai started to prophesy?
5. What proves that the book of Haggai belongs in the Bible canon?
6. Of what does the prophecy consist, and what emphasis is put on Jehovah's name?

to the people according to the messenger's commission from Jehovah, saying: 'I am with you people,' is the utterance of Jehovah." —Hag. 1:13.

7 This was a very important time in the history of God's people, and Haggai's work proved to be most beneficial. He was not the least backward in performing his task as a prophet and he did not mince words with the Jews. He was straightforward in telling them that it was a time to quit procrastinating and to get down to business. It was time to rebuild Jehovah's house and to restore pure worship, if they wanted to enjoy any prosperity from the hand of Jehovah. The whole tenor of the book of Haggai is to show that if one is to enjoy blessings from Jehovah he must serve the true God and do the work Jehovah commands to be done.

CONTENTS OF HAGGAI

8 **The first message** (1:1-15). This is directed to Governor Zerubbabel and High Priest Joshua, but in the hearing of the people. The people have been saying, "The time has not come, the time of the house of Jehovah, for it to be built." Jehovah through Haggai asks a searching question: "Is it the time for you yourselves to dwell in your paneled houses, while this house is waste?" (1:2, 4) They have sown much in a material way, but it has benefited them little in the way of food, drink and clothing. "Set your heart upon your ways," admonishes Jehovah. (1:7) It is high time to bring in lumber and build the house, that Jehovah may be glorified. The Jews are taking good care of their own houses, but Jehovah's house lies waste. Therefore he has withheld the dew of heaven and the increase of the field and his blessing from upon man and his toil.

9 Ah, they get the point! Haggai has not prophesied in vain. Rulers and people begin "to listen to the voice of Jehovah their God." Fear of Jehovah replaces fear of man. Jehovah's assurance through his messenger Haggai is: "I am with you people." (1:12, 13) It is Jehovah himself that rouses up the spirit of the governor, the spirit of the high priest and the spirit of the remnant of his people. They get to work, just twenty-three days after the start of Haggai's prophesying, and despite the official ban of the Persian government.

10 **The second message** (2:1-9). Less than a month passes after building activity is revived, and Haggai gives his second inspired message. This is addressed to Zerubbabel, Joshua and the remaining ones of the people. Evidently some of the Jews who returned from the captivity and who had seen the former temple of Solomon felt that this temple would be nothing by comparison. But what is the utterance of Jehovah of armies? 'Be strong, and work, for I am with you people.' (2:4) Jehovah reminds them of his covenant with them, and tells them not to be afraid. He strengthens them with the promise that he will rock all the nations, and cause their desirable things to come in, and fill his house with glory. The glory of this later house will be even greater than that of the former, and in this place he will give peace.

11 **The third message** (2:10-19). Two months and three days later Haggai addresses the priests. He uses an allegory to drive home his point. Will a priest's carrying holy flesh make holy any other food he touches? The answer is "No." Does the touching of something unclean, such as a dead body, make the one touching it unclean? The answer is "Yes." Haggai then applies the allegory. The people of the land are unclean by reason of their neglect of pure worship. Whatever they offer appears unclean to Jehovah God. Because of this Jehovah has not blessed their labors, and in addition he has sent on them scorching heat, mildew and hail. Let them change their ways, and from now on Jehovah will bless them.

12 **The fourth message** (2:20-23). This Haggai delivers on the same day as the third message, but it is directed to Zerubbabel. Again Jehovah speaks of "rocking the heavens and the earth," but this time extends this theme to the complete annihilation of the kingdoms of the nations. Many will be brought down, "each one by the sword of his brother." (2:22) Haggai concludes his prophecy with assurance of Jehovah's favor for Zerubbabel.

WHY BENEFICIAL

13 Jehovah's four messages communicated through Haggai were beneficial to the Jews of that day. They were encouraged to go right to work, and in four and a half years the temple was completed, to advance true worship in Israel. (Ezra 6:14, 15) Jehovah blessed their zealous activity. It was during this time of temple building that Darius the king of Persia examined the state records and reaffirmed the decree of Cyrus. The temple work was thus completed with his official backing.—Ezra 6: 1-13.

7. What did Haggai encourage the Jews to do, and what was his theme?
8. Why are the Jews not being blessed materially by Jehovah?
9. What spirit is roused in the people?
10. What do some Jews feel about the temple they are building, but what does Jehovah promise?
11. (a) By what allegory does Haggai point out the priests' neglect? (b) What has resulted therefrom?
12. What final message does Haggai direct to Zerubbabel?
13. Of what immediate benefit was Haggai's prophesying?

14 The prophecy also contains wise counsel for this day. How so? For one thing it underscores the need for the creature to put the interests of God's worship ahead of his own personal interests. It also drives home the point that selfishness is self-defeating, that it is futile to pursue materialism; it is the peace and blessing of Jehovah that make rich. (Hag. 1:3-6, 9-11; 2:9; Prov. 10:22) It also stresses the fact that the service of God itself does not make one clean unless it is pure and whole-souled, and that it may not be contaminated by loose conduct. (Hag. 2:10-14; Col. 3:23; Rom. 6:19) It shows that God's servants must not be pessimistic, looking back to "good old days," but forward-looking, 'setting their heart upon their ways' and seeking to bring glory to Jehovah. Then Jehovah will be with them. —Hag. 2:3, 4; 1:7, 8, 13; Phil. 3:13, 14; Rom. 8:31.

15 Once they got busy in the temple work, the Jews were favored and prospered by Jehovah. Obstacles vanished. The work was accomplished in quick time. Fearless, zealous activity for Jehovah will always be rewarded. Difficulties, real or imagined, can be overcome by exercising courageous faith. Obedience to "the word of Jehovah" gets results.—Hag. 1:1.

14. What wise counsel does the prophecy provide for this day?
15. What does it show as to the results of zealous obedience?

16 What of the prophecy that Jehovah will 'rock the heavens and the earth'? The apostle Paul gives the application of Haggai 2:6 in these words: "But now [God] has promised, saying: 'Yet once more I will set in commotion not only the earth but also the heaven.' Now the expression 'Yet once more' signifies the removal of the things being shaken as things that have been made, in order that the things not being shaken may remain. Wherefore, seeing that we are to receive a kingdom that cannot be shaken, let us continue to have undeserved kindness, through which we may acceptably render God sacred service with godly fear and awe. For our God is also a consuming fire." (Heb. 12:26-29) Haggai (2:21, 22) shows that the rocking is in order to "overthrow the throne of kingdoms and annihilate the strength of the kingdoms of the nations." In quoting the prophecy Paul speaks, in contrast, of God's kingdom "that cannot be shaken." In contemplation of this Kingdom hope, let us then 'be strong and work,' rendering God sacred service. Let us be mindful, too, that before Jehovah overthrows the nations of earth, something precious is to be stirred up and come out of them, for survival: " 'I will rock all the nations, and the desirable things of all the nations must come in; and I will fill this house with glory,' Jehovah of armies has said."—2:4, 7.

16. What relation does the prophecy have to the Kingdom hope, and to what service should it stir us today?

Bible Book Number Thirty-eight— Zechariah

Writer:	**Zechariah**
Place Written:	**Jerusalem Rebuilt**
Writing Completed:	**519 B.C.E.**
Time Covered:	**521-519 B.C.E.**

AT A standstill! That was the state of the construction work on Jehovah's temple in Jerusalem when Zechariah began to prophesy. Whereas Solomon had built the original temple in seven and a half years (1 Ki. 6:37, 38), the repatriated Jews had been back in Jerusalem for sixteen years and the building was yet far from completion. The work had finally stopped altogether following the ban by Artaxerxes (likely Gaumata). But now, despite this official ban, the work was once more getting under way due to Jehovah's using Haggai and Zechariah to stir up the people to renew the construction and to stay with it until completed.—Ezra 4:23, 24; 5:1, 2.

2 The task before them looked mountainous. (Zech. 4:6, 7) They were few, the opposers many, and although they had a prince of the Davidic line, Zerubbabel, they had no king and were under foreign domination. How easy to sink into a weak, self-centered attitude, when really the time demanded vigorous faith and energetic action! Zechariah was used to draw their attention to God's present purposes and even grander future purposes, thus strengthening them for the work to be done. (Zech. 8:9,

1. What was the situation as to the temple in Jerusalem when Zechariah began to prophesy?
2. Why did the task look mountainous, but to what did Zechariah draw their attention?

13) It was no time to be like their unappreciative forefathers.—Zech. 1:5, 6.

3 Who was Zechariah? There are about thirty different persons mentioned in the Bible with the name Zechariah. However, the writer of the book that bears this name is identified as "Zechariah the son of Berechiah the son of Iddo the prophet," and apparently he was a priest. (Zech. 1:1; Ezra 5:1; Neh. 12:12, 16) His name (Hebrew: *Z'khar·yah'*) means "Jehovah Has Remembered" or "Remembered by Jehovah." The book of Zechariah makes it very plain that "Jehovah of armies" remembers his people, to deal well with them for his own name's sake. The dates mentioned in the book give it a coverage of about two years. (Zech. 1:1; 7:1) It was in the second year of Darius that the temple building was resumed and Zechariah commenced prophesying. Secular history establishes that Darius I, Hystaspis, king of Medo-Persia, began to reign in 522 B.C.E. Hence Zechariah's prophecy would no doubt be spoken and also recorded during the years 521-519 B.C.E.—Ezra 4:24.

4 Students of the book of Zechariah will find ample proof of its authenticity. Take the case of Tyre. It was after a thirteen-year-long siege that Babylonian king Nebuchadnezzar ruined Tyre. Yet Zechariah, many years later, again predicted its fall. Why? Because before the mainland city of Tyre was destroyed, its people removed their possessions to a rocky island fortress that they had established not far from the shore. It was this island Tyre that Alexander the Great overthrew at the time of his famous causeway-building feat; he ruthlessly burned her, thus fulfilling Zechariah's prophecy of some two centuries earlier.[a]—Zech. 9:2-4.

5 The most convincing proof of the book's divine inspiration, however, is to be found in the fulfillment of its prophecies concerning the Messiah, Christ Jesus, as can be seen by comparing Zechariah 9:9 with Matthew 21:4, 5 and John 12:14-16, Zechariah 12:10 with John 19:34-37, and Zechariah 13:7 with Matthew 26:31 and Mark 14:27. Also, there are the similarities to be noted between Zechariah 8:16 and Ephesians 4:25, Zechariah 3:2 and Jude 9, and Zechariah 14:5 and Jude 14. How marvelous the harmony of God's Word!

6 There are some Bible critics who say that the change in writing style from chapter nine onward indicates that the latter section is the work of another or of two other writers. The change in style, however, is certainly no greater than the change in subject matter would justify. Whereas the first eight chapters deal with matters of more present importance to the people of Zechariah's day, in chapters 9 to 14 the prophet looks forward into a more distant future. Some have queried why it is that Matthew 27:9 quotes Zechariah (11:12) but attributes his words to Jeremiah. In Matthew's time it appears that the Bible section known as the Prophets began with Jeremiah (instead of Isaiah, as in our present Bibles); hence Matthew, in referring to Zechariah as "Jeremiah," could have been following the Jewish practice of including a whole section of Scripture under the name of the first book of the section. Jesus himself used the designation "Psalms" to include all the books known as the Writings.—Luke 24:44.[b]

7 Up to chapter 6, verse 8, the book consists of a series of eight visions, similar in type to those of Daniel and Ezekiel, relating generally to the temple's reconstruction. These are followed by pronouncements and prophecies regarding sincere worship, restoration and Jehovah's day of war.

CONTENTS OF ZECHARIAH

8 **Vision of the four horsemen** (1:1-17). "Return to me . . . and I shall return to you," says Jehovah, and then he asks, "My words and my regulations that I commanded my servants, the prophets, did they not catch up with your fathers?" (1:3, 6) The people admit they have received their just dues. Zechariah's first vision now appears. At night four horsemen stand among trees near Jerusalem, having returned from inspecting the whole earth, which they found undisturbed and at ease. But Jehovah's angel, who interviews them, *is* disturbed over Jerusalem's condition. Jehovah himself declares his great indignation against the nations that helped toward Zion's calamity, and that he will "certainly return to Jerusalem with mercies." His own house will be built in her, and his cities "will yet overflow with goodness."—1:16, 17.

9 **Vision of the horns and craftsmen** (1:18-21). Zechariah sees the four horns that dispersed Judah, Israel and Jerusalem. Then Jehovah shows him four craftsmen, explaining that these will come to cast down the horns of the nations that oppose Judah.

a *Archaeology and Bible History,* 1950, J. P. Free, pages 262, 263.

b *The Jewish Encyclopedia,* 1910, Vol. III, page 143.

3. (a) How is Zechariah identified, and why is his name appropriate? (b) When was the prophecy spoken and recorded?
4, 5. (a) Why did Zechariah predict Tyre's fall long after the city's destruction? (b) The fulfillment of what particular prophecies convincingly proves the book's inspiration?
6. (a) What accounts for the change of style from chapter 9 onward? (b) What appears to be the reason for Matthew's referring to Zechariah as "Jeremiah"?
7. How is the book arranged?
8. What does the vision of the four horsemen show concerning Jerusalem and the nations?
9. How does Jehovah explain the vision of the horns and craftsmen?

10 **Vision of Jerusalem's prosperity** (2:1-13). A man is seen measuring Jerusalem. The city will be blessed with expansion, and Jehovah will be a wall of fire all around her and a glory in the midst of her. He calls out, "Hey there, Zion! Make your escape," and adds the warning, "He that is touching you is touching my eyeball." (2:7, 8) With Jehovah residing in her, Zion will rejoice and many nations will join themselves to Jehovah. All flesh is commanded to keep silence before Jehovah, "for he has aroused himself from his holy dwelling."—2:13.

11 **Vision of Joshua's deliverance** (3:1-10). High Priest Joshua is shown on trial, with Satan opposing him and Jehovah's angel rebuking Satan. Is not Joshua "a log snatched out of the fire"? (3:2) Joshua is declared cleansed and his befouled garments are changed for clean "robes of state." He is urged to walk in the ways of Jehovah, who is 'bringing in his servant Sprout,' and who puts before Joshua a stone upon which are seven eyes.—3:4, 8.

12 **Vision of the lampstand and olive trees** (4:1-14). The angel awakens Zechariah to see a gold lampstand of seven lamps, flanked by two olive trees. He hears this word of Jehovah to Zerubbabel: 'Not by military force, nor by power, but by God's spirit.' The "great mountain" will be leveled before Zerubbabel, and the temple headstone will be brought forth to the cry: "How charming! How charming!" Zerubbabel has laid the temple foundations, and Zerubbabel will finish the work. The seven lamps are Jehovah's eyes that "are roving about in all the earth." (4:6, 7, 10) The two olive trees are Jehovah's two anointed ones.

13 **Vision of the flying scroll** (5:1-4). Zechariah sees a flying scroll, thirty feet long and fifteen feet wide. The angel explains that this is the curse that is going forth because of all those stealing and swearing falsely in Jehovah's name.

14 **Vision of the ephah measure** (5:5-11). The lid is lifted from an ephah measure (about 1.1 bushels, U.S.), revealing a woman named "Wickedness." She is thrust back into the ephah, which is then lifted toward heaven by two winged women, to be carried to Shinar (Babylon) and "deposited there upon her proper place."

15 **Vision of the four chariots** (6:1-8). Look! From between two copper mountains four chariots appear, with different-colored horses. They are the four spirits of the heavens. At the angel's command, they go walking about in the earth.

16 **The Sprout, insincere fasting** (6:9–7:14). Jehovah now instructs Zechariah to place a grand crown on High Priest Joshua's head. He speaks prophetically of the "Sprout" who will build Jehovah's temple and rule as a priest on his throne.

17 Two years after Zechariah started prophesying, a delegation arrives from Bethel to ask the temple priests whether certain periods of weeping and fasting should continue to be observed. Through Zechariah Jehovah asks the people and the priests whether they are really sincere in their fasting. What Jehovah desires is 'obedience, true justice, loving-kindness and mercies.' (7:7, 9) Because they resist his prophetic words with stubborn shoulders and emery-stone hearts he will hurl them tempestuously throughout all the nations.

18 **Restoration, "ten men"** (8:1-23). Jehovah declares he will return to Zion and reside in Jerusalem, which will be called "the city of trueness." Old people will sit and children will play in her public squares. This is not too difficult for Jehovah the true and righteous God! Jehovah promises the seed of peace to the remnant of this people, saying: "Do not be afraid. May your hands be strong." (8:3, 13) These things they should do: Speak truthfully with one another and judge with truth, keeping hearts free from calamitous schemes and false oaths. Why, the time will come when the people of many cities will certainly invite one another to go up earnestly to seek Jehovah, and "ten men" out of all the languages will "take hold of the skirt of a man who is a Jew" and go along with God's people.—8:23.

19 **Pronouncements against nations, false shepherds** (9:1–11:17). In the book's second section, chapters 9 to 14, Zechariah turns from the allegorical visions to the more customary prophetic style. He begins with a severe pronouncement against various cities, including the rocky island city of Tyre. Jerusalem is told to shout in joyful triumph, for, "Look! Your king himself comes to you. He is righteous, yes, saved; humble, and riding upon an ass." (9:9) Cutting off war chariots and bow, this one will speak peace to the nations, and will rule to the ends of the earth. Jehovah will fight for his people against Greece, and save them. "For O how great his goodness is, and how great his handsomeness is!" (9:17) Jehovah, the Rain-giver, condemns the diviners and false shep-

10. How is Jehovah associated with Jerusalem's prosperity?
11. How is High Priest Joshua vindicated, and what course is urged upon him?
12. What encouragement and assurance are given concerning the temple building?
13-15. What is seen in the visions of the flying scroll, the ephah measure and the four chariots?
16. What is prophesied concerning the "Sprout"?
17. As to worship, what does Jehovah desire, and what is to result to those resisting his words?
18. What glorious promises of restoration does Jehovah make?
19. What severe pronouncements follow, but what is said concerning Jerusalem's king?

herds. He will make the house of Judah superior and those of Ephraim like a mighty man. As for the redeemed ones, "their heart will be joyful in Jehovah . . . and in his name they will walk about."—10:7, 12.

[20] Zechariah is now assigned to shepherd the flock, which has been sold into slaughter by compassionless shepherds who say: "May Jehovah be blessed, while I shall gain riches." (11:5) The prophet takes two staffs and names them "Pleasantness" and "Union." Breaking "Pleasantness," he symbolizes a covenant broken. Then he calls for his wages, and they weigh him out thirty pieces of silver. Jehovah orders Zechariah to throw it into the treasury and, with superlative sarcasm, says, "the majestic value with which I have been valued." (11:13) Now staff "Union" is cut up, breaking the brotherhood of Judah and Israel. A sword will come upon the false shepherds who have neglected Jehovah's sheep.

[21] **Jehovah wars, becomes king** (12:1–14:21). Another pronouncement begins. Jehovah will make Jerusalem a bowl that causes peoples to reel, and a burdensome stone that scratches those lifting it. He will annihilate all nations that come against Jerusalem. Upon the house of David will Jehovah pour out the spirit of favor and entreaties, and the people will look upon the one they pierced through, wailing over him "as in the wailing over an only son." (12:10) Jehovah of armies declares a cutting-off of all idols and false prophets; the very parents of such a one must wound him so that in shame he removes his prophet's garb. Jehovah's associate shepherd is to be struck and the flock scattered, but he will refine a "third part" to call upon his name. Jehovah will say: "It is my people," and it will answer: "Jehovah is my God."—13:9.

[22] "Look! There is a day coming, belonging to Jehovah." All nations will attack Jerusalem and half the city will go into exile, leaving behind a remnant. Then Jehovah will go forth and war against those nations, "as in the day of his warring, in the day of fight." (14:1, 3) The mountain of olive trees, on the east of Jerusalem, will split from east to west, making a valley for refuge. In that day living waters will flow east and west from Jerusalem, in summer and in winter, and "Jehovah must become king over all the earth." (14:9) While Jerusalem enjoys security, Jehovah will scourge those warring against her. As they stand, their flesh, eyes and tongues will rot away. Confusion will hit them. The hand of each one will turn against his neighbor's. Those left alive of all the nations will have to "go up from year to year to bow down to the King, Jehovah of armies."—14:16.

WHY BENEFICIAL

[23] All who study and meditate on the prophecy of Zechariah will be benefited in gaining faith-strengthening knowledge. No less than fifty-two times does Zechariah draw attention to "Jehovah of armies" as the One that fights for and protects his people, filling them with power according to their need. When mountainlike opposition threatened the completion of the temple building, Zechariah declared: "This is the word of Jehovah to Zerubbabel, saying, '"Not by a military force, nor by power, but by my spirit," Jehovah of armies has said. Who are you, O great mountain? Before Zerubbabel you will become a level land.'" The temple was completed with the help of Jehovah's spirit. Likewise today, obstacles will melt if tackled with faith in Jehovah. It is just as Jesus told his disciples: "If you have faith the size of a mustard grain, you will say to this mountain, 'Transfer from here to there,' and it will transfer, and nothing will be impossible for you."—Zech. 4:6, 7; Matt. 17:20.

[24] In chapter 13, verses 2 to 6, Zechariah gives a prophetic illustration of the loyalty that marks Jehovah's organization. This must transcend every human relationship, such as that of close flesh-and-blood relatives. If the son in a family should prophesy falsehood in the name of Jehovah, that is, speak contrary to the Kingdom message and try wrongly to influence others in the congregation of God's people, the parents must reject this one, considering him spiritually dead. The same position must be taken with regard to any intimate associate who prophesies falsely, so that he may become ashamed and wounded at heart because of his wrong action.

[25] As our introductory paragraphs showed, Jesus' entry into Jerusalem as king, "humble, and riding upon an ass," his betrayal for "thirty silver pieces," the scattering of his disciples at that time and his being pierced on the stake by the soldier's spear, were all foretold by Zechariah in exact detail. (Zech. 9:9; 11:12; 13:7; 12:10) The prophecy also names "the Sprout" as the builder of the temple of Jehovah. A comparison of Isaiah 11:1-10, Jeremiah 23:5 and Luke 1:32, 33 shows this one to be Jesus Christ, who "will rule as king over the

20. What symbols are enacted with the staffs "Pleasantness" and "Union"?
21. (a) What is Jehovah's judgment on those who fight against Jerusalem? (b) What scattering and refining are foretold?
22. What is to result to the nations and to Jerusalem in 'the day belonging to Jehovah'?
23. How is the record of Zechariah strengthening to faith?
24. What illustration of loyalty is given in chapter 13?
25. How does the prophecy link with other scriptures in identifying Messiah, "the Sprout," and his office as High Priest and King under Jehovah?

house of Jacob forever." Zechariah describes "the Sprout" as "a priest upon his throne," which ties in with the apostle Paul's words: "Jesus . . . has become a high priest according to the manner of Melchizedek forever," also, "He has sat down at the right hand of the throne of the majesty in the heavens." (Zech. 6:12, 13; Heb. 6:20; 8:1) Thus the prophecy points to "the Sprout" as High Priest and King at God's right hand in the heavens, while at the same time proclaiming Jehovah as Sovereign Ruler over all: "And Jehovah must become king over all the earth. In that day Jehovah will prove to be one, and his name one."—Zech. 14:9.

26 Referring to that time, the prophet repeats the phrase "in that day" twenty times, and it even concludes his prophecy. An examination of its many occurrences shows it to be the day when Jehovah cuts off the names of the idols and removes the false prophets. (Zech. 13:2, 4) It is the day when Jehovah wars on the aggressor nations and spreads confusion in their ranks as he annihilates them and provides 'the valley of his mountains' as a refuge for his own people. (Zech. 14:1-3, 13; 12:8, 9; 14:4, 5) Yes, "Jehovah their God will certainly save them in that day like the flock of his people," and they will call one to the other from under the vine and fig tree. (Zech. 9:16; 3:10; Mic. 4:4) It is the glorious day when Jehovah of armies "will reside in the midst" of his people and when "living waters will go forth from Jerusalem." These words of Zechariah identify events "in that day" as harbingers of "a new heaven and a new earth" of Kingdom promise. —Zech. 2:11; 14:8; Rev. 21:1-3; 22:1.

27 "Who has despised the day of small things?" asks Jehovah. Look! This prosperity is to embrace the entire earth: 'Many peoples and mighty nations will actually come to seek Jehovah of armies in Jerusalem, and ten men out of all the languages of the nations will take hold of the skirt of a man who is a Jew, saying: "We will go with you people, for we have heard that God is with you people."' "In that day" even the bells of the horse will bear the words "Holiness belongs to Jehovah!" These heartwarming prophecies are most beneficial to consider, for they show Jehovah's name will indeed be sanctified through his Kingdom Seed!—Zech. 4:10; 8:22, 23; 14:20.

26. To what glorious "day" does the prophecy repeatedly refer?

27. How does the prophecy focus attention on Jehovah's sanctification?

Bible Book Number Thirty-nine— Malachi

Writer:	**Malachi**
Place Written:	**Jerusalem Rebuilt**
Writing Completed:	**a. 443 B.C.E.**
Time Covered:	**Undetermined**

WHO was Malachi? There is not a single fact recorded regarding his ancestry or personal history. However, from the tenor of his prophecy it is quite evident that he was most zealous in his devotion to Jehovah God, upholding His name and pure worship, and that he felt strong indignation toward those who profess to serve God but who serve only themselves. The name of Jehovah is mentioned forty-eight times in the four chapters of his prophecy.

2 His name in Hebrew is *Mal·a·khi'*, which means "My Messenger," or, if the name is an abbreviation (as some think) of *Mal·a·khi·yah'* (Greek: *Malakhias*), it means "Messenger [Angel] of Jehovah." The Hebrew Scriptures, the *Septuagint Version,* and the chronological order of the books all place Malachi last among the twelve "minor" prophets. According to the tradition of the Great Synagogue, he lived after the prophets Haggai and Zechariah and was a contemporary of Nehemiah.

3 When was the prophecy written? It was during the administration of a governor, which places it in the time of the restoration of Jerusalem following the seventy years' desolation of Judah. (Mal. 1:8) But which governor? Since the temple service is mentioned, but without reference to building the temple, it must have been after the time of Governor Zerubbabel, during whose tenure of office the temple was completed. There is only one other governor of this period mentioned in the Scriptures, and he is Nehemiah. Does the prophecy fit Nehemiah's time? Nothing is stated in Mal-

1. What indicates Malachi's zeal for Jehovah?
2. What does Malachi's name mean, and when, apparently, did he live?

3. What indicates that the prophecy was written after 443 B.C.E.?

achi concerning the rebuilding of Jerusalem and its wall, which eliminates the early part of Nehemiah's governorship. However, much is said concerning the abuses by the priesthood, tying Malachi in with the situation that existed when Nehemiah came a second time to Jerusalem, following his recall to Babylon by Artaxerxes in 443 B.C.E., the thirty-second year of the king's reign. (Mal. 2:1; Neh. 13:6) Similar passages in Malachi and Nehemiah indicate that the prophecy applies to this particular time.—Mal. 2:4-8, 11, 12—Neh. 13:11, 15, 23-26; Mal. 3:8-10—Neh. 13:10-12.

4 The book of Malachi has always been accepted by the Jews as authentic. Quotations from it in the Greek Scriptures, a number of which show fulfillments of his prophecy, prove that Malachi was inspired and part of the canon of Hebrew Scriptures that was recognized by the Christian congregation.—Mal. 1:2, 3—Rom. 9:13; Mal. 3:1—Matt. 11:10 and Luke 1:76 and 7:27; Mal. 4:5, 6—Matt. 11:14 and 17:10-13, Mark 9:11-13 and Luke 1:17.

5 Malachi's prophecy indicates that the religious zeal and enthusiasm aroused by the prophets Haggai and Zechariah at the time of rebuilding the temple had passed away. Priests had become careless, proud and self-righteous. Temple services had become a mockery. Tithes and offerings had lapsed due to a feeling that God was not interested in Israel. The hopes centered in Zerubbabel had not been realized and, contrary to some expectations, Messiah had not come. The Jews' spiritual state was at a very low ebb. What ground was there for encouragement and hope? How could the people be made aware of their true state and be awakened to return to righteousness? The prophecy of Malachi supplied the answer.

6 Malachi's manner of writing is direct and forceful. He first states the proposition and then answers the objections of those whom he addresses. Finally, he asserts his original proposition. This adds strength and vividness to his argument. Instead of soaring to heights of eloquence, he uses an abrupt, strongly argumentative style.

CONTENTS OF MALACHI

7 **Jehovah's commandment to the priests** (1:1–2:17). Jehovah first expresses his love for his people. He has loved Jacob and hated Esau. Let Edom try to build its devastated places; Jehovah will tear them down and they will be called "the territory of wickedness," the people denounced by Jehovah, for Jehovah will "be magnified over the territory of Israel."—1:4, 5.

8 Now Jehovah addresses directly the 'priests who are despising his name.' As they try to justify themselves, Jehovah points to their blind, lame and sick sacrifices, and asks, Will even the governor approve such offerings? Jehovah himself has no delight in them. His name must be exalted among the nations, but these men are profaning him by saying: "The table of Jehovah is something polluted." A curse will come on them because they have cunningly sidestepped their vows in offering worthless sacrifices. " 'For I am a great King,' Jehovah of armies has said, 'and my name will be fear-inspiring among the nations.' "—1:6, 12, 14.

9 Jehovah now gives a commandment to the priests, saying that if they do not take this counsel to heart he will send a curse upon them and upon their blessings. He will scatter the dung of their festivals upon their faces because of their failure to keep the covenant of Levi. "For the lips of a priest are the ones that should keep knowledge, and the law is what people should seek from his mouth; for he is the messenger of Jehovah of armies." (2:7) Malachi confesses the great sin of Israel and Judah. They have dealt treacherously with one another and have profaned the holiness of Jehovah, their Father and Creator, by taking the daughter of a foreign god as bride. They have gone to the extreme in wearying Jehovah. They have even asked, "Where is the God of justice?"—2:17.

10 **The true Lord and the messenger** (3:1-18). The prophecy now reaches a climax in the words of "Jehovah of armies": "Look! I am sending my messenger, and he must clear up a way before me. And suddenly there will come to His temple the true Lord, whom you people are seeking, and the messenger of the covenant in whom you are delighting. Look! He will certainly come." (3:1) As a refiner, he will cleanse the sons of Levi, and Jehovah will become a speedy witness against the wicked who have not feared Him. Jehovah does not change, and, because they are sons of Jacob, he will mercifully return to them if they return to him.

11 They have been robbing God, but now let them test him by bringing their tithes into the storehouse, that there may be food in his house, confident that he will pour forth from the floodgates of the heavens the very fullness of his blessing. They will become a land of delight, pronounced happy by all nations. Their

4. What proves the book to be authentic and inspired?
5. What low spiritual condition called forth Malachi's prophecy?
6. What is Malachi's style of writing?
7. What love and hatred does Jehovah express?
8. How have the priests polluted Jehovah's table, and why will a curse come on them?
9. In what duties have the priests failed, and how have they profaned Jehovah's holiness?
10. For what work of judgment does the Lord come to his temple?
11. How should they now test God, and what blessings will follow?

words had been strong against Jehovah, but some have been paying attention and listening to him. "And a book of remembrance began to be written up before him for those in fear of Jehovah and for those thinking upon his name." (3:16) They will certainly become Jehovah's in the day of his producing a special property.

12 **The great and fear-inspiring day of Jehovah** (4:1-6). This is the coming day that will devour the wicked, leaving neither root nor bough. But the sun of righteousness will shine forth to those who fear Jehovah's name, and they will be healed. Jehovah admonishes them to remember the law of Moses. Before his great and fear-inspiring day Jehovah promises to send Elijah the prophet. "And he must turn the heart of fathers back toward sons, and the heart of sons back toward fathers; in order that I may not come and actually strike the earth with a devoting of it to destruction." —4:6.

WHY BENEFICIAL

13 The book of Malachi helps in understanding the unchanging principles and merciful love of Jehovah God. At the outset it emphasizes Jehovah's great love for his people "Jacob." He declared to the sons of Jacob: "I am Jehovah; I have not changed." Despite their great wickedness, he was ready to return to his people if they would return to him. A merciful God indeed! (Mal. 1:2; 3:6, 7; Rom. 11:28; Ex. 34:6, 7) Through Malachi Jehovah stressed that a priest's lips "should keep knowledge." All who are entrusted with the teaching of God's Word should pay heed to this point, making sure that it is accurate knowledge that they impart. (Mal. 2:7; Phil. 1:9-11) Jehovah does not tolerate hypocrites, those who try to make out that "doing bad is good in the eyes of Jehovah." No one should think that he can deceive Jehovah by making the mere pretense of an offering to this great King. (Mal. 2:17; 1:14; Col. 3:23, 24) Jehovah will be a speedy witness against all who violate his righteous laws and principles; no one may expect to act wickedly and "get away with it." Jehovah will judge them. (Mal. 3:5; Heb. 10:30, 31) The righteous may have full assurance that Jehovah will remember their deeds and reward them. They should pay attention to the law of Moses, even as Jesus did, for it contains many things that are fulfilled in him.—Mal. 3:16; 4:4; Luke 24:44, 45.

14 As the last book of the inspired "minor" prophets Malachi points forward to events surrounding the coming of the Messiah, whose appearing more than four centuries later provided the reason for the writing of the Christian Greek Scriptures. As recorded at Malachi 3:1, Jehovah of armies said: "Look! I am sending my messenger, and he must clear up a way before me." Speaking under inspiration, the aged Zechariah showed that this had a fulfillment in his son John the Baptist. (Luke 1:76) Jesus Christ confirmed this, stating at the same time: "There has not been raised up a greater than John the Baptist; but a person that is a lesser one in the kingdom of the heavens is greater than he is." John had been sent, as Malachi foretold, to 'prepare the way,' so that he was not of the class with whom Jesus later made a covenant for a kingdom. —Matt. 11:7-12; Luke 7:27, 28; 22:28-30.

15 Then, at Malachi 4:5, 6, Jehovah promised: "Look! I am sending to you people Elijah the prophet." Who is this "Elijah"? Both the angel who appeared to Zechariah and Jesus apply these words likewise to John the Baptist, showing that he was the one to "restore all things" and "to get ready for Jehovah a prepared people" to receive the Messiah. However, Malachi says also that "Elijah" is the forerunner of "the great and fear-inspiring day of Jehovah," thus indicating a still future fulfillment in a day of judgment.—Matt. 17:11; Luke 1:17; Matt. 11:14; Mark 9:12; Rev. 11:15, 19.

16 Looking forward to that day, Jehovah of armies says: "From the sun's rising even to its setting my name will be great among the nations . . . For I am a great King, . . . and my name will be fear-inspiring among the nations." Fear-inspiring indeed! For 'the day will burn like the furnace, and all the presumptuous ones and all those doing wickedness must become as stubble.' Yet, happy are those who fear Jehovah's name, for to them "the sun of righteousness will certainly shine forth, with healing in its wings." This reminds also of Jesus' words: "At that time the righteous ones will shine as brightly as the sun in the kingdom of their Father." In pointing forward to that glorious and blessed day, Malachi encourages us to be wholehearted in bringing our offerings into Jehovah's house: " 'Test me out, please, in this respect,' Jehovah of armies has said, 'whether I shall not open to you people the floodgates of the heavens and actually empty

---

12. What is promised concerning Jehovah's fear-inspiring day?
13. What does Malachi have to say as to (a) Jehovah's mercy and love? (b) the responsibility of teachers of God's Word? (c) those who violate God's laws and principles?
14. (a) To what, particularly, does Malachi point forward? (b) How was Malachi 3:1 fulfilled in the first century A.D.?
15. Who is the "Elijah" of Malachi's prophecy?
16. To what blessed day does Malachi point forward, and what warm encouragement does he give?

out upon you a blessing until there is no more want.' "—Mal. 1:11, 14; 4:1, 2; Matt. 13:43; Mal. 3:10.

[17] While continuing to warn of 'a devoting of the earth to destruction,' yet this last book of the Prophets calls for optimism and rejoicing in line with Jehovah's words to his people: "All the nations will have to pronounce you happy, for you yourselves will become a land of delight."—Mal. 4:6; 3:12.

17. Malachi's warnings are tempered with what call for optimism?

Bible Book Number Forty— Matthew

Writer:	**Matthew**
Place Written:	**Palestine**
Writing Completed:	**c. A.D. 41**
Time Covered:	**2 B.C.E.—A.D. 33**

FROM the time of the rebellion in Eden Jehovah has held before mankind the comforting promise that he will provide deliverance for all lovers of righteousness through the Seed of his "woman." This Seed or Messiah he purposed to bring forth from the nation of Israel. As the centuries passed he caused to be recorded scores of prophecies through the inspired Hebrew writers, showing that the Seed would be Ruler in the kingdom of God and that he would act for the vindication of Jehovah's name, clearing it forever of the reproach that has been heaped upon it. Many details were provided through these prophets concerning this one who would be Jehovah's vindicator and who would bring about deliverance from fear, oppression, sin and death. With the completion of the Hebrew Scriptures the hope in Messiah was firmly established among the Jews.

[2] In the meantime the world scene had been changing. God had maneuvered the nations in preparation for Messiah's appearance, and the circumstances were admirable for spreading the news of that event far and wide. The fifth world power, Greece, had provided a common language, a universal means of communication among the nations. Rome, the sixth world power, had welded its subject nations into one world empire and had provided roads to make all parts of the empire accessible. Many Jews had been scattered throughout this empire, so that others had learned of their expectation of a coming Messiah. And now, more than 4,000 years after the Edenic promise, Messiah had appeared! The long-awaited promised Seed had come! The most important events thus far in the history of mankind unfolded as Messiah faithfully carried out the will of his Father here on earth.

[3] It was time again for inspired writings to be made to record these momentous happenings. The spirit of Jehovah inspired four faithful men to write independent accounts, thus providing a fourfold witness that Jesus was the Messiah, the Promised Seed and King, and giving the details of his life, his ministry, his death and his resurrection. These accounts are called "Gospels," the word "gospel" meaning "good news." While the four are parallel and often cover the same incidents, they are by no means mere copies of one another. The first three Gospels are often called "synoptic," meaning "like view," since they take a similar approach in recounting Jesus' life on earth. But each one of the four writers, Matthew, Mark, Luke and John, tells his own story of the Christ. Each one has his own particular theme, his own objective, reflects his own personality and keeps in mind his immediate readers. The more we search their writings the more we appreciate the distinctive features of each and that these four inspired Bible books form independent, complementary and harmonious accounts of the life of Jesus Christ.

[4] The first to put the good news about the Christ into writing was Matthew, his name being a form of the Hebrew *Mat·tith·yah'*, meaning "Gift of Jah." He was one of the twelve apostles chosen by Jesus and had a close, intimate relationship with him, as the Master traveled throughout the land of Palestine preaching and teaching about God's kingdom. Before becoming a disciple of Jesus, Matthew was a tax collector, an occupation the Jews thoroughly loathed since it was a constant

1. (a) What promise has Jehovah held before mankind from Eden onward? (b) How did this hope become firmly established among the Jews?
2. At Messiah's appearance, how were circumstances admirable for spreading the good news?
3. (a) What provision did Jehovah make for recording the details of Jesus' life? (b) What is distinctive about each of the Gospels, and why are all four of these necessary?
4. What is known of the writer of the first Gospel?

reminder to them that they were no longer free but under the domination of imperial Rome. Matthew was formerly called Levi and was the son of Alphaeus. He readily responded to Jesus' invitation to follow him.—Matt. 9:9; Mark 2:14; Luke 5:27-32.

5 While the Gospel credited to Matthew does not name him as the writer, the overwhelming testimony of early church historians stamps him as such. Indeed, no ancient book has its writer more clearly and unanimously established than the book of Matthew. From the early historian Papias (c. A.D. 130) onward we have a line of early witnesses to the fact that Matthew wrote this Gospel and that it is an authentic part of the Word of God. M'Clintock and Strong's *Cyclopœdia* states: "Passages from Matthew are quoted by Justin Martyr, by the author of the letter to Diognetus (see in Otto's *Justin Martyr,* vol. ii), by Hegesippus, Irenaeus, Tatian, Athenagoras, Theophilus, Clement, Tertullian, and Origen. It is not merely from the matter, but the manner of the quotations, from the calm appeal as to a settled authority, from the absence of all hints of doubt, that we regard it as proved that the book we possess had not been the subject of any sudden change."[a] The fact that Matthew was an apostle and, as such, had God's spirit upon him assures that what he wrote would be a faithful record.

6 Matthew wrote his account in Palestine. The exact year is not known, but subscriptions at the end of some manuscripts (all later than the tenth century) say that it was A.D. 41.[b] There is evidence to indicate that Matthew originally wrote his Gospel in the popular Hebrew of the time and later translated it into Greek. In his *Catalogue of Ecclesiastical Writers,* Jerome says: "Matthew, who is also Levi, and who from a publican came to be an apostle, first of all the Evangelists, composed a Gospel of Christ in Judaea in the Hebrew language and characters, for the benefit of those of the circumcision who had believed."[c] Jerome adds that the Hebrew text of this Gospel was preserved in his day (c. A.D. 340-420) in the library that Pamphilus had collected in Caesarea.

7 In the early third century, Origen wrote: "The first Gospel was written by Matthew, and arranged for believing Jews in the Hebrew language."[d] That it was written primarily with the Jews in mind is indicated by its genealogy, which shows Jesus' legal descent starting from Abraham, and its many references to the Hebrew Scriptures as pointing forward to the coming Messiah. Careful examination of Matthew's quotations from the Hebrew Scriptures reveals that he quoted directly from the Hebrew. Jerome confirms this in the above-cited *Catalogue,* saying: "It is to be remarked that, wherever the Evangelist makes use of the testimonies of the old Scripture, he does not follow the authority of the seventy translators, but of the Hebrew."[e] So it is reasonable to believe that Matthew used the divine name "Jehovah" in the form of the tetragrammaton whenever it appeared in these quotations. That is why the book of Matthew in the *New World Translation* contains the name "Jehovah" eighteen times, as does the Hebrew version of Matthew produced by F. Delitzsch in the nineteenth century. Matthew would have had the same attitude as Jesus toward the divine name, and would not have been restrained by a prevailing Jewish superstition about not using that name. —Matt. 6:9; John 17:6, 26.

8 Since Matthew had been a tax collector, it was natural that he would be explicit in his mention of money, figures and values. (Matt. 17:27; 26:15; 27:3) He keenly appreciated God's mercy in allowing him, a despised tax collector, to become a minister of the good news and an intimate associate of Jesus. Therefore, we find Matthew alone of the Gospel writers giving us Jesus' repeated insistence that mercy is required in addition to sacrifice. (9:9-13; 12:7; 18:21-35) Matthew was greatly encouraged by Jehovah's undeserved kindness and appropriately records some of the most comforting words Jesus uttered: "Come to me, all you who are toiling and loaded down, and I will refresh you. Take my yoke upon you and become my disciples, for I am mild-tempered and lowly in heart, and you will find refreshment for your souls. For my yoke is kindly and my load is light." (11:28-30) How refreshing were these tender words for this former tax collector, toward whom, no doubt, his fellow countrymen had directed little but insults!

9 Matthew particularly stressed the theme of Jesus' teaching as being "the kingdom of the heavens." To him Jesus was the Preacher-King. He used the term "kingdom" so frequently (fifty-six times in all) that his Gospel might be called the Kingdom Gospel. Matthew was

a 1875, Vol. V, pages 887, 895.
b *Clarke's Commentary,* Vol. V, page 33.
c Foreword to *New World Translation of the Christian Greek Scriptures,* 1950 Edition, pages 17, 18.
d *A Religious Encyclopedia,* 1894, Phillip Schaff, Vol. III, page 1435.

5. How is Matthew established as the writer of the first Gospel?
6, 7. (a) When and in what language was Matthew's Gospel first written? (b) What indicates it was written primarily for the Jews? (c) How often does the *New World Translation* use the name "Jehovah" in this Gospel, and why?
8. How is the fact that Matthew had been a tax collector reflected in the contents of his Gospel?
9. What theme and style of presentation characterize Matthew?

concerned more with a logical presentation of Jesus' public discourses and sermons than with a strict chronological sequence. For the first eighteen chapters Matthew's highlighting of the Kingdom theme led him to depart from a chronological arrangement. However, the last ten chapters (19 to 28) generally follow a chronological sequence, as well as continuing to stress the Kingdom.

10 Forty-two percent of Matthew's Gospel account is not to be found in any of the other three Gospels.[a] This includes at least ten parables or illustrations: The weeds in the field (13:24-30), the hidden treasure (13:44), the pearl of high value (13:45, 46), the dragnet (13:47-50), the unmerciful slave (18:23-35), the workers and the denarius (20:1-16), the father and two children (21:28-32), the marriage of the king's son (22:1-14), the ten virgins (25:1-13) and the talents (25:14-30). In all, the book gives the account from the birth of Jesus, 2 B.C.E., until his meeting with his disciples just prior to his ascension, A.D. 33.

CONTENTS OF MATTHEW

11 **Introducing Jesus and news of the "kingdom of the heavens"** (1:1–4:25). Logically, Matthew begins with Jesus' genealogy. The attention of the Jewish reader is thus arrested to recognize Jesus' legal right as heir to Abraham and David. Then we read the account of Jesus' miraculous conception, his birth in Bethlehem, the visit of the astrologers, Herod's angry slaying of all the boys in Bethlehem under two years old, Joseph and Mary's flight into Egypt with the young child, and their subsequent return to dwell in Nazareth. Matthew is careful to draw attention to the fulfillments of prophecy to establish Jesus as the foretold Messiah. —Matt. 1:23—Isa. 7:14; Matt. 2:1-6—Mic. 5:2; Matt. 2:13-18—Hos. 11:1 and Jer. 31:15; Matt. 2:23—Isa. 11:1, *NW* footnote, 1958 Ed.

12 Matthew's account now skips down through nearly thirty years. John the Baptist is preaching in the wilderness of Judea: "Repent, for the kingdom of the heavens has drawn near." (3:2) He is baptizing the repentant Jews in the river Jordan and warning the Pharisees and Sadducees of wrath to come. Jesus comes from Galilee and is baptized. Immediately God's spirit descends on him and a voice from the heavens says: "This is my Son, the beloved, whom I have approved." (3:17) Jesus is then led into the wilderness, where, after fasting forty days, he is tempted by Satan the Devil. Three times he turns Satan back by quotations from God's Word, saying finally: "Go away, Satan! For it is written, 'It is Jehovah your God you must worship, and it is to him alone you must render sacred service.' "—4:10.

13 "Repent, for the kingdom of the heavens has drawn near." These electrifying words are now proclaimed in Galilee by the anointed Jesus. He calls four from their nets to follow him and become "fishers of men," and travels with them "throughout the whole of Galilee, teaching in their synagogues and preaching the good news of the kingdom and curing every sort of disease and every sort of infirmity among the people."—4:17, 19, 23.

14 **The Sermon on the Mount** (5:1–7:29). As crowds begin to follow him, Jesus goes up into the mountain, sits down and begins teaching his disciples. He opens this thrilling discourse with nine "happinesses": happy are those who are conscious of their spiritual need, those who mourn, the mild-tempered, those who hunger and thirst for righteousness, the merciful, the pure in heart, the peaceable, those persecuted for righteousness' sake and those reproached and lyingly spoken against. "Rejoice and leap for joy, since your reward is great in the heavens." He calls his disciples "the salt of the earth" and "the light of the world" and explains the righteousness, so different from the formalism of the scribes and Pharisees, that is required for entering the kingdom of the heavens. "You must accordingly be perfect, as your heavenly Father is perfect."—5:12-14, 48.

15 Jesus warns against hypocritical gifts and prayers. He teaches his disciples to pray for the sanctification of the Father's name, for His kingdom to come and for their daily sustenance. Throughout the sermon Jesus holds the Kingdom to the fore. He cautions those who follow him not to worry about or work merely for material riches, for the Father knows their actual needs. "Keep on, then," he says, "seeking first the kingdom and his righteousness, and all these other things will be added to you."—6:33.

16 The Master counsels on relations with others, saying: "All things, therefore, that you want men to do to you, you also must likewise do to them." The few that find the road to life

[a] *Introduction to the Study of the Gospels*, 1896, B. F. Westcott, page 201.

10. How much of the contents is to be found only in Matthew, and what period does the Gospel cover?
11. (a) How does the Gospel logically open, and what early events are related? (b) What are some of the prophetic fulfillments that Matthew draws to our attention?
12. What occurs at Jesus' baptism and immediately thereafter?
13. What electrifying campaign now gets under way in Galilee?
14. In his sermon on the mountain, of what states of happiness does Jesus speak, and what does he say about righteousness?
15. What does Jesus have to say about prayer and about the Kingdom?
16. (a) How does Jesus counsel on relations with others, and what does he say concerning those who obey God's will and those who do not? (b) What effect does his sermon have?

will be those who are doing the will of his Father. The workers of lawlessness will be known by their fruits and rejected. The one who obeys his sayings Jesus likens to "the discreet man, who built his house upon the rock-mass." What effect does this discourse have on the listening crowds? They are "astounded at his way of teaching," for he teaches "as a person having authority, and not as their scribes."—7:12, 24-29.

17 **Kingdom preaching expanded** (8:1–11:30). Jesus performs many miracles, healing lepers, paralytics and the demon-possessed. He even demonstrates authority over the wind and waves by calming a storm, and he raises a girl from the dead. What compassion Jesus feels for the crowds as he sees how skinned and thrown about they are, "like sheep without a shepherd"! As he says to his disciples, "the harvest is great, but the workers are few. Therefore, beg the Master of the harvest to send out workers into his harvest."—9:36-38.

18 Jesus selects and commissions the twelve apostles. He gives them definite instructions on how to do their work and emphasizes the central doctrine of their teaching: "As you go, preach, saying, 'The kingdom of the heavens has drawn near.'" He gives them wise and loving admonition: "You received free, give free." "Prove yourselves cautious as serpents and yet innocent as doves." They will be hated and persecuted, even by close relatives, but Jesus reminds them: "He that finds his soul will lose it, and he that loses his soul for my sake will find it." (10:7, 8, 16, 39) On their way they go, to teach and preach in their assigned cities! Jesus identifies John the Baptist as the messenger sent forth before him, the promised "Elijah," but "this generation" accept neither John nor him, the Son of man. So, woe to this generation and the cities that have not repented at seeing his powerful works! But those who become his disciples will find refreshment for their souls.

19 **Pharisees refuted and denounced** (12:1-50). The Pharisees try to find fault with Jesus on the sabbath issue, but he refutes their charges and launches into a scathing condemnation of their hypocrisy. He tells them: "Offspring of vipers, how can you speak good things, when you are wicked? For out of the abundance of the heart the mouth speaks." (12:34) No sign will be given them except that of Jonah the prophet: the Son of man will be three days and nights in the heart of the earth.

20 **Seven Kingdom illustrations** (13:1-58). Why does Jesus speak in illustrations? To his disciples he explains: "To you it is granted to understand the sacred secrets of the kingdom of the heavens, but to those people it is not granted." He pronounces them happy because they see and hear. What a wealth of refreshing instruction he now provides for them through the illustrations of the sower, the weeds in the field, the mustard grain, the leaven, the hidden treasure, the pearl of high value and the dragnet—all portraying some likeness of "the kingdom of the heavens"! However, the people stumble at him, and Jesus tells them: "A prophet is not unhonored except in his home territory and in his own house."—13:11, 57.

21 **Further ministry and miracles of "the Christ"** (14:1–17:27). Jesus is deeply affected by the report of the beheading of John the Baptist at the order of spineless Herod Antipas. He miraculously feeds a crowd of 5,000 and more, walks on the sea, turns back further criticism from the Pharisees, who, he says, are 'overstepping the commandment of God because of their tradition,' heals the demon-possessed, the "lame, maimed, blind, dumb, and many otherwise," and again feeds more than 4,000 from seven loaves and a few little fishes. (15:3, 30) Responding to a question by Jesus, Peter identifies him, saying: "You are the Christ, the Son of the living God." Jesus commends Peter and declares: "On this rock-mass I will build my congregation." (16:16, 18) Jesus now begins to speak of his approaching death and of his resurrection on the third day. But he also promises that some of his disciples "will not taste death at all until first they see the Son of man coming in his kingdom." (16:28) Six days later Jesus takes Peter, James and John up into a lofty mountain to see him transfigured in glory. In a vision they behold Moses and Elijah conversing with him, and hear a voice from heaven saying: "This is my Son, the beloved, whom I have approved; listen to him." After coming down from the mountain Jesus tells them that the promised "Elijah" has already come, and they perceive that he is speaking about John the Baptist.—17:5.

22 **Jesus counsels his disciples** (18:1-35). While at Capernaum Jesus talks to the disciples about humility, the great joy of recovering a stray sheep, and settling offenses between brothers. Peter asks, 'How many times must I forgive my brother?' and Jesus answers: "I say to you, not, Up to seven times, but, Up to seventy

17. How does Jesus show his authority as Messiah, and what loving concern does he express?
18. (a) What instruction and admonition does Jesus give his apostles? (b) Why is it woe to "this generation"?
19. When the Pharisees question his conduct on the sabbath, how does Jesus denounce them?
20. (a) Why does Jesus speak in illustrations? (b) What Kingdom illustrations does he now give?
21. (a) What miracles does Jesus perform, and as what do they identify him? (b) What vision is given concerning the kingdom of the Son of man?
22. What does Jesus counsel on forgiveness?

seven times." To add force to this Jesus gives the illustration of the slave whose master forgave him a debt of sixty million denarii ($10,200,000). This slave later had a fellow slave imprisoned because of a debt of only one hundred denarii ($17), and, as a result, the merciless slave was likewise handed over to the jailers. Jesus makes the point: "In like manner my heavenly Father will also deal with you if you do not forgive each one his brother from your hearts."—18:22, 35.

23 **Closing days of Jesus' ministry** (19:1–22:46). The tempo of events quickens and tension mounts as the scribes and Pharisees become more incensed at Jesus' ministry. They come to trip him up on a matter of divorce but fail; Jesus shows that the only Scriptural ground for divorce is fornication or adultery. A rich young man comes to Jesus, asking the way to everlasting life, but goes away grieved when he finds he must sell all he has and be a follower of Jesus. After giving the illustration of the workers and the denarius Jesus speaks again of his death and resurrection, and says: "The Son of man came, not to be ministered to, but to minister and to give his soul a ransom in exchange for many."—20:28.

24 We have now entered the last week of Jesus' human life. He makes his triumphal entry into Jerusalem as 'King, mounted upon the colt of an ass.' (21:4, 5) He cleanses the temple of the money-changers and other profiteers, and the hatred of his foes mounts as he tells them: "The tax collectors and the harlots are going ahead of you into the kingdom of God." (21:31) His pointed illustrations of the vineyard and the marriage feast hit home. He skillfully answers the Pharisees' tax question by telling them to pay back "Caesar's things to Caesar, but God's things to God." (22:21) Likewise he turns back a "catch question" by the Sadducees and upholds the resurrection hope. Again the Pharisees come to him with a question on the Law, and Jesus tells them that the greatest commandment is to love Jehovah completely, and the second is to love one's neighbor as oneself. Jesus then asks them, 'How can the Christ be both David's son and his Lord?' Nobody can answer, and thereafter no one dares to question him.—22:45, 46.

25 **'Woe to you, hypocrites!'** (23:1–24:2). Speaking to the crowds at the temple, Jesus delivers another scathing denunciation of the scribes and Pharisees. Not only have they disqualified themselves from entering into the Kingdom, but they exert all their wiles to prevent others from entering. Just like whitewashed graves, they appear beautiful on the outside, but inside they are full of corruption and decay. Jesus concludes with this judgment: "Your house is abandoned to you." (23:38) As he leaves the temple, Jesus prophesies its destruction.

26 **Jesus gives "sign" of his presence** (24:3–25:46). On the Mount of Olives his disciples question him about 'the sign of his presence and the conclusion of the system of things.' In answer Jesus points forward to a time of total wars, 'nation against nation and kingdom against kingdom,' food shortages, earthquakes, lawlessness, the earthwide preaching of "this good news of the kingdom," the appointment of "the faithful and discreet slave . . . over all his belongings," and many other features of the composite sign that is to mark 'the arrival of the Son of man in his glory to sit down on his glorious throne.' (24:3, 7, 14, 45; 25:31) Jesus concludes this important prophecy with the illustrations of the ten virgins and the talents, which hold forth joyful rewards to the alert and faithful, and the illustration of the sheep and the goats, which shows goatish people departing "into everlasting cutting-off, but the righteous ones into everlasting life."—25:46.

27 **Events of Jesus' final day** (26:1–27:66). After celebrating the passover Jesus institutes something new with his faithful apostles, inviting them to partake of unleavened bread and wine as symbols of his body and his blood. Then they go to Gethsemane, where Jesus prays. There Judas comes with an armed crowd and betrays Jesus with a hypocritical kiss. Jesus is taken to the high priest, where he is given a mock trial. True to Jesus' prophecy, Peter disowns him when put to the test. Judas, feeling remorse, throws his betrayal money into the temple and goes off and hangs himself. In the morning Jesus is led before the Roman governor Pilate, who hands him over to be impaled under pressure from the priest-incited mob who cry: "His blood come upon us and upon our children." The governor's soldiers make fun of his kingship and then lead him out to Golgotha, where he is staked between two robbers, with a sign over his head reading, "This is Jesus the King of the Jews." (27:25, 37) After hours of torture Jesus finally dies at three in the afternoon and is then laid in the new memorial tomb belonging to Joseph of Arimathea. It has been the most eventful twenty-four hours in all history!

---

23. What does Jesus explain concerning divorce and the way to life?
24. As Jesus enters the last week of his human life, what encounters does he have with religious opposers, and how does he deal with their questions?
25. How does Jesus forcefully denounce the scribes and Pharisees?
26. What prophetic sign does Jesus provide concerning his coming again in kingly glory?
27. What events mark Jesus' final day on earth?

28 **Jesus' resurrection and final instructions** (28:1-20). Matthew now climaxes his account with the very best of news. The dead Jesus is resurrected—he lives again! Early on the first day of the week Mary Magdalene and "the other Mary" come to the tomb and hear the angel's announcement of this joyful fact. To confirm it, Jesus himself appears to them. The enemies even try to fight the fact of his resurrection, bribing the soldiers who had been on guard at the tomb to say, "His disciples came in the night and stole him while we were sleeping." Later, in Galilee, Jesus has another meeting with his disciples. What is his departing instruction for them? This: "Go . . . make disciples of people of all the nations, baptizing them in the name of the Father and of the Son and of the holy spirit." Would they have guidance in this preaching work? The last utterance of Jesus that Matthew records gives this assurance: "Look! I am with you all the days until the conclusion of the system of things." —28:13, 19, 20.

WHY BENEFICIAL

29 The book of Matthew, first of the four Gospels, truly provides an excellent bridge from the Hebrew Scriptures into the Christian Greek Scriptures. Unmistakably it identifies the Messiah and King of God's promised kingdom, makes known the requirements for becoming his followers and sets out the work that lies ahead for these on earth. First John the Baptist, then Jesus and finally his disciples went preaching, "The kingdom of the heavens has drawn near." Moreover, Jesus' command reaches right down to the conclusion of the system of things: "And this good news of the kingdom will be preached in all the inhabited earth for a witness to all the nations; and then the end will come." Truly it was, and still is, a grand and wonderful privilege to share in this Kingdom work of 'making disciples of people of all the nations,' working after the pattern of the Master.—Matt. 3:2; 4:17; 10:7; 24:14; 28:19.

30 Matthew's Gospel is indeed "good news." Its inspired message was "good news" to those who heeded it in the first century of the Common Era, and Jehovah God has seen to it that it has been preserved as "good news" until this day. Even non-Christians have been compelled to acknowledge the power of this Gospel, as, for example, the Hindu leader, Mahatma Gandhi, who is reported to have said to Lord Irwin, a former viceroy of India: "When your country and mine shall get together on the teachings laid down by Christ in this Sermon on the Mount, we shall have solved the problems not only of our countries but those of the whole world."[a]

31 However, the whole world, including that part claiming to be Christian, continues with its problems. It has been left to a small minority of true Christians to treasure, study, obey and derive the inestimable benefits of applying the Sermon on the Mount and all the other sound counsel of the good news "according to Matthew." It is profitable to study again and again Jesus' fine admonitions on finding the real happiness, on morals and marriage, the power of love, acceptable prayer, spiritual versus material values, seeking the kingdom first, respect for holy things and on watchfulness and obedience. Matthew chapter ten gives Jesus' service instructions to those who take up preaching the good news of the "kingdom of the heavens." The many parables of Jesus carry vital lessons for all who 'have ears to hear.' Moreover, Jesus' prophecies, such as his detailed foretelling of 'the sign of his presence,' build strong hope and confidence in the future. —Matt. 5:1–7:29; 10:5-42; 13:1-58; 18:1–20:16; 21:28–22:40; 24:3–25:46.

32 Matthew's Gospel abounds with fulfilled prophecies. Many of his quotations from the inspired Hebrew Scriptures were for the purpose of showing these fulfillments. They provide indisputable evidence that Jesus is the Messiah, for it would have been utterly impossible to prearrange all these details. Compare, for example, Matthew 13:14, 15 with Isaiah 6:9, 10, Matthew 21:42 with Psalms 118: 22, 23 and Matthew 26:31, 56 with Zechariah 13:7. Such fulfillments give us strong assurance, too, that all the prophetic forecasts of Jesus himself, as recorded by Matthew, would in due course come true as Jehovah's glorious purposes with regard to "the kingdom of the heavens" reach their fruition.

33 How exact God was in foretelling the life of the King of the kingdom, even to minute details! How exact was the inspired Matthew in faithfully recording the fulfillment of these prophecies! As they reflect on all the prophetic fulfillments and promises recorded in the book of Matthew, lovers of righteousness can indeed exult in the knowledge and hope of "the king

a *Treasury of the Christian Faith,* S. J. Corey.

28. With what "best of news" does Matthew climax his account, and with what commission does he conclude?
29. (a) How does Matthew bridge over from the Hebrew to the Greek Scriptures? (b) What privilege enjoyed by Jesus is still open to Christians today?
30. What particular portion of this Gospel has gained recognition for its practical value?
31. Who have shown real appreciation for the counsel in Matthew, and why is it profitable to study this Gospel again and again?
32. (a) Illustrate how fulfilled prophecy proves Jesus' Messiahship. (b) What strong assurance do these fulfillments give us today?
33. In what knowledge and hope can lovers of righteousness now exult?

dom of the heavens" as Jehovah's instrument for sanctifying his name. It is this kingdom by Jesus Christ that brings untold blessings of life and happiness to the mild-tempered and spiritually hungry ones "in the re-creation, when the Son of man sits down upon his glorious throne." (Matt. 19:28) All of this is stimulating good news "according to Matthew."

Bible Book Number Forty-one— Mark

Writer:	**Mark**
Place Written:	**Rome**
Writing Completed:	**c. A.D. 60-65**
Time Covered:	**A.D. 29-33**

WHEN Jesus was arrested at Gethsemane, and the apostles fled, he was followed by 'a certain young man wearing a fine linen garment over his naked body." When the crowd tried to seize him too, "he left his linen garment behind and got away naked." This young man is generally believed to be Mark. He is described in Acts as "John who was surnamed Mark," and must have come from a comfortably situated family in Jerusalem, for they had their own house and servants. His mother Mary was also a Christian, and the early congregation used her home as a meeting place. On the occasion when he was delivered by the angel from prison Peter went to this house and found the brothers assembled there.—Mark 14:51, 52; Acts 12:12, 13.

2 The missionary Barnabas, a Levite from Cyprus, was the cousin of Mark. (Acts 4:36; Col. 4:10) When Barnabas came with Paul to Jerusalem in connection with famine relief, Mark also got to know Paul. These associations in the congregation and with zealous visiting ministers no doubt instilled in Mark the desire to enter missionary service. So we find him as companion and attendant to Paul and Barnabas on their first missionary journey. For some reason, however, Mark left them in Perga, Pamphylia, and returned to Jerusalem. (Acts 11:29, 30; 12:25; 13:5, 13) Because of this Paul refused to take Mark along on the second missionary tour, and this resulted in a break between Paul and Barnabas. Paul took Silas, while Barnabas took his cousin Mark and sailed with him to Cyprus.—Acts 15:36-41.

3 Mark proved himself in the ministry and became a valuable help, not only to Barnabas, but later also to the apostles Peter and Paul. Mark was with Paul about A.D. 60 during his first imprisonment in Rome. (Philem. 1, 24) Then we find Mark with Peter in Babylon between the years A.D. 62 and 64. (1 Pet. 5:13) Paul is again a prisoner in Rome probably in the year 65 (A.D.), and in a letter he asks Timothy to bring Mark with him "for he is useful to me for ministering." (2 Tim. 1:8; 4:11) This is the latest mention of Mark in the Bible record.

4 The composition of the shortest Gospel is credited to this Mark. He was a co-worker with Jesus' apostles and one who placed his own life in the service of the good news. But Mark was not one of the twelve apostles and he was not an immediate companion of Jesus. Where did he get the intimate details that make his account of Jesus' ministry really live from beginning to end? According to the earliest tradition of Papias, Irenaeus, Origen and Tertullian, this source was Peter, with whom Mark was closely associated. Did not Peter call him "my son"? (1 Pet. 5:13) Peter was an eyewitness of practically all that Mark recorded, so he could have learned from Peter many descriptive points that are lacking in the other Gospels. For example, Mark speaks of the "hired men" that worked for Zebedee, the leper entreating Jesus "on bended knee," the demonized man "slashing himself with stones" and Jesus' giving his prophecy on the end of the world while sitting on the Mount of Olives "with the temple in view."—Mark 1:20, 40; 5:5; 13:3.

5 Peter himself was a man of deep emotions and so could appreciate and describe to Mark the feelings and emotions of Jesus. So it is that Mark frequently records how Jesus felt and reacted; for example, that he looked "around upon them with indignation, being thoroughly grieved," that he "sighed deeply" and that he "groaned deeply with his spirit." (3:5; 7:34; 8:12) It is Mark who tells us of Jesus' sentiments toward the rich young ruler, saying that

1. What is known concerning Mark and his family?
2, 3. (a) What no doubt stirred Mark to enter missionary service? (b) What association did he have with other missionaries, particularly with Peter and Paul?

4-6. (a) How was Mark able to get the intimate details for his Gospel? (b) What indicates his close association with Peter? (c) Give examples of Peter's characteristics in the Gospel.

he "felt love for him." (10:21) And what warmth we find in the account that Jesus not only stood a young child in their midst but also "put his arms around it," and that on another occasion "he took the children in his arms"! —9:36; 10:13-16.

6 Some of Peter's characteristics are to be seen in Mark's style, which is impulsive, living, vigorous, vital and descriptive. It seems he can hardly relate events fast enough. For example, the word "immediately" occurs again and again, carrying the story along in dramatic style.

7 Although Mark had access to the Gospel of Matthew and his record contains only 7 percent that is not contained in the other Gospels, it would be a mistake to believe that Mark simply condensed Matthew's Gospel and added a few special details. Whereas Matthew had portrayed Jesus as the promised Messiah and King, Mark now considers his life and works from another angle. He portrays Jesus as the miracle-working Son of God, the conquering Savior. Mark puts stress on the activities of Christ rather than on his sermons and teachings. Only a small proportion of the parables and one of Jesus' longer discourses are reported, and the Sermon on the Mount is omitted. It is for this reason that Mark's Gospel is shorter, though it contains just as much action as the others. At least nineteen miracles are specifically referred to.

8 While Matthew wrote his Gospel for the Jews, Mark wrote primarily for the Romans. How do we know this? The law of Moses is mentioned only when reporting conversation that referred to it, and the genealogy of Jesus is left out. The gospel of Christ is represented as of universal importance. He makes explanatory comments on Jewish customs and teachings with which non-Jewish readers might be unfamiliar. (2:18; 7:3, 4; 14:12; 15:42) Aramaic expressions are translated. (3:17; 5:41; 7:11, 34; 14:36; 15:22, 34) He qualifies Palestinian geographic names and plant life with explanations. (1:5, 13; 11:13; 13:3) The value of Jewish coins is given in Roman money. (12:42, *NW* footnote, 1950 Ed.) He uses more Latinisms than the other Gospel writers, examples being *speculator* (body guardsman), *praetorium* (governor's palace) and *centurion* (army officer). —Mark 6:27; 15:16, 39.

9 Since Mark wrote primarily for the Romans, he most likely did his writing in Rome. Both earliest tradition and the contents of the book allow for the conclusion that it was composed in Rome during either the first or the second imprisonment of the apostle Paul, and hence about A.D. 60 or 65. In those years Mark was in Rome. All the leading authorities of the second and third centuries confirm that Mark was the writer. The Gospel was already in circulation among Christians by the middle of the second century. Its appearance in all the early catalogues of the Christian Greek Scriptures confirms the authenticity of Mark's Gospel.

10 However, the long and short conclusions that are sometimes added after chapter 16, verse 8, are not to be regarded as authentic. They are missing in most of the ancient manuscripts, such as the Sinaitic and the Vatican No. 1209. The fourth-century scholars, Eusebius and Jerome, are in agreement that the authentic record closes with the words "they were in fear." The other conclusions were probably added with a view to smoothing over the abruptness with which the Gospel ends.

11 That Mark's account is accurate is to be seen in the fact that his Gospel is in full harmony, not only with the other Gospels, but also with all the Holy Scriptures from Genesis to Revelation. Moreover, Jesus is shown again and again as one having authority, not only in his spoken word, but over the forces of nature, over Satan and the demons, over sickness and disease, yes, over death itself. So Mark opens his narrative with the impressive introduction: "The beginning of the good news about Jesus Christ." His coming and ministry meant "good news," and hence the study of Mark's Gospel must be beneficial to all readers. The events described by Mark cover the period from spring A.D. 29 to spring A.D. 33.

CONTENTS OF MARK

12 **Baptism and temptation of Jesus** (1:1-13). Mark begins the good news by identifying John the baptizer. He is the foretold messenger, sent to proclaim: "Prepare the way of Jehovah, you people, make his roads straight." Of the One soon to come, the baptizer says, 'He is stronger than I.' Yes, he will baptize, not with water, but with holy spirit. Jesus now comes from Nazareth of Galilee, and John baptizes him. The spirit descends on Jesus like a dove, and a voice is heard out of the heavens: "You are my Son, the beloved; I have approved you." (1:3, 7, 11) Jesus is tempted by Satan in the wilderness, and angels minister to him. All

7. What distinguishes Mark's Gospel from that of Matthew?
8. What features indicate Mark's Gospel was written for the Romans?
9. Where and when was the book of Mark written, and what confirms its authenticity?
10. How are the "long" and "short" conclusions of Mark to be regarded, and why?
11. (a) What proves Mark's Gospel to be accurate, and what authority is emphasized? (b) Why is this "good news," and what period does Mark cover?
12. What is packed into the first thirteen verses of Mark?

these dramatic events are packed into Mark's first thirteen verses.

13 **Jesus begins ministry in Galilee** (1:14–6:6). After John is arrested, Jesus goes preaching the good news of God in Galilee. What a startling message he has! "The kingdom of God has drawn near. Be repentant, you people, and have faith in the good news." (1:15) He calls Simon and Andrew, and James and John from their fishing nets to be his disciples. On the sabbath he begins to teach in the synagogue at Capernaum. The people are astounded, for he teaches "as one having authority, and not as the scribes." He demonstrates his authority as "the Holy One of God" by driving an unclean spirit out of a possessed man, and by healing Simon's mother-in-law who was sick with a fever. The news spreads like wildfire, and by nighttime "the whole city" has gathered outside Simon's house. Jesus cures many that are sick and expels many demons.—1:22, 24, 33.

14 Jesus declares his mission: "That I may preach." (1:38) Throughout the whole of Galilee he preaches. Wherever he goes he expels demons and heals the sick, including a leper, and a paralytic to whom he says: "Your sins are forgiven." 'This is blasphemy. Who can forgive sins but God?' reason some of the scribes in their hearts. Discerning their thoughts, Jesus proves "that the Son of man has authority to forgive sins" by telling the paralytic to get up and go home. The people glorify God. When the tax collector Levi (Matthew) becomes his follower, Jesus tells the scribes: "I came to call, not righteous people, but sinners." He shows himself to be "Lord even of the sabbath." —2:5, 7, 10, 17, 28.

15 Jesus now forms the group of twelve apostles. His relatives manifest some opposition, and then some scribes from Jerusalem accuse him of expelling demons by means of the ruler of the demons. Jesus asks them, "How can Satan expel Satan?" and warns them: "Whoever blasphemes against the holy spirit has no forgiveness forever, but is guilty of everlasting sin." During the discussion his mother and brothers come seeking him, and Jesus is moved to declare: "Whoever does the will of God, this one is my brother and sister and mother." —3:23, 29, 35.

16 Jesus starts teaching "the sacred secret of the kingdom of God" by illustrations. He speaks of the sower of seed that falls on various kinds of soil (illustrating the different kinds of hearers of the word) and of the lamp shining from its lampstand. He likens the kingdom to a man who sows seed: "Of its own self the ground bears fruit gradually, first the grass blade, then the stalk head, finally the full grain in the head." (4:11, 28) He also illustrates the kingdom of God by a mustard grain, which, though the tiniest of all seeds, grows large with great branches for shelter.

17 As they cross the Sea of Galilee Jesus miraculously causes a violent wind to abate, and the stormy sea becomes calm at his command: "Hush! Be quiet!" (4:39) Over in the country of the Gerasenes Jesus expels a "Legion" of demons from one man and permits them to enter into a herd of about two thousand swine, which, in turn, rush over a precipice and are drowned in the sea. (5:8-13) After this Jesus crosses back to the opposite shore. A woman is healed of a flow of blood, incurable for twelve years, merely by touching Jesus' outer garment, as he is on the way to raise the twelve-year-old daughter of Jairus to life again. Truly, the Son of man has authority over both life and death! However, the people in Jesus' home territory dispute his authority. He wonders at their lack of faith, but continues "round about to the villages in a circuit, teaching."—6:6.

18 **Galilean ministry expanded** (6:7–9:50). The twelve are sent out two by two with instructions and authority to preach and teach, to cure people and expel demons. The name of Jesus is becoming well known, some thinking it is John the Baptist raised from the dead. This possibility worries Herod, during whose birthday party John had been beheaded. The apostles return from their preaching tour and make a report of their activity to Jesus. A great crowd follows Jesus around Galilee and he is 'moved with pity for them, because they are as sheep without a shepherd.' So he starts to teach them many things. (6:34) He lovingly provides material food, too, feeding five thousand men with five loaves of bread and two fishes. Shortly after, when the disciples in their boat are hard put battling against a windstorm as they make for Bethsaida, he comes walking to them on the sea and calms the wind. No wonder that even his disciples are "much amazed"!—6:51.

19 In the district of Gennesaret Jesus gets into a discussion with the scribes and Pharisees from Jerusalem about eating with unwashed hands, and rebukes them for 'letting go the

13. In what ways does Jesus early demonstrate his authority as "the Holy One of God"?
14. How does Jesus give proof of his authority to forgive sins?
15. What does Jesus declare about those who deny his miracles, and what does he say about family ties?
16. By illustrations, what does Jesus teach about the Kingdom, especially as to its growth?
17. How do Jesus' miracles demonstrate the extent of his authority?
18. (a) How is Jesus' ministry expanded? (b) What moves Jesus to teach and to perform miracles?
19, 20. How does Jesus give reproof to the scribes and Pharisees? (b) What circumstances lead to Peter's also being reproved?

commandment of God and holding fast the tradition of men.' He says it is not what enters from outside that defiles a man, but it is what issues from inside, out of the heart, namely, "injurious reasonings." (7:8, 21) Going north into the regions of Tyre and Sidon, he performs a miracle for a Gentile, expelling a demon from the daughter of a Syrophoenician woman.

20 Back in Galilee, Jesus feels pity again for the crowd following him and feeds four thousand men with seven loaves and a few little fishes. He warns his disciples of the leaven of the Pharisees and the leaven of Herod, but at the time they fail to get the point. Then, another miracle—the healing of a blind man at Bethsaida. In a discussion on the way to the villages in Caesarea Philippi, Peter convincingly identifies Jesus as "the Christ," but then objects strongly when Jesus speaks of the approaching sufferings and death of the Son of man. For this Jesus reproves him: "Get behind me, Satan, because you think, not God's thoughts, but those of men." (8:29, 33) Jesus exhorts his disciples to follow him continually for the sake of the good news; if they become ashamed of him, he will be ashamed of them when he arrives in the glory of his Father.

21 Six days later, when up on a lofty mountain, Peter, James and John are privileged to see "the kingdom of God already come in power," as they behold Jesus transfigured in glory. Jesus again demonstrates his authority by expelling a speechless spirit from a boy, and a second time he speaks of his coming suffering and death. He counsels his disciples not to allow anything to hinder them from entering into life. Does your hand make you stumble? Cut it off! Your foot? Cut it off! Your eye? Throw it away! It is far better to enter into the kingdom of God maimed than to be pitched whole into Gehenna.

22 **Ministry in Perea** (10:1-52). Jesus comes to the frontiers of Judea and "across the Jordan" (into Perea). Pharisees now question him about divorce, and he uses the opportunity to state godly principles for marriage. A rich young man questions him about inheriting everlasting life, but is grieved at hearing that, to have treasure in heaven, he must sell his possessions and become Jesus' follower. Jesus tells his disciples: "It is easier for a camel to go through a needle's eye than for a rich man to enter into the kingdom of God." He encourages those who have forsaken all on account of the good news, promising them "a hundredfold now . . . with persecutions, and in the coming system of things everlasting life."—10:25, 30.

23 They now set out on the way to Jerusalem. Jesus tells the twelve a third time about the suffering before him, and also of his resurrection. He asks them if they are able to drink the same cup that he is drinking, and tells them: "Whoever wants to be first among you must be the slave of all." On their way out of Jericho a blind beggar calls from the roadside: "Son of David, Jesus, have mercy on me!" Jesus makes the blind man see—his last miraculous healing as recorded by Mark.—10:44, 47, 48.

24 **Jesus in and around Jerusalem** (11:1-15:47). The account moves quickly! Jesus rides upon a colt into the city, and the people acclaim him as King. The next day he cleanses the temple. The chief priests and the scribes become fearful of him and seek his death. "By what authority do you do these things?" they ask. (11:28) Jesus skillfully turns the question back on them, and tells the parable of the cultivators who killed the heir of the vineyard. They see the point, and leave him.

25 Next they send some of the Pharisees to catch him on the tax question. Calling for a denarius, he asks: "Whose image and inscription is this?" They reply: "Caesar's." Jesus then says: "Pay back Caesar's things to Caesar, but God's things to God." No wonder they marvel at him! (12:16, 17) Now the Sadducees, who do not believe in the resurrection, try to catch him with the question: 'If a woman had seven husbands in succession, whose wife will she be in the resurrection?' Jesus promptly replies that those who rise from the dead will be "as angels in the heavens," for they will not marry. (12:25) "Which commandment is first of all?" asks one of the scribes. Jesus answers: "The first is, 'Hear, O Israel, Jehovah our God is one Jehovah, and you must love Jehovah your God with your whole heart and with your whole soul and with your whole mind and with your whole strength.' The second is this, 'You must love your neighbor as yourself.'" (12:28-31) After this nobody dares to question him. Jesus' authority as the perfect teacher is upheld. The great crowd listens with pleasure, and Jesus warns them against the pompous scribes. Then he commends to his disciples the poor widow who put more into the temple treasury chest than all the others, for her two small coins were "all of what she had, her whole living."—12:44.

26 Seated on the Mount of Olives with the

21. (a) Who see "the kingdom of God already come in power," and how? (b) How does Jesus emphasize putting the Kingdom first?
22. What counsel highlights Jesus' ministry in Perea?
23. What conversation and miracle ensue on the way to Jerusalem?
24, 25. (a) By what actions does Jesus testify to his authority? (b) With what arguments does he answer his opponents? (c) What warning does Jesus give the crowd, and what does he commend to his disciples?
26. What is the only long discourse recorded by Mark, and with what admonition does it end?

temple in view, Jesus tells four of his disciples privately of the "sign" of the conclusion of these things. (This is the only long discourse recorded by Mark, and parallels that of Matthew chapters 24 and 25.) It closes with Jesus' admonition: "Concerning that day or the hour nobody knows, neither the angels in heaven nor the Son, but the Father. But what I say to you I say to all, Keep on the watch."—13:32, 37.

27 At nearby Bethany a woman anoints Jesus with costly perfumed oil. Some protest this is a waste, but Jesus says it is a fine deed, a preparation for his burial. At the appointed time Jesus and the twelve assemble in the city for the passover. He identifies his betrayer, institutes the memorial supper with his faithful disciples and they depart for the Mount of Olives. On the way Jesus tells them that they will all be stumbled. "I will not be," exclaims Peter. But Jesus says to him: "This night, before a cock crows twice, even you will disown me three times." On reaching the spot named Gethsemane, Jesus withdraws to pray, asking his disciples to watch. His prayer is climaxed with the words: *"Abba,* Father, all things are possible to you; remove this cup from me. Yet not what I want, but what you want." Three times Jesus returns to his disciples, and three times he finds them sleeping, even "at such a time as this"! (14:29, 30, 36, 41) But the hour has come! Look!—the betrayer!

28 Judas draws close and kisses Jesus. This is the sign for the chief priests' armed men to arrest him. They bring him to the court of the high priest, where many bear false witness against him, but their testimonies are not in agreement. Jesus himself keeps silent. Finally, the high priest questions him: "Are you the Christ the Son of the Blessed One?" Jesus replies, "I am." The high priest cries, 'Blasphemy!' and they all condemn him to be liable to death. (14:61-64) In the courtyard below Peter has denied Jesus three times. A cock crows a second time, and Peter, recalling Jesus' words, breaks down and weeps.

29 Immediately at dawn the Sanhedrin consults and sends Jesus bound to Pilate. He quickly recognizes that Jesus is no criminal and tries to release him. However, at the insistence of the mob, incited by the chief priests, he finally hands Jesus over to be impaled. He is brought to Golgotha (meaning "Skull Place") and impaled, with the charge against him written above: "The King of the Jews." Passersby reproach him: "Others he saved; himself he cannot save!" At noon (the sixth hour) a darkness falls over the whole land until three o'clock. Then Jesus cries out with a loud voice, "My God, my God, why have you forsaken me?" and expires. At seeing these things an army officer remarks: "Certainly this man was God's Son." Joseph of Arimathea, one of the Sanhedrin but a believer in the kingdom of God, asks Pilate for Jesus' body and lays it in a tomb quarried out of rock.—15:26, 31, 34, 39.

30 **Events after Jesus' death** (16:1-8). Very early on the first day of the week three women go out to the tomb. To their surprise they find that the large stone at the entrance has been rolled away. "A young man" who is sitting inside tells them that Jesus is raised up. He is no longer there, but is going ahead of them into Galilee. They flee from the tomb, trembling and in fear.

WHY BENEFICIAL

31 All readers of Mark, from early Christian times until now, have been able to identify through this vivid pen picture of Jesus Christ the fulfillment of many prophecies of the Hebrew Scriptures concerning the Messiah. From the opening quotation, "Look! I am sending forth my messenger before your face," to Jesus' agonized words on the stake, "My God, my God, why have you forsaken me?" the entire account of his zealous ministry, as recorded by Mark, is in accord with what the Hebrew Scriptures foretold. (Mark 1:2; 15:34; Mal. 3:1; Ps. 22:1) Moreover, his miracles and his marvelous works, his healthful teaching and flawless refutations, his utter dependence on Jehovah's Word and spirit and his tender shepherding of the sheep—all these things mark him as the One who came with authority as the Son of God. He taught "as one having authority," authority received from Jehovah, and he emphasized "preaching the good news of God," namely, that "the kingdom of God has drawn near," as his primary work here on earth. His teaching has proved to be of inestimable benefit to all who have paid heed to it.—Mark 1:22, 14, 15.

32 Jesus said to his disciples: "To you the sacred secret of the kingdom of God has been given." Mark uses this expression "kingdom of God" fifteen times and sets out many guiding principles for those who would gain life through the Kingdom. Jesus stated: "Whoever loses his soul for the sake of me and the good news will save it." Every hindrance to gaining

---

27. Describe the events leading up to Jesus' betrayal in Gethsemane.
28. What are the circumstances of Jesus' arrest and trial before the high priest?
29. What record does Mark make of Jesus' final trial and execution, and how is the Kingdom shown to be at issue?
30. On the first day of the week, what happens at the tomb?
31. (a) How does Mark testify to Jesus' being the Messiah? (b) What proves Jesus' authority as the Son of God, and what did he emphasize?
32. How many times does Mark use the expression "kingdom of God," and what are some of the guiding principles he sets out for gaining life through the Kingdom?

life must be removed: "It is finer for you to enter one-eyed into the kingdom of God than with two eyes to be pitched into Gehenna." Jesus further declared: "Whoever does not receive the kingdom of God like a young child will by no means enter into it," and, "How difficult a thing it will be for those with money to enter into the kingdom of God!" He said that the one who discerns that keeping the two great commandments is worth far more than all the whole burnt offerings and sacrifices is "not far from the kingdom of God." These and other Kingdom teachings of Mark's Gospel contain much good admonition that we can apply in our daily lives.—Mark 4:11; 8:35; 9:43-48; 10:13-15, 23-25; 12:28-34.

33 The good news "according to Mark" can be read through entirely in from one to two hours, giving the reader a thrilling, quick and dynamic review of Jesus' ministry. Such straight reading of this inspired account, as well as closer study and meditation on it, will always prove beneficial. Mark's Gospel is of benefit to persecuted Christians today in the same way as in the first century, for true Christians now face "critical times hard to deal with" and have need for such inspired guidance as is found in this record concerning our Exemplar, Jesus Christ. Read it, thrill to its dramatic action, and draw encouragement to follow in the steps of the Chief Agent and Perfecter of our faith, Jesus, with the same invincible joy that he showed. (2 Tim. 3:1; Heb. 12:2) Yes, see him as a man of action, be imbued with his zeal and copy his uncompromising integrity and courage amid trial and opposition. Gain comfort from this rich portion of the inspired Scriptures. Let it benefit you in your pursuit of everlasting life!

33. (a) How may we gain benefit from Mark's Gospel? (b) To what course should Mark encourage us, and why?

Bible Book Number Forty-two— Luke

Writer:	**Luke**
Place Written:	**Caesarea**
Writing Completed:	**c. A.D. 56-58**
Time Covered:	**3 B.C.E.—A.D. 33**

THE Gospel of Luke was written by a man with a keen mind and a kind heart, and this fine blend of qualities, with the guidance of God's spirit, has resulted in an account that is both accurate and full of warmth and feeling. In the opening verses he says, "I resolved also, because I have traced all things from the start with accuracy, to write them in logical order to you." His detailed, meticulous presentation fully bears out this claim.—Luke 1:3.

2 Although Luke is nowhere named in the account, ancient authorities are agreed that he was the writer. Internal evidence also points strongly to Luke. Paul speaks of him at Colossians 4:14 as "Luke the beloved physician," and his work is of the scholarly order one would expect from a well-educated doctor. His fine choice of language and his extensive vocabulary, larger than that of the other three Gospels combined, make possible a most careful and comprehensive treatment of his vital subject. His account of the prodigal son is regarded by some as the best short story ever written.

3 Luke uses more than three hundred medical terms, or words to which he gives a medical meaning, that are not used in the same way (if they are used at all) by the other writers of the Christian Greek Scriptures.[a] For example, when speaking of leprosy Luke does not always use the same term as the others. To them leprosy is leprosy, but to the physician there are different stages of leprosy, as when Luke speaks of "a man full of leprosy." Lazarus, he says, was "full of ulcers." No other Gospel writer says that Peter's mother-in-law had "a *high* fever." (Luke 5:12; 16:20; 4:38) Although the other three tell us of Peter's cutting off the ear of the slave of the high priest, only Luke mentions that Jesus healed him. (22:51) It is like a doctor to say of a woman that she had "a spirit of weakness for eighteen years, and she was bent double and was unable to raise herself up at all." And who but "Luke the beloved physician" would have recorded in such detail the first aid rendered to a man by the Samaritan who "bound up his wounds, pouring oil and wine upon them"?—13:11; 10:34.

4 When did Luke write his Gospel? Acts 1:1

1. What kind of Gospel did Luke write?
2, 3. What external and internal evidence points to the physician Luke as writer of this Gospel?

a *The Medical Language of Luke,* 1954, W. K. Hobart, pages xi-xxviii.

4. When, probably, was Luke written, and what circumstances support this view?

ndicates that the writer of Acts (who was also uke) had earlier composed "the first account," he Gospel. Acts was most probably completed bout A.D. 61 while Luke was in Rome with aul, awaiting his appeal to Caesar. So the ospel account was probably written by Luke n Caesarea about A.D. 56-58, after returning vith Paul from Philippi at the end of his third nissionary journey and while Paul was waiting wo years in prison at Caesarea before being aken to Rome for his appeal.[a] During this time, ince Luke was there in Palestine, he was well ituated to 'trace all things from the start with ccuracy' concerning the life and ministry of esus. Thus Luke's account appears to have receded Mark's Gospel.

[5] Luke was not, of course, an eyewitness of ll the events he records in his Gospel, not eing one of the twelve and probably not even believer until after Jesus' death. However, he vas very closely associated with Paul in the nissionary field. (2 Tim. 4:11; Philem. 24) So, s might be expected, his writing shows evience of Paul's influence, as can be seen by omparing their two accounts of the Lord's vening meal, at Luke 22:19, 20 and 1 Cointhians 11:23-25. As further sources of mateial, Luke could have referred to Matthew's ospel and possibly to notes left by John's now eceased brother James and, through Paul, to otes made by Mark. In 'tracing all things with ccuracy' he would be able personally to interiew many eyewitnesses of the events of Jesus' ife, such as the surviving disciples, and posibly Jesus' mother Mary. We can be sure that e left no stone unturned in assembling the eliable details.

[6] It becomes clear on examining the four ospel writings that they do not simply repeat ne another's narratives, nor do they write olely to provide several witnesses for this most ital Bible record. Luke's account is most inlividualistic in its treatment. In all, 59 percent f his Gospel is unique with him. He records eventeen parables and seven miracles that are ot mentioned in the other Gospel accounts, levoting one third of his Gospel to narrative nd two thirds to the spoken word; his Gospel s the longest of the four. Matthew wrote for he Jews, and Mark for the Romans. Luke's ospel was addressed to the "most excellent heophilus" and through him to "men of good vill" of all the nations. (Luke 2:14) In giving is account a universal appeal, he traces the enealogy of Jesus back to "Adam, the son of God," and not just to Abraham, as does Matthew in writing specially for the Jews. He particularly notes the prophetic words of Simeon, that Jesus would be the means of "removing the veil from the nations," and tells that "all flesh will see the saving means of God."—3:38; 2:29-32; 3:6.

[7] Throughout his writing Luke proves to be an outstanding narrator, his accounts being well arranged and accurate. These qualities of accuracy and fidelity in Luke's writings are strong proof of their authenticity. A legal writer recently observed: "While romances, legends and false testimony are careful to place events related in some distant place and some indefinite time, thereby violating the first rules we lawyers learn of good pleading, that 'the declaration must give time and place,' the Bible narratives give us the date and place of the things related with the utmost precision."[b] In proof he cited Luke 3:1, 2: "In the fifteenth year of the reign of Tiberius Caesar, when Pontius Pilate was governor of Judea, and Herod was district ruler of Galilee, but Philip his brother was district ruler of the country of Ituraea and Trachonitis, and Lysanias was district ruler of Abilene, in the days of chief priest Annas and of Caiaphas, God's declaration came to John the son of Zechariah in the wilderness." There is no indefiniteness here as to time or place, but Luke names no less than seven public officials so that we can establish the time of the beginning of John's (and Jesus') ministry.

[8] Luke also gives us two pointers for fixing the time of Jesus' birth when he says, at Luke 2:1, 2: "Now in those days a decree went forth from Caesar Augustus for all the inhabited earth to be registered; (this first registration took place when Quirinius was governor of Syria)." This was when Joseph and Mary went up to Bethlehem to be registered, and Jesus was born while they were there. We cannot but agree with the commentator who says: "It is one of the most searching tests of Luke's historical sense that he always manages to achieve perfect accuracy."[c] We must acknowledge as just Luke's claim to have "traced all things from the start with accuracy."

[9] Luke also points out how the prophecies of the Hebrew Scriptures were accurately fulfilled in Jesus Christ. He quotes Jesus' inspired testi-

a *The Encyclopædia Britannica,* 1946, Vol. 3, page 528.

b *A Lawyer Examines the Bible,* 1943, I. H. Linton, page 38.

c *Modern Discovery and the Bible,* 1943, A. Rendle Short, page 159.

5. From what sources may Luke have 'traced with accuracy' the events of Jesus' life?
6. How much of Luke's Gospel is unique with him, and for whom especially did he write? Why do you so answer?
7. What testifies strongly to the authenticity of Luke's Gospel?
8. How does Luke indicate the time of Jesus' birth "with accuracy"?
9. What prophecy of Jesus, recorded by Luke, had a remarkable fulfillment A.D. 70?

mony on this. (Luke 24:27, 44) Further, he accurately records Jesus' own prophecies concerning future events, and many of these have already had remarkable fulfillments in all their foretold detail. For example, Jerusalem was surrounded by siege works of pointed stakes and perished in a frightful holocaust A.D. 70, just as Jesus foretold. (Luke 19:43, 44; 21:20-24; Matt. 24:2) The secular historian, Flavius Josephus, who was an eyewitness with the Roman army, testifies that the countryside was denuded of trees to a distance of eleven miles to provide stakes, that the siege wall was five miles long, that many women and children died from famine, and that more than one million Jews lost their lives and 97,000 were taken captive. To this day, the Arch of Titus in Rome portrays the Roman victory procession with spoils of war from Jerusalem's temple.[a] We can be sure that other inspired prophecies recorded by Luke will be just as accurately fulfilled.

CONTENTS OF LUKE

10 **Luke's introduction** (1:1-4). Luke records that he has traced all things from the start with accuracy, and that he has resolved to write them in logical order so that the "most excellent Theophilus . . . may know fully the certainty" of these things.

11 **The early years of Jesus' life** (1:5–2:52). An angel appears to the aged priest Zechariah with the joyful news that he will have a son whom he is to call John. But until the boy is born Zechariah will not be able to speak. As promised, his wife Elizabeth becomes pregnant, though also "well along in years." About six months later the angel Gabriel appears to Mary and tells her that she will conceive by "power of the Most High" and bear a son who is to be called Jesus. Mary visits Elizabeth, and, after a happy greeting, declares exultantly: "My soul magnifies Jehovah, and my spirit cannot keep from being overjoyed at God my Savior." She speaks of Jehovah's holy name and of his great mercy toward those who fear him. At John's birth Zechariah's tongue is loosed to declare also God's mercy and that John will be a prophet who will make Jehovah's way ready.—1:7, 35, 46, 47.

12 In due course, Jesus is born at Bethlehem, and an angel announces this "good news of a great joy" to shepherds watching their flocks at night. Circumcision is carried out according to the Law, and then, when Jesus' parents "present him to Jehovah" at the temple, the aged Simeon and the prophetess Anna speak concerning the child. Back in Nazareth, he 'continues growing and getting strong, being filled with wisdom, and God's favor continues with him.' (2:10, 22, 40) At the age of twelve, on a visit from Nazareth to Jerusalem, Jesus amazes the teachers with his understanding and his answers.

13 **Preparation for the ministry** (3:1–4:13) In the fifteenth year of the reign of Tiberius Caesar, God's declaration comes to John the son of Zechariah, and he goes "preaching baptism in symbol of repentance for forgiveness of sins," that all flesh may "see the saving means of God." (3:3, 6) When all the people are baptized at the Jordan, Jesus is also baptized, and, as he prays, the holy spirit descends on him and his Father expresses approval from heaven. Jesus Christ is now about thirty years of age. (Luke supplies his genealogy.) Following his baptism, the spirit leads Jesus about in the wilderness for forty days, where the Devil tempts him without success and then retires "until another convenient time." —4:13.

14 **Jesus' Galilean ministry** (4:14–9:62). In the synagogue of his hometown of Nazareth Jesus makes clear his commission, reading and applying to himself the prophecy of Isaiah 61:1, 2: "Jehovah's spirit is upon me, because he anointed me to declare good news to the poor, he sent me forth to preach a release to the captives and a recovery of sight to the blind, to send the crushed ones away with a release, to preach Jehovah's acceptable year." (4:18, 19) The people's initial pleasure at his words turns to anger as he continues his discourse, and they attempt to do away with him. So he moves down to Capernaum, where he heals many people. Crowds follow him and try to detain him, but he tells them: "Also to other cities I must declare the good news of the kingdom of God, because for this I was sent forth." (4:43) He goes on to preach in the synagogues of Judea.

15 In Galilee, Jesus provides Simon, James and John with a miraculous catch of fish. He tells Simon Peter: "From now on you will be catching men alive." So they abandon everything and follow him. Jesus continues in prayer and in teaching, and 'Jehovah's power is there for him to do healing.' (5:10, 17) He calls Levi (Matthew), a despised tax collector, who honors Jesus with a big feast, attended also

---

a *Wars of the Jews*, Josephus, v, 12, ¶2, 3; vi, 1, ¶1; vi, 9, ¶3; vii, 1, ¶1; see also Study 9, paragraph 25.

---

10. What does Luke set out to do?
11. What joyful events are related in the first chapter of Luke?
12. What is stated concerning Jesus' birth and childhood?
13. What does John preach, and what occurs at Jesus' baptism and immediately thereafter?
14. Where does Jesus make clear his commission, what is it, and how do his hearers respond?
15. Describe the calling of Peter, James and John; also Matthew.

by "a great crowd of tax collectors." (5:29) This results in the first of a number of encounters with the Pharisees that leave them maddened and conspiring to do him harm.

16 After a whole night of prayer to God, Jesus chooses twelve apostles from among his disciples. Further works of healing follow. Then he gives the sermon recorded at Luke 6:20-49, paralleling in shorter form the Sermon on the Mount at Matthew chapters 5 to 7. Jesus draws the contrast: "Happy are you poor, because yours is the kingdom of God. But woe to you rich persons, because you are having your consolation in full." (6:20, 24) He admonishes his hearers to love their enemies, to be merciful, to practice giving and to bring forth good out of the good treasure of the heart.

17 Returning to Capernaum, Jesus receives a request from an army officer to cure an ailing slave. He feels unworthy to have Jesus under his roof, and asks Jesus to "say the word" from where he is. Accordingly, the slave is healed, and Jesus is moved to comment: "I tell you, Not even in Israel have I found so great a faith." (7:7, 9) For the first time Jesus raises a dead person, the only son of a widow of Nain, for whom he "was moved with pity." (7:13) As the news concerning Jesus spreads through Judea, John the Baptist sends to him from prison to ask, "Are you the Coming One?" In answer Jesus tells the messengers: "Go your way, report to John what you saw and heard: the blind are receiving sight, the lame are walking, the lepers are being cleansed and the deaf are hearing, the dead are being raised up, the poor are being told the good news. And happy is he who has not stumbled over me." —7:19, 22, 23.

18 Accompanied by the twelve, Jesus goes "from city to city and from village to village, preaching and declaring the good news of the kingdom of God." He gives the illustration of the sower, and rounds out the discussion by saying: "Therefore, pay attention to how you listen; for whoever has, more will be given him, but whoever does not have, even what he imagines he has will be taken away from him." (8:1, 18) Jesus continues to perform wonderful works and miracles. He also gives the twelve authority over the demons and to cure sicknesses and sends them forth "to preach the kingdom of God and to heal." Five thousand are miraculously fed. Jesus is transfigured on the mountain and the following day heals a demon-possessed boy whom the disciples could not cure. He cautions those who want to follow him: "Foxes have dens and birds of heaven have roosts, but the Son of man has nowhere to lay down his head." To be fit for the kingdom of God one must set his hand to the plow and not look back.—9:2, 58.

19 **Jesus' later Judean ministry** (10:1–13:21). Jesus sends out seventy others into the "harvest," and they are filled with joy at the success of their ministry. As he is preaching, a man, wanting to prove himself righteous, asks Jesus: "Who really is my neighbor?" In answer, Jesus gives the illustration of the good Samaritan. A man, lying on the roadside half-dead from a beating by robbers, is ignored by a passing priest and a Levite. It is a despised Samaritan who stops, tenderly cares for his wounds, lifts him up on his ass and brings him to an inn and pays for him to be taken care of. Yes, it is "the one that acted mercifully toward him" who was the neighbor.—10:29, 37.

20 In Martha's house, Jesus mildly rebukes her for becoming overly anxious about her household chores, and commends Mary for choosing the better part, sitting down and listening to his word. To his disciples he teaches the model prayer and also the need for persistence in prayer, saying: "Keep on asking, and it will be given you; keep on seeking, and you will find." Later he expels demons and declares happy "those hearing the word of God and keeping it." While at a meal he clashes with the Pharisees over the Law, and pronounces woes upon them for taking away "the key of knowledge."—11:9, 28, 52.

21 As he is again with the crowds a certain one urges Jesus: "Tell my brother to divide the inheritance with me." He goes to the heart of the problem in replying: "Keep your eyes open and guard against every sort of covetousness, because even when a person has an abundance his life does not result from the things he possesses." Then he gives the illustration of the wealthy man who tore down his barns to build bigger ones, only to die that very night and leave his wealth to others. Jesus concisely makes the point: "So it goes with the man that lays up treasure for himself but is not rich toward God." In commending the heavenly treasures to his disciples, Jesus tells them: "Have no fear, little flock, because your Father has approved of giving you the kingdom." His healing on the sabbath, of a woman who has been sick for eighteen years, leads to a further clash with his opposers, who are put to shame.—12:13, 15, 21, 32.

16. (a) Following what does Jesus choose the twelve apostles? (b) What points are highlighted by Luke in giving a parallel version of the Sermon on the Mount?
17. (a) What miracles does Jesus next perform? (b) How does Jesus answer the messengers of John the Baptist as to his being the Messiah?
18. With what illustrations, works and words of counsel does the Kingdom preaching continue?
19. How does Jesus illustrate true love of neighbor?
20. (a) What point does Jesus make with Martha and Mary? (b) What stress does he lay on prayer?
21. What warning does Jesus give against covetousness, and what does he commend to his disciples?

22 **Jesus' later Perean ministry** (13:22–19:27). Jesus uses colorful illustrations in pointing his hearers to the kingdom of God. He shows that those who seek prominence and honor will be abased. Let the one who spreads a feast invite the poor who cannot repay; he will be happy and be "repaid in the resurrection of the righteous ones." Next, there is the illustration of the man spreading a grand evening meal. One after another the invited ones make excuses: One has bought a field, another has purchased some oxen, and another has just married a wife. In anger the householder sends out to bring in "the poor and crippled and blind and lame," and declares that none of those first invited will have so much as "a taste" of his meal. (14:14, 21, 24) He gives the illustration of the lost sheep that is found, saying, "I tell you that thus there will be more joy in heaven over one sinner that repents than over ninety-nine righteous ones who have no need of repentance." (15:7) The illustration of the woman who sweeps her house to recover one drachma coin (15c) makes a similar point.

23 Jesus then tells of the prodigal son who asked his father for his share in the property and then squandered it "by living a debauched life." Falling into dire need, the son came to his senses and returned home to throw himself upon his father's mercy. His father, moved with pity, "ran and fell upon his neck and tenderly kissed him." Fine clothing was provided, a big feast prepared and "they started to enjoy themselves." But the elder brother objected. In kindness his father set him straight: "Child, you have always been with me, and all the things that are mine are yours; but we just had to enjoy ourselves and rejoice, because this your brother was dead but has become alive, and he was lost but has been found."—15:13, 20, 24, 31, 32.

24 On hearing the illustration of the unrighteous steward, the money-loving Pharisees sneer at Jesus' teaching, but he tells them: "You are those who declare yourselves righteous before men, but God knows your hearts; because what is lofty among men is a disgusting thing in God's sight." (16:15) By the illustration of the rich man and Lazarus he shows how great is the chasm that is fixed between those favored and those disapproved by God. Jesus warns the disciples that there will be causes for stumbling, but "woe to the one through whom they come!" He speaks of difficulties to appear "when the Son of man is to be revealed." "Remember the wife of Lot," he tells them. (17:1, 30, 32) By an illustration he gives assurance that God will certainly act in behalf of those who "cry out to him day and night." (18:7) Then by another illustration he reproves the self-righteous: A Pharisee, praying in the temple, thanks God that he is not like other men. A tax collector, standing at a distance and not willing even to raise his eyes to heaven, prays: "O God, be gracious to me a sinner." How does Jesus evaluate this? He declares the tax collector to be more righteous than the Pharisee, "because everyone that exalts himself will be humiliated, but he that humbles himself will be exalted." (18:13, 14) Jesus is entertained at Jericho by the tax collector Zacchaeus and gives the illustration of the ten minas, contrasting the result of faithfully using entrusted interests with that of hiding them away.

25 **Final public ministry in and around Jerusalem** (19:28–23:35). As Jesus rides into Jerusalem on a colt and is hailed by the multitude of the disciples as "the One coming as the King in Jehovah's name," the Pharisees call on him to rebuke them. Jesus replies: "If these remained silent, the stones would cry out." (19:38, 40) He gives his memorable prophecy of Jerusalem's destruction, saying that she will be built around with pointed stakes, distressed, dashed to the ground with her children and that not one stone will be left on another. Jesus teaches the people in the temple, declaring the good news and answering the subtle questions of the chief priests, the scribes and the Sadducees by skillful illustrations and argumentation. Jesus gives a powerful portrayal of the great sign of the end, mentioning again the surrounding of Jerusalem with encamped armies. Men will become faint out of fear at the things coming to pass, but when these things occur his followers are to 'raise themselves erect and lift their heads up, because their deliverance is getting near.' They are to keep awake to succeed in escaping what is destined to occur.—21:28.

26 It is now Nisan 14, A.D. 33. Jesus holds the passover and then introduces "the new covenant" to his faithful disciples, associating this with the symbolic meal, which he commands them to observe in remembrance of him. He also tells them: "I make a covenant with you, just as my Father has made a covenant with me, for a kingdom." (22:20, 29) That same night, as Jesus prays at the Mount of Olives, 'an angel from heaven appears to him and strengthens him. But getting into an agony, he

22. By what pointed illustrations did Jesus instruct concerning the Kingdom?
23. What is illustrated in the account of the prodigal son?
24. What truths does Jesus emphasize in the illustrations of the rich man and Lazarus and the Pharisee and the tax collector?
25. How does Jesus enter upon the final stage of his ministry, and what prophetic warnings does he give?
26. (a) What covenants does Jesus introduce, and with what does he associate them? (b) How is Jesus strengthened under trial, and what rebuke does he give at the time of his arrest?

continues praying more earnestly; and his sweat becomes as drops of blood falling to the ground.' The atmosphere grows tense as Judas the betrayer leads in the mob to arrest Jesus. The disciples cry: "Lord, shall we strike with the sword?" One of them does lop off the ear of the high priest's slave, but Jesus rebukes them and heals the wounded man.—22:43, 44, 49.

27 Jesus is hustled along to the high priest's house for questioning, and in the chill of the night Peter mingles with the crowd around a fire. On three occasions he is challenged with being a follower of Jesus, and three times he denies it. Then the cock crows. The Lord turns and looks upon Peter, and Peter, recalling how Jesus had foretold this very thing, goes out and weeps bitterly. After being haled into the Sanhedrin hall Jesus is now led before Pilate and accused of subverting the nation, forbidding payment of taxes and "saying he himself is Christ a king." Learning that Jesus is a Galilean, Pilate sends him to Herod, who happens to be in Jerusalem at the time. Herod and his guards make fun of Jesus and send him back for trial before a frenzied mob. Pilate 'surrenders Jesus to their will.'—23:2, 25.

28 **Jesus' death, resurrection and ascension** (23:26–24:53). Jesus is impaled between two evildoers. One taunts him, but the other manifests faith and asks to be remembered in Jesus' kingdom. Jesus promises: "Truly I tell you today, You will be with me in Paradise." (23:43) Then an unusual darkness falls, the curtain of the sanctuary is rent down the middle, and Jesus cries out: "Father, into your hands I entrust my spirit." At this he expires, and his body is taken down and laid in a tomb carved in the rock. On the first day of the week the women who had come with him from Galilee go to the tomb but cannot find Jesus' body. Just as he himself foretold, he has arisen on the third day!—23:46.

29 Appearing unidentified to two of his disciples on the road to Emmaus, Jesus speaks of his sufferings and interprets the Scriptures to them. Suddenly they recognize him, but he disappears. Now they comment: "Were not our hearts burning as he was speaking to us on the road, as he was fully opening up the Scriptures to us?" They hurry back to Jerusalem to tell the other disciples. Even while they are speaking these things Jesus appears in their midst. They cannot believe it for sheer joy and wonderment. Then he 'opens up their minds fully to grasp' from the Scriptures the meaning of all that has happened. Luke concludes his Gospel account with a description of the ascension of Jesus to heaven, thus linking up with the opening verses of his book of Acts.—24:32, 45.

WHY BENEFICIAL

30 The good news "according to Luke" builds confidence in the Word of God and strengthens faith to stand against the buffetings of an alien world. Luke supplies many examples of accurate fulfillments of the Hebrew Scriptures. Jesus is shown drawing his commission in specific terms from the book of Isaiah, and Luke seems to use this as a theme throughout the entire book. (Luke 4:17-19; Isa. 61:1, 2) This was one of the occasions of Jesus' quoting from the Prophets. He also quoted from the Law, as when rejecting the Devil's three temptations, and from the Psalms, as when asking his adversaries, "How is it they say that the Christ is David's son?" Luke's account contains many other quotations from the Hebrew Scriptures. —Luke 4:4, 8, 12; 20:41-44; Deut. 8:3; 6:13, 16; Ps. 110:1.

31 When Jesus rode into Jerusalem on a colt as foretold at Zechariah 9:9, the multitudes hailed him joyously, applying to him the scripture at Psalm 118:26. (Luke 19:35-38) In one place two verses of Luke are sufficient to cover six points that the Hebrew Scriptures prophesied concerning Jesus' reproachful death and his resurrection. (Luke 18:32, 33; Ps. 22:7; Isa. 50:6; 53:5-7; Jonah 1:17) Finally, after his resurrection, Jesus forcefully brought home to the disciples the importance of the entire Hebrew Scriptures. "He now said to them: 'These are my words which I spoke to you while I was yet with you, that all the things written in the law of Moses and in the Prophets and Psalms about me must be fulfilled.' Then he opened up their minds fully to grasp the meaning of the Scriptures." (Luke 24:44, 45) Like those first disciples of Jesus Christ, we too can be enlightened and gain strong faith by paying attention to the fulfillments of the Hebrew Scriptures, so accurately explained by Luke and the other writers of the Greek Scriptures.

32 Throughout his account Luke continually points his reader to the kingdom of God. From the beginning of the book, where the angel promises Mary that the child she will bear "will rule as king over the house of Jacob forever, and there will be no end of his kingdom," to the closing chapters, where Jesus speaks of taking the apostles into the covenant for the

27. (a) Wherein does Peter fail? (b) What charges are laid against Jesus, and under what circumstances is he tried and sentenced?
28. (a) What does Jesus promise to the goodwill thief? (b) What does Luke record concerning Jesus' death, burial and resurrection?
29. With what joyful account does Luke's Gospel conclude?
30, 31. (a) How does Luke build confidence in the Hebrew Scriptures as inspired of God? (b) What words of Jesus does he quote to support this?
32. How does Luke's account highlight the Kingdom and what our attitude should be toward the Kingdom?

Kingdom, Luke highlights the Kingdom hope. (Luke 1:33; 22:28, 29) He shows Jesus setting the lead in Kingdom preaching and sending out the twelve apostles, and later the seventy, to do this very work. (4:43; 9:1, 2; 10:1, 8, 9) The single-minded devotion needed in order to enter the Kingdom is underlined by Jesus' pointed words: "Let the dead bury their dead, but you go away and declare abroad the kingdom of God," and, "No man that has put his hand to a plow and looks at the things behind is well fitted for the kingdom of God."—9:60, 62.

33 Luke emphasizes the matter of prayer. His Gospel is outstanding in this. It tells of the multitude praying while Zechariah was in the temple, of John the Baptist being born in answer to prayers for a child and of Anna the prophetess praying night and day. It describes Jesus' praying at the time of his baptism, his spending the whole night in prayer before choosing the twelve and his praying during the transfiguration. Jesus admonishes his disciples "always to pray and not to give up," illustrating this by a persistent widow who continually petitioned a judge until he gave her justice. Only Luke tells of the disciples' request for Jesus to teach them to pray, of the angel's strengthening Jesus as he prayed at the Mount of Olives, and he alone records the words of Jesus' final prayer: "Father, into your hands I entrust my spirit." (Luke 1:10, 13; 2:37; 3:21; 6:12; 9:28, 29; 18:1-8; 11:1; 22:39-46; 23:46) As in the day when Luke recorded his Gospel, so today prayer is a vital provision for strengthening all who are doing the divine will.

34 With his keenly observant mind and his fluent, descriptive pen, Luke gives warmth and vibrant life to Jesus' teaching. The love, kindness, mercy and compassion of Jesus toward the weak, oppressed and downtrodden show up in sharp contrast to the cold, formal, narrow, hypocritical religion of the scribes and Pharisees. (Luke 4:18; 18:9) Jesus gives constant encouragement and help to the poor, the captives, the blind and the crushed ones, thus providing splendid precedents for those who are seeking to "follow his steps closely."—1 Pet. 2:21.

35 Just as Jesus, the perfect, wonder-working Son of God, manifested loving concern for his disciples and all men of goodwill, we also should strive to minister God's Word in love, yes, "because of the tender compassion of our God." (Luke 1:78) To this end the good news "according to Luke" is indeed most beneficial and helpful. We can be truly grateful to Jehovah for inspiring Luke, "the beloved physician," to write this accurate, upbuilding and encouraging account, pointing as it does to salvation through the Kingdom by Jesus Christ, "the saving means of God."—Luke 3:6.

33. Give examples of Luke's emphasis on prayer. What lesson can we draw from this?

34. What qualities of Jesus does Luke stress as fine precedents for his followers?

35. Why can we be truly grateful to Jehovah for his provision of Luke's Gospel?

Bible Book Number Forty-three— John

Writer:	**Apostle John**
Place Written:	**Ephesus, or near**
Writing Completed:	**c. A.D. 98**
Time Covered:	**After Prologue, A.D. 29-33**

THE Gospel records of Matthew, Mark and Luke had been circulating for over thirty years and had come to be treasured by first-century Christians as the works of men inspired by holy spirit. Now, as the close of the century neared and the number of those who had been with Jesus dwindled, the question may well have arisen, Was there still something to be told? Was there still someone who could from personal memories fill in precious details of the ministry of Jesus? Yes, there was. The aged John had been singularly blessed in his association with Jesus. He was apparently among the first of John the Baptist's disciples to be introduced to the Lamb of God and one of the first four to be invited by the Lord to join him full time in the ministry. (John 1:35-39; Mark 1:16-20) He continued in intimate association with Jesus throughout his ministry, and was the disciple "Jesus loved" who reclined in front of Jesus' bosom at the last supper. (John 13:23; Matt. 17:1; Mark 5:37; 14:33) He was present at the heartbreaking scene of execution, when Jesus entrusted to him the care of his fleshly mother, and it was he that outstripped Peter as they ran to the tomb to investigate the report that Jesus had risen. —John 19:26, 27; 20:2, 3.

1. What do the Scriptures show as to the closeness of John's association with Jesus?

2 Mellowed by almost seventy years in the active ministry and charged with the visions and meditations of his recent lonely imprisonment on the Isle of Patmos, John was well equipped to write of things he had long treasured in his heart. Holy spirit now energized his mind to recall and set down in writing many of those precious, life-giving sayings so that each one reading 'might believe that Jesus is the Christ the Son of God, and that, because of believing, he might have life by means of his name.'—John 20:31.

3 Christians of the early second century accepted John as the writer of this account and also treated this writing as an unquestioned part of the canon of the inspired Scriptures. Clement of Alexandria, Irenaeus, Tertullian and Origen, all of the late second and early third centuries, testify to John's writership. Moreover, much internal evidence that John was the writer is to be found in the book itself. Obviously the writer was a Jew, well acquainted with their customs and their land. (John 2:6; 4:5; 5:2; 10:22, 23) The very intimacy of the account indicates that he was not only an apostle, but one of the inner circle of three—Peter, James and John—who accompanied Jesus on special occasions. (Matt. 17:1; Mark 5:37; 14:33) Of these, James (the son of Zebedee) is eliminated because he was martyred by Herod Agrippa I about A.D. 44, long before this book was written. (Acts 12:2) Peter is eliminated because he is mentioned along with the writer at John 21:20-24.

4 In these closing verses the writer is referred to as the disciple "Jesus used to love," this and similar expressions being used several times in the record, though the name of the apostle John is never mentioned. Jesus is here quoted as saying about him: "If it is my will for him to remain until I come, of what concern is that to you?" (John 21:20, 22) This suggests that the disciple referred to would long survive Peter and the other apostles. All this fits the apostle John. It is of interest that John, after being given the Revelation vision of Jesus' coming, concludes this remarkable prophecy with the words: "Amen! Come, Lord Jesus." —Rev. 22:20.

5 Although John's writings themselves give no definite information on the matter, it is generally believed that John wrote his Gospel after his return from exile on the island of Patmos. (Rev. 1:9) Roman emperor Nerva, A.D. 96-98, recalled many who had been exiled at the close of the reign of his predecessor, Domitian. After writing his Gospel, about A.D. 98, John is believed to have died peacefully at Ephesus in the third year of Emperor Trajan, A.D. 100.

6 As to Ephesus or vicinity as the place of writing, the historian Eusebius (c. A.D. 260-340) quotes Irenaeus as saying: "John, the disciple of the Lord, who had even rested on his breast, himself also gave forth the gospel, while he was living at Ephesus in Asia."[a] That the book was written outside Palestine is supported by its references to Jesus' opponents by the general term, "the Jews," rather than "Pharisees," "chief priests," and so forth, in many places. (John 1:19; 12:9) Also, the Sea of Galilee is explained by its Roman name, Sea of Tiberias. (6:1; 21:1) For the sake of the non-Jews, John gives helpful explanations of the Jewish festivals. (6:4; 7:2; 11:55) The place of his exile, Patmos, was near Ephesus, and his acquaintance with Ephesus, as well as the other congregations of Asia Minor, is indicated by Revelation chapters 2 and 3.

7 Bearing on the authenticity of John's Gospel are important manuscript finds of the past half century. One of these is a fragment of John's Gospel found in Egypt, now known as the Rylands Papyrus 457 (P^{52}), containing John 18:31-33, 37, 38, and preserved at the John Rylands Library, Manchester, England. As to its bearing on the tradition of John's writership at the end of the first century, the late Sir Frederic Kenyon said in his book *The Bible and Modern Scholarship*, 1948, page 21: "Small therefore as it is, it suffices to prove that a manuscript of this Gospel was circulating, presumably in provincial Egypt where it was found, about the period of A.D. 130-150. Allowing for even a minimum time for the circulation of the work from its place of origin, this would throw back the date of composition so near to the traditional date in the last decade of the first century that there is no longer any reason to question the validity of the tradition."

8 John's Gospel is remarkable for its introduction, which reveals the Word, who was "in the beginning with God," as the One through whom all things came into existence. After making known the precious relationship between Father and Son, John launches into a masterly portrayal of Jesus' works and discourses, especially from the viewpoint of the intimate love that binds in union everything in God's great arrangement. This account of

a *Eusebius, The Ecclesiastical History,* V, viii, 4, translated by Kirsopplake, 1926.

2. How was John equipped and energized to write his Gospel, and for what purpose?
3, 4. What is the external and internal evidence for (a) the Gospel's canonicity, and (b) John's writership?
5. When is John believed to have written his Gospel?
6. What evidence indicates the Gospel was written outside Palestine, at or near Ephesus?
7. Of what importance is the Rylands Papyrus 457?
8. (a) What is remarkable about the introduction of John's Gospel? (b) What proof does it supply that Jesus' ministry was three and a half years in duration?

Jesus' life on earth covers the period A.D. 29-33, and is careful to make mention of the four passovers that Jesus attended during his ministry, thus providing one of the lines of proof that his ministry was three and a half years in duration. Three of these passovers are mentioned as such. (John 2:13; 6:4; 12:1 and 13:1) One of them is referred to as "a festival of the Jews," but the context places it shortly after Jesus' words about there being "yet four months before the harvest," thus indicating the festival to be the passover, which took place about the beginning of the harvest.—4:35; 5:1.

9 The good news "according to John" is largely supplementary, containing 92 percent new material not covered in the other three Gospels. Even so, John concludes with the words: "There are, in fact, many other things also which Jesus did, which, if ever they were written in full detail, I suppose, the world itself could not contain the scrolls written."—John 21:25.

CONTENTS OF JOHN

10 **Prologue: Introducing "the Word" (1:1-18).** With beauteous simplicity, John states that in the beginning "the Word was with God," that life itself was by means of him and that he became "the light of men" and that John (the Baptist) bore witness about him. (1:1, 4) The light was in the world, but the world did not know him. Those who did receive him became God's children, being born from God. Just as the Law was given through Moses, so "the undeserved kindness and the truth came to be through Jesus Christ."—1:17.

11 **Presenting "the Lamb of God" to men** (1:19-51). John the baptizer confesses *he* is not the Christ but says there is one coming behind him 'the lace of whose sandal he is not worthy to untie.' The next day, as Jesus comes toward him, John identifies him as "the Lamb of God that takes away the sin of the world." (1:27, 29) Next he introduces two of his disciples to Jesus, and one of these, Andrew, brings his brother Peter to him. Philip and Nathanael also accept Jesus as 'the Son of God, the King of Israel.'—1:49.

12 **Jesus' miracles prove him "the Holy One of God"** (2:1–6:71). Jesus performs his first miracle in Cana of Galilee, turning water into the best of wine at a wedding feast. This is the "beginning of his signs, . . . and his disciples put their faith in him." (2:11) Jesus goes up to Jerusalem for the passover. Finding peddlers and money changers in the temple, he takes a whip and drives them out with such vigor that his disciples recognize the fulfillment of the prophecy: "The zeal for your house will eat me up." (John 2:17; Ps. 69:9) He predicts that the temple of his own body will be broken down and raised up again in three days.

13 The fearful Nicodemus comes to Jesus at night and confesses that Jesus is sent from God. Jesus tells him that one must be born from water and spirit to enter the kingdom of God. Believing in the Son of man from heaven is necessary for life. "For God loved the world so much that he gave his only-begotten Son, in order that everyone exercising faith in him might not be destroyed but have everlasting life." (John 3:16) The light that has come into the world is in conflict with darkness, "but he that does what is true comes to the light," concludes Jesus. John the Baptist then learns of Jesus' activity in Judea and declares that, while he himself is not the Christ, yet "the friend of the bridegroom . . . has a great deal of joy on account of the voice of the bridegroom." (3:21, 29) Jesus must now increase, and John decrease.

14 Jesus sets out again for Galilee. On the way, dust-laden and "tired out from the journey," he sits down to rest at Jacob's fountain in Sychar, while his disciples are off buying food in the city. It is midday, the sixth hour. A Samaritan woman approaches to draw water, and Jesus asks for a drink. Then, weary though he is, he begins to speak to her about the real "water" that truly refreshes, imparting everlasting life to those who worship God "with spirit and truth." The disciples return and urge him to eat, and he declares: "My food is for me to do the will of him that sent me and to finish his work." He spends two days longer in the area, so that many of the Samaritans come to believe that "this man is for a certainty the savior of the world." (4:24, 34, 42) On reaching Cana of Galilee, Jesus heals a nobleman's son without even going near his bedside.

15 Jesus goes up again to Jerusalem for the Jews' festival. He heals a cripple on the sabbath, and this raises a great storm of criticism. Jesus counters: "My Father has kept working until now, and I keep working." (5:17) The Jewish leaders now claim that Jesus has added blasphemy, that of making himself equal to God, to his crime of sabbath-breaking.

9. What shows John's Gospel to be supplementary, and yet does it fill out all the details of Jesus' ministry?
10. What does John say about "the Word"?
11. As what does John the Baptist identify Jesus, and as what do John's disciples accept him?
12. (a) What is Jesus' first miracle? (b) What does he do when up at Jerusalem for the first passover during his ministry?
13. (a) What does Jesus show to be necessary for gaining life? (b) How does John the Baptist speak of himself in relationship to Jesus?
14. What does Jesus explain to the Samaritan woman at Sychar, and what results from his preaching there?
15. What charges are made against Jesus in Jerusalem, but how does he answer his critics?

Jesus answers that the Son cannot do a single thing of his own initiative, but is entirely dependent on the Father. He makes the marvelous statement that "all those in the memorial tombs will hear his voice and come out" to a resurrection. But to his faithless audience Jesus says: "How can you believe, when you are accepting glory from one another and you are not seeking the glory that is from the only God?"—5:28, 29, 44.

16 When Jesus miraculously feeds five thousand men with five loaves and two small fishes, the crowd consider seizing him and making him king, but he withdraws into a mountain. Later, he reproves them for going after "the food that perishes." Rather, they should work "for the food that remains for life everlasting." He points out that exercising faith in him as the Son is the partaking of the bread of life, and adds: "Unless you eat the flesh of the Son of man and drink his blood, you have no life in yourselves." Many of his disciples are offended at this and leave him. Jesus asks the twelve: "You do not want to go also, do you?" and Peter replies: "Lord, whom shall we go away to? You have sayings of everlasting life; and we have believed and come to know that you are the Holy One of God." (6:27, 53, 67-69) However, Jesus, knowing that Judas will betray him, says that one of them is a slanderer.

17 **"The light" conflicts with darkness** (7:1–12:50). Jesus goes up secretly to Jerusalem, and appears halfway through the feast of tabernacles, teaching openly in the temple. The people argue as to whether he is really the Christ. Jesus tells them: "I have not come of my own initiative, but he that sent me is real, . . . that One sent me forth." On another occasion he cries out to the crowd: "If anyone is thirsty, let him come to me and drink." Officers sent to arrest Jesus return empty-handed and report to the priests: "Never has another man spoken like this." Infuriated, the Pharisees answer that none of the rulers have believed, nor is any prophet to be raised up out of Galilee. —7:28, 29, 37, 46.

18 In a further speech Jesus says: "I am the light of the world." To the malicious charges that he is a false witness, that he has been born out of wedlock and that he is a Samaritan and demon-possessed, Jesus forcefully replies: "If I glorify myself, my glory is nothing. It is my Father that glorifies me." When he declares, "Before Abraham came into existence, I have been," the Jews make another abortive attempt on his life. (8:12, 54, 58) Frustrated, they later examine a man whose sight Jesus has miraculously restored, and throw him out.

19 Again Jesus speaks to the Jews, this time concerning the fine shepherd who calls his sheep by name and who surrenders his soul in behalf of the sheep, 'that they might have life in abundance.' "And I have other sheep, which are not of this fold; those also I must bring, and they will listen to my voice, and they will become one flock, one shepherd." (10:10, 16) He tells the Jews that no one can snatch the sheep out of the hand of his Father, and that he and his Father are one. Again they seek to stone him to death. In answer to their charge of blasphemy, he reminds them that in the book of Psalms (82:6) certain mighty ones of earth are referred to as "gods," whereas he has referred to himself as God's Son. He urges them at least to believe his works.—John 10:34.

20 From Bethany, near Jerusalem, comes news that Lazarus, brother of Mary and Martha, is ill. By the time Jesus arrives there Lazarus is dead and already four days in the tomb. Jesus performs the stupendous miracle of recalling Lazarus to life, causing many to put faith in him. This precipitates a special meeting of the Sanhedrin, where high priest Caiaphas is compelled to prophesy that Jesus is destined to die for the nation. As the chief priests and Pharisees take counsel to kill him, Jesus retires temporarily from the public scene.

21 Six days before the passover Jesus comes again to Bethany on his way to Jerusalem, and is entertained by Lazarus' household. Then, the day after the sabbath, on Nisan 9, seated upon a young ass, he makes an entry into Jerusalem amid the acclamations of a great crowd; and the Pharisees say to one another: "You are getting absolutely nowhere. See! The world has gone after him." By the illustration of a grain of wheat Jesus intimates that he must be planted in death in order for fruitage to be produced for everlasting life. He calls on his Father to glorify His name, and a voice is heard from heaven: "I both glorified it and will glorify it again." Jesus urges his hearers to avoid the darkness and to walk in the light, yes, to become "sons of light." As the forces of darkness close in on him he makes a strong public appeal for the people to put faith in him 'as a light that has come into the world.'—12:19, 28, 36, 46.

16. (a) What does Jesus teach concerning food and life? (b) How does Peter express the conviction of the apostles?
17. What effect has Jesus' teaching in the temple at the feast of tabernacles?
18. What opposition do the Jews bring against Jesus, and how does he reply?
19. (a) How does Jesus speak of his relationship with his Father and his care for his sheep? (b) How does he answer the Jews when they threaten him?
20. (a) What outstanding miracle does Jesus next perform? (b) To what does this lead?
21. (a) How do the people and the Pharisees respond to Jesus' entry into Jerusalem? (b) How does Jesus illustrate his death and its purpose, and what does he urge upon his hearers?

22 **Jesus' parting counsel to the faithful apostles** (13:1–16:33). While the evening meal of the passover with the twelve is in progress, Jesus rises and, removing his outer garments, takes a towel and foot basin and proceeds to wash the feet of his disciples. Peter protests, but Jesus tells him he too must have his feet washed, and admonishes the disciples to follow this pattern of humility, for "a slave is not greater than his master." He speaks of the betrayer and then dismisses Judas. After Judas goes out Jesus begins to speak intimately with the others. "I am giving you a new commandment, that you love one another; just as I have loved you, that you also love one another. By this all will know that you are my disciples, if you have love among yourselves."—13:16, 34, 35.

23 Jesus speaks wonderful words of comfort for this critical hour. They must exercise faith in God, and also in him. In his Father's house there are many abodes, and he will come again and receive them home to himself. "I am the way and the truth and the life," says Jesus. "No one comes to the Father except through me." Comfortingly he tells his followers that by exercising faith they will do greater works than he, and that he will grant whatever they ask in his name, that his Father may be glorified. He promises them another helper, "the spirit of the truth," which will teach them all things and bring back to their minds all that he has told them. They should rejoice that he is going away to his Father, for, says Jesus, "the Father is greater than I am."—14:6, 17, 28.

24 Jesus speaks of himself as the true vine and his Father as the cultivator. He urges them to remain in union with him, saying: "My Father is glorified in this, that you keep bearing much fruit and prove yourselves my disciples." (15:8) And how may their joy become full? By loving one another just as he has loved them. He calls them friends. What a precious relationship! The world will hate them as it has hated him, and will persecute them, but Jesus will send the helper to bear witness about him and to guide his disciples into all truth. Their present grief will give way to rejoicing when he sees them again, and their joy no one will take from them. Consoling are his words: "The Father himself has affection for you, because you have had affection for me and have believed that I came out as the Father's representative." Yes, they will be scattered, but, says Jesus, "I have said these things to you that by means of me you may have peace. In the world you will have tribulation, but take courage! I have conquered the world."—16:27, 33.

25 **Jesus' prayer on behalf of his disciples** (17:1-26). In prayer Jesus acknowledges to his Father: "This means everlasting life, their taking in knowledge of you, the only true God, and of the one whom you sent forth, Jesus Christ." Having finished his assigned work on earth, Jesus now asks to be glorified alongside his Father with the glory he had before the world was. He has made the Father's name manifest to his disciples and asks him to watch over them 'on account of His own name.' He requests the Father, not that they be taken out of the world, but to keep them from the wicked one and to sanctify them by His word of truth. Jesus broadens out his prayer to embrace all those who will yet exercise faith through hearing the word of these disciples, "in order that they may all be one, just as you, Father, are in union with me and I am in union with you, that they also may be in union with us, in order that the world may believe that you sent me forth." He asks that these also may share with him in his heavenly glory, for he has made the Father's name known to them, that His love may abide in them.—17:3, 11, 21.

26 **Christ tried and impaled** (18:1–19:42). Jesus and his disciples go now to a garden across the Kidron valley. It is here that Judas appears with a soldier band and betrays Jesus, who mildly submits. However, Peter defends him with a sword and is reproved: "The cup that the Father has given me, should I not by all means drink it?" (18:11) Jesus is then led away bound to Annas, the father-in-law of the acting high priest. John and Peter follow closely, and John gets them access to the courtyard of the high priest, where Peter three times denies knowing Christ. Jesus is first tried before Annas and then before Caiaphas the acting high priest. For another trial Jesus is brought before Roman governor Pilate, with the Jews clamoring for the death sentence.

27 To Pilate's question, "Are you a king?" Jesus replies: "You yourself are saying that I am a king. For this I have been born, and for this I have come into the world, that I should bear witness to the truth." (18:37) Pilate, finding no real evidence against Jesus, offers to release him, as it was the custom to free some prisoner at the passover, but the Jews call for the robber Barabbas instead. Pilate has Jesus

22. What pattern and new commandment does Jesus provide at the passover meal?
23. As comfort, what hope and what promised helper does Jesus discuss?
24. How does Jesus discuss the relationship of the apostles with himself and the Father, with what blessings for them?
25. (a) What does Jesus acknowledge in prayer to his Father? (b) What does he request with regard to himself, his disciples and those who will exercise faith through their word?
26. What does the account say concerning Jesus' arrest and trial?
27. (a) What questions as to kingship and authority are raised by Pilate, and how does Jesus comment? (b) What stand on kingship do the Jews take?

scourged, and again tries to release him, but the Jews cry: "Impale him! Impale him! . . . because he made himself God's son." When Pilate tells Jesus he has authority to impale him, Jesus answers: "You would have no authority at all against me unless it had been granted to you from above." Again the Jews cry out: "Take him away! Take him away! Impale him! . . . We have no king but Caesar." At this Pilate hands him over to be impaled. —19:6, 7, 11, 15.

28 Jesus is taken away "to the so-called Skull Place, which is called *Golgotha* in Hebrew," and impaled between two others. Above him Pilate fastens the title "Jesus the Nazarene the King of the Jews," written in Hebrew, Latin and Greek, for all to see and understand. (19:17, 19) Jesus entrusts his mother to the care of John, and, after receiving some sour wine, exclaims: "It has been accomplished!" Then he bows his head and expires. (19:30) In fulfillment of the prophecies, the executional squad casts lots for his garments, refrains from breaking his legs and jabs his side with a spear. (John 19:24, 32-37; Ps. 22:18; 34:20; 22:17; Zech. 12:10) Afterward, Joseph of Arimathea and Nicodemus prepare the body for burial and place it in a new memorial tomb nearby.

29 **Appearances of the resurrected Christ** (20:1–21:25). John's array of evidence as to the Christ concludes on the happy note of the resurrection. Mary Magdalene finds the tomb empty, and Peter and another disciple (John) run there, to see only the bandages and head cloth remaining. Mary, who has remained near the tomb, speaks with two angels and finally, as she thinks, with the gardener. When he answers "Mary!" she immediately recognizes it to be Jesus. Next, Jesus manifests himself to his disciples behind locked doors, and tells them of the power they will receive through holy spirit. Thomas, who was not present, refuses to believe, but eight days later Jesus again appears, and gives him the proof, at which Thomas exclaims: "My Lord and my God!" (20:16, 28) Days later Jesus again meets his disciples, at the Sea of Tiberias, provides them a miraculous catch of fish, and then breakfasts with them. Three times he asks Peter whether he loves him. As Peter insists that he does, Jesus says pointedly: "Feed my lambs," "Shepherd my little sheep," "Feed my little sheep." Then he foretells by what sort of death Peter will glorify God. Peter asks about John, and Jesus says: "If it is my will for him to remain until I come, of what concern is that to you?" —21:15-17, 22.

WHY BENEFICIAL

30 Powerful in its directness, and convincing in its intimate, heartwarming portrayal of the Word, who became Christ, the good news "according to John" gives us a close-up view of this anointed Son of God in word and in action. Though John's style and vocabulary are of the simplest, such as to mark him as an "unlettered and ordinary" man, yet there is tremendous power in his expression. (Acts 4:13) His Gospel soars to its greatest heights in making known the intimate love between Father and Son, and the blessed, loving relationship to be found in union with them. John uses the words "love" and "loved" more often than the other three Gospels combined.

31 In the beginning what a glorious relationship existed between the Word and God the Father! In God's providence "the Word became flesh and resided among us, and we had a view of his glory, a glory such as belongs to an only-begotten son from a father; and he was full of undeserved kindness and truth." (John 1:14) Then, throughout the account, Jesus emphasizes his relationship to be one of subjection in unquestioning obedience to the will of the Father. (4:34; 5:19, 30; 7:16; 10:29, 30; 11:41, 42; 12:27, 49, 50; 14:10) His expression of this intimate relationship reaches its glorious climax in the moving prayer recorded in John chapter 17, where Jesus reports to his Father that he has finished the work He gave him to do in the earth, and adds: "So now you, Father, glorify me alongside yourself with the glory that I had alongside you before the world was."—17:5.

32 What of Jesus' relationship with his disciples? Jesus' role as the sole channel through which God's blessings are extended to these and to all mankind is continually kept to the fore. (14:13, 14; 15:16; 16:23, 24) He is referred to as "the Lamb of God," "the bread of life," "the light of the world," "the fine shepherd," "the resurrection and the life," "the way and the truth and the life" and "the true vine." (1:29; 6:35; 8:12; 10:11; 11:25; 14:6; 15:1) It is under this illustration of "the true vine" that Jesus makes known the marvelous unity that exists, not only between his true followers and himself, but also with the Father. By bearing much fruit they will glorify his Father. "Just as the Father has loved me and I have loved you, remain in my love," counsels Jesus.—15:9.

28. What takes place at *Golgotha*, and what prophecies are there fulfilled?
29. (a) What appearances does the resurrected Jesus make to his disciples? (b) What points does Jesus make in his final remarks to Peter?
30. How does John give special emphasis to the quality of love?
31. What relationship is stressed throughout the Gospel, and how does it reach its climactic expression?
32. By what expressions does Jesus show his own relationship with his disciples and that he is the sole channel through which blessings of life come to mankind?

33 Then how fervently does he pray to Jehovah that all these loved ones, and also 'those putting faith in him through their word,' may be one with his Father and himself, sanctified by the word of truth! Indeed, the entire purpose of Jesus' ministry is wonderfully expressed in the final words of this prayer to his Father: "I have made your name known to them and will make it known, in order that the love with which you loved me may be in them and I in union with them."—17:17, 20, 26.

34 Though Jesus was leaving his disciples in the world, he was not going to leave them without a helper, "the spirit of the truth." Moreover, he gave them timely counsel on their relationship with the world, showing them how to overcome as "sons of light." (14:16, 17; 3: 19-21; 12:36) "If you remain in my word, you are really my disciples," said Jesus, "and you will know the truth, and the truth will set you free." In contrast, he said to the sons of darkness: "You are from your father the Devil, and you wish to do the desires of your father. . . . he did not stand fast in the truth, because truth is not in him." Let us be determined, then, always to stand fast in the truth, yes, to "worship the Father with spirit and truth," and to draw strength from Jesus' words: "Take courage! I have conquered the world."—8:31, 32, 44; 4:23; 16:33.

35 All of this has a relation, also, to God's kingdom. Jesus testified when on trial: "My kingdom is no part of this world. If my kingdom were part of this world, my attendants would have fought that I should not be delivered up to the Jews. But, as it is, my kingdom is not from this source." Then, in answer to Pilate's question, he said: "You yourself are saying that I am a king. For this I have been born, and for this I have come into the world, that I should bear witness to the truth. Everyone that is on the side of the truth listens to my voice." (18:36, 37) Happy indeed are those who listen and who are "born again" to "enter into the kingdom of God" in union with the King. Happy are the "other sheep" who listen to the voice of this Shepherd-King and gain life. There is, indeed, cause for gratitude for the provision of John's Gospel, for it was written "that you may believe that Jesus is the Christ the Son of God, and that, because of believing, you may have life by means of his name."—3:3, 5; 10:16; 20:31.

33. What purpose of his ministry does Jesus express in prayer?
34. What beneficial counsel did Jesus give on how to overcome the world?
35. (a) How is all of this related to God's kingdom? (b) Why does John's Gospel give cause for happiness and gratitude?

Bible Book Number Forty-four—Acts

Writer:	**Luke**
Place Written:	**Rome**
Writing Completed:	**c. A.D. 61**
Time Covered:	**A.D. 33–c. 61**

IN THE forty-second book of the inspired Scriptures Luke gives an account covering the life, activity and ministry of Jesus and his followers up to the time of his death. The historical record of the forty-fourth book of the Scriptures, the Acts of the Apostles, continues the history of early Christianity by describing the founding of the congregation by the operation of the holy spirit and the expansion of the witness, first among the Jews and then to men of goodwill of all the nations. The greater part of the material in the first twelve chapters covers the activities of Peter and the remaining sixteen chapters, the activities of Paul. Luke had an intimate association with Paul, accompanying him on many of his travels.

2 The book is addressed to Theophilus. Since he is referred to as "most excellent," it appears he occupied some official position. The account provides an accurate historical record of the establishment and growth of the Christian congregation. It commences with Jesus' appearances to his disciples following his resurrection, and then records important events of the period A.D. 33 to about 61, covering about twenty-eight years in all.

3 From ancient times the writer of the Gospel of Luke has been credited with the writing of Acts. Both books are addressed to Theophilus. Also, by repeating the closing events of his Gospel in the opening verses of Acts, Luke binds the two accounts together as the work of the same author. It appears that Luke com-

1, 2. (a) What historic events and activities are described in Acts? (b) What time period does the book cover?
3. Who wrote Acts, and when was the writing completed?

pleted Acts A.D. 61, probably toward the close of a two-year stay in Rome while in the company of the apostle Paul. Since it records events down to that year, it could not have been completed earlier, and the fact that it leaves Paul's appeal to Caesar undecided indicates its being completed by that year.

4 From the most ancient times Acts has been accepted by Bible scholars as canonical. Parts of the book are to be found among some of the oldest extant papyrus manuscripts of the Greek Scriptures, notably the Michigan 1571 and Chester Beatty I manuscripts. Both of these are of the third century A.D., indicating that Acts was circulating with other books of the inspired Scriptures, and hence as part of the catalogue, at an early date. Luke's writing in the book of Acts reflects the same remarkable accuracy as we have already noted marks his Gospel. Sir William M. Ramsay rates the writer of Acts "among the historians of the first rank," and he explains what this means by saying: "The first and the essential quality of the great historian is truth. What he says must be trustworthy."[a]

5 Illustrating the accurate reporting that so characterizes Luke's writings, we quote Edwin Smith, commander of a flotilla of British warships in the Mediterranean during World War I, writing in *The Rudder* magazine, March, 1947: "The ancient vessels were not steered as those in modern times by a single rudder hinged to the stern post, but by two great oars or paddles, one on each side of the stern; hence the mention of them in the plural number by St. Luke. [Acts 27:40] . . . We have seen in our examination that every statement as to the movements of this ship, from the time when she left Fair Havens until she was beached at Malta, as set forth by St. Luke has been verified by external and independent evidence of the most exact and satisfying nature; and that his statements as to the time the ship remained at sea correspond with the distance covered; and finally that his description of the place arrived at is in conformity with the place as it is. All of which goes to show that Luke actually made the voyage as described, and has moreover shown himself to be a man whose observations and statements may be taken as reliable and trustworthy to the highest degree."[b]

6 Archaeological findings also confirm the accuracy of Luke's statements. For example, a document has been recovered from the ruins of the ancient theater of Ephesus, which is dated by archaeologists A.D. 160, and reads in part: "Whereas Artemis [Diana], the goddess who presides over this city, is set at naught, not only in our native town, which she has made more glorious than all the other cities . . . so that in many places her sacrifices and honours have been neglected."[c] So what Demetrius, the image-making silversmith, feared most actually became a documented reality! —Acts 19:27.

7 Further, the various speeches made by Peter, Stephen, Cornelius, Tertullus, Paul and others, as recorded by Luke, are all different in style and composition. Even the speeches of Paul, spoken before different audiences, changed in style to suit the occasion. This indicates that Luke recorded only what he himself heard or what other eyewitnesses reported to him. Luke was no fiction writer.

8 Very little is known of the personal life of Luke. Luke himself was not an apostle but was associated with those who were. (Luke 1:1-4) In the three instances where Luke is mentioned by name Mark is said to be in his company. (Col. 4:10, 14; 2 Tim. 4:11; Philem. 24) For some years he was the constant companion of the apostle Paul, who called him "the beloved physician." There is a shifting back and forth in the account between "they" and "we," indicating that Luke first joined up with Paul at Troas during Paul's second missionary tour, that he remained behind at Philippi until Paul returned some years later, and that he then rejoined Paul and stuck with him down to the end.—Acts 16:8, 10; 17:1; 20:4-6; 28:16.

CONTENTS OF ACTS

9 **Events till Pentecost** (1:1-26). As Luke opens this second account, the resurrected Jesus tells his eager disciples that they will be baptized in holy spirit. Will the kingdom be restored at this time? No, not that. But they will receive power and become witnesses "to the most distant part of the earth." As Jesus is lifted up out of their sight, two men in white tell them: "This Jesus who was received up from you into the sky will come thus in the same manner."—1:8, 11.

10 **The memorable day of Pentecost** (2:1-42). The disciples are all assembled in Jerusalem.

a *St. Paul the Traveller,* 1895, W. M. Ramsay, page 4.
b Quoted in *Awake!* of July 22, 1947, pages 22, 23.
c *Modern Discovery and the Bible,* 1949, A. Rendle Short, page 213.

4. What proves the book to be canonical and authentic?
5. Illustrate Luke's accurate reporting.
6. What example shows how archaeological finds support the accuracy of the account?
7. How do the speeches recorded show the record to be factual?
8. What do the Scriptures tell us of Luke and his associations with Mark and Paul?
9. What things are the disciples told at the time of Jesus' ascension?
10. (a) What strange things happen on the day of Pentecost? (b) What explanation does Peter give, and with what result?

Suddenly a rushing wind fills the house. Tongues as if of fire rest on those present. They are filled with holy spirit and begin speaking in different languages about "the magnificent things of God." (2:11) Onlookers are perplexed. Now Peter stands up and speaks. He explains that this outpouring of the spirit is in fulfillment of the prophecy of Joel (2:28-32), and that Jesus Christ, now resurrected and exalted to God's right hand, 'has poured out this which they see and hear.' Stabbed to the heart, about three thousand embrace the word and are baptized.—2:33.

11 **The witness expands** (2:43–5:42). Daily, Jehovah continues to join to them those being saved. Outside the temple Peter and John come upon a crippled man who has never walked in his life. "In the name of Jesus Christ the Nazarene, walk!" commands Peter. Immediately the man begins "walking and leaping and praising God." Peter then appeals to the astonished people to repent and turn around, "that seasons of refreshing may come from the person of Jehovah." Annoyed that Peter and John are teaching Jesus' resurrection, the religious leaders arrest them, but the ranks of the believers swell to about five thousand men.—3:6, 8, 19.

12 The next day, at their trial, Peter and John testify outspokenly that salvation is only through Jesus Christ, and, when commanded to stop their preaching work, they reply: "Whether it is righteous in the sight of God to listen to you rather than to God, judge for yourselves. But as for us, we cannot stop speaking about the things we have seen and heard." (4:19, 20) They are released, and all the disciples continue to speak the word of God with boldness. Due to the circumstances they pool their material possessions and make distributions according to the need. However, a certain Ananias and his wife Sapphira sell some property and secretly keep back part of the price. Peter exposes them, and they drop dead because they have played false to God and the holy spirit.

13 Again the outraged religious leaders throw the apostles into jail, but this time Jehovah's angel releases them. The next day they are again brought before the Sanhedrin and charged with 'filling Jerusalem with their teaching.' They reply: "We must obey God as ruler rather than men." Though flogged and threatened, they still refuse to stop, and 'every day in the temple and from house to house they continue without letup teaching and declaring the good news about the Christ, Jesus.'—5:28, 29, 42.

14 **Stephen's martyrdom** (6:1–8:1a). Stephen is one of seven appointed by holy spirit to distribute food to tables. He also witnesses powerfully to the truth, and so zealous is his support of the faith that his enraged opponents have him brought before the Sanhedrin on the charge of blasphemy. In making his defense, Stephen tells first of Jehovah's long-suffering toward Israel. Then, in fearless eloquence, he comes to the point: 'Obstinate men, you are always resisting the holy spirit, you who received the Law as transmitted by angels but have not kept it.' (7:51-53) This is too much for them. They rush on him, throw him outside the city and stone him to death. Saul looks on in approval.

15 **Persecutions, Saul's conversion** (8:1b–9:30). The persecution that begins that day against the congregation in Jerusalem scatters all except the apostles, throughout the land. Philip goes to Samaria, where many accept the word of God. Peter and John are sent there from Jerusalem so that these believers may receive holy spirit "through the laying on of the hands of the apostles." (8:18) An angel then directs Philip south to the Jerusalem-Gaza road, where he finds a eunuch of the royal court of Ethiopia riding in his chariot and reading the book of Isaiah. Philip enlightens him as to the meaning of the prophecy and baptizes him.

16 Meanwhile, Saul, "still breathing threat and murder against the disciples of the Lord," sets out to arrest those 'belonging to The Way' in Damascus. Suddenly a light from heaven flashes around him, and he falls to the ground, blinded. A voice from heaven tells him: "I am Jesus, whom you are persecuting." After three days in Damascus a disciple named Ananias ministers to him. Saul recovers his sight, gets baptized and becomes filled with holy spirit, so that he becomes a zealous and able preacher of the good news. (9:1, 2, 5) In this amazing turn of events the persecutor becomes the persecuted and has to flee for his life, first from Damascus, and then from Jerusalem.

17 **The good news goes to non-Jews** (9:31–12:25). The congregation now 'enters into a period of peace, being built up; and as it walks in the fear of Jehovah and in the comfort of the holy spirit it keeps on multiplying.' (9:31) At Joppa, Peter raises the beloved Tabitha (Dorcas) from the dead, and it is from here that he receives the call to go to Caesarea, where an army officer named Cornelius awaits him. He preaches to Cornelius and his household and they believe, and the holy spirit is

11. How does Jehovah prosper the preaching work?
12. (a) What answer do the disciples give when commanded to stop preaching? (b) For what are Ananias and Sapphira punished?
13. With what are the apostles charged, how do they reply, and what do they continue to do?
14. How does Stephen meet martyrdom?
15. What results from persecution, and what preaching experiences does Philip have?
16. How does the conversion of Saul come about?
17. How does the good news first go to uncircumcised Gentiles?

poured out upon them. Having perceived "that God is not partial, but in every nation the man that fears him and works righteousness is acceptable to him," Peter baptizes them—the first uncircumcised Gentile converts. Peter later explains this new development to the brothers in Jerusalem, at which they glorify God.—10: 34, 35.

18 As the good news spreads rapidly, Barnabas and Saul get to teaching quite a crowd in Antioch, 'and it is first in Antioch that the disciples are by divine providence called Christians.' (11:26) Once again persecution breaks out. Herod Agrippa I has James the brother of John killed with the sword. He also throws Peter into prison, but once again Jehovah's angel sets him free. Too bad for the wicked Herod! Because he fails to give glory to God, he is eaten up with worms and dies. On the other hand, 'the word of Jehovah goes on growing and spreading.'—12:24.

19 **Paul's first evangelizing trip, with Barnabas** (13:1–14:28). Barnabas and "Saul, who is also Paul," are set apart and sent forth from Antioch by holy spirit. (13:9) On the island of Cyprus many become believers, including the proconsul Sergius Paulus. On the mainland of Asia Minor they make a circuit of six or more cities, and everywhere it is the same story: A clear division appears between those who gladly accept the good news and the stiff-necked opponents who incite rock-throwing mobs against Jehovah's messengers. After making appointments in the newly formed congregations, Paul and Barnabas return to Antioch in Syria.

20 **Settling the circumcision issue** (15:1-35). With the great influx of non-Jews the question arises as to whether these should be circumcised. Paul and Barnabas take the issue to the apostles and the older brothers in Jerusalem, where James presides and arranges to send out the unanimous decision by formal letter: "The holy spirit and we ourselves have favored adding no further burden to you, except these necessary things, to keep yourselves free from things sacrificed to idols and from blood and from things strangled and from fornication." (15:28, 29) The encouragement of this letter causes the brothers in Antioch to rejoice.

21 **Ministry expands with Paul's second trip** (15:36–18:22). "After some days" Barnabas and Mark sail for Cyprus, while Paul and Silas set out through Syria and Asia Minor. The young man Timothy joins Paul at Lystra, and they journey on to Troas on the Aegean seacoast. Here in a vision Paul sees a man entreating him: "Step over into Macedonia and help us." (16:9) Luke joins Paul and they take a ship to Philippi, the principal city of Macedonia, where Paul and Silas are thrown into prison. This results in the jailer's becoming a believer and getting baptized. On their release they push on to Thessalonica, and there the jealous Jews incite a mob against them. So by night the brothers send Paul and Silas out to Beroea. Here the Jews show noble-mindedness by receiving the word "with the greatest eagerness of mind." (17:11) Leaving Silas and Timothy with this new congregation, as he had left Luke in Philippi, Paul continues on south to Athens.

22 In this city of idols high-minded Epicurean and Stoic philosophers deride Paul as a "chatterer" and a "publisher of foreign deities," and take him up to the Areopagus, or Mars Hill. With skillful oratory Paul argues in favor of seeking the true God, the "Lord of heaven and earth," who guarantees a righteous judgment by the one whom he has resurrected from the dead. Mention of the resurrection divides his audience, but some become believers.—17: 18, 24.

23 Next, in Corinth, Paul stays with Aquila and Priscilla, plying with them the trade of tentmaking. Opposition to his preaching compels him to move out of the synagogue and to hold his meetings next door, in the home of Titius Justus. Crispus, the presiding officer of the synagogue, becomes a believer. After an eighteen months' stay in Corinth, Paul departs with Aquila and Priscilla for Ephesus, where he leaves them, and continues on to Antioch in Syria, thus completing his second evangelizing tour.

24 **Paul revisits congregations, third tour** (18: 23–20:38). A Jew named Apollos comes to Ephesus from Alexandria, Egypt, speaking boldly in the synagogue about Jesus, but Aquila and Priscilla find it necessary to correct his teaching before he goes on to Corinth. Paul is now on his third journey and in due course comes to Ephesus. Learning that the believers here have been baptized with John's baptism, Paul explains baptism in Jesus' name. He then baptizes about twelve men, lays his hands upon them, and they receive the holy spirit.

25 During Paul's three-year stay in Ephesus, 'the word of Jehovah keeps growing and prevailing in a mighty way,' and many give up their worship of the city's patron goddess, Artemis (Diana). (19:20) Angered at the pros-

18. (a) What next occurs in Antioch? (b) What persecution breaks out, but does it achieve its object?
19. How extensive is Paul's first missionary journey, and what is accomplished?
20. By what decision is the circumcision issue settled?
21. (a) Who are associated with Paul on his second missionary trip? (b) What events mark the visit to Macedonia?
22. What results from Paul's skillful speech on Mars Hill?
23. What is accomplished at Corinth?
24, 25. (a) At the time of Paul's starting his third journey, what takes place in Ephesus? (b) What commotion marks the conclusion of Paul's three-year stay?

pective loss of business, the makers of silver shrines throw the city into such an uproar that it takes hours to disperse the mob. Soon afterward Paul leaves for Macedonia and Greece, visiting the believers along the way.

26 Paul stays three months in Greece before returning by way of Macedonia, where Luke rejoins him. They cross over to Troas, and here, as Paul is discoursing into the night, a young man falls asleep and tumbles out of a third-story window. He is picked up dead, but Paul restores him to life. The next day Paul and his party leave for Miletus, where Paul stops over en route to Jerusalem, to have a meeting with the older men and overseers from Ephesus. He assures them they will see his face no more. How urgent, then, it is for them to take the lead and shepherd the flock of God, 'among which the holy spirit has appointed them overseers'! He recalls the example he has set among them, and admonishes them to keep awake, not sparing themselves in giving on behalf of the brothers.—20:28.

27 **Paul arrested and tried** (21:1–26:32). Though warned against setting foot in Jerusalem, Paul does not turn back. His companions acquiesce, saying: "Let the will of Jehovah take place." (21:14) There is great rejoicing when Paul reports to James and the older men concerning God's blessing on his ministry among the nations. But when Paul appears in the temple he is given a different reception. Jews from Asia stir up the whole city against him, and Roman soldiers rescue him just in the nick of time.

28 What is all the uproar about? Who is this Paul? What is his crime? The puzzled military commander wants to know the answers. Because of his Roman citizenship Paul escapes the whipping rack and is brought before the Sanhedrin. Ah, a divided court of Pharisees and Sadducees! Paul therefore raises the question of the resurrection, setting them one against another. As the dissension becomes violent, the Roman soldiers have to snatch Paul from the midst of the Sanhedrin before they pull him to pieces. He is sent secretly by night to Governor Felix in Caesarea with heavy soldier escort.

29 Charged with sedition by his accusers, Paul ably defends himself before Felix. But Felix holds out in hope of getting bribe money for Paul's release. Two years pass. Porcius Festus succeeds Felix as governor and a new trial is ordered. Again, serious charges are made, and again Paul declares his innocence. But Festus, to gain favor with the Jews, suggests a further retrial before him in Jerusalem. Paul therefore declares: "I appeal to Caesar!" (25:11) More time passes. Finally, King Herod Agrippa II pays a courtesy visit to Festus, and Paul is again brought into the judgment hall. So forceful and convincing is his testimony that Agrippa is moved to say to him: "In a short time you would persuade me to become a Christian." (26:28) Agrippa likewise recognizes Paul's innocence and that he could be released if he had not appealed to Caesar.

30 **Paul goes to Rome** (27:1–28:31). The prisoner Paul is taken on a boat for the first stage of the journey to Rome. The winds being contrary, progress is slow. At the port of Myra they change ships. On reaching Fair Havens, in Crete, Paul recommends wintering there, but the majority advise setting sail. They have hardly put to sea when a tempestuous wind seizes them and drives them along unmercifully. After two weeks their vessel is finally pounded to pieces on a shoal off the coast of Malta. True to Paul's previous assurance, not one of the 276 aboard loses his life! The inhabitants of Malta show extraordinary human kindness, and during that winter Paul cures many of them by the miraculous power of God's spirit.

31 The next spring Paul reaches Rome, and the brothers come out on the roadway to meet him. The sight of them causes Paul to 'thank God and take courage.' Though still a prisoner, Paul is permitted to stay in his own hired house with a soldier guard. Luke ends his account with Paul's kindly receiving all those who come in to him, "preaching the kingdom of God to them and teaching the things concerning the Lord Jesus Christ with the greatest freeness of speech, without hindrance."—28:15, 31.

WHY BENEFICIAL

32 The book of Acts adds testimony to that of the Gospel accounts in confirming the authenticity and inspiration of the Hebrew Scriptures. As Pentecost approached Peter cited the fulfillment of two prophecies "which the holy spirit spoke beforehand by David's mouth about Judas." (Acts 1:16, 20; Ps. 69:25; 109:8) Peter also told the astonished Pentecost crowd that they were actually witnessing fulfillment of prophecy: "This is what was said through the prophet Joel."—Acts 2:16-21; Joel 2:28-32; compare also Acts 2:25-28, 34, 35 with Psalms 16:8-11 and 110:1.

26. (a) What miracle does Paul perform at Troas? (b) What counsel does he give the overseers from Ephesus?
27. What receptions greet Paul's return to Jerusalem?
28. (a) What question does Paul raise before the Sanhedrin, and with what result? (b) Where is he then sent?
29. Charged with sedition, what series of trials or hearings does Paul have, and what appeal does he make?
30. What experiences attend Paul's voyage as far as Malta?
31. How is Paul greeted on arrival at Rome, and in what does he busy himself there?
32. Before and at Pentecost, how did Peter testify to the authenticity of the Hebrew Scriptures?

33 To convince another crowd outside the temple, Peter again called upon the Hebrew Scriptures, first quoting Moses and then saying: "And all the prophets, in fact, from Samuel on and those in succession, just as many as have spoken, have also plainly declared these days." Later, before the Sanhedrin, Peter quoted Psalm 118:22 in showing that Christ, the stone that they rejected, had become "the head of the corner." (Acts 3:22-24; 4:11) Philip explained to the Ethiopian eunuch how the prophecy of Isaiah 53:7, 8 had been fulfilled, and on being enlightened this one humbly requested baptism. (Acts 8:28-35) Likewise, speaking to Cornelius concerning Jesus, Peter testified: "To him all the prophets bear witness." (Acts 10:43) When the matter of circumcision was being debated, James backed up his decision by saying: "With this the words of the Prophets agree, just as it is written." (Acts 15:15-18) The apostle Paul relied on the same authorities. (Acts 26:22; 28:23, 25-27) The evident ready acceptance by the disciples and their hearers of the Hebrew Scriptures as God's Word sets the seal of inspired approval on those writings.

34 Acts is most beneficial in showing how the Christian congregation was founded and how it grew under power of holy spirit. Throughout this dramatic account we observe God's blessings of expansion, the boldness and joy of the early Christians, their uncompromising stand in the face of persecution and their willingness, as exemplified in Paul's answering the calls to enter foreign service and to go into Macedonia. (Acts 4:13, 31; 15:3; 5:28, 29; 8:4; 13:2-4; 16:9, 10) The Christian congregation today is no different, for it is bound together in love, unity and common interest as it speaks "the magnificent things of God" under guidance of holy spirit.—2:11, 17, 45; 4:34, 35; 11:27-30; 12:25.

35 The book of Acts shows just how the Christian activity of proclaiming God's kingdom should be carried out. Paul himself was an example, saying: "I did not hold back from telling you any of the things that were profitable nor from teaching you publicly and from house to house." Then he goes on to say: "I *thoroughly* bore witness." This theme of 'thorough witnessing' strikes our attention throughout the book, and it comes impressively to the fore in the closing paragraphs, where Paul's wholehearted devotion to his preaching and teaching, even under prison bonds, is borne out in the words: "And he explained the matter to them by bearing thorough witness concerning the kingdom of God and by using persuasion with them concerning Jesus from both the law of Moses and the Prophets, from morning till evening." May we ever be as single-hearted in our Kingdom activity!—20:20, 21; 28:23; 2:40; 5:42; 26:22.

36 Paul's discourse to the overseers from Ephesus contains much practical counsel for overseers today. Since these have been appointed by holy spirit, it is most important that they 'pay attention to themselves and to all the flock,' shepherding them tenderly and guarding them against oppressive wolves that seek their destruction. No light responsibility this! They have need to keep awake and build themselves up on the word of God's undeserved kindness. As they labor to assist those who are weak, they "must bear in mind the words of the Lord Jesus, when he himself said, 'There is more happiness in giving than there is in receiving.' "—20:17-35.

37 The other discourses of Paul also sparkle with clear expositions of Bible principles. For example, there is the classic argumentation of his talk to the Stoics and Epicureans on Mars Hill. First he quotes the altar inscription, "To an Unknown God," and uses this as his reason for explaining that the One God, the Lord of heaven and earth, who made out of one man every nation of men, "is not far off from each one of us." Then he quotes the words of their poet, "For we are also his progeny," in showing how ridiculous it is to suppose that they sprang from lifeless idols of gold, silver or stone. Thus Paul tactfully establishes the sovereignty of the living God. It is only in his concluding words that he raises the issue of the resurrection, and even then he does not mention Christ by name. He got across his point of the supreme sovereignty of the one true God, and some became believers as a result.—17:22-34.

38 The book of Acts encourages continuous, diligent study of "all Scripture." When Paul first preached in Beroea, the Jews there, because "they received the word with the greatest eagerness of mind, carefully examining the Scriptures daily as to whether these things were so," were commended as being "noble-minded." (Acts 17:11) Today, as then, this eager searching of the Scriptures in association with Jehovah's spirit-filled congregation will result in the blessings of conviction and strong faith. It is by such study that one may come to a clear appreciation of the divine principles. A fine statement of some of these principles is recorded at Acts 15:29. Here the governing

33. How did Peter, Philip, James and Paul all show the Hebrew Scriptures to be inspired?
34. What does Acts reveal concerning the Christian congregation, and is this any different today?
35. How does Acts show how the witness was to be given, and what quality in the ministry is emphasized?
36. What practical counsel by Paul applies forcefully to overseers today?
37. By what tactful argumentation did Paul get across his point on Mars Hill?
38. What blessings will result from the kind of study encouraged in Acts?

body of apostles and older brothers in Jerusalem made known that, while circumcision was not a requirement for spiritual Israel, there were definite prohibitions on idolatry, blood and fornication.

39 Those early disciples really studied the inspired Scriptures, and could quote and apply them as needed. They were strengthened through accurate knowledge and by God's spirit to meet fierce persecutions. Peter and John set the pattern for all faithful Christians when they boldly told the opposing rulers: "Whether it is righteous in the sight of God to listen to you rather than to God, judge for yourselves. But as for us, we cannot stop speaking about the things we have seen and heard." And when brought again before the Sanhedrin, which had "positively ordered" them not to keep teaching on the basis of Jesus' name, they said unequivocally: "We must obey God as ruler rather than men." This fearless testimony resulted in a fine witness to the rulers, and led the famous Law teacher Gamaliel to make his well-known statement in favor of freedom of worship, which led to the apostles' release. —4:19, 20; 5:28, 29, 34, 35, 38, 39.

39. (a) How were the disciples strengthened to meet persecutions? (b) What bold testimony did they give? Was it effective?

40 Jehovah's glorious purpose concerning his kingdom, which runs like a golden thread throughout the entire Bible, stands out very prominently in the book of Acts. At the outset Jesus is shown during the forty days prior to his ascension "telling the things about the kingdom of God." It was in answer to the disciples question about the restoration of the kingdom that Jesus told them that they must first be his witnesses to the ends of the earth. (1:3, 6, 8) Starting in Jerusalem, they preached the Kingdom with unflinching boldness. Persecutions brought the stoning of Stephen and scattered many of them into new territories. (7:59, 60) It is recorded that Philip declared "the good news of the kingdom of God" with much success in Samaria, and that Paul and his associates proclaimed "the kingdom" in Asia, Corinth, Ephesus and Rome. All these early Christians set sterling examples of unswerving reliance on Jehovah and his sustaining spirit. (8:5, 12; 14:5-7, 21, 22; 18:1, 4; 19:1, 8; 20:25; 28:30, 31) Viewing their indomitable zeal and courage and noting how abundantly Jehovah blessed their efforts, we also have wonderful incentive to be faithful in "bearing thorough witness concerning the kingdom of God."—28:23.

40. What incentive does Acts give us to bear thorough witness to the Kingdom?

Bible Book Number Forty-five— Romans

Writer:	**Paul**
Place Written:	**Corinth**
Writing Completed:	**c. A.D. 56**
Time Covered:	**Undetermined**

IN ACTS we watched Saul, violent persecutor of Jewish Christians, become Paul, Christ's zealous apostle to the non-Jewish nations. With Romans we begin the fourteen books of the Bible that the holy spirit inspired this former Pharisee, now a faithful servant of God, to write. By the time he wrote Romans, Paul had already completed two long preaching tours, and was well along on the third. He had written five other inspired letters: First and Second Thessalonians, Galatians and First and Second Corinthians. Yet in our modern Bibles Romans logically precedes the others, since it discusses the new equality between Jews and non-Jews, the two classes to whom Paul preached. It explains a turning point in God's dealings with his people and shows that the inspired Hebrew Scriptures had long foretold that the good news would be proclaimed also to the non-Jews.

2 Paul, using Tertius as secretary, laces rapid argument and an astounding number of Hebrew Scripture quotations into one of the most forceful books of the Christian Greek Scriptures. With remarkable beauty of language, he discusses the problems that arose when first-century Christian congregations were composed of both Jews and Greeks. Did Jews have priority because of being Abraham's descendants? Did mature Christians, exercising their liberty from Mosaic law, have the right to stumble weaker Jewish brothers who still held to ancient customs? In this letter Paul firmly es-

1. Why does Romans logically precede Paul's other letters in our modern Bibles?

2. (a) What problems does Paul here discuss? (b) What is firmly established by this letter?

tablished that Jews and non-Jews are on an equality before God and that justification comes, not through the Mosaic law, but through faith in Jesus Christ and by God's undeserved kindness. At the same time God requires Christians to show proper subjection to the various authorities under which they find themselves.

3 How did the Roman congregation get started? There had been a sizable Jewish community in Rome at least since the time of Pompey's capturing Jerusalem in 63 B.C.E. At Acts 2:10 it is specifically stated that some of these Jews were in Jerusalem at Pentecost A.D. 33, where they heard the good news preached. The converted sojourners stayed in Jerusalem to learn from the apostles, and later those from Rome would no doubt return there, some probably at the time when persecution broke out in Jerusalem. (Acts 2:41-47; 8:1, 4) Further, the people of that day were great travelers, and this may explain Paul's intimate acquaintance with so many members of the Roman congregation, some of whom may have heard the good news in Greece or Asia as a result of his own preaching.

4 The first reliable information about this congregation is found in Paul's letter. It is clear from this that the congregation was made up of both Jewish and non-Jewish Christians, and that their zeal was praiseworthy. He tells them: "Your faith is talked about throughout the whole world," and, "Your obedience has come to the notice of all." (Rom. 1:8; 16:19) Suetonius, writing in the second century, reports that during the rule of Claudius (A.D. 41-54) the Jews were banished from Rome. They later returned, however, as evidenced by the fact that Aquila and Priscilla, whom Paul met in Corinth and who had left Rome at the time of Claudius' decree, were back in Rome at the time Paul wrote to the congregation there. —Acts 18:2; Rom. 16:3.

5 The letter's authenticity is firmly established. It is, as its introduction says, from "Paul, a slave of Jesus Christ and called to be an apostle, . . . to all those who are in Rome as God's beloved ones, called to be holy ones." (Rom. 1:1, 7) Its outside documentation is among the earliest to be found for the Christian Greek Scriptures. Peter uses so many similar expressions in his first letter, written probably six to eight years later, that many authorities think he must have already seen a copy of Romans. Romans was clearly regarded as a part of Paul's writings and cited as such by Clement of Rome, Polycarp of Smyrna and Ignatius of Antioch, all of whom lived in the late first and early second centuries.

6 The book of Romans is found, together with eight others of Paul's letters, in a codex called "Chester Beatty Papyrus No. 2." In his book *The Story of the Bible*, 1947, page 29, Sir Frederic Kenyon wrote: "Thus one of the Chester Beatty papyri, of the first half of the third century, contained when complete all four Gospels and the Acts; another, which is at least as early and may be of the end of the second century, contained all the epistles of St. Paul; another contained the books of Ezekiel, Daniel and Esther." The Chester Beatty Greek Biblical papyri are older than the well-known Sinaitic Manuscript and Vatican Manuscript No. 1209, both of the fourth century A.D. These, too, contain Romans and most of the other canonical letters of Paul.

7 When and from where was Romans written? There is no disagreement among Bible commentators that this letter was written from Greece, most probably from Corinth, when Paul visited there for some months toward the end of his third missionary journey. The internal evidence points to Corinth. Paul wrote the letter from the home of Gaius, who was a member of the congregation there, and recommends Phoebe of the nearby congregation of Cenchreae, Corinth's seaport, who apparently carried this letter to Rome. (Rom. 16: 1, 23; 1 Cor. 1:14) At Romans 15:23 Paul wrote: "I no longer have untouched territory in these regions," and indicates in the following verse that he intends to branch out his missionary work west, toward Spain. He could well write this way toward the end of his third tour, at the beginning of A.D. 56.

CONTENTS OF ROMANS

8 **God's impartiality toward Jew and Gentile** (1:1–2:29). What does the inspired Paul tell the Romans? In his opening words he identifies himself as an apostle chosen by Christ to bring 'obedience by faith' among the nations. He expresses his fervent desire to visit the holy ones in Rome, to enjoy "an interchange of encouragement" with them, and to declare among them the good news that is "God's power for salvation to everyone having faith." As it had long ago been written, the righteous one will live "by means of faith." (1:5, 12, 16, 17) Both Jews and Greeks, he shows, merit God's wrath. Man's ungodliness is inexcusable because God's invisible qualities are clearly seen through his creation. Yet the nations foolishly make gods

3. How did the congregation in Rome get started, and what may account for Paul's knowing so many there?
4. (a) What information does the letter provide concerning the Roman congregation? (b) Why did Aquila and Priscilla leave Rome, only to return later?
5. What facts establish the authenticity of Romans?
6. How does an ancient papyrus testify to the canonicity of Romans?
7. What evidence is there as to place and time of writing?
8. (a) What does Paul say about his mission? (b) How does he show both Jews and Greeks merit God's wrath?

of created things. However, the Jews should not judge the nations harshly, since they also are guilty of sins. Both classes will be judged according to their deeds, for God is not partial. Fleshly circumcision is not the determining factor; "he is a Jew who is one on the inside, and his circumcision is that of the heart."—2:29.

9 **By faith all are declared righteous** (3:1–4:25). "What, then, is the superiority of the Jew?" It is great, for the Jews were entrusted with God's sacred pronouncements. Yet "Jews as well as Greeks are all under sin," and no one is "good" in God's sight. Seven quotations are made from the Hebrew Scriptures to prove this point. (Rom. 3:1, 9-18; Ps. 14:1-3; 5:9; 140:3; 10:7; Prov. 1:16; Isa. 59:7, 8; Ps. 36:1) The law shows up man's sinfulness, so "by works of law no flesh will be declared righteous." However, through God's undeserved kindness, and the release by ransom, both Jews and Greeks are being declared righteous "by faith apart from works of law." (Rom. 3:20, 28) Paul supports this argument by citing the example of Abraham, who was counted righteous, not because of works or circumcision, but because of his exemplary faith. Thus Abraham became the father, not only of the Jews, but of "all those having faith."—4:11.

10 **No longer slaves to sin but to righteousness through Christ** (5:1–6:23). Through the one man Adam sin entered into the world, and sin brought death, "and thus death spread to all men because they had all sinned." (5:12) Death ruled as king from Adam down to Moses. When the Law was given through Moses, sin abounded and death continued to reign. But God's undeserved kindness now abounds even more, and through Christ's obedience many are declared righteous for everlasting life. Yet this is no license for living in sin. Persons baptized into Christ must be dead to sin. Their old personality is impaled, and they live with reference to God. Sin no longer rules over them, but they become slaves to righteousness, with holiness in view. "The wages sin pays is death, but the gift God gives is everlasting life by Christ Jesus our Lord."—6:23.

11 **Dead to the Law, alive by spirit in union with Christ** (7:1–8:39). Paul uses the example of a wife who is bound to her husband as long as he lives, but is free to marry another if he dies, to show how through Christ's sacrifice Christian Jews were made dead to the Law, and were free to become Christ's and bear fruit to God. The holy Law made sin more evident, and the sin brought death. Sin, dwelling in our fleshly bodies, wars against our good intentions. As Paul says: "For the good that I wish I do not do, but the bad that I do not wish is what I practice." Thus, "the one working it out is no longer I, but the sin dwelling in me."—7:19, 20.

12 What can save man from this miserable state? God can make those who belong to Christ alive through his spirit! They are adopted as sons, become heirs of God and joint heirs with Christ, and are declared righteous and glorified. To them Paul says: "If God is for us, who will be against us? Who will separate us from the love of the Christ?" No one! Triumphantly he declares: "We are coming off completely victorious through him that loved us. For I am convinced that neither death nor life nor angels nor governments nor things now here nor things to come nor powers nor height nor depth nor any other creation will be able to separate us from God's love that is in Christ Jesus our Lord."—8:31, 35, 37-39.

13 **"Israel" saved through faith and by God's mercy** (9:1–10:21). He expresses "great grief" for his fellow Israelites, but recognizes that not all fleshly Israel is really "Israel," since God has the authority to choose as sons whomsoever he wishes. As shown by God's dealings with Pharaoh and by the illustration of the potter, "it depends, not upon the one wishing nor upon the one running, but upon God, who has mercy." (9:2, 6, 16) He calls sons "not only from among Jews but also from among nations," as Hosea (2:23) long before foretold. Israel fell short because of seeking to gain God's favor, "not by faith, but as by works," and of stumbling over Christ, the "rock-mass of offense." (Rom. 9:24, 32, 33) They had "a zeal for God; but not according to accurate knowledge." For those exercising faith for righteousness Christ is the end of the Law, while for salvation one must publicly declare "that Jesus is Lord," and exercise faith "that God raised him up from the dead." (10:2, 9) Preachers are sent forth to enable people of all nations to hear, to have faith, and to call upon the name of Jehovah in order to be saved.

14 **Illustration of the olive tree** (11:1-36). Due to undeserved kindness a remnant of natural Israel has been chosen, but because the majority stumbled "there is salvation to people of the nations." (11:11) Using the illustration of an olive tree, Paul shows non-Jews that they

9. (a) In what are the Jews superior, and yet what scriptures does Paul quote to show that all are under sin? (b) How, then, will a man be declared righteous, and what example supports this argument?
10. (a) How did death come to rule as king? (b) What has resulted through Christ's obedience, but what warning is sounded with regard to sin?
11. (a) How does Paul illustrate the Christian Jews' release from the Law? (b) What did the Law make evident, and so what things are at war in the Christian?
12. How do some become joint heirs with Christ, and in what are these completely victorious?
13. (a) According to prophecy who are included in the real Israel of God, and this is according to what divine principle? (b) Why did fleshly Israel fall short, but what is necessary for salvation?
14. What does Paul illustrate by the olive tree?

should not rejoice over the rejection of Israel, since, if God did not spare the unfaithful natural branches, neither will he spare the wild olive branches grafted in from among the nations.

[15] **Making over the mind; the superior authorities** (12:1–13:14). Present your bodies as living sacrifices to God, Paul counsels. No longer be "fashioned after this system of things," but be "transformed by making your mind over." Do not be haughty. The body of Christ, like a human body, has many members, which have different functions, but they work together in unity. Return evil for evil to no one. Leave vengeance to Jehovah. Conquer "the evil with the good."—12:2, 21.

[16] Be in subjection to superior authorities; it is the arrangement of God. Keep doing good and do not be owing anyone a single thing, except to love one another. Salvation approaches, so "put off the works belonging to darkness" and "put on the weapons of the light." (13:12) Walk in good behavior, not according to the desires of the flesh.

[17] **Welcome all impartially with toleration** (14:1–15:33). Tolerate those who, because their faith is weak, abstain from certain foods or observe feast days. Neither judge, nor, by your own eating and drinking, stumble your brother, since God judges everyone. Pursue peace and upbuilding things, and bear the weaknesses of others.

[18] The apostle writes: "All the things that were written aforetime were written for our instruction," and gives four more Hebrew Scripture quotations as final proof that the inspired prophets had long before foretold that God's promises would extend to the non-Jewish nations. (Rom. 15:4, 9-12; Ps. 18:49; Deut. 32:43; Ps. 117:1; Isa. 11:1, 10) "Therefore," Paul admonishes, "welcome one another, just as the Christ also welcomed us, with glory to God in view." (Rom. 15:7) Paul expresses appreciation for the undeserved kindness given to him by God to be a public servant to the nations, "engaging in the holy work of the good news of God." He is always seeking to open up new territories rather than "building on another man's foundation." And he is not yet finished, for he plans, after taking contributions to Jerusalem, an even greater preaching tour to distant Spain, and on his way there to bring "a full measure of blessing from Christ" to his spiritual brothers in Rome.—15:16, 20, 29.

[19] **Concluding salutations** (16:1-27). Paul sends personal greetings to twenty-six members of the Roman congregation by name, as well as to others, and exhorts them to avoid persons who cause divisions and to "be wise as to what is good, but innocent as to what is evil." All is for God's glory "through Jesus Christ forever. Amen."—16:19, 27.

15. What is involved in presenting living sacrifices to God?
16. How must Christians walk before authorities and others?
17. What is counseled concerning toleration, judging and building up the weak?
18. (a) What further quotations does Paul make in showing God's acceptance of the non-Jews? (b) How does Paul himself take advantage of God's undeserved kindness?

WHY BENEFICIAL

[20] The book of Romans presents a logical basis for belief in God, stating that "his invisible qualities are clearly seen from the world's creation onward, because they are perceived by the things made, even his eternal power and Godship." But more than this, it goes on to exalt his righteousness, and to make known his great mercy and undeserved kindness. This is beautifully brought to our attention through the illustration of the olive tree, in which the wild branches are grafted in when the natural branches are lopped off. In contemplation of this severity and kindness of God, Paul exclaims: "O the depth of God's riches and wisdom and knowledge! How unsearchable his judgments are and past tracing out his ways are!"—Rom. 1:20; 11:33.

[21] It is in this connection that the book of Romans explains the further development of God's sacred secret. In the Christian congregation there is no longer a distinction between Jew and Gentile, but persons of all nations may share in Jehovah's undeserved kindness through Jesus Christ. "There is no partiality with God." "He is a Jew who is one on the inside, and his circumcision is that of the heart by spirit, and not by a written code." "There is no distinction between Jew and Greek, for there is the same Lord over all, who is rich to all those calling upon him." For all of these it is faith, and not works, that is counted to them as 'righteousness.'—Rom. 2:11, 29; 10:12; 3:28.

[22] The practical counsel contained in this letter to the Christians in Rome is equally beneficial to Christians today who have to meet similar problems in an alien world. The Christian is exhorted to "be peaceable with all men," including those outside the congregation. Every soul must "be in subjection to the superior authorities," for these constitute an arrangement of God and are an object of fear, not to the law-abiding, but to those who do bad deeds.

19. What salutations and exhortation conclude the letter?
20. (a) What logical reason does Romans give for belief in God? (b) How are God's righteousness and mercy illustrated, and what does this lead Paul to exclaim?
21. How does Romans show the further development of God's sacred secret?
22. What practical counsel does Romans give concerning relations with those outside the congregation?

Christians are to be in law-abiding subjection, not only on account of the fear of punishment, but on account of Christian conscience, therefore paying their taxes, rendering their dues, meeting their obligations, owing no one anything, "except to love one another." Love fulfills the law.—Rom. 12:17-21; 13:1-10.

23 Paul emphasizes the matter of public testimony. While it is with the heart that one exercises faith for righteousness, it is with the mouth that one makes public declaration for salvation. "Everyone who calls on the name of Jehovah will be saved." But in order for this to take place it is necessary for preachers to go forth and "declare good news of good things." Happy is our portion if we are among these preachers whose sound has now gone out "to the extremities of the inhabited earth"! (Rom. 10:13, 15, 18) And in preparation for this preaching work, may we try to become as familiar with the inspired Scriptures as was Paul, for in this one passage (10:11-21) he makes quotation upon quotation from the Hebrew Scriptures. (Isa. 28:16; Joel 2:32; Isa. 52:7; 53:1; Ps. 19:4; Deut. 32:21; Isa. 65:1, 2) He could well say: "All the things that were written aforetime were written for our instruction, that through our endurance and through the comfort from the Scriptures we might have hope."—Rom. 15:4.

24 Wonderfully practical advice is given on relations within the Christian congregation. Whatever their previous national, racial or social background, all must make over their minds to render God sacred service according to his "good and acceptable and perfect will." (Rom. 11:17-22; 12:1, 2) What practical reasonableness breathes through all of Paul's counsel in Romans 12:3-16! Here indeed is excellent admonition for building zeal, humility and tender affection among all in the Christian congregation. In the closing chapters Paul gives strong admonition on watching and avoiding those who cause divisions, but he also speaks of the mutual joy and refreshment that come from clean associations in the congregation. —16:17-19; 15:7, 32.

25 As Christians we must continue to watch our relations with one another. "For the kingdom of God does not mean eating and drinking, but means righteousness and peace and joy with holy spirit." (Rom. 14:17) This righteousness, peace and joy is especially the portion of the "joint heirs with Christ," who are to be "glorified together" with him in the heavenly kingdom. Note, too, how Romans points to a further step in the fulfillment of the Kingdom promise given in Eden, saying: "The God who gives peace will crush Satan under your feet shortly." (Rom. 8:17; 16:20; Gen. 3:15) Believing these great truths, may we continue to be filled with all joy and peace, and abound in hope. Let our determination be to come off victorious with the Kingdom Seed, for we are convinced that nothing in heaven above or in earth below "nor any other creation will be able to separate us from God's love that is in Christ Jesus our Lord."—Rom. 8:39; 15:13.

23. How does Paul emphasize the importance of public declaration, and what example does he give as to preparation for the ministry?
24. What advice does Paul give with a view to building zeal and happy relations within the congregation?
25. (a) What proper view and further understanding does Romans give concerning God's kingdom? (b) In what ways should the study of Romans benefit us?

Bible Book Number Forty-six— 1 Corinthians

Writer:	**Paul**
Place Written:	**Ephesus**
Writing Completed:	**c. A.D. 55**
Time Covered:	**Undetermined**

CORINTH was "a renowned and voluptuous city, where the vices of the East and West met."[a] Situated on the narrow isthmus between the Peloponnesus and continental Greece, Corinth commanded the land route to the mainland. In the days of the apostle Paul it teemed with an estimated population of about 400,000. To the east lay the Aegean Sea and to the west, the Gulf of Corinth and the Ionian Sea. So Corinth, the capital of the province of Achaia, with its two ports of Cenchreae and Lechaeum, held a position of strategic importance commercially. It was also a center of Greek learning. "Its wealth," it has been said, "was so celebrated as to be proverbial; so were the vice and profligacy of its inhabitants."[b] Among its pagan religious practices was the worship of

a *Pocket Bible Handbook,* 1944, H. H. Halley, page 444.

b Smith's *Dictionary of the Bible,* 1915, page 188.

1. What kind of city was Corinth in the days of Paul?

Venus, which was carried on in a most licentious manner. Public prostitution was a part of the city's religion.

2 It was to this thriving but morally decadent metropolis of the Roman world that the apostle Paul traveled about A.D. 50. During his stay of eighteen months a Christian congregation was established there. (Acts 18:1-11) What love Paul felt toward these believers to whom he had first carried the good news about Christ! By letter he reminded them of the spiritual bond that existed, in saying: "Though you may have ten thousand tutors in Christ, you certainly do not have many fathers; for in Christ Jesus I have become your father through the good news."—1 Cor. 4:15.

3 Deep concern for their spiritual welfare moved Paul to write his first letter to the Corinthian Christians while in the course of his third missionary tour. A few years had passed since he had resided in Corinth. It was now about A.D. 55, and Paul was in Ephesus. Apparently he had received a letter from the relatively new congregation in Corinth, and it required a reply. Furthermore, disturbing reports had reached Paul. (1 Cor. 7:1; 1:11; 5:1; 11:18) So distressing were these that the apostle did not even refer to their letter of inquiry until the opening verse of chapter seven of his letter. Especially because of the reports he had received did Paul feel compelled to write to his fellow Christians in Corinth.

4 But how do we know Paul wrote First Corinthians at Ephesus? For one thing, in concluding the letter with greetings, the apostle includes those of Aquila and Prisca (Priscilla). (1 Cor. 16:19) Acts 18:18, 19 shows that they had transferred from Corinth to Ephesus. Since Aquila and Priscilla were residing there and Paul included them in the closing greetings of First Corinthians, he must have been in Ephesus when he wrote the letter. A point that leaves no uncertainty, however, is Paul's statement at 1 Corinthians 16:8: "But I am *remaining* in Ephesus until the festival of Pentecost." So First Corinthians was written by Paul at Ephesus, apparently near the end of his stay there.

5 The authenticity of First Corinthians, and also of Second Corinthians, is unquestionable. These letters were ascribed to Paul and accepted as canonical by the early Christians, who included them in their collections. In fact, it is said that First Corinthians is alluded to and quoted at least six times in a letter from Rome to Corinth dated about A.D. 95 and called First Clement. With apparent reference to First Corinthians, the writer urged the recipients of this letter to "take up the epistle of the blessed Paul the apostle."[a] First Corinthians is also directly quoted by Justin Martyr, Athenagoras, Irenaeus and Tertullian. There is strong evidence that a corpus, or collection, of Paul's letters, including First and Second Corinthians, "was formed and published in the last decade of the first century."[b]

6 Paul's first letter to the Corinthians gives us an opportunity to look inside the Corinthian congregation itself. These Christians had problems to face and questions to be resolved. There were factions within the congregation, for some were following men. Some were living in religiously divided households. Should they remain with their unbelieving mates or separate? And what of eating meat sacrificed to idols? Should they partake of it? The Corinthians needed advice regarding the conducting of their meetings, including the celebration of the Lord's evening meal. What should be the position of women in the congregation? Then, too, there were those in their midst who denied the resurrection. Problems were many. Particularly, though, was the apostle interested in bringing about a spiritual restoration of the Corinthians.

7 Because conditions inside the congregation and the environment outside in ancient Corinth, with its prosperity and licentiousness, are not without modern parallels, Paul's sterling counsel penned under divine inspiration, commands our attention. What he said is so full of meaning for our own day that thoughtful consideration of his first letter to his beloved Corinthian brothers and sisters will prove beneficial indeed. Recall now the spirit of the time and place. Think searchingly, as the Corinthian Christians must have done, while we review the penetrating, stirring, inspired words of Paul to his fellow believers in Corinth of old.

CONTENTS OF FIRST CORINTHIANS

8 **Paul exposes sectarianism, exhorts unity** (1:1–4:21). Paul has good wishes for the Corinthians. But what of the factions, the dissensions among them? "Does the Christ exist divided?" (1:13) The apostle is thankful that he has baptized so few of them, so they cannot say they have been baptized in his name. Paul preaches Christ impaled. This is a cause of

a *The Interpreter's Bible,* 1944, Vol. 10, page 13.
b *The Interpreter's Bible,* 1944, Vol. 9, page 356.

2. How was the Corinthian congregation established, and hence what bond did it have with Paul?
3. What moved Paul to write his first letter to the Corinthians?
4. What proves that Paul wrote this letter from Ephesus?
5. What establishes the authenticity of the letters to the Corinthians?
6. What problems existed in the Corinthian congregation, and in what was Paul especially interested?
7. With what attitude of mind should we consider First Corinthians, and why?
8. (a) How does Paul expose the folly of sectarianism in the congregation? (b) What does Paul show is necessary in order to understand the things of God?

stumbling to the Jews and foolishness to the nations. But God chose the foolish and weak things of the world to put to shame the wise and strong. So Paul does not use extravagant speech but lets them see the spirit and power of God through his words, that their faith may not be in men's wisdom but in God's power. We speak the things revealed by God's spirit, says Paul, "for the spirit searches into all things, even the deep things of God." These cannot be understood by the physical man, but only by the spiritual.—2:10.

9 They are following men—some Apollos, some Paul. But who are these? Only ministers through whom the Corinthians became believers. The ones planting and watering are not anything, for "God kept making it grow," and they are his "fellow workers." The test of fire will prove whose works are durable. Paul tells them, "You people are God's temple," in whom his spirit dwells. "The wisdom of this world is foolishness with God." Hence, let no one boast in men, for indeed all things belong to God. —3:6, 9, 16, 19.

10 Paul and Apollos are humble stewards of God's sacred secrets, and stewards should be found faithful. Who are the brothers at Corinth to boast, and what do they have that they did not receive? Have they become rich, begun ruling as kings, and become so discreet and strong, while the apostles, who have become a theatrical spectacle to both angels and to men, are yet foolish and weak, the offscouring of all things? Paul is sending Timothy to help them remember his methods in connection with Christ and become his imitators. If Jehovah wills, Paul himself will come shortly and get to know, not just the speech of those who are puffed up, but their power.

11 **On keeping the congregation clean** (5:1–6:20). A shocking case of immorality has been reported among the Corinthians! A man has taken his father's wife. He must be handed over to Satan, because a little leaven ferments the whole lump. They must quit mixing in company with anyone called a brother who proves to be wicked.

12 Why, the Corinthians have even been taking one another to court! Would it not be better to be defrauded? Since they are going to judge the world and angels, can they not find someone among them to judge between brothers? More than that, they should be clean, for fornicators, idolaters and the like will not inherit God's kingdom. That is what some of them were, but they have been washed clean and sanctified. "Flee from fornication," says Paul. "For you were bought with a price. By all means, glorify God in the body of you people." —6:18, 20.

13 **Counsel on singleness and marriage** (7:1-40). Paul answers a question about marriage. Because of the prevalence of fornication, it may be advisable for a man or a woman to be married, and those who are married should not be depriving each other of conjugal dues. It is well for the unmarried and widows to remain single, like Paul; but if they do not have self-control, let them marry. Once they marry, they should remain together. Even if one's mate is an unbeliever, the believer should not depart, for in that way the believer may save the unbelieving mate. As to circumcision and slavery, let each one be content to remain in the state in which he was called. With regard to the married person, he is divided because he wants to gain the approval of his mate, whereas the single person is anxious only for the things of the Lord. Those who marry do not sin, but those who do not marry do better.

14 **Doing all things for the sake of the good news** (8:1–9:27). What about food offered to idols? An idol is nothing! There are many "gods" and "lords" in the world, but for the Christian there is only "one God the Father," and "one Lord, Jesus Christ." (8:5, 6) Yet someone may be offended if he observes you eating meat sacrificed to an idol. Under these circumstances, Paul advises, refrain from it, so as not to cause your brother to stumble.

15 Paul denies himself many things for the sake of the ministry. As an apostle he has a right "to live by means of the good news," but has refrained from doing so. But necessity is laid upon him to preach; in fact, he says, "Woe is me if I did not declare the good news!" So he has made himself a slave to all, becoming "all things to people of all sorts," that he "might by all means save some," doing all things "for the sake of the good news." To win the contest and the incorruptible crown he browbeats his body, so that after preaching to others he himself "should not become disapproved somehow."—9:14, 16, 19, 22, 23, 27.

16 **Warning against injurious things** (10:1–11:1). What of the "forefathers"? These were under the cloud and were baptized into Moses. Most of them did not gain God's approval, but

9. By what argument does Paul show that no one should boast in men?
10. Why is the boasting of the Corinthians out of place, and what steps is Paul taking to remedy the situation?
11. What immorality has arisen among them, what must be done about it, and why?
12. (a) What does Paul argue about taking one another to court? (b) Why should they flee from fornication?
13. (a) Why does Paul counsel some to marry? But once married, what should they do? (b) How does the single person "do better"?
14. What does Paul say about "gods" and "lords," yet when is it wise to refrain from food offered to idols?
15. How does Paul conduct himself in the ministry?
16. (a) What warning should Christians take from the "forefathers"? (b) As to idolatry, how may they do all things for God's glory?

were laid low in the wilderness. Why? They desired injurious things. Christians should take warning from this and refrain from idolatry and fornication, from putting Jehovah to the test and murmuring. The one who thinks he is standing should beware that he does not fall. Temptation will come, but God will not let his servants be tempted beyond what they can bear; he will provide a way out so they can endure it. "Therefore," writes Paul, "flee from idolatry." (10:14) We cannot be partakers of the table of Jehovah and the table of demons. However, should you be eating in a home, do not inquire regarding the source of the meat. If someone advises you that it has been sacrificed to idols, though, refrain from eating on account of that one's conscience. "Do all things for God's glory," writes Paul. "Become imitators of me, even as I am of Christ."—10:31; 11:1.

17 **Headship; the Lord's evening meal** (11:2-34). Paul sets out the divine principle of headship: The head of the woman is the man, the head of the man is Christ, the head of Christ is God. Therefore the woman should have "a sign of authority" upon her head when she prays or prophesies in the congregation. Paul cannot commend the Corinthians, for divisions exist among them when they meet together. In this condition, how can they properly partake of the Lord's evening meal? He reviews what occurred when Jesus instituted the memorial of his death. Each must scrutinize himself before partaking, lest he bring judgment against himself for failure to discern "the body."—11:10, 29.

18 **Spiritual gifts, love and its pursuit** (12:1–14:40). There are varieties of spiritual gifts, yet the same spirit; varieties of ministries and operations, yet the same Lord and the same God. Likewise there are many members in the one united body of Christ, each member needing the other, as in the human body. God has set every member in the body as he pleases, and each has his work to do, so "there should be no division in the body." (12:25) Users of spiritual gifts are nothing without love. Love is long-suffering and kind, not jealous, not puffed up. It rejoices only with the truth. "Love never fails." (13:8) Spiritual gifts, such as prophesying and tongues, will be done away with, but faith, hope and love remain. Of these, the greatest is love.

19 "Pursue love," Paul admonishes. Spiritual gifts are to be used in love for the upbuilding of the congregation. For this reason prophesying is to be preferred over speaking in tongues. He would rather speak five words with understanding to teach others than ten thousand in an unknown language. Tongues are for a sign to unbelievers, but prophesying is for the believers. They should not be "young children" in their understanding of these matters. As for women, they should be in subjection in the congregation. "Let all things take place decently and by arrangement."—14:1, 20, 40.

20 **The certainty of the resurrection hope** (15:1–16:24). The resurrected Christ appeared to Cephas, to the twelve, to upward of five hundred brothers at one time, to James, to all the apostles and last of all to Paul. 'If Christ has not been raised up,' writes Paul, 'our preaching and faith are in vain.' (15:14) Each one is raised in his own order, Christ the firstfruits, then afterward those who belong to him during his presence. Finally he hands over the kingdom to his Father after all enemies have been put under his feet. Even death, the last enemy, is to be brought to nothing. Of what use is it for Paul to face perils of death continually if there is no resurrection?

21 But how are the dead to be raised? As the sown grain must die in order for the body of a plant to develop, so is the resurrection of the dead. "It is sown a physical body, it is raised up a spiritual body. . . . flesh and blood cannot inherit God's kingdom." (15:44, 50) Paul tells a sacred secret: Not all will fall asleep in death, but during the last trumpet they will be changed in the twinkling of an eye. When this that is mortal puts on immortality, death will be swallowed up forever. "Death, where is your victory? Death, where is your sting?" From the heart Paul exclaims: "But thanks to God, for he gives us the victory through our Lord Jesus Christ!"—15:55, 57.

22 In conclusion Paul counsels on orderliness in collecting their contributions for sending to Jerusalem to aid needy brothers. He tells of his coming visit via Macedonia and indicates that Timothy and Apollos may also visit. "Stay awake," Paul exhorts. "Stand firm in the faith, carry on as men, grow mighty. Let all your affairs take place with love." (16:13, 14) Paul sends greetings from the congregations in Asia, and then writes a final greeting in his own hand, conveying his love.

---

17. (a) What principle does Paul set out concerning headship? (b) How does he tie in the question of division in the congregation with a discussion of the Lord's evening meal?
18. (a) While there are varieties of gifts and ministries, why should there be no division in the body? (b) Why is love preeminent?
19. What counsel does Paul give for building up the congregation, and for orderly arrangement of things?
20. (a) What evidence does Paul give as to Christ's resurrection? (b) What is the order of the resurrection, and what enemies are to be put down?
21. (a) How are those who are to inherit God's kingdom raised? (b) What sacred secret does Paul reveal, and what does he say about victory over death?
22. What closing counsel and exhortation does Paul give?

WHY BENEFICIAL

23 This letter of the apostle Paul is most beneficial in enlarging our understanding of the Hebrew Scriptures, from which it makes many quotations. In the tenth chapter he points out that the Israelites under Moses drank from a spiritual rock-mass, which meant the Christ. (1 Cor. 10:4; Num. 20:11) Then he goes on to refer to the disastrous consequences of desiring injurious things, as exemplified by the Israelites under Moses, and adds: "Now these things went on befalling them as examples, and they were written for a warning to us upon whom the ends of the systems of things have arrived." Never let us become self-reliant, thinking that we cannot fall! (1 Cor. 10:11, 12; Num. 14:2; 21:5; 25:9) Again, he draws an illustration from the communion sacrifices in Israel to show how to share worthily in the altar of Jehovah. Then he quotes from Psalm 24:1, saying, "To Jehovah belong the earth and that which fills it," to back up his argument that it is proper to eat everything sold in the meat market.—1 Cor. 10:18, 26; Ex. 32:6; Lev. 7:11-15.

24 In showing the superiority of "the things that God has prepared for those who love him," and the futility of "the reasonings of the wise men" of this world, Paul again draws on the Hebrew Scriptures. (1 Cor. 2:9; 3:20; Isa. 64:4; Ps. 94:11) He quotes as authority for his instructions in chapter five on disfellowshiping the wrongdoer Jehovah's law to 'clear what is bad from your midst.' (Deut. 17:7) In discussing his right to live by the ministry, Paul again referred to the law of Moses, which said that working animals must not be muzzled to prevent their eating and that the Levites on temple service were to receive their portion from the altar.—1 Cor. 9:8-14; Deut. 25:4; 18:1.

25 What benefits of inspired instruction we have received from Paul's first letter to Corinthian Christians! Meditate upon the counsel given against divisions and following men. (Chapters 1-4). Recall the case of immorality and how Paul emphasized the need for virtue and cleanliness within the congregation. (Chapters 5 and 6) Consider his inspired advice relative to singleness, marriage and separation. (Chapter 7) Think of the apostle's discussion of foods offered to idols and of how the necessity of guarding against stumbling others and falling into idolatry was so forcefully brought to the fore. (Chapters 8-10) Admonition concerning proper subjection, a consideration of spiritual gifts, that most practical discussion on the excellence of love, the enduring, unfailing quality—these things, too, have passed in review. And how well the apostle accentuated the need for orderliness in Christian meetings! (Chapters 11-14) What a marvelous defense of the resurrection he penned under inspiration! (Chapter 15) All this and more has moved before the mind's eye—and it is so valuable to Christians in our own day!

26 This letter adds notably to our understanding of the glorious Bible theme of the kingdom of God. It gives a stern warning that unrighteous persons will not enter the Kingdom, and lists many of the vices that would disqualify a person. (1 Cor. 6:9, 10) But most important, it explains the relation between the resurrection and God's kingdom. It shows that Christ, "the first fruits" of the resurrection, must "rule as king until God has put all enemies under his feet." That includes the bruising under his feet of the archenemy, the old Serpent, Satan, as foretold in the first Kingdom promise in Eden. Then, when he has put down all enemies, including death, "he hands over the kingdom to his God and Father, . . . that God may be all things to everyone." Grand, indeed, is the resurrection prospect of those who are to share incorruptibility with Christ Jesus in the heavenly kingdom. It is on the basis of the resurrection hope that Paul admonishes: "Consequently, my beloved brothers, become steadfast, unmovable, always having plenty to do in the work of the Lord, knowing that your labor is not in vain in connection with the Lord."—1 Cor. 15:20-28, 58; Gen. 3:15; Rom. 16:20.

---

23. (a) How does Paul illustrate the disastrous consequences of wrong desire and self-reliance? (b) To what authority does he refer in counseling on the Lord's evening meal and proper foods?
24. What other references does Paul make to the Hebrew Scriptures in support of his arguments?
25. What are some of the outstanding points of beneficial instruction contained in First Corinthians?
26. (a) What long-foretold work does the resurrected Christ accomplish when he rules as king? (b) On the basis of the resurrection hope what powerful encouragement does Paul give?

Bible Book Number Forty-seven— 2 Corinthians

Writer:	**Paul**
Place Written:	**Macedonia**
Writing Completed:	**c. A.D. 55**
Time Covered:	**Undetermined**

IT WAS now probably late summer or early fall of A.D. 55. There were still some matters in the Christian congregation at Corinth that were causing concern to the apostle Paul. Not many months had passed since the writing of his first letter to the Corinthians. Since then Titus had been dispatched to Corinth to assist in the collection being undertaken there for the holy ones in Judea and possibly also to observe the reaction of the Corinthians to the first letter. (2 Cor. 8:1-6; 2:13) How did they take it? What comfort it brought Paul to know that it had moved them to sorrow and repentance! Titus had returned to Paul in Macedonia with this good report, and now the apostle's heart was filled to overflowing with love for his beloved Corinthian fellow believers.—2 Cor. 7:5-7; 6:11.

2 So Paul wrote again to the Corinthians. This heartwarming and forceful second letter was written from Macedonia, and was delivered apparently by Titus. (2 Cor. 9:2, 4; 8:16-18, 22-24) One of the matters of concern that moved Paul to write was the presence among the Corinthians of "superfine apostles," whom he also described as "false apostles, deceitful workers." (2 Cor. 11:5, 13, 14) The spiritual welfare of the comparatively young congregation was in jeopardy, and Paul's authority as an apostle was under attack. His second letter to Corinth thus filled a great need.

3 It may be noted that Paul said: "This is the third time I am ready to come to you." (2 Cor. 12:14; 13:1) He had planned to visit them a second time when he wrote his first letter, but though he got ready, this "second occasion for joy" did not materialize. (1 Cor. 16:5; 2 Cor. 1:15) Actually, then, Paul had been there only once before, for eighteen months in A.D. 50-52, when the Christian congregation was founded in Corinth. (Acts 18:1-18) However, Paul later realized the fulfillment of his wish to visit Corinth once more. While in Greece for three months, probably in 56 (A.D.), he spent at least part of the time in Corinth, and it was from there that he wrote his letter to the Romans.—Rom. 16:1, 23; 1 Cor. 1:14.

4 Second Corinthians has always been reckoned along with First Corinthians and the other Pauline epistles as an authentic part of the Bible canon. Again we are enabled to look inside the congregation at Corinth, and derive benefit from Paul's inspired words given for their and our admonition.

CONTENTS OF SECOND CORINTHIANS

5 **Help from the "God of all comfort"** (1:1–2:11). Paul includes Timothy in the opening salutation. "Blessed," says Paul, is "the Father of tender mercies and the God of all comfort, who comforts us in all our tribulation," that we, in turn, may be able to comfort others. Though Paul and his companions have been under extreme pressure and in danger for their lives, God has rescued them. The Corinthians can help, too, with prayers on their behalf. It is with confidence in his sincerity and in God's undeserved kindness that he is writing to them. God's promises have become "Yes" by means of Jesus, and He has anointed his servants and given them "the token of what is to come, that is, the spirit" in their hearts.—1:3, 4, 20, 22.

6 It appears that the man who was the object of Paul's comments in his first letter, chapter five, was ousted from the congregation. He has repented and is showing sorrow. Paul therefore tells the Corinthians to extend genuine forgiveness and to confirm their love for the penitent one.

7 **Qualified as ministers of the new covenant** (2:12–6:10). Paul compares the ministry to a triumphal procession with Christ. (The Corinthians were familiar with the processions of victorious armies in that day, when the odor of sweet incense was burned along the route.) There is a strong contrast between the "odor" of the Christian to those who will gain life and the "odor" to those who are perishing. "We are not peddlers of the word of God," affirms Paul.—2:17.

8 Paul and his fellow workers need no docu-

1, 2. (a) What led to Paul's writing his second letter to the Corinthians? (b) From where did Paul write, and about what was he concerned?
3, 4. (a) What visits did Paul himself make to Corinth? (b) How does this letter benefit us now?
5. (a) What does Paul write concerning comfort? (b) What has come about through Christ that is of further assurance?
6. What does Paul counsel should be done for the disfellowshiped wrongdoer who is now repentant?
7. To what does Paul compare the ministry, and what does he affirm?
8. (a) What credentials did Paul and his fellow workers have as ministers? (b) How is the ministry of the new covenant superior?

ments, written letters of recommendation, to or from the Corinthians. The Corinthian believers themselves are letters of recommendation, written "by us as ministers," and inscribed, not on tablets of stone, but "on fleshly tablets, on hearts," declares Paul. God has adequately qualified the ministers of the new covenant. The written code was an administration of death, with fading glory, and it was temporary. The administration of the spirit, however, leads to life, is lasting and is of abounding glory. When "Moses is read," a veil rests upon the hearts of the sons of Israel, but when there is a turning to Jehovah, the veil is removed and they are "transformed into the same image from glory to glory."—3:3, 15, 18.

9 Then Paul continues: 'We have this ministry due to the mercy that was shown to us. We have renounced underhanded things, and have not adulterated God's word, but have recommended ourselves by making the truth manifest. If the message of good news is veiled, it is because the god of this world has blinded the minds of unbelievers. Our hearts, however, are illuminated with the glorious knowledge of God by the face of Christ. How great this treasure that we have! It is in earthen vessels, so that the power beyond what is normal may be God's. Under persecution and stress, yes, in the face of death itself, we exercise faith and do not give up, for the momentary tribulation works out for us a glory that is of more and more surpassing weight and is everlasting. So we keep our eyes on the things unseen.'—4:1-18.

10 'We know,' writes Paul, 'that our earthly house will give way to an everlasting one in the heavens. In the meantime we press on in faith and are of good courage. Though absent from Christ, we seek to be acceptable to him.' (5:1, 7-9) Those in union with Christ are a "new creation" and have a ministry of reconciliation. They are "ambassadors substituting for Christ." (5:17, 20) In every way Paul recommends himself as a minister of God. How? 'By the endurance of much in the way of tribulations, beatings, labors, sleepless nights, by purity, by knowledge, by long-suffering, by kindness, by holy spirit, by love free from hypocrisy, by truthful speech, by God's power, as poor but making many rich, as having nothing and yet possessing all things.'—6:4-10.

11 **"Perfecting holiness in God's fear"** (6:11–7:16). Paul tells the Corinthians: 'Our heart has widened out to receive you.' They, too, should widen out their tender affections. But now comes a warning! "Do not become unevenly yoked with unbelievers." (6:14) What fellowship does light have with darkness, or Christ with Belial? As a temple of a living God, they must separate themselves and quit touching the unclean thing. Says Paul: "Let us cleanse ourselves of every defilement of flesh and spirit, perfecting holiness in God's fear."—7:1.

12 Paul states further: "I am filled with comfort, I am overflowing with joy in all our affliction." (7:4) Why? Not only because of the presence of Titus, but also because of the good report from Corinth, that of their longing, their mourning and their zeal for Paul. He realizes that his first letter caused temporary sadness, but rejoices that the Corinthians were saddened for repentance to salvation. He commends them for cooperating with Titus.

13 **Generosity will be rewarded** (8:1–9:15). In connection with contributions for the needy "holy ones," Paul cites the example of the Macedonians, whose generosity out of deep poverty was really beyond their ability; and he now hopes to see the same kind of giving on the part of the Corinthians as a demonstration of the genuineness of their love for the Lord Jesus Christ, who became poor that they might be rich. This giving according to what they have will result in an equalizing, so that the one with much will not have too much, and the one with little, not too little. Titus and others are being sent to them in connection with this kind gift. Paul has been boasting about the generosity and readiness of the Corinthians, and he does not want them put to shame by any failure to complete the bountiful gift. Yes, "he that sows bountifully will also reap bountifully." Let it be from the heart, for "God loves a cheerful giver." He is also able to make his undeserved kindness abound toward them and to enrich them for every sort of generosity. "Thanks be to God for his indescribable free gift."—9:6, 7, 15.

14 **Paul argues his apostleship** (10:1–13:14). Paul acknowledges that he is lowly in appearance. But Christians do not war according to the flesh; their weapons are spiritual, "powerful by God" for overturning reasonings contrary to the knowledge of God. (10:4) Some, seeing things just at their face value, say that the apostle's letters are weighty but his speech contemptible. Let them know that Paul's actions will be just the same as his word by letter. The Corinthians should realize that Paul is not boasting about accomplishments in someone else's territory. He has personally carried the good news to them. Furthermore,

9. How does Paul describe the treasure of the ministry?
10. (a) What does Paul say of those in union with Christ? (b) How does Paul recommend himself as a minister of God?
11. What counsel and warning does Paul give?
12. Why did Paul rejoice at the report from Corinth?
13. (a) What examples of generosity does Paul cite? (b) What principles does Paul discuss in connection with giving?
14. What points does Paul make in support of his apostleship?

if there is to be any boasting, let it be in Jehovah.

15 Paul feels his responsibility to present the Corinthian congregation to the Christ as a chaste virgin. Just as Eve was seduced by the serpent's cunning, so there is danger that their minds may be corrupted. With force, therefore, Paul speaks out against the "superfine apostles" of the Corinthian congregation. (11:5) They are false apostles. Satan himself keeps transforming himself into an angel of light, so it is no wonder if his ministers do the same. But as to being ministers of Christ, how do they compare with Paul's record? He has endured much: imprisonment, beatings, shipwreck three times, many dangers, going often without sleep or food. Yet through it all he never lost sight of the needs of the congregations and always felt incensed when someone was stumbled.

16 So if anyone has reason to boast it is Paul. Could the other so-called apostles at Corinth tell about being caught away into paradise, to hear unutterable things? Yet Paul speaks about his weaknesses. That he might not feel overly exalted, he was given "a thorn in the flesh." God did not remove this when he entreated Him, but said: "My undeserved kindness is sufficient for you." Paul would rather boast in his weaknesses, that "the power of the Christ" may remain over him like a tent. (12:7, 9) No, Paul has not proved inferior to the "superfine apostles," and the Corinthians have seen the proofs of apostleship that he produced among them "by all endurance, and by signs and portents and powerful works." He is not seeking their possessions, just as Titus and his other fellow workers whom he sent did not take advantage of them.—12:12.

17 All things are for their upbuilding. However, Paul expresses fears that, when he arrives in Corinth, he will find some who have not repented of works of the flesh. He warns the sinners in advance that he will take appropriate action and spare none, and advises all in the congregation to keep testing whether they are in the faith in union with Jesus Christ. Paul and Timothy will pray to God for them. He bids them rejoice and be restored to unity, so that the God of love and peace will be with them, and concludes by sending greetings from the holy ones and his own best wishes for their spiritual blessing.

15. (a) With what illustrations does Paul speak out against the false apostles? (b) What is Paul's own record?
16. (a) Of what might Paul boast, but why would he rather speak of his weaknesses? (b) How has Paul produced proofs of his apostleship?
17. What final admonition does Paul give the Corinthians?

WHY BENEFICIAL

18 How stimulating and encouraging is Paul's appreciation for the Christian ministry as expressed in Second Corinthians! Let us view it as he did: A triumphal procession in company with the Christ! The Christian minister who has been adequately qualified by God is no peddler of the Word, but serves out of sincerity. What recommends him is, not some written document, but the fruitage he bears in the ministry. However, while the ministry is indeed glorious, this is no cause for his becoming puffed up. God's servants as imperfect humans have this treasure of service in frail earthen vessels, that the power may plainly be seen to be God's. So this calls for humility in accepting the glorious privilege of being God's ministers, and what an undeserved kindness from God it is to serve as "ambassadors substituting for Christ"! How appropriate, then, was Paul's exhortation "not to accept the undeserved kindness of God and miss its purpose"!—2 Cor. 2:14-17; 3:1-5; 4:7; 5:18-20; 6:1.

19 Paul certainly provided a splendid example for Christian ministers to copy. For one thing, he valued and studied the inspired Hebrew Scriptures, repeatedly quoting and applying them. (2 Cor. 6:2, 16-18; 7:1; 8:15; 9:9; 13:1; Isa. 49:8; Lev. 26:12; Isa. 52:11; Ezek. 20:41; 2 Sam. 7:14; Hos. 1:10) Moreover, as an overseer he displayed deep concern for the flock, saying: "For my part I will most gladly spend and be completely spent for your souls." He gave himself entirely in behalf of the brothers, as the record clearly shows. (2 Cor. 12:15; 6:3-10) He was untiring in his labors, as he taught, exhorted and set things straight in the Corinthian congregation. He warned plainly against fellowship with darkness, telling them: "Do not become unevenly yoked with unbelievers." Because of his loving concern for the Corinthians he did not want to see their minds become corrupted, "as the serpent seduced Eve by its cunning," and so he heartily admonished them: "Keep testing whether you are in the faith, keep proving what you yourselves are." He stirred them to Christian generosity, showing them that "God loves a cheerful giver," and he himself expressed the most appreciative thanks to God for His indescribable free gift. Truly his brothers at Corinth were inscribed in love on the fleshly tablet of Paul's heart, and his unstinted service in their interests was everything that should mark a zealous, wide-awake overseer. What an outstanding model for us today!—2 Cor. 6:14; 11:3; 13:5; 9:7, 15; 3:2.

18. What right view should Christians take of the ministry?
19. In what various ways did Paul provide an outstanding model for Christian ministers today, especially for overseers?

20 The apostle Paul sets our minds in the right direction in pointing to "the Father of tender mercies and the God of all comfort" as the real source of strength in time of trial. He it is that "comforts us in all our tribulation," that we may endure for salvation into his new world. Paul points also to the glorious hope of "a building from God, a house not made with hands, everlasting in the heavens," and says: "Consequently if anyone is in union with Christ, he is a new creation; the old things passed away, look! new things have come into existence." Second Corinthians does indeed contain wonderful words of assurance for those who, like Paul, will inherit the heavenly kingdom. —2 Cor. 1:3, 4; 5:1, 17.

20. (a) How does Paul set our minds in the right direction? (b) To what glorious hope does Second Corinthians point?

Bible Book Number Forty-eight— Galatians

Writer:	**Paul**
Place Written:	**Corinth or Syrian Antioch**
Writing Completed:	**c. A.D. 50-52**
Time Covered:	**Undetermined**

THE congregations of Galatia addressed by Paul at Galatians 1:2 apparently included Pisidian Antioch, Iconium, Lystra and Derbe— places in different districts, but all within this Roman province. Acts, chapters thirteen and fourteen, tells of Paul's and Barnabas' first missionary journey through this area, which led to the organizing of the Galatian congregations, made up of varying nationalities, such as Phrygians, Greeks, Romans, Gauls and a minority of Jews. This was shortly after Paul's visit to Jerusalem about A.D. 46.—Acts 12:25.

2 In the year 49 (A.D.) Paul and Silas started out on Paul's second missionary tour into the Galatian territory, which resulted in 'the congregations being made firm in the faith and increasing in number day by day.' (Acts 16:5; 15:40, 41; 16:1, 2) However, hot on their heels came false teachers, Judaizers, who persuaded some in the Galatian congregations to believe that circumcision and observance of the law of Moses were an essential part of true Christianity. In the meantime Paul had journeyed on past Mysia into Macedonia and Greece, eventually arriving in Corinth, where he spent more than eighteen months with the brothers. Then, in A.D. 52, he departed by way of Ephesus for Syrian Antioch, his home base, arriving there in the same year.—Acts 16:8, 11, 12; 17:15; 18:1, 11, 18-22.

3 Where and when did Paul write the letter to the Galatians? No doubt he wrote it as soon as word reached him concerning the activity of the Judaizers. This could have been in Corinth, Ephesus or Syrian Antioch. It could well have been during his eighteen-month stay in Corinth, A.D. 50-52, as information would have time to reach him there from Galatia. Ephesus is unlikely, as he stayed there only briefly on his return journey. However, he then "passed some time" at his home base of Syrian Antioch, apparently in the summer of A.D. 52, and since there was ready communication between this city and Asia Minor, it is possible that he received the report concerning the Judaizers and wrote his letter to the Galatians from Syrian Antioch at this time.—Acts 18:23.

4 The letter describes Paul as "an apostle, neither from men nor through a man, but through Jesus Christ and God the Father." It also discloses many facts about Paul's life and apostleship, proving that, as an apostle, he worked in harmony with the apostles in Jerusalem, and that he even exercised his authority in correcting another apostle, Peter. —Gal. 1:1, 13-24; 2:1-14.

5 What facts argue the authenticity and canonicity of Galatians? *The Encyclopædia Britannica* says: "The authenticity of this letter has never been questioned save by occasional critics who have refused to admit the genuineness of any of the Pauline letters."[a] It is included in the following important Bible manuscripts of rank: Sinaitic, Alexandrine, Vatican No. 1209, Codex Ephraemi rescriptus, Codex Bezae, the Chester Beatty No. 2 and the Pe-

1. Which congregations are addressed in Galatians, and how and when were they organized?
2. (a) What resulted from Paul's second tour in Galatia, but what followed thereafter? (b) In the meantime, how did Paul proceed with his journey?
3. From where and when may Galatians have been written?

a 1959 Edition, Vol. 9, page 969.

4. What does the letter disclose as to Paul's apostleship?
5. What facts argue for the authenticity and canonicity of Galatians?

shitta. Moreover, it is entirely in harmony with the other Greek Scripture writings and also with the Hebrew Scriptures, to which it frequently refers.

6 In Paul's powerful and hard-hitting letter "to the congregations of Galatia," he proves (1) that he is a true apostle (a fact that the Judaizers had sought to discredit), and (2) that justification is by faith in Christ Jesus, not by the works of the Law, and that therefore circumcision is unnecessary for Christians. Though it was Paul's custom to have a secretary write down his epistles, he himself wrote Galatians in 'large letters with his own hand.' (Gal. 6:11) The contents of the book were of the greatest importance, both to Paul and the Galatians. *The Westminster Bible Dictionary*, 1944, page 191, even calls Galatians "the Magna Charta of Christian liberty."

CONTENTS OF GALATIANS

7 **Paul argues his apostleship** (1:1–2:14). After greeting the congregations in Galatia, Paul marvels that they are being so quickly removed to another sort of good news, and firmly declares: "Even if we or an angel out of heaven were to declare to you as good news something beyond what we declared to you as good news, let him be accursed." The good news that he has declared is not something human, neither was he taught it, "except through revelation by Jesus Christ." Previously, as a zealous exponent of Judaism, Paul had persecuted the congregation of God, but then God called him through His undeserved kindness to declare the good news about his Son to the nations. It was not until three years after his conversion that he went up to Jerusalem, and then, of the apostles, he saw only Peter, as well as James the brother of the Lord. He was unknown in person to the congregations of Judea, though they used to hear of him and "began glorifying God" because of him.—1:8, 12, 24.

8 After fourteen years Paul went up to Jerusalem again, and explained privately the good news that he is preaching. They did not even require his companion Titus, though a Greek, to be circumcised. When they saw that Paul had entrusted to him the good news for those who are uncircumcised, just as Peter had it for those who are circumcised, James and Cephas and John gave Paul and Barnabas the right hand of sharing together, to go to the nations, while they themselves went to the circumcised. When Cephas came to Antioch and failed to walk straight "according to the truth of the good news" for fear of the circumcised class, Paul rebuked him before them all.—2:14.

9 **Declared righteous by faith, not law** (2:15–4:31). We Jews know, argues Paul, "that a man is declared righteous, not due to works of law, but only through faith toward Christ Jesus." He now lives in union with Christ and is alive by faith to do the will of God. "If righteousness is through law, Christ actually died for nothing."—2:16, 21.

10 Are the Galatians so senseless as to believe that, having started by receiving the spirit due to faith, they can finish serving God by works of law? It is the hearing by faith that counts, as with Abraham, who "put faith in Jehovah, and it was counted to him as righteousness." Now, according to God's promise, "those who adhere to faith are being blessed together with faithful Abraham." They have been released from the curse of the Law by Christ's death on the stake. Christ is the seed of Abraham, and the Law made 430 years later does not abolish the promise concerning that seed. What, then, was the purpose of the Law? It was "our tutor leading to Christ, that we might be declared righteous due to faith." Now we are no longer under the tutor, nor is there now any distinction between Jew and Greek, for all are one in union with Christ Jesus, and "are really Abraham's seed, heirs with reference to a promise."—3:6, 9, 24, 29.

11 God sent forth his Son to release those under law, that they "might receive the adoption as sons." (4:5) So why turn back to the slavery of the weak and beggarly elementary things? Since they are now observing days and months and seasons and years, Paul is afraid his work on their behalf has been wasted. On his first visit to them they received Paul like an angel of God. Has he now become their enemy because he tells them the truth? Let those who want to be under law hear what the Law says: Abraham acquired two sons by two women. The one woman, the servant girl, Hagar, stands in symbol of the covenant from Mount Sinai, which brings forth children for slavery, and corresponds to earthly Jerusalem. The other son was born by the free woman through a promise, and this woman corresponds with the Jerusalem above, which is free, and she is our mother. "What," asks Paul, "does the Scripture say?" This: "By no means shall the son of the servant girl be an heir with the son of the free woman." And we are children, not of a servant girl, "but of the free woman." —4:30, 31.

---

6. (a) What two points does the letter establish? (b) What was unusual about the writing of this letter?
7, 8. (a) What does Paul argue concerning the good news? (b) How was Paul confirmed as apostle to the uncircumcised, and how did he demonstrate his authority in connection with Cephas?
9. On the basis of what is the Christian declared righteous?
10. What is it that counts for God's blessing, and so what was the purpose of the Law?
11. (a) What release are the Galatians ignoring? (b) How does Paul illustrate the Christian's freedom?

12 **Stand fast in Christ's freedom!** (5:1–6:18). Circumcision or lack of it means nothing, but it is faith operating through love that counts. The entire Law is fulfilled in the saying: "You must love your neighbor as yourself." Keep walking by the spirit, for "if you are being led by spirit, you are not under law." As to the works of the flesh, Paul forewarns "that those who practice such things will not inherit God's kingdom." In glowing contrast he describes the fruitage of the spirit, against which there is no law, and adds: "If we are living by spirit, let us go on walking orderly also by spirit," and put away egotism and envy.—5:14, 18, 21, 25.

13 If a man takes some false step before he is aware of it, those spiritually qualified must try to restore him "in a spirit of mildness." The law of Christ is fulfilled by carrying the burdens of one another, but let each one carry his own load in proving what his own work is. One will reap according to what he sows; either corruption from the flesh, or everlasting life from the spirit. Those who want the Galatians to be circumcised are only out to please men and avoid persecution. The thing of vital concern is not circumcision or uncircumcision, but a new creation. Peace and mercy will be upon those who walk orderly according to this rule of conduct, even upon "the Israel of God." —6:1, 16.

WHY BENEFICIAL

14 The letter to the Galatians reveals Paul as the devastating persecutor who became the alert apostle to the nations, always ready to contend on behalf of the interests of his brothers. (Gal. 1:13-16, 23; 5:7-12) Paul showed by example that an overseer should move quickly to handle problems, quashing false reasonings by logic and Scripture.—Gal. 1:6-9; 3:1-6.

15 The letter was beneficial to the congregations in Galatia in clearly establishing their freedom in Christ and discrediting the perverters of the good news. It made plain that justification is by faith and that circumcision was no longer of any value. (Gal. 2:16; 3:8; 5:6) By setting aside such fleshly distinctions it served to unify Jew and Gentile in the one congregation. This freedom from the Law was not to serve as an inducement for the desires of the flesh, for the principle still held: "You must love your neighbor as yourself." It continues to hold as a guidepost to Christians today.—Gal. 5:14.

16 Paul's letter helped the Galatians on many points of doctrine, drawing on the Hebrew Scriptures for powerful illustrations. It gave the inspired interpretation of Isaiah 54:1-6, identifying Jehovah's woman as "the Jerusalem above." It explained the "symbolic drama" of Hagar and Sarah, showing that the heirs of God's promises are those made free by Christ, and not those remaining in bondage to the Law. (Gal. 4:21-26; Gen. 16:1-4, 15; 21:1-3, 8-13) It clearly explained that the Law covenant had a temporary and subsidiary relationship to the Abrahamic covenant. It also pointed out that the time interval between the making of the two covenants was 430 years, which is important to Bible chronology. (Gal. 3:17, 18, 23, 24) The record of these things has been preserved for building up Christian faith today.

17 Most important, Galatians unmistakably identifies the Kingdom Seed, to which all the prophets looked forward. "Now the promises were spoken to Abraham and to his seed . . . who is Christ." Those who become sons of God through faith in Christ Jesus are shown to be adopted into this seed. "If you belong to Christ, you are really Abraham's seed, heirs with reference to a promise." (Gal. 3:16, 29) The fine admonition given in Galatians should be heeded by these Kingdom heirs and those who labor with them: 'Stand fast in the freedom for which Christ has set you free!' 'Do not give up in doing what is fine, for in due season we shall reap if we do not tire out.' 'Work what is good, especially toward those related to us in the faith.'—Gal. 5:1; 6:9, 10.

18 Finally, there is the powerful warning that those who practice the works of the flesh "will not inherit God's kingdom." Let all, then, turn completely from worldly filth and strife and set their hearts entirely upon bringing forth the fruitage of the spirit, which is "love, joy, peace, long-suffering, kindness, goodness, faith, mildness, self-control."—Gal. 5:19-23.

---

12. (a) By what must the Galatians now walk? (b) What important contrast does Paul make?
13. How is the law of Christ fulfilled, and what is of vital concern?
14. What example does Paul here set for overseers?
15. How was the letter beneficial to the Galatian congregations, and what guidepost does it provide for Christians today?
16. What faith-building explanations of the Hebrew Scriptures are to be found in Galatians?
17. (a) What important identification does Galatians make? (b) What fine admonition is given the Kingdom heirs and their colaborers?
18. What final powerful warning and admonition are given?

Bible Book Number Forty-nine— Ephesians

Writer:	**Paul**
Place Written:	**Rome**
Writing Completed:	**c. A.D. 60-61**
Time Covered:	**Undetermined**

IMAGINE that you are in prison. You are there because of being persecuted for your zealous activity as a Christian missionary. Now that you can no longer travel and visit the congregations to strengthen them, what are you going to do? Can you not write letters to those who have become Christians through your preaching work? Are they not probably wondering how you are, and are they not perhaps in need of encouragement? Of course they are! So you begin to write. You are now doing exactly what the apostle Paul did when he was imprisoned in Rome the first time, about A.D. 59-61. He had appealed to Caesar, and, although awaiting trial and under guard, he had freedom for some activity. Paul wrote his letter "To the Ephesians" from Rome, probably A.D. 60 or 61, and sent it by Tychicus, who was accompanied by Onesimus.—Eph. 6:21; Col. 4:7-9.

2 Paul identifies himself as the writer in the very first word and four times refers or alludes to himself as "the prisoner in the Lord." (Eph. 1:1; 3:1, 13; 4:1; 6:20) Arguments against Paul's writership have come to nothing. The Chester Beatty Papyrus No. 2 (P^{46}), written early in the third century, contains eighty-six leaves out of a codex of Paul's epistles, and among them is the epistle to the Ephesians, thus showing that it was grouped among his letters at that time.

3 Early ecclesiastical writers confirm that Paul wrote the letter and that it was "to the Ephesians." For example, Irenaeus, of the second century, quoted Ephesians 5:30 as follows: "As the blessed Paul says in the epistle to the Ephesians, that we are members of his body." Clement of Alexandria, of the same period, quoted Ephesians 5:21 in reporting: "Wherefore, also, in the epistle to the Ephesians he writes, Be subject one to another in the fear of God." Origen, writing in the first half of the third century, quoted Ephesians 1:4 in saying: "But also the apostle in the epistle to the Ephesians, uses the same language when he says, Who chose us from the foundation of the world."[a] Eusebius, another authority on early Christian history (c. A.D. 260-340), includes Ephesians in the Bible canon, and most other early theological writers make references to Ephesians as part of the inspired Scriptures.[b]

4 The Chester Beatty Papyrus, as well as the Vatican No. 1209 and Sinaitic Manuscripts, omit the words "in Ephesus" in chapter 1, verse 1, and thus do not indicate the destination of the letter. This fact, together with the absence of greetings to individuals in Ephesus (though Paul had labored there for three years), has led some to surmise that the letter may have been addressed elsewhere, or at least that it may have been a circular letter to the congregations in Asia Minor, including Ephesus. However, most other manuscripts include the words "in Ephesus," and, as we have noted above, the early church writers accepted it as a letter to the Ephesians.

5 Some background information will help us to understand the purpose of this letter. In the first century of the Common Era Ephesus was noted for its sorcery, magic, astrology and the worship of the great goddess Artemis (Diana). Around the statue of the goddess there had been erected a magnificent temple that took 220 years to complete. The Roman historian Pliny says that the temple was 220 feet wide and 425 feet long, and was supported by 127 columns sixty feet in height, each column having been erected by a king or prince. The roof was covered with large white marble tiles. Gold is said to have been used instead of mortar between the joints of the marble blocks. The temple attracted tourists from all over the earth, and visitors numbering as many as 700,000 would throng into the city during festivals. The silversmiths of Ephesus carried on a lucrative business selling small silver shrines of Artemis to pilgrims as souvenirs.[c]

a *Origin and History of the Books of the Bible,* 1868, C. E. Stowe, page 357.
b *The New Bible Dictionary,* 1962, edited by J. D. Douglas, page 197.
c M'Clintock and Strong's *Cyclopædia,* 1882, Vol. 3, page 244.

1. When and under what circumstances did Paul write the letter to the Ephesians?
2, 3. (a) What conclusively proves Paul's writership and, at the same time, the canonicity of Ephesians?
4. What has led some to surmise the letter was addressed elsewhere, but what evidence supports Ephesus as its destination?
5. What was noteworthy about the Ephesus of Paul's day?

6 Paul had stopped in Ephesus on his second missionary journey for a short visit of preaching, and then had left Aquila and Priscilla there to continue the work. (Acts 18:18-21) He returned on his third missionary journey and stayed for about three years, preaching and teaching "The Way" to many. (Acts 19:8-10; 20:31) Paul worked hard while in Ephesus. In his book *Daily Life in Bible Times,* 1943, page 308, A. E. Bailey writes: "Paul's general practice was to work at his trade from sunrise to 11 a.m. (Acts 20:34, 35) at which hour Tyrannus had finished his teaching; then from 11 a.m. to 4 p.m. to preach in the hall, hold conferences with helpers, . . . then lastly to make a house-to-house evangelistic canvass that lasted from 4 p.m. till far into the night. (Acts 20:20, 21, 31) One wonders when he found time to eat and sleep."

7 In the course of this zealous preaching Paul exposed the use of images in worship. This stirred up the wrath of those making and selling them, such as the silversmith Demetrius, and in the uproar Paul finally had to leave the city.—Acts 19:23–20:1.

8 Now, while in prison, Paul is thinking of the problems faced by the Ephesian congregation, surrounded by pagan worshipers and in the shadow of the awe-inspiring temple of Artemis. These Christians no doubt needed the impressive description of Jehovah's spiritual temple, which Paul now gives them, grander than anything made by men. The "sacred secret" being revealed to the Ephesians, showing them that they, too, would become a part of the heavenly structure for administering God's will, was unquestionably a great inspiration and comfort to them. Paul emphasizes the union of Jew and Gentile in Christ. He exhorts to oneness, to unity. Thus we can now appreciate the purpose, value and obvious inspiration behind this book.

CONTENTS OF EPHESIANS

9 **God's undeserved kindness by means of Christ** (1:1–2:22). Paul, the apostle, sends greetings. God is to be blessed for his glorious undeserved kindness. This has to do with His choosing of them to be in union with Jesus Christ, by means of whom they have the release by ransom through his blood. Furthermore, God has made his love abound toward them by making known the sacred secret of his will. For he has purposed an administration, "to gather all things together again in the Christ," in union with whom they were also assigned as heirs. (1:10) As a token of this in advance they have been sealed by holy spirit. His prayer is that they will be firmly convinced of the hope to which they have been called and realize that God will use the same power toward them that he did in resurrecting Christ and in placing him far above every government and authority and making him head over all things to the congregation.

10 God out of the richness of his mercy and his great love has made them alive, though they were dead in their trespasses and sins, and has seated them together "in the heavenly places in union with Christ Jesus." (2:6) This is all due to undeserved kindness and faith, and not as a result of any works of their own. Christ is their peace who has broken down the wall, the Law of commandments, that had fenced off Gentiles from Jews. Now both peoples have the approach to the Father through Christ. Therefore the Ephesians are no longer aliens, but are "fellow citizens of the holy ones" and are growing into a holy temple for Jehovah to inhabit by his spirit.—2:19.

11 **"The sacred secret of the Christ"** (3:1-21). God has now revealed to his holy apostles and prophets the "sacred secret of the Christ . . . that people of the nations should be joint heirs and fellow members of the body and partakers with us of the promise in union with Christ Jesus through the good news." (3:4, 6) By God's undeserved kindness Paul has become a minister of this, to declare the unfathomable riches of the Christ and make men see how the sacred secret is administered. It is through the congregation that the greatly diversified wisdom of God is made known. Because of this Paul prays that they will be made mighty with power through God's spirit in order that they may fully know the love of Christ, which surpasses knowledge and realize that God can "do more than superabundantly beyond all the things we ask or conceive."—3:20.

12 **Putting on "the new personality"** (4:1–5:20). They should walk worthily of their calling, in lowliness of mind, long-suffering and love, and in the uniting bond of peace. For there is but one spirit, one hope, one faith, and "one God and Father of all persons, who is over all and through all and in all." (4:6) Therefore Christ, the "one Lord," has given prophets, evangelizers, shepherds and teachers, "with a view to the training of the holy ones, for ministerial work, for the building up of the body of the Christ." So, writes Paul, "speaking the truth, let us by love grow up in all things into him

6. What was the extent of Paul's activity in Ephesus?
7. What resulted from Paul's zealous preaching?
8. In what points was Paul's letter most timely?
9. How has God made his love abound, and what is Paul's prayer?
10. How have the Ephesians become "fellow citizens of the holy ones"?
11. What is the "sacred secret," and for what does Paul pray in behalf of the Ephesians?
12. (a) How should Christians walk, and why? (b) What gifts has Christ given, and for what purpose? (c) What is involved in putting on "the new personality"?

who is the head, Christ," as a body harmoniously joined together and cooperating in every member. (4:5, 12, 15) The immoral, unprofitable and ignorant ways of the old personality are to be put away; one should be made new in the force actuating his mind and "put on the new personality which was created according to God's will in true righteousness and loyalty." Because all belong to one another they are to speak the truth and put away wrath, stealing, rotten sayings, malicious bitterness—not grieving God's holy spirit. Instead, let them become 'kind to one another, tenderly compassionate, freely forgiving one another, just as God also by Christ freely forgave them.' —4:24, 32.

13 All should become imitators of God. Fornication, uncleanness and greediness should not even be mentioned among them, for those who do these things have no inheritance in the Kingdom. Paul admonishes the Ephesians: "Go on walking as children of light." "Keep strict watch" on how you walk, buying out the opportune time, "because the days are wicked." Yes, they must "go on perceiving what the will of Jehovah is," and speak about the praises of God in a thankful way.—5:8, 15-17.

14 **Proper subjection; Christian warfare** (5:21–6:24). Let wives be in subjection to husbands, even as the congregation is in subjection to the Christ, and let husbands continue loving their wives, "just as the Christ also loved the congregation." Likewise, "the wife should have deep respect for her husband."—5:25, 33.

15 Let children live at unity with parents, in obedience and responding to godly discipline. Slaves and masters, also, should conduct themselves so as to be pleasing to God, for the Master of all "is in the heavens, and there is no partiality with him." Finally, let all "go on acquiring power in the Lord and in the mightiness of his strength," putting on the complete armor from God so as to be able to stand firm against the Devil. "Above all things, take up the large shield of faith," also "the sword of the spirit, that is, God's word." Carry on prayer, and keep awake. Paul asks that they pray also for him, that he may with all freeness of speech "make known the sacred secret of the good news."—6:9, 10, 16, 17, 19.

WHY BENEFICIAL

16 The epistle to the Ephesians touches almost every aspect of the Christian's life. In view of the present-day upsurge of distressing problems and delinquency in the world, Paul's sound, practical advice is of real benefit to those who desire to live godly lives. How should children conduct themselves toward parents, and parents toward children? What are the responsibilities of a husband toward his wife, and of a wife toward her husband? What must the individuals in the congregation do in order to maintain unity in love, and Christian purity in the midst of a wicked world? Paul's counsel covers all these questions, and he goes on to show what is involved in putting on the new Christian personality. Through the study of Ephesians all will be able to gain real appreciation of the kind of personality that is pleasing to God and that is "created according to God's will in true righteousness and loyalty."—Eph. 4:24-32; 6:1-4; 5:22-33, 15-20, 3-5.

17 The letter also shows the purpose of appointments and assignments in the congregation. This is "with a view to the training of the holy ones, for ministerial work, for the building up of the body of the Christ," with maturity in view. By cooperating fully in these congregational arrangements the Christian can "by love grow up in all things into him who is the head, Christ."—Eph. 4:12, 15.

18 The letter to the Ephesians greatly benefited the early congregation in sharpening their understanding of "the sacred secret of the Christ." Here it was made plain that, along with believing Jews, "people of the nations" were being called to be "joint heirs and fellow members of the body and partakers . . . of the promise in union with Christ Jesus through the good news." The wall of partition, "the Law of commandments," that had fenced off Gentile from Jew had been abolished, and now by the blood of the Christ all had become fellow citizens of the holy ones and members of the household of God. In striking contrast to the pagan temple of Artemis, these were being built up together in union with Christ Jesus into a place for God to inhabit by spirit—"a holy temple for Jehovah."—Eph. 3:4, 6; 2:15, 21.

19 With regard to the "sacred secret," Paul also spoke of "an administration . . . to gather all things together again in the Christ, the things in the heavens and the things on the earth. Yes, in him, in union with whom we were also assigned as heirs." Thus the glorious hope of inheritance in God's kingdom is again brought to the fore. In this connection Paul prayed on behalf of the Ephesians, the eyes of

13. For one to be an imitator of God, what must he do?
14. What are the mutual responsibilities of husbands and wives?
15. What does Paul counsel with regard to children and parents, slaves and masters, and the Christian's armor?
16. What questions find a practical answer in Ephesians, and what is said about the personality that is pleasing to God?
17. What does the letter show as to arrangements and cooperation in the congregation?
18. What is made plain with regard to the "sacred secret" and the spiritual temple?
19. What hope and encouragement does Ephesians continue to hold forth to this day?

whose hearts had been enlightened, that they might fully grasp the hope to which God had called them and see "what the glorious riches are which he holds as an inheritance for the holy ones." These words must have greatly encouraged them in their hope. And the inspired letter to the Ephesians continues to be upbuilding to the congregation in this day, that 'in everything it may be filled with all the fullness that God gives.'—Eph. 1:9-11, 18; 3:19.

Bible Book Number Fifty— Philippians

Writer:	**Paul**
Place Written:	**Rome**
Writing Completed:	**c. A.D. 60-61**
Time Covered:	**Undetermined**

WHEN the apostle Paul received the call in a vision to carry the good news into Macedonia, he and his companions, Luke, Silas and young Timothy, were quick to obey. From Troas in Asia Minor they traveled by ship to Neapolis and set out at once for Philippi, some eight miles inland over a mountain pass. The city is described by Luke as "the principal city of the district of Macedonia." (Acts 16:12) It was named Philippi after the Macedonian king Philip II (father of Alexander the Great), who captured the city 356 B.C.E. Later it was taken by the Romans. It was the site of decisive battles in 42 B.C.E. that helped to strengthen the position of Octavius, who later became Augustus Caesar. In commemoration of the victory he favored the Philippians with Roman citizenship.

2 It was Paul's custom on arrival in a new city to preach first to the Jews. However, on his first arrival in Philippi about A.D. 50 he found these few in number and apparently without a synagogue, for they used to meet for prayer on a riverbank outside the town. Paul's preaching quickly bore fruit, one of the first converts being Lydia, a businesswoman and Jewish proselyte who readily embraced the truth about the Christ and insisted that the travelers stay at her house. "She just made us come," writes Luke. Opposition was soon encountered, however, and Paul and Silas were beaten with rods and then imprisoned. While they were in the prison an earthquake occurred, and the jailer and his family, listening to Paul and Silas, became believers. The next day they were released from prison, and they visited and encouraged the brothers at the home of Lydia before leaving the city. Paul carried with him vivid memories of the tribulations surrounding the birth of the new congregation in Philippi.—Acts 16:9-40.

3 A few years later, in the course of his third missionary tour, Paul was able to visit the Philippian congregation again. Then, about ten years after first establishing the congregation, he was moved by a touching expression of their love to write them the inspired letter that has been preserved in the Holy Scriptures under the name of that beloved congregation.

4 That Paul did write the letter, as stated in its first verse, is generally accepted by Bible commentators, and with good reason. Polycarp in his own letter to the Philippians, dated about A.D. 107, refers to the fact that Paul had written to them. The letter is quoted as from Paul by such early Bible commentators as Ignatius, Irenaeus, Tertullian and Clement of Alexandria. It is cited in the Muratorian fragment of the second century and in all other early canons, and appears in the Chester Beatty Papyrus No. 2 of the early third century, side by side with eight others of Paul's letters.

5 The place and date of writing can be established with reasonable certainty. At the time, Paul was a prisoner in the custody of the Roman emperor's bodyguard, and there was a great deal of Christian activity going on around him. He closed his letter with greetings from the faithful in Caesar's household. These facts combine to point to Rome as the place from which the letter was sent.—Phil. 1:7, 13, 14; 4:22; Acts 28:30, 31.

6 But when was the letter written? It seems that Paul had already been in Rome long enough for the news of and reasons for his imprisonment as a Christian to spread right through the emperor's praetorian guard, and to

1. (a) How did the Philippians come to hear the good news? (b) What is of interest about the city of Philippi?
2. What progress did Paul make with his preaching in Philippi, and what events attended the birth of the congregation there?
3. What later contacts did Paul have with the Philippian congregation?
4. What identifies the writer, and what proves the authenticity of the letter?
5. What points to Rome as the place of writing?
6. What evidence is there for the time of writing?

many others. Also, there had been time for Epaphroditus to come from Philippi with a gift for Paul, for news of Epaphroditus' illness in Rome to get back to Philippi again, and for expressions of sorrow at this to come from Philippi to Rome. (Phil. 2:25-30; 4:18) Since Paul's first imprisonment in Rome was probably A.D. 59-61, he very likely wrote this letter A.D. 60 or 61, a year or more after his first arrival in Rome.

7 The birthpangs experienced in begetting these children at Philippi through the word of truth, their affection and generosity that followed Paul through many of his travels and hardships with gifts of needed things, and the fact that Jehovah had so signally blessed the initial missionary labors in Macedonia, all combined to forge a strong bond of mutual love between Paul and the Philippian brothers. Now their kind gift, followed by their anxious inquiry about Epaphroditus, and the progress of the good news in Rome, stirred Paul to write them a warm and affectionate letter of upbuilding encouragement.

CONTENTS OF PHILIPPIANS

8 **Defense and advancement of the good news** (1:1-30). Paul and Timothy send greetings, and Paul thanks God for the contribution the Philippians have made to the good news "from the first day until this moment." He is confident they will carry their good work to a completion, for they are sharers with him in the undeserved kindness, including "the defending and legally establishing of the good news." He yearns for all of them in tender affection and says: "This is what I continue praying, that your love may abound yet more and more . . . that you may make sure of the more important things." (1:5, 7, 9, 10) Paul wants them to know that his "affairs have turned out for the advancement of the good news," in that his prison bonds have become public knowledge and the brothers have been encouraged to speak the word of God fearlessly. While there is gain for Paul to die now, yet he knows that for the sake of their advancement and joy it is more necessary for him to remain. He counsels them to behave in a manner worthy of the good news, for, whether he comes to them or not, he wants to hear that they are fighting on in unity, and 'in no respect being frightened by their opponents.'—1:12, 28.

9 **Keeping the same mental attitude as Christ** (2:1-30). Paul encourages the Philippians to lowliness of mind, 'keeping an eye, not in personal interest upon just their own matters, but also in personal interest upon those of the others.' They should be of the same mental attitude as Christ Jesus, who, though existing in God's form, emptied himself to become a man and humbled himself in obedience as far as death, so that God has exalted him and given him a name above every other name. Paul exhorts them: "Keep working out your own salvation with fear and trembling." "Keep doing all things free from murmurings and arguments," and keep "a tight grip on the word of life." (2:4, 12, 14, 16) He hopes to send Timothy to them, and is confident that he himself will also come shortly. For the present, he is sending them Epaphroditus, who has recovered from his sickness, that they may rejoice again.

10 **"Pursuing down toward the goal"** (3:1–4:23). 'We of the real circumcision,' says Paul, 'must look out for the dogs, for those who mutilate the flesh.' If anyone has grounds for confidence in the flesh, Paul has more so, and his record as a circumcised Jew and a Pharisee proves it. Yet all of this he has considered loss 'on account of the excelling value of the knowledge of Christ Jesus his Lord.' Through the righteousness that is by faith he hopes to "attain to the earlier resurrection from the dead." (3:2, 3, 8, 11) Therefore, says Paul, "forgetting the things behind and stretching forward to the things ahead, I am pursuing down toward the goal for the prize of the upward call of God by means of Christ Jesus." Let as many as are mature have the same mental attitude. There are those whose god is their belly, who have their minds upon things on the earth, and whose end is destruction, but "as for us," Paul affirms, "our citizenship exists in the heavens." —3:13, 14, 20.

11 'Rejoice in the Lord,' Paul exhorts, 'and let your reasonableness become known to all men. Continue considering the things that are true and of serious concern, things that are righteous, chaste, lovable, well spoken of, virtuous and praiseworthy. Practice what you learned and accepted and heard and saw in connection with me, and the God of peace will be with you.' (4:4-9) Paul rejoices greatly in their generous thoughts toward him, though he has the strength for all things "by virtue of him who imparts power." He thanks them warmly for their gift. From the start of his declaring the good news in Macedonia, they have excelled in giving. In turn, God will fully

7. (a) What bond existed between Paul and the Philippians, and what stirred him to write? (b) What kind of letter is this?
8. (a) How does Paul express his confidence in and affection for the Philippian brothers? (b) What does Paul say about his prison bonds, and what counsel does he give?
9. How may the Philippians keep Christ's mental attitude?
10. How has Paul pursued toward the goal, and what does he admonish for others?
11. (a) What are the things to be considered and practiced? (b) What expression does Paul make with regard to the Philippians' generosity?

supply all their "need to the extent of his riches in glory by means of Christ Jesus." (4:13, 19) He sends greetings from all the holy ones, including those of the household of Caesar.

WHY BENEFICIAL

12 How beneficial the book of Philippians is for us! We certainly desire Jehovah's approval and the same kind of commendation from our Christian overseers that the congregation at Philippi received from Paul. This can be ours if we follow the fine example of the Philippians and the loving counsel of Paul. Like the Philippians, we should manifest generosity, be concerned to aid our brothers when in difficulty, and share in the defending and legally establishing of the good news. (Phil. 1:3-7) We should continue "standing firm in one spirit, with one soul fighting side by side for the faith of the good news," shining as "illuminators" in among a crooked and twisted generation. As we do these things and continue considering the things of serious concern, we may become a joy to our brothers in the same way that the Philippians became a crowning joy to the apostle Paul.—1:27; 2:15; 4:1, 8.

13 "Unitedly become imitators of me," says Paul. Imitate him in what way? One way is to be self-sufficient under all circumstances. Whether Paul had an abundance or was in want, he learned to adjust himself uncomplainingly to the circumstances, so as to continue zealously and with rejoicing in God's ministry. All should be like Paul, too, in showing tender affection for faithful brothers. With what affectionate joy he spoke of the ministry of Timothy and Epaphroditus! And how close he felt to his Philippian brothers, whom he addressed as "beloved and longed for, my joy and crown"!—Phil. 3:17; 4:1, 11, 12; 2:19-30.

14 How else may Paul be imitated? By "pursuing down toward the goal"! All who have set their minds on the 'things of serious concern' are vitally interested in Jehovah's marvelous arrangement in heaven and earth, wherein 'every tongue will openly acknowledge that Jesus Christ is Lord to the glory of God the Father.' The fine counsel in Philippians will encourage all who hope for eternal life in connection with God's kingdom to pursue that goal. The letter to the Philippians, however, is addressed primarily to those whose "citizenship exists in the heavens" and who eagerly await being "conformed to [Christ's] glorious body." "Forgetting the things behind and stretching forward to the things ahead," let all of these imitate the apostle Paul in "pursuing down toward the goal for the prize of the upward call," their glorious inheritance in the kingdom of the heavens!—Phil. 4:8; 2:10, 11; 3:13, 14, 20, 21.

12. How may we today, like the brothers at Philippi, gain God's approval and become a joy to our brothers?
13. In what ways may we unitedly imitate Paul?
14. What fine counsel does the letter to the Philippians give with regard to the goal of life and the Kingdom, and to whom especially is the letter addressed?

Bible Book Number Fifty-one— Colossians

Writer:	**Paul**
Place Written:	**Rome**
Writing Completed:	**c. A.D. 60-61**
Time Covered:	**Undetermined**

LEAVING Ephesus behind them, two men traveled east through Asia Minor along the Maeander (Menderes) River. On reaching the tributary called Lycus, in the country of Phrygia, they swung southeast to follow the river up through the mountain-enclosed valley. Before them was a beautiful sight: Fertile green pastures with large flocks of sheep. (Wool products were a principal source of income for the region.[a]) Proceeding up the valley, the travelers passed, on the right, the wealthy city of Laodicea, center of Roman administration for the district. To their left, across the river, they could see Hierapolis, famous for its temples, medicinal baths and gay entertainment. There were Christian congregations in both these cities, and also in the small town of Colossae, about ten miles farther up the valley.

2 Colossae was the destination of the travelers. They were both Christians. One of them, at least, knew the region well, as he was from Colossae. His name was Onesimus, and he was a slave returning to his master, who was a member of the congregation there. Onesimus'

a *The Westminster Bible Dictionary,* 1944, J. D. Davis, page 114.

1. Where was the town of Colossae located?
2. (a) Who were the two envoys sent by Paul to Colossae? (b) What is known concerning the Colossian congregation?

companion was Tychicus, a freeman, and both were envoys from the apostle Paul, carrying a letter from him addressed to the "faithful brothers in union with Christ at Colossae." As far as we know, Paul never visited Colossae. The congregation, which consisted mainly of non-Jews, was probably founded by Epaphras, who had labored among them and who was now with Paul in Rome.—Col. 1:2, 7; 4:12.

3 The apostle Paul was the writer of this letter, as he states in its opening and closing words. (Col. 1:1; 4:18) His conclusion states also that he wrote it from prison. This would be the time of his first imprisonment in Rome, A.D. 59-61, when he wrote a number of letters of encouragement, the letter to the Colossians being dispatched along with that to Philemon. (Col. 4:7-9; Philem. 10, 23) It appears it was written about the same time as the letter to the Ephesians, as many ideas and phrases are the same.

4 There are no grounds for doubting the authenticity of the letter to the Colossians. Its presence with other Pauline epistles in the Chester Beatty Papyrus No. 2 (originally a codex) of the third century shows that it was accepted by the early Christians as one of Paul's letters. Its genuineness is testified to by the same early authorities who also testify to the authenticity of Paul's other letters.

5 What prompted Paul to write a letter to the Colossians? For one thing Onesimus was going back to Colossae. Epaphras had recently joined Paul, and no doubt his report on conditions at Colossae provided a further reason for the letter. (Col. 1:7, 8; 4:12) A certain danger threatened the Christian congregation there. The religions of the day were in the process of dissolution, and new religions were constantly being formed by fusing parts of old ones. There were heathen philosophies involving asceticism, spiritism and doing penance, and these, combined with Jewish abstinence from foods and observance of days, may have influenced some in the congregation. Whatever the problem, it appears to have been sufficient reason for Epaphras' making the long journey to Rome to see Paul. However, that the congregation as a whole was not in immediate danger is indicated by Epaphras' encouraging report on their love and steadfastness. On hearing the report, Paul came strongly to the defense of accurate knowledge and clean worship by writing this letter to the Colossian congregation. It emphasized the God-given superiority of Christ in the face of heathen philosophy, worship of angels and Jewish traditions.

3. What does the letter itself reveal as to the writer, and the time and place of writing?
4. What testifies to the genuineness of the letter?
5. (a) What prompted Paul's writing to the Colossians? (b) What does the letter emphasize?

CONTENTS OF COLOSSIANS

6 **Have faith in Christ, the head of the congregation** (1:1-2:7). After the opening greetings from Timothy and himself, Paul gives thanks for the Colossians' faith in Christ and for their love. They have learned of the undeserved kindness of God as a result of Epaphras' preaching the good news among them. Since hearing the report concerning them Paul has not ceased praying that they may be filled with "the accurate knowledge of his will in all wisdom and spiritual discernment, in order to walk worthily of Jehovah" and "to endure fully and be long-suffering with joy." (1:9-11) The Father has delivered them into "the kingdom of the Son of his love," who is the image of the invisible God, and through whom and for whom all things have been created. He is the head of the congregation and the firstborn from the dead. Through his blood God saw good to reconcile all things again to himself, yes, including the once-alienated Colossians, 'provided, of course, that they continue in the faith.'—1:13, 23.

7 Paul rejoices to fill up the sufferings of the Christ on behalf of the congregation, whose minister he became. This was in order to preach fully on their behalf the word of God concerning 'the sacred secret, the glorious riches of which God has now been pleased to make known to his holy ones.' 'It is Christ we are publicizing,' says Paul, 'admonishing and teaching in all wisdom, that we may present every man complete in union with Christ.'—1:27, 28.

8 Paul's struggle on behalf of the Colossians, the Laodiceans and others is in order that they may be comforted and harmoniously joined together in love, with a view to their gaining 'an accurate knowledge of the sacred secret of God, namely, Christ, in whom are carefully concealed all the treasures of wisdom and of knowledge.' He does not want to see them deluded by persuasive arguments, but, rather, they should go on walking in union with Christ, "rooted and being built up in him and being stabilized in the faith."—2:2, 3, 7.

9 **Become dead to works of the flesh, but alive to Christ** (2:8-4:18). Paul now sounds a warning. "Look out: perhaps there may be someone who will carry you off as his prey through the philosophy and empty deception according to the tradition of men." Though they were dead in their trespasses and uncircumcision, God has made them alive together with Christ, blotting

6. (a) What prayer does Paul make on the Colossians' behalf? (b) What does Paul discuss as to Jesus' position and ministry in connection with the congregation?
7. What is Paul preaching, and for what purpose?
8. Why does Paul struggle on behalf of his brothers?
9. Against what kind of worship does Paul warn, and why should the Colossians not subject themselves to the Law?

out the handwritten document of the Law, which was against the Jews. "Therefore let no man judge" them with respect to the Law or its observances, which are but a shadow of the reality, Christ. Also, if they have died together with Christ toward the elementary things of the world, why do they subject themselves to the decrees: "Do not handle, nor taste, nor touch," according to the commands and teachings of men? A showy self-imposed form of worship, mock humility, severe treatment of the body—these are of no value in combating desires of the flesh.—2:8, 16, 21.

10 Rather, Paul counsels: "Go on seeking the things above, where the Christ is seated at the right hand of God. Keep your minds fixed on the things above, not on the things upon the earth." This can be done by stripping off the old personality and putting on the new personality, which through accurate knowledge makes no fleshly distinction between Jew and Greek, "but Christ is all things and in all." It means becoming clothed "as God's chosen ones" with the tender affections of compassion, kindness, lowliness of mind, mildness and long-suffering. Says the apostle: "As Jehovah freely forgave you, so do you also. But, besides all these things, clothe yourselves with love, for it is a perfect bond of union." In word or in work, everything should be done "in the name of the Lord Jesus, thanking God the Father through him."—3:1, 2, 11-14, 17.

11 As to family relationships, let wives be subject to husbands and let husbands love their wives, let children obey parents and let not fathers exasperate their children. Slaves are to be obedient to their masters in fear of Jehovah, and masters are to deal righteously with their slaves. Let all persevere in prayer and go on walking in wisdom toward those on the outside. Tychicus and Onesimus will relate to them personally the things concerning Paul and his fellow workers for the kingdom of God. They send greetings to Colossae, and Paul also greets the brothers at Laodicea, asking that they exchange the letters he is sending. Paul writes a concluding greeting in his own hand: "Continue bearing my prison bonds in mind. The undeserved kindness be with you."—4:18.

WHY BENEFICIAL

12 We can imagine how quickly the news of the arrival of the two brothers from Rome circulated among the brothers at Colossae. With keen anticipation they would assemble, possibly at Philemon's house, to hear the reading of Paul's letter. (Philem. 2) What refreshing truths it provided on the exact position of Christ and the need for accurate knowledge! How clearly were philosophies of men and Jewish traditions put in their place, and the peace and the word of the Christ exalted! Here was nourishment for mind and heart for all in the congregation—overseers, husbands, wives, fathers, children, masters, slaves. Certainly there was good advice for Philemon and Onesimus as they entered once again into the relation of master and slave. What a fine lead to the overseers in restoring the flock to right doctrine and a sharp appreciation of their privilege of working whole-souled as to Jehovah! And the upbuilding counsel to the Colossians on getting free from the enslaving thoughts and practices of the world remains as a living message for the congregation today. —Col. 1:9-11, 17, 18; 2:8; 3:15, 16, 18-25; 4:1.

13 Excellent advice for the Christian minister is set out at Colossians 4:6: "Let your utterance be always with graciousness, seasoned with salt, so as to know how you ought to give an answer to each one." Gracious words of truth will prove appetizing to men of goodwill, and work to their permanent benefit. Also, the wide-awake prayer of the Christian, expressed from an appreciative heart, will bring rich blessings from Jehovah: "Be persevering in prayer, remaining awake in it with thanksgiving." And what joy and upbuilding refreshment is to be found in Christian association! "Keep on teaching and admonishing one another," says Paul, "singing in your hearts to Jehovah." (Col. 4:2; 3:16) You will find many other gems of sound, practical instruction as you search through the letter to the Colossians.

14 Concerning the observances of the Law, the letter says: "Those things are a shadow of the things to come, but the reality belongs to the Christ." (Col. 2:17) It is this reality of the Christ that is highlighted in Colossians. The letter refers frequently to the glorious hope reserved in the heavens for those in union with Christ. (Col. 1:5, 27; 3:4) Such ones can be most thankful that the Father has already delivered them from the authority of the darkness and transplanted them "into the kingdom of the Son of his love." Thus they have become subject to the One who is "the image of the invisible God, the first-born of all creation; because by means of him all other things were created in the heavens and upon the earth, the things visible and the things invisible, no matter whether they are thrones or lordships or

---

10. How may one keep seeking the things above and be clothed with the "new personality"?
11. (a) What counsel is given concerning family and other relations? (b) What greetings are conveyed in conclusion?
12. What refreshing truths did Paul's letter provide? With what benefit to the congregation?
13. What does Paul admonish with regard to gracious words, prayer and Christian association?
14. (a) What reality is highlighted in Colossians? (b) How is the Kingdom hope emphasized?

governments or authorities." This One is eminently qualified to rule in righteousness in the kingdom of God. Thus it is that Paul admonishes the anointed Christians: "If, however, you were raised up with the Christ, go on seeking the things above, where the Christ is seated at the right hand of God."—Col. 1:12-16; 3:1.

Bible Book Number Fifty-two— 1 Thessalonians

Writer:	**Paul**
Place Written:	**Corinth**
Writing Completed:	**c. A.D. 50**
Time Covered:	**Undetermined**

IT WAS about the year 50 (A.D.), while on his second preaching tour, that the apostle Paul visited the Macedonian city of Thessalonica and there established the Christian congregation of Thessalonians. Within a year, while in Corinth accompanied by Silvanus (Silas of the book of Acts) and Timothy, Paul was moved to write his first letter to the Thessalonians to comfort them and build them up in the faith. It was late A.D. 50 or early A.D. 51. This letter apparently enjoys the distinction of being the first of Paul's writings to become part of the Bible canon, and, with the probable exception of Matthew's Gospel, the first book of the Christian Greek Scriptures to be put into writing.

2 The evidence supporting the letter's authenticity and integrity is overwhelming. Paul identifies himself by name as the writer, and the book is internally harmonious with the rest of the inspired Word. (1 Thess. 1:1; 2:18) The epistle is mentioned by name in many of the earliest catalogues of the inspired Scriptures, including the Muratorian fragment.[a] The book is either quoted or alluded to by many of the early church writers, including Irenaeus (c. A.D. 170), who mentions it by name. The Chester Beatty Papyrus No. 2, of the early third century, contains First Thessalonians, and another papyrus of the third century (P^{30}), now in Ghent, France, contains fragments of both First and Second Thessalonians.[b]

3 A glance at the brief history of the congregation at Thessalonica, prior to the writing of this letter, establishes the background for Paul's deep concern for the brothers in that city. From the very beginning the congregation underwent severe persecution and opposition. At Acts chapter 17, Luke reports the arrival of Paul and Silas at Thessalonica, "where there was a synagogue of the Jews." For three sabbaths he preached to them, reasoning with them from the Scriptures, and there are indications that he stayed there even longer than this, for he had time to set himself up in his trade and, above all, to establish and organize a congregation.—1 Thess. 2:9; 1:6, 7.

4 The record in Acts 17:4-7 graphically relates the effect of the apostle's preaching in Thessalonica. Jealous about the success of Paul's Christian ministry, the Jews organized a mob and threw the city into an uproar. They assaulted Jason's house and dragged him and other brothers to the city rulers, crying out: "These men that have overturned the inhabited earth are present here also, and Jason has received them with hospitality. And all these men act in opposition to the decrees of Caesar, saying there is another king, Jesus." Jason and the others were compelled to provide bond before they were released. For the sake of the brothers in the congregation, as well as for their own personal safety, Paul and Silas were dispatched by night to Beroea. But the congregation at Thessalonica was now established.

5 Fiery opposition from the Jews pursued Paul to Beroea and threatened to stop his preaching there. He then moved on to Athens, in Greece. Still he longed to know how his brothers in Thessalonica were faring under tribulation. Twice he attempted to return to them, but each time 'Satan cut across his path.' (1 Thess. 2:17, 18) Filled with concern for the young congregation, and painfully aware of the tribulation they were undergoing, Paul sent Timothy back to Thessalonica to comfort the brothers and make them more firm in the faith.

a See chart, "Early Catalogues of the Christian Greek Scriptures," page 302.
b *Light from the Ancient Past*, 1946, J. Finegan, page 339.

1. (a) How did First Thessalonians come to be written? (b) When was this, and what distinction does the letter thus enjoy?
2. What evidence is there for the writership and authenticity of the letter?
3, 4. What resulted from the early success of Paul's ministry at Thessalonica?
5. How did Paul show his concern for and loving interest in the Thessalonian congregation?

When Timothy returned with his heartwarming report, Paul was overjoyed with the news of their stalwart integrity amid violent persecution. Their record by now had become an example to believers throughout all Macedonia and Achaia. (1 Thess. 1:6-8; 3:1-7) Paul was thankful to Jehovah God for their faithful endurance, but he also realized that as they continued to grow to maturity, they needed further guidance and counsel. Therefore, while in the company of Timothy and Silvanus, Paul wrote his first letter to the Thessalonians from Corinth.

CONTENTS OF FIRST THESSALONIANS

6 **Thessalonians an example to other believers** (1:1-10). Paul begins his letter to the Thessalonians with warm commendation of their faithful work, loving labor and endurance in hope. The good news preached among them had not been with speech alone, but 'also with power and strong conviction.' Imitating the example given them, they had accepted the word "with joy of holy spirit," and had themselves become an example to all the believers in Macedonia and in Achaia, and even beyond. They had turned completely from their idols, "to slave for a living and true God, and to wait for his Son from the heavens."—1:5, 6, 9, 10.

7 **Paul's loving concern for the Thessalonians** (2:1–3:13). After insolent treatment in Philippi, Paul and his companions had mustered up boldness to preach to the Thessalonians. This they had done, not as men pleasers, nor as flatterers, nor as seeking glory from men, but, to the contrary, says Paul, "we became gentle in the midst of you, as when a nursing mother cherishes her own children. So, having a tender affection for you, we were well pleased to impart to you, not only the good news of God, but also our own souls, because you became beloved to us." (2:7, 8) They kept exhorting them, as a father does his children, to go on walking worthily of God, who is calling them to his kingdom and glory.

8 Paul commends them for their ready acceptance of the good news for what it is, "the word of God." They are not alone in being persecuted by their own countrymen, for the first believers in Judea suffered similar persecutions at the hands of the Jews. Anxious about their welfare, Paul, on two occasions, wanted to come to them in person, but was thwarted by Satan. To Paul and his co-workers the Thessalonian brothers are a crown of exultation, their 'glory and joy.' (2:13, 20) When he could no longer bear the lack of news concerning them, Paul sent Timothy to Thessalonica to make firm their faith and to comfort them. Now Timothy has just returned with the good news of their spiritual prosperity and love, and this has brought comfort and joy to the apostle. Paul gives thanks to God, and prays that the Lord may give them increase, that they may abound in love to one another and that their hearts may be "unblamable in holiness" before God the Father at the presence of the Lord Jesus.—3:13.

9 **Serving in sanctification and honor** (4:1-12). Paul commends the Thessalonians for walking so as to please God, and exhorts them to keep on doing it more fully. Each one "should know how to get possession of his own vessel in sanctification and honor, not in covetous sexual appetite." In this, no one should encroach upon his brother's rights. For God called them, "not with allowance for uncleanness, but in connection with sanctification. So, then, the man that shows disregard is disregarding, not man, but God." (4:4, 5, 7, 8) Paul commends them because they are showing love one to another, and exhorts them to keep doing this in fuller measure, making it their aim to live quietly and to mind their own business and work with their hands. For they must walk decently "as regards people outside."—4:12.

10 **The resurrection hope** (4:13-18). With regard to those sleeping in death, the brothers must not sorrow as do those who have no hope. If they have faith that Jesus rose again, so, too, God through Jesus will raise those who have fallen asleep in death. At the presence of the Lord he will descend from heaven with a commanding call, "and those who are dead in union with Christ will rise first." Afterward, those surviving will "be caught away in clouds to meet the Lord in the air," to be always with the Lord.—4:16, 17.

11 **Keeping awake as Jehovah's day approaches** (5:1-28). "Jehovah's day is coming exactly as a thief in the night." It is when people are saying "Peace and security!" that sudden destruction will be instantly upon them. Let the Thessalonians, therefore, stay awake, as "sons of light and sons of day," keeping their senses and having "on the breastplate of faith and love and as a helmet the hope of salvation." (5:2, 3, 5, 8) This is a time for them to keep comforting and building one another up. Let all give "more than extraordinary consideration in love" to those working hard and presid-

6. For what does Paul commend the Thessalonians?
7. What attitude had Paul and his companions displayed while among the Thessalonians, and to what had they exhorted them?
8. How have they become an exultation to Paul, and what does he pray on their behalf?
9. What does Paul exhort concerning sanctification and love one to another?
10. What attitude should the brothers have with regard to those who have fallen asleep in death?
11. Why should the Thessalonians stay awake, and what should they keep doing?

ng among them. On the other hand, the disorderly must be admonished, the weak built up, and long-suffering shown to all. Yes, writes Paul, "always pursue what is good toward one another and to all others."—5:13, 15.

12 Finally, Paul counsels on a number of vital matters: 'Always be rejoicing. Pray incessantly, giving thanks for everything. Maintain the fire of the spirit. Have respect for prophesyings. Make sure of all things and hold fast what is fine. Abstain from every form of wickedness.' (5:16-22) Then he prays for the very God of peace to sanctify them completely and that they may remain blameless in spirit, soul and body at the presence of the Lord Jesus Christ. He closes the letter with warm words of encouragement and solemn instruction that the letter be read to all the brothers.

WHY BENEFICIAL

13 In this letter Paul demonstrated a spirit of loving concern for his brothers. He and his fellow ministers had set a noble example of tender affection, imparting not only the good news of God, but even their own souls, in behalf of their beloved brothers in Thessalonica. Let all overseers endeavor to forge such ties of love with their congregations! Such expression of love will incite all to show love for one another, even as Paul said: "Moreover, may the Lord cause you to increase, yes, make you abound, in love to one another and to all, even as we also do to you." This love expressed willingly among all of God's people is most upbuilding. It makes hearts "firm, unblamable in holiness before our God and Father at the presence of our Lord Jesus with all his holy ones." It sets Christians apart from a corrupt and immoral world, to walk in holiness and sanctification, and so please God.—1 Thess. 3:12, 13; 2:8; 4:1-8.

14 This letter provides an excellent model of tactful, loving counsel in the Christian congregation. Zealous and faithful as were the Thessalonian brothers, there were points of correction to make. However, in each case Paul commends the brothers on their good qualities. For example, in warning against moral uncleanness, he first commends them on walking so as to please God, and then urges them to do it "more fully," each one keeping his vessel in sanctification and honor. Then, after commending them on their brotherly love, he exhorts them to continue in this way "in fuller measure," minding their own business and living decent lives before those on the outside. Tactfully Paul directs his brothers to "pursue what is good toward one another and to all others."—1 Thess. 4:1-7, 9-12; 5:15.

15 On four occasions Paul makes mention of the "presence" of Jesus Christ. Apparently the newly converted Christians at Thessalonica were very much interested in this teaching. While in their city Paul had no doubt preached boldly concerning Jesus' kingdom, as indicated by the accusation brought against him and his companions: "All these men act in opposition to the decrees of Caesar, saying there is another king, Jesus." (Acts 17:7; 1 Thess. 2:19; 3:13; 4:15; 5:23) The Thessalonian brothers had set their hope on the Kingdom and, having faith toward God, were waiting "for his Son from the heavens, whom he raised up from the dead, namely, Jesus," to deliver them from the wrath to come. Likewise, all who hope in God's kingdom today need to heed the fine counsel of First Thessalonians to abound in love, with hearts firm and unblamable, so that they may 'go on walking worthily of God who is calling them to his kingdom and glory.'—1 Thess. 1:8, 10; 3:12, 13; 2:12.

12. On what vital matters does Paul finally give counsel, and how does he close his letter?
13. In what were Paul and his companions a noble example, and what effect does the willing expression of love have in the congregation?
14. In what way is this letter an excellent example of tactful, loving counsel?
15. What indicates that Paul zealously preached the Kingdom hope while at Thessalonica, and what fine counsel did he give in this connection?

Bible Book Number Fifty-three—2 Thessalonians

Writer:	**Paul**
Place Written:	**Corinth**
Writing Completed:	**c. A.D. 51**
Time Covered:	**Undetermined**

THE apostle Paul's second letter to the Thessalonians followed closely on the first one. That it was written shortly after the first letter, and also from the same city of Corinth, is indicated by the fact that the same brothers, Silvanus and Timothy, again join with Paul in greeting the congregation at Thessalonica. They were all traveling servants of the early Christian congregation, and there is no record that all three came together again after this association in Corinth. (2 Thess. 1:1; Acts 18: 5, 18) The subject matter and nature of the discussion indicate that Paul felt an urgent need to correct the congregation promptly with regard to an error into which it had fallen.

2 The letter's authenticity is just as well attested as in the case of First Thessalonians. It is also quoted by Irenaeus as well as other early writers, including Justin Martyr (about A.D. 140), who apparently refers to 2 Thessalonians 2:3 when writing of "the man of lawlessness [sin]." It appears in the same early catalogues as First Thessalonians. Though it is now missing from the Chester Beatty Papyrus No. 2, it was almost certainly contained in the first two of seven leaves that are missing after First Thessalonians.

3 What was the purpose of this letter? From the counsel that Paul offered the Thessalonians, we learn that some in the congregation were contending that the presence of the Lord was imminent, that these speculators were actively preaching this theory of theirs, and that they were creating no little stir in the congregation. It appears that some were even using this as an excuse for not working to provide for themselves. (2 Thess. 3:11) In his first letter Paul had made references to the presence of the Lord, and, doubtless, when these speculators heard the letter read, they were quick to seize on it to support their theories, twisting Paul's words and reading into them meanings that were never intended.

4 It seems that Paul had received a report on this condition, probably from the person who delivered his first letter to the congregation, and he would therefore be very anxious to correct the thinking of his brothers for whom he had such great affection. So in the year 51 (A.D.) Paul, in association with his two companions, sent a letter from Corinth to the congregation in Thessalonica. In addition to correcting the wrong viewpoint on Christ's presence, Paul gives warm encouragement to stand firm in the truth.

1. What indicates the time and place of writing, and what prompted the second letter to the Thessalonians?
2. What attests the authenticity of this letter?
3, 4. (a) What problem had arisen in the Thessalonian congregation? (b) When and where was the letter written, and what did Paul seek to accomplish by it?

CONTENTS OF SECOND THESSALONIANS

5 **The revelation of the Lord Jesus** (1:1-12). Paul and his companions thank God on account of the fine growth of the Thessalonians' faith and their love toward one another. Their endurance and faith under persecutions are proof of God's righteous judgment that they are counted worthy of the Kingdom. God will repay tribulation to those who make it for the congregation, and give relief to those who suffer. This will be "at the revelation of the Lord Jesus from heaven with his powerful angels . . . at the time he comes to be glorified in connection with his holy ones." (1:7, 10) Paul and his companions always pray for the Thessalonians, that God may count them worthy of His calling, and that the name of the Lord Jesus may be glorified in them and they in union with him.

6 **Apostasy to come before Jesus' presence** (2:1-12). The brothers should not become excited by any message that the day of Jehovah is here. "It will not come unless the apostasy comes first and the man of lawlessness gets revealed, the son of destruction." They know now "the thing that acts as a restraint," but the mystery of this lawlessness is already at work. When this restraint is removed, "then, indeed, the lawless one will be revealed, whom the Lord Jesus will do away with by the spirit of his mouth and bring to nothing by the manifestation of his presence." The lawless one's presence is according to the operation of Satan with powerful works and deception, and God is permitting an operation of error to go to those who did not accept the love of the truth, that they may get to believe the lie.—2:3, 6, 8.

5. For what do Paul and his companions thank God, what assurance do they give, and what do they pray?
6. What must come before the day of Jehovah, and how?

7 **Stand firm in faith** (2:13–3:18). Paul continues: "We are obligated to thank God always for you, brothers loved by Jehovah, because God selected you from the beginning for salvation by sanctifying you with spirit and by your faith in the truth." To this end the good news was declared to them. The brothers should therefore stand firm and maintain their hold on the traditions they were taught, that Jesus Christ and the Father, who lovingly gave everlasting comfort and hope, may make them "firm in every good deed and word." (2:13, 17) Paul asks for their prayers, "that the word of Jehovah may keep moving speedily and being glorified." (3:1) The Lord, who is faithful, will make them firm and keep them from the wicked one, and it is Paul's prayer that the Lord continue directing their hearts successfully into love of God and into endurance for the Christ.

8 Strong admonition follows: "Now we are giving you orders, brothers, in the name of the Lord Jesus Christ, to withdraw from every brother walking disorderly and not according to the tradition you received from us." (3:6) The apostle reminds them of the example his missionary group gave, laboring night and day so as not to become an expense to them, so that they were able to give the order: "If anyone does not want to work, neither let him eat." But now they hear that certain disorderly ones are not working and are meddlers. These should get to earning their own food.—2 Thess. 3:10; 1 Thess. 4:11.

9 The brothers should not give up in doing right. But if anyone is not obedient to Paul's letter, the congregation should shame him by no longer associating with him, at the same time admonishing him as a brother. Paul expresses the prayer that the Lord of peace may give them "peace constantly in every way," and concludes his letter with greetings in his own hand.—2 Thess. 3:16.

7. How may they stand firm and find protection from the wicked one?
8. What strong admonition is given, and wherein have Paul and his group set the example?
9. What does Paul say about doing right and shaming the disobedient, and how does he end his letter?

WHY BENEFICIAL

10 This short inspired letter to the Thessalonians touches on a vast array of Christian truth, all of which is beneficial for consideration. Consider the following basic teachings and principles that are called to attention: Jehovah is the God of salvation, and he sanctifies by spirit and faith in the truth (2:13); the Christian must endure suffering to be counted worthy of the kingdom of God (1:4, 5); Christians are gathered together to the Lord Jesus Christ at his appearing (2:1); Jehovah will bring righteous judgment on those who disobey the good news (1:5-8); those called will be glorified in union with Christ Jesus, in accordance with God's undeserved kindness (1:12); they are called through the preaching of the good news (2:14); faith is a vital requirement (1:3, 4, 10, 11; 2:13; 3:2); it is proper to work in order to provide for oneself in the ministry; otherwise a person may become lazy and start to meddle in things that do not concern him (3:8-12); the love of God is associated with endurance (3:5). What a treasure of upbuilding information can be found in one short inspired letter!

11 In this letter Paul showed deep concern for the spiritual welfare of his brothers in Thessalonica and for the unity and prosperity of the congregation. He set them right on the timing of the Lord's return, showing that "the man of lawlessness" must first appear, to sit down in "the temple of The God, publicly showing himself to be a god." However, those "counted worthy of the kingdom of God" may have absolute assurance that the Lord Jesus will in due course be revealed from heaven, taking vengeance in flaming fire "at the time he comes to be glorified in connection with his holy ones and to be regarded in that day with wonder in connection with all those who exercised faith."—2:3, 4; 1:5, 10.

10. What are some of the basic teachings and principles covered in Second Thessalonians?
11. What important information and assurance are presented in connection with the Kingdom?

Bible Book Number Fifty-four— 1 Timothy

Writer:	**Paul**
Place Written:	**Macedonia**
Writing Completed:	**c. A.D. 61-64**
Time Covered:	**Undetermined**

LUKE'S account of Paul's life in the book of Acts ends with Paul in Rome awaiting the outcome of his appeal to Caesar. He is shown as dwelling in his own hired house, preaching the kingdom of God to all who came to him, and doing so "with the greatest freeness of speech, without hindrance." (Acts 28:30, 31) But in his second letter to Timothy Paul writes: "I am suffering evil to the point of prison bonds as an evildoer," and speaks of his death as imminent. (2 Tim. 2:9; 4:6-8) What a change! In the first instance he was treated as an honorable prisoner, in the second, as a felon. What had happened in between Luke's comment on Paul's situation A.D. 61 at the end of two years in Rome and Paul's own writing of his condition to Timothy, which appears to have been written shortly before his death?

2 The difficulty of fitting the writing of Paul's letters to Timothy and Titus into the period covered by the book of Acts has led reputable Bible commentators to the conclusion that Paul was successful in his appeal to Caesar and was released about A.D. 61. *The Encyclopedia Americana* comments that this is "the natural inference," and then states: "After his release (61 A.D.) Paul appears to have undertaken another missionary journey, possibly to Spain (Rom. 15:24, also the tradition in Clem. Rom.) He afterward revisited the East and while there (according to what seems the most probable theory) wrote 1 Timothy and Titus. Again arrested, he was brought to Rome for a second trial. Before this took place he wrote a letter to Timothy (2 Timothy) beseeching him to come to him as soon as possible. It was probably about 64 or 65 that the great Apostle was executed by command of Nero."[a] (Some authorities put his death as late as A.D. 67.) It is, then, to the period between his release from his first imprisonment A.D. 61 and when he was rearrested and imprisoned in Rome again A.D. 64 that the writing of First Timothy belongs.

a 1956, Vol. 24, page 160.

1, 2. (a) What contrast is seen between the descriptions of Paul's imprisonment in Acts and Second Timothy? (b) What events appear to have marked Paul's last years, and hence when does it appear that First Timothy was written?

3 It is thought that on his release Paul went first westward to Spain and then returned to the Aegean area for further missionary activity before his being martyred in Rome. Clement of Rome wrote (c. A.D. 90-100) that Paul preached "both in the East and West, . . . taught righteousness to the whole world and came to the extreme limit of the West." This expression "limit of the West" is understood to refer to Spain and the Atlantic seacoast.[b]

4 From where did Paul write his first letter to Timothy? First Timothy 1:3 indicates that Paul arranged for Timothy to attend to certain congregational matters in Ephesus while he himself went his way to Macedonia. From here, it appears, he wrote the letter back to Timothy in Ephesus.

5 The two letters to Timothy have been accepted from the earliest times as written by Paul and as being part of the inspired Scriptures. The early Christian writers, including Polycarp, Ignatius and Clement of Rome, all agree on this, and the letters are included in the catalogues of the first few centuries as Paul's writings. One authority writes: "There are few New Testament writings which have stronger attestation, . . . Objection to authenticity must therefore be regarded as modern innovations contrary to the strong evidence of the early church."[c]

6 Paul wrote this first letter to Timothy to set out clearly certain organizational procedures in the congregation. There was also a need for him to warn Timothy to be on guard against false teachings and to strengthen the brothers to resist such 'false knowledge.' The commercial city of Ephesus would also provide the temptations of materialism and "love of money," and so it would be timely to give some advice on this also. Timothy certainly had a

b *The New Schaff-Herzog Encyclopedia of Religious Knowledge,* 1956, Vol. VIII, page 404.
c *The New Bible Dictionary,* 1962, edited by J. D. Douglas, page 1282.

3, 4. (a) What areas were probably covered in Paul's later missionary activity? (b) From where did he write First Timothy?
5. What testimony is there to the authenticity of the letters to Timothy?
6. (a) For what several reasons did Paul write First Timothy? (b) What was Timothy's background, and what indicates him to have been a mature worker?

fine background of experience and training to be used for this work. He was born of a Greek father and a God-fearing Jewish mother, and his first contact with Christianity was about A.D. 47 or 48. He was probably in his early teens when Paul and Barnabas called on his mother in the course of Paul's first missionary tour. Later, when Paul visited Lystra on his second missionary tour, he found that Timothy was well reported on; so he arranged for Timothy to travel with Silas and himself. (Acts 16:1-3) He is mentioned by name in eleven of Paul's fourteen letters as well as in the Acts of the Apostles. Paul always took a fatherly interest in him and on several occasions assigned him to visit and serve different congregations—an evidence he had done good work in the missionary field and had progressed on to maturity.—1 Tim. 1:2; 5:23; 6:20; 1 Thess. 3:2; Phil. 2:19.

CONTENTS OF FIRST TIMOTHY

7 **Exhortation to faith with a good conscience** (1:1-20). After greeting Timothy as "a genuine child in the faith," Paul encourages him to remain in Ephesus. He is to correct those teaching a "different doctrine," which is leading to useless questions rather than to a dispensing of faith. Paul says the objective of this mandate is "love out of a clean heart and out of a good conscience and out of faith without hypocrisy," and adds: "By deviating from these things certain ones have been turned aside into idle talk."—1:2, 3, 5, 6.

8 Though Paul was formerly a blasphemer and a persecutor, nevertheless, the undeserved kindness of the Lord "abounded exceedingly along with faith and love that is in connection with Christ Jesus," so that he was shown mercy. He had been the foremost of sinners, and so he became a demonstration of the long-suffering of Christ Jesus, who "came into the world to save sinners." How worthy is the King of eternity to receive honor and glory forever! Paul charges Timothy to wage a fine warfare, "holding faith and a good conscience." He must not be like those who have made shipwreck of the faith, such as Hymenaeus and Alexander, whom Paul has disciplined on account of blasphemy.—1:14, 15, 19.

9 **Counsel on worship and organization in the congregation** (2:1–6:2). Prayers are to be made concerning all sorts of men, including those in high station, to the end that Christians may live peaceably in godly devotion. It is the will of God, the Savior, that "all sorts of men should be saved and come to an accurate knowledge of truth. For there is one God, and one mediator between God and men, a man Christ Jesus, who gave himself a corresponding ransom for all." (2:4-6) Paul was appointed an apostle and teacher of these things. So he calls on the men to pray in loyalty, and the women to dress modestly and sensibly, as befits those who reverence God. A woman must learn in silence and not exercise authority over a man, "for Adam was formed first, then Eve."—2:13.

10 The man who reaches out to be an overseer is desirous of a fine work. Paul then lists the qualifications for overseers and ministerial servants. An overseer must be "irreprehensible, a husband of one wife, moderate in habits, sound in mind, orderly, hospitable, qualified to teach, not a drunken brawler, not a smiter, but reasonable, not belligerent, not a lover of money, a man presiding over his own household in a fine manner, having children in subjection with all seriousness; . . . not a newly converted man, . . . he should also have a fine testimony from people on the outside." (3:2-7) There are similar requirements for ministerial servants, and they should be tested as to their suitability before serving. Paul writes these things in order that Timothy may know how he ought to conduct himself in the congregation of God, which is "a pillar and support of the truth."—3:15.

11 In later times some will fall away from the faith, through the teachings of demons. Hypocritical men speaking lies will forbid marriage and command to abstain from foods that God created to be partaken of with thanksgiving. As a fine minister, Timothy must turn down false stories and 'old women's tales.' On the other hand, he should be training himself with godly devotion as his aim. "To this end we are working hard and exerting ourselves," says Paul, "because we have rested our hope on a living God, who is a Savior of all sorts of men, especially of faithful ones." Therefore Timothy must keep on giving these commands and teaching them. He is to let no man look down on his youth, but, to the contrary, become an example in conduct and godly service. He is to be absorbed in these things, and to pay constant attention to himself and to his teaching, for in staying by these things he will 'save both himself and those listening to him.'—4:7, 10, 16.

12 Paul counsels Timothy on how to deal with individuals: older men as fathers, younger men

7. Why is Paul encouraging Timothy to stay in Ephesus?
8. What did Paul's being shown mercy emphasize, and what fine warfare does he encourage Timothy to wage?
9. (a) What prayers are to be made, and why? (b) What is said as to women in the congregation?
10. What are the qualifications for overseers and ministerial servants, and why does Paul write these things?
11. (a) What errors will appear later? (b) To what should Timothy give attention, and why?
12. What counsel is given as to dealing with widows and others in the congregation?

as brothers; older women as mothers, younger women as sisters. Suitable provision is to be made for those who are really widows. However, a widow's family should care for her if possible. To fail in this would be to disown the faith. When at least sixty years of age a widow may be put on the list if there is witness borne to her for fine works. On the other hand, younger widows, who let their sexual impulses control them, should be turned down. Rather than gadding about and gossiping, let them marry and bear children, so as to give no inducement to the opposer.

13 The older men who preside in a fine way should be reckoned worthy of double honor, "especially those who work hard in speaking and teaching." (5:17) An accusation is not to be admitted against an older man, except on the evidence of two or three witnesses. Persons who practice sin are to be reproved before all onlookers, but there is to be no prejudgment or bias in these things. Let slaves respect their owners, giving good service, and especially to brothers, who are "believers and beloved." —6:2.

14 **On "godly devotion along with self-sufficiency"** (6:3-21). The man that does not assent to healthful words is puffed up with pride, and his mental disease leads to violent disputes over trifles. On the other hand, "godly devotion along with self-sufficiency" is a means of great gain. One should be content with sustenance and covering. The determination to be rich is a snare leading to destruction, and the love of money is "a root of all sorts of injurious things." Paul urges Timothy, as a man of God, to flee these things, to pursue Christian virtues, to fight the fine fight of the faith and to "get a firm hold on the everlasting life." (6:6, 10, 12) He must observe the commandment "in a spotless and irreprehensible way" until the manifestation of the Lord Jesus Christ. Those who are rich should "rest their hope, not on uncertain riches, but on God," in order to get a firm hold on the real life. Paul, in closing, encourages Timothy to guard his doctrinal trust and to turn away from defiling speeches and from "the contradictions of the falsely called 'knowledge.'"—6:14, 17, 20.

WHY BENEFICIAL

15 This letter provides a stern warning for those who dabble in vain speculations and philosophical arguments. "Debates about words" are allied to pride and mental disease, and are to be avoided, for Paul tells us that they obstruct Christian growth, furnishing only "questions for research rather than a dispensing of anything by God in connection with faith." (1 Tim. 6:3-6; 1:4) Along with the works of the flesh, these disputings are "in opposition to the healthful teaching according to the glorious good news of the happy God."—1 Tim. 1:10, 11.

16 The Christians in money-greedy Ephesus apparently needed counsel on fighting materialism and its distractions. Paul gave that counsel. The world has freely quoted him in saying, 'The love of money is the root of all evil,' but how few pay heed to his words! To the contrary, true Christians need to heed this advice all the time. It means life to them. They need to flee from the hurtful snare of materialism, resting their hope, "not on uncertain riches, but on God, who furnishes us all things richly for our enjoyment."—1 Tim. 6:6-12, 17-19.

17 Paul's letter shows that Timothy himself was a fine example of what a young Christian should be. Though young in years, he was mature in spiritual growth. He had reached out to qualify as an overseer, and was richly blessed in the privileges he enjoyed. But like all zealous young ministers today, he needed to keep pondering over these things and to be absorbed in them, so as to make continued advancement. Timely is Paul's advice to all who seek continued joy in making Christian progress: "Pay constant attention to yourself and to your teaching. Stay by these things, for by doing this you will save both yourself and those who listen to you."—1 Tim. 4:15, 16.

18 This inspired letter instills appreciation of God's orderly arrangements. It shows how both men and women may do their part in maintaining theocratic harmony in the congregation. (1 Tim. 2:8-15) Then it goes on to discuss the qualifications for overseers and ministerial servants. Thus holy spirit indicates the requirements to be met by those who serve in special capacities. It also encourages all dedicated ministers to meet these standards, saying: "If any man is reaching out for an office of overseer, he is desirous of a fine work." (1 Tim. 3:1-13) The overseer's proper attitude toward the age-groups and sexes in the congregation is appropriately discussed, also the handling of accusations before witnesses. In emphasizing that the older men who work hard in speaking and teaching are worthy of double honor, Paul calls twice on the Hebrew Scriptures as authority: "For the scripture says: 'You must not

13. What consideration should be shown to older men, how are persons who practice sin to be handled, and what responsibility falls upon slaves?
14. What does Paul have to say about pride and love of money in connection with "godly devotion with self-sufficiency"?
15. What warning is given against speculations and arguments?
16. What counsel did Paul give on materialism?
17. What advice to Timothy is timely for all zealous young ministers today?
18. What orderly arrangements in the congregation are clearly defined, and how does Paul use the Hebrew Scriptures as authority?

muzzle a bull when it threshes out the grain'; also: 'The workman is worthy of his wages.'" —1 Tim. 5:1-3, 9, 10, 19-21, 17, 18; Deut. 25:4; Lev. 19:13.

19 After giving all this fine counsel Paul adds that the commandment should be observed in a spotless and irreprehensible way 'until the manifestation of the Lord Jesus Christ as the King of those who rule as kings and Lord of those who rule as lords.' On the basis of this Kingdom hope, the letter closes with a powerful exhortation for Christians "to work at good, to be rich in fine works, to be liberal, ready to share, safely treasuring up for themselves a fine foundation for the future, in order that they may get a firm hold on the real life." (1 Tim. 6:14, 15, 18, 19) Beneficial indeed is all the fine instruction of First Timothy!

19. How is the Kingdom hope brought to the fore, and what exhortation is given on this basis?

Bible Book Number Fifty-five— 2 Timothy

Writer:	**Paul**
Place Written:	**Rome**
Writing Completed:	**c. A.D. 65**
Time Covered:	**Undetermined**

ONCE again Paul was a prisoner in Rome. However, the circumstances of this second imprisonment were much more severe than those of the first. It was approximately A.D. 64-65. A great fire had swept through Rome in July, A.D. 64, causing extensive damage in ten of the city's fourteen regions. According to the Roman historian Tacitus, Emperor Nero was unable to "banish the sinister belief that the conflagration was the result of an order. Consequently, to get rid of the report, Nero fastened the guilt and inflicted the most exquisite tortures on a class hated for their abominations, called Christians by the populace. . . . An immense multitude was convicted, not so much of the crime of firing the city, as of hatred against mankind. Mockery of every sort was added to their deaths. Covered with the skins of beasts, they were torn by dogs and perished, or were nailed to crosses, or were doomed to the flames and burnt, to serve as a nightly illumination, when daylight had expired. Nero offered his gardens for the spectacle . . . there arose a feeling of compassion; for it was not as it seemed, for the public good, but to glut one man's cruelty, that they were being destroyed."[a]

2 It was shortly following the outbreak of this wave of violent persecution that Paul again found himself a prisoner in Rome. This time he was in chains. He did not expect to be released, but awaited only final judgment and execution. Visitors were few. Indeed, for anyone to identify himself openly as a Christian was to run the risk of arrest and death by torture. Hence Paul could write appreciatively concerning his visitor from Ephesus: "May the Lord grant mercy to the household of Onesiphorus, because he often brought me refreshment, and he did not become ashamed of my chains. On the contrary, when he happened to be in Rome, he diligently looked for me and found me." (2 Tim. 1:16, 17) Writing under the shadow of death, Paul styles himself "an apostle of Christ Jesus through God's will according to the promise of the life that is in union with Christ Jesus." (2 Tim. 1:1) He knew that life in union with Christ awaited him. He had preached in many of the chief cities of the known world, from Jerusalem to Rome, and perhaps even as far as Spain. (Rom. 15:24, 28) He had run the course faithfully to the finish. —2 Tim. 4:6-8.

3 The letter was probably written about A.D. 65, immediately prior to Paul's martyrdom. Timothy was probably still at Ephesus, for Paul had encouraged him to stay there. (1 Tim. 1:3) Twice he urges Timothy to come to him quickly, and he asks him to bring Mark with him, and also the cloak and scrolls that he left at Troas. (2 Tim. 4:9, 11, 13, 21) Written at so critical a time, his letter contained powerful encouragement for Timothy, and it has continued to provide beneficial encouragement for true Christians in all ages since.

4 The book of Second Timothy is authentic and canonical for the same reasons already discussed under First Timothy. It was recognized

a *The Complete Works of Tacitus,* 1942, edited by Moses Hadas, pages 380, 381.

1. What persecution flared up in Rome about A.D. 64, and for what apparent reason?
2. Under what circumstances did Paul write Second Timothy, and why does he speak appreciatively of Onesiphorus?
3. When was the letter written, and how has it benefited Christians through the ages?
4. What proves the book to be authentic and canonical?

and used by early writers and commentators, including Polycarp in the second century of the Christian era.

CONTENTS OF SECOND TIMOTHY

5 **"Holding the pattern of healthful words"** (1:1–3:17). Paul tells Timothy that he never forgets him in his prayers, and that he is longing to see him. He recollects 'the faith without hypocrisy' that is in Timothy, and which dwelt first in his grandmother Lois and his mother Eunice. Timothy should stir up like a fire the gift within him, 'for God gave not a spirit of cowardice, but that of power and of love and of soundness of mind.' Let him therefore be unashamed in witnessing and suffering evil for the good news, because God's undeserved kindness has been made clearly evident through the manifestation of the Savior, Christ Jesus. Timothy should "keep holding the pattern of healthful words" that he heard from Paul, guarding it as a fine trust.—1:5, 7, 13.

6 Timothy is to commit the things he learned from Paul to "faithful men, who, in turn, will be adequately qualified to teach others." Timothy should prove himself a fine soldier of Christ Jesus. A soldier shuns business entanglements. Moreover, the one crowned at the games contends according to the rules. Let Timothy give constant thought to Paul's words, in order to gain discernment. The important things to remember, and to remind others of, are: "Jesus Christ was raised from the dead and was of David's seed"; salvation and everlasting glory in union with Christ, reigning as kings with him, are the rewards for the chosen ones who endure. Timothy is to do his utmost to present himself as an approved workman to God, shunning empty speeches that violate what is holy, and which spread like gangrene. Just as in a large house an honorable vessel is kept separate from one lacking honor, so, admonishes Paul, "flee from the desires incidental to youth, but pursue righteousness, faith, love, peace, along with those who call upon the Lord out of a clean heart." The slave of the Lord needs to be gentle toward all, qualified to teach, instructing with mildness. —2:2, 8, 22.

7 "In the last days" there will be critical times hard to deal with, persons proving false to their show of godly devotion, "always learning and yet never able to come to an accurate knowledge of truth." But Timothy has closely followed Paul's teaching, his course of life and his persecutions, out of which the Lord delivered him. "In fact," he adds, "all those desiring to live with godly devotion in association with Christ Jesus will also be persecuted." Timothy, however, should continue in the things he learned from infancy, which are able to make him wise for salvation, for *"all scripture is inspired of God and beneficial."* —3:1, 7, 12, 16.

8 **Fully accomplishing the ministry** (4:1-22). Paul charges Timothy to preach the word with urgency. The time will come when men will not put up with healthful teaching and will turn to false teachers, but let Timothy keep his senses, 'do the work of an evangelist, fully accomplish his ministry.' As the time for his release approaches, Paul exults that he has fought the fine fight, that he has run the course to the finish and observed the faith. Now he looks confidently forward to the reward, "the crown of righteousness."—4:5, 8.

9 Paul urges Timothy to come to him quickly, and gives instructions concerning the journey. When Paul made his first defense everyone forsook him, but the Lord infused power into him that the preaching might be fully accomplished among the nations. Yes, he is confident that the Lord will deliver him from every wicked work and save him for his heavenly kingdom.

WHY BENEFICIAL

10 "All Scripture is inspired of God and beneficial." Beneficial for what? Paul tells us in his second letter to Timothy: "For teaching, for reproving, for setting things straight, for disciplining in righteousness, that the man of God may be fully competent, completely equipped for every good work." (2 Tim. 3:16, 17) Thus the benefit of "teaching" is emphasized in this letter. All lovers of righteousness today will want to heed the letter's wise counsel in striving to become teachers of the Word and in doing their utmost to become God's approved workmen "handling the word of the truth aright." As in the Ephesus of Timothy's day, so in this modern age, there are those who dabble in "foolish and ignorant questionings," who are "always learning and yet never able to come to an accurate knowledge of truth," and who reject "healthful teaching" in favor of teachers who tickle their ears the way they selfishly want it. (2 Tim. 2:15, 23; 3:7; 4:3, 4) To avoid this contaminating worldly influence,

5. What kind of faith dwells in Timothy, and yet what should he keep doing?
6. What counsel does Paul give on teaching, and how can Timothy be an approved workman and an honorable vessel?
7. Why are the inspired Scriptures to be especially beneficial in "the last days"?
8. What does Paul urge upon Timothy, and in this connection how does he himself exult?
9. What confidence in the Lord's power does Paul express?
10. (a) What particular benefit of "all Scripture" is emphasized in Second Timothy, so what should Christians strive to become? (b) What influence is to be avoided, and how may this be done? (c) For what does there continue to be an urgent need?

it is necessary to "keep holding the pattern of healthful words" in faith and love. Moreover, there is the urgent need for more and more persons to become like the "man of God" Timothy, "adequately qualified to teach others," both inside and outside the congregation. Happy are all those who shoulder this responsibility, becoming 'qualified to teach with mildness,' and who preach the word "with all long-suffering and art of teaching"!—2 Tim. 1:13; 2:2, 24, 25; 4:2.

11 As Paul stated, Timothy had known the holy writings "from infancy," due to the loving instruction of Lois and Eunice. "From infancy" also indicates the time to start Bible instruction for young people today. But what if, in later years, early fires of zeal start to die out? Paul's advice is to stir up that fire again in the spirit of "power and of love and of soundness of mind," keeping faith without hypocrisy. "In the last days," he said, there will be critical times, with problems of delinquency and false teachings. That is why it is so necessary for young people especially, and all others, to 'keep their senses in all things, and fully accomplish their ministry.'—2 Tim. 3:15; 1:5-7; 3:1-5; 4:5.

11. What advice is given with regard to the young?

12 The prize is worth contending for. (2 Tim. 2:3-7) In this connection, Paul calls attention to the Kingdom Seed, saying: "Remember that Jesus Christ was raised up from the dead and was of David's seed, according to the good news." His hope was to remain in union with that Seed. Farther on he speaks of his approaching execution in words of triumph: "From this time on there is reserved for me the crown of righteousness, which the Lord, the righteous judge, will give me as a reward in that day, yet not only to me, but also to all those who have loved his manifestation." (2 Tim. 2:8; 4:8) How happy all those who can look back over many years of faithful service and say the same! However, this requires serving *now* in integrity, with love for the manifestation of Jesus Christ and demonstrating the same confidence as when Paul wrote: "The Lord will deliver me from every wicked work and will save me for his heavenly kingdom. To him be the glory forever and ever. Amen." —2 Tim. 4:18.

12. (a) How did Paul call attention to the Kingdom Seed, and what hope did he express? (b) How can God's servants today have the same mental attitude as Paul?

Bible Book Number Fifty-six— Titus

Writer:	**Paul**
Place Written:	**Macedonia (?)**
Writing Completed:	**c. A.D. 61-64**
Time Covered:	**Undetermined**

1 "PAUL, a slave of God and an apostle of Jesus Christ . . . to Titus, a genuine child according to a faith shared in common." (Titus 1:1, 4) So begins Paul's letter to his co-worker and long-time associate Titus, whom he had left in Crete to organize the congregations on a better footing. Titus had a big task on his hands. This island, which was said to have been the ancient abode of "the father of gods and men," was also the source of the saying, "to Crete a Cretan," meaning "to outwit a knave."[a] The untruthfulness of its people was proverbial, so that Paul even quoted their own prophet as saying: "Cretans are always liars, injurious wild beasts, unemployed gluttons." (Titus 1:12) The Cretans of Paul's day have also been described as follows: "The character of the people was unsteady, insincere, and quarrelsome; they were given to greediness, licentiousness, falsehood, and drunkenness, in no ordinary degree; and the Jews who had settled among them appear to have gone beyond the natives in immorality."[b] It was in just such an environment that the congregations of Crete had sprung up; and hence it was especially needful for the believers "to repudiate ungodliness and worldly desires and to live with soundness of mind and righteousness and godly devotion," as Paul exhorted.—Titus 2:12.

2 The book of Titus itself gives very little information about the association of Paul and

a M'Clintock and Strong's *Cyclopædia*, 1882, Vol. II, page 564; *The New Schaff-Herzog Encyclopedia of Religious Knowledge*, 1958, Vol. III, page 306.

b M'Clintock and Strong's *Cyclopædia*, 1881, Vol. X, page 442.

1. (a) In what environment had the Cretan congregations sprung up? (b) What did the Christians in Crete need to do, and what task was entrusted to Titus?

2, 3. (a) What association did Titus have with Paul? (b) From where did Paul likely write Titus, and for what purpose?

Titus except that the expression "a genuine child according to a faith shared in common" may indicate that Titus received the truth through Paul's preaching. (Titus 1:4) From the references to him in Paul's other letters, however, much information can be gleaned. Titus, who was a Greek, often accompanied Paul, and on at least one occasion went up to Jerusalem with him. (Gal. 2:1-5) Paul refers to him as "a sharer with me and a fellow worker." It was Titus whom Paul had sent to Corinth after writing his first letter to the Corinthians from Ephesus. While in Corinth, Titus was connected with the collection that was being made for the brothers in Jerusalem, and subsequently he went back at Paul's direction to complete the collection. It was on the return journey to Corinth from his meeting with Paul in Macedonia that Titus was used to carry the second letter from Paul to the Corinthians.—2 Cor. 8:16-24; 2:13; 7:5-7.

3 After his release from his first imprisonment in Rome, Paul was again associated with Timothy and Titus during the final years of his ministry. This appears to have included service in Crete, Greece and Macedonia. Finally, Paul is spoken of as going to Nicopolis, in northwest Greece, where he was apparently arrested and taken to Rome for his final imprisonment and execution. It was during the visit to Crete that Paul had left Titus there to "correct the things that were defective and . . . make appointments of older men in city after city," in harmony with Paul's instructions. Paul's letter appears to have been written shortly after he left Titus in Crete, most likely from Macedonia. (Titus 1:5; 3:12; 1 Tim. 1:3; 2 Tim. 4:13, 20) It seems to have served a purpose similar to that of First Timothy, namely, to encourage Paul's colaborer and to give him authoritative backing in his duties.

4 The letter must have been written between Paul's release from prison, about A.D. 61, and his later arrest at the beginning of Nero's persecutions, about A.D. 64. The weight of evidence for the authenticity of the letter to Titus is the same as for the contemporary letters to Timothy, the three Bible books often being termed Paul's "pastoral letters." The style of writing is similar. Irenaeus and Origen both quote from Titus, and many other ancient authorities also testify to the book's canonicity. It is found in the Sinaitic and Alexandrine Manuscripts. In the John Rylands Library there is a papyrus fragment, P^{32}, which is a codex leaf of the third century of the Christian era containing Titus 1:11-15 and 2:3-8. There is no question that the book is an authentic part of the inspired Scriptures.

4. When must the letter have been written, and what is the evidence for its authenticity?

CONTENTS OF TITUS

5 **Overseers to exhort by healthful teaching** (1:1-16). After an affectionate greeting, Paul sets out the qualifications for overseers. It is emphasized that an overseer must be "free from accusation," a lover of goodness, righteous, loyal, a man "holding firmly to the faithful word as respects his art of teaching, that he may be able both to exhort by the teaching that is healthful and to reprove those who contradict." This is needful in view of the "deceivers of the mind" who are even subverting entire households for the sake of dishonest gain. So Titus must "keep on reproving them with severity, that they may be healthy in the faith, paying no attention to Jewish fables." Defiled persons may declare publicly that they know God, but they disown him by their works of disobedience.—1:6-10, 13, 14.

6 **Living with soundness of mind, righteousness and godly devotion** (2:1–3:15). The aged men and aged women should be serious and reverent. The younger women should love their husbands and their children, and subject themselves to their husbands, "so that the word of God may not be spoken of abusively." The younger men should be an example of fine works and wholesome speech. Slaves in subjection should exhibit "good fidelity to the full." God's undeserved kindness, leading to salvation, has been manifested, encouraging soundness of mind, righteousness and godly devotion in those whom God has cleansed through Christ Jesus to be "a people peculiarly his own, zealous for fine works."—2:5, 10, 14.

7 Paul stresses the need for subjection and obedience to governments and for "exhibiting all mildness toward all men." Paul and his fellow Christians were once as bad as other men. Not owing to any works of their own, but because of God's kindness, love and mercy and by holy spirit they have been saved and have become heirs to a hope of everlasting life. So those who believe God should "keep their minds on maintaining fine works." They are to shun foolish questionings and strife over the Law, and as for a man that promotes a sect, they are to reject him after a first and second admonition. Paul asks Titus to come to him at Nicopolis and, after giving other missionary instructions, stresses again the need for fine works, in order not to be unfruitful.—3:2, 7, 8.

WHY BENEFICIAL

8 The Cretan Christians lived in an environ-

5. (a) What overseer qualifications does Paul emphasize, and why is this needful? (b) Why must Titus reprove with severity, and what is said of defiled persons?
6. What advice is given on Christian conduct?
7. What does Paul stress in connection with subjection, salvation, and fine works?
8. What in Paul's counsel in the letter to Titus is "fine and beneficial" for us today, and why?

ment of lying, corruption and greed. Should they just go along with the crowd? Or should they take definite steps to separate themselves completely to serve as a people sanctified to Jehovah God? In making known through Titus that the Cretans should "keep their minds on maintaining fine works," Paul said: "These things are fine and beneficial to men." It is "fine and beneficial" today also, in a world that has sunk into a mire of untruthfulness and dishonest practices, that real Christians "learn to maintain fine works," being fruitful in God's service. (Titus 3:8, 14) All of Paul's condemnation of the immorality and wickedness that threatened the congregations in Crete stands as a warning to us now when 'the undeserved kindness of God instructs us to repudiate ungodliness and worldly desires and to live with soundness of mind and righteousness and godly devotion amid this system of things.' Christians should also be "ready for every good work" in showing obedience to governments, maintaining a good conscience. —Titus 2:11, 12; 3:1.

9 Titus 1:5-9 supplements 1 Timothy 3:2-7 in showing what holy spirit requires of overseers. This lays emphasis on the overseer "holding firmly to the faithful word" and being a teacher in the congregation. How necessary this is in bringing all along to maturity! In fact, this need for right teaching is emphasized several times in the letter to Titus. Paul admonishes Titus to "keep on speaking what things are fitting for healthful teaching." The aged women are to be "teachers of what is good," and slaves are 'to adorn the teaching of their Savior, God, in all things.' (Titus 1:9; 2:1, 3, 10) Paul stresses the need for Titus as an overseer to be firm and fearless in his teaching, saying: "Keep on speaking these things and exhorting and reproving with full authority to command." And in the case of those who disobey, he says: "Keep on reproving them with severity, that they may be healthy in the faith." Thus Paul's letter to Titus is especially "beneficial for teaching, for reproving, for setting things straight, for disciplining in righteousness." —Titus 2:15; 1:13; 2 Tim. 3:16.

9. How is the importance of right teaching underlined, and especially as a responsibility of the overseer?

10 The letter to Titus stimulates our appreciation for the undeserved kindness of God and encourages us to turn from the ungodliness of the world, "while we wait for the happy hope and glorious manifestation of the great God and of our Savior Christ Jesus." So doing, those who have been declared righteous through Christ Jesus may become "heirs according to a hope of everlasting life" in the kingdom of God.—Titus 2:13; 3:7.

10. In what does the letter to Titus encourage us, and what happy hope does it stimulate?

Bible Book Number Fifty-seven— Philemon

Writer:	**Paul**
Place Written:	**Rome**
Writing Completed:	**c. A.D. 60-61**
Time Covered:	**Undetermined**

THIS very tactful and loving letter of Paul is of great interest to Christians today. Not only is it the shortest epistle preserved from the hand of "the apostle to the nations," but in the whole Bible only Second and Third John contain less material. Also, it is the only "private" letter of Paul, in the sense of not being addressed officially to a congregation or a responsible overseer, but to a private person, and dealing solely with the special problem Paul wanted to discuss with this Christian brother, the apparently well-to-do Philemon, who lived in the Phrygian city of Colossae, in the very heart of Asia Minor.

2 The purpose of the letter is clearly revealed: During his first imprisonment in Rome (A.D. 59-61) Paul had great freedom to preach the kingdom of God. Among those who listened to his preaching was Onesimus, a runaway slave from the household of Philemon, Paul's friend. As a result, Onesimus became a Christian, and Paul decided, with Onesimus' consent, to send him back to Philemon. It was at this time, also, that Paul wrote the letter to the congregation in Colossae, in which he gave good counsel to Christian slaves and slave-owners on how to conduct themselves properly in this relationship. (Col. 3:22–4:1) However, over and above this, Paul composed a letter to Philemon, in which he personally pleaded on Onesimus' behalf. It was a letter written with his own hand—an unusual thing for Paul. (Philem. 19) This personal touch added greatly to the weight of his plea.

1. What are some of the characteristics of the letter to Philemon?
2. Against what background and for what purpose was the letter written?

3 The letter was most likely penned about A.D. 60-61, as Paul had apparently preached in Rome long enough to make converts. Also, because he expresses hope, in verse 22, of being released, we can conclude that the letter was written after some time had elapsed of his imprisonment. The epistle to the Ephesians was written at the same time, and it appears that these three letters, one for Philemon and those for the congregations in Ephesus and Colossae, were dispatched with Tychicus and Onesimus.—Eph. 6:21, 22; Col. 4:7-9.

4 That Paul was the writer of Philemon is evident from the first verse, where he is mentioned by name. He was acknowledged as such by Origen, Tertullian and Eusebius.[a] The authenticity of the book is also supported by its being listed, with others of Paul's epistles, in the Muratorian fragment of the second century of the Christian era.

CONTENTS OF PHILEMON

5 **Onesimus sent back to his master "as more than a slave"** (Vss. 1-25). Paul sends warm greetings to Philemon, to Apphia, "our sister," to Archippus, "our fellow soldier," and to the congregation in Philemon's house. He commends Philemon (whose name means "Affectionate") for the love and faith he has toward the Lord Jesus and the holy ones, which have refreshed them, thus bringing Paul joy and comfort. Paul, an aged man and a prisoner, now expresses himself with great freeness of speech concerning his "child" Onesimus, to whom he became a "father" while in prison bonds. Onesimus (whose name means "Profitable") had formerly been useless to Philemon, but now he is useful to both Philemon and Paul.

6 The apostle would like to keep Onesimus to minister to him in prison, but would not do so without Philemon's consent. So he is sending him back, "no longer as a slave but as more than a slave, as a brother beloved." He asks that he be received kindly, the same way Paul himself would be received. If Onesimus has wronged Philemon, let it be charged to Paul's account, for, Paul tells Philemon, "you owe me even yourself." (Vss. 16, 19) Paul hopes he may soon be released, and that he may visit Philemon, and concludes with greetings.

a M'Clintock and Strong's *Cyclopœdia,* 1883, Vol. VIII, page 83.

3. When was the letter most likely penned, and how was it forwarded?
4. What proves writership and authenticity of Philemon?
5. (a) With what greetings and commendation does the letter open? (b) What does Paul tell Philemon of his slave Onesimus?
6. What kind of treatment does Paul recommend for Onesimus, and with what tactful reasoning?

WHY BENEFICIAL

7 As shown by this letter, Paul was not preaching a "social gospel," trying to do away with the existing system of things and its institutions, such as slavery. He did not arbitrarily set even Christian slaves free, but, rather, he sent the runaway slave Onesimus on a journey taking him over 900 miles from Rome to Colossae, right back to his master Philemon. Thus Paul adhered to his high call as an apostle, abiding strictly by his divine commission of "preaching the kingdom of God . . . and teaching the things concerning the Lord Jesus Christ."—Acts 28:31; Philem. 8, 9.

8 The letter to Philemon is revealing in that it shows the love and unity that existed among the Christians of the first century. It reveals for Christians today the practical application of Christian principles among Christian brothers. On the part of Paul we find the expression of brotherly love, respect for civil relations and for the property of another, effective tactfulness and commendable humility. Instead of trying to compel Philemon to forgive Onesimus by the weight of the authority he possessed as a leading overseer in the Christian congregation, Paul humbly appealed to him upon the basis of Christian love and his personal friendship. Overseers today can benefit from the tactful manner in which Paul approached Philemon.

9 Paul obviously expected Philemon to comply with his request, and his doing so would be a practical application of what Jesus said at Matthew 6:14 and of what Paul said at Ephesians 4:32. Christians today can likewise be expected to be kind and forgiving toward an offending brother. If Philemon could be forgiving toward a slave that he owned and that he was legally free to mistreat as he pleased, Christians today should be able to forgive an offending brother—a far less difficult task.

10 The operation of Jehovah's spirit is very evident in this letter to Philemon. It is manifested in the masterful way in which Paul handled a very touchy problem. It is evident in the fellow feeling, the tender affection and the trust in a fellow Christian that are exhibited by Paul. It is seen in the fact that the letter to Philemon, like the other Scriptures, teaches Christian principles, encourages Christian unity and magnifies the love and faith that abound among "the holy ones," who hope in God's kingdom and in whose conduct is reflected the loving-kindness of Jehovah.

7. As regards Onesimus, how was Paul adhering to his high call as an apostle?
8. What practical application of Christian principles does the letter illustrate?
9. By complying with Paul's request, what fine precedent would Philemon set, of interest to Christians today?
10. How is the operation of Jehovah's spirit evident in the letter to Philemon?

Bible Book Number Fifty-eight— Hebrews

Writer:	**Paul**
Place Written:	**Rome**
Writing Completed:	**c. A.D. 61**
Time Covered:	**Undetermined**

PAUL is best known as the apostle "to the nations." But was his ministry confined to the non-Jews? Not at all! Just before Paul was baptized and commissioned for his work, the Lord Jesus said to Ananias: "This man [Paul] is a chosen vessel to me to bear my name to the nations as well as to kings and *the sons of Israel.*" (Acts 9:15; Gal. 2:8, 9) The writing of the book of Hebrews was truly in line with Paul's commission to bear the name of Jesus to the sons of Israel.

2 However, some critics doubt Paul's writership of Hebrews. One objection is that Paul's name does not appear in the letter. But this is really no obstacle, as many other canonical books fail to name the writer, who is often identified by internal evidence. Moreover, some feel that Paul may have deliberately omitted his name in writing to the Hebrew Christians in Judea, since his name had been made an object of hatred by the Jews there. (Acts 21:28) Neither is the change of style from his other epistles any real objection to Paul's writership. Whether addressing pagans, Jews or Christians, Paul always showed his ability to "become all things to people of all sorts." Here his argument is presented to Jews as from a Jew, arguments that they could fully understand and appreciate.—1 Cor. 9:22.

3 The internal evidence of the book is all in support of Paul's writership. The writer was in Italy and was associated with Timothy. These facts fit Paul. (Heb. 13:24, 23) Furthermore, the doctrine is typical of Paul, though the arguments are presented from a Jewish viewpoint, designed to appeal to the strictly Hebrew congregations to which the letter was addressed. On this point *Clarke's Commentary,* Volume 6, page 681, says concerning Hebrews: "That it was written to *Jews,* naturally such, the whole structure of the epistle proves. Had it been written to the *Gentiles,* not one in ten thousand of them could have comprehended the argument, because unacquainted with the Jewish system; the knowledge of which the writer of this epistle everywhere supposes." This helps to account for the difference of style, as compared with Paul's other letters.

4 The discovery in 1931 of the Chester Beatty Papyrus No. 2 has provided further evidence of Paul's writership. Commenting on this papyrus codex, written only about a century and a half after Paul's death, Sir Frederic Kenyon, the eminent British textual critic, said: "It is noticeable that Hebrews is placed immediately after Romans (an almost unprecedented position), which shows that at the early date when this manuscript was written no doubt was felt as to its Pauline authorship."[a] On this same question M'Clintock and Strong's *Cyclopædia* states pointedly: "There is no substantial evidence, external or internal, in favor of any claimant to the authorship of this epistle except Paul."[b]

5 Apart from the fact that the early Christians accepted it, the contents of the book also prove that it is "inspired of God." It continually points the reader toward the Hebrew Scripture prophecies, making numerous references to the early writings, and shows how these were all fulfilled in Christ Jesus. In the first chapter alone no less than seven quotations from the Hebrew Scriptures are used as the point is developed that the Son is now superior to the angels. It constantly magnifies Jehovah's Word and his name, pointing to Jesus as the Chief Agent of life and to his kingdom as mankind's only hope.

6 As to the time of writing, it has already been shown that Paul wrote the letter while in Italy. In concluding the letter he says: "Take note that our brother Timothy has been released, with whom, if he comes quite soon, I shall see you." (Heb. 13:23) This seems to indicate that Paul was expecting an early release from prison and hoped to accompany Timothy, who had also been imprisoned but who had already been released. Thus the final year of

a *The Story of the Bible,* 1949, Sir Frederic Kenyon, page 116.
b 1882, Vol. IV, page 147.

1. In line with what commission did Paul write the letter to the Hebrews?
2. How may arguments against Paul's writership be refuted?
3. What internal evidence both supports Paul's writership and indicates he wrote Hebrews primarily for the Jews?
4. What do reliable authorities say as to writership?
5. How do the contents of the book prove it to be inspired?
6. What does the evidence indicate as to place and time of writing?

Paul's first imprisonment in Rome is suggested as the date of writing, namely, A.D. 61.

7 During the "time of the end" of the Jewish "system of things" a period of crucial testing came upon the Hebrew Christians in Judea, and especially in Jerusalem. With the growth and spread of the good news, the Jews were becoming bitter and fanatical in the extreme in their opposition to the Christians. Only a few years earlier the mere appearance of Paul in Jerusalem had stirred up a riot, with the religious Jews screaming at the top of their voices: "Take such a man away from the earth, for he was not fit to live!" More than forty Jews had bound themselves with a curse neither to eat nor to drink until they had done away with him, and it required a strong escort of heavily armed troops to bring him down by night to Caesarea. (Acts 22:22; 23:12-15, 23, 24) In this atmosphere of religious fanaticism and hatred of Christians the congregation had to live, preach and keep themselves firm in the faith. They had to have sound knowledge and understanding of how Christ fulfilled the Law in order to keep from falling back to Judaism and its observing of the Mosaic law with the offering of animal sacrifices, all of it now nothing more than empty ritual.

8 No one was better able to understand the pressure and persecution to which the Jewish Christians were exposed than the apostle Paul. No one was better equipped to supply them with powerful arguments and refutations of Jewish tradition than Paul, the former Pharisee. Drawing on his vast knowledge of the Mosaic law, learned at the feet of Gamaliel, he presented incontestable proof that Christ is the fulfillment of the Law, its ordinances and its sacrifices, which had now been replaced by far more glorious realities, bringing inestimably greater benefits under a new and better covenant. His keen mind lined up proof after proof in clear and convincing array. The end of the law covenant and the coming in of the new covenant, the superiority of Christ's Melchizedekian priesthood over the Aaronic priesthood, the real value of Christ's sacrifice compared with the offerings of bulls and goats, the entry of Christ into the holy place in the heavens rather than on earth—all of these strikingly new teachings, hateful in the extreme to the orthodox Jews, were here presented to the Jewish Christian converts with such abundant evidence from the Hebrew Scriptures that no reasonable Jew could fail to be convinced.

7. With what kind of opposition were the Jewish Christians faced, and hence what was needful for them?
8. Why was Paul admirably equipped to write this letter, and what array of arguments did he present for the benefit of believing Jews?

9 Armed with this letter, the Judean Christians had a new and powerful weapon to stop the mouths of the persecuting Jews, and a persuasive argument with which to convince and convert honest Jews seeking God's truth. The letter shows Paul's deep love for his own people and his burning desire to help them in a practical way in their time of great need.

CONTENTS OF HEBREWS

10 **The exalted position of Christ** (1:1–2:18). The opening words focus attention on Christ: "God, who long ago spoke on many occasions and in many ways to our forefathers by means of the prophets, has at the end of these days spoken to us by means of a Son." This Son is the appointed heir of all things and the reflection of his Father's glory. Having made a purification for our sins, he has now "sat down on the right hand of the majesty in lofty places." (1:1-3) Paul quotes scripture upon scripture to prove Jesus' superiority over the angels.

11 Paul writes that "it is necessary for us to pay more than the usual attention." Why so? Because, argues Paul, if there was severe retribution for disobeying "the word spoken through angels, . . . how shall we escape if we have neglected a salvation of such greatness in that it began to be spoken through our Lord?" God made "the son of man" a little lower than angels, but now we behold this Jesus "crowned with glory and honor for having suffered death, that he by God's undeserved kindness might taste death for every man." (2:1-3, 6, 9) In bringing many sons to glory, God first made this Chief Agent of their salvation "perfect through sufferings." He it is who brings the Devil to nothing, and emancipates "all those who for fear of death were subject to slavery all through their lives." Jesus thus becomes "a merciful and faithful high priest." And wonderfully, since he himself suffered under test, "he is able to come to the aid of those who are being put to the test."—2:10, 15, 17, 18.

12 **Entering into God's rest by faith and obedience** (3:1–4:16). Jesus is counted worthy of more glory than Moses. Therefore, Christians, of all people, should take warning from the Israelites' example of unfaithfulness, for fear of developing "a wicked heart lacking faith by drawing away from the living God." (Heb. 3: 12; Ps. 95:7-11) Just as God rested from his

9. What powerful weapon did this letter become, and how was it a demonstration of Paul's love?
10. What does the letter state with regard to Christ's position?
11. (a) Why does Paul counsel paying more than the usual attention to the things they have heard? (b) Because of his experiences and his exalted position, what things is Jesus able to accomplish?
12. What course must Christians avoid if they are to enter into God's rest?

creative works, so there is a "rest" promised to the people of God. Natural Israel could not enter into that rest "because of lack of faith" and "because of disobedience." "So there remains a sabbath resting for the people of God. For the man that has entered into God's rest has also himself rested from his own works, just as God did from his own." The pattern of disobedience shown by Israel is to be avoided. "For the word of God is alive and exerts power and is sharper than any two-edged sword . . . and is able to discern thoughts and intentions of the heart." (Heb. 3:19; 4:6, 9, 10, 12) Therefore let them hold on to confessing Jesus, the great high priest who has passed through the heavens, that they may find mercy.

13 **Mature view of superiority of Christ's priesthood** (5:1–7:28). The Christ did not glorify himself, but it was the Father who said: "You are a priest forever according to the manner of Melchizedek." (Heb. 5:6; Ps. 110:4) First, he was perfected in obedience through suffering, so as to become responsible for everlasting salvation to all those obeying him. Concerning him Paul has "much to say and hard to be explained," but the Hebrews are still babes in need of milk, when, in fact, they ought to be teachers. "Solid food belongs to mature people, to those who through use have their perceptive powers trained to distinguish both right and wrong." The apostle urges them to "press on to maturity."—Heb. 5:11, 14; 6:1.

14 It is impossible for those who have known the word of God and who have fallen away to revive themselves again to repentance, "because they impale the Son of God afresh for themselves and expose him to public shame." Only through faith and patience can they inherit the promise made to Abraham—a promise made sure and firm by two unchangeable things: God's word and his oath. Their hope, which is as "an anchor for the soul, both sure and firm," has been established by Jesus' entry "within the curtain" as forerunner and high priest like Melchizedek.—6:6, 19.

15 This Melchizedek was both "king of Salem" and "priest of the Most High God." Even the family head Abraham paid tithe to him, and through him Levi, who was still in the loins of Abraham, did so. Melchizedek's blessing of Abraham thus extended to the unborn Levi, and this showed that the Levitical priesthood was inferior to that of Melchizedek. Further, if perfection came through the Levitical priesthood of Aaron, would there be need for another priest "according to the manner of Melchizedek"? Moreover, since there is a change of priesthood, "there comes to be of necessity a change also of the law."—7:11, 12.

16 The Law, in fact, made nothing perfect, but proved to be weak and ineffective. Because they kept dying, its priests were many, but the Melchizedekian high priest by "continuing alive forever has his priesthood without any successors. Consequently, he is able also to save completely those who are approaching God through him, because he is always alive to plead for them." This high priest, Jesus, is "loyal, guileless, undefiled, separated from the sinners," whereas the high priests appointed by the Law are weak, having first to offer sacrifices for their own sins before they can intercede for others. So the word of God's sworn oath "appoints a Son, who is perfected forever."—7:24-26, 28.

17 **The superiority of the new covenant** (8:1–10:39). Jesus is shown to be the "mediator of a correspondingly better covenant, which has been legally established upon better promises." (8:6) Paul quotes in full Jeremiah 31:31-34, showing that the laws of the new covenant are written in their minds and hearts, that all will know Jehovah and that Jehovah will "by no means call their sins to mind any more." This "new covenant" has made the former one obsolete, and it is "near to vanishing away." —Heb. 8:12, 13.

18 Paul describes the yearly sacrifices at the tent of the former covenant as "legal requirements . . . imposed until the appointed time to set things straight." However, when Christ came as high priest, it was with his own precious blood, and not that of goats and of young bulls. Moses' sprinkling of the blood of animals had validated the former covenant and cleansed the typical tent, but better sacrifices were necessary for the heavenly realities in connection with the new covenant. "For Christ entered, not into a holy place made with hands, which is a copy of the reality, but into heaven itself, now to appear before the person of God for us." Nor does he have to make yearly sacrifices, as did Israel's high priest, for "now he has manifested himself once for all time at the conclusion of the systems of things to put sin away through the sacrifice of himself." —9:10, 24, 26.

19 In summary, Paul says that, "since the Law has a shadow of the good things to come,"

13. (a) How did Christ become "a priest forever," responsible for everlasting salvation? (b) Why does Paul urge the Hebrews to press on to maturity?
14. How may they inherit the promise, and how has their hope been established?
15. What shows that Jesus' priesthood, being according to the order of Melchizedek, would be superior to that of Levi?
16. Why is the priesthood of Jesus superior to that under the Law?
17. In what is the new covenant superior?
18. What comparison does Paul make on the matter of sacrifice in connection with the two covenants?
19. (a) What has the Law been unable to do, and why? (b) What is God's will in connection with sanctification, and what strong admonition does Paul give on holding fast their faith?

its repetitious sacrifices have not been able to remove the consciousness of sin. However, Jesus came into the world to do God's will. "By the said 'will,'" says Paul, "we have been sanctified through the offering of the body of Jesus Christ once for all time." Therefore, let the Hebrews hold fast the public declaration of their faith without wavering, and "consider one another to incite to love and fine works," not forsaking the gathering of themselves together. If they continue to sin willfully after receiving the accurate knowledge of the truth, "there is no longer any sacrifice for sins left." He tells them: "Keep on remembering the former days in which, after you were enlightened, you endured a great contest under sufferings." Let them not throw away their freeness of speech, which has a great reward, but let them endure so as to receive the fulfillment of the promise, and "have faith to the preserving alive of the soul."—10:1, 10, 24, 26, 32, 39.

20 **Faith defined and illustrated** (11:1–12:3). Faith! Yes, that is what is needed. First, Paul defines it: "Faith is the assured expectation of things hoped for, the evident demonstration of realities though not beheld." Then, in one inspiring chapter, he paints in quick succession brief word pictures of men of old who lived, worked, fought, endured and became heirs of righteousness through faith. "By faith" Abraham, dwelling in tents with Isaac and Jacob, awaited "the city having real foundations," the builder of which is God. "By faith" Moses continued steadfast, "as seeing the One who is invisible." "What more shall I say?" says Paul. "For the time will fail me if I go on to relate about Gideon, Barak, Samson, Jephthah, David as well as Samuel and the other prophets, who through faith defeated kingdoms in conflict, effected righteousness, obtained promises." Others, too, were tried through mockings, scourgings, bonds and tortures, but refused release "in order that they might attain a better resurrection." Truly, "the world was not worthy of them." All of these had witness borne to them through their faith, but they have yet to receive the fulfillment of the promise. "So, then," continues Paul, "because we have so great a cloud of witnesses surrounding us, let us also put off every weight and the sin that easily entangles us, and let us run with endurance the race that is set before us, as we look intently at the Chief Agent and Perfecter of our faith, Jesus."—11:1, 8, 10, 27, 32, 33, 35, 38; 12:1, 2.

21 **Endurance in the contest of faith** (12:4–29). Paul exhorts them to endure in the contest of faith, for Jehovah is disciplining them as sons. Now is the time to strengthen enfeebled hands and knees and to keep making straight paths for their feet. They must strictly guard against the entry of any poisonous root or defilement that could cause their rejection, as in the case of Esau, who did not appreciate sacred things. At the literal mountain Moses said: "I am fearful and trembling," because of the fearsome display of flaming fire, the cloud and the voice. But the Hebrew Christians have approached something far more awe-inspiring—Mount Zion and a heavenly Jerusalem, myriads of angels, the congregation of the firstborn, God the Judge of all, and Jesus the mediator of a new and better covenant. Now there is all the more reason to listen to divine warning! At that time God's voice shook the earth, but now he has promised to set both heaven and earth in commotion. Paul drives home the point: "Wherefore, seeing that we are to receive a kingdom that cannot be shaken, let us . . . acceptably render God sacred service with godly fear and awe. For our God is also a consuming fire." —12:21, 28, 29.

22 **Various exhortations on matters of worship** (13:1-25). Paul concludes on a note of upbuilding counsel: Let brotherly love continue, do not forget hospitality; let marriage be honorable among all; keep free from the love of money; be obedient to those taking the lead among you, and do not be carried away by strange teachings. Finally, "through him [Jesus] let us always offer to God a sacrifice of praise, that is, the fruit of lips which make public declaration to his name."—13:15.

WHY BENEFICIAL

23 As a legal argument in support of Christ, the letter to the Hebrews is an unchallengeable masterpiece, perfectly constructed and freely documented with proof from the Hebrew Scriptures. It takes the various features of the Mosaic law—the covenant, the blood, the mediator, the tent of worship, the priesthood, the offerings—and shows them to have been nothing more than a perfect pattern made by God pointing forward to far greater things to come, all culminating in Christ Jesus and his sacrifice, the fulfillment of the Law. The Law "which is made obsolete and growing old is near to vanishing away," said Paul. But "Jesus Christ is the same yesterday and today, and forever." (Heb. 8:13; 13:8; 10:1) How joyful those Hebrews must have felt on reading their letter!

24 But of what value is this to us today, in

20. (a) What is faith? (b) What glowing word pictures of faith does Paul now paint?
21. (a) How may Christians endure in the contest of faith? (b) What stronger reason for listening to divine warning does Paul now give?
22. With what upbuilding counsel does Paul conclude his letter?
23. What does Paul argue as to the Law, and how does he support his argument?
24. What arrangement is explained in Hebrews that is of immeasurable benefit to us today?

our different circumstances? Since we are not under the Law, can we find anything beneficial in Paul's argument? Most certainly, yes. Here is outlined for us the great new covenant arrangement based on the promise to Abraham that through his seed all families of the earth would bless themselves. This is our hope for life, our only hope, the fulfillment of Jehovah's ancient promise of blessing through Abraham's seed, Jesus Christ. Although not under the Law, we are born in sin as Adam's seed and we need a merciful high priest, one with a valid sin offering, one who can enter right into Jehovah's presence in heaven and there mediate for us. Here we find him, the One who can lead us to life in Jehovah's new system of things, the One who can sympathize with our weaknesses, having "been tested in all respects like ourselves," and who invites us to "approach with freeness of speech to the throne of undeserved kindness, that we may obtain mercy and find undeserved kindness for help at the right time."—Heb. 4:15, 16.

25 Furthermore, in Paul's letter to the Hebrews we find heart-stirring evidence that prophecies recorded long ago in the Hebrew Scriptures were later fulfilled in a marvelous way. All of this is for our instruction and comfort today. For example, in Hebrews Paul five times applies the words of the Kingdom prophecy at Psalm 110:1 to Jesus Christ as the Kingdom Seed, who "has sat down at the right hand of the throne of God" to wait "until his enemies should be placed as a stool for his feet." (Heb. 12:2; 10:12, 13; 1:3, 13; 8:1) Further, Paul quotes Psalm 110:4 in explaining the important office filled by the Son of God as "a priest forever according to the manner of Melchizedek." Like Melchizedek of old, who in the Bible record is "fatherless, motherless, without genealogy, having neither a beginning of days nor an end of life," Jesus is both king and "a priest perpetually" to administer the everlasting benefits of his ransom sacrifice to all who obediently place themselves under his rule. (Heb. 5:6, 10; 6:20; 7:1-21) It is to this same king-priest that Paul refers in quoting Psalm 45:6, 7: "God is your throne forever, and the scepter of your kingdom is the scepter of uprightness. You loved righteousness, and you hated lawlessness. That is why God, your God, anointed you with the oil of exultation more than your partners." (Heb. 1:8, 9) As Paul quotes from the Hebrew Scriptures and shows their fulfillment in Christ Jesus we see the pieces of the divine pattern falling into place for our enlightenment.

26 As the letter to the Hebrews clearly shows, Abraham looked forward to the Kingdom, "the city having real foundations, the builder and creator of which city is God"—the city "belonging to heaven." "By faith" he reached out for the kingdom, and he made great sacrifices that he might attain its blessings by "a better resurrection." What a striking example we find in Abraham and in all those other men and women of faith—the "so great a cloud of witnesses" that Paul portrays in Hebrews chapter 11! As we read this record our hearts exult and leap for joy, in appreciation of the privilege and hope we have along with such faithful integrity-keepers. Thus we are encouraged to "run with endurance the race that is set before us."—Heb. 11:8, 10, 16, 35; 12:1.

27 Quoting from Haggai's prophecy (2:6), Paul calls attention to God's promise: "Yet once more I will set in commotion not only the earth but also the heaven." However, God's kingdom by Christ Jesus the Seed will remain forever. "Wherefore, seeing that we are to receive a kingdom that cannot be shaken, let us continue to have undeserved kindness, through which we may acceptably render God sacred service with godly fear and awe." This stirring record assures us that Christ appears a second time "apart from sin and to those earnestly looking for him for their salvation." Through him, then, "let us always offer to God a sacrifice of praise, that is, the fruit of lips which make public declaration to his name." May the great name of Jehovah God be forever sanctified through his King-Priest, Jesus Christ! —Heb. 12:26, 28; 9:28; 13:15.

25. What enlightening applications does Paul here make of the Hebrew Scriptures?

26. What encouragement does Hebrews give to run the race in faith and with endurance?

27. What glorious Kingdom prospects are highlighted in Hebrews?

Bible Book Number Fifty-nine—James

Writer:	**James (Jesus' brother)**
Place Written:	**Jerusalem**
Writing Completed:	**Before A.D. 62**
Time Covered:	**Undetermined**

"HE HAS gone out of his mind." That is what Jesus' relatives thought of him. During the time of his earthly ministry, "his brothers were, in fact, not exercising faith in him," and James, along with Joseph, Simon and Judas, was not counted as one of Jesus' early disciples. (Mark 3:21; John 7:5; Matt. 13:55) On what grounds can it be said, then, that James the brother of Jesus wrote the Bible book that bears the name James?

2 The record shows that the resurrected Jesus appeared to James, and this no doubt convinced him beyond question that Jesus was the Messiah. (1 Cor. 15:7) Acts 1:12-14 tells that even before Pentecost Mary and the brothers of Jesus were assembling for prayer with the apostles in an upper chamber in Jerusalem. But did not one of the apostles called James write the letter? No, for, at the outset, the writer identifies himself, not as an apostle, but as 'a slave of the Lord Jesus Christ.' Moreover, Jude's introductory words, similar to those of James, mention Jude (or Judas) also as "a slave of Jesus Christ, but a brother of James." (Jas. 1:1; Jude 1) From this we can safely conclude that James and Jude, the fleshly half brothers of Jesus, wrote the Bible books that bear their names.

3 James was eminently qualified to write a letter of counsel to the Christian congregation. He was greatly respected as an overseer in the Jerusalem congregation. Paul speaks of "James the brother of the Lord" as one of the "pillars" in the congregation along with Cephas and John. (Gal. 1:19; 2:9) His prominence is indicated by Peter's sending immediate word to "James and the brothers" after his release from prison. And was it not James that acted as spokesman for "the apostles and the older brothers" when Paul and Barnabas journeyed to Jerusalem to request a decision regarding circumcision? Incidentally, this decision and the letter of James both start with the identical salutation, "Greetings!"—another indication that they had a common writer.—Acts 12:17; 15:13, 22, 23; Jas. 1:1.

1. What raises a question as to James' writership of this book?
2. But what argues that Jesus' half brother was the writer?
3. What were James' qualifications for writing?

4 The historian Josephus tells us that it was High Priest Ananus, a Sadducee, the last son of the chief priest Annas who shared in instigating Jesus' execution, that was responsible for the stoning of James to death, after the death of the Roman procurator Festus and before his successor, Albinus, took office, which was about A.D. 62.[a] But when did James write his letter? After the outpouring of the holy spirit A.D. 33 it required time for Christianity to spread out so that James could address his letter from Jerusalem to "the twelve tribes that are in the dispersion." (Jas. 1:1, *NW* footnote, 1950 Ed.) It would require time, also, for the alarming conditions mentioned in the letter to develop. Further, the letter indicates that the Christians were no longer small groups, but they were organized into congregations with mature "older men" who could pray for and support the weak. Also, sufficient time had elapsed for a measure of complacency and formalism to creep in. (Jas. 2:1-4; 4:1-3; 5:14; 1:26, 27) It is most probable, therefore, that James wrote his letter at a late date, perhaps shortly before his death A.D. 62, if Josephus' account is true.

5 As to the authenticity of James, it is contained in the Vatican No. 1209, the Sinaitic and the Alexandrine Manuscripts. It is included in at least ten ancient catalogues prior to the Council of Carthage, A.D. 397.[b] It was widely quoted by church writers in the fourth century. A deep inner harmony with the rest of the inspired Scriptures is very evident in James' writings.

6 Why did James write this letter? A careful consideration of the letter discloses that internal conditions were causing difficulties among the brothers. Christian standards were being lowered, yes, even ignored to the point where some had become "adulteresses" with respect to friendship with the world. Eager to invent supposed contradictions, some have claimed

a *Antiquities*, XX, 9, 1; *Webster's Biographical Dictionary*, 1943, page 517.
b See chart, page 302.

4. What indicates that the letter was written shortly before A.D. 62?
5. What proves the book to be authentic?
6. (a) What circumstances called for James to write his letter? (b) Rather than contradict, how does James supplement Paul's arguments on faith?

that James' letter encouraging faith by works nullifies Paul's writings regarding salvation by faith and not by works. However, the context reveals that James refers to faith supported by works, not just words, whereas Paul clearly means works of the Law. Actually, James supplements the arguments of Paul, going one step farther to define how faith is made manifest. James' counsel is most practical in its coverage of the day-to-day problems of the Christian.

7 Illustrations from everyday life, including animals, boats, farmers, vegetation, and so on, give colorful backing to James' arguments on faith, patience and endurance. This copying of Jesus' successful teaching method makes his counsel extremely forceful. This letter impresses one with James' keen discernment of the motives prompting individuals.

CONTENTS OF JAMES

8 **Patient endurance as "doers of the word"** (1:1-27). James opens with words of encouragement: "Consider it all joy, my brothers, when you meet with various trials." Through patient endurance they will be made complete. If one lacks wisdom he should ask God for it, not in doubt, like a wind-tossed wave of the sea, but in faith. The lowly will be exalted, but the rich will fade away like the flower that perishes. Happy is the man that endures trial, for "he will receive the crown of life, which Jehovah promised to those who continue loving him." God does not tempt man with evil things to cause his downfall. It is one's own wrong desire that becomes fertile and gives birth to sin, and this, in turn, brings forth death.—1:2, 12.

9 Whence come all good gifts? From the never-varying 'Father of celestial lights.' "Because he willed it," says James, "he brought us forth by the word of truth, for us to be a certain first fruits of his creatures." Christians, then, should be swift to hear, slow to speak, slow to wrath, and should put away all filthiness and moral badness and accept the implanting of the word of salvation. "Become doers of the word, and not hearers only." For he who peers into the mirrorlike law of freedom, and persists in it, "will be happy in his doing it." The formal worship of the man that does not bridle his tongue is futile, but "the form of worship that is clean and undefiled from the standpoint of our God and Father is this: to look after orphans and widows in their tribulation, and to keep oneself without spot from the world."—1:17, 18, 22, 25, 27.

10 **Faith perfected by right works** (2:1-26). The brothers are making distinctions, preferring the rich above the poor. But is it not true that "God chose the ones who are poor respecting the world to be rich in faith and heirs of the kingdom"? Are not the rich oppressors? The brothers should practice the kingly law, "You must love your neighbor as yourself," and shun favoritism. Let them also practice mercy, for, as regards the Law, whoever offends in one point offends in all. Faith without works is meaningless, as when telling a needy brother or sister to "keep warm and well fed," without giving practical aid. Can faith be shown apart from works? Was not Abraham's faith perfected by his works in offering Isaac on the altar? Likewise, Rahab the harlot was "declared righteous by works." So faith without works is dead.—2:5, 8, 16, 19, 25.

11 **Controlling the tongue to teach wisdom** (3:1-18). The brothers should be wary about becoming teachers, lest they receive heavier judgment. Everyone stumbles many times. As a bridle controls a horse's body, and a small rudder a large boat, so that little member, the tongue, has great power. It is like a fire that can set a great woodland on fire! Wild animals can be tamed more easily than the tongue. With it men bless Jehovah, yet curse their fellowman. This is not proper. Does a fountain produce both bitter and sweet water? Can a fig tree produce olives? a vine, figs? salt water, sweet water? James asks: "Who is wise and understanding among you?" Let him show his works with meekness, and avoid contentiousness, animalistic bragging against the truth. For "the wisdom from above is first of all chaste, then peaceable, reasonable, ready to obey, full of mercy and good fruits, not making partial distinctions, not hypocritical."—3:13, 17.

12 **Shun sensual pleasure, friendship with the world** (4:1-17). "From what source are there fights among you?" James answers his own question: "Your cravings for sensual pleasure"! Their motives are wrong. Those that would be friends of the world are "adulteresses," and become God's enemies. Rather, "oppose the Devil, and he will flee from you. Draw close to God, and he will draw close to you." Jehovah will exalt the humble. So let them quit judging one another. And, because no one can be sure of his life from one day to the next, they ought to say: "If Jehovah wills, we shall live and also do this or that." Pride is wicked, and it is a sin

7. How does James copy Jesus' teaching methods, and with what effect?
8. What will result from patient endurance, but what from wrong desire?
9. What is involved in being "doers of the word," and what form of worship is approved by God?

10. (a) What distinctions are to be shunned? (b) What is the relationship of works to faith?
11. (a) By use of what illustrations does James warn concerning the tongue? (b) How are wisdom and understanding to be shown?
12. (a) What wrong conditions exist in the congregation, and what is their source? (b) What attitude should be avoided and what quality cultivated to gain Jehovah's approval?

to know what is right and not to do it.—4:1, 4, 7, 8, 15.

13 **Happy those who endure in righteousness!** (5:1-20). 'Weep and howl, you rich men!' declares James. 'The rust of your wealth will be witness against you. Jehovah of armies has heard the calls for help from the reapers that you have deprived. You have lived in luxury and sensual pleasure, and have condemned and murdered the righteous one.' However, in view of the nearness of the Lord's presence, let the brothers exercise patience, like the farmer waiting for his harvest, and consider the pattern of the prophets, "who spoke in the name of Jehovah." Happy are those who have endured! They should recall the endurance of Job, and the outcome Jehovah gave, "that Jehovah is very tender in affection and merciful." —5:1-6, 10, 11.

14 Let them stop swearing oaths. Rather, let their *Yes* mean Yes, and their *No*, No. They should openly confess their sins and pray for one another. As shown by Elijah's prayers, "a righteous man's supplication . . . has much force." If anyone is misled from the truth, the one who turns him back "will save his soul from death and will cover a multitude of sins." —5:16, 20.

WHY BENEFICIAL

15 Though James only twice mentions the name Jesus (1:1; 2:1), he makes much practical application of the teachings of the Master, as a careful comparison of James' letter and the Sermon on the Mount reveals. At the same time, Jehovah's name appears thirteen times (*New World Translation*), and his promises are emphasized as rewards for faith-keeping Christians. (Jas. 4:10; 5:11) James draws repeatedly on the Hebrew Scriptures for illustrations and apt quotations in order to develop his practical counsel. He identifies the source by his expressions: "according to the Scriptures," "and the scripture was fulfilled," "the scripture says," and goes on to apply these scriptures to Christian living. (Jas. 2:8, 23; 4:5) In making plain points of counsel and building faith in God's Word as a harmonious whole, James makes deft references to Abraham's works of faith, to Rahab's demonstration of faith by works, to Job's faithful endurance and to Elijah's reliance on prayer.—Jas. 2:21-25; 5:11, 17, 18; Gen. 22:9-12; Josh. 2:1-21; Job 1: 20-22; 42:10; 1 Ki. 17:1; 18:41-45.

16 Invaluable is James' counsel to be doers of the word and not just hearers, to keep proving faith by works of righteousness, to find joy in enduring various trials, to keep on asking God for wisdom, always to draw close to him in prayer and to practice the kingly law, "You must love your neighbor as yourself." (Jas. 1:22; 2:24; 1:2, 5; 4:8; 5:13-18; 2:8) Strong are his warnings against teaching error, the injurious use of the tongue, making class distinctions in the congregation, craving sensual pleasure and trusting in corruptible riches. (Jas. 3:1, 8; 2:4; 4:3; 5:1, 5) James makes it very plain that friendship with the world amounts to spiritual adultery and enmity with God, and he gives the definition of the practical form of worship that is clean in God's sight: "to look after orphans and widows in their tribulation, and to keep oneself without spot from the world." (Jas. 4:4; 1:27) All this counsel, so practical and easy to understand, is just what could be expected from this "pillar" of the early Christian congregation. Its kindly message continues as a guidepost for Christians in this turbulent twentieth century, for it is "wisdom from above" that produces "the fruit of righteousness."—Jas. 3:17, 18.

17 James was anxious to help his brothers reach their goal of life in God's kingdom. So he urges them: "You too exercise patience; make your hearts firm, because the presence of the Lord has drawn close." They are happy if they go on enduring trial, because God's approval means receiving "the crown of life, which Jehovah promised to those who continue loving him." (Jas. 5:8; 1:12) Referring evidently to Jesus' words found at Luke 22:29, James says also: "Listen, my beloved brothers. God chose the ones who are poor respecting the world to be rich in faith and heirs of the kingdom, which he promised to those who love him." Thus God's promise of the crown of life in his heavenly kingdom is emphasized as strong reason for enduring in faithful works. Surely this wonderful letter will encourage all to reach out for the goal of everlasting life in Jehovah's new world ruled by the Kingdom Seed, our Lord Jesus Christ.—Jas. 2:5.

13. (a) Why is it woe for the rich? (b) How does James illustrate the need for patience and endurance, and what results therefrom?
14. What closing counsel is given concerning confessing sin and concerning prayer?
15. How does James make application of the Hebrew Scriptures? Illustrate.
16. What counsel and warnings does James give, and from what source is such practical wisdom?
17. What strong reason is presented for enduring in faithful works?

Bible Book Number Sixty— 1 Peter

Writer:	**Peter**
Place Written:	**Babylon**
Writing Completed:	**c. A.D. 62-64**
Time Covered:	**Undetermined**

AS THE early Christians declared abroad the excellencies of God, the Kingdom work prospered and increased throughout the Roman Empire. However, some misunderstandings arose concerning this zealous group. For one thing, their religion had originated from Jerusalem and from among the Jews, and some confused them with the politically-minded Jewish zealots who chafed under the Roman yoke and were a constant trouble to local governors. Moreover, the Christians were "different" in that they refused to sacrifice to the emperor or to mix in with the pagan religious ceremonies of the day. They were spoken against, and had to undergo many trials on account of the faith. At the right time, and with forethought denoting divine inspiration, Peter wrote his first letter, encouraging the Christians to stand firm, and counseling them on how to conduct themselves under Nero, the "Caesar" of that time. This letter proved to be most timely in view of the storm of persecution that broke out almost immediately thereafter.

2 Peter's writership is established by the opening words. Moreover, Irenaeus, Clement of Alexandria, Origen and Tertullian all quote the letter, naming Peter as writer.[a] The authenticity of First Peter is as well attested as any of the inspired letters. Eusebius tells us that the elders of the church made free use of the letter; there was no question as to its authenticity in his time (c. A.D. 260-340). Ignatius, Hermas and Barnabas, of the early second century, all make references to it. First Peter is completely in harmony with the rest of the inspired Scriptures, and sets out a powerful message for the Jewish and non-Jewish Christians residing as "temporary residents scattered about in Pontus, Galatia, Cappadocia, Asia, and Bithynia."

3 When was the letter written? Its tone indicates that the Christians were experiencing trials from either the pagans or unconverted Jews, but that Nero's campaign of persecution, launched A.D. 64, had not yet begun. It is evident that Peter wrote the letter just prior to this, probably between A.D. 62 and 64. The fact that Mark was still with Peter strengthens this conclusion. In A.D. 60 Mark was with Paul in Rome but was due to travel to Asia Minor, and at the time of Paul's second imprisonment in A.D. 65 Mark was due to join Paul again in Rome. (1 Pet. 5:13; Col. 4:10; 2 Tim. 4:11) In the interval he would have the opportunity to be with Peter in Babylon.

4 Where was First Peter written? Whereas Bible commentators agree on the authenticity, canonicity, writership and approximate date of writing, they differ as to the place of writing. Some claim it was the famous Babylon of Asia, on the Euphrates River. Others argue that it was Babylon in Egypt, now called Old Cairo. The Roman Catholic Church is quick to assert that Peter wrote from Rome, Babylon being a "mystical name for Rome." On this, Halley's *Pocket Bible Handbook*, 1944, page 506, says: "The Roman Catholic tradition that Peter founded the church in Rome and was its bishop for 25 years has no historical foundation whatever. It was a fiction invented centuries later when the Roman bishops were becoming ambitious to be overlords of Christendom." *The Westminster Dictionary of the Bible* (1944, page 473), although it supports the view of many early writers that Peter was executed in Rome, has this to say concerning Peter: "Legend was early busy with his life; the Roman legend of his 25 years' episcopate in Rome has its roots in early apocryphal stories originating among the heretical Ebionites, and is discredited not less by its origin and manifest internal inconsistencies than by all authentic history."

5 The inspired Scriptures, including the two letters written by Peter, make no mention of his going to Rome. Paul speaks of being in Rome but never refers to Peter's being there. Although he mentions thirty-five names in his letter to the Romans and sends greetings by name to twenty-six, why does Paul fail to mention Peter? And in this letter to the Romans, why does Paul give instruction that Peter as "vicegerent of Christ" would normally be ex-

a M'Clintock and Strong's *Cyclopædia*, 1883, Vol. VIII, page 15.

1. Why did the Christians have to undergo trials, and why was Peter's first letter timely?
2. What proves Peter to be the writer, and to whom was the letter addressed?
3. What evidence is there as to time of writing?

4, 5. (a) What disproves the claim that Peter wrote his first letter from Rome? (b) What indicates he wrote from the literal Babylon?

pected to give his flock? Simply because Peter was not there at the time! (Rom. 16:3-15) The "Babylon" from which Peter wrote his first letter appears, then, to have been the literal Babylon on the banks of the Euphrates River in Mesopotamia. Circumcised Jews had been living in that city from Nebuchadnezzar's day. According to the orderly division of territory among the apostles, Paul traveled west and finally reached Rome, whereas Peter worked among the "circumcised" in the Near East, including the Jewish settlements in Babylon. —Gal. 2:7-9.

CONTENTS OF FIRST PETER

6 **The new birth to a living hope through Christ** (1:1-25). At the outset Peter directs his readers' attention to the "new birth to a living hope" and the unfading inheritance reserved for them in the heavens. This is according to God's mercy, through the resurrection of Jesus Christ. Therefore they are greatly rejoicing, though grieved by various trials, so that the tested quality of their faith "may be found a cause for praise and glory and honor at the revelation of Jesus Christ." The prophets of old, yes, even angels, have inquired concerning this salvation. Hence, they should brace up their minds for activity and set their hope on this undeserved kindness, becoming holy in all their conduct. Is this not proper in view of their being delivered, not with corruptible things, but "with precious blood, like that of an unblemished and spotless lamb, even Christ's"? Their "new birth" is through the word of the living and enduring God, Jehovah, which endures forever and which has been declared to them as good news.—1:3, 7, 19, 23.

7 **Maintaining fine conduct among the nations** (2:1–3:22). As living stones, Christians are built up a spiritual house, offering up spiritual sacrifices acceptable to God through Jesus Christ, the foundation cornerstone who became a stone of stumbling to the disobedient. Those exercising faith have become 'a royal priesthood, a holy nation, to declare abroad the excellencies of the one that called them out of darkness into his wonderful light.' As temporary residents among the nations, let them abstain from fleshly desires and maintain fine conduct. Let them be subject to "every human creation," whether to a king or to his governors. Yes, let them "honor men of all sorts, have love for the whole association of brothers, be in fear of God, have honor for the king." Likewise, let servants be in subjection to their owners, with a good conscience, bearing up under unjust suffering. Even Christ, though sinless, submitted to reviling and suffering, leaving "a model . . . to follow his steps closely."—2:9, 13, 17, 21.

8 Subjection applies also to wives, who through chaste conduct together with deep respect may even win over unbelieving husbands without a word. Their concern should not be external adornment, but as with the obedient Sarah, "let it be the secret person of the heart in the incorruptible apparel of the quiet and mild spirit, which is of great value in the eyes of God." Husbands should honor wives as "a weaker vessel" and as "heirs with them of the undeserved favor of life." All Christians should show brotherly love. "He that would love life . . . let him turn away from what is bad and do what is good; let him seek peace and pursue it. For the eyes of Jehovah are upon the righteous ones." Rather than fear men, they should always be ready to make a defense of their hope. It is better to suffer for doing good, if it is God's will, than for doing evil. "Why, even Christ died once for all time concerning sins, a righteous person for unrighteous ones, that he might lead you to God, he being put to death in the flesh, but being made alive in the spirit." Just as God made provision for the salvation of Noah and his family in the ark, so now there is a provision for salvation through baptism and through the resurrection of Jesus Christ.—3:4, 7, 10-12, 18.

9 **Rejoicing in doing God's will as a Christian, despite suffering** (4:1–5:14). Christians should have the same mental disposition as Christ, living only to do God's will, and no longer that of the nations, even though these speak of them abusively for not continuing to run with them "to the same low sink of debauchery." Since the end of all things has drawn close, they should be sound in mind, prayerful, and have intense love for one another, doing all things that God may be glorified. As trials burn among them, they should not be puzzled, but rejoice as sharers in the sufferings of the Christ. However, let none suffer as an evildoer. Since judgment starts at the house of God, "let those who are suffering in harmony with the will of God keep on commending their souls to a faithful Creator while they are doing good."—4:4, 19.

10 The older men should shepherd the flock of God willingly, yes, eagerly. Being examples to the flock will assure them of the unfadable crown of glory at the manifestation of the

6. Of what hope does Peter write, and on what basis is the "new birth" to this hope possible?
7. (a) Into what house are Christians being built, and for what purpose? (b) As temporary residents, how should they conduct themselves?
8. (a) What sound admonition is given wives and husbands? (b) What provision for salvation has God made for those now seeking to do what is good?
9. What mental disposition should Christians have? Despite what?
10. What counsel is given to older men, and to younger men, and with what powerful assurance does the letter end?

Chief Shepherd. Let younger men be in subjection to the older men, all having lowliness of mind, "because God opposes the haughty ones, but he gives undeserved kindness to the humble ones." Let them be solid in the faith and watchful of that "roaring lion," the Devil. Again powerful words of assurance ring out, as Peter concludes his exhortation: "But, after you have suffered a little while, the God of all undeserved kindness, who called you to his everlasting glory in union with Christ, will himself finish your training, he will make you firm, he will make you strong. To him be the might forever. Amen."—5:5, 8, 10, 11.

WHY BENEFICIAL

11 The first letter of Peter contains sound advice for overseers. Following up on Jesus' own counsel at John 21:15-17 and that of Paul at Acts 20:25-35, Peter again shows the work of the overseer to be a shepherding work, to be done unselfishly, willingly and eagerly. The overseer is an undershepherd, serving in subjection to the Chief Shepherd and accountable to him for the flock of God, whose interests he must care for as an example and in all humility.—1 Pet. 5:2-4.

12 Many other aspects of Christian subjection are touched on in Peter's letter, and excellent advice is given. At 1 Peter 2:13-17, proper subjection to the rulers, such as a king and governors, is counseled. However, this is to be a relative subjection, being for the Lord's sake and coupled with "fear of God," whose slaves Christians are. House servants are exhorted to be in subjection to their owners, and to bear up if they have to suffer "because of conscience toward God." Also, wives are given invaluable admonition concerning subjection to husbands, including unbelieving ones, it being shown that their chaste, respectful conduct is "of great value in the eyes of God" and may even win their husbands to the truth. Here Peter uses the illustration of Sarah's faithful submission to Abraham to underscore the point. (1 Pet. 2: 18-20; 3:1-6; Gen. 18:12) Husbands, in turn, should exercise their headship with proper consideration for the "weaker vessel." Still on this topic, Peter exhorts: "In like manner, you younger men, be in subjection to the older men." And then he emphasizes the need for lowliness of mind, humility, a Christian quality that is emphasized throughout his letter. —1 Pet. 3:7-9; 5:5-7; 2:21-25.

13 At a time when fiery trials and persecutions were beginning to flare up again, Peter provided strengthening encouragement, and his letter is indeed invaluable to all who face such trials today. Notice how he draws on the Hebrew Scriptures in quoting Jehovah's words: "You must be holy, because I am holy." (1 Pet. 1:16; Lev. 11:44) Then, again, in a passage that is rich in its references to other inspired Scripture, he shows how the Christian congregation is built as a spiritual house of living stones on the foundation of Christ. And for what purpose? Peter answers: "You are 'a chosen race, a royal priesthood, a holy nation, a people for special possession, that you should declare abroad the excellencies' of the one that called you out of darkness into his wonderful light." (1 Pet. 2:4-10; Isa. 28:16; Ps. 118:22; Isa. 8:14; Ex. 19:5, 6; Isa. 43:21; Hos. 1:10; 2:23) It is to this "royal priesthood," the general priesthood comprising the entire holy nation of God, that Peter holds forth the Kingdom promise of "an incorruptible and undefiled and unfading inheritance," "the unfadable crown of glory," "everlasting glory in union with Christ." Thus, these are greatly encouraged to go on rejoicing, that they may "rejoice and be overjoyed also during the revelation of his glory." —1 Pet. 1:4; 5:4, 10; 4:13.

---

11. How does Peter follow up Jesus' and Paul's counsel in giving advice to overseers?

12. (a) What relative subjection must be rendered to rulers and to owners? (b) What does Peter admonish regarding wifely submission and the husband's headship? (c) What Christian quality is emphasized throughout the letter?

13. (a) How does Peter in his letter make clear the purpose of God's calling out the Christian congregation? (b) To what joyful inheritance does he point forward, and who attain to it?

Bible Book Number Sixty-one— 2 Peter

Writer:	**Peter**
Place Written:	**Babylon (?)**
Writing Completed:	**c. A.D. 64**
Time Covered:	**Undetermined**

WHEN Peter composed his second letter he realized he was to face death soon. He anxiously desired to remind his fellow Christians of the importance of accurate knowledge to aid them to maintain steadfastness in their ministry. Would there be any reason to doubt that the apostle Peter was the writer of the second letter bearing his name? The letter itself erases any doubts that may have arisen as to writership. The writer says he is "Simon Peter, a slave and apostle of Jesus Christ." (1:1) He refers to this as "the second letter I am writing you." (3:1) He speaks of himself as an eyewitness to the transfiguration of Jesus Christ, a privilege that Peter shared with James and John, and writes of this with all the feeling of an eyewitness. (1:16-21) He mentions that Jesus had foretold his death.—2 Pet. 1:14; John 21:18, 19.

2 However, some critics have pointed to the difference in style of the two letters as a reason for discounting the second letter as the work of Peter. But this should pose no real problem, for the subject and the purpose in writing were different. Also, Peter wrote his first letter "through Silvanus, a faithful brother," and if Silvanus were given some latitude in formulating the sentences, this could account for the difference of style in the two letters, since Silvanus apparently did not have a part in writing the second letter. (1 Pet. 5:12) Its canonicity has also been disputed on the grounds that it "is poorly attested in the Fathers." However, as may be observed from the chart "Early Catalogues of the Christian Greek Scriptures," Second Peter was regarded as part of the Bible catalogue by eleven authorities prior to the Third Council of Carthage.[a]

3 When was Peter's second letter written? It is most probable that it was written A.D. 64 from Babylon or its vicinity, shortly after the first letter, but there is no direct evidence, particularly as to the place. At the time of writing, most of Paul's letters were circulating among the congregations and were known to Peter, who considered them as inspired of God and compared them with "the rest of the Scriptures." Peter's second letter is addressed "to those who have obtained a faith, held in equal privilege with ours," and includes those to whom the first letter was addressed and others to whom Peter had preached. Just as the first letter had circulated in many areas, so the second letter also took on a general character. —2 Pet. 3:15, 16; 1:1; 3:1; 1 Pet. 1:1.

CONTENTS OF SECOND PETER

4 **Making sure of the calling to the heavenly kingdom** (1:1-21). Peter is quick to show loving concern for "those who have obtained a faith." He desires that undeserved kindness and peace be increased to them "by an accurate knowledge of God and of Jesus our Lord." God has freely given them "the precious and very grand promises," through which they may become sharers in the divine nature. Therefore by earnest effort let them supply to their faith virtue, knowledge, self-control, endurance, godly devotion, brotherly affection and love. If these qualities overflow in them, they will never become inactive or unfruitful with regard to accurate knowledge. The brothers should do their utmost to make sure of their calling and choosing, and their entrance into the everlasting kingdom of their Lord. Knowing that 'the putting off of his tabernacle is soon to be,' Peter is disposed to remind them of these things so that they may make mention of them after his departure. Peter was an eyewitness of Christ's magnificence in the holy mountain when these words "were borne to him by the magnificent glory: 'This is my son, my beloved, whom I myself have approved.'" Thus the prophetic word is made more sure, and should be heeded, for it is not by man's will, "but men spoke from God as they were borne along by holy spirit."—1:1, 2, 4, 14, 17, 21.

5 **Strong warning against false teachers** (2:1-22). False prophets and teachers will bring in destructive sects, promote loose conduct and bring reproach upon the truth. But their destruction is not slumbering. God did not hold back from punishing the angels that sinned,

a See chart on page 302.

1. What facts prove Peter's writership?
2. What argues for the canonicity of Second Peter?
3. When and where does the letter appear to have been written, and to whom was it addressed?

4. (a) How should the brothers strive to become fruitful with regard to accurate knowledge, and in view of what promises? (b) How is the prophetic word made more sure, and why should it be heeded?
5. What warning does Peter give against false teachers, and what powerful illustrations does he use as to the certainty of God's judgments against such men?

from bringing a deluge in Noah's day or from reducing Sodom and Gomorrah to ashes. Just as he delivered preacher Noah and righteous Lot, so "Jehovah knows how to deliver people of godly devotion out of trial, but to reserve unrighteous people for the day of judgment to be cut off." For these are daring, self-willed, like unreasoning animals, ignorant, abusive talkers, delighting in deceptive teachings, adulterous, covetous, and like Balaam in loving the reward of wrongdoing. They promise freedom, but are themselves the slaves of corruption. It would have been better for them not to have known the path of righteousness, for the saying has happened to them: "The dog has returned to its own vomit, and the sow that was bathed to rolling in the mire."—2:9, 22.

6 **Keeping close in mind the day of Jehovah** (3:1-18). Peter is writing to arouse their clear thinking faculties, that they may remember the sayings previously spoken. Ridiculers will come in the last days, saying: "Where is this promised presence of his?" It escapes the notice of these men that God destroyed the world of ancient times by waters, and that "by the same word the heavens and the earth that are now are stored up for fire," against the day of destruction of the ungodly men. Just as a thousand years are with Jehovah as one day, so "Jehovah is not slow respecting his promise," but is patient, not desiring any to be destroyed. Hence Christians should watch their conduct and practice deeds of godly devotion as they await and keep close in mind the presence of the day of Jehovah, through which the heavens will be dissolved by fire and the elements melt with intense heat. But there are to be "new heavens and a new earth" according to God's promise.—3:4, 7, 9, 13.

7 Hence they should do their utmost "to be found finally by him spotless and unblemished and in peace." They should consider the patience of their Lord as salvation, just as the beloved Paul wrote them. With this advance knowledge let them be on guard not to fall from their own steadfastness. "No," concludes Peter, "but go on growing in the undeserved kindness and knowledge of our Lord and Savior Jesus Christ. To him be the glory both now and to the day of eternity."—3:14, 18.

WHY BENEFICIAL

8 How essential is accurate knowledge! Peter himself weaves into his arguments accurate knowledge that he has acquired from the Hebrew Scriptures, which he testifies to have been inspired by holy spirit: "For prophecy was at no time brought by man's will, but men spoke from God as they were borne along by holy spirit." He points out, also, that Paul's wisdom was "given him." (2 Pet. 1:21; 3:15) We benefit greatly by considering all these inspired Scriptures, and holding fast to accurate knowledge. Thus we will never become complacent, like those whom Peter describes as saying: "All things are continuing exactly as from creation's beginning." (2 Pet. 3:4) Nor will we fall into the traps of the false teachers such as Peter describes in chapter two of his letter. Rather, we should constantly consider the reminders provided by Peter and the other Bible writers, so as to remain "firmly set in the truth," and patiently and steadfastly to "go on growing in the undeserved kindness and knowledge of our Lord and Savior Jesus Christ."—2 Pet. 1:12; 3:18.

9 As an aid to increasing in "accurate knowledge of God and of Jesus our Lord" Peter recommends earnest effort to build up those Christian qualities listed in chapter 1, verses 5 to 7, and then in verse 8 he adds: "For if these things exist in you and overflow, they will prevent you from being either inactive or unfruitful regarding the accurate knowledge of our Lord Jesus Christ." Truly this is splendid encouragement to activity as God's ministers in these critical days!

10 How important it is to exert oneself to the utmost in order to be assured of sharing in "the precious and very grand promises" of Jehovah God! So it is that Peter exhorts the anointed Christians to keep eyes fixed on the Kingdom goal, saying: "Do your utmost to make the calling and choosing of you sure for yourselves; for if you keep on doing these things you will by no means ever fail. In fact, thus there will be richly supplied to you the entrance into the everlasting kingdom of our Lord and Savior Jesus Christ." Then Peter calls attention to the magnificence of Jesus' Kingdom glory, of which he had been an eyewitness through the transfiguration vision, and adds: "Consequently we have the prophetic word made more sure." True, every prophecy concerning the magnificent kingdom of Jehovah will come to certain fulfillment. Thus it is with confidence that we echo Peter's words quoted from Isaiah's prophecy: "There are new heavens and a new earth that we are awaiting according to his promise, and in these righteousness is to dwell."—2 Pet. 1:4, 10, 11, 19; 3:13; Isa. 65:17, 18.

6. (a) Why does Peter write, and what does he say concerning God's promise? (b) In contrast to ridiculers, how must Christians show themselves watchful?
7. Having this advance knowledge, how should Christians exert themselves?
8. (a) How does Peter testify to the inspiration of both the Hebrew and the Greek Scriptures? (b) How will we be benefited by holding fast to accurate knowledge?
9. What earnest effort are we encouraged to make, and why?
10. (a) What promises does Peter emphasize, and what does he exhort in connection therewith? (b) What assurance does he give concerning the Kingdom prophecies?

Bible Book Number Sixty-two— 1 John

Writer:	**Apostle John**
Place Written:	**Ephesus, or near**
Writing Completed:	**c. A.D. 98**
Time Covered:	**Undetermined**

JOHN, the beloved apostle of Jesus Christ, had a strong love for righteousness. This helped give him a keen insight into the mind of Jesus. We are therefore not surprised that a theme of love dominates his writings. He was no sentimentalist, however, for Jesus referred to him as one of the "Sons of Thunder [Boanerges]." (Mark 3:17) In fact, it was in defense of truth and righteousness that he wrote his three letters, for the apostasy foretold by the apostle Paul had become evident. John's three letters were indeed timely, for they were an aid in strengthening the early Christians in their fight against the encroachments of "the wicked one."—2 Thess. 2:3, 4; 1 John 2:13, 14; 5:18, 19.

2 Judging from the contents, these letters belong to a period much later than the Gospels of Matthew and Mark—later, also, than the missionary letters of Peter and Paul. Times had changed. There is no reference to Judaism, the big threat to the congregations in the days of their infancy; and there does not appear to be a single direct quotation from the Hebrew Scriptures. On the other hand, John talks about the "last hour" and the appearance of "many antichrists." (1 John 2:18) He refers to his readers by expressions such as "my little children," and to himself as "the older man." (1 John 2:1, 12, 13, 18, 28; 3:7, 18; 4:4; 5:21; 2 John 1; 3 John 1) All of this suggests a late date for his three letters. Also, 1 John 1:3, 4 seems to indicate that John's Gospel was written about the same time. It is generally believed that John's three letters were completed by A.D. 98, shortly before the apostle's death, and that they were written in the vicinity of Ephesus.

3 That First John was actually written by John the apostle is indicated by its close resemblance to the fourth Gospel, which he unmistakably wrote. For example, he introduces the letter by describing himself as an eyewitness who has seen "the word of life . . . the everlasting life which was with the Father and was made manifest to us," expressions strikingly similar to those with which John's Gospel opens. Its authenticity is attested by the Muratorian Canon and by Irenaeus, and it is quoted by Polycarp, Papias and others, all of the second century A.D.[a] However, it is to be noted that some translations have added to chapter 5 the following words at the end of verse 7 and the beginning of verse 8: "In heaven, the Father, the Word and the holy spirit; and these three are one. And there are three witness bearers on earth." But this text is not found in any Greek manuscript of First John prior to the fifteenth century, and has obviously been added to bolster the trinity doctrine. Most modern translations omit these words.[b]

4 John writes to protect his "beloved ones," his "young children," against the wrong teachings of the "many antichrists" that have gone out from among them and that are trying to seduce them away from the truth. Apparently these were the forerunners of the "Gnostics," a group that claimed special knowledge of a mystical sort from God.[c] John's statements on sin, and in support of Jesus' sacrifice for sins, indicate that these "modernist" teachers were self-righteously claiming themselves to be without sin and having no need of Jesus' ransom sacrifice. Their self-centered "knowledge" had made them selfish and loveless, a condition that John exposes as he continually emphasizes true Christian love. Moreover, John is apparently combating their false doctrine as he expounds that Jesus is the Christ, that he had a prehuman existence, and that he came in the flesh as the Son of God to provide salvation for believing men. (1 John 1:7-10; 2:1, 2; 4:16-21; 2:22; 1:1, 2; 4:2, 3, 14, 15) John brands these false teachers plainly as "antichrists," and gives a number of ways in which the children of God and the children of the Devil can be recognized.—1 John 2:18, 22; 4:3.

---

1. (a) What quality permeates John's writings, yet what shows he was no sentimentalist? (b) Why were his three letters timely?
2. (a) What indicates these letters were written much later than Matthew, Mark and the missionary letters? (b) When and where do the letters appear to have been written?
3. (a) What testifies to the writership and authenticity of First John? (b) What text was added later, but what proves it to be spurious?

a *The New Bible Dictionary,* 1962, J. D. Douglas, page 644.
b *New World Translation of the Christian Greek Scriptures,* 1950 Edition, page 786.
c *The New Bible Dictionary,* 1962, J. D. Douglas, pages 642, 473.

4. Against whom is John seeking to protect his fellow Christians, and what false teaching does he refute?

5 Since no particular congregation is addressed, the letter was evidently intended for the entire Christian association. The lack of a greeting at the beginning and a salutation at the end would also indicate this. Some have even described this writing as a tract rather than a letter. The use of the plural "you" throughout (as indicated by capitals in the *New World Translation*) shows that the writer directed his words to a group rather than to an individual.

CONTENTS OF FIRST JOHN

6 **Walking in the light, not in the darkness** (1:1–2:29). "We are writing these things," says John, "that our joy may be in full measure." Since "God is light," only those "walking in the light" are having "a sharing with him" and with one another. These are cleansed from sin by "the blood of Jesus his Son." On the other hand, those who "go on walking in the darkness" and who claim, "We have no sin," are misleading themselves and the truth is not in them. If sins are confessed, God will be faithful to forgive them.—1:4-8.

7 Jesus Christ is identified as "a propitiatory sacrifice" for sins, one who is a "helper with the Father." He that claims to know God but does not observe his commandments is a liar. He that loves his brother remains in the light, but he that hates his brother is walking in the darkness. John strongly counsels not to love the world or the things in the world, for, he says, "If anyone loves the world, the love of the Father is not in him." Many antichrists have come, and "they went out from us," explains John, for "they were not of our sort." The antichrist is the one that denies that Jesus is the Christ. He denies both the Father and the Son. Let the "little children" stay with what they have learned from the beginning, so as to "abide in union with the Son and in union with the Father," according to the anointing received from him, which is true.—2:1, 2, 15, 18, 19, 24.

8 **Children of God do not practice sin** (3:1-24). Because of the Father's love they are called "children of God," and at Christ's manifestation they are to be like him and to "see him just as he is." Sin is lawlessness, and those who are remaining in union with Christ do not practice it. The one who does carry on sin originates with the Devil, whose works the Son of God will break up. The children of God and the children of the Devil are thus evident: those originating with God have love for one another, but those originating with the wicked one are like Cain who hated and slew his brother. John tells the "little children" that they have come to know love because "that one surrendered his soul" for them, and admonishes them not to 'shut the door of tender compassions' on their brothers. Let them "love, neither in word nor with the tongue, but in deed and truth." To determine whether they "originate with the truth," they must check what is in their hearts and see if they "are doing the things that are pleasing in [God's] eyes." They must observe his commandment to "have faith in the name of his Son Jesus Christ and be loving one another." Thus they will know that they are remaining in union with him, and he with them by spirit.—3:1, 2, 16-19, 22, 23.

9 **Loving one another in union with God** (4:1–5:21). The inspired expressions are to be tested. Those that deny that Christ came in the flesh do "not originate with God," but are the antichrist's. They originate with the world and are in union with it, but the inspired expression of truth is from God. "God is love." And says John: "The love is in this respect, not that we have loved God, but that he loved us and sent forth his Son as a propitiatory sacrifice for our sins." How great the obligation, then, to love one another! Those who do, have God remain in union with them, and thus love has been made perfect that they "may have freeness of speech," throwing fear outside. "As for us," says John, "we love, because he first loved us." "The one who loves God should be loving his brother also."—4:3, 8, 10, 17, 19, 21.

10 Showing love as children of God means observing his commandments, and this results in conquering the world, through faith. God gives witness concerning those putting faith in the Son of God, that He gave them "everlasting life, and this life is in his Son." Thus they may have confidence toward him, that he will hear them in whatever they ask him according to his will. Though all unrighteousness is sin, yet there is a sin that does not incur death. Everyone born from God does not make a practice of sin. Though "the whole world is lying in the power of the wicked one . . . the Son of God has come," and he has given the "intellectual capacity" for gaining knowledge of the true God, with whom they are now in union "by means of his Son Jesus Christ." Let them guard themselves from idols!—5:11, 19, 20.

---

5. What indicates that this writing was intended for the entire Christian congregation?
6. What contrast does John make between those who walk in the light and those who are in darkness?
7. (a) How does one show that he knows and loves God? (b) How is the antichrist identified?
8. (a) What distinguishes the children of God and those of the Devil? (b) How have they come to know love, and what check must they continually make on their hearts?
9. (a) What test is to be made of the inspired expressions? (b) What emphasizes the obligation to love one another?
10. (a) How may the children of God conquer the world, and what confidence do they have? (b) What attitude must they have toward sin and idolatry?

WHY BENEFICIAL

11 Just as in the closing years of the first century of the Christian era, so today there are "many antichrists" against whom true Christians must be warned. These must hold fast to 'the message which they heard from the beginning, having love for one another,' and remain in union with God and the true teaching, practicing righteousness with freeness of speech. (1 John 2:18; 3:11; 2:27-29) Most important also is the warning against "the desire of the flesh and the desire of the eyes and the showy display of one's means of life," those materialistic, worldly evils that have engulfed most professing Christians. True Christians will shun the world and its desire, knowing that "he that does the will of God remains forever." In this age of worldly desire, sectarianism and hatred, how beneficial it is, indeed, to study God's will through the inspired Scriptures, and to do that will!—2:15-17.

12 It is for our benefit that First John makes clear the contrasts between the light that emanates from the Father and the truth-destroying darkness from the evil one, between the life-giving teachings of God and the deceptive lies of the antichrist, between the love that pervades the entire congregation of those in union with the Father and the Son and the murderous Cain-like hatred that is in those who "went out from us . . . that it might be shown up that not all are of our sort." (2:19; 1:5-7; 2:8-11, 22-25; 3:23, 24, 11, 12) Having this appreciation, it should be our fervent desire to 'conquer the world.' And how may we do this? By having strong faith and by having "the love of God," which means observing his commandments.—5:3, 4.

13 "The love of God"—how wonderfully is this motivating force highlighted throughout the letter! In chapter two we find the sharp contrast made between the love of the world and the love of the Father. Later it is called to our attention that "God is love." (4:8, 16) And what a practical love this is! It found its magnificent expression in the Father's sending forth "his Son as Savior of the world." (4:14) This should stir in our hearts an appreciative, fearless love, in line with the apostle's words: "As for us, we love, because he first loved us." (4:19) Our love should be of the same kind as that of the Father and the Son—a practical love. Just as Jesus surrendered his soul for us, so "we are under obligation to surrender our souls for our brothers," yes, to open the door of our tender compassions so as to love our brothers, not in mere words only, but "in deed and truth." (3:16-18) As John's letter so clearly shows, it is this love, combined with the true knowledge of God, that binds those who go on walking with God in unbreakable union with the Father and the Son. (2:5, 6) It is to the Kingdom heirs in this blessed bond of love that John says: "And we are in union with the true one, by means of his Son Jesus Christ. This is the true God and life everlasting." —5:20.

11. How may Christians today combat antichrists and worldly desires?
12. What contrasts does First John make for our benefit, and how may we conquer the world?
13. (a) How is the love of God highlighted as a practical force? (b) Of what kind should the Christian's love be, resulting in what union?

Bible Book Number Sixty-three— 2 John

Writer:	**Apostle John**
Place Written:	**Ephesus, or near**
Writing Completed:	**c. A.D. 98**
Time Covered:	**Undetermined**

JOHN's second letter is short—it could have been written on a single sheet of papyrus —but it is full of meaning. It is addressed "to the chosen lady and to her children." Although "Kyria" (Greek for "Lady") did exist as a proper name at the time, most Bible scholars feel that no individual by that name was being addressed, but rather that John was writing to a Christian congregation, referring to it as "the chosen lady." This may even have been a device to confuse any enemy into whose hands the letter might fall. Likewise, it is probable that the greetings mentioned in the last verse are those of the members of a sister congregation. The fact that the plural form of "you" often appears also indicates that the letter was not directed to an individual Christian sister, but rather to a group. One thing is certain: the second letter was not intended to be as general in scope as the first, for it was written either to an individual or at most to one congregation.

1. What indicates Second John may have been written to a congregation rather than to an individual?

2 There is no reason to doubt that John wrote this letter. The writer calls himself the "older man." This certainly fits John, not only because of his advanced age, but also because, as one of the "pillars" (Gal. 2:9) and the last surviving apostle, he was truly an "older man" in the Christian congregation. He was well known, and no further identification would be required for his readers. His writership is also indicated by the similarity in style to that of the first letter and John's Gospel. Like the first letter, it appears to have been written in or around Ephesus, about A.D. 98. Concerning Second and Third John, M'Clintock and Strong's *Cyclopædia,* 1876, Vol. IV, page 955, comments: "From their general similarity, we may conjecture that the two epistles were written shortly after the first epistle from Ephesus. They both apply to individual cases of conduct the principles which had been laid down in their fullness in the first Epistle." As to proof of authenticity, it is quoted by Irenaeus, of the second century, and was accepted by Clement of Alexandria, of the same period.[a] Also, John's letters are listed in the Muratorian Canon.

3 The reason for the letter is again the onslaught on the Christian faith by false teachers, against whom John wants to warn his readers, so that they can recognize them and stay clear of them, while continuing to walk in the truth, in mutual love.

CONTENTS OF SECOND JOHN

4 **Love one another; reject apostates** (Vss. 1-13). After expressing his love in the truth for 'the chosen lady and her children,' John rejoices that he has found some of them walking in the truth, as commanded by the Father. He requests that they show their love for one another by continuing to walk according to God's commandments. For deceivers and antichrists have gone forth into the world, who do not confess Jesus Christ as coming in the flesh. He that pushes ahead beyond the teaching of Christ does not have God, but he that remains in this teaching "has both the Father and the Son." Anyone that does not bring this teaching is not to be received into their homes, nor even greeted. John has many things to write them, but, rather, he hopes to come and speak with them face to face, that their joy may be "in full measure."—Vss. 9, 12.

WHY BENEFICIAL

5 It appears that in John's day, as in modern times, there were some who were not content to stay with the plain, simple teachings of Christ. They wanted something more, something that would tickle their "ego," something that would exalt them and put them in a class with worldly philosophers, and they were willing to contaminate and divide the Christian congregation in order to gain their selfish ends. John valued the harmony of the congregation that rests in love and in right teaching in union with the Father and the Son. We should place like store on the unity of the congregation today, even refusing fellowship or greetings to those who apostatize to another teaching beyond that received through the inspired Scriptures. By continuing to walk according to God's commandments, and in the full measure of joy to be found in true Christian association, we can be assured that "there will be with us undeserved kindness, mercy and peace from God the Father and from Jesus Christ the Son of the Father, with truth and love." (2 John 3) Certainly John's second letter underlines the blessedness of such Christian oneness.

a *The New Bible Dictionary,* 1962, J. D. Douglas, page 644.

2. (a) What evidence points to the apostle John as writer? (b) What suggests that the letter was written in or near Ephesus, about A.D. 98, and what proves its authenticity?
3. Why did John write the letter?
4. Why particularly does John admonish loving one another, and how must they treat those who push ahead beyond the teaching of Christ?
5. (a) What situation arose in John's day, as seen also in modern times? (b) Like John, how can we today show appreciation for the unity of the congregation?

Bible Book Number Sixty-four— 3 John

Writer:	**Apostle John**
Place Written:	**Ephesus, or near**
Writing Completed:	**c. A.D. 98**
Time Covered:	**Undetermined**

THIS letter is written to Gaius, a faithful Christian whom John truly loved. The name Gaius was a common one in the days of the early church. It appears four times in other parts of the Christian Greek Scriptures, referring to at least two and probably three different men. (Acts 19:29; 20:4; Rom. 16:23; 1 Cor. 1:14) There is no information available that would definitely identify the Gaius to whom John wrote with any of these others. All that we know of Gaius is that he was a member of a Christian congregation, that he was a special friend of John's and that the letter was addressed to him personally, for which reason the word "you" appears always in the singular.

2 Since the style of the opening and closing greetings is the same as that of Second John and the writer again identifies himself as "the older man," there can be no question that the apostle John also wrote this letter. The similarity of contents and language also suggests that it was written, as in the case of the other two letters, in or near Ephesus, about A.D. 98. Due to its brevity, it was seldom quoted by early writers, but along with Second John it is to be found in early catalogues of the inspired Scriptures.[a]

3 In his letter John expresses appreciation of Gaius' hospitality shown toward traveling brothers, and mentions some trouble with a certain ambitious Diotrephes. The Demetrius mentioned seems to be the one who brought this letter to Gaius, so it is possible he was sent out by John and was in need of Gaius' hospitality on his journey, which the letter should secure. As in the case of Gaius, we know nothing about Diotrephes and Demetrius beyond what we read here. However, the letter gives an interesting glimpse of the close international brotherhood of the early Christians. Among other things this included the custom, it appears, of providing free board and lodging in the congregation for those traveling 'in behalf of the name,' although these might not be personally known to their hosts.

a See chart, "Early Catalogues of the Christian Greek Scriptures," page 302.

1. To whom was Third John addressed, and what is known of him?
2. What identifies the writer, as well as time and place of writing?
3. What does John express through this letter, and what interesting glimpse do we gain of the brotherhood of the early Christians?

CONTENTS OF THIRD JOHN

4 **The apostle counsels hospitality and good works** (Vss. 1-14). John rejoices at hearing that Gaius is still "walking in the truth." He commends him for doing a faithful work, that of showing loving care for visiting brothers. "We . . . are under obligation," says John, "to receive such persons hospitably, that we may become fellow workers in the truth." John wrote previously to the congregation, but the self-exalting Diotrephes receives nothing from them with respect. John, if he comes, will call him to account for his 'chattering with wicked words.' The beloved Gaius is advised to "be an imitator, not of what is bad, but of what is good." Demetrius is cited as a praiseworthy example. Rather than write of many things, John hopes soon to see Gaius face to face. —Vss. 4, 8, 10, 11.

WHY BENEFICIAL

5 The apostle John shows himself to be an exemplary overseer in his zeal to safeguard the congregation against contaminating influences. The spirit of love and hospitality that permeated the congregation was commendable, and indeed it was their obligation to preserve this happy condition, that the local brothers and "strangers" who came among them might serve together as "fellow workers in the truth." However, Diotrephes apparently had other ideas. He had lofty eyes, a thing hateful to Jehovah, and he was disrespectful of theocratic authority, even chattering wickedly about the apostle John. (Prov. 6:16, 17) He was putting a roadblock in the way of the congregation's Christian hospitality. No wonder John was so outspoken against this evil and in favor of genuine Christian love in the congregation. We should be just as zealous today for maintaining humility, walking in the truth, and practicing godly love and generosity, in line with the principle stated by John: "He that does good originates with God. He that does bad has not seen God."—3 John 11.

4. For what does John commend Gaius, what unruly conduct does he condemn, and what sound advice does he give?
5. (a) How did John show himself to be an exemplary overseer, and what spirit was it important to preserve? (b) Why was John so outspoken against Diotrephes? (c) For what should we be zealous today, in line with what principle stated by John?

Bible Book Number Sixty-five— Jude

Writer:	**Jude (Jesus' brother)**
Place Written:	**Palestine (?)**
Writing Completed:	**c. A.D. 65**
Time Covered:	**Undetermined**

THE Christian brothers of Jude were in danger! During the time that had elapsed since the death and resurrection of Christ Jesus foreign elements had wormed their way into the Christian congregation. The enemy had filtered in for the purpose of undermining the faith, just as the apostle Paul had warned about fourteen years previously. (2 Thess. 2:3) How should the brothers be alerted and placed on guard against the danger? The letter of Jude, vigorous and robust in its forthright statement, provided the answer. Jude himself stated the position clearly in verses 3 and 4: 'I found it necessary to write you because certain men have slipped in, ungodly men, turning the undeserved kindness of our God into an excuse for loose conduct.' The very foundations of sound doctrine and morality were being threatened. Jude felt called upon to fight for the interests of his brothers, that they, in their turn, might put up a hard fight for the faith.

2 But who was Jude? The opening words tell us that the letter was written by "Jude, a slave of Jesus Christ, but a brother of James, to the called ones." Was Jude, or Judas, whose name means "Lauded," an apostle, since two of Jesus' original twelve apostles were named Judas? (Luke 6:16) Jude does not speak of himself as an apostle, but instead speaks of the apostles in the third person as "they," manifestly excluding himself. (Jude 17, 18) Moreover, he calls himself "a brother of James," evidently meaning the writer of the letter of James, who was a brother of Jesus. As one of the "pillars" of the congregation in Jerusalem, this James was well known, and hence Jude identifies himself with him. This makes Jude also a brother of Jesus, and he is listed as such. (Gal. 1:19; 2:9; Matt. 13:55; Mark 6:3) However, Jude did not make capital of his fleshly relationship with Jesus, but humbly placed the emphasis on his spiritual relationship as "a slave of Jesus Christ."—Jude 1; 1 Cor. 7:22; 2 Cor. 5:16; Matt. 20:27.

3 The authenticity of this Bible book is supported by mention of it in the Muratorian Canon, of the second century. Also Clement of Alexandria (c. A.D. 150-220) quotes from it, calling it a production of a prophetic mind. Origen refers to it as a work of 'few verses, yet full of mighty words of heavenly grace.'[a] Tertullian also refers to it as authentic. There is no doubt that it belongs with the other inspired Scriptures.

4 Jude writes "to the called ones," specifying no particular congregation or individual, so his epistle is a general letter to be circulated widely to all Christians. Though it is not stated, the most likely place of writing is Palestine. It is also difficult to fix the date with certainty. However, it must have been well along in the development of the Christian congregation, for Jude calls attention to "the sayings that have been previously spoken by the apostles of our Lord Jesus Christ," and apparently quotes 2 Peter 3:3. (Jude 17, 18) Moreover, there is a strong similarity between Jude and the second chapter of Second Peter. This indicates that he wrote about the same time as Peter, both being deeply concerned over the danger to the congregation at that time. Hence A.D. 65 is suggested as an approximate date. This date is also supported in that Jude does not mention Cestius Gallus' moving in to put down the Jews' revolt A.D. 66, nor does he mention the fall of Jerusalem A.D. 70. Jude in his epistle refers to specific divine judgments executed against sinners, and it is logical that, had Jerusalem already fallen, he would have enforced his argument by mention of this execution of judgment, especially since Jesus foretold the event.—Jude 5-7; Luke 19:41-44.

CONTENTS OF JUDE

5 **Warnings against fornication and disregard for lordship** (Vss. 1-16). After conveying loving greetings to "the called ones," Jude says he intended writing "about the salvation we hold in common," but has now found it necessary to write them "to put up a hard fight for

a *The New Bible Dictionary,* 1962, J. D. Douglas, page 675.

1. Because of what conditions inside the congregation did Jude find it necessary to write his vigorous letter in behalf of his brothers?
2. (a) Who was Jude? (b) What relationship with Jesus did he esteem the most?
3. What proves the book's authenticity?
4. What kind of letter is this, where was it probably written, and what is suggested as to the time of writing?
5. (a) Why does Jude find it necessary to write the called ones "to put up a hard fight for the faith"? (b) What warning examples does Jude cite?

the faith." Why so? Because ungodly men have slipped in, turning God's undeserved kindness into an excuse for loose conduct. These men, says Jude, are "proving false to our only Owner and Lord, Jesus Christ." (Vss. 1, 3, 4) He reminds them that, though Jehovah saved a people out of Egypt, he afterward "destroyed those not showing faith." Also, he has reserved "for the judgment of the great day" those angels that forsook their proper dwelling place. Likewise the everlasting punishment on Sodom and Gomorrah and their neighbor cities is a warning example as to the fate of those who 'commit fornication excessively and go out after flesh for unnatural use.'—Vss. 5-7.

6 Now, in like manner, ungodly men "are defiling the flesh and disregarding lordship and speaking abusively of glorious ones." Why, even Michael the archangel did not speak abusively to the Devil when disputing over Moses' body, simply saying: "May Jehovah rebuke you." Yet these men use abusive speech, and go on corrupting themselves like unreasoning animals. They have gone in the way of Cain, Balaam and the rebellious Korah. They are like hidden rocks below water, like waterless clouds, like fruitless trees twice-dead and uprooted, like wild waves that foam up their shame, and like stars with no set course. For these "the blackness of darkness stands reserved forever."—Vss. 8, 9, 13.

7 **Counsel on remaining in God's love** (Vss. 17-25). Enoch prophesied that Jehovah will execute judgment against these ungodly ones. They are murmurers and complainers, and they selfishly admire personalities. The apostles of the Lord Jesus Christ used to warn that "in the last time there will be ridiculers, proceeding according to their own desires for ungodly things." These troublemakers are "animalistic men, not having spirituality." Let the "beloved ones," therefore, build themselves up in the faith, and keep themselves in God's love, while they await the mercy of Christ "with everlasting life in view." In their turn, let them extend mercy and aid to those who waver. Jude closes by ascribing glory through the Lord Jesus Christ to "God our Savior," the One who can guard them from stumbling.—Vss. 18-21, 25.

WHY BENEFICIAL

8 Jude himself found the inspired Scriptures beneficial for warning, exhorting, encouraging, instructing and admonishing the "beloved ones." In exposing the gross sin of the ungodly intruders, he used expressive illustrations from the Hebrew Scriptures, such as those of the backsliding Israelites, the angels that sinned and the inhabitants of Sodom and Gomorrah, showing that all who practice like vices will suffer a like punishment. He compared corrupt men to unreasoning animals, and said that they were going in the path of Cain, rushing into the error of Balaam and perishing like Korah for their rebellious talk. He also drew vivid pictures from "the book of nature." Jude's forthright letter itself became a part of "all Scripture," to be studied along with other Scripture admonishing right conduct "in the last time."—Jude 17, 18, 5-7, 11-13; Num. 14:35-37; Gen. 6:4; 18:20, 21; 19:4, 5, 24, 25; 4:4, 5, 8; Num. 22:2-7, 21; 31:8; 16:1-7, 31-35.

9 Oppositions and trials from the outside had failed to check the growth of Christianity, but now the brothers were endangered by corruption from within. Hidden rocks beneath the surface threatened to wreck the entire congregation. Realizing that this danger could be even more devastating, Jude argued strongly in favor of 'putting up a hard fight for the faith.' His letter is as timely today as it was back there. The same warning is still needed. Faith still must be guarded and fought for, immorality uprooted, doubters helped with mercy and 'snatched out of the fire,' if that be possible. In the interest of moral integrity, spiritual effectiveness and true worship, Christians today must continue to build themselves up in the most holy faith, standing by right principles and drawing close to God in prayer. They need also to have proper regard for "lordship," respecting Jehovah's arrangement of matters in the Christian congregation.—Jude 3, 23, 8.

10 "Animalistic men, not having spirituality," will never enter God's kingdom, and will only endanger others who are on the way to everlasting life. (Jude 19; Gal. 5:19-21) The congregation must be warned against them, and it must get rid of them! Thus "mercy and peace and love" will be increased toward the beloved ones, and they will keep themselves in God's love, 'while they are waiting for the mercy of their Lord Jesus Christ with everlasting life in view.' God the Savior will set the Kingdom heirs "unblemished in the sight of his glory with great joy." Certainly these join with Jude in ascribing to Him through Jesus Christ the "glory, majesty, might and authority."—Jude 2, 21, 24, 25.

---

6. In what are ungodly men indulging, and how does Jude illustrate the wrongness and the outcome of their conduct?
7. (a) What judgment awaits the ungodly ones, and how did the apostles warn concerning them? (b) In view of the hope of everlasting life what should the "beloved ones" do for themselves and others?
8. What use did Jude make of the inspired Scriptures, and of "the book of nature," in admonishing his brothers?
9. Why is Jude's warning still needed at this time, and how must Christians continue to build themselves up?
10. (a) How must the congregation treat animalistic men, and in what will this result? (b) What reward awaits the Kingdom heirs, and in what do these join Jude?

Bible Book Number Sixty-six— Revelation

Writer:	**Apostle John**
Place Written:	**Patmos**
Writing Completed:	**c. A.D. 96**
Time Covered:	**Undetermined**

ARE the symbolisms of Revelation intended to terrify? Far from it! The prophecy's fulfillment may bring terror to the wicked, but God's faithful servants will agree with the inspired introduction and the angel's comment at the end: "Happy is he who reads aloud and those who hear the words of this prophecy." "Happy is anyone observing the words of the prophecy of this scroll." (Rev. 1:3; 22:7) Though written before the four other inspired books by John, Revelation is correctly placed last in the collection of sixty-six inspired books making up our Bible, for it is the Revelation that takes its readers far into the future in providing an all-embracing vision of God's purposes toward mankind and bringing the grand theme of the Bible, the sanctification of Jehovah's name by the Kingdom Seed, to a glorious climax.

2 According to the title verse, this is "a revelation by Jesus Christ, which God gave him, . . . and he sent forth his angel and presented it in signs through him to his slave John." So John was merely the writer, but not the originator, of the material. Therefore John is not the revelator, nor is the book a revelation of John. (Rev. 1:1) This unveiling to God's slave of His wonderful purposes for the future makes its title most appropriate, for the book's Greek name *A·po·ka'lyp·sis* (Apocalypse) means "Uncovering; Disclosing."

3 Who was this John referred to as the writer of Revelation in chapter one? We are told that he was a slave of Jesus Christ and a brother and sharer in tribulation, exiled on the isle of Patmos. Obviously he was well known to his first readers, to whom no further identification was necessary. He must be the apostle John. This conclusion is supported by most ancient historians. Papias, who wrote in the first part of the second century, held the book to be of apostolic origin. Justin Martyr, in the middle of the second century, stated: "A man from among us, by name John, one of the apostles of Christ, in a Revelation made to him has prophesied that the believers in one Christ shall live a thousand years in [New] Jerusalem." Irenaeus speaks explicitly of the apostle John as the writer, as do Clement of Alexandria and Tertullian, all of the late second century. Origen, noteworthy Biblical scholar of the third century, said: "John who leaned on the bosom of Jesus has left us one gospel, and he wrote also the Apocalypse." He speaks of this John as being "the son of Zebedee" and "condemned to the isle of Patmos for bearing this testimony to the word of truth."[a]

4 The fact that John's other writings put so much emphasis on love does not mean that he could not have written the very forceful and dynamic Revelation. He and his brother James were the ones so filled with indignation against the Samaritans of a certain city that they wanted to call down fire from heaven. That is why they were given the surname "Boanerges," or "Sons of Thunder." (Mark 3:17; Luke 9:54) This divergence in style should cause no difficulty when we remember that in Revelation the subject matter is different. What John saw in these visions was unlike anything he had ever seen before.

5 As to the authenticity of the Revelation, Hastings' *Dictionary of the Bible*, 1902, Volume IV, page 240, says: "Hardly any other book in the NT [Christian Greek Scriptures] is so well attested in the 2nd century." The book exhibits a remarkable unity in literary style, in grammatical construction and in doctrine. Its outstanding harmony with the rest of the prophetic Scriptures unquestionably proves it to be an authentic part of God's inspired Word.

6 According to the earliest testimony, John wrote the Revelation about A.D. 96, approximately twenty-six years after Jerusalem's destruction. This would be toward the close of the reign of Emperor Domitian. In verification of this, Irenaeus says of the Apocalypse: "It

a *Notes on the Book of Revelation*, 1852, by Albert Barnes, page xiv.

1. (a) Regarding the symbolisms of Revelation, with what will God's servants agree? (b) Why is Revelation correctly placed last in the Bible?
2. By what means did the Revelation come to John, and why is the title of the book most appropriate?
3. Whom does Revelation itself indicate to be the writer, and how do ancient historians support this?
4. What explains the divergence in style in Revelation, as compared with John's other writings?
5. What proves Revelation to be an authentic part of the inspired Scriptures?
6. When did John write the Revelation, and under what circumstances?

was seen no long time ago, but almost in our age, at the end of the reign of Domitian." Melito, Clement of Alexandria, Eusebius and Jerome all concur in this testimony.[a] Domitian was the brother of Titus, who led the Roman armies to destroy Jerusalem. He became emperor at the death of Titus, fifteen years before the book of Revelation was written. He demanded that he be worshiped as god and assumed the title *Dominus ac Deus noster* (meaning: "Our Lord and God"). Emperor worship did not disturb those who worshiped false gods, but it could not be indulged in by the early Christians, who refused to compromise their faith on this point.[b] Thus, toward the close of Domitian's rule, severe persecution came upon the Christians, as a result of which John was exiled to Patmos. When Domitian was assassinated A.D. 96, he was succeeded by the more tolerant Emperor Nerva, and John was released. It was during this imprisonment on Patmos that John received the visions that he wrote down.

7 We must appreciate that what John saw and was told to write to the congregations was not just a series of unrelated visions, haphazardly recorded. No, the entire book of Revelation, from beginning to end, gives us a coherent picture of things to come, going from one vision to another until the full disclosure of God's Kingdom purposes are reached at the end of the visions. We should therefore see the book of Revelation as a whole, and as made up of related, harmonious parts, transporting us far into the future from John's time. The book can be divided into four sections: (1) The introduction (1:1-9); (2) The messages to the seven congregations (1:10–3:22); (3) The visions of things to come (4:1–22:7); (4) The conclusion (22:8-21).

CONTENTS OF REVELATION

8 **The introduction** (1:1-9). John explains the divine Source and the angelic channel through which the revelation is given, and goes on to address the seven congregations in the district of Asia. Jesus Christ has made them "to be a kingdom, priests to his God and Father," Jehovah God, the Almighty. John reminds them that he is a sharer with them "in the tribulation and kingdom and endurance in company with Jesus," being in exile on Patmos.—1:6, 9.

9 **The messages to the seven congregations** (1:10–3:22). By inspiration John finds himself in the Lord's day. A strong, trumpetlike voice tells him to write what he sees in a scroll, and send it to the seven congregations, in Ephesus, Smyrna, Pergamum, Thyatira, Sardis, Philadelphia and Laodicea. Turning toward the voice, John sees "someone like a son of man" in the midst of seven lampstands, having seven stars in his right hand. This One identifies himself as "the First and the Last," the One who became dead but is now living forever and ever, and who has the keys of death and of Hades. He is therefore the resurrected Jesus Christ. He explains: "The seven stars mean the angels of the seven congregations, and the seven lampstands mean seven congregations." —1:13, 17, 20.

10 John is told to write the angel of the congregation of Ephesus, which, despite its labor, endurance and refusal to put up with bad men, has left its first love and should repent and do the former deeds. The congregation in Smyrna is told that, despite tribulation and poverty, it is in fact rich and should not be afraid: "Prove yourself faithful even to death, and I will give you the crown of life." The congregation in Pergamum, dwelling "where the throne of Satan is," keeps holding fast to Christ's name, but has apostates in its midst, and these must repent or be put to the sword. In Thyatira the congregation has "love and faith and ministry and endurance," yet tolerates "that woman Jezebel." However, faithful ones who hold fast will receive "authority over the nations."—2:10, 13, 19, 20, 26.

11 The congregation in Sardis has the reputation of being alive, but is dead because its deeds are not fully performed before God. Those who conquer, however, will not have their names blotted out of the book of life. The congregation in Philadelphia has kept Christ's word, so he promises to keep the congregation "from the hour of test, which is to come upon the whole inhabited earth." The one who conquers he will make a pillar in the temple of his God, and he will write upon him the name of his God and of the city of his God, "the new Jerusalem." Referring to himself as "the beginning of the creation by God," Christ tells the Laodicean congregation it is neither hot nor cold, and will be vomited out of his mouth. Though boasting of riches, they are actually poor, blind and naked. They need white outer garments, and eyesalve in order to see. Christ

---

a *Notes on the Book of Revelation,* 1852, by Albert Barnes, pages xv-xvii.
b *Word Pictures in the New Testament,* 1933, by A. T. Robertson, Vol. VI, pages 271, 272.

7. As what should we see the book of Revelation, and into what four sections can it be divided?
8. What does John say about the origin of the Revelation, and what things does he say he shares in common with the seven congregations?
9. (a) What is John instructed to do? (b) Whom does he see in the midst of the lampstands, and what does this One explain?
10. What commendation and counsel are given to the congregations in Ephesus, Smyrna, Pergamum and Thyatira?
11. What messages are sent to the congregations in Sardis, Philadelphia and Laodicea?

will come in and dine with anyone who opens the door to him. To the one that conquers he will grant to sit down with him on his throne, even as he has sat down with his Father on His throne.—3:10, 12, 14.

12 **The vision of Jehovah's holiness and glory** (4:1-11). John now begins to record the visions of "things that must take place," which continue into chapter 22. The first vision takes us before Jehovah's heavenly throne of splendor. The scene is dazzling in its beauty, like precious gems for brilliance. Around the throne sit twenty-four older persons wearing crowns. Four living creatures ascribe holiness to Jehovah, and he is worshiped as worthy "to receive the glory and the honor and the power" because of being the Creator of all things.—4:1, 11.

13 **The Lamb opens the seven seals of the scroll** (5:1–8:2). "The one seated upon the throne" holds a scroll with seven seals. But who is worthy to open the scroll? It is "the Lion that is of the tribe of Judah, the root of David," that is worthy! This One, who is also "the Lamb that was slaughtered," takes the scroll from Jehovah.—5:1, 5, 12.

14 The Lamb proceeds to open the seals. First, a horseman on a white horse goes forth "conquering and to complete his conquest." Then the rider of a fiery-colored horse takes peace away from the earth, and another on a black horse rations out grain. A pale horse is ridden by Death, and Hades follows closely. The fifth seal is opened, and "those slaughtered because of the word of God" are seen calling for the avenging of their blood. (6:2, 9) At the opening of the sixth seal there is a great earthquake, sun and moon are darkened, and the mighty ones of the earth call upon the mountains to fall on them and hide them from Jehovah and the wrath of the Lamb.

15 After this four angels are seen holding back the four winds of the earth until the slaves of God are sealed in their foreheads. Their number is 144,000. Afterward John sees an innumerable great crowd out of all nations standing before God and the Lamb, to whom they attribute salvation, rendering service day and night in God's temple. The Lamb himself 'will shepherd and guide them to fountains of waters of life.'—7:17.

16 The seventh seal is then opened. There is silence in heaven. Then seven trumpets are handed to the seven angels.

17 **The angels sound the seven trumpets** (8:3–13:18). As the first three trumpets are successively blown, calamities rain down upon the earth, the sea, and upon the rivers and fountains of waters. At the fourth trumpet, a third of the sun, moon and stars is darkened. At the sound of the fifth, a star from heaven releases a plague of locusts that attack those "who do not have the seal of God on their foreheads." This is "one woe," and two more are coming. —9:4, 12.

18 The sixth trumpet heralds the untying of four angels who come forth to kill. "Two myriads of myriads" of horsemen bring further calamity and slaughter, but still men do not repent of their evil deeds. (9:16) Another strong angel descends from heaven and declares that, "in the days of the sounding of the seventh angel . . . the sacred secret of God according to the good news" is to be brought to a finish. John is given a little scroll to eat. It is "sweet as honey" in his mouth, but makes his belly bitter. (10:7, 9) Two witnesses prophesy 1,260 days in sackcloth; then they are killed by "the wild beast that ascends out of the abyss," and their corpses are left three and a half days "on the broad way of the great city." Those dwelling on the earth rejoice over them, but this turns to fright when God raises them to life. In that hour there is a great earthquake. "The second woe is past."—11:7, 8, 14.

19 Now the seventh angel blows his trumpet. Heavenly voices announce: "The kingdom of the world has become the kingdom of our Lord and of his Christ." The "twenty-four older persons" worship God and give thanks, but the nations become wrathful. It is God's appointed time to judge the dead and to reward his holy ones, and "to bring to ruin those ruining the earth." His temple sanctuary is opened, and in it is seen the ark of his covenant.—11:15, 16, 18.

20 Following the announcement of the Kingdom's establishment, the vision immediately shows "a great sign" in heaven. It is a woman who gives birth to "a son, a male, who is to shepherd all the nations with an iron rod." "A great fiery-colored dragon" stands ready to devour the child, but the child is caught away to God's throne. Michael wars against the dragon, and down to the earth he hurls this "original serpent, the one called Devil and Satan." It is "woe for the earth"—the third

12. As John begins to record the "things that must take place," what magnificent vision first comes to his attention?
13. Who only is worthy to open the scroll with seven seals?
14. What procession of visions accompanies the opening of the first six seals?
15. What is seen next with regard to the slaves of God, and "a great crowd"?
16. What follows the opening of the seventh seal?
17. What attends the successive blowing of the first five trumpets, and what is the first of the three woes?
18. What does the sixth trumpet herald, and what events culminate in the announcement that the second woe is past?
19. What important announcement occurs at the sounding of the seventh trumpet, and for what is it now the appointed time?
20. What sign and warfare are seen in heaven, what is the outcome, and how does this involve the third woe?

"woe"! The dragon persecutes the woman, and goes off to make war with the remaining ones of her seed.—12:1, 3, 5, 9, 12; 8:13.

21 The vision now shows a wild beast with seven heads and ten horns ascending out of the sea. It gets its power from the dragon. One of its heads was as though slaughtered to death, but got healed, and all the earth admired the beast. It utters blasphemies against God and wages war with the holy ones. But, look! John sees another wild beast, this one ascending out of the earth. It has two horns like a lamb, but begins speaking like a dragon. It misleads earth's inhabitants, and tells them to make an image to the first wild beast. All are compelled to worship this image or be killed. Without the mark or number of the wild beast, none can buy or sell. Its number is 666.

22 **"The everlasting good news" and related visions** (14:1-20). In happy contrast, John sees, and, look! the Lamb on Mount Zion, and with him 144,000 having the names of the Lamb and of the Father on their foreheads. "They are singing as if a new song before the throne," having been "bought from among mankind as a first fruits to God and to the Lamb." Another angel appears in midheaven, bearing "everlasting good news to declare as glad tidings" to every nation, and declaring: "Fear God and give him glory." And still another angel announces: "Babylon the great has fallen!" Another, a third, proclaims that those who worship the wild beast and its image will drink of God's wrath. One "like a son of man" thrusts in his sickle, and another angel, too, thrusts in his sickle and gathers the vine of the earth, hurling it into "the great wine press of the anger of God." As the winepress is trodden outside the city, blood comes up as high as the bridles of the horses, for a distance of two hundred miles.—14:3, 4, 6-8, 14, 19.

23 **The angels with the seven last plagues** (15:1–16:21). Those who have gained the victory over the wild beast glorify Jehovah, the "King of eternity," for his great and wonderful works. Seven angels come out of the sanctuary in heaven, and are given seven golden bowls full of the anger of God. The first six are poured out into the earth, the sea, the rivers and fountains of waters, and upon the sun, the throne of the wild beast and the river Euphrates, drying up its water to make way for "the kings from the rising of the sun." Demonic expressions gather 'the kings of the entire inhabited earth to the war of the great day of God the Almighty' at Har-Magedon. The seventh bowl is poured out upon the air, and, amid terrifying natural phenomena, the great city splits into three parts, the cities of the nations fall, and Babylon receives 'the cup of the wine of the anger of God's wrath.'—15:3; 16:12, 14, 19.

24 **God's judgment upon Babylon** (17:1–18:24). Look! It is God's judgment upon "Babylon the Great, the mother of the harlots," "with whom the kings of the earth committed fornication." Drunk with the blood of the holy ones, she rides a scarlet-colored wild beast having seven heads and ten horns. This beast "was, but is not, and yet is about to ascend out of the abyss." Its ten horns battle with the Lamb, but because he is "Lord of lords and King of kings" he conquers them. The ten horns turn on and devour the harlot, and another angel, whose glory lights the earth, declares: "She has fallen! Babylon the great has fallen!" God's people are commanded to get out of her, lest they share in her plagues. The kings and other mighty ones of the earth weep over her, saying: "Too bad, too bad, you great city, Babylon you strong city, because in one hour your judgment has arrived!" Her great riches have been devastated. As a great millstone is hurled into the sea, so with a swift pitch has Babylon been hurled down, never to be found again. At last the blood of God's holy ones has been avenged!—17:2, 5, 8, 14; 18:2, 10.

25 **The Lamb makes war in righteousness** (19:1–20:15). Four times heaven resounds to the call: "Praise Jah, you people!" Praise Jah because he has executed judgment on the great harlot! Praise Jah because Jehovah has begun to reign as king! Rejoice and be overjoyed because "the marriage of the Lamb has arrived and his wife has prepared herself"! Now the "King of kings and Lord of lords" leads heavenly armies in righteous warfare. Kings and strong men become carrion for the birds of heaven, and the wild beast and false prophet are hurled alive into the fiery lake that burns with sulphur. (19:1, 3, 4, 6, 7, 16) "The dragon, the original serpent, who is the Devil and Satan," is seized and bound for a thousand years. Those having part in the first resurrection become 'priests of God and of the Christ, and rule as kings with him for the thousand years.' Thereafter Satan will be let loose, and will go out to mislead the nations of earth, but will be hurled, with those who follow him, into the

---

21. What two wild beasts next appear in the vision, and how do they influence men on the earth?
22. What does John see on Mount Zion, what do the angels bear and proclaim, and how is the vine of the earth disposed of?
23. (a) Who are next seen to glorify Jehovah, and why? (b) Where are the seven bowls of God's anger poured out, and what world-shaking developments follow?
24. (a) How is God's judgment executed on Babylon? (b) What announcements and lament accompany her fall?
25. (a) What joyful praise resounds through heaven? (b) How decisive is the warfare waged by the Lamb, and what follows during and at the end of the thousand years?

lake of fire. The dead, great and small, are judged before God's great white throne. Death and Hades are hurled into the lake of fire, which "means the second death," and with them is hurled anyone not found written in the book of life.—20:2, 6, 14.

26 **The glory of the New Jerusalem** (21:1–22:7). The thrilling vision of "a new heaven and a new earth" follows. The New Jerusalem comes down out of heaven, and God tents with mankind, wiping out every tear from their eyes. No more death, mourning, outcry or pain! Yes, God is "making all things new," and confirms his promise, saying: "Write, because these words are faithful and true." Those conquering will inherit these things, but not the cowards, or those lacking faith, or those who are immoral or practice spiritism or idolatry. John is now shown "the Lamb's wife," the heavenly Jerusalem, with its twelve gates and twelve foundation stones bearing the names of the twelve apostles. It is foursquare, and its majestic splendor is represented by the jasper, gold and pearl in it. Jehovah and the Lamb are the temple of this city, and are also its light. Only those written in the Lamb's scroll of life may enter into it.—21:1, 5, 9.

27 A pure river of water of life issues from the throne down the broad way of the city, and on each side are trees of life producing new crops of fruit each month, and with leaves for healing. The throne of God and of the Lamb will be in the city, and his slaves will see his face. "Jehovah God will shed light upon them, and they will rule as kings forever and ever." Again the assurance is given: "These words are faithful and true." Happy, indeed, all those who observe the words of the prophecy!—22:5, 6.

28 **The conclusion** (22:8-21). Having heard and seen these things, John falls down to worship the angel, who reminds him to worship only God. The words of the prophecy are not to be sealed, "for the appointed time is near." Happy are those gaining entrance into the city, for outside are the filthy and "everyone liking and carrying on a lie." Jesus states that he himself sent this witness to the congregations through his angel, and that he is "the root and the offspring of David, and the bright morning star." "And the spirit and the bride keep on saying: 'Come!' And let anyone hearing say: 'Come!' And let anyone thirsting come; let anyone that wishes take life's water free." And let no one add to or take away from the words of this prophecy, lest his portion be taken away "from the trees of life and out of the holy city."—22:10, 15-17, 19.

WHY BENEFICIAL

29 What a glorious finale the Revelation does provide for the Bible's inspired collection of sixty-six books! Nothing has been omitted. There are no loose ends. Now we see clearly the end as well as the beginning. The last part of the Bible closes out the record begun in the first part. As Genesis 1:1 described God's creation of the material heavens and earth, so Revelation 21:1-4 shows how a new heavens and a new earth will bring untold blessings to mankind, as prophesied also in Isaiah 65:17, 18; 66:22 and 2 Peter 3:13. Just as the first man was told he would positively die if disobedient, so God positively guarantees that, for the obedient ones, "death will be no more." (Gen. 2:17; Rev. 21:4) When the serpent first appeared as mankind's deceiver, God foretold the bruising of his head, and the Revelation discloses how "the original serpent, who is the Devil and Satan," is finally hurled into destruction. (Gen. 3:1-5, 15; Rev. 20:2, 10) Whereas disobedient man was driven away from the Edenic tree of life, symbolic trees of life appear "for the curing of the nations" of obedient mankind. (Gen. 3:22-24; Rev. 22:2) Just as a river issued out of Eden to water the garden, so a symbolic river, life-giving and life-sustaining, is pictured as flowing from God's throne. This parallels the earlier vision of Ezekiel, and it also calls to mind Jesus' words about "a fountain of water bubbling up to impart everlasting life." (Gen. 2:10; Rev. 22:1, 2; Ezek. 47:1-12; John 4:13, 14) In contrast to being driven from God's presence, as were the first man and woman, the faithful overcomers will see his face. (Gen. 3:24; Rev. 22:4) It is beneficial indeed to consider these thrilling visions of Revelation!

30 Note, too, how Revelation ties together the prophecies concerning wicked Babylon. Isaiah had foreseen the fall of the literal Babylon long before it happened, and had declared: "She has fallen! Babylon has fallen!" (Isa. 21:9) Jeremiah (51:6-12) also prophesied against Babylon. But the Revelation speaks in symbol of "Babylon the Great, the mother of the harlots and of the disgusting things of the earth." She, too, must be overthrown, and John sees it in vision, declaring: "She has fallen! Babylon the great has fallen!" (Rev. 17:5; 18:2) Do you recall Daniel's vision of a kingdom set

26. (a) What thrilling vision follows, and who will inherit these things? (b) What description is given of the heavenly Jerusalem?
27. (a) What life-sustaining things are seen in the city, and what about its light? (b) With what joyful assurance does this vision close?
28. (a) What do the angel and Jesus himself tell John concerning the prophecy? (b) With what pressing invitation and warning does the Revelation conclude?
29. By what examples can we appreciate that Revelation closes out the record begun in the first part of the Bible?
30. (a) How does Revelation tie together the prophecies concerning Babylon? (b) What parallels are to be noted in the Daniel and Revelation visions of the Kingdom, and of the beasts?

up by God, that will crush other kingdoms and stand "to times indefinite"? Note how this ties in with the heavenly proclamation in Revelation: "The kingdom of the world has become the kingdom of our Lord and of his Christ, and he will rule as king forever and ever." (Dan. 2:44; Rev. 11:15) And just as Daniel's vision described 'someone like a son of man coming with the clouds of heaven to receive a lasting rulership and dignity and kingdom,' so Revelation identifies Jesus Christ as "The Ruler of the kings of the earth," and as "coming with the clouds, and every eye will see him." (Dan. 7:13, 14; Rev. 1:5, 7) There are certain parallels to be observed, also, between the beasts of Daniel's visions and the beasts of Revelation. (Dan. 7:1-8; Rev. 13:1-3; 17:12) The Revelation provides a vast field, indeed, for faith-strengthening study.

31 What a wondrous, many-featured vision the Revelation does provide concerning God's kingdom! It brings into brilliant focus what the prophets of old and Jesus and his disciples said concerning the Kingdom. Here we have the completed view of the sanctification of Jehovah's name through the Kingdom: "Holy, holy, holy is Jehovah God, the Almighty," and worthy "to receive the glory and the honor and the power." Indeed, he it is that 'takes his great power and begins ruling as king' through Christ. How zealous this regal Son, the "King of kings and Lord of lords," is shown to be in striking the nations and treading "the press of the wine of the anger of the wrath of God the Almighty"! As the grand Bible theme of Jehovah's sanctification builds up to its climax, it is emphasized that everyone and everything sharing in his Kingdom purposes must be holy. The Lamb Jesus Christ, who "has the key of David," is spoken of as holy, and so are the angels of heaven. Those having part in the first resurrection are said to be "happy and holy," and it is stressed that "anything not sacred and anyone that carries on a disgusting thing" will in no way enter "the holy city Jerusalem." Those who have been bought by the blood of the Lamb "to be a kingdom and priests to our God" thus have powerful encouragement to maintain sanctification before Jehovah. The "great crowd," too, must 'wash their robes and make them white in the blood of the Lamb,' that they may render sacred service.—Rev. 4:8, 11; 11:17; 19:15, 16; 3:7; 14:10; 20:6; 21:27, 2, 10; 22:19; 5:9, 10; 7:9, 14, 15.

32 The vision of this magnificent and holy kingdom of heaven crystallizes in our minds as we note certain features that are called to our attention only in the book of Revelation. Here we have the complete vision of the Kingdom heirs on Mount Zion with the Lamb, singing a new song that only they can master. It is only the Revelation that tells us the number of those bought from the earth to enter the Kingdom—144,000—and this number is sealed out of the twelve symbolic tribes of Israel. It is only the Revelation that shows that these "priests and kings," who share with Christ in the first resurrection, will also rule with him "for the thousand years." It is only the Revelation that gives us the complete view of "the holy city, New Jerusalem," showing its radiant glory with Jehovah and the Lamb as its temple, with its twelve gates and foundation stones, and the kings that reign in it forever by the eternal light that Jehovah sheds upon them.—Rev. 14:1, 3; 7:4-8; 20:6; 21:2, 10-14, 22; 22:5.

33 It can truly be said that this vision of "the holy city" sums up all that the Scriptures have foretold from ancient times concerning the Kingdom Seed. Abraham looked forward to a seed in which 'all the families of the earth would certainly bless themselves' and to "the city having real foundations, the builder and creator of which city is God." Now, in the Revelation vision, this city of blessing is clearly identified for us as the "New Jerusalem, coming down out of heaven from God." Here is Jehovah's instrument, "the holy city," the long-promised Kingdom, by means of which he dwells again with mankind, so that they may become "his peoples" in a happy, sinless, deathless condition such as man enjoyed before the rebellion in Eden. And by way of emphasis, the Revelation twice tells us that God will "wipe out every tear from their eyes."—Gen. 12:3; 22:15-18; Heb. 11:10; Rev. 21:2-4; 7:17.

34 Yes, what a grand conclusion to the inspired Scriptures! How marvelous these "things that must shortly take place"! (Rev. 1:1) The name of Jehovah, "the God of the inspired expressions of the prophets," is sanctified. (Rev. 22:6) The prophetic writings of sixteen centuries are shown in fulfillment and the works of faith of seven thousand years rewarded! The "original serpent" is dead, his hosts are destroyed, and wickedness is no more. God's kingdom rules as "a new heavens" to his praise. The blessings of a righteous new earth, filled and subdued according to Jehovah's purpose stated in the first chapter of the Bible, stretch for a

31. (a) What complete view does Revelation give of Jehovah's sanctification through the Kingdom? (b) What is emphasized with regard to holiness, and whom does this affect?
32. What features of the Kingdom are called to our attention only in the book of Revelation?

33. (a) How does the vision of "the holy city" sum up all that had been foretold concerning the Kingdom Seed? (b) What blessings does the Kingdom assure for mankind on earth?
34. (a) What marvelous overall vision does Revelation give of the divine purposes fulfilled? (b) How has "all Scripture" been proved to be "inspired of God and beneficial," and why is it now the time to study and obey God's Word?

glorious eternity before mankind. (Gen. 1:28) All Scripture has indeed proved to be "inspired of God and beneficial for teaching, for reproving, for setting things straight, for disciplining in righteousness." Jehovah has used it to lead fully competent, completely equipped men of faith to this marvelous day. Now, therefore, is the time to study these Scriptures to strengthen *your* faith. Obey their commands in order to receive God's blessings. Follow them on the straight path that leads to everlasting life. By doing so, you too can say, in the assured confidence with which the last book of the Bible closes: "Amen! Come, Lord Jesus."—2 Tim. 3:16; Rev. 22:20.

35 What incomparable joy we now can have by hailing "the kingdom of our Lord and of his Christ," the Seed, as this brings eternal sanctification to the matchless name of "Jehovah God, the Almighty"!—Rev. 11:15, 17.

35. How can we now have incomparable joy, and why?

Part Two—

Studies on the Inspired Scriptures and Their Background

Study One—
A Visit to The Promised Land

The regions of the land, its physical features, its mountains and valleys, its rivers and lakes, its climate, soil and varieties of vegetation.

THE boundaries of the ancient "Land of Promise" were set by Jehovah God himself. (Ex. 23:31; Num. 34:1-12; Josh. 1:4) In modern times this area is known as the land of Palestine, a name derived from "Philistia," which originally applied just to the territory of the Philistines, who were enemies of God's people. However, since Jehovah promised this land to faithful Abraham and his descendants, the designation "Promised Land" is most appropriate. (Gen. 15:18; Deut. 9:27, 28) This land is remarkable in the variety of its geography, wrapping up in this small area many of the distinct features and extremes that are to be found throughout the earth. If Jehovah could give as an inheritance to his ancient witnesses such a Land of Promise with all its beauteous variety, then certainly he can yet give to his dedicated worshipers a glorious New World paradise extending earthwide, with mountains and valleys, rivers and lakes, to bring them delight. Let us now pay keen attention to the geographical features of the Land of Promise, as we visit on an imaginary tour.

GENERAL SIZE

2 According to its God-given boundaries as stated in Numbers 34:1-12, the land promised to Israel was to be a thin strip of territory. It was to be about 300 miles from north to south, and about 35 miles wide, on the average. It was not until the reigns of Kings David and Solomon that the entire area promised was occupied militarily, with the placing of many subject peoples under control. However, the portion actually settled by the Jews is generally described as that covering from Dan to Beersheba, which was a distance of about 150 miles from north to south. (1 Ki. 4:25) The distance from Mount Carmel to the Sea of Galilee is about thirty-two miles across the country, and in the south where the Mediterranean shoreline curves gradually to the southwest, it is some fifty miles from Gaza to the Dead Sea. This settled area west of the Jordan River was only about 6,000 square miles. However, the Israelites additionally settled in lands to the east of Jordan (lands not included in the original promised boundaries), to make the total of settled territory about 10,000 square miles.

NATURAL REGIONS

3 Our visit to the Promised Land will take us through the following natural divisions of the country. The outline below provides the key to the accompanying map, which shows the approximate boundaries of the areas discussed.[a]

Geographical Regions

- A. The Seacoast of the Great Sea.—Josh. 15:12.
- B. The Plains West of Jordan
  - 1. The Plain of Asher.—Judg. 5:17.
  - 2. The Ridge of Dor.—Josh. 12:23.
  - 3. The Pasture Grounds of Sharon.—1 Chron. 5:16.
  - 4. The Plain of Philistia.—Gen. 21:32; Ex. 13:17.
  - 5. The Central East-West Valley
    - a. The Plain of Megiddo (Esdraelon).—2 Chron. 35:22.
    - b. The Low Plain of Jezreel.—Judg. 6:33.
- C. The Mountainous Regions West of Jordan
  - 1. Hills of Galilee.—Josh. 20:7; Isa. 9:1.
  - 2. The Mount Carmel Range.—1 Ki. 18:19, 20, 42.
  - 3. The Mountains of Samaria.—Jer. 31:5; Amos 3:9.
  - 4. The Shephelah.—Josh. 11:2; Judg. 1:9.
  - 5. The Mountainous Region of Judah.—Josh. 11:21.
  - 6. The Wilderness of Judah (Jeshimon).—Judg. 1:16; 1 Sam. 23:19.
  - 7. The Negeb.—Gen. 12:9; Num. 21:1.
  - 8. The Wilderness of Paran.—Gen. 21:21; Num. 13:1-3.

a *Geography of the Bible,* 1957, by Denis Baly, page 127.

1. (a) Why is the designation "Promised Land" most appropriate? (b) What glorious prospect may we have in mind as we examine the geography of the land?
2. In how much of the Promised Land did the Jews settle, and in what additional territory?
3. With the help of the map "Natural Regions of the Promised Land (and Adjoining Territory)," briefly state the location and relationship of the natural divisions of the land under the following headings: (a) The Plains West of Jordan, (b) The Mountainous Regions West of Jordan, (c) The Hills and Tablelands East of the Jordan.

D. The Great Arabah (the Rift Valley). —2 Sam. 2:29; Jer. 52:7.
 1. The Huleh Basin
 2. Region Around the Sea of Galilee (Gennesaret).—Matt. 14:34; John 6:1.
 3. District of the Jordan Valley (The *Ghor*).—1 Ki. 7:46; 2 Chron. 4:17; Luke 3:3.
 4. The Salt (Dead) Sea (Sea of the Arabah).—Num. 34:3; Deut. 4:49; Josh. 3:16.
 5. The Arabah (southward from the Salt Sea).—Deut. 2:8.

E. The Hills and Tablelands East of the Jordan (Transjordan).—Josh. 13:9, 16, 17, 21; 20:8.
 1. The Land of Bashan.—1 Chron. 5:11; Ps. 68:15.
 2. The Land of Gilead.—Josh. 22:9.
 3. The Land of Ammon and of Moab. —Josh. 13:25; 1 Chron. 19:2; Deut. 1:5.
 4. The Mountain Plateau of Edom.—Num. 21:4; Judg. 11:15.

F. The Mountains of Lebanon.—Josh. 13:5.

A. THE SEACOAST OF THE GREAT SEA

4 Beginning our visit from the west, we view first the seacoast stretching along the beautiful, blue Mediterranean. There are no natural ports below Mount Carmel, because of large stretches of sand dunes; but north of Carmel there are several good natural harbors. It was for this reason that the Phoenicians who lived in the country along this part of the coast became such famous seafaring people. The average annual temperature along the sunny seacoast is a pleasant 67° F., though the summers are fairly hot, averaging over 78° in Gaza in July.

B-1 THE PLAIN OF ASHER

5 This coastal plain stretches north from Mount Carmel for about twenty-five miles. Its greatest width is about eight miles, and it is part of the land that was assigned to the tribe of Asher. (Josh. 19:24-30) It was a fertile strip of plain, and produced well, supplying food for Solomon's royal tables.—Gen. 49:20; 1 Ki. 4:7, 16.

B-2 THE RIDGE OF DOR

6 This strip of coastland borders the Carmel range for about twenty miles. It is only two miles wide. It actually amounts to a ridge of land lying between Carmel and the Mediterranean. In its southern part there is the city of Dor, and to the south of this begin the sand dunes. The hills behind Dor produced choice food for Solomon's banquets. Solomon's own daughter was married to the deputy from this region.—1 Ki. 4:7, 11.

B-3 THE PASTURE GROUNDS OF SHARON

7 In view of the proverbial beauty of its flowers, it is appropriate that Sharon is mentioned in Isaiah's prophetic vision of the restored land of Israel. (Isa. 35:2) This was a fertile, well-watered land. It was a plain that varied from ten to twelve miles in width, extending for about forty miles southward from the Ridge of Dor. In Hebrew times oak forests grew in its northern part. Many flocks grazed there after the grain was cut. It is for this reason that it was called the pasture grounds of Sharon. In King David's time the royal herds were kept in Sharon. (1 Chron. 27:29) Today extensive citrus groves are to be found in this area.

B-4 THE PLAIN OF PHILISTIA

8 This section of land lies south of the pasture grounds of Sharon, extending some fifty miles along the coast and about fifteen miles inland. (1 Ki. 4:21) The sand dunes along the shoreline penetrate for about two miles. This is a rolling plain, which rises steppelike from 100 feet to more than 300 feet toward Gaza in the south, and at some places even higher. The soil is rich, but rains are not very plentiful, and there is always the danger of drought.

B-5 THE CENTRAL EAST-WEST VALLEY

9 The Central East-West Valley is actually made up of two parts, the valley plain of Megiddo, or Esdraelon, to the west, and the Low Plain of Jezreel to the east. (2 Chron. 35:22; Judg. 6:33) This entire central valley offered easy cross-country travel from the Jordan rift valley to the Mediterranean coast, and became an important trade route. The Plain of Megiddo is drained by the river Kishon, which makes its way out through a narrow gap between Mount Carmel and the hills of Galilee into the Plain of Asher and thence to the Mediterranean. This river all but dries up during the summer months, but at other times wells up into a torrent.—Judg. 5:21.

10 The Low Plain of Jezreel drains southeasterly toward the Jordan. This valley corri-

4. What are the characteristics and climate of the seacoast?
5, 6. Describe briefly (a) The Plain of Asher, (b) The Ridge of Dor.
7. (a) How is Sharon referred to in prophecy, and why? (b) In Hebrew times for what was this region used?
8. Where is the Plain of Philistia, and what are its features?
9. (a) What two parts comprise the Central East-West Valley, and of what practical value was it? (b) By using the diagrams of "Typical Cross Sections of the Promised Land," describe the general topography of this area.
10. (a) Describe the Low Plain of Jezreel. (b) With what Biblical events is this area associated?

dor of Jezreel Plain is about two miles wide and covers a distance of nearly twelve miles. The elevation starts at about 300 feet, and then drops down steadily to 400 feet below sea level near Beth-shan. The entire central valley is very fertile, the Jezreel section being one of the richest parts of the entire country, Jezreel itself meaning "God will sow seed." (Hos. 2:22) The Scriptures speak of the pleasantness and beauty of this district. (Gen. 49:15) Both Megiddo and Jezreel were strategic in the battles fought by Israel and surrounding nations, and it was here that Barak, Gideon, King Saul and Jehu fought.—Judg. 5:19-21; 7:12; 1 Sam. 29:1; 31:1, 7; 2 Ki. 9:27.

C-1 HILLS OF GALILEE

11 It was in the southern section of the hills of Galilee (and around the Sea of Galilee) that Jesus performed the greater part of his work of witnessing to Jehovah's name and kingdom. (Matt. 4:15-17; Mark 3:7) Most of Jesus' followers came from Galilee, including all eleven of his faithful apostles. (Acts 2:7) In this district, what is sometimes called Lower Galilee, the country is truly delightful, the hills rising no higher than 2,000 feet. There is no lack of rain over this pleasant land, and hence no desert. In springtime every hillside is ablaze with flowers and every valley basin is rich with grain. On the small plateaus there is rich soil for farming, and the hills are well suited for olive trees and vines. Towns of Bible fame in this area are Nazareth, Cana and Nain. (Matt. 2:22, 23; John 2:1; Luke 7:11) Galilee gave Jesus a rich background to draw on in speaking his illustrations.—Matt. 6:25-32; 9:37, 38.

12 In the northern section, or Upper Galilee, the hills rise to well over 3,000 feet, becoming, in effect, the foothills of the Lebanon Mountains. Upper Galilee is aloof and windswept, and rain is heavy. In Bible times the westward slopes were heavily forested. This region was assigned to the tribe of Naphtali.—Josh. 20:7.

C-2 THE MOUNT CARMEL RANGE

13 The spur of Mount Carmel juts out majestically into the Mediterranean Sea. Carmel is actually a hilly range, of about thirty miles' length, that rises as high as 1,742 feet above the sea. It extends from the mountains of Samaria to the Mediterranean, and its headland, which forms the main ridge at the northwest end, is unforgettable in its grace and beauty. (Song of Sol. 7:5) The name *Carmel* means "Garden Park; Fruitful Field," which truly fits this fertile promontory, bedecked with its famous fruit and olive trees. Isaiah 35:2 uses it as a symbol of the fruitful glory of the restored land of Israel: 'The splendor of Carmel must be given it.' It was here that Elijah challenged the priests of Baal and that "the fire of Jehovah came falling" in proof of his supremacy, and it was from the top of Carmel that Elijah called attention to the small cloud that became a great downpour, thus miraculously ending the drought on Israel.—1 Ki. 18:17-46.

C-3 THE MOUNTAINS OF SAMARIA

14 The southern part of this region is the more mountainous, rising to above 3,300 feet in the east. (1 Sam. 1:1) Here there is a greater and more dependable rainfall than in Judah to the south. This region was settled by the descendants of Ephraim, Joseph's younger son. It is rich, fertile country, and to this day the hills abound with olive groves and with orchards bearing luscious summer fruits. The northern part of this region, which was allotted to the half tribe of Manasseh, the older son of Joseph, comprises valley basins and small plains surrounded by mountains. The hilly land is not so fertile, though there are vineyards and olive groves. (Jer. 31:5) However, the larger valley basins are excellent for grain growing and general farming. Many cities dotted this region in Bible times. During the time of the northern kingdom, Manasseh supplied the three successive capitals of Shechem, Tirzah and Samaria, and the entire region came to be called Samaria, after the capital. —1 Ki. 12:25; 15:33; 16:24.

15 Moses' blessing on Joseph was truly fulfilled toward this land. "As to Joseph he said: 'May his land be continually blessed from Jehovah with the choice things of heaven, with dew, . . . and with the choice things, the products of the sun, and with the choice things, the yield of the lunar months, and with the choicest from the mountains of the east, and with the choice things of the indefinitely lasting hills.'" (Deut. 33:13-15) Yes, this was delightful country. Its mountains were heavily forested, its valleys were productive and it became filled with prosperous and well-populated cities. (1 Ki. 12:25; 2 Chron. 15:8) In later times Jesus preached in the land of Samaria, as did his disciples, and Christianity found many supporters there.—John 4:4-10; Acts 1:8; 8:1, 14.

11, 12. (a) To what extent did Galilee feature in the ministry of Jesus, and who came from this district? (b) Contrast Upper Galilee with Lower Galilee.
13. (a) What actually is Carmel? (b) What mention is made of it in the Bible?
14. Which tribes settled in the mountains of Samaria, and for what crops is this area suitable?
15. (a) How was Moses' blessing on Joseph fulfilled here? (b) How was this land further blessed from Jesus' time?

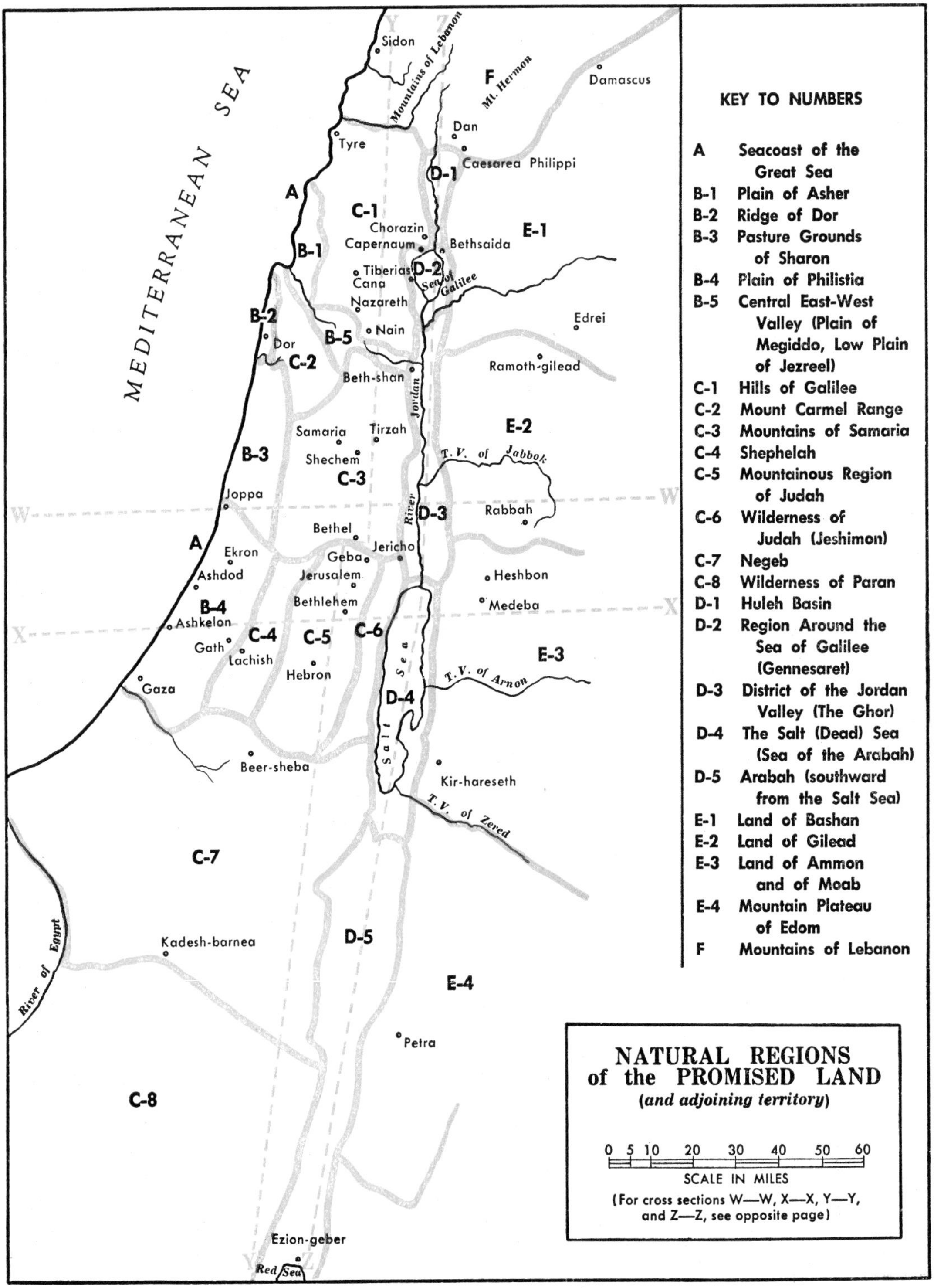
NATURAL REGIONS of the PROMISED LAND
(and adjoining territory)
KEY TO NUMBERS
A Seacoast of the Great Sea
B-1 Plain of Asher
B-2 Ridge of Dor
B-3 Pasture Grounds of Sharon
B-4 Plain of Philistia
B-5 Central East-West Valley (Plain of Megiddo, Low Plain of Jezreel)
C-1 Hills of Galilee
C-2 Mount Carmel Range
C-3 Mountains of Samaria
C-4 Shephelah
C-5 Mountainous Region of Judah
C-6 Wilderness of Judah (Jeshimon)
C-7 Negeb
C-8 Wilderness of Paran
D-1 Huleh Basin
D-2 Region Around the Sea of Galilee (Gennesaret)
D-3 District of the Jordan Valley (The Ghor)
D-4 The Salt (Dead) Sea (Sea of the Arabah)
D-5 Arabah (southward from the Salt Sea)
E-1 Land of Bashan
E-2 Land of Gilead
E-3 Land of Ammon and of Moab
E-4 Mountain Plateau of Edom
F Mountains of Lebanon
0 5 10 20 30 40 50 60
SCALE IN MILES
(For cross sections W—W, X—X, Y—Y, and Z—Z, see opposite page)
MEDITERRANEAN SEA
Sidon
Mountains of Lebanon
Mt. Hermon
Damascus
Tyre
Dan
Caesarea Philippi
Chorazin
Capernaum
Bethsaida
Tiberias
Cana
Sea of Galilee
Nazareth
Nain
Edrei
Dor
Beth-shan
Ramoth-gilead
Jordan
Samaria
Tirzah
Shechem
T. V. of Jabbok
Joppa
River
Rabbah
Bethel
Jericho
Ekron
Geba
Ashdod
Jerusalem
Heshbon
Bethlehem
Medeba
Ashkelon
Gath
Lachish
Hebron
Salt Sea
T. V. of Arnon
Gaza
Beer-sheba
Kir-hareseth
T. V. of Zered
Kadesh-barnea
River of Egypt
Petra
Ezion-geber
Red Sea

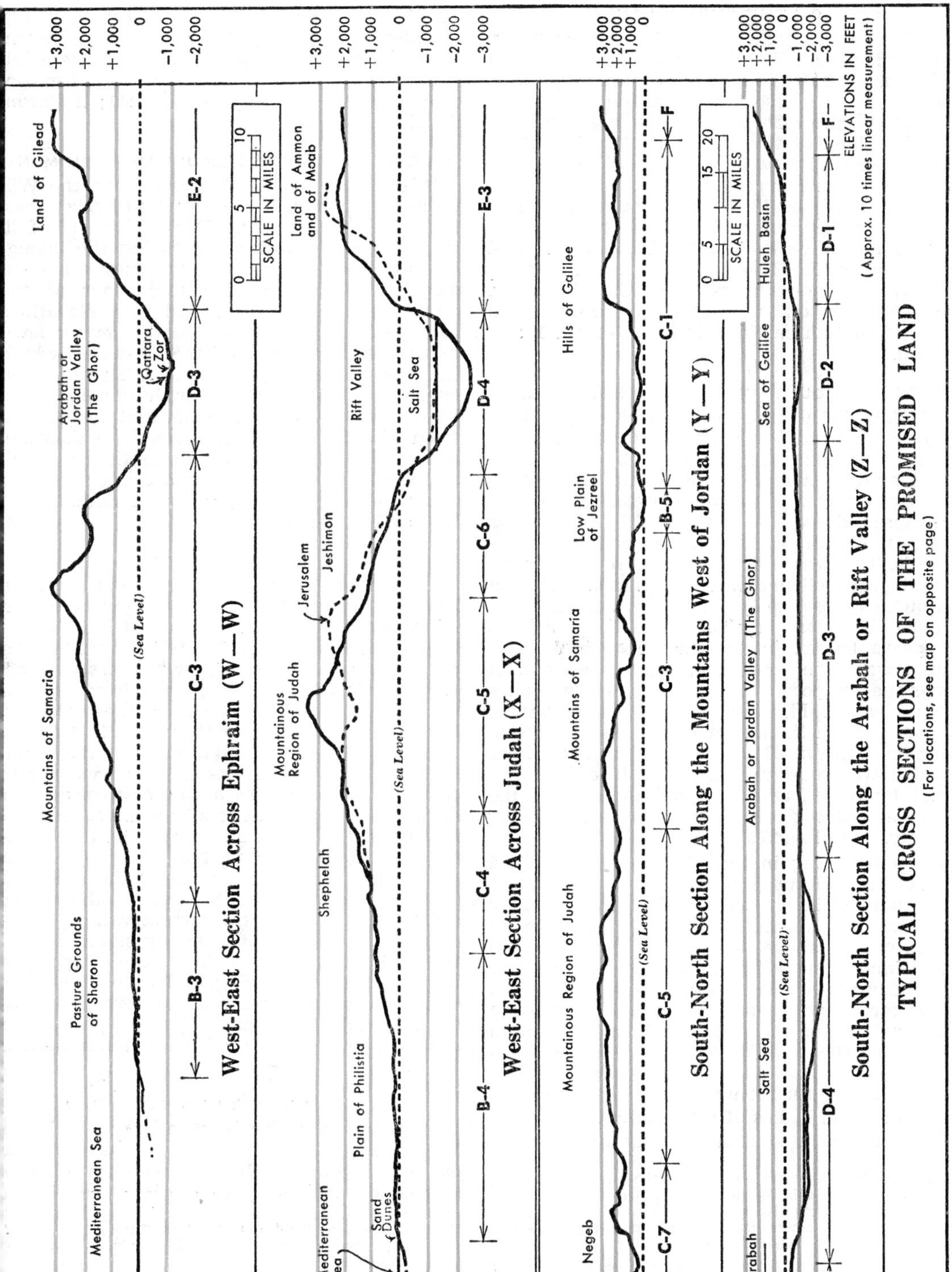

TYPICAL CROSS SECTIONS OF THE PROMISED LAND

(For locations, see map on opposite page)

C-4 THE SHEPHELAH

16 While the name *Shephelah* means "Lowland," it is actually a hilly area reaching to an altitude of 1,500 feet in the southern portion, and cut by frequent valleys that run from east to west. (2 Chron. 26:10) It rises due east of "the land of the Philistines," and is to be considered a "lowland" only by comparison with the higher mountains of Judah farther to the east. (Josh. 12:8) Its hills, which were covered with sycamore trees, now support vineyards and olive groves. (1 Ki. 10:27) It had many cities. In Bible history it served as the buffer zone between Israel and the Philistines, or whatever other invading armies tried to enter Judah from that direction.—2 Ki. 12:17; Obad. 19.

C-5 THE MOUNTAINOUS REGION OF JUDAH

17 This is a high rocky area about fifty miles long and less than twenty miles wide, with elevations varying from 2,000 to 3,340 feet above sea level. In Bible times the area was covered with timber growth, and on the western side particularly the hills and valleys were rich with grainfields, olive trees and vineyards. This was a district that produced much good grain, oil and wine for Israel. The area around Jerusalem particularly has suffered much deforestation since Bible times and so appears barren in comparison with what it once was. The land of Judah has an annual average temperature of 63° F., which makes for pleasant highland living. In the winter snow falls on the higher elevations in the center, such as at Bethlehem. In ancient times Judah was considered a good place for cities and fortresses, and in troublesome times the people could flee to these mountains for safety.—2 Chron. 27:4.

18 Outstanding in the history of Judah and of Israel is Jerusalem, also called Zion, after the name of its citadel. (Ps. 48:1, 2) Originally it was the Canaanite city of Jebus, lying on high ground above the junction of the valleys of Hinnom and Kidron. After David captured it and made it the capital, it was extended to the northwest, covering also the Tyropoeon Valley. In time the valley of Hinnom came to be called *Gehenna.* Because of the Jews' making idolatrous sacrifices there, it was declared unclean, and turned into a dump for rubbish and the dead bodies of vile criminals. Thus its fires became a symbol of total annihilation. (2 Ki. 23:10; Jer. 7:31-33) Jerusalem drew only a limited water supply from the pool of Siloam, west of the valley of Kidron, and Hezekiah protected this by building an outer wall to contain it within the city.—Isa. 22:11; 2 Chron. 32:2-5.

C-6 THE WILDERNESS OF JUDAH (JESHIMON)

19 Jeshimon is the Bible name for the Wilderness of Judah. It means "the (desert) desolation." (1 Sam. 23:19, *NW* footnote, 1955 Edition) How descriptive and fitting this name! The wilderness consists of the rugged eastern slopes of barren chalky formations of the Judean mountains, which fall from elevations of 3,000 feet to about 1,000 feet below sea level as they approach toward the Dead Sea, where there is a wall of jagged cliffs. There are no cities, and few settlements in Jeshimon. It was to this wilderness of Judah that David fled from King Saul, it was between this wilderness and the Jordan that John the Baptist preached, and it was to this region that Jesus retired in order to fast for forty days.—1 Sam. 23:14; Matt. 3:1; Luke 4:1.

C-7 THE NEGEB

20 South of the mountains of Judah lies "the Negeb," where the patriarchs Abraham and Isaac resided for many years. (Gen. 13:1-3; 24:62) The Bible also refers to the southeastern part of this area as "the wilderness of Zin." (Josh. 15:1) The semiarid Negeb stretches from the district of Beer-sheba in the north to Kadesh-barnea in the south. (Gen. 21:31; Num. 13:1-3, 26; 32:8) The land drops from the mountains of Judah in a series of ridges, which run east and west, in such a way as to present a natural barrier against traffic or invasion from the south. The land falls away from the mountains in the eastern part of the Negeb to a desert plain in the west, along the seacoast. Summer finds the land as barren as the desert, except near some of the torrent valleys. However, water may be obtained by sinking wells. (Gen. 21:30, 31) The modern state of Israel is irrigating and developing the Negeb. The "river of Egypt" marked the southwestern boundary of the Negeb as well as marking off part of the southern boundary of the Promised Land.—Gen. 15:18.

C-8 THE WILDERNESS OF PARAN

21 South of the Negeb and merging with the Wilderness of Zin lies the Wilderness of Paran. On leaving Sinai the Israelites crossed this wilderness on their way to the Promised Land,

16. (a) What characterizes the Shephelah? (b) Of what importance was this district in Bible times?
17. (a) How productive was the mountainous region of Judah in Bible times, and how about today? (b) For what was Judah considered a good place?
18. (a) When did Jerusalem become the capital of Israel and Judah? (b) What are some interesting features of the city?
19. (a) How does Jeshimon fit the meaning of its name? (b) What Bible events took place in this region?
20. Describe the Negeb.
21. Where is Paran, and what part did it play in Bible history?

and it was from Paran that Moses sent out the twelve spies.—Num. 12:16-13:3.

D. THE GREAT ARABAH (THE RIFT VALLEY)

22 One of the most unusual land formations on this earth is the great Rift Valley. In the Bible, that part that cuts through Palestine from north to south is called "the Arabah." (Josh. 18:18) At 2 Samuel 2:29 this split in the earth's crust is described as a gully. To its north is Mount Hermon. (Song of Sol. 4:8) From the foot of Hermon the Rift Valley drops rapidly southward to about 2,580 feet *below* sea level at the bottom of the Dead Sea. From the southern end of the Dead Sea the Arabah continues, rising to 650 feet above sea level about forty-eight miles farther south, and thereafter descends rapidly into the tepid waters of the eastern prong of the Red Sea. The accompanying section maps show the relation of the Rift Valley to the surrounding country.

D-1 THE HULEH BASIN

23 Beginning at the foot of Mount Hermon, the Rift Valley quickly falls off over 1,600 feet to the Huleh region, which is at about sea level. (The lake that was here in times past has been identified with the "waters of Merom," referred to at Joshua 11:5, 7, but some commentators consider these "waters of Merom" to have been springs some ten miles west of the Jordan and between the Huleh region and the Sea of Galilee.) This district is well watered and remains beautifully green even through the hot summer months. It was in this area that the Danites settled in their city of Dan, which served as an idolatrous center of worship from the time of the judges into that of the ten-tribe kingdom of Israel. (Judg. 18:29-31; 2 Ki. 10:29) It was at Caesarea Philippi, a town near the location of ancient Dan, that Jesus confirmed to his disciples that he was the Christ, and many believe that it was on nearby Mount Hermon that the transfiguration took place six days later. From Huleh the Rift Valley rapidly descends to the Sea of Galilee, which is over 680 feet below sea level.—Matt. 16:13-20; 17:1-9.

D-2 REGION AROUND THE SEA OF GALILEE (GENNESARET)

24 The Sea of Galilee and its surroundings are delightful. Interest in this region is heightened by the many remembrances it carries concerning Jesus' ministry. (Matt. 4:23) The "sea" is also called the Lake of Gennesaret, or Chinnereth, and the Sea of Tiberias. (Luke 5:1; Josh. 13:27; John 21:1) It is in reality a heart-shaped lake, almost thirteen miles long by seven miles wide at its broadest point. It is closely shut in by hills on almost every side. The surface of the lake is over 680 feet below sea level, resulting in pleasant, warm winters and very long, hot summers. In the days of Jesus it was the center of a highly developed fishing industry, and the thriving cities of Chorazin, Bethsaida, Capernaum and Tiberias were located on or near the lake shore. The peacefulness of the lake is quickly disturbed by storms. (Luke 8:23) The little plain of Gennesaret (or Chinnereth), triangular in shape, is located to the northwest of the lake. The soil is rich, producing almost every kind of crop known to the Promised Land. In the spring the gaily colored slopes glow with a brilliance that is nowhere surpassed in the land of Israel.

D-3 DISTRICT OF THE JORDAN VALLEY (THE GHOR)

25 This entire gulley-like descending valley is also called "the Arabah." (Deut. 3:17) The Arabs today refer to it as the *Ghor*. The valley starts from the Sea of Galilee and is generally broad—being about twelve miles wide in places. The Jordan River itself lies about 150 feet below the valley plain, turning and twisting in a course of two hundred miles, to cover the sixty-five miles to the Dead Sea. It averages from 100 to 150 feet in width. Leaping over and down twenty-seven cascading rapids, it falls about six hundred feet by the time it reaches the Dead Sea. The lower Jordan is fringed by a thicket of trees and shrubs, principally tamarisks, oleanders and willows, among which lions and their whelps lurked in Bible times. This is today known as the *Zor*, and is partly flooded in the spring. (Jer. 49:19) Rising above each side of this narrow jungle-like strip is the *Qattara*, an inhospitable border of desolate land of little plateaus and dissected slopes leading up to the plains of the *Ghor* itself. The plains in the northern part of the *Ghor* or Arabah are well cultivated. Even in the southern part, toward the Dead Sea, the plateau of the Arabah, which is today very arid, at one time is said to have produced forty-nine different kinds of dates, as well as many other tropical fruits. The most famous city in the Jordan valley was Jericho.—Josh. 6:2, 20; Mark 10:46.

---

22. By using the map on page 272 and the diagrams on page 273, along with this paragraph, briefly describe the main features of the Great Arabah (Rift Valley) in their relationship to each other, and in their relationship to the surrounding territory.
23. With what was the Huleh region associated in Bible times?
24. (a) By what other names is the Sea of Galilee called in the Bible? (b) What were its surroundings like in Jesus' day?
25. What are the main features of the Jordan Valley?

D-4 THE SALT (DEAD) SEA

26 This is one of the most remarkable bodies of water on the face of this earth. It is fittingly called "Dead," for nothing lives in the sea, nor is there any vegetation by its shore. The Bible calls it the Salt Sea, or the Sea of Arabah, since it is located in the rift valley of the Arabah. (Gen. 14:3; Josh. 12:3) The sea is approximately forty-seven miles from north to south, and nine miles across. Its surface is, on an average, 1,287 feet below that of the Mediterranean Sea, and this is the lowest point on the earth's surface. In its northern part it has a depth of about 1,300 feet. On each side the sea is shut in by steep and barren hills. Although the Jordan River brings in fresh water, there is no water outlet, except by evaporation, and this is as fast as the water intake. The trapped water contains 25 percent of solid matter, mostly salt, and is poisonous to fish and painful to human eyes. Visitors to most of the area around the Dead Sea are often overwhelmed by a sense of desolation and destruction. It is a place of the dead. Though the entire region was once "well-watered . . . like the garden of Jehovah," around the Dead Sea it is now largely "a desolate waste" and has been for close on 4,000 years, as striking testimony to the unchangeableness of Jehovah's judgments, as executed there against Sodom and Gomorrah. —Gen. 13:10; 19:27-29; Zeph. 2:9.

D-5 THE ARABAH (SOUTHWARD FROM THE SALT SEA)

27 This final section of the Rift Valley runs southward for another one hundred miles. This region is virtually all desert. Rain is rare, and the sun beats down without mercy. The Bible calls this also the Arabah. (Deut. 2:8) About forty-eight miles south of the Salt Sea, it reaches its highest point at 650 feet above sea level, and then descends southward again to the Gulf of Aqabah, the eastern prong of the Red Sea. It was here, at the port of Ezion-geber, that Solomon built a fleet of ships. (1 Ki. 9:26) For much of the period of the kings of Judah, this part of the Arabah was under control of the kingdom of Edom.

E. THE HILLS AND TABLELANDS EAST OF THE JORDAN

28 "The side of the Jordan toward the east" rises rapidly from the Rift Valley to form a series of tablelands. (Josh. 18:7; 13:9-12; 20:8) To the north is the land of Bashan (E-1), which, together with half of Gilead, was given to the tribe of Manasseh. (Josh. 13:29-31) This was cattle country, a land for the farmers, a fertile plateau averaging about 2,000 feet above sea level. (Ps. 22:12; Ezek. 39:18; Isa. 2:13; Zech. 11:2) In Jesus' day this area exported much grain, and today the main crop is wheat. Next, to the south, there lies the land of Gilead (E-2), the lower half of which was assigned to the tribe of Gad. (Josh. 13:24, 25) A dome-like mountainous region reaching to 3,300 feet, watered by good rains in the winter and heavy dews in the summer, it was also good livestock country and was specially renowned for its balsam. Today it is noted for its choice grapes. (Num. 32:1; Gen. 37:25; Jer. 46:11) It was to the land of Gilead that David fled from Absalom, and in the western part Jesus preached in "the regions of Decapolis."—2 Sam. 17:26-29; Mark 7:31.

29 The "land of the sons of Ammon" (E-3) lies immediately south of Gilead, and half of this was given to the tribe of Gad. (Josh. 13: 24, 25; Judg. 11:12-28) It is a rolling tableland, best suited to sheep grazing. (Ezek. 25:5) Yet farther to the south is the "land of Moab." The Moabites themselves were great sheep-herders, and to this day sheep raising is the principal occupation of that area. (2 Ki. 3:4) Then, southeast of the Dead Sea, we come to the mountainous plateau of Edom (E-4). The ruins of its great trading strongholds, such as Petra, remain to this day.—Gen. 36:19-21; Obad. 1-4.

30 To the east of these hills and tablelands lies the extensive rocky wilderness that effectively cut off direct travel between Palestine and Mesopotamia, causing the caravan routes to detour many miles northward. To the south this wilderness meets up with the sand dunes of the great Arabian desert.

F. THE MOUNTAINS OF LEBANON

31 Dominating the landscape of Palestine are the mountains of Lebanon. There are really two ranges of mountains running parallel. The foothills of the Lebanon range proper continue into Upper Galilee. In many places these hills reach right down to the seacoast. The highest peak in this range is about 10,000 feet above sea level. The highest peak in the adjoining Anti-Lebanon range is the beautiful Mount Hermon, over 9,000 feet. Its snows provide a major source for the Jordan River, and dew during the dry months. (Ps. 133:3) The Leb-

26. (a) What are some of the remarkable facts about the Dead Sea? (b) What striking testimony does this region give concerning Jehovah's judgments?
27. What kind of territory makes up the southern Arabah, and who controlled this in ancient times?
28. Of what value have been the lands of Bashan and Gilead as to agriculture, and how did these regions figure in Bible history?
29. What lands lay to the south in Transjordan, and for what were they noted?
30. By what are the tablelands bounded on the east?
31. (a) What comprises the mountains of Lebanon? (b) What features of Lebanon survive to this day?

anon Mountains were specially noted for their gigantic cedars, the wood of which featured in the construction of Solomon's temple. (1 Ki. 5:6-10) While only a few groves of cedars remain today, the lower slopes still support vineyards, olive groves and fruit orchards, just as they did in Bible times.—Hos. 14:5-7.

32 As we thus conclude our visit to Jehovah's Land of Promise, sandwiched as it is between the forbidding wilderness and the Great Sea, we can form a mental picture of the glory that once clothed it in the days of Israel. Truly, it was "a very, very good land . . . flowing with milk and honey." (Num. 14:7, 8; 13:23) Moses referred to it in these words: "Jehovah your God is bringing you into a good land, a land of torrent valleys of water, springs and watery deeps issuing forth in the valley plain and in the mountainous region, a land of wheat and barley and vines and figs and pomegranates, a land of oil olives and honey, a land in which you will not eat bread with scarcity, in which you will lack nothing, a land the stones of which are iron and out of the mountains of which you will mine copper. When you have eaten and satisfied yourself, you must also bless Jehovah your God for the good land that he has given you." (Deut. 8:7-10) May all who love Jehovah now likewise give thanks that he purposes to make the entire earth a glorious paradise, after the pattern of his ancient Land of Promise.—Ps. 104:10-24.

32. How did Moses correctly describe the Land of Promise?

Study Two— Time and The Holy Scriptures

Describing time divisions used in the Bible, the calendars in common use, absolute dates for the Bible and interesting points with regard to "the stream of time."

MAN is deeply conscious of the passing of time. With each tick of the clock, he progresses a step farther down time's corridor. He is wise, indeed, if he makes proper use of his time. As King Solomon wrote: "For everything there is an appointed time, even a time for every affair under the heavens: a time for birth and a time to die; a time to plant and a time to uproot what was planted; a time to kill and a time to heal; a time to break down and a time to build; a time to weep and a time to laugh." (Eccl. 3:1-4) How fleeting is this passage of time! The seventy years of the normal life-span are far too short for taking in the abundance of knowledge and for enjoying all the other good things Jehovah has provided for man on this earth. "Everything he has made pretty in its time. Even time indefinite he has put in their heart, that mankind may never find out the work that the true God has made from the start to the finish."—Eccl. 3:11; Ps. 90:10.

2 Jehovah himself lives in an eternity of time. As for his creatures, it has pleased him to set them in the stream of time. The angels of heaven, yes, even the rebellious Satan, are fully aware of the passage of time. (Dan. 10:13; Rev. 12:12) Of mankind it is written, "Time and unforeseen occurrence befall them all." (Eccl. 9:11) Happy is the man who at all times includes God in his thoughts, and who welcomes God's provision of "food at the proper time"!—Matt. 24:45.

1, 2. What did Solomon write concerning time, and in view of the fleeting nature of time, what should we do with it?

3 **Time Is One-Directional.** Though time is universal, no man living is able to say what it is. It is as unfathomable as space. No one can explain where the stream of time began, or where it is flowing. These things belong to the limitless knowledge of Jehovah, who is described as being God "from time indefinite to time indefinite."—Ps. 90:2.

4 However, time has certain characteristics that can be understood. Its apparent rate of flow can be measured. Another characteristic is that it moves in one direction only. Like traffic in a one-way street, time moves relentlessly in that one direction—onward, ever onward. Whatever the speed of its forward motion, time can never be thrown into reverse. We live in a momentary present. However, this present is in motion, flowing continually into the past. There is no stopping.

5 **The Past.** The past is gone, it is history, and it can never be repeated. Any attempt to call

3. What do time and space have in common?
4. What can be said as to the movement of time?
5. Why may it be said that the past has been won or lost?

back the past is as impossible as trying to make a waterfall tumble uphill, or an arrow fly back to the bow that shot it. Our mistakes have left their mark in the corridor of time, a mark that only Jehovah can wipe out. (Isa. 43:25) In like manner, a man's good deeds of the past have made a record that "will come back to him" with blessing from Jehovah. (Prov. 12:14; 13:22) The past has been won or lost. No longer is there any control over it. Of the wicked it is written: "For like grass they will speedily wither, and like green new grass they will fade away."—Ps. 37:1, 2.

6 **The Future.** The future is different. It is always flowing toward us. By the help of God's Word, we can identify obstacles that loom ahead of us, and prepare to meet them. We can store up for ourselves "treasures in heaven." (Matt. 6:20) These treasures will not be swept away by the stream of time. They will stay with us, and will endure into an eternal future of blessing. We are interested in the wise use of time, as it affects that future. —Eph. 5:15, 16.

7 **Time Indicators.** Our modern-day watches and clocks indicate time by small hands. These, in turn, are kept in motion by revolving cogwheels, energized by wound springs. In similar manner Jehovah, the Creator, has set in revolving motion giant time indicators—the earth spinning on its axis, the moon revolving around the earth, and the earth revolving around the sun. Moreover, he has made this great timepiece luminous, by light from the sun, so that from his standpoint on earth, man may be accurately advised of the time. "And God went on to say: 'Let luminaries come to be in the expanse of the heavens to make a division between the day and the night; and they must serve as signs and for seasons and for days and years.'" (Gen. 1:14) Thus, as a multitude of objects with interlocking purposes, these heavenly bodies move in their perfect cycles, unendingly and unerringly measuring the one-directional movement of time.

8 **Day.** The word "day" in the Bible is used with several different meanings, even as it has a variety of applications in modern times. As the earth makes one complete rotation on its axis, it measures out one day of twenty-four hours. In this first sense, *day* is made up of daytime and nighttime, a total of twenty-four hours. (John 20:19) However, the daylight period itself, of about twelve hours, is also called *day*—a second sense. "And God began calling the light *Day,* but the darkness he called *Night.*" (Gen. 1:5) This also gives rise to the time term *night,* the period of approximately twelve hours of darkness. (Ex. 10:13) A third sense is where the word *day(s)* refers to a period of time contemporaneous with some outstanding person. For example, Isaiah saw his vision "in the *days* of Uzziah, Jotham, Ahaz and Hezekiah" (Isa. 1:1), and the *days* of Noah and Lot are mentioned as being prophetic. (Luke 17:26-30) Another sense is where one *day* with Jehovah is spoken of as a thousand years. (2 Pet. 3:8) A fifth sense is that of the creative *day,* an even longer period of time. (Gen. 2:2, 3; Ex. 20:11) The Bible context indicates the sense in which the word "day" applies.

9 **Hour.** The division of the day into twenty-four hours, with subdivisions of sixty minutes and sixty seconds, was an innovation of post-Flood times. Instead of the decimal system, as we have it today, early Babylonian (Chaldean) and Egyptian civilizations used the duodecimal system, based on twelves and sixties. From this our modern-day hours, minutes and seconds originated. There is no mention of division into hours in the Hebrew Scriptures.[a] However, the "steps" mentioned at 2 Kings 20:11 and Isaiah 38:8 in connection with the "sign" that Jehovah gave King Hezekiah may refer to a sundial method of keeping time that Ahaz had previously imported from Babylon, whereby shadows were projected by the sun on a series of steps.

10 However, there is frequent mention of the "hour" in the Christian Greek Scriptures, and it appears that this measure of time was about the same length as it is today. (John 12:23; Matt. 20:2-6) Hours were counted from sunrise, or about 6 a.m. The Bible mentions the "third hour," which would be about 9 a.m. The "sixth hour" is also mentioned, as the time when darkness fell on Jerusalem at Jesus' impalement. This would correspond to our twelve o'clock noon. Jesus' expiration in death on the torture stake is stated to have occurred "about the ninth hour," or about 3 p.m.—Mark 15:25; Luke 23:44; Matt. 27:45, 46.[b]

11 **Week.** It was early in his history that man began to count his days in cycles of seven.

---

a The word "hour" appears in the *AV* translation of Daniel 3:6, 15; 4:19, 33; 5:5, from the Aramaic; however, Strong's *Concordance, Hebrew and Chaldee Dictionary,* gives the meaning of the word as "a look, i.e. a moment"; it is translated "moment" in *NW*.
b See *NW* footnotes, 1950 Edition.

---

6. How is the future different, and why especially should we be interested in it?
7. What time indicators has Jehovah provided for man?
8. In what different senses is the word "day" used in the Bible?
9. (a) How did hours, minutes and seconds originate? (b) Are hours mentioned in the Hebrew Scriptures?
10. Of what length was the "hour" used in Jesus' time, and how does the use of this term help us fix the time of Jesus' death?
11. How old is the use of the "week" as a measurement of time?

In doing this he followed the example of his Creator, who proceeded to crown his six creative days with a seventh day-period. Noah counted days in cycles of seven. In Hebrew, "week" literally means "sevened," or a cycle of seven.—Gen. 2:2, 3; 8:10, 12; 29:27.

12 **Lunar Months.** The Bible speaks of "lunar months." (Ex. 2:2; Deut. 21:13; 33:14; Ezra 6: 15) Our modern months are not lunar months, because they are not determined by the moon. They are merely twelve arbitrary divisions of the solar year. However, the word "month" is derived from "moon," which is *luna* in the Latin language. A "lunar month" is a month that is actually determined by the new moon. There are four phases of the moon, which make up one lunation of slightly more than twenty-nine and a half days. One has only to look at the shape of the moon to tell approximately the day of the lunar month.

13 Rather than using strictly lunar months, Noah appears to have recorded events by months of thirty days each. By the log that Noah kept on the ark, and from which his sons wrote their history, we understand that the waters of the Flood kept overwhelming the earth for a period of five months, or "a hundred and fifty days." It was after twelve months and ten days that the earth had dried off, so that the ark's passengers could go out. Thus those epoch-making events were accurately recorded as to time.—Gen. 7:11, 24; 8:3, 4, 14-19.

14 **Seasons.** In preparing the earth for habitation, Jehovah made the wise and loving provision of the seasons. (Gen. 1:14) These follow as a consequence of the earth's being tilted or inclined at a 23½° angle to the plane of its travel around the sun. This results in first the Southern Hemisphere and then the Northern Hemisphere being tilted toward the sun, so that the seasons come and go in their procession. This change of the seasons provides for variety and contrast and controls the times for planting and harvesting. God's Word assures us that this arrangement for change and contrast of the seasons through the year is to continue forever. "For all the days the earth continues, seed sowing and harvest, and cold and heat, and summer and winter, and day and night, will never cease."—Gen. 8:22.

15 The year in Palestine can be generally divided into the rainy season, running from October to April, and the dry season, from May to September. The rainy season may be further divided into the early or "autumn rain" (October-November), the heavy winter rains and colder weather (December-February), and the late or "spring rain" (March-April). (Deut. 11:14; Joel 2:23) These divisions are approximate, the seasons overlapping due to variations in climate in different parts of the land. The early rain softens up the dry ground, so that October-November is "plowing time" and for "sowing of seed." (Ex. 34:21; Lev. 26:5) During the heavy winter rains from December to February snowfalls are not uncommon, and in January and February the temperature may drop below freezing on the higher elevations, including Jerusalem. The Bible speaks of Benaiah, one of David's mighty men, killing a lion "on a day of snowfall."—2 Sam. 23:20.

16 The months of March and April (approximately the Hebrew months of Nisan and Ziv) are the months of the "spring rain." (Zech. 10:1) This is the *late* rain, which is needed to make the grain planted in autumn swell, so that a good harvest may result. (Hos. 6:3; Jas. 5:7) This is also the season of the early harvest, and God commanded Israel to offer the firstfruits of the harvest on Nisan 16. (Lev. 23:10; Ruth 1:22) It is a time of beauty and delight. "Blossoms themselves have appeared in the land, the very time of vine trimming has arrived, and the voice of the turtledove itself has been heard in our land. As for the fig tree, it has gained a mature color for its early figs; and the vines are abloom, they have given their fragrance."—Song of Sol. 2: 12, 13.

17 With the month of May the dry season begins, but, almost throughout this period, and especially on the coastal plains and the western slopes of the mountains, an abundance of dew sustains the summer crops. (Deut. 33:28) During May all the grain is harvested, and it was at the end of this month or the beginning of June that the Feast of Weeks (Pentecost) was celebrated. (Lev. 23:15-21) Then as the weather becomes warmer and the ground drier the grapes on the vines ripen and are harvested, followed by the other summer fruits, such as olives, dates and figs. (2 Sam. 16:1) With the ending of the dry season and the beginning of the early rains all the produce of the land has been harvested, and it was then (about the beginning of October) that the Feast of Tabernacles was held.—Ex. 23:16; Lev. 23:39-43.

---

12. What is a "lunar month," and how does it differ from our modern months?
13. How was the Flood accurately recorded as to time?
14. (a) How did Jehovah make provision for the seasons? (b) How long will the arrangement of seasons continue?
15, 16. (a) How may the rainy season in Palestine be subdivided? (b) Describe the seasons of the early and the late rains. (c) What relationship did these have to agricultural activity?
17. (a) How are the crops sustained during the dry season? (b) Consider the chart, "The Year of the Israelites," and divide off the year according to seasons as discussed in paragraphs 15-17. (c) When was the early harvest? the grain harvest? the time when all the fruits were gathered in? What festivals coincided with these events?

THE YEAR OF THE ISRAELITES

Name of Month	*Corresponds to*	*Sacred Year*		*Secular Year*		*Citations*	*Festivals*	
Abib or Nisan	March - April	1st	Month	7th	Month	Ex. 13: 4; Neh. 2: 1	Nisan 14 Nisan 15-21 Nisan 16	Passover Festival of unfermented cakes Offering of firstfruits
Ziv or Iyyar	April - May	2d	"	8th	"	1 Ki. 6: 1		
Sivan	May - June	3d	"	9th	"	Esther 8: 9	Sivan 6	Feast of weeks (Pentecost)
Tammuz	June - July	4th	"	10th	"	Jer. 52: 6		
Ab	July - August	5th	"	11th	"	Ezra 7: 8		
Elul	August - September	6th	"	12th	"	Neh. 6: 15		
Ethanim or Tishri	September - October	7th	"	1st	"	1 Ki. 8: 2	Ethanim 1 Ethanim 10 Ethanim 15-21 Ethanim 22	Day of the trumpet blast Day of atonement Festival of booths Solemn assembly
Bul or Heshvan	October - November	8th	"	2d	"	1 Ki. 6: 38		
Chislev	November - December	9th	"	3d	"	Neh. 1: 1		
Tebeth	December - January	10th	"	4th	"	Esther 2: 16		
Shebat	January - February	11th	"	5th	"	Zech. 1: 7		
Adar	February - March	12th	"	6th	"	Esther 3: 7		
V^e^adar	(Intercalary month)	13th	"					

18 **Year.** Our study of time in the Bible now brings us to the *year*. From the beginning of man's history there is mention of the *year*. (Gen. 1:14) The Hebrew word for "year" is *shanáh*, which literally means "repetition."[a] This was appropriate since each year the cycle of seasons was repeated. An earthly year is the time it takes for the earth to make one complete revolution or trip around the sun. The actual time that it takes for us here on earth to complete this trip is 365 days 5 hours 48 minutes 46 seconds, or approximately 365 ¼ days. This is called the true solar year, "sun" in Latin being *sol*.

19 **Bible Years.** According to the ancient Biblical reckoning, the year ran from autumn to autumn. This was particularly suited to an agricultural life, the year beginning with plowing and sowing about October 1, and ending with the gathering in of the harvest. Noah counted the year as beginning in the autumn. He recorded the Deluge as beginning "in the second month," which would correspond to the latter half of October and the first half of November. (Gen. 7:11)[b] To this day, many peoples of the earth still start their new year in the autumn. At the time of the exodus from Egypt, in 1513 B.C.E., Jehovah decreed that Abib (Nisan) should become "the start of the months" for the Jews, so that they now had a "sacred year," running from spring to spring. (Ex. 12:2) However, the Jews in this day observe a secular or civil year beginning in the autumn, Tishri being the first month.

a *Young's Concordance*, under "year."
b See *NW* footnote, 1953 Edition.

18. (a) Why is the meaning of the Hebrew word for "year" appropriate? (b) What is the true solar year as regards the earth?
19. (a) How were ancient Bible years reckoned? (b) What "sacred year" did Jehovah later decree?

20 **Lunisolar Year.** Up until the time of Christ most nations used lunar years for counting time, using various ways of adjusting the year to coincide more or less with the solar year. The common lunar year of twelve lunar months has 354 days, with the months having twenty-nine or thirty days, depending on the appearance of each new moon. The lunar year is therefore about eleven days short of the true solar year of 365 ¼ days. The Hebrews followed the lunar year. Just how they adjusted this year to coincide with the solar year and the seasons is not explained in the Bible, but they must have added additional or *intercalary* months when needed. The arrangement of intercalary months was later systematized in the fifth century B.C.E. into what is now known as the Metonic cycle. This allowed for the intercalary month to be added seven times every nineteen years, and in the Jewish calendar it was added after the twelfth month Adar and called *V^e^Adar*, or "second Adar." As the lunar calendar is thus adjusted to the sun, the years, of twelve or thirteen months, are known as "bound years" or "lunisolar years."

21 **Julian and Gregorian Calendars.** A calendar is a system of fixing the beginning, length and divisions of the secular or civil year, and arranging these divisions in order. The Julian Calendar was introduced by Julius Caesar in 46 B.C.E., to give the Roman people a solar-year time arrangement in place of the lunar year. The Julian Calendar consists of 365 days in a year, with the exception that on each fourth year ("leap year") one day is added, to make it 366 days. However, in the course of

20. How was the lunar year adjusted to correspond with the solar year, and what are "lunisolar years"?
21, 22. (a) What is the Julian Calendar? (b) Why is the Gregorian Calendar more accurate? (c) What is now the time difference between the two?

time it was found that the Julian Calendar fell behind about one day in each 128 years. This was because the Julian Calendar is actually 11 minutes longer than the true solar year. Thus, in 1582, Pope Gregory XIII introduced a slight revision, instituting what is now known as the Gregorian Calendar. This provides that centuries not divisible by 400 are not to be considered leap years. For example, no day was added in 1900 to make it a leap year, but it is planned to add a leap-year day in the year 2000, as this is divisible by 400. The Gregorian Calendar is now the one in general use in Western countries.

22 Historians usually employ the Julian Calendar for events prior to the sixteenth century of the Common Era, but the Gregorian Calendar in dating events after A.D. 1600. As an illustration, the Memorial of Jesus' death for 1963 was celebrated on April 8, 1963, according to the Gregorian Calendar, but this same day was March 26 according to the Julian Calendar. Today, there is a thirteen-day difference between the two calendars.

23 **A Bible "Time."** A prophetic "time" in the Bible, whether literal or symbolic, is always taken as a year of twelve months, each month having thirty days, for a total of 360 days. Note what one authority says in commenting on Ezekiel 4:5 and Daniel 12:11: "We must suppose that Ezekiel knew a year of 360 days. This is neither a true solar year nor is it a lunar year. It is an 'average' year in which each month has 30 days. . . . The 1290 days in Daniel must be interpreted as 3 ½ x 360 days + 30 days (of an intercalary month)."[a]

24 A study of Revelation 11:2, 3 and 12:6, 14 reveals how one "time" is reckoned as 360 days.

25 **No Zero Year.** Ancient peoples, including the learned Greeks, the Romans and the Jews of Jesus' day, had no conception of a *zero*. To them, everything began from *one*. When you studied Roman numerals at school (I, II, III, IV, V, X, etc.) did you learn a figure for *zero?* No, because the Romans had none. It was for this reason that the Christian era began, not with a *zero,* but with A.D. 1. This also gave rise to the ordinal arrangement of numbers, such as first (1st), second (2d), third (3d), tenth (10th), hundredth (100th), and so forth. In modern mathematics, which was largely designed by the Arabs, man conceives of everything as starting from nothing, or *zero*. The zero was invented by the Hindus about A.D. 150, and then introduced by the Arabs into Europe some centuries later.[b]

26 Thus it is that whenever *ordinal* numbers are used, we must always subtract one to get the full number. For example, this is called the twentieth century. Does this mean there have been a full twenty centuries? No, it means nineteen full centuries plus some years. To express full numbers the Bible, as well as modern mathematics, has the *cardinal* numbers, such as 1, 2, 3, 10, 100, and so forth. These are also called "whole numbers."

27 Now, since the Christian era did not begin with the year zero, but began with A.D. 1, and the calendar for the years before the Christian era did not count back from a zero year, but began with 1 B.C.E., the figure used for the year in any date is in reality an ordinal number. That is, A.D. 1960 really represents 1959 full years since the beginning of the Christian era, and the date July 1, 1960, represents 1959 ½ years since the beginning of the Christian era. The same principle applies to B.C.E. dates. So to figure how many years elapsed between October 1, 607 B.C.E., and October 1, A.D. 1914, add 606 years (plus the last three months of the previous year) to 1913 (plus the first nine months of the next year), and the result is 2519 (plus twelve months), or 2520 years. Or if you want to figure what date would be 2520 years after October 1, 607 B.C.E., remember that 607 is an ordinal number; it really represents 606 full years, and since we are counting, not from December 31, 607 B.C.E., but from October 1, 607 B.C.E., we must add to 606 the three months at the end of 607 B.C.E. Now subtract 606 ¼ from 2520 years. The remainder is 1913 ¾. That means that 2520 years from October 1, 607 B.C.E., takes us 1913 ¾ years into the Christian era. Nineteen hundred and thirteen full years brings us to the beginning of A.D. 1914; ¾ of a year in addition brings us to October 1, A.D. 1914.

28 **Absolute Dates.** Reliable Bible chronology is based on certain *absolute dates*. An *absolute date* is a calendar date that is proved by secular history to be the actual date of an event recorded in the Bible. It can then be used as the starting point from which a series of Bible events can be located on the calendar with certainty. Once this *absolute date* is fixed, calculations forward or backward from this date are made from accurate records in the Bible

a *Biblical Calendars,* 1959, by J. Van Goudoever, page 75.

b *Mathematics for the Million,* 1940, by Lancelot Hogben, pages 51, 281, 288.

23, 24. What is a prophetic "time"?
25. How did the various ancient peoples start their counting?
26. How do ordinal numbers differ from cardinal numbers?
27. How would you figure (a) the years from October 1, 607 B.C.E., to October 1, 1914 A.D.? (b) 2,520 years from October 1, 607 B.C.E.?
28. What are absolute dates, and why are they of great value?

itself, such as the stated life-spans of people, or the duration of the reigns of kings. Thus, starting from a pegged point, we can use the reliable internal chronology of the Bible itself in dating many Bible events.

29 **Absolute Date for the Hebrew Scriptures.** A prominent event recorded both in the Bible and in pagan secular history is the overthrow of the city of Babylon by the Medes and Persians under Cyrus. The Bible records this event at Daniel 5:30. The pagan record was made by King Nabonidus, and it has been dated by him in what is known as the Nabonidus Chronicle, discovered in 1879 and now preserved in the British Museum, London.[a] Modern authorities have set this absolute date for the fall of Babylon as October 11-12, 539 B.C.E., according to the Julian Calendar, or October 5-6 by the Gregorian Calendar. (Like the Hebrew day, the Babylonian day began at 6 p.m.)[b]

30 Following the overthrow of Babylon, as the Bible record shows, "Darius the Mede himself received the kingdom." And since Daniel refers to "the first year of Darius," the inference is that he was king for at least one full year. (Dan. 5:31; 9:1) But apparently by late in 538 B.C.E. Cyrus acceded to the throne, and during his first year, at least before spring of 537 B.C.E., he issued his famous edict, or decree, permitting the Jews to return to Jerusalem to rebuild the house of Jehovah. This would give ample opportunity for the Jews to resettle in their homeland, and to come up to Jerusalem to restore the worship of Jehovah in "the seventh month," or about October 1, 537 B.C.E.—Ezra 1:1-3; 3:1-6.

31 **Absolute Date for the Christian Greek Scriptures.** An absolute date for the Christian Greek Scriptures is determined by Tiberius Caesar's succession to Emperor Augustus. This was August 19, A.D. 14, according to the Julian Calendar. It is stated in Luke 3:1, 3 that John the Baptist began his ministry in the fifteenth year of Tiberius' reign. From the absolute date we can therefore calculate the fifteenth year of Tiberius' actual rule to have run from August 19, A.D. 28, to August 18, A.D. 29. Soon after this, Jesus, who was about six months younger than John the Baptist, came to be baptized, when he was "about thirty years old." (Luke 3:2, 21-23; 1:34-38) This agrees with the fact that, according to Daniel 9:25, sixty-nine "weeks" (prophetic "weeks" of seven years each, thus totaling 483 years) would elapse after the decree was issued for the rebuilding of Jerusalem with its wall until the appearance of Messiah. That decree was issued by Artaxerxes I in 455 B.C.E., taking effect in the latter part of that year. And 483 years later, in the latter part of A.D. 29, when Jesus was baptized by John he was also anointed by holy spirit from God, thus becoming the Messiah or Anointed One. That Jesus was baptized and began his ministry in the latter part of the year also agrees with the fact that he was to be cut off "at the half of the week" (or after three and a half years). (Dan. 9:27) Since he died in the spring, his ministry of three and a half years must have begun toward the fall of A.D. 29. Incidentally, these two lines of evidence also prove that Jesus was born in the autumn of 2 B.C.E., and not, as some commentators say, several years before that, since Luke 3:23 shows that Jesus was about thirty years of age when he commenced his work.

32 **How Time Moves Faster.** There is an old saying that "a watched kettle never boils." It is true that when we are watching time, when we are conscious of it, when we are waiting for something to happen, then it passes ever so slowly. However, if we are busy, if we are interested and preoccupied in what we are doing, then it really appears that "time flies." Moreover, with old people, time seems to pass much more quickly than with young people. Why is this? One year added to the life of a one-year-old means a 100-percent increase in life's experiences. One year added to the life of a fifty-year-old means just 2 percent more. To the child, a year seems a long, long time. The older person, if busy and in good health, finds the years flying faster and faster. He comes to a deeper understanding of Solomon's words: "There is nothing new under the sun." On the other hand, young people still have the slower, formative years with them. Instead of "striving after wind" with a materialistic world, they may use these years profitably in piling up a wealth of godly experience. Timely are Solomon's further words: "Remember, now, your grand Creator in the days of your young manhood, before the calamitous days proceed to come, or the years have arrived when you will say: 'I have no delight in them.'"—Eccl. 1:9, 14; 12:1.

33 **Time when Living Forever.** However, there are joyous days ahead that will be far from calamitous. Lovers of righteousness, whose 'times are in Jehovah's hand,' may look for-

a See Study 9, paragraphs 17, 18.
b *Babylonian Chronology*, 1956, Parker and Dubberstein, pages 13, 14, 29.

29. What absolute date is provided for the Hebrew Scriptures?
30. When was Cyrus' decree issued, allowing opportunity for what?
31. How does an absolute date along with fulfilled prophecy fix the time of Jesus' baptism, and of his birth?
32. (a) Why does the speed of time appear to vary? (b) What advantage do young people therefore have?
33. How may humans come to appreciate more fully Jehovah's view of time?

ward to everlasting life in the realm of God's kingdom. (Ps. 31:14-16; Matt. 25:34, 46) Under the Kingdom, death will be no more. (Rev. 21:4) Idleness, illness, boredom and vanity will have vanished. There will be work to do, absorbing and intriguing, challenging man's perfect abilities, and bringing intense satisfaction in accomplishment. The years will seem to flow faster and faster, and appreciative and retentive minds will be continually enriched with memories of happy events. As millenniums pass, humans on this earth will no doubt come to appreciate more fully Jehovah's view of time: 'For a thousand years in Jehovah's eyes are but as yesterday when it is past.'—Ps. 90:4.

34 Viewing the stream of time from our present human standpoint, and taking into account God's promise of a new world of righteousness, how joyous in prospect are the blessings of that day: "For there Jehovah commanded the blessing to be, even life to time indefinite"! —Ps. 133:3.

34. With regard to time, what blessing has Jehovah commanded?

Study Three—Measuring Events in the Stream of Time

The counting of time in Bible days, and a discussion of the chronology of outstanding events of both the Hebrew and Greek Scriptures.

IN GIVING Daniel the vision of the "king of the north" and the "king of the south," Jehovah's angel several times used the expression "the time appointed." (Dan. 11:27, 29, 35) There are many other scriptures, too, that indicate Jehovah is an accurate timekeeper, who accomplishes his purposes exactly on time. (Luke 21:24; 1 Thess. 5:1, 2) In his Word the Bible he has provided a number of "guideposts" that help us locate important happenings in the stream of time. In recent years much progress has been made in the understanding of Bible chronology. Archaeological and other research continues to shed light on various problems, enabling us to determine the timing of key events of the Bible record.—Prov. 4:18.

2 **Ordinal and Cardinal Numbers.** In the previous study (paragraphs 25 and 26) we learned that there is a difference between cardinal numbers and ordinal numbers. Now, let us apply this understanding to Jeremiah 52:31. Here it speaks of "the thirty-seventh year of the exile of Jehoiachin the king of Judah." Note that "thirty-seventh" is an *ordinal* number. This indicates thirty-six full years plus some months. The exile of Jehoiachin began early in the year 617 B.C.E. The thirty-seventh year began, not after thirty-seven years had passed, but after thirty-six full years had elapsed, or early in the year 581. However, it is noted that the event spoken of in this verse occurred "in the twelfth month, on the twenty-fifth day of the month," or almost a full year after the beginning of the thirty-seventh year. Since this year began early in 581, the twelfth month would carry us over into the early part of 580 B.C.E. (In contrast to the ordinal number thirty-seventh, thirty-six is used as a *cardinal* number. It does not end with "th," and so represents a full thirty-six.)

3 **Regnal and Accession Years.** The Bible refers to state records of the governments of Judah and Israel, as well as to state matters of Babylon and Persia. In all four of these kingdoms, state chronology was accurately reckoned according to the rulerships of the kings, and the same system of reckoning has been carried over into the Bible. Very often the Bible gives the name of the document quoted, as, for example, "the book of the affairs of Solomon." (1 Ki. 11:41) The reign of a king would cover part of an accession year, to be followed by a complete number of regnal years. In all these countries the *regnal* years were the official years in the kingship, and were generally counted from Nisan to Nisan, or from spring to spring. When a king succeeded to the throne, the intervening months until the next spring month of Nisan were referred to as his *accession* year, during which he filled out the regnal term of rulership for his predecessor. However, his own official regnal term was counted as beginning on the next Nisan 1.

1. (a) What indicates that Jehovah is an accurate timekeeper? (b) What recent progress has been made in understanding Bible chronology?
2. Give an example of reckoning with ordinal numbers.
3. (a) What state records assist in reckoning Bible dates? (b) How were regnal and accession years observed in ancient times?

4 As an example, it appears that Solomon had an *accession* year starting sometime before Nisan of 1037 B.C.E., while David was still living. Shortly afterward David died. (1 Ki. 1:39, 40; 2:10) However, David's last regnal year continued down to the spring of 1037 B.C.E., still being counted as part of his forty years' administration. Solomon had an accession year lasting until the spring of 1037 B.C.E., and this could not be counted as a regnal year, as he was still filling out his father's term of administration. Therefore Solomon's first full regnal year did not begin until Nisan, 1037 B.C.E. (1 Ki. 2:12) Eventually, forty full regnal years were credited to Solomon's administration as king. (1 Ki. 11:42) By keeping the *regnal* years apart from *accession* years in this way, it is possible to calculate Bible chronology accurately.

COUNTING BACK TO ADAM'S CREATION

5 **Starting from the Absolute Date.** The absolute date for this calculation is that of Cyrus' overthrow of the Babylonian dynasty, 539 B.C.E.[a] Cyrus issued his decree of liberation for the Jews during his first year, before spring of 537 B.C.E. Ezra 3:1 reports that the sons of Israel were back in Jerusalem by the seventh month, or the early autumn. So the autumn of 537 is reckoned for the date of the restoration of Jehovah's worship in Jerusalem.

6 This restoration of Jehovah's worship in the autumn of 537 marked the end of a prophetic period. What period? It was the "seventy years" during which the Promised Land "must become a devastated place," and concerning which Jehovah also said, "In accord with the fulfilling of seventy years at Babylon I shall turn my attention to you people, and I will establish toward you my good word in bringing you back to this place." (Jer. 25:11, 12; 29:10) Daniel, who was well acquainted with this prophecy, acted in harmony with it as the "seventy years" drew to a close. (Dan. 9:1-3) The "seventy years" that ended in the autumn of the year 537 must have begun, then, in the autumn of 607 B.C.E. The facts bear this out. Jeremiah chapter 52 describes the momentous events of the siege of Jerusalem, the Babylonian breakthrough and the capture of King Zedekiah, 607 B.C.E. Then, as verse 12 states, "in the fifth month, on the tenth day," that is, Ab 10, the Babylonians burned the temple and the city. However, this was not yet the starting point of the "seventy years." Some vestige of Jewish sovereignty still remained in the person of Gedaliah, whom the king of Babylon had appointed as governor of the remaining Jewish settlements. "In the seventh month" Gedaliah and some others were assassinated, so that the remaining Jews fled in fear to Egypt. Then only, from about October 1, 607, was the land in the complete sense "lying desolated . . . to fulfill seventy years."—2 Ki. 25:22-26; 2 Chron. 36:20, 21.

7 **From 607 to 997 B.C.E.** The calculation for this period back from the fall of Jerusalem to the time of the division of the kingdom after Solomon's death presents many difficulties. However, a comparison of the reigns of the kings of Israel and of Judah as recorded in First and Second Kings indicates that this time period covers 390 years. A strong evidence that this is the correct figure is the prophecy of Ezekiel 4:1-13. As shown in this prophecy itself, it is pointing to the time when Jerusalem would be besieged and its inhabitants taken captive by the nations, which occurred in 607 B.C.E. So the forty years spoken of in the case of Judah terminated with Jerusalem's desolation. The 390 years spoken of in the case of Israel did not end when Samaria was destroyed, because that was long past when Ezekiel prophesied, and the prophecy plainly says that it is pointing to the siege and destruction of Jerusalem. So it, too, terminated in 607 B.C.E. Counting back from this date, we see that the "error of the house of Israel" began in 997 B.C.E. It was in that year, then, that Jeroboam, on the death of Solomon, broke with the house of David and "proceeded to part Israel from following Jehovah, and he caused them to sin with a great sin."—2 Ki. 17:21.

8 **From 997 to 1513 B.C.E.** Since the last of Solomon's forty full regnal years ended in the spring of 997, it follows that his first regnal year must have commenced in the spring of 1037 B.C.E. (1 Ki. 11:42) The Bible record says that Solomon began to build the house of Jehovah in Jerusalem in the second month of the fourth year of his reign. This means three full years and one complete month of his reign had elapsed, bringing us to April-May, 1034 B.C.E., for the start of the temple building. However, the same scripture at 1 Kings 6:1 states that this was also "the four hundred and eightieth year after the sons of Israel came out from the land of Egypt." Again, 480th is an *ordinal* number, representing 479 complete years.

a Study 2, paragraphs 29, 30.

4. Show how Bible chronology may be counted according to regnal years.
5. How is the date for the restoration reckoned?
6. (a) What foretold period ended in the autumn of 537? (b) When must that period have begun, and how do the facts support this?
7. (a) How may the years be calculated back to Solomon's death? (b) What support is supplied by Ezekiel's prophecy?
8. (a) How are the years then reckoned back to the exodus? (b) What change affects Bible chronology about this time?

Hence, 479 added to 1034 gives the date 1513 B.C.E. as the year that Israel came out of Egypt.[a] Paragraph 19 of Study Two explains how from the year 1513 B.C.E. Abib (Nisan) was to be reckoned as "the first of the months of the year" for Israel (Ex. 12:2), and that previously a year beginning in the autumn, with the month Tishri, was followed. *The New Schaff-Herzog Encyclopedia of Religious Knowledge,* 1957, Vol. 12, page 474, comments: "The reckoning of the regnal years of the kings is based upon the year which began in the spring, and is parallel to the Babylonian method in which this prevailed." Whenever the change, from commencing the year from the autumn to commencing the year from the spring, began to be applied to periods of time in the Bible, this would involve a loss or gain of six months somewhere in the counting of time.

9 **From 1513 to 1943 B.C.E.** At Exodus 12:40, 41, Moses records that "the dwelling of the sons of Israel, who had dwelt in Egypt, was four hundred and thirty years." From the above wording it is apparent that not all this "dwelling" was in Egypt. This time period begins with Abraham's departure from Haran for Canaan, at which time Jehovah's covenant with Abraham went into effect. The first 215 years of this "dwelling" was in Canaan, and then an equal period was spent in Egypt, until Israel became completely independent of all Egyptian control and dependency, in 1513 B.C.E.[b] The *New World Translation* footnote (1953 Edition) on Exodus 12:40 shows that the Samaritan *Pentateuch* and the *Septuagint,* both of which are based on Hebrew texts older than the Masoretic, add the words "and in the land of Canaan" to "Egypt." Galatians 3:17, which also mentions the 430 years, confirms that this period started with the making of the Abrahamic covenant, at the time that Abraham moved into Canaan. This was therefore in 1943 B.C.E., when Abraham was seventy-five years old.—Gen. 12:4.

10 Another line of evidence supports the above reckoning: At Acts 7:6 mention is made of the seed of Abraham as being afflicted four hundred years. Since Jehovah removed the affliction by Egypt in 1513 B.C.E., the beginning of affliction must have been in 1913 B.C.E. This was five years after the birth of Isaac, and corresponds with Ishmael's "poking fun" at Isaac on the occasion of his weaning.—Gen. 15:13; 21:8, 9.

11 **From 1943 to 2370 B.C.E.** We have seen that Abraham was seventy-five years old when he entered Canaan in 1943 B.C.E. Now it is possible to date the stream of time farther back, to the days of Noah. This is done by use of the time periods supplied for us in Genesis 11:10 to 12:4. This reckoning, which gives a total of 427 years, is made as follows:

From the beginning of the Flood to Arpachshad's birth	2 years
Then to the birth of Shelah	35 "
To the birth of Eber	30 "
To the birth of Peleg	34 "
To the birth of Reu	30 "
To the birth of Serug	32 "
To the birth of Nahor	30 "
To the birth of Terah	29 "
To the death of Terah, when Abraham was 75 years old	205 "
Total	427 years

Adding 427 years to 1943 B.C.E. brings us to 2370 B.C.E. Thus the timetable of the Bible shows that the flood of Noah's day began in 2370 B.C.E.

12 **From 2370 to 4026 B.C.E.** Going still farther back in the stream of time, we find that the Bible dates the period from the Flood all the way to Adam's creation. This is determined by Genesis 5:3-29; 7:11, and the time count is summarized below:

From Adam's creation to the birth of Seth	130 years
Then to the birth of Enosh	105 "
To the birth of Kenan	90 "
To the birth of Mahalalel	70 "
To the birth of Jared	65 "
To the birth of Enoch	162 "
To the birth of Methuselah	65 "
To the birth of Lamech	187 "
To the birth of Noah	182 "
To the Flood	600 "
Total	1,656 years

Adding 1,656 years to our previous date of 2370, we arrive at 4026 B.C.E. for the creation of Adam, perhaps in the fall, since it is in the fall that the year began on the most ancient calendars.

a *The Watchtower,* 1948, pages 92-94.
b From Abraham's leaving Haran to Isaac's birth is 25 years; then to Jacob's birth, 60 years; Jacob was 130 years old when he went down to Egypt.—Gen. 12:4; 21:5; 25:26; 47:9.

9. (a) How is the record dated back to the Abrahamic covenant? (b) How are the first 215 years of this period accounted for? (c) How old was Abraham when he left Haran?
10. What other line of evidence supports the chronology of Abraham's time?
11. How does the Bible timetable carry us back to the date of the Flood?
12. What is the time count back to Adam's creation?

13 Of what significance is this today? It means that by the fall of 1963 mankind has dwelt upon this earth 5,988 years. Does this mean, then, that by 1963 we had progressed 5,988 years into the "day" on which Jehovah "has been resting from all his work"? (Gen. 2:3) No, for the creation of Adam does not correspond with the beginning of Jehovah's rest day. Following Adam's creation, and still within the sixth creative day, Jehovah appears to have been forming further animal and bird creations. Also, he had Adam name the animals, which would take some time, and he proceeded to create Eve. (Gen. 2:18-22; see also *NW*, 1953 Ed., footnote on vs. 19) Whatever time elapsed between Adam's creation and the end of the "sixth day" must be subtracted from the 5,988 years in order to give the actual length of time from the beginning of the "seventh day" until now. It does no good to use Bible chronology for speculating on dates that are still future in the stream of time. —Matt. 24:36.

14 How about scientific claims that man has been on this earth for hundreds of thousands or even millions of years? None of them can be substantiated by written records from those early times, as Biblical events are. The fantastic dates given to "prehistoric man" are based on erroneous assumptions, and these assumptions have been pointed out by reliable scientific sources. But since the more reasonable conclusions are not considered to be as sensational, they are often reported only in scientific journals and not in the public press. The fact is that reliable secular history, together with its chronology, extends back only a few thousand years. The earth has undergone many changes and upheavals, such as the worldwide deluge of Noah's day, which have greatly disturbed rock strata and fossil deposits, making any pseudoscientific pronouncements on dates, prior to the Flood, highly conjectural.[a] In contrast to all the contradictory hypotheses and theories of men, the Bible appeals to reason through its explicit, harmonious account of the origins of mankind and its carefully documented history of Jehovah's chosen people.

15 Study of the Bible and contemplation of the works of the great Timekeeper, Jehovah God, should make us feel very humble. Mortal man is small indeed in comparison with the Omnipotent God, whose stupendous act of creation, performed countless millenniums ago, is so simply stated in Scripture: "In the beginning God created the heavens and the earth." —Gen. 1:1.

13. (a) How long, then, is the history of mankind on this earth? (b) Why does this not correspond with the length of Jehovah's rest day?
14. Why is the Bible account of the origins of mankind to be preferred to the hypotheses of professed scientists?

a *Awake!*, October 22, 1962, pages 9-11; March 8, 1958, pages 12-16; April 22, 1958, pages 17-22; February 22, 1952, pages 13-16.

15. How should Bible study humble us?

Questions on chart covering "Main Events of Jesus' Earthly Sojourn": (a) Name some of the outstanding events in Jesus' ministry up till the time of the imprisonment of John the Baptist. (b) Give the place and year for the following events: (1) The calling of Simon and Andrew, James and John. (2) The choosing of the twelve apostles. (3) The sermon on the mount. (4) The transfiguration. (5) The raising of Lazarus from the dead. (6) Jesus' visit to the home of Zacchaeus. (c) Name some of the outstanding miracles of Jesus, and when and where they occurred. (d) What are some of the principal events concerning Jesus that occurred from Nisan 8 to Nisan 16, A.D. 33? (e) What were some of the outstanding parables that Jesus gave during his earthly ministry?

MAIN EVENTS OF JESUS' EARTHLY SOJOURN

As Recorded in the Four Gospels, and Set in Chronological Order

Abbreviations used: Beth., Bethlehem; Cap., Capernaum; J., Jordan; Jer., Jerusalem; Naz., Nazareth; NE, northeast; S.G., Sea of Galilee; SE, southeast.

TIME	PLACE	EVENT	MATTHEW	MARK	LUKE	JOHN
3 B.C.E	Temple, Jerusalem	Birth of John the Baptist foretold to Zechariah			1:5-25	
c. 2 B.C.E.	Nazareth; Judea	Birth of Jesus foretold to Mary, who visits Elizabeth			1:26-56	
2 B.C.E.	Judean hill country	Birth of John the Baptist; his desert life (later)			1:57-80	
		Genealogies of Jesus	1:1-17		3:23-38	
2 B.C.E., c. Oct. 1	Bethlehem	Birth of Jesus	1:18-25		2:1-7	1:14
	Near Bethlehem	Angel announces good news; shepherds visit babe			2:8-20	
	Bethlehem, Jerusalem	Jesus circumcised (8th day), presented in temple (40th day)			2:21-38	
c. A.D. 1	Jer.; Beth.; Naz.	Astrologers; flight to Egypt; babes killed; Jesus' return	2:1-23		2:39, 40	
A.D. 12	Jerusalem	Twelve-year-old Jesus at the passover; goes home			2:41-52	
29, spring	Wilderness, Jordan	Ministry of John the Baptist	3:1-12	1:1-8	3:1-18	1:6-8, 15-28

TIME	PLACE	EVENT	MATTHEW	MARK	LUKE	JOHN
		Beginning of Christ's Ministry				
29, fall	Jordan River	Baptism of Jesus	3:13-17	1:9-11	3:21-23	1:32-34
	Wilderness of Judah	Temptation of Jesus (40 days)	4:1-11	1:12, 13	4:1-13	
	Bethany beyond J.	John the Baptist's testimony concerning Jesus				1:15, 29-34
	Upper Jordan Valley	First disciples of Jesus				1:35-51
	Cana of Galilee; Capernaum	Jesus' first miracle; he visits Capernaum				2:1-12
30, Passover	Jerusalem	Passover celebration; drives traders from temple				2:13-25
	Jerusalem	Jesus' discussion with Nicodemus				3:1-21
	Judea; Aenon	Jesus' disciples baptize; John to decrease				3:22-36
	Tiberias	John imprisoned; Jesus goes from Judea to Galilee	4:12; 14:3-5	1:14; 6:17-20	3:19, 20; 4:14	4:1-3
	Sychar, in Samaria	En route to Galilee, Jesus teaches the Samaritans				4:4-42
		Great Galilean Ministry				
	Galilee	First announces, "The kingdom of the heavens has drawn near"	4:17	1:14, 15	4:14, 15	4:43-45
	Cana; Naz.; Cap.	Heals boy; reads commission; rejected, he moves to Cap.	4:13-16		4:16-31	4:46-54
	S.G., near Cap.	Call of Simon and Andrew, James and John	4:18-22	1:16-20	5:1-11	
	Capernaum	Heals demoniac, Peter's mother-in-law, many others	8:14-17	1:21-34	4:31-41	
	Galilee	First tour of Galilee, with the four now called	4:23-25	1:35-39	4:42, 43	
	Galilee	Leper healed; multitudes flock to Jesus	8:2-4	1:40-45	5:12-16	
	Capernaum	Heals paralytic	9:1-8	2:1-12	5:17-26	
	Capernaum	Call of Matthew; feast with tax collectors	9:9-17	2:13-22	5:27-39	
	Judea	Preaches in Judean synagogues			4:44	
31, Passover	Jerusalem	Jesus attends feast; heals man; rebukes Pharisees				5:1-47
	Returning from Jerusalem?	Disciples pluck ears of grain on the sabbath	12:1-8	2:23-28	6:1-5	
	Galilee; S.G.	Heals hand on sabbath; retires to seashore; heals	12:9-21	3:1-12	6:6-11	
	Mountain near Capernaum	The twelve are chosen as apostles		3:13-19	6:12-16	
	Near Capernaum	The sermon on the mount	5:1–7:29		6:17-49	
	Capernaum	Heals army officer's servant	8:5-13		7:1-10	
	Nain	Raises widow's son			7:11-17	
	Galilee	John in prison sends disciples to Jesus	11:2-19		7:18-35	
	Galilee	Cities reproached; revelation to babes; yoke kindly	11:20-30			
	Galilee	Feet anointed by sinful woman; parable of debtors			7:36-50	
	Galilee	Second preaching tour of Galilee, with the twelve			8:1-3	
	Galilee	Demoniac healed; league with Beelzebub charged	12:22-37	3:19-30		
	Galilee	Scribes and Pharisees seek a sign	12:38-45			
	Galilee	Christ's disciples his close relatives	12:46-50	3:31-35	8:19-21	
	Sea of Galilee	Parables of sower, weeds, others; explanations	13:1-53	4:1-34	8:4-18	
	Sea of Galilee	Windstorm stilled in the crossing of the lake	8:18, 23-27	4:35-41	8:22-25	
	Gadara, SE of Sea of Galilee	Two demoniacs healed; swine possessed by demons	8:28-34	5:1-20	8:26-39	
	Probably Capernaum	Jairus' daughter raised; woman healed	9:18-26	5:21-43	8:40-56	
	Capernaum?	Heals two blind men, and a dumb demoniac	9:27-34			
	Nazareth	Revisits city where reared, and is again rejected	13:54-58	6:1-6		
	Galilee	Third tour of Galilee, expanded as apostles sent	9:35–11:1	6:6-13	9:1-6	
	Tiberias	John the Baptist beheaded; Herod's guilty fears	14:1-12	6:14-29	9:7-9	
Passover of 32 near (John 6:4)	Cap.; NE side Sea of Galilee	Apostles return from preaching tour; 5,000 fed	14:13-21	6:30-44	9:10-17	6:1-13
	NE side S.G.; Gennesaret	Attempt to crown Jesus; he walks on sea; cures	14:22-36	6:45-56		6:14-21
	Capernaum	Identifies "bread of life"; many disciples fall away				6:22-71
32, Passover	Probably Capernaum	Traditions that make void God's Word	15:1-20	7:1-23		7:1

TIME	PLACE	EVENT	MATTHEW	MARK	LUKE	JOHN
	Phoenicia; Decapolis	Near Tyre, Sidon; then to Decapolis; 4,000 fed	15:21-38	7:24–8:9		
	Magadan	Sadducees and Pharisees again seek a sign	15:39–16:4	8:10-12		
	NE side S.G.; Bethsaida	Warns against leaven of Pharisees; heals blind	16:5-12	8:13-26		
	Caesarea Philippi	Jesus the Messiah; foretells death, resurrection	16:13-28	8:27–9:1	9:18-27	
	Probably Mt. Hermon	Transfiguration before Peter, James and John	17:1-13	9:2-13	9:28-36	
	Caesarea Philippi	Jesus heals demoniac disciples could not heal	17:14-20	9:14-29	9:37-43	
	Galilee	Jesus again foretells his death and resurrection	17:22, 23	9:30-32	9:43-45	
	Capernaum	Tax money miraculously provided, and paid	17:24-27			
	Capernaum	Greatest in Kingdom; settling faults; mercy	18:1-35	9:33-50	9:46-50	
	Galilee; Samaria	Leaves Galilee for festival of tabernacles; everything set aside for ministerial service	8:19-22		9:51-62	7:2-10
		Later Judean Ministry				
32, Festival of tabernacles	Jerusalem	Jesus' public teaching at festival of tabernacles				7:11-52
	Jerusalem	Teaching after festival; cures blind				8:12–9:41
	Probably Judea	The seventy sent to preach; their return, report			10:1-24	
	Judea; Bethany	Tells of good Samaritan; at home of Martha, Mary			10:25-42	
	Probably Judea	Again teaches model prayer; persistence in asking			11:1-13	
	Probably Judea	Refutes false charge; shows generation condemnable			11:14-36	
	Probably Judea	At Pharisee's table, Jesus denounces hypocrites			11:37-54	
	Probably Judea	Discourse on God's care, ministers' faithfulness			12:1-59	
	Probably Judea	Heals crippled woman on sabbath; three parables			13:1-21	
32, Festival of dedication	Jer.; beyond Jordan	Jesus at dedication; Fine Shepherd				10:1-39
		Later Perean Ministry				
	Beyond Jordan	Many put faith in Jesus				10:40-42
	Perea (or, Beyond J.)	Teaches in cities, villages, moving Jerusalemward			13:22	
	Perea	Kingdom entrance; Herod's threat; house desolate			13:23-35	
	Probably Perea	Humility; parable of grand evening meal			14:1-24	
	Probably Perea	Counting the cost of discipleship			14:25-35	
	Probably Perea	Parables: lost sheep, lost coin, prodigal son			15:1-32	
	Probably Perea	Parables: unrighteous steward, rich man and Lazarus			16:1-31	
	Probably Perea	Forgiveness and faith; good-for-nothing slaves			17:1-10	
	Bethany	Lazarus raised from the dead by Jesus				11:1-46
	Jerusalem; Ephraim	Caiaphas' counsel against Jesus; Jesus withdraws				11:47-54
	Samaria; Galilee	Heals and teaches en route through Samaria, Galilee			17:11-37	
	Samaria or Galilee	Parables: importunate widow, Pharisee and tax collector			18:1-14	
	Perea	Swings down through Perea; teaches on divorce	19:1-12	10:1-12		
	Perea	Jesus receives and blesses children	19:13-15	10:13-16	18:15-17	
	Perea	Rich young man; parable of laborers in vineyard	19:16–20:16	10:17-31	18:18-30	
	Probably Perea	Third time Jesus foretells his death, resurrection	20:17-19	10:32-34	18:31-34	
	Probably Perea	Request for James and John's seating in Kingdom	20:20-28	10:35-45		
	Jericho	Passing through Jericho, he heals two blind men	20:29-34	10:46-52	18:35-43	
	Outskirts of Jericho	Jesus visits Zacchaeus; parable of the ten minas			19:1-28	
		Final Public Ministry in and Around Jerusalem				
Nisan 8, 33	Bethany	Jesus arrives at Bethany six days before passover				11:55–12:1
Nisan 9	Bethany	Jews come to see Jesus and Lazarus				12:9-11
	Bethany-Jerusalem	Christ's triumphal entry into Jerusalem	21:1-11, 14-17	11:1-11	19:29-44	12:12-19

TIME	PLACE	EVENT	MATTHEW	MARK	LUKE	JOHN
Nisan 10	Bethany-Jerusalem	Barren fig tree cursed; second temple cleansing	21:18, 19, 12, 13	11:12-17	19:45, 46	
	Jerusalem	Chief priests and scribes scheme to destroy Jesus		11:18	19:47, 48	
	Jerusalem	Discussion with Greeks; unbelief of Jews				12:20-50
Nisan 11	Bethany-Jerusalem	Barren fig tree found withered	21:19-22	11:19-25		
	Jerusalem, temple	Christ's authority questioned; parable of two sons	21:23-32	11:27-33	20:1-8	
	Jerusalem, temple	Parables of wicked cultivators, marriage feast	21:33–22:14	12:1-12	20:9-19	
	Jerusalem, temple	Catch questions on tax, resurrection, commandment	22:15-40	12:13-34	20:20-40	
	Jerusalem, temple	Jesus' silencing question on Messiah's descent	22:41-46	12:35-37	20:41-44	
	Jerusalem, temple	Scathing denunciation of scribes and Pharisees	23:1-39	12:38-40	20:45-47	
	Jerusalem, temple	The widow's mite		12:41-44	21:1-4	
	Mount of Olives	Jerusalem's fall; second presence; world's end	24:1-51	13:1-37	21:5-36	
	Mount of Olives	Parables of ten virgins, talents; sheep and goats	25:1-46			
Nisan 12	Jerusalem	Religious leaders plot Jesus' death	26:1-5	14:1, 2	22:1, 2	
	Bethany	Feast at Simon the leper's house; Mary anoints Jesus	26:6-13	14:3-9		12:2-8
	Jerusalem	Judas bargains with priests for Jesus' betrayal	26:14-16	14:10, 11	22:3-6	
Nisan 13 (Thursday afternoon)	Near and in Jerusalem	Arrangements for the passover	26:17-19	14:12-16	22:7-13	
Nisan 14	Jerusalem	Passover feast eaten with the twelve	26:20, 21	14:17, 18	22:14-18, 24-27	
	Jerusalem	Jesus washes the feet of his apostles				13:1-20
	Jerusalem	Judas identified as traitor, and he withdraws	26:21-25	14:18-21	22:21-23	13:21-30
	Jerusalem	Memorial supper instituted with the eleven	26:26-29	14:22-25	22:19, 20, 23-30	[1 Cor. 11:23-25]
	Jerusalem	Denial by Peter and dispersion of apostles foretold	26:31-35	14:27-31	22:31-38	13:31-38
	Jerusalem	Helper; mutual love; tribulation; Jesus' prayer				14:1–17:26
	Gethsemane	Agony in the garden; Jesus' betrayal and arrest	26:30, 36-56	14:26, 32-52	22:39-53	18:1-12
	Jerusalem	Trial by Annas, Caiaphas, Sanhedrin; Peter denies	26:57–27:1	14:53–15:1	22:54-71	18:13-27
	Jerusalem	Judas the betrayer hangs himself	27:3-10		[Acts 1: 18, 19]	
	Jerusalem	Before Pilate, then Herod, and then back to Pilate	27:2, 11-14	15:1-5	23:1-12	18:28-38
	Jerusalem	Delivered to death, after Pilate seeks his release	27:15-30	15:6-19	23:13-25	18:39–19:16
Died 3 p.m., Friday	Golgotha, Jerusalem	Jesus' death on the stake, and accompanying events	27:31-56	15:20-41	23:26-49	19:16-30
	Jerusalem	Jesus' body removed from the stake and buried	27:57-61	15:42-47	23:50-56	19:31-42
Nisan 15	Jerusalem	Priests and Pharisees get guard for sepulcher	27:62-66			
Nisan 16	Jerusalem, and vicinity	Jesus' resurrection, and events of that day	28:1-15	16:1-8	24:1-49	20:1-25
	Jerusalem; Galilee	Subsequent appearances of Jesus Christ	28:16-20	[1 Cor. 15:5-7]	[Acts 1: 3-8]	20:26–21:25
Ziv (Iyyar) 25	Mount of Olives, near Bethany	Jesus' ascension, 40th day of resurrected living	[Acts 1: 9-12]		24:50-53	

JESUS' EARTHLY RESIDENCE

16 The four inspired accounts of Jesus' earthly life appear to have been written in this order: Matthew (c. A.D. 41), Luke (c. A.D. 56-58), Mark (c. A.D. 60-65) and John (c. A.D. 98). As explained in the previous chapter, Luke 3:1-3 combines with the absolute date A.D. 14 for the start of Tiberius Caesar's reign to give A.D. 29 as the starting point for Jesus' remarkable ministry on this earth. Though the events in Matthew do not always follow in chronological sequence, in most instances the other three books appear to present the actual order of the momentous happenings that followed. These are epitomized in the accompanying chart. It will be noted that John's account, which was written more than thirty years after the other three, fills in essential gaps in the history that are not covered by the others. Especially noteworthy is John's apparent mention of the four passovers of Jesus' earthly ministry, which confirms a ministry of three-and-a-half years, ending A.D. 33.—John 2:13; 5:1; 6:4; 12:1 and 13:1. See also Bible Book

16. (a) In what order were the four Gospels written? (b) How may we date the start of Jesus' ministry? (c) What sequence do events follow in the different Gospels, and what is to be noted about John's account?

Number 43, paragraph 8, and *The New Bible Dictionary,* 1962, J. D. Douglas, pages 225, 227.

17 Jesus' death in A.D. 33 is also confirmed by astronomy. According to the law of Moses, Nisan 15 was always a special sabbath regardless of the day on which it fell. If it coincided with an ordinary sabbath, then the day became known as a "great" sabbath, and John 19:31 shows that such a sabbath followed the day of Jesus' death, which was therefore on a Friday. Astronomical tables for A.D. 28-34 show that during those years it was only in A.D. 30 and A.D. 33 that the full moon of Nisan 14 was seen on a Friday.[a] The year A.D. 30 is ruled out, as it would allow for a ministry of only six months' duration. Therefore the year must have been A.D. 33, and astronomy is seen to support the other evidence for this date.

18 **The "Seventieth Week," A.D. 29 to A.D. 36.** Time features of Jesus' ministry are also covered by Daniel 9:24-27, which foretells the passage of sixty-nine weeks of years (483 years) "from the going forth of the word to restore and to rebuild Jerusalem until Messiah the Leader." According to Nehemiah 2:1-8, this word went forth "in the twentieth year of Artaxerxes," king of Persia. When did Artaxerxes commence his reign? The Greek historian Thucydides of Artaxerxes' time (who is supported by the Greek biographer Plutarch of the first century A.D. as well as by the Roman historian Nepos of the first century B.C.E.) writes of General Themistocles' fleeing to Persia when Artaxerxes had "lately come to the throne." Another Greek historian of the first century A.D., Diodorus Siculus, records the date of Themistocles' death as 471 B.C.E. After fleeing his country, Themistocles had asked Artaxerxes' permission to study the Persian language for one year before appearing before him, which was carried out. Hence Themistocles' flight may reasonably be dated 473 B.C.E., and the beginning of Artaxerxes' reign as 474 B.C.E.[b]

19 Thus "the twentieth year of Artaxerxes" would be 455 B.C.E. Counting 483 years (the "sixty-nine weeks") from this point, and remembering that there was no "zero" year in crossing into the Common Era, we arrive at A.D. 29 for the appearance of "Messiah the Leader." Jesus became the Messiah when he was baptized and anointed with holy spirit in the autumn of that year. The prophecy also indicates that "at the half of the [seventieth] week he will cause sacrifice and gift offering to cease." This occurred when the typical Jewish sacrifices lost their validity, due to Jesus' sacrifice of himself. "The half" of this "week" takes us along three-and-a-half years to the spring of A.D. 33, when Jesus was put to death. However, "he must keep the covenant in force for the many" for the entire seventieth week. This shows Jehovah's special favor as continuing with the Jews during the seven years A.D. 29-36. Then, only, was the way opened for uncircumcised Gentiles to become spiritual Israelites, as indicated by the conversion of Cornelius A.D. 36.—Acts 10:30-33, 44-48; 11:1.

a *The Watchtower,* 1959, pages 489-492.
b *The Watchtower,* 1946, page 360.

17. How does astronomy support the date of Jesus' death?
18. (a) What did Daniel prophesy in regard to 'sixty-nine weeks'? (b) According to Nehemiah, when did this period begin? (c) How do we arrive at the date for the beginning of Artaxerxes' reign?
19. (a) Counting from "the twentieth year of Artaxerxes," how do we determine the date of Messiah's appearance? (b) How was the prophecy of the "seventy weeks" fulfilled from this date?

COUNTING THE YEARS IN APOSTOLIC TIMES

20 **Between A.D. 33 and A.D. 49.** The year 44 (A.D.) may be accepted as a useful date for this period. Josephus' *Jewish Wars* and his *Antiquities* are in agreement that Herod Agrippa I reigned for three years after the accession of Emperor Claudius of Rome A.D. 41. The historical and archaeological evidence indicates that this Herod died following Nisan, A.D. 44.[c] Looking now at the Bible record, we find that it was just prior to Herod's death that Agabus prophesied "through the spirit" concerning a great famine to come, that the apostle James was put to the sword and that Peter was jailed (at passover time) and miraculously released. All these events may be dated A.D. 44. —Acts 11:27, 28; 12:1-11, 20-23.

21 Secular history shows that Herod Agrippa was followed by Roman procurators, Cuspius Fadus and Tiberius Alexander, and that it was during the rule of the latter that the foretold famine came, about A.D. 46. It must have been about this time, then, that Paul and Barnabas "carried out the relief ministration in Jerusalem." (Acts 12:25) After returning to Syrian Antioch, they were set aside by holy spirit to make the first missionary tour, which covered Cyprus and many cities and districts of Asia Minor. This would probably extend from the spring of A.D. 47 to the autumn of A.D. 48, with one winter spent in Asia Minor. It appears Paul spent the following winter back in Syrian Antioch, and this brings us to the spring of A.D. 49.—Acts 13:1–14:28.

22 The record in Galatians chapters 1 and 2 appears to tie in with this chronology. Here

c *The Encyclopædia Britannica,* 1946, Vol. 3, page 527.

20. How does secular history combine with the Bible record in timing Herod's death and preceding events?
21. On what basis can we approximately date Paul's first missionary tour?
22. How may the two visits of Paul to Jerusalem mentioned in Galatians chapters 1 and 2 be dated?

Paul speaks of making two other special visits to Jerusalem after his conversion, the one "three years later," and the other "after fourteen years." (Gal. 1:17, 18; 2:1) If these two time periods are taken to be ordinals, according to the custom of the day, and if Paul's conversion was early in the apostles' time, as the record seems to indicate, then we may reckon the three years and the fourteen years consecutively as A.D. 34-36 and A.D. 36-49.

23 Paul's second Jerusalem visit mentioned in Galatians seems to have been concerned with the circumcision issue, as Titus who accompanied Paul is said not to have been required even to be circumcised. If this corresponds with the visit to obtain the ruling on circumcision described in Acts 15:1-35, then A.D. 49 fits nicely as lying between Paul's first and second missionary tours. Moreover, according to Galatians 2:1-10, Paul used this occasion to lay before the "outstanding men" of the Jerusalem congregation the good news that he was preaching, 'for fear he was running in vain,' a thing he would logically do in reporting to them after his very first missionary tour. Paul made this visit "as a result of a revelation."

24 **Paul's Second Missionary Journey, A.D. 49-52.** After his return from Jerusalem, Paul spent time in Syrian Antioch, so that it must have been well along in the summer of A.D. 49 that he left there on his second tour. (Acts 15:35, 36) This was much more extensive than the first, and would require him to winter in Asia Minor. It was probably in the spring of A.D. 50 that he answered the Macedonian's call and crossed over into Europe. Then he preached and organized new congregations in Philippi, Thessalonica, Beroea and Athens. This would bring him to Corinth, in the province of Achaia, in the autumn of A.D. 50, after having made a journey of about 1,300 miles, mostly on foot. (Acts 16:9, 11, 12; 17:1, 2, 10, 11, 15, 16; 18:1) According to Acts 18:11, Paul stayed there eighteen months, bringing us to early A.D. 52. With winter ended, Paul could sail for Caesarea, via Ephesus; after going up to greet the congregation, apparently in Jerusalem, he arrived back at his home base of Syrian Antioch, probably in the summer of A.D. 52.—Acts 18:12-22.

25 An archaeological discovery supports A.D. 50-52 as the dates of Paul's first visit in Corinth. This is a fragment of an inscription, a rescript from Emperor Claudius to the Delphians of Greece, which contains the words "in Gallio's proconsulship . . . Claudius being Imperator for the 26th time." Other inscriptions show that Claudius was acclaimed emperor for the twenty-third time after January 25, 51, and for the twenty-seventh time before August 1, 52. The proconsuls' term ran for a year, starting with the beginning of summer. Thus Gallio's year as proconsul of Achaia must have run from the summer of A.D. 51 to the summer of A.D. 52. "Now while Gallio was proconsul of Achaia, the Jews rose up with one accord against Paul and led him to the judgment seat." After Gallio's acquitting Paul, the apostle stayed "quite some days longer," and then sailed away to Syria. (Acts 18:11, 12, 17, 18) All of this seems to confirm the spring of A.D. 52 as the conclusion of Paul's eighteen-month stay in Corinth. Another time marker is found in the statement that, on arrival in Corinth, Paul "found a certain Jew named Aquila, a native of Pontus who had recently come from Italy, and Priscilla his wife, because of the fact that Claudius had ordered all the Jews to depart from Rome." (Acts 18:2) According to the historian Paulus Orosius, of the early fifth century, this expulsion order was given on January 25, A.D. 50, in Claudius' ninth year. Thus Aquila and Priscilla could have reached Corinth some time before the autumn of that year, allowing for Paul's stay there from the autumn of A.D. 50 to the spring of A.D. 52.[a]

26 **Paul's Third Missionary Journey, A.D. 52-56.** After the passage of "some time" in Syrian Antioch, Paul was on his way into Asia Minor again, and it is likely that he reached Ephesus by the winter of A.D. 52-53. (Acts 18:23; 19:1) Paul spent "three months" and then "two years" teaching in Ephesus, and after this he left for Macedonia. (Acts 19:8-10) Later, he reminded the overseers from Ephesus that he had served among them "for three years," but this may well be a round figure, the actual time being about two-and-a-half years. (Acts 20:31) It appears that Paul left Ephesus after "the festival of Pentecost" early in A.D. 55, traveling all the way through to Corinth, Greece, in time to spend three winter months there. Then he returned north as far as Philippi by passover time A.D. 56. From here he sailed by way of Troas and Miletus to Caesarea, and journeyed up to Jerusalem, arriving by Pentecost of A.D. 56.—1 Cor. 16:5-8; Acts 20:1-3, 6, 15, 16; 21:8, 15-17.

27 **The Closing Years, A.D. 56-100.** It was

---

23. What evidence suggests that both Galatians chapter 2 and Acts chapter 15 have reference to Paul's visit to Jerusalem, A.D. 49?
24. During what years did Paul make his second missionary journey, and why, no doubt, did he not reach Corinth till late in A.D. 50?
25. (a) How does archaeology support A.D. 50-52 for Paul's first visit in Corinth? (b) How does the fact that Aquila and Priscilla "had recently come from Italy" confirm this?

a *The Encyclopædia Britannica,* 1946, Vol. 3, page 528; *The New Bible Dictionary,* 1962, J. D. Douglas, pages 226-228.

26. What dates mark the successive stages of Paul's third missionary journey?
27. What is the timing of events down to the end of Paul's first captivity in Rome?

shortly after his arrival in Jerusalem that Paul was arrested. He was taken to Caesarea, and remained in custody there for two years, until Felix was replaced by Festus as governor. (Acts 21:33; 23:23-35; 24:27) This appears to have been A.D. 58. *The Encyclopœdia Britannica* mentions two schools of critics who argue A.D. 55 and A.D. 60-61 for Festus' arrival, but adds: "It can be said confidently that the truth is between these two extremes, for the arguments urged in each case appear less to prove one extreme than to disprove its opposite."[a] We therefore accept A.D. 58 as the date of Festus' arrival, and of Paul's subsequent departure for Rome. After shipwreck and wintering in Malta, the journey was completed in the spring of A.D. 59, and the record indicates that Paul remained in captivity in Rome, preaching and teaching, for a period of two years, or until A.D. 61.—Acts 27:1; 28:1, 11, 16, 30, 31.

28 While the historical record of Acts takes us no farther than this, the indications are that Paul was released and continued his missionary journeying, possibly visiting Spain in the west, and traveling to Crete, Greece and Macedonia. It is reasonable to allow three years for this ministry, which brings us to A.D. 64-65 for Paul's final imprisonment and execution in Rome. Secular history gives July, A.D. 64, as the date of the great fire in Rome, following which Nero's persecution burst upon the Christians. Paul's imprisonment in "chains" and subsequent execution fit logically into this period.—2 Tim. 1:16; 4:6, 7.

29 The five books written by the apostle John are located at the end of a time of persecution, that by Emperor Domitian, who is said to have acted like a madman during the last three years of his reign, which covered A.D. 81-96. It was while in exile on the isle of Patmos that John wrote down the Revelation about A.D. 96.[b] His Gospel and three letters followed from Ephesus or vicinity after his release, and this last of the apostles died about A.D. 100.

30 It is thus seen that a comparison of events of secular history, with the Bible's internal chronology and prophecy, helps us to picture more clearly Bible events in the stream of time. The harmony of the Bible chronology adds to our confidence in the Holy Scriptures as the Word of God.

---

a *The Encyclopœdia Britannica,* 1946 Edition, Vol. 3, page 528; and Young's *Analytical Concordance to the Bible,* page 342, under "Festus."

b *Notes on the Book of Revelation,* 1852, by Albert Barnes, pages xxix, xxx.

---

28. What dates may logically be assigned to the closing events of Paul's life?
29. When did the apostolic age end, and with the writing of which Bible books?
30. Of what benefit is this study of Bible chronology?

Questions on "Chart of Outstanding Historical Dates" and "Table of the Books of the Bible": (a) By comparing the two charts, name some of the prophets and Bible writers who lived (1) prior to the setting up of the Kingdom of Israel in 1117 B.C.E., (2) during the time of the kingdoms of Israel and Judah, and (3) during and after the captivity in Babylon until the completion of the Hebrew Scripture canon. (b) Locate the time of writing of Paul's letters in relation to his missionary tours. (c) What other interesting points do you note as to the time of writing of other books of the Christian Greek Scriptures? (d) Relate the following persons to some prominent event in Bible history, stating whether they lived before or after the event, or associate them with other persons living at the same time: Shem, Samuel, Methuselah, Lot, Saul, David, Job, Hoshea king of Israel, Solomon, Aaron, Zedekiah king of Judah. (e) What outstanding events occurred during the lifetime of (1) Noah, (2) Abraham, (3) Moses? (f) Match the following dates (B.C.E.) with the outstanding events listed below: 4026, 2370, 1943, 1513, 1473, 1117, 997, 740, 607, 539, 537, 455.

Creation of Adam
Law covenant made at Sinai
Jerusalem destroyed
Jews return to Jerusalem after Cyrus' decree
Inspired Bible writing begins
The Flood begins
Babylon falls to Medes and Persians
First king of Israel anointed
Abraham enters Canaan; Abrahamic covenant made
Kingdoms of Israel and Judah split
Northern kingdom subjugated by Assyria
Jerusalem's walls rebuilt by Nehemiah
Israelites delivered from Egypt
Joshua leads Israel into Canaan
Jerusalem's 70-year desolation ends

CHART OF OUTSTANDING HISTORICAL DATES

DATE	EVENT	REFERENCE
4026 B.C.E.	Adam's creation (in the fall)	Gen. 2:7
a. 4026 B.C.E.	Edenic covenant made, first prophecy	Gen. 3:15
b. 3896 B.C.E.	Cain slays Abel	Gen. 4:8
3896 B.C.E.	Birth of Seth	Gen. 5:3
3404 B.C.E.	Birth of righteous Enoch	Gen. 5:18
3339 B.C.E.	Birth of Methuselah	Gen. 5:21
3152 B.C.E.	Birth of Lamech	Gen. 5:25
3096 B.C.E.	Death of Adam	Gen. 5:5
3039 B.C.E.	Transference of Enoch; ends his period of prophesying	Gen. 5:23, 24; Jude 14

2970 B.C.E.	Birth of Noah	Gen. 5:28, 29
2490 B.C.E.	God's pronouncement as to mankind	Gen. 6:3
2470 B.C.E.	Birth of Japheth	Gen. 5:32; 9:24; 10:21
2468 B.C.E.	Birth of Shem	Gen. 7:11; 11:10
2370 B.C.E.	Death of Methuselah	Gen. 5:27
	Flood waters fall (in November)	Gen. 7:6, 11
2369 B.C.E.	Making of the covenant after the Flood	Gen. 8:13; 9:16
2368 B.C.E.	Birth of Arpachshad	Gen. 11:10
a. 2239 B.C.E.	Building of the Tower of Babel	Gen. 11:4
2020 B.C.E.	Death of Noah	Gen. 9:28, 29
2018 B.C.E.	Birth of Abraham	Gen. 11:26, 32; 12:4
1943 B.C.E.	Abraham enters Canaan; Abrahamic covenant made; beginning of the 430-year period to law covenant	Gen. 12:4, 7; Ex. 12:40; Gal. 3:17
b. 1933 B.C.E.	Lot rescued; Abraham visits Melchizedek	Gen. 14:16, 18; 16:3
1932 B.C.E.	Ishmael born	Gen. 16:15, 16
1919 B.C.E.	Covenant of circumcision made	Gen. 17:1, 10, 24
	Judgment of Sodom and Gomorrah	Gen. 19:24
1918 B.C.E.	Birth of Isaac the true heir; beginning of the "about 450 years"	Gen. 21:2, 5; Acts 13:17-20
1913 B.C.E.	Weaning of Isaac; Ishmael sent away; beginning of the 400-year affliction	Gen. 21:8; 15:13; Acts 7:6
1881 B.C.E.	Death of Sarah	Gen. 17:17; 23:1
1878 B.C.E.	Marriage of Isaac and Rebekah	Gen. 25:20
1868 B.C.E.	Death of Shem	Gen. 11:11
1858 B.C.E.	Birth of Esau and Jacob	Gen. 25:26
1843 B.C.E.	Death of Abraham	Gen. 25:7
1818 B.C.E.	Esau marries first two wives	Gen. 26:34
1795 B.C.E.	Death of Ishmael	Gen. 25:17
1781 B.C.E.	Jacob flees to Haran; his vision at Bethel	Gen. 28:2, 13, 19
1774 B.C.E.	Jacob marries Leah and Rachel	Gen. 29:23-30
1767 B.C.E.	Birth of Joseph	Gen. 30:23, 24
1761 B.C.E.	Jacob returns to Canaan from Haran	Gen. 31:18, 41
c. 1761 B.C.E.	Jacob wrestles angel; is named Israel	Gen. 32:24-28
1750 B.C.E.	Joseph sold as a slave by his brothers	Gen. 37:2, 28
1738 B.C.E.	Death of Isaac	Gen. 35:28, 29
1737 B.C.E.	Joseph made prime minister of Egypt	Gen. 41:40, 46
1728 B.C.E.	Jacob with his whole family enters Egypt	Gen. 45:6; 46:26; 47:9
1711 B.C.E.	Death of Jacob	Gen. 47:28
1657 B.C.E.	Death of Joseph	Gen. 50:26
b. 1613 B.C.E.	Job's trial	Job 1:8; 42:16
a. 1600 B.C.E.	Egypt attains prominence as First World Power	Ex. 1:8
1593 B.C.E.	Birth of Moses	Ex. 2:2, 10
1553 B.C.E.	Moses offers himself as a deliverer; flees to Midian	Ex. 2:11, 14, 15; Acts 7:23
c. 1514 B.C.E.	Moses at the burning thornbush	Ex. 3:2
1513 B.C.E.	Passover; Israelites leave Egypt; Red Sea deliverance; Egypt's power shaken; end of 400-year period of affliction	Ex. 12:12; 14:27, 29, 30; Gen. 15:13, 14
	Law covenant made at Mt. Sinai (Horeb)	Ex. 24:6-8
	End of the 430-year period from Abrahamic covenant	Gal. 3:17; Ex. 12:40
	Moses compiles Genesis in wilderness; Bible writing begins	John 5:46
1512 B.C.E.	Tabernacle construction completed	Ex. 40:17
	Consecration of the Aaronic priesthood	Lev. 8:34-36
	Moses completes Exodus and Leviticus	Lev. 27:34; Num. 1:1
c. 1473 B.C.E.	Moses completes the book of Job	Job 42:16, 17

1473 B.C.E.	Moses completes Numbers on Moab plains	Num. 35:1; 36:13
	Covenant of the Repeated Law in Moab	Deut. 29:1
	Moses writes Deuteronomy	Deut. 1:1, 3
	Moses dies on Nebo in Moab	Deut. 34:5, 7
	Israel enters Canaan under Joshua	Josh. 4:19
1467 B.C.E.	End of Joshua's war operations in Canaan; end of the "about 450 years" of Acts 13:17-20	Josh. 11:23; 14:7, 10-15
c. 1433 B.C.E.	Book of Joshua completed	Josh. 1:1; 24:26
	Death of Joshua	Josh. 24:29
1117 B.C.E.	Samuel anoints Saul as king of Israel	1 Sam. 10:24; Acts 13:21
1107 B.C.E.	Birth of David at Bethlehem	1 Sam. 16:1; 2 Sam. 5:4
c. 1100 B.C.E.	Samuel completes the book of Judges	Judg. 21:25
c. 1090 B.C.E.	Samuel completes the book of Ruth	Ruth 4:18-22
c. 1077 B.C.E.	Book of 1 Samuel completed	1 Sam. 31:6
1077 B.C.E.	David becomes king of Judah at Hebron	2 Sam. 2:4
1070 B.C.E.	David becomes king over all Israel; takes Jerusalem; makes it capital	2 Sam. 5:3-7
a. 1070 B.C.E.	The Ark brought into Jerusalem; Kingdom covenant made with David	2 Sam. 6:15; 7:12-16
c. 1040 B.C.E.	Gad and Nathan complete 2 Samuel	2 Sam. 24:18
1037 B.C.E.	Solomon succeeds David as king of Israel	1 Ki. 1:39; 2:12
1034 B.C.E.	Construction of Solomon's temple begun	1 Ki. 6:1
1027 B.C.E.	Solomon's temple in Jerusalem completed	1 Ki. 6:38
c. 1020 B.C.E.	Solomon completes the Song of Solomon	Song of Sol. 1:1
c. 1000 B.C.E.	Solomon completes the book of Ecclesiastes	Eccl. 1:1
997 B.C.E.	Rehoboam succeeds Solomon, kingdom split; Jeroboam begins reign as king of Israel	1 Ki. 11:43; 12:19, 20
993 B.C.E.	Shishak assaults Jerusalem and takes treasures from temple	1 Ki. 14:25, 26
980 B.C.E.	Abijam succeeds Rehoboam as king of Judah	1 Ki. 15:1, 2
978 B.C.E.	Asa succeeds Abijam as king of Judah	1 Ki. 15:9, 10
977 B.C.E.	Nadab succeeds Jeroboam as king of Israel	1 Ki. 14:20
976 B.C.E.	Baasha succeeds Nadab as king of Israel	1 Ki. 15:33
953 B.C.E.	Elah succeeds Baasha as king of Israel	1 Ki. 16:8
952 B.C.E.	Zimri succeeds Elah as king of Israel	1 Ki. 16:15
	Tibni and Omri succeed Zimri as kings of Israel	1 Ki. 16:21
948 B.C.E.	Omri rules as king of Israel alone	1 Ki. 16:22, 23
941 B.C.E.	Ahab succeeds Omri as king of Israel	1 Ki. 16:29
938 B.C.E.	Jehoshaphat succeeds Asa as king of Judah	1 Ki. 22:41, 42
922 B.C.E.	Ahaziah succeeds Ahab as king of Israel	1 Ki. 22:51, 52
921 B.C.E.	Jehoram of Israel succeeds Ahaziah as king	2 Ki. 3:1
917 B.C.E.	Jehoram of Judah succeeds Jehoshaphat as king	2 Ki. 8:16, 17
910 B.C.E.	Ahaziah succeeds Jehoram as king of Judah	2 Ki. 8:25, 26
909 B.C.E.	Queen Athaliah usurps throne of Judah	2 Ki. 11:1-3
	Jehu succeeds Jehoram as king of Israel	2 Ki. 9:24, 27; 10:36
903 B.C.E.	Jehoash succeeds Ahaziah as king of Judah	2 Ki. 12:1
881 B.C.E.	Jehoahaz succeeds Jehu as king of Israel	2 Ki. 13:1
867 B.C.E.	Jehoash succeeds Jehoahaz as king of Israel	2 Ki. 13:10
866 B.C.E.	Amaziah succeeds Jehoash as king of Judah	2 Ki. 14:1, 2
852 B.C.E.	Jeroboam II succeeds Jehoash as king of Israel	2 Ki. 14:23
c. 852 B.C.E.	Jonah completes the book of Jonah	Jonah 1:1, 2
826 B.C.E.	Uzziah (Azariah) succeeds Amaziah as king of Judah	2 Ki. 15:1, 2
c. 820 B.C.E.	Joel completes the book of Joel	Joel 1:1
c. 811 B.C.E.	Amos completes the book of Amos	Amos 1:1
789 B.C.E.	Zechariah succeeds Jeroboam II as king of Israel	2 Ki. 15:8
788 B.C.E.	Shallum succeeds Zechariah as king of Israel	2 Ki. 15:13, 17
	Menahem succeeds Shallum as king of Israel	
777 B.C.E.	Pekahiah succeeds Menahem as king of Israel	2 Ki. 15:23
775 B.C.E.	Pekah succeeds Pekahiah as king of Israel	2 Ki. 15:27

c. 775 B.C.E.	Isaiah begins to prophesy	Isa. 1:1; 6:1
774 B.C.E.	Jotham succeeds Uzziah (Azariah) as king of Judah	2 Ki. 15:32, 33
759 B.C.E.	Ahaz succeeds Jotham as king of Judah	2 Ki. 16:1, 2
748 B.C.E.	Hoshea succeeds Pekah as king of Israel	2 Ki. 17:1
745 B.C.E.	Hezekiah succeeds Ahaz as king of Judah	2 Ki. 18:1, 2
a. 745 B.C.E.	Hosea completes the book of Hosea	Hos. 1:1
740 B.C.E.	Assyria, Second World Power, subjugates Israel, takes Samaria	2 Ki. 17:6, 13, 18
732 B.C.E.	Sennacherib invades Judah	2 Ki. 18:13
c. 732 B.C.E.	Isaiah completes the book of Isaiah	Isa. 1:1
b. 716 B.C.E.	Micah completes the book of Micah	Mic. 1:1
c. 716 B.C.E.	Compiling of Proverbs completed	Prov. 25:1
716 B.C.E.	Manasseh succeeds Hezekiah as king of Judah	2 Ki. 21:1
661 B.C.E.	Amon succeeds Manasseh as king of Judah	2 Ki. 21:19
659 B.C.E.	Josiah succeeds Amon as king of Judah	2 Ki. 22:1
b. 648 B.C.E.	Zephaniah completes the book of Zephaniah	Zeph. 1:1
647 B.C.E.	Jeremiah begins preaching	Jer. 1:1, 2
b. 633 B.C.E.	Nahum completes the book of Nahum	Nah. 1:1
c. 633 B.C.E.	Nineveh falls to Chaldeans and Medes	Nah. 3:7
	Babylon now in line to become Third World Power	
628 B.C.E.	Jehoahaz, successor of Josiah, rules as king of Judah	2 Ki. 23:31
	Jehoiakim succeeds Jehoahaz as king of Judah	2 Ki. 23:36
c. 628 B.C.E.	Habakkuk completes the book of Habakkuk	Hab. 1:1
625 B.C.E.	Nebuchadnezzar rules as king of Babylon	Jer. 25:1
620 B.C.E.	Nebuchadnezzar makes Jehoiakim tributary king	2 Ki. 24:1
618 B.C.E.	Jehoiachin becomes king after Jehoiakim in Judah	2 Ki. 24:6, 8
617 B.C.E.	Nebuchadnezzar takes first Jewish captives to Babylon Zedekiah is made king of Judah	Dan. 1:1-4; 2 Ki. 24:12-18
613 B.C.E.	Ezekiel begins prophesying	Ezek. 1:1-3
609 B.C.E.	Nebuchadnezzar attacks Judah third time; begins siege of Jerusalem	2 Ki. 25:1, 2
607 B.C.E.	Fifth month (Ab 7-10), temple razed and Jerusalem destroyed	2 Ki. 25:8-10; Jer. 52:12-14
	Seventh month, Jews abandon Judah; Seven Gentile Times begin to count	2 Ki. 25:25, 26
	Jeremiah writes Lamentations	Lam., preamble *LXX*
c. 607 B.C.E.	Obadiah completes the book of Obadiah	Obad. 1
591 B.C.E.	Ezekiel completes the book of Ezekiel	Ezek. 40:1; 29:17
c. 580 B.C.E.	Books of 1 and 2 Kings and Jeremiah completed	Jer. 52:31; 2 Ki. 25:27
539 B.C.E.	Babylon falls to the Medes and Persians; Medo-Persia becomes the Fourth World Power	Dan. 5:30, 31
537 B.C.E.	Decree of Cyrus the Persian, permitting Jews to return to Jerusalem, takes effect; Jerusalem's 70-year desolation ends	2 Chron. 36:22, 23; Jer. 25:12; 29:10
536 B.C.E.	Daniel completes the book of Daniel	Dan. 10:1
	Foundation of temple laid by Zerubbabel	Ezra 3:8-10
522 B.C.E.	Ban put on temple-building work	Ezra 4:23, 24
521 B.C.E.	Haggai completes the book of Haggai	Hag. 1:1
519 B.C.E.	Zechariah completes the book of Zechariah	Zech. 1:1
516 B.C.E.	Zerubbabel completes second temple	Ezra 6:14, 15
c. 474 B.C.E.	Mordecai completes the book of Esther	Esther 3:7; 9:32
468 B.C.E.	Ezra and priests return to Jerusalem	Ezra 7:7
c. 460 B.C.E.	Ezra completes the books of 1 and 2 Chronicles and Ezra; final compilation of Psalms	Ezra 1:1; 2 Chron. 36:22; Ps. 137
455 B.C.E.	Jerusalem's walls rebuilt by Nehemiah; prophecy of 70 weeks begins fulfillment	Neh. 1:1; 2:1, 11; 6:15; Dan. 9:24
a. 443 B.C.E.	Nehemiah completes the book of Nehemiah	Neh. 5:14
	Malachi completes the book of Malachi	Mal. 1:1
406 B.C.E.	Jerusalem fully rebuilt to ancient glory	Dan. 9:25

332 B.C.E.	Greece, Fifth World Power, rules Judea	Dan. 8:21
c. 280 B.C.E.	The Greek *Septuagint* translation begun	
165 B.C.E.	Renewal of temple after desecration by Greek idolatry; Festival of Dedication	John 10:22
63 B.C.E.	Rome, Sixth World Power, rules Jerusalem	John 19:15; Rev. 17:10
37 B.C.E.	Herod (appointed king by Rome) takes Jerusalem by storm	
17 B.C.E.	Herod begins rebuilding the temple in Jerusalem	John 2:20
2 B.C.E.	Birth of John the Baptist and of Jesus	Luke 1:60; 2:7
A.D. 29	John and Jesus begin their ministries	Luke 3:1, 2, 23
A.D. 33	Nisan 14, Jesus becomes sacrifice for the new covenant; is impaled	Luke 22:20; 23:33
	Nisan 16, the resurrection of Jesus	Matt. 28:1-10
	Sivan 6, Pentecost; outpouring of spirit; Peter opens the way for Jews to Christian congregation; uses first key	Acts 2:1-17; Matt. 16:19; Acts 2:38
A.D. 36	End of the 70 weeks of years; Peter uses second key, uncircumcised people of the nations enter the Christian congregation	Dan. 9:24-27; Acts 10:1, 45
c. A.D. 41	Matthew writes the Gospel entitled "Matthew"	
c. A.D. 47-48	Paul's first missionary tour	Acts 13:1–14:28
c. A.D. 49	Governing body rules against circumcision for the believers from the nations	Acts 15:28, 29
c. A.D. 49-52	Paul's second missionary tour	Acts 15:36–18:22
c. A.D. 50	Paul writes 1 Thessalonians from Corinth	1 Thess. 1:1
c. A.D. 50-52	Paul writes his letter to the Galatians from Corinth or Syrian Antioch	Gal. 1:1
c. A.D. 51	Paul writes 2 Thessalonians from Corinth	2 Thess. 1:1
c. A.D. 52-56	Paul's third missionary tour	Acts 18:23–21:17
c. A.D. 55	Paul writes 1 Corinthians from Ephesus and 2 Corinthians from Macedonia	1 Cor. 15:32; 2 Cor. 2:12, 13
c. A.D. 56	Paul writes the letter to the Romans from Corinth	Rom. 16:1
c. A.D. 56-58	Luke writes the Gospel entitled "Luke"	Luke 1:1, 2
c. A.D. 60-61	From Rome Paul writes: Ephesians	Eph. 3:1
	Philippians	Phil. 4:22
	Colossians	Col. 4:18
	Philemon	Philem. 1
c. A.D. 60-65	Mark writes the Gospel entitled "Mark"	
c. A.D. 61	Paul writes the letter to the Hebrews from Rome	Heb. 13:24; 10:34
	Luke completes the book of Acts in Rome	
c. A.D. 61-64	Paul writes 1 Timothy from Macedonia	1 Tim. 1:3
	Paul writes Titus from Macedonia (?)	Titus 1:5
b. A.D. 62	James, Jesus' brother, writes the letter of "James" from Jerusalem	Jas. 1:1
c. A.D. 62-64	Peter writes 1 Peter from Babylon	1 Pet. 1:1; 5:13
c. A.D. 64	Peter writes 2 Peter from Babylon (?)	2 Pet. 1:1
c. A.D. 65	Paul writes 2 Timothy from Rome	2 Tim. 4:16-18
	Jude, Jesus' brother, writes "Jude"	Jude 1, 17, 18
A.D. 70	Jerusalem and its temple destroyed by the Romans	Dan. 9:27; Matt. 23:37, 38; Luke 19:42-44
c. A.D. 96	John, on Patmos, writes Revelation	Rev. 1:9
c. A.D. 98	John writes the Gospel entitled "John" and his letters 1, 2 and 3 John; Bible writing completed	John 21:22, 23
c. A.D. 100	John, the last of the apostles, dies	2 Thess. 2:7

NOTE: It should be borne in mind that, while many of these dates are firmly established, in the case of some, approximate dates are given, based on the available evidence. The purpose of the chart is not to fix unalterable dates for each event, but to help Bible students to locate events in the stream of time and see their relationship to one another.

Symbols: "a" for "after"; "b" for "before"; "c" for "circa or about."

TABLE OF THE BOOKS OF THE BIBLE

(Indicating the writer, the place of writing, the time of completion of writing, and the time covered by the events of the book)

[Names of writers of some books and of places where written are uncertain. Many dates are only approximate, the symbol a. meaning "after," b. meaning "before" and c. meaning "circa" or "about."]

Books of the Hebrew Scriptures before the Common or Christian Era

Name of Book	The Writer	Place Written	Writing Completed (B.C.E.)	Time Covered (B.C.E.)
Genesis	Moses	Wilderness	1513	46,026-1657
Exodus	Moses	Wilderness	1512	1657-1512
Leviticus	Moses	Wilderness	1512	1 month (1512)
Numbers	Moses	Plains of Moab	1473	1512-1473
Deuteronomy	Moses	Plains of Moab	1473	2 months (1473)
Joshua	Joshua	Canaan	c. 1433	1473–c. 1433
Judges	Samuel	Israel	c. 1100	c. 1433-1190
Ruth	Samuel	Israel	c. 1090	11 years of judges' rule
1 Samuel	Samuel; Gad; Nathan	Israel	c. 1077	c. 1190-1077
2 Samuel	Gad; Nathan	Israel	c. 1040	1077–c. 1040
1 Kings	Jeremiah	{ Jerusalem, Israel and Egypt	{ 1 roll c. 580	c. 1040-917
2 Kings	Jeremiah			922–c. 580
1 Chronicles	Ezra	Jerusalem (?)	{ 1 roll c. 460	1077-1037
2 Chronicles	Ezra	Jerusalem (?)		1037-537
Ezra	Ezra	Jerusalem	c. 460	537-467
Nehemiah	Nehemiah	Jerusalem	a. 443	456–a. 443
Esther	Mordecai	Shushan, Elam	c. 474	c. 484-474
Job	Moses	Wilderness	c. 1473	between 1657-1473
Psalms	David and others		c. 460	
Proverbs	Solomon; Agur; Lemuel		c. 716	
Ecclesiastes	Solomon	Jerusalem	c. 1000	
Song of Solomon, The	Solomon	Jerusalem	c. 1020	
Isaiah	Isaiah	Jerusalem	c. 732	c. 775-732
Jeremiah	Jeremiah	Jerusalem; Egypt	c. 580	647–c. 580
Lamentations	Jeremiah	Near Jerusalem	607	
Ezekiel	Ezekiel	Babylon	591	613-591
Daniel	Daniel	Babylon	536	618-536
Hosea	Hosea	Samaria (District)	a. 745	b. 811–a. 745
Joel	Joel	Judah	c. 820 (?)	
Amos	Amos	Judah	c. 811	
Obadiah	Obadiah		c. 607	
Jonah	Jonah		c. 852	
Micah	Micah	Judah	b. 716	c. 774-716
Nahum	Nahum	Judah	b. 633	
Habakkuk	Habakkuk	Judah	c. 628	
Zephaniah	Zephaniah	Judah	b. 648	
Haggai	Haggai	Jerusalem rebuilt	521	112 days (521)
Zechariah	Zechariah	Jerusalem rebuilt	519	521-519
Malachi	Malachi	Jerusalem rebuilt	a. 443	

Books of the Greek Scriptures Written During the Common (Christian) Era

Name of Book	The Writer	Place Written	Writing Completed (A.D.)	Time Covered
Matthew	Matthew	Palestine	c. 41	2 B.C.E.–A.D. 33
Mark	Mark	Rome	c. 60-65	29-33
Luke	Luke	Caesarea	c. 56-58	3 B.C.E.–A.D. 33
John	Apostle John	Ephesus, or near	c. 98	After prologue, A.D. 29-33
Acts	Luke	Rome	c. 61	33–c.61
Romans	Paul	Corinth	c. 56	
1 Corinthians	Paul	Ephesus	c. 55	
2 Corinthians	Paul	Macedonia	c. 55	
Galatians	Paul	Corinth or Syrian Antioch	c. 50-52	
Ephesians	Paul	Rome	c. 60-61	
Philippians	Paul	Rome	c. 60-61	
Colossians	Paul	Rome	c. 60-61	
1 Thessalonians	Paul	Corinth	c. 50	
2 Thessalonians	Paul	Corinth	c. 51	
1 Timothy	Paul	Macedonia	c. 61-64	
2 Timothy	Paul	Rome	c. 65	
Titus	Paul	Macedonia (?)	c. 61-64	
Philemon	Paul	Rome	c. 60-61	
Hebrews	Paul	Rome	c. 61	
James	James (Jesus' brother)	Jerusalem	b. 62	
1 Peter	Peter	Babylon	c. 62-64	
2 Peter	Peter	Babylon (?)	c. 64	
1 John	Apostle John	Ephesus, or near	c. 98	
2 John	Apostle John	Ephesus, or near	c. 98	
3 John	Apostle John	Ephesus, or near	c. 98	
Jude	Jude (Jesus' brother)	Palestine (?)	c. 65	
Revelation	Apostle John	Patmos	c. 96	

Study Four— The Bible and Its Canon

The origin of the word "Bible"; determining which books rightfully belong in the Divine Library; rejection of the Apocrypha.

SINCE the inspired Scriptures are commonly referred to as the Bible, it is of interest to inquire into the origin and meaning of the word "Bible." It is derived from the Greek word *bi·bli′a,* which is the diminutive plural form of *bi′blos.* This is the word the Greeks used for the pith of the stem of the papyrus plant from which, in ancient times, a "paper" for writing was produced. (The Phoenician port of Gebal, through which papyrus was imported from Egypt, came to be called Byblos by the Greeks. See Joshua 13:5, *NW* footnote, 1953 Ed.) All written communications upon this type of material became known by the neuter plural word *bi·bli′a.* Thus in Greek *bi·bli′a* came to describe any writings, scrolls, books, documents, scriptures or even a library collection of little books.

2 Surprisingly, the word *Bible* itself is not found in the translated text of any English or other-language publication of the Holy Scriptures. However, by the second century B.C.E., the collection of the inspired books of the Hebrew Scriptures was referred to as *ta bi·bli′a* in the Greek language. At Daniel 9:2 the prophet wrote: "I myself, Daniel, discerned by the *books* . . ." Here the *Septuagint* has *bi′blois,* the dative form of *bi′bloi.* At 2 Timothy 4:13, Paul wrote: "When you come, bring . . . the scrolls [Greek: *ta bi·bli′a*]." In their several grammatical forms, the Greek words *bi·bli′on* and *bi′blos* occur forty-five times in the Christian Greek Scriptures and are translated "scroll(s)" or "book(s)." *Bi·bli′a* was later used in Latin as a singular word, and from the Latin the word "Bible" came into the English language.

3 **It Is God's Word.** While various men were used in the inspired writing of it, and still others have shared in translating it from the original tongues into the spoken languages of today, the Bible is, in the fullest sense, *God's* Word, His own inspired revelation to men. The inspired writers themselves viewed it this way, as evidenced by their use of phrases such as "expression of Jehovah's mouth" (Deut. 8:3), "sayings of Jehovah" (Josh. 24:27), "commandments of Jehovah" (Ezra 7:11), "law of Jehovah" (Ps. 19:7), "word of Jehovah" (Isa. 38:4), 'utterance of Jehovah' (Matt. 4:4), and "Jehovah's word" (1 Thess. 4:15).

THE DIVINE LIBRARY

4 What man knows today as the Bible is in fact a collection of ancient divinely inspired documents. These were composed and compiled in written form over a period of sixteen centuries. All together this collection of documents forms what Jerome well described in Latin as the *Bibliotheca Divina,* or the Divine Library. This library has a catalogue, or official listing of publications. As in the case of other specialized libraries, this catalogue is limited to the right publications pertaining to the scope of that library. All unauthorized books are excluded. Jehovah God is the Great Librarian who sets the standard that determines which writings should be listed. So the Bible has a set catalogue that today comprises sixty-six books, all products of his guiding holy spirit.

5 The collection or list of books accepted as genuine and inspired Scriptures is often referred to as the Bible *canon.* Originally this word "canon" referred to a reed used as a measuring rod if a piece of wood were not at hand, and then to a tool, a carpenter's level or a scribe's ruler. The apostle Paul referred to a "rule of conduct" (Greek: *ka·non′*) as well as to a literal rule or boundary line. (Gal. 6:16; 2 Cor. 10:13) So canonical books are those that are true and inspired and worthy to be used as a straightedge in determining the right faith and doctrine. If we use books that are not "straight" as a plumbline, our "building" will not be true and it will fail the test of the Master Surveyor.

6 **Determining Canonicity.** What are some of the divine indications that have determined the canonicity of the sixty-six books of the Bible? First of all, the documents must deal with Je-

1, 2. (a) What is the general meaning of the Greek word *bi·bli′a?* (b) How are this and associated words used in the Christian Greek Scriptures? (c) How did the word Bible come into the English language?
3. How did writers of the Bible testify to its being God's inspired Word?

4. Of what is the Bible composed, and who has determined this?
5. What is the Bible "canon," and how did this designation originate?
6. What are some of the factors determining a book's canonicity?

hovah's affairs in the earth, turning men to his worship and stimulating deep respect for his work and purposes in the earth. They must give evidence of inspiration, that is, be products of holy spirit. (2 Pet. 1:21) There must be no appeal to superstition or creature worship, but, rather, an appeal to love and service of God. There would have to be nothing in any of the individual writings that would conflict with the internal harmony of the whole, but, rather, each book must, by its unity with the others, support the one authorship, that of Jehovah God. In addition to these basic essentials there are other specific indications for inspiration, and therefore for canonicity, according to the nature of each book's contents, and these have been discussed in the introductory material to each of the Bible books. Also, there are special circumstances that apply to the Hebrew Scriptures and others to the Christian Greek Scriptures that help in determining the establishing of the Bible canon.

THE HEBREW SCRIPTURES

7 It should not be thought that acceptance of what constituted inspired Scriptures had to wait till the completion of the Hebrew canon in the fifth century B.C.E. The writings of Moses under the direction of God's spirit were from the very beginning accepted by the Israelites as inspired, of divine authorship. When completed, the Pentateuch constituted the "canon" up till that time. Further revelations concerning Jehovah's purposes given to men under inspiration would need to follow logically and be in harmony with the fundamental principles concerning true worship that are set forth in the Pentateuch. This we have seen to be true in considering the different Bible books, especially as these deal directly with that grand theme of the Bible, the kingdom of the promised Seed.

8 The Hebrew Scriptures, especially, abound with prophecy. Jehovah himself, through Moses, provided the basis for establishing the genuineness of prophecy, whether it was indeed from God or not, and so aiding in determining a prophetic book's canonicity. (Deut. 18:20-22) An examination of each of the prophetic books of the Hebrew Scriptures along with the Bible as a whole and secular history establishes beyond doubt that "the word" they spoke did "occur or come true," either completely or in a miniature or partial way when it had to do with things yet future, yet sufficiently to establish the prophecy as genuine and inspired.

9 While quotations by Jesus and the inspired writers of the Christian Greek Scriptures provide a very direct way of establishing the canonicity of many of the books of the Hebrew Scriptures, this test does not apply to all of them, such as to Esther and Ecclesiastes. In considering the matter of canonicity, then, one other most important factor must be kept in mind, one that applies to the entire Bible canon. Just as Jehovah inspired men to write down his divine communications for their instruction, upbuilding and encouragement in his worship and service, so it logically follows that Jehovah would direct and guide the collating of the inspired writings and the establishing of the Bible canon so that there would be no doubt as to what composed his Word of truth, what would constitute the enduring measuring line of true worship. Indeed, only in this way could creatures on earth continue to be given 'a new birth through the word of God,' and be able to testify to the fact that "the saying of Jehovah endures forever."—1 Pet. 1:23, 25.

10 **Establishing the Hebrew Canon.** Jewish tradition credits Ezra with beginning the compiling and cataloguing of the canon of the Hebrew Scriptures, and says that this was completed by Nehemiah and the Great Synagogue, which continued in existence until about 300 B.C.E. Ezra was certainly well equipped for such a work, being one of the inspired Bible writers himself as well as a priest, scholar and official copyist of sacred writings. (Ezra 7:1-11) There is no reason to doubt the traditional view that the canon of the Hebrew Scriptures was fixed by the end of the fifth century B.C.E.

11 While today we list thirty-nine books of the Hebrew Scriptures, the traditional Jewish canon, while including these same books, counts them as twenty-four, listing them as follows:

The Law (The Pentateuch)
1. Genesis
2. Exodus
3. Leviticus
4. Numbers
5. Deuteronomy

The Prophets
6. Joshua
7. Judges
8. Samuel (First and Second together as one book)
9. Kings (First and Second together as one book)
10. Isaiah
11. Jeremiah
12. Ezekiel
13. The Minor Prophets (Hosea, Joel, Amos, Obadiah, Jonah, Micah, Nahum, Habakkuk, Zephaniah, Haggai, Zechariah and Malachi, as one book.)

The Writings (Hagiographa)
14. Psalms
15. Proverbs
16. Job
17. Song of Solomon
18. Ruth
19. Lamentations
20. Ecclesiastes
21. Esther
22. Daniel
23. Ezra (Nehemiah was included with Ezra)
24. Chronicles (First and Second together as one book)

---

7. By what progressive steps was the Hebrew canon completed, and in harmony with what?
8. What establishes the canonicity of the prophetic books of the Bible?
9. What important factor must be borne in mind when considering the question of the Bible canon?
10. By about what time was the canon of the Hebrew Scriptures fixed?
11. How does the traditional Jewish canon list the Hebrew Scriptures?

Some authorities, by putting Ruth with Judges and Lamentations with Jeremiah, counted the number of books as twenty-two, though still holding to exactly the same canonical writings.[a] (This made the number of inspired books equal the number of letters in the Hebrew alphabet.)

12 This was the catalogue or canon that was accepted as inspired Scriptures by Christ Jesus and the early Christian church. It was from these writings only that the inspired writers of the Christian Greek Scriptures quoted as being the word of God, introducing such quotations by expressions like "as it is written." (Rom. 15:9) Jesus, in speaking of the complete inspired Scriptures written up till the time of his ministry, referred to the things recorded in "the law of Moses and in the Prophets and Psalms." (Luke 24:44) Here "Psalms," as the first book of the Hagiographa, is used to refer to this whole section. The last historical book to be included in the Hebrew canon was that of Nehemiah. That this was under the direction of God's spirit is seen in that this book alone provides the starting point for reckoning Daniel's outstanding prophecy that "from the going forth of the word to restore and to rebuild Jerusalem" until the coming of the Messiah would be a period of sixty-nine prophetic weeks. (Dan. 9:25; Neh. 2:1-8; 6:15) Also the book of Nehemiah provides the historical background for the last of the prophetic books, Malachi. That Malachi belongs in the canon of the inspired Scriptures cannot be doubted, since it is quoted a number of times even by the Son of God Jesus himself, as evidenced by the Christian Greek Scriptures. (Matt. 11:10, 14) While similar quotations are made from the majority of the books of the Hebrew canon, all written prior to Nehemiah and Malachi, the Christian Greek Scriptures make no quotations from any so-called inspired writings written *after* their time and down to the time of Christ. This confirms the traditional view of the Jews and also the belief of the Christian congregation of the first century A.D., that the Hebrew canon ended with the writings of Nehemiah and Malachi.

APOCRYPHAL BOOKS OF THE HEBREW SCRIPTURES

13 What are the apocryphal books? These are writings that some have tried to include in the Bible catalogue, but which have been rejected because they do not bear evidence of having been inspired of God. "Apocrypha" means "hidden," "secret," "uncanonical." The term is applied to books of doubtful authorship or authority, or which, while being reckoned of some value for personal reading, lacked evidence of divine inspiration. Such books were kept apart and not read publicly, hence the thought of "hidden." It was at the Council of Carthage, A.D. 397, that it was proposed that seven of the apocryphal books be added to the Hebrew Scriptures, along with additions to the canonical books of Esther and Daniel. However, it was not until as late as A.D. 1546, at the Council of Trent, that the Roman Catholic Church definitely confirmed the acceptance of these additions into its catalogue of Bible books. These additions were: Tobit, Judith, an addition to Esther, Wisdom, Ecclesiasticus, Baruch, three additions to Daniel, First Maccabees and Second Maccabees.

14 The book of First Maccabees, while not in any way to be reckoned as an inspired book, contains information that is of historical interest. It appears to give a fairly accurate account of the struggle of the Jews for independence during the second century B.C.E. under the leadership of the family of the Maccabees. For the rest, the apocryphal books are full of myths and superstitions, and abound with errors. They were never referred to or quoted by Jesus or the writers of the Christian Greek Scriptures.

15 The Jewish historian Flavius Josephus, of the first century A.D., in his work "Against Apion" (i, 8), refers to all the books that were recognized by the Hebrews as sacred. He wrote: "We have not an innumerable multitude of books among us, disagreeing from and contradicting one another, but only twenty-two books [the equivalent of our thirty-nine today, as shown in paragraph eleven], which contain the records of all past times; which are justly believed to be divine. . . . It is true, our history hath been written since Artaxerxes very particularly, but hath not been esteemed of the like authority with the former by our forefathers, because there hath not been an exact succession of prophets since that time." Thus Josephus shows he was aware of the existence of apocryphal books and specifically excluded them from the Hebrew canon.[b]

16 Jerome, who completed the Latin Vulgate translation of the Bible A.D. 404, was quite definite in his position on the apocryphal

a *The Jewish Encyclopedia,* 1910, Vol. III, pages 141, 142.

b *The Life and Works of Flavius Josephus,* translated by Whiston.

12. What further confirms the Hebrew canon, and with what writings did it end?
13. (a) What are the "apocryphal" books? (b) How did they come to be accepted in the Roman Catholic canon?
14. (a) In what way is First Maccabees of interest? (b) What authorities never referred to the Apocrypha, and why?
15, 16. How did Josephus and Jerome indicate that the apocryphal books are not canonical?

books. After listing the inspired books, using the same counting as Josephus, numbering the thirty-nine inspired books of the Hebrew Scriptures as twenty-two, he writes in his *Prologus Galeatus* to the *Vulgate:* "Thus there are twenty-two books . . . This prologue of the Scriptures can serve as a fortified approach to all the books which we translate from the Hebrew into Latin; so that we may know that *whatever is beyond these must be put in the apocrypha.*"[a]

THE CHRISTIAN GREEK SCRIPTURES

17 The Roman Catholic Church claims responsibility for the decision as to which books should be included in the Bible canon, and reference is made to the Councils of Hippo (A.D. 393) and Carthage (A.D. 397), where catalogues of books were formulated. The opposite is true, however, for the canon, including the list of books making up the Christian Greek Scriptures, was already settled by then, not by the decree of any council, but by the usage of Christian congregations throughout the ancient world. Says one authority: "It goes without saying that the Church, understood as the entire body of believers, created the Canon . . . it was not the reverse; it was not imposed from the top, be it by bishops or synods."[b] Our examination of the evidence will describe how this came about.

18 **The Evidence of Early Catalogues.** A glance at the accompanying chart reveals that a number of fourth-century catalogues of the Christian Scriptures, dated prior to the above-mentioned councils, agree exactly with our present canon, and some others omit only Revelation. Before the end of the second century there is universal acceptance of the four Gospels, Acts and twelve of the apostle Paul's letters. Only a few of the smaller writings were doubted in certain areas, this being due no doubt to such writings being limited in their initial circulation for one reason or another, and thus taking longer to become established as canonical.

19 One of the most interesting early catalogues is the fragment discovered by L. A. Muratori in the Ambrosian Library, Milan, Italy, and published by him in 1740. Though the beginning is missing, its reference to Luke as the third Gospel indicates that it first mentioned Matthew and Mark. The Muratorian Fragment, which is in Latin, dates to the latter part of the second century, and is probably a translation from a Greek original. It is a most interesting document, as the following partial translation shows: "The third book of the Gospel is that according to Luke. Luke, the well-known physician, wrote it in his own name, . . . The fourth book of the Gospel is that of John, one of the disciples. . . . And so to the faith of believers there is no discord, even although different selections are given from the facts in the individual books of the Gospels, because in all [of them] under the one guiding Spirit all the things relative to his nativity, passion, resurrection, conversation with his disciples, and his twofold advent, the first in the humiliation arising from contempt, which took place, and the second in the glory of kingly power, which is yet to come, have been declared. What marvel is it, then, if John adduces so consistently in his epistles these several things, saying in person: 'what we have seen with our eyes, and heard with our ears, and our hands have handled, those things we have written.' For thus he professes to be not only an eyewitness but also a hearer and narrator of all the wonderful things of the Lord, in their order. Moreover, the acts of all the apostles are written in one book. Luke [so] comprised them for the most excellent Theophilus, . . . Now the epistles of Paul, what they are, whence or for what reason they were sent, they themselves make clear to him who will understand. First of all he wrote at length to the Corinthians to prohibit the schism of heresy, then to the Galatians [against] circumcision, and to the Romans on the order of the Scriptures, intimating also that Christ is the chief matter in them—each of which it is necessary for us to discuss, seeing that the blessed Apostle Paul himself, following the example of his predecessor John, writes to no more than seven churches by name in the following order: to the Corinthians (first), to the Ephesians (second), to the Philippians (third), to the Colossians (fourth), to the Galatians (fifth), to the Thessalonians (sixth), to the Romans (seventh). But though he writes twice for the sake of correction to the Corinthians and the Thessalonians, that there is one church diffused throughout the whole earth is shown [?i.e., by this sevenfold writing]; and John also in the Apocalypse, though he writes to seven churches, yet speaks to all. But [he wrote] out of affection and love one to Philemon, and one to Titus, and two to Timothy; [and these] are held sacred in the honorable esteem of the Church. . . . Further, an epistle of Jude and two bearing the name of John are counted . . . We receive

---

a *Origin and History of the Books of the Bible,* 1868, Prof. C. E. Stowe, pages 580, 581.
b *The Problem of the New Testament Canon,* 1962, Kurt Aland, page 18.

---

17. What responsibility does the Roman Catholic Church claim, but what do the facts show?
18. What important conclusions can be drawn from the accompanying chart showing early catalogues of the Christian Greek Scriptures?
19. (a) What outstanding document has been located in Italy, and what is its date? (b) How does this define the accepted canon of that time?

the apocalypses of John and Peter only, which [latter] some of us do not wish to be read in church."—*The New Schaff-Herzog Encyclopedia of Religious Knowledge*, 1956, Vol. VIII, page 56.

[20] It is noted that toward the end of the Muratorian Fragment mention is made of just two epistles of John. However, on this point the above-mentioned encyclopedia, page 55, notes: "Having already treated the first, though only incidentally, in connection with the Fourth Gospel, and there declared his unquestioning belief in its Johannine origin, the author felt able here to confine himself to the two smaller letters." As to the apparent absence of any mention of Peter's first epistle, this authority

20. (a) How is the omission of one of John's and one of Peter's letters explained? (b) How closely, then, does this catalogue correspond with our present-day catalogue?

Outstanding Early Catalogues of the Christian Greek Scriptures

Name and Place	Approximate Date A.D.	Matthew	Mark	Luke	John	Acts	Romans	1 Cor.	2 Cor.	Galatians	Ephesians	Philippians	Colossians	1 Thess.	2 Thess.	1 Timothy	2 Timothy	Titus	Philemon	Hebrews	James	1 Peter	2 Peter	1 John	2 John	3 John	Jude	Revelation
Muratorian Fragment, Italy	170	(A)	(A)	A	A	A	A	A	A	A	A	A	A	A	A	A	A	A	A			A?	D?	A	A	A?	A	A
Irenaeus, Asia Minor	180	A	A	A	A	A	A	A	A	A	A	A	A	A	A	A	A	A		D		A	A	A	A			A
Clement of Alexandria	190	A	A	A	A	A	A	A	A	A	A	A	A	A	A	A	A	A		DA		A		DA	DA		DA	A
Tertullian, N. Africa	200	A	A	A	A	A	A	A	A	A	A	A	A	A	A	A	A	A	A	D		A		A			A	A
Origen, Alexandria	230	A	A	A	A	A	A	A	A	A	A	A	A	A	A	A	A	A	A	DA	DA	A	DA	A	DA	DA	DA	A
Eusebius, Palestine	310	A	A	A	A	A	A	A	A	A	A	A	A	A	A	A	A	A	A	DA	DA	A	DA	A	DA	DA	DA	DA
Cyril of Jerusalem	348	A	A	A	A	A	A	A	A	A	A	A	A	A	A	A	A	A	A	A	A	A	A	A	A	A	A	
Cheltenham List, N. Africa	360	A	A	A	A	A	A	A	A	A	A	A	A	A	A	A	A	A	A		?	A	DA	A	DA	DA	?	A
Athanasius, Alexandria	367	A	A	A	A	A	A	A	A	A	A	A	A	A	A	A	A	A	A	A	A	A	A	A	A	A	A	A
Epiphanius, Palestine	368	A	A	A	A	A	A	A	A	A	A	A	A	A	A	A	A	A	A	A	A	A	A	A	A	A	A	DA
Gregory Nazianzus, Asia Minor	370	A	A	A	A	A	A	A	A	A	A	A	A	A	A	A	A	A	A	A	A	A	A	A	A	A	A	
Amphilocius, Asia Minor	370	A	A	A	A	A	A	A	A	A	A	A	A	A	A	A	A	A	A	DA	A	A	D	A	D	D	D	D
Philastrius, Italy	383	A	A	A	A	A	A	A	A	A	A	A	A	A	A	A	A	A	A	D	A	A	A	A	A	A	A	D
Jerome, Italy	394	A	A	A	A	A	A	A	A	A	A	A	A	A	A	A	A	A	A	DA	DA	A	DA	A	DA	DA	DA	DA
Augustine, N. Africa	397	A	A	A	A	A	A	A	A	A	A	A	A	A	A	A	A	A	A	A	A	A	A	A	A	A	A	A
Third Council of Carthage, N. Africa	397	A	A	A	A	A	A	A	A	A	A	A	A	A	A	A	A	A	A	A	A	A	A	A	A	A	A	A

A – Accepted without query as Scriptural and Canonical.
D – Doubted in certain quarters.
DA – Doubted in certain quarters but cataloguer accepted as Scriptural and Canonical.
? – Scholars uncertain of the reading of the text.

continues: "The most probable hypothesis is that of the loss of a few words, perhaps a line, in which 1 Peter and the Apocalypse of John were named as received." Therefore, from the standpoint of the Muratorian Fragment, this encyclopedia concludes: "The New Testament is regarded as definitely made up of the four Gospels, the Acts, thirteen epistles of Paul, the Apocalypse of John, probably three epistles of his, Jude, and probably 1 Peter, while the opposition to another of Peter's writings was not yet silenced."

21 Origen, about the year 230 (A.D.), accepted among the inspired Scriptures the books of Hebrews and James, both missing from the Muratorian Fragment. While he indicates that some doubted their canonical quality, this also shows that all the congregations by this time were in agreement about the canonicity of most of the Greek Scriptures, only a few doubting some of the less well known epistles. Later, Athanasius, Jerome and Augustine reaffirmed the conclusions of earlier lists by defining the canon and listing the same twenty-seven books that we now have.[a]

22 The majority of the catalogues in the chart are specific lists showing which books are accepted as canonical. Those of Irenaeus, Clement of Alexandria, Tertullian and Origen are completed from the quotations they made, which reveal how they regarded the writings referred to. These are further supplemented from the records of the early historian Eusebius. However, the fact that these writers do not mention certain ones of the canonical writings does not argue against their canonicity. It is just that they did not happen to make reference to such books in their writings, not having occasion to do so because of the subjects under discussion or because of choice. But why do we not find exact lists earlier than the Muratorian Fragment?

23 It was not until men like Marcion came along in the middle of the second century that the need arose to catalogue the books Christians should accept. Marcion constructed his own canon to suit his doctrines, taking only certain of the apostle Paul's letters and an expurgated form of the Gospel of Luke. This, together with the mass of apocryphal literature by now spreading throughout the world, made it imperative to pronounce a clear-cut distinction between what could be received as Scripture and what could not.

24 **Apocryphal Writings.** Internal evidence confirms the clear division that was made between the inspired Christian writings and works that were spurious or uninspired. The apocryphal writings are much inferior and often fanciful and childish. They are frequently inaccurate. Note the following statements by scholars on these noncanonical books:

"There is no question of any one's having excluded them from the New Testament: they have done that for themselves."—M. R. James, *The Apocryphal New Testament,* page xii.

"We have only to compare our New Testament books as a whole with other literature of the kind to realise how wide is the gulf which separates them from it. The uncanonical gospels, it is often said, are in reality the best evidence for the canonical."—G. Milligan, *The New Testament Documents,* page 228.

"It cannot be said of a single writing preserved to us from the early period of the Church outside the New Testament that it could properly be added today to the Canon." —K. Aland, *The Problem of the New Testament Canon,* page 24.

25 **Inspired Penmen.** This further point is of interest. All the writers of the Christian Greek Scriptures in one way or another were closely associated with the original governing body of the Christian congregation, which included the apostles who had been personally selected by Jesus himself. Matthew, John, Peter and Paul were apostles. While Paul was not present at the special outpouring of spirit at Pentecost, the three other apostles were, as were James and Jude and probably Mark. (Acts 1:14) Peter makes specific mention of the letters of Paul as to their being counted in with "the rest of the Scriptures." (2 Pet. 3:15, 16) Mark and Luke were close associates and traveling companions of Paul and Peter. (Acts 12:25; 1 Pet. 5:13; Col. 4:14; 2 Tim. 4:11) All these writers were endowed with miraculous abilities by holy spirit, either by special outpouring as at Pentecost and in the case of Paul (Acts 9:17, 18) or, no doubt as in the case of Luke, through the laying on of the apostles' hands. (Acts 8:14-17) All the writing of the Christian Greek Scriptures was done during the time that the special gifts of the spirit were operative.

26 Faith in the Almighty God, who is the Inspirer and Preserver of his Word, makes us confident that he is the One who has guided

a *The Books and the Parchments,* 1950, F. F. Bruce, page 110.

21. (a) Of what interest are Origen's comments on the inspired writings? (b) What did later writers reaffirm?
22, 23. (a) How were the lists of the catalogues in the chart prepared? (b) Why were there apparently no such lists prior to the Muratorian fragment?

24. (a) What characterizes the apocryphal "New Testament" writings? (b) What do scholars say of these?
25. What facts about the individual writers of the Christian Greek Scriptures argue for the inspiration of these writings?
26. (a) What do we accept as God's Word, and why? (b) How should we show appreciation for these Scriptures?

the gathering together of its various parts. So we confidently accept the twenty-seven books of the Christian Greek Scriptures along with the thirty-nine of the Hebrew Scriptures as the one Bible, by the one author, Jehovah God. His Word in its sixty-six books is our guide and its complete harmony and balance testify to its completeness. All praise to Jehovah God, the Creator of this incomparable Book! It can equip us completely and put our feet on the way to life. Let us use it wisely at every opportunity.

Study Five— The Hebrew Text of The Holy Scriptures

How the Hebrew Scriptures were copied, preserved as to textual integrity, and transmitted down to this day as the inspired Word of God.

THE 'words of Jehovah' captured in writing may be likened to "waters of truth" collected in a remarkable reservoir of inspired documents. How grateful we can be that, throughout the period of these heavenly communications, Jehovah caused these "waters" to be so gathered together, to become an inexhaustible source of life-giving information! Other treasures of the past, such as regal crowns, heirlooms and monuments of men, have tarnished, eroded or collapsed with the passage of time, but the treasure-like sayings of our God will last to time indefinite. (Isa. 40:8) However, questions arise as to whether there has been contamination of these "waters of truth" after they have been taken into the "reservoir." Have they remained unadulterated? How faithfully have they been transmitted from the original-language texts, so as to be made available to peoples of every language on earth today? We will find it a thrilling study to examine the section of this reservoir known as the Hebrew text, noting the care taken to preserve its accuracy, together with the wonderful provisions made for its transmission and availability to all nations of mankind through versions, or new translations.

2 The original documents in the Hebrew and Aramaic languages were produced by God's co-writers, from Moses in 1513 B.C.E. down to shortly after 443 B.C.E. As far as is known today, none of these original writings are now in existence. However, from the beginning great care was exercised in preserving the inspired writings, including authorized copies thereof. About 642 B.C.E., in King Josiah's time, "the very book of the law" of Moses was found stored away in the house of Jehovah. It had by this time been faithfully preserved for 871 years. Bible writer Jeremiah manifested such great interest in this discovery that he made written record of it at 2 Kings 22:8-10, and about the year 460 Ezra again referred to the same incident. (2 Chron. 34:14-18) He was interested in these things, because "he was a skilled copyist in the law of Moses, which Jehovah the God of Israel had given." (Ezra 7:6) No doubt Ezra had access to other scrolls of the Hebrew Scriptures that had been prepared up to his time, possibly including originals of some of the inspired writings. Indeed, Ezra seems to have been the custodian of the divine writings in his day.—Neh. 8:1, 2.

1. (a) In what way do the 'words of Jehovah' differ from other treasures of the past? (b) What questions arise as to the preservation of God's Word?
2. How were the inspired writings preserved down to Ezra's day?

ERA OF MANUSCRIPT COPYING

3 From Ezra's time forward there was an increased demand for copies of the Hebrew Scriptures. Not all the Jews returned to Jerusalem and Palestine in the restoration of 537 B.C.E. and thereafter. Instead, thousands remained in Babylon, while others scattered themselves in migrations and for business reasons, so that they were to be found in most of the large commercial centers of the ancient world. Many Jews would make annual pilgrimages back to Jerusalem for the various temple festivals, and there they would share in the services conducted in Biblical Hebrew. In Ezra's time the Jews in these many faraway lands began to build local assembly halls known as "synagogues," where readings and discussions of the Hebrew Scriptures took place. Because of the many scattered places of worship, copyists had to multiply the supply of handwritten manuscripts.

3. What need now arose for additional copies of the Scriptures, and how was this filled?

4 These synagogues had a rear room known as the *genizah*, which was used as a storage room. In the course of time, the Jews assembled in these *genizahs* discarded manuscripts that had become torn or worn with age, replacing them with new ones for current synagogue use. From time to time the contents of these *genizahs* were solemnly buried in the earth, in order that the text—containing the holy name of Jehovah—might not be desecrated. Over the centuries thousands of old Hebrew Bible manuscripts disappeared from use in this way. However, the well-stocked *genizah* of the synagogue in old Cairo was spared this treatment, probably because it was walled up and forgotten. About A.D. 1890, when the synagogue was being repaired, the contents of the *genizah* were reexamined and its treasures were either sold or donated. From this source, fairly complete manuscripts have found their way to the various libraries of Europe and America. However, these manuscripts are, for the most part, comparatively recent, belonging to the Middle Ages.

5 Today, there have been counted and catalogued in various libraries of the world more than 1,700 handwritten copies in the Hebrew language of various parts of the Hebrew Scriptures. Until recently there were no such manuscripts (except for a few fragments) older than the tenth century A.D. Then in A.D. 1947 there was discovered in the Dead Sea area a scroll of the book of Isaiah, and in subsequent years additional priceless scrolls of the Hebrew Scriptures came to light as caves in the Dead Sea area surrendered rich treasures of manuscripts that had been hidden for over two thousand years. Experts have now dated some of these as having been copied in the last few centuries B.C.E. The comparative study of these more than 1,700 manuscripts of the Hebrew Scriptures gives a sound basis for establishing the Hebrew text, and reveals faithfulness in the text's transmission.

THE HEBREW LANGUAGE

6 What men call today the "Hebrew language" was, in its early or *proto* form, the language that Adam spoke in the garden of Eden. For this reason it could be referred to as man's language. Hebrew could also be called one of Jehovah's languages, because he used it to speak to Adam. (Gen. 1:28-30; 2:16, 17; 3:9-19) It was the language spoken in Noah's day, though with an increased vocabulary. In still further expanded form it was the basic language that survived when Jehovah confused mankind's speech at the tower of Babel. (Gen. 11:1, 7-9) Hebrew belongs to the Semitic group of languages, of which it is the family head. It appears to be related to the language of Canaan in Abraham's time, and from their Hebraic branch the Canaanites formed various dialects. At Isaiah 19:18 it is referred to as "the language of Canaan." Moses in his time was a scholar learned, not only in the wisdom of the Egyptians, but also in the Hebrew language of his forefathers. For this reason he was in position to read the ancient documents, both pre-Flood and post-Flood, that came into his hands, and to compile them into what is now known as the Bible book of Genesis.

7 Later, in the days of the Jewish kings, Hebrew came to be known as the "Jews' language." (2 Ki. 18:26, 28) In Jesus' time, the Jews spoke a newer or expanded form of Hebrew, and this still later became a rabbinic Hebrew. However, it should be noted that in the Christian Greek Scriptures it is still referred to as the "Hebrew" language, not the Aramaic. (John 5:2; 19:13, 17; Acts 22:2; Rev. 9:11) From earliest times, Biblical Hebrew was the binding language of communication, understood by most of Jehovah's pre-Christian witnesses and by some of his Christian witnesses.

8 The Hebrew Scriptures served as a reservoir of crystal-clear waters of truth, communicated and collected under divine inspiration. However, only those able to read Hebrew could avail themselves directly of these divinely provided waters. How could men of the multitongued nations also find a way to imbibe these waters of truth, thus gaining divine guidance and refreshment of soul? (Rev. 22:17) The only way was by translation from the Hebrew into other languages, thus broadening the flow of the stream of divine truth to all the multitudes of mankind. We can be truly thankful to Jehovah God that, from about the fourth century B.C.E. down to the present time, portions of the Bible have been translated into more than 1,180 languages. What a boon this has proved to be for all righteously inclined men, who have indeed been enabled to find their "delight" in these precious waters!—Ps. 1:2; 37:3, 4.

9 Does the Bible itself give authority or justification for translating its text into other languages? Certainly it does! God's word to Is-

4. (a) What were the "genizahs," and how were they used? (b) What valuable find was made in one of these about A.D. 1890?
5. (a) What ancient Hebrew manuscripts have now been catalogued, and how old are they? (b) What does a study of them reveal?
6. (a) What was the early history of the Hebrew language? (b) How was Moses qualified to compile Genesis?
7. (a) What later development of Hebrew took place? (b) As what did Biblical Hebrew serve?
8. Having in mind the purpose of the Scriptures, for what can we be truly thankful?
9. (a) What authority for translation does the Bible itself give? (b) What further good purpose have ancient Bible translations served?

rael, "Be glad, you nations, with his people," and Jesus' prophetic command to Christians, "This good news of the kingdom will be preached in all the inhabited earth for a witness to all the nations," must of necessity be fulfilled. For this to take place, translation of the Scriptures is a necessity. Looking back over twenty-four centuries of Bible translating, there can be no question that Jehovah's blessing has accompanied this work. Moreover, ancient translations of the Bible that have survived in manuscript form have also served to confirm the high degree of textual faithfulness of the Hebrew reservoir of truth.—Deut. 32:43; Matt. 24:14.

EARLIEST TRANSLATED VERSIONS

10 **The Samaritan Pentateuch.** Dating farthest back into antiquity, there is the version known as the Samaritan Pentateuch, which, as the name implies, contains only the first five books of the Hebrew Scriptures. In the strict sense, it is not a translation, but, rather, a transliteration of the Hebrew text into the characters of the Samaritan alphabet. It provides a useful pointer to the Hebrew text of the time. This transliteration was made by the foreigners imported by the king of Assyria to replace the Israelites of the ten-tribe kingdom when these went into captivity 740 B.C.E. These foreigners, later known as Samaritans, incorporated the worship of Israel with that of their own pagan gods, and accepted the Pentateuch, making their transliteration of it, about the fourth century B.C.E. As they read its text they would, in fact, be pronouncing Hebrew. It contains about six thousand variations from the Hebrew text, the majority of which are of trifling importance. Sir Frederic Kenyon evaluates the Samaritan Pentateuch as follows: "These variations, though sufficient to arouse our interest, are not serious enough to cause any disquietude as to the substantial integrity of the text."[a] A few manuscript copies have survived till this day, but the oldest are of the tenth and twelfth centuries A.D. Some references are made to the Samaritan Pentateuch in footnotes of the *New World Translation*.[b]

11 **The Aramaic Targums.** The Aramaic word for "interpretation" or "paraphrase" is *targum*. From Nehemiah's time forward, Aramaic came to be used as the common language of many of the Jews living in the territory of Persia, and so it was necessary to accompany readings of the Hebrew Scriptures by translations into that language. About the fourth century B.C.E., these loose, oral paraphrases came to be called Targums, and they were put down in writing about the first century of the Common Era. Though they are only loose paraphrases of the Hebrew text, and not an accurate translation, yet they supply a rich background to the text and give help in determining some difficult passages. Frequent references are made to the Targums in footnotes of the *New World Translation*.[c]

12 **The Septuagint Version.** The most important of the early versions of the Hebrew Scriptures, and the first actual written translation from the Hebrew, is the Greek *Septuagint* (meaning: "Seventy"). Its translation commenced about 280 B.C.E., according to tradition, by some seventy Jews of Alexandria, Egypt, and it was completed sometime in the second century B.C.E. It served as Scripture for the Greek-speaking Jews, and was used extensively down to the time of Jesus and his apostles. In the Christian Greek Scriptures most of the 365 direct quotations and approximately 375 references to the Hebrew Scriptures are based on the *Septuagint*.

13 There are still available for study today a considerable number of fragments of the *Septuagint* written on papyrus. These contain only a few chapters or verses of the original manuscripts, but they are valuable in that they belong to the early Christian times, and thus help in telling us the contents of the original *Septuagint* texts. The Fouad papyrus collection (No. 266) was discovered in Egypt in 1939, and has been found to be as old as the second or first century B.C.E. It covers the second half of the book of Deuteronomy, and the fragments that remain of this manuscript contain the divine name in many places, written always in old Hebrew characters.[d] Other *papyri* date down to the fourth century A.D., when the more durable *vellum*, a fine grade of calfskin, began to be used for writing manuscripts.

14 It is of interest that the divine name, in

a *Our Bible and the Ancient Manuscripts*, 1941, page 51.
b See footnotes, *NW*, 1953 Edition, "Sam," at Genesis 4:8; Exodus 6:2; 7:9; 8:15 and 12:40. This last rendering helps in understanding Galatians 3:17.
c See footnotes, "T," at Deuteronomy 33:13; Psalm 100:3 and Isaiah 49:5, *NW*, 1953, 1957 and 1958 Editions.
d See footnotes at Deuteronomy 18:5; 25:15 and 26:2, *NW*, 1953 Edition.

10. (a) What is the Samaritan Pentateuch, how accurate is it, and why is it useful to us today? (b) Give an example of its use in the *New World Translation*.
11. (a) What are the Targums, and of what benefit are they in connection with the text of the Hebrew Scriptures?
12. What is the *Septuagint*, and why is it so important?
13. (a) What valuable fragments of the *Septuagint* have survived to this day? (b) How do footnotes in the *New World Translation* comment on these?
14. (a) What does Origen testify as to the *Septuagint*? (b) When and how was the *Septuagint* tampered with? (c) What witness must the early Christians have given in using the *Septuagint*?

the form of the tetragrammaton, also appears in the *Septuagint* of Origen's six-column *Hexapla,* of about A.D. 245. Commenting on Psalm 2:2, Origen wrote of the *Septuagint:* "In the most faithful manuscripts THE NAME is written in Hebrew characters, that is, not in modern, but in archaic Hebrew."[a] The evidence appears conclusive that the *Septuagint* was tampered with at an early date, *Ky'ri·os* (Lord) and *Theos'* (God) being substituted for the tetragrammaton. Since the early Christians appear to have used manuscripts containing the divine name, it cannot be supposed that they followed Jewish tradition in failing to pronounce "THE NAME" during their ministry. They must have witnessed to Jehovah's name from the Greek *Septuagint Version.*

15 There are hundreds of *vellum* manuscripts of the Greek *Septuagint* still in existence. A number of these, produced between the fourth and tenth centuries A.D., are important because of the large sections of the Hebrew Scriptures that they cover. They are known as "uncials," because they are written entirely in large or capital letters. The remainder are called "minuscules," because they are written in a smaller, cursive style of handwriting. These were copied from the ninth up to the fifteenth century. The outstanding uncial manuscripts of the fourth and fifth centuries, namely, the Vatican No. 1209, the Sinaitic and the Alexandrine, all contain the Greek *Septuagint Version* with some slight variations.[b] Frequent references are made to the *Septuagint* in the footnotes and comments in the *New World Translation,* First Edition, under the symbol *LXX.* See, for example, the Foreword to the *Christian Greek Scriptures,* 1950 Edition.

16 **The Latin Vulgate.** This version has been the mother text used by a multitude of Catholic translators, in producing other versions in the many languages of Western Christendom. How did the *Vulgate* originate? The Latin word *vulgatus* means "common, that which is popular." When the *Vulgate* version was first produced it was in the common or popular Latin of the day, so that it could be easily understood by the ordinary people of the Western Roman Empire. The scholar Jerome, who made this translation, had previously made a partial translation of the *Septuagint* into Latin. However, his translation of the Vulgate Bible was made direct from the original Hebrew and Greek languages, and was thus not a version of a version. Jerome's careful work of translation occupied him from A.D. 382 to 404, and the completed manuscript was published the following year. While the completed work included apocryphal books, that were by this time in the copies of the *Septuagint,* Jerome clearly distinguished between which were the canonical books and which were not. The *New World Translation* refers many times to Jerome's *Vulgate* in its footnotes.[c]

a Foreword to the *New World Translation of the Christian Greek Scriptures,* 1950 Edition, page 15.

b The *New World Translation* notes these variations by symbol *LXX*ℵ for Sinaitic, *LXX*A for Alexandrine and *LXX*B for Vatican. See footnotes at 1 Kings 14:2; 1 Chronicles 7:34 and 12:19, *NW,* 1955 Edition.

15. (a) Using the chart on page 313, describe the *vellum* manuscripts of the *Septuagint.* (b) What references does the *New World Translation* make to these?
16. (a) What is the Latin *Vulgate,* and why is it so valuable? (b) Give an example of the *New World Translation's* reference to it.

THE HEBREW-LANGUAGE TEXTS

17 **The Sopherim.** The men who copied the Hebrew Scriptures from the days of Ezra up to the time of Jesus were called *scribes* or *sopherim.* In the course of time these began to take liberties in making textual changes. In fact, Jesus himself roundly condemned these would-be custodians of the Law for assuming powers that did not belong to them.—Matt. 23:2, 13.

18 **The Masorah Reveals Alterations.** The scribal successors of the *sopherim* in the centuries after Christ came to be known as the Masoretes. These took note of the alterations made by the earlier *sopherim,* recording them in the margin of the Hebrew text. These marginal notes came to be known as the Masorah. The Masorah listed the fifteen extraordinary points of the *sopherim,* namely, fifteen words or phrases in the Hebrew text that had been marked by dots above and below. Some of these extraordinary points do not affect the English translation or the interpretation, but others do and are of importance. The *sopherim* allowed their superstitious fear of pronouncing the name Jehovah to ensnare them into altering it to read *Adonay* (Lord) at 134 places and to read *Elohim* (God) at seventeen places. The Masorah (marginal comments on the text by the Masoretes) lists these changes. Also, the *sopherim* or early scribes are charged with making at least eighteen emendations (corrections), according to a note in the Masorah, though there evidently were even more. The Masorah also lists thirty-two passages that have different readings according to an important codex, and which are called *Severin.* Here again, some of these readings affect only such minor matters as spelling, but others make

c See footnotes, "Vg," at Exodus 6:3 and 37:6, *NW,* 1953 Edition.

17. Who were the *sopherim,* and for what did Jesus condemn them?
18. (a) Who were the Masoretes, and what valuable comments have they made on the Hebrew text? (b) What are some examples of their corrections, as noted in the *New World Translation?*

SOURCES FOR THE TEXT OF THE NEW WORLD TRANSLATION OF THE HEBREW SCRIPTURES

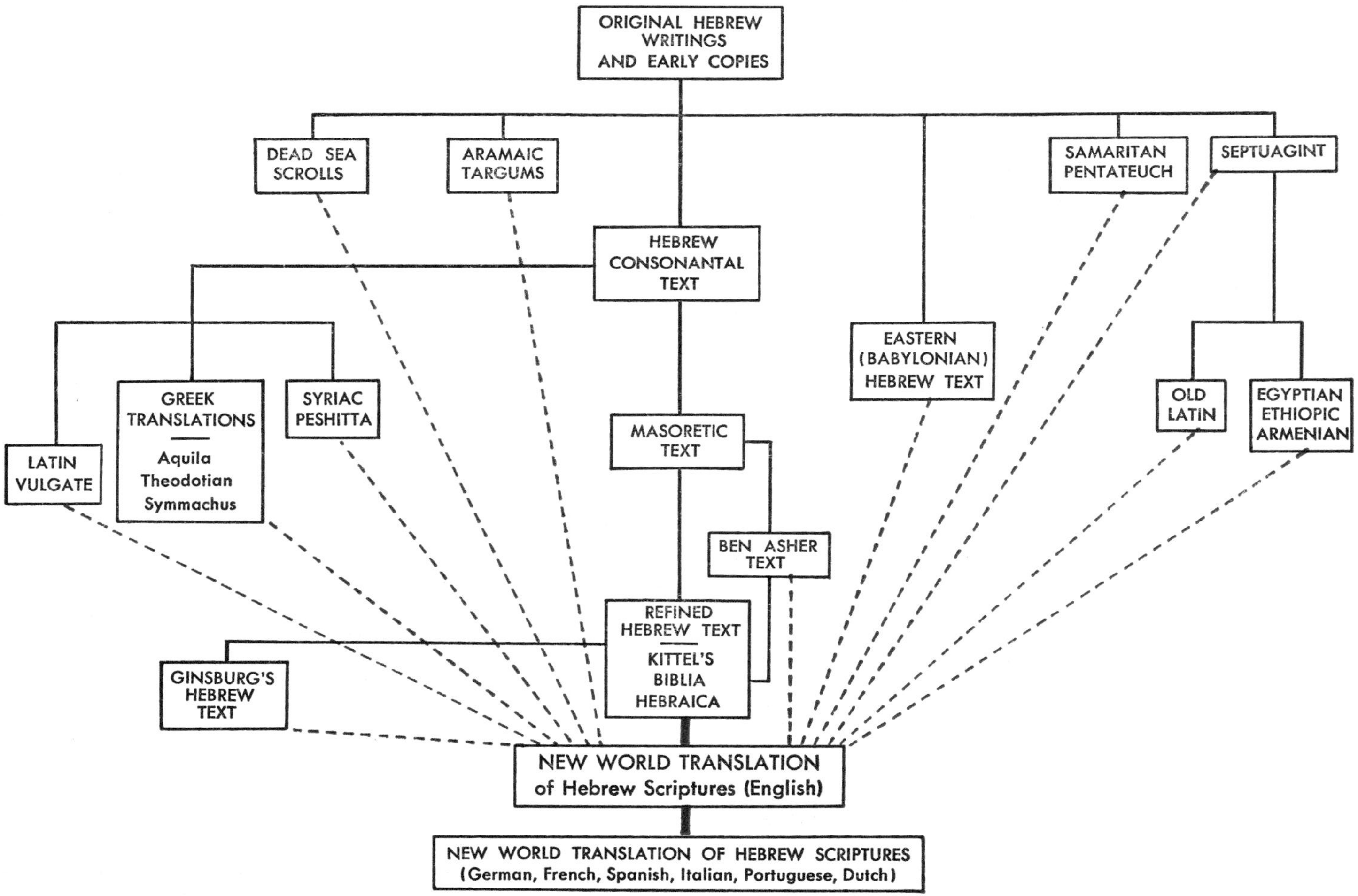

SOURCES FOR THE NEW WORLD TRANSLATION OF THE CHRISTIAN GREEK SCRIPTURES

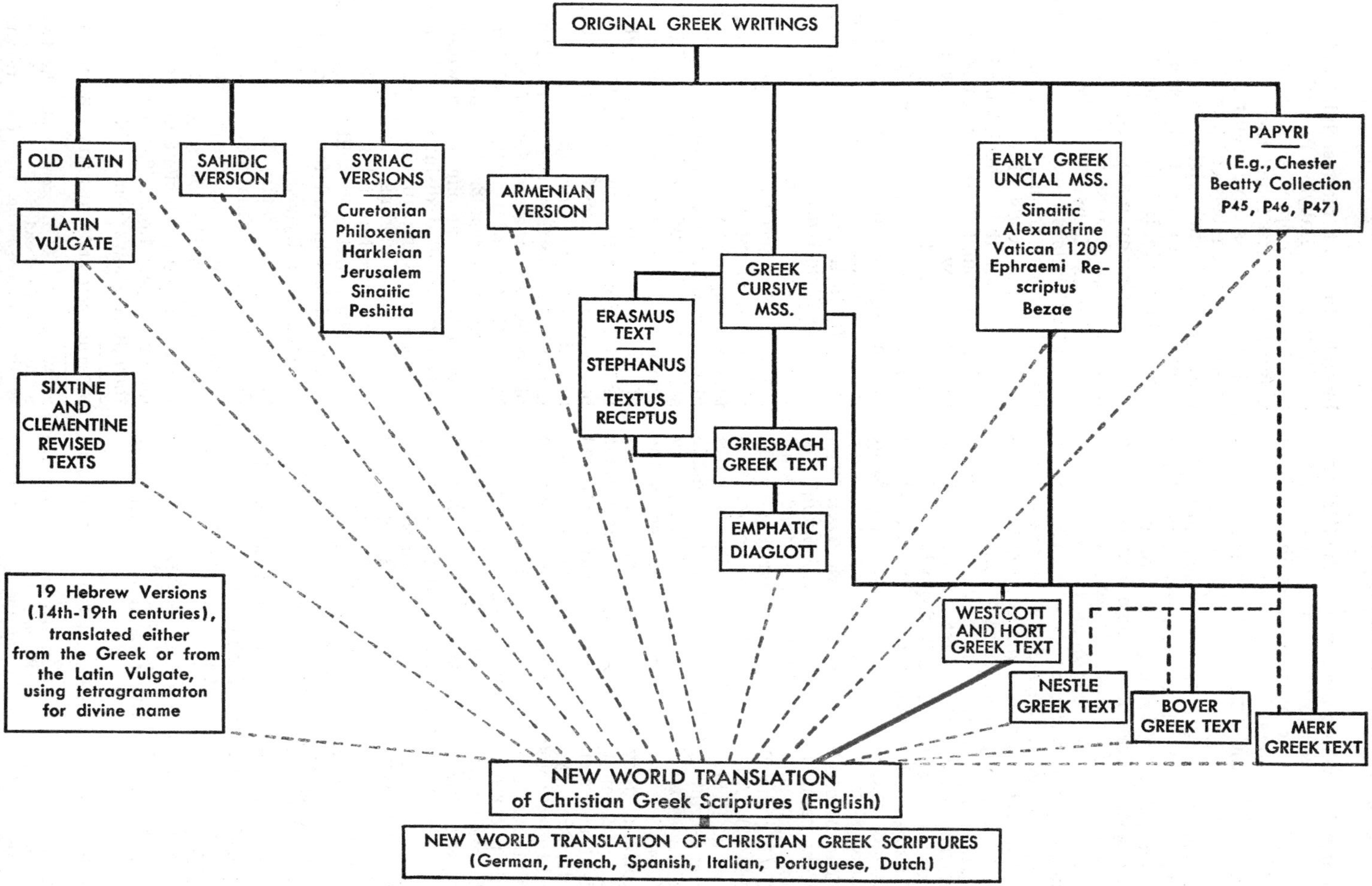

ORIGINAL GREEK WRITINGS
OLD LATIN
LATIN VULGATE
SIXTINE AND CLEMENTINE REVISED TEXTS
SAHIDIC VERSION
SYRIAC VERSIONS
Curetonian
Philoxenian
Harkleian
Jerusalem
Sinaitic
Peshitta
ARMENIAN VERSION
ERASMUS TEXT
STEPHANUS
TEXTUS RECEPTUS
GREEK CURSIVE MSS.
GRIESBACH GREEK TEXT
EMPHATIC DIAGLOTT
EARLY GREEK UNCIAL MSS.
Sinaitic
Alexandrine
Vatican 1209
Ephraemi Re-scriptus
Bezae
PAPYRI
(E.g., Chester Beatty Collection P45, P46, P47)
19 Hebrew Versions (14th-19th centuries), translated either from the Greek or from the Latin Vulgate, using tetragrammaton for divine name
WESTCOTT AND HORT GREEK TEXT
NESTLE GREEK TEXT
BOVER GREEK TEXT
MERK GREEK TEXT
NEW WORLD TRANSLATION of Christian Greek Scriptures (English)
NEW WORLD TRANSLATION OF CHRISTIAN GREEK SCRIPTURES (German, French, Spanish, Italian, Portuguese, Dutch)

note of points where the sense of the Scripture verses is involved. Most of these corrections made in the Masorah are noted in the *New World Translation*.[a]

19 **The Consonantal Text.** The Hebrew alphabet is made up of twenty-two consonants, with no vowels. Originally the reader had to supply the vowel sounds from his knowledge of the language. Hebrew writing was like an abbreviated script. Even in modern English there are many standard abbreviations that people use wherein only consonants appear. For example, there is *ltd.* as an abbreviation for *limited.* Similarly, the Hebrew language comprised a series of words made up only of consonants. Thus, by "consonantal text" we mean the Hebrew text without any vowel markings. The consonantal text of the Hebrew manuscripts became fixed in form between the first and second centuries A.D. Alterations were no longer made, as in the previous period of the *sopherim.*

20 **The Masoretic Text: Western Text.** The Hebrew name for the Masoretes, *Baalei Hamasorah,* means literally "lords of tradition." Following the Targum-Talmud writing period of 100-500 (A.D.), it was the Masoretes who served as Hebrew scholars and scribal copyists of manuscripts till about 900 (A.D.). They made no changes whatsoever in the texts that they handled, but recorded marginal notes in the Masorah as they saw fit. They exercised great care to take no textual liberties. The Masoretes devised a system of markings called "vowel points," and by these vowel points they indicated the vowel sounds as handed down by oral tradition. A system of accent marks further assured correct pronunciation. The Hebrew text now presented in printed editions of the Hebrew Bible is known as the "Masoretic Text." The name derives from the Palestinian or Western Masoretes who produced the manuscripts of this text together with its marginal notes, the Masorah. Footnotes in the *New World Translation,* First Edition, refer many times to the Masoretic Text, under the symbol "M."

21 **The Eastern (Babylonian) Text.** During the past hundred years archaeological finds, and especially those at the Old Cairo Genizah, have brought to light manuscripts and fragments containing the Babylonian or Eastern text of the Hebrew Scriptures. A number of these manuscripts have found their way to libraries in Russia. Claims have been made that some of these date from between the sixth and ninth centuries, but such claims are not generally accepted. Others are to be seen, also, in libraries in Berlin, Britain and the United States.

22 Of the many manuscripts of the Eastern text catalogued, one of the most important is the Codex Babylonicus Petropolitanus of A.D. 916. Scholars have eagerly examined this line of textual transmission, to see whether there are any wide differences in renderings from those of the Palestinian Masoretic text, and have found that the variations are remarkably few in number. For example, the Babylonian text of Ezekiel shows only sixteen real variations. Likewise, the British Museum has a copy of the Babylonian text of the Pentateuch, which has been found to be substantially in full agreement with the Masoretic text. The *New World Translation* makes reference to this text.[b]

23 **Dead Sea Scrolls.** In the year 1947 an exciting new chapter in Hebrew manuscript history was opened with the discovery in a cave at Qumran, in the Dead Sea area, of the Isaiah scroll, together with other non-Biblical scrolls. Shortly thereafter a complete photostatic copy of this well-preserved Isaiah scroll was published for scholars to study. It is reckoned to be of the second or first century B.C.E. Here, indeed, was an incredible find—a Hebrew manuscript one thousand years older than the oldest extant manuscript of the recognized Masoretic text of Isaiah! In 1952 other caves in Qumran surrendered further quantities of ancient scrolls, among which were some seventy tightly rolled, disintegrating Bible scrolls. In 1956 the Qumran Cave No. 11 gave up a scroll of the Psalms. Experts are now busy, carefully unrolling all these Bible scrolls. It is promised that these will later be photostated and published in full for scholars to examine.

24 One authority reports that his investigation of the lengthy Psalm 119 in this Dead Sea Scroll of the Psalms shows it to be in almost complete verbal agreement with the Masoretic text of Psalm 119. Other glimpses of this remarkable find of ancient manuscripts indicate no great variations. The Isaiah scroll itself, though it shows some differences in spelling

a See footnotes at Genesis 16:5; 18:3; Leviticus 11:42; Numbers 33:8 and Deuteronomy 3:20, *NW,* 1953 Edition, also pages 396-398, 417-419, of the Appendix of the 1960 Edition.

b See footnote at Ezekiel 6:14, *NW,* 1960 Edition.

19. What is the Hebrew consonantal text, and when did it become fixed in form?
20. What is the Masoretic text, and how is it referred to in the *New World Translation?*
21, 22. (a) What manuscripts of the Babylonian text have become available? (b) How does this text compare with the Masoretic text?
23. What series of Hebrew manuscript finds has been made near the Dead Sea?
24. How do these manuscripts compare with the Masoretic text, and what use does the *New World Translation* make of them?

and in grammatical construction, does not vary as to doctrinal points. The published Isaiah scroll was examined as to its variations in the preparation of the *New World Translation,* and references are made to it.[a]

25 The major lines of transmission of the Hebrew Scriptures have now been discussed. Principally, these are the Samaritan Pentateuch, the Aramaic Targums, the Greek *Septuagint Version,* the Western (Masoretic) Hebrew text, the Eastern (Babylonian) Hebrew text, and the Hebrew text of the Dead Sea Scrolls. As a result of study and comparison of these texts, we are assured that the Hebrew Scriptures have come down to us, in this twentieth century, substantially in the form in which inspired servants of God first wrote them down.

THE REFINED HEBREW TEXT

26 It was not until the end of the eighteenth century that scholars began to make a critical study of the Hebrew text. In 1776-1780 Bishop Kennicott published at Oxford the readings of no less than 634 Hebrew manuscripts. Then in 1784-1788 the Italian scholar De Rossi published collations (comparisons) of 825 more manuscripts. Hebrew scholar Baer, of Germany, also produced a master text. In more recent times, C. D. Ginsburg devoted many years to producing a critical master text of the Hebrew Bible. This first appeared in 1894, with a final revision in 1926. The New World Bible Translation Committee consulted the valuable 1926 edition of the Ginsburg text in preparing its English version of the Hebrew Scriptures, and the Ginsburg text was followed as the main reading in several places.[b] Joseph Rotherham used the 1894 edition of this text in producing his excellent English translation, *The Emphasised Bible,* in 1902, and Professor Max L. Margolis and co-workers used the texts of Ginsburg and of the German scholar Baer in producing their translation of the Hebrew Scriptures in 1917.

27 In 1906 Hebrew scholar Rudolph Kittel released in Germany the first edition (and later, a second edition) of his refined Hebrew text entitled *Biblia Hebraica,* or "The Hebrew Bible." In this book Kittel offered a textual study through an extended footnote service, collating or comparing the many Hebrew manuscripts of the Masoretic text available at that time. He used the generally accepted Ben Chayyim text as the basic text. When the far older, superior Ben Asher Masoretic texts, which had been standardized about A.D. 930, became available, Kittel set out to produce an entirely different third edition of the *Biblia Hebraica.* This work was completed by his associates after his death. Twelve editions of Kittel's monumental work had appeared up until 1961.

28 Kittel's *Biblia Hebraica,* the 7th, 8th and 9th editions (1951-1955), provided the basic text used for the Hebrew section of the *New World Translation* in English. This translation thus not only offers an accurate rendering of the most widely recognized, reliable Hebrew text, but also makes available in its footnotes of the first edition invaluable collations (comparisons) presented in Kittel's footnotes on important variations in the Hebrew text.

29 Kittel's presentation of the full Masorah, which captures all the many textual alterations of pre-Christian scribes, has enabled the *New World Translation* to restore these as part of the Hebrew text itself, thus to become part of the translated English text. This has brought about further restorations of the divine name, Jehovah. A vast field of Biblical scholarship has therefore been made available through the *New World Translation's* use of the *Biblia Hebraica.*

30 Accompanying this Study is a chart that sets out the sources for the text of the Hebrew Scriptures in the *New World Translation.* This chart briefly shows the development of the Hebrew text leading to Kittel's *Biblia Hebraica,* which was the main source used. The secondary sources that were consulted are shown by the dotted lines. This is not intended to indicate that in the case of such versions as the *Latin Vulgate* and the *Septuagint* the original works were consulted. In such cases, as with the inspired Hebrew writings themselves, the originals are not now extant. These sources were consulted by means of reliable editions of the texts, or from dependable ancient translations and critical commentaries. By consulting these various sources the New World Bible Translation Committee was able to present an authoritative and reliable version of the original inspired Hebrew Scriptures. These sources are all

a See footnotes DSIa, at Isaiah 3:17; 7:14 and 21:16, *NW,* 1958 Edition.
b See footnotes at Leviticus 11:42 and Joshua 21:37, *NW,* 1953 Edition.

25. What Hebrew texts have now been discussed, and of what does their study assure us?
26. (a) When did critical study of the Hebrew text begin, and what was its object? (b) How has the Ginsburg text been of outstanding use?
27, 28. (a) What is the *Biblia Hebraica,* and how has it been developed? (b) How has the *New World Translation* used this text?
29. What feature of the *Biblia Hebraica* was of particular value in restoring the divine name?
30. (a) Using the accompanying chart showing sources for the text of the *New World Translation of the Hebrew Scriptures,* trace the history of the Hebrew text through to the *Biblia Hebraica* as the main source of the *New World Translation.* (b) What are some of the other sources to which the New World Bible Translation Committee made reference, and how are these sources related to the original Hebrew text?

indicated in the footnotes of the first editions of the *New World Translation*.

31 The *New World Translation of the Hebrew Scriptures* is thus a result of age-long Biblical scholarship and research. It is founded on a text of great integrity, and is the richly endowed product of faithful textual transmission. With a flow and style that are arresting, it offers a translation that is at once honest and accurate. Thanks be to Jehovah, the communicating God, that His Word is more alive, and exerts greater power today, than ever before in the history of mankind! (Heb. 4:12) May men of goodwill continue to build faith through the study of God's precious Word, and be aroused to do Jehovah's will during these momentous days. —2 Pet. 1:12, 13.

31. (a) Of what, therefore, is the *New World Translation of the Hebrew Scriptures* the result? (b) What thanks and hope may we thus express?

SOME LEADING PAPYRUS MANUSCRIPTS

Symbol	Name of Manuscript	Date	Language	Located At	Approximate Contents	Illustrations of Use in *New World Translation*. (See footnotes in the separate volumes for scriptures cited.)
OF THE HEBREW SCRIPTURES						
	Nash Papyrus	2d or 1st cent. B.C.E.	Hebrew	Cambridge, England	Fragments of Deuteronomy, chapters 5, 6	
957	Rylands 458	2d cent. B.C.E.	Greek	Manchester, England	Fragments of Deuteronomy, chapters 23-28	Foreword to Christian Greek Scriptures, page 12, footnote "a."
	Fouad 266	2d or 1st cent. B.C.E.	Greek	Cairo, Egypt	Deuteronomy, chapters 18, 20, 24, 25, 31, 32	Deut. 18:5; 25:15; Foreword to Christian Greek Scriptures, pages 12-14.
DSIa	Isaiah Scroll	2d or 1st cent. B.C.E.	Hebrew	Jerusalem	Isaiah	Isa. 3:17; 7:14
	Aquila fragment	2d cent. A.D.	Greek	Cambridge, England	1 Kings 20: 7-17; 2 Kings 23: 11-27; parts of Psalms	1 Ki. 20:13; Ps. 22:23; 91:2
	Fragment of Septuagint	1st cent. A.D.	Greek	Published by L'Ecole Pratique d'Etudes Biblique, Paris, France	Micah 4:3-7; Habakkuk 1:14–2:5; 2:13-15	Mic. 4:4 (See reference to Appendix on footnote "c.")
963	Chester Beatty 6	2d cent. A.D.	Greek	Part at Ann Arbor, Michigan, U.S.A.	Portions of Numbers and Deuteronomy	
OF THE CHRISTIAN GREEK SCRIPTURES						
P1	Oxyrhynchus 2	3d cent. A.D.	Greek	Philadelphia, Pa., U.S.A.	Parts of Matthew chapter 1	
P22	Oxyrhynchus 1228	3d cent. A.D.	Greek	Glasgow, Scotland	Fragments of John chapters 15, 16	
P37	Michigan 1570	3d cent. A.D.	Greek	Ann Arbor, Mich., U.S.A.	Parts of Matthew chapter 26	
P45	Chester Beatty 1	3d cent. A.D.	Greek	Dublin, Ireland; Vienna, Austria	Fragments of Matthew, Mark, Luke, John, Acts	Luke 10:42; John 10:18
P46	Chester Beatty 2	3d cent. A.D.	Greek	Dublin, Ireland; Ann Arbor, Mich., U.S.A.	Nine of Paul's letters	Rom. 8:28; 1 Cor. 2:16
P47	Chester Beatty 3	3d cent. A.D.	Greek	Dublin, Ireland	Revelation 9:10–17:2	Rev. 13:18; 15:3
P52	Rylands 457	2d cent. A.D.	Greek	Manchester, England	John 18:31-33, 37, 38	
P66	Bodmer 2	c. A.D. 200	Greek	Geneva, Switzerland	John 1:1–6:11; 6:35–14:26	
P72	Bodmer 7, 8	3d cent. A.D.	Greek	Geneva, Switzerland	Jude, 1 and 2 Peter	
P75	Bodmer 14, 15	c. A.D. 200	Greek	Geneva, Switzerland	Luke 3:18–18:18; 22:4–John 15:8 (with gaps)	

SOME LEADING VELLUM MANUSCRIPTS

Symbol	Name of Manuscript	Date	Language	Located At	Approximate Contents	Illustrations of Use in *New World Translation.* (See footnotes in the separate volumes for scriptures cited.)
OF THE HEBREW SCRIPTURES (IN HEBREW)						
	Aleppo Sephardic Codex	c. A.D. 930	Hebrew	Formerly at Aleppo, Syria. Now in Israel.	Hebrew Scriptures (Model Ben Asher Text)	Foreword to Hebrew Scriptures, Vol. I, page 19.
	British Museum Codex Or4445	10th cent. A.D.	Hebrew	London, England	Pentateuch	
Ca	Cairo Karaite Codex	c. A.D. 895	Hebrew	Cairo, Egypt	Earlier and Later Prophets	Josh. 21:37; 2 Sam. 8:3
B 19A	Leningrad Codex	A.D. 1008	Hebrew	Leningrad, Russia	Hebrew Scriptures	Josh. 21:37; 2 Sam. 8:3
B_3	Codex Babylonicus Petropolitanus	A.D. 916	Hebrew	Leningrad, Russia	Later Prophets	Ezek. 6:14
OF THE SEPTUAGINT AND CHRISTIAN GREEK SCRIPTURES						
ℵ	Sinaiticus	4th cent. A.D.	Greek	London, England	Part of Hebrew Scriptures and all of Greek Scriptures, some apocryphal writings	1 Chron. 12:19; John 5:3; 2 Cor. 12:4
A	Alexandrinus	5th cent. A.D.	Greek	London, England	All of Hebrew and Greek Scriptures (some small portions lost or damaged), and some apocryphal writings	1 Ki. 14:2; Acts 13:20; Heb. 3:6
B	Vatican 1209	4th cent. A.D.	Greek	Vatican City	Originally complete Bible. Now missing: Gen. 1:1–46:28; Ps. 106–138; latter part of Hebrews after 9:14, 2 Timothy, Titus, Philemon, Revelation	1 Chron. 7:34; John 1:18; 7:52
C	Ephraemi Rescriptus	5th cent. A.D.	Greek	Paris, France	Parts of Hebrew Scriptures (64 leaves) and portions of all books of the Greek Scriptures except 2 Thessalonians and 2 John (145 out of 238 original leaves of codex)	Acts 8:36; Rom. 16:23
D	Bezae (Cantabrigiensis)	5th or 6th cent. A.D.	Greek-Latin	Cambridge, England	Most of four Gospels and Acts, few verses of 3 John	Matt. 18:22
D_2	Bezae (Claromontanus)	6th cent. A.D.	Greek-Latin	Paris, France	Pauline Epistles (including Hebrews)	Gal. 5:12 (Reference is shown just to symbol "D.")

Study Six—
The Christian Greek Text of The Holy Scriptures

The copying of the text of the Greek Scriptures, and its transmission in Greek and other languages to this day; the reliability of the modern text.

THE early Christians were worldwide educators and publishers of the written 'word of Jehovah.' They took seriously Jesus' words made just before his ascension: "You will receive power when the holy spirit arrives upon you, and you will be witnesses of me both in Jerusalem and in all Judea and Samaria and to the most distant part of the earth." (Acts 1:8) As Jesus had foretold, the first 120 disciples received the holy spirit, with its energizing force, on the day of Pentecost, A.D. 33. That same day, Peter spearheaded the new educational program by giving thorough witness, with the result that many heartily embraced the message, and about three thousand more were added to the newly founded Christian congregation.—Acts 2:14-42.

2 Stirred as no other group had been in all history, these disciples of Jesus Christ launched a teaching program that overflowed into every corner of the then-known world. Yes, these devoted witnesses of Jehovah were eager to use their feet, walking from house to house, from city to city, and from country to country, declaring "good news of good things!" (Rom. 10:15) This "good news" told about Christ's ransom provision, the resurrection hope and the promised kingdom of God. (1 Cor. 15:1-3, 20-22, 50; Jas. 2:5) Never before had such a witness concerning things unseen been presented to mankind, so that it became an "evident demonstration of realities though not beheld," a display of *faith,* to the many who now accepted Jehovah as their Sovereign God on the basis of Jesus' sacrifice.—Heb. 11:1; 1 Tim. 1:14-17.

3 These Christian ministers, men and women, were enlightened ministers of God. They could read and write. They were educated in the Holy Scriptures. They were people informed as to world happenings. They were accustomed to travel. They were locust-like in that they permitted no obstacle to hinder their forward movement in spreading the good news. (Acts 2:7-11, 41; Joel 2:7-11, 25) In that first century of the Common Era, they worked among people who were in many ways very much like people of the twentieth century.

4 As progressive preachers of "the word of life," the early Christians made good use of whatever Bible scrolls they could obtain. (Phil. 2:15, 16; 2 Tim. 4:13) Four of them, namely, Matthew, Mark, Luke and John, were inspired by Jehovah to put "the good news about Jesus Christ" into writing. (Mark 1:1; Matt. 1:1) Some of them, such as Peter, Paul, John, James and Jude, wrote letters under inspiration. (2 Pet. 3:15, 16) Others became copyists of these inspired communications, and these were interchanged with benefit among the multiplying congregations. (Col. 4:16) Further, "the apostles and older men in Jerusalem" made doctrinal pronouncements that received the witness of God's spirit and were recorded for later use. This central governing body also sent out letters of instruction to the far-flung congregations. (Acts 5:29-32; 15:2, 6, 22-29) And for this they had to provide their own mail service.

5 In order to expedite the distribution of the Scriptures, as well as provide them in a form convenient for reference, the early Christians soon started to use the codex form of manuscript in place of scrolls. The codex is similar in form to the modern book, in which the leaves may be turned readily in looking up a reference, whereas this might necessitate considerable unrolling in the case of a scroll. Moreover, the codex form made it possible to bind canonical writings together, whereas those in scroll form were usually kept in separate rolls. The early Christians were pioneers in the use of the codex. They may even have been its inventors. While the codex was only slowly adopted by non-Christian writers, the great majority of Christian papyri of the second and third centuries are in codex form.

6 **The Medium of Koiné Greek.** The so-called "classical period" of the Greek language ex-

---

1. How did the Christian educational program get started?
2. What "good news" was now proclaimed, and of what was this work of witnessing a demonstration?
3. What characterized the Christian ministers and the people of the first century?
4. Under Jehovah's inspiration and leading, what writing was done in the days of the early congregation?
5. (a) What is a codex? (b) To what extent did these Christians use the codex, and what were its advantages?
6. (a) What were the periods of the classical and the *koiné* Greek? (b) How and to what extent did *koiné* Greek come into general use?

tended from the ninth to the fourth centuries B.C.E. This was the period of the Attic and Ionic dialects. It was during this time, and especially in the fifth and fourth centuries B.C.E., that many Greek dramatists, poets, orators, historians, philosophers and scientists flourished, of whom Homer, Herodotus, Socrates, Plato and others became famous. The period from 330 B.C.E. to A.D. 330 marked the ascendancy of what is known as the *koiné*, or common, dialect of Greek. Its development was due largely to the military operations of Alexander the Great, whose army was made up of soldiers from all parts of Greece. These spoke different Greek dialects. Through the mingling of their dialects, a common dialect, the *koiné* Greek, developed and came into general use. Alexander's conquest of Egypt, and of Asia as far as India, spread the *koiné* Greek among many peoples. It became the international language, continuing as such for many centuries. *Koiné* Greek became the language of the *Septuagint*, which was translated from the Hebrew in Alexandria, Egypt, during the third and second centuries B.C.E.

7 In the days of Jesus and the apostles, *koiné* Greek was the international language of the Roman realm. The Bible itself testifies to this fact. When Jesus was nailed to the stake, it was necessary for the inscription over his head to be posted not only in Hebrew, the language of the Jews, but also in Latin, the official language of the land, and in Greek, which was spoken on the streets of Jerusalem almost as frequently as in Rome, Alexandria or Athens itself. (John 19:20; Acts 6:1) Acts 9:29 shows that Paul preached the good news in Jerusalem to Jews who spoke the Greek language. *Koiné* Greek was a dynamic, living, well-developed tongue—a language ready at hand and well suited for Jehovah's purpose in further communicating the divine Word.

THE GREEK TEXT AND ITS TRANSMISSION

8 In the preceding study, we learned that Jehovah preserved his 'waters of truth' in a reservoir of written documents—the inspired Hebrew Scriptures. However, what of the Scriptures written down by the apostles and other disciples of Jesus Christ? Have these been preserved for us with like care? An examination of the vast reservoir of manuscripts preserved in the *koiné* Greek and its versions into other languages shows that they have. As already explained, this part of the Bible canon comprises twenty-seven books. Consider the lines of textual transmission of these twenty-seven books, showing how the original Greek text has been preserved down to this present day.

9 **The Fountain of Greek Manuscripts.** The entire catalogue of twenty-seven canonical Greek Scripture books was written in the *koiné* Greek of the day. However, the book of Matthew was apparently written first in Biblical Hebrew, to serve the Jewish people. The fourth-century Bible translator Jerome confirms this, and says that it was later translated into the Greek.[a] Matthew himself probably made this translation, he, without doubt, knowing Hebrew, Latin and Greek, having been a Roman civil servant, a tax collector.—Mark 2:14-17.

10 The other Christian Bible writers, Mark, Luke, John, Paul, Peter, James and Jude, all wrote their documents in the *koiné* Greek, the common, living language that was understood by the Christians and most other people of the first century. The last of the original documents was written by John about A.D. 98. As far as is known, none of these twenty-seven original manuscripts in *koiné* Greek have survived to this day. However, from this original fountainhead, there have flowed to us copies of the originals, copies of copies and families of copies, to form a vast reservoir of manuscripts of the Christian Greek Scriptures.

11 **A Reservoir of 13,600 Manuscripts.** A tremendous fund of manuscript copies of all twenty-seven canonical books is available today. Some of these cover extensive portions of Scripture; others are mere fragments. According to one authority, there are more than 4,600 manuscripts in the original Greek.[b] In addition there are over 8,000 manuscripts in Latin and about 1,000 in other languages—a total exceeding 13,600 manuscripts all together. Dating from the second to the fifteenth centuries, they all help in determining the true, original text. The oldest of these many manuscripts is the papyrus fragment of the Gospel of John in the John Rylands Library in Manchester, England, known by the number P^{52}, and which is dated about A.D. 150. Thus this copy was written only some fifty years after the original. When we consider that for ascertaining the text of most classical authors only a handful of manuscripts are available, and seldom within centuries of the original writings, we can appreciate what a wealth of

a See Bible Book Number 40, paragraphs 6 and 7.
b *The New Bible Dictionary*, 1962, J. D. Douglas, page 1264.

7. (a) How does the Bible testify to the use of *koiné* Greek in the time of Jesus and his apostles? (b) Why was it well suited for communicating God's Word?
8. Why do we now examine the reservoir of Greek Scripture manuscripts?
9. (a) In what language were the Christian Scriptures written? (b) What exception is noted with Matthew?
10. How have the Bible writings come down to us?
11. (a) What fund of manuscript copies is available today? (b) How do these contrast with classical works as to quantity and age?

evidence there is to assist in arriving at an authoritative text of the Christian Greek Scriptures.

12 **Papyrus Manuscripts.** As with early copies of the *Septuagint,* the first manuscripts of the Christian Greek Scriptures were written on papyrus, and this continued to be used for Bible manuscripts until about A.D. 300. The Bible writers also apparently used papyrus when they sent letters to the Christian congregations.

13 Great quantities of papyrus writings have been located in the province of Fayum, in Egypt. Papyri were first discovered there in 1778. In 1891 a further quantity of papyri from Egypt's Fayum was acquired by the British Museum. One of the most important of all modern-day manuscript finds was a papyri discovery made public in 1931. It consisted of portions of eleven codices, containing portions of eight different books of the inspired Hebrew Scriptures and fifteen books of the Greek Scriptures, all in Greek. These papyri range in date of writing from the second to the fourth century of the Common Era. Much of the Christian Greek Scripture portions of this find are now in the Chester Beatty Collections and are listed as P^{45}, P^{46} and P^{47}, the symbol "P" standing for "Papyrus."

14 The table just preceding this study lists some of the outstanding ancient Bible papyri of the Hebrew and Christian Greek Scriptures. In the last column there are cited passages in the *New World Translation of the Holy Scriptures* where these papyri manuscripts give support to the renderings made, as indicated also in the footnotes of the first edition.

15 These papyri discoveries supply proof that the Bible canon was completed at a very early date. A codex (P^{45}) among the Chester Beatty papyri binding together the four Gospels and Acts, and another (P^{46}) bringing within the lids of one codex nine of the fourteen letters of Paul, show that the inspired Christian Greek Scriptures were assembled shortly after the death of the apostles. Since these codices had circulated widely and found their way down into Egypt by the early part of the third century, it is apparent that these Scriptures had been collected into their standard form by the second century, at the latest. Thus with the second century there must have come the closing of the canon of the Christian Greek Scriptures, the completion of the canon of the entire Bible.

12. On what were the first manuscripts written?
13. What important papyrus find was made public in 1931?
14, 15. (a) What are some outstanding papyri of the Greek Scriptures listed in the table on page 312? (b) Indicate how the *New World Translation* has made use of these. (c) What do the early papyrus codices prove?

16 **Vellum Manuscripts.** As we learned in the previous study, the more durable vellum, a fine grade of calfskin, began to be used in place of papyrus in writing manuscripts from the fourth century on. The most important Bible manuscripts known to exist today are recorded on vellum. We have already discussed the vellum manuscripts of the Hebrew Scriptures. The table on page 313 lists some of the outstanding vellum manuscripts for both the Christian Greek and the Hebrew Scriptures. Those listed of the Greek Scriptures were written entirely in capital letters and are referred to as "uncials." *The New Bible Dictionary* reports 241 uncial manuscripts of the Christian Greek Scriptures, and these date from the fourth to the tenth century. Then there are the more than 4,360 "cursive" manuscripts, made in a running style of writing.[a] These, also on vellum, were written from the ninth to the fifteenth century. The "uncial" manuscripts are very reliable, and were extensively used by the New World Bible Translation Committee in making accurate renderings from the Greek text. This is indicated in the table of Leading Vellum Manuscripts.

ERA OF TEXTUAL CRITICISM AND REFINING

17 **Erasmus' Text.** Throughout the long centuries of the "dark ages," when the Latin language dominated and Western Europe was under the iron control of the Roman Catholic Hierarchy, scholarship and learning were at a low ebb. However, with the European invention of printing from movable type in the fifteenth century and the Reformation of the early sixteenth century, the shackles were broken and there was a rebirth of interest in Greek learning and Biblical matters. It was during this early revival of learning that the famous Dutch scholar Desiderius Erasmus produced his first edition of a master Greek text of the "New Testament." This was printed in Basel, Switzerland, in 1516, one year before the Reformation started in Germany. The first edition had many errors, but an improved text was presented in succeeding editions in 1519, 1522, 1527 and 1535. Erasmus had, at the most, only eight late cursive manuscripts available to him for collating and preparing his master text.

18 Erasmus' refined Greek text became the basis for better translations into several of

a *The New Bible Dictionary,* 1962, J. D. Douglas, page 1264.

16. (a) What vellum manuscripts have survived to this day? (b) To what extent have the "uncial" manuscripts been used in the *New World Translation,* and why?
17. (a) What two events led to increased study of the Greek text of the Bible? (b) For what work is Erasmus noted?
18. What did Erasmus' text make possible, and who made good use of it?

the Western European languages. This made possible the production of versions superior to those that had been translated previously from the Latin *Vulgate.* First to use the Erasmus text was Martin Luther of Germany, who completed his translation of the Christian Greek Scriptures into German in 1522. In the face of much persecution, William Tyndale of England followed with his English translation from the Erasmus text, completing this while in exile on the continent of Europe in 1525. Brucioli of Italy translated Erasmus' text into Italian in 1532. With the advent of Erasmus' Greek text, there was now opening up an era of textual criticism and better Bible translations.

19 **Division into Chapters and Verses.** Robert Estienne, or Stephanus, of Paris, was prominent as a printer and editor in the sixteenth century. Being an editor, he saw the practical benefit of using a system of chapters and verses for ready reference, and so introduced this system in his Greek-Latin New Testament in 1551. Verse divisions were first made for the Hebrew Scriptures in 1448, but it was Stephanus' Latin Bible of 1555 that first showed the present divisions for the complete Bible. This was followed in subsequent English-language Bibles and made possible the production of Bible concordances such as that by Alexander Cruden in 1737, and the two exhaustive concordances to the Authorized Version of the English Bible—Robert Young's, first published in Edinburgh in 1873, and James Strong's, published in New York in 1894.

20 **The "Received Text."** Stephanus also issued several editions of the Greek "New Testament." This was based mainly on Erasmus' text, with corrections according to the Complutensian Polyglott of 1522 and fifteen late cursive manuscripts of the previous few centuries. Stephanus' third edition of his Greek text in 1550 became in effect the *textus receptus* (Latin for "received text") upon which were based the many other early English versions, including the *Authorized Version* of 1611.

21 **Refined Greek Texts.** Other Greek scholars produced increasingly refined texts. Outstanding was that produced by J. J. Griesbach, who had access to the hundreds of Greek manuscripts that had become available toward the end of the eighteenth century. The chief edition of Griesbach's entire Greek text was published in 1796-1806. His master text was the basis for Sharpe's English translation in 1840, and is the Greek text printed in *The Emphatic Diaglott,* first published complete in 1865. Other excellent texts were produced by Count Constantine Tischendorf (1872) and Hermann von Soden (1910), the latter serving as the basis for Moffatt's English version of 1913.

22 **Westcott and Hort Text.** The Greek master text that has reached the highest universal acceptance is that produced by the Cambridge University scholars, Bishop B. F. Westcott and Professor F. J. A. Hort, in 1881. Proofs of Westcott and Hort's Greek text were consulted by the British Revision Committee, of which Westcott and Hort were members, for their revision of the New Testament of 1881. This is the master text that underlies the 1950 and 1961 editions of the *New World Translation* of the Christian Greek Scriptures, thus assuring the greatest possible accuracy. This text is also the foundation for the following translations into English: *Rotherham* (1897), the *American Standard* (1901), *Goodspeed* (1923 and 1948) and the *Revised Standard Version* (1946). This last translation also used Nestle's text.

23 Nestle's Greek text (the eighteenth edition, 1948) was also used by the New World Bible Translation Committee for the purpose of comparison. The Committee also referred to those by Catholic Jesuit scholars Joseph M. Bover (1943) and Augustinus Merk (1948).[a]

24 **Ancient Versions from the Greek.** In addition to the Greek manuscripts, there are also available for study today many manuscripts of translations of the Christian Greek Scriptures into other languages. Some thirty-eight of these are in Old Latin and there are about 8,000 of Jerome's Latin *Vulgate* translation. The New World Bible Translation Committee referred to these, as well as to the Sahidic, Armenian and Syriac versions.[b]

25 From the fourteenth century onward, translations of the Greek Scriptures into the Hebrew language have been produced. These are of interest in that a number of them have made restorations of the divine name into

---

a See footnote references to Appendix at Matthew 1:1 and 1 John 5:8; also footnote on James 1:12, *NW*, 1950 Edition.

b See footnotes at Luke 24:40; Acts 26:5; Colossians 2:18; James 1:26; Matthew 23:13; Acts 7:53; John 5:3; Acts 15:33; 19:23; 2 John 11; Matthew 16:2; Acts 27:37; Revelation 3:16; 16:13, *NW*, 1950 Edition.

---

19. What is the history of chapter and verse division, and what has this made possible?
20. What was the "Received Text," and for what did it become the basis?
21. What refined texts have been produced since the eighteenth century, and how have they been used?
22. (a) What Greek text has reached the highest universal acceptance? (b) As a basis for what English translations has it been used?
23. What other texts were used for the *New World Translation?*
24. To what ancient versions has the *New World Translation* also referred? What are some examples?
25. Of what special interest are the Hebrew language versions that are referred to in the *New World Translation?*

the Christian Scriptures. The *New World Translation* makes many references to these Hebrew versions under the symbols J[1] to J[19]. For details, see the Foreword of the *New World Translation of the Christian Greek Scriptures,* 1950 Edition, pages 30 to 33.

TEXTUAL VARIATIONS AND THEIR MEANING

26 Among the more than 13,600 manuscripts of the Christian Greek Scriptures there are many textual variations. The 4,600 manuscripts in the Greek language alone show many such differences. On the basis of similar differences, these manuscripts were first divided into three main families, these families relating to the three general locations where these texts originated, namely, the Alexandrian, the Byzantine and the Caesarean areas. A fourth family, named the "Western," was later identified. We can well understand that copies made from early manuscripts would contain each its own distinctive scribal errors, and that these errors would be recopied in the area to which a manuscript was sent, thus becoming characteristic of other manuscripts in that area. It was in this way that families of similar manuscripts grew up. However, are not the thousands of scribal errors to be viewed with alarm? Do they not indicate lack of faithfulness in the transmission of the text? Not at all!

27 Dr. Hort, who was co-producer of the Westcott and Hort text, says that "variations are but secondary incidents of a fundamentally single and identical text. . . . The great bulk of the words of the New Testament stand out above all discriminative processes of criticism, because they are free from variation, and need only to be transcribed. If comparative trivialities . . . are set aside, the words in our opinion still subject to doubt can hardly amount to more than a thousandth part of the whole New Testament."[a] Since the Westcott and Hort Greek text contains approximately 140,000 words, and it is only one word in a thousand that brings serious textual difficulties, this means that there were only 140 places in the entire Greek text where Westcott and Hort had to handle major textual problems. This is only one tenth of one percent of textual corruption of the original Christian Greek Scriptures.

28 **Evaluation of Textual Transmission.** What, then, is the net evaluation as to textual integrity and authenticity, after these many centuries of textual transmission? Not only are there thousands of manuscripts to compare, but discoveries of older Bible manuscripts during the past few decades take the Greek text back as far as the year 150 (A.D.), just fifty years short of the death of the apostle John about A.D. 100. These manuscript evidences provide strong assurance that we now have a dependable Greek text in refined form. Note the evaluation that the former Director of the British Museum, Sir Frederic Kenyon, puts on this matter:

29 "The interval then between the dates of original composition and the earliest extant evidence becomes so small as to be in fact negligible, and the last foundation for any doubt that the Scriptures have come down to us substantially as they were written has now been removed. Both the *authenticity* and the *general integrity* of the books of the New Testament may be regarded as finally established. General integrity, however, is one thing, and certainty as to details is another."[b]

30 As to the last observation on "certainty as to details," the quotation in an earlier paragraph by Dr. Hort covers this. It is the work of the textual refiners to rectify such details, and this they have done to a large degree. For this reason, the Westcott and Hort refined Greek text is generally accepted as one of high excellence. The *New World Translation* of the Greek Scriptures, being based on this excellent Greek text, is thus able to give its readers the faithful "saying of Jehovah," as this has been so wonderfully preserved for us in the Greek reservoir of manuscripts. —1 Pet. 1:24, 25.

31 Of further interest are the comments of Sir Frederic Kenyon in his book, *Our Bible and the Ancient Manuscripts,* 1941, on page 179: "We must be content to know that the general authenticity of the New Testament text has been remarkably supported by the modern discoveries which have so greatly reduced the interval between the original autographs and our earliest extant manuscripts, and that the differences of reading, interesting as they are, do not affect the fundamental doctrines of the Christian faith." As shown on page 309 in the chart of "Sources for the New

---

a *The New Testament in the Original Greek,* 1935, Westcott and Hort, pages 564, 565.

b *The Bible and Archaeology,* 1940, pages 288, 289.

---

26. How did textual variations and manuscript families arise?
27. What assurance do we have as to the integrity of the Greek text?
28, 29. (a) What must be our net evaluation of the refined Greek text? (b) What authoritative statement do we have on this?
30. Why can we look with confidence to the *New World Translation* as providing for its readers the faithful "saying of Jehovah"?
31. (a) What have modern discoveries shown as to the text of the Greek Scriptures? (b) How does the chart on page 309 indicate the principal source for the *New World Translation of the Christian Greek Scriptures,* and what are some of the secondary sources that were used?

World Translation of the Christian Greek Scriptures," the *New World Translation* has drawn from numerous sources in order to present an accurately translated English text. Valuable footnotes back up all these faithful renderings. The *New World Translation* has made use of the cream of Bible scholarship of the centuries in producing its fine English translation. What confidence we may have today that the Christian Greek Scriptures, as they are now available to us, do indeed contain the "pattern of healthful words" as written down by the disciples of Jesus Christ! May we keep holding to these precious words in faith and in love!—2 Tim. 1:13.

32 Both this and the preceding study have been devoted to a discussion of the manuscripts and text of the Holy Scriptures. Why has this been given such exhaustive treatment? The purpose has been to show conclusively that the texts of both the Hebrew and the Greek Scriptures are essentially the same as the authentic, original text that Jehovah inspired faithful men of old to record. Those original writings were inspired. The copyists, though skilled, were not inspired. (Ps. 45:1; 2 Pet. 1:20, 21; 3:16) Hence it has been necessary to sift through the vast reservoir of manuscript copies, in order to identify clearly and unmistakably the pure "waters of truth" as they originally poured forth from the Great Fountainhead, Jehovah. All thanks goes to Jehovah for the marvelous gift of His Word, the inspired Bible, and the refreshing Kingdom message that flows forth from its pages!

32. Why has considerable space been devoted here to a discussion of the manuscripts and text of the Holy Scriptures, and with what satisfying result?

Study Seven— The Bible in Modern Times

The history of the Bible societies; the Watch Tower Society's work in printing and publishing Bibles; the production of the "New World Translation."

THE Holy Scriptures, in all the sixty-six inspired books that we know today as the Bible, contain the "word of Jehovah" put down in writing. (Isa. 66:5) Through many centuries this "word" flowed freely over the line of communication, from Jehovah to his prophets and servants on earth. These divine messages accomplished their immediate purpose, as well as giving powerful foregleams of events certain to take place in the then-distant future. It was not always required of God's prophets that they put down in writing the "word of Jehovah" that was relayed to them. For example, some of the utterances of Elijah and Elisha that were made for the generation of their time have not been preserved in written form. On the other hand, the prophets Moses, Isaiah, Jeremiah, Habakkuk and others received specific orders to 'write down,' or to 'write in a book or scroll' the "word of Jehovah" that was revealed to them. (Ex. 17:14; Isa. 30:8; Jer. 30:2; Hab. 2:2; Rev. 1:11) "The sayings previously spoken by the holy prophets" were thus preserved, along with other holy writings, to arouse the clear thinking faculties of Jehovah's servants, and especially to provide guidance concerning "the last days." —2 Pet. 3:1-3.

2 Much copying of the inspired Hebrew Scriptures was done from Ezra's time, and, again, from the first century of the Common Era the Bible was copied and recopied by the early Christians and used in witnessing concerning Jehovah's purposes with regard to his Christ throughout the length and breadth of the then-known world. With the invention of printing in the fifteenth century, further impetus was given to multiplying and distributing copies of the Bible. Much translation and printing were undertaken by private groups in the sixteenth and seventeenth centuries. As early as A.D. 1800 the Bible had appeared in whole or in part in seventy-one languages.

BIBLE SOCIETIES

3 Greater momentum was given this work in the nineteenth and twentieth centuries, when well-endowed Bible societies began to take a

1. (a) For what two purposes were divine communications given, and why therefore were some not recorded? (b) What specific orders did Jehovah give to many of the prophets, and with what benefit for "the last days"?

2. What periods in history have been noted for increased activity in Bible copying and translation?
3. What factor has greatly contributed to the increase in Bible distribution since the beginning of the nineteenth century?

hand in this gigantic task of distributing the Bible. One of the earliest of these Bible societies was the British and Foreign Bible Society, which was organized in London in 1804. This Society has expanded until today it has more than 5,000 "auxiliaries and branches" outside Britain, all of them sharing in a vast work of Bible distribution. The organizing of this Bible society was the signal for the establishment of many more such societies.[a]

4 With so many Bible societies operating, the work of spreading the Bible flourished. By the year 1900 the Bible had appeared in whole or in part in 567 languages, and by 1928 in 856 languages. By 1938 the 1,000-mark was passed, and now in the 1960's the Bible is represented in more than 1,180 languages. It is estimated that the total distribution of the Bible by all these societies has exceeded two billion copies. Jehovah's refreshing "word of life" has overspread all the earth! Thus it has become possible for men of all nations to answer the call: "Praise Jehovah, all you nations, and let all the peoples praise him." (Rom. 15:11) The chart on page 321 showing "Some Leading Bible Translations in Seven Principal Languages" gives further information on modern-day Bible distribution.

5 Though making the Bible available to the multitudes of the earth is a commendable work, yet the putting of these Bibles to use in giving the people Bible understanding is an even more important task. It was conveying "the sense" of the word that was important in Jewish and apostolic times, when few Bibles were available, and this is still the most important thing. (Matt. 13:23; Neh. 8:8) However, this work of teaching God's Word to the peoples of all the earth has been speeded up by the wide distribution of the Bible. As Jehovah's witnesses in this twentieth century press forward with their globe-encircling work of Bible education, they are grateful that many Bibles are now available in many lands and in many languages.

a Among the many Bible societies formed since 1804 are the following: the American Bible Society (1816), formed out of already existing local societies; the Edinburgh Bible Society (1809) and the Glasgow Bible Society (1812), both later incorporated (1861) into the National Bible Society of Scotland. By 1920 Bible societies had also been formed in Switzerland, Ireland, France, Finland, Sweden, Denmark, Norway, the Netherlands, Iceland, Russia and Germany.

4. (a) What statistics prove that the "word of life" has indeed overspread the earth? (b) What helpful information is supplied on the chart on page 321 about the different Bible versions listed? Illustrate this by reference to some specific Bible version.
5. What is even more important than Bible distribution, yet for what are Jehovah's witnesses thankful?

JEHOVAH'S WITNESSES AS BIBLE PUBLISHERS

6 Jehovah's witnesses are a Bible-publishing people. This was so in the days of Ezra. It was so in the days of the early disciples of Jesus Christ, who saturated the ancient world with their handwritten copies of the Bible—to such an extent that the rich legacy we have received of their manuscript writings surpasses that of any other ancient literature. Now, in these modern times, the same kind of energetic Bible-publishing activity characterizes the witnesses of Jehovah.

7 It was in the year 1884 that Jehovah's witnesses obtained a charter for carrying on their Bible-publishing work, the corporation then formed being now known as the Watch Tower Bible and Tract Society of Pennsylvania. At first Bibles were purchased from other Bible societies for redistribution by these witnesses, who were even then developing their characteristic house-to-house ministry. The *Authorized (King James) Version* of 1611 in English was used as their basic version for Bible study.

8 True to its name, the Watch Tower Bible and Tract Society has engaged in distributing Bibles, as well as publishing books, tracts and other Christian literature. This has been for the purpose of instruction in the correct teachings of God's Word. Its Bible education has helped lovers of righteousness to cut loose from false religious tradition and worldly philosophy, and to return to the freedom of Bible truth as revealed through Jesus and other devoted spokesmen for Jehovah. (John 8:31, 32) From the time that the magazine *The Watchtower* began to be published in 1879, the English-language publications of the Watch Tower Society have up to now quoted, cited and referred to more than seventy different Bible translations in English and other languages. Thus the Society has recognized the value of them all, and has made use of the good in them all, as profitable in clearing away religious confusion and setting forth the message of God.

9 **Rotherham and Holman Bibles.** In 1896 Jehovah's witnesses, by means of the Watch Tower Society, entered directly into the field as publishers and distributors of the Bible. In that year printing rights were obtained from the British Bible translator, Joseph B. Rother-

6. What activity characterizes Jehovah's witnesses today, as in ancient times?
7. What charter did Jehovah's witnesses obtain, and when, and how did they start to develop their ministry at that time?
8. (a) How has the Watch Tower Bible and Tract Society been true to its name? (b) How has the Society made use of the many Bible translations, and to what end?
9. How did the Society enter the field of Bible publishing?

SOME LEADING BIBLE TRANSLATIONS IN SEVEN PRINCIPAL LANGUAGES

Name of Version	Originally Published	Basic Text for Hebrew Scriptures	Divine Name Rendered	Basic Text for Greek Scriptures	Apocrypha	Comparative Nine-Year Distribution (1953-61 inclusive, by twenty-four Bible societies)
ENGLISH				**Total English Bibles**		— **107,693,750[a]**
Douay	1610	Vulgate	Lord (ADONAI, twice)	Vulgate	Yes	
Authorized (King James)	1611	M.T.[b]	LORD (Jehovah, few)	Received Text	No	
English Revised	1885, 1895	M.T.	LORD	(Westcott and Hort)	Yes	
Rotherham	1878-1902	Ginsburg M.T.	Yahweh	Westcott and Hort, Tregelles	No	
American Standard	1901	M.T.	Jehovah	Westcott and Hort	No	
Moffatt	1913-1925	M.T.	Eternal	Von Soden	No	
An American Translation	1927	M.T.	LORD (Yahweh, few)	Westcott and Hort	Yes	
Revised Standard	1952	M.T.	LORD	Westcott and Hort, Nestle	Yes[c]	
New World	1950-1961	Kittel M.T.	Jehovah	Westcott and Hort	No	
SPANISH				**Total Spanish Bibles**		— **35,917,670**
Valera	1602	M.T.	Jehová	Received Text	No	
Scío	1790-1793	Vulgate	Señor (ADONAI)	Vulgate	Yes	
Torres Amat	1824	Vulgate	Señor (Jehová, few)	Vulgate	Yes	
Moderna	1893	M.T.	Jehová	Scrivener	No	
Bover-Cantera	1947, 1951	Kittel M.T.	Yahveh	Greek[d]	Yes	
Nácar-Colunga	1944	M.T.	Yavé	Greek	Yes	
Straubinger	1948-1951	M.T.	Yahvé	Greek	Yes	
PORTUGUESE				**Total Portuguese Bibles**		— **17,286,637**
Almeida	1681-1691	M.T.	Jehovah	Beza-Latin, Received Text	No	
Figueiredo	1778-1790	Vulgate	Senhor	Vulgate	Yes	
Brasileira	1917	Ginsburg M.T.	Jehovah	Nestle	No	
Matos Soares	1932	Vulgate	Senhor	Vulgate	Yes	
Almeida (Revised)	1945	Kittel M.T.	Senhor, Jeová[e]	Nestle	No	
GERMAN				**Total German Bibles**		— **11,424,822**
Luther	1522, 1534	Soncino M.T.	HErr	Erasmus	Yes	
Allioli	1830-1833 (?)	Vulgate	Herr	Vulgate	Yes	
Elberfelder	1855-1871	M.T.	Jehova	Received Text	No	
Schlachter	1905	M.T.	Herr, Jehova	Greek	No	
Menge	1926	M.T.	HErr	Greek	No	
Aschaffenburger	1957	Vulgate and Hebrew	Herr	Vulgate and Greek	Yes	
FRENCH				**Total French Bibles**		— **2,706,044**
Segond	1873-1880	M.T.	Éternel	Tischendorf	No	
Darby (Pau)	1859, 1885	M.T.	Éternel	Greek	No	
Crampon	1894-1905	M.T.	Jéhovah[f]	Merk	Yes	
Synodale	1910	M.T.	Éternel	Nestle, Gebbert	No	
Lienart	1950	(Pirot-Clamer)	Yahweh	Merk	Yes	
Jerusalem	1952-1955	Vulgate and Hebrew	Yahvé	Vulgate and Greek	Yes	
DUTCH (NETHERLANDS)				**Total Dutch Bibles**		— **1,796,131**
Statenvertaling	1637	Byzantine Greek	HERE	Received Text	No	
Leidsche Vertaling	1912	M.T.	Jahwe	Nestle	No	
Himmelreich	1938	M.T.	Jahve	Merk and Vulgate	Yes	
Canisiusvertaling	1939	M.T.	Jahweh	Nestle	Yes	
Nieuwe Vertaling (complete)	1951	M.T.	HERE	Greek	No	
ITALIAN				**Total Italian Bibles**		— **1,674,698**
Brucioli	1530-1532	Pagnini Latin	Signore	Erasmus	Yes	
Diodati	1607, 1641	Hebrew and Latin	Signore	Greek and Latin	No	
Riveduta	1925	M.T.	Eterno	Greek	No	
Ricciotti	1940	Vulgate	Signore	Vulgate	Yes	
Tintori	1945	Vulgate	Signore	Vulgate	Yes	
Nardoni	1960	M.T.	Signore, Jahweh	Greek	Yes	

FOOTNOTES:

a Total distribution of all Bibles in each language. This includes only those handled by the twenty-four Bible societies from which figures were collated and does not include other channels of printing and distribution.

b "M.T." refers to the Masoretic Text. When it stands alone this indicates that no special edition of the Masoretic Text is specified.

c Some versions that have translated the apocrypha do not include it in all editions.

d "Greek" indicates translation made from the Greek, but no special text indicated.

e In the 1959 revision only Senhor is used.

f Yahweh in later revisions.

ham, to publish in the United States the Twelfth Edition Revised of his *New Testament*. On the title page of these printed copies there appeared the name of the Watch Tower Bible and Tract Society, Allegheny, Pennsylvania; the Society's headquarters being located there at the time. In 1901 arrangements were made for a special printing of the *Holman Linear Bible*, containing marginal explanatory notes from the Society's publications of 1895 to 1901. The Bible text itself presented the *Authorized* and *Revised Versions* of the "Old" and "New Testaments." The entire edition of five thousand copies had been distributed by the year 1903.

10 **The Emphatic Diaglott.** In 1902 the Watch Tower Society came to be the copyright owners, sole publishers and distributors of *The Emphatic Diaglott*. This excellent version of the Christian Greek Scriptures was prepared by the English-born Bible translator Benjamin Wilson, of Geneva, Illinois, being completed in 1864. The book entitled "The English Bible in America," published in 1961 by the New York American Bible Society and The New York Public Library, gives the following accurate description of this Bible: "1865. The Emphatic Diaglott: Containing the Original Greek text of what is commonly styled the New Testament, according to the recension of Dr. J. J. Griesbach, with an interlineary word for word English Translation; a new Emphatic Version, based on the Interlineary Translation, on the renderings of eminent critics, and on the various readings of the Vatican Manuscript together with illustrative and explanatory footnotes and a copious set of references to the whole of which is added a valuable alphabetical appendix. By Benjamin Wilson . . . Published by the Author: Geneva, Illinois. . . . In 1902 the text was endorsed by the Watch Tower Bible and Tract Society and offered at reduced price with a year's subscription to *Zion's Watch Tower*. . . . [1926] printing was begun in the organization's old plant but finished in their new one. Editions were printed every few years. . . . The text has been reset, breathings and accents having been added to the Greek text." (Pages 265, 369) By 1963 the Watch Tower Society had published 202,147 copies of this scholarly work.

11 **A Bible Students Edition.** In 1907 the Watch Tower Society published a "Bible Students Edition" of the Bible. This volume contained a clear printing of the Authorized Version of the Bible, and included excellent marginal notes, together with a valuable appendix designed by Jehovah's witnesses. The Appendix, which was later enlarged to over 550 pages, was called the "Berean Bible Teachers Manual," and was also published in separate book form. Part 1 contained brief comments on many of the verses of the Bible, with references to *The Watchtower* and to the Society's textbooks, *Studies in the Scriptures*. Part 2 comprised collections of scriptures on various doctrinal subjects, "for the assistance of Bible Students especially in their presentations of the truth to others." This was similar in form to the Society's later publication, *"Make Sure of All Things."* Part 3 contained a topical index, and part 4 was devoted to "difficult texts explained and spurious passages noted." A scripture index followed, and a final section contained a comparative chronology and twelve helpful maps. This excellent Bible was bound in leather, and served Jehovah's witnesses for decades in their public preaching work.

A BIBLE PRINTING SOCIETY

12 For thirty years, the Watch Tower Society had engaged outside firms to do the actual printing of its Bibles. However, in December, 1926, *The Emphatic Diaglott* became the first Bible version to be printed on the Society's own presses at Brooklyn, New York. The printing of this edition of the Christian Greek Scriptures fostered the hope that a complete Bible would someday be printed on the Society's presses.

13 **The Authorized Version.** World War II underlined the need for independent publication of the Bible itself. While the global conflict was at its height, the Society succeeded in purchasing plates of the complete Authorized Version of the Bible. It was on September 18, 1942, at the New World Theocratic Assembly of Jehovah's witnesses, with key assembly point at Cleveland, Ohio, that the Society's president spoke on the subject "Presenting 'The Sword of the Spirit.'" As climax to this address, he released this first complete Bible printed in the Watch Tower Society's Brooklyn factory. In its Appendix it provided a list of proper names with their meanings, a specially prepared "Concordance of Bible Words and Expressions," and other helps. Appropriate running heads were provided at the top of each page. As examples, "Jephthah's earnest vow" replaced the traditional "Jephthah's rash vow" at Judges 11, and "Prehuman existence and human birth of God's Word"

10. What excellent version of the Greek Scriptures has the Society published, and what are some of its features?
11. When did the Society publish the "Bible Students Edition," and what did this contain?
12. When did the Society enter the field of Bible printing?
13. (a) What was the first complete Bible printed by the Society, and when was it released? (b) What helps did it contain? (c) How extensive has been its distribution?

appeared at John chapter 1. Up until 1963 the Society had printed and distributed 1,436,949 copies of this Bible.

14 **The American Standard Version.** A fine Bible translation of the twentieth century is the *American Standard Version* of 1901. As well as being a greatly improved translation by comparison with the *Authorized Version* of 1611, it has the most commendable feature of rendering God's name as "Jehovah" at 6,823 places in the Hebrew Scriptures. After long negotiations, the Watch Tower Society was able to purchase, in 1944, the *use* of the plates of the complete American Standard Version of the Bible for printing on its own presses. On August 10, 1944, at Buffalo, New York, the key city of seventeen simultaneous assemblies of Jehovah's witnesses linked together by private telephone lines, the Society's president delighted his large audience by releasing the Watch Tower edition of the *American Standard Version*. The Appendix included a most helpful, expanded "Concordance of Bible Words, Names, and Expressions." A pocket edition of the same Bible was published in 1958. By 1963 the printing in the two editions was 884,944 copies.

15 Thus Jehovah's witnesses are not only preaching the good news of God's established kingdom in some 189 countries and islands throughout the earth, but they have become printers and publishers, on a large scale, of the priceless Book that contains that Kingdom message, the Holy Scriptures inspired by Jehovah God.

"NEW WORLD TRANSLATION OF THE HOLY SCRIPTURES"

16 Jehovah's witnesses acknowledge their indebtedness to all the many Bible versions that they have used in attaining to the truth of the Word of God. However, all these translations, even down to the very latest, have their defects. There are inconsistencies or unsatisfactory renderings, infected with sectarian traditions or worldly philosophies, and hence not in full harmony with the sacred truths that Jehovah has recorded in his Word. Particularly since 1946 the president of the Watch Tower Bible and Tract Society had been in quest of a faithful translation of the Scriptures from the original languages—a translation just as understandable to modern readers as the original writings were understandable to the ordinary intelligent people of the Bible era itself.

17 On September 3, 1949, at the Brooklyn headquarters of the Society, the president announced to the Board of Directors the existence of a "New World Bible Translation Committee" that had completed a translation of the Christian Greek Scriptures. The committee's document was read, by which it assigned the possession, control and publication of the translation manuscript to the Society, in recognition of the Society's unsectarian work of promoting Bible knowledge throughout the earth. Portions of the manuscript were also read, as examples of the nature and quality of the translation. The directors were unanimous in accepting the gift of the translation, and arrangements were made for its printing. Typesetting began on September 29, 1949, and by early summer of 1950, tens of thousands of copies were completed in bound form.

18 **Releasing the "New World Translation" in Its Parts.** It was on Wednesday, August 2, 1950, on the fourth day of their world assembly at Yankee Stadium, New York, that a totally surprised audience of 82,075 of Jehovah's witnesses heartily accepted the release of the *New World Translation of the Christian Greek Scriptures*. Encouraged by the initial enthusiastic reception, as well as by later expressions of appreciation of the translation's merits, the Committee next undertook the extensive work of translating the Hebrew Scriptures. This appeared in five additional volumes, released successively from 1953 to 1960. The set of six volumes formed a library of the entire Bible in modern English. Each volume also contained valuable aids to Bible study. A vast storehouse of Scriptural data and information was thus made available to the modern-day student of the Bible. Diligent effort had been made to draw on every reliable source of textual information, so that the *New World Translation* would express clearly and accurately the powerful message of the original inspired Scriptures. The total number of these volumes printed came to 3,589,949 copies by 1963.

19 Among the Bible-study aids in the six-part first edition of the *New World Translation*, which in 1963 was published in one volume of 3,646 pages, is the invaluable collection of textual footnotes, giving background to the renderings. In these notes powerful arguments in defense of the Scriptures are made avail-

14. What improved translation of the Bible was printed by the Society in 1944, and what features does this Bible have?
15. In what twofold work are Jehovah's witnesses thus engaged?
16. (a) How have the many Bible versions been useful, and yet what defects do they contain? (b) Since 1946, what had the president of the Watch Tower Society been seeking?
17. How did the Society come to be publishers and printers of the *New World Translation?*
18. (a) How did the *New World Translation* appear in its parts? (b) What effort had been made in preparing these volumes, and what was the distribution by 1963?
19. What valuable aids does the first edition of the *New World Translation* contain in (a) its footnotes, (b) its marginal references, and (c) its forewords and appendixes?

able. A valuable chain-reference system is also included. These chains of important doctrinal words were designed to direct the student to a series of key texts on these subjects. There is an abundance of cross references in the margins of the pages. These direct the reader to (a) parallel words, (b) parallel thoughts, ideas and events, (c) biographical information, (d) geographical information, (e) fulfillments of prophecies, and (f) direct quotations in or from other parts of the Bible. The volume also contains important forewords, photostatic copies of some ancient manuscripts, helpful appendixes and indexes, and maps of Bible lands and locations. This first edition of the *New World Translation* will continue to provide a "gold mine" for personal Bible study, and for beneficial teaching of goodwill persons as ministers make return visits. This special edition, in a printing of 150,000 copies, was released June 30, 1963, at the opening of the "Everlasting Good News" Assembly of Jehovah's Witnesses at Milwaukee, Wisconsin, U.S.A.

20 **One-Volume Revised Edition Released.** In the summer of 1961, at a series of assemblies of Jehovah's witnesses held in the United States and Europe, the complete *New World Translation of the Holy Scriptures* in one volume was released for distribution. It was accepted with joy by the hundreds of thousands who attended these assemblies, and who marveled that so fine a volume was to be distributed for the sum of only one dollar. Bound in green cloth, it contains 1,472 pages, and has an excellent concordance, as well as an appendix on Bible topics, and maps. In less than three years the total published equaled 3,662,400 copies, including the 1963 printing of a pocket edition of this Bible.

21 This one-volume revised edition of the *New World Translation* has a readable print and prominent verse-numberings. Two columns are printed on a page, with a type smaller than that of the first edition, so that a greater amount of material can readily be scanned in its context. In order to aid the reader in locating quickly any desired material, carefully designed running heads are provided at the top of each page, describing the material below, and these are especially planned to aid the minister in the field in quickly locating texts in answer to questions that may be put to him.

22 For example, the minister may be trying to locate counsel on the training of children. Coming to page 750 in the Proverbs, he sees first the key phrase, "A name." Since this is the first heading, it indicates that the subject will appear early on that page, and that is where he finds it, in Proverbs 22:1. The scripture identified by the next running head, "Train a boy," he finds farther down the page, at verse 6. The third heading reads, "Use rod." This material is located near the bottom of the first column, in verse 15. The last two running heads on this page, "Rob" and "Riches," could be expected to apply to material in the second column, and this is to be found at verse 22 and at chapter 23, verse 4. Though there are no cross-references in the Revised Edition Bible, these running page headings can be a great aid to the minister who knows the general locations of texts for which he is searching. They can open up the Bible for quick action.

23 At the back of this Bible there is a 104-page word-index, called "Important Bible Words for Quick Reference." Here are to be found some 6,400 important Bible words together with lines of context. In fact, a concordance service is thus made available, including the wide range of new, descriptive words used in the text. For those accustomed to the *Authorized Version* renderings, help is given in making scores of transitions from old English Bible words to the more modern Bible terms. Take for example the word "grace" in the *Authorized Version*. This is listed in the index, referring the student to "undeserved kindness," the up-to-date expression used in the new translation. The word-index further contains key doctrinal words and subjects, making possible detailed study directly from the Bible texts. A minister who is called upon to preach on any of these outstanding subjects could immediately use the brief portions of context supplied in this concordance. A good selection of the outstanding proof references explaining key doctrinal words is listed. Additionally, principal citations are offered for outstanding proper names, geographical as well as those of prominent Bible characters. Invaluable aid is thus rendered to all Bible readers and ministers using this translation.

24 A scholarly appendix to the Revised Edition offers further accurate information beneficial for ministerial teaching. A number of Scripture verses are specifically commented on in conjunction with the treatment of related Bible subjects. For example, in dealing with the word "souls" at Genesis 1:20, the appendix goes on to list 199 quotations from the Hebrew Scriptures to show the various ways in

20. (a) What were the circumstances of the release of the revised *New World Translation?* (b) What are some of its features, and what has been its distribution?
21, 22. (a) What are some of the advantages of this edition? (b) Illustrate the use of the running heads.

23. What concordance service is provided, and to what practical uses may this be put?
24. Illustrate one of the ways in which the appendix to the *New World Translation* is of help.

which the word "soul" (Hebrew: *neph'esh*) is used. (In addition to the eight subjects thus treated in the one-volume edition, a number of other excellent treatments of Bible subjects are to be found in the appendixes of Volumes I and V of the Hebrew Scriptures, and of the volume of the Christian Greek Scriptures.) Diagrams and maps are also provided. Thus the *New World Translation* is outstanding for the range of services that it provides for placing accurate knowledge quickly at the disposal of its readers.

25 **Aid to Pronouncing Bible Names.** In the English text itself, both editions of the *New World Translation* render aid in the pronunciations of proper names. The system is the same as that designed by a modern expert for the *Revised Standard Version* of 1952. The proper name is broken down into syllables that are kept apart by a dot or by the accent mark (′). The accent mark follows the syllable on which major emphasis should be put in pronouncing the word. If the accented syllable ends in a vowel, then the vowel is long in its pronunciation. If a syllable ends in a consonant, then the vowel in that syllable is pronounced short.

26 As an example, note Job 4:1. Here it speaks of "El′i·phaz the Te′man·ite." While the accent in both cases falls on the first syllable, the letter "e" is to be pronounced differently in these two cases. In "El′i·phaz" the accent mark falling after the consonant "l" makes the vowel "e" short, as in "end." Whereas, in "Te′man·ite" the accent falling directly after the vowel "e" makes it long, as the first "e" in "Eden." When the two vowels "a" and "i" are combined, as in *Mor′de·cai* at Esther 2:5 and *Si′nai* at Exodus 19:1, the "ai" is pronounced simply as a long "i."

27 **A Fresh Translation.** Outstanding among the many features of the entire eleven-year production of the *New World Translation* is that of its being a fresh translation from the original Bible languages of Hebrew, Aramaic and Greek. By no means is it a revision of any other English translation, nor does it copy any other version as to style, vocabulary or rhythm. For the Hebrew-Aramaic section, the well-refined and universally accepted text of Rudolf Kittel's *Biblia Hebraica*, editions of 1951 and 1955, was used. The Greek section was translated from the Greek master text prepared by Westcott and Hort, published in 1881, which is widely accepted in Christendom. Descriptions of these excellent master texts are presented in Studies Five and Six of this volume. The Translation Committee has made a fresh approach to translation of the Bible, and this has resulted in a clear and living text, opening up the way to a deeper, more satisfying understanding of the Word of God.

28 Note one critic's evaluation of this translation: "Original renderings of the Hebrew Scriptures into the English language are extremely few. It therefore gives us much pleasure to welcome the publication of the first part of the New World Translation [of the Hebrew Scriptures], Genesis to Ruth. This version has evidently made a special effort to be thoroughly readable. No one could say it is deficient in freshness and originality. Its terminology is by no means based upon that of previous versions."—Alexander Thomson, in *The Differentiator*, June 1954, page 131.

29 **A Literal Translation.** Faithfulness as to translation is also demonstrated in its being literal. This requires an almost word-for-word correspondency between the rendering in English and the Hebrew and Greek texts. The degree of literalness should be as high as the original-language idiom permits in its presentation in intelligible English. Furthermore, literalness requires that the word order of most of the renderings in English should be the same as in the Hebrew or Greek, thus preserving the emphasis of the original writings. Through literal translation, the flavor, color and rhythm of the original writings may be accurately communicated.

30 There have been occasional departures from the literal text, for the purpose of conveying difficult Hebrew or Greek idioms in understandable English. However, in the six-part first edition of the *New World Translation* these have been called to the reader's attention by means of footnotes that give the literal rendering for those readers who might prefer it.

31 Many Bible translators have abandoned literalness for what they consider to be elegance of language and form. They argue that literal renderings are wooden, stiff and confining. However, their abandonment of literal translation has brought about many departures from the accurate, original statements of truth. They have in effect watered down the very thoughts of God. For example, there is the Dean Emeritus of a large American University who has charged Jehovah's witnesses with

25, 26. Explain and illustrate how the *New World Translation* indicates the pronunciations of proper names.
27. (a) What fresh approach to translation was made with this Bible, and with what result? (b) On what texts is it based?
28. How does one critic evaluate this translation?
29. To what extent is the *New World Translation* literal, and with what benefit?
30. How have occasional departures from the literal text been noted?
31. (a) What results from abandoning literal translation? (b) Illustrate.

destroying the beauty and elegance of the Bible. By the Bible he meant the *Authorized Version,* which has long been venerated as a standard of beautiful English. He said: 'Look what you have done to Psalm 23. You have destroyed its swing and beauty by your "Je/ho/vah is / my / shep/herd." Seven syllables instead of six. It is shocking. It is off balance. There is no rhythm. The King James has it right with its six balanced syllables—"The / Lord / is / my shep/herd." ' It was protested to the professor that it was more important to put it the way that David, the Bible writer, put it. Did David use the general term "Lord," or did he use the divine name? The professor admitted that David used the divine name, but he still argued that, for the sake of beauty and elegance, the word "Lord" would be warranted. What a lame excuse for removing Jehovah's illustrious name from this psalm to his praise!

32 Thousands of renderings have been sacrificed in this way on the altar of man's conception of language beauty, resulting in inaccuracies in the many Bible versions. Thanks be to God that he has now provided the *New World Translation,* with its clear and accurate Bible text! May his great name, Jehovah, be sanctified in the hearts of all who read it!

32. For what may we thank God, and what is our hope and prayer?

Study Eight—Advantages of the New World Translation

A discussion of its modern language, its uniformity, careful verb renderings and dynamic expression of the inspired Word of God.

IN RECENT years a number of modern Bible translations have been published that have done much to help lovers of God's Word to get quickly to the sense of the original writings. However, the trend has been to eliminate the use of the divine name from the sacred record. On the other hand, the *New World Translation* dignifies and honors the worthy name of the Most High God by restoring it to its rightful place in the text. The name now appears in 6,962 places in the Hebrew Scripture section, as well as 237 places in the Greek Scripture section, a total of 7,199 places all together. The pronunciation *Yahweh* may be a more correct one, but the Latinized form *Jehovah* continues to be used because it is the most commonly accepted form of English translation of the tetragrammaton, or four-letter Hebrew name, יהוה.

2 However, the *New World Translation* is not the first version to restore the divine name in the Christian Greek Scriptures. From the fourteenth century onward, some nineteen Jewish translators have seen fit to do this, including Catholic translator Jonah in 1668. Wilson's *Emphatic Diaglott* of 1864 and some thirty-eight missionary versions in languages other than English have also made restorations in the so-called "New Testament." A series of studies of the Gospels by Abbé Geslin, Professor of Holy Scripture at the Seminary of Sées, Orne, France, presents the text in Latin and French. In the French translation, in verses where the *New World Translation* has the name Jehovah, Abbé Geslin uses Jéhovah nine times in Matthew, once in John, and Iahweh twice in Luke.[a] Wherever the divine name is rendered, there is no more any doubt as to which "lord" is indicated. It is the Lord of heaven and earth, Jehovah, whose name is sanctified by being kept unique and distinct in the *New World Translation of the Holy Scriptures.*[b]

3 The *New World Translation* adds further to the sanctification of Jehovah's name by presenting his inspired Scriptures in clear, understandable language that brings the intended meaning plainly to the reader's mind. It uses simple, modern language, is as uniform as possible in its renderings, conveys accurately the action or state expressed in the Hebrew and Greek verbs, and distinguishes between

1. (a) What trend does the *New World Translation* correct, and how? (b) Why is *Jehovah* used rather than *Yahweh?*
2. (a) What precedents are there for restoring the divine name in the Christian Greek Scriptures? (b) What doubt is thus removed?

a The studies are published as a series of volumes under the general title of "La demi-heure d'Écriture Sainte." The Gospel of Matthew was published in 1924. The texts where the divine name appears are: Matthew 1:20, 22, 24; 2:13, 15, 19; 3:3; 5:33; 21:42; Luke 20:37, 42; John 1:23.

b Foreword to the *New World Translation of the Christian Greek Scriptures,* 1950 Edition, pages 10-25.

3. By what means does the *New World Translation* help to convey the force, beauty and sense of the original writings?

the plural and singular in its use of the pronoun "you" and when using the imperative form of the verb. In these and other ways the *New World Translation* brings to light in modern speech the force, beauty and sense of the original writings.

RENDERED IN MODERN LANGUAGE

4 The older Bible translations contain many obsolete words that belong to the sixteenth and seventeenth centuries. Though not understood now, they were readily understood then. For example, one man who had much to do with putting them in the English Bible was William Tyndale, who is reported as saying to one of his religious opponents: 'If God spare my life, ere many years I will cause a boy who drives the plow to know more of the Scriptures than you do.' Tyndale's translation of the Greek Scriptures was easy enough for a plowboy to understand in his time. However, many of the words he used have now become archaic, so that 'a boy who drives the plow' can no longer clearly grasp the meaning of many words in the King James and other old versions of the Bible. Thus it has become necessary to take off the shrouds of archaic language and to restore the Bible to the simple spoken language of the common man.

5 It was the language of the common man that was used in writing the inspired Scriptures. The apostles and other early Christians did not use the classical Greek of the philosopher Plato. They used everyday Greek, the *koiné* or common Greek. Hence the Greek Scriptures, like the Hebrew Scriptures before them, were written in the language of the people. It is highly important, then, that translations of the original Scriptures should also be in the language of the people, so as to be readily understood. It is for this reason that modern translations like the *New World Translation* turn from the archaic language of three or four centuries ago, and use clear, expressive modern speech so that readers will really get to know what the Bible is about.

6 To give some idea of the extent of change in the English language between the seventeenth and twentieth centuries, note the following comparisons from the *King James Version* and *New World Translation*. "Suffered" in the *King James Version* becomes "allowed" in the *New World Translation* (Gen. 31:7), "was bolled" becomes "had flower buds" (Ex. 9:31), "spoilers" becomes "pillagers" (Judg. 2:14), "ear his ground" becomes "do his plowing" (1 Sam. 8:12), "when thou prayest" becomes "when you pray" (Matt. 6:6), "sick of the palsy" becomes "paralytic" (Mark 2:3), "quickeneth" becomes "makes . . . alive" (Rom. 4:17), "shambles" becomes "meat market" (1 Cor. 10:25), "letteth" becomes "acting as a restraint" (2 Thess. 2:7), and so on. From this the service of the *New World Translation* in using current words in place of obsolete words can well be appreciated.

UNIFORMITY OF RENDERINGS

7 The *New World Translation* makes every effort to be consistent in its renderings. For a given Hebrew or Greek word there has been assigned one English word, and this has been used as uniformly as the idiom or context permits in giving the full English understanding. For example, there is the Hebrew word *neph'esh,* which is consistently translated *soul.* The Greek word *psy·khe'* is translated *"soul"* in every occurrence.

8 At some places a problem has arisen over the translation of *homonyms.* These are words in the original languages that are spelled the same but which have different meanings, and hence the difficulty is to supply the word with the correct meaning when translating. In English there are *homonyms* such as *Polish* and *polish,* and *lead* (the sheep) and *lead* (pipe), which are spelled identically, but are distinctly different words. As a Bible example there is the Hebrew *rab,* which represents three distinctly different words, and these are therefore rendered differently in the *New World Translation. Rab* most commonly has the meaning of "many," as at Exodus 5:5. However, there is also the word *rab* that is used in titles, such as in *Rabshakeh* at 2 Kings 18:17, and that means "chief," as when rendered "his *chief* court-official" at Daniel 1:3. The third word *rab* means "archers," and is so rendered at Jeremiah 50:29. Word experts, such as L. Koehler and W. Baumgartner, have been accepted as authorities by the translators in separating these identically spelled words.

9 As to this feature of uniformity, note what Hebrew and Greek scholar Alexander Thomson has to say in his review on the *New World Translation of the Christian Greek Scriptures:* "The translation is evidently the work of skilled and clever scholars, who have sought to bring out as much of the true sense of the Greek text as the English language is capable of expressing. The version aims to keep to one

4. (a) What noble purpose did one early Bible translator express? (b) However, what has become necessary with the passage of time?
5. In what language should the Bible appear, and why?
6. Illustrate the benefit of using current expressions in the place of obsolete words.
7. How is the *New World Translation* consistent in its renderings?
8. (a) Give examples of *homonyms.* (b) How have these been handled in the translation?
9. How does one Hebrew and Greek scholar appraise the *New World Translation?*

English meaning for each major Greek word, and to be as literal as possible. The word usually rendered 'justify' is generally translated very correctly as 'declare righteous.' The word for the Cross is rendered 'torture stake' which is another improvement. Luke 23:43 is well rendered, 'Truly I tell you today, You will be with me in Paradise.' This is a big improvement upon the reading of most versions." On the translation of the Hebrew Scriptures, the same reviewer makes this comment: "The New World Version is well worth acquiring. It is lively and lifelike, and makes the reader think and study. It is not the work of Higher Critics, but of scholars who honour God and His Word."—*The Differentiator*, April 1952, pages 52-57, and June 1954, page 136.

10 The consistency of the *New World Translation* has won many a technical Bible discussion in the field. On one occasion, a society of freethinkers in New York asked the Watch Tower Society to send two speakers to address their group on Biblical matters, which request was granted. These learned men held to a Latin maxim, *falsum in uno falsum in toto*, meaning that an argument proved false in one point is totally false. During the discussion, one man challenged Jehovah's witnesses on the reliability of the Bible. He asked that Genesis 1:3 be read to the audience, and this was done, from the *New World Translation:* "And God proceeded to say: 'Let light come to be.' Then there came to be light." Confidently, he next called for Genesis 1:14, and this also was read from the *New World Translation:* "And God went on to say: 'Let luminaries come to be in the expanse of the heavens . . .' " "Stop," he said, "what are you reading? My Bible says God made light on the first day, and again on the fourth day, and that is inconsistent." Though he claimed to know Hebrew, it had to be pointed out to him that the Hebrew word translated "light" in verse 3 was *ōr*, whereas the word in verse 14 was different, being *mᵉ·o·roth′*, which means "luminaries." The learned man sat down defeated. The faithful consistency of the *New World Translation* had won the point, upholding the Bible as reliable and beneficial.

CAREFUL VERB RENDERINGS

11 The *New World Translation* gives special attention to conveying the sense of the action of the Greek and Hebrew verbs. In doing so the *New World Translation* endeavors to preserve the peculiar charm, simplicity, forcefulness and manner of expression of the original-language writings. It has thus been necessary to use auxiliary verbs to convey carefully the actual states of the actions. It is due to the power of their verbs that the original Scriptures are so dynamic and so full of action.

12 The Hebrew verb does not have "tenses" in the sense that that term is applied to most languages of the West. In English there are quite a number of tenses, the present, past, future, past perfect, future perfect, and so forth. The Hebrew verb, on the other hand, basically expresses just two "states." These are (1) the "perfect" state, used to speak of an action that is completed, and (2) the "imperfect" state, to describe an action that has begun but has not yet been completed. These states of the Hebrew verb may be used with reference to actions in the past or in the future, the context determining the time. The perfect or completed sense of the verb is used to speak of a future action or state as if it had already occurred and were past, this to show its future certainty or the obligation of it to occur.

13 The conveying of the state of the Hebrew verb accurately into English is most important, otherwise the meaning may be distorted and a completely different thought conveyed. For an example of this, consider some of the expressions in Genesis 2:2, 3. In many translations, speaking of God's resting on the seventh day, the expressions "he rested," "he desisted," "he had desisted," "he then rested," "God rested," and "he had rested" are used. From these readings one would conclude that God's resting on the seventh day was completed in the past, and that the Hebrew verb in this case is therefore in the "perfect" state. But this is not so. Note how the *New World Translation* brings out the sense of the imperfect state of the verb used, and so conveys the accurate understanding of the passage: "And by the seventh day God came to the completion of his work that he had made, and he proceeded to rest on the seventh day from all his work that he had made. And God proceeded to bless the seventh day and make it sacred, because on it he has been resting from all his work that God has created for the purpose of making." So the original Hebrew does not convey the thought that God "rested," that is, completed the action back at that time, but rather conveys the idea of an action commenced and still continuing, not yet completed. The expression "he has been resting" thus gives the right sense.

10. Illustrate how the consistency of this translation upholds Bible truth.
11. What dynamic feature of the original Scriptures is preserved in the *New World Translation?* How?
12. (a) In what does Hebrew differ from Western languages? (b) Explain the two "states" of the Hebrew verb.
13. How does proper regard to state of the Hebrew verb help in a correct understanding of Genesis 2:2, 3?

14 One of the reasons for errors in translating the verb states has been a mistaken view of an important verbal form called today "waw consecutive." *Waw* (ו) is the Hebrew conjunction that basically means "and." It never stands alone, but is always joined with some other word, frequently with the Hebrew verb to form one word with it. It has been, and still is, claimed that this relationship has the power to convert the verb from one state to another, that is, from the imperfect to the perfect, as has been done by many translations, including modern ones, at Genesis 2:2, 3, or from the perfect to the imperfect. This effect has been described by the term "waw conversive." This wrong application of this verbal form has led to much confusion and to mistranslation of the Hebrew text. While giving due place to the force of the waw consecutive, the *New World Translation* does not recognize that it has any power to change the state of the verb. Rather, the attempt is always made to bring out the proper and distinctive force of the Hebrew states of the verb, perfect or imperfect. In that way the truth of the original is more accurately translated.[a]

15 Similar care has been exercised in the translating of the Greek verbs. In Greek the verb tenses express not only the time of an action or state, but also the kind of action, whether starting out, or continuing, or repetitious, or completed. Attention to such senses contained in the verb forms leads to a precise translation with the full force of the action described. For example, giving the sense of the continuative idea where this occurs in the Greek verb not only brings out the true color of a situation but also makes admonitions and counsel more powerful. The *continuing* disbelief of the Pharisees and Sadducees is brought home by Jesus' words: "A wicked and adulterous generation *keeps on seeking* for a sign." And the need for continuing action in right things is well expressed by these texts: "*Continue to love* your enemies." "*Keep on,* then, *seeking* first the kingdom." "*Keep on asking,* and it will be given you; *keep on seeking,* and you will find; *keep on knocking,* and it will be opened to you."—Matt. 16:4; 5:44; 6:33; 7:7.

16 The Greek has a peculiar tense called the "aorist," which means "not bounded" as to time. Verbs in the aorist may be rendered in a variety of ways according to their context. One way in which it is used is to denote one act of a certain kind, though not related to any particular time. Such an example is found at 1 John 2:1, where many versions render the verb "sin" so as to allow for the thought of a continuing course of sin, whereas the *New World Translation* reads, "commit a sin," that is, a single act of sin. This conveys the correct thought, that if a Christian should commit an act of sin, he has an advocate or helper with the heavenly Father, Jesus Christ. Thus 1 John 2:1 in no way contradicts, but only contrasts with, the condemnation of the 'practice of sin' at 1 John 3:6-8 and 5:18.

17 The imperfect tense in Greek may express not only an action that continues, but also an attempt to do something. Hebrews 11:17 in the *Authorized Version* reads: "By faith Abraham, when he was tried, offered up Isaac: and he that had received the promises offered up his only begotten son." The *New World Translation,* taking into account the imperfect tense, translates the last part of the verse: "attempted to offer up his only-begotten son." *The New English Bible* expresses a similar thought by the words: "he was on the point of offering up his only son."

18 Careful attention to other parts of speech, such as to the cases of nouns, has led to the clearing up of apparent contradictions. For example, at Acts 9:7, in recounting the remarkable experience of Saul on the road to Damascus, a number of translations say that his traveling companions "heard the voice" but did not see anyone. Then at Acts 22:9, where Paul is relating this incident, the same translations read that, although they saw the light, "they did not hear the voice." However, in the first reference the Greek word for "voice" is in the genitive case, but in the second instance it is in the accusative case, as it is at Acts 9:4. Why the difference? None is conveyed in the above translations into English, yet the Greek, by the change of case, indicates something different. The men heard literally "of the voice," but not hearing it the way Paul did, that is, hearing the words and understanding them. Thus, the *New World Translation,* noting the use of the genitive at Acts 9:7, reads that the men who were with him were "hearing, indeed, the sound of a voice, but not beholding any man."

a Foreword to the *New World Translation of the Hebrew Scriptures,* Vol. I, 1953 Edition, pages 12-18.

14. Avoiding the mistaken view of the "waw consecutive," what does the *New World Translation* endeavor to do as to the Hebrew verbs?
15. (a) With what care have the Greek verbs been translated? (b) Illustrate the benefit of presenting the continuative idea correctly.
16. By taking account of the Greek aorist tense, how is John's comment on "sin" at 1 John 2:1 correctly expressed?
17. Besides showing continuing action, what else may the Greek imperfect tense express? Illustrate.
18. What has resulted from careful attention to other parts of speech? Give an example.

PLURAL "YOU" INDICATED

19 The old English forms of the second person singular, "thee," "thou" and "thy," have been retained in many modern translations in cases where God is being addressed. However, in the languages in which the Bible was written there was no special form of the personal pronoun for use in address to God, but the same form was used as when addressing one's fellowman. So the *New World Translation* has dropped these now sanctimonious usages, and employs the normal conversational "you" in all cases. In order to distinguish the second person plural "you" and verbs whose plural number is not readily apparent in English, the words are printed entirely in capital letters. Often it is helpful to the reader to know whether a given Scripture text refers to "you" as an individual, or to "YOU" as a group of persons, a congregation.

20 For example, at Romans 11:13 Paul is speaking to the many: "Now I speak to YOU who are people of the nations." However, at verse 17 the Greek changes to the singular "you," and the application is brought down pointedly to the individual: "However, if some of the branches were broken off but you . . . were grafted in . . . "

SIX OTHER "NEW WORLD TRANSLATIONS"

21 In 1961 it was announced that the Watch Tower Society was proceeding to render the *New World Translation* into six more widely used languages, namely, French, Spanish, Italian, Portuguese, German and Dutch. This translation work was entrusted to skilled and dedicated translators, all working together at the Watch Tower Society's headquarters in Brooklyn, New York. They have served as a large international committee working under competent direction. Thus uniformity and excellence of renderings have been assured. It was in July 1963, at the "Everlasting Good News" Assembly of Jehovah's Witnesses at Milwaukee, Wisconsin, U.S.A., that the first-fruits of this translation work became available when the *New World Translation of the Christian Greek Scriptures* was released simultaneously in the above six languages.[a] Now other sections of the earth's multitongued inhabitants could begin to enjoy the advantages of this modern translation.

GRATEFULNESS FOR POWERFUL INSTRUMENT

22 The *New World Translation* is indeed a powerful instrument for demonstrating that "all Scripture is inspired of God and beneficial." From the points discussed in this Study, it can be appreciated that it is accurate and reliable, and that it is able to provide genuine enjoyment to those who desire to hear God speak to man stirringly in modern, living language. The language of the *New World Translation* is spiritually arousing, and quickly puts the reader in tune with the dynamic expression of the original, inspired Scriptures. No longer is it necessary to read and reread the verses in order to understand obscure expressions. It speaks out with power and clarity from the very first reading. That it has met with ready acceptance is indicated by the need to print 3,662,400 copies of the complete one-volume revised edition from the time of its release on June 23, 1961, up till 1963.

23 The *New World Translation of the Holy Scriptures* is a faithful translation of God's Word, "the sword of the spirit." As such it is indeed an effective weapon in the spiritual warfare of the Christian, to aid in 'overturning strongly entrenched false teachings and reasonings raised up against the knowledge of God.' How well it enables us to declare with better understanding the things beneficial and upbuilding, the glorious things related to God's kingdom of righteousness—yes, "the magnificent things of God"!—Eph. 6:17; 2 Cor. 10:4, 5; Acts 2:11.

[a] With a combined printing of 980,000. With this printing, the total quantity of complete Bibles or Bible volumes (including *King James Version, American Standard Version, Diaglott* and *New World Translation*) printed by the Watch Tower Society came to 10,906,389. Most of this printing was done in the thirteen years from 1950 to 1963.

19, 20. (a) What has the *New World Translation* done as to sanctimonious forms of address, and why? (b) Illustrate how the singular "you" may be distinguished from the plural.

21. (a) How has it become possible for others of earth's population to enjoy the benefits of the *New World Translation?* (b) What is the total of Bibles printed by the Watch Tower Society by 1963?

22, 23. In what outstanding ways does this translation of the inspired Scriptures benefit the Christian?

Study Nine—Archaeology Supports the Inspired Record

The evidence in archaeological discoveries and in ancient records of secular history that confirms the accuracy of the Bible record.

BY "Bible archaeology" is meant the scientific study of the peoples and events of Bible times through fossils, writings, implements, buildings and other remains that are found in the earth. This has required much exploration and the moving of millions of tons of dirt in order to discover the artifacts of ancient Bible locations. By "artifact" is meant any object showing human workmanship, such as will give evidence of man's activity and life. Artifacts may include such items as pottery, ruins of buildings, clay tablets, written inscriptions, documents, monuments, chronicles recorded on stone, and many others.

2 By the early twentieth century, archaeology had been reduced to a careful science, with expeditions to Bible lands being sponsored by major universities and museums in Europe and America. As a result, the museums have been filled with a wealth of evidence testifying to the genuineness of the Bible record. Bible archaeology has built up a solid bulwark of proof in support of the Bible's authenticity, showing that the Word of God is accurate right down to the tiniest detail.

3 **The Tower of Babel.** The Tower of Babel is no mere figment of the imagination, but it was a mighty construction work. Archaeologists confirm that such towers were built in and around Babylon, and it is thought the most probable site of the Tower of Babel is the ruined temple of Etemenanki, which was within Babylon's walls. One authority refers to the unearthing of ancient records and inscriptions concerning this structure, saying: "It was so high, apparently, that its pinnacle was in fact constantly toppling, and there are many records of its repair. In several of these we find the ominous words 'Its top shall reach the heavens.' Nebuchadrezzar, for instance, writes: 'I raised the summit of the Tower of stages at Etemenanki so that its top rivalled the heavens.' George Smith [in *Chaldean Account of Genesis* (1880)] also quotes a remarkable fragment relating to the collapse of such a ziggurat: 'The building of this temple offended the gods. In a night they threw down what had been built. They scattered them abroad, and made strange their speech. The progress they impeded.'—a passage which is certainly reminiscent of the Bible story."[a] —Gen. 11:1-9.

4 **Destruction of Sodom and Gomorrah.** Heeding the divine warning, Lot and his family fled Sodom, and just in the nick of time! "Then Jehovah made it rain sulphur and fire from Jehovah, from the heavens, upon Sodom and upon Gomorrah." (Gen. 19:12-26) These cities were located in "the Low Plain of Siddim, that is, the Salt Sea," on a section of land that is now submerged at the south end of the Dead Sea. There were "pits upon pits of bitumen [asphalt]" in this area. (Gen. 14:3, 10) Geologists who have examined the location report that a sudden subsidence, accompanied by volcanic action, occurred there about 1900 B.C.E. This apparently resulted in a catastrophic explosion followed by a rain of sulphur and a destructive fire that engulfed the entire District. Thereafter the waters of the Dead Sea spread over the area, so that the ruins of Sodom and Gomorrah are now submerged. Remains of submerged forests of the District, which was once "like the garden of Jehovah," are still visible along the southern shore, having been wiped out with man and city in this terrible expression of Jehovah's judgment.—Gen. 13:10.[b]

5 American divers have in recent years made interesting finds under the waters of the Dead Sea. The New York *Times* of April 29, 1960, reported the following: "Find in Dead Sea Linked to Sodom—Dr. Ralph E. Baney of Kansas City, Mo., head of a four member expedition, . . . told an interviewer of finding extensive underwater remnants of the civilization that flourished and languished 4,000 years ago. The evidence indicated that the cities of the once fertile plain had been engulfed after a

a *Bible and Spade,* 1938, S. L. Caiger, page 29.
b *The Bible as History,* 1956, Werner Keller, pages 93-96 London Ed., pages 78-81 New York Ed.

1. What is meant by (a) "Bible archaeology"? (b) "artifacts"?
2. To what does Biblical archaeology testify?
3. What ancient ruins and records confirm the Bible account of the Tower of Babel?
4. What conclusions of geologists support the Bible account of the destruction of Sodom and Gomorrah?
5. What further evidence did an expedition to the Dead Sea in 1960 report?

levee collapsed in an earthquake." This confirms the Bible account regarding the existence of these cities whose ruin Abraham viewed from afar on the morning of the catastrophe, as he looked out toward the Siddim area from his position to the west of the Dead Sea: "Now Abraham made his way early in the morning to the place where he had stood before Jehovah. Then he looked down toward Sodom and Gomorrah and toward all the land of the District and saw a sight. Why, here thick smoke ascended from the land like the thick smoke of a kiln!"—Gen. 19:27, 28.

6 **The Hittites.** In his book *Prophets, Idols and Diggers,* John Elder writes: "One of the striking confirmations of Bible history to come from the science of archaeology is the 'recovery' of the Hittite peoples and their empires. Here is a people whose name appears again and again in the Old Testament, but who in secular history had been completely forgotten and whose very existence was considered to be extremely doubtful." Remarkable, indeed, has been the rediscovery of the ancient empire of these descendants of Canaan, who are mentioned forty-seven times in the Bible under the name "Hittite(s)," and fourteen times under the name of their father, "Heth." (Gen. 10:15; Josh. 11:1-9; 1 Ki. 10:29) Up until 1871, there was not one reference to be found to the Hittites in the non-Biblical histories of the world, and they were scorned by "higher critics" as being a Bible myth. However, from 1871 archaeologists began to find references to them in Egyptian writings, and evidences of their existence in the past began to be found throughout Asia Minor, and in Palestine.—*The Watch Tower,* as of September 15, 1902, page 285, ¶3.

7 Then, from 1906, all the extent and former glory of the Hittite Empire began to be appreciated. Excavations by German archaeologists at Boghazkeui, the site of an ancient Hittite capital, which is located about ninety miles east of Ankara, Turkey, uncovered a multitude of artifacts of every sort, including some 10,000 clay tablets written in Hittite cuneiform script and other languages of that day. These finds have shown that the Hittites worshiped a Pantheon of a "thousand gods," and that their empire flourished throughout Asia Minor and extended its control over the greater part of the Land of Promise during 2000-1200 B.C.E. Several of the two hundred paragraphs of Hittite laws, translated and published in London in 1951, give informative background to the discussion between Abraham and the Hittites, at the purchase of the field of Machpelah. (Gen. 23:1-20) Now that Hittite law can be understood, the steps of negotiation become very clear, right down to mentioning all the trees in the field. This is indeed remarkable confirmation of that legal transaction of 1881 B.C.E.[a]

8 **Jehovah's Word Vindicated at Jericho.** It was by a miracle that Jehovah caused Jericho's double-walled fortifications to "fall down flat" before the Israelites under Joshua, in 1473 B.C.E. This enabled the Israelites to enter, so that "they burned the city with fire and everything that was in it." (Josh. 6:20-24) A British expedition headed by Professor John Garstang made a thorough excavation of the ruins of Jericho, and their findings support everything in the Bible record. To quote Professor Garstang: "The main defences of Jericho followed the upper brink of the city mound, and comprised two parallel walls, the outer six feet and the inner twelve feet thick. . . . Investigations along the west side show continuous signs of destruction and conflagration. The outer wall suffered most, its remains falling down the slope. The inner wall is preserved only where it abuts upon the citadel, or tower, to a height of eighteen feet; elsewhere it is found largely to have fallen, together with the remains of buildings upon it, into the space between the walls which was filled with ruins and debris. Traces of intense fire are plain to see, including reddened masses of brick, cracked stones, charred timbers and ashes. Houses alongside the wall were found burnt to the ground, their roofs fallen upon the domestic pottery within. . . . It looks, in short, as though Jericho was finally burnt after deliberate preparation; that it was in fact devoted as a holocaust, precisely in the manner described in the Book of Joshua." Charred food, including a store of bread and unbaked dough, testified to a sudden disaster breaking into the everyday life of the people. The metallic ring of the shattered pottery indicated a second baking by a fiery holocaust. There was every evidence of a fierce and well-prepared conflagration. There had been virtually no plundering. The ruins showed that some houses had been built on rafters that spanned the walls. Since the only part of the walls to survive was near the citadel, this must have been the location of Rahab's house—on the northwest corner—and this would also fit in with the earlier escape of the spies to the mountainous region of Judah. The archaeologists

---

6, 7. (a) What mention is made of the Hittites in the Bible, yet why did "higher critics" formerly regard them as mythological? (b) What striking revelations has archaeology since brought to light, and have such findings helped in a better understanding of events in the Bible?

a *The Encyclopædia Britannica,* 1946, Vol. XI, pages 598B-605; *The Watchtower,* 1955, pages 201-203.

8. How has archaeology joined hands with the Bible account of the destruction of Jericho?

confirm that Jericho remained a ruin for five hundred years after its destruction, in harmony with the curse that Joshua placed upon it.[a] Thus archaeology has joined hands with the dramatic account in the Bible, which lives as the record of a genuine eyewitness.—Josh. 2:15, 22; 6:26.

9 **The Water Tunnels at the Fountain of Gihon.** Similar findings authenticate the account of David's capture of Jebus. In 1867 (A.D.) Charles Warren came across an old water tunnel running from the fountain of Gihon back into the hill, finally leading upward into the old city of Jebus. Here, apparently, was the way in which David's men first penetrated the city. (2 Sam. 5:6-10) It was in 1909-1911 that the entire system of tunnels leading from the Gihon spring was cleared. One massive tunnel, six feet high and chiseled for 1,777 feet through solid rock, leading from Gihon to the pool of Siloam in the Tyropoeon Valley (within the city) is apparently that built by Hezekiah. It must have been truly a remarkable feat of engineering for those times![b]—2 Ki. 20:20; 2 Chron. 32:30.

10 **Shishak's Victory Relief.** Shishak, king of Egypt, is mentioned seven times in the Bible. Because King Rehoboam left the law of Jehovah, Jehovah permitted Shishak to invade Judah, in 993 B.C.E., but not to bring it to complete ruin. (1 Ki. 14:25-28; 2 Chron. 12:1-12) Until recent years there appeared to be only the Bible record of this invasion. Then there came to light a large document of the Pharaoh whom the Bible calls Shishak. This was in the form of an imposing relief in hieroglyphics and pictures on the outer wall of the vast Egyptian temple at Karnak. The first European of note to view it was Napoleon Bonaparte, A.D. 1799. However, the meaning had to remain a secret until about 1830, when the French scholar Jean Champollion found the key to the hieroglyphics. This made it possible to decipher the Karnak writings, which proved to be Shishak's victory document. On this gigantic relief there is depicted the Egyptian god Amun, holding in his right hand a sickle-shaped sword, bringing to Pharaoh Shishak 156 manacled Palestinian prisoners, who are attached by cords to his left hand. Each prisoner represents a city or village, the name of which is shown in hieroglyphics. Among those that can still be read and identified are Rabbith (Josh. 19:20), Taanach, Beth-shean and Megiddo (Josh. 17:11), Shunem (Josh. 19:18), Rehob (Josh. 19:28), Hapharaim (Josh. 19:19), Gibeon (Josh. 18:25), Beth-horon (Josh. 21:22), Aijalon (Josh. 21:24), Socoh (Josh. 15:35) and Arad (Josh. 12:14). The document also makes reference to "The Field of Abram," this being the earliest mention of Abraham in Egyptian records.[c]

Copy of the Moabite (Mesha) Stone (original in the Louvre of Paris), with the letters in transcription, in a language which is virtually Hebrew. This inscription is the oldest known in the Hebrew-Phoenician form of writing.

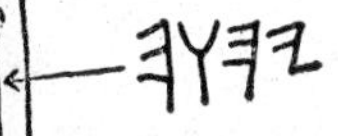

Enlargement of the Tetragrammaton in an ancient lettering, as appearing in the eighteenth line, to the right.

11 **The Moabite Stone.** In 1868 the German missionary F. A. Klein made a remarkable discovery of an ancient inscription in Trans-jordan. This has become known as the Moabite Stone. A cast was made of its writing, but the stone itself was broken up by the Arabs before it could be moved. However, most of the pieces were recovered, and the stone is now preserved in the Louvre, Paris, with a copy in the British Museum, London. It was originally erected at Dibon, in Moab, and gives King Mesha's version of his revolt against Israel. (2 Ki. 1:1; 3:4, 5) It reads, in part: "I am Mesha, son of Chemosh . . . , king of Moab, the Dibonite. . . . Omri, king of Israel . . . oppressed Moab many days because Chemosh [the god of Moab] was angry with his land. And his son succeeded him, and he also said, I will oppress Moab. In my days, he spoke.

a *The Story of Jericho,* 1940, by John Garstang and J. B. E. Garstang, pages 133, 136-150.
b *Light from the Ancient Past,* 1946, J. Finegan, pages 149, 158, 159.

c *Light from the Ancient Past,* page 113; *The Bible as History,* 1956, by Werner Keller, pages 228, 229 N.Y. Ed.; pages 223, 224 London Ed.

9. How do discoveries at Gihon support the Bible record?
10. What striking confirmation of Shishak's invasion and Bible place names has been found at Karnak?
11, 12. What is the history of the Moabite Stone, and in what ways does it give confirmation of the Bible?

But I saw my desire upon him and upon his house, and Israel perished forever."[a] "And Chemosh said unto me, Go, take Nebo against Israel. And I went by night and fought against it from the break of dawn until noon. And I took it and slew the whole of it. . . . And I took thence the vessels of *Yahweh* and I dragged them before Chemosh."[b] Note the mention of the divine name in the last sentence. This can be seen in the picture of the Moabite Stone on page 333, to the right of the document, in line 18, as the tetragrammaton written in the Hebrew-Phoenician characters. This is the oldest document known in this form of writing.

12 In further confirmation of the authenticity of the Scriptural record, the Moabite Stone also mentions the following Bible places: Ataroth and Nebo (Num. 32:34, 38), the Arnon, Aroer, Medeba and Dibon (Josh. 13:9), Bamoth-baal, Beth-baal-meon, Jahaz and Kiriathaim (Josh. 13:17-19), Bezer (Josh. 20:8), Horoniam (Isa. 15:5), Beth-diblathaim and Kerioth.—Jer. 48:22, 24.

13 **King Sennacherib's Prism.** The Bible records in considerable detail the invasion by the Assyrians under King Sennacherib in the year 732 B.C.E. (2 Ki. 18:13 to 19:37; 2 Chron. 32:1-22; Isa. 36:1 to 37:38) It was during 1847-1851 that the English archaeologist A. H. Layard excavated the ruins of Sennacherib's great palace at Kuyunjik in the territory of ancient Assyria. The palace was found to have seventy-one rooms, with 9,880 feet of walls lined with sculptured slabs. The yearly reports of events, or annals, of Sennacherib were recorded on clay cylinders or "prisms." The final edition of these annals, apparently made shortly before his death, appears on what is known as the Taylor Prism, preserved in the British Museum, but the Oriental Institute of the University of Chicago has an even finer copy on a prism that was discovered near the site of ancient Nineveh, the capital of the Assyrian Empire.

King Sennacherib's Prism (Courtesy of the Oriental Institute, University of Chicago)

14 In these last annals Sennacherib gives his own boastful version of his invasion of Judah: "As for Hezekiah, the Jew, who did not submit to my yoke, 46 of his strong, walled cities, as well as the small cities in their neighborhood, which were without number,—by escalade [assault ladder] and by bringing up siege engines, by attacking and storming on foot, by mines, tunnels and breaches, I besieged and took. [Note that he correctly omits to claim taking Jerusalem.] 200,150 people, great and small, male and female, horses, mules, asses, camels, cattle and sheep, without number, I brought away from them and counted as spoil. Himself, like a caged bird, I shut up in Jerusalem, his royal city. . . . I added to the former tribute, and laid upon him as their yearly payment, a tax in the form of gifts . . . 30 talents of gold and 800 talents of silver, . . . [and] all kinds of valuable treasures." As for this tribute imposed by Sennacherib upon Hezekiah, the Bible confirms the thirty talents of gold, but mentions only three hundred talents of silver. Moreover, it shows that this was *before* Sennacherib threatened Jerusalem with siege. In Sennacherib's slanted report for Assyrian history, he purposely omits mention of his crushing defeat in Judah, when in one night Jehovah's angel destroyed 185,000 of his soldiers, thus forcing him to flee back to Nineveh like a whipped dog. Nevertheless, this boastful, pagan "prism" record indicates an immense invasion of Judah before Jehovah turned the Assyrians back after threatening Jerusalem.[c]—2 Ki. 18:14; 19:35, 36.

15 **The Lachish Letters.** The famous fortress city of Lachish is mentioned twenty-three times in the Bible. It was located about thirty miles southwest of Jerusalem. The ruins have been extensively excavated. In 1935, in a guardroom of the double gatehouse, there were found eighteen ostraca, or pieces of pottery inscribed with writing. These turned out to be a number of letters written in the ancient Hebrew-Phoenician script. This collection of eighteen is now known as the Lachish Letters, and they are in the possession of the Wellcome Trustees in Britain. Lachish was one of the last strongholds of Judah to

a *Light from the Ancient Past,* pages 157, 158.
b *The Bible and Archaeology,* 1940, Sir Frederic Kenyon, page 166.

c *Light from the Ancient Past,* pages 176, 177.

13. What does the Bible record concerning Sennacherib, and what have excavations of his palace revealed?
14. What does Sennacherib record, in support of the Bible account, but what does he fail to mention, and why?

15, 16. (a) What are the Lachish Letters, and what do they reflect? (b) How do they support Jeremiah's writings?

hold out against Nebuchadnezzar, being reduced to a pile of charred ruins in 609-607 B.C.E. The letters reflect the urgency of the times. They appear to be letters written from remaining outposts of Judean troops to Ya'osh, a military commander at Lachish. One of these reads in part: "May YHWH [Tetragrammaton, Jehovah] let my lord hear even now tidings of good. . . . we are watching for the signal-stations of Lachish, according to all the signs which my lord gives, because we do not see Azekah." This is a striking confirmation of Jeremiah 34:7, which mentions Lachish and Azekah as the last two fortified cities left remaining. According to this letter, Azekah had now fallen. The divine name, in the form of the tetragrammaton, appears frequently in the letters, showing that the Jews were not at that time averse to using the name.

16 Another letter commences as follows: "May the Lord [YHWH] cause my lord to hear tidings of peace! . . . And it hath been reported to thy servant saying, 'The commander of the host, Coniah son of Elnathan, hath come down in order to go into Egypt and unto Hodaviah son of Ahijah and his men hath he sent to obtain [supplies] from him.'" This letter confirms that Judah went down to Egypt for assistance, in violation of Jehovah's command, and to her own destruction. (Isa. 31:1; Jer. 46:25, 26) The Elnathan of this letter may be the one mentioned at Jeremiah 36:12. Hoshaiah is named as the writer of one of these letters, and may be the Hoshaiah of Jeremiah 42:1 and 43:2. Three other persons referred to in the letters appear to be mentioned in the Bible book of Jeremiah. They are Gemariah (36:10), Neriah (32:12) and Jaazaniah (35:3). Thus, in many respects, the Lachish Letters give striking support to Jeremiah's writings in the Bible.[a]

17 **The Nabonidus Chronicle.** In the latter half of the nineteenth century excavations near modern Baghdad produced many finds of clay tablets and cylinders that threw much light on the history of ancient Babylon. One of these was the very valuable document known as the Nabonidus Chronicle, or Nabunaid Chronicle, which is now in the British Museum. King Nabonidus of Babylon was the father of his coregent Belshazzar. He outlived his son, who was killed on the night that troops of Cyrus the Persian took Babylon, October 5-6, 539 B.C.E. (Dan. 5:30, 31) Nabonidus' remarkably well-dated record of the fall of Babylon is our means of establishing on what day this event occurred. Following is a translation of a small part of the Nabonidus Chronicle: "In the month of Tashritu [Tishri, Hebrew 7th month], when Cyrus attacked the army of Akkad in Opis on the Tigris . . . the 15th day, Sippar was seized without battle. Nabonidus fled. The 16th day [October 11-12, 539 B.C.E., Julian or October 5-6, Gregorian] Gobryas (Ugbaru), the governor of Gutium and the army of Cyrus entered Babylon without battle. Afterwards Nabonidus was arrested in Babylon when he returned (there). . . . In the month of Arahshmanu [Heshvan, Hebrew 8th month], the 3rd day [October 28-29, Julian], Cyrus entered Babylon, green twigs were spread in front of him—the state of 'Peace' (Sulmu) was imposed upon the city. Cyrus sent greetings to all Babylon. Gobryas, his governor, installed (sub-)governors in Babylon. . . . In the month of Arahshmanu on the night of the 11th day [November 5-6, 539 B.C.E., Julian] Gobryas died."[b]

The Nabonidus Chronicle
(Courtesy of the Trustees of the British Museum)

18 It may be noted that Darius the Mede is not mentioned in this chronicle, and, thus far, no mention has been found of this Darius in any historical document outside the Bible. Some have therefore suggested that he might be the Gobryas mentioned in the above account, but there is objection to this. In any event, secular history definitely establishes that Cyrus

a *Light from the Ancient Past,* pages 160-162; *The Bible and Archaeology,* pages 195-197.

b *Ancient Near Eastern Texts Relating to the Old Testament,* 1955, J. B. Pritchard, pages 305-307.

17, 18. What does the Nabonidus Chronicle describe, and why is it of special value?

was a key figure in the conquest of Babylon and that he thereafter ruled there as king.

19 **The Cyrus Cylinder.** Some time after he began ruling as king of the Persian world power, Cyrus recorded on a clay cylinder his capture of Babylon in 539 B.C.E., mentioning also some of the evils that he corrected there. This outstanding document was found at the ancient site of Sippar, on the Euphrates and about twenty miles from Baghdad, and is also preserved in the British Museum. A part of the translated text follows: "I am Cyrus, king of the world, the great king, the powerful king, king of Babylon, king of Sumer and Akkad, king of the four quarters of the world . . . When I made my triumphal entrance into Babylon, with joy and rejoicing I took up my lordly residence in the royal palace, Marduk, the great lord, moved the noble heart of the inhabitants of Babylon to me, while I gave daily care to his worship. My numerous troops marched peacefully into Babylon. . . . The needs of Babylon and all its cities I gladly took heed to . . . the gods, who dwelt in them, I brought them back to their places, and caused them to dwell in a habitation for all time. All their inhabitants I collected and restored them to their dwelling places. . . . May all the gods, whom I brought into their cities pray daily for long life for me."[a]

20 The Cyrus Cylinder thus makes known the king's policy of restoring captive peoples and their gods to their former places, in harmony with which he issued his decree for the Jews to return to Jerusalem and rebuild the house of Jehovah there. Once again the Bible stands vindicated as true, this time by the testimony of Cyrus, whom Jehovah had foretold by name two hundred years previously as the one who would take Babylon and bring about the restoration of Jehovah's people.—Isa. 44:28; 45:1; 2 Chron. 36:23.

ARCHAEOLOGY AND THE CHRISTIAN GREEK SCRIPTURES

21 As with the Hebrew Scriptures, so with the Christian Greek Scriptures, archaeology has brought to light many interesting artifacts in support of the inspired record.

22 **Denarius Coin with Tiberius' Inscription.** The Bible shows clearly that Jesus' ministry took place during the rule of Tiberius Caesar. (Luke 3:1) Some of Jesus' opposers tried to trap him on the matter of paying head tax to Caesar. The record reads: "Detecting their hypocrisy, he said to them: 'Why do you put me to the test? Bring me a denarius to look at.' They brought one. And he said to them: 'Whose image and inscription is this?' They said to him: 'Caesar's.' Jesus then said: 'Pay back Caesar's things to Caesar, but God's things to God.' And they began to marvel at him." (Mark 12:15-17) Now, archaeology has come up with a silver denarius coin, bearing the head of Tiberius Caesar! It was put in circulation A.D. 15.[b] This is consistent with Tiberius' ruling as emperor from August 19, A.D. 14, and brings added confirmation to the record stating that John the Baptist's ministry commenced in the fifteenth year of Tiberius, or the spring of A.D. 29.—Luke 3:1, 2.

23 **Pontius Pilate Inscription.** It was in 1961 that the first archaeological find was made with reference to Pontius Pilate. This was a stone slab located at Caesarea, which bore the Latin names *Pontius Pilatus* and *Tiberius*.[c]

24 **The Areopagus.** Paul delivered one of his most famous recorded speeches in Athens, Greece, A.D. 50. (Acts 17:16-34) This was on the occasion when he was brought to the Areopagus before the council composed of city fathers. The Areopagus, or Hill of Ares ("Mars Hill"), is the name of a bare, rocky hill, about 370 feet high, immediately northwest of the Acropolis of Athens. Steps cut in the rock lead to the top, where rough, rock-hewn benches, forming three sides of a square, can still be seen. The Areopagus still remains, to confirm the Bible's recorded setting for Paul's historic speech.

25 **The Arch of Titus.** Jerusalem and its temple were destroyed by the Romans under Titus, A.D. 70. The next year, in Rome, Titus celebrated his triumph, together with his father, Emperor Vespasian. Seven hundred Jewish prisoners were marched in the triumphal procession. Loads of the spoils of war were also paraded, including temple treasures. Titus himself became emperor, from A.D. 79 to 81, and after his death a large monument, the Arch of Titus, was completed and dedicated *divo Tito* ("to the deified Titus"). His triumphant procession is represented in bas-relief, carved on each side of the passage through the Arch. On the one side there are depicted the Roman soldiers, without weapons

a *Cuneiform Parallels to the Old Testament,* 1912, R. W. Rogers, pages 380-383.

b *Harper's Bible Dictionary,* 1952, pages 456, 758.

c *The New Bible Dictionary,* 1962, J. D. Douglas, page 997.

19. Where was the Cyrus Cylinder found, where is it preserved, and what is recorded on it?
20. How does this harmonize with and vindicate the Bible?
21. What does archaeology have to tell us in connection with the Greek Scriptures?
22. How does archaeology support Jesus' discussion of the tax question?
23. What find has been made with reference to Pontius Pilate?
24. What still remains to confirm the setting of Acts 17:16-34?
25. To what does the Arch of Titus continue to testify, and how?

and crowned with laurels, carrying the sacred furniture from Jerusalem's temple. This includes the seven-branched lampstand and the table of showbread, upon which the sacred trumpets are seen resting. The relief on the other side of the passage shows the victorious Titus, standing in a car drawn by four horses, and conducted by a woman representing the city of Rome.[a] Each year thousands of sightseers view this triumphal Arch of Titus, which still stands in Rome as silent testimony to the fulfillment of Jesus' prophecy and the terrible execution of Jehovah's judgment upon rebellious Jerusalem.—Matt. 23:37–24:2; Luke 19:43, 44; 21:20-24.

26 In the same way that the discovery of ancient manuscripts has helped to restore the pure, original text of the Bible, so the discovery of the multitude of artifacts has brought convincing confirmation that the things stated in the Bible text are historically, chronologically and geographically reliable, right down to the minutest details. Thus archaeology has confounded the critics of the Bible. The noted British scholar, the late Sir Frederic Kenyon, who was director and principal librarian of the British Museum for many years, had the following to say concerning the Bible: "The evidence of archaeology has been to re-establish its authority, and likewise to augment its value by rendering it more intelligible through a fuller knowledge of its background and setting. Archaeology has not yet said its last word; but the results already achieved confirm what faith would suggest, that the Bible can do nothing but gain from an increase of knowledge."[b]

a *Light from the Ancient Past,* pages 249, 250.

26. (a) In what way has archaeology worked hand in hand with manuscript discoveries? (b) What view does Sir Frederic Kenyon express concerning archaeology and the Bible?

27 However, archaeology is not alone in testifying to the integrity of the Bible record. Other fields of secular knowledge and research bring accumulating proofs of the authenticity of the Bible, as we will see in the next Study.

b *The Bible and Archaeology,* page 279.

27. Is archaeology alone in testifying to the Bible's integrity?

Study Ten— The Bible— Authentic and True

The Bible's coverage of history, geography and human origins; its accuracy as to science, culture and customs; the candor, harmony and integrity of its writers; and prophecy.

THE Bible is generally accepted as a great literary masterpiece of transcendent poetic beauty and a remarkable accomplishment for the men who were its writers. But it is much more than that. The writers themselves testified to the fact that what they wrote originated with Jehovah, the Almighty God himself. This is the underlying reason for the Bible's beauty of expression and, more importantly, its surpassing value as the book of life-giving knowledge and wisdom. Jesus, the Son of God, testified that the words he spoke "are spirit and are life," and he quoted copiously from the ancient Hebrew Scriptures. "All Scripture is inspired of God," said the apostle Paul, who spoke of the Hebrew Scriptures as "the sacred pronouncements of God." —John 6:63; 2 Tim. 3:16; Rom. 3:1, 2.

2 The apostle Peter testified that the prophets of God were moved by holy spirit. King David wrote: "The spirit of Jehovah it was that spoke by me, and his word was upon my tongue." The prophets credited their utterances to Jehovah. Moses warned against any addition to or taking away from the sacred words given him by Jehovah. Peter counted Paul's writings as inspired, and Jude quoted Peter's statement as inspired authority. Finally John, the writer of Revelation, wrote as he was directed by the spirit of God and warned that anyone adding to or taking away from this prophetic revelation would be accountable, not to man but directly to God.—1 Pet. 1:10-12; 2 Pet. 1:19-21; 2 Sam. 23:2; Deut. 4:2; 2 Pet. 3:15, 16; Jude 17, 18; Rev. 1:1, 10; 21:5; 22: 18, 19.

3 These devoted slaves of God all testified that the Bible is inspired and true. There are many other proofs of the authenticity of the Holy Scriptures, some of which we will discuss under the twelve headings that follow.

1. (a) As what is the Bible generally accepted? (b) However, what is the underlying reason for the Bible's preeminence?
2, 3. How do the Bible's writers testify to its inspiration?

4 **(1) Historical Accuracy.** From the earliest times the canonical books of the Hebrew Scriptures have been received by the Jews as inspired and as wholly trustworthy documents. Thus, in David's time, the events recorded from Genesis to First Samuel were fully accepted as the true history of the nation and God's dealings with them, and this is illustrated by the 78th Psalm, which refers to more than thirty-five of these details. Opponents of the Bible have strongly attacked the Pentateuch, especially as to authenticity and authorship. But step by step the critics have had to retreat as modern research has brought new facts to light. For example, it is now clear that Moses compiled the first thirty-six chapters of Genesis from documents written and kept by his predecessors, some evidently being carried by Noah through the flood, so that he finally had eleven documents from which to compile the account of mankind's history as it related to God's dealings with them.[a]

5 To the Jews' acceptance of Moses as writer of the Pentateuch may be added the testimony of heathen writers, some of them enemies of the Jews. Hecataeus of Abdera, Manetho the Egyptian historian, Lysimachus of Alexandria, Eupolemus, Tacitus and Juvenal, all ascribe to Moses the institution of the code of laws distinguishing the Jews from other nations, and the majority distinctly note that he committed his laws to writing. Numenius, the Pythagorean philosopher, even mentions Jannes and Jambres as the Egyptian priests who withstood Moses. (2 Tim. 3:8) These authors cover a period extending from the time of Alexander (4th century B.C.E.), when the Greeks first became curious about Jewish history, to that of Emperor Aurelian (3d century A.D.). Many other ancient writers mention Moses as a leader, ruler or lawgiver.[b] As we have seen from the previous study, archaeological discoveries confirm the historical accuracy of many events recorded in the Bible where God's people became involved with the surrounding nations.

6 But what of the Christian Greek Scriptures? Not only do they verify the Hebrew Scripture account, but they themselves are proved to be historically accurate as well as authentic and of equal inspiration with the Hebrew Scriptures. The writers declare to us what they heard and saw, for they were eyewitnesses of and often participators in the very events that they recorded. They were believed by thousands of their contemporaries. Their testimony finds abundant support in the words of heathen writers, among whom are Juvenal, Tacitus, Seneca, Suetonius, Pliny the Younger, Lucian, Celsus and Josephus the Jewish historian.

7 Writing in *The Union Bible Companion,* S. Austin Allibone says: "Sir Isaac Newton . . . was also eminent as a critic of ancient writings, and examined with great care the Holy Scriptures. What is his verdict on this point? 'I find,' says he, 'more sure marks of authenticity in the New Testament than in any profane history whatever.' Dr. Johnson says that we have more evidence that Jesus Christ died on Calvary, as stated in the Gospels, than we have that Julius Caesar died in the Capitol. We have, indeed, far more. Ask anyone who professes to doubt the truth of the Gospel history what reason he has for believing that Caesar died in the Capitol, or that the Emperor Charlemagne was crowned Emperor of the West by Pope Leo III in 800 . . . How do you know that such a man as Charles I ever lived, and was beheaded, and that Oliver Cromwell became ruler in his stead? . . . Sir Isaac Newton is credited with the discovery of the law of gravitation . . . We believe all the assertions just made respecting these men; and that because we have historical evidence of their truth. . . . If, on the production of such proof as this, any still refuse to believe, we abandon them as stupidly perverse or hopelessly ignorant. What shall we say, then, of those who, notwithstanding the abundant evidence now produced of the authenticity of the Holy Scriptures, profess themselves unconvinced? . . . Surely we have reason to conclude that it is the heart rather than the head which is at fault;—that they do not wish to believe that which humbles their pride, and will force them to lead different lives."[c]

8 The superiority of Christianity as a religion whose followers worship 'with truth' is highlighted by George Rawlinson, who says: "Christianity—including therein the dispensation of the Old Testament, which was its first stage—is in nothing more distinguished from the other religions of the world than in its

a *New Discoveries in Babylonia About Genesis,* 1949, P. J. Wiseman, pages 45-47.

b *The Historical Evidences of the Truth of the Scripture Records,* 1862, George Rawlinson, pages 54, 254-258.

c *The Union Bible Companion,* 1871, S. A. Allibone, pages 29-31.

4. (a) How was Moses able to write an accurate account of history up till his time? (b) How were such historical records always viewed by the Jews?
5. What have ancient writers testified concerning Moses and the law code of the Jews?
6. What testimony supports the historical accuracy of the Greek Scriptures?
7. (a) What argument does one commentator present as to the Bible's superior claims to authenticity? (b) What does he point to as being at fault with those who refuse the evidence?
8. In what way is the Christianity of the Bible shown to be in contrast with all other religions?

objective or historical character. The religions of Greece and Rome, of Egypt, India, Persia, and the East generally, were speculative systems, which did not even seriously postulate an historical basis. . . . But it is otherwise with the religion of the Bible. There, whether we look to the Old or the New Testament, to the Jewish dispensation or to the Christian, we find a scheme of doctrine which is bound up with facts; which depends absolutely upon them; which is null and void without them; and which may be regarded as for all practical purposes established if they are shown to deserve acceptance. . . . Dr. Stanley tersely expresses the contrast between the Christian and other religions in this respect, when he says of Christianity, that it 'alone, of all religions, claims to be founded not on fancy or feeling, but on Fact and Truth.' "[a]

9 **(2) Geographical and Geological Accuracy.** Many writers have commented on the remarkable accuracy of the Bible description of the Promised Land and neighboring territories. As an example, an Oriental traveler, Dr. Stanley, said concerning the Israelites' wilderness trek: "Even if the precise route of the Israelites were unknown, yet the peculiar features of the country have so much in common that the history would still receive many remarkable illustrations. . . . The occasional springs, and wells, and brooks, are in accordance with the notices of the 'waters' of Marah, the 'springs' of Elim, the 'brook' of Horeb; the 'well' of Jethro's daughters, with its 'troughs' or tanks. The vegetation is still that which we should infer from the Mosaic history." In the account of Egypt the accuracy is seen not only in the general description of the territory —its rich grain lands, its Nile River, edged with reeds (Gen. 41:47-49; Ex. 2:3), its waters derived from 'rivers, canals, reedy pools and impounded waters' (Ex. 7:19), its 'flax, barley, wheat and spelt' (Ex. 9:31, 32)—but also in the names and sites of towns.[b]

10 Such is the reliance placed on the geological and geographical record in the Bible by some modern-day scientists that they have followed it as a guide and have been well rewarded. One of the Israeli Republic's leading geologists, Dr. Ben Tor, followed through on the scripture: "For Jehovah your God is bringing you into a good land, . . . a land the stones of which are iron." (Deut. 8:7, 9) A few miles from Beer-sheba he found immense cliffs saturated with red-black ore. Here was an estimated fifteen million tons of low-grade iron ore. Recently, engineers discovered a mile-long outcropping of excellent ore, 60 to 65 percent pure iron. Israel's noted authority on reforestation, Dr. Joseph Weitz, said: "The first tree Abraham put in the soil of Beersheba was a tamarisk. Following his lead, four years ago we put out two million in the same area. Abraham was right. The tamarisk is one of the few trees we have found that thrives in the south where yearly rainfall is less than six inches."—Gen. 21:33.[c]

11 As to small details such as chronological and geographical statements in the Bible, Professor R. D. Wilson writes in *A Scientific Investigation of the Old Testament,* p. 213: "Whenever there is sufficient documentary evidence to make an investigation, the statements of the Bible in the original text have stood the test. . . . The chronological and geographical statements are more accurate and reliable than those afforded by any other ancient documents; the biographical and other historical narratives harmonize marvellously with the evidence afforded by extra-Biblical documents."

12 **(3) Races and Languages of Mankind.** In his book, *After Its Kind,* 1927, page 21, Byron C. Nelson says: "It was *man* that was created, not the Negro, the Chinese, the European. Two human beings whom the Bible knows as Adam and Eve were created, out of whom by natural descent and variation have come all the varieties of men that are on the face of the earth. All races of men, regardless of color or size, are one natural species. They all think alike, feel alike, are alike in physical structure, readily intermarry, and are capable of reproducing others of the same character. All races are descended from two common ancestors who came full-formed from the hand of the Creator." This is the testimony of Genesis 1:27, 28; 2:7, 20-23; 3:20; Acts 17:26 and Romans 5:12.

13 As to the Bible's account of the origin of the races of mankind, Sir Henry Rawlinson, archaeologist, in speaking of the different races in western Asia, says: "It is pleasing to remark, that if we were to be guided by the mere intersection of linguistic paths, and independently of all reference to the Scriptural record, we should still be led to fix on the plains of Shinar, as the focus from which the various lines had radiated."[d] Thus the 4,000-

a *The Historical Evidences of the Truth of the Scripture Records,* pages 25, 26, 232, 233.
b *Ibid.*, pages 288, 289.

c *Reader's Digest,* March 1954, pages 27, 30.
d *The Historical Evidences of the Truth of the Scripture Records,* page 287.

9. Illustrate the accuracy of the Bible's geographical references.
10. How have modern scientists been rewarded in following the Bible record?
11. What does Professor Wilson testify concerning Bible accuracy?
12. How do the facts fit the Bible record of the origin of mankind?
13. What modern scientific support is there for Genesis 11:1-9?

year-old record of Genesis 11:1-9, concerning Jehovah's confusing the tongues and scattering mankind from Babel in Shinar, finds modern scientific support.

14 **(4) Practicality.** If there were no other proofs of authenticity available, the Bible's righteous principles and moral standards would alone set it apart as a product of the divine mind. Its practicality extends to every phase of daily living. No other book gives us a rational view of the origin of all things, including mankind, and of the Creator's purpose toward earth and man. (Gen., chapter 1; Isa. 45:18) The Bible tells us why man dies, why wickedness exists. (Gen., chapter 3; Rom. 5:12; Job, chapters 1, 2; Ex. 9:16) It sets out the highest standard of justice. (Num. 35:16, 32; Deut. 19:15-21) It even contains instruction for kings and rulers. (Deut. 17:15-20) It gives right counsel on business dealings (Lev. 19:35, 36; Prov. 20:10; 22:22, 23; Matt. 7:12), clean morals (Lev. 20:10-16; Gal. 5:19-23; Heb. 13:4), relationships with others (Matt. 7:12; 1 Tim. 5:1, 2; Prov. 12:15; 15:1; 29:11; 27:1, 2, 5, 6; Lev. 19:18), marriage (Matt. 19:4, 5, 9; 1 Cor. 7:2, 9, 10, 26, 38, 39; Gen. 2:22-24), family relationships and duties of husband, wife and children (Deut. 6:4-9; Eph. 6:1-4; 5:21-33; Prov. 13:24; Col. 3:18-21; 1 Pet. 3:1-6), proper attitude toward rulers (Rom. 13:1-10; Tit. 3:1; 1 Pet. 2:13, 14; 1 Tim. 2:1, 2), honest work and master-slave and employer-employee relationships (Eph. 4:28; Col. 3:22-24; 4:1; 1 Pet. 2:18-21), proper associations (Heb. 10:24, 25; 1 Cor. 15:33; Prov. 1:10-16; 5:3-11; 2 Tim. 2:22), settling disputes (Matt. 18:15-17; Eph. 4:26) and many other things that vitally affect our everyday lives.

15 The Bible also provides valuable pointers to physical and mental health. (Prov. 17:22; 15:17) Sir George Vickers, writing in the British medical journal *The Lancet*, March 12, 1955, stated: "The most significant discovery of mental science is the power of love to protect and restore the mind." However, this "discovery" is but a belated recognition of what the Bible had long ago stated on this point. Love, the basis of the two greatest commandments, has the greatest curative power.—Matt. 22:37, 39; 1 Cor. 13:1-13; 1 John 4:18; John 13:34, 35.

16 **(5) Scientific Accuracy.** Though the Bible is not a treatise on science, where it touches on scientific matters it is found to be in accurate harmony with true scientific discovery and knowledge. Its record of the order of creation, including animal life (Gen., chapter 1), the earth's being round or spherical (Isa. 40:22) and the fact that it is hung in space on "nothing" antedate scientific discoveries of these truths. (Job 26:7) Modern physiology has demonstrated the truth of the Scriptural statement that "not all flesh is the same flesh," the cellular structure of the flesh of one kind being different from that of another, man having his own unique "flesh." (1 Cor. 15:39)[a] In the field of zoology, Leviticus 11:6 classes the hare with the cud-chewing animals. This was once scoffed at, but science now finds that the rabbit reingests its food by a process labeled "pseudorumination."[b]

17 The statement that the 'life of the flesh is in the blood' has in modern times come to be recognized as a basic truth of medical science. (Lev. 17:11-14) The Mosaic law indicated which animals, birds and fish were "clean" for human consumption, and excluded risky foods. (Lev., chapter 11) It was not until World War I that medical science came up-to-date with Moses' program of hygiene and took effectual precautions to eliminate water-borne and insect-borne diseases such as dysentery and typhoid fever, which had long plagued armies in the field.[c]—Deut. 23:12-14.

18 The Bible recommends a little wine for "the sake of your stomach" and for "sickness." (1 Tim. 5:23) Dr. Salvatore P. Lucia, professor of medicine at the University of California School of Medicine, in *Wine as Food and Medicine* writes: "Wine is the most ancient dietary beverage and the most important medicinal agent in continuous use throughout the history of mankind."[d] Even a passing remark, such as Job's "I escape with the skin of my teeth" (Job 19:20) is scientifically accurate, as tooth enamel is made up of skin cells.[e]

19 **(6) Culture and Customs.** A. Rendle Short writes in *Modern Discovery and the Bible*, 1943, pages 159-161, about the book of Acts: "It was the Roman custom to govern the provinces of their farflung empire by continuing as far as they safely could the local system of administration, and consequently the authorities in different districts went by many

a *Scientific American*, September 1961, pages 51, 54, 146.
b *Proceedings of the Zoological Society of London*, 1940, Vol. 110, pages 159-163.
c *Basis for Belief in a New World*, page 42.
d *Awake!*, March 8, 1960, page 15.
e *Scientific American*, June 1953, in an article entitled "The Skin of Your Teeth," page 39.

14. (a) What alone would set the Bible apart as inspired of God? (b) What rational view is presented only in the Bible, and how does its practicality extend to every phase of daily living?
15. What belated "discovery" has science made that supports the Bible's practical counsel as to physical and spiritual health?
16. What are some of the Bible statements of truth that far outdate their discovery by science?
17. With what information in the Mosaic law has medical science recently come up-to-date?
18. What other illustrations of the Bible's scientific accuracy are given?
19. How may the "perfect accuracy" of Luke's writings be illustrated?

different names. No one, unless he were either an observant traveller or a painstaking student of records, could possibly give all these gentry their correct denomination. It is one of the most searching tests of Luke's historical sense that he always manages to achieve perfect accuracy. In several cases it is only the evidence of a coin, or an inscription, that has given us the necessary information to check him; the recognized Roman historians do not adventure themselves on such a difficult terrain. Thus Luke calls Herod and Lysanias tetrarchs; so does Josephus. Herod Agrippa, who slew James with the sword and cast Peter into prison, is called a king; Josephus tells us how he became friendly at Rome with Gaius Caesar (Caligula) and was rewarded with a royal title when Caligula came to be emperor. The governor of Cyprus, Sergius Paulus, is called proconsul. . . . Not long before, Cyprus had been an imperial province, and governed by a propraetor or legatus, but in Paul's time, as is shown by Cyprian coins, both in Greek and Latin, the correct title was proconsul. A Greek inscription found at Soloi on the north coast of Cyprus is dated 'in the proconsulship of Paulus,' probably the same as Sergius Paulus. . . . At Thessalonica the city magnates took the quite unusual title of politarchs, a name unknown to classical literature. It would be quite unfamiliar to us, except from Luke's use of it, if it were not for the fact that it appears in inscriptions. . . . Achaia under Augustus was a senatorial province, under Tiberius it was directly under the emperor, but under Claudius, as Tacitus tells us, it reverted to the senate, and therefore Gallio's correct title [Acts 18:12] was proconsul. . . . Luke is equally happy, equally accurate, in his geography and his travel experiences."

[20] Paul's letters accurately reflect the background of his time and indicate that he was an eyewitness of the things written. For example, Philippi was a military colony whose citizens were especially proud of their Roman citizenship. Paul admonished the Christians there that their citizenship was in the heavens. (Acts 16:12, 21, 37; Phil. 3:20) Ephesus was a city noted for magical arts and spiritistic practices. Paul instructed Christians there how to arm themselves against becoming prey to the demons, and at the same time gave an accurate description of the armor of a Roman soldier. (Acts 19:19; Eph. 6:13-17) The custom of Roman victors, of leading a triumphant march with a procession of captives, some naked, is used in illustration. (2 Cor. 2:14; Col. 2:15) At 1 Corinthians 1:22 the differing outlooks of Jews and Greeks are pointed out. In such matters, the Christian writers reflect the accuracy of Moses, the writer of the Pentateuch, of which George Rawlinson says: "The *ethological* accuracy of the Pentateuch as respects Oriental manners and customs generally, has never been questioned."[a]

[21] **(7) Candor of Bible Writers.** Throughout the Bible, the unhesitating candor of its writers is strong proof of its reliability. Moses, for example, straightforwardly tells of his own sin and God's judgment that he and his brother Aaron should not enter the Promised Land. (Num. 20:7-13; Deut. 3:23-27) The sins of David on two occasions as well as the apostasy of his son Solomon are openly exposed. (2 Sam., chapters 11, 12 and 24; 1 Ki. 11:1-13) Jonah writes about his own disobedience and its result. The entire nation of Israel was condemned by nearly all the writers of the Hebrew Scriptures, all of whom were Jews, for its disobedience to God, in the very record the Jews cherished and accepted as the pronouncements of God and the true history of their nation. The Christian writers were no less candid. All four of the Gospel writers revealed Peter's denial of Christ. And Paul called attention to Peter's serious error on a matter of faith in making a separation between Jews and Gentiles in the Christian congregation at Antioch. It builds confidence in the Bible as truth, when we realize that its writers spared no one, not even themselves, in the interests of making a faithful record.—Matt. 26:69-75; Mark 14:66-72; Luke 22:54-62; John 18:15-27; Gal. 2:11-14; John 17:17.

[22] **(8) Harmony of Writers.** The fact that the Bible was written over a period of more than 1,600 years by about forty writers, with no disharmony, and the phenomenon of its being so widely distributed in such tremendous numbers despite the fiercest opposition and the most energetic efforts to destroy it, prove that it is what it claims to be, the Word of the Almighty God, and that it is indeed "beneficial for teaching, for reproving, for setting things straight, for disciplining in righteousness."—2 Tim. 3:16.

[23] Its inspiration is shown by the thorough consistency with which it emphasizes the theme of sanctification of Jehovah's name by his kingdom under Christ. A few of the outstanding instances are:

a *The Historical Evidences of the Truth of the Scripture Records*, page 290.

20. How do Paul's writings accurately reflect the times in which he lived and wrote?

21. (a) Give examples of the candor of the Bible writers. (b) How does this build confidence in the Bible as truth?
22. What else proves that the Bible is indeed God's Word, and for what purpose was it written?
23. What consistent theme also proves the Bible's inspiration? Illustrate.

Gen. 3:15	Promise of the Seed to destroy the Serpent
Gen. 22:15-18	All nations to be blessed by means of Abraham's seed
Ex. 3:15; 6:3	God emphasizes his memorial name Jehovah
Ex. 9:16; Rom. 9:17	God declares purpose to have name published
Ex. 18:11; Isa. 36:18-20; 37:20, 36-38; Jer. 10:10, 11	Jehovah greater than all other gods
Ex. 20:3-7	God respects name, demands exclusive devotion
Job chaps. 1, 2	Jehovah's rightful sovereignty and man's attitude and integrity toward it
Job 32:2; 35:2; 36:24; 40:8	God's vindication brought to the fore
Isa. 9:7	God zealously supports everlasting kingdom of his Son
Dan. 2:44; 4:17, 34; 7:13, 14	The importance of God's kingdom by the "son of man"
Ezek. 6:10; 38:23	People "will have to know that I am Jehovah." This statement appears more than sixty times in the prophecy of Ezekiel
Mal. 1:11	God's name to be great among the nations
Matt. 6:9, 10, 33	Sanctification of God's name by his kingdom is of first importance
John 17:6, 26	Jesus declared God's name
Acts 2:21; Rom. 10:13	Jehovah's name to be called on for salvation
Rom. 3:4	God to be proved true, though every man a liar
1 Cor. 15:24-28	God to be all things to everyone by means of the kingdom under Christ
Heb. 13:15	Christians must make public declaration to Jehovah's name
Rev. 15:4	Jehovah's name to be glorified by all nations
Rev. 19:6	Jehovah's name praised when he takes Kingdom power

24 **(9) Integrity of Witnesses.** Of the weight that may be accorded the testimony of early Christians, the writers of the Christian Scriptures as well as a great number of others, George Rawlinson says: "The early converts knew that they might at any time be called upon to undergo death for their religion. They preached and taught with the sword, the cross, the beasts, and the stake ever before their eyes. . . . and every early writer advocating Christianity, by the fact of his advocacy, braved the civil power, and rendered himself liable to a similar fate. When faith is a matter of life and death, men do not lightly take up with the first creed which happens to hit their fancy; nor do they place themselves openly in the ranks of a persecuted sect, unless they have well weighed the claims of the religion which it professes, and convinced themselves of its being the truth. It is clear that the early converts had means of ascertaining the historic accuracy of the Christian narrative very much beyond ourselves; they could examine and cross-question the witnesses—compare their several accounts—inquire how their statements were met by their adversaries—consult Heathen documents of the time—thoroughly and completely sift the evidence. All this together—and it must be remembered that the evidence is *cumulative*—constitutes a body of proof such as is seldom producible with respect to any events belonging to remote times; and establishes beyond all reasonable doubt the truth of the Christian Story. In no single respect . . . has that story a mythic character. It is a single story, told without variation, whereas myths are fluctuating and multiform; it is blended inextricably with the civil history of the times, which it everywhere represents with extraordinary accuracy, whereas myths distort or supersede civil history; it is full of prosaic detail, which myths studiously eschew; it abounds with practical instruction of the plainest and simplest kind, whereas myths teach by allegory. . . . Simple earnestness, fidelity, painstaking accuracy, pure love of truth, are the most patent characteristics of the New Testament writers, who evidently deal with facts, not with fancies. . . . They write 'that we may know the certainty of those things' which were 'most surely believed' in their day."[a]

25 An enthralling field covered by this Book is that of divine prophecy. The authenticity of the Bible has been in no way as strikingly demonstrated as in the fulfillment of multitudes of prophecies, all showing the remarkable forevision of Jehovah in foretelling the future. This prophetic word is indeed a "lamp shining in a dark place," and paying attention to it will strengthen the faith of those who desire to survive until all Kingdom prophecy is fulfilled in God's everlasting new world

24. (a) How does the integrity of the early Christians establish the truthfulness of "the Christian story"? (b) What other proof is there that the Bible writers recorded facts, not myths?

a *The Historical Evidences of the Truth of the Scripture Records,* pages 225-228.

25. What outstandingly demonstrates the authenticity of the Bible?

of righteousness. The three tables that follow add further proof of the Bible's authenticity in showing many of these prophetic fulfillments, as well as the harmony of the entire Hebrew and Greek Scriptures. With the passage of time, the Bible shines forth more and more brilliantly as being truly "inspired of God and beneficial."—2 Pet. 1:19; 2 Tim. 3:16.

Questions on chart of "Outstanding Prophecies Concerning Jesus and Their Fulfillment": (a) What prophecies concerning his birth put Jesus in line for Messiahship? (b) What prophecies were fulfilled at the beginning of Jesus' ministry? (c) How did Jesus fulfill prophecy by the way he carried on his ministry? (d) What prophecies were fulfilled during the last few days before Jesus' trial? (e) How was prophecy fulfilled at the time of his trial? (f) What prophecies marked his actual impalement and death and his resurrection? (g) By Jesus' begettal by holy spirit and by his resurrection what was Jesus shown to be according to prophecy?

Questions on chart of "Examples of Other Bible Prophecies Fulfilled": (a) What foretold events occurred after the nation of Israel came into the land of Canaan? (b) What prophecies of judgment against Israel and Judah came to pass, and when? (c) What was foretold of a restoration? Was this fulfilled? (d) Which nations are listed against whom specific messages of judgment came, and how were these prophetic judgments fulfilled? (e) What are some of the outstanding events of history foretold by Daniel? by Jesus?

Questions on chart of "Some Quotations and Applications of the Hebrew Scriptures by Writers of the Greek Scriptures": (a) How do references to Genesis in the Greek Scriptures support its account of creation? (b) What applications are made of references in Genesis to Abraham and to Abraham's seed? (c) What quotations are made from the book of Exodus as to the Ten Commandments and other aspects of the Law? (d) Where do we find the original declarations of the two great commandments? (e) Name some of the basic principles stated in the Pentateuch that are quoted in the Greek Scriptures. How are they applied? (f) What passages in the Psalms, quoted in the Greek Scriptures, magnify Jehovah (1) as Creator and Owner of the earth? (2) as the One who shows interest in the righteous and cares for them? (g) How do the Christian Greek Scriptures apply passages from Isaiah and the other prophets to (1) the preaching of the good news? (2) the fact that some would reject the good news? (3) the fact that, in addition to a remnant of Israel, people of the nations would become believers? (4) the benefits of exercising faith in the good news?

(10) OUTSTANDING PROPHECIES CONCERNING JESUS AND THEIR FULFILLMENT

Gen. 49:10	Born of the tribe of Judah	Matt. 1:2-16; Luke 3:23-33; Heb. 7:14
Ps. 132:11; Isa. 9:7; 11:1, 10	From the family of David the son of Jesse	Matt. 1:1, 6-16; 9:27; 15:22; 20:30, 31; 21:9, 15; 22:42; Mark 10:47, 48; Luke 1:32; 2:4; 3:23-32; 18:38, 39; Acts 2:29-31; 13:22, 23; Rom. 1:3; 15:8, 12
Mic. 5:2	Born in Bethlehem	Matt. 2:1, 5, 6; Luke 2:4-11; John 7:42
Isa. 7:14	Born of a virgin	Matt. 1:18-23; Luke 1:30-35
Jer. 31:15	Babes killed after his birth	Matt. 2:16-18
Mal. 3:1; 4:5; Isa. 40:3	Way prepared before	Matt. 3:1-3; 11:10-14; 17:10-13; Mark 1:2-4; Luke 1:17, 76; 3:3-6; 7:27; John 1:20-23; 3:25-28; Acts 13:24; 19:4
Hos. 11:1	Called out of Egypt	Matt. 2:15
Dan. 9:25	Appeared as Messiah at end of "sixty-nine weeks"	Presented himself for baptism and was anointed on schedule, A.D. 29 (Luke 3:1, 21, 22)
Isa. 61:1, 2	Commissioned	Luke 4:18-21
Isa. 9:1, 2	Ministry caused people in Naphtali and Zebulun to see great light	Matt. 4:13-16
Ps. 78:2	Spoke with illustrations	Matt. 13:11-13, 31-35; Mark 4:11, 33, 34
Isa. 53:4	Carried our sicknesses	Matt. 8:16, 17
Isa. 53:1	Not believed in	John 12:37, 38; Rom. 10:11, 16
Ps. 69:9	Zealous for Jehovah's house	Matt. 21:12, 13; Mark 11:15-18; Luke 19:45, 46; John 2:13-17
Isa. 42:1-4	As Jehovah's servant would not wrangle in streets	Matt. 12:14-21
Ps. 69:4	Hated without cause	Luke 23:13-25; John 15:24, 25; 1 Pet. 2:22
Zech. 9:9; Ps. 118:26	Entry into Jerusalem on colt of an ass; hailed as king and one coming in Jehovah's name	Matt. 21:1-9; Mark 11:7-11; Luke 19:28-38; John 12:12-15

Isa. 28:16; 53:3; Ps. 69:8; 118:22, 23	Rejected, but becomes chief cornerstone	Matt. 21:42, 45, 46; Mark 9:12; 12:10, 11; Luke 20:17; John 1:10, 11; Acts 3:14; 4:11; 1 Pet. 2:7
Isa. 8:14, 15	Becomes stone of stumbling	Matt. 21:44; Luke 20:17, 18; Rom. 9:31-33; 1 Pet. 2:8
Ps. 41:9; 109:8	One apostle unfaithful, betrays him	Matt. 26:47-50; Mark 14:43-46; Luke 22:47, 48; John 13:18, 26-30; 17:12; 18:2-5; Acts 1:16-20
Zech. 11:12	Betrayed for thirty pieces of silver	Matt. 26:15; 27:3-10; Mark 14:10, 11; Luke 22:3-6
Zech. 13:7	Disciples scatter	Matt. 26:31, 56; Mark 14:27, 50; John 16:32
Ps. 2:1, 2	Roman powers and leaders of Israel act together against anointed of Jehovah	Matt. 27:1, 2; Mark 15:1, 15; Luke 23:10-12; Acts 4:25-28
Isa. 53:8, ftn.[a]	Tried and condemned	Matt. 26:57-68; 27:1, 2, 11-26; Mark 14:53-65; 15:1-15; Luke 22:54, 66-71; 23:1-25; John 18:12-14, 19-24, 28-40; 19:1-16
Ps. 27:12	Use of false witnesses	Matt. 26:59-61; Mark 14:56-59
Isa. 53:7	Silent before accusers	Matt. 27:12-14; Mark 14:61; 15:4, 5; Luke 23:9; John 19:9
Isa. 50:6; Mic. 5:1	Struck, spat on	Matt. 26:67; 27:26, 30; Mark 14:65; 15:19; Luke 22:63; John 18:22; 19:3
Ps. 22:16 (and *NW* footnote)	Impaled	Matt. 27:35; Mark 15:24, 25; Luke 23:33; John 19:18, 23; 20:25, 27
Ps. 22:18	Lots cast for garments	Matt. 27:35; Mark 15:24; Luke 23:34; John 19:23, 24
Isa. 53:12	Numbered with sinners	Matt. 26:55, 56; 27:38; Mark 14:48, 49; 15:27; Luke 22:37, 52; 23:32, 33
Ps. 22:7, 8	Reviled while on stake	Matt. 27:39-43; Mark 15:29-32; Luke 23:35-39
Ps. 69:21	Given vinegar and gall	Matt. 27:34, 48; Mark 15:23, 36; Luke 23:36; John 19:29, 30
Ps. 22:1	Forsaken to enemies by God	Matt. 27:46; Mark 15:34
Ps. 34:20; Ex. 12:46	No bones broken	John 19:33, 36
Isa. 53:5; Zech. 12:10	Pierced	Matt. 27:49; John 19:34, 37; Rev. 1:7
Dan. 9:26, 27	Cut off "at the half of the week." Brings end to sacrifices under Mosaic law	Died Nisan 14, A.D. 33, after 3½-year ministry; John 19:14-16; Col. 2:13-17; Heb. chaps. 9, 10
Gen. 3:15	As Seed, bruised in the heel	Acts 3:15
Isa. 53:5, 8, 11, 12	Dies sacrificial death to carry away sins and open way to righteous standing with God	Matt. 20:28; John 1:29; Rom. 3:24; 4:25; 1 Cor. 15:3; Heb. 9:12-15; 1 Pet. 2:24; 1 John 2:2
Isa. 53:9	Buried with the rich	Matt. 27:57-60; Mark 15:42-46; Luke 23:50-53; John 19:38-42
Jonah 1:17; 2:10	In grave parts of three days, then resurrected	Matt. 12:39, 40; 16:21; 17:23; 20:19; 27:64; 28:1-7; Mark 8:31; 9:31; 10:34; 16:1-7; Luke 9:22; 18:33; 24:6, 7, 21, 46; Acts 10:40; 1 Cor. 15:3-8
Ps. 16:8-11, ftn.	Raised before corruption	Acts 2:25-31; 13:34-37
Ps. 2:7	Jehovah declares him His Son by spirit begetting and by resurrection	Matt. 3:16, 17; Mark 1:9-11; Luke 3:21, 22; Acts 13:33; Rom. 1:4; Heb. 1:5; 5:5

a Footnotes to scriptures that are referred to on these charts are found in the First Edition of the *New World Translation*.

Gen. 3:15; 22:18	Jesus as principal Seed becomes basis for blessing all believing mankind and is to crush Satan under his heel	John 3:16; Gal. 3:16; Rev. 12:5, 7-9; 20:2, 3, 10

(11) EXAMPLES OF OTHER BIBLE PROPHECIES FULFILLED

Gen. 9:25	Canaanites to become servants to Israel	Josh. 9:23, 27; Judg. 1:28; 1 Ki. 9:20, 21; 2 Chron. 8:7, 8
Gen. 15:13, 14; Ex. 3:21, 22	Israel to come out of Egypt with much property when God judges enslaving nation	Ex. 12:35, 36; Ps. 105:37
Gen. 17:20; 21:13, 18	Ishmael to produce twelve chieftains and become a great nation	Gen. 25:13-16; 1 Chron. 1:29-31
Gen. 25:23; 27:39, 40	Edomites to dwell away from fertile soils, to serve Israelites and at times to revolt	Gen. 36:8; Deut. 2:4, 5; 2 Sam. 8:14; 2 Ki. 8:20; 1 Chron. 18:13; 2 Chron. 21:8-10
Gen. 48:19, 22	Ephraim to become greater than Manasseh, and each tribe to have an inheritance	Num. 1:33-35; Deut. 33:17; Josh. 16:4-9; 17:1-4
Gen. 49:7	Simeon and Levi to become scattered in Israel	Josh. 19:1-9; 21:41, 42
Gen. 49:10	Kingly leadership to come from Judah	2 Sam. 2:4; 1 Chron. 5:2; Matt. 2:6; Heb. 7:14
Deut. 17:14	Israel to request a monarchy	1 Sam. 8:4, 5, 19, 20
Deut. 28:52, 53, 64-66, 68	Israel to be punished for unfaithfulness; cities besieged, sent into slavery	Fulfilled on Samaria in 740 B.C.E. (2 Ki. 17:5-23), on Jerusalem in 607 B.C.E. (Jer. 52:1-27), and on Jerusalem again A.D. 70
Josh. 6:26	Penalty for rebuilding Jericho	1 Ki. 16:34
1 Sam. 2:31, 34; 3:12-14	Eli's line cursed	1 Sam. 4:11, 17, 18; 1 Ki. 2:26, 27, 35
1 Ki. 9:7, 8; 2 Chron. 7:20, 21	Temple to be destroyed, if Israel turned apostate	2 Ki. 25:9; 2 Chron. 36:19; Jer. 52:13; Lam. 2:6, 7
1 Ki. 13:1-3	Jeroboam's altar to be polluted	2 Ki. 23:16-18
1 Ki. 14:15	Overthrow of ten-tribe kingdom of Israel	2 Ki. 17:6-23; 18:11, 12
Isa. 13:17-22; 45:1, 2; Jer. 50:35-46; 51:37-43	Destruction of Babylon; gates of Babylon to be left open; Medes and Persians to conquer under Cyrus	Dan. 5:22-31; secular history corroborates. Cyrus took Babylon when gates left open.[a]
Isa. 23:1, 8, 13, 14; Ezek. 26:4, 7-12	Mainland city of Tyre to be destroyed by Chaldeans under Nebuchadnezzar	Secular history records this accomplished by Nebuchadnezzar after 13-year siege[b]
Isa. 44:26-28	Rebuilding of Jerusalem and temple, and Cyrus' part in it	2 Chron. 36:22, 23; Ezra 1:1-4
Jer. 25:11; 29:10	Restoration of a remnant to be after seventy years' desolation	Dan. 9:1, 2; Zech. 7:5; 2 Chron. 36:21-23
Jer. 48:15-24; Ezek. 25:8-11; Zeph. 2:8, 9	Moab to be laid waste	Moab now an extinct nation[c]
Jer. 49:2; Ezek. 25:1-7; Zeph. 2:8, 9	Ammonite cities to become desolate heaps	Ammon now an extinct nation[d]
Jer. 49:17, 18; Ezek. 25:12-14; 35:7, 15; Obad. 16, 18	Edom to be cut off as though it had never been	Became extinct as a nation after death of the Herods
Dan. 2:31-40; 7:2-7	Four kingdoms of Babylon, Persia, Greece and Rome depicted. Many prophetic details foretold.	Secular history confirms fulfillments in rise and fall of these powers[e]

a *The History of Herodotus,* translated by George Rawlinson, 1928, page 71.
b Rollin's *Ancient History,* Vol. I, page 472; M'Clintock and Strong's *Cyclopædia,* 1881, Vol. X, page 617.
c *The Encyclopedia Americana,* 1956, Vol. 19, page 277.
d *The Encyclopedia Americana,* 1956, Vol. 1, page 579.
e *"Your Will Be Done on Earth,"* pages 104-125, 166-176, 188-195, 220-229.

Dan. 8:1-8, 20-22; 11:1-19	After kingdom of Persia a mighty one of Greece would rule. His kingdom to be divided into four, out of which would come two powers, the king of the north and the king of the south.	Alexander the Great conquered Persian Empire. At his death four generals took over. Eventually Seleucid and Ptolemaic powers developed and were continually at war with each other.[a]
Dan. 11:20-24	Ruler to decree registration. In days of his successor the "Leader of the covenant" would be broken.	Registration decree in Palestine during reign of Caesar Augustus. Jesus killed during reign of his successor, Tiberius Caesar.[a]
Zeph. 2:13-15; Nah. 3:1-7	Nineveh to become a desolation	Became a mound of rubbish[b]
Zech. 9:3, 4	Island city of Tyre to be destroyed	Accomplished by Alexander in 332 B.C.E.[c]
Matt. 24:2, 16-18; Luke 19:41-44	Jerusalem to be surrounded by staked fortifications and demolished	Fulfilled by Romans A.D. 70[d]
Matt. 24:7-14; Mark 13:8; Luke 21:10, 11, 25-28; 2 Tim. 3:1-5	Great time of trouble foretold before complete end of this system of things; to include world war, food shortages, earthquakes, pestilence, delinquency. Preaching of Kingdom good news to all the nations.	Unprecedented time of trouble on earth since first world war in 1914. Kingdom preaching being done in 189 lands by 1963.

(12) SOME QUOTATIONS AND APPLICATIONS OF THE HEBREW SCRIPTURES BY WRITERS OF THE GREEK SCRIPTURES

(NOTE: This list does not include references that are listed in the "Outstanding Prophecies Concerning Jesus" on the preceding pages.)

Gen. 1:3	God commands light to shine	2 Cor. 4:6
Gen. 1:26, 27	Man made in God's likeness, male and female	Jas. 3:9; Mark 10:6
Gen. 2:2	God rests from earthly creative work	Heb. 4:4
Gen. 2:7	Adam made a living soul	1 Cor. 15:45
Gen. 2:24	Man to leave his parents, stick to his wife and the two become one flesh	Matt. 19:5; Mark 10:7, 8; 1 Cor. 6:16; Eph. 5:31
Gen. 12:3; 18:18	All nations to be blessed by means of Abraham	Gal. 3:8
Gen. 15:5	Abraham's seed to be many	Rom. 4:18
Gen. 15:6	Faith counted to Abraham as righteousness	Rom. 4:3; Gal. 3:6; Jas. 2:23
Gen. 17:5	Abraham father of those with faith out of "many nations"	Rom. 4:16, 17
Gen. 18:10, 14	A son promised to Sarah	Rom. 9:9
Gen. 18:12	Sarah calls Abraham "lord"	1 Pet. 3:6
Gen. 21:10	Prophetic picture of Sarah, Hagar, Isaac and Ishmael	Gal. 4:30
Gen. 21:12	Seed of Abraham to be through Isaac	Rom. 9:7; Heb. 11:18
Gen. 22:16, 17	God swears by himself to bless Abraham	Heb. 6:13, 14
Gen. 25:23	God's favor to Jacob over Esau foretold	Rom. 9:12
Ex. 3:6	God is the God, not of the dead, but of the living	Matt. 22:32; Mark 12:26; Luke 20:37
Ex. 9:16	God's reason for allowing Pharaoh to remain	Rom. 9:17
Ex. 13:2, 12	Firstborn dedicated to Jehovah	Luke 2:23
Ex. 16:18	God equalizes matters in the gathering of manna	2 Cor. 8:15
Ex. 19:5, 6	Israel in line to be kingdom of priests	1 Pet. 2:9
Ex. 19:12, 13	The awesomeness of Jehovah at Mount Sinai	Heb. 12:18-20

a *"Your Will Be Done on Earth,"* pages 121, 122, 172-174, 194, 195, 220-263.
b See Bible Book Number 34, paragraphs 5, 6.
c M'Clintock and Strong's *Cyclopædia,* 1881, Vol. X, pages 618, 619.
d See Bible Book Number 42, paragraph 9.

Ex. 20:12-17	5th, 6th, 7th, 8th, 9th and 10th commandments	Matt. 5:21, 27; 15:4; 19:18, 19; Mark 10:19; Luke 18:20; Rom. 13:9; Eph. 6:2, 3; Jas. 2:11
Ex. 21:17	Penalty for breaking fifth commandment	Matt. 15:4; Mark 7:10
Ex. 21:24	Eye for eye and tooth for tooth	Matt. 5:38
Ex. 22:28	"You must not speak injuriously of a ruler of your people"	Acts 23:5
Ex. 24:8	The making of the law covenant—"the blood of the covenant"	Heb. 9:20; Matt. 26:28; Mark 14:24
Ex. 25:40	Moses instructed in the pattern of the tabernacle and its furnishings	Heb. 8:5
Ex. 32:6	Israelites rise up to revel and have a good time	1 Cor. 10:7
Ex. 33:19	God shows mercy on whomever he pleases	Rom. 9:15
Lev. 11:44	"You must be holy, because I am holy"	1 Pet. 1:16
Lev. 12:8	Offering by a poor person after birth of a son	Luke 2:24
Lev. 18:5	He that keeps the law will live by it	Gal. 3:12
Lev. 19:18	Love your neighbor as yourself	Matt. 19:19; 22:39; Mark 12:31; Rom. 13:9; Gal. 5:14; Jas. 2:8
Lev. 26:12	Jehovah was God of Israel	2 Cor. 6:16
Num. 16:5	Jehovah knows those who belong to him	2 Tim. 2:19
Deut. 6:4, 5	Love Jehovah with whole heart and soul	Matt. 22:37; Mark 12:29, 30; Luke 10:27
Deut. 6:13	"It is Jehovah your God you must worship"	Matt. 4:10; Luke 4:8
Deut. 6:16	"You must not put Jehovah your God to the test"	Matt. 4:7; Luke 4:12
Deut. 8:3	Man must not live by bread alone	Matt. 4:4; Luke 4:4
Deut. 18:15-19	God to raise up a prophet like Moses	Acts 3:22, 23
Deut. 19:15	Everything must be established by two or three witnesses	John 8:17; 2 Cor. 13:1
Deut. 23:21	"You must pay your vows to Jehovah"	Matt. 5:33
Deut. 24:1	Mosaic law provision for divorce	Matt. 5:31
Deut. 25:4	"You must not muzzle a bull when it is threshing"	1 Cor. 9:9; 1 Tim. 5:18
Deut. 27:26	Israelites who did not abide by law were cursed	Gal. 3:10
Deut. 29:4	Not many Jews listened to the good news	Rom. 11:8
Deut. 30:11-14	The need to have the "word" of faith in one's heart and preach it	Rom. 10:6-8
Deut. 31:6, 8	God will by no means forsake his people	Heb. 13:5
Deut. 32:17, 21	God incited jealousy of Jews by inviting Gentiles. Israelites incited Jehovah to jealousy through idolatry	Rom. 10:19; 1 Cor. 10:20-22
Deut. 32:35, 36	Vengeance is Jehovah's	Heb. 10:30
Deut. 32:43	"Be glad, you nations, with his people"	Rom. 15:10
1 Sam. 13:14; 16:1	David a man agreeable to God's own heart	Acts 13:22
1 Sam. 21:6	David and his men eat loaves of presentation	Matt. 12:3, 4; Mark 2:25, 26; Luke 6:3, 4
1 Ki. 19:14, 18	Only a remnant of Jews remained faithful to God	Rom. 11:3, 4
2 Chron. 20:7	Abraham called God's "friend" ("lover")	Jas. 2:23
Job 41:11	"Who has first given to [God]?"	Rom. 11:35
Ps. 5:9	"Their throat is an opened grave"	Rom. 3:13
Ps. 8:2	God furnishes praise "out of the mouth of babes"	Matt. 21:16
Ps. 8:4-6	"What is man that you keep him in mind?" God subjected all things under Christ's feet	Heb. 2:6, 7; 1 Cor. 15:27
Ps. 10:7	"Their mouth is full of cursing"	Rom. 3:14
Ps. 14:1-3	"There is not a righteous [man]"	Rom. 3:10-12
Ps. 18:49	Gentile nations to glorify God	Rom. 15:9
Ps. 19:4, ftn.	No lack of opportunity to hear the truth of God's existence as testified to by all creation	Rom. 10:18
Ps. 22:22	"I will declare your name to my brothers"	Heb. 2:12

Ps. 24:1	The earth belongs to Jehovah	1 Cor. 10:26
Ps. 32:1, 2	"Happy is the man whose sin Jehovah will by no means take into account"	Rom. 4:7, 8
Ps. 34:12-16	"The eyes of Jehovah are upon the righteous"	1 Pet. 3:10-12
Ps. 36:1	"There is no fear of God before their eyes"	Rom. 3:18
Ps. 40:6-8	God no longer approved of sacrifices under the Law; one offering of body of Jesus, according to God's will, brings sanctification	Heb. 10:6-10
Ps. 44:22	"We have been accounted as sheep for slaughtering"	Rom. 8:36
Ps. 45:6, 7	"God is [Christ's] throne forever"	Heb. 1:8, 9
Ps. 51:4	God vindicated in his words and judgments	Rom. 3:4
Ps. 68:18	When Christ ascended on high he gave gifts in men	Eph. 4:8
Ps. 69:22, 23	Peace table of Israelites becomes a trap	Rom. 11:9, 10
Ps. 78:24	The bread from heaven	John 6:31-33
Ps. 82:6	"You are gods"	John 10:34
Ps. 94:11	"Jehovah knows that the reasonings of the wise men are futile"	1 Cor. 3:20
Ps. 95:7-11	Disobedient Israelites did not enter into God's rest	Heb. 3:7-11; 4:3, 5, 7
Ps. 102:25-27	"You . . . O Lord, laid the foundations of the earth"	Heb. 1:10-12
Ps. 104:4	"He makes his angels spirits"	Heb. 1:7
Ps. 110:1	The Lord to sit at Jehovah's right hand	Matt. 22:43-45; Mark 12:36, 37; Luke 20:42-44; Heb. 1:13
Ps. 110:4	Christ a priest forever according to the manner of Melchizedek	Heb. 7:17
Ps. 112:9	"He has distributed widely . . . his righteousness continues forever"	2 Cor. 9:9
Ps. 116:10	"I exercised faith, therefore I spoke"	2 Cor. 4:13
Ps. 117:1	"Praise Jehovah, all you nations"	Rom. 15:11
Ps. 118:6	"Jehovah is my helper; I will not be afraid"	Heb. 13:6
Ps. 140:3	"Poison of asps is behind their lips"	Rom. 3:13
Prov. 26:11	"The dog has returned to its own vomit"	2 Pet. 2:22
Isa. 1:9	Except for a remnant, Israel would have been like Sodom	Rom. 9:29
Isa. 6:9, 10	Israelites did not pay attention to the good news	Matt. 13:13-15; Mark 4:12; Luke 8:10; Acts 28:25-27
Isa. 8:17, 18	"Look! I and the young children, whom Jehovah gave me"	Heb. 2:13
Isa. 10:22, 23	Only a remnant of Israel to be saved	Rom. 9:27, 28
Isa. 22:13	"Let us eat and drink, for tomorrow we are to die"	1 Cor. 15:32
Isa. 25:8	"Death is swallowed up forever"	1 Cor. 15:54
Isa. 28:11, 12	People did not believe even though spoken to "with the tongues of foreigners"	1 Cor. 14:21
Isa. 28:16	No disappointment for those who rest their faith in Christ the foundation in Zion	1 Pet. 2:6; Rom. 10:11
Isa. 29:13	Hypocrisy of scribes and Pharisees described	Matt. 15:7-9; Mark 7:6-8
Isa. 29:14	God makes the wisdom of wise men perish	1 Cor. 1:19
Isa. 40:6-8	The word spoken by Jehovah endures forever	1 Pet. 1:24, 25
Isa. 40:13	'Who has become Jehovah's counselor?'	Rom. 11:34
Isa. 42:6; 49:6	"I have appointed you as a light of nations"	Acts 13:47
Isa. 45:23	Every knee shall bend to Jehovah	Rom. 14:11
Isa. 49:8	The acceptable time to be heard, in the "day of salvation"	2 Cor. 6:2
Isa. 52:7	Feet of carriers of good news beautiful	Rom. 10:15
Isa. 52:11	"Get out from among them, and separate yourselves"	2 Cor. 6:17
Isa. 52:15	Good news announced to the Gentiles	Rom. 15:21
Isa. 54:1	"Be glad, you barren woman who does not give birth"	Gal. 4:27
Isa. 54:13	"And they will all be taught by Jehovah"	John 6:45
Isa. 56:7	Jehovah's house to be a house of prayer for all nations	Matt. 21:13; Mark 11:17; Luke 19:46

Isa. 59:7, 8	Wickedness of men described	Rom. 3:15-17
Isa. 65:1, 2	Jehovah became manifest to Gentile nations	Rom. 10:20, 21
Isa. 66:1, 2	"The heaven is my throne, and the earth is my footstool"	Acts 7:49, 50
Jer. 5:21	Having eyes, but not seeing	Mark 8:18
Jer. 9:24	"He that boasts, let him boast in Jehovah"	1 Cor. 1:31; 2 Cor. 10:17
Jer. 31:31-34	God to make a new covenant	Heb. 8:8-12; 10:16, 17
Dan. 9:27; 11:31	"The disgusting thing that causes desolation"	Matt. 24:15
Hos. 1:10; 2:23	Gentiles also to become God's people	Rom. 9:24-26
Hos. 6:6	"I want mercy, and not sacrifice"	Matt. 9:13; 12:7
Hos. 13:14	"Death, where is your sting?"	1 Cor. 15:54, 55
Joel 2:28-32	"Everyone who calls on the name of Jehovah will be saved"	Acts 2:17-21; Rom. 10:13
Amos 9:11, 12	God to rebuild the booth of David	Acts 15:16-18
Hab. 1:5	"Behold it, you scorners, and wonder at it"	Acts 13:40, 41
Hab. 2:4	"My righteous one will live by reason of faith"	Rom. 1:17; Heb. 10:38
Hag. 2:6	Heavens and earth to be shaken	Heb. 12:26, 27
Mal. 1:2, 3	Jacob loved, Esau hated	Rom. 9:13

The Inspired Scriptures Bring Eternal Benefits

OUR review of "all Scripture . . . inspired of God" has opened before our eyes a glorious vision of Jehovah's sovereignty and his Kingdom purposes. We have noted that the Bible is one Book, and that the powerful theme appearing in its opening pages is developed and explained through the writings that follow, until, with its closing chapters, the glorious reality of God's grand purpose by means of his kingdom is made clearly to appear. What a remarkable book the Bible is! Starting from the awe-inspiring creation of the material heavens and of the earth with its plant and creature life, the Bible then gives us the one inspired and authentic account of God's dealings with humankind until our time, and, yes, carries us through to the complete realization of Jehovah's most glorious creation of "a new heaven and a new earth." (Rev. 21:1) With his purpose completely vindicated by means of the Kingdom of the Seed, Jehovah God is seen in the relationship of a kind Father to a happy united human family, which joins in with all the heavenly hosts in praising Him and sanctifying his holy name.

2 How wonderfully is this theme of the "Seed" developed throughout the Scriptures! Almost six thousand years ago, as the first inspired prophecy, God gave the promise that 'the seed of the woman' would bruise the serpent in the head. (Gen. 3:15) More than two thousand years pass, and God tells faithful Abraham: "By means of your seed all nations of the earth will certainly bless themselves." Over 800 years later, Jehovah gives a like promise to Abraham's descendant, loyal King David, showing that the Seed will be a kingly One. As time passes, Jehovah's prophets thrillingly join in to foretell the glories of his Kingdom rule. (Gen. 22:18; 2 Sam. 7:12, 16; Isa. 9:6, 7; Dan. 2:44; 7:13, 14) Then the Seed himself appears, more than four thousand years after the first promise in Eden. This One, who is also 'the seed of Abraham,' is Jesus Christ, "Son of the Most High," and to him Jehovah gives "the throne of David his father."—Gal. 3:16; Luke 1:31-33.

3 Though this Seed, God's anointed King, is bruised in death by the "serpent's" earthly seed, yet God raises him from the dead and exalts him to his own right hand, where he awaits God's due time to 'crush Satan's head.' (Gen. 3:15; Heb. 10:13; Rom. 16:20) Then the Revelation brings the entire vision to its glorious climax by describing Christ's entry into Kingdom power and his hurling of "the original serpent, the one called Devil and Satan," from heaven down to earth. For a short time the Devil brings woe to the earth and wages war with 'the remaining ones of the seed of God's woman.' But Christ, as "King of kings," smites the nations. The original serpent, Satan, is abyssed, and then finally destroyed forever. With the name of Jehovah forever sanctified, He and his Christ rule in the heavenly "New

1. What glorious vision has our review of "all Scripture" opened before our eyes?
2, 3. How is the theme of the Seed developed throughout the Scriptures?

Jerusalem," for the blessing of all the families of the earth. Thus the magnificent theme of the inspired Scriptures unfolds before us in all its thrilling grandeur!—Rev. 11:15; 12:1-12, 17; 19:11-16; 20:1-3, 7-10; 21:1-5; 22:3-5.

BENEFITING BY THIS INSPIRED RECORD

4 How can we gain the greatest benefit from the Holy Scriptures? We can benefit by letting the Bible go to work in our lives. By daily study and application of the inspired Scriptures, we can get guidance from God. "The word of God is alive and exerts power," and it can be a marvelous power for righteousness in our lives. (Heb. 4:12) If we continually study and follow the leadings of God's Word, we will come to "put on the new personality which was created according to God's will in true righteousness and loyalty." We will be made new in the force actuating our minds, and we will be transformed by making our minds over, so as to prove to ourselves "the good and acceptable and perfect will of God."—Eph. 4:23, 24; Rom. 12:2.

5 We can learn much by observing how other faithful servants of God have benefited from studying and meditating upon God's Word. For example, there was Moses, 'the meekest of all men,' who was always teachable and willing to learn. (Num. 12:3) We should always have the same prayerful appreciation of Jehovah's sovereignty as he had. It was Moses who said: "O Jehovah, you yourself have proved to be a real dwelling for us during generation after generation. Before the mountains themselves were born, or you proceeded to bring forth as with labor pains the earth and the productive land, even from time indefinite to time indefinite you are God." Moses was thoroughly acquainted with God's wisdom, for he was used by Jehovah in writing the opening books of the Bible, and hence he understood the importance of daily seeking wisdom from Jehovah. Thus, he prayed to God: "Show us just how to count our days in such a way that we may bring a heart of wisdom in." Though "the days of our years" may be few, just seventy years, or eighty in the case of "special mightiness," we are wise if we feast daily upon his Word, for then "the pleasantness of Jehovah our God" will "prove to be upon us," as it was upon his faithful servant, Moses.—Ps. 90:1, 2, 12, 10, 17.

6 How necessary it is to meditate daily on God's Word! Jehovah made this plain to Moses' successor, Joshua, telling him: "Only be courageous and very strong to take care to do according to all the law that Moses my servant commanded you. Do not turn aside from it to the right or to the left, in order that you may act wisely everywhere you go. This book of the law should not depart from your mouth, and you must in an undertone read in it day and night, in order that you may take care to do according to all that is written in it; for then you will make your way successful and then you will act wisely." Did Joshua's continual reading of Jehovah's law 'make his way successful'? Jehovah's blessing on his courageous campaign in Canaan supplies the answer. —Josh. 1:7, 8; 12:7-24.

7 Consider, too, the beloved David, another who deeply treasured wisdom from Jehovah. What heartfelt appreciation he showed for Jehovah's "law," "reminder," "orders," "commandment," and "judicial decisions"! As David expressed it: "They are more to be desired than gold, yes, than much fine gold; and sweeter than honey and the flowing honey of the combs." (Ps. 19:7-10) This exulting theme is expanded and repeated with soul-stirring beauty throughout the 119th Psalm. As we daily study God's Word and abide by its wise counsels, may we ever be able to say to Jehovah: "Your word is a lamp to my foot, and a light to my roadway. Your reminders are wonderful. That is why my soul has observed them." —Ps. 119:105, 129.

8 In the days of his faithfulness, David's son Solomon also lived by God's Word, and in his sayings, too, we can find moving expressions of appreciation that we will do well to make our very own. Through daily reading and application of the Bible we will come to understand fully the inner depth of meaning of Solomon's words: "Happy is the man that has found wisdom, and the man that gets discernment. Length of days is in its right hand; in its left hand there are riches and glory. Its ways are ways of pleasantness, and all its roadways are peace. It is a tree of life to those taking hold of it, and those keeping fast hold of it are to be called happy." (Prov. 3:13, 16-18) Daily study and obedience to God's Word lead to the greatest happiness, together with "length of days"—eternal life in Jehovah's new world.

9 Not to be overlooked among those who have cherished and obeyed the inspired Scriptures are God's faithful prophets. Jeremiah, for example, had the "toughest" of assignments. (Jer. 6:28) As he said: "The word of Jehovah became for me a cause for reproach and for jeering all day long." But he had been well

4. How can we gain the greatest benefit from the Holy Scriptures, and why?
5. What can we learn from Moses' attitude and example?
6. How may we, like Joshua, make our way successful?
7. How did David express his appreciation for the wisdom from God, and how is the same appreciation expressed in Psalm 119?
8. What sayings of Solomon should we make our very own?
9. What encouragement may we draw from the example of Jeremiah?

fortified by his studies of God's Word, and, in fact, he himself was used to write four books of the inspired Scriptures—First and Second Kings, Jeremiah and Lamentations. So, what happened when discouragement seemed to envelop Jeremiah, and he thought he would desist from preaching "the word of Jehovah"? Let Jeremiah himself answer: "In my heart it proved to be like a burning fire shut up in my bones; and I got tired of holding in, and I was unable to endure it." He was compelled to speak out Jehovah's word, and in doing so he found that Jehovah was with him "like a terrible mighty one." If we study and keep studying God's Word so that it becomes just as much a part of us as it was of Jeremiah, then Jehovah's invincible power will likewise be with us, and we will be able to triumph over every obstacle in continuing to speak of His glorious Kingdom purposes.—Jer. 20:8, 9, 11.

10 Now, what of our greatest example, "the Chief Agent and Perfecter of our faith, Jesus"? Was he familiar with the inspired Scriptures after the manner of all the prophets and other faithful men before him? Certainly he was, as his many quotations and his course of life in harmony with the Scriptures clearly show. It was with God's Word in mind that he made his dedication to do his Father's will here on this earth: "Here I have come, in the roll of the book it being written about me. To do your will, O my God, I have delighted, and your law is within my inward parts." (Heb. 12:2; Ps. 40:7, 8; Heb. 10:5-7) Thus God's Word played a key role in Jehovah's sanctifying Jesus, or setting him apart for his service. Jesus prayed that his followers might likewise be sanctified: "Sanctify them by means of the truth; your word is truth. Just as you sent me forth into the world, I also sent them forth into the world. And I am sanctifying myself in their behalf, that they also may be sanctified by means of truth."—John 17:17-19.

11 Being sanctified "by means of the truth," the spirit-begotten and anointed footstep followers of Jesus must 'remain in his word' so as to be really his disciples. (John 8:31) Thus Peter, in writing to "those who have obtained a faith," stressed the need for continued study and attention to God's Word: "For this reason I shall be disposed always to remind you of these things, although you know them and are firmly set in the truth that is present in you." (2 Pet. 1:1, 12) Continual reminders, such as are found in the daily reading and study of God's Word, are important also to all who hope to be of the "great crowd" whom John saw in vision after describing the 144,000 sealed ones of the tribes of spiritual Israel. For, unless they keep on taking in life's water of truth, how can this "great crowd" intelligently "keep on crying with a loud voice, saying: 'Salvation we owe to our God, who is seated on the throne, and to the Lamb' "?—Rev. 7:9, 10; 22:17.

12 We cannot escape it! The way to gain the greatest benefit from the inspired Scriptures, the way to find salvation to everlasting life in God's new world, is to study those Scriptures and live by them every day of our lives. We must constantly meditate on God's Word, with the same prayerful attitude of appreciation as expressed by the psalmist: "I shall remember the practices of Jah; for I will remember your marvelous doing of long ago. And I shall certainly meditate on all your activity." (Ps. 77:11, 12) Meditating on Jehovah's 'marvelous doing and activity' will stir us also to be active in fine works, with everlasting life in view. The purpose of this book, *"All Scripture Is Inspired of God and Beneficial,"* is to encourage everyone loving righteousness to share in the eternal and satisfying benefits that accrue from continued study and application of the Word of God.

IN "CRITICAL TIMES"

13 This modern age is the most critical in human history. It is explosive with awesome possibilities. Indeed, it can truly be said that the very survival of the human race is in peril. Most appropriate, then, are the words of the apostle Paul: "But know this, that in the last days critical times hard to deal with will be here. For men will be lovers of themselves, lovers of money, self-assuming, haughty, blasphemers, disobedient to parents, unthankful, disloyal, having no natural affection, not open to any agreement, slanderers, without self-control, fierce, without love of goodness, betrayers, headstrong, puffed up with pride, lovers of pleasures rather than lovers of God, having a form of godly devotion but proving false to its power; and from these turn away." —2 Tim. 3:1-5.

14 Why turn away from such ones? Because their godless way is due to end in destruction! Rather, let us, along with all men of goodwill, turn to the healthful teaching of the inspired Scriptures, making these Scriptures the very foundation of our daily living. Let us heed the words of Paul to young Timothy: "You, however, continue in the things that you learned and were persuaded to believe." (2 Tim. 3:14) Yes, "continue" in them, says Paul. Doing so,

---

10. What role did the Scriptures play in Jesus' life, and what did he pray on behalf of his disciples?
11. (a) What did Peter stress with regard to God's Word? (b) Why is study of the Bible also important to the "great crowd"?
12. Why, then, must we constantly meditate on God's Word?
13. In what "critical times" are we living?
14. In view of the times, what advice of Paul will we heed?

we must humbly let the Scriptures teach us, reprove us, set things straight for us, and discipline us in righteousness. Jehovah knows what is needful for us, for his thoughts are so much higher than our thoughts, and by his inspired Scriptures he tells us what is beneficial for us, that we may be fully equipped and competent for the good work of witnessing to his name and kingdom. So it is that Paul gives this outstanding advice in the context of describing the "critical times" that come "in the last days": "All Scripture is inspired of God and beneficial for teaching, for reproving, for setting things straight, for disciplining in righteousness, that the man of God may be fully competent, completely equipped for every good work." May all of us survive these "critical times" by giving heed to this inspired advice!—2 Tim. 3:16, 17; Isa. 55:8-11.

15 Obedience to the inspired Scriptures should be our goal. It was through disobedience to the word and command of Jehovah that the first man fell into sin and death, "and thus death spread to all men." So man lost the opportunity that might have been his in the Edenic paradise to "actually take fruit also of the tree of life and eat and live to time indefinite." (Rom. 5:12; Gen. 2:17; 3:6, 22-24) But through the obedience of Christ and on the basis of the sacrifice of this "Lamb of God" Jehovah will cause "a river of water of life, clear as crystal," to flow forth for the benefit of all those of mankind who dedicate themselves to Him in obedience. As the apostle John saw it in vision: "On this side of the river and on that side there were trees of life producing twelve crops of fruit, yielding their fruits each month. And the leaves of the trees were for the curing of the nations." —Rev. 22:1, 2; Rom. 5:18, 19.

16 Once again the way to everlasting life lies open to mankind. Happy, then, are those who heed the inspired scripture: "You must choose life in order that you may keep alive, you and your offspring, by loving Jehovah your God, by listening to his voice and by sticking to him; for he is your life and the length of your days." (Deut. 30:19, 20) Blessed is Jehovah, the God and Father of our Lord Jesus Christ, who makes this grand provision for life through the sacrifice of his Son and by means of his everlasting kingdom. How great is our joy and gratitude that we can read and reread, study and restudy, and meditate on these precious truths, for truly "all Scripture is inspired of God and beneficial," leading on to eternal life in the New World where everything will be 'holiness to Jehovah.'—Zech. 14:20; Rev. 4:8; John 17:3.

15. (a) What has resulted from disobedience? (b) What glorious opportunity has been opened up by the obedience of Christ?

16. Of what eternal benefit are the inspired Scriptures?

If you do not yet have a copy of the "New World Translation of the Holy Scriptures" you will want to obtain one now for use in regular Bible reading and study. See page 267 for a description of the various editions of this fine translation.

PALESTINE
IN THE
Time OF Christ
Sidon
ABILENE
Damascus
Mt. Hermon
PHOENICIA
Tyre
Caesarea
Philippi
ITURAEA
TRACHONITIS
GREAT SEA
Ptolemais
GALILEE
Chorazin
Capernaum
Bethsaida
SEA OF GALILEE
Magadan
Cana
Tiberias
Mt.
Carmel
Plain of Esdraelon
Nazareth
Mt. Tabor
Nain
DEC
Gadara
Bethany across the

The Architecture of Modern Italy

Italy 1750

SWITZERLAND
AUSTRIA
Simplon
Lombardy
Veneto
Belluno
Gallarate
Bergamo
Possagno
Monza
Treviso
Trieste
Novara
Milan
Brescia
Verona
Venice
Turin
Padua
Mantua
Piedmont
Parma
Ferrara
Modena
Genoa
Bologna
Liguria
Faenza
Carrara
Pistoia
San Marino
Florence
Urbino
Livorno
Ancona
Tuscany
Papal States
ADRIATIC SEA
Follonica
Montalcino
Perugia
Elba
Civitavecchia
Tivoli
Rome
Subiaco
Terracina
Minturno
Gaeta
Caserta
Kingdom of
Two Sicilies
Naples
Portici/Herculaneum
Amalfi
SARDINIA
Paestum
TYRRHENIAN SEA
Palermo

The Architecture of Modern Italy

Volume I: The Challenge of Tradition, 1750–1900

Terry Kirk

Princeton Architectural Press
New York

FOR MARCELLO

Published by
Princeton Architectural Press
37 East Seventh Street
New York, New York 10003

For a free catalog of books, call 1.800.722.6657.
Visit our web site at www.papress.com.

Printed and bound in China
08 07 06 5 4 3 2 First edition

Project Coordinator: Mark Lamster
Editing: Elizabeth Johnson, Linda Lee, Megan Carey
Layout: Jane Sheinman

Special thanks to: Nettie Aljian, Dorothy Ball, Nicola Bednarek, Janet Behning, Penny (Yuen Pik) Chu, Russell Fernandez, Clare Jacobson, John King, Nancy Eklund Later, Katharine Myers, Lauren Nelson, Scott Tennent, Jennifer Thompson, and Joseph Weston of Princeton Architectural Press —Kevin C. Lippert, publisher

Library of Congress Cataloging-in-Publication Data
Kirk, Terry.
The architecture of modern Italy / Terry Kirk.
v. cm.
Includes bibliographical references.
Contents: v. 1. The challenge of tradition, 1750–1900 — v. 2. Visions of Utopia, 1900–present.
ISBN 1-56898-438-3 (set : alk. paper) — ISBN 1-56898-420-0 (v. 1 : alk. paper) — ISBN 1-56898-436-7 (v. 2 : alk. paper)
1. Architecture—Italy. 2. Architecture, Modern. I. Title.
NA1114.K574 2005
720'.945—dc22

2004006479

Contents

Acknowledgments 9

Introduction 10

Chapter 1

Architecture of the Italian Enlightenment, 1750–1800

The Pantheon Revisited 14
Rome of the Nolli Plan 20
Alessandro Galilei and San Giovanni Laterano 22
Nicola Salvi and the Trevi Fountain 24
Luigi Vanvitelli and the Reggia at Caserta 28
Fernando Fuga and the Albergo dei Poveri 40
Giovanni Battista Piranesi 47
Giacomo Quarenghi 59
The Grand Tour and the Impact of Archeology 62
Collecting and Cultural Heritage 65
The Patronage of Pope Pius VI 73
Giuseppe Piermarini and Milan in the Eighteenth Century 77
Venice's Teatro La Fenice and Conclusions on Neoclassicism 83

Chapter 2
Napoleon in Italy, 1800–1815

Napoleon's Italic Empire 86
Milan 91
Venice 98
Turin 101
Naples 105
Trieste 107
The Neoclassical Interior 110
Rome 112
Napoleon's Interest in Archeology 120
Political Restoration and Restitution of Artworks 123
Napoleonic Neoclassicism 125

Chapter 3
Restoration and Romanticism, 1815–1860

Giuseppe Jappelli and the Romantic Ideal 126
Villa Rivalry: The Borghese and the Torlonia of Rome .136
Italian Opera Stage Design and Theater Interiors 143
Antonio Canova's Temple in Possagno 147
Pantheon Progeny and Carlo Barabino 153
Romanticism in Tuscany 156
Alessandro Antonelli 160
Construction in Iron 166
Architectural Restoration of Monuments 169
Revivalism and Camillo Boito 176

Chapter 4
Unification and the Nation's Capitals, 1860–1900

Turin, the First Capital 186
Florence, the Interim Capital .190
Naples *Risanata* 196
Milan, the Industrial Capital 199
Cathedral Facades and Town Halls 204
Palermo and National Unification 217
The Last of Papal Rome 219
Rome, the Capital of United Italy 222
Monumental Symbols of the New State 231
A New Urban Infrastructure for Rome 241
A National Architecture 246
Rome, a World Capital 252

Bibliography 260

Credits 275

Index 276

ACKNOWLEDGMENTS

The author would like to thank by name those who supported the gestation of this project with valuable advice, expertise, and inspiration: Marcello Barbanera, Eve Sinaiko, Claudia Conforti, John Pinto, Marco Mulazzani, Fabio Barry, Allan Ceen, Nigel Ryan, Jeffery Collins, Lars Berggren, Elisabeth Kieven, Diana Murphy, Lucy Maulsby, Catherine Brice, Flavia Marcello, and Andrew Solomon.

Illustrations for these volumes were in many cases provided free of charge, and the author thanks Maria Grazia Sgrilli, the FIAT Archivio Storico, and the Fondazione Ente Cassa di Risparmio di Roma; the archives of the following studios: Albini Helg & Piva, Armando Brasini, Costantino Dardi, Mario Fiorentino, Gino Pollini, Gio Ponti, and Aldo Rossi; and personally the following architects: Carlo Aymonino, Lodovico Belgioioso, Mario Botta, Massimiliano Fuksas, Vittorio Gregotti, Zaha Hadid, Richard Meier, Manfredi Nicoletti, Renzo Piano, Paolo Portoghesi, Franco Purini, and Gino Valle.

The author would also like to acknowledge the professional support from the staffs of the Biblioteca Hertziana, the Biblioteca dell'Istituto Nazionale di Archeologia e Storia dell'Arte, the Biblioteca Nazionale Centrale Vittorio Emanuele II, and the generous financial support of The American University of Rome.

INTRODUCTION

"Modern Italy" may sound like an oxymoron. For Western civilization, Italian culture represents the classical past and the continuity of canonical tradition, while modernity is understood in contrary terms of rupture and rapid innovation. Charting the evolution of a culture renowned for its historical past into the modern era challenges our understanding of both the resilience of tradition and the elasticity of modernity.

We have a tendency when imagining Italy to look to a rather distant and definitely premodern setting. The ancient forum, medieval cloisters, baroque piazzas, and papal palaces constitute our ideal itinerary of Italian civilization. The Campo of Siena, Saint Peter's, all of Venice and San Gimignano satisfy us with their seemingly unbroken panoramas onto historical moments untouched by time; but elsewhere modern intrusions alter and obstruct the view to the landscapes of our expectations. As seasonal tourist or seasoned historian, we edit the encroachments time and change have wrought on our image of Italy. The learning of history is always a complex task, one that in the Italian environment is complicated by the changes wrought everywhere over the past 250 years. Culture on the peninsula continues to evolve with characteristic vibrancy.

Italy is not a museum. To think of it as such—as a disorganized yet phenomenally rich museum unchanging in its exhibits—is to misunderstand the nature of the Italian cultural condition and the writing of history itself. To edit Italy is to overlook the dynamic relationship of tradition and innovation that has always characterized its genius. It has never been easy for architects to operate in an atmosphere conditioned by the weight of history while responding to modern progress and change. Their best works describe a deft compromise between Italy's roles as Europe's oldest culture and one of its newer nation states. Architects of varying convictions in this context have striven for a balance, and a vibrant pluralistic architectural culture is the result. There is a surprisingly transparent top layer on the palimpsest of Italy's cultural history. This book explores the significance of the architecture and urbanism of Italy's latest, modern layer.

This book is a survey of architectural works that have shaped the Italian landscape according to the dictates of an emerging modern state. The idea of Italy had existed as a collective cultural notion for centuries, but it was not until the late nineteenth century that Italy as a political state became a reality. It was founded upon the strength of the cultural tradition that brought together diverse regional entities in a political whole for the first time since antiquity. The architecture and the traditions it drew upon provided images and rallying points, figures to concretize the collective ideal. Far from a degradation of tradition—as superficial treatments of the period after the baroque propose—Italy's architectural culture reached a zenith of expressive power in the service of this new nation by relying expressly on the wealth of its historical memory. Elsewhere in Europe, the tenets of a modern functionalism were being defined, tenets that are still used rather indiscriminately and unsuccessfully to evaluate the modern architecture of Italy. The classical tradition, now doubly enriched for modern times by the contributions of the intervening Renaissance, vied in Italy with forces of international modernism in a dynamic balance of political and aesthetic concerns. An understanding of the transformation of the Italian tradition in the modern age rests upon a clarification of contemporary attitudes toward tradition and modernity with respect to national consciousness.

Contemporary scholarship has demonstrated the benefits of breaking down the barriers between periods. Notions of revolution are being dismantled to reconstruct a more continuous picture of historical development in the arts. Yet our vision of modern Italian architecture is still characterized by discontinuities. Over the last fifty years, scholars have explored individual subjects from Piranesi to the present, and have contributed much to our knowledge of major figures and key monuments, but these remain isolated contributions in a largely fragmentary overview. Furthermore, many of these scholars were primarily professional architects who used their historical research to pursue timely political issues that may seem less interesting to us now than their ostensible content. My intention is to strive for a nonpolemical evaluation of cultural traditions within the context of the modern Italian political state, an evaluation that bears upon a reading of the evolution of its architecture.

The Architecture of Modern Italy surveys the period from the late baroque period in the mid-eighteenth century down to the Holy Year 2000. Its linear narrative structure aligns Italy's modern architectural culture for the first time in a chronological continuum. The timeline is articulated by the rhythms of major political events—such as the changes of governing regimes—that marshal official architecture of monuments, public buildings, and urban planning and set the pace for other building types as well. The starting point of this history will not be justified in terms of contrast against the immediately preceding period; indeed, we set ourselves down in the flow of time more or less arbitrarily. Names and ideas will also flow from one chapter to the next to dismantle the often artificial divisions by style or century.

This study is initiated with Piranesi's exploration of the fertile potential of the interpretation of the past. Later, neoclassical architects developed these ideas in a wide variety of buildings across a peninsula still politically divided and variously inflected in diverse local traditions. The experience of Napoleonic rule in Italy introduced enduring political and architectural models. With the growing political ideal of the *Risorgimento*, or resurgence of an Italian nation, architecture came to be used in a variety of guises as an agent of unification and helped reshape a series of Italian capital cities: Turin, then Florence, and finally Rome. Upon the former imperial and recent papal capital, the image of the new secular nation was superimposed; its institutional buildings and monuments and the urban evolution they helped to shape describe a culminating moment in Italy of modern progress and traditional values balanced in service of the nation. Alongside traditionalist trends, avant-garde experimentation in Art Nouveau and Futurism found many expressions, if not in permanent built form then in widely influential architectural images. Under the Fascist regime, perhaps the most prolific period of Italian architecture, historicist trends continued while interpretations of northern European modernist design were developed, and their interplay enriches our understanding of both. With the reconstruction of political systems after World War II, architecture also was revamped along essential lines of construction and social functions. Contemporary architecture in Italy is seen in the context of its own rich historical endowment and against global trends in architecture.

Understanding the works of modern Italy requires meticulous attention to cultural context. Political and social changes, technological advance within the realities of the Italian economy, the development of new building types, the influence of related arts and sciences (particularly the rise of classical archeology), and theories of restoration are all relevant concerns. The correlated cultures of music production, scenography, and industrial design must be brought to bear. Each work is explored in terms of its specific historical moment, uncluttered by anachronistic polemical commentary. Primary source material, especially the architect's own word, is given prominence. Seminal latter-day scholarship, almost all written in Italian, is brought together here for the first time. Selected bibliographies for each chapter subheading credit the original thinkers and invite further research.

1.1 Giovanni Battista Piranesi, Pantheon, Rome. Engraving from *Vedute di Roma*, c. 1748

Chapter 1

ARCHITECTURE OF THE ITALIAN ENLIGHTENMENT, 1750–1800

THE PANTHEON REVISITED

The Pantheon is one of the most celebrated and most carefully studied buildings of Western architecture. In the modern age, as it had been in the Renaissance, the Pantheon is a crucible of critical thinking. Preservation of the Pantheon had been undertaken in the seventeenth century and continued in the eighteenth during the pontificate of Clement XI. Floodwater stains had been removed and some statues placed in the altars around the perimeter. Antoine Derizet, professor at Rome's official academy of arts, the Accademia di San Luca, praised Clement's operation as having returned the Pantheon "to its original beauty." A view of the interior painted by Giovanni Paolo Panini recorded the recent restorations. From a lateral niche, between two cleaned columns, Panini directs our vision away from the Christianized altar out to the sweep of the ancient space. The repeated circles of perimeter, marble paving stones, oculus, and the spot of sunlight that shines through it emphasize the geometrical logic of the rotunda. Panini's painted view reflects the eighteenth-century vision of the Pantheon as the locus of an ideal geometrical architectural beauty.

Not everything in Panini's view satisfied the contemporary critical eye, however. The attic, that intermediate level above the columns and below the coffers of the dome, seemed discordant—ill proportioned, misaligned, not structurally relevant. A variety of construction chronologies were invented to explain this "error." The incapacity of eighteenth-century critics to interpret the Pantheon's original complexities led them to postulate a theory of its original

1.2 Giovanni Paolo Panini, Pantheon, c. 1740

state and, continuing Clement XI's work, formulate a program of corrective reconstruction.

In 1756, during the papacy of Benedict XIV, the doors of the Pantheon were shut, and behind them dust rose as marble fragments from the attic were thrown down. What may have started as a maintenance project resulted in the elimination of the troublesome attic altogether. The work was carried out in secret; even the pope's claim of authority over the Pantheon, traditionally the city's domain, was not made public until after completion. Francesco Algarotti, intellectual gadfly of the enlightened age, happened upon the work in progress and wrote with surprise and irony that "they have dared to spoil that magnificent, august construction of the Pantheon.... They have even destroyed the old attic from which the cupola springs and they've put up in its place some modern gentilities." As with the twin bell towers erected on the temple's exterior in the seventeenth century, Algarotti did not know who was behind the present work.

The new attic was complete by 1757. Plaster panels and pedimented windows replaced the old attic pilaster order, accentuating lines of horizontality. The new panels were made commensurate in measure to the dome's coffers and the fourteen "windows" were reshaped as statue niches with cutout figures of statues set up to test the effect. The architect responsible for the attic's redesign, it was later revealed, was Paolo Posi who, as a functionary only recently hired to Benedict XIV's Vatican architectural team, was probably brought in after the ancient attic was dismantled. Posi's training in the baroque heritage guaranteed a certain facility of formal invention. Francesco Milizia, the eighteenth century's most widely respected architectural critic, described Posi as a decorative talent, not an architectural mind. Whatever one might think of the design, public rancor arose over the wholesale liquidation of the materials from the old attic. Capitals, marble slabs, and ancient stamped bricks were dispersed on the international market for antiquities. Posi's work at the Pantheon was sharply criticized, often with libelous aspersion that revealed a prevailing sour attitude toward contemporary architecture in Rome and obfuscated Posi's memory. They found the new attic suddenly an affront to the venerated place.

Reconsidering Posi's attic soon became an exercise in the development of eighteenth-century architects in Rome. Giovanni Battista Piranesi, the catalytic architectural mind who provided us with the evocative engraving of the Pantheon's exterior, drew up alternative ideas of a rich, three-dimensional attic of clustered pilasters and a meandering frieze that knit the openings and elements together in a bold sculptural treatment. Piranesi, as we will see in a review of this architect's work, reveled in liberties promised in the idiosyncrasies of the original attic and joyously contributed some of his own. Piranesi had access to Posi's work site and had prepared engravings of the discovered brick stamps and the uncovered wall construction, but these were held from public release. In his intuitive and profound understanding of the implications of the Pantheon's supposed "errors," Piranesi may have been the only one to approach without prejudice the Pantheon in all its complexity and contradiction.

The polemical progress of contemporary architectural design in the context of the Pantheon exemplifies the growing difficulties at this moment of reconciling creativity and innovation with the past and tradition. History takes on a weight and gains a life of its own. The polemic over adding to the Pantheon reveals a moment of transition from an earlier period of an innate, more fluid sense of continuity with the past to a period of shifting and uncertain relationship in the present. The process of redefining the interaction of the present to the past, of contemporary creativity in an historical context, is the core of the problem of modern architecture in Italy and the guiding theme of this study.

1.3 Giovanni Battista Piranesi, Pantheon, design for the attic, 1756

ROME OF THE NOLLI PLAN

The complex layering found at the Pantheon was merely an example of the vast palimpsest that is Rome itself, and there is no better demonstration of this than the vivid portrait of the city engraved in 1748. The celebrated cartographer Giovanni Battista Nolli and his team measured the entire city in eleven months using exact trigonometric methods. At a scale of 1 to 2,900, the two-square-meter map sacrifices no accuracy: interior spaces of major public buildings, churches, and palazzi are shown in detail; piazza furnishings, garden parterre layouts, and scattered ruins outside the walls are described with fidelity. Buildings under construction in the 1740s were also included: Antoine Derizet's Church of Santissimo Nome di Maria at Trajan's Column, the Trevi Fountain, Palazzo Corsini on Via della Lungara. In the city's first perfectly ichnographic representation Nolli privileges no element over another in the urban fabric. All aspects are equally observed and equally important. Vignettes in the lower corners of the map, however, present selected monuments of ancient and contemporary Rome: columns, arches, and temples opposite churches, domes, and new piazzas. *Roma antica* and *Roma moderna* face one another in a symbiotic union.

The Nolli plan captures Rome in all its richness, fixing in many minds the date of its publication as the apex of the city's architectural splendor. It is an illusory vision, however, as Rome, like all healthy cities, has never been in stasis. Nolli's inclusion of contemporary architecture emphasizes its constant evolution. His plan is neither a culmination nor a conclusion but the starting point for contemporary architecture. The architecture of modern Italy is written upon this already dense palimpsest.

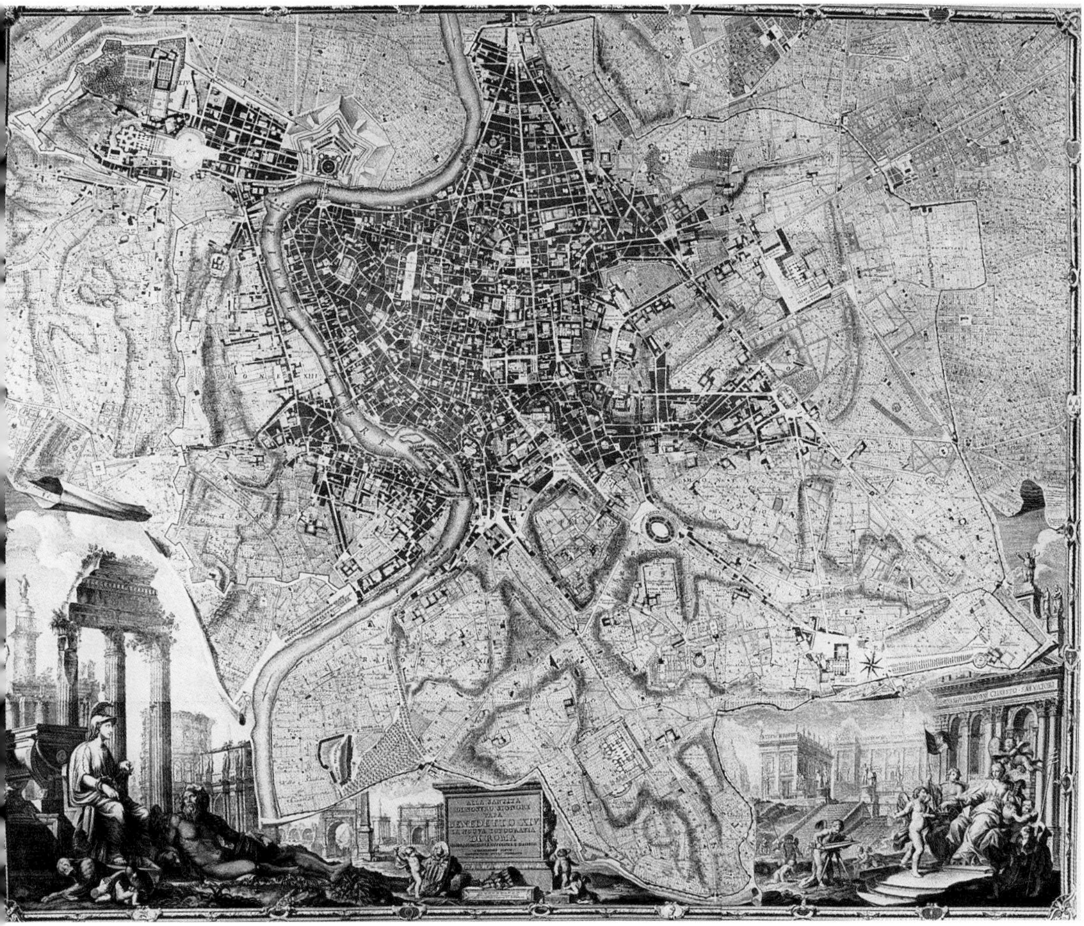

.4 Giovanni Battista Nolli, *La Nuova pianta di Roma*, 1748

ALESSANDRO GALILEI AND SAN GIOVANNI LATERANO

One of the contemporary monuments featured in Nolli's vignettes was a new facade for the church of San Giovanni Laterano. The basilica, along with its baptistery, was erected by the Emperor Constantine in the year 315. It was, and still is, the pre-eminent liturgical seat in the Christian capital, where the relics of Saints Peter and Paul—specifically, their heads—are preserved. The popes resided at the Lateran through the Middle Ages and it remains today the cathedral of the city of Rome, though it does not enjoy a pre-eminent urban position or architectural stature; indeed its peripheral site along the city's western walls and eccentric orientation facing out across the open countryside make the maintenance of its rightful stature, let alone its aging physical structure, extremely difficult. The Church of Saint Peter's, on the other hand, also Constantinian in origin, had been entirely reconceived under Pope Julius II in the Renaissance and became the preferred papal seat. Meanwhile, the Lateran remained in constant need of repair, revision, and reform. Pope Sixtus V reconfigured the site by adding an obelisk, a new palace and benediction loggia on the side and later Pope Innocent X set Francesco Borromini to reintegrate the body of the church, its nave, and its double aisles, but his plans for the facade and eastern piazza were left unexecuted. Dozens of projects to complete the facade were proposed over the next seventy-five years until Pope Clement XII announced in 1731 an architectural competition for it.

Clement XII's idea of a competition was a novelty for Rome, with a published program and projects presented anonymously before an expert jury. It would indeed provide an opportunity for exposure of new ideas and for stimulating discussion. In 1732, nearly two dozen proposals were put on display in a gallery of the papal summer palace on the Quirinal Hill. All the prominent architects of Rome participated, as well as architects from Florence, Bologna, and Venice. Participants drew up a variety of alternatives ranging, as tastes ran, between a stern classicism to fulsome baroque images after Borromini. Jury members from the Accademia di San Luca found the projects that followed Borrominian inspiration excessively exuberant and preferred the sobriety of the classical inheritance, and Alessandro

Galilei emerged the winner. These expressed opinions delineated a polemical moment dividing the baroque from a new classicism.

Galilei was a remote relation of the famous astronomer and followed the papal court from Florence to Rome. Galilei had been active in the rediscovery of classic achievements in the arts and letters in the eighteenth century re-examining Giotto, Dante, and Brunelleschi with renewed appreciation. For example, when asked in 1723 for his opinion on a new baroque-style altar for the Florentine baptistry, Galilei favored preserving the original Romanesque ambience of the interior despite the tastes of his day. A renewed classical sense stigmatized the frivolities of the rococo as uncultivated, arbitrary, and irrational. Clement XII's competition for San Giovanni may merely have been a means to secure the project less flagrantly for Galilei and to introduce a rigorous cultural policy to Rome.

Roman architects petitioned the pope, livid that their talent went unrewarded, and Clement responded with, in effect, consolation prizes to some of them with commissions for other papal works. Construction on the Lateran facade was begun in 1733.

Galilei's facade of San Giovanni Laterano is a tall and broad structure in white travertine limestone. The structure is entirely open to the deep shadowed spaces of a loggia set within a colossal Corinthian order. In a manuscript attributed to Galilei, the architect articulates his guiding principles of clear composition and reasoned ornament, functional analysis and economy. Professional architects, Galilei insists, trained in mathematics and science and a study of antiquity, namely the Pantheon and Vitruvius, can assure good building. Galilei's handling of the composition has the rectilinear rigor and interlocking precision one might expect from a mathematician. The ponderous form is monumental merely by the means of its harmonious proportions of large canonical elements. It is a strong-boned, broad-shouldered architecture, a match for Saint Peter's. It demonstrates in its skeletal sparseness and subordination of ornamentation the rational architectural logic attributed to Vitruvius. Galilei's images are derived primarily from sources in Rome: the two masterpieces of his Florentine forefather Michelangelo, Saint Peter's and the Palazzo dei Conservatori at the Capitoline. Galilei's classicism is a constant strain among architects in Rome who built their monumental church facades among the vestiges of the ancient temples. Galilei refocused that tradition upon Vitruvius and in his measured austerity contributed a renewed objectivity to Roman architecture of the eighteenth century.

Galilei's austere classicism is emblematic of a search for a timeless and stately official idiom at a point in time where these qualities were found lacking in contemporary architecture. Reason, simplicity, order, clarity—the essential motifs of this modern discussion—set into motion a reasoned disengagement from the baroque. With Galilei's monumental facade, guided in many ways by the pressures of Saint Peter's, the Cathedral of Rome takes its rightful position, as Nolli's vignette suggests, a triumphal arch over enthroned *Roma moderna*.

NICOLA SALVI AND THE TREVI FOUNTAIN

Alongside serious official architectural works on major ecclesiastical sites, eighteenth-century Rome also sustained a flourishing activity in more lighthearted but no less meaningful works. The Trevi Fountain ranks perhaps as the most joyous site in Rome. Built from 1732 to 1762 under the patronage of popes Clement XII, Benedict XIV, and Clement XIII, the great scenographic water display is often described as the glorious capstone of the baroque era. This is indeed where most architectural histories (and tourist itineraries) of Italian architecture end. It is one of those places, like the Pantheon, where the entire sweep of Rome's culture can be read.

The history of the Trevi Fountain reaches back to antiquity. The waters that feed the fountain today flow through the Aqua Virgo aqueduct originally constructed by Agrippa in 19 B.C. The aqueduct passes mostly underground and was obstructed in the Middle Ages to prevent barbarian infiltration, so it was easily repaired in the Renaissance. The water inspired a succession of baroque designers with ideas for a fountain. As at San Giovanni, a similar architectural competition was opened by Clement XII. With Clement's own favored Florentine architect, Galilei, already loaded up with projects,

1.5 Alessandro Galilei, San Giovanni Laterano facade, Rome, 1732–35

1.6 Nicola Salvi with Luigi Vanvitelli, then Giuseppe Panini, Trevi Fountain, Rome, 1732–62. Engraving by Giovanni Battista Piranesi, from *Vedute di Roma*, c. 1748 the pope took this opportunity to calm the waters over the Lateran competition with a bit of artistic diplomacy. Nicola Salvi, born and bred a Roman, was awarded the commission in 1732.

Salvi was endowed with a remarkably broad education in literary and artistic culture that earned him positions in a range of Roman intellectual societies, including the Virtuosi del Pantheon, a sort of well-rounded genius club that met in the temple. His participation in the Lateran competition featured his ability for flexibility and fusion, both innovative and traditionalist, combining qualities of architectural grandeur drawn from ancient and baroque examples. The same balance and profundity is found in his singular masterpiece, the Trevi Fountain.

The Trevi Fountain is an architectural, sculptural, and aquatic performance that spills off the flank of a pre-existing palace into a low, irregular piazza. A colossal Corinthian order on a rusticated base sews the broad facade together around a central arch motif that marks the terminus of the Aqua Virgo. Sculptural figures and panels in relief adorn the central section. The figure of Ocean on an oyster-shell chariot rides outward and gestures commandingly to Tritons and their sea horses in the churning water below. The water rushes in at eye level on the piazza across a cascade of rough-hewn travertine blocks tumbling down from the palace's rustication into a deep-set pool. Sweeping steps bring us down to the water while rich sculptural flourishes draw our eye upward to the papal arms above.

Salvi has deftly combined formal references to imperial arches of triumph and the colossal order of the Renaissance, elements featured in both vignettes of Nolli's map, with the scenographic unity characteristic of the baroque. The architectonic structure is packed with all the sculptural decoration it can hold, not more. The sculptures were contracted to various artists who despite their legal protests were forced to subordinate their work to Salvi's commanding architectural scansion.

One stumbles upon the site on this edge of the eighteenth-century city quite by surprise, as the engraved image by Piranesi of the fountain and the piazza shows. Attracted perhaps by the splashing sounds, we are drawn into a delightful episode in the urban fabric. The jump in scale of Salvi's construction provides a powerful impact for this unexpectedly grand public event, like the grandiose architectures of contemporary festivals or the fantasies of the lyric opera stage. Here water has taken center stage in an engaging spectacle of cascading forms. Water is the source of salubrity and fertility and nourishes all growing things, represented by all the accompanying sculptures here and focused by Ocean's magisterial presence. Classical allegory is the basis here of a contemporary philosophical program typical of Enlightenment interests in the natural sciences. Thirty species of flora minutely described and artfully disposed upon the rocks emphasize an encyclopedic spirit. The natural and the artificial, the tectonic and the fluid, are intermingled in continual transformation one into the other. The themes of this poem in stone and water suggest an exaltation of water's vital energy in the cycle of self-renewal, time and decay, ruin and regeneration.

At Levi, Christ turned water into wine; at the Trevi, Clement XII turned wine into water: construction of the fountain was financed with proceeds from the lottery and a tax on wine. Salvi hired a learned and sensitive building contractor for the work, Nicola Giobbe, and he also relied on close collaboration with Luigi Vanvitelli. When Salvi's health gave way following a stroke in 1744 (due to too many subterranean visits to the aqueduct, it was thought), the direction of the work was eventually shifted to Giuseppe Panini, son of the famous painter, who oversaw its completion in 1762.

The response to the Trevi Fountain was overwhelmingly positive. Salvi was catapulted to fame, receiving invitations to finish up the cathedral of Milan with a new facade and build a palace for the royal family in Naples. Even the stern critic Milizia who preferred utilitarian works conceded that the Trevi was "superb, grandiose, rich and altogether of a surprising beauty... nothing in this century in Rome is more magnificent." The Trevi Fountain cannot be considered either a precursor of neoclassical rigor nor a pure product of baroque exuberance. Salvi's subtle shift toward a knowledgeable, historicist ensemble is evidence of a significant transformation in architectural ideas at this moment in the mid-eighteenth century. The Trevi is a culmination of a grand cultural tradition in Roman architecture and yet subtly innovative in its Enlightenment philosophical implications. The Trevi Fountain was the most widely influential modern construction in its day, emulated by architects across Europe. It enthuses still today an almost fanatical fascination among all who encounter it.

LUIGI VANVITELLI AND THE REGGIA AT CASERTA

Clement XII's consolation prize of the Trevi Fountain commission to Salvi was coupled with another commission to the second runner-up in the Lateran competition, Luigi Vanvitelli. Vanvitelli was the son of a Dutch landscape painter working in Italy, Gaspar Van Wittel, who Italianized his son's last name. Luigi trained like many in his day in scenography yet found employ in civil engineering. His participation in the competition for the facade of the Lateran assured his reputation although the bulk of his work continued to be in rather utilitarian tasks. He built the bastions and quarantine hospital in the pope's Adriatic port of Ancona, his consolation prize, and reorganized Michelangelo's Church of Santa Maria degli Angeli in Rome, itself a reintegration of the ancient Baths of Diocletian, which stirred criticism comparable to the contemporaneous Pantheon restorations. As head architect of the building commission at Saint Peter's, called the *Fabbrica*, his restoration project of Michelangelo's dome was contested yet successful. In Vanvitelli, the indispensable professional qualifications of engineer and architect, scenographer and coordinator were recognized by, among many, King Carlos III of Naples.

Naples and the southern reaches of the Italian peninsula, ancient Magna Graecia, had been ruled over by a succession of foreign powers. The early eighteenth century brought the Bourbon monarchy to Naples under Carlos III. Born the son of King Felipe V of Spain and Elisabetta Farnese, Carlos inherited not only the traditions arcing back through the French Bourbons to King Louis XIV, his great-grandfather, but also through his maternal line to the Farnese and Medici dynasties of Italy. Carlos III became, in 1734, the absolute monarch of the new and autonomous Kingdom of Two Sicilies which bordered the papal states to the south. Naples, which for over two centuries had languished, was now under Carlos's rule to be promoted to rank with Madrid, Paris, and Rome. Carlos instigated ameliorative policies in architecture, urbanism, and regional infrastructure that became a primary function of his reign. By ordering landed aristocrats to be physically present at the capital's urban court, Carlos stimulated the local economy in construction while simultaneously directing Naples toward a more cosmopolitan image. The king set the example by supporting the arts, undertaking archeological excavations at the buried ancient city of Herculaneum, and building several royal palaces.

Carlos had lived in many of his parents' residences, yet the structures available to the new monarch in Naples were not up to those standards either in the nature of their planning or in their less-than-imposing scale. At Portici, the Herculaneum excavation site on the bay of Naples, he began a great royal palace more for the good fishing than the promise of archeological finds the site promised. On a hill above Naples at Capodimonte he had a hunting lodge built that outstripped in its ambitious scope that modest program. Both palaces were in large part the work of a Sicilian architect, Giovanni Antonio Medrano, but both projects proved insufficient in Carlos's eye on aesthetic, representational, and functional grounds.

Finding local architects lacking, Carlos turned to Rome's prominent architectural culture for the professionals he required. Nicola Salvi was first on his wish list, but with the architect in ill health and concerned for the ongoing fountain project, he deferred, recommending instead his collaborator Vanvitelli. Benedict XIV may have been loath to see not only Vanvitelli but also another of his prized architects, Ferdinando Fuga, summoned by the powerful new monarch to the south, but the pope sent them along at the close of the Holy Year of 1750 as a diplomatic payment of cultural tokens.

Carlos set his two new architects to the major buildings of his two-fold economic and political scheme: two palaces for opposite ends of the sociopolitical scale, the Reggia or royal court palace at Caserta from Vanvitelli and the *regium pauperum hospitalium*, or royal poor-man's hospice at Naples from Fuga. Following schemes of his

French Bourbon forefathers, Carlos consolidated the charitable institutions for the poor in a grand architectural project, like Jacques-Germain Soufflot's Hotel Dieu in Lyons, and brought together the governing institutions of the upper realm in an ambitious work comparable to the palace at Versailles.

Like Versailles, the site of Carlos's new Reggia lies several dozen kilometers beyond the capital city limits at Caserta, amidst the king's favorite hunting grounds. More crucially, the site was safe from civil unrest, coastal attack, and volcanic eruption. For the entirely unimpeded site Vanvitelli drew up his first ideas for a great palace, but so did the king: as a contemporary noted, "with compass and slate in hand, Carlos drew out the first sketches of the great palace." Carlos's specific design directives can be deduced by noting all the changes Vanvitelli subsequently adopted and conscientiously adhered to in his second project proposal: a square construction with four internal courtyards and a great central dome. This design had many inspirations: the project Carlos's father had commissioned for Buen Retiro outside Madrid, as well as El Escorial; elements from his mother's Palazzo Pitti in Florence; the Palazzo Farnese in Rome; the Farnese ducal residence at Colorno; and most importantly, the Louvre, Versailles, and their gardens. Vanvitelli procured all this pertinent comparative material and dutifully shaped the project according to the royal vision. In 1751, he was summoned to the Portici residence where in a private audience, Vanvitelli tells us, the king and the queen delighted over his solutions, each asking questions and voicing desires for the apartments, the gardens, the fountains and, Queen Amalia extemporized, on a whole new, orderly city to rise up around. *Maestà*, the courtier-architect obsequiously responded, "this lesson that you deign to give me will be kept well in mind and executed without alteration."

On 20 January 1752, the foundation stone for the Reggia at Caserta was laid with pompous ceremony. This and the entire palace project were minutely described by Vanvitelli in a lavish publication of 1756 distributed by the royals to visiting dignitaries. As the architect puts it, the fourteen engraved plates and elucidating text broadcast the sublimity of Carlos's idea, which feared no comparison with the great palaces of Europe or antiquity. Vanvitelli's text is a guide to the sculptural elements and their monumental architectural vessel. Like the founding legends of western European civilization expounded by the Neapolitan philosopher Giambattista Vico, the rhythms, repetitions, gestures, and metaphors of Caserta are Vanvitelli's architectural poems of the ideal of Bourbon absolutism.

Vanvitelli coordinated the ongoing spectacle of construction of palace and gardens, along with the aqueduct that would serve them. A 40-kilometer conduit, the Acquedotto Carolino, passes through mountains, like the Aqua Virgo, and over valleys on arches modeled on the Roman-era Pont du Gard in France. Aqueduct building, the stuff of ancient emperors, provided aesthetic and functional benefits to the palace as well as to the city of Naples—a grand watercourse was to connect Carlos's two great works in a single stream.

The Reggia's ground plan measures over 250 by 200 meters, a magnificent rectilinear block of stately proportions. Two ranges of state rooms bisect within to define four rectangular courtyards. Its 1,200 rooms are arranged according to a rational geometric disposition that conjoins the symmetry, distribution, and dimension of the great palaces of Renaissance reason and Vico's notion of geometry as the visible manifestation of monarchic rule. The facade is articulated with a colossal Composite order. Its thirty-seven bays are broken up in central and terminal pavilions originally to have been accented with a cupola, corner towers, and acroterial sculpture, references to Carlos's Farnese inheritance and boyhood homes. Unlike Louis's Versailles, the walls of Caserta are not dissolved in windows; instead, Vanvitelli, like Galilei before him, exalts the rectilinear solidity of construction and achieves a sweeping monumentality worthy of the Sun King's descendant. Vanvitelli has balanced Carlos's French memories with the requisites of Italian design tradition.

The facade of the palace announces its monarchic functions. The deep central niche on the upper floor, which emphasizes the wall's solidity, is ideal for royal appearances. As Vanvitelli declared, the central area of the palace "must show off those characteristics that might give to those who enter some notion of the Personage who resides there." The various statues and inscriptions planned for the entrance declare his virtues: Justice, the measure of our well-being, and Peace, which increases our prosperity, Clemency that sustains the miserable, and Magnificence that sustains the arts "as was known," Vanvitelli wrote, "of Rome in the times of Augustus, Trajan, Hadrian, in Paris in the celebrated reign of Louis XIV, and now in Naples." The towers, which were not executed due to later financial constraints, would have lightened the facade's horizontality with bright vertical accents. For the central cupola the architect may have been thinking of Saint Peter's, but this suggestion would have been overridden by the patron's own more pertinent reference to El Escorial. Here, this cupola does not mark a chapel within the palace. Whereas Felipe erected a palace for the lord, Carlos, his son, erects a palace for the realm, inverting ecclesiastical models and confirming a theme of divinization of the monarch. The crowning construction was to have been a pierced belvedere, an airy temple seen from the vast piazza and axial road approaching the palace, rising high and framing the equestrian statue on the pediment as if the royal simulacrum were in triumphal procession.

Entering the palace, the visitor's eye is drawn along a central axis through the ground floor and clear out the back to the garden. This is a grand covered street, a triumphant way that threads three vestibules each of which radiates diagonal glimpses into the courtyards. Many sources for Vanvitelli's inspiration for these surprising and dramatic vestibules have been suggested, but only Vanvitelli's first training in scenography can explain the effect of infinite space achieved by the fleeting diagonal planes across the rectangular courtyards. Every view to and through the Reggia suggests the infinite power of its resident, even the interior vistas. That power is also manifest in the materials used in the construction. The dozens of monolithic columns that punctuate the great masses of supporting wall, especially in the vestibules, were a particular passion of Carlos, both for their representational value as achievements of the classical past and for their local provenance from archeological sites across his realm. Even the materials manifest the monarch's sovereignty across space and time, territory and its history.

These connections are made explicit in the few but significant sculptural elements realized at Caserta. At the central ground floor vestibule is a colossal figure of resting Hercules, loosely adapted from

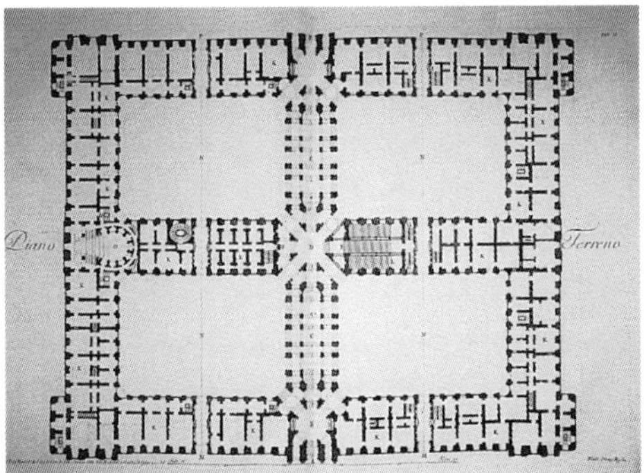

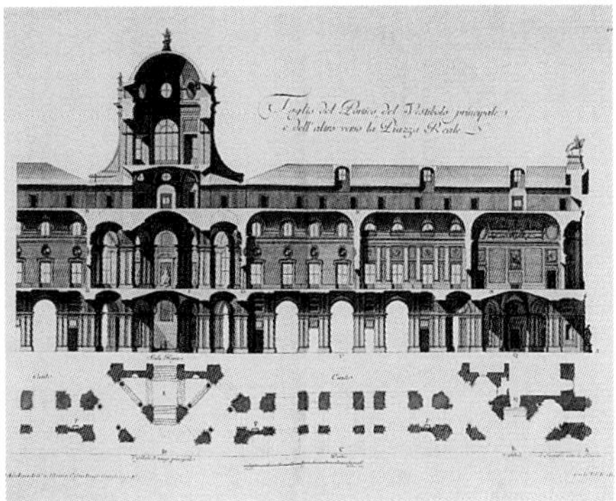

1.7–1.9 Luigi Vanvitelli, Reggia, Caserta, 1751–. Front elevation, ground floor plan, partial longitudinal section, from *Dichiarazione dei disegni del reale palazzo di Caserta*, 1756

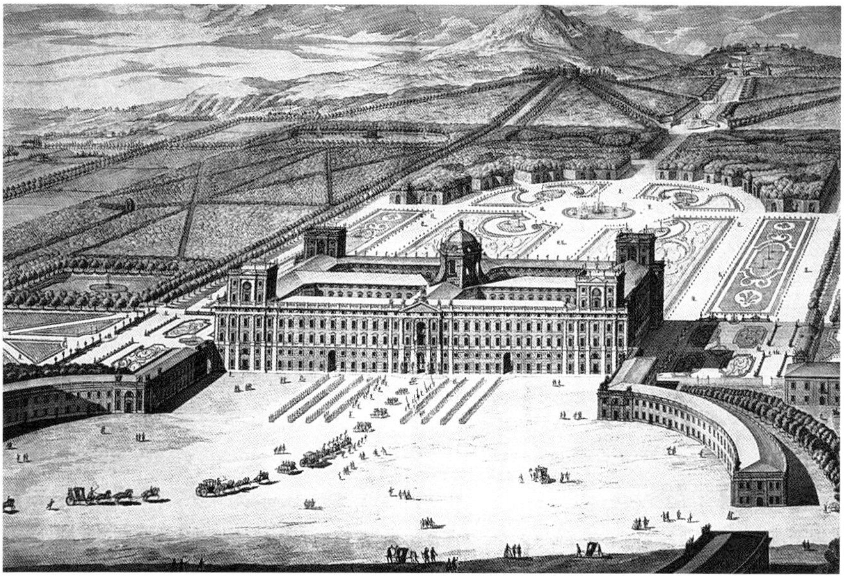

1.10 and 1.11 Luigi Vanvitelli, Reggia, Caserta, 1751–. *Scalone d'onore* and aerial view from *Dichiarazione*, 1756

the ancient "Farnese Hercules." According to Vico, Hercules plays a major role in the origin of civilization and in many ways: wanderer to foreign shores, tamer of beasts and land, huntsman and planter, builder of gardens and cities. This reflects Carlos in all his endeavors. The stair climbs its first ramp between lions and up to a tall scenic wall with a statue symbolizing Royal Majesty. Here, approaching petitioners are exhorted to truthfulness and meritoriousness by flanking allegories. The stairs bifurcate and continue to climb within this large space vaulted by two domical shells, the first pierced to reveal the second painted empyrean of Apollo's realm. A musicians' gallery tucked away above allows for ethereal accompaniment to the ascent. Here, Vanvitelli maintains an extraordinary equilibrium of baroque theatricality and classical measure.

The upper vestibule is similar to the one directly below, but bathed in intense light. Approached at oblique angles, this vestibule is invested with a centrifugal force that sends the visitor off to the four corners of the palace. Carlos ordered Vanvitelli to model the chapel after Jules-Hardouin Mansart's at Versailles by emphasizing the structural integrity of the free-standing polychrome marble shafts. Vanvitelli also paired the columns as Claude Perrault had done on the recent facade at the Louvre. Vanvitelli too strikes a balance between the forces of tradition and the drive for innovation.

The royal apartments emanate from the central vestibule, the king's toward the principal facade, the queen's toward the gardens, in a strict subdivision of title and gender. The visitor proceeds through sequences of antechambers to the royal presences, shaping, as at Versailles, the rituals of absolute monarchy through the controlled movement of its courtiers. Although the decoration of these interiors fell to the successors of Carlos and Vanvitelli, the *fuga di stanze*, or flight of aligned rooms along its 250-meter axes is more impressive than any later gilding. The court theater on the ground floor was completed entirely under Vanvitelli's direction. Within its tiny 10-meter breadth, completely subsumed like the chapel within the overall geometry of the building, Vanvitelli's colossal columnar order unifies the space. Placed on the ground floor, the stage may be opened at the back to a garden vista.

The gardens at Caserta are an integral element in the experience of Bourbon self-imagery. Parterres and boxwood extend the geometry of the palace's architecture outward. The central axis, noted upon our first approach, shoots thousands of meters up the hillside; the abundant waters of the aqueduct cascade toward us, bursting rambunctiously from a mountain cataract, stepping down enormous water chains and flowing into long, low pools. Vanvitelli's son, Carlo, strove to complete the key features of the sculptural program of his father's gardens. The Ovidian themes of fertility and metamorphosis that Vanvitelli listed in his publication were carefully determined as a Vichian mythopoeic historiography of the land. The fountain sculptures reference both the king's passion for hunting here and the site's historical association with the virginal goddess of the hunt, Diana. At the top of the park, a dramatic ensemble of statues play out the scene of Actaeon's fateful encounter with the goddess in her bath who in her ire flings drops of water onto the hapless hunter who is transformed into a stag and devoured by his dogs. In other ensembles along the water chain, Adonis departs on his fatal hunt and Venus uses his blood to seminate the earth with anemones. The statues describe the region's mythic foundations in the acts of gods.

All elements of this monarchic project are concatenated along the water's course, garden, palace, and on to the new city of Caserta. In front of the palace, a vast elliptical piazza opens, delineated by the severe forms of barracks and service buildings. Its geometry begs a comparison to Bernini's piazza at Saint Peter's but here the architectural gesture is stern and military beneath the monarch at his loggia controlling with his gaze this place and the model town that expands from it, the center of a wisely governed realm. From here a radiating *trevium* and an orderly grid of streets were planned with decorous, uniform blocks to guarantee light and air to the residential units. Contemporary interests in urban planning exhorted the monarch to the organization of cities, a duty that brings with it not only considerable public utility but also effective political propaganda.

Caserta was designed not to replace the capital city but, like Versailles, to rise alongside as an ideal image of the monarch's rule.

1.12 Luigi Vanvitelli with Carlo Vanvitelli, Reggia, Caserta, 1751–. Garden fountains

The axis of the palace and garden was to continue over the horizon to Naples along a single road carrying with it the waters of the aqueduct in flanking canals. The union of monumental aesthetic and functional utility characterizes the particular strengths of Vanvitelli's vast plan and the absolute power of Carlos's rule. Contemporaries hailed Caserta as the greatest project of its kind. Milizia gushed with praise calling it "a rare complex of grandeur, of regularity, of rhythm, of variety, of contrasts, of richness, of facility, of elegance." Antoine-Chrysostôme Quatremère de Quincy, the French critic, lauded its unity of conception and unity of execution, others its sublime effect of symmetry and expansion, huge dimensions, and controlled singular vision. While concepts of the sublime were being developed across Europe, Vanvitelli himself described Caserta as "a true mirror in which His Royal Highness can see himself . . . and the sublime Ideas conceived by his magnificence," and claimed that it would "show to Italy, and to all Europe, what sublimity the thoughts of his Majesty reach."

Vanvitelli was the last architect of such absolutist ambition and Caserta the swan song of the absolutist rule that sustained such visionary building. Caserta is as much connected to the traditions of the Renaissance and the baroque as it is a response to the innovating classical shift of Vanvitelli's generation. But Caserta stands, even in its abbreviated form, as a confirmation of the highest aspirations of late-eighteenth-century culture and a prototype for a whole line of "megapalaces," buildings of power, logic, largeness, magnificence, and manipulation.

In celebration of his achievements, the festival decorations erected in the streets and squares of his capital presented Carlos III as a modern Hercules, the mythic builder of a new civilization. Far from abandoning the city to its own squalor, the king began to set out systems of urban improvement for the city of Naples, encouraging private building. He commissioned a map of the city, like Nolli's of Rome, a clear testimony of an urban consciousness. He built the Teatro San Carlo, repaired churches like Santa Chiara, established public museums for the Herculaneum finds and the Farnese sculpture collection, supplied warehouses, barracks, and hospices, and opened an ancient-style forum, the Foro Carolino.

Vanvitelli brought to Naples what Carlos most needed, a grand architectural imagery—clear, solid, geometric, with its severe grandeur and rich magnificence "fusing," as the visiting Frenchman Jérôme Richard summarized in 1764, "the majestic beauty of ancient architecture with the pleasantness of modern architecture." Vanvitelli's impact in the hitherto provincial world of Neapolitan architects was, as he immodestly said himself, "a lesson in proper modern architecture." As Michelangelo had done for Rome itself in the sixteenth century, Vanvitelli defined an imperial idiom for his day that dismantled regional inflections through the Herculean force of classicism. Vanvitelli's command of objective functional requirements may certainly have predisposed him to classical solutions, reducing the perceived excesses of baroque space with the rigor of columns, but his classicism is neither self-consciously historicist nor artificially aesthetisized but the result of a continuously evolving and solid Italian tradition in architecture almost two millennia in the making.

Carlos's ameliorative policies and architectural visions were stopped short by his ascension to the Spanish throne and departure for Madrid in 1759, leaving behind the regency of his eight-year-old son, Ferdinando IV. Vanvitelli's career, which depended upon Carlos, was in jeopardy under Ferdinando's lax interest and his regent's stringent spending. During his reign, only Caserta's theater was inaugurated, along with some small apartments on the main floor. Efforts to build up parts of the new town, then to be called Ferdinandopoli, were undertaken, although not to Vanvitelli's original plans. Ferdinando, however, established a worker's colony specializing in silk production nearby at San Leucio in 1769, and examples of its work line the walls of the Caserta apartments. The collective community at San Leucio figures as the Bourbon monarchy's most effective socioeconomic effort—it sustained local crafts, educated its inhabitants, and eliminated the need to import silk. The notions of social ameliorative policies had been at the core of Bourbon works, and Carlos had all along a second grand project under way in town.

FERNANDO FUGA AND THE ALBERGO DEI POVERI

While Vanvitelli developed the worldly Caserta, to Ferdinando Fuga fell a more mundane but no less instrumental element of Bourbon rule: the Albergo dei Poveri in Naples. Born a Florentine, Fuga came to Rome to study at the Accademia di San Luca. He had proposed a project for the Lateran facade as early as 1722 and participated in the Trevi competition as well. His fortunes brightened when the Florentine pope Clement XII made him architect of the papal palaces. Fuga enlarged the Corsini properties along Via della Lungara, and for the papal summer palace at the Quirinal he extended the Via Pia wing to an indeterminate length with what is called simply the long sleeve, "La Manica Lunga." He finished the stables at the Quirinal, built a prison at San Michele a Ripa, extended the hospital of Santo Spirito and designed its cemetery. The Palazzo della Consulta, 1732–37, a multipurpose building opposite the Quirinal Palace, is his most representative work, combining a carefully coordinated plan behind a lively polychrome facade.

The pope's big spending throughout the papal states was understood as an opportunity to revive a slumped economy. Monumental facades for unfinished churches, public fountains, administrative offices, hospitals, even land reclamation and port reconstruction were the signs of papal magnanimity, *magnificienza*, well-balanced schemes for social well-being. A rich intellectual climate, drawing in Clement's case from Tuscan circles, sustained this development. For example, Lione Pascoli, the pope's economist, developed a utilitarian understanding of architectural programs as efficacious instruments of social policy. There was in Pascoli's notion little concern for style or form beyond clearly ordered space and structure. Corsini's enlightened circle advanced an erudite return to the order of Renaissance and classical topoi and a rationalization in all ways of thought. Fuga, like Alessandro Galilei and Nicola Salvi, propelled these values as architectural principles in his work.

Under Clement's successor, Benedict XIV, Fuga's career did not falter. Indeed, the full range of his talents was exercised, from the most spirited light baroque splendor of the new arcaded facade for Santa Maria Maggiore to a sober Doric-style pavilion for serving coffee in the Quirinal gardens. They called it with self-conscious cosmopolitan airs a *caffèaus*. This addition to the garden provided the pope with a casual location for encounters, for example, with King Carlos III of Naples in 1744, for which the palace throne room would have been unwantedly officious. Fuga's accomplishments were even more obvious than Luigi Vanvitelli's for they demonstrated capabilities of adaptation to a wide variety of circumstances and program, to site and to patrons' tastes while solving difficult functional and representational problems with brilliance and economy. Already in 1748, Carlos had hand-picked Fuga, at the height of his fame, for a mammoth job in his building scheme for Naples.

Regium totius regni pauperum hospitalium, the royal hospice for all the realm's paupers, better known as the Albergo dei Poveri, was not a second prize to Vanvitelli's Reggia but an integral component of Carlos's social, political, and architectural vision that in fact may predate the maturation of the ideas for Caserta.

The population of Naples had grown dramatically in the eighteenth century, necessitating a reorganization of its antiquated charitable institutions. In the first years of Carlos's reign, the idea of a large, single, specifically designed hospice for the poor and orphaned, like Rome's San Michele a Ripa, was guided by a clear program for the moral and economic health of the capital. The Neapolitan hospice was to have been the largest in Europe, planned to accommodate and sustain, equip and reintegrate eight-thousand souls at a time. The Albergo dei Poveri addresses both the aesthetics of magnificence in civil architecture and the functionality of a framework for social sustenance.

Because the project relied upon the growing technical proficiency of economic planners and even medical experts, Fuga's job as architectural designer was enriched if complicated by the opinions of many special consultants. As in the case of Luigi Vanvitelli's evident qualifications, Carlos needed above all decisive project managers. Fuga was given power of executive decision on the means of production, which did not put him in an easy relationship to the local workmen. They took every opportunity to make the Florentine architect's work more difficult. Fuga often fled to Rome, leaving the Albergo to young assistants. Although Fuga forged no

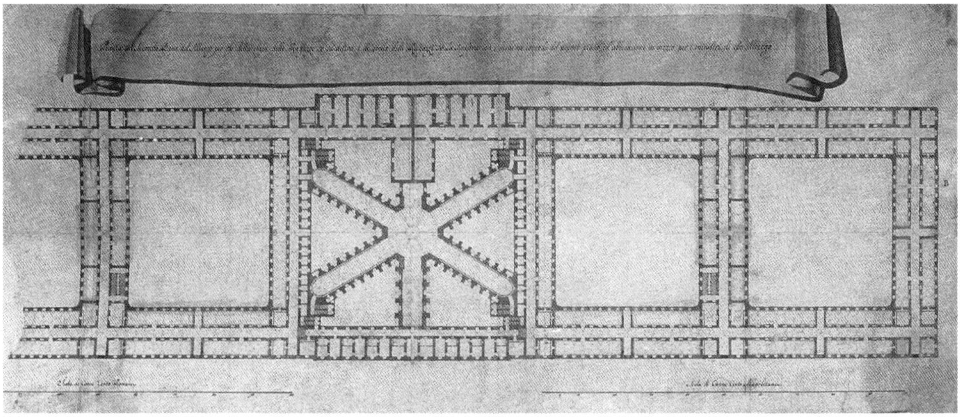

1.13 Ferdinando Fuga, Caffèaus, Palazzo Quirinale, Rome, 1741–43. Giovanni Paolo Panini, *King Carlos III of Naples Visiting Pope Benedict XIV in the Quirinal Gardens Caffèaus in 1744*, 1746
1.14 Ferdinando Fuga, Albergo dei Poveri, Naples, 1751–. Second-floor plan

school or theory of architecture, he left behind in Naples a *modus operandi* of a high level of professionalism. Already in 1748, Fuga's project was ready to go. An enormous square, 276 by 268 meters, was to be divided four-square by cross branches within, much like Caserta, but larger. A church space was placed so that its dome might rise from the facade plane for greater visibility. Not one but three nave spaces were to be fit within the body of the wings—left, right, and down the center. Fuga could have drawn from a plethora of sources for his plan, but we should not underestimate the influence that Carlos had upon this project "with compass in hand." As the royal vision of things directed Vanvitelli's work, so too Fuga considered Carlos's basic archetype for magnificence. The four-square configuration with dome and towers of Fuga's first design proposal recalls the same rigorous geometry and elemental components that Carlos gave to the architects of all his projects, confirming the related nature of his architectural endeavors. The original site designated to accommodate such a mammoth construction was, however, too low and swampy and was rejected for hygienic reasons. That it was close to the military installations of the port was also a problem for reasons of security, though it is unclear whether it would be the poor or the port in danger. With the designation in 1751 of a new site along the Via Foria, Fuga had to rework the plans.

Complications such as this frustrated Fuga, but nothing could have been more of an aggravation to him than to have seen Vanvitelli at this time invited to the more seductive and flattering Caserta project. It was clear that Carlos was more interested in Caserta after Vanvitelli's private audiences at Portici, and Fuga reacted bitterly. Vanvitelli criticized the Albergo plans and perhaps, by his authority, triggered further changes shouldered by Fuga. In turn, Fuga tried to wrench the Caserta commission from Vanvitelli by criticizing the impractical nature and lack of economy of the designs. The rivals bragged to one another about their buildings, exaggerating their comparative sizes.

In May 1751, plans for both the Reggia and the Albergo dei Poveri were presented to the monarch, Vanvitelli in his first encounter, Fuga already having re-adapted the building to the new site on the slope beneath the Capodimonte lodge. The higher site afforded the desired light, air, and requisite salubrity encouraged by medical consultants. Water slews and aqueducts from the hill behind, perhaps to have been linked to the Acquedotto Carolino, would supply the site. The cornerstone was laid on 7 December 1751, coinciding again with one of Vanvitelli's preliminary design deadlines for the Reggia at Caserta.

The new site for the Albergo, however, required a horizontal reconfiguration of the plan on the slope along five aligned courtyards. The longitudinal development of Fuga's second plan more closely resembles the Roman hospice at San Michele a Ripa on which Fuga had worked. The resemblance moreover to Soufflot's recently completed Hôtel Dieu in Lyons is a particularly compelling connection, even more since the great French architect was actually in Naples during the gestation of the Albergo project and may have been consulted for his expertise. Fuga's new building, however, was to be three times the size: 634 meters long, eight stories high, and containing over 750,000 cubic meters of interior space. A single central entrance on the Via Foria facade brings all beneath the *Regium totius* inscription into a vestibule where, according to more Latin inscriptions, men and boys are directed to the left, women and girls to the right. This immediate and irrevocable division by gender, akin to the front and back apartments for the king and queen at Caserta, is emphatically, graciously, and more obviously indicated to the illiterate by the statuesque gestures of the images of King Carlos and Queen Amalia to show the way. Routes through the building maintain strict segregation of sexes and ages with special skip-floor stair columns and interrupted corridors that carefully restrict movement within. Fuga conceived the systematic circulation spaces to eliminate all promiscuity in every sense. Paths of movement are regulated in invariable schedules of eating and sleeping, working and praying. There is within the Albergo dei Poveri a rigorous geometric control of movement through space dissimilar only in quality to the ritualized movement of the royal court through Vanvitelli's equally considered Caserta plan.

Segregation was only the first part of the Albergo's program of controlled movement. Once divided, the users were brought together in the central symbolic space of a church. Experts on religious reform, such as the Neapolitan philosopher Ludovico Antonio Muratori, expounded upon the efficacy of evangelical instruction in combating indigence. Hence, at the heart of Fuga's Albergo, the central of the five courtyards was to be filled with a church with five radiating naves, four on the diagonals with their separate entrances on the corners of the courtyard for the four categories of inmate, men, women, boys, and girls, the central nave for the public entering from the front vestibule. Each space was focused upon the central domed tribune area without affording views from the fenced-in individual naves to the whole complex. The controlled visibility and focus on the altar was a feature Fuga had also employed at his prison in Rome. Here the fully radiating plan, a multiplication of his first three-naved version, recalls models the architect could have brought in, such as Michelangelo's unexecuted although well-studied plan for San Giovanni dei Fiorentini in Rome, and others that Carlos III and Soufflot could have suggested. The structures of the naves closely resemble the heavily buttressed Gothic vessel of the Church of Santa Chiara in Naples, which Carlos was then having Fuga restore as a royal funerary chapel.

From the Albergo's sparse nave spaces, the inmates would be encouraged to participate by visiting one of the confessionals built between the wall's buttresses. Special passageways through the walls allowed the priests to access these confessionals, themselves not mingling among the inconstant of soul. Bathrooms were conveniently located nearby for the inconstant of body. As by then a century of French development in the building types of confinement had taught, the centralizing gaze assured patients of the presence of providence, but the conscious surveillance of their peripheral positions from the center would, according to Enlightenment philosophy of mind and body, invest the individuals therein with a responsible consciousness. They would become through prayer and work agents of their own reform and reintegration to society. The architectural design would guarantee it.

If the building's plan fulfills the functional necessities of its social goals, the facade addresses, within the limits of economy, the aesthetics of civic architecture and magnificence. The facade was originally to have been 101 bays long, longer than the Manica

Lunga, each of its five segments larger than the Palazzo Farnese in Rome, and so sparse in its ornamentation as to bring to mind the unadorned mass of the Palazzo Farnese in Parma, once young Carlos's ducal seat. Fuga employed the lowest, most economical pilaster strips and trabeation lines to delineate wall cells and rhythm for suggestions of central and terminal pavilions. The wall is stripped down to its barest essentials. The triangular pediment that only meekly ornaments the mighty face was added by later architects who shied from Fuga's severity.

The Albergo dei Poveri, even in the small fraction of the building eventually completed, exercises an immense visual power at its scale—larger than the eye can take in. The Albergo impresses itself upon the city and the region not by any alignments that were sacrificed at this site but merely by the scale of its conception. Fuga's achievement of sober grandiosity and equilibrated articulations has made the most monumental effect from the most parsimonious means. The true monumentality of the Albergo dei Poveri is expressed in a perfect match of his form and its program. Although largely incomplete, it is the most ambitious utopian attempt of the Enlightenment.

After thirty years of fitful construction, it was clear that the economic support of Ferdinando's regency would not see the building completed. "At less expense and in shorter time, one could have eliminated all poverty in the abundant Realm of Naples. It's a continual refrain," Milizia complained, "that with these Hospices one does not eliminate the poor. But this is not the business of the Architect but of good Government." In 1764, a famine pressed the building into partial service, and the central church space was never built, nor were the workshops for the education of the inmates. The program never rehabilitated or reintegrated anyone, and the Albergo became known crudely as a *reclusorio*, jokingly as a *seraglio*, and effectively as a prison for the poor. Fuga's Albergo passed immediately from a utopian vision to a grandiose ruin, inhabited by a variegated society of squatters. The palace for the proletariat did not ameliorate the situation in Naples as Milizia predicted but defined with greater clarity the distance between it and the palace of the privileged at Caserta.

Architecture in both Carlos's great building projects was employed judiciously as an instrument to stabilize and regulate society. If Caserta is the last in the line of symbols of absolute rule, the Albergo dei Poveri is the progenitor of architectural instruments of social control in the centuries to follow.

GIOVANNI BATTISTA PIRANESI

Into this context of shifting patterns of making and thinking about architecture, Giovanni Battista Piranesi burst upon the scene as a wholly innovative interpreter of his cultural heritage. Although Piranesi built little, through his protean production of architectural images he became the initiator of an influential train of thought that courses through the architecture of modern Italy.

Piranesi was educated in Venice, where the Palladian heritage combined with his own family traditions in stonecutting and hydraulic engineering. The architectural culture of the time was dominated by the polymath Carlo Lodoli, thirty years Piranesi's senior, who led the debate among Venetians on the relationship between past antiquity and present architecture. Lodoli's criterion of functional and material rigor repudiated the validity of the Vitruvian canon as codified, for example, in Palladio's masterly drawings. Ornament, not to be denied its communicative usefulness, would be conscientiously applied to architectural structure in a purely decorative manner: "nothing that doesn't appear to represent what is actually its function." While the French theorist Antoine Laugier hypothesized theoretical principles in a primitive hut, Lodoli discussed instead concrete achievements in ancient engineering of the Etruscan civilization. Lodoli found material beauty in an architecture born of necessity and usefulness and fostered in the minds of his followers an image of, as he is to have said, "an eternally youthful flowering of architecture."

Piranesi's first practical engagement with architecture came in the theater. The complex perspectival illusions of the eighteenth-century stage were Piranesi's basic training, which he also put to use making urban views, *vedute*, of Venice he sold to tourists. Both modes of expression, scenography and *vedutismo*, emphasize the personal experience of architectural space and led to Piranesi's production of the architectural fantasies, or *capricci*, popular at the time. Piranesi's etchings proved a highly fertile experiment nurturing a visual and visceral approach to architecture. Picturing theatrical space, emphasizing point of view, charging lighting effects, and creating episodic sequences of changing views encouraged a reconsideration of the very mode of perceiving and re-creating the reality of architecture. "Perspective," wrote Piranesi in his first publication, is "the source of architecture's most important beauty," and by perspective, *prospettiva*, he meant the viewing of form in space. In an analysis of his architectural views and, eventually, his built work, we will see that in his visual fashion Piranesi challenges traditional ways of seeing architecture.

In 1740, Piranesi had the chance to go to Rome for the first time thanks to a connection to the powerful Rezzonico family. He was struck by Rome: the drama of its monumental baroque spaces, the scale and texture of the looming ruins, and the painterly play of the Roman sun. He engraved the Trevi Fountain and assisted Giuseppe Vasi in the production of *vedute* for the market of tourists, architectural students, and intellectuals in Rome. Piranesi met both Nicola Salvi, his master builder Giobbe, and Luigi Vanvitelli, whom he praised in his own volume of etched views, *Prima parte di Architettura e Prospettive* of 1743. He aspired to inherit from them the position of papal architect.

In the meantime, Piranesi was drawn to Rome's ruins. "Those living speaking ruins filled my spirit with images such as even the masterfully wrought drawings of the immortal Palladio, which I kept before me at all times, could not arouse in me. So the idea came to me to tell the world of some of these buildings." Piranesi set to work to activate the antiquarian world of Roman buildings and ruins as a challenge to contemporary art and life. His *veduta* of the Pantheon provides us with an impression heightened by the towering scale of the building in its environment, the stark contrasts of light and textures, and, in a scenographic touch, a contrast of the eminent nobility of the ancient structure against the squalid details around it.

In characteristically uncircumspect brashness, Piranesi rebuffed the mediocrity of contemporary architects and patrons with the expressly pedagogical thrust of his images.

With little opportunity at twenty-three years of age to build, the *architetto veneziano*, as Piranesi signed his works, turned to the production of architectural images to bridge the gap between ancient grandeur and contemporary work. This was not a new idea, but his was a new method. Reaching across Europe from his shop, strategically located opposite the French Academy on Via del Corso, Piranesi's etchings of ancient vestiges living in the modern city inspired an entire generation to see Rome in a new sensibility of innovative inquiry. Contrary to the philological tradition in archeological research, Piranesi's etchings of familiar sites stressed the visual values of perspective and chiaroscuro, of overall composition and material construction, ornament, architectural organism, and urban context. His approach is charged with a novel sense of immediacy by his interpretive genius for archeological remains. The grandeur of public building ensembles was evident to Piranesi down to the smallest corroded fragment. Piranesi did not seek to reactivate the functionality or purity of ancient forms but the visual, visceral impact of the ruins, which move us precisely because they are signs of a closed historical cycle beyond our power to reclaim. Piranesi's is a speculative archeology, akin not to the early Renaissance intellectual method of considering past achievement but, if anything, to the empathetic attitudes of the later mannerists Pirro Ligorio and Baldassarre Peruzzi, whom Piranesi extolled by name.

Piranesi acknowledged the divergence of his images from Vitruvian and Palladian views on ancient architecture. He begs us to understand that in antiquity, as much as among the moderns, architects fruitfully diverged from their works of theory into realms of unfettered imagination to open a dialog between past and present. As Vico proposed, myths, fantasy, and individual genius were fundamental in reviving a dimension of historical truth. Both Vico and Piranesi demonstrated that the heroic origins of Roman magnificence, both moral and formal, lay in Etruscan, Italic virtue, not the Greco-Vitruvian classical tradition.

1.15 Giovanni Battista Piranesi, Ruins of the Forum of Nerva, Rome. From *Vedute di Roma*, c. 1748
1.16 Giovanni Battista Piranesi, *Invenzioni capric[ciosi] di carceri*, plate XIV, 1760

Piranesi was, as few others, a profound architectural thinker on the past who was also an active creator in the present, both archeologist and artist, analyzer and synthesizer of his cultural heritage. His *Invenzioni capric[ciosi] di carceri* are an example of this unique fusion. Fourteen plates first produced in 1745 on the popular stage theme of prison scenes were drawn from his rich experience of ruins to forge a poetic architectural vision without precedent. These experiments in the visualization of architectural space press to radical conclusions the compositional, or decompositional, impulses unleashed by his training in scenography. "Before terror, audacity grows," reads an equivocal inscription in the etching. The *Carceri* are not conventional perspective scenes. Piranesi disintegrates the traditional quantitative control of space by collapsing Euclidean geometry. The scenes are characterized by multiple viewpoints, random episodes, spatial distortions, an ambiguity of scale, and disproportionate fragments. Robert Adam, the young English architect then in Rome, described them as "amazing and ingenious fantasies . . . the greatest fund for inspiring and instilling in any lover of architecture that can be imagined." Piranesi's vertiginous visions liberate the mind from the traditional architectural order in a systematic critique of the syntax of architecture itself.

Piranesi's contemporaries, however, engaged him on a more prosaic level. Among the scholars and architects re-evaluating antiquity's heritage, two foreigners, Julien-David Leroy and Johann Joachim Winckelmann, stand out in polemical contrast to Piranesi for their arguments of the superiority of Greek artistic culture to any Roman derivation. The Greco-Roman controversy was a debate on the origins of architecture tinged by the aesthetic shift from the rococo toward an astringency of taste. It also took on nationalist meaning. Piranesi pugnaciously defended Roman genius by connecting it to autonomous Etruscan, as opposed to Greek, origins and found in local Italic sources the origins of a Lodolian functionalist austerity, an impetuous and rather peevish retort to the foreigners. Piranesi's Roman position, although never rigorous or definitive, is advanced in his publication of 1761, *Della Magnificenza ed Architettura de' Romani*, dedicated to the reigning Rezzonico pope, Clement XIII, and *Il Campo Marzio dell'Antica Roma* of the following year. In the first publication, he conjoined the moral and the material by celebrating the magnificence of the Romans as a people and their public works of architecture and engineering. The second publication demonstrated the mythic proportions of the ancient city. Piranesi's defense of the indigenous origins of architectural genius is qualitatively different from his French and German rivals' positions because Piranesi defends his own national patrimony thus becoming an early champion of *Italianità* or *Romanità*, as the patriotic sentiment in the arts will come to be called.

In order to evolve a contemporary system of architecture, Piranesi embraced indeed a more widely based study of the past. At the height of his polemic exchanges, Piranesi published his most explicit critique of contemporary attitudes toward architecture, his *Parere su l'Architettura*, illustrated with more loosely drawn images of immense variety and vitality tapping the widest array of sources, from Etruria to Egypt. The *Parere* defended an all-inclusive historicism that can be summed up in one strange word Piranesi liked to use: *sbizzararsi*, or to let yourself go in a momentary and explosive moment of capriciousness. Piranesi was finally given the opportunity to put his ideas to the test in an architectural project for an actual site.

In the 1760s, attention returned to the continuing renovation of San Giovanni Laterano. Pope Clement XIII confronted the care of the only remaining Constantinian part left at the Lateran: the apse. The pope seems to have solicited drawings for a new apse and high altar from the head of the Vatican *Fabbrica*, Carlo Marchionni. Piranesi, counting on his Venetian connections, also worked up a series of drawings to present. He proposed rebuilding the liturgical focus of the basilica with a barrel-vaulted choir and a broad semicircular presbytery area with an ambulatory behind a columnar screen, the whole crowned with a dramatically illuminated half dome.

All the surfaces of Piranesi's project are covered with profuse ornament. The sources of his invention range from the elevated altar screens of Palladio's Venetian churches to the mannerist ornament of Peruzzi and Ligorio. The spatial complexities, leaps of scale, intense lighting effects explored in his etchings, especially the *Carceri*, can be seen to bear upon his project for San Giovanni. Given the context of Piranesi's work on the interior, Borromini is by far the most decisive

1.17 Giovanni Battista Piranesi, San Giovanni Laterano, project for a new apse, Rome, 1763–67

source of influence and guidance for Piranesi. The *Parere* was republished at this time in a second edition in which Piranesi praised the baroque master. Piranesi's ornament is drawn, like Borromini's, from arcane sources of antiquity, exceptional examples used in a syntactical looseness with the polemical intention of distancing the architect from canons and unleashing an intensely personal and creative vocabulary.

Piranesi's contemporaries did not understand him. Luigi Vanvitelli thought him mad. "If they really will let Piranesi build anything, we'll see what the mind of a crazy man with no foundation can produce." Vanvitelli, the stately classicist, was not propelled by the same passions that drove Piranesi. Rebuilding the apse at San Giovanni was not at this time undertaken, perhaps because of the uncertain stability of the ground. Perhaps the project was not pursued because of its high costs, as the pope's treasurer Gianangelo Braschi noted, or because of Rezzonico's own shifting tastes. The aging pope eventually hired the coolly neoclassical sculptor Antonio Canova for his tomb in Saint Peter's. Piranesi's ideas for the Lateran remained on paper and the beautiful finished drawings that show what he could do as an architect were eventually presented not to the pope, who may never have requested them in the first place, but to his twenty-six-year-old nephew Giovanni Battista Rezzonico, Piranesi's only effective patron.

During the gestation of the Lateran project, a less monumental but more concrete commission would become Piranesi's only major built work: Santa Maria del Priorato in Rome. This is the only commission of which Piranesi speaks directly in any of his written works, in *Diverse maniere di adornare camini* published in 1769, which he dedicated to Rezzonico. The young Rezzonico, made Grand Prior of the Order of the Knights of Malta by his uncle only a few years earlier, hired Piranesi in 1764 to lay out the order's estate and restore the priory's funerary chapel on the Aventine hill. As at the Lateran, the goal of this project was to intervene in an ailing pre-existing structure and at the same time transform it into a more dignified setting. The small church, the surrounding villa garden terraces, and a new entrance piazza providing access and introduction to the site are the elements that Piranesi "renewed rather than merely restored," as he stated.

The Martial Order of Knights Hospitaller moved their funerary chapel to this quiet place in the fourteenth century from the Church of Saint Basil of Capadoccia, which once stood upon the ruins of Augustus's Temple of Mars. The Aventine hill was attractive to the order in this phase of its history for its reserved geographical position above the riverbank opposite the Ripa port and the San Michele hospice, and for the various accreted memories of the hill itself. The knights' tombs were placed in a modest chapel erected in the sixteenth century. Over the next two hundred years, the gardens and adjoining villa structures were embellished. A planted avenue of arched ilex shrubs famously frames a view to the cupola of Saint Peter's all the way across the city, spied today by tourists who peek through the gate's keyhole. Besides this long, purely visual connection, the site and access to the church itself are particularly eccentric. There is no clear approach up the steep slope of the hill, nor any comprehensive view of the complex once arrived.

Piranesi's project was conceived in a series of discrete events starting with an introductory piazza and culminating in an apotheosis at the altar of the church interior. The Piazza dei Cavalieri di Malta is not a normal piazza in the urban sense, like Vanvitelli's Foro Carolino, because its perimeter is defined not by buildings or colonnades but by a low boundary wall that only loosely delimits the void on three sides. Here, Piranesi invites us to meditate on the brotherhood of knights. At this site outside the city limits returning ancient soldiers consigned their arms for purification and safekeeping. Piranesi relives that memory imaginatively in connection to the valorous warriors' return to Rome. Reliefs on the boundary wall and entrance screen to the gardens feature ornaments inspired by those on the base of the Column of Trajan. Pairs of obelisks, used in Piranesi's Venice to honor the success of naval leaders, here with prows and rudders, specify the knights' campaigns defending the seas. Emblems regarding the patron, the Rezzonico double-headed eagle and towers, are also woven in among a plethora of lyres, cameos, birds' wings, and pan pipes, drawn from Piranesi's own recherché collection. Each symbol pertains to more than one of four themes: antique or martial, the patron or the artist. The wreathed eagle is at once the Rezzonico seal and an ancient symbol of glory from imperial monuments, and also included in

Piranesi's synoptic table of exemplary Etruscan decorative inventions published in *Diverse maniere*. Simultaneous saturated readings of these motifs communicate the site's ancient history and the history of the knights; they eulogize the order's heroic past while introducing a funeral note, acknowledge the Grand Prior patron, and all the while advance the artist's own polemical agenda on contemporary creativity.

Piranesi shored up the foundations of the chapel, its facade, and its vault, often embedding ancient materials found on the site. He applied to the reconfigured facade a series of compounded motifs molded in inexpensive white stucco reprising the themes announced at the piazza. Sheathed swords are hung high on the pilasters as quiet trophies of battle. Beside the door, weightless strings of symbols hung as garlands bring together a deceptively nonlinear sequence of motifs again combining the Maltese and martial, Rezzonico and Piranesian. The Ionic capitals are carved with figures of sphinxes flanking Rezzonico towers elaborated, Piranesi informs us, from examples in the Villa Borghese antiquities collection and illustrated in his *Magnificenza*. His *ordine ionico moderno* is the product of a creative transformation of ancient examples and natural elements into abundant ornament held in congruence to its architectural frame. There is a comparable plastic treatment of the manipulated motifs around the oculus where a fluted sarcophagus, wings, reeds, pipes, prows, and paddles appear all at once transformed and unified in as compactly integrated a meaning as in its formal composition. The inventions of ornamental incrustations are called by Piranesi and his workmen *scherzi*, a joking playfulness that brings to mind earlier *capricci* and the tradition of mannerist grotesques and similar to many passages in the plates of his enigmatic *Parere*. Like the reliefs in the piazza, the facade is imaginatively enlivened with etched collages of diverse motifs equivocal and fragmentary that communicate encoded messages along Piranesi's route through Maltese memory. The interior presents, finally, the complete and climactic expression of all the episodic meanings. By extending and elevating the presbytery and puncturing the apse with a window in the back and the crossing with a lantern, Piranesi subtly reconfigured the spatial and lighting effects of the interior, incurring no structural alterations to the original chapel. A progressively enriched ornament intensifies the sensation of the space. Along the

.18 and 1.19 Giovanni Battista Piranesi, Santa Maria del Priorato, Rome, 1764–66

vault's crown a central panel of superabundant symbols composed with the intensity of a collector's cabinet of precious objects brings together all references to the order, its religious duties, and military achievements. The priory altar is a fitting climax of the episodes that lead to it. Saint Basil is hoisted in apotheosis upon the nude form of a perfect sphere emerging from a pile of sarcophagi and ships prows. The iconography of the piazza, the facade and the nave is reiterated here in a compounded three-dimensional *capriccio* of enormous scale. The immense variety of Piranesi's brain explodes at the altar in monstrous potency. Pope Clement XIII visited the church in October 1766 and was impressed—or pressed—enough to grant Piranesi the knighthood of the *Sperone d'Oro* he so avidly desired.

Piranesi's articulated speculations on design caught up with his fervent practice with the publication of *Diverse maniere di adornare camini* in 1769. In it he concocted elaborate chimneypieces precisely because this element had no ancient precedent. These plates are lessons in composition and decoration that draw on the widest variety of sources to get architecture "out of the old monotonous track." Piranesi elaborates upon the extraordinary variety possible with the creative license: "Mankind is too fond of variety to be always pleased with the same decorations. We are alternatively pleased with the gay and the serious, and even with the pathetic, even the horror of a battle has its beauty, and out of fear springs pleasure." This text was published in three languages and contains images of the interiors Piranesi executed in Rome for the Rezzonico clan, none of which survive today. Here are also the only surviving records of the interior of his Caffè degli Inglesi, an Egyptian extravaganza painted for the cosmopolitan community at Piazza di Spagna. With the artistic license, Piranesi defended the "Sanctuary of Art" against the reduction of architecture to mere building. He adopted as his battle cry this line from Sallust: *Novitatem meum contemnunt, ego illorum ignavium*, "They condemn my novelty, I their timidity."

Piranesi's license frees us to address the fullness of historical legacy as the font of an imaginative process. Academies, however, swayed by a growing austerity of taste in reaction to the rococo and in response to discoveries in classical archeology, painted Piranesi's reputation black. His influence was more subtle than a mere taking up again of antiquity but was in the character with which antiquity was taken up. Piranesi's rich imaginative approach to his cultural heritage would guide architects for generations to come.

GIACOMO QUARENGHI

At the same time as Piranesi was working on Santa Maria del Priorato, a similar commission for the rehabilitation of a small church in Subiaco outside Rome was undertaken by Giacomo Quarenghi. The two events demonstrate the variegated nature of the process of renewal in mid-eighteenth-century architecture. Quarenghi, like Piranesi, came to architecture through interests in *veduta* painting and arrived in Rome from his native Bergamo during the Rezzonico papacy in 1763. His first teachers, Derizet and Posi, didn't impress him as much as Palladio. After having happened upon a fresh re-edition of Palladio's *Quattro libri di architettura*, Quarenghi tells us he burned all his drawings and returned to the ancient ruins "from which one can learn the good and perfect manner." Quarenghi's goal of a renewal of architecture through a study of the past may have been similar to Piranesi's but his method was entirely different, trusting the good sense of Renaissance masters and his own sense of reason.

In 1768, the Benedictines, under the protection of a Rezzonico cardinal, decided to modernize the interior of their Gothic abbey church of Santa Scholastica at Subiaco. When the solicited project proved too costly and too Borrominian to the congregation, some of the monks from Bergamo had "a new project of Simple Architecture" prepared by their fellow countryman, Quarenghi. He measured the irregular medieval interior and, in 1770, initiated the reconstruction of Santa Scholastica. The nave walls were straightened and wrapped with semicircular chapels. Thermal-style window openings in the austere barrel vault bring light across the smooth interior surfaces simply and sparingly decorated. As for Piranesi, Quarenghi casually informed his stuccoist that the bas-relief details could be pulled from one of the madman's recent books.

1.20 Giacomo Quarenghi, Santa Scholastica, Subiaco, 1770–76

Quarenghi was theoretically inclined toward Piranesi's "Grecian" rivals, particularly Winckelmann and Anton Raffael Mengs. Both had drafted treatises on the simple and noble beauty of ancient art the year Quarenghi arrived in Rome. Quarenghi translated these ideals into architecture. Palladio's clarity of wall, mass, volume, and light also helped to define Quarenghi's forms. At Santa Scholastica, there is a solemn simplicity, a quiet but secure rhythm of volumetric essentials.

The realization of such a serene space, however, was fraught with enervating conflict for its irascible architect. Quarenghi had to threaten his stuccoist with legal action for not having followed his instructions, and he wrangled with the administration over the simple rectangular statuary niches that he wanted even though there were no funds for statues to put in them. "I tried to give the architecture a noble and severe character," Quarenghi tenaciously wrote in Winckelmannian terms, using "only ornament adapted to the idea of the church." The interior was readied for the visit in 1773 of Gianangelo Braschi, Subiaco's titular cardinal, who was unimpressed. Subiaco is also rather remote and Quarenghi's work there had only a limited impact. When it was finally inaugurated in October 1776, Braschi was pope, and Quarenghi was soon looking elsewhere for work.

In 1779 the Russian ambassador to Rome was dispatched to round up "two good Italian architects" for Catherine the Great because, she complained, "all of mine have become too old or too blind or too lazy." Quarenghi jumped at the opportunity. At thirty-five and with only Subiaco to show for himself, he left Rome for St. Petersburg. In a few years, Quarenghi delineated classical St. Petersburg with granite buildings more austere, sharp, and simplified than at Subiaco. Nineteen public institutions were erected: academies, baths, theaters, palaces, commercial "galleries," even a church for the Knights of Malta.

If Piranesi's work was strictly personal but fervently native, Quarenghi's architecture was international and ultimately impersonal in its pared-down simplicity. In Russia, he was introduced to the severe and grandiose drawings of the contemporary French architect, Claude-Nicolas Ledoux, which he assiduously studied. Quarenghi developed the qualities of a style called "Neo-Classical." Although they are derived from an experience of Italian architecture, the style seems to have been assembled elsewhere. Only from a vantage point outside Italy could the classical continuity seem "neo."

THE GRAND TOUR AND THE IMPACT OF ARCHEOLOGY

Foreign influence on Italian culture intensified in the eighteenth century in the form of high-style tourism. The careful study of the roots of Western civilization in antiquity flourished among Europe's educated classes of diplomats, aristocrats, patrons, and artists, for whom a visit to Italian soil was obligatory. Their "Grand Tour" culminated with an extended stay in Rome, which became a sort of open international academy. English, French, Germans, Danes, Dutch, Russian, Poles, Swedes, and eventually Americans all came to Italy claiming its treasures as an international cultural heritage. Indeed, the Grand Tour had become a vast social phenomenon of intellectual and cultural exchange in a new atmosphere of cosmopolitanism. Such attention would have enormous consequences upon the Italians' self-consciousness and evaluation of their own history.

Veduta painters, like Gaspar Van Wittel, Luigi Vanvitelli's father, flourished. Giovanni Paolo Panini welcomed the world to his Rome with panoramic paintings of ancient and modern sites. It was in this international economic context that Piranesi worked. So thrilling were Piranesi's visual images, so sublime the sense of monumentality communicated through his widely circulated prints, that many travelers who prepared their itineraries upon them found the actual sites a disappointment. As Piranesi's images suggested, ancient ruins required imagination if they were to be brought to life, especially as modern archeological excavation was not yet developed into a modern science. Whereas Panini painted the cosmopolitan piazzas of the contemporary city, foreign painters like Nicolas Poussin imagined Elysian Fields with Arcadian shepherds. Prevailing theories in art, codified in the European academies, dwelled upon the concept of a classical ideal of recognizable, recurrent schemata and established traditional images. The Grand Tourist expected to find them in Italy. Under such intense and inspired scrutiny, Italy and especially Rome developed a cultural consciousness. The idea of Italy was formed in the light of tourists' mental images of it.

Italians also had their Grand Tour. Carlo Rezzonico, another papal relation, traveled the breadth of Europe in the 1780s admiring art, architecture, gardens, and natural landscapes, even Gothic buildings. Italians traveled less assiduously to other Italian cities. There was less urgency and far less diligence in examining the vestiges of one's native culture, especially in the case of well-documented architecture. When Italians traveled abroad, more likely they traveled, like Quarenghi, to practice their professions in the host countries, not to learn from them. Music masters, librettists, scenographers, singers, painters, plasterers, architects, and urban planners brought to the European courts Italian classical traditions. Many, like the artisans Robert Adam brought back with him to London, stayed abroad for their entire careers. Through the export of objects and skilled labor, Italy was the producer of classical beauty and culture for all of Europe, a heady proposition for eighteenth-century Italians but one that created among them a brain drain.

Beyond Rome, the Grand Tourist was drawn to Naples with the promise of recent archeological discoveries such as Herculaneum and Pompeii. The bronzes, marbles, inscriptions, coins, papyruses, and all sorts of quotidian objects dug up were stored in the closed cabinets of Carlos III's "Museo Ercolense" at Portici. By 1755, the king established an academy to care for the finds and their eventual publication. When the more easily excavatable site at Pompeii was gradually unearthed in the 1760s, it offered the Grand Tourist the opportunity to contextualize a mental image of the classical world in actual environments.

Direct experience of Herculaneum's objects and Pompeii's spaces was disorienting for most early visitors. The fresh, unfiltered impressions fell so far outside the prevailing aesthetic that most of the unearthed artifacts were deemed negligible. Carlos III, who had aspirations to utilize the finds in interior decorations, was paradoxically responsible for their meager immediate impact. He imposed strict rules on the visitor to the Bourbon museums and archeological sites: sketching was prohibited and time was limited. The academy he established exercised a monopoly on all visual imagery and was slow to publish the six volumes of *Le Antichità di Ercolano.* Moreover, they were not for sale but, like Carlos's other publicity folio on Caserta, were proffered as calculated diplomatic gestures. Only when Ferdinando IV transferred the treasures to Naples, refitting the old university building for the purpose in 1777, could one identify the birth of a real public archeological museum. Archeology, if it can be so called under Bourbon rule, was placed in the service of governing and had scant effect on contemporary architectural imagination.

Grand Tourists to Naples continued on to Paestum. The Doric temples of the ancient Greek colony were not well known but had not been entirely forgotten. Carlos III thought of purloining their columns for a royal palace project, but the very stout proportions of their archaic order did not appeal to his taste, nor to anyone else's until Soufflot approached them, free of prejudice, in 1750. Only Soufflot was able to get permission to draw there on site; others had to content themselves with the engravings and cork models tendered exclusively through the king's authorized dealers.

The Doric appealed almost exclusively to foreign visitors at first. Piranesi, evidently the only Italian ready for such a jolt, ventured in the last year of his life to prepare a publication of Paestum views that was published in French in 1778. Johann Wolfgang Goethe, visiting nine years later, confessed a certain stupefaction before the stones, which he didn't immediately recognize as architecture at all. "Our eyes and, through them, our whole sensibility have become so conditioned to a more slender style of architecture that these crowded masses of stumpy conical columns appear offensive and even terrifying." It proved hard to "see" the Doric order of the Paestum temples except as a theoretical alternative, a line of enquiry pursued in French treatises, like Laugier's, and built in English garden follies. The Doric column became an emblem of architecture's primal origins and was almost exclusively a foreign purview.

The only use of the Doric in Italy in the late eighteenth century was by a Frenchman. At the Villa Giulia of Palermo, the city's first public gardens (where Goethe was want to read from Homer), a botanical academy building was designed by Léon Dufourny. Dufourny, a student of Julien-David Leroy, had recently returned from ten months in the field measuring the Doric temples of Sicily, and eagerly accepted the invitation to design "the first major edifice in which the Doric order, buried amongst the ruins of the temples of Greece and her colonies, is recuperated in all its purity." The building, which incorporates a lecture hall, library, and herbarium, features Doric columns at the entrance. Dufourny, who upon returning to his native Paris founded a museum of the history of architecture, had initiated in Palermo the significant ideological movement to recompose principal theories of architecture in light of archeological investigation.

The Palermitano architect Giuseppe Venanzio Marvuglia, enthused by Dufourny's ideas, added flanking pavilions to the botanical academy. He also designed a villa in Palermo in the Chinois manner for Ferdinando IV, *La Favorita*, which has a "Fountain of Hercules" in the garden consisting of a single free-standing Doric column. Marvuglia's variegated production belies a less theoretical focus than his foreign contemporary, suggesting that the concerns of Italian architects were quite different from the interests of the rather radical foreigners present in Italy at the time.

COLLECTING AND CULTURAL HERITAGE

In Rome, the popes could not monopolize the archeological culture as the Bourbon king managed, so they sought to intervene with creative policies for the protection and potentializing of this cultural heritage. With intense demand for antiquities, especially among the British, economic incentive aggravated the likelihood of illicit digging for new items and of Roman aristocrats selling off their collections for cash. Pope Clement XIII, through his commissioner of antiquities, Ridolfino Venuti, renewed the enforcement of limiting excavation licenses to registered agents, the right to entail one third of everything found by them, and strict export regulations. The consequent amassing of objects in papal possession helped to boost the initiative of a public art museum in Rome. An account of the relationship between private and public collecting in Rome illustrates the crucial importance of formulating a policy for the protection of this heritage.

Cardinal Alessandro Albani, the papal nephew, maintained a high profile that was manifest in a superb collection of antiquities, pieces of which were sold conspicuously, for example, to King Augustus III of Poland in 1728. Alarmed, Pope Clement XII purchased as a precautionary measure against their dispersal all of Albani's remaining pieces for display in Michelangelo's buildings on the Capitoline Hill. The Palazzo Nuovo was opened as a public museum according to the Corsini pope "for the curiosity of foreign visitors and dilettantes and for the use of scholars." Albani began to amass a second collection of finds from Hadrian's Villa. His honorable image as a protector and promoter of the arts is largely accepted by historians today, but contemporaries interpreted his actions as bald speculation on Rome's cultural assets. Albani trafficked in antiquities, often collaborating with Baron Stosch until the latter was expelled from Rome on charges of espionage. Albani's interest in antiquities is obvious on the financial level as it is on the aesthetic level. Indeed, he delighted in the works. The exquisite images of Emperor Hadrian's homosexual lover Antinous were tucked away in the intimate spaces of his villa, where he could spy them in private.

In 1747, a new villa was planned for his second collection at a suburban site along the Via Salaria. Nolli surveyed the land for him and may have also designed the parterres and hemicycle included in the upper corner of his map. A two-floor *palazzina* was begun at the other end of the garden in 1755. This is a narrow building, much like the Palazzo Nuovo at the Capitoline that houses Albani's first collection. Low wings extend left and right and finish in pavilions whose small temple facades are entirely constructed of ancient elements. Caryatids, herms, statues, reliefs, decorative masks, columns, basins, and colored marbles fill every available space in profusion. The designer was the papal architect Carlo Marchionni, a man of extraordinary compositional virtuosity, but Albani himself is often given credit. The emulation of the Palazzo Nuovo could have been the cardinal's idea, worked out with facility and success by the able Marchionni. Like Nolli before him, Marchionni was one in a succession of experts the cardinal hired to create this precious reliquary of vestiges of ancient Rome.

The Villa Albani was admired for its exceptional fusion of the ancient and the modern, right down to the nature of the statues' restoration. The current specialist in the field, Bartolomeo Cavaceppi, reintegrated—made whole again—the ancient fragments with new and virtuosically carved additions. Ancient works were in turn fluidly assimilated in a wholly contemporary setting with, as an inscription at the villa says, a *romano animo*, a Roman spirit. Winckelmann praised the Villa Albani as "a most modern place . . . the most beautiful building of our time." The sycophantic talk was, perhaps, required of Winckelmann as he too was on Albani's payroll, hired in 1758 to advise on the disposition of the collection.

Without genuine ruins on the property nor a proper view to any, Albani's team concocted a sham ruin on the grounds. The artifice, the first of its kind in an Italian villa, was praised precisely for its English—and hence cosmopolitan—inspiration. Its curious disintegrated composition suggests the influence, if not the direct intervention, of Piranesi. The engraver featured thirty-four pieces from Albani's collection among his publications, perhaps jockeying for the enviable position left vacant after Winckelmann's death in 1768. Piranesi may also have designed some over-door reliefs and a fountain for the gardens. He flatteringly included an engraving of the villa in his *vedute* series. Piranesi's strong aestheticizing approach to antiquity and his keen business acumen may have appealed to Albani, but in the end the cardinal hired Giovanni Battista Visconti and his son Ennio Quirino to write the catchy copy for the collection's catalog. Venuti, Winckelmann, and then the two Viscontis all had better qualifications than Piranesi; they were all in turn the papal Commissioner of Antiquities and could be counted on to cover Albani's commerce at the highest level.

The Villa Albani was a sumptuous showroom of antiquities, staffed by professional publicists who hyped the objects and raised

1.21 Carlo Marchionni and others, Villa Albani, Rome, 1755–63. Engraving by Giovanni Battista Piranesi, *Vedute di Roma*, c. 1769

their value considerably. The pieces, like the caryatids, were not so integral to the structure that they could not easily be extracted and sold. Pope Clement XIII, who visited the villa in the summer of 1763, recognized another Albani lode ready for liquidation. This pope, in strapped finances, could do nothing, but his successor, Clement XIV would.

The necessity of government intervention against the wholesale spoliation of Rome's cultural heritage led Clement XIV to institute a veritable public trust at the Vatican in 1770. The Museum Clementinum, later expanded by his successor Pius VI (hence Museo Pio-Clementino), is a direct response to the threat of cultural dispersal triggered by the pressures of the Grand Tour and speculation on artistic goods. We witness here the birth of the modern public art museum distinguished from the private collections for its accessibility to the general public as well as the intention of the collection as a long-term cultural depository.

The papal collections had been, like Carlos III's Herculaneum museum, preserved in closed cabinets along the corridors leading to the Belvedere Villa on the Vatican Hill. The hallways grew unexpectedly crowded when Clement XIV, like Clement XII before him, felt compelled to purchase Roman collections on the block. An acquisition policy was put into place, funded by the lottery, guided by the Viscontis, and fulfilled by antiquities dealers including Cavaceppi and Piranesi. Meanwhile, choice works flowed in from the exercise of papal prerogative on excavation finds all across the territory as well as eminent domain over any bishop's collection. During Clement XIV's papacy, forty-seven statues, fifty-nine busts, seven sarcophagi, sixteen vases and candelabra, twenty-three animal figures, twenty-eight ancient altars, forty-one reliefs, and 124 inscriptions were acquired.

In 1771, a reorganization of the Belvedere Villa was projected by the in-house architect, Alessandro Dori. The original Renaissance loggia was rearranged and outfitted with statues on pedestals, busts on shelves, and generous ornament in a manner similar to that of Villa Albani. A portico was applied to the unadorned walls of the pre-existing courtyard of the Belvedere complex. The vaulted, top-lit portico provides adequately sumptuous cover for the statues. There is no reason to suppose that at this first phase of the museum's development the elegant architectural handling was designed to be anything substantially different from the Villa Albani, a perfectly modern reliquary that might extol the integrity of this world capital's cultural assets. Dori died only a year into the project. Marchionni was busy, so the museum project was continued and completed in 1774 by Dori's successor, Michelangelo Simonetti.

When Gianangelo Braschi, Clement XIV's treasurer and perhaps the driving force behind the project, was elected Pope Pius VI in 1775, he directed Simonetti to organize the complex with new rooms and new routes. The courtyard's oblique cross axis was extended through a series of new monumental galleries. The former jumble of incidental spaces and clashing axes were elegantly reconfigured into the semblance of a coherent plan and a coherent institution, promptly renamed Museo Pio-Clementino. Ancient models, such as the Pantheon, were adapted freely by Simonetti to the museum's spatial requirements and although the architecture is in no way a reconstruction of ancient forms, hypothetical or otherwise, the gracious volumes effectively draw out the nature of the ancient art on display. As with Albani at his villa, Pius availed himself of a curatorial team headed by Giovanni Battista Visconti, and Simonetti could be counted upon to carry out the team's directives. Indeed, Giacomo Quarenghi, bitter that he had not impressed Braschi at Subiaco, spat that they had advanced a common "Measurer named Simonetti who now passes for a famous Architect." For the first time in Rome, architecture had conformed in theme and function to the display of specific works of art in a secular setting, not the other way around. The Museo Pio-Clementino is not a lavish reliquary as captivating as its treasures, but a space designed to elicit appropriate responses consonant with the art. With a print series of interior views, a gallery guide, and eventually a complete catalog of the collection, the Museo Pio-Clementino became Rome's first planned public art museum, the most durable and successful promotion of visual culture in eighteenth-century Europe, unmatched in its artistic patrimony.

The museum's first major visitor was King Gustav III of Sweden on New Year's Day, 1784. Because the visiting monarch was a

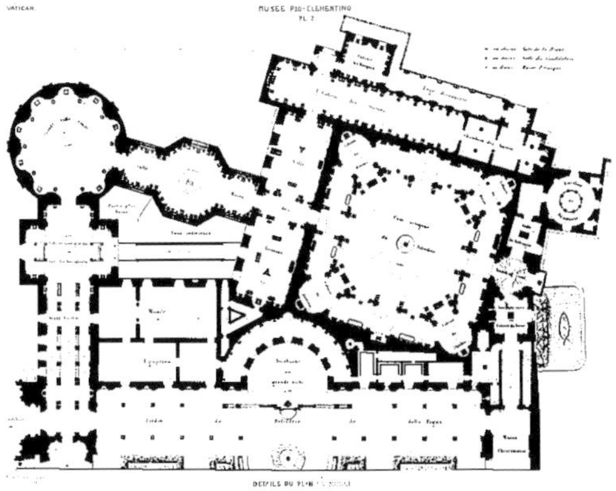

1.22 and 1.23 Alessandro Dori, then Michelangelo Simonetti, Museo Pio-Clementino, Rome, 1771–84. Plan from Paul Letarouilly, *Le Vatican et la Basilique de Saint-Pierre de Rome*, 1882; painting by Bénigne Gagnereaux, *King Gustav III of Sweden visiting the Museo Pio-Clementino*, 1785.

Lutheran, Pius VI opted diplomatically to "happen upon" him in a casual manner, strolling through a cosmopolitan place, much as Benedict XIV used his coffeehouse in the Quirinal gardens for Carlos III's visit. The moment was immortalized in a painting commissioned by the traveling sovereign from a French painter in Rome, Bénigne Gagnereaux. The painter significantly altered Simonetti's architecture, however, making the vaults more lofty and eliminating the rotunda's clerestory level beneath the dome, thereby avoiding the problem posed by the Pantheon's attic. Pius asked for a copy of this painting, a most complete portrait of him in his institution, international host and cultural guardian.

Pius's efforts had an effect on the plebeian crowds who were offered free entrance during Holy Week and on the aristocratic elite who hurried to update their own holdings. The efficacy of Pius's model is seen in the revitalization of the Villa Borghese. Prince Marcantonio IV Borghese inherited this patrimony in 1763, the year Villa Albani was completed, and undertook a complete revamping to maintain the pre-eminence of his family's cultural stature. His team of mostly foreign designers was coordinated by Antonio Asprucci, assisted by his son Mario. The prince participated in the design process with on-site visits and open-ended discussions with his idea men to assure the project's up-to-date qualities. The villa interiors were enriched with columns and a profusion of colored marbles, vault paintings, and furniture to complement the art works. The Aspruccis struck a measured and melodic marriage between the solemnity of the antique and the extravagance of the baroque. The Egyptian room of 1786 is typical. Ancient fragments of porphyry, granite, and basalt were reintegrated on an Egyptian theme, and new statues and decorative elements were commissioned. Of course, Egyptian things were no novelty in Rome. There were the obelisks in the piazzas, a special cabinet in the Capitoline museum, even Albani had a reference to the Nile in his garden, and Piranesi referred to Egypt in his English caffè and *Camini* prints, but never before had Egypt been re-examined with such intensity and precision.

The interior work was a clever attempt to boost the collection without buying any new pieces. Borghese could not outbid Albani or Pius VI, so he found ways to reposition his existing collection, including a replanting of the gardens. Marcantonio helped delineate the serpentine outline of an artificial lake and select the sites for several new "ruins." On a man-made island in the lake, Mario Asprucci concocted a Temple to Aesculapius, and Christoph Unterperger, the animal painter at the villa, mocked up a Temple to Faustina reusing real ancient architectural fragments. Charles Percier, a young Parisian student at the French Academy, designed an aqueduct carried on stout Doric columns, and Asprucci *padre*, the ancient-style hippodrome called the "Piazza di Siena." Marcantonio brought in the Scottish landscape painter Jacob More to make sure everything in this picturesque garden was right.

Marcantonio rendered the Villa Borghese not only a more gentle but also a more public place. Continuing a family tradition, he opening many of the grounds' minor structures for popular reception, festivities, and relaxation. At the Villa Borghese of the late eighteenth century, collecting, interior decoration, architecture, and landscape design all conjoined to enhance the continuity of Roman culture under enlightened aristocratic patronage.

THE PATRONAGE OF POPE PIUS VI

Pope Pius VI pursued a wide program of arts patronage. The Braschi pope had been the financial advisor on the Lateran apse project and the Museum Clementinum, and the titular cardinal at Santa Scholastica. By the time his turn as pope came, he had firm ideas about cultural heritage, in particular the mediation between forces of tradition and necessities for innovation. The Basilica of Saint Peter had no proper sacristy. Michelangelo hadn't planned one, and there was no satisfactory solution in any of the proposals that had been pouring in since then. Pius put the job of developing a new project to his *Fabbrica* architect, Carlo Marchionni, by then seventy-four years old. The new sacristy stands a dozen meters to the south of the basilica's exterior wall, connected by bridges at the level of the cathedral floor. The rich materials employed were supposed to have been representations of the wealth of the papal states and the genius of her artisans, but the structural iron elements Marchionni used had to be imported. Marchionni's skill is seen in the handling of the material and decorative complexity of the sacristy surfaces, a virtuosic synthesis of High Renaissance and baroque motifs from Michelangelo to Bernini, earlier masters at Saint Peter's.

Marchionni's task was complicated by the proximity of Michelangelo's exterior, which was many times larger, richer, and more interesting than the sacristy needed to be. He treated the three essential parts of his construction, the blocky canons' residence, the vaulted sacristy proper, and the linking galleries, with increasing surface decoration and in declining elevation as they cascade quietly toward the basilica. Its careful proportions and self-effacing asymmetry have proven a masterly deferential gesture. But what makes the project work is the historicism of Marchionni's outlook. Pius required a sacristy consonant with the layered complexity of the cathedral's own evolution across the sixteenth and seventeenth centuries. In a mixture of styles and details, Marchionni created an architectural amalgam commensurate with the history of the cathedral itself.

While the new sacristy is a distinctive and distinctively sumptuous symbol of Pius's patronage, this former accountant also pursued a wide range of invigorating programs employing art, architecture, and even hydraulic engineering to glorify his papacy and Rome. New bells and clocks for Saint Peter's facade, repairs to the Lateran nave ceiling, a new wing for the Santo Spirito hospital, a tapestry workshop at San Michele, and a cotton warehouse in the ruins of the Baths of Diocletian all underscored his progressive "Christian Enlightenment." Pius's imperial display is most evident in the triumphal arches erected in his honor, from a temporary one designed by Francesco Milizia to commemorate his election, to a permanent one in Subiaco, his former abbey seat.

But the project most redolent of Pius's attempts to achieve imperial glory was his plan to drain the Pontine Marshes. The inland bogs, just 100 kilometers south of Rome along the Appian

1.24 Carlo Marchionni, Sacristy, Saint Peter's Cathedral, Rome, 1776–84
1.25 Cosimo Morelli, Palazzo Braschi, Rome, 1790–

Way, troubled both Julius Caesar and Pope Julius II, who had put their best men to devising ways to reclaim the 800 square kilometers of swamp. Pius VI, with modern science at his command, had a drainage canal dug and a highway, the Linea Pio, laid. Terracina, the dreary medieval town overlooking the area, was revamped with a papal residence and public buildings for trade and commerce. Even a museum was planned to display the artifacts dredged up below. Pius IV combined the agricultural and the antiquarian in a complete program of economic and spiritual recovery of a long fallow land.

But it would be myopic to call the Pontine Marsh reclamation a clamoring success for the region. Pius's own nephew turned out to be the primary economic beneficiary. Nepotism was still a papal prerogative and Pius, who had no brothers with sons of the Braschi name, encouraged his sister's offspring to hyphenate theirs. Luigi Braschi-Onesti was made a duke, married to a Roman noblewoman and set up for display in the papal limelight. A palace was built, the Palazzo Braschi. Architects of the capital rushed to offer their services even before the site was purchased in 1790. Cosimo Morelli, official architect of the papal legations, designed the palazzo to fill the boundaries of the roughly triangular site to maximum volume with no particular attention to Piazza Navona behind it. Like Marchionni and probably under similar directives, Morelli undertook a historicist amalgam of all that made the Roman Renaissance palazzo great, then rather perfunctorily he knocked everything up a notch. The effect of its extra tall floors and obvious details is an aesthetic equivalent of the duke's fabricated stature in Roman society. Despite the shortcomings of the overall conception, the staircase within justifies Morelli's reputation. The scenographic masterpiece is studded with ancient sculpture and granite columns.

The Palazzo Braschi is the last in a long line of nepotistic papal palaces in Rome. The consciousness of its constructed role required of Morelli a historicist operation perhaps less brilliantly achieved than Marchionni's but of the same ilk. While Pope Pius VI was building the Palazzo Braschi in Rome, French revolutionaries were dismantling the Bastille in Paris. But Pius, who was bereaved by

Louis XVI's beheading, should not be seen in the clarity of historical hindsight as a pathetic anachronism but as a man convinced that the traditions of Rome would never wane.

GIUSEPPE PIERMARINI AND MILAN IN THE EIGHTEENTH CENTURY

Milan, under Hapsburg rule from Vienna, was guided by the best of Enlightenment governing policies. Although Empress Marie Therese's attitude was paternalistic, her effect on intellectual and artistic life in Lombardy was undeniably positive. Archduke Ferdinand, her son, was dispatched to wed Maria Beatrice d'Este, and when he arrived in Milan he found the city lacking in buildings he thought worthy of his image. He promptly set about rectifying this situation. In a half-century of Hapsburg administration, palaces, villas, thoroughfares and gardens, academies of learning, and public theaters came into being. Pietro Verri wrote to his brother, "since you have left Milan many changes have occurred that could not have been imagined before.... They're tearing down [the church of] La Scala to build a theater. At [the Jesuit monastery of] the Brera they're setting up a painting school.... In no other country have there been as many changes over these twelve years while no other country is so contrary to change as ours." Ferdinand wanted his own palace on the order of Shönbrunn, or Caserta, for Milan, so a serious headhunting campaign for an architect began. Luigi Vanvitelli was brought to Milan in 1769 to consult on the conversion of the Palazzo Ducale, whose medieval structures needed a complete overhaul. Vanvitelli, used to working on a *tabula rasa*, told them to knock everything down, but Wenceslaus Kaunitz, the minister who held the purse strings in Vienna, vetoed the idea. Vanvitelli had little patience for petty patrons but satisfied his contract by leaving behind one of his trusted minions, Giuseppe Piermarini.

Piermarini had gone to Rome in 1755 to study with Paolo Posi, but he found his work less than satisfying and drew up some of his own solutions for the Pantheon's attic. Vanvitelli's reputation attracted him to Naples, where he worked on secondary projects and not, it seems, on the Reggia at Caserta. But in this industrious atmosphere he learned the indispensable tools of the trade: patron relations and the cosmopolitan classicism that appealed to them. Thus, Vanvitelli could boastfully claim to the Milanese, perhaps a bit nonplused by his bait-and-switch, that Giuseppe "will make it known that my tutelage has not been in vain in his learning the most difficult profession of architecture." Indeed, Vanvitelli sowed Europe with his pupils, sending Antonio Rinaldi and Luigi Rusca to Russia, and Francesco Sabbatini to Spain along with his own sons, Francesco and Pietro.

Piermarini was duly invested in 1769 as the Imperial Royal Architect of Hapsburg Lombardy over which he held a kind of architectural monopoly. He supervised dozens of projects while his example significantly raised the standards of professionalism in the region. Piermarini understood implicitly Kaunitz's economic limits, and managed to provide both infrastructural and stylistic coherence to Milan.

The restructuring of the Palazzo Ducale in 1773 is indicative of Piermarini's strengths. Pre-existing foundations were used to reconfigure the old building with a generous forecourt opening toward the cathedral. A distribution of half-columns and pilasters lend the exterior a stately economy, with balanced horizontal and vertical accents. Interior decorations, finished in 1778 by Piermarini's trusted stuccoist Giocondo Albertolli, lend verve exactly where the architecture is in danger of becoming monotonous. Piermarini also built Ferdinand a country house in Monza outside Milan with a tree-lined avenue 15 kilometers long to link the Villa Reale to the capital.

In the spirit of Hapsburg enlightened rule, Piermarini was also put in charge of the reform of key cultural institutions, both administratively and architecturally. For the new Accademia Virgiliana at Mantua, in which all that city's scientific, literary, and artistic groups were conglomerated, Piermarini restructured the building with its baroque theater behind a classical facade. Similar decrees changed Milan's old educational institutions of the arts. In 1776, the expropriated Jesuit monastery of the Brera was designated as the seat for a new Accademia di Belle Arti. Piermarini was in charge not only of the architectural adaptation but also the building of the faculty. He gathered a distinguished group of professionals including Albertolli for the chair of *Ornato*, a concept of artistic decorum on the measure of everything from domestic interiors to urban planning. Through his power over these institutions, Piermarini systematically engineered the regeneration of the region's architectural practice.

Milan's entire urban structure became a venue for the Hapsburg program in architectural and social improvements. The city's system of canals was improved; roads were straightened, widened, and leveled. The road from Vienna and the Corso di Porta Orientale were embellished with new toll gates and public gardens. By 1778, Milan was endowed with its first comprehensive urban design, drawn up principally by Piermarini and Albertolli. Throughout Italy, the state—in the person of its ruler—usually took the lead in building and planning, but only in Milan do we find also a social class independent and prosperous enough to respond in spontaneous private initiative. Whether they were poor charges in Fuga's Albergo dei Poveri or in Marie Therese's wealthy Milan, the Enlightenment approach was the same: to stimulate subjects to become active agents of their own reform. Piermarini took on many private commissions that are each shining examples of how enlightened rule stimulated independent initiative. With Piermarini's expertise, Prince Alberigo Barbiano di Belgioioso d'Este, protector of the Brera and captain of the archduke's royal guard, was happy to do his part. For his new palazzo, he dumped several rather splendiferous proposals in favor of Piermarini's more contained classical design. Within the dense medieval fabric of the city, before a narrow but regular piazza, Piermarini produced for Belgioioso a miniature Caserta. The facade is underscored by continuous horizontal striations while the pilasters draw vertical accents at its three entrances for a discrete tripartite scansion. Here, the elements of the Reggia are subtly rearranged to modest but entirely effective results. Piermarini's sense of control is carried throughout the building in evenly distributed rooms largely decorated by Albertolli. The Palazzo Belgioioso has smaller and more domestic spaces than in the patrician palaces of the previous generation, and its style served as a model for generations to come.

1.26 Giuseppe Piermarini with Giocondo Albertolli, Palazzo and Piazza Belgioioso, Milan, 1772–81. Engraving by Domenico Aspari, *Vedute di Milano*, 1788

1.27 Giuseppe Piermarini, Teatro alla Scala, Milan, 1776–78. Painting by Angelo Inganni, 1852

1.28 Teatro alla Scala. Interior view during a recital by Renata Tebaldi, 1974

Belgioioso may also have gotten Piermarini the commission for what would be the architect's most famous work: the Teatro alla Scala. The world-renowned theater lies at the heart of Enlightenment Milan, a cultural locus and catalyst of paramount importance. The origins of this theater lie in the burnt ruins of an earlier theater once located within the old Palazzo Ducale. This popular auditorium burned during Piermarini's renovation work on the palace, in February 1776. No one was particularly surprised. Theater fires were frequent, and the archduke purportedly didn't like the idea of such a venue in the palace in the first place. The fire, perhaps an arson, provided the opportunity to modernize not only the theater's interior appointments but also its urban profile.

In the eighteenth century, Milanese theaters were managed by clubs of private individuals, usually noble devotees, who were given opera boxes, or *palchi*, in exchange for financing. In the case of the former Teatro Ducale, the *palchettisti* included Alberigo Belgioioso. In March 1776, the *palchettisti*, discreetly guided by Archduke Ferdinand, formulated a proposal for a new theater to be built of masonry at a new site by Piermarini. Authorization came through Kaunitz in July, Piermarini's first plans were ready in September, and construction began in December. Twenty months later, on 3 August 1778, the Teatro alla Scala was completed.

The name of the theater derives from the ducal chapel of Santa Maria della Scala, which was demolished by the duke expressly for the purpose of locating the new theater on its site (hence "*alla* [at the] Scala"). The overlay of secular culture on religious memory is particularly indicative of Enlightenment operations in Milan. This site was a step out of the shadow of the Palazzo Ducale and into the tangle of streets where the theater could become the focus of a new urban center. Indeed, in anticipation of traffic congestion, the city's *Ornato* commission insisted on a *porte-cochère* at the theater's doorstep. The Scala exterior displays a balance of horizontal and vertical elements that tend toward an economical minimalism. The *porte-cochère*, however, was given a greater monumentality at the request of the *palchettisti* and its less convincing impression reveals the uneasy interplay between patrons' requests and the architect's refined design sense. Piermarini may have learned how to deal graciously with clients but he didn't match Vanvitelli in finessing their ideas into great architecture. The exterior lost that shimmering coherence of the Belgioioso palace. Pietro Verri opined that the theater looked good on paper but rather forced in reality. But no one had reservations over Piermarini's superb interior.

The scientific nature of Enlightenment endeavor made theater design one of its distinctive hallmarks. Piermarini, as was his method, gleaned examples from the already prodigious technical literature on theater architecture, acoustic engineering, and fireproof construction. Various treatises on the subject posited the traditional half-round ancient model revived by Palladio against the innovative science of acoustics that called for elliptical, horseshoe, and bell shapes. In a lavish commemorative volume on La Scala, a Vanvitellian promotional touch, Piermarini published a synoptic table comparing all the major theaters of Italy. For La Scala, Piermarini synthesized the current technical knowledge in the rather unusual curve of the auditorium. It is clear he did not invent anything new here, but everyone confessed that it proved a perfect solution. Masonry construction was used in the auditorium structure, leaving wooden surfaces only on the box divisions and fronts and the coved ceiling. Ornament, controlled for acoustic purposes, was originally designed by Albertolli in harmony with Piermarini's quiet classicism, but it has been altered repeatedly over the decades. The distribution was praised on both sides of the proscenium arch. There are spaces for a multitude of interrelated functions serving their purposes with varying degrees of pageantry or economy: opera and ballet production, scenery and costume workshops, gaming rooms and caffès, shops and offices. The Teatro alla Scala established a model of methodological mediation in the building type and was imitated by countless others across Italy. The original aspiration of the *palchettisti* to make a theater "by its magnificence and by its size . . . superior to any other in Italy" has indeed been excelled by La Scala's status today as a world-famous cultural institution.

Piermarini brought the spirit of classicism to life in Milan. His role in the progress of Lombard architecture is comparable to Vanvitelli's in Naples: giving rigor to the baroque with classical discipline. This was brought about through formal, constructive, and procedural clarification not only in architecture but also in decoration, urbanism, and education. Piermarini renewed Milan through the classical traditions while addressing its current needs to lift it to capital rank.

VENICE'S TEATRO LA FENICE AND CONCLUSIONS ON NEOCLASSICISM

An overview of Italian architecture of the late eighteenth century testifies to the vigorous continuity of tradition combined with the innovations brought on by the Enlightenment. A glance to late-eighteenth-century Venice provides an idea of the classical renewal in architecture. In Palladio's homeland, one needn't think of a "neoclassicism" at all but of an unbroken tradition. Giannantonio Selva is a typical product of the Palladian heritage. Selva was a student of mathematics who traveled more widely than most in his day. From the ruins of Paestum to the gardens at Stowe, England, Selva was witness to the gamut of eighteenth-century cultural phenomena. His mental bank of images paid out in a career in theatrical scenography. When in 1787 the Venetian gentlemen's club *Nobile Società* undertook the initiative to build yet another theater in that city, they held a competition and Selva won. A site was found in the city's tight fabric at Campo San Fantin. There was hope of creating a new cultural center there.

A competition program detailing the complex's various functional requirements was published in 1789 and distributed through academies all across Italy, attracting dozens of projects. The *Società* members favored Selva, even though, as other competitors brought to their attention in a lawsuit, it did not fulfill the program requirements. The Teatro "La Fenice" was built from scratch in eighteen months and inaugurated on 16 May 1792. The exterior of the theater, confined as it is to a short end facing the small *campo*, has sober Palladian rhythms and is noteworthy in its rejection of extraneous surface decoration. Selva's auditorium was modeled without apology on Piermarini's La Scala, and again excellent acoustics and financial gain resulted. There are four levels of wooden-fronted *palchi*, instead of La Scala's five, and broad box partitions to accommodate the local tradition of dining during a performance. La Fenice's original interior decorations were neoclassical but lightened by a rococo touch, but they were altered, as was the custom, by each successive scenographer on staff.

The creation of a theater displays all the complex crosscurrents of the age—Palladian traditions, scientific advance, commercial interests, lingering rococo taste—and the creation of a self-image of modern society all blended into one elusive, ever changing expression. La Fenice would have been better named "La Chimera" rather than "the Pheonix."

The architectural forms of late-eighteenth-century classicism, from Galilei to Selva, are clearer in structural representation, simpler in volumetric clarity, and more linear and planar than the earlier baroque. Francesco Milizia, who promulgated his ideas through rigorous criticism of contemporary architecture, spelled out principles of composition, structure, and ornament more severe than contemporary tastes. His principles helped to redefine an architecture for the public weal that was commodious, solid, and grand.

A tendency toward purer architectural form made the re-emerging classical style once again, as it was in the Renaissance, adaptable to a wide range of new building types. The strong, forthright forms of public architecture provided the appropriate impact for the underlying pedagogic aim of the arts during the Enlightenment. The reforms of Bourbon Naples, of Hapsburg Milan, even papal Rome, were manifest in contemporary architecture of more stoic, secular images. As Diderot explained in his *Encyclopédie*, the edifying effect of the arts would make virtue more attractive. Museums and theaters were of paramount importance in the *risorgimento*, or resurgence of the arts, as contemporaries called it.

This was not a "revolutionary" architecture. In most cases patron, artist, and style were lodged firmly within the continuities of the old regimes. The term "neoclassicism" seems out of place in Italy, where scientific reconstruction of architectural principles independent of

Renaissance precedent were rare and the idea of a "true style" was expressed only by foreigners looking for it. This was a perennial return to a hardly absent classicism. The essence of tradition—recognizable schema established by recurrent use—exerts a remarkable force on the Italian consciousness. The result was a judicious balance of tradition and innovation at Caserta, La Scala, Villa Albani, Museo Pio-Clementino. The Roman palimpsest of Nolli's map favored cultural continuity. As Salvi's Trevi Fountain shows, to trace upon the layered surface of Italian cities one is profoundly influenced by what lies below.

2.1 Giuseppe Camporese, Andrea Vici, and Paolo Bargigli, *Festa della Federazione*, in Piazza of Saint Peter, Rome, 20 March 1798. Painting by Felice Giani

Chapter 2

NAPOLEON IN ITALY, 1800–1815

NAPOLEON'S ITALIC EMPIRE

Napoleon Bonaparte brought the ideals and imagery of the French Revolution to Italy. In March 1796, as an offensive army commander against the Austrian empire in Lombardy, he entered Italian territory to secure free passage across Piedmont from the Savoyard monarch. A chain of rebellions in the neighboring regions of Reggio Emilia and the papal legations of Ferrara and Bologna spurred Napoleon to further territorial consolidations. By the end of the year, a Cisalpine Republic was formed and Pope Pius VI was dispensed with in an armistice at Bologna. The subsequent Treaty of Tolentino, signed on 19 February 1797, demanded disarmament, concessions, and passage south to Bourbon domain. A republic in Rome was proclaimed on 15 February 1798, and the pope was finally exiled to France, where he died the following year. His nephew scampered to meet the French but was promptly taken hostage. Napoleon was hailed as the liberator of Italy, galvanizing hitherto scattered or incomplete movements of reform in a sweeping political maneuver. The French Revolution and Napoleon's meteoric appearance sparked an enthusiastic spirit of transformation that lit up Italy.

The force of the revolution politicized the arts in a way that they had never been in the eighteenth century. Republican ideals were projected onto the forms of established classicism. Napoleon himself did not discriminate in artistic matters, but he clearly understood art's pedagogic value. He promoted art institutions and established procedures of state patronage that would disseminate images across the land. Classicism, or neoclassicism as he would see it, contained simultaneously the rational underpinnings of a military engineer and the efficacious imagery of a propagandist.

Nowhere better than in the staged political festivals is the synthesis of classical art and revolutionary politics under Napoleon more clearly demonstrated. Public festivals were effective instruments in transmitting ideology and releasing social tensions while shaping the collective consciousness. In republican Rome, grand allegorical processions were performed, illustrating crucial episodes of the revolution. *Tableaux vivants* of the fall of the Bastille were reenacted on the grounds of the Villa Borghese, and forests of *Alberi della Libertà*, poles erected and laden with the symbols of revolutionary spirit, rose up everywhere.

On 20 March 1798, a *Festa della Federazione* was staged in the piazza of Saint Peter's. The event was ostensibly mounted by the "Roman Consuls" to pledge their union as a French *département*. Lavish adornments included a "patriotic altar" designed by three architects, Giuseppe Camporese, Andrea Vici, and Paolo Bargigli with the help of numerous sculptors. The "altar" consisted of a majestic stepped dais, 30 meters in diameter with four Doric columns of *papier-mâché* and trumpeting figures on globes. At the center, a statue symbolizing Rome stood between *Liberté* and *Egalité*, like three graces of the revolution. St. Peter's facade was clouded by burning urns; its bells were drowned out by patriotic hymns sung by legions of citizens. There was no passive participation in this fashioning of a collective consciousness. Although the forms were ephemeral, they were significant for their secularization of architectural ideas and their influence on built reality in Italy.

The French rhetoric of liberty and equality marked a promising advance in Enlightenment progress. A rationalist spirit was turned on to political and religious institutions by a secularist and materialist intellectual class seeking the benefits of free enterprise. In reality, Italians were free only as far as French foreign policy would allow, as was most evident in the south where plutarchies formed in the absence of any bourgeoisie. The Neapolitan republic lasted only 150 days, yet the experience of political action was invaluable. Trenchant *campanilismo*, the sense of local allegiance defined metaphorically by the distance at which one's parish church bells could be heard, was dismantled for the first time in modern Italian history and replaced with a sensation of a national consciousness.

Concerted forces of the old order—King Ferdinando IV, who retreated to Sicily, and General Suvarov, head of an Austro-Russian army—temporarily regained control, but by May 1800 Napoleon was once again in Italy. He retook Lombardy, reconstructed the Cisalpine Republic, and eventually marched through all the peninsula's regions including Austrian Tyrol and along the Istrian coast toward Trieste. Contrary to his first ebullient apparition of 1796, Napoleon's new goals for Italy were to establish more stable, long-lasting changes to the civil landscape. His legal code was applied uniformly across the former patchwork of customs, and a territorial organization set up with prefects assigned to public works projects, such as the new Simplon alpine pass. In January 1802, the "Repubblica Italiana" was named, and two years later, at Napoleon's coronation as emperor, Italy became a kingdom. Napoleon appointed his siblings to governing positions across his empire. Joseph, Napoleon's elder brother, was made king of Naples and then later of Spain; Elisa, his sister, became the grand duchess of Tuscany; and a stepson, Eugène de Beauharnais, viceroy at Milan. Pauline was wed to a Borghese prince in Rome, and Caroline Bonaparte's husband, Joachim Murat, succeeded Joseph at Naples. In the regions not significantly prepared in Enlightenment reform, the applications of Napoleonic administration came as a shock. While Naples' Albergo dei Poveri was finally if incompletely up and running, all the good will of Murat could do little to bridge effectively the gulf of social and economic differences in his charge.

Not all of Napoleon's policies promoted Italy's best interests. The concessions exacted of Rome by the Treaty of Tolentino specified the removal of one hundred artworks among the paintings and statues of its public collections at the Capitoline and Vatican. Dominique-Vivant Denon, Napoleon's art advisor in Paris, selected pieces from Albani's and Braschi's collections for a Musée Napoléon at the Louvre. Pauline made many works available from the Borghese collection for her brother's purchase. When the convoys from Venice, Florence, and Rome arrived in Paris, triumphal processions were staged and the citizens of Paris applauded themselves as guardians of the art of the free world. The conflict between the revolutionary rhetoric of freedom and liberty and this cultural spoliation did not escape Napoleon's critics, particularly Quatremère de Quincy, who protested that works of art and their historical context of origin could not be separated.

2.2 Arrival of a convoy of statues and works of art at the Champs de Mars for the Musée Napoléon, Paris, 1798. Engraving by De Vinck

For Italians, being for the first time on the bitter end of such a triumphal procession sharpened a consciousness of the fragility of their cultural heritage. Artworks, the icons of history itself, had become commodities to be sold or stolen. In return, the modernity Napoleon promoted in the form of reasoned urban development was perhaps of far greater importance for Italy's continued livelihood. The architecture and urbanism Napoleon left behind describes the benefits.

MILAN

When Napoleon arrived in Milan, a considerable upheaval in Milanese society was expected. After the benevolent Hapsburg rule, the Milanese had much to lose, not so much in terms of their historical patrimony, but in advancements in social progress. Napoleon, however, continued many of the programs of public works improvement begun under Austrian rule, and private initiative soon picked up. Viceroy Beauharnais, like Archduke Ferdinand before him, pursued public building projects to elevate and affirm Milan's capital status.

Beauharnais gathered an entirely new group of architects to carry out the projects. Piermarini's monopoly now broken, Jacobin radicals from all over flocked to take up the opportunities offered in Milan. Piermarini's subtlety, his pilasters and linearism, became anathema; a bold, columnar architecture reflected the new political order. Luigi Canonica, Piermarini's student, adapted the Brera program of instruction to a more simplified formal repertory. Giuseppe Bossi, second in command at the Brera, impelled young designers to careers of political action through the arts. Architecture was a means of achieving social goals, he claimed, inciting civil virtues to unify the people. For Bossi, the forms of antiquity manifested the politically correct symbolism of republican virtue. Paraphrasing Napoleon, Bossi declared that a state cannot have life without the arts, and further clarified his position by contrasting the present resurgence of the classical style against the muddled Middle

Ages, in which, many held, there was no art and no nation.

A *Festa della Federazione* was also staged in Milan, complete with a triumphal arch, patriotic altar, and liberty trees. Monuments to Napoleon's triumphs were planned: a commemorative column modeled on Trajan's, and a Temple to Immortality with columns "in the Paestum order." Indeed, the Milanese praised Napoleon and aimed to prove themselves worthy of his approbation. Projects of economic and urban development were drawn up by the local governors, including a new forum. They claimed that in this public form, "decorum and calm will reign. The Foro Bonaparte will present a spectacle of Roman Magnificence. To the pomp and display of the ancients will be united the good taste and amenities of the moderns." The initiative was wholly homegrown and Napoleon never intervened in the project. In fact, this enterprise coincided with the Cisalpine state's bid for independence, a move Napoleon would never allow. The Milanese projects can thus be seen as a tactic of architectural self-expression intended to gain Napoleon's favor and their promised independence.

After the battles for Milan's liberation, Napoleon commanded the demolition of its obsolete fortification at the Castello Sforzesco. The dismantled bastions were used to fill the surrounding moats, providing a cleared and level ground for political festivities. The remaining fortress was to be converted for civil functions and the core of the new forum. Within a month, Luigi Canonica devised a basic program that combined military, commercial, and commemorative functions, and the building commission was swept away by the galvanic vision of an unsolicited project from a radical newcomer, Giovanni Antonio Antolini.

Antolini had studied in Rome and had attempted a sacristy project for the Vatican, but was assigned only minor works in the Pontine. Cosimo Morelli, a fellow Romagnolo, helped the younger man attain projects in the Tiber basin managing bridges and dams. He also studied the Doric order. In search of better opportunities, he rushed to the liberated territories at Napoleon's advent and put his ideas to work on an ephemeral arch of triumph in Faenza. Antolini then headed for Milan to design their *Festa della Federazione* and found steady employment, again, in hydraulic engineering on the city's canals commission. The Foro Bonaparte project was drawn up when Antolini was nearing forty-five, confident in his vision but anxious to see it realized.

Antolini's proposal called for a colonnade of stripped Doric columns forming a circular precinct around the castle, 570 meters in diameter. The route from the Simplon pass enters Milan at this point. The castle, refurbished with a colossal marble portico, was to be accompanied by a ring of fourteen monumental public buildings linked along the colonnade. A customs house, an exchange, a theater, communal baths, a museum, a "pantheon," and eight citizens' assembly halls called, didactically, *scuole* or schools, animated the vast program of "modern amenities" of commerce and socialization. The specificity of Antolini's proposal as depicted in the superb engravings of Alessandro Sanquirico, scenographer at La Scala, appeared palpable to the commission.

Antolini's vision was not embroidered with academic refulgence but simplified in neoclassical stringency. The volumes were articulated, the surfaces made austere, and the space rigorously symmetrical. Antolini was clearly influenced by the ancient forms Jacques-Louis David employed for his famous *Oath of the Horatii*, which had once been exhibited in Rome. The commissioners' report expounded on the project's inherent heroic profile, its stout Doric proportions equated with stolid republican virtues. The metaphoric value of the column made clear in the festival ephemera was joined to the rational functionalism of permanent useful construction, thus uniting the Doric style to public utility. Similar to Ledoux's salts complex at Chaux, then under construction but still unpublished, the Foro Bonaparte combined science, art, and commerce. Antolini's gigantic proposal was a large-scale urban plan guided by a clear governing ideology and its architectural form was considered an active promoter of society. Antolini presented his project in Paris in May 1801. Unlike Etienne-Louis Boullée's visionary drawings to which Antolini's work might easily have been compared, the Foro Bonaparte was imminently realizable. Milanese confidence in the project preceded the presentation, and on 30 April 1801 the cornerstone was placed. The ceremony, orchestrated by Paolo Bargigli, included a Doric temple, burning urns, and a truncated

Column of Trajan surmounted by a statue of Napoleon. Speeches noted that the project would promote commercial strength and social stability. In June 1802, construction was halted by the Parisian supervisors who had assessed its escalating costs. At the same time, Napoleon was seeking to present a more moderate governmental imagery in architecture, as proposed to him by Charles Percier and Pierre Fontaine, his official architects. The commission was asked to rework the Foro project under more utilitarian and less celebratory aims.

The Milanese were embarrassed by the reprimand, and enthusiasm for Antolini suddenly shrank. He was shunted off to Bologna where, as a doddering professor of architecture, he ruminated unceasingly before his bemused students on the lost opportunity "to give a proper order and form to the fundamental ideas and to create the theoretical metaphysics of architecture." Nonetheless, Antolini's unexecuted plan exerted a magnetic influence on Milanese urban planning. Despite its rejection, the Foro Bonaparte was included in the 1807 city map as if completed. The area, however, would be laid out in far more modest fashion and cost by Luigi Canonica.

Under a revised financial scheme, just disencumbering the castle was deemed a sufficient recognition of the progress the French brought to Milan. Canonica carried on the project with Piermarinian professionalism closely following economized directives. He traveled to Paris to study the examples of Napoleon's official architecture. Canonica cannot boast any masterpieces among the city gates, houses, villas, and dozen theaters he built, including an enlargement of La Scala, but his ubiquitous work brought Percier and Fontaine's adaptable architecture to the Italian cityscape.

In the end, only the most minimal suggestions of the original forum idea were executed by Canonica. Ten thousand trees were planted in substitution for a colonnade, and behind the castle, a vast parade ground, the *piazza d'armi*, was opened at the entrance of the Simplon route. Napoleon decreed the construction of an ancient-style arena in 1806 and Canonica worked it into the Foro Bonaparte plans. The wide, low grandstands were constructed from the rubble of the former bastion. With a capacity of up to four thousand

3 Giovanni Antonio Antolini, Foro Bonaparte, Milan, 1801. Engraving by Alessandro Sanquirico, 1806
4 Luigi Canonica, Arena, Foro Bonaparte, Milan, 1806–7
5 Luigi Cagnola, Arco delle Vittorie napoleoniche (now Arco della Pace), Milan, 1807–38

citizen-spectators, it was the largest such structure since antiquity. A triumphal arch served as an entrance and a stately "pulvinar," or imperial tribune, was made of reclaimed ancient columns. A screen of shade trees completed the ellipse.

The encouragement of an imperial imagery coincided with Napoleon's crowning as Emperor of Italy on 26 May 1805. The Milanese, anxious to please their exacting overlord, were confident that a triumphal arch "in imitation of those decreed by the Senate and built by the people of Rome for the Caesars" would effectively commemorate this occasion. A celebratory archway could double as a utilitarian city gate and as such ranked among the indispensable projects impervious to cutbacks.

In 1806 Luigi Cagnola designed a temporary structure in celebration of Viceroy Beauharnais's marriage to Amalia Augusta of Bavaria. The edifice was admired and led to Cagnola being commissioned for Milan's second permanent arch. Cagnola was an erudite aristocrat with a cultivated interest in the arts. He collaborated on an illustrated translation of a Winckelmann text and designed Ledoux-inspired toll houses for his own pleasure. His diplomatic career in Vienna was terminated with the rise of the French, so the future marquis retreated to Venice to study Palladian architecture. Cagnola returned to his native Milan under the second republic to take a seat on the city council and *Ornato* board. He was primarily interested in issues of celebratory urban decor, but his personal tastes coincided with Canonica's.

Cagnola's triumphal arch for Napoleon, the "Arco delle Vittorie napoleoniche," was begun in 1807 at the entrance to the Foro Bonaparte. Urbanistically, it was the only construction that recalls Antolini's original ideas and archeological spirit. Building materials from new quarries were meticulously selected, as were the collaborating sculptors from the Brera. Like many projects conceived under Napoleonic rule, the arch was completed by later governors with some slight but significant alterations to its name and iconography.

Continuities across successions of regimes were common in the slow development of urban plans. The Napoleonic *Ornato* board, consisting of Canonica, Cagnola, Albertolli, and Paolo Landriani, a

2.6 Giovanni Perego, Palazzo Belloni (now Rocca Saporiti), Milan, 1812

scenographer from La Scala, integrated Antolini's forum and open piazzas at the Teatro alla Scala and the Duomo in their 1807 plans of the city. The design of piazzas with avenues lined with uniform facades coincided with Parisian development under Napoleon. In Italy a constant exchange of ideas among designers of scenography and urban architecture was prevalent. The art of scenography, a staple of eighteenth-century architects and nineteenth-century academies, animated public space first through public spectacles and then in permanent urban architecture. Gaetano Belloni, manager at La Scala, hired Giovanni Perego, Landriani's student in theater design and decorator of La Scala's interior appointments, to design his palace in 1812. Its showy display of columns demonstrates the interplay of stage design and architecture recurrent in Napoleonic-era concepts of the city.

VENICE

Napoleon consolidated his power in Venice in 1805, during his later imperial phase, and arrived in the city two years later. Giannantonio Selva orchestrated the pageant of Napoleon's flotilla down the Grand Canal with an arch on *papier-mâché* columns. The impressive water welcome was similar to the pomp conferred on many other dignitaries of great import. But at La Fenice a new spirit was evident: Selva added an imperial box to the auditorium for Napoleon.

During his visit, Napoleon reviewed issues of Venice's economic recovery, urban infrastructure, and accommodations for his governors. The Doges' Palace was not considered for conversion as it was indelibly associated with the eclipsed aristocratic republic. Instead, Napoleon authorized the reworking of Sansovino's famous Renaissance-era administrative buildings: the Procuratie Nuove next to the Library of Saint Mark. Antolini was summoned in August 1806 to consult with Selva on the architectural possibilities. Ideas for an enlarged entranceway to the complex from the Piazza San Marco, however, created numerous problems with Sansovino's original facade. Beauharnais authorized the demolition of the western end of

2.7 Giuseppe Maria Soli, Ala Napoleonica, Piazza di San Marco, Venice, 1808–13

the piazza facing San Marco, Venice's newly designated cathedral. Construction of Antolini's Palazzo Reale was begun in December 1807, but it was heavily criticized and construction was halted due to its poorly laid foundations. Consultants were brought in: Canonica from Milan and Giuseppe Maria Soli from Bologna. Canonica opined that Antolini should go and Soli offered to take over. Soli finished the project by stretching a uniform two-story arcade across the end expanse, eliminating the grand central accent Antolini considered. By extending and replicating Sansovino's Procuratie arcade in a new wing, Soli's addition is called, simply, the Ala Napoleonica. The high pitch of the roofline was hidden behind a tall attic faced with politically keyed decorations. Panels with olive branches and laurel wreaths alternate with antique-style statues of divinities, emperors, and illustrious statesmen reminiscent of those on Sansovino's library. The exterior was finished in 1813 and featured a central bas-relief with Napoleon enthroned as Jupiter in a magnificent cortege, iconography derived from a spectacle presented on the Fenice stage the year before.

Soli positioned a monumental stair within to the right of the central axis, as at Caserta, leaving a vestibule clear through at the ground level. The only large ceremonial spaces within the entire complex are found at the top of these stairs. The viceroyal audience chamber was decorated in an imperial manner, according to Percier and Fontaine's authoritative publication, the *Receuil des décorations intérieures* of 1801. Unlike Antolini's project—and several others that were proposed—Soli did not try to reshape the piazza but deftly lent coherence to an urban space that had been evolving for centuries. Although he did not resolve the building's conflicted relationship to the Gothic Procuratie Vecchie (except to align their top edges), it is clear that his aspiration was to unify the piazza with symmetry and consonance by using Sansovino's classical imagery. In the long tradition of shaping this public space to the requisites of ruling representation, Soli's work proved in its understanding of historical precedent to have been the least invasive intervention here in the heart of Venice.

Elsewhere in the city, Napoleon's efforts at modernization were more marked and on every count much appreciated. Through the city's new *Ornato* board, headed by Selva, plans for a public garden beyond the arsenal and a basin-side promenade accessed from San Marco were realized. Selva laid out the gardens in geometrical alignments that expressed, he explained, rational order and clarity as opposed to the effete nature of the picturesque English aristocratic garden. Structures for public service were installed: a restaurant, public baths, a belvedere tempietto, and benches. The public gardens, like the cemetery on the isle of San Michele also created under Napoleonic administration, were guided by a clear program of public service and socialization. The program also extended to various institutions. An academy of fine arts was established, headed by Francesco Leopoldo Cicognara. The school was housed according to Selva's plans in expropriated ecclesiastical properties of Santa Maria della Carità. Eventually, despite much appropriation of artworks by Napoleon for the Louvre, a gallery for the history of Venetian painting was opened to the public. Napoleon's operations in Venice and in Italy as a whole were eminently urban. He reinvigorated society not through empty political symbols but in long-lasting structural modernizations that connected with the historical city in graceful and useful ways.

TURIN

Napoleon's operations in Turin exemplified the effective symbiosis of modernity and tradition in Italy under his aegis. Turin, the Savoy monarchic capital, was thoroughly demilitarized by Napoleon. The city walls were dismantled within a year and public promenades planned by the local architect Ferdinando Bonsignore.

Migration to Turin from the countryside caused the population to leap to seventy thousand, requiring serious consideration of the city's infrastructure. Turin was already endowed with an efficient grid pattern of streets, the inheritance of its ancient Roman military *castrum*. The city planning commission on which Bonsignore sat developed a proposal in 1808 for an extension of this grid while introducing public gardens and a pleasant variety of geometric

2.8 Giuseppe Frizzi, Piazza Vittorio Emanuele I, Turin, 1825–29; with Claude La Ramée Pertinchamp, Ponte Vittorio Emanuele, 1810; and Ferdinando Bonsignore, Church of La Gran Madre di Dio, 1818–31

piazzas at the principal points of entry to the city. As in Napoleonic Paris, street names were registered, house numbers assigned, and clear building codes established. French military engineer Claude La Ramée Pertinchamp built Turin's first stone bridge over the Po in 1810, attracting urban expansion to the riverbank.

Even after the departure of the French, the restored Savoy king, Vittorio Emanuele I, continued Napoleonic city planning projects. It was thought that the king himself designed the broad rectangular piazza aligned on the French bridge. His edict defined the piazza's perimeter and implemented tax breaks to individuals willing to build there, but only if they used a prescribed facade prototype. A decade later, the project, still lacking public interest, was revised by the city commission. The open space was reduced and the facades simplified by the city architect Giuseppe Frizzi. By the late 1820s construction was finished. The simple, decorous masses of the residential blocks exemplified the economy of Torinese urban solutions. The ground floor arcades, similar to Percier and Fontaine's Rue de Rivoli buildings in Paris, perpetuate the long-standing Piedmontese tradition of continuous commercial space under cover. Despite this lineage, the Piazza Vittorio Emanuele bears the stamp of Napoleonic planning in the unprecedented scale of its conception and in its harnessing of private initiative in the creation of rational and uniform public space. Years later, Bonsignore completed the Church of La Gran Madre di Dio on the axis of the piazza. His design, refined in consultation with Luigi Cagnola, was an elaboration upon the Pantheon and commands the piazza's vista. It stands, despite its dedication to the restored king, as a reminder of the literally broadened spatial consciousness with which Napoleon invested this city.

NAPLES

In Naples, all projects of Bourbon reform were continued by the Napoleonic administration into the nineteenth century, guided not by royal pleasure but by a bureaucratic mandate of the civic council established in 1806. The Foro Carolino was completed, the Albergo dei Poveri staffed, the cemetery enlarged, and streets all around these sites "rectified." Joseph Bonaparte founded the botanical gardens next to the Albergo, assembling several private collectors' cabinets for public display. Giuliano de Fazio designed its greenhouse in 1809 with heavy Doric columns, after the similar project in Palermo. Private construction among Naples's nascent professional class showed its first tentative signs of life under Napoleonic induction.

While a new generation of decorators worked diligently in the vast interiors of Caserta, Joseph took up residence in the old Palazzo Reale downtown. From his front windows, he viewed a motley array of structures set around an open area known as the *largo*. The unimpressive view was fantastically transformed in many public celebrations, such as Ferdinando IV's temporary return in 1799 and the coronation of Murat in 1808. The new king decreed an architectural competition to rebuild the *largo* definitively as the "Foro Murat." The encompassing churches were demolished and each competition contestant proposed appropriately civil institutions as substitutes: a courthouse, an exhibition hall, a temple of illustrious persons. The proposal by the local architect, Leopoldo Laperuta, was favored and construction of his half-elliptical Corinthian colonnade progressed. Yet it remained only at its foundations when Murat fell and Ferdinando returned from Sicily in 1814.

The forum project continued under the new administration, only its name was changed to "Foro Ferdinandeo." Another competition was declared and its jurying was deferred to outside experts: the academicians in Rome, Bonsignore in Turin, and Cagnola in Milan. Cagnola then autocratically demoted all the competition entries and advanced a project drawn up by one of his own students, Pietro Bianchi. Ferdinando, like his father Carlos, was prepared to overthrow any local talent for the semblance of a cosmopolitan foreign architect, and Bianchi was invited to Naples.

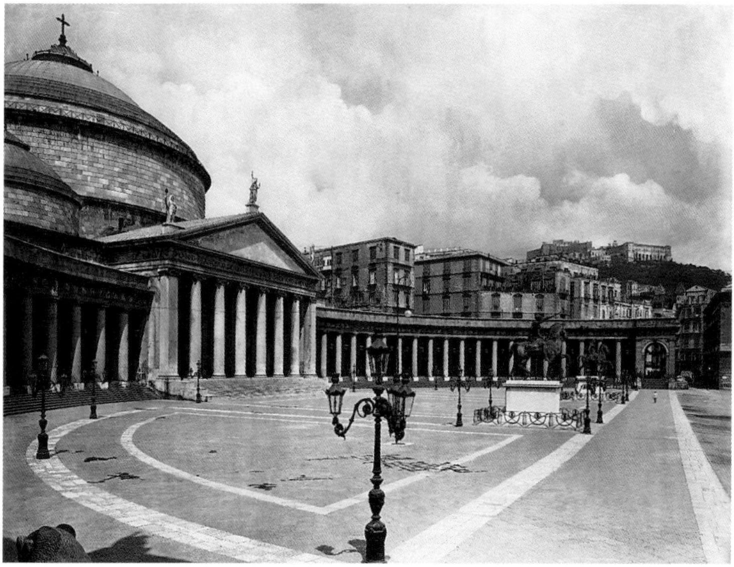

2.9 Pietro Bianchi, Foro Murat (later Foro Ferdinandeo, now Piazza del Plebiscito), with the Church of San Francesco di Paola, Naples, 1817–31
2.10 Antonio Niccolini, Teatro San Carlo, Naples, 1809–10

On Laperuta's foundations, Bianchi erected a Doric order that framed an Ionic portico for the restored ecclesiastical seat, San Francesco di Paola. The crisp volumes of the church's exterior constituted an interpretation of the Pantheon, contemporaneous with Bonsignore's in Turin. With subsidiary domed chapels and motifs drawn from Saint Peter's, paradigms of Christian and classical architecture were merged. Bianchi's work was solid if unsubtle, correct in geometry if poor in poetry. It pleased few besides Ferdinando.

Across from the new forum, the Teatro San Carlo, built for Carlos in 1737 by Giovanni Antonio Medrano, was also a site of continual transformation and updating with each successive regime. The theater's interior was redesigned numerous times by its staff scenographers. The exterior, the inelegant stairs, and ballrooms were, Murat believed, also due for a face-lift. In 1809 Antonio Niccolini, head of the scenography team at San Carlo, suggested holding an architectural competition, which he himself won. Niccolini rebuilt the front portion of the theater. Behind the ample ground floor vestibule, stairs climb commodiously to grand rooms of the long Ionic loggia. The unusual proportions were characteristic of the unabashed originality of Niccolini's designs; the theater was a spectacular visceral display of virtuosity with no clear precedent. Everybody in Naples liked it, so much so that when a fire destroyed the by-then stale interior in 1816, Niccolini was immediately commissioned to rebuild it. The reconstruction of the tired horseshoe-shaped auditorium took seven months. The Teatro di San Carlo was a continually evolving laboratory for Niccolini's scenographic experiments, visions of architectural adaptations, and wider urbanistic proposals.

TRIESTE

Since the beginning of the eighteenth century, Trieste had provided the Austrian empire with important southern access to the Adriatic, and it was the recipient of much Hapsburg urban and economic rationalization. Trieste was declared a free port in 1719. The town was weeded out of unnecessarily crowded constructions, the port rebuilt, and the salt flats to the west, once a source of income for the region, reclaimed. In 1736, an infrastructural framework of interlocking canals and street systems, the "Borgo Teresiano," was planned. It represented an abstract, rational, and rudimentary framework for a city, the kind Milizia praised as more important for a successful city than even fine architecture. Upon this egalitarian grid, merchants from the Italian and Istrian coasts, Greeks, Germans, Arabs, and Dutch settled in what was a spontaneous generation of the collective civil society Enlightenment rhetoric exalted. Casanova took refuge here, Lorenzo da Ponte shifted through, and Winckelmann met his assassin in Trieste. The lack of any strong local tradition allowed free reign in the new city for the building of entirely innovative social and urban structures. The merchants of the flourishing port were wary of Napoleon's approach in 1797, but the Treaty of Campoformio, which ceded Trento and the Veneto regions to Austria, bolstered Trieste by eliminating its rivalry with Venice under uniform Hapsburg control.

Trieste was endowed with representative public buildings, such as a grand merchants' exchange designed by Antonio Mollari in 1802. Its crisp, tetrastyle portico stands as a visual anchor in the irregular piazza at the juncture between the old and new towns. The construction of a public theater expressed the new-found civic consciousness of the Triestines. They consulted with Piermarini in Milan and eventually hired Selva in 1798 to build a theater comparable to La Fenice. When Selva's facade was found to lack monumentality a competition, won by Matthäus Pertsch, followed to alter it. German born, Pertsch studied at the Brera under Piermarini, and brought to the Trieste theater the robust *porte-cochère* and colossal columnar order that had made La Scala a monumental event in its urban fabric.

2.11 Pietro Nobile, Canal Grande with the Church of Sant'Antonio Taumaturgo, Trieste, 1808–31

Pertsch had come to Trieste to build the palace of a wealthy Greek merchant, Demetrios Carciotti. The Palazzo Carciotti fills an entire city block with warehouses and stables, proprietor's quarters facing the port, and sixteen rentable residential units along the sides. Finished in 1806, the facade was synthesized from Palladian models, combining a colossal Ionic colonnade, a balustrade with statuary, and a pure hemispherical cupola. Pertsch introduced to Trieste a decorous register of private building emulated throughout the next century.

Pietro Nobile designed the church of Sant'Antonio at the center of the new city development. Nobile was one of Trieste's few native architects. He studied at the local naval academy and was sent on scholarship to the Accademia di San Luca in Rome in 1798. He spent two years at the academy in Vienna and when he returned to Trieste in 1807 assumed the directorship of the office of public works. As the only architect working in Trieste with experience in Rome, Nobile's work stood out for the purity of its archeological spirit. Unlike Antolini's exactly contemporaneous Foro Bonaparte designs, Nobile's stern forms have none of the political meanings normally associated with neoclassicism. His masterpiece was a church at the top of the Canal Grande modeled on the Pantheon. Its monumental scale, clarity and simplicity of form, and rigorous archeological style earned him an invitation to head the Viennese academy, in 1818, where he spoke of lucid Mediterranean classicism to northern Europeans nostalgic for Italy.

The variety of Trieste's architects—Mollari, Pertsch, and Nobile—demonstrates the diverse routes to neoclassicism in Italy. Its architecture showed the signs of cross-currents that flowed through its society: Palladian traditions from the peninsula, the cosmopolitan classicism of Piermarini from Milan, archeological purism from Rome, and the northern Europeans' classical idea of Italy. Trieste was a crucible in which a particular neoclassicism was forged, an alchemic amalgam of Enlightenment components, economic, social, intellectual, and architectural. It was not a rigid, exclusive system, but a fluid expressive universal language, decorous and dignified, adaptable to a variety of building types and urban conditions, ordered and rational and perfectly reflective of Triestine society at the turn of the century.

THE NEOCLASSICAL INTERIOR

Given the alacrity of Napoleon's movement into Italy, the ephemeral constructions of staged festivals were key in directing long-term urban design. Interior decoration was another medium prevalent among Napoleon's agents in Italy, especially his sisters, to set the tone of governing. Elisa Bonaparte was made Grand Duchess of Tuscany in 1809, deposing Ferdinando III of the Lorraine who had sustained the flourishing Tuscan intellectual culture of the Enlightenment. When he fled to Austria, taking with him a single Raphael painting, his own purchase, he left the rest of the famous Palazzo Pitti collection because it "belonged to the nation." Elisa, in her turn in residence at the Pitti, fashioned herself as a patron of the arts in the Florentine tradition. She increased productivity at the quarries at Carrara with a special financing institution and assigned an academy for sculpture with the production of Bonaparte portrait busts and statues. With no real power at her disposal but considerable funds, she poured her energies into collecting and decorating, outfitting the Palazzo Pitti with new interiors.

Napoleon planned a visit to Florence in 1810 and Elisa, in consultation with Fontaine in Paris, set about reconfiguring and redecorating the *piano nobile* apartments in a manner appropriate to her exigent brother. The new spaces designed by the Florentine Giuseppe Cacialli feature a clean columnar architecture of geometrical volumes, comparable to Robert Adam's work in England, derived from ancient sources like the Roman baths and Hadrian's Villa. The smaller scale and reasoned functionality of the Napoleonic apartments at the Pitti contrasted with the earlier baroque gallery spaces. Napoleon's interiors were characterized, like his governing, by efficient standardization and efficacious references to antiquity. Percier and Fontaine supplied visual material, through their publications, for the redecoration of imperial residences across Italy: Viceroy Beauharnais's apartments in the Procuratie Nuove in Venice, for example, and interiors at the Reggia of Caserta for Murat. The emperor, however, never made the trip to see them.

A Roman residence was also diligently undertaken. The Palazzo Quirinale was designated and imperial quarters, as at the Pitti, were

2.12 Giuseppe Cacialli, Napoleonic apartments, Palazzo Pitti, Florence, 1810

planned. Denon, surrounded by the riches of Italian painting and sculpture in the new Musée Napoléon, devised the iconographic program from his office in Paris. Raffael Stern, a Roman architect, was appointed *architecte du palais imperiale* in 1811. Felice Giani, Jean-Auguste-Dominique Ingres, several students of Jacques-Louis David, and the famous Dane Bertel Thorvaldsen, among many others, were employed to decorate the Quirinal. The teams set to work on subjects of ancient virtue and leadership—Romulus, Ossian, Julius Caesar, Charlemagne, and Alexander the Great—each a historical metaphor for Napoleon's rule.

ROME

A larger architectural restructuring of the Quirinal palace and gardens was also considered. The idea of a megapalace for Napoleon on a hill in Rome was contemporaneous with and comparable to Percier and Fontaine's palace planned on the heights of the Chaillot in Paris for Napoleon's son and heir. In Rome, as in all the Italian cities that fell under Napoleon's spell, eager architects rushed forward with visionary projects. Scipione Perosini sought Napoleon's attention with a gigantic project for the Capitoline Hill. Centered on the Senate House, facets of ancient, medieval, and Renaissance Rome were reconstituted in a gargantuan field of columns and halls stretching across the Forum Romanum to the Colosseum. The planning was patently French and academic in its resemblance to the visions of young designers under Boullée's inspiration. As Antolini and the Milanese had presented a plan that their Parisian supervisors might readily recognize, appreciate, and fund, Perosini's imperial palace sought to spark megalomaniacal aspirations, but his proposal was too grand and the project was never taken seriously.

Napoleon's direct interventions in the city of Rome were far more realistic and reasonable than Perosini hoped. Rome was in many respects revered by the French, who occupied it only quite late in their reign. Pope Pius VII, who had been elected in the March 1800 conclave held in Venice during Rome's first republican

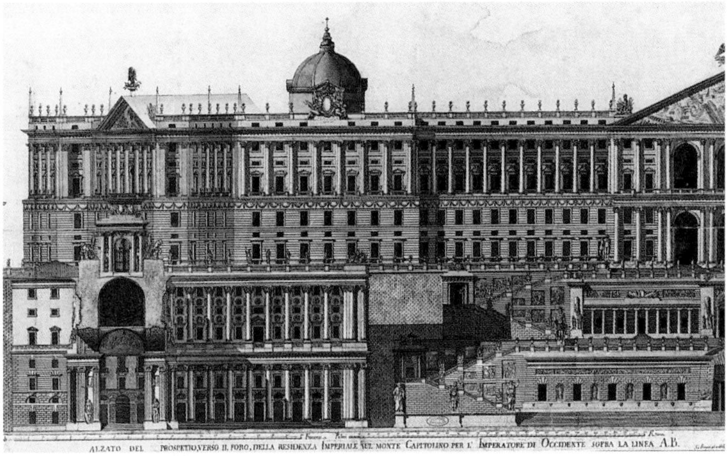

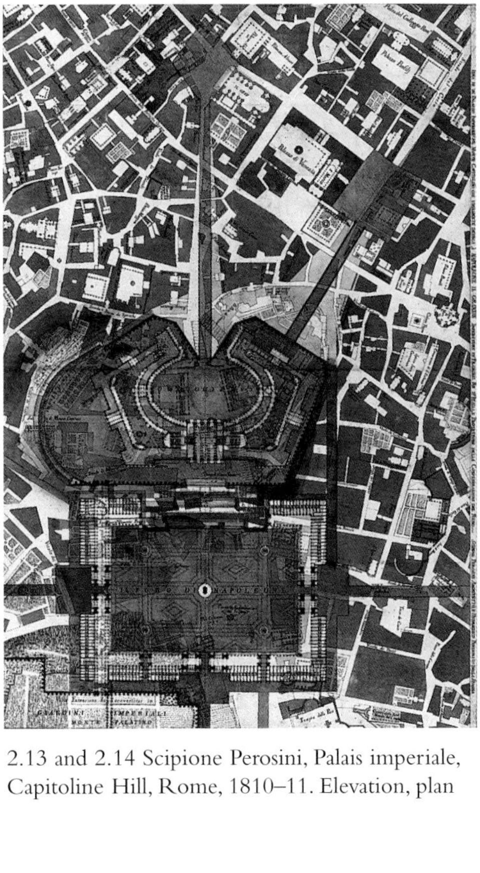

2.13 and 2.14 Scipione Perosini, Palais imperiale, Capitoline Hill, Rome, 1810–11. Elevation, plan

interlude, struck a concord with Napoleon in his moderate phase. Napoleon assured the pontiff that France and its dominions would observe Catholicism as the state religion, and Pius VII ministered Napoleon's coronation at Notre Dame in 1804. But the pope's wavering sympathies irritated the new emperor, who occupied Rome in May 1809 and deported Pius to Fontainebleau, where the papacy would serve as an instrument of French power.

Napoleonic administration of Rome over the next five years brought a considerable influx of money for building and urban management and left indelible effects on Rome. A myriad of interrelated economic and architectural projects were drafted, each focused on the social goals central to Napoleon's investment in Italy. Large-scale archeological excavations were done by squads of unemployed locals. Commissions were formed among the professional and upper classes to shape projects supervised by the French prefect, Camille de Tournon. Napoleon often took direct interest in the projects although he never ventured to Rome to see the results. French administrative offices were accommodated in the papal chancellery, the Palazzo della Cancelleria. Tribunals were set up in the deconsecrated church. Public works on the river banks were deliberated, and enlargements of public piazzas at the Pantheon, the Trevi Fountain, the Palazzo Venezia, and the Vatican "Borgo" were drafted. Public parks and promenades were planted, archeological sites cleared, markets and slaughterhouses erected. On architectural and urbanistic matters, the Commission des Embellissements, the first public bureaucratic instrument of its kind in Rome, was formed by the triumvirate of Giuseppe Camporese, collaborator on the 1798 *Festa della Federazione*, Carlo Fea, Visconti's successor at the Vatican curatorial staff, and Giuseppe Valadier. As an instrument of socialization, public space for promenades was a main priority for Napoleon and in 1811 he established a public garden above the Piazza del Popolo on the Pincian Hill. Valadier, who had already been working on such a plan, was well prepared for the project's direction and was given the job.

Giuseppe Valadier was of the third generation in the famous family of Provençal goldsmiths in Rome. His family's reputation and his father's contacts assisted in his rich education and early rise. While yet a teenager, he had traveled to Milan as his father's courier and admired the cosmopolitan classicism of Piermarini's architecture. Before his twentieth birthday, he was appointed to the architectural team at the Vatican during the construction of Marchionni's sacristy. Like Morelli, he quickly advanced his position by working on projects across the papal provinces. In November 1786, Valadier was sent to rebuild the cathedral at Urbino that had been damaged by an earthquake. He reformed the church in a classical Palladian mode akin to Quarenghi's handling at Subiaco a decade earlier. Valadier successfully balanced his fine classical training and rational temperance to prevail as a prominent professional.

The brusk arrival of the revolution and the flush of new architectural blood marginalized Valadier's talents, but he found continuing support among private patrons. In the more moderate times that followed, Valadier studied Percier and Fontaine's *Receuil*, as is evident in the French-inspired interior decorations he completed for the Palazzo Braschi. Valadier's broad education and equilibrated character made him employable on a wide range of tasks, and as such he was Napoleon's key architect in Rome on the most important French projects.

The Piazza del Popolo was Rome's principal point of entry. Grand Tourists arrived along the Via Flaminia, passing through the city walls at the northern gate in to this piazza. Despite many significant interventions, including a new Renaissance facade for the Church of Santa Maria del Popolo, the relocation of an Egyptian obelisk to a point on axis with the three radiating streets, the space itself lacked definition.

Like the Pantheon's attic, the oddly formed piazza was an eyesore to eighteenth-century scholars trained on classical integration. In 1772 Anton Raffael Mengs, then president of the Accademia di San Luca, sponsored a student competition for a redrafting of the piazza with "decorous constructions disposed in good symmetry." Valadier was too young to have participated, but he returned to the intriguing project twenty years later on his own accord. His proposal, presented to Pope Pius VI in 1794, called for a large barracks complex useful at a city gate. Two Doric colonnades shaped the trapezoidal space, focusing axial movement while governing circulation between severe architectural phalanxes. The newly arrived would pass through the Piazza del Popolo at an initial military check point before proceeding across town to the embrace of Saint Peter's colonnades. The marked shift of attention in the piazza away from its famous church to a military presence may have been triggered by an anxiety in Rome against the revolutionary forces emanating from French territory. Once the French arrived, Valadier promptly redirected his project to Napoleon's needs.

The insertion of a public promenade on the Pincian Hill would affect the nature of the piazza in ways unprecedented in the history of Roman urbanism. Valadier's earlier Doric colonnade was replaced in his new project with a garden fence that traced the original trapezoid. Tree-lined avenues radiated from looping paths leading east to the walls and west to the riverbank. A small barracks building stood opposite the Church of Santa Maria at the gateway. The project ignored the realities of the site's steep slope to the east. The Pincian Hill rises 30 meters from the piazza floor, an impossible incline for the abstract curves. Valadier cunningly drew up a project designed to attract the attention of his Parisian overseers with patently French-style planning. This was a more clever wooing than Antolini attempted for his Foro or Perosini for the imperial palace. Valadier even hedged his proposal with English-style shrubs, pools, and hillocks as at Villa Borghese nearby. His proposal was successfully received. This project dated October 1810 is certainly suggested when Napoleon decreed in 1811 the *promenade du côté de la Porte du Peuple*, the *Jardin du Grand César*.

Valadier set to work developing the promenade and resolving its altimetric problems. His drawings of a switchback system of ramps up the slope were reviewed by de Tournon. The garden layout began to lose its ideal geometric coherence, so thicker plantings were projected to mask the asymmetries and diagonal ramps. While the gardens began to take shape on Valadier's drawing board, new ideas for the piazza it bordered were also generated. In all of the evolving project ideas for the gardens and piazza a prominently demarcated east-west cross axis fixed on the obelisk remained constant.

By January 1812 the commission had drawings ready to send to Paris for further review. Valadier struggled, however, between the

2.15 Piazza del Popolo, Rome. Engraving by Giuseppe Vasi, *Vedute di Roma*, c. 1747
2.16 Giuseppe Valadier, Piazza del Popolo, proposed project, Rome, 1794. Engraving by Vincenzo Feoli

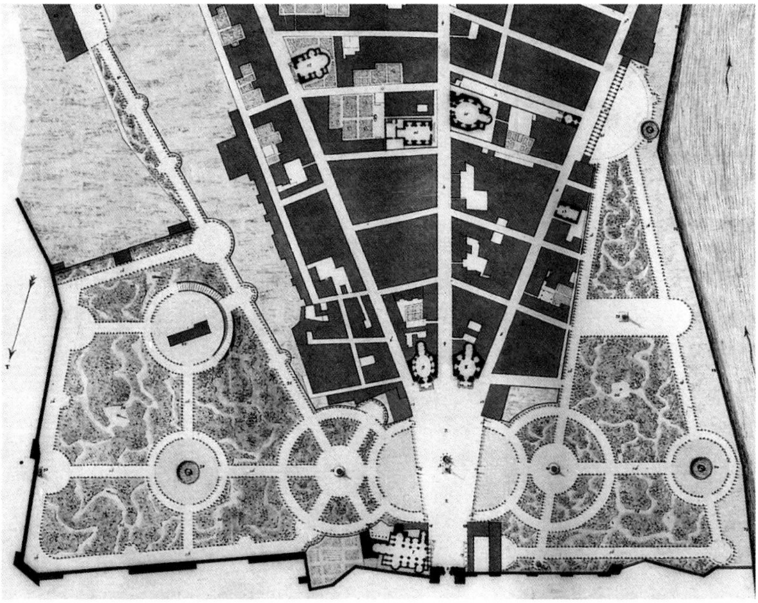

2.17 Giuseppe Valadier, Piazza del Popolo and Jardin du Grand César, proposed project, Rome, 1810.
2.18 Giuseppe Valadier with Louis-Martin Berthault, Piazza del Popolo and Pincian Hill gardens,, Rome, 1813–25

French requirements of clarity and the irregularities of the site. The Conseil des Bâtiments Civils sent Louis-Martin Berthault, Empress Josephine's personal architect and specialized garden designer, to aid in resolving these problems. He created precise drawings of the existing conditions and proposed a series of rigid stairs up the hill, a martial version of the "Spanish" Steps nearby. This dismayed de Tournon, who trusted instead the experience of the local designer. In resolution, a collaboration between Valadier and Berthault was set. Berthault introduced many good ideas that had not occurred to Valadier, like a strong vertical link up the face of the crossing terraces. More importantly, the Parisian garden designer eliminated Valadier's fence, dismantling the demarcation between garden and piazza. The simple act brought the garden's lowest circular geometries to shape the unresolved piazza space. Trees were planted around the semicircular perimeters. The integration of such a green space into the structure of the city was for Rome entirely new. The distinction between garden and city became gentle and fluid and subtly controlled through rising levels and sight lines. The exedra walls and plantings hide the ascending ramps crossing back and forth. A cascading water chain, tapping Camillo Borghese's supply, was implemented. Never before in Rome had garden greenery been called to play such an important complementary role to built urban form. The new geometry of the Piazza del Popolo brought the initial piazza of Rome in closer formal relationship to the Piazza of Saint Peter's. The designs of the *Festa della Federazione* staged at Saint Peter's also offer us keys to reading the sculptural iconography planned for the Piazza del Popolo. There are trophies on rostral columns, ancient deities and river gods, seasons, sphinxes, dolphins and figures of Dacian captives, spoils from Trajan's Forum.

Berthault left Valadier to carry out the project, but in January 1814, the French left Rome altogether after Napoleon's fall at Leipzig. Pius VII was returned to his restored seat, and he entered the city at a Piazza del Popolo still under construction. As in so many of the long-term projects initiated by Napoleon, Pius VII maintained continuities of administrative structures and on-going planning projects without interruption, and in this case, with nearly imperceptible changes to the program. Like all Napoleon's projects for Italian cities, the Piazza del Popolo and the Pincian garden promenade fulfilled its primary function of genteel socialization of the population. The French brought to the fore the inherent social program of architecture, endowing Rome with a multivalent public space, completing the long evolution of the Piazza del Popolo with a solution as dynamically innovative as it was thoroughly in tune with the tradition and meanings of the place.

NAPOLEON'S INTEREST IN ARCHEOLOGY

Napoleonic-era administration in Rome also had a decisive effect on the progress of archeology in developing clear programs and methods for uncovering, restoring, and assessing ancient remains. Large government subsidies were poured in through the Commission des Embellissements for the excavation and restoration of the Roman Forum. All post-antique accretions around the Forum's fragmentary vestiges were stripped and the lower register of the monuments disinterred to remove the layers of the valley's sediment and reveal the stratum of ancient times. On 21 April 1811, the anniversary of Romulus's legendary founding of the city, triumphant citizens marched once again on the Sacred Way. In unexcavated sections, trees were planted in green colonnades to form public promenades. Like the Piazza del Popolo and the Pincian gardens, the disencumbered Forum was reconceived as a social space, focused on the experience of ancient history. Its monuments stood free from the passage of time in a easily accessible presentation.

French interests in Roman ruins had a further agenda. Rome was declared an imperial city second only to Paris. French academicians assiduously studied the ancient Roman monuments and their urban relationships, as evidenced by the Arc du Carousel constructed in Paris. Architectural ideas were not the only commodity in this exchange. In addition to the acquisition of several prominent Roman artworks, Napoleon attempted to transport the colossal Column of Emperor Trajan. This proving impossible, he had a bronze version made with scenes of his own exploits and erected it

.19 Excavations at the Column of Trajan, Rome, with boundary wall by Pietro Bianchi, 1812–13

in Place Vendôme in Paris. The original, left *in situ* and restored by Percier, was the locus of intense activity. The built-up area around the column was cleared for excavation by expropriating several convents. In 1813 the granite columns of a basilica and its marble floor were uncovered and the ensemble of Trajan's magnificent complex began to emerge. Valadier proposed enclosing the perimeter of the excavated site within a circus form, half-rounded on both ends, but this was rejected in favor of Pietro Bianchi's plan for a rectangle for the basilica and a half-circle around the column base. The project was continued after the French retreat without interruption under Pius VII.

The investigations around the Column of Trajan were the first in a continual series of excavations that changed irreparably the nature of the city of Rome. In the eighteenth century, the ground was a storehouse from which goods were extracted, reintegrated, and displayed in collections. In the next century, following on the experience of uncovered Pompeii, the original architectural and urbanistic environment of the archeological site became increasingly significant. Carlo Fea helped to define new goals of understanding the topography of antiquity. Visitors were encouraged to climb to the top of Trajan's Column to grasp the layout of the ancient buildings poking through. In this, the first large-scale excavation in the center of the historic city, a distinction between the present and the pre-existing was drawn. What had to Piranesi's eyes been held together by the resonances of history and myth was now revealed through science and observation. The living city was pushed back and the city that once lived laid bare.

POLITICAL RESTORATION AND RESTITUTION OF ARTWORKS

With Napoleon's fall and the restoration of former political boundaries in 1815 came the restitution of pillaged artworks. Meanwhile, Pius VII's legislation on the trafficking of antiquities (first the *Chirografo* of 1802, then the Pacca Edict of 1820) had helped to restock the Vatican collections and refine its museological approach. The Pacca Edict was based upon the idea of an essential relationship between an object and its place of origin, as Quatremère de Quincy had articulated, and was Europe's most advanced legal instrument in the protection of cultural goods. When Elisa Bonaparte relocated from the Pitti to Trieste in 1814, for example, she could take with her only the works she had commissioned. With the restitution of the works to the Vatican collection, the halls of the Belvedere at the Vatican swelled and Pius VII planned a new extension.

Antonio Canova headed the Vatican commission with the help of Fea, Thorvaldsen, and Filippo Aurelio Visconti. In 1816, Raffaele Stern designed the "Braccio Nuovo," or new wing, of the museum. Stern integrated the statues, busts, bas-reliefs, and mosaics in a strongly suggestive classical environment. The vaulted basilican hall is top-lit and lined with semicircular niches for an ideal presentation of the sculptures. Ancient space is more markedly evoked here than in Simonetti's earlier Museo Pio-Clementino. The Braccio Nuovo was described at its conception as "an example of the way to construct and to decorate typical of the Golden age of Augustus," whose statue, discovered later in the century at Prima Porta, was installed there. The Braccio Nuovo ranked among the most sophisticated museums. The guarantee of broad public accessibility was one of the conditions for the works' restitution set by the international treaties so regular public opening hours throughout the year were established. The latest rooms of the Vatican shaped the public art museum as an evocative experience tuned to the historical context of the pieces on display.

2.20 Raffaele Stern, Braccio Nuovo of the Vatican Museums, Rome, 1816–22

NAPOLEONIC NEOCLASSICISM

The rationalizing spirit of the eighteenth-century Enlightenment gave birth to the elements that constituted nineteenth-century Napoleonic neoclassicism. Political and social, scientific and moral, matters of theory and taste, the general trend of classical renewal—all these elements of the earlier century were brought together by Napoleon's influence. If in 1815 the restored political landscape seemed only slightly different after Napoleon's passing, the architectural landscape was obviously altered. Although the bulk of the built work was ephemeral and much else finished after his fall, the eighteen-year period of his reign was formative in the development of modern Italy. New building types were created, the didactic nature of architectural projects explored, a rigor in archeological methods found, and a number of interventions in historical places carried out. Moreover, a national Italian spirit and imagery began to emerge that proved to be adaptable to a wide variety of cultural requirements. Napoleon's imperial classicism was conceived in the mythic image of ancient Rome, and effects of standardization of form, reduction, and simplification were inevitable. Valadier, like Canonica, Cagnola, Bianchi, Nobile, and Bonsignore, met the imperative of maximum visual effect within economizing limitations. The solid imagery and usefulness of function came about not only through a faith in the indisputable authority of antiquity but also in a practical, empirical process of problem solving.

3.1 Giuseppe Jappelli, Spectacle in honor of King Franz I of Austria in the Palazzo della Ragione, Padua
20 December 1815. Drawing by Giacinto Maina

Chapter 3

RESTORATION AND ROMANTICISM, 1815–1860

GIUSEPPE JAPPELLI AND THE ROMANTIC IDEAL

The restoration of former, pre-Napoleonic political boundaries was, for many Italians, not a recovery but a disconcerting regression. Below the apparently placid surface of the redrawn political map of Italy churned an undercurrent that only a few polyvalent minds navigated with success. Giuseppe Jappelli was one such figure. An architect, landscape designer, engineer, inventor, scenographer, and philosopher, he was the Renaissance man of Italy's dawning industrial age.

Jappelli studied stage design in Bologna, yet his drawings show sympathies to the rigors of Carlo Lodoli's teachings on functionalism. By 1803, he was working for a cartographer, and in 1807 he was appointed to the civil corps of the French army engineering defense systems. Upon Napoleon's arrival in Padua, Jappelli offered his services in the design of festivals of political consensus. He enlisted in the French army in 1813 and rose to captain under Beauharnais's command, but the brevity of his Napoleonic engagement was followed by the dull Austrian dominion that seemed a setback to the thirty-year-old professional.

But soon Jappelli designed ephemera for the festival celebrating Austrian Emperor Franz I's visit to Padua on 20 December 1815. For a single day, the Palazzo della Ragione's Gothic interior was transformed into a spectacular Arcadian landscape—"a serenade in a northern European villa garden," according to its official Paduan promoters. Pine and cypress trees were latched to the walls. Painted flats of laurel and orange groves could be glimpsed through rose trellises lit by crystal candelabra. The fictive view stretched to a distant forest landscape with an alabaster temple, a mossy grotto, and a mighty body of water beyond. There were statues, fountains, an imperial "pulvinar" and a Trajanic column the visitors could climb beneath the canvas twilight sky.

The illusion, constructed *pittorescamante*, was a three-dimensional, mechanical stage setting for a mythic drama. Actors playing the indigenous Paduan people pleaded with Truth in her temple for reassurance against the potentially threatening waters of the Brenta river, symbolized by an ogre that burst from the cavern in a spontaneous cascade of floodwaters. Truth announced the arrival of a great monarch who would decree the waters be used for prosperity not calamity, and a joyous chorus spelled out "Caesar" in garlands.

The scenery, cycling waterfall, and fire-safe illumination system earned Jappelli applause from the event's eight thousand spectators. Jappelli's artistic and mechanical ingeniousness "promised your eye what your feet couldn't do," wrote one observer. To Franz, it was also a political message: he should pick up infrastructural matters where Napoleon had left off.

The formal language of Napoleonic neoclassicism, however, was adjusted to serve now a different northern European overlord. Rigid classicism was subsumed within a romantic, picturesque landscape, and the traditional forms served evocative purposes. Andrea Cittadella-Vigodarzere, an eyewitness, described the experience in fairy-tale terms, conjuring a faraway place and time that bewitched the senses. Unlike Vanvitelli's projects for Carlos, or Antolini's for Napoleon, Jappelli's romantic vision reached heights of the sublime not through reference to monarchic magnificence but through the potent force of Nature. Emotion complemented the achievements of the rational mind in an exploration of new categories of aesthetic experience. Romanticism, as Friedrich Schlegel defined it in 1798, was "a progressive, universal poetry," "always becoming, never completed." With Jappelli's architecture, romanticism manifests itself not as a style, but as an attitude, a mood with respect to form and its experience.

Cittadella-Vigodarzere offered Jappelli the opportunity to explore these romantic notions in a garden for his villa at Saonara. Work was begun in 1816, the year the region was struck with famine. With considerable earth moving carried out by locals eager

3.2 Giuseppe Jappelli, Chapel of the Templars at Saonara gardens, near Padua, 1816. Lithograph by Andrea Gloria, *Territorio padovano illustrato*, 1862

for work, Jappelli formed artificial hillocks and ponds, grottoes and pathways—the fabricated accidents of a naturalistic landscape. The boundaries of the garden were obscured, its vistas contained, the experience turned in upon itself in a series of controlled atmospheric episodes. Cittadella-Vigodarzere wrote that Jappelli drew inspiration from nature and from "other kinds of marvelous things, from history, from science, or from poetry." For example, the visitor might happen upon the suggestively named Chapel of the Templars, a "Gothic ruin" set in the willows and wild overgrowth. Jappelli employed fragments from a dismantled medieval building to create this scene of mysterious ritual. The gardens of Saonara were a museum of the senses not to be viewed from a single suspended point of view, as at Caserta's palace balcony, but from within, through time, individually and intimately. Jappelli was hailed "the William Kent of Italy," a painter of landscapes full of pleasing variety. Jappelli was a voracious reader and able synthesizer of the latest technical and theoretical literature on the picturesque, particularly from northern Europe. This material was summed up in Milizia's publications and elaborated by Ercole Silva in *Dell'arte dei giardini*, published in Milan while Pollack was also finishing a picturesque garden for the Villa Belgioioso.

Jappelli's garden work had a significant impact for his architecture. In Padua, he developed a series of projects of communal utility and public decorum: programs for a new market loggia and municipal seat, a unified university seat, and a radial prison. Only his slaughterhouse was built, in 1818. Like the other projects, it was an outgrowth of Napoleonic-era reforms in commerce and hygiene. Its Doric portico has none of the Palladian repose one might expect of an architect from this region, but it is inflected with the somber, darkly expressionist energy of Ledoux. A central rotunda, originally open to the sky like a primitive Pantheon, was the site of the butchering and evoked in the minds of its nineteenth-century observers associations with pagan ritual. The public administration, however, was too dampened under disinterested Austrian command to take up Jappelli's other proposals. He had to rely, as he would throughout his career, upon private initiative.

Of all Jappelli's many projects, the Caffè Pedrocchi is his masterpiece. Antonio Pedrocchi took over his father's corner coffee bar in Padua in 1799. There were nearly seventy such businesses in the city, but Pedrocchi's was located next to the university building. When the sea blockade during the Napoleonic wars forced many intellectual and industrious Venetians to Padua, Pedrocchi's became the venue for impromptu activities of all kinds, similar to the coffeehouses in Trieste and London. Pedrocchi provided services to complement the new clientele, supplying newspapers to his customers, inviting them to occupy tables without ordering, even offering free glasses of water, toothpicks, and umbrellas when it rained. Soon his finances were flush enough that he could undertake a remodeling of his caffè to accommodate the requirements of his innovative management program. The new Caffè Pedrocchi was the first coffeehouse in Italy to be conceived according to a clear programmatic plan, a free-standing structure in a key urban setting that would become something more than a caffè: a *stabilimento*, an establishment.

By 1818 Pedrocchi had purchased his entire block and had the church next door demolished to clear a piazza at one side. Ancient Roman remains were excavated from pits dug for his ice caverns, attracting speculation about a buried city like Pompeii. In 1826, after a first architect failed to match Pedrocchi's vision, Jappelli was hired. Dismantling much construction, he reshaped the area for maximum accessibility and internal flow. Contrary to all other examples of the building type, from Fuga's Caffèaus on the Quirinal to local rival businesses in Padua, Jappelli's plan broke down the divisions of traditional rooms in favor of open, continuous interior spaces. Entrance porches made fluid connections at the ends toward the little piazzas to pull pedestrians off the street. The exterior elevations were simple in their geometric and planar classicism. Pietro Selvatico Estense, head of Padua's *Ornato* board for public decorum, reviewed the plans and wrote, "one has to recognize in this building the rare merit of responding perfectly to its purpose without concealing them in conventional servitude to preconceived rules." The Pedrocchi was full of practical gadgets, a showplace of modern technology: it was the first public establishment in Padua equipped with gas illumination and steam-run kitchens, an intercom between floors, and a special contraption—Jappelli's invention—for preparing hot chocolate.

Businessmen met at Pedrocchi's in an octagonal ground floor room set apart for them. It was named the Exchange, *la Borsa*, or trading room. The caffè provided a place for any gathering for which the municipal hall or cathedral, the open marketplace or palace waiting room, the university or the brothel would have been inappropriate. The caffè was the new space of the bourgeoisie, a new democracy, "welcoming," the management specified, "anyone whose honest life and polite manners assure conformity to civil society." The Pedrocchi offered the opportunity to realize an autonomous and dynamic new expression for Padua's evolving society. In no small part the result of Enlightenment and Napoleonic inculcation, it is significant that the caffè is a building type developed by private initiative. Pedrocchi was praised at its inauguration in 1831 for having taken such concern in creating an establishment from which society at large profited.

The upstairs rooms were completed in the next decade as the "Casino Pedrocchi." Catered soirées were held in rooms each of a different geometric shape and historical style. There was an Etruscan-style cloakroom; a Moorish ladies' lounge; an octagonal hall painted with frescoes of Athenian themes; a round conversation room wrapped with panoramic *vedute* of the Roman Forum and the Column of Trajan; refreshment parlors in Egyptian, Pompeian, Renaissance, and baroque styles. At the center, a large Empire-style ballroom of white and gold musical motifs was dedicated not to Napoleon but to the Italian conqueror of the Paris opera stage, Gioachino Rossini. The simultaneity of historical styles is a distinct feature of the Casino's experience. Jappelli and his decorators ranged freely through a variety of historical material. Like Jappelli's gardens, the Casino interiors lead us into a synchronic event for the sensations, an exploration of a new category of aesthetic expression with an enchanting effect upon the imagination. The Casino rooms were inaugurated in 1842 with a congress of Italian scientists presided by Cittadella-Vigodarzere, who praised the place for its

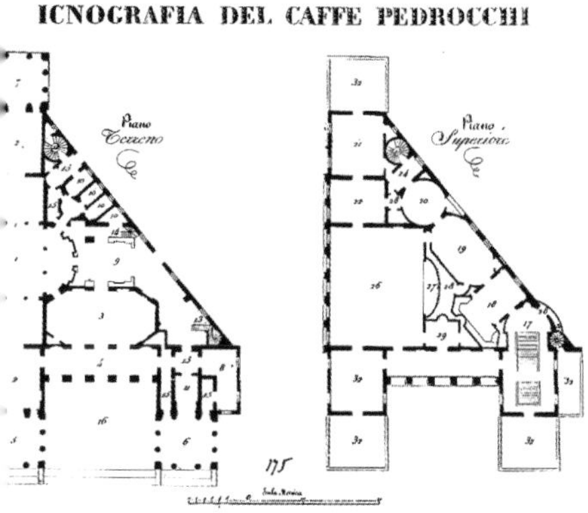

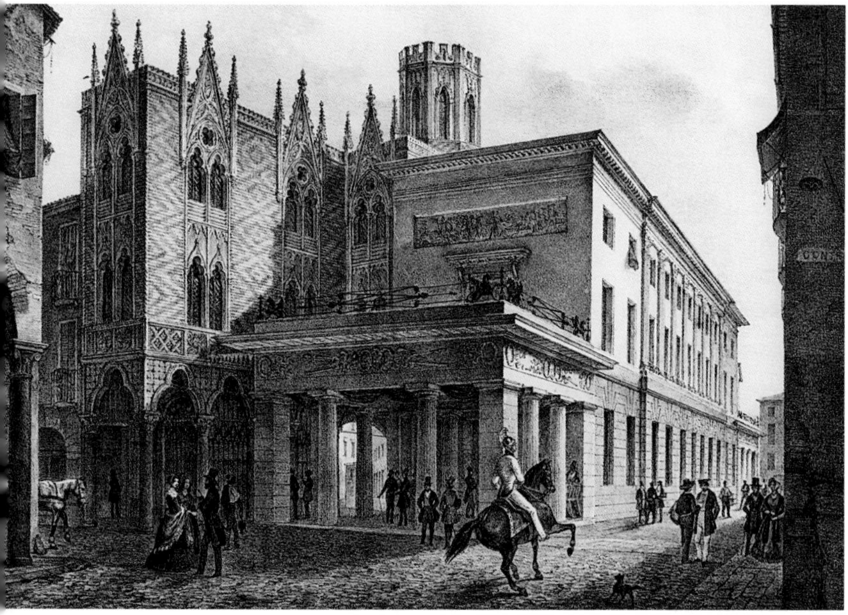

3 and 3.4 Giuseppe Jappelli, Caffè Pedrocchi, Padua, 1826–31. Ground floor and upper
oor plans; interior view
5 Giuseppe Jappelli, Caffè Pedrocchi and "Il Pedrocchino," Padua, 1837–39

balance of artistic fantasy and applied technology. A social club was formed to manage the Casino's many activities. Like the caffè clientele below, the club membership cut across class lines.

The *stabilimento* continued to grow, and in 1837 a neighboring property was acquired to house an annexed pastry shop, "il Pedrocchino." This is said to be Italy's first major building of the Gothic revival. Jappelli's sources were both Venetian and Elizabethan, references he had assimilated through publications as well as a trip to England. (In 1836 he had been sent to England to shop for train locomotives for the chamber of commerce.) The Pedrocchino was designed simultaneously with the casino interiors to which it is linked by a bridge and a Gothic reading room. Selvatico as the city supervisor explained the unexpected use of Gothic here on formal and functional premises: the tiny plot would not have allowed for the symmetry of the classical, only an agile Gothic verticality. What was the point, asked Selvatico, of "refrying Palladio or Quarenghi, or adapting ancient forms sometimes to buildings whose purpose the ancients would not have known." Selvatico claims that both the Pedrocchi and the Pedrocchino, two structures in different styles built at the same time, by the same architect, at the same place, demonstrate the guiding logic of forms reconciled with functions.

At the end of his life, Jappelli returned to Venice to assist in his native city's problematic modernization with studies for a railway viaduct, marsh reclamation, and a mechanized, floating port depot. He was among the few who had the technological mind and preparation to propose such concrete contributions for an ailing Venice. He met with resistance from the ossifying academies of art of the region, and no biographer grasped the immensity of his talents. They were at a loss for words: he was "the Gessner of building," "the Ariosto of landscape." Cicognara called him *un architetto e filosofo profondissimo*.

Romanticism, which rose as a cultural language across restored Europe, reassessed the roles of reason and intuition in the creative process. The era needed a philosopher-architect. Positivist Enlightenment progress manifest in Napoleon's classical hegemony was called into question through the exploration of new aesthetic experiences of the sublime and the picturesque. In architectural terms, this meant the evocative suggestion available through historical style. Piranesi had opened the way to stylistic diversity, and in the nineteenth century architects explored the implications. Classicism, which had enjoyed the preeminence of imperial instrumentalization, lost its authority, but was not replaced outright. Instead, a plurality of historical material, an eclecticism, was brought forth as a philosophical proposition, a synthesis of the best of all precedents in an effort to regenerate creativity in architecture.

The theory of eclecticism resonated in Italy on a political level during the Restoration. Vincenzo Gioberti in his *Primato morale e civile degli Italiani* of 1843 extolled the superiority of Italian cultures, which he emphasized in the plural. He broadened the cultural basis of Italian national identity from the classic to include also the early Christian. Leopoldo Cicognara focused in his *Storia della scultura* from the Middle Ages to the present on the growth of national consciousness through the arts, but the absence of a *patria*, fatherland, or a single *nazione*, or birthplace, among the Italians of the twelfth century, remarks the author, had caused disunity and weakness, and had rendered them vulnerable to subjection to foreign interests. Napoleon had said as much regarding the art of nations, but the restored Austrian censors denied Cicognara permission for a second edition of his inflammatory remarks. But the progress toward a national identity paralleled artistic developments.

What courses through Italy of the ninteenth century and is exemplified in the work of Giuseppe Jappelli is a search for a new architecture expressive of contemporary progress and aspiration. There were many questions to ask, yet there were few certain answers. The arrival of industrial change challenged the old order. Railroad tracks were laid across Caserta's noble axis. Archeological digs cleared the ground of Piranesi's *vedute*. A disconcerting dichotomy between scientific progress and artistic tradition became evident. There were new materials, new building types, new functions for art, diversified methods of construction, and new roles for the architect to fill. Jappelli was the era's pioneer.

VILLA RIVALRY: THE BORGHESE AND THE TORLONIA OF ROME

After the Napoleonic interlude, Pius VII was restored to his capital on 24 May 1815. Pius continued construction of the Piazza del Popolo and the Vatican Braccio Nuovo, but the recent vicissitudes had left the state of private architecture impoverished. Palazzo Braschi was stripped and rented out, Villa Borghese depleted and forsaken by its heirs. Prince Camillo Borghese was coaxed back to Rome with the prospect of taking up his father's passion for the villa gardens and maintaining the Borghese tradition of keeping their villa open to the public. By 1820 some neighboring properties were purchased and Camillo's interest was sparked by a set of drawings commissioned of a young architect, Luigi Canina. Canina had studied architecture in Turin but avoided the normal civil engineering career track there by leaving for Rome in 1810 on an old-fashioned Grand Tour on which he engraved *vedute*, toured ruins with Englishmen and archeologists, and pondered how the Pantheon might be improved with a Doric portico.

Canina's plan for the Villa Borghese extension draws a wide avenue straight up from a new entrance on the Via Flaminia outside the Porta del Popolo. Massive landfill was required to allow a gradual ascent to the higher plateau. From the earlier work on the villa grounds by Asprucci, Canina extrapolated a pattern of a strong visual structure of carriage routes with picturesque paths in the interstices. Canina thought, however, that the English artificial landscape was ill-adapted to Rome's clime and customs. It was associated with aristocratic elitism and failed to capture the imagination of Romans, who would find its usual follies puny compared with their authentic remains. So, Canina's garden constructions all serve real purposes of connecting the disparate parts of the grounds. There is an "Arch of Septimius Severus" with a reintegrated ancient statue on top and a set of Egyptian pylons designed according to recent archeological research. Both passageways were also cleverly designed viaduct bridges over a dirty public right of way channeled in the landfill underneath. The bleating of sheep herded to the slaughterhouse on the riverbank was overridden by the chatter of socialites flocking

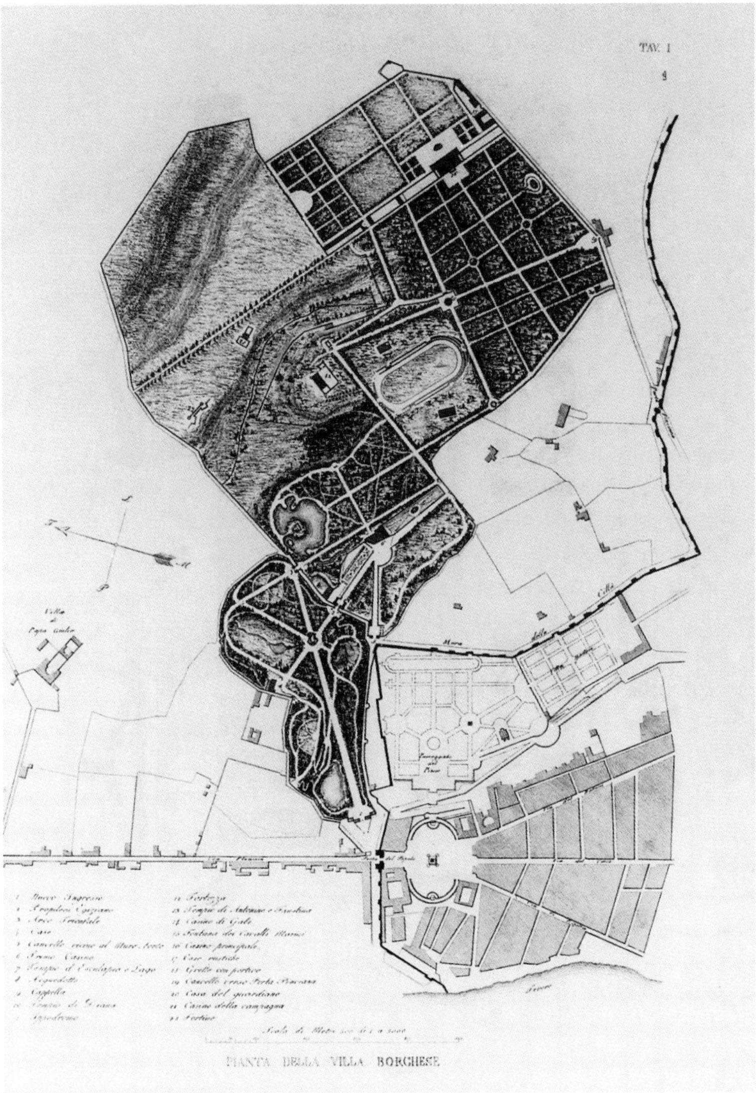

3.6 Luigi Canina, Villa Borghese extension to Via Flaminia, Rome, 1822–34. Site plan. Engraving by Canina, *Le nuove fabbriche della Villa Borghese denominata Pinciana*, 1828

through the villa gateways. For the villa's new entrance on Via Flaminia, Canina designed a refined Ionic propylaeum, by far the grandest public welcome to any of Rome's patrician villas. Canina's three constructions here are in Greek, Roman, and Egyptian styles, emblematic of his idea of a triadic classical heritage. His compilations of historical prototypes at the villa are not intended as faithful archeological reproductions, but examples of form adapted to contemporary requirements of utility and legible representation. Canina went on to excavate the Forum, write a treatise on classical architecture, and opine that the style of the iron Crystal Palace in London could have been much improved by his research on Pompeian wall-painting motifs.

Soon, another family and another villa typical of nineteenth-century society came to rival the Borghese: the villa of the Torlonia family. Giovanni, born to French immigrants in Rome, carried his father's modest financial concern to the highest rank of economic prominence. Through the period of fluctuating allegiances of the revolution, Torlonia played upon either the guarantee of his French origins or the convenience of his Roman birth to win the confidence of clients on both sides of the political swing. He floated Pius VI a loan to pay off the indemnities of the Treaty of Tolentino and helped Roman nobility liquidate properties to match the onerous "contributions" to the public festivals. Noting his tracts and titles and monopoly on transactions of tobacco and salt, Stendhal wrote that "from the most vulgar condition Mr. Torlonia has risen by his own know-how to a most brilliant position." This acute and ironical observer also tell us of Giovanni's audacious arriviste prophecy that his children would be richer than all the princes of Rome combined and that among their children a Torlonia would reign as pope.

Investing in real estate, Giovanni Torlonia accrued enormous wealth; investing in architecture, he gained social status. One of the apartment buildings at Giuseppe Valadier's Piazza del Popolo was Torlonia's, along with a string of money-making theaters in Rome, including the Tordinona and Argentina. The family had a palace at Piazza Venezia, a chapel at San Giovanni Laterano, and a suburban villa on the ancient Via Nomentana not far from the Albani. Valadier was hired in 1802 to design the main villa structure, which he did with inspiration and materials taken from ancient Roman constructions. He reworked the grounds, helped collect and install sculptures, and all for a wisely spent 32,000 *scudi*, a tenth of what Cardinal Albani had spent on his.

Giovanni passed a fortune of more than 30 million *scudi*, the bank, the palace, and the villa on to his son, Alessandro. If Giovanni Torlonia liked to compare himself to Cosimo de' Medici, Alessandro played the role of Lorenzo the Magnificent, carrying the family name to the most conspicuous ranks of patronage in the arts. Alessandro's idea of patronage was born of his compulsion to measure himself against the Roman tradition, especially the Borghese. He was the most active employer of contemporary artists during the rather dull period of the restoration in Rome, commissioning altars, church decorations, and facades. He set about his patronage with the same aggressive enterprising techniques he used in the banking business. He modeled himself on Alessandro Albani—the coincidence of their first names appealed to his sense of historical connection. Indeed, the new Torlonia altar for the Church of Il Gesù was spurred by no particular religious sympathies for the Jesuit order but by the fact that Alessandro Farnese's name was inscribed on that monument. He mimicked papal patterns of patronage by funding excavations, erecting obelisks, and collecting Egyptian art just as the current pope, Gregory XVI, was adding the Museo Egiziano to the Vatican complex. If Torlonia patronage was a calculated instrument of their economic rise, it was also a necessary component of their self-representation. On a concrete level, it was an instrument to be used with managerial efficiency. Alessandro set stringent financial and legal controls on his artists. Torlonia's choices belie little feeling for their work, and when dealing with his artists he adopted an affectedly familiar tone with them that was not always appreciated.

For the villa, Alessandro needed a project coordinator, like Borghese's Asprucci. His choice was Giovanni Battista Caretti, who had studied with Albertolli at the Brera and then at the Accademia di San Luca. He had taken on a three-year stint decorating places in Poland and returned to Rome in 1826 when he found employ in

3.7 Giuseppe Valadier, then Giovanni Battista Caretti, then Giuseppe Jappelli, Villa Torlonia, Rome, 1802–42. Engraving by Gaetano Cottafavi, 1842

the Torlonia pool. By 1832, Caretti had added a monumental Ionic portico to Valadier's villa structure, and the interiors were done up in a variety of alternative historical styles. To allude to another namesake from history, and to amplify his self-image, Alessandro had a chamber decorated with a relief showing the life of Alexander the Great.

On several trips to Britain and on a tour of gardens in Italy, including Saonara, Torlonia had seen the best his era could offer in landscape design and wanted to outdo the Borghese with Rome's most genuinely picturesque garden. In response, Caretti supplied a temple to Saturn, a *caffèaus*, sham ruins, and an amphitheater—a panorama of structures explicitly inspired by Hadrian's Villa. Even the boundary wall with its teetering pile of counterfeit antiquities, broken columns, and statues is a simulated stratification. The noble portico of the enlarged palazzo lords over the scene. "With a single sweep of his gaze," writes Giuseppe Checchetelli, an observant if sycophantic contemporary, Torlonia "could enjoy the product of his greatness . . . just as Hadrian who from a single point in his villa took in all the monuments of various styles his powerful will had collected." Piranesi's influence can be detected here in an assemblage of symbolic elements drawn from an array of historical materials. To continue the works, Torlonia sought out top names, like Giovanni Antolini, whom he unsuccessfully tried to coax down from Bologna. He settled for Quintiliano Raimondi, who constructed a theater to draw the public onto the villa grounds. Raimondi demonstrated little sensibility for landscape, so Torlonia purchased the expertise of Giuseppe Jappelli, who was tempted by the enormous amounts of cash Torlonia was prepared to spend on the project. The rear parts of the Villa Torlonia are Jappelli's only creation outside his native Veneto region, though he came to regret taking it on.

Jappelli introduced accidents of terrain to isolate the small area he had to work with. A little Mount Olympus sprang up behind Caretti's temples, and its spiraling paths took one into secluded forest valleys behind. Jappelli tucked into his fantastical landscape a Gothic ruin, a secret grotto of sylvan nymphs, an arena for medieval jousts, a Moorish pavilion of exotic pleasures, and a rustic farmstead. As at Saonara, Jappelli's garden is essentially a literary inspiration, his architecture stock settings for romantic adventures. The cement *campo da tornei* simulated the wooden surfaces of a temporary structure for a knights' tournament. The Moorish pavilion was a marvelous hothouse of painted iron and mirror panels, orchid planters and goldfish tanks built into the window sills, and a minaret fitted with a dining table raised on a screw mechanism that transforms into a poof. The *capanna svizzera*, a rustic Swiss hut, was dramatized with faux-fir half-timbering and brick-like stucco surfaces. It was stocked with genuine Swiss milk cows. The forced asymmetries of its design and the affectedly picturesque rusticity may have been encouraged by Torlonia himself, who brought Jappelli's attention to John Nash's Blaise Hamlet cottages in England.

Jappelli found Torlonia a most unappealing patron, willing to push the picturesque to absurdly grandiose proportions. In a series of bitter letters back home, Jappelli lamented that the garden's Romantic sensibility was lost in Rome's sunny weather. Jappelli found Rome lax and backward, closed-minded in its proud classical inheritance, and Torlonia's ambition a ludicrous product of retardataire tradition. He returned to Padua the day his contract was fulfilled. What Jappelli left behind, however, was Rome's most fascinating architectural experiment, structurally and technologically innovative, theoretically and philosophically exploratory.

Torlonia's ego was not bruised by Jappelli's huffy departure. He continued to build and acquire, erecting two obelisks in a panegyric public festival at which even Pope Gregory XVI and King Ludwig of Bavaria were left flabbergasted. Torlonia eventually bought the Villa Albani, lock, stock, and barrel. Before he died, richer than all the princes of Rome combined, he saw his daughter wed to a Borghese with special authorization that the husband might take the Torlonia name. Their offspring, however, was too mad or too self-absorbed to think about becoming pope.

ITALIAN OPERA STAGE DESIGN AND THEATER INTERIORS

The architecture of the mid-nineteenth century in Italy was enriched by a symbiotic relationship with the art of scenography. A number of artists were involved in both media. For Italian architecture, theater culture, as it had been since the Renaissance, was a progressive laboratory of experiment. The theater itself was an ubiquitous building type of the early modern era. Cosimo Morelli built numerous theaters across the papal states. At the Foro Bonaparte, Giovanni Antolini invested his theater with a strict program of civic morality. In the nineteenth century, theaters were built even in the tiniest towns as important institutions of evolving civic consciousness.

The theater industry evolved too, making its way from the palace (as at Caserta), through independent societies of noblemen (as at La Scala), and into the hands of impresarios (as at San Carlo and La Fenice). The nineteenth-century audience also shifted from courtly hierarchies toward a heterogeneous group. New men of the merchant class filled the *platea*; tiers of boxes were sometimes reconfigured as open galleries for the ladies. On the stage, the lyric opera evolved from utopian classical visions of courtly authority into an open-ended exploration of a new bourgeois society.

Italians were the undisputed leaders in scenographic arts, and brought their talents to the European capitals. Pietro Gonzaga designed Piranesian scenes for the Scala stage in its first two decades before following Quarenghi to Russia in 1792. There he published a treatise, *La musique des yeux*, that promoted greater homogeneity of visual imagery and dramatic content. Domenico Ferri designed all Gioachino Rossini's operas for the Parisian stage, and the Quaglio dynasty of designers commanded a slew of German venues.

Eighteenth-century treatises on theater architecture and acoustics, in addition to Piermarini's synthesis of that knowledge at La Scala, allowed theoretical attention to turn now to stage design. In Naples, Antonio Niccolini founded Italy's first academy of scenography in 1821, where he stressed the unity of the staged experience. The opera stage was his full-scale laboratory of visual imagery where he explored the possibilities of various historical styles and visceral effects of lighting and scale. While libretti and music repertory expanded, the scenographer had to exercise creative genius with discretion and erudition on an ever wider range of historical source material. Contemporary archeological studies supplied some ideas, but the scenographic art, Niccolini insisted, remained within the realm of poetry. In 1844 he overhauled the Teatro San Carlo's interior decorations. An eclectic by profession, Niccolini was an active architect, engineer, urban planner outside his duties at San Carlo, and many ideas that appear in his architectural projects were first developed on the San Carlo opera stage.

In addition to Naples, Venice and Milan were the great capitals of Italian theater culture. At La Scala, Gonzaga left a series of his students in command, including Paolo Landriani who also brought his talents to the city *Ornato* board in 1807 and taught at the Brera. Alessandro Sanquirico met the scenic demands of operas by Rossini, Donizetti, and Bellini. His sets for Meyerbeer's *Il crociato in Egitto*, which premiered in 1824, took the audience on Maltese ships to a sultan's palace, distant ports, and daunting Piranesi-inspired prisons. Productions of this opera also opened in Trieste, Padua, Florence, and London. Publications of Sanquirico's sketches established the standard for grand opera elsewhere. In 1829 he redecorated La Scala's interiors. At La Fenice, Giuseppe Borsato, who had worked with the original architect, Selva, was the staff scenographer and overhauled its interior decorations once again in 1828. Francesco Bagnara, a colleague of Jappelli in garden projects, designed sets at La Fenice for the burgeoning mid-century opera repertory, including twenty-one Rossini operas. Giuseppe Bertoja and his son Pietro were responsible for the staging of dozens of Verdi's operas at La Fenice later in the century. Staff scenographers were called upon to apply their art to the interior decorations of the auditoriums, which were usually refreshed every twenty years.

On the night of 13 December 1836, a fire gutted La Fenice. Before the cinders were cool, engineer Tommaso Meduna had prepared the cost estimates for its reconstruction. Because questions of acoustics and sight lines had been resolved in Selva's original design, the idea of rebuilding the essential horseshoe-shaped hall went unquestioned. Niccolini had proceeded similarly after the last San Carlo fire. Tommaso brought in his brother, Giambattista Meduna, a trained architect who improved the access stairwells and corridors, lowered the box partitions, and introduced new ventilation systems. Eventually the stage's oil lamps were substituted with gas, improving safety but altering the quality of the light on the scenes and in the auditorium.

In 1853, not two decades after reconstruction, another competition was held to redecorate La Fenice's interior once again. The style, according to the program, was not as important as its effect, which was to be a *splendidezza di ornamenti*. Giambattista Meduna's winning project covered Selva's neoclassical framework—which Meduna himself had rebuilt sixteen years earlier—with a lacy veil of frivolity. Like all the period's theater interiors, it was unabashedly modish, wearing its neo-rococo pinks and blues with the aplomb of a guest at a costume ball. No one imagined that this delightful cream puff might last long until another confection would be whipped up to take its place, but it survived to the end of the twentieth century. The essential features of Romanticism were thoroughly explored on the lyric opera stage, and the crossover of scenographers into the field of architecture fostered a remarkable evolution of architecture in the nineteenth century toward patently scenographic methods and effects.

Scenographers created illusions that explored the sublimity of natural phenomena, emotive energies, and evocative moods. The content of the dramas to which the scenographer's art gave form were by and large romances: historical dramas not of mythic gods and allegories but tales of heroism, love, adventure, and tragedy based on Italian medieval legends. Crusaders and figures from Dante made many appearances. The genre of Romantic drama gave voice to a bourgeois society just now gaining its self-consciousness by drawing on allusions to national origins and local heroism. The power of music helped overcome political and regional barriers. Most regions of the divided peninsula were represented on the opera stage, from *I Lombardi* to *I Vespri Siciliani*. Specific historical events and places were seen: the Venetian arsenal, Milan's Romanesque churches, medieval

3.8 Giambattista Meduna, Teatro La Fenice, Venice, interior redecorations, 1853–54

castles, Renaissance palaces. Verdi was the most frequently performed opera composer of the 1850s, and his operas were received as proto-nationalist fodder. He co-opted scenic talent, even deriving musical inspiration from visual imagery, and he was the first composer to specify the scenic effects required. Verdi's choice of themes of struggle, virtue, and hope, along with an emphasis on the choral voice, strummed the chords of a nascent national consciousness. His libretti were often censored, but his music rose above the controls to become unofficial patriotic hymns. The political voice of the Italian opera is key to understanding the Romantic era in Italy. Architecture took many of its leads from scenography. It therefore may not be surprising that the most renowned building of the Romantic period in Italy was not conceived by an architect at all.

ANTONIO CANOVA'S TEMPLE IN POSSAGNO

Giuseppe Verdi's mythic status in the mid-nineteenth century is the product of an Italian cultural phenomenon linking the cult of indigenous genius to a collective consciousness of imminent nationhood. The phenomenon began with Antonio Canova. Canova, the neoclassical sculptor, had come to Rome in 1780, two years after Piranesi's death. Selva took him to see the statues set up by Visconti in the Museo Pio-Clementino. Canova fell in with Anton Raffael Mengs at Villa Albani and with a circle of English artists on their Grand Tour, making the requisite visits to Herculaneum, Pompeii, and Paestum. He set up his studio near Piazza del Popolo in 1783. Canova's fame was established with the Rezzonico tomb in Saint Peter's, the project Piranesi felt entitled to, and continued in a series of sculptural masterworks. He was elected to the academy in 1800, decorated with the *Sperone d'Oro* by Pius VII, and made inspector of antiquities in 1802. Canova addressed Winckelmann's noble antiquarianism and debated theoretical issues in letters to Giacomo Quarenghi. He was praised by Quatremère de Quincy, courted by Catherine the Great, and, despite his wariness of politics, appointed the official sculptor of Napoleon's empire.

Canova's great success was based upon work that exhibited a formal refinement infused with a delicate sensuality. His sculptures of Cupids, Psyches, Venuses, and graces were without rivals in supreme beauty. Canova drew from ancient models combining the features of an array of studied prototypes in a process called *imitazione*. His monumental statue groups, portraits, and tombs communicated heroic and sublime tones, lyric meditations on fame, greatness, tragedy, or death. Canova's creative process is key to understanding the nature of Romantic-era art and architecture in Italy. His initial ideas were produced in drawings or clay or plaster figurines full of an inspired impulsiveness of creative genius. They were then meticulously executed in marble with the help of a workshop of technicians. Without compromising the initial immediacy, Canova achieved what contemporaries appreciated as a meditative serenity of ideal form—"the visible virtue of the soul," as the artist once boasted to a friend.

Canova's talents were co-opted by a slew of political figures: Pius VI, Ferdinando IV, Napoleon, Pius VII, George Washington. He elevated each to noble heights while buoying himself and his art above their clashing politics. During the radical Republicanism in Rome, Canova retreated to his sleepy Veneto birthplace, Possagno. He always avoided direct political or ideological engagement, insisting foremost on aesthetic integrity; however, many of Canova's masterpieces stirred feelings of Italian national pride. His *Venus Italica* was designed for the inner sanctum of Italian art at the Uffizi Gallery after the Medici Venus had been carted off by the French. Leopoldo Cicognara in his history of sculpture since the Middle Ages places Canova at the apex of the *Risorgimento*, or resurgence, of Italian culture. After the restoration of the peninsula's former political boundaries, Canova and his art remained, along with opera and Romantic poetry, one of the major focuses of an Italian collective consciousness. Indeed, Canova represented in person the interests of Italian national culture when he was dispatched to Paris in 1815 to recover those works of art Napoleon had taken. Restitution and restoration meant for Canova a comforting retrieval of peace and a revival of Christian values to which the artist, nearing sixty, was drawn.

Canova was in the habit of giving overly generous and self-serving gifts. In 1809, when the meek hometown parishioners of Possagno asked their illustrious native son for help in sprucing up the local church, he retorted that anything spent on the old building would be wasted. He painted an altarpiece for them, a Lamentation of Christ, but so grand as to throw the modest place into embarrassing contrast. Canova had already tried his hand at architecture: the sanctuary of the Madonna del Còvolo, a small strictly by-the-book Palladian chapel at Crespano del Grappa. In the summer of 1818, he offered Possagno a design for a new parish church construction, a majestic hillside "temple," he called it.

Canova confessed that architecture was, technically, not his specialty. Although the design for the Possagno temple was undoubtedly his, from its brilliant flash of inspiration through to its exacting execution, he availed himself of expert technicians, as he did with his sculpture production. Pietro Bosio was Canova's draftsman. Trained at the Brera and a student of Raffael Stern, Bosio came to Canova's attention for his meticulousness, not his individuality, a requisite for all the minions in the Canova workshop. Selva may have suggested to Canova a basic design idea and helped Canova review Bosio's drawings, but Selva died only months into the project and Antonio Diedo carried on the consultancy. A contemporary chronicler of the project, Gerolamo Luciolli, wrote two years later that Canova himself was taking sole care of the entire enterprise.

The cornerstone for the new church was laid in Possagno on 11 July 1819, amid rustic banquet festivities during which Canova was honored like a demigod. The architect-donor was an exacting taskmaster, however, requiring manual labor from the parishioners on Sundays. The idea was that the temple might rise as if from the spontaneous ardor of the people, as they imagined the Gothic cathedrals did, and in turn focus the moral being of the population as Enlightenment theory proposed.

The Tempio Canoviano is a domed rotunda with a columned front and an apse at the back, isolated above the village of Possagno against a verdant backdrop of the Dolomite foothills. Inside, the

Pantheon model is followed with some significant alterations: the purity of the volume is accentuated by the elimination of subsidiary divisions like an attic level. Canova's synthesis of major historical archetypes is immediately striking. His method was, he explained, "to follow in the execution of this work the example of a few illustrious and distinguished monuments without actually inventing anything new. There is nothing here that is not antique in its essence." In the same reductive process toward pure form and concentrated sentiment that marked his sculpture, Canova's creative impulse conjoined the revered features of architectural history: the Greek columns, the Roman vault, the Christian apse, in a symbolic synthesis.

Luciolli, witness to the project's inception, extolled Canova's "sublime idea" of uniting three diverse formal archetypes. Today, scholars grimace as they excuse the inelegant junctures of the composition, blaming Bosio, Selva, or Canova's own inexperience. But the clear original ideas and meticulous control that characterizes all of Canova's work prohibited any laxity. Melchiore Missirini, who was the first to write on the completed structure in 1833, comments exactingly on the *legamento*, or tying together, of the three parts of the composition. It is a perfect juncture, he says, unlike the original Pantheon in Rome. Possagno's geometric alignments work in perfect correspondence: cornice lines connect, heights of pediment and cylinder match, the rotunda's inner diameter determines the portico's width, yet the parts remain distinct. There is a poetry in their contrast. Each part—Greek portico, Roman dome, Christian apse—is emblematic of a progress of civilization, like Canina's historiography at Villa Borghese, now for Canova with a layer of Christian values. The synthesis of the three forms may also be read as an architectural iconography of Trinitarianism, as suggested by the portico's inscription.

This new parish church is located outside the loosely defined village, up a path rising on the temple's left side. In numerous period views, the village is either minuscule or altogether omitted, leaving the pristine construction set in sharp contrast against a natural background. The temple is a titanic vision, a scenography of the sublime. In the continuum of Italian architecture, at the crucial moment of the Restoration, Possagno stands as an emblem of the passage from trenchant neoclassicism to exploratory Romanticism.

3.9 Antonio Canova, Tempio Canoviano, Possagno, 1819–31. Engraving by Melchior Missirini, *Del tempio eretto in Possagno da Antonio Canova*, 1833

Eager to advance the project while his stomach ailments grew threatening, Canova came to Possagno in September 1822. Visiting his doctor in Venice, Canova died on 12 October, and his dying wish was that the Tempio be finished. Four days later, his funeral at Saint Mark's was celebrated under anxious Austrian vigilance to deter a patriotic gathering. The cortège up the Grand Canal was hijacked at the Accademia di Belle Arti for a second unauthorized funeral. Leopoldo Cicognara, president of the academy, orchestrated the event: the coffin was set up in the gallery space upstairs, and eulogies were spoken that equated art, society, and politics in the resurgence of Italian culture. The artist's heart and hand, separated from the corpse at its autopsy, would remain in Venice, parsimoniously distributed like the relics of a Christian saint. Borsato designed a porphyry urn for the heart and a tomb was concocted from Canova's own famous designs in the Church of Santa Maria dei Frari, but the Possagnesi claimed the body. Canova may have wanted to have been buried in the Pantheon's walls like Raphael, but the Possagno parish church became his tomb site. The "Tempio Canoviano" was completed in 1831 as a shrine to Canova himself, confirming his cult status.

A gallery in Possagno was built to contain all the plaster working models from Canova's studio at the time of his death. The Gipsoteca was designed by Francesco Lazzari in emulation of Stern's Braccio Nuovo as a classical basilica space. The Gipsoteca is attached to Canova's birthplace, a construction lying on the edge of the village but aligned exactly with the mighty Temple above, connected now by a wide avenue, revealing finally Canova's not so disingenuous oblique siting of the church. Shrines to Canova began popping up everywhere, and almost all of them, like Possagno, were interpretations of the Pantheon.

PANTHEON PROGENY AND CARLO BARABINO

The Pantheon, in fact, had many progeny. In addition to the Pantheonic churches of Naples, Turin, and Trieste already mentioned, another rose in Milan: San Carlo al Corso of 1844, by Carlo Amati. Funerary chapels in new public cemeteries at Brescia, Verona, and Genoa all elaborated on the Pantheon model, but nowhere was the famous ancient prototype slavishly reproduced. The paradigm was not in itself a perfect image, as the critical response to it attests; it was an example of a synthesis of eclectic parts and served as a point of departure for many architects.

Among the best of the Pantheon progeny is the chapel in the civic cemetery of Genoa designed by Carlo Barabino and completed in 1851. Here, too, distinct prototypes are conjoined: a Doric portico, domed rotunda, and a lobed altar tribune area. The dramatic force of their juxtaposition is rendered through the reduced purity of elements. Like Possagno, the Genovese ensemble presents the major elements of its composition without gentle transitions; only aligned entablatures strap the forms together. They stand crisp and white against the backdrop of cypresses.

The idea for the cemetery itself dated back to 1797. Napoleonic legislation on burial practices took the control of death away from the Church. "Monumental" cemeteries, as they were called, were founded in Brescia and Verona, Bologna and Ferrara, Venice, Turin, Rome, and Milan, to name only the most prominent. Genoa's project was troubled over the site, costs, and local resistance, which delayed matters until a few weeks after the architect's death from cholera in 1835. Giovanni Battista Resasco, Barabino's closest collaborator, fleshed out the design and brought it to completion. The Pantheonic chapel is dedicated to the memory of illustrious men of Genoa, and Barabino is buried inside.

As the city architect since 1815, Barabino provided vital social spaces and new structures to bourgeois Genoa. He devised the city's first real expansion plan, providing incentives for development to draw building away from the crowded port area and up onto the hills. There were new, orderly thoroughfares and designated

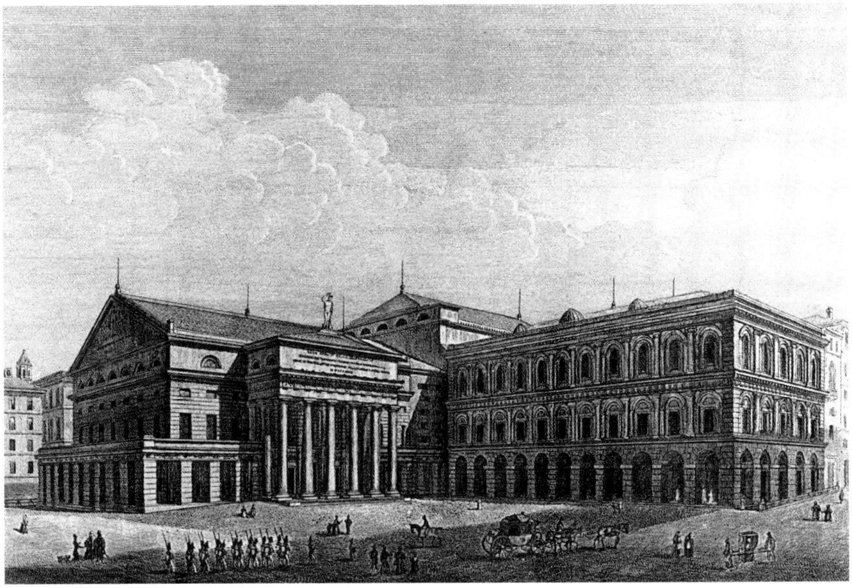

3.10 Carlo Barabino, Cimitero Monumentale, Staglieno, Genoa, 1835–51
3.11 Carlo Barabino, Teatro Carlo Felice, Genoa, 1826–28. Engraving by Luigi Garibbo

apartment block prototypes—a cross between John Nash's London and Charles Percier's Paris, both examples cited by Barabino. Bonsignore was sent down from Turin to supervise. A new street system was devised that circled the old town and led to a new piazza where Genoa's largest public theater rose.

Since 1799, the Genovese recognized the civic value of a monumental theater, a focus of self-expression, but such ambitions were effectively suppressed in Napoleon's designs for Italy. Under the new Piedmontese king's more happy reign, the project of the Teatro Carlo Felice found enthusiastic support on the city council and from wealthy *palchettisti*. Construction was begun in March 1826 and completed in just twenty-five months. Barabino developed a facade with an austere, abstract geometry and crisp interlocking volumes. The interior pathways are designed also to draw pedestrians from the surrounding streets into the auditorium placed obliquely to the main facade. The civic nature of the Teatro Carlo Felice was also evident in the novel handling of the auditorium's boxes. Their partitions were pulled back to create a sense of unity among them and better acoustics. The concerns of this society can be read in the subtlety of the auditorium's curve and the inflection of its boxes as they turn attention away from each other in the hall and toward the stage. The whole is a spacious and monumental contribution for a city long associated with a crowded and boisterous port. Barabino can be credited with providing Genoa with its first collective social symbols: its public cemetery, major piazza, and new theater of well-tuned civic imagery.

ROMANTICISM IN TUSCANY

Siena in the heart of Tuscany had always been bypassed on any Grand Tour, but the nineteenth century and the Romantic era significantly invigorated the cultural self-image of the region. Isolated in the hills with its unfinished cathedral and oddly shaped *campo*—all "detestably Gothic" to early modern eyes—Siena had lost its political autonomy and its artistic voice to Florence in the sixteenth century. With the exception of some minor works by Vanvitelli and hometown son Paolo Posi, the modern era left Siena behind. But from this provincial backwater emerged a fervent Romantic genius: Agostino Fantastici. Fantastici went to Rome where he filled his sketchbook with images drawn from Piranesi's plates and from the Villa Borghese. After the excitement in Napoleonic Rome died down, Fantastici returned to his native region to rebuild the cathedral of Montalcino. Its high altar is remarkably similar to Piranesi's heterogeneous syntheses. He modernized the palace interiors of Sienese noblemen and designed the fittings for the shops and caffès of its bourgeoisie.

Fantastici's most complete expression was the Villa "Il Pavone" for Mario Bianchi Bandinelli. Mario's father, Giulio, was the Napoleonic *maire* of the city, and his palace, refurbished in 1802, was the mirror of cosmopolitan aspiration. When Giulio died in 1824, an era of pomp died with him and his son retreated to introspective moodiness at his suburban villa. Taken together, the Bandinellis express the shift from Napoleonic neoclassicism to Restoration Romanticism—the former official, public, and confident, the latter intimate, private, and exploratory.

Fantastici was commissioned in 1825 to rebuild the villa and gardens. A doleful pyramid faces the entrance gates. Inside, a sequence of atmospheric, tree-filled spaces lead to a melancholic pond and an Etruscan-like tomb. The villa rises in the sun above, a shining rational beacon over the shadowy hermit's retreat below. The scene was illustrated by the villa's decorative painter, Alessandro Maffei, complete with a romantic figure lost in the pages of a Gothic novel. Visitors to "Il Pavone" were led through the experience of "the most varied scenes and of the greatest magical and picturesque effect nature can provide," according to Fantastici, In his *Vocabolario*, or dictionary of architectural terms, Fantastici also explained that points of view were to be carefully planned "from which a building should create its true and best appearance."

The rebuilt villa structure is characterized by its pure volumes, a composition of simple forms that, Fantastici suggests, "could be best appreciated by moonlight." Inside, Fantastici's furnishing and Maffei's wall paintings referenced Hadrian's Villa. Egyptian allusions here and in the garden may owe something to the patron's freemasonry practices, but things remain enigmatic in Fantastici's charged poetic atmosphere of color, shadow, and suggestion. Although Fantastici had few followers of his inimitable poetry, he helped, like Piranesi before him, to reinvigorate hopes of productivity in the arts.

Elsewhere in Tuscany, Romantic sensibility was focused on public and patriotic aims. At the Villa Puccini (no relation to the later composer) outside Pistoia, built from 1824 to 1844, dozens of little constructions were arranged across several acres of land, including: a ruined Temple of Pythagoras, a medieval tower, a hermitage, a rustic hut, a caffè, and a "Teatro Napoleonico." There were monuments to Dante and Tasso, Vico, Linneaus, Gutenberg, Galileo, Machiavelli, Michelangelo, Raphael, the Madonna, Canova, Columbus, and Cleopatra. Lording over it all was a "Pantheon" with a roof terrace from which twenty-six sites throughout this theme park could be admired.

Niccolò Puccini, with the assistance of friends and architects, was responsible for the garden's creation. Luigi de Cambray Digny and the garden designer Alessandro Gherardesca, a jack of all styles, discussed the project at dinner parties with a circle of Puccini's intellectual friends. Puccini got them all involved in his philanthropic effort to elevate the lower classes "who talked only of girls and card games." The guide to the gardens reads like a Gothic romance; each scene suggests virtuous achievements in civilization's march of progress, a great "school of mutual instruction." The undercurrent of Italian patriotism that courses through lyric opera pools here in Puccini's energetic philanthropy under the tolerant reign of the grand dukes of Lorraine.

Patriotic messages are reiterated in another Pistoia monument, a Pantheon to Illustrious Men. Conceived at the same time as Puccini's park, this city monument just within the walls at Piazza San Francesco faces an open space once used as the Foro Bonaparte. The somber temple was finished up in 1826 to the designs left by Cosimo Rossi-Melocchi. The plasticity of Rossi-Melocchi's interpretation of traditional classical form recalls the liberties explored by Niccolini in Naples with Doric columns of exaggerated entasis. What was once the gathering place of the marginalized poor in Franciscan care, then for citizens drilled in Napoleonic consensus, is now a Romantic corner of meditation on national glories as yet unfulfilled.

Tuscany under the restored grand dukes of Lorrain enjoyed a considerable cultural efflorescence. When Ferdinando III was restored, he set about planning improvements to his grand duchy. Pasquale Poccianti typified the well-trained Florentine professional with his systematic knowledge of architecture and engineering issues. As head architect of the Lorraine, Poccianti continued works in the Palazzo Pitti with a new main vestibule, a reorganization of the piazza, apartments on the second floor, and a new grand staircase. The grand dukes of Lorraine, successors to the Medici, also continued work at the Church of San Lorenzo, asking Poccianti for a facade design that might conclude Brunelleschi's unfinished exterior, plus a funerary chapel of their own and an expansion of the famous library in the cloister. Only the last project, a Pantheonic rotunda, was realized,

Poccianti was also Tuscany's prime engineer, and it was in this complementary role that he was sent to Livorno to design that port city's aqueduct and cisterns. Representative of the endeavor is the monumental "Cisternone." Rising above a severe portico of Tuscan columns an enormous half-dome structure open to the front holds back in its coffered concavity the mass of the water tanks behind. The large scale, austere forms, fine stone, and impeccable execution are entirely unexpected qualities for a work of such pure utility. The Pantheon's dome is nowhere else so closely reproduced, but here vivisected like an abstract representation of the paradigm. The half dome recalls ancient fallen vaults, the Serapeum at Hadrian's Villa, Palladian drawings of ancient baths, and motifs developed by Ledoux,

12 Agostino Fantastici, Villa Il Pavone, Siena, 1825–35. Watercolor by Alessandro Maffei, 1841
13 Cosimo Rossi-Melocchi, Pantheon degli Uomini illustri, Pistoia, 1826
14 Pasquale Poccianti, "Il Cisternone," Livorno, 1827–42

all of which may have been suggested to Poccianti. The dome space is apparently inaccessible and functionless, and can be read only as a symbol, an absence, a poignant inverse to the volume of water behind. Poccianti's formal language, like Barabino's in Genoa, is rigorous to the point of abstraction. Unlike his Florentine architecture, Poccianti's Livorno engineering explored a formal poetic language beyond the confines of former neoclassical doctrine and opened, even for engineering work, dynamic new possibilities of imagery.

ALESSANDRO ANTONELLI

Alessandro Antonelli explored the intersection of architecture and engineering. As Turin's top student, he won the university's first Rome Prize in 1826. He gravitated to the lectures on applied geometry and construction at Rome's new engineering faculty. Antonelli's Roman credentials did not after all help much in the workaday atmosphere of Piemontese building, where he at first made only modest inroads. Among minor provincial church restorations, he distinguished himself in Turin with a series of apartment block constructions for developers in the area of Piazza Vittorio Emanuele I. At a time of sluggish and small-scale building, Antonelli wisely lent his ordered and rational manner to this modest bourgeois building type. Among his most popular was the *Casa delle colonne* of 1853, with its Doric trabeation and clear internal planning. A skeletal system permits an infinite extension of the composition and a variety of interior divisions for the various classes within. For the developer, Antonelli's equations were clear: maximum return on the plot with minimal outlay of material.

Antonelli was able to explore issues of construction and style more deeply while completing the Church of San Gaudenzio in Novara. The sixteenth-century structure had remained without its intended crossing dome until Antonelli was commissioned in 1840 to erect one. After a year of studying the pre-existing parts, Antonelli

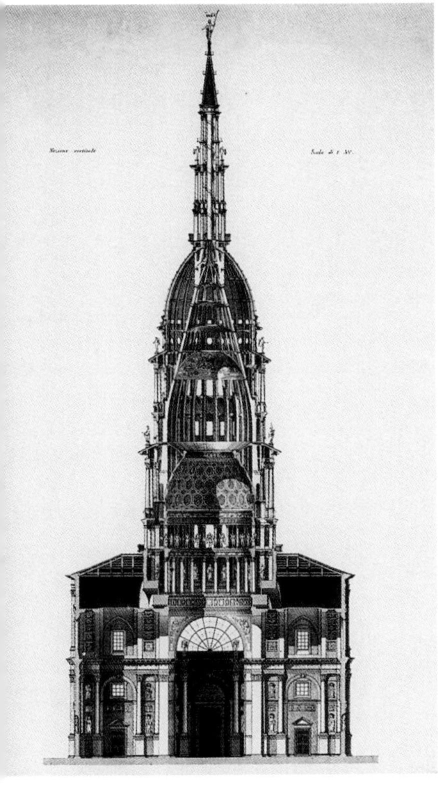

3.15 Alessandro Antonelli, Casa Ponzio Vaglia or "Casa delle colonne," Turin, 1853
3.16 Alessandro Antonelli, San Gaudenzio, Novara, 1841–78

presented a project for a tall structure formed of three nested domes, the inner coffered with a wide oculus giving up to a second inverted parabolic cone with its inner face frescoed. The third, classically styled outer drum and hemisphere rose to a height of 42 meters. Construction was begun in 1844, but like many of Antonelli's public commissions, it was often set back by financial and bureaucratic problems.

Antonelli's stacked dome construction relied upon examples built by Wren in London and Soufflot in Paris, as well as research on ancient and Renaissance domes in recent technical literature, so he was confident after one of the construction hiatuses to propose, in 1860, adding a little more height to the construction. The new stacked double drum would reach a height of 80 meters. Doubts grew on the stability of such an attenuated structure, but the project had garnered so much popular support that the commissioners let themselves be convinced by Antonelli's impassioned vision. After numerous successive elaborations and refinements, the structure's lantern, finished in 1878, rose 125 meters above the pavement.

One of Antonelli's interim reports explained this "tubular" construction system with allusions to vegetal stems. Rigidity and lightness were guaranteed by the series of five perforated parabolic cones that stiffen the walls like the structure of a bamboo shoot. The structural walls could then be reduced to the thickness of a single brick. The towering composition whirls upward with an effect that feels decidedly Gothic. Soufflot was already famous for having fused classical formal repose and Gothic structural lightness in his Sainte Geneviève, known in Antonelli's time as the *Panthéon* of Paris. According to his contemporaries, Antonelli achieved the same synthesis, "taking away from Classical architecture its usual gravity to give it the ease of that architecture commonly known as Gothic."

Far from an eclectic, Antonelli synthesized traditions that many take as irremediably dichotomous; his understanding of Gothic and classical was not a division of disparate styles but a continuity of related structural possibilities. Antonelli did not make explicit mathematical calculations. He worked in a fluid manner, keeping his projects in continual modification while he rethought the design possibilities. Each stage of construction was in complete equilibrium, and therefore could change direction with the architect's intuition. At every successive phase Antonelli stretched the design process, defied convention, and dismantled the old-fashioned idea of stylistic coherence.

Antonelli's career was characterized by continual exploration in projects that evolved slowly over decades, often pushing the mundane to monumental heights. In 1862, he received the commission for a synagogue in Turin whose program called for classrooms, offices, and apartments in addition to the large meeting hall, all on a small lot on a side street behind Piazza Vittorio Emanuele I. The Jewish community in Turin, five thousand strong, expressed the desire that their first temple might also be their "perennial and eternal reminder of gratitude" to the liberal society that had emancipated them. The architectural expression of synagogues had up to that time in Italy remained indeterminate, taking form in a passive manner through pressures of dominant tastes, economic constraints, and the realities of the religious politics of Catholic states. Now open to exploration, Antonelli excluded the option of an exotic style with a bogus iconography. To signify this religious institution's difference, he started with the functional disposition of the required spaces and structures to house them. His first project piled a few uniform levels and flexible modular floor areas on the lot with the meeting hall, as was the rule, on the top. In order that the hall might remain unencumbered, Antonelli envisioned a dome to cover the hall rising from the square plan in four curved planes. His square dome would have risen decorously into the skyline alongside other unusual domes in Turin, like Guarini's over the Chapel of the Holy Shroud six blocks away.

Contemporaneous with the exploratory extensions of the San Gaudenzio project, Antonelli began at the synagogue to follow his intuition, remaining always one step ahead of his masons. He elaborated upon the tubular concept here in a wall system that resembles a mesh of cell membranes. The structural elements are trimmed to their barest essentials. He evolved a vault technology toward zero internal resistance, and this dome encloses a maximum amount of space with a minimum of material, surpassing

Michelangelo's Vatican dome eight times on a solid-to-void ratio. Traditional materials are used in the precise and frank construction of the lower floors. Iron is also used as at San Gaudenzio but it does not appear as an autonomous structural element. Antonelli was aware of the advances in iron technology; but he wanted to explore the potentials of traditional masonry, preferring it over rusting metal and rotting wood for reasons of durability that would pay back its higher costs, he said, in the long run.

But the money ran out nonetheless in 1869. It seemed to the congregation that commissioned him that Antonelli, quite unscrupulously, had outstretched the original program and budget to pursue his own ambitious agenda. He had doubled the dome to a monstrous height—construction was halted at 77 meters. They pondered the aesthetic impact and called in consultants to assess its stability. Antonelli tried in vain to win the rabbis over but they bailed out, selling the outlandish construction to the city in 1877. No one was sure what would be done with it, but it was shaping up as a most monumental pile, a *mole*, the Torinesi began to call it. By June 1878, the erstwhile synagogue was designated as Turin's National Monument and Museum of Italian Independence. At 77 meters and still rising, the Mole had a shot at being the tallest construction in the world, and Antonelli, who kept tabs on such feats, was brought back to continue climbing. He was eighty years old.

The dome was capped at a height of 81 meters with a lantern and finally a towering spire doubling the building's height again. At slightly over 163 meters, the Mole is indeed the tallest masonry construction in Europe. Super tall structures like the Eiffel Tower sprang up at world's fairs as exciting proof of industrial progress. The Mole is also a monument to a heroic vision, and like Eiffel's it was officially named after its architect. The Mole Antonelliana is the culmination of a continuous Italian tradition in construction and the ultimate expression of the age of Romanticism. Inside, the space overhead is so lofty and of such overwhelming volume that the rushing absence of scale makes the mind spasm. Antonelli has invested architecture with a sense of continual becoming, unpredictable in its outcomes. The Mole Antonelliana is a dynamic conception, a culmination of the

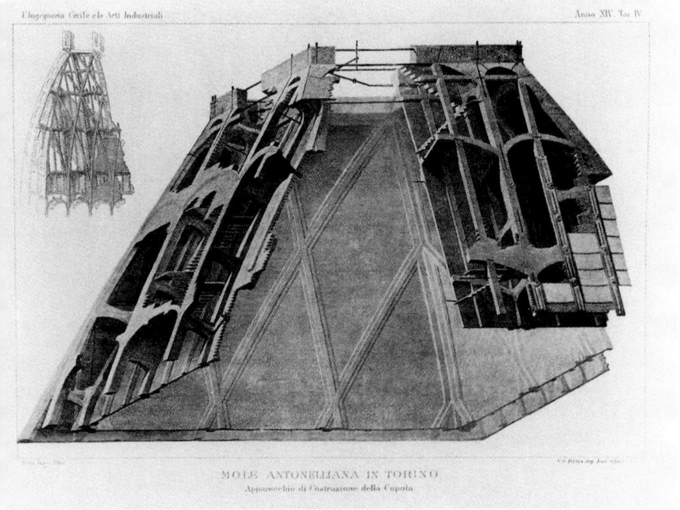

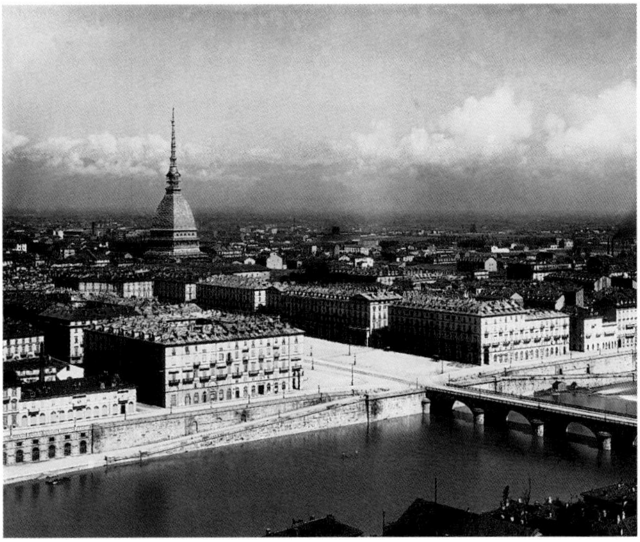

17–3.19 Alessandro Antonelli, Mole Antonelliana, Turin, 1862–1900. Axonometric drawing; photograph during •nstruction, 1877; view with Piazza Vittorio Emanuele I

exploratory characteristics of the nineteenth century and a fountainhead of the twentieth, never fully finished, never fully functional—just like the modern world of Antonelli's day.

CONSTRUCTION IN IRON

As Antonelli was extending the potential of masonry construction, iron was making inroads into Italian architecture. Indeed, iron had always been present, but in an ancillary and hidden role. Vanvitelli used it to reinforce Saint Peter's dome in 1743. Milizia, however, was opposed to the belts and latches, the rods and chains that were in common use to make, for example, stone lintels stretch further. Valadier had accepted iron for the fixtures in neoclassical design and also noted that for public works where economy, speed, and lightness were needed iron would be a great help. But the peninsula lagged behind England and France in the quantity and quality of its iron production. Italy's metallurgy was grounded in artisinal processes and remained an industry that varied by region, some with no iron production at all. While Italy continued to export its aesthetic expertise, its new material technology was of foreign supply. Antonelli's iron was imported from France but remained hidden behind his patriotic pursuit of masonry achievement. Iron took on a vaguely antipatriotic tinge. Iron construction was confined to new building types: railway stations, markets, and bridges.

In 1832, Italy's first iron suspension bridges were opened over the Garigliano River at Minturno north of Naples and, shortly thereafter, at the Calore River on the route south to Paestum. The rivers at Florence, Turin, and Rome were soon bridged quickly and easily with the new technology. The iron suspension links were in these cases hung from masonry pylons affecting more often than not Egyptian styling—papyrus columns or obelisks. The Neapolitan bridges were conceived by a local engineer, Luigi Giura, and made of locally produced material, but all the others were made on commission to French builders.

3.20 Carlo Reishammer, Church of San Leopoldo, Follonica, 1838

Naples also led in railway construction, opening Italy's first line in 1839 with service to Portici. Its two modest stations employed exposed iron in light canopies over the tracks. Milan's first train station—providing service to Monza—was designed in 1840 by Giovanni Milani. It was typical of early stations, a hybrid mixture of iron construction over the tracks framed by service buildings that were classically dressed in the style of Piermarini. Longer-ranging rail lines were a rarity on the peninsula, divided at it was into separate states. Austrian reluctance to concede links to its territory stalled the construction of a railway viaduct bridge across the shallow lagoon out to Venice until 1846 (it was also built by Giovanni Milani). Meanwhile, there was no use of new iron technology on the Adriadic coast, in the deep south, or on the islands.

Only Tuscany managed to establish a healthy iron industry, relying on a plant at Follonica that was conveniently situated halfway between its mineral supply (on the Isle of Elba) and its marketplace (Livorno). Grand Duke Leopoldo II provided support to reclaim the malarial swamps along Follonica's coast and to renew its traditional foundries with the latest furnace technology from England. Production expanded quickly under the direction of Florentine-born architect Carlo Reishammer. Reishammer's constructions in Follonica included a Palladian-style portal to the foundry, the Gothic filagree of the town's clock tower, and the Church of San Leopoldo of 1838. Onto the rather plain masonry box of San Leopoldo, Reishammer riveted a deep porch made entirely of iron components. Inside, all the liturgical fixtures are of iron, from the pulpit to the Stations of the Cross. Reishammer also built in Livorno. Its new toll gates of 1840 demonstrate the aesthetic possibilities of iron. Reishammer worked as an architectural designer for industrial material and he held together the roles of architect and engineer which over the arc of the nineteenth century were beginning to split into dichotomous specialized professions.

ARCHITECTURAL RESTORATION OF MONUMENTS

In the nineteenth century, the restoration of ancient monuments became a critical and creative act guided by the values that Romanticism vested in the historical past. Objects that time or vicissitudes had reduced could be reconstituted and recovered for contemporary cultural fruition. The Colosseum was the literal arena for early modern restoration theory and practice in Rome. Since the 1348 earthquake that toppled the southern portions of the Flavian amphitheater, the outer rings of the ancient structure had been gradually peeling away. In 1703, another collapse brought more arches to the ground and a renewed supply of authentic ancient travertine for new buildings. Benedict XIV put a stop to the material spoliation by recognizing the Colosseum as a site of Christian martyrdom.

Pius VII began digging out the structure and clearing the granaries built around it, but the ragged eastern edge threatened imminent collapse. Wooden trusses were thrown up until Pius could get his architect, Raffaele Stern, to begin work in 1806. A commission, headed by Carlo Fea, considered trimming off the damaged portion and reusing the old stones to prop up the remaining stable parts, but their consciences were disturbed by the idea of eliminating even fractured bits. They could screw the blocks back up with iron or dismantle and re-erect them with pins, but this proved too daunting. At half the cost and in half the time, Stern simply filled in the falling arches and erected a supporting brick-and-mortar buttress that halted the structure's movement. "The buttress executed in the present circumstances," wrote Stern, "brings us as close as possible to our great forefathers." The purely functional brick buttress was "the only modern work that can stand up to comparison to ancient construction."

Attention turned to other teetering ruins, like the nearby Arch of Titus, whose slipping keystone required intervention. The French had cleared away the buildings alongside the ancient arch, like those convents that crowded the Column of Trajan, but what little remained of the original construction required extra support. In

1817, Pius VII sent Stern to deal with the arch. Stern dismantled it block by block and ordered new travertine and iron pins with which to reset the few original white marble fragments. Pietro Bosio, Canova's details expert, was called upon to determine the nature of the missing forms for the travertine infill. Work was halted in December 1818 for financial reasons, and before they were cleared up and work resumed Stern was mysteriously murdered. The direction of the work passed to Valadier, who finished it in 1824.

Fea was outspoken in his support of this, Rome's first scientific restoration. "One will be also be able to see its true ancient form while distinguishing the ancient from the modern," Fea assured. Unlike the technique of "reintegration" of eighteenth-century practice, the nineteenth-century replacement parts for the Arch of Titus deliberately lack the touches of individual artistic virtuosity that Piranesi or Cavaceppi would have added. Valadier tells us in his publication of 1822 that this was an operation "to recompose the pieces as they had been soundly constructed originally, an operation that is called restoration, not building." In the early nineteenth century in Rome, restoration was codified as a scientific retrieval of a precise historical image disencumbered of accretions. This shift of restoration theory is exemplified by the second and radically different buttress added to the western edge of the Colosseum in 1822.

Once Valadier finished with the Arch of Titus, Pius VII sent him on to the Colosseum. Stern's earlier buttress was by then seen as "disagreeable to the eye," the regrettably dull result of a structural emergency and limited finances. So Valadier's western buttress features an open series of arches meticulously modeled upon the original first-century design. These are stacked up in a diminishing series against the damaged edge. Although constructed of brick, the bases, capitals, and cornices are made of travertine like the originals. When this part of the construction was finished in 1829, all the brickwork was stuccoed over. "We have faithfully imitated the ancient design and, having given it a patina all over imitating the antique, it seems entirely built of travertine." Pius VII himself said: "If each of our predecessors had added just a single arch to the Colosseum, by now it would have been returned to its original form." The idea of rebuilding the Colosseum soon became a reality. In the 1840s, Luigi

3.21 Raffaele Stern, eastern (distant) buttress of the Colosseum, Rome, 1804–6; Giuseppe Valadier, western buttress, 1822–29; Raffaele Stern, then Giuseppe Valadier, restoration of the Arch of Titus, 1818–24

Canina, who had written his dissertation on the amphitheater, began rebuilding the missing chunks of the inner rings on the south, to the point of replicating the ancient brick patterns.

The new theory of restoration was tested in the debate over the Church of San Paolo fuori le mura in Rome. On the night of 15 July 1823, a fire devastated the nave of the early Christian basilica. The Church of Saint Paul was, like Saint Peter's and Saint John's, originally built by Emperor Constantine; it was rebuilt in the fourth century and continually added to over the centuries. Now, seventeen of the nave's forty-two marble columns had fallen, bringing down with them a quarter of the church's fabled fresco cycle. The great apse and its mosaics were undamaged. When Pope Leo XII was elected later in the summer, he took the matter of San Paolo in hand, opening an international fund-raising campaign.

San Paolo had never sparked much interest among architects, though it remained important as a site of pilgrimage and veneration. For this reason, a popular reaction rose up "to conserve respectfully the traces of the magnificent layout," as Abbot Angelo Uggeri put it. This churchman was also a dilettante architect and academician at San Luca, and was the first to present a project for the church's reconstruction. He called for a rebuilding *in pristinum* with improvements by which some elements of the old fabric could be rebuilt with ideally classical features. Carlo Fea supported Uggeri's idea. Architects, including Valadier, however, saw the opportunity here for the kind of reconception of the site that had transformed, for example, Saint Peter's in the Renaissance. Valadier delivered a proposal that while preserving the untouched apse planned a new building within the sturdy walls of the transept—a renewal of the medieval building rather than a restoration. To repair the old structure, Valadier claimed, would have been needlessly expensive for a building of such "deprecated irregularities" from the "decadent period of architecture." If anyone were curious about the former structure, a scale model could be made and put in a museum. Here, it is important to distinguish, Valadier was not restoring a remnant from antiquity as at the Arch of Titus or the Colosseum, but giving a renewed imagery to a living institution.

In 1824 Leo XII decided to undertake the Valadier project, despite heated protest from the new specialists in restoration. Carlo Fea furiously denounced the radical changes Valadier planned. He evoked the public will that San Paolo should be put back as it was. "Forfend any innovations!" he railed. "Away the projects of ambitious architects and the academies! ... The fine arts are in the service of Religion, not vice versa." Thus the battlefield was marked out between the erudite archeologists and the innovative architects over the methodology of architectural restoration.

Leo XII set up a special commission to look into the commotion, and Abbot Uggeri, appointed as secretary, succeeded in overturning Valadier's directorship. Leo XII was brought about face to a reactionary position.

At San Paolo fuori le mura, for the first time in Italy, the theory of restoration honed for ancient ruins was applied to architecture in the broader sense. Valadier was dismissed and Pasquale Belli was brought in from the Vatican architectural staff to direct the works. Fea trumpeted victoriously that "in Rome the Archeologists are the premier masters." Under Belli's direction the nave walls were all pulled down saving mosaics but not the frescoes of later date. The first granite replacement columns for the magnificent plan of the nave arrived in 1831. But Belli was soon displaced by Luigi Poletti, an architect with broad vision who had trained under Antolini and Stern.

With his bold personality, Poletti managed to cut through the debilitating network of conflicting committees that had ruined Valadier. When necessary he appealed directly to the pope, by then Gregory XVI. The rebuilding of the basilica's original ground plan would include a magnificent forecourt, a baptistry, and a bell tower. Inside, Poletti rebuilt the columns and walls in their former locations and to their former proportions, but everything in a totally renewed manner, his biographer tells us, "to give a new San Paolo all the splendor of magnificence and of the perfection of construction of materials." Poletti rebuilt San Paolo as if its original builders had returned and, in their spirit, availed themselves of all the erudition compiled in the interim, revisiting the design and correcting its errors.

Poletti's San Paolo is an idealized image of its own past, an evocative simulacrum of itself. Its pure space and brilliant surfaces shine with surreal precision, transporting us to a storybook-perfect history. Whereas Valadier had quipped that scholars and the curious could be satisfied with a model as a record of the former structure, the Romantic generation that buried Valadier made the new building itself a didactic model. Saint Paul's reconstruction *com'era, dov'era*—as it was, where it was—significantly influenced the nature of architectural restoration in Italy for the next century.

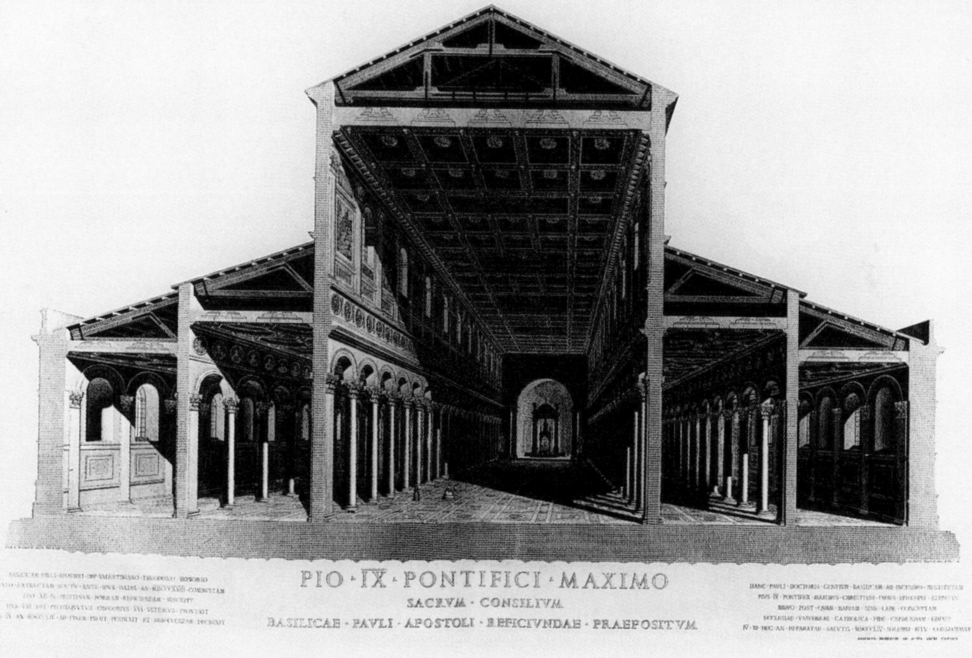

.22 Luigi Poletti, San Paolo fuori le mura, reconstruction, Rome, 1831–54. Engraving by Giuseppe Bianchi, 1854

REVIVALISM AND CAMILLO BOITO

In other European countries in the nineteenth century, the Gothic Revival was associated primarily with issues of architectural restoration and national imagery. This was not the case in Italy, where architects confronted Gothic architecture only in rare instances, such as the completion of the cathedral of Milan. Under construction continuously since the late Middle Ages, the Duomo still lacked a facade. Portals had been added in the late Renaissance not consonant with the building's original Gothic forms. The clash of styles only became more irksome to later generations.

Attention to civic imagery under Archduke Ferdinand's rule at the end of the eighteenth century encouraged many architects to propose solutions to the variegated facade, many of which tried to diminish the impact of the classical intrusions. In 1807 Napoleon sanctioned funds for the execution of Carlo Amati's project for the facade, which reshaped the buttresses and completed the finials in the Gothic style of the cathedral's flanks. Amati, the designer of San Carlo al Corso nearby and a committed classicist, admitted that when he was forced to study the Gothic structure he was moved by its intelligence. "Whoever takes the time to examine with an erudite eye any of these monuments will not forget the architectonic sensibility of their execution and the shrewd selection of material components. Our century cannot avoid confessing that it would not be capable of surpassing them." Until Alessandro Antonelli of Turin came along to take that challenge seriously, Gothic inspiration could only be found on the lyric opera stage and in picturesque gardens.

Jappelli, with his Pedrocchino, was not the first to revive Gothic styling. Amati had erected a turreted garden folly at Monza in 1815, and in Rome an Englishman, Charles Andrew Mills, had his villa on the Palatine Hill redecorated in 1818 with Gothic-style appliqués. Significantly, the few large-scale examples of Gothic Revival architecture in Italy are each associated with the post-Napoleonic political restoration. At Hautecombe, for example, in the French department of the Savoie, the ancestral seat of the Piemontese dynasty, King Carlo Felice restored the abbey that had been sacked in

3.23 Carlo Amati, Duomo facade, Milan, 1807–; with Giuseppe Piermarini, Palazzo Ducale, 1773, at right.

the revolution. Neither the patron nor his architect in charge, Ernesto Melano, had any previous inclination toward Gothic design, yet they opted to retain the historical style that would effectively elicit the memories of the dynastic shrine. In Rome, the convent chapel for the Sisters of the Sacred Heart was erected in Gothic Revival form in 1841. This neo-Catholic order of French nuns was founded to redress the antireligious wave of the revolution. They adapted often donated buildings for their use, so the order had no architectural style of its own. Pietro Holl, a Roman-born architect, designed for them the city's first Gothic Revival chapel that opposes dramatically the temporal imperialism of the classical idiom. A third example is found at Gaeta, the Bourbon coastal installation at the border to the papal states. Its thirteenth-century church, supposedly founded by Saint Francis but gutted during the French occupation in 1809, became the object of intense interest after Pope Pius IX had taken temporary exile there during the Republican uprising in Rome of 1848. Ferdinando IV ordered its complete restoration to memorialize the pope's stay and the harmony of Catholic nations. Giacomo Guarinelli, its architect, tells us that the monarch insisted on maintaining the distinctive character of the old church, of which there was little left. Guarinelli was given a travel grant to study Gothic sites for inspiration, but instead spent the money on illustrated books. From those he concocted a cross between King's College Chapel and Cologne Cathedral, meeting the requirement for an iconography that would demonstrate international support of the pope's restoration to power.

The idea of a Gothic revival took a powerful hold over more liberal northern regions of the peninsula. In Padua, Pietro Selvatico championed Italian medieval architecture as a national heritage with the same moral vehemence as Pugin and Viollet-le-Duc. Selvatico, like his mentor Jappelli, wanted to dismantle the classical hegemony and allow imaginations to roam among the variety of historical styles. He started with Gothic architecture that offered such variety. Selvatico built little yet exercised his influence as a historian, critic, and teacher at the Venetian academy from 1850. He found in Venice's pre-Renaissance architecture the traces of the various cultures that filtered through the city. He was eclectic in his approach, exercising the right Piranesi had granted architects to address without prejudice their cultural heritage for contemporary needs. Romanesque architecture, with its classical derivations and varied inflections, captivated Selvatico. Indigenous examples were scattered all across the peninsula, each recalling a former city-state's fierce independence or a medieval maritime republic's efflorescence. The prospect of a neo-Romanesque revival envisioned a future of vibrant architecture, the fruit of Italian genius unhampered by foreign influences, colonial oppression, or preconceived aesthetic notions. Selvatico made explicit the idea that this revival architecture could be enlisted in the definition of an Italian social identity.

Camillo Boito, Selvatico's top student and successor at the Venice academy, took up the neo-Romanesque cause. Camillo and his brother Arrigo lived in Milan where they both wrote, Camillo on the connections between medieval architecture and Italy's current political resurgence, Arrigo libretti for Verdi's operas. Picking up from Selvatico, Boito's elaborations of a neo-Romanesque extolled the style's elastic qualities and indigenous origins. Boito's research is exactly contemporaneous with the linguistic theory of Graziadio Ascoli at the university in Milan, who found in Dante's Florentine language an archetype for a standard national idiom. "We firmly believe," wrote Boito in 1865, "that one can take a certain Italian style from along the past centuries and modify it so as to render it fit to represent the inclination of our society, serving its necessities and demands without losing however its national and its artistic character."

Boito's candidate for the national archetype was the fourteenth-century Lombard Romanesque exemplified in Milan's minor churches, an architecture of "that grand century in which Dante wrote and Giotto painted." He brought the discussion of a national Italian architecture to concrete terms. Lombard Romanesque was ductile in its applicability, adaptable to the formal requirements of a variety of building types, especially the smaller, casual private house. Its constructive principles were demonstrably logical, using economical material like brick. It was functional and free of the usual imperialist rhetoric.

Boito's Lombard Romanesque was not a revival style. An archeological return to the fourteenth century would not, he warned, provide an architecture fit for modern needs. Instead, Boito proposed the rediscovery of the process of making style. A contemporary style would be born of the symbiotic relationship between the *parte organica*, the structure, the materials, the work's disposition according to function, and the *parte simbolica*, the aesthetic considerations of decoration. In order to create the humus for the regeneration of Italian modern architecture, it would be necessary to strike a synthesis of utility and beauty. "When architects begin to follow scrupulously the demands of the architectonic organism," Boito often repeated, "then they will have laid the fundamental basis of Italian architecture; they will have discovered in large part its new symbolism. The heart of the matter is in the organism." Boito concretized this theoretical principle in a highly successful practice.

At Gallerata, on Milan's inchoate industrial periphery, Boito designed a municipal cemetery in 1865 and a hospital in 1869. Their plans are drawn from utilitarian considerations of spatial disposition and their forms recall the essential qualities of Romanesque monastic cells. There is no styling, but a simplification from which a reasoned aesthetic expression of function and structure and an essential if bitter beauty have been extracted. In Padua, Boito designed an elementary school building in the same manner: a thoroughly functional distribution of spaces and a correspondingly robust vertical structure in brick and stone. Inaugurated in 1881, the schoolhouse earned Boito gold-medal recognition at the second national architectural exposition in Milan and the design was propagated as a paradigm of its type in special photographs ordered by the ministry of education.

Also in Padua, across the street from the Palazzo della Ragione, Boito erected his most important building, the Palazzo delle Debite. The local Paduan *Ornato* board, which included Selvatico,

3.24 Camillo Boito, Scuola Carrarese, Padua, 1883. Photograph by L. Borlinetto, 1883
3.25 Camillo Boito, Palazzo delle Debite, Padua, 1873

called for the rehabilitation of the city's former debtors prison. Not only did the key site need a face-lift, but as debt was no longer a criminal offence, the historical memory of the place needed revamping too. In 1872, a general competition was held from which Boito's designs gained favor for their good distribution and facades that harmonized well with the Ragione next door. Boito boosted the volume of the block with a high ground floor portico for shops, typical of Padua's commercial streets, and upper floors with richly articulated walls and windows for private habitation. The formal elements were drawn from Paduan medieval examples including details elaborated from the Palazzo della Ragione. The Palazzo delle Debite assumes a prominent role in the new bourgeois city.

Boito was an authority on a variety of artistic matters. He sat on important juries for public competitions. In the field of architectural restoration he was a definitive voice. After the exploratory events earlier in the century, Boito was the first to formulate a systematic theory of architectural restoration in Italy. The fourth national congress of Italian engineers and architects of 1883 approved Boito's charter, which sought to consolidate threatened structures by replacing key missing features even in new materials, maintain fidelity to the original design when documentation existed, and retain stratifications of evolved buildings even at the expense of stylistic homogeneity. Boito did allow for ideal reconstruction, as in the case of the Arch of Titus or Saint Paul's, for the restoration of monuments of particular cultural import. Boito's influence on the eve of Italian national unification was widespread, especially through his students at the Brera, who were constantly confronted with the idea of a regenerating starting point for a new Italian architecture.

Medieval revivalism offered architects freedom and flexibility from the constraints of the codified norms of classicism. The Gothic Revival provided the fodder for nurturing theories of a social art of aesthetics and ethics, architecture and religion. Each European nation that could claim a role in the Gothic style's evolution developed its own revival and supporting reasoning. In Italy of the

Romantic era, the relationship of the architecture of the present to the historical past was dramatically reconfigured, reaching back to an idealized medieval epoch to define architecture's symbolic role. In Italy, the role of architecture in this crucial period of national resurgence was strongly social and political. The experiments of Romanticism in the arts found full fruition in the service of the new state under King Vittorio Emanuele II.

4.1 "Vittoria! Vittoria!," triumphal march for piano. Cover illustration of musical composition by Stefano Galinelli with Luigi Cagnola, Arco delle Vittorie napoleoniche, renamed Arco della Pace, Milan, 1807–38. Lithograph published by Ricordi, Milan, 1860

Chapter 4

UNIFICATION AND THE NATION'S CAPITALS, 1860–1900

Italy, hitherto an agglomeration of fiefdoms united only in collective imagination, became an unexpected geopolitical reality in 1860. King Vittorio Emanuele II's troops battling against Austrian forces along the Lombard border in the north and Garibaldi's march with his thousand men across Bourbon Sicily in the south coalesced to form the nation. One by one, the populations of the peninsular states declared their adherence to the guiding Savoy monarchy of Piedmont, which offered the nascent state a mature governing system, its only indigenous royal line, and a monumental city, Turin, as a capital.

Main streets and central piazza everywhere across the new country were dedicated to the king and others renamed "del Plebiscito," "dell'Indipendenza," "dell'Unità." Governing seats, monuments, and museums were forged in styles designed to evoke historical memory. National identity was fostered through the manipulation of architecture and the configuration of urban space as didactic instruments in building a collective consciousness of recent events. Camillo Cavour, united Italy's first prime minister, declared Rome as the inevitable locus of national expression of all the peninsula's Italian-speaking peoples, but the city of Rome was at this first stage of unification not yet included. Pope Pius IX, with support from the French, held on to his temporal capital for another ten years. Meanwhile, the Veneto region was finally taken from Austrian control in 1866. The drama of nationhood spilled into the streets, making of the cities themselves the scenographic setting of newly won *Italianità*.

TURIN, THE FIRST CAPITAL

Turin, whose urban infrastructure was already advanced under Savoy rule, adapted well to its role as the first national capital. New residential zones were grafted onto the edges of the orthogonal city plan, erasing the memory of former fortifications. The regular lots were filled with large and profitable blocks like those being designed by Alessandro Antonelli. Spurred by its politically liberal culture and industrial strength, Turin's population grew significantly, necessitating by the 1840s a master plan to discipline the speculative building industry. This was provided by Carlo Promis, Piedmont's inspector of antiquities. Like his friend Pietro Selvatico, Promis found neoclassicism inadequate for the variety of architectural requirements demanded by an increasingly modern culture. With his publication of *Fabbriche moderne*, he offered a set of practical building types to fit the needs of Italy's new patrons: speculators, municipal administrators, industrialists.

Promis's own career was dedicated to the public weal. For the crucial 1851 expansion of Turin, he drafted an urban plan that revisioned the city as a bourgeois capital with broad, tree-lined streets. New legal instruments for expropriation were employed to align development and encourage homogeneity and completeness of the urban fabric. Avoiding a rigid grid, he threaded several earlier developments together by joining them along the axes of the historical city core. "Turin has transformed into a true nineteenth-century city," Promis wrote, "carried through by an equalness of its building stock . . . there are no palaces but neither are there shacks or hovels, but bourgeois dwellings everywhere." In his own words, the plan's strengths were in its "uniformity, alignment, and visible measure in the principal streets and squares." Promis's Turin displays a regularity of imagery entirely without pomp or presumption, in which individual monuments defer to a solid collective urbanity. This restrained urban design solidified a sense of public decorum at the moment of Turin's transition from regional to national capital.

The emphatic role the train station played in Promis's plan, placed as it was on the central Via Nuova axis, encouraged the reconception of the structure in 1861. The engineer Alessandro

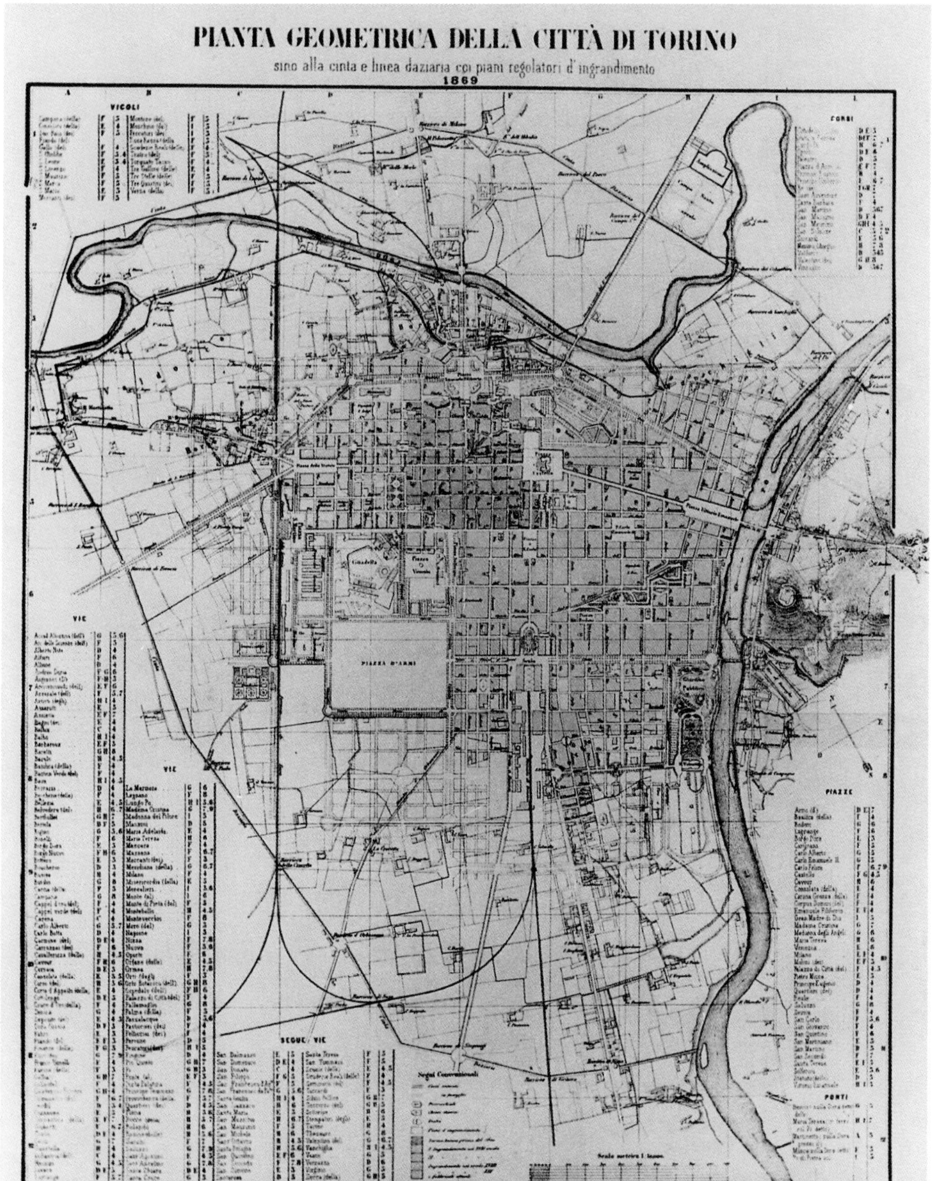

4.2 Carlo Promis, Turin city plan, 1869

4.3 Carlo Promis, Piazza Carlo Felice, Turin, 1848

4.4 Carlo Ceppi and Alessandro Mazzucchetti, Stazione Porta Nuova, Turin, 1861

Mazzucchetti, who designed all the stations along the Turin-Genoa line, collaborated with the architect Carlo Ceppi, who earned his degree under Promis. The new Stazione Porta Nuova terminus consists of two longitudinal buildings differentiated east and west by their complementary functions: ticketing and departure opposite arrival and baggage retrieval, with an impressive vaulted iron train shed between. The architects chose an eclectic combination of styles to, in Ceppi's words, "offer the greatest latitude for combinations and variations." Gothic design for the iron window tracery mingles among the classical stone arcades. The iron construction of the train shed, produced by an English manufacturing firm in Genoa, is expressed through to a transparent facade on the piazza "so that," Ceppi wrote, "the structure and internal distribution might be manifest to the eye of the observer of the external forms." As the new monumental entrance to Turin, the station and piazza are symbols of the capital's industrial and social progress.

Turin's status as the national capital was, however, short-lived. It was challenged in parliamentary debates by the idea of designating a more centrally located capital, one more historically resonant for the entire nation. French interests in maintaining the balance of European powers forced Vittorio Emanuele II into an international agreement not to threaten the pope's lands, so Rome was not an option. Milan was not central, Naples too vulnerable by sea, Venice not yet liberated. The onus fell to Florence, closer to the geographical center of the peninsula, prestigious in its cultural heritage, and sufficiently modernized under Lorraine rule to serve as an interim capital. At the news of Turin's demotion, rioting erupted among the city's real estate investors until the departing parliament promised to recompense the city's economy with government munitions contracts.

FLORENCE, THE INTERIM CAPITAL

No one believed Florence would long be needed as the national capital before Rome was taken. But nonetheless, Florence profited by upgrading its infrastructure. Florence was small but well run under Lorraine rule and Napoleon left no marks upon the city's fabric. During the Romantic era, however, in the spirit of redefining the rapport between present and past through building, a single significant project of urban reconfiguration had been undertaken, a project that exemplifies nineteenth-century Florentine urbanism. This grand project was the widening of the Via dei Calzaioli from the Piazza della Signoria to the Duomo through the heart of the city.

In 1841, Luigi de Cambray Digny, the grand-ducal architect who had been elected *gonfaloniere* (mayor), ordered the municipal *Ornato* board, the Ufficio d'Arte, to study the idea of broadening the street for reasons of improved traffic flow and heightened decorum of the city center. Expropriations shaved back nearly one hundred commercial addresses along three blocks to a uniform 10-meter width. Each property owner was responsible within six months for rebuilding his facade. Many are by Enrico Presenti, and all were reviewed by the Ufficio d'Arte to meet minimum height requirements, have acceptable window patterns, and demonstrate high-quality Renaissance-style decoration. The operation wiped away centuries of medieval stratification, and the upscale buildings quickly outpriced the street's former residents, who were supplanted by the rising bourgeois class. The result, seen in before-and-after views, demonstrates the willful creation of an ideal Renaissance city. Even the name of the street was enriched by the addition of a "u" to Calzaiuoli. Meanwhile, the historical patrimony of Florentine museums, palaces, and churches also underwent systematic restoration to render the city's architectural history a focus of civic pride.

Florence joined the nation by plebiscite in 1860 and dutifully dedicated a Piazza "dell'Indipendenza." More streets were widened and regularized, like the one from the train station to the Duomo, to provide commodious and decorous routes. Areas were lotted out for residential quarters, further clarifying the growing differentiation of classes and urban functions with a commercial center and residential

.5 and 4.6 Luigi de Cambray Digny and Enrico Presenti, Via dei Calzaiuoli widening, Florence, 1841–44. :omparative before and after lithographs by Ballagny da Simoncini

periphery. The planners on all these new projects were local architects, competent professionals descended in the school of Florentine professionals from Pasquale Poccianti. With the declaration of the moving of the capital, the Florentines feared that the stationing of the ten-thousand-person national bureaucracy in the city of only one hundred thousand might compromise its qualities, so Mayor Luigi Guglielmo de Cambray Digny, son of the architect, retained his father's *Ornato* experts to the exclusion of all non-Tuscan designers. In the words of Bettino Ricasoli, a Florentine in the national parliament, they would have hated "to see the city's *Toscanità* inundated by the ocean of *Italianità*."

To meet the deadline for the transfer of the capital, communal palaces and confiscated convents were adapted to the requirements of the arriving government. The Chamber of Deputies sat in the Palazzo Vecchio's Salone dei Cinquecento, the Senate in the Uffizi, the interior ministry in the Palazzo Medici-Riccardi, the defense ministry in the monastery of San Marco, and the royal court in the Palazzo Pitti. More ecclesiastical property, like the cloisters at Santa Croce, were requisitioned by parliamentary legislation. The demand on rental apartments drove prices up, brought about subdivision of large flats in more crowded quarters, and further aggravated the welfare of the lower class. Florentine noblemen, on the other hand, profited on their good names by offering for rent remodeled units in their palaces. Florence needed for the first time a comprehensive plan for its future growth, and an architect was chosen whose background intersected all aspects of the modern Florentine experience.

Giuseppe Poggi, born to a prominent family of professional jurists and son-in-law of Poccianti, garnered the trust of the Florentine aristocracy by renovating their historic palaces. He was successful for neither innovation nor overt creativity but for his impeccable taste, which appealed to patrician conservatives and the rising bourgeoisie that imitated them. Poggi's neo-Renaissance style, never hybrid or incorrect, guaranteed an understated and ideal *Toscanità*.

Poggi was assigned the task of working up Florence's first comprehensive master plan in 1864. Like Promis, Poggi had the unique opportunity to confirm collective notions of decorum and cultural identity for his native city. Florence's now constricted wall

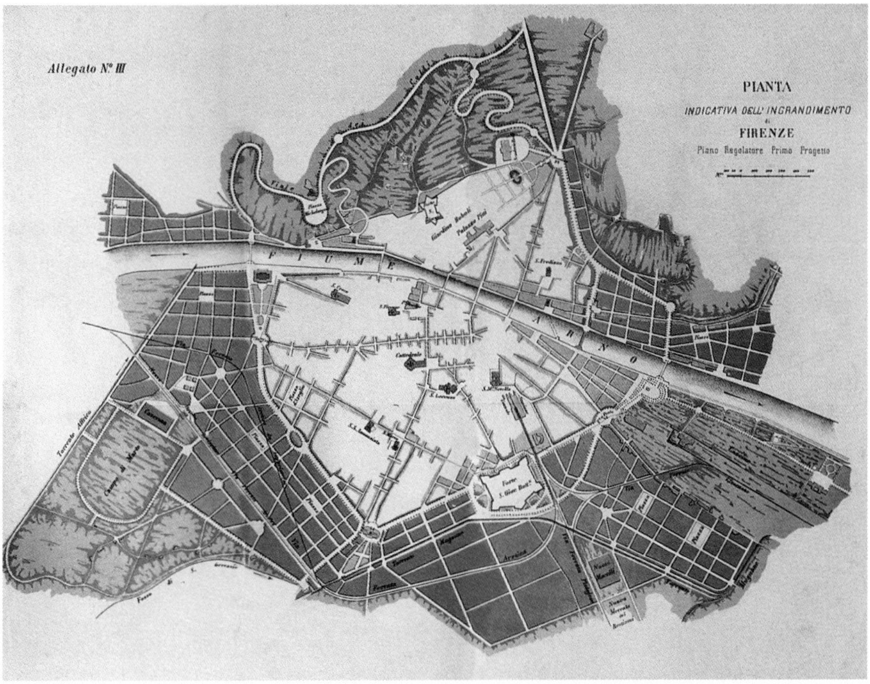

4.7 Giuseppe Poggi, Florence, master plan, 1865. From *Sui lavori per l'ingrandimento di Firenze, 1864–1877*, 1882
4.8 Giuseppe Poggi, Piazza Cesare Beccaria, Florence, 1865–. Drawing by Poggi and Nicola Sanesi

fortifications were demolished and a layout for controlled residential expansion was drawn up. Poggi's plan was approved in 1865, a few months before the scheduled arrival of the government from Turin. The path of the dismantled wall provided spaces for wide avenues, while most of the city gates were retained, isolated in the centers of new piazzas.

Poggi's piazzas were not like Haussmann's Parisian *rond points*, nor was his new circumferential boulevard, the Viale dei Colli, designated for any specific public function, like the Ringstrasse development of Vienna (two examples of which Poggi would have known). At Florence, the historic center remained the sole defining feature of the urban experience. Poggi introduced nothing new, he simply set a stylistic standard. Around the former Porta della Croce, for example, a group of identical concave facades were constructed to define the elliptical perimeter of a piazza.

Poggi's orthodox, classical language set an orderly tone, faultless if impassionate. Avenues were tied into a circuit across suspension bridges over the Arno and onto the hills of the left bank. The utility of the meandering Viale dei Colli was hotly debated, although it proved to be Poggi's most economical and successful intervention. Poggi claimed that the picturesque nature of the street "would be all that a romantic and rambling spirit could imagine," and its first visitors compared its bright and festive naturalness to the music of Rossini. Since the early Renaissance, Florentines had been climbing the hills to admire their city in *vedute*, and now Poggi programmed this experience in a novel contribution to the city's structure, connected with omnibus service from the train station. At its most dramatic moment, the street rises to a panoramic overlook near the church of San Miniato, with the entire city spread out for the eye in one sweeping vista. The self-referential nature of this viewing experience is accentuated by the dedication of the piazza overlook to Florence's revered native son, Michelangelo. A loggia was designed to display casts of his sculptures, as at Canova's shrine. A bronze *David* stands at the center of the piazza, a full-sized version of the souvenir simulacra sold to the tourists in stalls beneath it. As with so many other projects of the period, Poggi's shrine to Michelangelo demonstrated a collective cultural policy to make Florence more demonstrably Florentine.

The renewal of the old marketplace reiterated this idea. The area between the Via dei Calzaiuoli and Palazzo Strozzi around the Mercato Vecchio, once the Jewish ghetto, had been a concern of the Ufficio d'Arte since 1860. Not until the market could be moved to a new structure elsewhere could new planning begin. A commission sent in to study the sixteen city blocks found only misery and squalor. Noting concerns of hygiene and cultural prestige (fears of moral lassitude and political unrest were unspoken), the commission initiated a process it called *risanamento*, or curing, of the center. A dozen proposals for rebuilding the area were displayed in local shop windows, a perfectly suggestive frame for the bourgeois initiative. There was no discussion of restoration of the architecture. Most designs cleared away everything for new constructions and new configurations. In the end, only a handful of structures of artistic interest were saved, some shifted to new locations. In 1889, before the city had made any decisions, an equestrian monument of King Vittorio Emanuele II was placed at the center of the area. The final plan, by Mariano Falcini, called upon lingering memory of an ancient forum somewhere underneath his rectified street grid. The architecture, like that of the Via dei Calzaiuoli, was grand and confident in execution—keyed to the now national tenor of building in Italian cities.

Although the capital was soon transferred elsewhere, the remaking of Florence was nearly complete. Anchored in a cultural prestige it would never lose, Florence was nonetheless denied the economic base the presence of the government offered, and local building contractors went bankrupt in 1878. The bronze of Michelangelo's *David* and the equestrian statue of Emanuele II were symbolic gifts from the state to assure the city's economic rescue.

NAPLES *RISANATA*

National unification brought the promise of economic prosperity to most Italian cities. Naples's urban growth under the last Bourbons was guided by a *Consiglio edilizio*, or planning board, founded in 1839. Each of its six Neapolitan architects was responsible for a zone in the city. Antonio Niccolini planned to bore a traffic tunnel through Naples's steep hills to improve traffic flow to his theater, and Luigi Giura organized the area of the train station. "Spacanapoli," the city center, was left to its superb ancient Greek grid, but the labyrinthine medieval port area provided a daunting challenge to the planners. The wealthy had moved to new residential quarters strung along a serpentine route, the Corso Maria Teresa, along the coastal hills. Designed by Errico Alvino, the Corso, like Poggi's Viale dei Colli, offered a constantly changing panorama of city and bay.

In 1860, the Neapolitans joined united Italy, declaring their adhesion in the Bourbon Foro, which was promptly renamed the Piazza del Plebiscito. Naples was the nation's most populous city, but also its slowest growing, with a subsistence-level economy and a variety of social problems. Naples suffered its declassification from capital of a realm more deeply than any other annexed city. Garibaldi entered Naples in September 1860 and wasted no time formulating a scheme for the ailing city's recovery. Availing himself of the same technicians as the Bourbon council, Garibaldi decreed improvement plans for hygiene and commerce: there would be workers' housing in the hills, industrial expansion on the coast, crosstown arteries to better serve the port, and demolition of insalubrious quarters around the market.

The language of Garibaldi's decree made explicit the moral imperative and the geometrical means of his intervention. A straight line, a *rettifilo*, was to be drawn across the "underbelly" of the city, where over half its population lived in bestial conditions in huge flop houses (*fondaci*) and dark ground floor rooms (*bassi*). Reports to the Turin parliament linked the local hygienic predicament to social pathologies and promoted urban infrastructural instruments to rectify a potentially dangerous hotbed of political unrest.

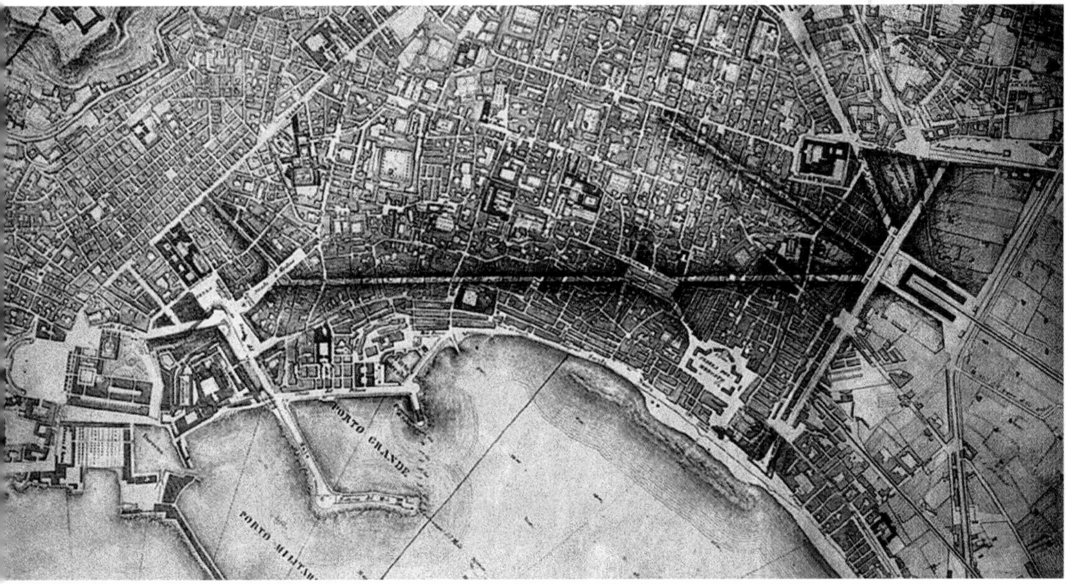

4.9 Errico Alvino, Il Rettifilo, urban renewal project, Naples, 1868
4.10 Il Rettifilo, Corso Umberto I, Naples. Photograph c. 1896

Projects proposed drastic linear solutions to the contorted situation. Alvino's *rettifilo* of 1868 was drawn from the train station to the symbolic center of the city near the Piazza del Plebiscito, cutting diagonally across the port area. The clarity of Alvino's proposal was typical of a nineteenth-century belief in the efficiency of clear urban solutions to social disorders. Alvino's Haussmannian slice—in Italian a *sventramento*, or gutting—met fierce criticism in Naples as a despotic marshaling of the populace into even more constricted and blighted quarters behind the rifle-straight facades of his grand avenue. Projects like Alvino's, however, floundered in a municipal administration tangled by rival interests and financial instability.

The plight of the abject city became a cause among writers and artists when a cholera epidemic swept the city in 1884. The head of the municipal engineering board, Adolfo Giambarba, secured government funds for an emergency plan through special legislation. The plan concentrated on the port and market areas. It would be the urban equivalent of a swampland reclamation, a *bonifica*, regularizing street levels of the sodden district and gutting the most dense zone with the diagonal slice Alvino planned. The cross streets that branch from the *rettifilo* were aimed at knocking out each of the infamous *fondaci*. Local contractors were so inexperienced on jobs of such magnitude, however, that their unrealistic construction bids were annulled and the city had to turn to a consortium of capitalists from the industrial north, who secured favorable terms for their loans.

The overblown architecture that lines the Via del Rettifilo concedes no thriftiness, however. These fulsome facades display an eclectic variety of mannerist decorations, all in stucco. At the Piazza Nicola Amore, the Rettifilo's midpoint, four bulky speculative apartment buildings by Pier Paolo Quaglia were erected. The highly self-conscious ostentation, a far cry from Alvino's reasoned neo-Renaissance designs, was the consortium's aesthetic sellout to an affluent market that might guarantee a return on its investment. There are no public buildings on the Rettifilo, with the exception of the rehabilitated Naples University building. In any other city, a major public building—a post office, museum, church, or city hall—would dominate. Instead, sixty-two churches and chapels were destroyed in the *sventramento* project, but even Benedetto Croce, philosopher and founder of Naples' preservation movement, was forced to admit:

> On these big and pompous buildings we have all said and will continue to say the worst from the artistic point of view. But, truly, who looks on them with eyes still offended by the former filth of dying Naples cannot hold to too subtle and refined an aesthetic taste. In these palazzi one had to recognize the execution machinery of a justice too long awaited.

In the end, the government-sponsored *risanamento* of Naples was manipulated into an instrument of private capitalist gain that only benefited a small portion of the citizens it was originally intended to help. Compounding problems, the glutted market of upscale apartments ate away at any profits, and further depressed the local economy. Indeed, the microeconomy of the back alley continues to characterize the Neapolitan experience. Programs of modern *risanamento* encouraged by the national government proved in the end to be both paternalistic and exploitative. Adding insult to injury, these failed interventions also allowed for the rise of systems of organized crime and corruption that still affect the political and commercial life of the city.

MILAN, THE INDUSTRIAL CAPITAL

In Milan, the idea of creating a space in front of the cathedral, a Piazza del Duomo, is as old as the Duomo itself. As it was, an irregular opening in the residential fabric extended obliquely from the cathedral's facade. Napoleon had charged Carlo Amati with the completion of the facade and the architect proposed surrounding the Gothic cathedral with a vast piazza of classical columns. Numerous projects followed. When, after the war for independence, the Milanese chose to place an equestrian statue of their newest liberator, King Vittorio Emanuele II, they were assured of a speedy realization

4.11 Giuseppe Mengoni, Galleria Vittorio Emanuele II, Milan, 1863–75

of the long-awaited project by force of a royal decree and a lottery to raise funds. There were no imperatives for a *risanamento* here, although the pretext of hygiene was expressed. In 1860, a preliminary design competition was held, called a *gara d'idee*, or collective brainstorming, in which 160 ideas were sent in and exhibited at the Brera. From these, the guiding committee formulated their criteria for a proper competition: a rectangular symmetrical piazza lined with porticoes, the gutting of the blocks to the north, the tracing of a new street to form a direct connection between the Duomo and La Scala, and the covering of that street. Eighteen proposals were received, including one from Camillo Boito, but the competition was won by a young architect from Bologna, Giuseppe Mengoni.

Mengoni, who studied scenography at the Bologna academy and traveled extensively across Europe, claimed to be an autodidact and fashioned himself as a Romantic genius. He was energetic, impulsive, fanatic about opera, virile, and mercurial. His Piazza del Duomo is a vast rectangular area, 120 meters across. The western area opposite the cathedral was to have been filled with a large block for city council chambers and administrative offices, the Palazzo dell'Indipendenza. The inventive style of the surrounding porticoes is typical of Mengoni and resists easy classification. In any case, his use of polychromatic stone smartly sets off the cathedral's whiteness.

Mengoni's masterpiece and the highlight of the Piazza del Duomo complex is the covered street, the Galleria Vittorio Emanuele II. Nearly 200 meters long, stretching from the Duomo to the Piazza della Scala under a transparent vault 30 meters high, the Galleria remains the largest such covered passage in all Europe. Mengoni, unlike Antonelli, was not a structural exhibitionist. The technology used here was common by the 1860s; the prefabricated iron elements were imported from the Parisian firm of Henry Joret. Behind the stucco facades of the ground floor commercial spaces, slim iron support columns can be found. The prodigious dome that rises from the octagonal intersection at the cross axis was a novelty in the composition of the galleria building type and is one of its most appealing aspects.

The Galleria was an immediate commercial success, thanks largely to its location between the theater and the cathedral and the

4.12 Emmanuele Rocco and Francesco Paolo Boubée, Galleria Umberto I, Naples, 1885–92

channeling of pedestrian traffic flow through the complex. License requests for eight hotels, five caffès, forty-two shops, a concert hall, public baths, and a pharmacy were received. The end result was a fluid space of encounter for the middle class, an augmentation of caffè society, a commercialization of theater life, and a secularization of the cathedral's neighborhood.

Mengoni also designed the new markets for Florence at San Lorenzo in 1874. The French-style, iron-and-glass-covered market hall is wrapped in a shell of gray rusticated stone, appropriately Florentine in style. Models of Mengoni's on-going projects were proudly displayed at the Vienna world's fair of 1873 and many Italian architects emulated his work. In 1855, a galleria was built directly across from the Teatro San Carlo in Naples by Emanuele Rocco and Francesco Paolo Boubée. The Galleria Umberto I closely followed Mengoni's model: it formed a direct pedestrian connection to a popular cultural institution (the opera house) and channeled traffic from an important city center (the Piazza del Plebiscito). Here too was an exuberant display of iron and glass technology capped by a lofty dome.

Although the two gallerias were speculative capitalist instruments, their dedications to royalty charged them with collective imagination. The general public was involved through lottery subscription, and its practical concerns and tastes were anticipated and served. Together, they managed to create a thoroughly cogent representation of contemporary Italian society (unlike Antonelli's folly in Turin). If Piranesi accused the patronage system of his day of lagging behind the genius of Italy's architects, by the mid-nineteenth century, the tables had turned: Mengoni and his followers were of the architects prepared to respond to the material and economic reality of Italian unity.

Milan's building industry flourished in the absence of any enforceable regulatory measures (or figures prepared to enforce them). This came to an end when developers' sights fell on the Piazza d'Armi, the former Foro Bonaparte, and the adjacent Castello Sforzesco. This rapaciousness spurred and was then thwarted by national preservation legislation. The area was saved as a public park, and the castle underwent an extensive restoration project by Luca Beltrami.

Further development was pushed out of the city core, as specified by an 1885 master plan drawn up by municipal engineer Cesare Beruto. Giovanni Battista Pirelli, an engineer who imagined an electric mass transportation system for the growing city, consulted on the project. The swath of Milan's peripheral expansion was rationalized in a concentric pattern expanding in all directions like the growth rings of a tree. Radial routes connected the periphery to the center. A *rettifilo*, dedicated to Dante, was lined with the opulent capitalist palaces of commercial culture.

Milan distinguished itself as a leading city of the new nation by its industrial strength. In 1881, it hosted the first national industrial exhibition, held in the Piazza d'Armi, which featured the Pirelli tire company (it was founded in 1872). A general electric company was created in 1883, followed by the Italian national commercial bank and the Breda metalworks. The opening of the San Gottardo tunnel in 1882 made Milan the most important Italian rail link to north-central Europe. But industry did not present a particularly attractive face, and despite Mengoni's rare success at giving it one, most cities in Italy looked to their cathedral facades to establish their identities, and a surprising number were still incomplete.

CATHEDRAL FACADES AND TOWN HALLS

After five hundred years, the cathedral of Florence, Santa Maria del Fiore, still had no facade. In the early fourteenth century, Arnolfo da Cambio, the Duomo's original architect, had evidently designed one encrusted with medieval statuary, but by the time Filippo Brunelleschi finished the great dome, tastes had changed. Arnolfo's incomplete work was dismantled and generations of aspirant designers fashioned wooden models to take its place. None proved fully satisfactory, and eventually, in 1688, the blank 65-meter-high surface was stuccoed over and painted up with Corinthian pilasters that faded only too slowly for the Florentines irked by its incongruity. The desire to complete the facade properly stimulated the first serious publications on Tuscan medieval architecture.

4.13 Santa Maria del Fiore, Florence. Photograph c. 1865

Giovanni Battista Silvestri, a young Sienese student who had assisted on such publications, pondered Arnolfo's lost composition and drew up a Gothic Revival design in 1822. Exuberant in detail, Silvestri's unbuilt proposal was the first to derive its form from the original pointed-arch nave construction behind it, and in doing so set a trend.

Florence's Santa Croce also lacked a facade, and in 1856 a design by Niccolò Matas was chosen to rectify this situation. Its three flat, triangular gables, or cuspids, were modeled on fourteenth-century examples from Orvieto and Siena. Gaetano Baccani constructed a new campanile in 1847 that fits easily in the historical skyline.

The Duomo, however, proved, a more difficult task. The physical irregularities of wall structure underneath the stucco and a tantalizing variety of visual documents suggested, but did not reveal, the intentions of the original builder. Only in 1858 did civic and ecclesiastical powers, Tuscan Grand Duke Ferdinando and Archbishop Giovacchino Limberti, join forces in a fund-rasing campaign for the job. The archbishop then arranged for a competition program to be drawn up by Baccani, head architect of the cathedral building commission, with the assistance of Emilio de Fabris, the grand duke's architecture advisor.

The events of national unification reinforced their efforts and under royal Savoy patronage a symbolic cornerstone was laid on 22 April 1860. Completion of this monument from the heyday of the city-state in the new era of national unity would provide a potent symbol for the new regime. Brunelleschi's cupola had always been a symbol of particular pride in Tuscany, and now the political shadow of the Duomo would be extended across all Italy. "To the former municipal aspirations, we now join the national idea," declared the initiative's spokesmen, "this sacred monument will represent two memorable epochs of our history: Italy of the communes and Italy of national unity."

Forty-two design proposals were submitted to the competition, which was open to all Europeans, and these were then exhibited to the public without the names or origins of their authors in 1863. A jury reflecting the national import of the project was assembled, including Boito from Milan (at twenty-seven, the youngest juror), Alvino from Naples, and Antonelli from Turin. (The pope declined to send a representative from Rome.) With Baccani as president, the jury found none of the entries satisfactory. Many projects lifted design ideas from other roughly comparable cathedrals, some had exotic northern European motifs, some had classical touches with a bewildering array of crowning elements. Only three, noncommittal prize awards were distributed, one each to Carlo Ceppi (designer of the Turin train station), Mariano Falcini (the Florentine), and Vilhelm Valdemar Petersen (a Dane).

The competition was therefore reopened in a second invitational round of ten "celebrated architects" that included six of the seven former jury members. When Ceppi refused to participate, de Fabris was invited. With so many jurors now contestants, a new panel needed to be formed, though the idea of their jurying their own projects did occur to them. The aged Pietro Selvatico was put in charge, but everyone he invited to the jury declined: Poggi, Promis, Mengoni, Resasco, and, setting sights higher, Viollet-le-Duc. He had to settle for a motley crew and at the last moment his eyesight failed him and Massimo d'Azeglio, the Florentine political representative in the national government, was pressured into presiding over the jury.

The public exhibition of the second competition entries opened in 1864. Antonelli proposed a characteristically bold articulation of the interior structure, with a gigantic vaulted portico extending off the facade. Petersen altered earlier peaked gables for a flat top. The exhibition became the locus of a litigious free-for-all of opinionated Florentines—like Guelfs versus Ghibellines, Alvino complained. Antonelli's project was dismissed with a sure epithet: "American." It was not easy for the jury to operate with any serenity, but they proceeded, oblivious to guiding principles that could have been gleaned from the previouis competition experience. After a few weeks' discussion, in January 1865, they chose de Fabris's design. According to the architect, its three tall gables were a characteristic feature of fourteenth-century churches, and their triangular planes consonant with the vault structures of the interior.

No one was convinced, least of all d'Azeglio, the jury president. Polemical bile continued to spill, while the lack of a conclusion jeopardized Florence's reputation on the eve of the transfer of the government. Finally, Viollet-le-Duc was secured as an expert

4.14 Santa Maria del Fiore, Florence, facade mock-up trials. Doctored photograph, 6 December 1883

consultant, and it was hoped his opinion would be definitive. Treading his characteristically subtle line between archeology and invention, the famous French theorist stated that they needed to imagine what *new* thing Arnolfo would have created. Everyone went back to the drawing boards for a third, exasperating competition. Selvatico, who had undergone successful cataract surgery, returned in person to guarantee an outcome. Viollet-le-Duc declined the invitation to join the official jury, but they managed to secure the involvement of the German architectural theorist Gottfried Semper. The same indefatigable architects were back: Petersen, Falcini, Mattas, Baccani, Alvino, Antonelli, Boito, and de Fabris. After the briefest public exhibition of their projects in 1867, the jury chose de Fabris again by the slightest of margins. Suspect irregularities, a three-month delay in the publication of the jury deliberations, and a premature notification to de Fabris that he had won, caused a shakedown and further delay.

Emilio de Fabris had studied off and on with Baccani in the 1820s, and traveled on scholarship between Rome and Venice, where he met Selvatico. Evidently, they maintained a long and fruitful friendship. When Baccani invited him to participate in the second competition, de Fabris's career was jump-started with an academic post and the commission to add new rooms at the Accademia to house Michelangelo's *David* (moved there in 1883 for safekeeping, and thereby leaving another simulacrum outside in the Piazza della Signoria). Selvatico had been behind de Fabris all along, finding him a malleable man—not too creative, not too principled—perfectly suited for the cathedral's messy collective design process. De Fabris's designs were successful for his uncanny knack at synthesizing so many propositions into one or two ideal images of Santa Maria del Fiore.

Four piers articulate the three portals of the facade, the central rising to an elaborate tabernacle with a statue of the Madonna and a horizontal range of statue niches. Above the corbelled balustrade that belts the entire church, gables of tall equilateral triangles with mosaic decorations and delicate turrets were to rise like those of Matas's Santa Croce facade. The patterns of green, white, and pink marble were derived from the pre-existing exteriors and intensified with more sculptural figures and highly detailed carving. An enormous presentation drawing was made to reinvigorate public subscription, but it had the adverse effect of reigniting public debate. Aversion to the crowning gables grew so intense that the works were stopped. This would not have been the first time the cathedral's builders balked before public opinion. Michelangelo's comment that the loggia around the base of Brunelleschi's cupola looked like a cricket's cage was enough to halt that project altogether. De Fabris compromised by working up a flatter "basilican" roofline. Once construction reached the balustrade, they put up plaster mock-ups of both alternatives to decide which of the different hats they preferred, as the architect blithely put it. De Fabris did not live to hear the public response, but would have been happy in either case. Luigi del Moro, specially trained by de Fabris, completed the facade in 1887 introducing still more changes.

The powerful facade is thickly laden with figures and decorations and has a boldness that recalls Viollet-le-Duc's incitement. It also conforms remarkably well to eyewitness accounts of Arnolfo's original facade, "all of cut stone and sculpted figures." The iconographical program of 138 figures included illustrious men (Arnolfo, Brunelleschi, Giotto, Dante, Raphael, Michelangelo, Galileo), and emblems of the founders and modern promoters of the Duomo itself (King Vittorio Emanuele II, Grand Duke Ferdinando, and eventually Pope Pius IX as well), and private donors down to the latest Torlonias.

The official unveiling was on 12 May 1887, and came with hyperbolic acclaim—"Our art is returned to the glories of the golden age." But Boito bitingly denounced the work and contemporary architecture in general as "a grab bag of many rich and of many impoverished minds." Searing criticism has never abated, culminating in today's snobbish Florentine conviction that if American tourists like it, it must be worthless. The jury was never very clear about what it wanted, leaving the work open to the vagaries of wavering public opinion. The cathedral is a preeminent public building, but the public, although many times evoked and appealed to, did not have a defined role in the decision-making process. The outcome of the crowning-element alternative was decided by a commission, not by plebiscite. The eminently public

4.15 Emilio de Fabris, Santa Maria del Fiore facade, Florence, 1870–86

nature of the Florentine Duomo facade design venture, compounded by its preeminent historical significance for the city and the nation, had set contemporary Italian architecture to its greatest challenge yet in establishing patterns of public architectural symbols.

The completion of unadorned cathedral facades became a priority for all Italian cities as each sought to clarify its identity within the mosaic of Italian national culture. Standing as the benchmarks of native authenticity were the facades at Orvieto, which had been restored at the beginning of the century by Valadier, and Siena, which was not quite as authentic as may be supposed. In 1834 a committee for the conservation of Sienese monuments had undertaken long-needed repairs. Weathered elements were taken down and substituted with newly carved ones by Alessandro Manetti. Sometimes they were, according to Manetti, "improved." The gradual process of substitution and adjustment was intended to return the facade by degrees to its original splendor. In 1869, a museum was established around the corner to house all the original elements stripped from the entirely rebuilt facade. In fact, much of Siena had undergone a similar process of material substitution and image clarification. All the structures around the Campo had been restored, enlarged, or rebuilt in medieval styles that would recall the civic virtues of the once great Sienese republic.

In 1876, Errico Alvino designed a facade for the Neapolitan Duomo, making the stock references to Siena and Orvieto. The collapse of the cathedral facade at Amalfi, on Christmas eve 1861, presented that city with an opportunity to recapture some of its former glory. At the time, scholarly study of Amalfi's history, its *storia patria*, was being written in broad terms of grandeur and decline that emphasized the city's architecture. The eleventh-century church had been redecorated in the baroque era, and when it came down no one, at first, bemoaned its loss, and it was announced that it was "the public and unanimous will to reproduce the old and elegant byzantine style of this, one of the most respected churches of this southern province." So reconstructed, it would remind "the erudite viewer of the long ago days of the rich and powerful Republic of Amalfi when the arts, industry and commerce were in eminent splendor." Alvino was hired for the design; the city council

4.16 Errico Alvino, Duomo facade, Amalfi, 1871–91

particularly liked the way he "divined" an entirely new and original image from the former elements. His drawings, ready in 1871, were displayed to drum up subscriptions in the parish. The work lagged after Alvino's death, however, and the new facade was not inaugurated until 1891. Its pointed arches, busy polychrome incrustation, and neo-Byzantine mosaics have no real precedent in the region and constituted a new Amalfitano imagery.

Among the many Italian cities busy fabricating their identities, Bologna stands out. The city of Antolini's exile and Mengoni's humble origins remained a sad, squalid place until it joined Italy by plebiscite in 1860. By the 1880s, the population of Bologna had regained its medieval-era levels and a master plan was in order. The ensuing design called for the dismantling of fortification walls, wrapping residential areas around the city for expansion, and drawing new arteries into the city center. The Via dell'Indipendenza, a rod-straight avenue lined with continuous porticoes, would bring traffic into the center from a new train station. There, markets were cleared and civic buildings isolated. In 1886, a competition was held to develop a facade for San Petronio, Bologna's primary church. The results were so problematic that it remains a cliff of mute bricks to this day.

Meanwhile, Alfonso Rubbiani began restoring the medieval buildings in Bologna's historic center. Medieval monuments left incomplete were invitations to Rubbiani, "a dynamic inheritance" with which he could reconstitute a distinct historical memory for Bologna. He saw medieval works as "ideas left to posterity to develop further"; "just a few remains," he said, "are enough to provoke a hundred ideas." He founded the Comitato per Bologna Storica e Artistica and an artisan's cooperative, Aemelia Ars, modeled on William Morris's utopian Arts and Crafts Movement, and through these two organs set about restoring the city's most emblematic historic buildings, in particular those around Piazza Maggiore. Between 1905 and 1912, he removed additions, realigned bays, regularized window openings, and reworked decorative schemes and exterior details, adding crenelations everywhere. Rubbiani relied on photographs, many taken for him by Pietro Poppi, upon which he drafted freehand his projected restitutions. His detractors complained of his intuitive "divinations"—using the same term as the Amalfitani,

4.17 Alfonso Rubbiani, Via del Santo Stefano houses restoration project, Bologna, 1904. Ink drawing on a photograph by Pietro Poppi
4.18 Francesco Azzurri, Palazzo Pubblico, San Marino, 1884–94

but as an epithet—and for supplanting historical vision with an arbitrary Romantic scenography. Undeterred, Rubbiani constructed a mythic city stage on which the people of Bologna could reinvent themselves.

Every Italian city council sought to manifest its contribution to national culture. Many restored their medieval architecture to recall the spirit of the medieval communes. There may not be a single medieval *palazzo comunale*, or city hall, that was not treated to a thoroughgoing restoration, from Belluno's (in 1835, under Selvatico's influence) to Treviso's (by Boito in 1872). Venice's Palazzo Ducale, serving as its municipal seat, was restored in 1876. No example puts this cultural trend into sharper focus than the experience of the independent state of San Marino. With the nation of Italy rising all around it, the minuscule republic, self-governing for as long as anyone could remember, was a living relic of the much idolized distant past. In "restoring" its Palazzo Pubblico, the republican authorities, guided by Antonio Tonnini, embarked upon a self-conscious program of cultural construction beginning with the refashioning of their featureless city hall. Tonnini, an amateur painter, directed his chosen architect, Francesco Azzurri, to supply only rough sketches that looked very much like Verdi's opera sets. Local craftsmen were given considerable latitude to interpret these images in a kind of cooperative design process. The original building was eventually entirely dismantled in 1884 and every single nondescript stone was replaced with a new, medievalized one. Though people called it a "restoration," the reality was that it was a wholly concocted invention, a simulacrum of a medieval governing seat that never was. By the 1940s, the entire city center had been remedievalized according to the stylistic lead established by the Palazzo Pubblico. Today, the proud citizens of San Marino think it has been like this for as long as anyone can remember.

PALERMO AND NATIONAL UNIFICATION

In contrast to many other Italian cities, Palermo enjoyed direct connections to European culture and trade, thanks to its coastal position, along with a well-developed entrepreneurial class. Its 1848 revolutionary government was one of the few to leave an indelible mark upon its city during that brief republican interlude—the broad "Strada della Libertà," which extended beyond the city walls. (The restored Bourbons renamed the street.) When Garibaldi entered the city in May 1860, he established a commission to demolish fortification walls, plan traffic arteries, and build markets and workers' housing. Architect Giovanni Battista Filippo Basile was nominated as the head of the new municipal development board in 1863; he had followed Garibaldi across Sicily, studying the island's ancient architecture along the way. For King Vittorio Emanuele II's entry into Palermo, he designed a triumphal arch, a Trajanic column, and a patriotic altar. Basile helped develop a master plan for Palermo with a *rettifilo*, Via Roma, through the lower port area, but its implementation was delayed by corrupt city administrators with vested interests in an unregulated real estate boom.

What Palermo lacked was prominent public buildings. As if to fend off an inevitable provincialism, given its peripheral location within the new nation, the Palermo city council decided to erect the country's largest theater, the Teatro Massimo Vittorio Emanuele II. An international design competition was convened. Charles Garnier and Karl Friedrich Schinkel were invited to serve on the jury, but declined. In the end, the city fathers cajoled Gottfried Semper, who built the acclaimed Dresden Theater, Mariano Falcini of Florence, and local engineer Saverio Cavallari to serve on the three-person panel. Of the thirty-five entries, they chose one by Basile: "encouraging proof of an incredibly robust renewal of the arts," according to Semper. Basile synthesized the century's cumulative design experience with a grand columnar exterior that brings to mind Sicily's ancient temples. The ample distribution and structural articulation of its spaces confirm a diligent study of Garnier and Semper. Iron was used in the construction of the central dome. The theater's stark classical styling had, for the architect, declaredly

4.19 Giovanni Battista Filippo Basile, Teatro Massimo, Palermo, 1866–97

political overtones, its "eminently Italic" elements "appropriate in this epoch of Italian renewal." The theater was slow in construction and was finished after the architect's death in 1897.

On the same street, but at the other end of the cultural spectrum, a popular *Politeama*, or multifunctional playhouse, was built and dedicated, appropriately, to Garibaldi. Giuseppe Damiani Almeyda, engineer in the city administration, combined references to the Colosseum with a circus-like polychromy. He also used iron extensively throughout the structure.

THE LAST OF PAPAL ROME

Rome was left out of the first invigorating decade of Italian national unity. The Church was stripped of its territories, leaving Rome and its immediate environs as the dwindling base of papal temporal power. Giovanni Maria Mastai Ferretti, who had been elected pope in 1846, chose the name Pius IX in memory of his predecessors who too had struggled with reformation and revolution. Some hoped that he might lead the nation instead of a king, but this idea was dashed in the virulent anticlericalism of the 1848 republican revolt in Rome and Pius's exile to Gaeta. Once reinstated, he turned reactionary and consolidated his supranational Christian consensus with an increase of canonizations, ecclesiastical councils, and pilgrimage jubilees. Correspondingly, Pius erected monuments, restored churches, and made improvements to Rome's public services. The proclamation of the Immaculate Conception of the Virgin Mary was commemorated by the erection of a column in Piazza di Spagna designed by Luigi Poletti in 1856. The Porta San Pancrazio on the Janiculum Hill was restored (it had been damaged during the French siege of Republican Rome). The Porta Pia, left unfinished by Michelangelo, was completed by Virginio Vespignani with an exterior facade modeled after the Arch of Titus. Vespignani, who finished San Paolo fuori le mura, was involved in many of Pius IX's design programs. He restored many churches in Rome to an image of supposed original purity to recall a strength of the earliest Christian community.

A Commissione di Belle Arti of lay city administrators funded and supervised all restoration work in consultation with an ecclesiastical Commissione Pontificia di Archeologia Sacra. Funds that came directly from the pope and his commissioners went to projects of strategic evangelical purpose. Vespignani was commissioned in 1862 to restore San Lorenzo fuori le mura, a complex of two basilicas joined and reoriented in the thirteenth century. The recovery of its Constantinian levels, including the original narthex, was facilitated by the stripping away of all later accretions. Renaissance ceilings and baroque tombs were removed, and the interior decorations, as at San Paolo, were entirely renovated. San Lorenzo was not restored to an authentic original state but transformed into an ideal image of the venerated place. Pius was buried there, fashioning himself the last martyr alongside Lawrence, one of Rome's first, in a tomb brilliantly decorated by the Venetian mosaicist and architect Raffaele Cattaneo.

Interest in the Lateran's restoration was renewed at this time, but now with the idea to faithfully preserve what Constantinian elements still remained. Andrea Busiri-Vici's plan to enlarge the presbytery by moving the apse back with the help of steam engines received the approval of the Commissione di Archeologia Sacra in 1877. But upon Pius's death, Busiri-Vici lost control of the project to Vespignani, who opted instead to demolish and entirely rebuild the apse in his idealizing style.

Pius's urban works were designed to project a sense of well-being. Iron suspension bridges were built over the Tiber; one to the Vatican was met at the Piazza Pia with a pair of matching buildings that rehearsed the symmetrical effect of the Piazza del Popolo entry. Pius built the grand Manifattura dei Tabacchi near the hospice of San Michele in Trastevere, in which he consolidated and monopolized the city's cigarette production. The architect for the new factory, Antonio Sarti, a student of Raffael Stern, designed in a grand classical style that reminded contemporaries of Vanvitelli's Caserta. They called it the *Reggia del Fumo*. Andrea Busiri-Vici organized the piazza in front, Piazza Mastai, bordered with quarter-round workers' housing.

The pope's charitable works were designed with enough pomp to fend off criticisms, but the reality was that he had built just as many barracks as seminaries, as many prisons as hospitals. In 1862, his

4.20 Salvatore Bianchi, Stazione Termini, Rome, 1866–74

minister of war, Frédéric de Mérode, whose family back in Brussels were major real estate developers, installed the papal armed forces on the Esquiline Hill, where the ancient emporers had housed the Praetorian Guard. De Mérode also purchased tracts on the Esquiline slopes, where he laid out a simple grid of streets in 1866. The development of his "Via Nuova" extrapolated geometry from the Renaissance streets in the vicinity, connecting the Via Sistina to the Baths of Diocletian.

De Mérode's development also helped to link Rome's first train station to the city. Pius's predecessor had thought the railroad locomotive the work of the devil, but after 1846 the papal states were laced with lines to Naples, to Civitavecchia, and to Ancona—some over viaduct bridges made with the latest steel technology. The lines were brought together in one station on the Esquiline plateau, alongside the Baths or "Terme" of Diocletian, hence "Stazione Termini." Architect Salvatore Bianchi, created two large masonry blocks (one for departures, one for arrivals) with a broad iron shed in between. Archeological remains uncovered at the site were preserved. One of the city's largest covered spaces, the long nave of iron and glass was big enough—and the architecture grand enough—for Pius to joke during construction that it could serve all of united Italy. Then, on 9 September 1870, freshly reinvigorated by the recent Vatican council on papal infallibility, Pius IX came to the train station to inaugurate a fountain. It would be his last public appearance in the city.

ROME, THE CAPITAL OF UNITED ITALY

Just a few days later, on 20 September, Rome joined the Italian nation as troops forced a breach in the walls at Porta Pia and the *Risorgimento* burst in. The event was restaged the next day for photographers. The march to Rome completed the unification of the peninsula and this event, like the architectural projects that followed, fulfilled a task of national image-making. The rowdy damage inflicted on Pius's gate presaged the treatment of the city of Rome itself,

21 The Breach of the Porta Pia, Rome. Restaged by the photographer D'Alessandri, 21 September 1870

which was to be boisterously reconfigured as the nation's capital. As the *Risorgimento* was a political process based upon the evocation of the past glories of Italian culture, so Rome would be called upon to concretize in architectural and urban configurations the collective memory of the nation. As Massimo d'Azeglio had said when unification was first forged, "We have created Italy, we must now create Italians."

La Terza Roma is the political slogan that expressed the taking of the city of Rome from papal temporal control, as the popes had done from the pagans, and designating it the capital of the modern secular government, a third great civilization. To its latest claimants, Rome appeared untouched by modernity, still laden with the symbols of the Church and its hierarchies. Its architectural forms and urban spaces and the itineraries that lead through them demanded reformation. The topography of Rome became the ground for strategic political symbolism, with the country's representatives proudly establishing their governmental seat, erecting buildings for their administration, and monuments to celebrate their accomplishments, all the while fostering a real-estate expansion of unprecedented force.

Rome's new political leadership used the entire city to legitimize its authority, as seen in the many prints that placed King Vittorio Emanuele II in command of all Rome's architectural patrimony. With its traditions of civil government from its imperial days and universal spirituality from its Christian tradition, Rome provided an ideal foundation for a national capital. The functional, urbanistic, and architectural transformations of the city, however, were constantly measured against its gloried past. Francesco Crispi, a leftist minority leader, spelled out this problem:

> Our work is still incomplete until we have proven to foreigners . . . that we are no lesser than our forefathers. . . . Whoever enters the great city finds the synthesis of two great ages, one more marvelous than the other. The monuments that celebrate these ages are the pride of the world, they are for the Italians a sharp reminder of their duties. We also need to establish Rome and to erect our monuments to civilization so that our descendants might be able to say that we were great like our forefathers.

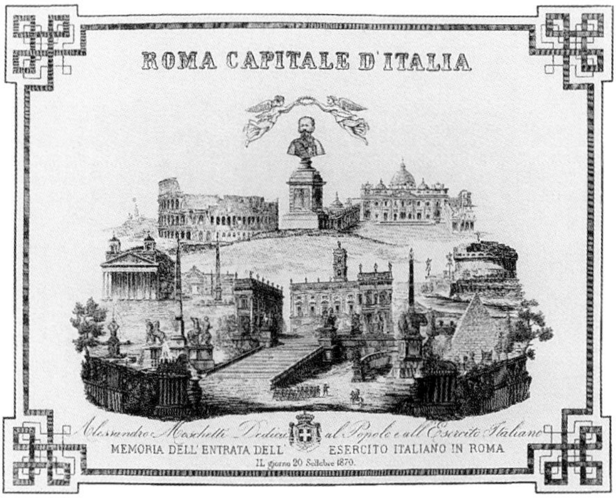

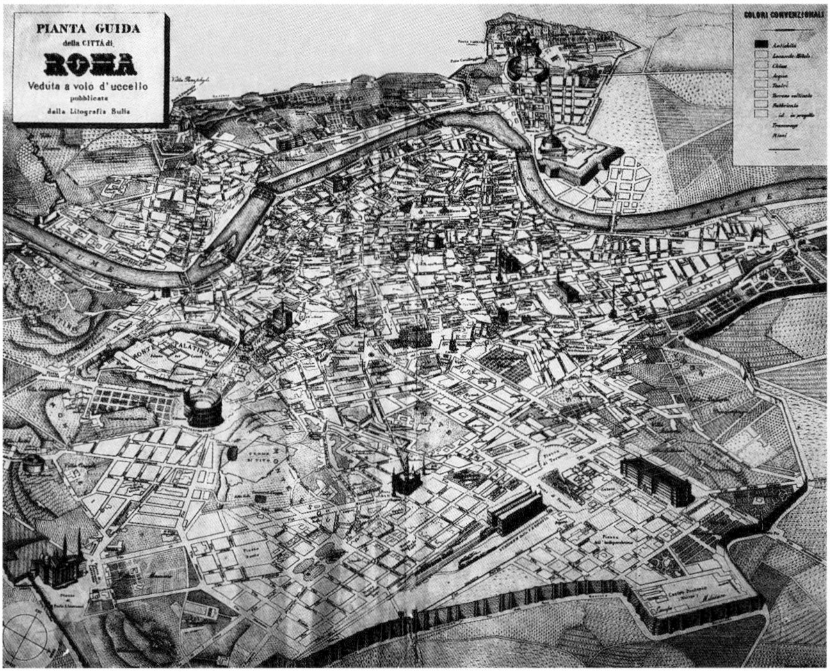

4.22 "Roma Capitale d'Italia, Memoria dell'entrata dell'esercito italiano a Roma," 1870. Engraving by Alessandro Moschetti
4.23 "Pianta Guida della Città di Roma, Veduta a volo d'uccello," Rome, 1884

Rome became the capital of Italy under a regime characterized by an acute historical consciousness.

The installation of the Italian government in Rome had an indelible effect upon the city. Buildings were demolished and quarters gutted, but these acts were never wanton. Only those structures that could be construed as symbols of papal military aspiration were considered for major alteration or elimination (the papal fortifications at the Castel Sant'Angelo around the Mausoleum of Hadrian, the fortified tower erected on the Capitoline by Pope Paul III, both strongholds connected to papal palaces). Contrary to exaggerated fears of anticlerical retaliation by the new government, the obliteration of ecclesiastical symbols would have been detrimental to the new administration; the nationalized, secular Rome derived its strength precisely from its proximity to the old images of the former great regimes, both imperial and papal. Primo Levi, an art critic and journalist at the time, advanced an idea of a new monument on the Capitoline Hill, writing: "Italian Rome needs to rise as a new personality, an unprecedented event, with its new institutions, with its original monuments, to demonstrate what the capital city of a grand people could be before the capital of two successive worlds." Rome was Italy's greatest asset politically and architecturally, and attitudes toward it expressed in acts of construction or demolition were shaped according to clear political goals.

In the first hours after the siege of Porta Pia, the military occupied key positions throughout the city including the Palazzo Montecitorio and Castel Sant'Angelo, until then the papal courthouse and political prisons. Meanwhile, the Roman populace, once assured of the success of the coup, gathered on the Capitoline to celebrate and declare their allegiance to the Italian nation. When Vittorio Emanuele II finally entered Rome by train, he took up residence overlooking the city in the Quirinal palace, just as Napoleon had planned.

These first acts of occupation were largely expedient but they had a lasting effect upon the city's modernization: Palazzo Montecitorio was adapted to the needs of the lower house of the legislature and Palazzo Quirinale became the permanent residence of the Italian head of state. Expropriations of ecclesiastical property were also an expedient means of housing the government ministries transferred from Florence. Some of the largest monastic complexes had already been adapted as office space by the former papal regime, and the national government used them accordingly: the Ministry of Finance in the Augustinian monastery of Santa Maria sopra Minerva, the public courts in Borromini's oratory at Chiesa Nuova. A commission of Roman architects was established to study long-term plans for the administrative offices, but their deliberations were not heeded. Meanwhile, private real estate developers backed by foreign banks bought up tracts around de Mérode's Via Nuova and the train station, and began building unhindered by preemptive planning or financial regulations of any kind. The local administration was unprepared to control the demographic and economic explosion that the arrival of the national governing bodies brought to the city; indeed, city councilors with vested interests colluded in delaying regulations on real estate speculation, and the shape of the city was left at first to these swifter forces.

The Esquiline plateau to the east of the historic city was the locus of the first real-estate development of modern Rome. With the Stazione Termini nearing completion (it was inaugurated in 1874), de Mérode sold his properties at 1,500 percent profit to other speculators who, striking deals with the new city planning commission, got the Via Nuova inserted into the earliest official urban planning schemes. It was then renamed, appropriately, "Via Nazionale." Straight and broad, evenly graded, tree-lined, and defined by rigorously boxy, large-scale volumes, this was the first boulevard of the new capital, an avenue to rank with the great thoroughfares of other European capitals. The pretentious stucco facades of its hotels and apartment houses, shops and offices are evidence of as much a leap in scale as a fall in quality of building in the late nineteenth century. As in Paris and Vienna, Naples and Turin, much of this second-rate architecture made first-rate urbanism. But unlike Paris or Vienna, the creation of Rome's first thoroughfare did not come at the expense of any earlier urban fabric. On the contrary, Via Nazionale and the other independent real estate developments across the city's eastern plateau were integrated into the pre-existing urban system first traced by Pope Sixtus V in the sixteenth century.

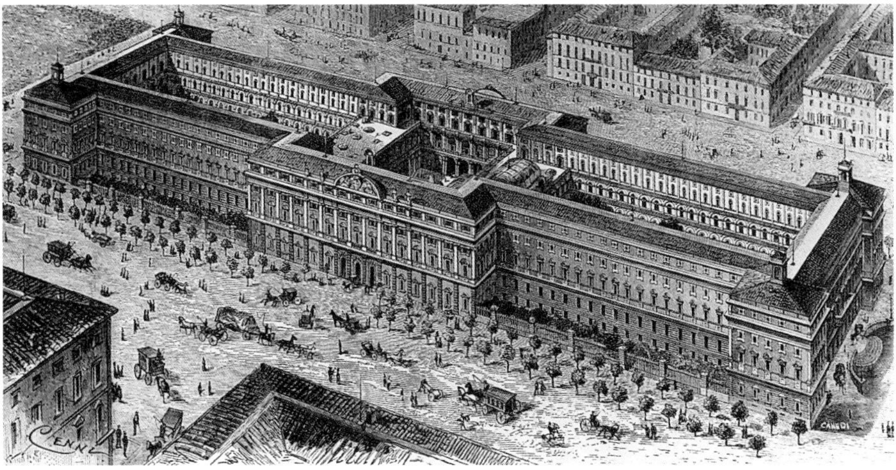

4.24 Via Nazionale, Rome. Photograph of the late nineteenth century, with George Edmund Street, Saint Paul's within the walls, 1872–75
4.25 Raffaele Canevari, Luigi Martinori, and Francesco Pieroni, Ministero delle Finanze, Rome, 1872–77

One of the more successful developments was the new Piazza Vittorio Emanuele II. The 163-acre site between Via Merulana and the train station was laid out by the Roman engineer Francesco de Mari in 1871, with a central rectangular piazza aligned along a vista looking out to Santa Croce in Gerusalemme. Archeological remains of an imperial-era water tower were preserved and the open space was planted as an English-style garden, Rome's first public garden-piazza. The symmetrical apartment blocks that surround the piazza, built by Gaetano Koch and others in the 1880s, elevate the new homes of the transplanted government bureaucrats with a monumental ensemble. By introducing ground floor arcades for shopping—functional and widely appreciated given the Roman climate—the Roman architects brought this building type, familiar from Turin and Bologna, to the capital. The square was praised in its day for its synthesis of a wide range of Roman public spaces, from the ancient Forum's basilica arcades and Michelangelo's open Capitoline facades to Bernini's Piazza of Saint Peter at the Vatican.

In similar real estate development schemes, former aristocratic preserves across the eastern plateau, like the Villa Ludovisi on the Pincian Hill, were sold off by their owners and stitched into the new urban fabric. When the Villa Borghese was threatened with similar development, it was bought by the state and maintained with only slight alterations as a public park. It was clear that with all these early piecemeal developments in progress the city needed a master plan, but the work of its commissions remained, like most municipal deliberations, ineffectual. The rapid turnover of administrations guaranteed unbridled economic exploitation and the inconclusiveness of official efforts to curb it. In its first decade, the planning of the new capital's development was largely a frenetic race to integrate the various real estate schemes already under way, as they were far more advanced than any institutional strategies advocated by the city itself.

The only individual with the vision and political clout to carry out an effective planning decision was Quintino Sella, a leading figure in the majority party of the right and its finance minister. He instigated the construction of his ministry's headquarters, the first new construction for a government agency in Rome, in 1872. The Ministry of Finance building was designed by the engineer Raffaele

Canevari with the assistance of Francesco Pieroni, the able draftsman who with Francesco Azzurri had drawn up the plates for Letarouilly's publications on the architecture of Renaissance Rome. The architectural language is, therefore, in a staid and competent neo-Renaissance style typical of mid-nineteenth-century palaces or barracks of papal Rome. Given the minister's stringent finance policy—the wars of independence were costly indeed—there is no hint of excess in its stucco-formed trabeation.

The site of the ministry, not far from Porta Pia, was along the renamed Via XX Settembre, which became the spine of a separate administrative city of roomy bureaucratic institutions, the *Città alta*. Sella's vision was for a new capital of modern science and administration to grow up alongside and independent of the older ecclesiastical city. Other government agencies—defense, agriculture, public works—followed suit and rose along Via XX Settembre. Today, they line the street like filing cabinets. The Ministry of Finance has remarkably little urban presence for a building of its size, and is wholly disconnected from the larger symbolic context of Rome, from its urban traditions, even from the ruins of the Baths of Diocletian immediately adjacent to its site. This is indicative of Sella's attitude—and that of his party—toward the pre-existing city: indifference both physically and symbolically. The *Città alta* was a city apart from historical Rome, which they would gladly have turned into a museum.

MONUMENTAL SYMBOLS OF THE NEW STATE

By the time Sella's building was finished in 1877, his urban conception was outmoded. The parliamentary right had fallen from power to Francesco Crispi's liberal left. Architectural critics panned the ministry buildings of the *Città alta* as miserly things that suggested dull bureaucracy rather than national spirit. Sella's idea of separate administrative city was shelved, but with no guiding figure emerging to take his place, the many new ministries, each with its own ambitious leader, were dispersed throughout the city without a cohesive plan.

The sudden death of King Vittorio Emanuele II in January 1878 was a catalyst for the demonstration of the symbolic power of architecture in service of the new state. Pius IX also died in the winter of 1878, and the funerals of the two leaders were designed to serve their respective causes of secular nationalism and Christian piety, one in mythic hyperbole at the Pantheon, the other in victimized understatement at Saint Peter's. The scenography for the state funeral in the Pantheon was designed by Luigi Rosso, who synthesized pagan and papal images: a catafalque of ermine and palm fronds filled the rotunda and new sculpture of mourning allegories were set on the temple's blank pediment along with an inscription for Vittorio Emanuele, the father of the country. Afterward, the much maligned bell towers were finally removed. The idea of burying Italy's first king in the center of the rotunda floor, comparable to the interment of the first Pope Peter under his dome, kept Emanuele's successor, Umberto I, and Pope Leo XIII in heated deliberations until 1884, when they agreed upon a sober bronze design by Manfredo Manfredi to be installed in the western niche. Italian compatriots made their "secular pilgrimage" to their new capital in large numbers to see the king's tomb. In the Pantheon, they found a crucible of national symbolism where the first, second, and third Romes were in perfect balance: imperial glory and Christian piety were seamlessly co-opted in this royal mausoleum.

King Vittorio Emanuele II served the nation best in his death, giving fodder to an even grander embodiment of the spirit of the state. Indeed, the Monument to Vittorio Emanuele II on the

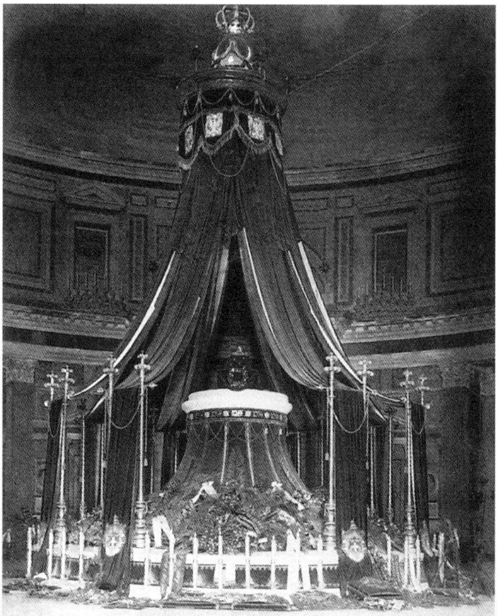

4.26 and 4.27 Luigi Rosso, decorations for the funeral of Vittorio Emanuele II, Pantheon, Rome, 16 February 1878

Capitoline Hill, the *Altare della Patria*, is the central architectural element of national self-representation. A few months after the king's funeral, the government passed a bill for a national monument to be erected with a budget almost twice that of Sella's Finance Ministry. An international competition for its design was opened in 1880 in which the choice of building type and site was left to the individual contestants. More than three hundred proposals were entered. Most, like Guglielmo Calderini's design for a monument in Piazza Vittorio, reflected the richness of Italian architectural inheritance with all manner of eclectic elements. The jury, which included Camillo Boito, sifted through the projects hoping to clarify what symbols and sites might after all be appropriate. Triumphal arches struck the jury as too militaristic in tone. Sites on the Esquiline were deemed too peripheral. The project proposed by Pio Piacentini and the sculptor Ettore Ferrari for a terraced hillside temple on the Capitoline, which they called a "forum," was favored with second prize in the competition.

The winning entry, however, was drafted by an Ecole des Beaux-Arts Rome Prize–winner then at the French Academy, Paul-Henri Nénot, who proposed a commemorative column and triumphal arch gateway for a site at the top of Via Nazionale. It was a compendium of classical monumental types from antiquity arranged in close formal correspondence to Bernini's colonnades at Saint Peter's (visible on the horizon in Nénot's aerial perspective drawing). The wide variety of responses to the architectural competition is evidence of a rather wayward architectural climate in Italy both on the part of architects as well as patrons. Architectural competitions were more often than not sloppy processes of trial and error. Typically, none of the entries in the first competition for the monument was deemed worthy of construction. Prime Minister Francesco Depretis, who chaired the jury, honored the French architect as a diplomatic gesture toward former political foes and simultaneously goaded the pride of local architects to a second, definitive competition restricted this time to Italian designers.

The site for the monument was designated for the northern slope of the Capitoline Hill on axis with the Via del Corso. Despite the increased costs for expropriation, Depretis insisted on the

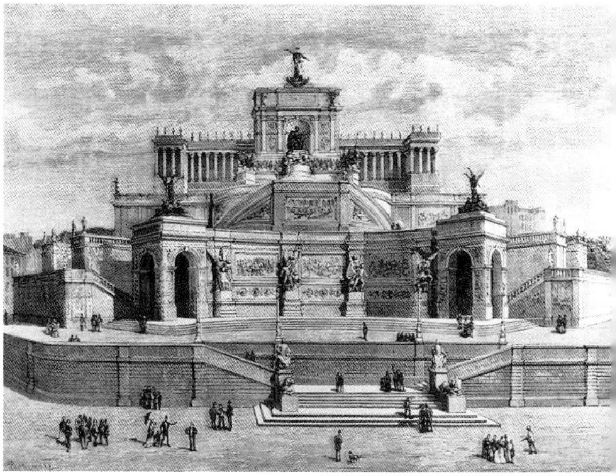

4.28–4.30 Monument to Vittorio Emanuele II, Rome, competition projects, 1881: Guglielmo Calderini, Pio Piacentini and Ettore Ferrari, and Paul-Henri Nénot

Capitoline for symbolic reasons. The Capitoline Hill, like the Pantheon, was to be again reappropriated, its history revised and focused for the third Rome. The construction of the monument on this site required the demolition of the tower of Pope Paul III and other structures connected to the Church of Santa Maria in Ara Ceoli and to the Palazzo Venezia, once a papal residence. Placing the national monument on this site would redraw the symbolic map of Rome, designating the Capitoline Hill—as it was in antiquity—the epicenter of the city.

The second competition for the monument opened in 1882 with a program that specified an equestrian statue of the monarch against a tall architectural backdrop on the hill. All 101 entries tended toward the gargantuan size characteristic of European monumental architecture of this period. The winner of the competition was a young architect who had studied with Luigi Rosso in Rome, Giuseppe Sacconi in collaboration with the sculptor Eugenio Maccagnani. It is, in the context of the competition, a comparatively restrained design of ramparts and terraces, with flights of steps that rise to a concave screen of Corinthian columns. Bronze quadrigas atop the end pavilions can be seen from most points in the city, and the structure below is covered with sculpture. Figures in the pediments and attic, processional reliefs, allegorical statue groups in white marble or gilded bronze, fountains, altars, pedestals and inscriptions—all these serve as the setting for a colossal equestrian statue of Vittorio Emanuele II at the center of the monument.

Construction was begun in 1885 with the assistance of dozens of sculptors selected from across the nation. Enrico Chiaradia designed an equestrian statue so colossal that the only space large enough for his studio was the concert auditorium in the ruins of the Mausoleum of Augustus. Work on the monument continued for three decades, long after Sacconi's premature death, under the direction of Manfredi, Piacentini, and Koch in a building works committee, much like a cathedral's *fabbrica*, and was still incomplete when it was inaugurated in 1911 during the celebrations of the nation's fiftieth anniversary.

The "Vittoriano" is characteristic of the late-nineteenth-century monument: big and white. It imposes itself upon its beholder with its colossal scale and explicit symbols. Above all, it is brilliantly white, constructed not of Roman travertine but of Brescian *botticcino* limestone, selected as much for its beauty as for the minister of public works's connections in the Brescian quarry business. The architectonic and decorative images of its decor are drawn from a wide repertory of forms, but each element conveys an appropriate meaning through the logic of its historical association. Sacconi's sources for the architectural setting ranged from the ancient sanctuary of Fortuna at Praenestae, known at the time through Palladio's reconstruction, to the "Spanish" Steps, a model with political resonance when we recall that the steps were originally to have been the setting for an equestrian statue of King Louis XIV.

The area of the Piazza Venezia beneath the monument was at this time enlarged by demolishing the Palazzo Torlonia and was dubbed the "Foro Italico," a forum like the ancient ones nearby. The sculptures on the monument, in particular the equestrian statue so similar to that of Marcus Aurelius in Michelangelo's Capitoline piazza, carry both ancient imperial and Renaissance connotations. Historical associations elicited by the forms are merged. This is the logic of Sacconi's historicist method. Ancient imperial glory and the continual revival of Italian culture, first in the Renaissance now in the *Risorgimento*, are compounded in every element of Sacconi's work in the service of the state.

The Vittoriano was the embodiment of national consciousness, a setting for the liturgy of the nation state enshrined in stone and bronze and renewed in continual ritual. It is the keystone of national symbolism, an instrument of influence that communicates the moral and political messages of the regime, those being to forge collective memory, and establish a historiography and hagiography of its players while counterbalancing ecclesiastical tradition. The statue groups of Thought and Action that flank the entrance frame the whole experience within the philosophical parameters of reasoned contemplation and active intervention. They also draw into the official register the complementary roles of Giuseppe Mazzini and Giuseppe Garibaldi, subsuming the revolutionary theorist and the military activist, problematic political contenders for the king's central authority, in this telling of Italy's resurgence. On the first terrace,

4.31–4.33 Giuseppe Sacconi, Monument to Vittorio Emanuele II, Rome, 1885–1911. Overview; detail; inauguration ceremony, 4 June 1911

4.34 Emilio Gallori, Monument to Giuseppe Garibaldi, Rome, 1882–95

dynamic sculpture groups symbolizing Strength, Concord, Sacrifice, and Law, like allegories on papal monuments in Saint Peter's, record the monarch's character while they broadcast desirable civic attributes—a call to collective virtue. From the outset, the monument was planned as a pedagogical instrument. Here, at the heart of the capital, an official Italian history would replace personal, local, and regional memory in an open-air civics lesson in the making of Italians on the altar of the nation.

With the monument to the king as a centerpiece, a series of other politically appropriate monuments were erected in Rome during the 1880s. An equestrian statue of Garibaldi was placed on the Janiculum Hill after his death in 1882. The location was somewhat removed, near the site of his defense of republican Rome against the French siege thirty-three years earlier. This was the work of parliamentary commissioners who wanted the rambuctious general in a position that would be clearly seen as subservient to the monarch. Even his horse stands demurely. But the sculptor, Emilio Gallori, has Garibaldi throwing a cautionary gaze over his left shoulder toward the cupola of Saint Peter's. The gesture was choreographed by Gallori's review board, which sought to calibrate the monument's political impact between pre-existing signs of religion and the new points of secular reference in the city.

Whereas the monument to Garibaldi was a national effort, some fringe figures were also added, through private initiative, to the register of Rome's heroes. Burned at the stake by the Inquisition in 1600, Giordano Bruno was resurrected by the more radical elements of nineteenth-century Italian society—in particular the freemasons—as a forefather in the struggle for freedom of thought. However, the idea of erecting the monument in the Campo dei Fiori, the site of his execution, irked a conservative city council that continually denied a building permit until a leftist majority gained control of the city administration (that the original design had Bruno gesturing in an admonishing way at his judges had not helped gain favor with the local politicians). By 1889, after the sculptor Ettore Ferrari adjusted his design, the monument was erected, with Bruno now calmly facing in the direction of the Vatican and with reliefs on the memorial's side emphasizing his role as a teacher and not a firebrand.

The monument to Camillo Cavour was also a finely calibrated political tool in this period of uncertain church-state relations. United Italy's first prime minister and proponent of the transfer of the capital to Rome, Cavour's posthumous memorial stakes its ground on the right bank of the Tiber close to the Vatican—a position that brings to mind his ecclesiastical policy: "a free Church in a free State." The project, however, was not a state initiative but that of the conservative city council of 1882, which sought to preempt the erection of any more potentially aggressive political symbol by the parliamentary majority that advocated tough policies. Sculptor Stefano Galletti kept Cavour's arms down at his sides to emphasize the statesman's calm deliberation. Personifications of Italy and Rome with Thought and Action accompany him, but the latter two needed to be shifted to opposite sides in the final composition so that Action might not seem to raise its sword in the direction of the Vatican.

The groundbreaking and inaugural ceremonies for all of these commemorative monuments were choreographed political events: the statues of Garibaldi and Cavour were unveiled on 20 September 1895, the twenty-fifth anniversary of the breaching of the Porta Pia; the Bruno inauguration was scheduled deliberately to trump Pope Leo XIII's tenth jubilee celebration.

The monument building in the capital was repeated at a reduced scale in every town in the nation, physically establishing a new and pervasive hagiography of the unified Italian state. Through their sitings, gazes, gestures, and unique histories, each of these monuments reveals a political negotiation between various local institutions and a more general attempt to reconcile church and state to the modern era.

A NEW URBAN INFRASTRUCTURE FOR ROME

Despite the evident political intentions described in the planning of monuments in Rome, no official master plan for the development of the city yet existed. Alessandro Viviani, director of the city planning office, provided the first. Never before had Rome had a global planner like Viviani, whose primary occupation was coordinating with the many agencies working at cross-purposes to develop projects in the city. Not even the Renaissance popes Julius II and Sixtus V had encroached upon the built-up core of the city. Viviani's first master plan, ready in 1873, concentrated on linking Sella's *Città alta* to the historical center, expanding the city to outlying areas in Testaccio and Trastevere, and tying in the Prati di Castello with new bridges. The gutting of the crowded area of the Vatican Borgo with the elimination of the so-called *spina* was also part of the plan. Viviani's efforts, however, came to naught due to the instability, inefficiency, and collusion of the city administration; Rome's first plan was not even presented to parliament for the consideration required to authorize expropriation. Infrastructural work demanded sums greater than the municipal coffers could bear and was ignored for ten more years. Instead, the city was left open to an unbridled building boom.

The national government intervened only for the construction of the Tiber Embankment walls in 1875. Although the river is small in comparison to those of other European capitals, the deforestation of its hinterland provokes raging flows in the fall. Historically, roughly every thirty years a devastating flood submerged the city, followed by famine and pestilence. To counter the threat, tall protective walls replaced the muddy riverbanks and nearby buildings, including Torlonia's Teatro Tordinona and, most sadly, the Porto di Ripetta. They were replaced with tree-lined thoroughfares, the "Lungotevere," that serve as a ring road around the city center.

For all their invasive impact upon the edges of the older city fabric, the embankments save the city from periodic flooding while improving hygienic conditions in the lower areas like the former

4.35 Alessandro Viviani, Master Plan, Rome, 1883

Ghetto. Massive public hydraulic engineering projects were, for the nineteenth century, symbols of modern progress, aspirations of former emperors and popes who had long dreamed of draining the Pontine Marshes and taming the torrents of rivers.

When it finally became clear that the city could not handle this scale of public building by itself, the national government stepped in to provide the financial help. With the funding bill of 1881, the state committed itself to help the city, but only after the city presented a comprehensive master plan. Viviani set to work again. He had to integrate a specific list of public buildings the national bill required: a courthouse, an academy of sciences (the lingering influence of Quintino Sella), barracks, a drilling ground and military hospital, a public hospital and a major exhibition building for the fine arts. The siting of the national buildings, however, was not left to Viviani but to the various heads of the institutions, who jockeyed for position within the politicized topography of Rome. The ministers of justice and public instruction chose sites in the historic center, while the two municipal projects, the hospital and the exhibition hall, were kept, more conservatively, up on the *Città alta*. Once these locations were designated, Viviani concentrated on traffic arteries and bridge connections. His master plan was ratified in 1883, and constitutes Rome's first ever all-inclusive development scheme. Although not all the interventions were carried out, it would be the basic guideline for all urban projects over the next twenty-five years.

Viviani's most controversial task was carving out a passage for modern traffic through the historic city center. This intervention, the Corso Vittorio Emanuele II, is a demonstration of the difficulty of Viviani's work and the subtlety of his accomplishment. The westward route from Piazza Venezia begins with the Via del Plebiscito and slips between pre-existing palaces and the Church of Il Gesù. Beyond this point, expropriation of buildings considered of lesser historic or artistic value was undertaken along a swerving path that dodges a selection of important monuments: the Palazzo della Valle and the Church of Sant'Andrea, the Palazzo Massimo alle Colonne, and the Chiesa Nuova among others. The flanks of the Palazzo della Cancelleria and the little Palazzo Regis were exposed and redressed with neo-Renaissance decor. The new apartment buildings along the

Corso Vittorio take their scale from the noble facades opposite them, patrician and ecclesiastical tradition here counterbalanced by the architecture of bourgeois democracy.

Viviani's urban planning solution was empirical, unlike the abstract slicing typical in Haussmann's Paris—a remarkably subdued intervention in which the famous piazzas along the way, like Piazza Navona, were left undisturbed. Consequently, the Corso Vittorio is a shifting route of constantly changing views leading to the cupola of Saint Peter's, the ultimate destination of the route. The path is also populated with commemorative monuments to secular cultural and government leaders. Like the Via Papale, the traditional route of ecclesiastical processions from Saint Peter's, the Corso Vittorio is a route tying the Vatican to the city. But now, inexorably and emphatically, that route leads to a secular and nationalist city center, the *Altare della Patria*.

The program of the Corso Vittorio was made explicit with the Ponte Vittorio, the bridge that links the reformed city and the Vatican. Proposals for this bridge date from 1887, though construction did not begin until 1910, as it was considered a lower priority than several of the other Tiber spans and, with all of the other monuments going up, there was a shortage of good travertine. The design was by Angelo Vescovali who, as architect for the ministry of public works, was responsible for five other bridges over the Tiber.

The elegant white bridge of three arches is laden with allegorical sculptures akin to those on the Vittoriano. They describe the king's military valor and fidelity and hail him as father of the country. Like the Corso Vittorio that leads to it, the bridge offers a panoramic and politically charged view of Rome. In the river below, the ruins of the Pons Trionphalis recall the achievement of ancient emperors and the failure of Pope Julius II to rebuild it to carry his street, the Via Giulia. Views from the bridge to the Castel Sant'Angelo and the Hospital of the Santo Spirito make plain the state's secular command of the military and the state structure of social welfare. As if in reprimand to the church, the state is ready to defend its position at the bridgehead. Winged Victories greet citizens coming from the city with laurel wreathes while those on the Vatican side brandish swords.

4.36 Corso Vittorio Emanuele II, Rome, 1888–1910
4.37 Angelo Vescovali, Ponte Vittorio Emanuele II, Rome, 1910–11

A NATIONAL ARCHITECTURE

The Corso and the Ponte Vittorio pulled the Vatican into a reconfigured urban system. The first monumental building constructed by the national government on the Vatican side of the Tiber attests to this same political intention. The Palazzo di Giustizia is the seat of the Italian Supreme Court together with all of the district courts in Rome and is the largest secular institutional building in the capital. In several respects it recalls Pope Julius II's Palazzo dei Tribunali, planned by Bramante for the Via Giulia. The Vatican's side of the Tiber was chosen for the modern courthouse by the minister of justice, Giuseppe Zanardelli. Prati had not been considered earlier because of its isolation across the unbridged river, its low flood plains, and its proximity to the Vatican, while territorial concession to the pope was still under discussion. Zanardelli's decisive move corresponds to his strong policy with regard to church-state relations. Once the bridges were financed, Viviani planned out the Prati area with axial vistas, grids, and a grand *trevium* clearly recalling the Piazza del Popolo into which it is tied. None of the vistas or thoroughfares in Prati lead to the Vatican, however, and like the street names chosen for them, they are assertions of the secular state upon this contested ground. The Palazzo di Giustizia is the anchor.

After a prolonged competition, Guglielmo Calderini's colossal neo-Cinquecento palazzo was chosen. This squat block of rusticated travertine is shaped with strong chiaroscuro effects in a lively architectural language while avoiding, according to the contemporary sensibility, the decadent excess of the baroque. All of the architect's sources, both declared and inferred, correspond to the chronological range of architects active in the *Fabbrica* of Saint Peter's, as if this construction were also the product of a century-long progress, the secular equivalent to the famous cathedral. Calderini, like Sacconi, used an architectural language enriched by relevant historical associations, in this case, in reference to Saint Peter's.

At the courthouse, images of ancient and modern Italian jurists, from Cicero to Vico, are presented like the saints arrayed before the Vatican. The allegorical groups are explicit and didactic. The brackets of the building's cornice are images of yoked bulls, symbolic of the

4.38 and 4.39 Guglielmo Calderini, Palazzo di Giustizia, Rome, 1889–1911

citizens of Italy who, instructed in civic virtues of strength, concord, sacrifice, and law at the Vittoriano, are here put *sub jugem legis*. Passages to and through this scenographic building, as in all the mature works of this period, unfold here like a triumphal procession, first through the entrance archway from the bridge and into a monumental courtyard. An exhilarating stair of Piranesian exuberance and complexity sweeps the visitor up to the vestibule before the courtrooms. A longitudinal space there called the *ambulatorio* replaces the usual *salle des pas perdus* of northern courthouse models. Calderini has proposed indigenous sources, each integrated in an historicist maneuver of considerable subtlety. He has retrieved the ancient forensic basilica, reappropriating the building type from its Christian converters, to rededicate the congregational space to its original civic function. The design of the Supreme Court chamber was kept strenuously secular in association with the top-light of an ancient *cella* and the architectural ornamentation associated with imperial audience halls. The fresco cycle by Cesare Maccari in the Supreme Court depicts great moments in the history and legacy of Roman jurisprudence, and was conspicuously modeled on the lunettes of Raphael's Stanza della Segnatura, thought at the time to have been Pope Julius II's own courtroom. As if to supplant ecclesiastical influence in the process of temporal justice, even the judges' benches seem to appropriate the qualities of choir stalls and confessionals. Throughout this rich structure, symbols of the new institution of secular, temporal justice are posited as equivalents to the now limited role of the Church in Italian governing.

The Palazzo di Giustizia's prominence in the Roman landscape corresponds to its broader impact on official public buildings across the country. All architects who had the opportunity to build for the public administration aspired to develop a valid national style, a topic of debate in architecture throughout the nineteenth century. Camillo Boito wrote a key article on the subject in 1872, *L'architettura della nuova Italia*, emphasizing the need to move freely toward an architecture that expresses the special character of contemporary society. After unification Boito realized that his earlier proposal of Lombard Romanesque and the medieval idiom of restored town halls and cathedral facades carried an inherent political message of regionalism and federalism antithetical to current centrist government policies. Calderini and his Palazzo di Giustizia, however, presented a powerful imagery that could be traced to any number of regions of the peninsula. That the Renaissance was considered the apogee of Italian culture only made the choice more appropriate. Boito, who adjudicated some of the nation's most prominent competitions, succumbed to the prevalent symbolic role of a grand sixteenth-century Renaissance classicism for the nation.

Calderini introduced his neo-Cinquecento style to his home town, Perugia, in the Hotel Cesaroni, now the seat of the Umbrian regional council. Calderini's pupil, Cesare Bazzani, brought the style to Florence when he won the competition for the National Library at Santa Croce in 1903. In Naples Alfonso Guerra's Stock Exchange on the Rettifilo of 1890 draws together a range of High Renaissance motifs from beyond the Neapolitan tradition and links it with a now larger national artistic heritage. One could cite other examples, from the Banco di Sicilia building in Palermo to the prefect's office of Genoa, for their reliance on Calderini's neo-Cinquecento style. The remarkable conformity of these examples is the result of the architects' involvement in competitions in the capital, which proved better than any academic institution to have been a decisive factor in the nationalization of an architectural idiom. On levels of political, cultural, and artistic theory, the sixteenth century was seen by nineteenth-century eyes as the apogee of Italian achievement. The Renaissance was successful in everything except national unification, which was where contemporary society and its architecture could surpass the historical model. The neo-Cinquecento style of national buildings of the 1890s is a bold, all-inclusive statement that draws together the heritage of the entire nation.

Architectural competitions played a key role in establishing this standard among both architects and their institutional clients. The Palazzo delle Esposizioni di Belle Arti in Rome was the locus of this process. The institution, located on Via Nazionale, was conceived as a permanent pavilion for triennial exhibitions of contemporary Italian art, not a museum for historical retrospectives. It was understood that from these public showings, qualified artists would be recognized and commissioned by an informed patronage. The city opened an architectural competition for the building's design in 1878, and the state secured its funding in 1881. This was the first competition in which the idea of the appropriate style for the capital was openly addressed. Pio Piacentini's winning project features a triumphal arch entrance between flanks of top-lit galleries that are laid out in such a way as to be fully functional even today. Statues of Italian artists from antiquity through the early nineteenth century stand on the parapet as forefathers in artistic traditions. Piacentini captured the grandeur and scale of the ancients in a building that serves contemporary functions. It was inaugurated by King Umberto I in 1883 in time to exhibit the entries to the architectural competition for the Palazzo di Giustizia.

Two years later, the Banca d'Italia was erected, also on the Via Nazionale, to the designs of Gaetano Koch, the era's most acclaimed architect. Koch's greatest success was the national bank, built after he won a limited competition against Pio Piacentini in 1885. Koch's designs had been preferred over Piacentini's Florentine image because the latter alluded to the origins of banking among early-Renaissance Tuscan families, while Koch's more generically grand, sixteenth-century classicism suggested a pan-regional identification. The bank has two distinct functions—official business on the left and public branch access on the right—and this duality was expressed throughout Koch's design. The building was also equipped with the most modern technology, including elevators and air conditioning. Koch's neo-Cinquecento handling is grander and richer, more vigorous and rigorous than Calderini's and became a benchmark itself.

Koch was also responsible for the Piazza dell'Esedra, a high-profile site at the top of Via Nazionale. With the introduction of train travel, this site had become the principal point of entry to the city. Koch's generous sweeping arcades hearken to the Piazza del Popolo and the Piazza of Saint Peter, which it would now precede along one continuous crosstown thoroughfare. The strength of Koch's design is its use of the adjacent Baths of Diocletian, in part revitalized as a national museum of ancient art. Most of Vanvitelli's eighteenth-

4.40 Pio Piacentini, Palazzo delle Esposizioni, Rome, 1878–82
4.41 Gaetano Koch, Banca d'Italia, Rome, 1885–92
4.42 Gaetano Koch, Piazza dell'Esedra, Rome, 1888–89

century facade was stripped off the Baths to reveal more of the ancient construction, though the church spaces inside were retained. The overall effect was again to reinforce the connection between ancient, modern, and ecclesiastical Rome. The fountain outside, however, was a different matter. Pius's fountain was relocated here and cavalierly transformed with bronzes by the sculptor Mario Rutelli. A muscular youth wrestles with a big fish that thrusts an obelisk-sized spray into the air. Its mist glistens the flanks of luxuriating nereids below. Too scandalous to be properly inaugurated, the scaffolding was brought down during the night of Carnevale in the otherwise Holy Year of 1900.

ROME, A WORLD CAPITAL

As Rome provided a point of dissemination of national imagery, it also became a point of convergence of imported images and institutions. The whole length of Via Nazionale had only one new religious institution: Saint Paul's within the Walls. Modern Rome's first permanent structure for a non-Catholic sect, it was erected by American Episcopalian expatriates. It was also the first work of a non-Italian architect in the modern city. The Americans turned to George Edmund Street, who was well known to them for his work in ecclesiastical architecture outside the Roman Catholic realm. Street had always been inspired by Italian examples, but his characteristic striated construction in courses of brick and travertine strikes a strident tone here, an effect amplified by a bell tower that was the tallest element along the Via Nazionale. There is no dome, no great facade, and its casual asymmetry plays counterpoint to its boxy classical neighbors. A hammer-beamed wooden ceiling over the nave, mosaics by the pre-Raphaelite designer Edward Burne-Jones, and terracotta tiles by William Morris all go against any aesthetic standards established by Roman Catholic tradition. Saint Paul's is a symbol of the opening of the Roman landscape to freedom of religious observance, and a number of other churches followed, such as All Saints' on Via del Babuino, also by Street, and two Waldensian churches, one on Piazza Cavour and the other near Piazza Venezia.

The most significant ecumenical event in Roman architecture of this period, however, was the triumphant rebuilding of the Jewish synagogue. The Jewish Ghetto of Rome was definitively dismantled in 1870, with emancipation under Italian rule. There are no markers or monuments to the Ghetto's former existence, only a name that lingers in popular nomenclature. Nothing in the district of any architectural note had been built since the middle of the sixteenth century, and now the entire area was to be cleared—rebuilding was deemed necessary with the construction of the Tiber Embankment. The Jews, reluctant to move from the area that had been their traditional home since the age of the Emperor Titus, set aside one of the new blocks along the Lungotevere for their synagogue. An architectural competition for the building was won by Osvaldo Armanni and Vincenzo Costa.

Construction began in 1885 but was finished only by the turn of the century. The architects sought an architectural idiom that might distinguish this institution from the many Catholic symbols that loom up around the former Ghetto. The variegated origins of Italy's Jewish population also encouraged a free amalgamation of various, vaguely eastern Mediterranean sources; it was important that the sources be quite distinct from the broad Western classical tradition that buttresses the constructions of the Catholic faith. The synagogues of Turin, Trieste, and Florence, for example, were all in exotic, non-Western styles.

Armanni and Costa elaborated on Babylo-Assyrian motifs that hearkened to a tradition older than Rome itself and seemed to trace a history back to the time of the Torah. Employing the prevalent historicist method, a "Jewish" architectural style was constructed from a range of appropriate pre-Roman sources. The synagogue rises from a centralized plan in a blocky ziggurat form up to its most salient feature, a square dome lined with aluminum. Antonelli had developed the image of a square dome for the original Turin synagogue and it became a fortuitous and distinctive motif for the Jewish community. The square dome, in counterbalance to the established Catholic images everywhere, helps to distinguish this alternative religious building at a glance.

4.43 and 4.44 Osvaldo Armanni and Vincenzo Costa, Tempio israelitico, Rome, 1889–1904. Tiber island view; interior
4.45 Giulio de Angelis, Magazzini Boccioni, Via del Corso, Rome, 1886–90

Rome was also opened to the new commercial building that had already marked the other cities of the peninsula. Giulio de Angelis built two remarkable structures in the heart of Rome. The city's first *galleria*, the Galleria Sciarra of 1883, although of a modest scale, is very much in the spirit of Mengoni's work in Milan, with slender iron columns and neo-Renaissance frescoes. A department store, the Magazzini Boccioni, also by de Angelis was built at a prominent site on the corner of the Via del Corso and the newly opened Via del Tritone, opposite the Palazzo Chigi. There, the architect broadly adapted the classical language of the palazzo to a new iron structure wrapped with a thin wall of stone. De Angelis was praised by his contemporaries for creating an imagery that confirmed Italian cultural identity in an evolving material and technological world.

A new plan for Rome, spreading now far beyond the city's ancient walls, was developed under the populist mayor Ernesto Nathan and ratified in 1909. Viviani's inner-city arteries were here extended under the design direction of Edmondo Sanjust de Teulada. Beyond the city walls, Sanjust planned a ring road encircling the city that followed the curves of the natural topography. Elsewhere, such as in Prati, elegant radial boulevards were planned. Most importantly, the Sanjust plan thoroughly integrated green areas with Rome's urban expansion and the concept of zoning for low-density garden city development and designated areas for major public building complexes.

Before implementation of the plan began, the area north of Prati, the former *piazza d'armi*, or military drilling ground, was designated as a world's fair site. The year 1911 marked the fiftieth anniversary of Italian national unity, and an international exhibition seemed an ideal way to celebrate the achievement. Mayor Nathan had turned down the invitation to host the Olympic Games of 1908 to concentrate on urgent housing issues, but the idea of a world's fair came at the right time. He called it Rome's "great secular jubilee."

A display of industrial progress was mounted in Turin while major exhibitions were also coordinated in Florence. The central cultural events took place in Rome, with the fine arts exhibition in the verdant valley behind the Villa Giulia and the "ethnographic" exhibition of Italian culture across the river in the open area above the Prati. An archeological exhibition was mounted in the newly rehabilitated halls of the Baths of Diocletian, and the Castel Sant'Angelo was converted into a museum of Italian military genius. The organizational efforts fostered significant advances in Italian museology, a broadened accessibility to cultural goods with publications and reproductions, and research that stimulated contemporary arts and industry. All Rome was readied for the exposition, which would emphatically demonstrate the "civil progress" of Italy in the modern era.

It was, however, not a world's fair in the strict sense because here only Italy was allowed to show off. The eleven foreign countries that sent representatives to Rome were confined to the section of the fine arts exhibition where Italy would easily shine over her guests. The pavilions designed for the fair displayed the common grandiloquent sumptuousness typical of the international exhibitions in which a temporary construction was to encapsulate national character: Carrère and Hastings built for the U.S. in a Federal style, Edwin Lutyens for the U.K. adapted Wren's facade of Saint Paul's. Josef Hoffmann's Austrian pavilion was noted for its serene spatial functionality and refined, indeed stripped, classical language. The works of these top-rate foreign architects did not have, however, much impact upon the ideas or trends of contemporary architecture within Italy.

The centerpiece of the fine arts division of the fair was the Italian pavilion, intended from the outset to remain as a permanent Galleria Nazionale d'Arte Moderna. Cesare Bazzani won the design competition in 1908 with a low and broad building set opposite the pedestrian entrance to the fairgrounds from the Villa Borghese public gardens. The architect learned a great deal from Piacentini's exhibition building of the previous generation on Via Nazionale, and adapted his general planning scheme to a larger, grander building. Bazzani's neo-Cinquecento style, a large-scale reminiscence of the Villa Giulia close-by, is softened in this park setting with naturalistic decorative details.

Other structures realized for the fair were also intended to be permanent additions to the Roman infrastructure and were coordinated with the Sanjust plan, in particular a stadium built along Via Flaminia and a new bridge, the Ponte Risorgimento. The latter

4.46 Cesare Bazzani, Galleria Nazionale d'Arte Moderna, Rome, 1908–11

4.47 Marcello Piacentini, Foro delle Regioni and Salone delle Feste at the Esposizione Universale, Rome, 1911

was an innovative work for Rome, a reinforced concrete structure that spanned the river in one low and elegant arch. It was conceived by the French engineer François Hennebique, using his patented construction system. The bridge gave access to the Italian ethnographic displays. Marcello Piacentini, son of Pio, designed the central architectural setting that consisted of a triumphal arch entrance from the bridge that led into a sweeping arcaded space called the "Forum of the Regions." The open space culminated in a colossal festivities hall covered with a high, square dome. The correspondence of Piacentini's design to the Vatican complex nearby was an unmistakable response to the mayor's frank declaration of the fair as a secular equivalent to ecclesiastical celebrations. Following the precepts of his father's generation, Marcello Piacentini amalgamated a national imagery in a culmination of Roman classicism.

All around rose the pavilions erected by the fourteen regions of the peninsula. They presented fusions of elements from famous architectural works that constituted the "classical" models of their cultures: the Umbrian pavilion was a free interpretation of Perugia's Palazzo del Popolo; Emilia-Romagna's, a mixture of the d'Este Castle at Ferrara, the Palazzo Bentivoglio of Bologna, and the Tempio Malatesta of Rimini. Over forty individual Italian ethnic groups were represented in smaller dioramas

Once Italy had been made, its architecture was called upon to make Italians. The Enlightenment of the eighteenth century invested architecture with the power of moral reform, and Romantic thought focused this reform on the goal of national unification. In Rome, the representational role of architecture was paramount in the shaping of a collective identity. The power of these architectural instruments of persuasion relied upon the inheritance of an indigenous classicism in which artistic, civil, and national identities were indissolubly united. The collective memory of the new nation was shaped efficiently by the capital's monumental architecture.

BIBLIOGRAPHY

References for further study have been organized according to the chapter and sub-chapter headings and in chronological order to identify available primary source material, then the important foundation studies that followed, and finally the latest, most up-to-date publications offering, in most cases, exhaustive bibliography and illustrations.

GENERAL TEXTS

1898 Willard, Ashton, *History of Modern Italian Art* (Longmans and Green, New York).

1956 Lavagnino, Emilio, *L'arte moderna dai neoclassici ai contemporanei, Storia dell'Arte Classica e Italiana* vol. 5 (Unione Tipografico, Turin).

1960 Maltese, Corrado, *Storia dell'arte in Italia, 1785–1943* (Einaudi, Turin).

1964 De Fusco, Renato, *L'idea di architettura, Storia della critica da Viollet-le-Duc a Persico* (Communità, Milan).

1966 Meeks, Carroll, *Italian Architecture, 1750–1914* (Yale University Press, New Haven).

1975 Patetta, Luciano, *L'architettura dell'eclettismo, Fonti, teorie, modelli, 1700–1900* (Marzotta, Milan).

1977 Sica, Paolo, *Storia dell'urbanistica, L'Ottocento* (Laterza, Bari/Rome).

1978 De Guttry, Irene, *Guida di Roma moderna dal 1870 ad oggi* (De Luca, Rome).

1982 Restucci, Amerigo, "Città e architettura nell'ottocento," in *Storia dell'arte italiana* vol. 2, part 2 (Einaudi, Turin): 670–792.

1985 Magnago Lampugnani, Vittorio, ed., *L'avventura delle idee nell'architettura, 1750–1980* (Electa, Milan).

1985 Tintori, Silvano, *Piano e pianificatori dall'età napoleonico al fascismo* (Angeli, Milan).

1989 Strappa, Giuseppe, ed., *Tradizione e innovazione nell'architettura di Roma Capitale, 1870–1930* (Kappa, Rome).

1994 Alisio, Giancarlo, et al., eds., *I disegni d'archivio negli studi di storia dell'architettura* (Electa Napoli, Naples).

1994 Villari, Sergio, "L'architettura dell'Ottocento," in De Fusco, Renato, ed., *L'Italia e la formazione della civiltà europea, Dall'architettura a design* (UTET, Turin), 169–88.

1997 Alisio, Giancarlo, ed., *Civiltà dell'Ottocento, Architettura e urbanistica* (Electa Napoli, Naples).

1999 Zucconi, Guido, *La città contesa, Dagli ingegneri sanitari agli urbanisti* (Jaca, Milan).

CHAPTER 1

ARCHITECTURE OF THE ITALIAN ENLIGHTENMENT, 1750–1800

1768 Milizia, Francesco, *Le Vite de' più celebri architett d'ogni nazione e d'ogni tempo, precedute da un saggio sopra l'architettura* (Monaldini, Rome).

1785 Milizia, Francesco, *Roma: Delle belle arti di disegno* (Remondini, Bassano).

1912 Hautcoeur, Louis, *Rome et la renaissance de l'anquité à la fin du XVIIIème siècle* (Fontemoing, Paris).

1955 Kaufmann, Emil, "Piranesi, Algarotti and Lodoli: A Controversy in XVIII Century Venice," in *Gazette des Beaux-Arts* 2: 21–28.

1957 De Benedetti, Michele, "La teoria dell'architettura funzionale del Lodoli e la pratica dell'architettura in Italia," in *Atti del V congresso nazionale di storia dell'architettura* (Centro di Studi per la Storia dell'Architettur Rome): 157–63.

1966 Grassi, Liliana, *Razionalismo architettonico dal Lodoli a Pagano* (Bignami, Milan).

1979 Dacos, Nicole, "Arte italiana e arte antica," in *Storia dell'arte italiana* 1, 3 (Einaudi, Turin) 5–70. Reprinted in English as *History of Italia*

Art vol.1, part 3 (Polity, Cambridge, UK, 1996), 113–213.
)82 Gabetti, Roberto, "Architettura italiana del '700," in *Storia dell'arte italiana* vol. 2, part 2 (Einaudi, Turin): 670–724.
)83 Rykwert, Joseph, *The First Moderns: The Architecture of the Eighteenth Century* (MIT Press, Cambridge, MA).
)88 Matteucci, Anna Maria, *L'Architettura del Settecento* (UTET, Turin).
)89 Simoncini, Giorgio, ed., *Francesco Milizia, architetti di età barocca e tardobarocca* (Testo e Immagine, Turin).
)93 Kieven, Elisabeth, and Joseph Connors, *Von Bernini bis Piranesi* (Hatje, Stuttgart).
)00 Bowron, Edgar Peters, and Joseph Rishel, *Art in Rome in the Eighteenth Century* (Philadelphia Museum of Art, Philadelphia).
)00 Curcio, Giovanna, and Elisabeth Kieven, eds., *Storia dell'architettura italiana: il settecento* (Electa, Milan).

HE PANTHEON REVISITED

781 Milizia, Francesco, *Dell'arte di vedere nelle belle arti del disegno secondo i principii di Sulzer e di Mengs* (Pasquali, Venice).
)92 Kelly, Cathie, "Paolo Posi, Alessandro Dori, and the Palace for the Papal Family on the Quirinal Hill," in Millon, Henry, and Susan Scott Munshower, eds., *An Architectural Progress in the Renaissance and Baroque, Sojourns in and out of Italy* (Pennsylvania State University, University Park, PA), 816–57.
)96 Pasquali, Susanna, *Il Pantheon, Architetture e antiquaria nel settecento a Roma* (Panini, Modena).

OME OF THE NOLLI PLAN

)80 Insolera, Italo, *Roma, Immagine e realtà dal X al XX secolo* (Laterza, Bari/Rome).
991 Ceen, Allan, *Rome 1748: Roma, La Pianta Grande di Roma di Giambattista Nolli* (Aronson, Highmount, NY).
998 Bevilacqua, Mario, *Roma nel secolo dei lumi, Architettura erudizione scienza nella Pianta di G. B. Nolli "celebre geometra"* (Electa Napoli, Naples).

LESSANDRO GALILEI AND SAN GIOVANNI ATERANO

)59 Schiavo, Armando, "Il concorso per la facciata di San Giovanni in Laterano e il parere della Congregazione," in *Bollettino dell'Unione Storia ed Arte* 3: 3.
1961 Golzio, Vincenzo, "La facciata di San Giovanni in Laterano e l'architettura del Settecento," in Bruhns, Leo, et al., eds., *Miscellanea Bibliothecae Hertzianae* (Schroll, Munich): 450–63.
1987 Kieven, Elisabeth, "Rome in 1732: Alessandro Galilei, Nicola Salvi, Ferdinando Fuga," in Hager, Hellmut, and Susan Scott Munshower, eds., *Light on the Eternal City* vol. 2 (Pennsylvania State University, University Park, PA), 255–76.
1991 Pietrangeli, Carlo, *San Giovanni in Laterano* (Nardini, Florence).

NICOLA SALVI AND THE TREVI FOUNTAIN

1832 Fea, Carlo, *Delle acque antiche* vol. 2, *Dei condotti antico-moderni delle Acque Vergine* (Stamperia della R.C.A, Rome).
1956 Schiavo, Armando, *La Fontana di Trevi e le altre opere di Nicola Salvi* (Poligrafico dello Stato, Rome).
1971 Benedetti, Sandro, "Per un'architettura dell'Acadia, Roma 1730," *Controspazio* 3, no. 7/8: 2–17.
1986 Pinto, John, *The Trevi Fountain* (Yale University Press, New Haven).
1991 Muratore, Giorgio, et al., *Fontana di Trevi* (Editalia, Rome).

LUIGI VANVITELLI AND THE REGGIA AT CASERTA

1756 Vanvitelli, Luigi, *Dichiarazione dei disegni del reale palazzo di Caserta* (Reale, Naples).
1939 Pane, Roberto, *Architettura dell'età barocca a Napoli* (Politecnica, Naples).
1953 Battisti, Eugenio, "Lione Pascoli, Luigi Vanvitelli e l'urbanistica italiana del 700," in *Atti dell'VIII congresso nazionale di storia dell'architettura* (Centro di Studi, perla Storia dell' Architettura, Rome): 51–64.
1953 Schiavo, Armando, *Il progetto di Luigi Vanvitelli per Caserta e la sua reggia* (Crescenzi, Rome).
1961 De Fusco, Renato, "Un centro comunitario del '700 in Campania," in *Comunità* 86: 56.
1963 Fagiolo dell'Arco, Marcello, *Funzioni simboli valori della Reggia di Caserta* (Dell'Arco, Rome).
1964 Strazzullo, Franco, *I primi anni di Luigi Vanvitelli a Caserta* (Laurenziana, Naples).
1973 De Fusco, Renato, et al., *Luigi Vanvitelli* (Scientifiche Italiane, Naples).
1978 De Seta, Cesare, "Luigi Vanvitelli: l'antico ed il neoclassico," in *Prospettiva* 15: 40–46.
1983 De Seta, Cesare, "Luigi Vanvitelli e Giovan Battista Piranesi: un'ipotesi integrativa del ruolo sociale dell'artista e metà Settecento," in Bettagno, Alessandro, ed., *Piranesi tra Venezia e*

l'Europa (Olschki, Florence,): 103–25.
1979 Wilton-Ely, John, "The Relationship between Giambattista Piranesi and Luigi Vanvitelli in Eighteenth-Century Architectural Practice," in De Seta Cesare, ed., *Vanvitelli e il '700 Europeo* 2 (Istituto di storia dell'architettura, Università di Napoli, Naples): 83–99.
1983 Hersey, George, *Architecture, Poetry and Number in the Royal Palace at Caserta* (MIT Press, Cambridge MA).
1998 De Seta, Cesare, ed., *Luigi Vanvitelli* (Electa Napoli, Naples).

FERNANDO FUGA AND THE ALBERGO DEI POVERI
1956 Pane, Roberto, *Ferdinando Fuga* (Scientifiche Italiane, Naples).
1966 Pane, Giulio, "Ferdinando Fuga e l'Albergo dei Poveri," *Napoli nobilissima* 5: 72–84.
1969 Strazzullo, Franco, *Architetti e Ingegneri Napoletani dal '500 al '700* (Benincasa, Naples).
1971 Alisio, Giancarlo, "Sviluppo urbano e struttura della città," in *Storia di Napoli* 8: 311–66.
1988 Kieven, Elisabeth, *Ferdinando Fuga e l'architettura romana del '700* (Multigrafica, Rome).
1995 Guerra, Andrea, et al., *Il Trionfo della miseria: gli alberghi dei poveri di Genova, Palermo e Napoli*(Electa, Milan).
1997 Giordano, Paolo, *Ferdinando Fuga a Napoli, L'Albergo dei Poveri, il Cimitero delle 366 fosse, i Granili* (Del Grifo, Lecce).

GIOVANNI BATTISTA PIRANESI
1743 Piranesi, Giovanni Battista, *Prima Parte di architettura e prospettive.*
1756 Piranesi, Giovanni Battista, *Le Antichità romane*, 4 vol. (Bouchard & Gravier, Rome)
1761 Piranesi, Giovanni Battista, *Invenzioni capric[ciosi] di carceri.*
1761 Piranesi, Giovanni Battista, *Della Magnificenza ed Architettura de' Romani.*
1762 Piranesi, Giovanni Battista, *Il Campo Marzio dell'antica Roma.*
1765 Piranesi, Giovanni Battista, *Osservazioni de Gio. Battista Piranesi sopra la lettre de M. Mariette*; 2nd ed. with *Parere su l'Architettura, con un Prefazione ad un nuovo Trattato della introduzione e del progresso delle belle arti in Europa ne' tempi.*
1769 Piranesi, Giovanni Battista, *Diverse maniere d'adornare i cammini ed ogni altra parte degli edifizj desunte dall'architettura Egizia, Etrusca, e Greca, con un Ragionamento apologetico in difesa dell'architettura Egizia e Toscana.*
1779 Bianconi, Gian Ludovico, "Elogio Storico del Cavaliere Giambattista Piranesi," *Antologia Romana*, 34–36: 265–84; reprinted in Bianconi, *Opere* 2 (Tipografia de'Classici Italiani, Milan, 1802): 127–40.
1915 Hermanin, Federico, *Giambattista Piranesi, architetto incisore* (Celanza, Turin).
1920 Muñoz, Antonio, *G. B. Piranesi*(Bestetti and Tuminelli, Milan/Rome).
1926 Galassi-Paluzzi, Carlo, "La romanità e il romanticismo di G. B. Piranesi," *Roma, Rivista di studi e vita romana* 4 (1926): 365–71.
1928 Wittkower, Rudolf, "Piranesi's Parere su l'Architettura," *Journal of the Warburg and Courthauld Institutes* 2, 2: 147–58.
1956 Fasolo, Vincenzo, "Il Campo Marzio di G. B. Piranesi," *Quaderni dell'Istituto di Storia dell'Architettura* (Rome) 15: 1–14.
1958 Vogt-Göknil, Ulya, *Giovanni Battista Piranesi: Carceri* (Origo, Zurich).
1968 Fischer, Manfred, "Die Umbaupläne des G. B. Piranesi für den chor von S. Giovanni in Laterano," *Münchner Jahrbuch der Bildenden Kunst* 19: 207–28.
1970 Messina, Maria Grazia, "Teoria dell'architettura in Giovanni Battista Piranesi, l'affermazione dell'eclettismo," *Controspazio* 2, 8\9: 6–13; 3, 6: 20–28.
1972 Nyberg, Dorothea, "The Drawings: Piranesi's Projects for San Giovanni in Laterano," in *Giovanni Battista Piranesi, Drawings and Etchings at Columbia University* (Avery Library, Columbia University, New York): 13–68.
1972 Tafuri, Manfredo, "G. B. Piranesi: l'architettura come 'utopia negativa'," *Angelus Novus* 20: 89–127; republished in English translation in *Architecture and Utopia, Design and Capitalist Development* (MIT Press, Cambridge MA, 1976).
1972 Wilton-Ely, John, ed., *Giovanni Battista Piranesi: The Polemical Works, Rome, 1757, 1761, 1765, 1769* (Gregg International Publishing, Ltd, Westmead, Farnborough UK).
1976 Wilton-Ely, John, "Piranesian Symbols on the Aventine," *Apollo* 103: 214–27.
1978 Bettagno, Alessandro, ed. *Piranesi, Incisioni, Rami, Legature, Architetture* (Neri Pozza, Vicenza).
1978 Brunel, Georges, ed., *Piranèse et les Francais* (Dell'Elefante, Rome).
1978 Stampfle, Felice, *Giovanni Battista Piranesi Drawings in the Pierpont Morgan Library* (Dover, New York).
1978 Wilton-Ely, John, *The Mind and Art of Giovanni Battista Piranesi* (Thames and Hudson, London).

79 MacDonald, William, *Piranesi's Carceri, sources of invention* (Smith College, Northampton MA).

83 Bettagno, Alessandro, ed., *Piranesi tra Venezia e l'Europa* (Olschki, Florence).

87 Tafuri, Manfredo, *The Sphere and the Labyrinth, Avant-Gardes and Architecture from Piranesi to the 1970s* (MIT Press, Cambridge MA).

92 Connors, Joseph, and John Wilton-Ely, *Piranesi architetto* (Dell'Elefante, Rome).

92 Rosa, Joseph, *Imagined and Real Landscapes of Piranesi, Critical Writings in America* (Columbia University School of Architecture, New York).

93 Brunotte, Ulrike, "The Construction of the Underworld, On the architecture of memory in cults and psychology," *Daidalos* 48: 78–86.

93 Denison, Cara D., Myra Nan Rosenfeld and Stephanie Wiles, eds., *Exploring Rome: Piranesi and His Contemporaries* (MIT Press, Cambridge MA).

93 Körte, Werner, "G. B. Piranesi als praktiker Architekt," *Zeitschrift für Kunstgeschichte* 3, 2: 16–33.

93 Raffone, Sandro, *Protopiro e Didascalo. . . da Giovanbattista Piranesi nel Parere sull'Architettura con un sunto antologico. . . ed un commento dove si ipotezza la sua continuità nell'architettura contemporanea* (Clean, Naples).

93 Wilton-Ely, John, *Piranesi as Architect and Designer* (Yale University Press, New Haven).

96 Debenedetti, Elisa, ed., *Giovanni Battista Piranesi, la raccolta di stampe della Biblioteca Fardelliana* (Biblioteca Fardelliana, Trapani).

98 Jatta, Barbara, ed., *Piranesi e l'Aventino* (Electa, Milan).

98 Panza, Pierluigi, *Piranesi architetto* (Guerini, Milan).

ACOMO QUARENGHI

21 Quarenghi, Giulio, *Fabbriche e disegni di Giacomo Quarenghi. . . illustrate dal Cav. Giulio suo figlio* (Tosi, Milan).

68 Ceschi, Carlo, "Il periodo romano di Giacomo Quarenghi," *Saggi e Memorie di Storia dell'Arte* 6: 135–47.

73 Arizzoli Clémentel, Pierre, "Giacomo Quarenghi à Subiaco, Lettres inédites," *Revue de l'Art* 19: 97–107.

80 Semenzato, Camillo, "Giacomo Quarenghi," *Bollettino del Centro Internazionale di Studi d'Architettura Andrea Palladio* 22, 1: 227–36.

91 Comencini, Italo, "Archi di trionfo pro e contro Napoleone progettati da Giacomo Quarenghi, (1744–1817)," *Medaglia* 19, 26: 25–32.

THE GRAND TOUR AND THE IMPACT OF ARCHEOLOGY

1973 Den Broeder, Frederick, ed., *Academy of Europe: Rome in the 18th Century* (University of Connecticut, Storrs CT).

1999 Clerici, Luca, *Viaggiatori italiani in Italia, 1700–1998, Per una bibliografia* (Bonnard, Milan).

1996 Bignamini, Ilaria, and Andrew Wilton, eds., *Grand Tour, The Lure of Italy in the Eighteenth Century* (Tate Gallery, London)].

2000 Hornsby, Clare, ed., *The Impact of Italy: The Grand Tour and Beyond* (The British School in Rome, London).

COLLECTING AND CULTURAL HERITAGE: THE VILLA OF CARDINAL ALBANI

1785 Morcelli, Stefano, Carlo Fea and Ennio Quirino Visconti, *Description de la Villa Albani* (Rome).

1967 Gaus, Joachim, *Carlo Marchionni, Ein Beitrag zur römischer Architektur des Settecento* (Boehlau, Köln).

1982 Beck, Herbert, and Peter Bol, eds., *Forschungen zur Villa Albani, Antike Kunst und die Epoche der Aufklärung* (Mam, Berlin).

1985 Debenedetti, Elisa, ed., *Committenza della famiglia Albani, Note sulla Villa Albani Torlonia* (Multigrafica, Rome).

1988 Debenedetti, Elisa, ed., *Carlo Marchionni, Architettura e scenografia contemporanea* (Multigrafica, Rome).

1991 Allroggen-Bedel, Agnes, "La Villa Albani, criteri di scelta e disposizione delle antichità," in Debenedetti, Elisa, ed., *Collezionismo e ideologia, mecenati, artisti e teorici dal classico al neoclassico* (Multigrafica, Rome): 205–22.

1993 Bevilacqua, Mario, "Nolli e Piranesi a Villa Albani," in Debenedetti, Elisa, ed., *Alessandro Albani patrono delle arti, Architettura, pittura e collezionismo nella Roma del '700* (Bonsignore, Rome): 71–82.

THE MUSEO PIO-CLEMENTINO AT THE VATICAN

1820 Visconti, Ennio Quirino, *Il Museo Pio Clementino* (Giegler, Milan).

1882 Letarouilly, Paul, *Le Vatican et al Basilique de Saint-Pierre* (Morel, Paris).

1959 Pietrangeli, Carlo, "I Musei Vaticani al tempo di Pio VI," *Bollettino dei Monumenti, Musei e Gallerie Pontifice* 1, 2: 7–45.

1966 Clark, Anthony, "The Development of the Collections and Museums of 18th Century

Rome," *Art Journal* 26, 2: 136–43.
2000 Collins, Jeffrey, "The God's Abode: Pius VI and the Invention of the Vatican Museums," in Hornsby, Clare, ed., *The Impact of Italy: The Grand Tour and Beyond* (The British School in Rome, London): 173–94.

VILLA BORGHESE IN THE LATE EIGHTEENTH CENTURY

1797 Visconti, Ennio Quirino, *Monumenti gabini della Villa Pinciana* (Fulgoni, Rome).
1978 Arizzoli-Clémentel, Pierre, "Charles Percier et la salle égyptienne de la Ville Borghèse," in Brunel, Georges, ed., *Piranèse et les Français* (Dell'Elefante, Rome): 1–24.
1992 Tullio, Maria Cristina, and Sandro Polci, eds., *Il Colle dei Giardini, Un itinerario romano fra giardini storici del Pincio dal XVI al XX secolo* (Mediocredito, Rome).
1995 Gonzalos Palacios, Alvar, "The Stanze of Apollo and Daphne in the Villa Borghese," *The Burlington Magazine* 137: 529–49.
1997 Campitelli, Alberta, *Villa Borghese* (Poligrafico e Zecca dello Stato, Rome).
1997 Di Gaddo, Beata, *L'Architettura di Villa Borghese* (Palombi, Rome).
1998 Robbiati, Cinzia, "I giardini di Villa Borghese: una nuova esperienza verso il culto della rovina," in Felicetti, Chiara, ed., *Cristoforo Unterperger* (De Luca, Rome): 110–14.
2000 Paul, Carol, *Making a Prince's Museum, Drawings for the Late-Eighteenth-Century Redecoration of the Villa Borghese* (Getty Research Institute, Los Angeles).

THE REDISCOVERY OF THE DORIC AT PAESTUM

1784 Paoli, Pasquale, *Le antichità di Pesto* (Rome).
1778 Piranesi, Giovanni Battista, *Différentes vues de trois grands édifices qui subsistent encore dans le milieu de l'ancienne ville de Pesto* (Rome).
1934 Caronia Roberti, Salvatore, *Venanzio Marvuglia (1729–1814)* (Ciuni, Palermo).
1938 Praz, Mario, "L'influsso delle scoperte di Ercolano sull'arte decorativa e sul gusto in Europa," *Emporium* 9: 159–70.
1984 Mauro, Eliana, "Realtà e apparenza in Villa Giulia e nell'Orto Botanico di Palermo," in Pirrone, Gianni, et al., *Il Giardino come labirinto della storia* (Centro Studi di Storia e Arte del Giardino, Palermo): 100–11.
1986 Burzotta, Pietro, "From the Botanical Gardens to the garden of the world," *Lotus International* 52: 112–27.
1986 Raspi Serra, Joselita, ed., *Paestum and the Dor[ic] Revival* (Centro Di, Florence).
1992 Arnold, Dana, "Count Gazola and the templ[e] at Paestum, An influential Grand Tour guide," *Apollo* 136, 366: 95–99.
1993 Franchi dell'Orto, Luisa, ed., *Ercolano 1738–1988, 250 anni di ricerca archeologica, At[ti] del Convegno Internazionale* (L'Erme di Bretschneider, Rome).

THE PATRONAGE OF POPE PIUS VI

1784 Cancellieri, Francesco Girolamo, *Sagrestia Vaticana eretta dal Regnante Pontefice Pio Sesto* (Casaletti, Rome).
1849 Letarouilly, Paul, *Edifices de Rome moderne* (Morel, Paris).
1926 Gambetti, Guido, *Cosimo Morelli: architetto imolese (1732–1812)* (Galeati, Imola).
1967 Pietrangeli, Carlo, et al., *Palazzo Braschi e il su[o] ambiente* (Capitolium, Rome).
1977 Matteucci, Anna Maria, and Deanna Lenzi, *Cosimo Morelli e l'architettura delle legazioni pontificie* (University Press Bologna).
1988 Ceccarelli, Simonetta, "Carlo Marchionni e la Sagrestia Vaticana," in Debenedetti, Elisa, ed., *Carlo Marchionni, Architettura e scenografia contemporanea* (Multigrafica, Rome): 57–133.
1989 Ricci, Emiliana, *Palazzo Braschi, Storia ed Architettura di un edificio settecentesco* (Palombi, Rome).
2004 Collins, Jeffrey, *Papacy and Politics in Eighteent[h] Century Rome: Pius VI and the Arts* (Cambridg[e] University Press, New York).

GIUSEPPE PIERMARINI AND MILAN IN THE EIGHTEENTH CENTURY

1782 Albertolli, Giocondo, *Ornamenti diversi invent[ati] disegnati ed eseguiti da Giocondo Albertolli* (Milan).
1811 Silva, Ettore, *Elogio dell'architetto Giuseppe Piermarini* (Corbetto, Monza).
1826 Piermarini, Giuseppe, *Teatro della Scala in Milano* (Rome).
1975 Mezzanotte, Gianni, *Architettura neoclassica in Lombardia* (Scientifiche Italiane, Naples).
1977 Brizio, Anna Maria, "Il rinnovamento urbanistico di Milano nella seconda metà del Settecento," in *Nuove idee e nuova art nel Settecento italiano* (Accademia dei Lincei, Rome): 361–408.
1977 Secchi, Luigi, *1778–1978, Il Teatro alla Scala, architettura, tradizione, società* (Electa, Milan).
1982 Mezzanotte, Gianni, *L'architettura della Scala nell'età neoclassica* (Profilo, Milan).

83 Pirovano, Carlo, ed., *Piermarini e il suo tempo* (Electa, Milan).

NICE'S TEATRO LA FENICE AND CONCLUSIONS ON EOCLASSICISM

15 Cicognara, Leopoldo, Antonio Diedo and Giannantonio Selva, *Fabbriche e i monumenti più cospicui di Venezia* (Antonelli, Venice).

36 Bassi, Elena, *Giovanni Antonio Selva architetto veneziano* (R. Università di Padova / Olschki, Florence).

87 Brusatin, Manlio, and Giuseppe Pavanello, eds., *Il Teatro La Fenice, i progetti, l'architettura, le decorazioni* (Albrizzi, Venice).

96 Muraro, Maria Teresa, *Gran Teatro La Fenice* (Corbo e Fiore, Venice).

96 Romanelli, Giandomenico, et al., *Gran Teatro La Fenice* (Biblos, Citadella).

97 Biggi, Maria Ida, *Il Concorso per la Fenice, 1789–1790* (Marsilio, Venice).

HAPTER 2

APOLEON IN ITALY, 1800–1815

13 Cicognara, Leopoldo, *Storia della scultura dal suo risorgimento in Italia fino al secolo di Napoleone* (Picotti, Venice).

40 Letarouilly, Paul, *Édifices de Rome moderne, ou Receuil des palais, maisons, églises, couvents et autres monuments publiés et particuliers les plus remarcables de la Ville de Rome* (Firmin Didot, Paris, 1840–1857).

55 Faldi, Italo, "La festa patriotica della Federazione in due dipinti di Felice Giani," *Bollettino dei Musei Comunali di Roma* 2, 1/2: 14–18.

64 Gabetti, Roberto, and Paolo Marconi, *L'Insegnamento dell'architettura nel sistema didattico franco-italiano* (Politecnico di Torino, Facoltà d'Architettura, Istituto Elementi di Architettura e Rilievo dei Monumenti, Turin).

64 Honour, Hugh, "The Italian Empire Style," *Apollo* 80, 31: 216–36.

69 Boyer, Ferdinand, *Le monde des arts en Italie et la France de la Révolution et de l'Empire* (Internazionale, Turin).

70 Oechslin, Werner, "Premesse all'architettura rivoluzionaria," *Controspazio* 2, 1/2: 2–15.

73 Starobinski, Jean, *1789, Les emblèmes de la raison / 1789* (Flammarion, Paris), *The Emblems of Reason* (University Press of Virginia, Charlottesville, 1979).

78 Pinelli, Antonio, "La rivoluzione imposta o della natura dell'entusiasmo, Fenomenologia della festa nella Roma giacobina," *Quaderni sul neoclassico, Miscellanea* 4: 97–146.

1983 Morachiello, Paolo, and Georges Teyssot, *Nascita delle città di stato, Ingegneri e architetti sotto il consolato e l'impero* (Officina, Rome).

1986 Soldini, Jean, "L'architettura neoclassica, la forma, i nessi e il ritrarsi del visibile," *Archivio storico ticinese* 27, 107/08: 89–104.

1989 Mainardi, Patricia, "Assuring the empire of the future, the 1798 Fete de la Liberté" *Art Journal* 48, 2: 155–63.

1989 Matteucci, Anna Maria, "Committenza e massoneria a Bologna in età neoclassica," in Cresti, Carlo, ed., *Massoneria e architettura* (Bastogi, Foggia): 143–53.

1989 Pinon, Pierre, "L'architecte P.-A. Paris à Rome et l'administration napoléonienne (1810–1812)," *Bulletin de la Société de l'Histoire de l'art francais*: 143–57.

1990 Boime, Albert, *Art in the Age of Bonapartism 1800–1815* (University of Chicago Press, Chicago).

MILAN

1806 Antolini, Giovanni Antonio, *Opera d'architettura, ossia progetto sul foro che doveva eseguirsi in Milano* (Parma).

1959 Mezzanotte, Paolo, "L'architettura dal 1796 alla caduta del Regno Italico," in *Storia di Milano*13, *L'Età di Napoleone (1796–1814)* (Treccani degli Alfieri, Milan): 477–522.

1966 Mezzanotte, Gianni, *Architettura neoclassica in Lombardia* (Scientifiche Italiane, Naples).

1969 Westfall, Carroll William, "Antolini's Foro Bonaparte in Milan," *Journal of the Warburg and Courthauld Institutes* 32: 366–85.

1976 Rossi Pinelli, Orietta, "Il Foro Bonaparte: Progetto e fallimento di una città degli eguali," *Ricerche di Storia dell'Arte* 3: 43–76.

1977 Finocchi, Anna, "La scuola d'ornato dell'Accademica di Brera e Giacomo Albertolli," in Borsi, Franco, et al., *Architettura in Emilia-Romagna dall'Illuminismo alla Restaurazione, Atti del convegno* (Istituto della Storia dell'Architettura, University di Firenze, Florence): 159–69.

1980 Folli, Maria Grazia, and Danilo Samsa, eds., *Milano Parco Sempione: spazio pubblico, progetto, architettura, 1796–1980* (Triennale, Milan).

1989 Scotti, Aurora, *Il Foro Bonaparte, un'utopia giacobina a Milano* (Franco Maria Ricci, Milan).

VENICE

1815 Cicognara, Leopoldo, Antonio Diedo and Giannantonio Selva, *Le fabbriche e monumenti*

più cospicui di Venezia (Alvisopoli, Venice).
1963 Bassi, Elena, "L'architettura neoclassica a Venezia," *Bollettino del Centro internazionale di studi di architettura Andrea Palladio* 5: 135–43.
1977 Borsi, Franco, et al., *Architettura in Emilia-Romagna dall'Illuminismo alla Restaurazione* (Istituto della Storia dell'Architettura, University di Firenze, Florence).
1978 Romanelli, Giandomenico, "La città, architettura e servizi," in Bassi, Elena, et al., *Venezia nell'età di Canova 1780–1830* (Assessorato alla Cultura e alle Belle Arti, Venice): 301–11.
1983 Pavanello, Giuseppe, and Giandomenico Romanelli, *Venezia nell'Ottocento, immagine e mito* (Electa, Milan).
1985 Bellavitis, Giorgio, and Giandomenico Romanelli, *Venezia* (Laterza, Bari/Rome).
1994 Franzoi, Umberto, "L'Ala Napoleonica," in Nepi Scire, Giovanna, et al., *Procuratie Nuove in Piazza San Marco* (Ediltalia, Rome): 117–56.

TURIN
1935 Olivero, Eugenio, *L'architettura in Torino durante la prima metà dell'Ottocento* (Accame, Turin).
1960 Cavallari-Murat, Augusto, "Breve storia dell'urbanistica in Piedmonte," in *Storia del Piemonte* 2 (Casanova, Turin): 929–47.
1969 Tamburini, L., "Il tempio della Gran Madre di Dio," *Torino* 2: 30–.
1976 Bergeron, C., "La Piazza Vittorio Veneto e la Piazza Gran Madre di Dio," *Studi piemontesi* 5: 211–19.
1980 Castelnuovo, Enrico, and Marco Rosci, *Cultura figurativa e architettonica negli Stati del Re di Sardegna 1773–1861* (Provincia di Torino).

NAPLES
1961 Venditti, Arnaldo, *Architettura neoclassica a Napoli* (Scientifiche Italiane, Naples).
1971 Alisio, Giancarlo, "Sviluppo urbano e struttura della città," in *Storia di Napoli* 8 (Soc. Ed. "Storia di Napoli"): 311–66.
1981 De Seta, Cesare, *Napoli* (Laterza, Bari/Rome).
1989 Scalvini, Maria Luisa, "Antonio Niccolini e il 'progetto grande' per Napoli, da Gioacchino Murat a Ferdinando II," in Carpeggiani, Paolo, and Luciano Patetta, eds., *Il Disegno di architettura, Atti del convegno* (Guerini, Milan): 79–86.
1995 Ossanna Cavadini, Nicoletta, ed., *Pietro Bianchi, 1787–1849, architetto archeologo* (Electa Napoli, Naples).
1997 Giannetti, Anna, and Rosanna Muzii, eds., *Antonio Niccolini, architetto e scenografo alla Cor di Napoli (1807–1850)* (Electa Napoli, Naple
1999 Capobianco, Fernanda, and Katia Fiorentino, *Tempio dei Borboni, La Chiesa di San Francesco Paola in Piazza del Plebiscito a Napoli* (Altrastampa, Naples).

TRIESTE
1814 Nobile, Pietro, *Progetti di varii monumenti architettonici immaginati per celebrare il trionfo de augusti alleati, la pace, la concordia dei popoli e la rinascente felicità d'Europa* (Governiale, Trieste)
1971 Semenzato, Camillo, "L'architettura neoclassi a Trieste," *Bollettino del Centro internazionale d studi di architettura Andrea Palladio* 13: 151–57
1984 Godoli, Ezio, *Trieste* (Laterza, Bari/Rome).
1988 Caputo, Fulvio, and Roberto Masiero, eds., *Trieste: architettura neoclassica, guida tematica* (Fachin, Trieste).
1988 Zanni, Nicoletta, "Ledoux a Trieste: 'Gloriett all'acquedotto," *Arte in Friuli, Arte a Trieste* 10 83–90.
1990 Caputo, Fulvio, ed., *Neoclassico, arte, architettur cultura a Trieste 1790–1840* (Marsilio, Venice).
1990 Caputo, Fulvio, and Roberto Masiero, eds., *Neoclassico, la ragione, l'architettura, la memoria, una città: Trieste* (Marsilio, Venice).
1991 De Vecchi, Fiorenza, "Pietro Nobile, funzionario presso la direzione delle fabbrich a Trieste," *Atii e memorie della Società Istriana d Archeologia e Storia Patria* 91: 53–78.
1991 Pacorig, Monica, "Massoneria e architettura nella Trieste neoclassica; il caso di Pietro Nobile," *Arte documento* 5: 226–31.

THE NEOCLASSICAL INTERIOR
1823 Caciali, Giuseppe, *Parte seconda dell'opera architettonica di Giuseppe Caciali la quale contien disegni dei nuovi ornamenti aggiunta e da aggiune all'I. e R. Palazzo Pitti* (Florence).
1829 Missirini, Melchiore, *Il trionfo di Alessandro. . . inventato e scolpito dal Cav. Alberto Thorvaldsen* (Aureli, Rome).
1940 Praz, Mario, *Gusto neoclassico* (Sansoni, Florence) / *On Neoclassicism* (Thames and Hudson, London, 1969).
1970 Ternois, Daniel, "Napoléon et la décoration d Palais Impérial de Monte Cavallo en 1811–1813," *Revue de l'Art* 7: 68–89.
1972 Praz, Mario, "Meaning and Diffusion of the Empire Style," in *The Age of Neo-Classicism* (Royal Academy and Victoria and Albert Museum, London): xxxix–xciv.
1978 Garzya, Chiara, *Interni neoclassici a Napoli*

(Sannitica, Naples).

79 Arizzoli-Clémentel, Pierre, "Les projets d'aménagement interieur et de décoration du palais Pitti pour Napoléon Ier et Marie-Louise, 1810–1814," in Cresti, M.V., ed., *Florence et la France, rapports sous la Révolution et l'Empire* (Centro Di, Florence / Quatre-Chemins, Paris): 289–340.

89 Natoli, Marina,and Maria Antonietta Scarpati, eds., *Il Palazzo Quirinale, il mondo artistico a Roma nel periodo napoleonico* (Poligrafico dello Stato, Rome).

91 Borsi, Franco, ed., *Il Palazzo del Quirinale* (Lavoro, Rome).

ME

07 Valadier, Giuseppe, *Progetti architettonici per ogni specie di fabriche in stili e usi diversi* (Feoli, Rome).

10 Valadier, Giuseppe, *Raccolta delle più insigne fabbriche di Roma antica e sue adjacenze* (De Romanis, Rome).

33 Valadier, Giuseppe, *Opere di architettura e di ornamento* (Rome).

37 Schultz-Battmann, Elfriede, *Giuseppe Valadier, ein klassizisticher Architekt Roms 1762–1839* (Zetzche, Dresden).

43 Apollonj-Ghetti, Bruno, "Il primo progetto del Valadier per la sistemazione della Piazza del popolo," *Capitolium* 7: 211–20.

46 Matthiae, Guglielmo, *Piazza del Popolo attraverso i documenti del primo ottocento* (Palombi, Rome).

61 Muñoz, Antonio, "Roma del primo ottocento," *L'Urbe* 24, 6: 3–8.

64 Marconi, Paolo, *Giuseppe Valadier* (Officina, Rome).

69 La Padula, Attilio, *Roma e la regione nell'epoca napoleonica, Contributo alla storia urbanistica della città e del territorio* (IEPI, Rome).

74 Ciucci, Giorgio, *La Piazza del Popolo, Storia architettura urbanistica* (Officina, Rome).

79 Debenedetti, Elisa, *Valadier diario architettonico* (Bulzoni, Rome).

85 Debenedetti, Elisa, ed., *Valadier, segno e architettura* (Multigrafica, Rome).

85 Pinon, Pierre, " 'Le grandi opere appartengano ai grandi sovrani', Un palazzo imperiale sul Campidoglio?," in *Forma, La Città antica e il suo avvenire* (De Luca, Roma): 28–29.

89 Natoli, Marina, and Maria Antoinette Scapati, eds., *Il mondo artistico a Roma nel periodo napoleonico* (Poligrafico dello Stato, Rome).

92 Pinon, Pierre, "Berthault ou Valadier? La place du Peuple et le jardin du Grand César à Rome," *Monuments historiques* 38, 180: 19–24.

NAPOLEON'S INTEREST IN ARCHEOLOGY

1973 Assunto, Rosaria, *L'antichità come futuro, studio sull'estetica del neoclassicismo europeo* (Mursia, Milan).

1987 Marino, Angela, "Progetto e tutela, La cultura archeologica a Roma in epoca napoleonica," in Spagnesi, Gianfranco, ed., *Esperienze di storia dell'architettura e di restauro* 1 (Enciclopedia Treccani, Rome): 309–14.

1987 Pinon, Pierre, "Naissance de la restauration moderne," *Monuments historiques de la France* 149: 49–51.

1990 Panza, Pierluigi, *Antichità e restauro nell'Italia del Settecento, Dal ripristino alla conservazione delle opere d'arte* (Francoangeli, Milan).

1992 Ridley, Ronald, *The Eagle and the Spade, Archeology in Rome during the Napoleonic Era* (Cambridge University Press, New York).

POLITICAL RESTORATION AND RESTITUTION OF ARTWORKS

1965 Boyer, Ferdinand, "Louis XVIII et la restitution des oeuvres d'art confisquées sous la Révolution e l'Empire," *Bulletin de la Socété de l'Histoire de l'Art Francais*: 201–07.

1978 Pinelli, Antonio, "Storia dell'arte e cultura della tutela, Le Lettres à Miranda di Quatremère-de-Quincy," *Ricerche di Storia dell'arte* 8: 42–62.

1985 Pietrangeli, Carlo, *I Musei Vaticani, cinque secoli di storia* (Quasar, Rome).

1991 Strazzulo, Franco, "Domenico Venuti e il recupero delle opere d'arte trafugate dai francesi a Napoli nel 1799," *Rendiconto dell'Accademia di archeologia, lettere e belle arti* 63: 13–26.

1993 De Angelis, Maria, "Il primo allestimento del Museo Chiaramonti in un manoscritto del 1808," *Bollettino dei Monumenti, Musei e Gallerie Pontificie* 13: 81–126.

1994 De Angelis, Maria, "Il 'Braccio Nuovo' del Museo Chiaramonti: Un prototipo di museo tra passato e futuro," *Bollettino dei Monumenti, Musei e Galleria Pontificie* 14: 187–256.

CHAPTER 3

RESTORATION AND ROMANTICISM, 1815–1860

1815 Cicognara, Leopoldo, *Dei quattro cavalli riportati sul pronao della Basilica di S. Marco, Narrazione storica* (Alvisopoli, Venice).

1883 De Gubernatis, Angelo, *Dizionario d'artisti italiani viventi, pittori, scultori, architetti* (Le

Monnier, Florence).
1952 Grassi, Liliana, "Architettura romantica," *Palladio* 2: 71–78.
1973 Gabetti, Roberto, and Andreina Griseri, *Architettura dell'eclettismo, Un Saggio su Giovanni Schellino* (Einaudi, Turin).
1989 Cresti, Carlo, ed., *Massoneria e architettura* (Bastogi, Foggia).
1992 Debenedetti, Elisa, ed, *Architettura, città, territorio, Realizzazioni e teorie tra illuminismo e romanticismo* (Bonsignore, Rome).

GIUSEPPE JAPPELLI AND THE ROMANTIC IDEAL

1816 *Descrizione della Festa Drammatica offerta nella gran Sala della Ragione alle LL. MM. II. RR. Francesco Primo e Maria Lodovica dalla Città Regia di Padova durante il loro soggiorno d'eterna ricordanza nel dicembre MDCCCXV* (Bettoni, Padova).
1869 Selvatico, Pietro, *Guida di Padova e dei principali suoi contorni* (Sacchetto, Padova).
1963 Gallimberti, Nino, *Giuseppe Jappelli* (La Stediv, Padova).
1977 Puppi, Lionello, and Fulvio Zulian, eds., *Padova, Case e Palazzi* (Neri Pozza, Vicenza).
1977 Romanelli, Giandomenico, "Jappelli per l'Università di Padova: un incompiuto manifesto di architettura," *Casabella* 41, 429: 41–7.
1980 Puppi, Lionello, *Il Caffè Pedrocchi di Padova* (Neri Pozza, Vicenza).
1982 Franco, Maria Teresa, "Un luogo per la società civile: il casino Pedrocchi," *Bollettino del Museo Civico di Padova* 71: 239–75.
1982 Mazza, Giuliana, ed., *Giuseppe Jappelli e il suo tempo* (Liviana, Padova).
1983 Bussadori, Paola, and Renato Roverato, *Il giardino romantico e Jappelli* (Comune di Padova).
1984 Mazza, Barbara, and Lionello Puppi, *Guida storica al Caffè Pedrocchi di Padova* (MP, Castelfranco Veneto).

VILLA RIVALRY: THE BORGHESE AND THE TORLONIA OF ROME

1828 Canina, Luigi, *Le nuove fabbriche della Villa Borghese denominata Pinciana* (Società Tipografica, Rome).
1832 Canina, Luigi, *L'architettura antica descritta e dimostrata coi monumenti . . . La storia, la teoria e le pratiche dell'architettura egiziana, greca, romana*, 10 vols. (the author, Rome).
1842 Checchetelli, Giuseppe, *Una giornata di osservazione nel palazzo e nella Villa di S. E. il Sig. Principe D. Alessandro Torlonia* (Piccinelli, Rome); reprinted in *Ricerche di storia dell'arte* 28/29 (1986): 39–81.
1842 Landesio, Eugenio, and Pietro Rosa, *Vedute principali della Villa Borghese* (Rome).
1986 Apolloni, Marco, with Alberta Campitelli, Antonio Pinelli, and Barbara Steindl, "La Vill di Alessandro Torlonia," *Ricerche di storia dell'a* 28/29: 5–35.
1990 Fagiolo dell'Arco, Marcello, "Villa Borghese Villa Torlonia, il modello di Villa Adriana ovvero il panorama della storia," in Tagliolini Alessandro , ed., *Il giardino italiano dell'Ottocen delle immagine, nella letteratura, nella memoria* (Guerini, Milan): 207–14.
1993 Steindl, Barbara, *Mäzenatentum in Rom des 19 Jahrhunderts: die Familie Torlonia* (Olms, Hildesheim).
1995 Sistri, Augusto, ed., *Luigi Canina (1795–1856 Architetto e teorico del classicismo* (Guerini, Milan).
1997 Lanzara Baldan Zenoni-Politeo, Giuliana, ed. *Il giardino dei sentimenti, Giuseppe Jappelli, architetto del paesaggio* (Guerini, Milan): 136–4
1997 Campitelli, Alberta, ed., *Villa Torlonia, L'ultima impresa del mecenatismo romano* (Poligrafico e Zecca dello Stato, Rome).

ITALIAN OPERA STAGE DESIGN AND THEATER INTERIORS

1830 Ferrario, Giulio, *Storia e descrizione de' principa teatri antichi e oderni, corredata de tavole col Sagg sull'architettura teatrale di Mr. Patte, illustrato con erudite osservazioni del chiarissimo architetto e pittore scenico Paolo Landriani* (the author, Milan).
1844 Niccolini, Antonio, *Sulle interne restaurazioni d Real Teatro San Carlo* (Naples).
1973 Fagiolo, Maurizio, *La scenografia dalle sacre rappresentazioni al futurismo* (Sansoni, Florence)
1987–88 Viale Ferrero, Mercedes, "Luogo teatrale e spazio scenico," and Morelli, Giovanni, "L'opera nella cultura nazionale italiana," in Bianconi, Lorenzo, and Giorgio Pestelli, eds., *Storia dell'opera italiana* 5 (EDT, Turin): 1–122 and 6: 393–454.
1995 Biggi, Maria Ida, *L'Immagine e la scena, Giusep Borsato, scenografo alla Fenice, 1809–1823* (Marsilio, Venice).
1995 Bucci, Moreno, ed., *Rapporti tra la scena e le ar figurative dalla fine dell'800* (Olschki, Florence).

NTONIO CANOVA'S TEMPLE IN POSSAGNO
813–18, 1823–25
Cicognara, Leopoldo, *Storia della scultura dal suo risorgimento in Italia fino al secolo di Napoleone*, 8 vols. (Picotti, Venice); *Storia della scultura dal suo risorgimento in Italia fino al secolo di Canova*, 8 vols. (Giachetti, Prato).
821 Luciolli, Gerolamo, *Descrizione del Tempio ideato dal marchese Canova e che per sola sua cura si sta costruendo a Possagno* (Venice).
833 Missirini, Melchiore, *Del tempio eretto in Possagno da Antonio Canova* (Antonelli, Venice).
834 Quatremère de Quincy, Antoine-Chrysostôme, *Canova et ses ouvrages* (Le Clere, Paris).
934 Bassi, Elena, "L'architetto Francesco Lazzari," *Rivista di Venezia* 13, 6: 239–50.
979 Argan, Giulio Carlo, Giandomenico Romanelli, and Giovanni Scarabello, *Canova, Cicognara, Foscolo* (Arsenale Cooperativa, Venice).
980 Wischermann, Heinfried, "Canovas Pantheon, Überlegungen zum Tempio Canoviano von Possagno," *Architectura* 10, 2: 134–63.
987 Paolin, Elide, ed., *Canova e Possagno* (Comunità Montana del Grappa / Asolo).
994 Barbieri, Franco, "Il Tempio canoviano di Possagno: fede e ragione," *Arte lombarda* 110/111, 3/4: 21–23.
998 Johns, Christopher, *Antonio Canova and the Politics of Patronage in Revolutionary and Napoleonic Europe* (University of California Press, Berkeley).
998 Mellini, Gian Lorenzo, "Per il Tempio di Possagno," *Labyrinthos* 17, 33/34: 217–40, reprinted in Mellini, Gian Lorenzo, *Canova, Saggio di filologia e di ermeneutica* (Skira, Milan 1999).

ANTHEON PROGENY AND CARLO BARABINO
827 *Piante e prospetti del Teatro Carlo Felice di Genova, inventato e diretto da Carlo Barabino* (Pagano, Genova).
977 De Negri, Emmina, *Ottocento e rinnovamento urbano: Carlo Barabino* (Sagep, Genova).
986 Botto, Ida Maria, ed., *Il Teatro Carlo Felice di Genova, Storia e progetti* (Sagep, Genova).
997 Sborgi, Franco, *Staglieno e la scultura funeraria ligure tra ottocento e novecento* (Artema, Turin).

OMANTICISM IN TUSCANY
845 Puccini, Niccolo, et al., *Monumenti del Giardino Puccini* (Cini, Pistoia).
974 Gurrieri, Francesco, et al., *Pasquale Poccianti architetto, 1774–1858, Studi e ricerche* (UNIEDIT, Florence).
1975 Borsi, Franco, with Gabriele Morolli, and Luigi Zangheri, *Firenze e Livorno e l'opera di Pasquale Poccianti nell'età granducale* (Officina, Rome).
1981 Danti, Cristina, "Per l'arte neoclassica e romantica a Siena," *Bulletino senese di storia patria* 88: 115–68.
1984 Di Giovine, Mirella, and Daniele Negri, *Il Giardino Puccini di Pistoia* (Comune di Pistoia).
1992 Cozzi, Mauro, Franco Nuti and Luigi Zangheri, *Edilizia in Toscana dal Granducato allo Stato unitario* (Edifir, Florence).
1992 Cresti, Carlo, ed., *Agostino Fantastici, Architetto senese, 1782–1845* (Allemandi, Turin).
1992 Matteoni, Dario, *Pasquale Poccianti e l'acquedotto di Livorno* (Laterza, Bari/Rome).
1994 Mazzoni, Gianni, ed., *Agostino Fantastici, Vocabolario di architettura: prima edizione completa dal manoscritto autografo* (Cadmo, Florence).
1999 Bonacchi Gazzarrini, Giuliana, *Il Pantheon nel giardino romantico di Scornio* (Polistampa, Florence).
2000 Matteoni, Dario, *Il Cisternone di Pasquale Poccianti* (Silvana, Milan).

ALESSANDRO ANTONELLI
1874 Antonelli, Alessandro, *Osservazioni all'Illustrissimo Signor Sindaco della Città di Torino sulla vertenza del Tempio Israelitico* (Torino).
1877 Caselli, Leandro, *La cupola della basilica di S. Gaudenzio in Novara, Architettura del Prof. Comm. Alessandro Antonelli, Dissertazione di Laurea* (Camilla and Bertolero, Turin); also published in *L'Ingegneria Civile e le Arti Industriali* 3 (1877) 1: 45–62.
1962 Gabetti, Roberto, "Problematica antonelliana," *Atti e rassegna tecnica della Società Ingegneri e Architetti in Torino* 16, 6: 159–94; reprinted as *Alessandro Antonelli* (Clup, Milan, 1989).
1989 Rosso, Franco, with Roberto Gabetti, and Vittorio Nascè, *Alessandro Antonelli, 1798–1888* (Stampatori, Turin).

CONSTRUCTION IN IRON
1970 Bruschi, Arnaldo, "Carlo Reishammer e 'l'architettura' della Fonderia di Follonica," *L'Architettura, cronache e storia* 15, 9/171: 622–26; 10/172: 686–96; 11/173: 762–66.
1977 Briano, Italo, *Storia delle Ferrovie in Italia* (Guerini, Milan).
1978 Lensi Orlandi, Giulio, *Ferro e architettura a Firenze* (Vallecchi, Florence).
1984 Zangheri, Luigi, ed., *L'Architettura di Giuseppe e*

Alessandro Manetti e Carlo Reishammer (Edam, Florence).
1985 Jodice, Romano, *L'architettura del ferro, l'Italia 1796–1914* (Bulzoni, Rome).

ARCHITECTURAL RESTORATION OF MONUMENTS

1822 Valadier, Giuseppe, *Narrazione artistica dell'operato finora nel restauro dell'arco di Tito* (De Romanis, Rome).
1823 Valadier, Giuseppe, *Progetto per la riedificazione della Basilica Ostiense, Della basilica di S. Paolo sulla via Ostiense* (Rome).
1825 Fea, Carlo, *Aneddoti sulla basilica ostiense di S. Paolo riuniti del 1823 dopo l'incendio* (Poggioli, Rome).
1865 Campori, Cesare, *Notizie biografiche del Comm. Prof. Luigi Poletti modenese, architetto di S. Paolo di Roma* (Vincenzi, Modena).
1959 Bonelli, Renato, "Il restauro come forma di cultura," in Bonelli, Renato, *Architettura e restauro* (Neri Pozza, Vicenza).
1971 Di Macco, Michela, *Il Colosseo, funzione simbolica storica urbana* (Bulzone, Rome).
1974 Gurrieri, Francesco, ed., *Teoria e cultura del restauro dei monumenti e dei centri antichi* (CLUSF, Florence).
1975 Marani, Stefano, "Intorno alla ricostruzione della basilica di S. Paolo f. l. m. a Roma," *Storia Architettura* 2, 3: 23–36.
1978 Marconi, Paolo, "Roma 1806–1829, un momento critico per la formazione della metodologia del restauro architettonico," *Ricerche di Storia dell'Arte* 8: 63–72.
1980 Fischer, Manfred, "«In pristinum» Brand und Wiederaufbau von S. Paolo fuori le mura in Rom, 1823–54," *Deutsche Kunst und Denkmalpflege* 38, 1/2: 6–19.
1986 Jonsson, Marita, "La cura dei monumenti alle origini, Restauro e scavo di monumenti antichi a Roma 1800–1830," *Skrifter Utgivna av Svenska Institutet i Rom, 8∞*,14: 9–190.
1992 Casiello, Stella, ed., *Restauro tra metamorfosi e teorie* (Electa Napoli, Naples).
1992 Dezzi Bardeschi, Marco, et al., *Luigi Poletti architetto (1792–1869)* (Nuova Alfa, Carpi).

REVIVALISM AND CAMILLO BOITO

1844 Marchi, Giuseppe, *Monumenti delle arti cristiane primitive nella metropoli del Cristianesimo* (Piccinelli, Rome).
1859 Selvatico, Pietro, *Scritti d'arte* (Barbera, Bianchi and Co., Florence), including "Prelezione al corso di storia architettonica," "Quale fosse l'educazione dell'architettura nel passato e quale sia al presente in Italia".
1880 Boito, Camillo, *Architettura del Medio Evo in Italia, con un introduzione sullo stile futuro dell'architettura italiana* (Hoepli, Milan).
1889 Broccoli, Angelo, "Del tempio monumentale nazionale di San Francesco di Assisi nella città di Gaeta," *Archivio Storico Campano* 1, 2/3: 124
1893 Boito, Camillo, *Questioni pratiche di belle arti, Restauri, concorsi, legislazione, professione, insegnamento* (Hoepli, Milan).
1916 Beltrami, Luca, et al., eds., *Camillo Boito* (Comitato per le onoranze alla sua memoria, Milan).
1959 Grassi, Liliana, *Camillo Boito* (Il Balcone, Milan).
1974 Bernabei, Franco, *Pietro Selvatico nella critica e nella storia delle arti figurative dell'ottocento* (Neri Pozza, Vicenza).
1979 Lipfert, David, "Gothic in Eighteenth-Centur Italy," in *Luigi Vanvitelli e il '700 Europa* 2 (Istituto di storia dell'architettura, Università d Napoli, Naples): 3–8.
1980 Castelnuovo, Enrico, and Marco Rosci, *Cultur figurativa e architettonica negli Stati del Re di Sardegna 1773–1861* (Provincia di Torino).
1989 Bossaglia, Rossana, and Valerio Terraroli, eds., *Neogotico nel XIX e XX secolo* (Mazzotta, Milan).
1990 Salvatore, Marcello, "Camillo Boito e le sue opere in Padova," in Bozzoni, Corrado, et al, eds., *Saggi in Onore di Renato Bonelli, Quaderni dell'Istituto di Storia dell'Architettura* 15/20, 2 (Multigrafica, Rome): 835–46.
1997 Simoncini, Giorgio, ed., *Presenze medievali nell'architettura di età moderna e contemporanea* (Guerini, Milan).
1997 Zucconi, Guido, *L'invenzione del passato: Camillo Boito e l'architettura neomediovale, 1855–1890* (Marsilio, Venice).
2000 Zucconi, Guido, and Francesca Castellani, *Camillo Boito, un'architettura per l'Italia unita* (Marsilio, Venice).

CHAPTER 4
UNIFICATION AND THE NATION'S CAPITALS, 1860–1900

1966 Borsi, Franco, *L'architettura dell'unità d'Italia* (Le Monnier, Florence).
1974 Cresti, Carlo, *Per un itinerario risorgimentale dell'architettura italiana* (CLUSF, Florence).
1976 Morachiello, Paolo, *Ingegneri e territorio nell'età della Destra, 1860–1875, Dal Canale Cavour all'Agro Romano* (Officina, Rome).
1982 Simoncini, Giorgio, ed., *Le capitali italiane dal*

Rinascimento all'unità, Urbanistica politica economia (CLUP, Milan).
)92 De Stefani, Lorenzo, *Le scuole di architettura in Italia il dibattito dal 1860 al 1933* (Francoangeli, Milan).
)93 Ricci, Giuliana, ed., *L'architettura nelle accademie riformate, Insegnamento, dibattito culturale, interventi pubblici* (Guerini, Milan).
)96 Isnenghi, Mario, ed., *I Luoghi della memoria, Simboli e miti dell'Italia unita* (Laterza, Bari/Rome).

URIN, THE FIRST CAPITAL
346 Promis, Carlo, "La Coltura e la civiltà, loro influenza sull'arte e segnamento sulla architettura," *Antologia Italiana* 1, 4: 1–17.
367 Mazzucchetti, Alessandro, *Scalo ferroviario eretto in Torino su disegni dell'Ingegner Alessandro Mazzucchetti* (Turin).
371 Promis, Carlo *Fabbriche moderne inventate da Carlo Promis ad uso degli studenti di architettura,* Castellazzi, Giovanni, ed. (Turin).
968 Scarzella, Paolo, "L'impronta di Carlo Promis come urbanista verso la metà dell'Ottocento," in Cavallari Murat, Augusto, ed., *Forma urbana ed architettura nella Torino barocca* 1, 2 (Istituto d'Architettura tecnica, Politecnico di Torino / UTET, Turin): 1086–98.
992 Massaia, Alberto, "Carlo Ceppi: un protagonaista dell'Ecletticismo a Torino," *Studi Piemontesi* 21, 2: 407–31.
993 Fasoli, Vilma, and Clara Vitulo, eds., *Carlo Promis, professore di architettura civile agli esordi della cultura politecnica* (Celid, Turin).
994 Comoli Mandracci, Vera, *Torino* (Laterza, Bari/Rome).

LORENCE, THE INTERIM CAPITAL
882 Poggi, Giuseppe, *Sui lavori per l'ingrandimento di Firenze, 1864–1877* (Barbera, Florence).
973 Fanelli, Giovanni, *Firenze, Architettura e città*, and *Atlante* (Vallecchi, Florence).
977 Cresti, Carlo, and Silvano Fei, "Le vicende del 'risanamento' del Mercato Vecchio a Firenze," *Storia urbana* 1, 2: 99–126.
989 Manetti, Renzo, and Gabriele Morelli, eds., *Giuseppe Poggi e Firenze, Disegni di architettura e città* (Alinea, Florence).
992 Corsani, Gabriele, "Giuseppe Poggi e il Viale dei Colli a Firenze," *Storia urbana* 16, 60: 37–58.
995 Cresti, Carlo, *Firenze, capitale mancata: architettura e città dal piano Poggi a oggi* (Electa, Milan).

NAPLES *RISANATA*
1894 Croce, Benedetto, "L'agonia di una strada," *Napoli Nobilissima* 3: 177–78.
1959 Russo, Giuseppe, *Il Risanamento e l'ampliamento della città di Napoli* (Società pel Risanamento, Naples).
1962 Bruno, Giuseppe, and Renato De Fusco, *Errico Alvino, architetto e urbanista napoletano dell'800* (Arte Tipografica, Naples).
1977 Marmo, Marcella, "Piano di 'Risanamento' e 'Ampliamento' dal 1885 a Napoli," *Storia urbana* 1, 2: 145–53.
1978 Alisio, Giancarlo, *Lamont Young, Utopia e realtà nell'urbanistica napoletana dell'Ottocento* (Officina, Rome).
1989 Biocca, Dario,"Urban renewal and economic crisis in Naples: 1884–1904" (Ph.D., University of California, Berkeley).

MILAN, THE INDUSTRIAL CAPITAL
1863 Mengoni, Giuseppe, *Progetto della nuova piazza del Duomo di Milano e della Via Vittorio Emanuele* (Milan).
1969 Geist, Johann Friedrich, *Passagen: Ein Bautyp des 19 Jahrhunderts* (Prestel, Munich).
1987 Fontana, Vincenzo, and Nullo Pirazzoli, *Giuseppe Mengoni, 1829–1877, un architetto di successo* (Essegi, Ravenna).
1992 Rozzi, Renato, et al., eds., *La Milano del Piano Beruto (1884–1889)* (Guerini, Milan).
1995 Gioeni, Laura, *L'affaire Mengoni: La piazza Duomo e la Galleria Vittorio Emanuele di Milano, I concorsi, la realizzazione, i restauri* (Guerini, Milan).
1997 Grelseri, Giuliano, ed., *La Galleria Vittorio Emanuele e l'Architetto Mengoni* (La Mandragora, Imola).
2000 Mozzarelli, Cesare, and Rosanna Pavone, *Milano 1848–1898, Ascesa e trasformazione della capitale morale* (Marsilio, Venice).

CATHEDRAL FACADES AND TOWN HALLS
1875 De Fabris, Emilio, *La facciata di S. Maria del Fiore: appendice artistica diretta alla Deputazione Promotrice e ai suoi concittadini* (Bencini, Florence).
1888 Del Moro, Luigi, *La facciata di Santa Maria del Fiore, illustrazione storica e artistica* (Ferroni, Florence).
1900 Beltrami, Luca, *Storia della facciata di S. Maria del Fiore in Firenze* (Allegretti, Milan).
1903 Beltrami, Luca, *Settantadue giorni ai lavori del Campanile di S. Marco* (Allegretti, Milan).
1913 Rubbiani, Alfonso, *Di Bologna riabbellita*

(Cappelli, Bologna).
1976 Dezzi Bardeschi, Marco, "Gottfried Semper e l'architettura dello storicismo in Italia: Il terzo concorso per la facciata del duomo di Firenze," in Börsche-Supan, Eva, et al., *Gottfried Semper und die Mitte des 19. Jahrhunderts* (Birkhäuser, Basel): 329.
1979 Mazzei, Otello, *Alfonso Rubbiani, La Mascheria e il volto della città, Bologna, 1879–1913* (Cappelli, Bologna).
1981 Dezzi Bardeschi, Marco, ed., *Firenze, Il Monumento e il suo doppio* (Alinari, Florence).
1981 Dezzi Bardeschi, Marco, and Franco Solmi, eds., *Alfonso Rubbiani: i veri e i falsi storici* (Galleria d'Arte Moderna and Comune di Bologna).
1987 Cova, Massimo, "Fotografie e restauro nell'opera di Alfonso Rubbiani," *Il Carrobbio* 13: 105–17.
1987 Cozzi, Mauro, Gabriella Carapelli and Carlo Cresti, *Il Duomo di Firenze, 1822–1887, L'avventura della facciata* (Il Bossolo, Florence).
1989 Bossaglia, Rossana, and Valerio Terraroli, eds., *Il neogotico nel XIX e XX secolo* (Mazzotta, Milan).
1989 Scalvini, Maria Luisa, "La facciata neogotica per il Duomo di Napoli nell'itinerario eclettico di Enrico Alvino," in Bossaglia, Rossana, and Valerio Terraroli, eds., *Il neogotico nel XIX e XX secolo* 2 (Mazzotta, Milan): 383–97.
1991 Contorni, Gabriella, "La materia e il metodo nel restauro dell'architettura policroma: Il Duomo di Siena," in Lambertini, Daniele, ed., *Il Bianco e il verde: architettura policroma fra storia e restauro* (Alinea, Florence): 87–97.
1991 Fiengo, Giuseppe, *Il Duomo di Amalfi, restauro ottocentesco della faciata* (Centro di cultura e storia amalfitana, Amalfi).
1991 Toscano, Gennaro, "Enrico Alvino e la ricostruzione della facciata del Duomo di Amalfi," in Lamberini, Daniele, ed., *Il Bianco e il verde: architettura policromia fra storia e restauro* (Alinea, Florence): 99–111.
1994 Fiengo, Giuseppe, et al., eds., *La parabola del restauro stilistico nella rilettura di sette casi emblematici* (Guerini, Milan).
1995 Zucconi, Guido, ed., *Un Palazzo medievale dell'ottocento, Architettura, arte e letteratura nel Palazzo Pubblico di San Marino* (Jaca, Milan).
1996 Verdon, Timothy, ed., *Alla riscoperta di Piazza del Duomo in Firenze, 5, La facciata di Santa Maria del Fiore* (Centro Di, Florence).
1999 Casiello, Stella, ed., *Falsi restauri, Trasformazioni architettoniche e urbane nell'ottocento in Campania* (Gangemi, Rome).
2001 *Aemelia Ars 1898–1903: Arts and Crafts a Bologna* (A+G Edizioni, Milan).
2001 Gresleri, Giuliano, and Pier Giorgio Massaretti, *Norma e arbitrio, Architetti e ingegneri a Bologna, 1850–1950* (Marsilio, Venice).
2002 Schiffini, Sandrino, and Stefano Zuffi, eds., *La storia d'Italia nei palazzi del Governo* (Electa, Milan).

PALERMO AND NATIONAL UNIFICATION

1894 Basile, Ernesto, "Il Teatro Massimo di Palermo," *L'Edilizia Moderna* 3, 2: 9–11.
1980 De Seta, Cesare, and Leonardo Di Mauro, *Palermo* (Laterza, Bari/Rome).
1983 Samonà, Antonio, *L'eclettico del secondo ottocento G. B. Filippo Basile, la cultura e l'opera architettonica teorica didattica* (ILAPalma, Palermo).
1984 Pirrone, Gianni, *Il Teatro Massimo di G. B. Filippo Basile a Palermo* (Officina, Roma).
1995 Basile, Giovan Battista Filippo, *Lezioni di architettura*, Giuffrè, Maria, and Giuseppe Guerrera, eds. (L'Epos, Palermo).
1995 Lo Nardo, Salvo, *Giovan Battista Filippo Basile, 1825–1891* (Panini, Modena).

THE LAST OF PAPAL ROME

1868 Busiri Vici, Andrea, *Progetti del nuovo coro, presbiterio e dipendenze dell'arcibasilica lateranense* (Tiberina, Rome).
1868 Letarouilly, Paul, *Les Edifices de Rome* (Morel, Paris).
1877 Busiri Vici, Andrea, *Illustrazione del progetto e disegni sul transferimento meccanico e totale conservazione dell'abside lateranense* (Tiberina, Rome).
1951 *La Nuova Stazione di Roma Termini delle Ferrovie Italiane dello Stato, raccolta di articoli pubblicati da "Ingegneria Ferroviaria"* (Collegio Ingegneri Ferroviari Italiani, Rome).
1974 Angeleri, Gianfranco, and Umberto Mariotti Bianchi, *I cento anni della vecchia Termini* (Banca Nazionale della Communicazione, Rome).
1978 Spagnesi, Gianfranco, *L'architettura a Roma al tempo di Pio IX* (Multigrafica, Rome).
1979 Fagiolo, Marcello, "La Roma di Pio IX: Revival della controriforma o autunno del medioevo?," in Borsi, Franco, ed., *Arte a Roma dal NeoClassico al Romanticismo* (Editalia, Rome): 87–120.
1990 Tolomeo, Maria Grazia, "Il monumento della Immacolata Concezione di Luigi Poletti, arte e architettura della restaurazione," *Bollettino dei*

Musei comunali di Roma 4: 87–101.
1993 Mulder, Suzanne, "Image Building by Means of Church Restorations, Conservations of Ancient Monuments, Evangelic Diligence and Church Policy Under the Pontificate of Pius IX During the Years 1850 – 1870," in Van Kessel, Peter, ed., *Power of Imagery, Essays on Rome, Italy and Imagination* (Apeiron / Nederlands Institute te Rome): 83–97.
1995 Pastorino, Armanda, and Laura Pastorino, "I restauri delle chiese ad impianto basilicale a Roma durante il pontificato di Pio IX," *Ricerche di storia dell'arte* 56: 60–72.
1996 Tamburrini, Filippo, "Andrea Busiri-Vici (1818–1911), architetto-ingegnere del capitolo Lateranese, le sue scoperte, i suoi progetti e le polemiche," *Archivium historiae pontificia* 34: 245–68.

ROME, THE CAPITAL OF UNITED ITALY

1897 Lanciani, Rodolfo, *Ruins and Excavations of Ancient Rome* (Houghton Mifflin, Boston).
1935 Negri, E., "Caratteri generali dell'architettura in Roma da G. Valadier a E. Basile",, Galassi Paluzzi, Carlo, ed., *Atti del III Congresso Nazionale di Studi Romani* 3 (Cappelli, Rome): 5–12.
1947–52 Piacentini, Marcello, "Le vicende edilizie di Roma dal 1870 a oggi," *L'Urbe* 10, 1: 18–25; 3: 18–23; 11, 2: 23–34; 3: 19–27; 4: 9–26; 6: 23–34; 12, 3: 19–33; 6: 29–32; 13, 3: 26–33; 5: 24–38; 6: 23–32; 15, 1:19–27; 3: 21–31.
1971 Accasto, Gianni, Vanna Fraticelli, and Renato Nicolini, *L'architettura di Roma Capitale, 1870–1970* (Golem, Rome).
1978 Schroeter, Eberhard, "Rome's First National State Architecture: The Palazzo delle Finanze," in Millon, Henry, and Linda Nochlin, eds., *Art and Architecture in the Service of Politics* (MIT Press, Cambridge MA): 128–49.
1979 Vannelli, Valter, *Economia dell'architettura in Roma liberale, Il centro urbano* (Kappa, Rome).
1980 Borsi, Franco, ed., *Arte a Roma dalla Capitale all'età umbertina* (Ediltalia, Rome).
1984 Ciucci, Giorgio, and Vanna Fraticelli, eds., *Roma Capitale 1870–1911, Architettura e urbanistica, Uso e trasformazione della città storica* (Marsilio, Venice).
1985 *I Ministri di Roma Capitale, Roma Capitale 1870–1911* (Marsilio, Venice).
1991 Tobia, Bruno, *Una patria per gli Italiani, Spazi, itinerari, monumenti nell'Italia unita (1870–1900)* (Laterza, Bari/Rome).
1993 Williams, Robin, "Rome as state image: The architecture and urbanism of the royal Italian government, 1870–1900" (Ph.D., Pennsylvania University, Philadelphia).
1995 Racheli, Alberto, *Restauro a Roma, 1870–1990, Architettura e città* (Marsilio, Venice).

MONUMENTAL SYMBOLS OF THE NEW STATE

1875 Boito, Camillo, "Spavento delle grandezze di Roma," *Nuova Antologia* 30:.
1907 Ojetti, Ugo, *Il monumento a Vittorio Emanuele in Roma e le sue avventure narrate da Ugo Ojetti con lettere e giudizi di Leonardo Bistolfi, Lodovico Pogliaghi, Benedetto Croce (ecc.) e illustrata da 19 incisioni* (Treves, Milan).

1911 Acciaresi, Piero, *Giuseppe Sacconi e l'opera sua massima* (Unione, Rome).
1946 Sapori, Francesco, *Il Vittoriano* (Libreria dello Stato, Rome).
1957 Venturoli, Marcello, *La Patria di marmo* (Nistri-Lischi, Pisa).
1983 Rodiek, Thomas, *Das Monument Nazionale Vittorio Emanuele II in Rom* (Lang, Frankfurt am Main).
1986 Porzio, Pier Luigi, ed., *Il Vittoriano, Materiali per una storia* (Palombi, Rome).
1986 Scheiwiller, Vanni, ed., *Processo all'altare della patria, Atti del processo al monumento in Roma a Vittorio Emanuele II, 27 gennaio 1986* (Scheiwiller, Milan).
1989 Porzio, Pier Luigi, "Il Vittoriano a Roma da acropoli del Risorgimento a Foro della Nazione," *Storia della città* 48: 83–86.
1996 Berggren, Lars, and Lennart Sjöstedt, *L'Ombra dei Grandi, Monumenti e politica monumentale a Roma (1870–1895)* (Artemide, Rome).
1998 Brice, Catherine, *Monumentalité publique et politique à Rome, Le Vittoriano* (Ecole Francaise a Rome).
1998 Tobia, Bruno, *L'Altare della Patria* (Il Mulino, Bologna).
2002 Magone, Fabio, Massimiliano Savorra, and Maria Luisa Scalvini, *Verso il Vittoriano, L'Italia unita e i concorsi di architettura, I disegni della Biblioteca Nazionale Centrale di Roma, 1881* (Electa Napoli, Naples).

A NEW URBAN INFRASTRUCTURE FOR ROME

1894 B[eltrami], L[uca], "Il Ponte Vittorio Emanuele a Roma," *L'Edilizia moderna* 3 (1894) 4: 28–29.
1933–34 Bianchi, Arturo, "Le vicende e le realizzazioni del Piano Regolatore," *Capitolium*, part V, 9 (1933): 498–515; part VII, 10 (1934): 278–98.
1971 Insolera, Italo, *Roma Moderna, Un secolo di storia urbanistica, 1870–1970* (Einaudi, Turin).

1973 Fried, Robert, *Planning the Eternal City, Roman Politics and Planning since WWII* (Yale University Press, New Haven).
1973 Kostof, Spiro, *The Third Rome, 1870–1950, Traffic and Glory* (University Art Museum, Berkely).
1974 Spagnesi, Gianfranco, *L'Esquilino e la Piazza Vittorio* (Editalia, Rome).
1976 Kostof, Spiro, "Drafting a master plan for Roma Capitale, An Exordium," *Journal of the Society of Architectural Historians* 25, 1: 4–20.
1991 Cambedda, Anna, and Luisa Cardilli, eds., *La Capitale a Roma, Città e arredo urbano, 1870–1945* (Carte Segrete, Rome).
1991 Cuccia, Giuseppe, *Urbanistica Edilizia Infrastruttura di Roma Capitale, 1870–1990, Una cronologia* (Laterza, Bari/Rome).

A NATIONAL ARCHITECTURE
1942 Piacentini, Marcello, "I grandi umbri: Guglielmo Calderini," *Nuova Antologia* 17, 1694: 281–84.
1983 Borsi, Franco, and Maria Cristina Buscioni, *Manfredo Manfredi e il classicismo della Nuova Italia*(Electa, Milan).
1990 Siligato, Rosella, and Maria Elisa Tittoni, eds., *Il Palazzo delle Esposizioni, Urbanistica e architettura* (Carte Segrete, Rome).
1991 Calderini, Guglielmo, *Scritti di architettura*, Barucci, Clementina, and Antonella Greco, eds. (Clear, Rome).
1995 Boco, Fedora, Terry Kirk and Giorgio Muratori, *Guglielmo Calderini dai disegni dell'Accademia di Belle Art di Perugia, Un architetto dell'Italia in costruzione* (Guerra, Perugia).
1996 Boco, Fedora, Terry Kirk and Giorgio Muratore, eds., *Guglielmo Calderini, La costruzione di un'architettura nel progetto di una capitale, Atti del convegno.*
1996 Kirk, Terry, "Roman Architecture before the Lateran Pact: Architectural Symbols of Reconciliation in the Competitions for the Palazzo di Giustizia, 1883–87," in Boco, Fedora, Terry Kirk and Giorgio Muratore, eds., *Guglielmo Calderini, La costruzione di un'architettura nel progetto di una capitale, Atti del convegno* (Guerra, Perugia): 83–125.
1997 Fabbri, Marcello, et al., *Il Palazzo di Giustizia di Roma* (Gangemi, Rome).
1997 Kirk, Terry, "Church, State and Architecture, The Palazzo di Giustizia of Nineteenth-Century Rome," (Ph.D., Columbia University, New York).

THE OPENING OF ROME
1953 Meeks, Carroll, "Churches by Street on the Via Nazionale and the Via del Babuino," *Art Quarterly* 16: 215–27.
1982 Millon, Judith Rice, *St. Paul's Within the Walls, Rome* (Bauhan, Dublin NH).

THE WORLD'S FAIR IN ROME
1908 Piacentini, Marcello, *Concorso per il progetto del Palazzo dell'Esposizione per le feste del 1911 in Roma, Relazione, architetto Marcello Piacentini* (Rome).
1911 *Guida ufficiale delle Esposizioni di Roma* (Rome).
1911 Rutelli, G., *L'Architettura italiana all'Esposizione Internazionale di Roma* (Palermo).
1980 Piantoni, Gianna, ed., *Roma 1911* (De Luca, Rome).
1999 Volpiano, Mauro, *Torino 1890, La prima esposizione italiana di architettura* (Celid, Turin).

ILLUSTRATION CREDITS

collection of the author: 1.4, 1.5, 1.12, 2.18, 3.7, 3.13, 3.20, 4.3, 4.15, 4.27, 4.28, 4.32, 4.33, 4.37

Archives Nationales de France, Paris, Atelier de photographie du Centre historique: 2.13, 2.14

Archivio Capitolino, Rome: 4.35

Archivio del Comitato per Bologna Storica e Artistica, Fondo Rubbiani: 4.17

Archivio di Stato, Naples, sezione disegni: 1.14

Archivio Storico Comunale, Naples: 4.9

Assessorato alla Cultura del Comune di Padova, Museo Civico: 3.1, 3.3, 3.4, 3.5, 3.24, 3.25

Bianchi Bandinelli collection, Villa di Geggiano (Siena): 3.12

Biblioteca Apostolica Vaticana, Rome: 1.3

Biblioteca dell'Istituto Nazionale di Archeologia e Storia dell'Arte, Rome: 2.17, 3.2, 3.6, 3.16, 4.26, 4.29, 4.30

Biblioteca di Storia Moderna e Contemporanea, Rome: 4.1

Biblioteca Hertziana, Rome: 1.7, 1.8, 1.9, 1.11, 1.22, 4.2

Biblioteca Nazionale Centrale Vittorio Emaneule II, Rome: 3.9, 3.17, 4.7, 4.23, 4.25, 4.47

Bibliothèque Nationale de France, Paris, Département des Estampse et Photographie: 2.2

Civiche Raccolte d'Arte Applicata ed Incisioni & Raccolta delle Stampe "Achille Bertarelli," Milan: 1.26, 2.3

Columbia University, New York, Avery Architectural and Fine Arts Library, Drawings and Archives Department: 1.17

E. Richter, Rome: 1.25

Fondazione Ente Cassa di Risparmio di Roma: 1.24

Francesco Jodice, Skira editore, Milan: 1.10

Fratelli Alinari, Florence: 1.20, 2.4, 2.6, 2.7, 2.8, 2.9, 2.10, 2.12, 3.10, 3.14, 3.19, 3.21, 3.23, 4.4, 4.10, 4.11, 4.12, 4.14, 4.16, 4.18, 4.19, 4.24, 4.31, 4.34, 4.36, 4.40, 4.41, 4.42, 4.43, 4.45

Giorgio Lotti, Milan: 1.28

Giuseppe d'Arvia, Rome: 4.38, 4.39

Istituto Centrale per il Catalogo e la Documentazione, Ministero per i Beni Culturali e Ambientali, Rome: 1.18, 1.19, 2.1, 2.5, 2.11, 2.20, 4.20, 4.44, 4.46

Istituto di Architettura Tecnica, Facoltà di Architettura, Politecnico di Torino: 3.15, 3.18

Istituto Nazionale per la Grafica, Rome: 1.1, 1.6, 1.15, 1.16, 1.21, 2.15, 2.16, 2.19, 3.22, 4.22

Istituto per la Storia del Risorgimento Italiano, Rome: 4.21

Mark Edward Smith, Venice: 3.8

Musei Comunali di Firenze, Fototeca: 4.5, 4.6, 4.8

Museo Nazionale di Capodimonte, Naples: 1.13

Museo Sant'Agostino, Genova, Collezione Topografica: 3.11

Museo Teatrale alla Scala, Milan: 1.27

Nationalmuseum, Stockholm: 1.23

Soprintendenza per i Beni Artistici e Storici delle Provincie di Firenze, Pistoia e Prato, Florence, Gabinetto Fotografico: 4.13

Statens Museum for Kunst, Copenhagen, photo: DOWIC: 1.2

INDEX

A
Accademia di San Luca, 15, 22, 40; 109
Albani, Cardinal Alessandro, 66–67
Albergo dei Poveri (Hospice of the Paupers), 41–47, **42,** 104
Alvino, Errico, 197, **213**
Amati, Carlo, 177
antiquities. *See also* archaeology; restoration (architectural): collection and preservation of, 65–69; as commodities, 91, 123; removal under Treaty of Tolentino, 89; restitution of after Napoleon, 123
Antolini, Giovanni Antonio, 92–95
Antonelli, Alessandro, 160–165
Arch of Titus, Rome: restoration of, 169–170, **171**
archaeology. *See also* restoration (architectural): early impact of, 63–65; excavation, 120, 122, 169–170; Napoleon's interest in, 120–122
archetypes (styles): synthesis of, 150
Arco delle Vittorie napoleoniche (Arco della Pace), Milan, **95, 184**
Armanni, Osvaldo, 253, 254
art museums. *See also* names of individual museums: concept of, 123
arts, "resurgence of," 84
artworks. *See* antiquities
Asprucci, Antonio, 72
Asprucci, Mario, 73
Azzurri, Francesco, 215

B
Banca d'Italia, Rome, **251**
Barbarino, Carlo, 153–155
Bargigli, Paolo, 86, 88
Basile, Giovanni Battista Filippo, 218
Bazzani, Cesare, 256, 257
Belli, Pasquale, 173
Benedict XIV, Pope, 17, **42**
Berthault, Louis-Martin, 118, 119
Bianchi, Pietro, 104, 105, 121, 122
Bianchi, Salvatore, 221
Boito, Camillo, 179–182; and contemporary style, 180
Bologna, city plan, 214
Bonaparte, Joseph, 104
Bonaparte, Napoleon. *See* Napoleon (Bonaparte)
Bonsignore, Ferdinando, 102, 103
Borghese, Camilo, 119
Borghese, Prince Marcantonio IV, 72–73
Borromini, Francesco, 22
Borsato, Giuseppe, 144
Bossi, Giuseppe, 91
Boubée, Francesco Paolo, 202, 203
Braccio Nuovo (of Vatican Museum), Rome, 123, **124**
bridges: Ponte Risorgimento, Rome, 256–258; Ponte Vittorio Emanuele II, Rome, **245**

C
Cacialli, Giuseppe, 110, 111
Caffe Pedrocci, Padua, 131–134, **133**
Cagnola, Luigi, 95, 96, 104, 184
Calderini, Guglielmo, 234, 247
Camporese, Giuseppe, 86, 88
Canal Grande, Trieste, **108,** 109
Canevari, Raffaele, 228, 230–231
Canina, Luigi, 136–138, **137**
Canonica, Luigi, 91, 94–96
Canova, Antonio, 123, 147, 151; cultural importance of, 148, 150; funeral of, 152
capital cities (historical): Florence, 190–195; Milan,

199–204; Naples, 196–199; Rome, 226, 252–259; Turin, 186–189
:aretti, Giovanni Battista, 139–141, 140
:arlos III, King of Naples, 28–39, **42**
Casa delle colonne," Turin, 160, **161**
:asa Ponzio Vaglia, Turin, **161**
Casino Pedrocchi," Padua, 132–134
athedral facades, 204–214
athedrals (Duomos) and churches. *See also* Duomo; individual names
:avaceppi, Bartolomeo, 67
:avour, Camillo, 240
emeteries: "monumental," 153
:eppi, Carlo, 188–189
:hapel of the Templars at Saonara Gardens, near Padua, **129**
hapels, Pantheonic, 153
:hiaradia, Enrico, 235
:hirografo, papal legislation (1802), 123
hurches and cathedrals (Duomos). *See* individual names
:icongnara, Leopoldo, 135
:imitero Monumentale, Staglieno, Genoa, 153–154, **154**
Cisternone," Livorno, 158–160, **159**
ities, capital. *See* capital cities (historical)
ity halls, 216
ity planning. *See* urban planning
ity plans: Bologna, 214; Florence, 192–194, **193,** 195; Milan, 204; Naples, **197,** 198–199; Palermo, 217; Rome, 20, **225**; Turin, **187**
lassical style, 109. *See also* neoclassicism; merged with Christian, 106
lassicism, austere, 23–24 See also neoclassicism
:lement XI, Pope, 15
:lement XII, Pope, 22–23, 24, 27, 40, 66
:lement XIV, Pope, 69
:olosseum, Rome: restoration of, 169, 170, **171**
:olumn of Trajan, Rome, 120–122, **121**
:ommission des Embellisements, 114, 120
onstruction materials, 164; iron, 166–168; masonry, 162, 163–164
:orso Vittorio Emanuele II, Rome, **245**
:osta, Vincenzo, 253, 254
:rispi, Francesco, 224
:ultural heritage: early preservation of, 65–66, 69–73

)

le Cambray Digny, Luigi (architect), 190–191
le Cambray Digny, Luigi Guglielmo (mayor), 192
le Fabris, Emilio, 206–211
le Mérode, Fredric, 222
)eriziet, Antoine, 20
lesign competitions, 22, 231–235; for monument to Vittorio Emanuele II, **234**
lome, stacked: construction of, 160–162; "Mole Antonelliana," 164–166
Dori, Alessandro, 69–70, 71
Doric style, 92–93, 104, 106
Doric temples, Paestum, 64–65
Dufourny, Leon, 65
Duomo, Milan, 176, **177**
Duomo facade, Amalfi, **213**

E

eighteenth-century classicism, 84–85
excavation, archaeological. *See* archaeology: excavation

F

Fabbrica (Vatican building commission), 28
Fantastici, Agostino, 156–157, 159
Fea, Carlo, 122
Ferrari, Ettore, 234
Festa della Federazione: Milan, 92; Rome, **86,** 88
flood control: Tiber Embankment, 241–242
Florence, 190–195; city plans, 192–194, **193,** 195
Foro Bonaparte, Milan, 93–96, **95**
Foro Carolino, Naples, 104
Foro delle Regioni, Rome, **258**
Foro Ferdinandeo (now Piazza del Plebiscito), Naples, 104, **105**
Foro Murat (now Piazza del Plebiscito), Naples, 104, **105**
Forum, Rome, 120
Forum of Nerva (ruins), Rome, **50**
foundries, iron, 168
Frizzi, Giuseppe, 102, 103
Fuga, Fernando, 40–46

G

Gagnereaux, Benigne, **71,** 72
Galilei, Alessandro, 23–24, 25
Gallerata, near Milan, 180
Galleria Nazionale d'Arte Moderna, Rome, 256, **257**
Galleria Sciarra, Rome, 255
Galleria Umberto I, Naples, **202,** 203
Galleria Vittorio Emanuele II, Milan, **200,** 201
Gallori, Emilio, 238, 239
garden design: effect of romantic attitudes upon, 128; naturalistic landscapes, 130; at Piazza del Popolo, Rome, 119; Villa Torlonia, Rome, 141–142
Garibaldi, Giuseppe: improvement decree (Naples), 196; monument to, Janiculum Hill, Rome, **238,** 239
Ghettos (slums). *See risanmento* (urban renewal)
Giani, Felice, 112
Gothic Revival, European, 176
Gothic style, 176–178
"Grand Tour," 62–65
Guarnelli, Giacomo, 178

H
height (construction), 164
Holl, Pietro, 178

I
"Il Cisternone," Livorno, **159**
"Il Pedrocchino" (pastry shop), Padua, **133,** 134
"Il Rettifilo" (urban renewal project), Naples, 196–198, **197**
independence (national). *See* unification (national)
industrial construction, 168
infrastructure. *See* bridges; roads
infrastructure planning. *See* urban planning
Ingres, Jean-Auguste-Dominique, 112
interior design, 110–112; theaters, 143–145
Invenzioni capriciosi di carceri (volume of prints), **50,** 51
Ionic style, 106
iron: in bridges, 166; construction with, 166–168
iron foundries, 168
Italian national consciousness: Boito's influence upon, 182; cultural basis of, 135; development of, 88, 147; Lombard Romanesque style and, 179–180
Italy, cultural evolution of, 10–11
Italy, unification and independence. *See* national unification (Italy)

J
Jappelli, Giuseppe, 126, 129, 132, 133, 140; public projects, Padua, 130

K
King Gustav III of Sweden visiting the Museo Pio-Clementino (painting), **71**
Koch, Gaetano, 229, 251

L
La Gran Madre di Dio (church), Turin, **102,** 103
La Nuova Pianta di Roma (city plan), **21**
La Scala, Milan, 77, 81–82
landscape design. *See* garden design
largo, Naples, 104
Le Vatican et la Basilique de Saint-Pierre de Rome (plan), **71**
Leo XII (pope), 173
Letarouilly, Paul, 71
Lombard Romanesque style, 180

M
Maccagnani, Eugenio, 235
Maffei, Alessandro, 157, **159**
Magazzini Boccione (department store), Rome, **254,** 255
Marchionni, Carlo, 66–68, 73–74, 75
Martinori, Luigi, 228
Marvuglia, Giuseppe Venanzio, 65
Mazzini, Giuseppe, 236
Mazzucchetti, Alessandro, 186–189
Medrano, Giovanni Antonio, 106
Meduna, Giambattista, 145, 146
Mengoni, Giuseppe, 200–203
Milan: city plans, 204; Hapsburg rule of, 77–81; industrial development, 204; Napoleonic influence, 91–98; *Ornato* Board, 96
Milizia, Francesco, 17
Ministerio delle Finanze, Rome, **228**
"Mole Antonelliana" (unfinished synagogue), Turin, 163–164, **165**
Mollari, Antonio, 107, 109
monuments: Arco delle Vittorie napoleoniche (Arco della Pace), **184**; to Camillo Cavour, Rome; Capitoline Hill, Rome, as site for, 233–235; to Giuseppe Garibaldi, Rome, **238**; theoretical aspects of, 236, 239, 240; "Vittoriano" (monument to Vittorio Emanuelle II), Rome, 235–239, **237**; to Vittorio Emanuele II (competing designs), **234**
monuments, restoration of, 161–175. *See also* archaeology restoration (architectural)
Morelli, Cosimo, 75, 76, 92
Moschetti, Alessandro, 225
Musée Napoleón, Paris, **90**
Museo Pio-Clementino, 69–72, **71,** 85, 123
museums. *See also* names of individual museums: art, 123

N
Naples: city plans, 196–199; gutting of *(sventramento),* 198 Napoleonic influence, 104–106; urban renewal projects, 196–199, **197**
Napoleon (Bonaparte), 87; conquest of Italy, 87–89; crowning as emperor of Italy, 96; fall from power, 123; monuments to, 88, 92–96, **95**; rationalist spirit under, 88–89
Napoleonic apartments, Palazzo Pitti, Florence, **111**
Napoleonic influence: interior design, 110–112; Milan, 91–99; Naples, 104–106; *Ornato* Board; Rome 112–120; Trieste, 107–110; Turin, 101–103; urban modernization program, 100–101; Venice, 98–101
national consciousness (Italy): Boito's influence upon, 182 cultural basis of, 135; effect of French Revolution on, 88; influence of Verdi operas on, 147; Lombard Romaneque style and, 179–180; under Napoleon, 88
national unification (Italy), 185, 222–224
Nénot, Paul-Henri, 234
neo-Renaissance style, 192
neo-Romanesque style, 179–180
neoclassicism, 83–85, 87, 109. *See also* classical style; effect of Romantic attitudes upon, 128
nepotism, papal, 76
Niccolini, Antonio, 105, 106
Nobile, Pietro, 108, 109
Nolli, Giovanni Battista, 20–22, 24

)
rnato boards, local, 96, 180, 190

acca Edict (1820), 123
aestum, 64
alais imperiale, Rome, **113**
alazzo Belgioso, Milan, **80**
alazzo Belloni (now Rocca Saporiti), Milan, **97**
alazzo Braschi, Rome, **75,** 76
alazzo della Ragione, Padua, **126**
alazzo delle Debite, Padua, **181,** 182
alazzo delle Esposizioni, Rome, **251**
alazzo di Giustizia, Rome, **247**
alazzo Ducale, Milan, 77–78, **177**
alazzo Nuovo, Rome, 66
alazzo Pitti, Florence, 110–112, **111**
alazzo Pubblico, San Marino, **215**, 216
alazzo Quirinale, Rome, **42,** 110–112, 226–227
alermo, city plan, 217
anini, Giovanni Paolo, 15–16, 62
anini, Giuseppe, 25, 27
antheon degli Uomini illustri, Pistoia, **159**
antheon (The), Rome, **14,** 15–19, **16**; decorated for state funeral, **232**; design for attic of, **19**; "progeny" of, 153
antheonic chapel. *See* cemeteries: "monumental"
erego, Giovanni, 97, 98
eriods, architectural, 11
erosini, Scipione, 113
ertinchamp, Claude La Remée, 102, 103
ertsch, Matthaus, 107–108
iacentini, Marcello, 258
iacentini, Pio, 234, 251
ianta Guida della Città di Roma, (city plan, 1884), Rome, **225**
iazza Belgioso, Milan, **80**
iazza Carlo Felice, Turin, **188**
iazza Cesare Beccaria, Florence, **193**
iazza del Duomo, Milan, 199, 201
iazza del Plebiscito, Naples, 104, **105,** 196
iazza del Popolo, Rome, 115–120, **117, 118**; gardens at, 116–119
iazza dell'Esedra, Rome, **251**
iazza di San Marco, Venice, **99**
iazza Vittorio Emanuele I, Turin, **102,** 103
iazzas. *See* names of individual piazzas
iermarini, Giuseppe, 77–83, 91, 177
ieroni, Francesco, 228, 230
incian Hill gardens. *See* garden design
iranesi, Giovanni Battista, 14, 18–19, 47–59, 62, 122; publications of, 51–52; *vedute* (urban views), 48–49
ius IX, Pope, 219–222
ius VI, Pope, 71–73, 73–76
Pius VII, Pope, 113–114
Poccianti, Pasquale, 158, 159
Poggi, Giuseppe, 192–194; stylistic contributions, 194
Poletti, Luigi, 173–174, 175
Pompeii, 63
Ponte Vittorio Emanuele I, Turin, **102**
Ponte Vittorio Emanuele II, Rome, **245**
Pontine Marshes, 75–76
Porta Pia (gate), Rome, **223**
Posi, Paolo, 17–18
Presenti, Enrico, 191
Promis, Carlo, 186–187, **188**
public buildings. *See also* individual building name: city halls, 216; Palermo, 217
public space, 114, 194, 259; *palazzo comunale* concept of, 216; in Venice, 101

Q
Quarenghi, Giacomo, 59–62, 70

R
railroad construction, 168
railroad stations, 186–189; Stazione Porta Nuova, Turin, **188,** 189; Stazione Termini, Rome, **221,** 222
Receuil des décorations intérieures (publication), 100
reconstruction. *See* restoration (architectural)
Reggia (palace) at Caserta, 28–39, **33, 34, 37**
Reishammer, Carlo, 167–168
restoration (architectural), 169–174. *See also* antiquities; archaeology; Boito's contribution to, 182
Rettifilo (urban renewal project), Naples, 196–198, **197**
revivalism, 176–182. *See also* specific style name
Rezzonico, Giovanni Battista, 54, 55
risanamento (urban renewal), 199; Florence, 195
Risorgimento (national resurgence), 12, 84, 222–224; Canova's importance in, 148
roads: Corso Vittorio Emanuele, Rome, **245**
Rocco, Emanuelle, 202, 203
"Roma Capitale d'Italia," (engraving), **225**
Roman ruins. *See* antiquities; archaeology
Romantic era: historical implications of, 182–183; and Verdi's opera, 147
romanticism, 128–130, 134–135; exploratory, 150; in Tuscany, 156–158
Rome: city plan (1748) by Nolli, **21**; city plans (1884), **225**; effects of government installation, 222–223, 226; final years of papal reign, 220–221; Napoleonic influence on, 112–120; Nolli plan for, **21**; plans under Mayor Nathan, 255; World's fair, 1911, 255–257
Rossi-Melocchi, Cosimo, 159
Rosso, Luigi, 232
Rubbiani, Alfonso, 214, 215
ruins. *See* antiquities; restoration (architectural)

S
Sacconi, Giuseppe, 235, 236–237
Saint Peter's Basilica, Rome, 73–74; sacristy of, **75**
Saint Peter's Square, Rome: *Festa della Federazione,* **86**
Salone delle Feste, **258**
Salvi, Nicola, 24–28
San Francesco di Paola, Naples, **105,** 106
San Gaudenzio, Novara, 160, **161,** 163
San Giovanni Laterano, 22, 23–24, **25,** 52, **53**; facade, **25**
San Leopoldo, Follonica, **167,** 168
San Lorenzo fuori le mura, Rome, 220
San Paolo fuori le mura, Rome, 172–175; restoration of, **175**; restoration theory and, 173–174
Santa Maria del Fiore, Florence, 204, **205, 208, 211**
Santa Maria del Priorato, Rome, 54, **57**
Santa Maria della Scala, Milan, 81
Santa Scholastica, Subaico, 59–61, **60**
Sant'Antonio Taumaturgo, Trieste, **108,** 109
Saonara Gardens, near Padua, **129**
scenography, 143–144
sculpture, neoclassical, 147–148
Scuola Carrarese, Padua, **181**
Sella, Quintino, 229, 230, 231
Selva, Giannantonio, 83–84, 107
Simonetti, Michaelangelo, 70–72
Soli, Giuseppe Maria, 99, 100
Stazione Porta Nuova, Turin, 187–189, **188**
Stazione Termini, Rome, **221,** 222
Stern, Raffaele, 112, 123, **124**, 169–170, 171
styles (architectural): Classical, 162; Gothic, 162, 176–178; neo-Renaissance, 192; neo-Romanesque, 179–180; romantic, 128–130, 134–135, 150, 156–158; utilitarian aspects, 180
synagogues, 163, **254,** See also "Mole Antonelliana," Turin

T
Teatro alla Scala, Milan, **80,** 81–82
Teatro Carlo Felice, Genoa, **154,** 155
Teatro La Fenice, Venice, 83–84, 144–145, **146**; reconstruction after fire, 144
Teatro Massimo Vittorio Emanuele II, Palermo, **218**
Teatro San Carlo, Naples, **105,** 106
Tempio Canoviano, Possagno, 149–151, **151**; as perfect synthesis of styles, 150
Tempio israelitico, Roma, **254**
theater design, 155; Teatro Massimo Vittorio Emanuele II, Palermo, 217
Thorvaldsen, Bertel, 112
Titus, Arch of, 169–170, **171**
Torlonia, Alessandro, 139–141, 142
Torlonia, Giovanni, 138–139
town halls, 214–216
train stations and terminals. *See* railroad stations
Trevi Fountain, Rome, 24–28, **25,** 85
Trieste: Napoleonic influence on, 107–112
Trieste theater, 107
Turin: as capital city, 186–189; city plan, 186, **187**; stone bridge over Po, 103

U
unification, national. *See* national unification (Italy)
urban planning: Florence, 190–192; industrial aspects (Milan), 204; infrastructure (roads and bridges), 243–245; Naples, 196; *risanamento,* 198–199; public financing for, 243; Rome under Mayor Nathan, 255; Viviani's contribution, 244
urban renewal. *See risanmento* (urban renewal)

V
Valadier, Giuseppe, 114–119, 138–139, 140, 171
Vanvitelli, Carlo, 36, **37**
Vanvitelli, Luigi, 25, 28–39, 77–78
Vatican Museums (Braccio Nuovo), Rome, 123, **124**
Venice: Napoleonic influence on, 98–101; *Ornato* Board, 101
Verdi, Giuseppe: effect on scenography, 147
Verri, Pietro, 82
Vescovali, Angelo, 245
Via dei Calziuoli (widening), Florence, **191**
Via del Corso, Rome, **254**
Via del Rettifilo, Naples, **197,** 198
Via del Santo Stefano houses (restoration), Bologna, **215**
Via Nazionale, Rome, 227–228, **228**
Viale dei Colli, Florence, 194
Vici, Andrea, 86, 88
Villa Albani, Rome, 66–67, **68,** 85
Villa Borghese, Rome, 72–73, 136–138; extension to Via Flaminia, **137**
Villa Il Pavone, Siena, **159**
Villa Puccini, near Pistoia, Tuscany, 157
Villa Torlonia, Rome, **140**
villas, rivalries among, 136–142
"Vittoriano," The (Monument to Vittorio Emanuelle II), Rome, **237**; designs for, **234**; political significance of, 236, 239
Vittorio Emanuelle II, King: death of, 231; funeral decorations for, **232**
Viviani, Alessandro, 241–244

W
Winckelmann, Johann Joachim, 107
works of art. *See* antiquities
World's Fair (1908), Rome, 255–258; "Forum of the Regions," **258,** 259; Italian pavilion, 256